Electrical Trainee Volume 1

NCCER Modules Published by Pearson

Trainee Guide ISBN: 0134290240

Electrical Concepts
Conductors & Cables

26105-14 - Intro. To the National Electrical Code

26109-14 - Conductors & Cables

26110-14 - Basic Electrical Construction Drawings

26201-14 - Alternating Current

26206-14 - Conductor Installations

26208-14 - Conductor Terminations & Splices

Conduits, Raceways, Boxes & Fittings

26107-14 - Hand Bending

26108-14 - Raceways & Fittings

26204-14 - Conduit Bending

26205-14 - Pull & Junction Boxes

26207-14 - Cable Tray

Residential and Commercial Wiring

26111-14 - Residential Electrical Services

26306-14 - Distribution Equipment

26308-14 - Commercial Electrical Services

5/11/16

Electrical Concepts
Conductors and Cables

Modules

26105-14
26109-14
26110-14
26201-14
26206-14
26208-14

Introduction to the *National Electrical Code®*

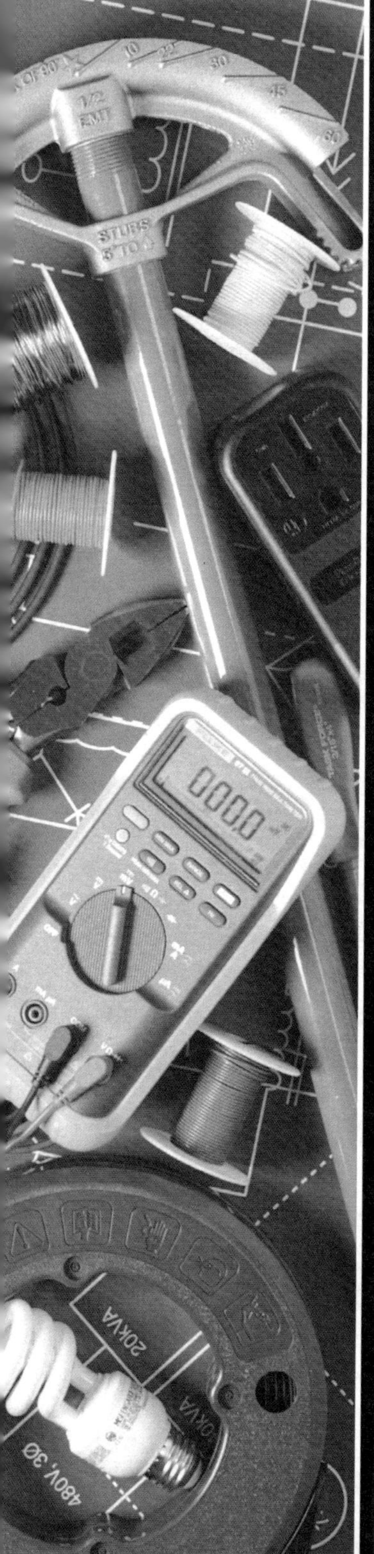

Brick Nanotechnology Center at Purdue University

The Gaylor Group's team of nearly 60 electricians followed strict cleanroom protocols to install electrical systems in this leading-edge nanotechnology facility while facing shared-space challenges and work restrictions.

26105-14

Trainees with successful module completions may be eligible for credentialing through NCCER's National Registry. To learn more, go to **www.nccer.org** or contact us at **1.888.622.3720.** Our website has information on the latest product releases and training, as well as online versions of our *Cornerstone* magazine and Pearson's product catalog.

Your feedback is welcome. You may email your comments to **curriculum@nccer.org,** send general comments and inquiries to **info@nccer.org,** or fill in the User Update form at the back of this module.

This information is general in nature and intended for training purposes only. Actual performance of activities described in this manual requires compliance with all applicable operating, service, maintenance, and safety procedures under the direction of qualified personnel. References in this manual to patented or proprietary devices do not constitute a recommendation of their use.

26105-14

INTRODUCTION TO THE *NATIONAL ELECTRICAL CODE*®

Objectives

When you have completed this module, you will be able to do the following:

1. Explain the purpose and history of the *NEC*®.
2. Describe the layout of the *NEC*®.
3. Demonstrate how to navigate the *NEC*®.
4. Describe the purpose of the National Electrical Manufacturers Association and the NFPA.
5. Explain the role of nationally recognized testing laboratories.

Performance Tasks

Under the supervision of the instructor, you should be able to do the following:

1. Use ***NEC Article 90*** to determine the scope of the *NEC*®. State what is covered by the *NEC*® and what is not.
2. Find the definition of the term *feeder* in the *NEC*®.
3. Look up the *NEC*® specifications that you would need to follow if you were installing an outlet near a swimming pool.
4. Find the minimum wire bending space required for two No. 1/0 AWG conductors installed in a junction box or cabinet and entering opposite the terminal.

Trade Terms

Articles
Chapters
Exceptions
Informational Note
National Electrical Manufacturers Association (NEMA)
National Fire Protection Association (NFPA)
Nationally Recognized Testing Laboratories (NRTLs)
Parts
Sections

Required Trainee Materials

1. Paper and pencil
2. Copy of the latest edition of the *National Electrical Code*®

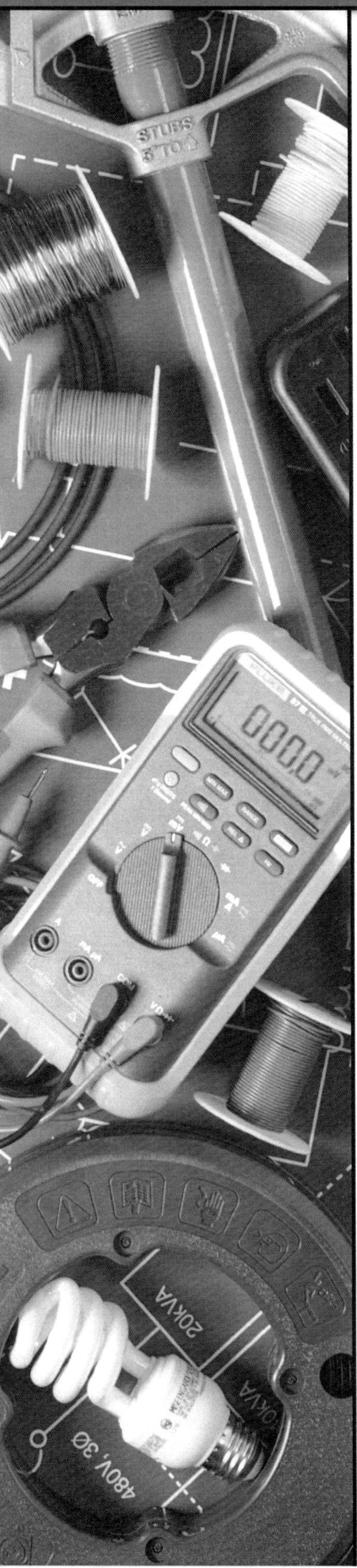

Contents

Topics to be presented in this module include:

Figures

1.0.0 INTRODUCTION

The *National Electrical Code*® (*NEC*®) is published by the National Fire Protection Association (NFPA). The *NEC*® is one of the most important tools for the electrician. When used together with the electrical code for your local area, the *NEC*® provides the minimum requirements for the installation of electrical systems. Unless otherwise specified, always use the latest edition of the *NEC*® as your on-the-job reference. It specifies the minimum provisions necessary for protecting people and property from electrical hazards. In some areas, however, local laws may specify different editions of the *NEC*®, so be sure to use the edition specified by your employer. Also, bear in mind that the *NEC*® only specifies minimum requirements, so local or job requirements may be more stringent.

2.0.0 PURPOSE AND HISTORY OF THE *NEC*®

The primary purpose of the *NEC*® is the practical safeguarding of persons and property from hazards arising from the use of electricity [*NEC Section 90.1(A)*]. A thorough knowledge of the *NEC*® is one of the first requirements for becoming a trained electrician. The *NEC*® is probably the most widely used and generally accepted code in the world. It has been translated into several languages. It is used as an electrical installation, safety, and reference guide in the United States. Compliance with *NEC*® standards increases the safety of electrical installations—the reason the *NEC*® is so widely used.

Although *NEC Section 90.1(A)* states, "This Code is not intended as a design specification or an instruction manual for untrained persons," it does provide a sound basis for the study of electrical installation procedures—under the proper guidance. The *NEC*® has become the standard reference of the electrical construction industry. Anyone involved in electrical work should obtain an up-to-date copy and refer to it frequently.

Think About It

The *NEC*®

Why do you think it's necessary to have a standard set of procedures for electrical installations? Find out who does the electrical inspection in your area. Who determines what will be inspected, when it will be inspected, and who will do the inspection?

All electrical work must comply with the currently adopted *NEC*® and all local ordinances. Like most laws, the *NEC*® is easier to work with once you understand the language and know where to look for the information you need.

NOTE

This module is not a substitute for the *NEC*®. You need to acquire a copy of the most recent edition and keep it handy at all times. The more you know about the *NEC*®, the better an electrician you will become.

2.1.0 History

In 1881, the National Association of Fire Engineers met in Richmond, Virginia. From this meeting came the idea to draft the first *National Electrical Code*. The first nationally recommended electrical code was published by the National Board of Fire Underwriters (now the American Insurance Association) in 1895.

In 1896, the National Electric Light Association (NELA) was working to make the requirements of the fire insurance organizations and electrical utilities fit together. NELA succeeded in promoting a conference that would result in producing a standard national code. The NELA code would serve the interests of the insurance industry, operating concerns, manufacturing, and industry.

The conference produced a set of requirements that was unanimously accepted. In 1897, the first edition of the *NEC*® was published, and the *NEC*® became the first cooperatively produced national code. The organization that produced the *NEC*® was known as the *National Conference on Standard Electrical Rules*. This group became a permanent organization, and its job was to develop the *NEC*®.

In 1911, the NFPA took over administration and control of the *NEC*®. However, the National Board of Fire Underwriters continued to publish the *NEC*® until 1962. From 1911 until now, the *NEC*® has experienced several major changes, as well as regular three-year updates. In 1923, the *NEC*® was rearranged and rewritten, and in 1937, it was editorially revised. In 1959, the *NEC*® adopted a numbering system in which each section of an article was identified with an article/section number.

2.1.1 Who Is Involved?

The creation of a universally accepted set of rules is an involved and complicated process. Rules made by a committee have the advantage that they usually do not leave out the interests of any of the groups represented on the committee. However,

What's wrong with these pictures?

26105-14_SA01.EPS

26105-14_SA02.EPS

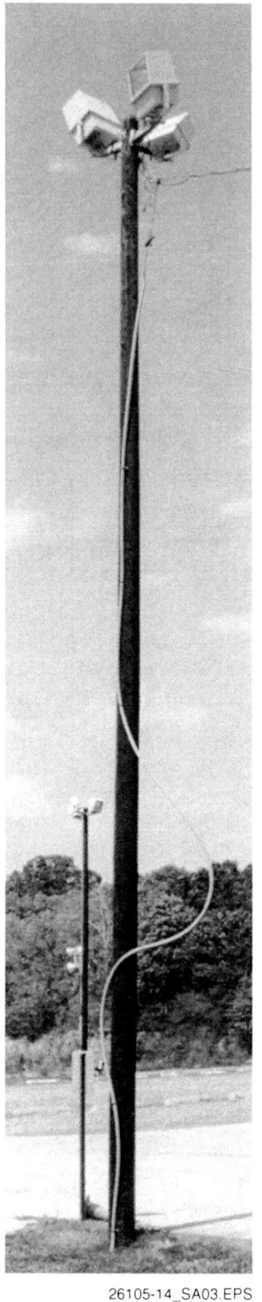

26105-14_SA03.EPS

since the rules must represent the interests and requirements of an assortment of groups, they are often quite complicated and wordy.

In 1949, the NFPA reorganized the *NEC®* into its present structure. The present structure consists of a Correlating Committee and Code Making Panels (CMPs). The Correlating Committee consists of principal voting members and alternates. The principal function of the Correlating Committee is to ensure that:

- No conflict of requirements exists
- Correlation has been achieved
- NFPA regulations governing committee projects have been followed
- A practical schedule of revision and publication is established and maintained

Each of the CMPs have members who are experts on particular subjects and have been assigned certain articles to supervise and revise as

Think About It

Code Changes

This photograph shows the first code book and the current code book. Code changes occur every three years. Who can suggest changes to the *National Electrical Code*®? What might be reasons for submitting changes?

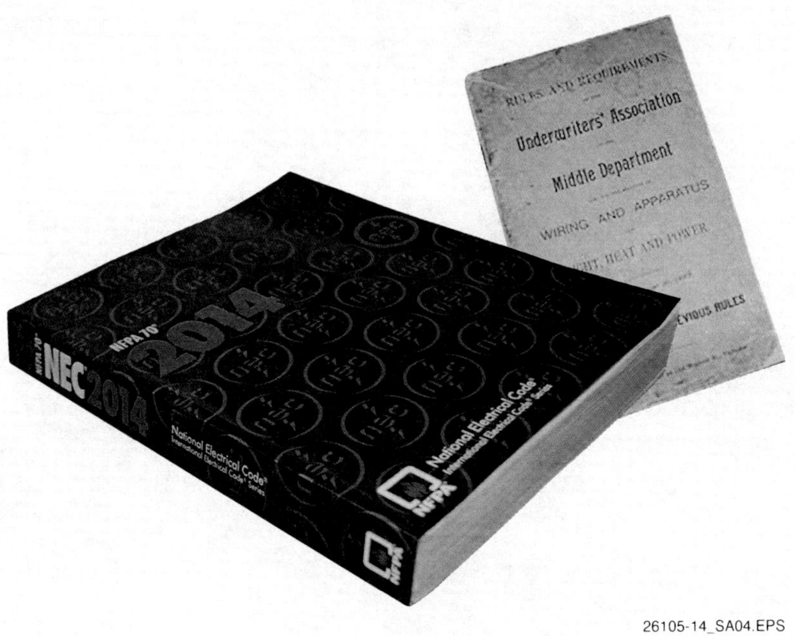

26105-14_SA04.EPS

required. Members of the CMPs represent special interest groups such as trade associations, electrical contractors, electrical designers and engineers, electrical inspectors, electrical manufacturers and suppliers, electrical testing laboratories, and insurance organizations.

Each panel is structured so that not more than one-third of its members are from a single interest group. The members of the *NEC*® Committee create or revise requirements for the *NEC*® through probing, debating, analyzing, weighing, and reviewing new input. Anyone, including you, can submit proposals to amend the *NEC*®. Sample forms for this purpose may be obtained from the Secretary of the Standards Council at NFPA Headquarters. The *NEC*® describes the code-making process in detail.

The NFPA membership is drawn from the fields listed above. In addition to publishing the *NEC*®, the duties of the NFPA include the following:

- Developing, publishing, and distributing standards that are intended to minimize the possibility and effects of fire and explosion
- Conducting fire safety education programs for the general public
- Providing information on fire protection, prevention, and suppression
- Compiling annual statistics on causes and occupancies of fires, large-loss fires (over one million dollars), fire deaths, and firefighter casualties
- Providing field service by specialists on electricity, flammable liquids and gases, and marine fire problems
- Conducting research projects that apply statistical methods and operations research to develop computer models and data management systems

3.0.0 The Layout of the *NEC*®

The *NEC*® begins with a brief history. *Figure 1* shows how the *NEC*® is organized.

3.1.0 Types of Rules

There are two basic types of rules in the *NEC*®: mandatory rules and permissive rules. It is important to understand these rules as they are defined in *NEC Section 90.5*. Mandatory rules contain the words "shall" or "shall not" and must be adhered to. Permissive rules identify actions that are allowed but not required and typically cover options or alternative methods. Permissive rules are indicated by the phrases "shall be permitted"

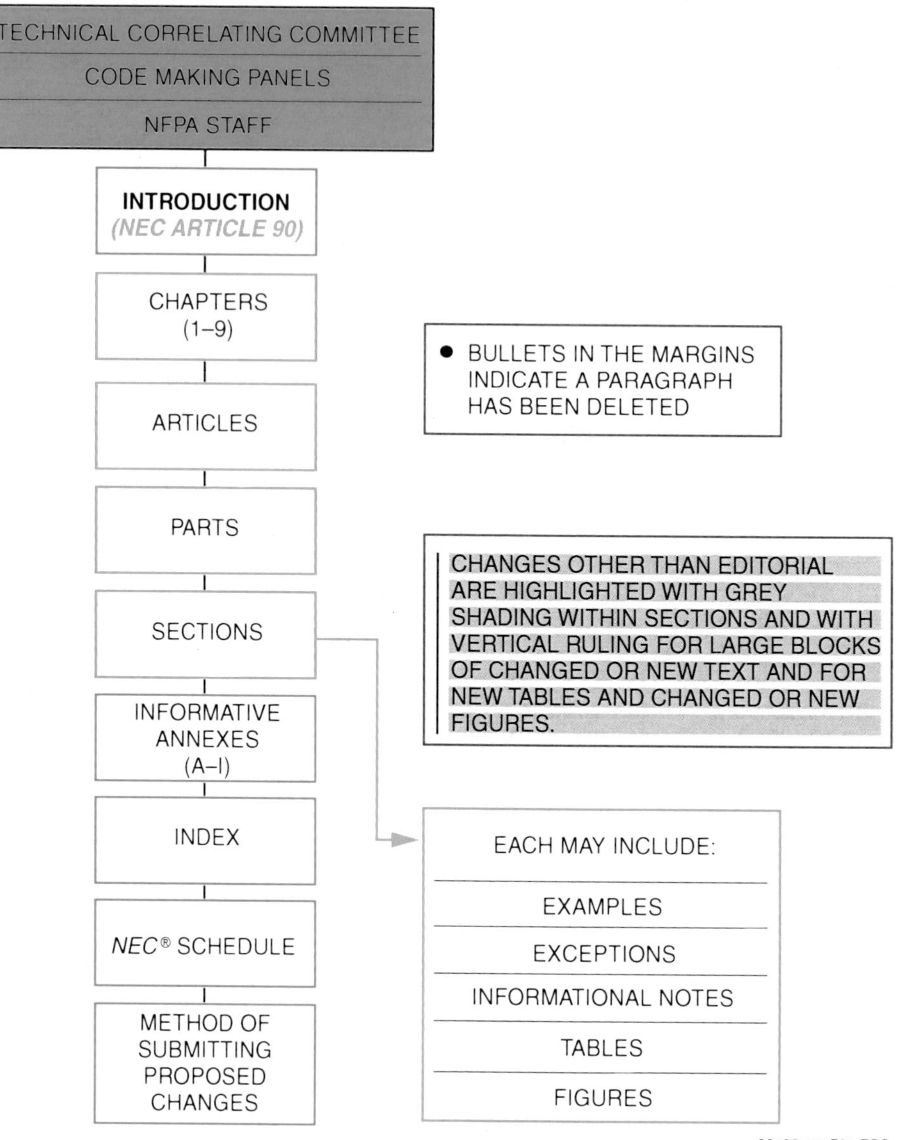

Figure 1 The layout of the *NEC*®.

or "shall not be required." Be aware that local ordinances may amend requirements of the *NEC*®. This means that a city or county may have additional requirements or prohibitions that must be followed in that jurisdiction.

3.2.0 *NEC*® Introduction

The main body of the text begins with an Introduction entitled *NEC Article 90*. This introduction gives you an overview of the *NEC*® (see *Figure 1*). Items included in this section are:

- Purpose of the *NEC*®
- Scope of the code book
- Code arrangement
- Enforcement
- Mandatory rules and explanatory material
- Formal interpretation
- Examination of equipment for safety
- Wiring planning
- Metric units of measurement

3.3.0 The Body of the *NEC*®

The remainder of the code is organized into nine **chapters**, followed by informative annexes, the index, a schedule for the next code cycle, and information on submitting proposed changes.

NEC Chapters 1 through 8 are subdivided into articles. Each chapter focuses on a general category of electrical application, such as *NEC Chapter 2, Wiring and Protection*. Each article emphasizes a more specific **part** of that category, such as *NEC Article 210, Branch Circuits, Part I General Provisions*. Each section gives examples of a specific application of the *NEC*®, such as *NEC Section 210.4, Multiwire*

On Site

NEC® Layout

Remember, chapters contain a group of articles relating to a broad category. An article is a specific subject within that category, such as *NEC Article 250*, *Grounding and Bonding*, which is in Chapter 2 relating to wiring and protection. When an article applies to different installations in the same category, it will be divided into parts using Roman numerals. Any specific requirements in any of the articles may also have exception(s) to the main rules.

Branch Circuits. *NEC Chapter 9* contains tables that are referenced by any of the articles in *NEC Chapters 1 through 8*. *Informative Annexes A through J* provide informational material and examples that are helpful when applying *NEC*® requirements.

The chapters of the *NEC*® are organized into four major categories:

- *NEC Chapters 1, 2, 3, 4* – The first four chapters present the rules for the design and installation of electrical systems. They generally apply to all electrical installations.
- *NEC Chapters 5, 6, and 7* – These chapters are concerned with special occupancies, equipment, and conditions. Rules in these chapters may modify or amend those in the first four chapters.
- *NEC Chapter 8* – This chapter covers communications systems, such as the telephone and television receiving equipment. It may also reference other articles, such as the installation of grounding electrode conductor connections as covered in *NEC Section 250.52*.
- *NEC Chapter 9* – This chapter contains tables that are applicable when referenced by other chapters in the *NEC*®.
- *Informative Annexes A through J* – These annexes contain helpful information that is not mandatory.
  - *Informative Annex A* contains a list of product safety standards. These standards provide further references for requirements that are in addition to the *NEC*® requirements for the electrical components mentioned.
  - *Informative Annex B* contains information for determining ampacities of conductors under engineering supervision.
  - *Informative Annex C* contains the conduit fill tables for multiple conductors of the same size and type within the accepted raceways.
  - *Informative Annex D* contains examples of calculations for branch circuits, feeders, and services as well as load calculations.
  - *Informative Annex E* contains information on types of building construction.
  - *Informative Annex F* provides information on critical operations power systems.
  - *Informative Annex G* is for informational purposes and covers supervisory control and data acquisition (SCADA) systems.
  - *Informative Annex H* contains the requirements for administration and enforcement of the *NEC*®.
  - *Informative Annex I* contains the recommended torque tables from *UL Standard 486-A–B*.
  - *Informative Annex J* contains the ADA Standards for accessible design.

3.4.0 Text in the *NEC*®

When you open the *NEC*®, you will notice several different types of text or printing used. Here is an explanation of each type of text:

- *Bold black letters* – Headings for each *NEC*® application are written in **bold** black letters.
- *Exceptions* – These explain the circumstances under which a specific part of the *NEC*® does not apply. Exceptions are written in *italics* under that part of the *NEC*® to which they pertain.
- *Informational Notes* – These explain something in an application, suggest other sections to read about the application, or provide tips

On Site

The *NEC*® as a Reference Tool

The *NEC*®, although carefully organized, is a highly technical document; as such, it uses many technical words and phrases. It's crucial for you to understand their meaning—if you don't, you'll have trouble understanding the rules themselves. When using the *NEC*® as a reference tool, you may have to refer to a number of articles to find your answer(s). *NEC*® definitions are covered in *NEC Article 100*. Many issues concerning the *NEC*® may be resolved by simply reviewing the definitions.

about the application. These are defined in the text by the term *Informational Note* before an indented paragraph.

- *Figures* – These may be included with explanations to give you a picture of what your application may look like.
- *Tables* – These are often included when there is more than one possible application of the *NEC*®. You would use a table to look up the specifications of your application.

4.0.0 Navigating the *NEC*®

To locate information for a particular procedure being performed, use the following steps:

Step 1 Familiarize yourself with *NEC Articles 90, 100, and 110* to gain an understanding of the material covered in the *NEC*® and the definitions used in it.

Step 2 Turn to the *Table of Contents* at the beginning of the *NEC*®.

Step 3 Locate the chapter that focuses on the desired category.

Step 4 Find the article pertaining to your specific application.

Step 5 Turn to the page indicated. Each application will begin with a bold heading.

NOTE

An index is provided at the end of the *NEC*®. The index lists specific topics and provides a reference to the location of the material within the *NEC*®. The index is helpful when you are looking for a specific topic rather than a general category.

Once you are familiar with *NEC Articles 90, 100, and 110,* you can move on to the rest of the *NEC*®. There are several key sections used often in servicing electrical systems.

4.1.0 *NEC Chapter 1, General*

NEC Article 100 contains a list of common definitions used in the *NEC*®. Definitions specific to a single article are included in the second section of each article. For example, *NEC Section 240.2* contains definitions specific to overcurrent protection.

Two definitions from *NEC Article 100* you should become familiar with are:

- *Labeled* – "Equipment or materials to which has been attached a label, symbol, or other identifying mark of an organization that is acceptable to the authority having jurisdiction and concerned with product evaluation, that maintains periodic inspection of production of labeled equipment or materials, and by whose labeling the manufacturer indicates compliance with appropriate standards or performance in a specified manner."
- *Listed* – "Equipment, materials, or services included in a list published by an organization that is acceptable to the authority having jurisdiction and concerned with evaluation of products or services, that maintains periodic inspection of production of listed equipment or materials, or periodic evaluation of services, and whose listing states that either the equipment, material, or service meets appropriate designated standards or has been tested and found suitable for a specified purpose."

Besides installation rules, you will also have to be concerned with the type and quality of materials that are used in electrical wiring systems. Nationally recognized testing laboratories are product safety certification laboratories. Underwriters Laboratories, Inc., also called UL, is one such laboratory. These laboratories establish and operate product safety certification programs to make sure that items produced under the service are safeguarded against reasonable foreseeable risks. Some of these organizations maintain a worldwide network of field representatives who make unannounced visits to manufacturing facilities to counter-check products bearing their seal of approval. The UL label is shown in *Figure 2*.

NEC Article 110 gives the general requirements for electrical installations. It is important for you to be familiar with this general information and the definitions.

Think About It

Junction Boxes

Find the rule in the *NEC*® that explains whether a junction box without devices can be supported solely by two or more lengths of rigid metal conduit (RMC). Explain the technical terminology in everyday language.

Think About It

NEC Article 90

After you've familiarized yourself with *NEC Article 90,* explain its intent. What part of electrical installation does it not cover?

26105-14_F02.EPS

Figure 2 Underwriters Laboratories label.

4.2.0 *NEC Chapter 2, Wiring and Protection*

NEC Chapter 2 discusses wiring design and protection, the information electrical technicians need most often. It covers the use and identification of grounded conductors, branch circuits, feeders, calculations, services, overcurrent protection, and grounding. This is essential information for all types of electrical systems. If you run into a problem related to the design or installation of a conventional electrical system, you can probably find a solution for it in this chapter.

NEC Article 200 contains important information on the use and identification of grounded conductors.

NEC Articles 210 and 215 cover the provisions and requirements for branch circuits, their ratings and required outlets, and installation and overcurrent protection requirements for feeders.

NEC Article 220 contains the requirements for calculating branch circuit, feeder, and service loads, including the calculation methods for farm loads.

NEC Articles 225 and 230 cover outside branch circuit, feeder, and service installation requirements.

NEC Article 240 covers the requirements for overcurrent protection and overcurrent protective devices, including the standard ratings for fuses and fixed-trip circuit breakers. *NEC Article 240, Part IX* covers overcurrent protection for installations over 1,000 volts.

NEC Article 250 covers the requirements for grounding and bonding electrical systems. It lists the systems required, permitted, and not permitted to be grounded and provides the requirements for grounding connection locations. It also covers accepted methods of grounding and bonding, including types and sizes of grounding and bonding conductors and electrodes.

On Site

Underwriters Laboratories®

The Chicago World's Fair was opened in 1893 and thanks to Edison's introduction of the electric light bulb, included a light display called the Palace of Electricity. But all was not perfect—wires soon sputtered and crackled, and, ironically, the Palace of Electricity caught fire. The fair's insurance company called in a troubleshooting engineer, who, after careful inspection, found faulty and brittle insulation, worn-out and deteriorated wiring, bare wires, and overloaded circuits. This engineer, William Henry Merrill, called for standards in the electrical industry and then set up a testing laboratory above a Chicago firehouse to do just that. An independent testing organization, Underwriters Electrical Bureau, was born. UL is now an internationally recognized authority on product safety testing and safety certification and standards development.

Think About It

Other Testing Laboratories

In addition to UL, there are several other recognized testing laboratories. How many can you name?

4.3.0 *NEC Chapter 3, General Requirements for Wiring Methods and Materials*

NEC Chapter 3 lists the rules on wiring methods and materials. The materials and procedures to use on a particular system depend on the type of building construction, the type of occupancy, the location of the wiring in the building, the type of atmosphere in the building or in the area surrounding the building, mechanical factors, and the relative costs of different wiring methods. The general requirements for conductors and wiring methods that form an integral part of manufactured equipment are not included in the requirements of the code per *NEC Article 300.1(B)*.

NEC Article 300 provides the general requirements for all wiring methods and materials, including information such as minimum burial depths and permitted wiring methods for areas above suspended ceilings.

NEC Article 310 contains a description of acceptable conductors for the wiring methods contained in *NEC Chapter 3*.

NEC Articles 312 and 314 give rules for boxes, cabinets, conduit bodies, and raceway fittings. Outlet boxes vary in size and shape, depending on their use, the size of the raceway, the number of conductors entering the box, the type of building construction, and the atmospheric conditions of the area. These articles should answer most questions on the selection and use of these items.

The *NEC*® does not describe in detail all types and sizes of outlet boxes. However, the manufacturers of outlet boxes provide excellent catalogs showing their products. Collect these catalogs, since these items are essential to your work.

NEC Articles 320 through 340 cover sheathed cables of two or more conductors, such as nonmetallic-sheathed and metal-clad cable.

NEC Articles 342 through 356 cover conduit wiring systems, such as rigid and flexible metal and nonmetallic conduit.

NEC Articles 358 through 362 cover tubing wiring methods, such as electrical metallic and nonmetallic tubing.

NEC Articles 366 through 390 cover other wiring methods, such as busways and wireways. *NEC Article 392* covers cable trays. *NEC Article 393* covers low-voltage suspended ceiling power distribution systems.

4.4.0 *NEC Chapter 4, Equipment for General Use*

NEC Article 400 covers the use and installation of flexible cords and cables, including the trade name, type letter, wire size, number of conductors, conductor insulation, outer covering, and use of each. *NEC Article 402* covers fixture wires, again giving the trade name, type letter, and other important details.

NEC Article 404 covers the requirements for the uses and installation of switches, switching devices, and circuit breakers where used as switches.

NEC Article 406 gives the rules for the ratings, types, and installation of receptacles, cord connectors, and attachment plugs (cord caps).

NEC Article 408 covers the requirements for switchboards, switchgear, and panelboards used to control light and power circuits.

Think About It

Disconnects

How would you proceed to find the *NEC*® rule for the maximum number of disconnects permitted for a service?

NEC Article 410 on luminaires is especially important. It gives installation procedures for luminaires in specific locations. For example, it covers luminaires near combustible material and luminaires in closets. However, the *NEC*® does not describe how many luminaires will be needed in a given area to provide a certain amount of illumination.

NEC Article 422 covers the use of electric appliances in any occupancy. It includes kitchen appliances, various heating appliances, cord-and-plug connected equipment, and other appliances.

NEC Article 424 covers fixed electric space-heating equipment. It includes heating cable, unit heaters, boilers, central systems, and other approved equipment.

NEC Article 430 covers electric motors, including electrical connections, motor controls, and overload protection.

NEC Articles 440 through 460 cover air conditioning and refrigerating equipment, generators, transformers, phase converters, and capacitors.

NEC Article 480 provides requirements related to battery-operated electrical systems. Storage batteries are seldom thought of as part of a conventional electrical system, but they often provide standby emergency lighting service. They may also supply power to security systems that are separate from the main AC electrical system.

4.5.0 *NEC Chapter 5, Special Occupancies*

NEC Chapter 5 covers special occupancy areas. These are areas where the sparks generated by electrical equipment may cause an explosion or fire. The hazard may be due to the atmosphere of the area or the presence of a volatile material in the area. Commercial garages, aircraft hangars, and service stations are typical special occupancy locations.

NEC Article 500 covers the different types of special occupancy atmospheres where an explosion is possible. The atmospheric groups were established to make it easy to test and approve equipment for various types of uses.

NEC Articles 501.10, 502.10, and 503.10 cover the installation of explosion-proof wiring. An explosion-proof system is designed to prevent the ignition of a surrounding explosive atmosphere when arcing occurs within the electrical system.

There are three main classes of special occupancy location:

- *Class I* – Areas containing flammable gases or vapors in the air. Class I areas include paint spray booths, dyeing plants where hazardous

Think About It

Sealing Requirements

Study *NEC Section 501.15.* Summarize key points. Discuss your interpretation with the rest of the class.

liquids are used, and gas generator rooms *(NEC Article 501)*.

- *Class II* – Areas where combustible dust is present, such as grain-handling and storage plants, dust and stock collector areas, and sugar-pulverizing plants *(NEC Article 502)*. These are areas where, under normal operating conditions, there may be enough combustible dust in the air to produce explosive or ignitable mixtures.
- *Class III* – Areas that are hazardous because of the presence of easily ignitable fibers or other particles in the air, although not in large enough quantities to produce ignitable mixtures *(NEC Article 503)*. Class III locations include cotton mills, rayon mills, and clothing manufacturing plants.

NEC Articles 511 and 514 regulate garages and fuel dispensing locations where volatile or flammable liquids are used. While these areas are not always considered critically hazardous locations, there may be enough danger to require special precautions in the electrical installation. In these areas, the *NEC®* requires that volatile gases be confined to an area not more than eighteen inches above the floor or tank. See *NEC Table 514.3(B)(2)*. So in most cases, conventional raceway systems are permitted above this level. If the area is judged to be critically hazardous, explosion-proof wiring (including seal-offs) may be required.

NEC Article 520 regulates theaters and similar occupancies where fire and panic can cause hazards to life and property. Projection rooms and adjacent areas must be properly ventilated and wired for the protection of operating personnel and others using the area.

NEC Chapter 5 also covers floating buildings, marinas, agricultural buildings, service stations, bulk storage plants, health care facilities, mobile homes and parks, and temporary installations.

4.6.0 *NEC Chapter 6, Special Equipment*

NEC Article 600 covers electric signs and outline lighting. *NEC Article 610* applies to cranes and hoists. *NEC Article 620* covers the majority of the electrical work involved in the installation and operation of elevators, dumbwaiters, escalators, and moving walks. The manufacturer is responsible for most of this work. The electrician usually just furnishes a feeder terminating in a disconnect means in the bottom of the elevator shaft. The electrician may also be responsible for a lighting circuit to a junction box midway in the elevator shaft for connecting the elevator cage lighting cable and exhaust fans. The articles in this chapter list most of the requirements for these installations.

NEC Article 630 regulates electric welding equipment. It is normally treated as a piece of industrial power equipment requiring a special power outlet, but there are special conditions that apply to the circuits supplying welding equipment. These are outlined in detail in this chapter.

NEC Article 640 covers wiring for sound recording and similar equipment. This type of equipment normally requires low-voltage wiring. Special outlet boxes or cabinets are usually provided with the equipment, but some items may be mounted in or on standard outlet boxes. Some sound recording systems require direct current. It is supplied from rectifying equipment, batteries, or motor generators. Low-voltage alternating current comes from relatively small transformers connected on the primary side to a 120V circuit within the building.

Other items covered in *NEC Chapter 6* include X-ray equipment *(NEC Article 660)*, induction and dielectric heat-generating equipment *(NEC Article 665)*, industrial machinery *(NEC Article 670)*, swimming pools and fountains *(NEC Article 680)*, and solar photovoltaic (PV) systems *(NEC Article 690)*.

4.7.0 *NEC Chapter 7, Special Conditions*

In most commercial buildings, the *NEC®* and local ordinances require a means of lighting public rooms, halls, stairways, and entrances. There must be enough light to allow the occupants to exit from the building if the general building lighting is interrupted. Exit doors must be clearly indicated by illuminated exit signs.

NEC Chapter 7 covers the installation of emergency and legally required standby systems. These circuits should be arranged so that they can automatically transfer to an alternate source

On Site

Different Interpretations

For as many trainees in class with you today, there will be as many different interpretations of the *NEC®*. However, a difference of opinion is not always a problem—discussing the *NEC®* will allow you to expand your own understanding of it. In your previous discussion about *NEC Section 501.15*, what differences of interpretation did you have to resolve?

of current, usually storage batteries or gasoline-driven generators. As an alternative in some types of occupancies, you can connect them to the supply side of the main service, so disconnecting the main service switch would not disconnect the emergency circuits. This chapter also covers fire alarms and a variety of other equipment, systems, and conditions that are not easily categorized elsewhere in the *NEC*®.

4.8.0 *NEC Chapter 8, Communications Systems*

NEC Chapter 8 is a special category for wiring associated with electronic communications systems including telephone, radio and TV, satellite dish, network-powered broadband systems, and community antenna systems.

4.9.0 Examples of Navigating the *NEC*®

Using your copy of the 2014 *NEC*®, follow along with these sample scenarios to familiarize yourself with the layout of the *NEC*®.

4.9.1 Installing Type SE Cable

Suppose you are installing Type SE (service-entrance) cable on the side of a home. You know that this cable must be secured, but you are not sure of the spacing between cable clamps. To find out this information, use the following procedure:

Step 1 Look in the *NEC*® *Table of Contents* and follow down the list until you find an appropriate category. (Or you can use the index at the end of the book.)

Step 2 *NEC Article 230* will probably catch your eye first, so turn to the page where it begins.

Step 3 Scan down through the section numbers until you come to *NEC Section 230.51, Mounting Supports.* Upon reading this section, you will find in paragraph *(A) Service-Entrance Cables* that "service-entrance cables shall be supported by straps or other approved means within 300 mm (12 in) of every service head, gooseneck, or connection to a raceway or enclosure and at intervals not exceeding 750 mm (30 in)."

After reading this section, you will know that a cable strap is required within 12 inches of the service head and within 12 inches of the meter base. Furthermore, the cable must be secured in between these two termination points at intervals not exceeding 30 inches.

4.9.2 Installing Track Lighting

Assume that you are installing track lighting in a residential occupancy. The owners want the track located behind the curtain of their sliding glass patio doors. To determine if this is an *NEC*® violation, follow these steps:

Step 1 Look in the *NEC*® *Table of Contents* and find the chapter that contains information about the general application you are working on. *NEC Chapter 4, Equipment for General Use,* covers track lighting.

Step 2 Now look for the article that fits the specific category you are working on. In this case, *NEC Article 410* covers luminaires, lampholders, and lamps.

Step 3 Next locate the section within *NEC Article 410* that deals with the specific application. For this example, refer to *Part XIV, Lighting Track.*

Step 4 Turn to the page listed.

Step 5 Read *NEC Section 410.2, Definitions,* to become familiar with track lighting. Then go to *NEC Section 410.151* and read the information contained therein. Note that paragraph *(C) Locations Not Permitted* under *NEC Section 410.151* states the following: "Lighting track shall not be installed in the following locations: (1) where likely to be subjected to physical damage; (2) in wet or damp locations; (3) where subject to corrosive vapors; (4) in storage battery rooms; (5) in hazardous (classified) locations; (6) where concealed; (7) where extended through walls or partitions; (8) less than 1.5 m (5 ft) above the finished floor except where protected from physical damage or track operating at less than 30 volts rms open-circuit voltage; (9) where prohibited by *NEC Section 410.10(D).*"

Step 6 Read *NEC Section 410.151(C)* carefully. Do you see any conditions that would violate any *NEC*® requirements if the track lighting is installed in the area specified? In checking these items, you will probably note condition (6), "where concealed." Since the track lighting is to be installed behind a curtain, this sounds like an *NEC*® violation. You need to check further.

Step 7 You need the *NEC*® definition of *concealed*. Therefore, turn to *NEC Article 100, Definitions* and find the main term *concealed*. It reads: "**Concealed**. Rendered inaccessible by the structure or finish of the building."

On Site

NFPA Codes and Standards

In addition to the *NEC*®, NFPA also publishes many other codes and standards. Two that are of interest to the electrician are *NFPA 70E*®, *Standard for Electrical Safety in the Workplace* and *NFPA 70B, Recommended Practice for Electrical Equipment Maintenance. NFPA 70E*® provides direction on the safe installation, operation, and maintenance of electrical equipment. *NFPA 70B* provides direction for performing electrical tests, inspection, and maintenance procedures. Both documents are excellent resources for the electrical professional.

Step 8 Although the track lighting may be out of sight if the curtain is drawn, it will still be readily accessible for maintenance. Consequently, the track lighting is really not concealed according to the *NEC*® definition.

When using the *NEC*® to determine electrical installation requirements, keep in mind that you will nearly always have to refer to more than one section. Sometimes the *NEC*® itself refers the reader to other articles and sections. In some cases, the user will have to be familiar enough with the *NEC*® to know what other sections pertain to the installation at hand. It can be a confusing situation, but time and experience in using the *NEC*® will make it much easier. A pictorial road map of some *NEC*® topics is shown in *Figure 3*.

5.0.0 Other Organizations

In support of the requirements of the *NEC*® there are other organizations that identify conformance standards for the manufacture and/or use of electrical products.

5.1.0 Nationally Recognized Testing Laboratories

Nationally Recognized Testing Laboratories (NRTLs) are product safety certification laboratories. These laboratories perform extensive testing of new products to make sure they are built to established standards for electrical and fire safety. They establish and operate product safety certification programs to make sure that items produced under the service are safeguarded against reasonably foreseeable risks. NRTLs maintain a worldwide network of field representatives who make unannounced visits to factories to check products bearing their safety marks.

Think About It

Conformance and Electrical Equipment

What other resources are available for finding information about the use of electrical equipment and materials?

5.2.0 National Electrical Manufacturers Association

The National Electrical Manufacturers Association (NEMA) was founded in 1926. It is made up of companies that manufacture equipment used for generation, transmission, distribution, control, and utilization of electric power. The objectives of NEMA are to maintain and improve the quality and reliability of products; to ensure safety standards in the manufacture and use of products; and to develop product standards covering such matters as naming, ratings, performance, testing, and dimensions. NEMA participates in developing the *NEC*® and advocates its acceptance by state and local authorities.

Think About It

Putting It All Together

Look around you at the electrical components and products used and the quality of the work. Do you see any components or products that have not been listed or labeled? If so, how might these devices put you in harm's way? Do you see any code violations?

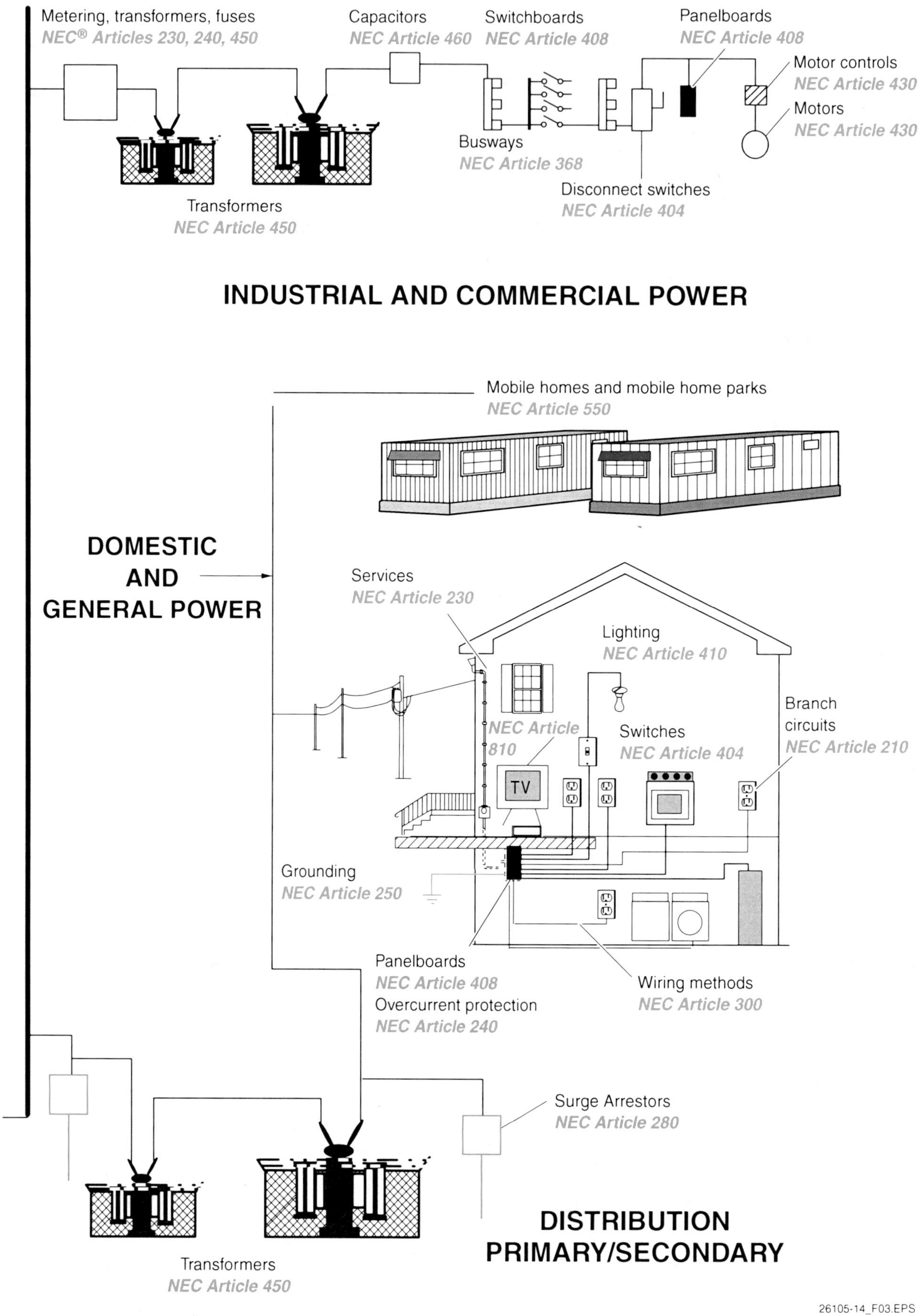

Metering, transformers, fuses
NEC® Articles 230, 240, 450

Capacitors
NEC Article 460

Switchboards
NEC Article 408

Panelboards
NEC Article 408

Motor controls
NEC Article 430

Motors
NEC Article 430

Busways
NEC Article 368

Disconnect switches
NEC Article 404

Transformers
NEC Article 450

INDUSTRIAL AND COMMERCIAL POWER

Mobile homes and mobile home parks
NEC Article 550

DOMESTIC AND GENERAL POWER

Services
NEC Article 230

Lighting
NEC Article 410

NEC Article 810

TV

Switches
NEC Article 404

Branch circuits
NEC Article 210

Grounding
NEC Article 250

Panelboards
NEC Article 408
Overcurrent protection
NEC Article 240

Wiring methods
NEC Article 300

Surge Arrestors
NEC Article 280

DISTRIBUTION PRIMARY/SECONDARY

Transformers
NEC Article 450

26105-14_F03.EPS

Figure 3 NEC® references for industrial, commercial, and residential power.

Summary

The *NEC*® specifies the minimum provisions necessary for protecting people and property from hazards arising from the use of electricity and electrical equipment. As an electrician, you must be aware of how to use and apply the *NEC*® on the job site. Using the *NEC*® will help you to safely install and maintain the electrical equipment and systems you come into contact with.

Review Questions

1. What word or phrase best describes the *NEC*® requirements for the installation of electrical systems?
   a. Minimum
   b. Most stringent
   c. Design specification
   d. Complete

2. All of the following groups are usually represented on the Code Making Panels *except* _____.
   a. trade associations
   b. electrical inspectors
   c. insurance organizations
   d. government lobbyists

3. Mandatory and permissive rules are defined in _____.
   a. *NEC Article 90*
   b. *NEC Article 100*
   c. *NEC Article 110*
   d. *NEC Article 200*

4. The general design and installation of electrical systems is covered in _____.
   a. *NEC Chapters 1, 2, and 7*
   b. *NEC Chapters 1, 2, 3, and 4*
   c. *NEC Chapters 6, 7, and 8*
   d. *NEC Chapters 5, 6, 7, and 9*

5. Devices such as radios, televisions, and telephones are covered in _____.
   a. *NEC Chapter 8*
   b. *NEC Chapter 7*
   c. *NEC Chapter 6*
   d. *NEC Chapter 5*

6. Examples of branch circuit calculations can be found in _____.
   a. *NEC Informative Annex A*
   b. *NEC Informative Annex C*
   c. *NEC Informative Annex D*
   d. *NEC Informative Annex G*

7. *NEC Article 110* covers _____.
   a. branch circuits
   b. definitions
   c. general requirements for electrical installations
   d. wiring design and protection

8. Cable trays are covered in _____.
   a. *NEC Article 330*
   b. *NEC Article 342*
   c. *NEC Article 368*
   d. *NEC Article 392*

Questions 9 through 12 are two-part questions that ask you to first locate an article in the *NEC*®, and then answer a question using the article.

9. Where in the *NEC*® would you find information on conductors for general wiring?
   a. *NEC Article 280*
   b. *NEC Article 310*
   c. *NEC Article 404*
   d. *NEC Article 340*

10. Within the article found in Question 9, locate information on stranded conductors. What size conductors must be stranded when installed in raceways?
    a. 14 AWG or larger
    b. 12 AWG or larger
    c. 10 AWG or larger
    d. 8 AWG or larger

11. Where in the *NEC*® would you find information on switchboards and panelboards?
    a. *NEC Article 285*
    b. *NEC Article 300*
    c. *NEC Article 408*
    d. *NEC Article 540*

12. Within the article found in Question 11, find the section that covers switchboard clearances. Assuming the switchboard does not have a noncombustible shield, what is the minimum clearance between the top of the switchboard and a combustible ceiling?

    a. 12 inches
    b. 18 inches
    c. 24 inches
    d. 36 inches

13. Installation procedures for luminaires are provided in _____.

    a. *NEC Article 410*
    b. *NEC Article 408*
    c. *NEC Article 366*
    d. *NEC Article 460*

14. Theaters are covered in _____.

    a. *NEC Article 338*
    b. *NEC Article 110*
    c. *NEC Article 430*
    d. *NEC Article 520*

15. *NEC Article 600* covers _____.

    a. track lighting
    b. electric signs and outline lighting
    c. X-ray equipment
    d. emergency lighting systems

Trade Terms Quiz

Fill in the blank with the correct term that you learned from your study of this module.

1. ____________ are the main topics of the *NEC*®.
2. Nine ____________ form the broad structure of the *NEC*®.
3. Certain articles in the *NEC*® are subdivided into lettered ____________.
4. Parts and articles are subdivided into numbered ____________.
5. Although they follow the applicable sections of the *NEC*®, ____________ allow alternative methods to be used under specific conditions.
6. A(n) ____________ is explanatory material that follows specific *NEC*® sections.
7. The ____________ is an organization that maintains and improves the quality and reliability of electrical products.
8. The ____________ publishes the *NEC*®; it also develops standards to minimize the possibility and effects of fire.
9. ____________ are organizations that are responsible for testing and certifying electrical equipment.

Trade Terms

Articles
Chapters
Exceptions
Informational Note
National Electrical Manufacturers Association (NEMA)
National Fire Protection Association (NFPA)
Nationally Recognized Testing Laboratories (NRTLs)
Parts
Sections

Module 26105-14
Supplemental Exercises

1. The *NEC*® is made up of ___________ chapters.

2. The *NEC*® provides the ___________ requirements for the installation of electrical systems.

3. *NEC Chapter 2* covers ___________.
   a. wiring and protection
   b. lighting
   c. occupancy
   d. emergency

4. Which of the following covers electric motors?
   a. *NEC Article 230*
   b. *NEC Article 330*
   c. *NEC Article 430*
   d. *NEC Article 130*

5. *NEC Article 520* covers ___________ and similar occupancies where fire and panic can cause hazards to life and property.

6. To size grounding conductors, refer to ___________.
   a. *NEC Chapter 1*
   b. *NEC Chapter 2*
   c. *NEC Chapter 3*
   d. *NEC Chapter 4*

7. Wiring methods are covered in ___________.
   a. *NEC Chapter 1*
   b. *NEC Chapter 2*
   c. *NEC Chapter 3*
   d. *NEC Chapter 4*

8. Gas stations are covered in ___________.
   a. *NEC Chapter 5*
   b. *NEC Chapter 6*
   c. *NEC Chapter 7*
   d. *NEC Chapter 8*

9. Emergency systems are covered in ___________.
   a. *NEC Chapter 6*
   b. *NEC Chapter 7*
   c. *NEC Chapter 8*
   d. *NEC Chapter 9*

10. Fire alarm systems are covered in ___________.
    a. *NEC Chapter 6*
    b. *NEC Chapter 7*
    c. *NEC Chapter 8*
    d. *NEC Chapter 9*

11. Definitions are covered in ____________.

12. Metric units of measurement are covered in ____________.

13. X-ray equipment is covered in ____________.

    a. *NEC Article 665*
    b. *NEC Article 660*
    c. *NEC Article 670*
    d. *NEC Article 650*

14. ____________ contains tables that specify the properties of conductors.

    a. *NEC Chapter 8*
    b. *NEC Chapter 9*
    c. *NEC Chapter 7*
    d. *NEC Chapter 6*

15. Electric signs are covered in ____________.

    a. *NEC Chapter 8*
    b. *NEC Chapter 7*
    c. *NEC Chapter 6*
    d. *NEC Chapter 9*

Cornerstone of Craftsmanship

Christine Thorstensen Porter

Intertek Testing Services

How did you choose a career in the electrical field?
It was "in the blood," literally. My father had his own electrical contracting company and was an instructor for our apprenticeship/training program. One day, my husband, who also worked for my dad, gave me a tool belt and sent me through the Construction Industry Training Council's (CITC) apprenticeship program in Seattle, Washington. Since my father taught many of the classes, the pressure was on. I felt that I had to perform well. My father was a major influence on me both as an electrician, and as a student leader. Eventually, I went into the estimating side of things in my dad's business.

In the fourth year of my apprenticeship program I was taking a lot of estimating and project management courses and applying the skills I gained in the field. My dad's business was high-end residential and some small commercial work. We'd have a crew on site from six months to a year until the projects were complete. A lot of the installations we did were data systems and computer-controlled security systems. When I took the Administrator's exam, that gave me my qualifications to supervise.

What positions have you held in the industry?
In 1981 I was a teaching assistant. That teacher started a new review class for electricians needing to pass journeyman and administrative exams; I took over his second-year apprenticeship/trainee class. To better prepare myself for my new teaching role, I took various classes offered by the International Association of Electrical Inspectors (IAEI), but I was dismayed and disappointed with the instructor because he merely read the *NEC®* to us, instead of giving us any insights as to how the *NEC®* could impact our installations, or why any particular *NEC®* rule was in place. So I also ended up getting involved with teaching classes for the IAEI.

My experience with IAEI gave me a solid grounding in the Code. It also led to more local involvement. In fact, I'm now the chairman of the city's Electrical Code Advisory Committee. I have also served on the Technical Advisory Committee for our state amendments to the *NEC®*.

What does your current job involve?
I teach the second-year electrical training program at CITC. I teach courses for IAEI. I perform inspections for Intertek Testing Services, and I serve on a variety of committees. In addition to chairing the Electrical Code Advisory Committee, I'm a Senior Associate member of the Puget Sound Chapter of IAEI; I sit on the city of Seattle's Construction Codes Advisory Board and am a subject matter expert for NCCER's *Contren®* Electrical curriculum.

Do you have any advice for someone just entering the trade?
I'd tell them that the electrical trade is extremely rich and diverse. There is so much that you can do. From installing all different types of systems, to project management, and to estimating, the field is wide open. The job never stays dull. The field changes with all the changes in technology. Because of that, there are so many new and emerging jobs within the trade. As far as becoming a success, I'd say to keep abreast of changes—changes in the Code and in technology—and stay connected. A good way to do that is to join associations such as IAEI. Network and continue your training. It never ends in this field. Also, spend time mentoring others. You learn more that way, by giving yourself.

Trade Terms Introduced in This Module

Articles: The articles are the main topics of the *NEC®*, beginning with *NEC Article 90, Introduction,* and ending with *NEC Article 840, Premises-Powered Broadband Communications Systems.*

Chapters: Nine chapters form the broad structure of the *NEC®*.

Exceptions: Exceptions follow the applicable sections of the *NEC®* and allow alternative methods to be used under specific conditions.

Informational Note: Explanatory material that follows specific *NEC®* sections.

National Electrical Manufacturers Association (NEMA): The association that maintains and improves the quality and reliability of electrical products.

National Fire Protection Association (NFPA): The publishers of the *NEC®*. The NFPA develops standards to minimize the possibility and effects of fire.

Nationally Recognized Testing Laboratories (NRTLs): Product safety certification laboratories that are responsible for testing and certifying electrical equipment.

Parts: Certain articles in the *NEC®* are subdivided into parts. Parts have letter designations (e.g., Part A).

Sections: Parts and articles are subdivided into sections. Sections have numeric designations that follow the article number and are preceded by a period (e.g., 501.4).

Additional Resources

This module presents thorough resources for task training. The following resource material is suggested for further study.

National Electrical Code® Handbook, Latest Edition. Quincy, MA: National Fire Protection Association.

Figure Credits

Associated Builders and Contractors, Inc., Module opener

John Traister, Figure 3

Topaz Publications, Inc., SA01, SA02, SA04

Tim Ely, SA03

NCCER CURRICULA — USER UPDATE

NCCER makes every effort to keep its textbooks up-to-date and free of technical errors. We appreciate your help in this process. If you find an error, a typographical mistake, or an inaccuracy in NCCER's curricula, please fill out this form (or a photocopy), or complete the online form at **www.nccer.org/olf**. Be sure to include the exact module ID number, page number, a detailed description, and your recommended correction. Your input will be brought to the attention of the Authoring Team. Thank you for your assistance.

Instructors – If you have an idea for improving this textbook, or have found that additional materials were necessary to teach this module effectively, please let us know so that we may present your suggestions to the Authoring Team.

NCCER Product Development and Revision
13614 Progress Blvd., Alachua, FL 32615
Email: curriculum@nccer.org
Online: www.nccer.org/olf

❑ Trainee Guide ❑ AIG ❑ Exam ❑ PowerPoints Other ______________________

Craft / Level: Copyright Date:

Module ID Number / Title:

Section Number(s):

Description:

Recommended Correction:

Your Name:

Address:

Email: Phone:

Conductors and Cables

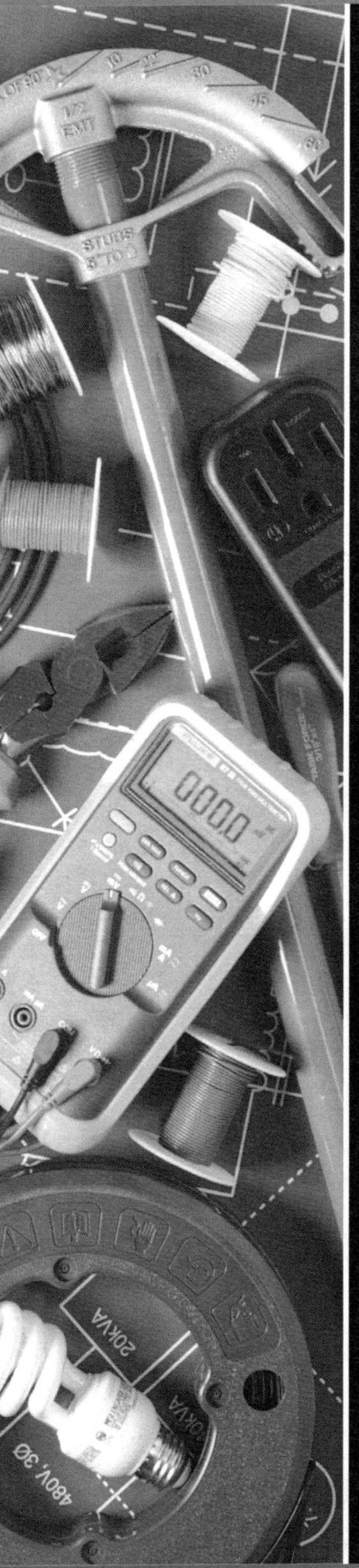

Forest Park-DeBaliviere Station

This MetroLink expansion project in downtown St. Louis used concrete in prolific ways, using more than 500 feet of concrete sewer bridges, installing three cut-and-cover tunnels totaling 1,400 linear feet, and constructing a pedestrian tunnel under a major thoroughfare. The expansion, which opened in August 2006, provides MetroLink customers with a new, eight-mile light rail line.

26109-14

Trainees with successful module completions may be eligible for credentialing through NCCER's National Registry. To learn more, go to **www.nccer.org** or contact us at **1.888.622.3720.** Our website has information on the latest product releases and training, as well as online versions of our *Cornerstone* magazine and Pearson's product catalog.

Your feedback is welcome. You may email your comments to **curriculum@nccer.org,** send general comments and inquiries to **info@nccer.org,** or fill in the User Update form at the back of this module.

This information is general in nature and intended for training purposes only. Actual performance of activities described in this manual requires compliance with all applicable operating, service, maintenance, and safety procedures under the direction of qualified personnel. References in this manual to patented or proprietary devices do not constitute a recommendation of their use.

26109-14

Conductors and Cables

Objectives

When you have completed this module, you will be able to do the following:

1. From the cable markings, describe the insulation and jacket material, conductor size and type, number of conductors, temperature rating, voltage rating, and permitted uses.
2. Determine the allowable ampacity of a conductor for a given application.
3. Identify the *NEC*® requirements for color coding of conductors.
4. Install conductors in a raceway system.

Performance Task

Under the supervision of the instructor, you should be able to do the following:

1. Install conductors in a raceway system.

Trade Terms

Ampacity
Capstan
Fish tape
Mouse
Wire grip

Required Trainee Materials

1. Paper and pencil
2. Copy of the latest edition of the *National Electrical Code*®
3. Appropriate personal protective equipment

Note:
NFPA 70®, *National Electrical Code*®, and *NEC*® are registered trademarks of the National Fire Protection Association, Inc., Quincy, MA 02269. All *National Electrical Code*® and *NEC*® references in this module refer to the 2014 edition of the *National Electrical Code*®.

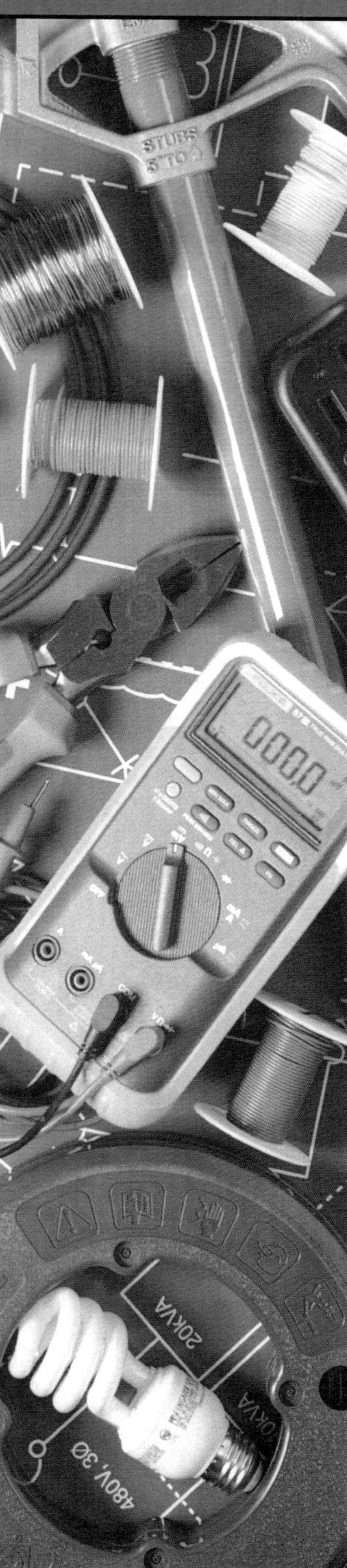

Contents

Topics to be presented in this module include:

Figures and Tables

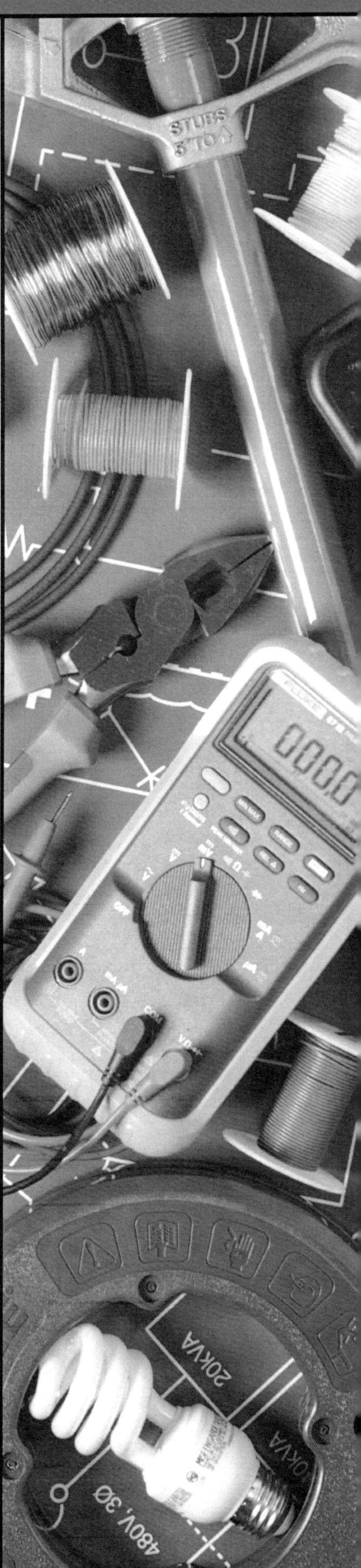

1.0.0 Introduction

As an electrician, you will be required to select the proper wire and/or cable for a job. You will also be required to pull this wire or cable through conduit runs in order to terminate it. This module describes the different types of conductors and conductor insulation. It also explains how these conductors are rated and classified by the *NEC®*. Different methods used for pulling these conductors through conduit runs are also discussed.

2.0.0 Conductors and Insulation

The term *conductor* is used in two ways. It is used to describe the current-carrying portion of a wire or cable, and it is used to describe a wire or cable composed of the current-carrying portion and an outer covering (insulation). In this module, the term *conductor*, if not specified otherwise, is used to describe the wire assembly, which includes the insulation and the current-carrying portion of the wire.

Conductors are uniquely identified by size and insulation material. Size refers to the cross-sectional area of the current-carrying portion of the wire. The ampacity is affected by the conductor material and size, insulation, and installation location.

2.1.0 Wire Size

Wire sizes are expressed in gauge numbers. The standard system of wire sizes in the United States is the American Wire Gauge (AWG) system.

2.1.1 AWG System

The AWG system uses numbers to identify the different sizes of wire and cable (*Figure 1*). The larger the number, the smaller the cross-sectional area of the wire. The larger the cross-sectional area of the current-carrying portion of a conductor, the higher the amount of current the wire can conduct. The AWG numbers range from 50 to 1; then 0, 00, 000, and 0000 (one aught [1/0], two aught [2/0], three aught [3/0], and four aught [4/0]). Any wire larger than 0000 is identified by its area in circular mils. Wire sizes smaller than No. 18 AWG are usually solid, but may be stranded in some cases. Wire sizes of No. 6 AWG or larger are stranded.

For wire sizes larger than No. 16 AWG, the wire size is marked on the insulation (*Figure 2*).

NEC Chapter 9, Table 8 has descriptive information on wire sizes. Again, note that all wires smaller than No. 6 are available as solid or stranded. Wire sizes of No. 6 or larger are shown only as stranded. Solid wire larger than No. 6 is manufactured; however, the *NEC®* only permits the use of solid wire in a raceway for sizes smaller than No. 8 per *NEC Section 310.106(C)*.

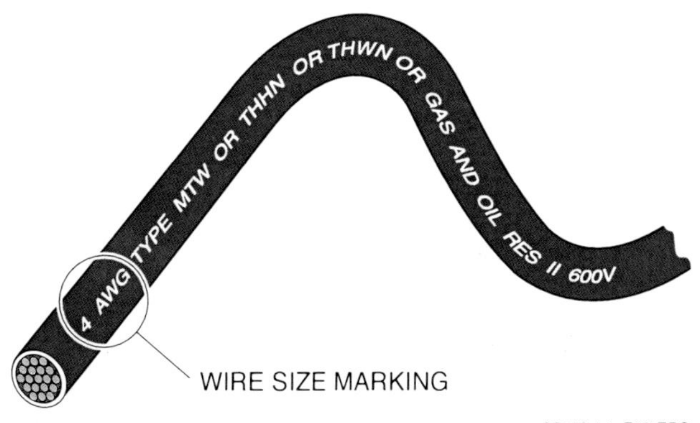

Figure 2 Wire size marking.

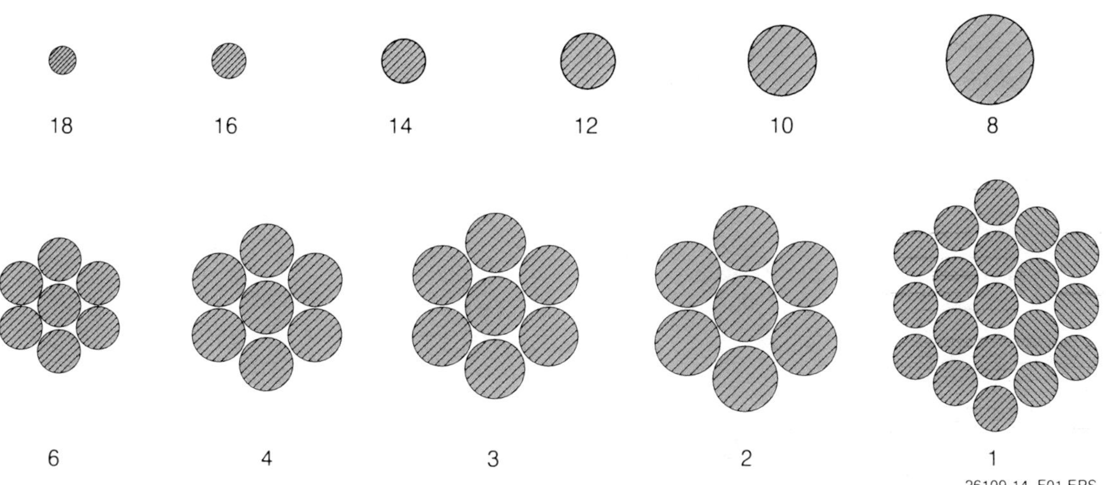

Figure 1 Comparison of wire sizes (enlarged) from No. 18 to No. 1 AWG.

Think About It

Wire Size

Why is wire size a critical factor in a wiring system? Other than load, what other factors may dictate wire size? What can happen when a wire isn't properly sized for the load?

2.1.2 Stranding

According to *NEC Chapter 9, Table 8,* wire sizes No. 18 to No. 2 have seven strands; wire sizes No. 1 to No. 4/0 have 19 strands; and wire sizes between 250 kcmil and 500 kcmil have 37 strands. The purpose of stranding is to increase the flexibility of the wire. Terminating solid wire sizes larger than No. 8 in pull boxes, disconnect switches, and panels would not only be very difficult, but might also result in damage to equipment and wire insulation.

Pulling solid wire in conduit around bends could pose a major problem and cause damage to equipment for wire sizes larger than No. 8. The reason for choosing 7, 19, and 37 strands for stranded conductors is that it is necessary to provide a flexible, almost round conductor. In order for a conductor to be flexible, individual strands must not be too large. *Figure 3* shows how these conductors are configured.

Aluminum conductors are designed with compact (compressed) stranding. See *Figure 4*.

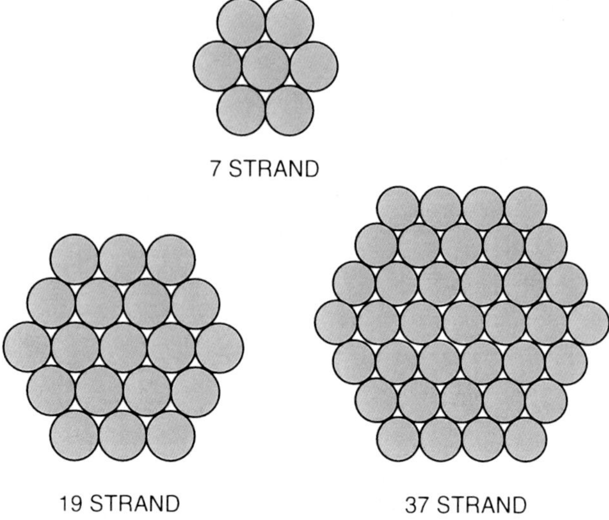

Figure 3 Strand configurations.

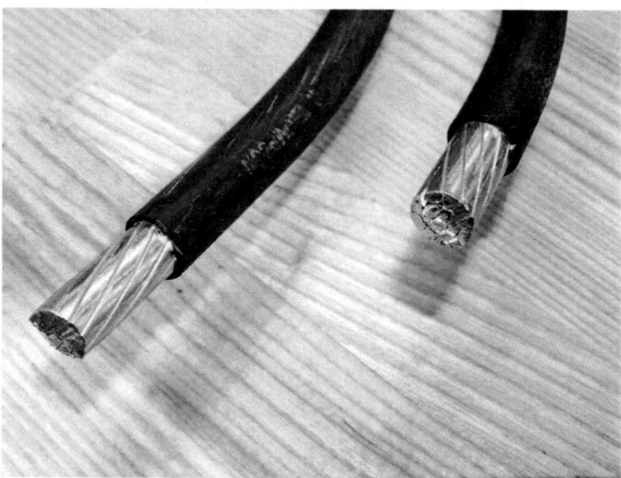

Figure 4 Aluminum conductors.

2.1.3 Circular Mils

A circular mil is a circle that has a diameter of 1 mil. A mil is 0.001 inch. When a wire size is 250 kcmil, the cross-sectional area of the current-carrying portion of the wire is the same as 250,000 circles having a diameter of 0.001 inch. This may seem to be a rather clumsy way of sizing wire at first; however, the alternative would be to size the wire as a function of its cross-sectional area expressed in square inches.

According to *NEC Chapter 9, Table 8,* the cross-sectional area of a 250 kcmil conductor is 0.260 square inch.

If a conductor is to be sized by cross-sectional area, it is much easier to express the wire size in circular mils (or thousands of circular mils) than in square inches.

2.2.0 Ampacity

Ampacity is the maximum current in amperes a conductor can carry continuously under the conditions of use without exceeding its temperature rating. The ampacity of conductors for given conditions are listed in *NEC Tables 310.15(B)(16) through 310.15(B)(21). NEC Table 310.15(B)(16)* covers conductors rated 2,000 volts and below where not more than three conductors are installed in a raceway or cable or are directly buried in the earth, based on an ambient temperature of 30°C (86°F).

NEC Table 310.15(B)(17) covers both copper conductors and aluminum or copper-clad aluminum conductors 2,000 volts and below where conductors are used as single conductors in free air, based on an ambient temperature of 30°C (86°F).

NEC Tables 310.15(B)(18) and 310.15(B)(19) apply to conductors rated at 150°C to 250°C (302°F to 482°F), used either in raceway or cable or as single conductors in free air, based on an ambient temperature of 40°C (104°F).

Example:

Determine the ampacity of a No. 12 Cu (copper) THW conductor.

Solution:

25 amps [from *NEC Table 310.15(B)(16)*].

2.3.0 Conductor Material

The most common conductor material is copper. Copper is used because of its excellent conductivity (low resistance), ease of use, and value. The value of a material as an ingredient for wire is determined by several factors, including conductivity, cost, availability, and workability.

2.3.1 Conductivity

Conductivity is a word that describes the ease (or difficulty) of travel presented to an electric current by a conductor. If a conductor has a low resistance, it has a high conductivity. Silver is one of the best conductors since it has very low resistance and high conductivity. Copper has high conductivity and a lower price than silver. Aluminum, another material with good conductivity, is also a good choice for conductor material. The conductivity of aluminum is approximately two-thirds that of copper.

2.3.2 Cost

Cost is always an issue that contributes to the selection of a material to be used for a given application. Often, a material that has low cost may be selected as a conductor material even though it has physical properties that are inferior to the more expensive material. Such is the case in the selection of copper over platinum. Here, the cost of platinum is very high, and very little thinking is required to determine that copper is a better choice. The choice between copper and aluminum is often more difficult to make.

2.3.3 Availability

The availability of some material is often a concern when selecting components for a job. As applied to wire, the mining industry often controls the availability of raw materials, which could produce shortages of some material. The availability of a substance such as copper or aluminum affects the price of the finished product (copper or aluminum wire).

Think About It

Overheating

What happens when insulation is overheated? What affects the ampacity of an insulated conductor?

2.3.4 Workability

It is a good idea to select a material that requires less expense for tools and is easier to work with. Aluminum conductors are lighter than copper conductors of the same size. They are also much more flexible than copper conductors and, in general, are easier to work with. However, terminating aluminum conductors often requires special tools and treatment of termination surfaces with an anti-oxidation material. Splicing and terminating aluminum conductors often requires a higher degree of training on the part of the electrician than do similar efforts with copper wire. This is partly due to the fact that aluminum expands and contracts with heat more than copper.

2.4.0 Conductor Insulation

The first attempt to insulate wire was made in the early 1800s during the development of the telegraph. This insulation was designed to provide physical protection rather than electrical protection. Electrical insulation was not an important issue because the telegraph operated at low-voltage DC. This early form of insulation was a substance composed of tarred hemp or cotton fiber and shellac and was used primarily for weatherproofing long-distance distribution lines to mines, industrial sites, and railroads.

Some early electrical distribution systems utilized the knob-and-tube technique of installing wire. The wire was often bare and was pulled between and wrapped around ceramic knobs that were affixed to the building structure. When it was necessary to pull wire through structural members, it was pulled through ceramic tubes. The structural member (usually wood) was drilled, the tube was pressed into the hole, and the wire was pulled through the hole in the tube. As dangerous as this may appear, older homes still exist that have knob-and-tube wiring that was installed in the early 1900s and is still operational. Knob-and-tube wiring was revised to use insulated conductors and was in use up to 1957 in some areas.

The grounded or neutral conductor in overhead services may be bare. Furthermore, the concentric grounded conductor in Type SE cable may be bare when used as a service-entrance cable. However, all current-carrying conductors (including the grounded conductor) must be insulated when used on the inside of buildings, or after the first overcurrent protection device.

NEC Table 310.104(A) presents application and construction data on the wide range of 600-volt insulated, individual conductors recognized by the *NEC*®, with the appropriate letter designation used to identify each type of insulated conductor.

2.4.1 Thermoplastic

Thermoplastic is a popular and effective insulation material. The following thermoplastics are widely used:

- *Polyvinyl chloride (PVC)* – The base material used for the manufacture of TW and THW insulation.
- *Polyethylene (PE)* – An excellent weatherproofing material used primarily for insulation of control and communications wiring. It is not used for high-voltage conductors (those exceeding 5,000 volts).
- *Cross-linked polyethylene (XLP)* – An improved PE with superior heat- and moisture-resistant qualities. Used for THHN, THWN, and THHW wiring as well as many high-voltage cables.
- *Nylon* – Primarily used as jacketing material. THHN building wire has an outer coating of nylon.
- *Teflon*® – A high-temperature insulation. Widely used for telephone wiring in a plenum (where other insulated conductors require conduit routing).

2.4.2 Thermoset

Many thermoplastic materials deform when heated. Thermoset materials maintain their form when heated. Thermoset insulations include RHH, RHW, XHH, XHHW, and SIS.

On Site

Terminating Aluminum Wire

Care must be taken to use listed connectors when terminating aluminum wire. All aluminum connections also require the use of anti-oxidizing compound. Some connectors are precoated with compound; others require the addition of it. Be sure to check the connectors before beginning the installation.

2.4.3 Letter Coding

Conductor insulation as applied to building wire is coded by letters. The letters generally, but not always, indicate the type of insulation or its environmental rating. The types of conductor insulation described in this module will be those indicated at the top of *NEC Table 310.15(B)(16)*. The various insulation designations are shown in *Table 1*.

NOTE

Any conductor used in a wet location (see definition under Location, Wet, in *NEC Article 100*) must be listed for use in wet locations. Any conduit run underground is assumed to be subject to water infiltration and is, therefore, in a wet location.

Table 1 Insulation Coding

Letter	Description
B	Braid
E	Ethylene or Entrance
F	Fluorinated or Feeder
H	Heat-Rated or Flame-Retardant
N	Nylon
P	Propylene
R	Rubber
S	Silicon or Synthetic
T	Thermoplastic
U	Underground
W	Weather-Rated
X	Cross-Linked Polyethylene
Z	Modified Ethylene Tetrafluoroethylene
TW	Weather-Rated Thermoplastic (60°C/140°F)
FEP	Fluorinated Ethylene Propylene
FEPB	Fluorinated Ethylene Propylene with Glass Braid
MI	Mineral Insulation
MTW	Moisture, Heat, and Oil-Resistant Thermoplastic
PFA	Perfluoroalkoxy
RHH	Flame-Retardant Heat-Rated Rubber
RHW	Weather-Rated, Heat-Rated Rubber (75°C/167°F)
SA	Silicon
SIS	Synthetic Heat-Resistant
TBS	Thermoplastic Braided Silicon
TFE	Extended Polytetrafluoroethylene
THHN	Heat-Resistant Thermoplastic
THHW	Moisture and Heat-Resistant Thermoplastic
THW	Moisture and Heat-Resistant Thermoplastic
THWN	Weather-Rated, Heat-Rated Thermoplastic with Nylon Cover
UF	Underground Feeder
USE	Underground Service Entrance
XHH	Thermoset
XHHW	Heat-Rated, Flame-Retardant, Weather-Rated Thermoset
ZW	Weather-Rated Modified Ethylene Tetrafluoroethylene

26109-14_T01.EPS

Think About It

Conductor Insulation

What are the functions of conductor insulation? Under what conditions does the NEC® allow uninsulated conductors?

2.4.4 Color Coding

A color code is used to help identify wires by the color of the insulation. This makes it easier to install and properly connect the wires. A typical color code is as follows:

- *Two-conductor cable* – One white or gray wire, one black wire, and a grounding wire (usually bare)
- *Three-conductor cable* – One white or gray, one black, one red, and a grounding wire
- *Four-conductor cable* – Same as three-conductor cable plus fourth wire (blue)
- *Five-conductor cable* – Same as four-conductor cable plus fifth wire (yellow)

The grounding conductor may be bare, green, or green with a yellow stripe. Power cable color codes are shown in *Figure 5*.

Think About It

Insulation Types

Use *NEC Table 310.104(A)* to identify two types of insulation that are suitable for use in wet locations.

The *NEC®* does not require color coding of ungrounded conductors except where more than one nominal voltage system is present [*NEC Section 210.5(C)*]. The ungrounded conductors may be any color with the exception of white, gray, or green; however, it is a good practice to color code conductors as described here. In fact, many construction specifications require color coding. Furthermore, on a four-wire, delta-connected secondary where the midpoint of one phase is grounded to supply lighting and similar loads, the phase conductor having the higher voltage to ground must be identified by an outer finish that is orange in color, by tagging, or by other effective means. Such identification must be placed at each point where a connection is made if the grounded conductor is also present. In most cases, orange tape is used at all termination points when such a condition exists.

2.4.5 Wire Ratings

A critical factor in selecting conductors is the conductor's maximum operating temperature. Consider how and where a conductor will be used so that the conductor's limiting (maximum) temperature rating will not be exceeded. A conductor's operating temperature is determined by the ambient temperature, current flow in the conductor (including harmonic current), current flow in bundled conductors (which raises the ambient temperature), and how fast or slow heat is dissipated into the surrounding medium (which is affected by the conductor insulation).

Another significant factor to consider when selecting and installing conductors is where the conductor will be terminated. The temperature

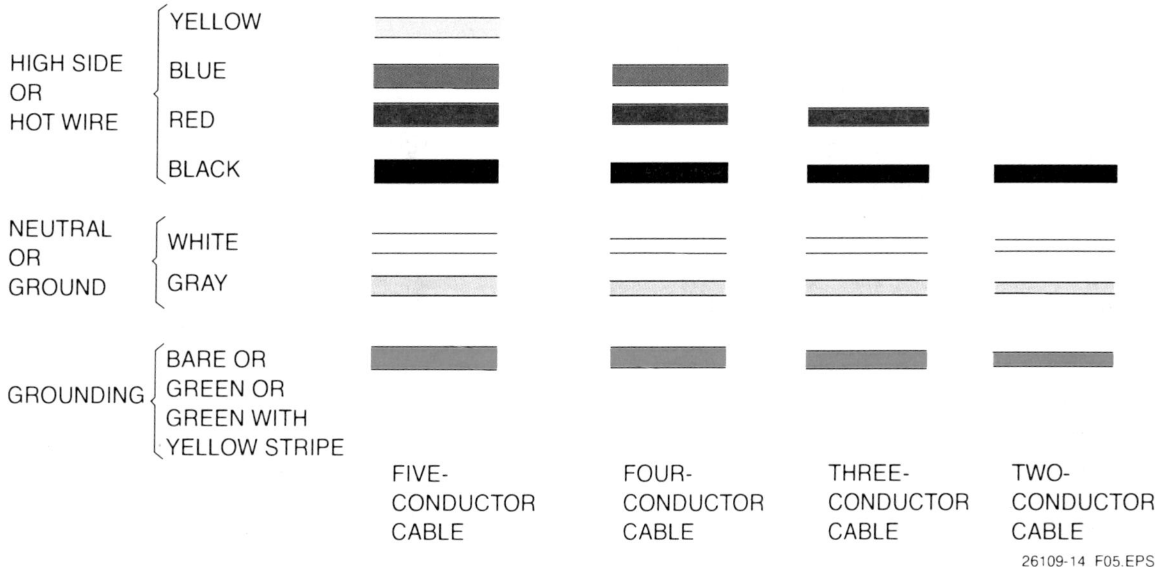

Figure 5 Typical power cable insulation color codes.

Think About It

Color Coding Ungrounded Conductors

Although the *NEC®* does not require the use of color-coded ungrounded current-carrying conductors, why might it be a good idea to use them anyway?

On Site

Color Coding

Color designations are good indicators, but never trust your life to them. Always protect yourself by testing circuits with a voltmeter.

rating of the termination may limit the allowable ampacity of the conductor.

The amount of current a conductor can safely carry, and thus the maximum safe temperature the conductor can reach, is determined in general by conductor size (diameter in circular mils), the ambient (surrounding) temperature, the number of conductors in a bundle, and where the conductors are installed (raceways, conduit, ducts, underground, etc.).

Conductor selection is based largely on the temperature rating of the wire. This requirement is extremely important and is the basis of safe operation for insulated conductors. As shown in *NEC Table 310.104(A)*, conductors have various ratings (60°C, 75°C, 90°C, etc.). Since *NEC Tables 310.15(B)(16) and 310.15(B)(17)* are based on an assumed ambient temperature of 30°C (86°F), conductor ampacities are based on the ambient temperature plus the heat (I^2R) produced by the conductor while carrying current. Therefore, the type of insulation used on the conductor is the first consideration in determining the maximum permitted conductor ampacity.

For example, a No. 3/0 THW copper conductor for use in a raceway has an ampacity of 200 according to *NEC Table 310.15(B)(16)*. In a 30°C ambient temperature, the conductor is subjected to this temperature when it carries no current. Since a THW-insulated conductor is rated at 75°C, this leaves 45°C (75 – 30) for increased temperature due to current flow. If the ambient temperature exceeds 30°C, the conductor maximum load-current rating must be reduced proportionally per *NEC Table 310.15(B)(2)(a)* so that the total temperature (ambient plus conductor temperature rise due to current flow) will not exceed the temperature rating of the conductor insulation (60°C, 75°C, etc.). For the same reason, the allowable ampacity must be reduced when more than three conductors are contained in a raceway or cable. See *NEC Section 310.15(B)(3)(a)*.

Using the ampacity tables – An important step in circuit design is the selection of the type of conductor to be used (TW, THW, THWN, RHH, THHN, XHHW, etc.). The various types of conductors are covered in *NEC Article 310*, and the ampacities of conductors are given in *NEC Tables 310.15(B)(16) through 310.15(B)(21)* for the varying conditions of use (e.g., in a raceway, in open air, at normal or higher-than-normal ambient temperatures). Conductors must be used in accordance with the data in these tables and notes.

2.5.0 Fixture Wires

Fixture wire is used for the interior wiring of fixtures and for wiring fixtures to a power source. Guidelines concerning fixture wire are given in *NEC Article 402*. The list of approved types of fixture wire is given in *NEC Table 402.3*. *Figure 6* shows one example of fixture wire. The wires are composed of insulated conductors with or without an outer jacket. The conductors range in size from No. 18 to No. 10 AWG.

The decision of which fixture wire to use depends primarily upon the operating temperature that is expected within the fixture. Therefore, it is the character of the insulation that will determine the wire selected. For instance, fixture wires insulated with perfluoroalkoxy (PFA) or extruded polytetrafluoroethylene (PTF) would be selected if the operating temperature of the fixture is expected to reach a maximum of 482°F. This is the highest operating temperature allowed for any fixture wire.

As indicated by *NEC Section 402.3*, fixture wires are suitable for service at 600 volts unless otherwise specified in *NEC Table 402.3*. The allowed ampacities of fixture wire are given in *NEC Table 402.5*.

Although the primary use for fixture wire is the internal wiring of fixtures, several of the wires listed in *NEC Table 402.3* may be used for wiring remote-control, signaling, or power-limited

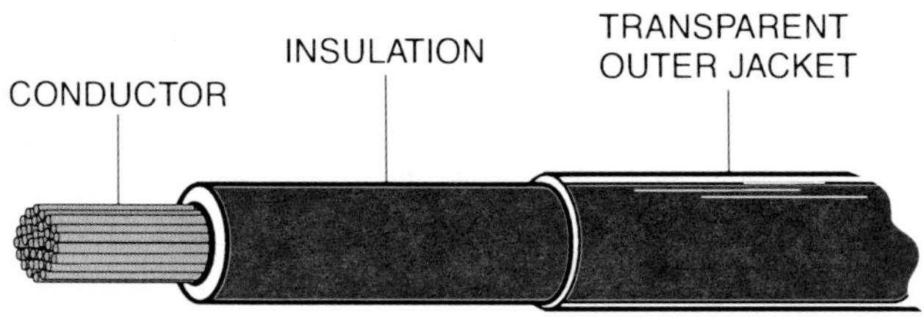

Figure 6 Fixture wire.

On Site

Cable Selection

There are two factors to be considered when determining the type of cable to be used for a specific application: the type of conductor insulation and the cable jacket. Both must be appropriate for the application.

circuits in accordance with *NEC Section 725.49.* Fixture wires may never be used as substitutes for branch circuit conductors.

2.6.0 Cables

Cables are two or more insulated wires and may contain a grounding wire covered by an outer jacket or sheath. Cable is usually classified by the type of covering it has, either nonmetallic (plastic) or metallic, also called armored cable.

Cable may also be classified according to where it can be used (see *NEC Table 400.4*). Because water is such a good conductor of electricity, moisture on conductors can cause power loss or short circuits. For this reason, cables are classified for either dry, damp, or wet locations. Cables can also be classified regarding exposure to sunlight and rough use.

2.6.1 Cable Markings

All cables are marked to show important properties and uses. Cable markings show the wire size, number of conductors, cable type, and voltage rating. In addition, a marking may be included to signify approved service or applications. This information is printed on nonmetallic cable (*Figure 7*).

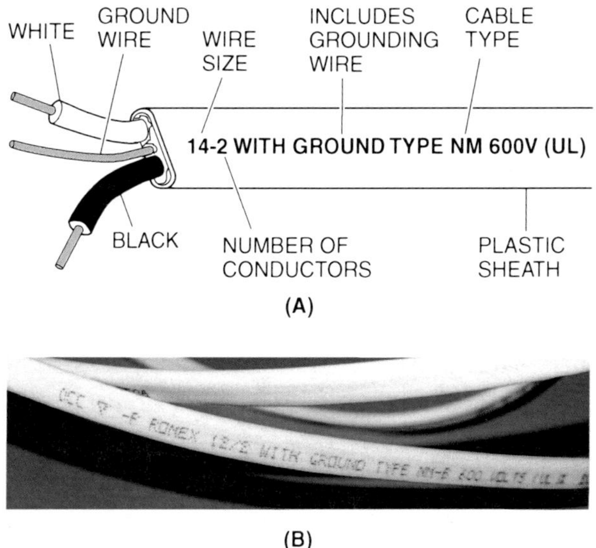

Figure 7 Nonmetallic cable markings.

On metallic cable, marking information is usually included on a tag.

2.6.2 Nonmetallic-Sheathed Cable

Nonmetallic-sheathed cable (Type NM and Type NMC) is widely used for branch circuits and feeders in residential and commercial systems. See *Figure 8*. Both types are commonly called Romex®, even though the cable manufacturer only calls Type NM cable Romex®. Guidelines for the use of nonmetallic-sheathed cable are given in *NEC Article 334.* This cable consists of two or three insulated conductors and one bare conductor enclosed in a nonmetallic sheath. The conductors may be wrapped individually with paper, and the spaces between the conductors may be filled with jute, paper, or other material to protect the conductors and help the cable keep its shape. The sheath covering both Type NM cable and Type NMC cable is flame-retardant and moisture-resistant. The sheath covering Type NMC cable has the additional characteristics of being fungus- and corrosion-resistant.

NEC Article 334 lists the allowed and prohibited uses for Type NM cable and Type NMC cable. Both are allowed to be installed in either exposed or concealed work. The primary difference in their applied uses is that Type NM cable is suitable for dry locations only, whereas Type NMC is permitted for dry, moist, damp, or corrosive locations.

Types NM and NMC cables may be used in one- and two-family dwellings, and in certain multifamily dwellings, depending on the type of construction. See *NEC Section 334.10*.

In general, NM and NMC cable cannot be used in ducts or plenums because toxic gases from burning cable insulation would be spread throughout the structure. NM and NMC cables cannot be installed exposed in the space above suspended ceilings. They cannot be used as service-entrance cable, embedded in concrete, or in hazardous locations. There are many other requirements for NM and NMC specified in *NEC Article 334*. Before installing this type of cable, be sure you read and understand the applicable sections of the *NEC®*.

2.6.3 Type UF Cable

Guidelines for the use of Type UF (underground feeder and branch circuit) cable are given in *NEC Article 340.* Type UF cable is very similar in appearance, construction, and use to Type NMC cable. The main difference between these two cables is that Type UF cable is suitable for direct burial, whereas Type NMC cable is not.

Some of the permitted uses of Type UF cable are: underground and direct burial; as a single-conductor cable; in wet, dry, or corrosive

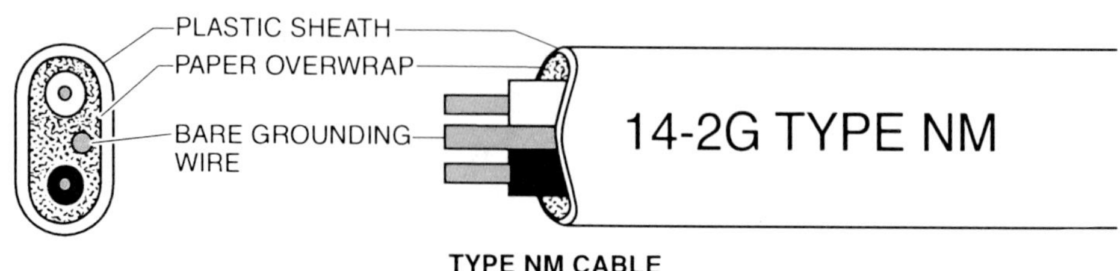

TYPE NM CABLE

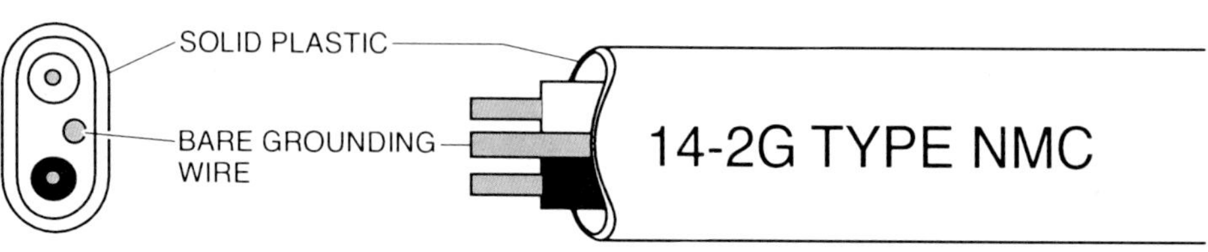

TYPE NMC CABLE

(A)

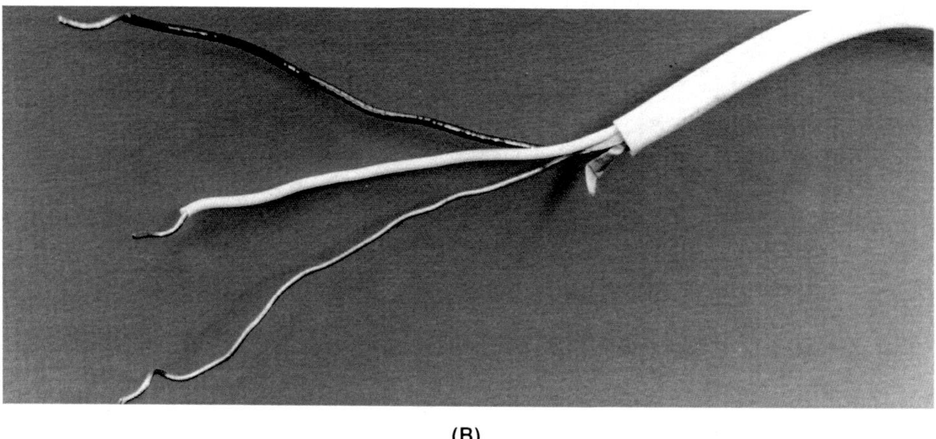

(B)

26109-14_F08.EPS

Figure 8 Nonmetallic-sheathed cable.

conditions; as a nonmetallic-sheathed cable; in solar photovoltaic systems; and in cable trays.

Typically, Type UF cable may not be used as service-entrance cable, in commercial garages, in theaters, in hoistways or elevators, or in hazardous locations. Type UF cable cannot generally be embedded in poured cement, concrete, or aggregate, exposed to sunlight (unless designed for that use), or used as an overhead cable. Refer to *NEC Article 340* for specifics on where and when to use Type UF cable.

2.6.4 Type NMS Cable

Refer to *NEC Sections 334.10* and *334.12* for the applications of Type NMS cable. Type NMS cable is a form of nonmetallic-sheathed cable that contains a factory assembly of power, communications, and signaling conductors enclosed within a moisture-resistant, flame-retardant sheath.

2.6.5 Type MV Cable

Type MV (medium-voltage) cable is covered in *NEC Article 328*. It consists of one or more insulated conductors encased in an outer jacket. This cable is suitable for use with voltages ranging from 2,001 to 35,000 volts. It may be installed in wet and dry locations and may be buried directly in the earth. See *Figure 9*.

2.6.6 Type MC Cable

Type MC (metal clad) cable consists of one or more insulated conductors encased in a metal tape or a metallic sheath. *NEC Article 330* covers Type MC cable. Further information can be found in *UL 1569, Standard for Metal Clad Cables*.

MC cable is used in a wide variety of applications, from small instrumentation cable up to medium voltage feeders. The conductors are

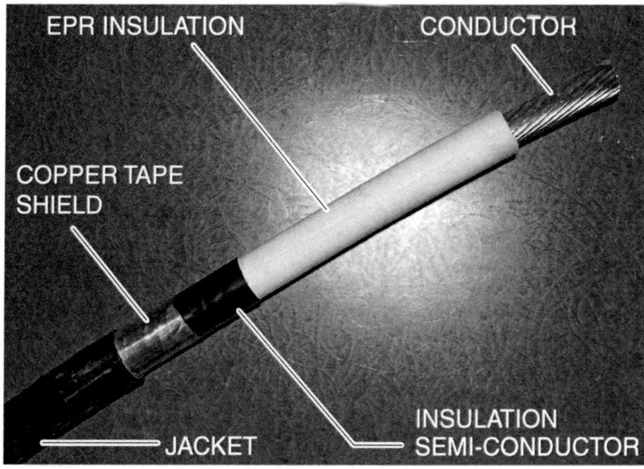

Figure 9 Type MV cable.

coated with a thermoset or thermoplastic insulation. Type MC cable can also be a composite of electrical conductors and optical fiber conductors.

Typical markings on the cable include the maximum rated voltage, AWG size (or circular mil area), and insulation type. If the outer covering will not accept markings, the markings will be on a tape inside the cable along the entire length of the cable. If on the outside, the markings typically have a 24-inch spacing.

The three types of MC cable are: interlocked metal tape, corrugated metal tube, and smooth metal tube. Cables with special uses will be marked accordingly. The outer covering may be a nonmetallic jacket over the metal sheath. One type of MC cable is shown in *Figure 10*.

Some of the typical uses for the three types of MC cable are for services, feeders, and branch circuits; for power, lighting, control, and signal circuits; indoors or outdoors; exposed or concealed; direct burial (if identified for that use); in any raceway; and other uses specified in *NEC Article 330*.

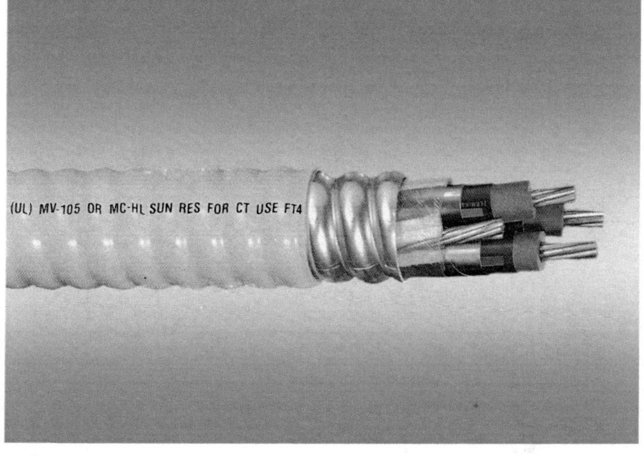

Figure 10 Type of MC cable.

Type MC cable may not be used in corrosive or damaging conditions unless the metal cladding protects the conductors, or some other protective material is used. Uses typically not permitted are in areas where the cable is subject to physical damage, direct burial, in concrete, or where subject to caustic materials.

Typically, UL does not recognize the interlocking metal cladding of Type MC cable as the only means of grounding equipment. For this reason, Type MC cable is not allowed in certain applications, such as patient care areas in hospitals.

Both armored (AC) and MC cables provide advantages during installation. The flexible metal sheath protects the conductors and allows them to bend around corners without kinking or damage to the conductor. Also, since the conductors are already protected by the sheathing, there is no need to pull conductors into a raceway, nor is there concern about conductor contact with pipes or other hard surfaces. Other advantages of metal clad cables are their relatively easy installation without the need for wire pullers, fish tapes, or lubricants.

There are some fundamental differences between Types AC and MC cables. The significant differences are:

- AC cable has a maximum of four conductors, plus a grounding conductor, and comes in sizes from 14 AWG to 1 AWG. Conversely, MC cable has no limitations on the number of conductors, and is sized from 18 AWG to 2,000 kcmil.
- AC cable has a bonding strip (16 AWG). This strip is in constant contact with the armor and, with the armor, forms an equipment ground. MC cable has no bonding strip. The MC cladding is not a ground, although it can supplement the ground.
- AC cable uses moisture-resistant and fire-retardant paper wraps on individual conductors. MC cables have no such paper wrap, but do incorporate a polyester tape used on the assembly.

2.6.7 High-Voltage Shielded Cable

Shielding of high-voltage cables protects the conductor assembly against surface discharge or burning due to corona discharge in ionized air, which can be destructive to the insulation and jacketing.

Electrostatic shielding of cables makes use of both nonmetallic and metallic materials (*Figures 11* and *12*).

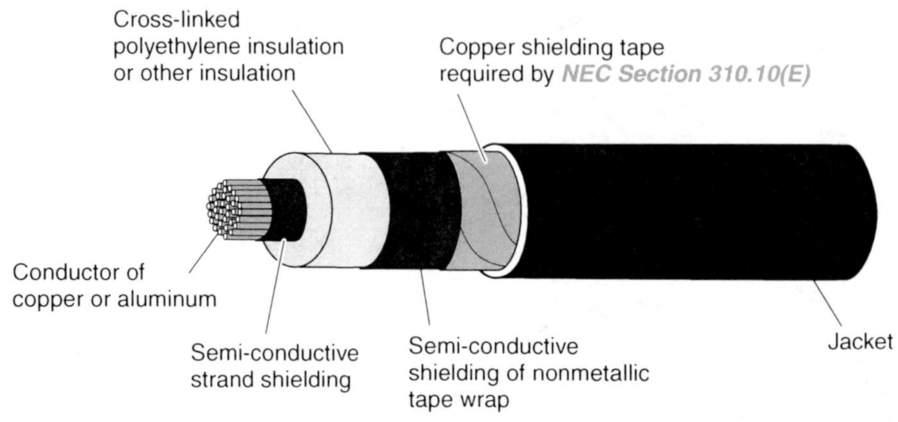

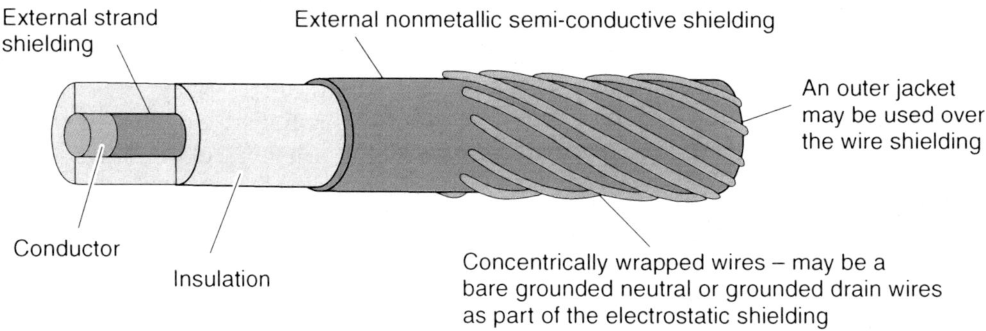

Figure 11 Various types of shielding.

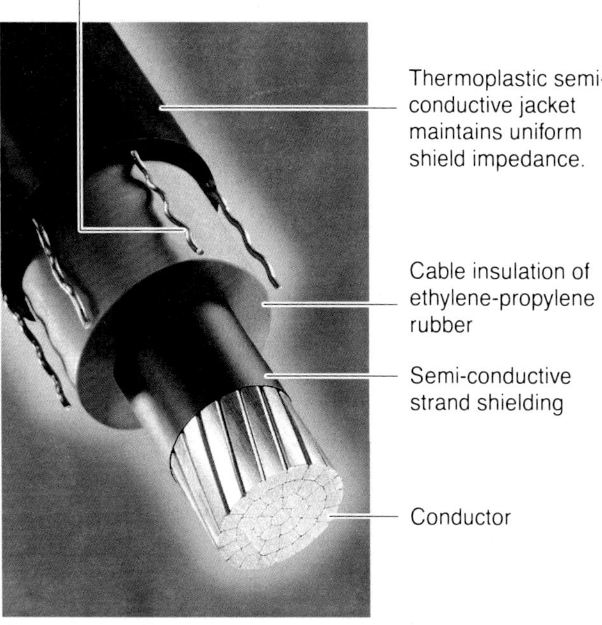

Figure 12 Corrugated drain wire shielding.

On Site

Type MC Cable

Metal clad cable (Type MC) is a type of cable that is widely used in both commercial and industrial environments. It is available in many configurations, with or without an outer jacket. Some of the special applications of MC cable include homerun cables, super neutrals, direct burial, and fire alarm cable.

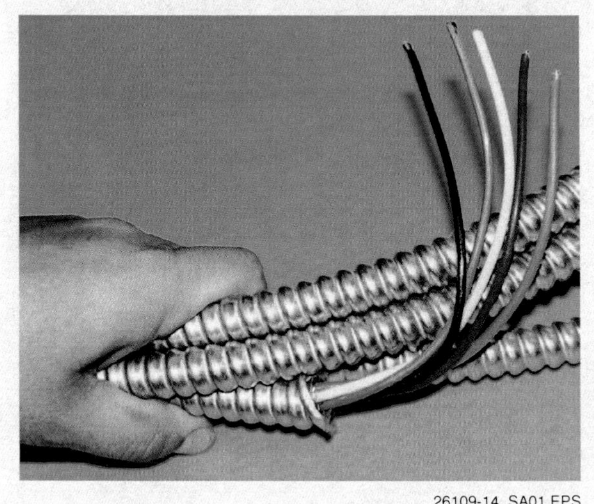

2.6.8 Channel Wire Assemblies

Channel wire assemblies (Type FC) comprise an entire wiring system, which includes the cable, cable supports, splicers, circuit taps, fixture hangers, and fittings (*Figure 13*). Guidelines for the use of this system are given in *NEC Article 322*. Type FC cable is a flat cable assembly with three or four parallel No. 10 special stranded copper conductors. The assembly is installed in an approved U-channel surface metal raceway with one side open. Tap devices can be inserted anywhere along the run. Connections from the tap devices to the flat cable assembly are made by pin-type contacts when the tap devices are fastened in place. The pin-type contacts penetrate the insulation of the cable assembly and contact the multi-stranded conductors in a matched phase sequence. These taps can then be wired to lighting fixtures or power outlets (*Figure 14*).

As indicated in *NEC Section 322.10,* this wiring system is suitable for branch circuits that only supply small appliances and lights. This system is suitable for exposed wiring only and may not be concealed within the building structure. It is ideal for quick branch circuit wiring at field installations.

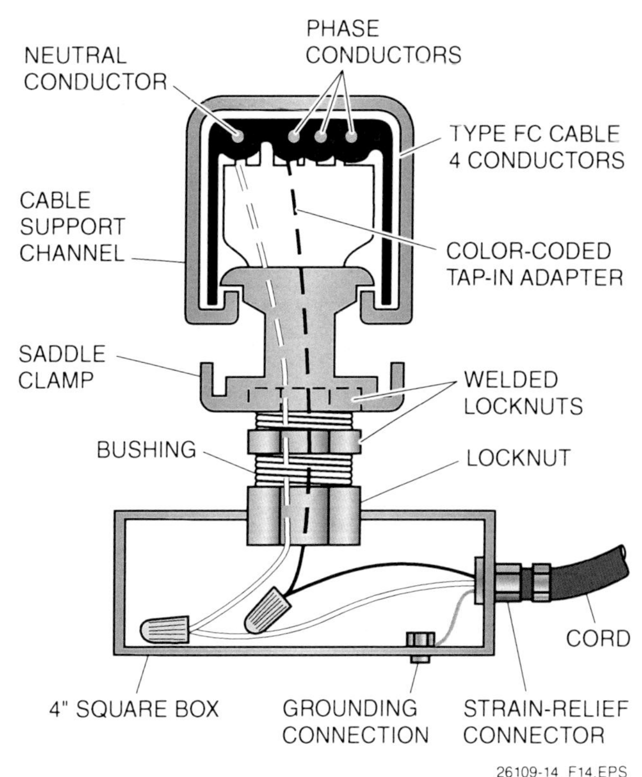

Figure 14 Type FC connection.

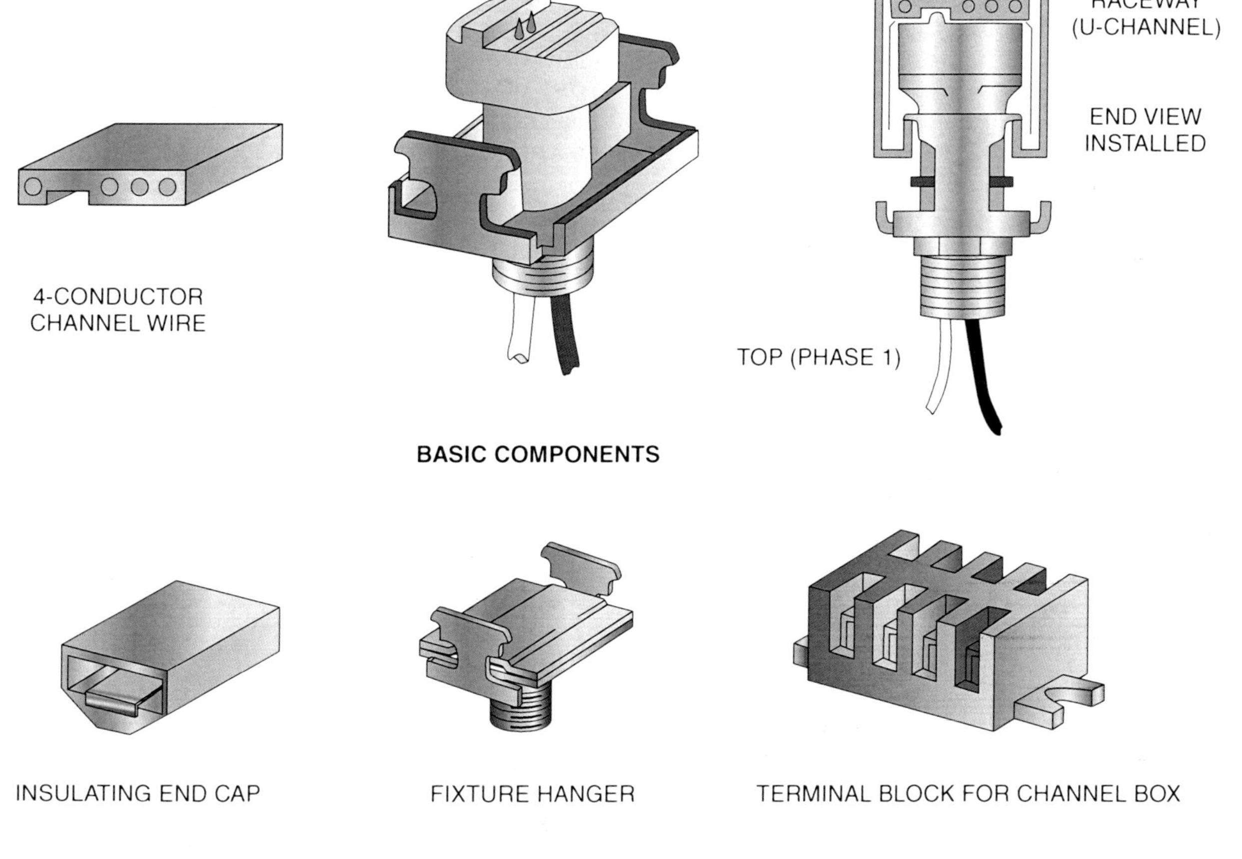

Figure 13 Channel wire components and accessories.

2.6.9 Flat Conductor Cable

Type FCC (flat conductor) cable comprises an entire branch wiring system similar in many respects to Type FC flat conductor assemblies. Guidelines for the use of this system are given in *NEC Article 324.* Type FCC cable consists of three to five flat conductors placed edge-to-edge, separated, and enclosed in a moisture-resistant and flame-retardant insulating assembly. Accessories include cable connectors, terminators, power source adapters, and receptacles.

This wiring system has been designed to supply floor outlets in office areas and other commercial and institutional interiors. It is meant to be run under carpets so that no floor drilling is required. This system is also suitable for wall mounting. As indicated in *NEC Article 324,* telephone and other communications circuits may share the same enclosure as Type FCC flat cable. The main advantage of the system is its ease of installation. It is the ideal wiring system for use when remodeling or expanding existing office facilities.

2.6.10 Type TC Cable

Guidelines for the use of Type TC (power and control tray) cable are given in *NEC Article 336.* Type TC cable consists of two or more insulated conductors twisted together, with or without associated bare or fully insulated grounding conductors, and covered with a nonmetallic jacket. The cables are rated at 600 volts. The cable is listed in conductor sizes No. 18 AWG to 2,000 kcmil copper or No. 12 AWG to 2,000 kcmil aluminum or copper-clad aluminum (*Figure 15*).

As the T in the letter designator indicates, this cable is tray cable. It can be used in cable trays and raceways. It may also be buried directly if the sheathing material is suitable for this use. Type TC cable is also good for use in sunlight when indicated by the cable markings.

26109-14_F15.EPS

Figure 15 Type TC cable.

2.6.11 SE and USE Cable

Guidelines for the use of Types SE (service-entrance) and USE (underground service-entrance) cable are given in *NEC Article 338.* The *NEC*® contains no specifications for the construction of this cable; it is left to UL to determine what types of cable should be approved for this purpose. Currently, service-entrance cable is labeled in sizes No. 12 AWG and larger for copper, and No. 10 AWG and larger for aluminum or copper-clad aluminum, with Types RH, RHW, RHH, or XHHW conductors. If the type designation for the conductor is marked on the outside surface of the cable, the temperature rating of the cable corresponds to the rating of the individual conductor. When this marking does not appear, the temperature rating of the cable is 75°C (167°F). Type SE cable is for aboveground installation only.

When used as a service-entrance cable, Type SE must be installed as specified in *NEC Article 230.* Service-entrance cable may also be used as feeder and branch circuit cable. Guidelines for the use of service-entrance cable are given in *NEC Section 338.10. Figure 16* shows SE cable with a bare aluminum conductor.

Type USE cable is for underground installation including burial directly in the earth. Type USE cable in sizes No. 4/0 AWG and smaller with all conductors insulated is suitable for all of the underground uses for which Type UF cable is permitted by the *NEC*®.

Type USE cable may consist of either single conductors or a multi-conductor assembly provided with a moisture-resistant covering, but it is not required to have a flame-retardant covering. This type of cable may have a bare copper conductor cabled with the assembly. Furthermore, Type USE single, parallel, or cabled conductor assemblies recognized for underground use may have a bare copper concentric conductor applied. These constructions do not require an outer overall covering. Guidelines for the use of Type USE cable are specified in *NEC Article 338.*

When used as a service-entrance cable, Type USE cable must be installed as specified in *NEC Article 230.* Take the time to read *NEC Article 230* to ensure proper installation. Type USE service-entrance cable may also be used as feeder and branch circuit cable.

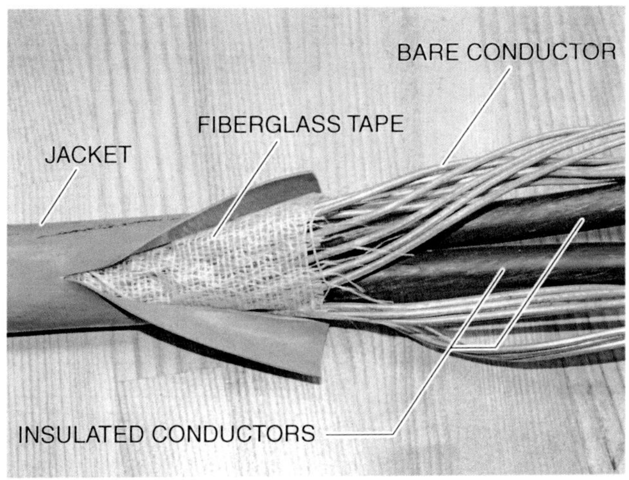

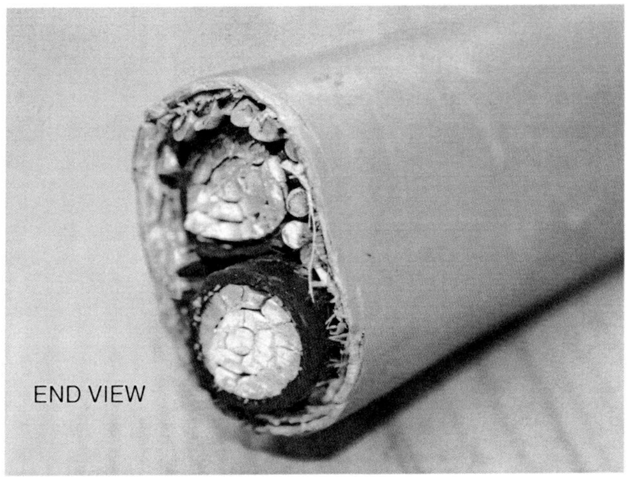

26109-14_F16.EPS

Figure 16 SE cable.

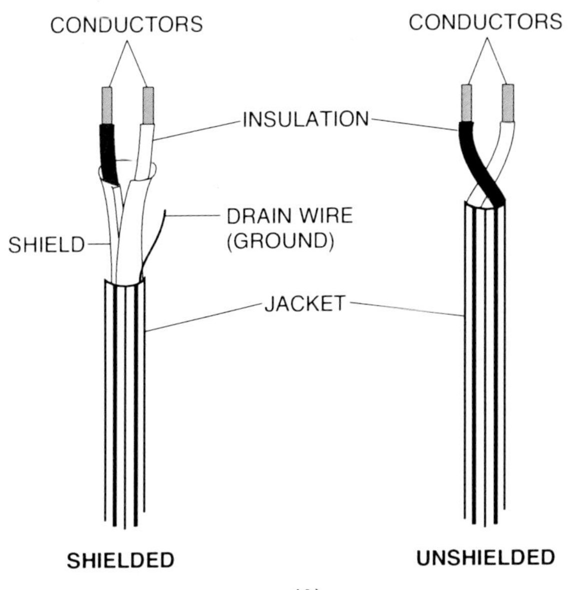

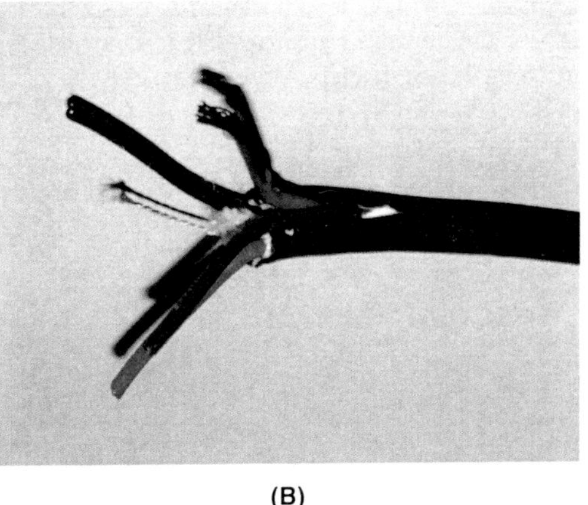

(B)

26109-14_F17.EPS

Figure 17 Instrumentation control cable.

2.7.0 Instrumentation Control Wiring

Instrumentation control wiring links the field-sensing, controlling, printout, and operating devices that form an electronic instrumentation control system. The style and size of instrumentation control wiring must be matched to a specific job.

Instrumentation control wiring usually has two or more insulated conductor wires. These wires may also have a shield and a ground wire. An outer layer called the jacket protects the wiring (*Figure 17*). Instrumentation conductor wires come in pairs. The number of pairs in a multi-conductor cable depends on the size of the wire used. A multi-pair cable typically has 12, 24, or 36 pairs of conductors.

2.7.1 Shields

Shields are provided on instrumentation control wiring to protect the electrical signals traveling through the conductors from electrical interference or noise. Shields are usually constructed of aluminum foil bonded to a plastic film (*Figure 18*). If the wiring is not properly shielded, electrical noise may cause erratic or erroneous control signals, false indications, and improper operation of control devices.

2.7.2 Shield Drain

A shield drain is a bare copper wire used in continuous contact with a specified grounding terminal. A shield drain allows connection of all the instruments within a loop to a common grounding point. Always refer to the loop diagram to determine whether or not the shield is to be terminated.

Typically, the shielding in instrumentation circuits is grounded at one end of the conductor only. The purpose of this is to drain induced

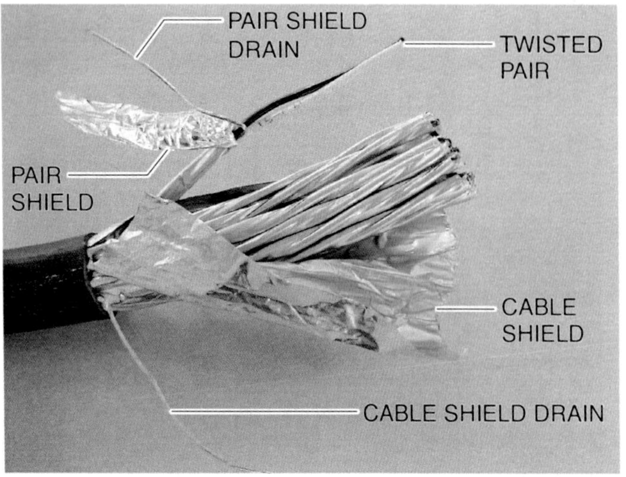

Figure 18 Multi-conductor instrumentation control cable with overall cable shield and individually shielded pairs.

charges to ground but not allow a circulating path for the flow of induced current. If the ground is not to be connected at the end of the wire you are installing, do not remove the ground wire. Fold it back and tape it to the cable. This is called floating the ground.

2.7.3 Jackets

A plastic jacket covers and protects the components within the wire. Polyethylene (PE) and polyvinyl chloride (PVC) jackets are the most commonly used (*Figure 19*). Some jackets have a nylon rip cord that allows the jacket to be peeled back without the use of a knife or cable cutter. This eliminates nicking of the conductor insulation when preparing for termination.

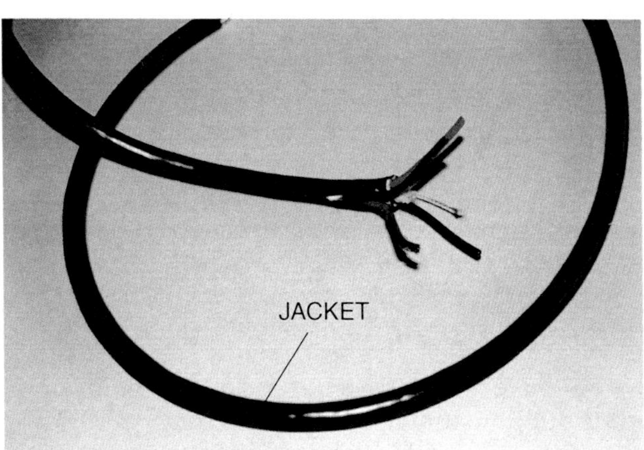

Figure 19 Wire jacket.

3.0.0 Installing Conductors in Conduit Systems

Conductors are installed in all types of conduit by pulling them through the conduit. This is done by using fish tape, pull lines, and pulling equipment.

3.1.0 Fish Tape

Fish tape can be made of flexible steel or nylon and is available in coils of 25 to 200 feet. It should be kept on a reel to avoid twisting. Fish tape has a hook or loop on one end to attach to the conductors to be pulled (*Figure 20*). Broken or damaged fish tape should not be used. To prevent electrical shock, fish tape should not be used near or in live circuits.

Fish tape is fed through the conduit from its reel. The tape usually enters at one outlet or junction box and is fed through to another outlet or junction box (*Figure 21*).

Sometimes fish tape can get hung up in very long conduit runs. These situations call for a rigid fishing tool known as a rodder. Rodders are available in various sizes and in lengths up to 1,000 feet. A typical rodder is shown in *Figure 22*.

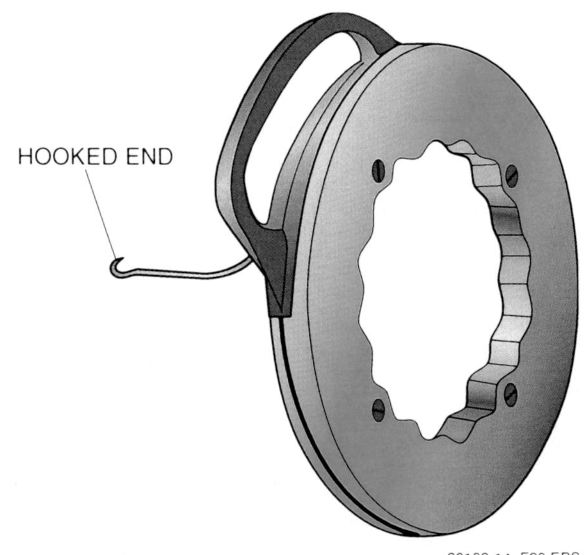

Figure 20 Fish tape.

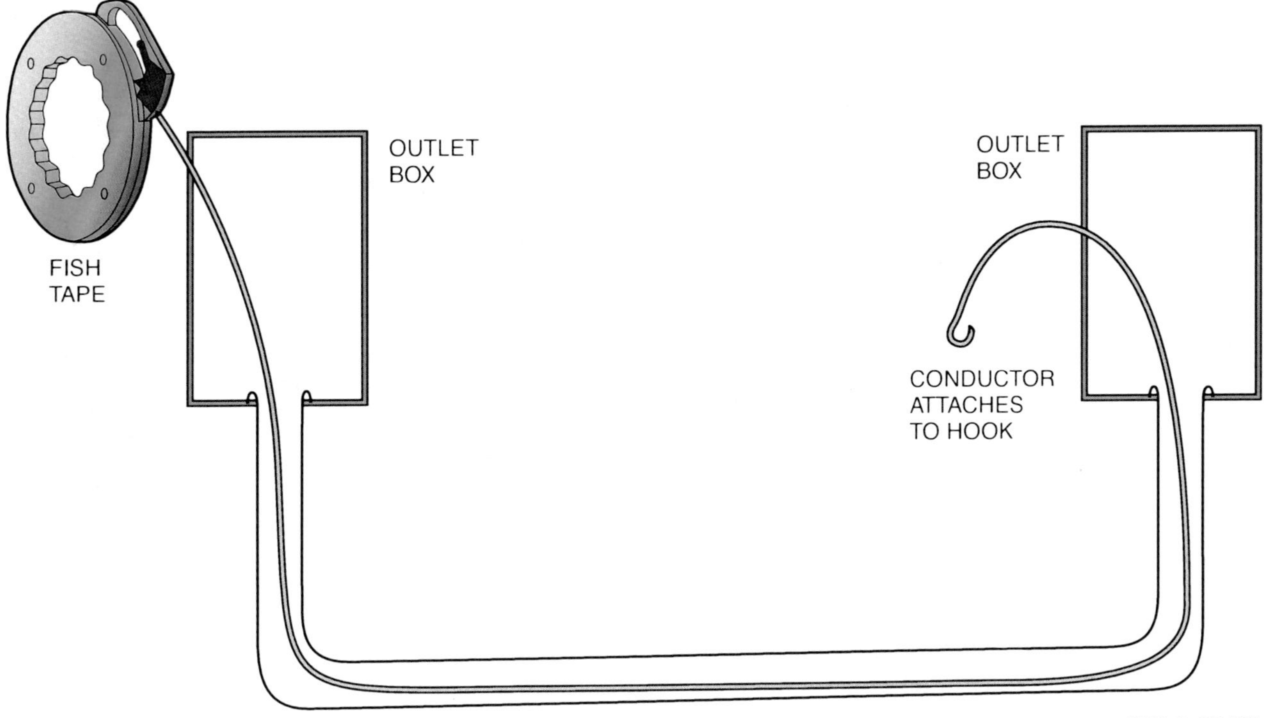

Figure 21 Fish tape installation.

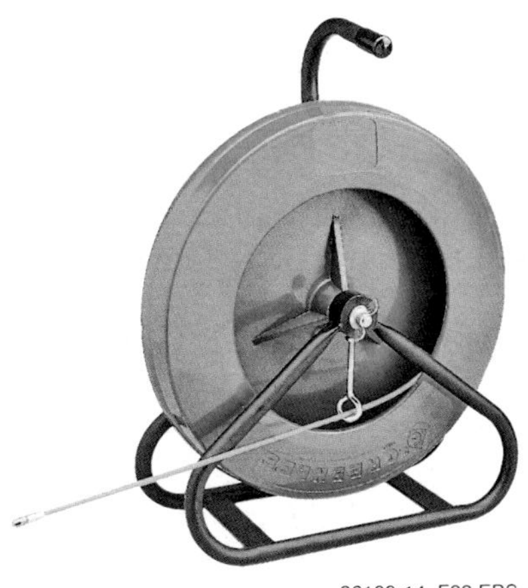

Figure 22 Rodder.

3.1.1 Power Conduit Fishing Systems

String lines can be installed by using different types of power systems. The power system is similar to an industrial vacuum cleaner and pulls a string or rope attached to a piston-like plug (sometimes called a **mouse**) through the conduit. Once the string emerges at the opposite end, either the conductor or a pull rope is then attached and pulled through the conduit, either manually or with power tools. See *Figure 23*.

The hose connection on these vacuum systems can also be reversed to push the mouse through the conduit. In other words, the system can either suck or blow the mouse through the conduit, depending on which method is best in a given situation. In either case, a fish tape is then attached to the string for retrieving through the conduit.

3.1.2 Connecting Wire to a String Line

Once the string is installed in the conduit run, a fish tape is connected to it and pulled back through the conduit. Conductors are then attached to the hooked end of the fish tape or else connected to a basket grip. In most cases, all required conductors are pulled at one time.

3.2.0 Wire Grips

Wire grips are used to attach the cable to the pull tape. One type of wire grip used is a basket grip (sometimes called Chinese Fingers). A basket grip is a steel mesh basket that slips over the end of a large wire or cable (*Figure 24*). The fish tape hooks onto the end and the pull on the fish tape tightens the basket over the conductor.

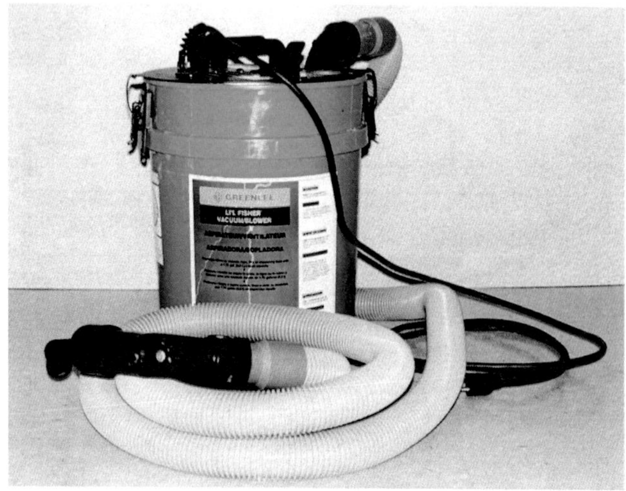

VACUUM BLOWER UNIT

FOAM PLUGS

26109-14_F23.EPS

Figure 23 Power fishing system.

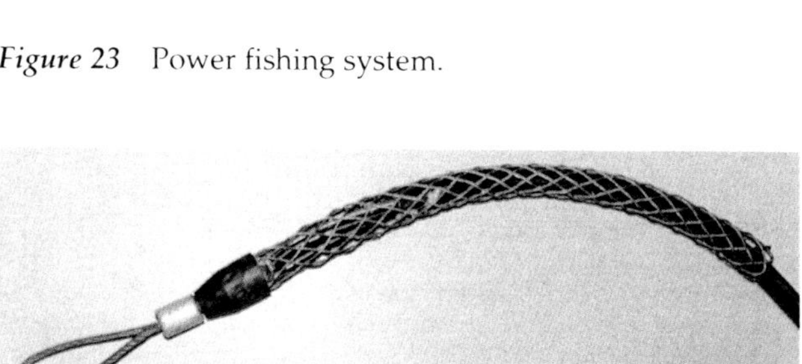

26109-14_F24.EPS

Figure 24 Basket grip.

3.3.0 Pull Lines

If a pull is going to be difficult because of bends in the conduit, the size of the conductors, or the length of the pull, a pull line should be used.

> **WARNING!**
>
> When using pull lines, exercise extreme caution and never stand in a direct line with the pulling rope. If the rope breaks, the line will whip back with great force. This can result in serious injury or death.

A pull line is usually made of nylon or some other synthetic fiber. It is made with a factory-spliced eye for easy connection to fish tape or conductors.

3.4.0 Safety Precautions

The following are several important safety precautions that will help to reduce the chance of being injured while pulling cable.

- To avoid electrical shock, never use fish tape near or in live circuits.
- Read and understand both the operating and safety instructions for the pull system before pulling cable.
- When moving reels of cable, use mechanical lifts for longer spools. For smaller spools, avoid back strain by using your legs to lift (rather than your back) and asking for help with heavy loads. Also, when manually pulling wire, spread your legs to maintain your balance and do not stretch.
- Be careful to avoid any pinchpoints in the capstans and sheaves.
- Select a rope that has a pulling load rating greater than the estimated forces required for the pull.
- Use only low-stretch rope such as multiplex and double-braided polyester for cable pulling. High-stretch ropes store energy much like a stretched rubber band. If there is a failure of the rope, pulling grip, conductors, or any other component in the pulling system, this potential energy will suddenly be unleashed. The whipping action of a rope can cause considerable damage, serious injury, or death.
- Inspect the rope thoroughly before use. Make sure there are no cuts or frays in the rope. Remember, the rope is only as strong as its weakest point.
- When designing the pull, keep the rope confined in conduit wherever possible. Should the rope break or any other part of the pulling system fail, releasing the stored energy in the rope, the confinement in the conduit will work against the whipping action of the rope by playing out much of this energy within the conduit.

On Site

Fish Tape Selection

Metal fish tape (A) generally comes in longer lengths and is the type used most often. Nylon fish tape (B) generally comes in shorter lengths and is more flexible than metal fish tape.

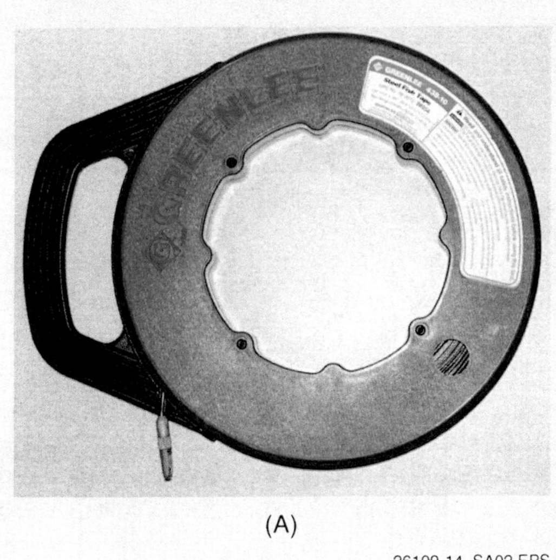

(A)

26109-14_SA02.EPS

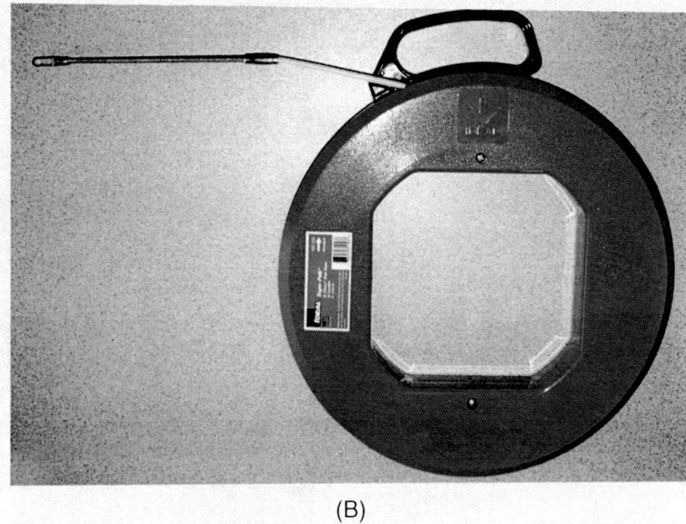

(B)

26109-14_SA03.EPS

- Do not stand in a direct line with the pulling rope. Some equipment is designed so that you may stand to one side for safety.
- Wrap up the pulling rope after use to prevent others from tripping over it.

3.5.0 Pulling Equipment

Many types of pulling equipment are available to help pull conductors through conduit. Pulling equipment can be operated both manually and electrically (*Figure 25*). A manually operated puller is used mainly for smaller pulling jobs where hand pulling is not possible or practical. It is also used in many locations where hand pulling would put an unnecessary strain on the conductors because of the angle of the pull involved.

Electrically driven power pullers are used where long runs, several bends, or large conductors are involved.

The main parts of a power puller are the electric motor, the chain or sprocket drive, the **capstan**, the sheave, and the pull line.

The pull line is routed over the sheave to ensure a straight pull. The pull line is wrapped around the capstan two or three times to provide a good grip on the capstan. The capstan is driven by the electric motor and does the actual pulling. The pull line is pulled by hand at the same speed at which the capstan is pulling. This eliminates the need for a large spool on the puller to wind the pull line.

Attachments to power pullers, such as special application sheaves and extensions, are available for most pulling jobs. Follow the manufacturer's instructions for setup and operation of the puller.

CAUTION

Before using power pullers, a qualified person must verify the amount of pull or tension that will be exerted on the conductors being pulled.

3.6.0 Feeding Conductors into Conduit

After the fish tape or pull line is attached to the conductors, they must be pulled back through the conduit. As the fish tape is pulled, the attached conductors must be properly fed into the conduit.

On Site

Straightening a Bent Fish Tape

To straighten a bent fish tape, drive five 16-penny (16d) nails into a 2 × 4 about 1 inch apart in a straight line. Then wind the fish tape through the nails in a slalom fashion, and pull it through. This will straighten the tape.

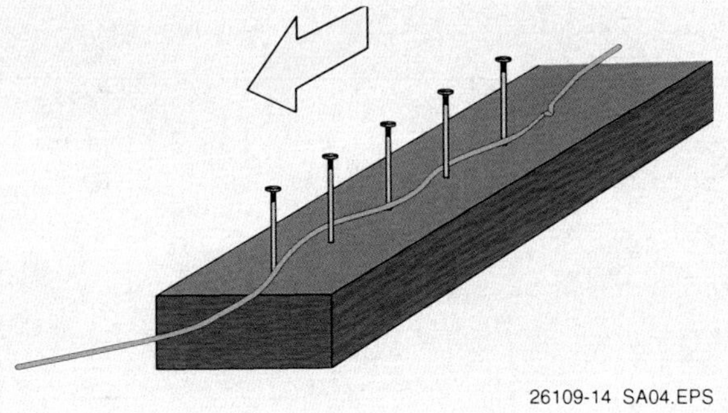
26109-14_SA04.EPS

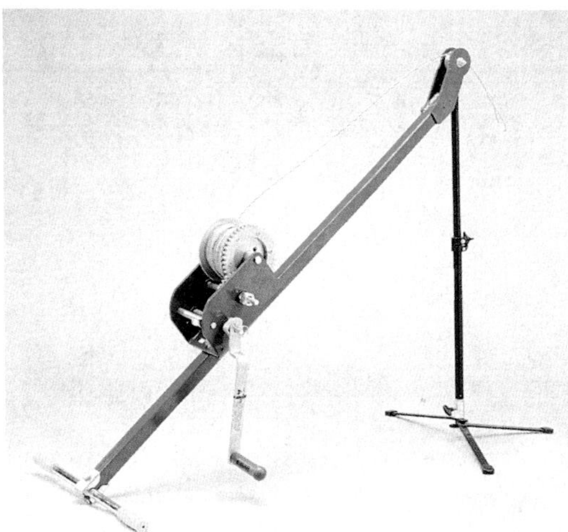
(A) MANUAL WIRE PULLER

(B) POWER PULLER

26109-14_F25.EPS

Figure 25 Pulling equipment.

Usually, more than one conductor is fed into the conduit during a wire pull. It is important to keep the conductors straight and parallel, and free from kinks, bends, and crossovers. Conductors that are allowed to cross each other will form a bulge and make pulling difficult. This could also damage the conductors.

Spools and rolls of conductors must be set up so that they unwind easily, without kinks and bends.

When several conductors must be fed into the conduit at the same time, a reel cart is used (*Figure 26*). The reel cart will allow the spools to turn freely and help prevent the wires from tangling.

3.7.0 Conductor Lubrication

When conductors are fed into long runs of conduit or conduit with several bends, both the conduit and the wires are lubricated with a compound designed for wire lubrication.

Several types of formulated compounds designed for wire lubrication are available in either dry powder, paste, or gel form. These compounds

On Site

Replacing the Hook on a Metal Fish Tape

The hook on a fish tape can be replaced using a propane torch. IMPORTANT: Always work in an appropriate environment and wear the necessary protective equipment. Hold the fish tape securely in a pair of pliers, heat the end with a propane torch until it softens, then use a second set of pliers to form a hook in the fish tape. Allow it to air cool.

26109-14_F26.EPS

Figure 26 Reel cart.

must be noncorrosive to the insulation material of the conductor and to the conduit itself. The compounds are applied by hand to the conductors as they are fed into the conduit. Battery-operated pumps are also available to lubricate the conduit prior to installing the conductors.

3.8.0 Conductor Termination

The amount of free conductor at each junction or outlet box must meet certain *NEC*® specifications. For example, there must be sufficient free conductor so that bends or terminations inside the box, cabinet, or enclosure may be made to a radius as specified in the *NEC*®. The *NEC*® specifies a minimum of six inches for connections made to wiring devices or for splices. Where conductors pass through junction or pull boxes, enough slack should be provided for splices at a later date.

When a box is used as a pull box, the conductors are not necessarily spliced. They may merely enter the pull box via one conduit run and exit via another conduit run. The purpose of a pull box, as the name suggests, is to facilitate pulling conductors on long runs. A junction box, however, is not only used to facilitate pulling conductors through the raceway system, but it also provides an enclosure for splices in the conductors.

On Site

Cleanup

A professional always takes the time to clean up the work area, removing excess lubricant from the boxes, bushings, and conductors. Completing a job in a professional manner is not only good business, it is also an *NEC*® requirement *(NEC Section 110.12)*.

Think About It

Putting It All Together

Think about the design of conductor installations. How does the location of pull points affect the ease of the pull?

Summary

This module introduced key concepts about conductors and cables.

Before selecting a conductor, you must understand wire ratings and why operating temperature is important. The conductor selection process requires that you also consider how and where the conductor will be terminated. The *NEC*® ampacity tables are based on operating temperature. The operating temperature of a conductor is affected by the conductor size (in circular mils), ambient temperature, number of conductors in the bundle, and where the conductors are installed.

Pulling wires and cables through conduit systems is an important part of your job as an electrician. The more you learn about the concepts involved in pulling cable, the safer and more efficient you will be.

Review Questions

1. A conductor's size refers to the cross-sectional area of both the current-carrying wire and the insulation.
   a. True
   b. False

2. The maximum size solid wire that should be terminated in pull boxes and disconnects is _____.
   a. No. 6
   b. No. 8
   c. No. 10
   d. No. 12

3. Compact stranding is used _____.
   a. when installing larger conduit sizes
   b. when decreasing the ampacity of an existing service
   c. with aluminum conductors
   d. in corrosive environments

4. The ampacity ratings of conductors can be found in _____.
   a. *NEC Chapter 1*
   b. *NEC Articles 348 through 352*
   c. *NEC 310.15(B)(16) through 310.15(B)(21)*
   d. *NEC Chapter 9*

5. To determine the ampacity of copper conductors where conductors are used as a single conductor in free air at ambient temperatures of 30°C, use _____.
   a. *NEC Table 310.15(B)(16)*
   b. *NEC Table 310.15(B)(17)*
   c. *NEC Table 310.15(B)(18)*
   d. *NEC Table 310.15(B)(19)*

6. All of the following help to determine how good a material will be for the construction of wire *except* _____.
   a. availability
   b. cost
   c. conductivity
   d. molecular weight

7. A type of thermoset insulation is _____.
   a. RHW
   b. THW
   c. THHW
   d. PVC

8. Polyethylene (PE) is used primarily for _____.
   a. the manufacture of TW and THW insulation
   b. insulation of control and communication wiring
   c. high-voltage cables
   d. high-temperature insulation

9. What letter must be included in the marking of a conductor if it is to be used in a wet, outdoor application?
   a. D
   b. O
   c. I
   d. W

10. What service conductor may be bare, green, or green with a yellow stripe?
    a. The grounding conductor of a multi-conductor cable
    b. The neutral conductor of a multi-conductor cable
    c. The ungrounded conductor of a multi-conductor cable
    d. The high leg of a four-wire, delta-connected secondary

11. What are the colors of insulation on the conductors for a three-conductor NM cable?
    a. One white or gray, one red, and one black
    b. Two white or gray and one red
    c. One white or gray, one red, one black, and a grounding conductor
    d. One green, one white or gray, one blue, and a grounding conductor

12. A conductor's operating temperature is *not* determined by _____.
    a. ambient temperature
    b. current flow
    c. current flow in bundled conductors
    d. the number of conductor strands

13. In some cases, fixture wires may be used as a substitute for branch circuit conductors.
    a. True
    b. False

14. Type NMC cable is suitable for all of the following *except* _____.
    a. dry locations
    b. damp locations
    c. corrosive locations
    d. embedding in concrete

15. The difference between AC cable and MC cable is _____.
    a. AC cable has a maximum of four conductors; MC has a maximum of six
    b. AC cable has a bonding strip; the MC ground is its metal cladding
    c. AC cable has fire-retardant wraps on individual conductors; MC cable does not
    d. AC cable is sized from 10 AWG to 4/0; MC is sized from 18 AWG to 2,000 kcmil

16. Type USE cable can be used for _____.
    a. aboveground installation only
    b. underground installation within a special PVC pipeline
    c. underground installation including direct burial
    d. indoor applications only

17. To prevent unwanted ground loops, instrumentation cable shielding is _____.
    a. not grounded at both ends of the wire
    b. grounded at both ends of the wire
    c. floated on both ends
    d. always ungrounded

18. A pulling line is usually made of _____.
    a. stranded wire
    b. wire rope
    c. steel tape
    d. nylon or other synthetic material

19. When feeding conductors into long runs of conduit, it is important to apply lubricant to the conductors only, and *not* to the conduit.
    a. True
    b. False

20. The *NEC*® specifies a minimum of _____ for connections made to wiring devices or for splices.
    a. 4"
    b. 6"
    c. 8"
    d. 10"

Trade Terms Quiz

Fill in the blank with the correct term that you learned from your study of this module.

1. A conductor's ____________ is the current the conductor can carry continuously without exceeding its temperature rating.
2. On a cable puller, the ____________ is the part on which the pulling rope is wrapped and pulled.
3. During a pull, cable may be attached to the pulling rope using a(n) ____________.
4. A(n) ____________ is a manually operated device that is used to pull a wire through conduit.
5. Composed of foam rubber, a(n) ____________ fits inside a piece of conduit and is propelled by compressed air or vacuumed through the conduit run, pulling a line or tape.

Trade Terms

Ampacity
Capstan
Fish tape
Mouse
Wire grip

Module 26109-14
Supplemental Exercises

1. The designation for one thousand circular mils is ____________________.

2. ____________________ is the maximum current in amperes a conductor can carry continuously under the conditions of use without exceeding its temperature rating.

3. True or False? *NEC Table 310.15(B)(16)* covers conductors rated up to 2,000V where not more than three conductors are installed in a raceway or cable.

4. True or False? Type NMC is suitable for direct burial.

5. Which of the following represents the largest wire size?

   a. 50
   b. 10
   c. 5
   d. 4/0

6. A(n) ____________________ is a circle which has a diameter of 1 mil.

7. True or False? All current-carrying conductors (including the grounded conductor) must be insulated when used on the inside of buildings.

8. True or False? Polyethylene is the base material used for the manufacture of TW and THW insulation.

9. Polyethylene is used primarily for insulation of ____________________.

   a. high-voltage conductors
   b. control and communications wiring
   c. THHN wiring
   d. XHHW wiring

10. What does the letter R stand for with regard to insulation coding?____________________

11. When conductors are installed where the ambient temperature is above ____________________, the conductor ampacity must be reduced proportionally with the increase in temperature.

    a. 25°C
    b. 30°C
    c. 45°C
    d. 60°C

12. Type UF cable ____________________.

    a. is commonly called *Romex®*
    b. is suitable for direct burial
    c. is commonly referred to as *BX®*
    d. consists of five conductors

13. Type MV cable is suitable for ________________.

    a. use in wet locations
    b. use in dry locations
    c. direct burial
    d. all of the above.

14. Some jackets have a(n) ________________ that allows the jacket to be peeled back without the use of a knife or cable cutter.

15. A(n) ________________ is a piston-like plug that is attached to a string or rope for pulling through conduit using a power fishing system.

Cornerstone of Craftsmanship

L. J. LeBlanc

Senior Electrician/Instructor
Pumba Electrical/Baton Rouge Community College

Provide a summary of how you got started in the construction industry.
I took electrical jobs to pay for college and attended night classes at trade school for four years.

Who inspired you to enter the industry? Why?
My dad was an electrician. I was working with him and wiring houses at an early age.

What do you enjoy most about your job?
Electrical work is constantly changing. I love the challenge of troubleshooting. By passing on the knowledge I've obtained, I have truly made a difference in my student's lives.

Do you think training and education are important in construction? If so, why?
Education is extremely important. One must stay abreast of the changes involved in the code.

How important are NCCER credentials to your career?
If you are going to train, you need to have credentials to show you are qualified to teach.

How has training/construction impacted your life and your career?
Pay scales are governed by education and accomplishments.

Would you suggest construction as a career to others? If so, why?
Construction jobs are high paying and the sky is the limit in this field if you are skilled and work hard.

How do you define craftsmanship?
A person signs his name with his work. The job you do not only represents you but your company as well. Installations should be done in a workmanlike manner.

Trade Terms Introduced in This Module

Ampacity: The maximum current in amperes a conductor can carry continuously under the conditions of use without exceeding its temperature rating.

Capstan: The turning drum of the cable puller on which the rope is wrapped and pulled.

Fish tape: A hand device used to pull a wire through a conduit run.

Mouse: A cylinder of foam rubber that fits inside the conduit and is then propelled by compressed air or vacuumed through the conduit run, pulling a line or tape.

Wire grip: A device used to link pulling rope to cable during a pull.

Additional Resources

This module presents thorough resources for task training. The following resource material is suggested for further study.

National Electrical Code® Handbook, Latest Edition. Quincy, MA: National Fire Protection Association.

Figure Credits

AGC of America, Module opener

Tim Dean, Figures 4, 16

Topaz Publications, Inc., Figures 7B (photo), 8B (photo), 15, 17B (photo), 18, 19, 23, 24, 26, SA01–SA03

Jim Mitchem, Figure 9

The Okonite Company, Figure 10

General Cable, Figure 12

Greenlee/A Textron Company, Figures 22, 25

NCCER CURRICULA — USER UPDATE

NCCER makes every effort to keep its textbooks up-to-date and free of technical errors. We appreciate your help in this process. If you find an error, a typographical mistake, or an inaccuracy in NCCER's curricula, please fill out this form (or a photocopy), or complete the online form at **www.nccer.org/olf**. Be sure to include the exact module ID number, page number, a detailed description, and your recommended correction. Your input will be brought to the attention of the Authoring Team. Thank you for your assistance.

Instructors – If you have an idea for improving this textbook, or have found that additional materials were necessary to teach this module effectively, please let us know so that we may present your suggestions to the Authoring Team.

NCCER Product Development and Revision

13614 Progress Blvd., Alachua, FL 32615

Email: curriculum@nccer.org

Online: www.nccer.org/olf

❑ Trainee Guide ❑ AIG ❑ Exam ❑ PowerPoints Other ______________________

Craft / Level: Copyright Date:

Module ID Number / Title:

Section Number(s):

Description:

Recommended Correction:

Your Name:

Address:

Email: Phone:

Basic Electrical Construction Drawings

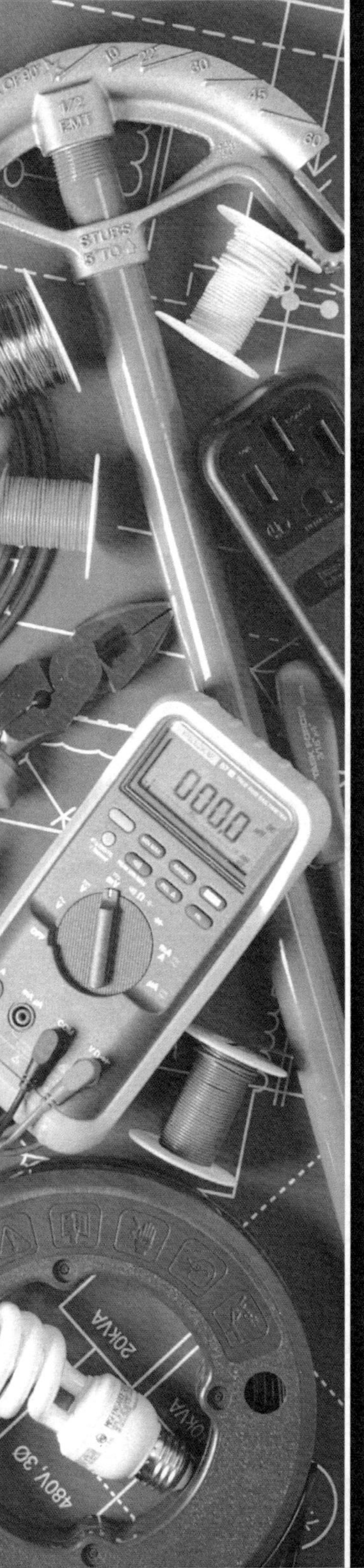

Fenway Park Pavilion Seat Expansion and EMC/State Street Club Project

This expansion illustrates the accomplishment of an ambitious concept in a sensitive historical environment. The $45 million project was completed within the six-month winter off-season and used precise phasing and logistics to ensure complete protection of Fenway Field. The contractor structurally lifted and shored the historic facility to accommodate the installation of a new ring of columns that would ultimately support the significant addition.

26110-14

Trainees with successful module completions may be eligible for credentialing through NCCER's National Registry. To learn more, go to **www.nccer.org** or contact us at **1.888.622.3720.** Our website has information on the latest product releases and training, as well as online versions of our *Cornerstone* magazine and Pearson's product catalog.

Your feedback is welcome. You may email your comments to **curriculum@nccer.org,** send general comments and inquiries to **info@nccer.org,** or fill in the User Update form at the back of this module.

This information is general in nature and intended for training purposes only. Actual performance of activities described in this manual requires compliance with all applicable operating, service, maintenance, and safety procedures under the direction of qualified personnel. References in this manual to patented or proprietary devices do not constitute a recommendation of their use.

26110-14

Basic Electrical Construction Drawings

Objectives

When you have completed this module, you will be able to do the following:

1. Explain the basic layout of a set of construction drawings.
2. Describe the information included in the title block of a construction drawing.
3. Identify the types of lines used on construction drawings.
4. Using an architect's scale, state the actual dimensions of a given drawing component.
5. Interpret electrical drawings, including site plans, floor plans, and detail drawings.
6. Interpret equipment schedules found on electrical drawings.
7. Describe the type of information included in electrical specifications.

Performance Tasks

Under the supervision of the instructor, you should be able to do the following:

1. Using an architect's scale, state the actual dimensions of a given drawing component.
2. Make a material takeoff of the lighting fixtures specified in Performance Profile Sheet 2 using the drawing provided on Performance Profile Sheet 3. The takeoff requires that all lighting fixtures be counted, and where applicable, the total number of lamps for each fixture type must be calculated.

Trade Terms

Architectural drawings
Block diagram
Blueprint
Detail drawing
Dimensions
Electrical drawing
Elevation drawing
Floor plan
One-line diagram
Plan view
Power-riser diagram
Scale
Schedule
Schematic diagram
Sectional view
Shop drawing
Site plan
Written specifications

Required Trainee Materials

1. Paper and pencil
2. Copy of the latest edition of the *National Electrical Code®*
3. Appropriate personal protective equipment

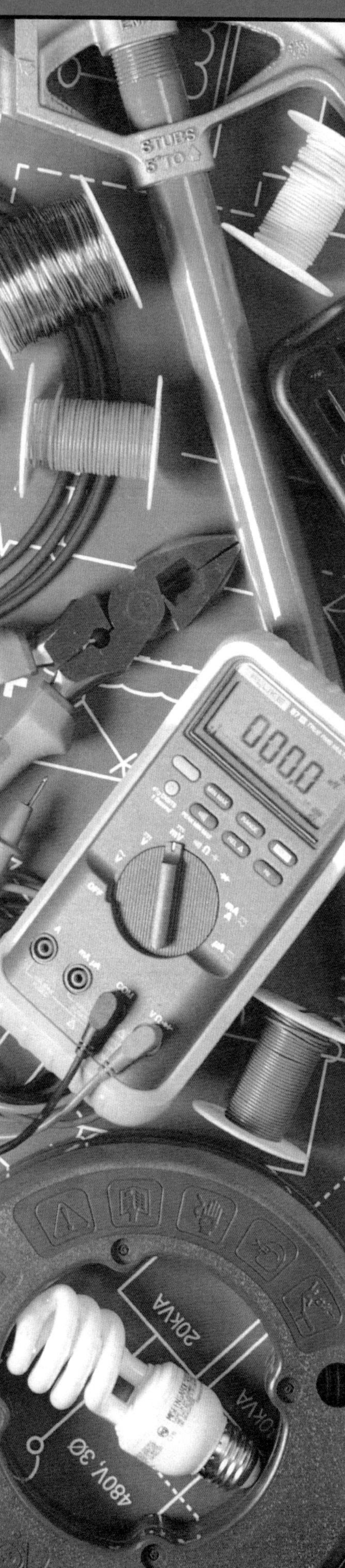

Contents

Topics to be presented in this module include:

Figures

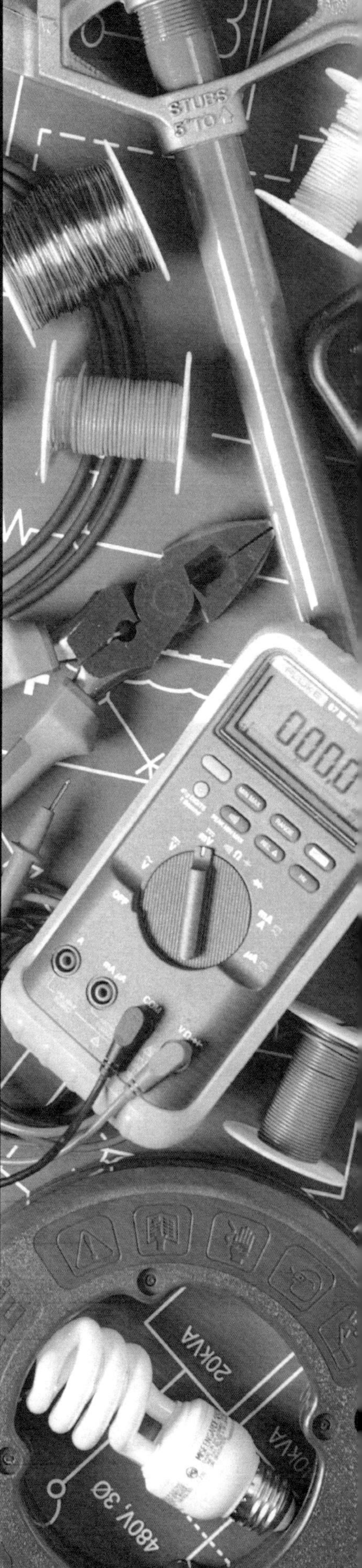

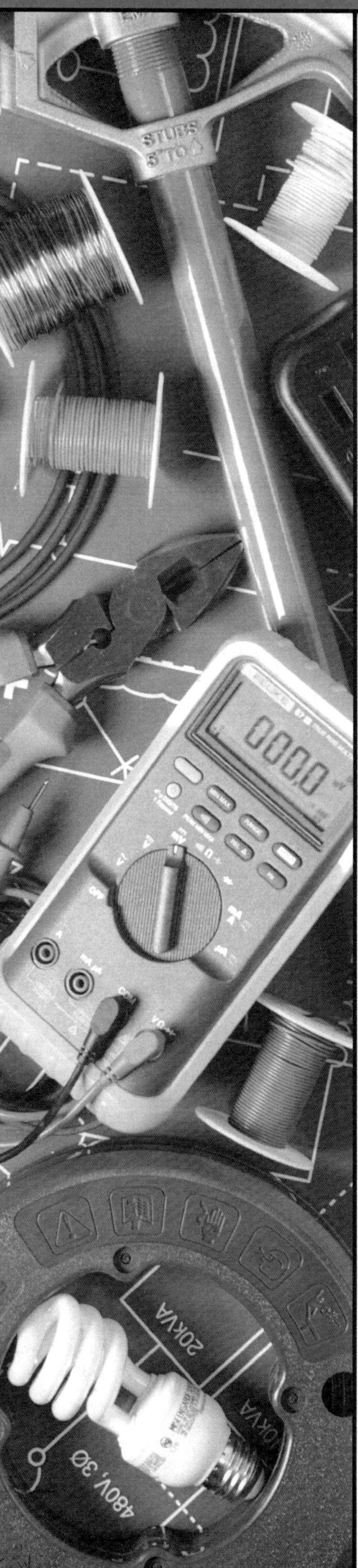
STUBS
5"TO
0000
20kVA
480V, 3Ø

1.0.0 Introduction to Construction Drawings

In all large construction projects and in many of the smaller ones, an architect is commissioned to prepare complete working drawings and specifications for the project. These drawings usually include:

- A **site plan** indicating the location of the building on the property.
- **Floor plans** showing the walls and partitions for each floor or level.
- Elevations of all exterior faces of the building.
- Several vertical cross sections to indicate clearly the various floor levels and details of the footings, foundation, walls, floors, ceilings, and roof construction.
- Large-scale **detail drawings** showing such construction details as may be required.

For projects of any consequence, the architect usually hires consulting engineers to prepare structural, electrical, and mechanical drawings, with the latter encompassing pipefitting, instrumentation, plumbing, and heating, ventilating, and air conditioning drawings.

1.1.0 Site Plan

This type of plan of the building site looks as if the site is viewed from an airplane and shows the property boundaries, the existing contour lines, the new contour lines (after grading), the location of the building on the property, new and existing roadways, all utility lines, and other pertinent details. The drawing **scale** is also shown. Descriptive notes may also be found on the site (plot) plan listing names of adjacent property owners, the land surveyor, and the date of the survey. A legend or symbol list is also included so that anyone who must work with the site plan can readily read the information. See *Figure 1*.

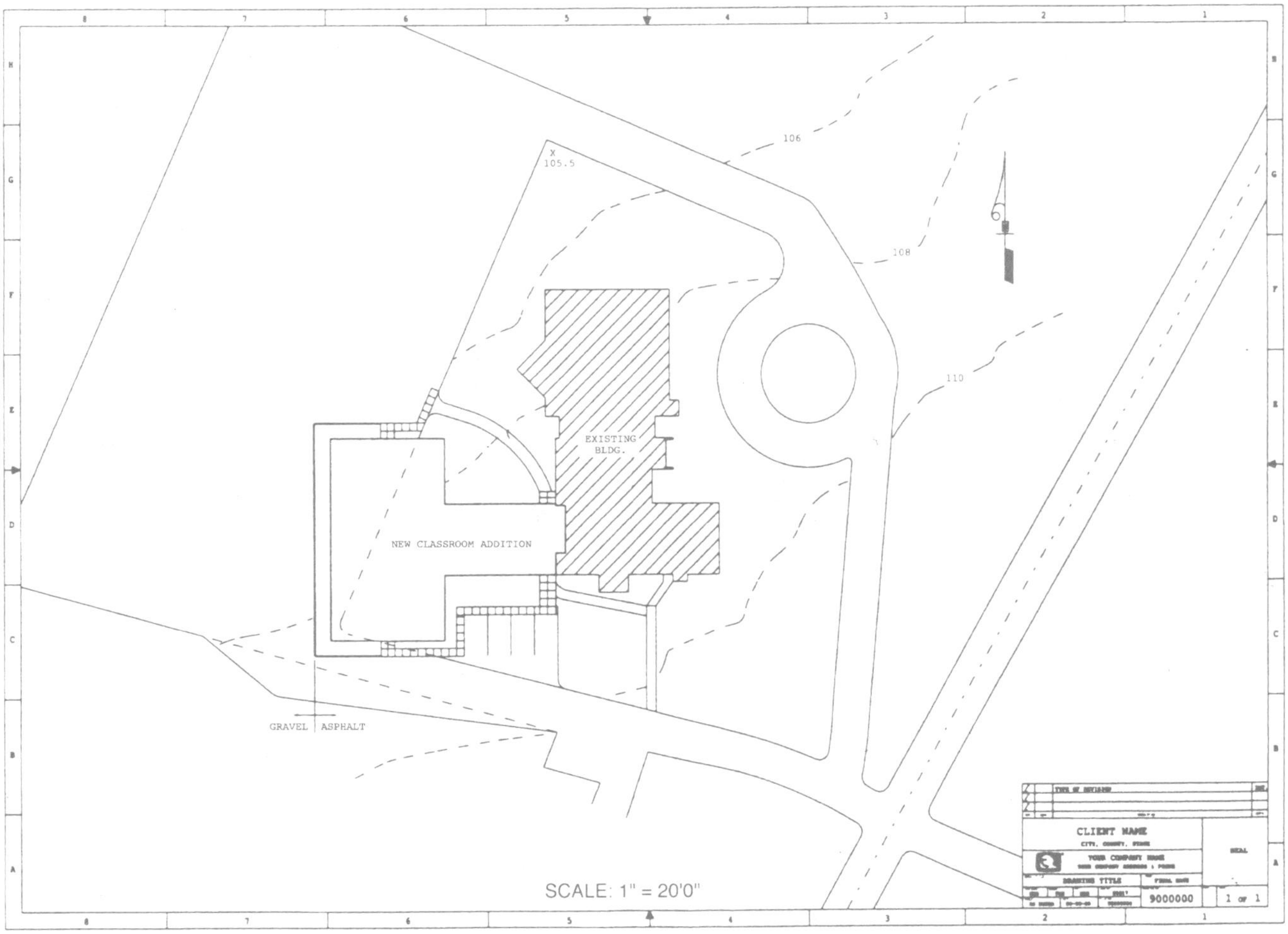

26110-14_F01.EPS

Figure 1 Typical site plan.

1.2.0 Floor Plans

The plan view of any object is a drawing showing the outline and all details as seen when looking directly down on the object. It shows only two dimensions, length and width. The floor plan of a building is drawn as if a horizontal cut were made through the building—at about window height—and then the top portion removed to reveal the bottom part. See *Figure 2*.

If a plan view of a home's basement is needed, the part of the house above the middle of the basement windows is imagined to be cut away. By looking down on the uncovered portion, every detail and partition can be seen. Likewise, imagine the part above the middle of the first floor windows being cut away. A drawing that looks straight down at the remaining part would be called the first floor plan or lower level. A cut through the second floor windows would be called the second floor plan or upper level. See *Figure 3*.

On Site

Then and Now

Years ago, blueprints were created by placing a hand drawing against light-sensitive paper and then exposing it to ultraviolet light. The light would turn the paper blue except where lines were drawn on the original. The light-sensitive paper was then developed, and the resulting print had white lines against a blue background. Modern blueprints usually have blue or black lines against a white background and are generated using computer-aided design programs. Newer programs offer three-dimensional modeling and other enhanced features.

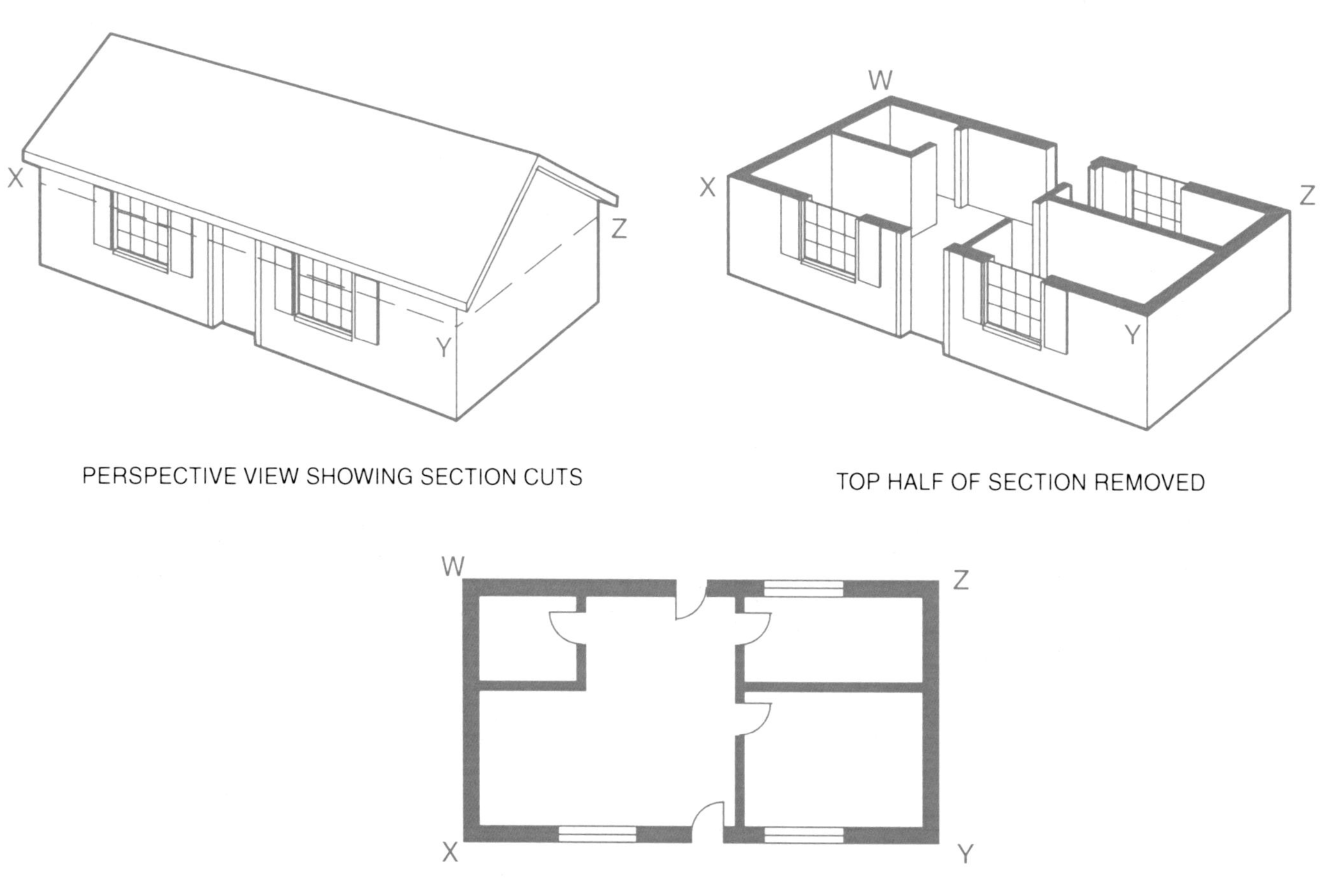

Figure 2 Principles of floor plan layout.

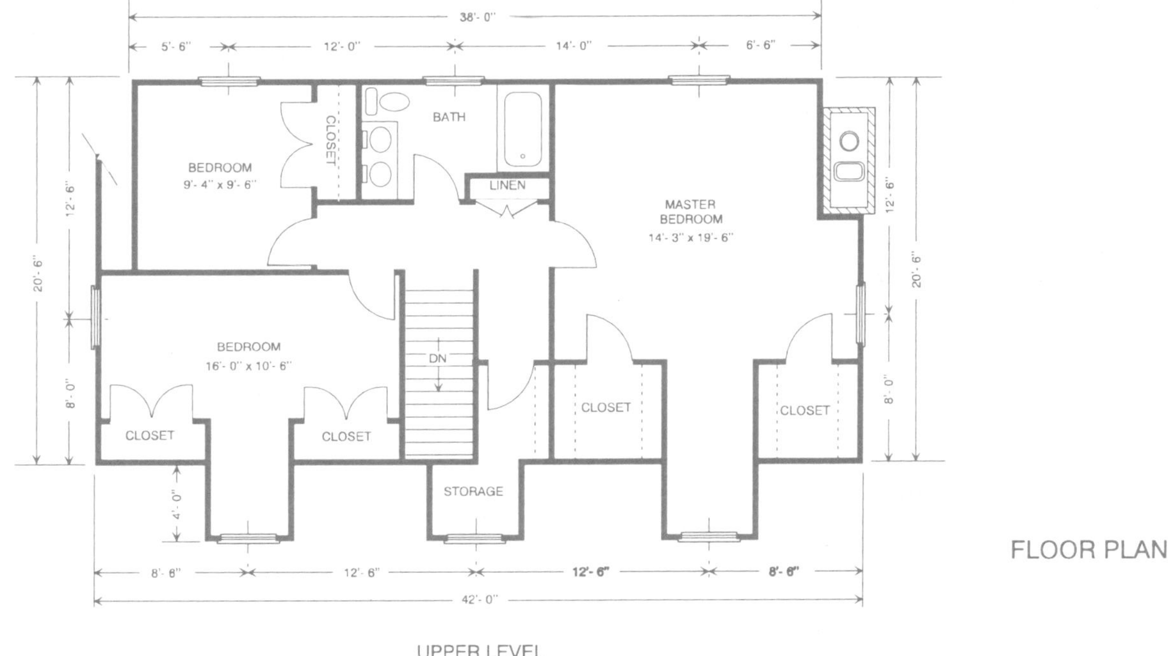

FLOOR PLAN

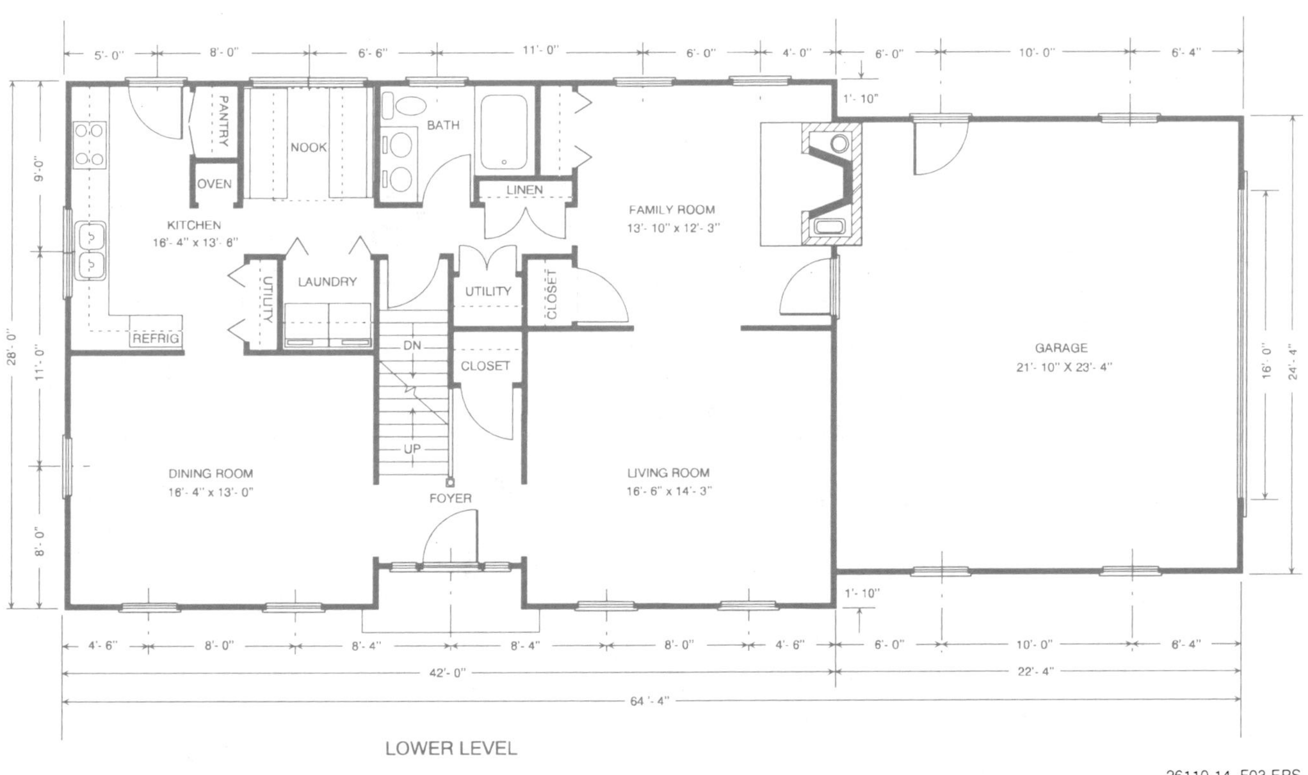

26110-14_F03.EPS

Figure 3 Floor plans of a building.

On Site

Using a Drawing Set

Always treat a drawing set with care. It is best to keep two sets, one for the office and one for field use. Be sure to use the most current revision. After you use a sheet from a set of drawings, refold the sheet with the title block facing up.

1.3.0 Elevations

The elevation is an outline of an object that shows heights and may show the length or width of a particular side, but not depth. *Figures 4* and *5* show elevation drawings for a building.

NOTE

Elevation drawings may also show the heights of windows, doors, and porches, the pitch of roofs, etc., because all of these measurements cannot be shown conveniently on floor plans.

1.4.0 Sections

A section or sectional view (*Figure 6*) is a cutaway view that allows the viewer to see the inside of a structure. The point on the plan or elevation showing where the imaginary cut has been made is indicated by the section line, which is usually a dashed line. The section line shows the location of the section on the plan or elevation. It is necessary to know which of the cutaway parts is represented in the sectional drawing. To show

FRONT ELEVATION

REAR ELEVATION

26110-14_F04.EPS

Figure 4 Front and rear elevations.

Figure 5 Left and right elevations.

this, arrow points are placed at the ends of the section lines.

In architectural drawings, it is often necessary to show more than one section on the same drawing. The different section lines must be distinguished by letters, numbers, or other designations placed at the ends of the lines. These section letters are generally large so as to stand out on the drawings. To further avoid confusion, the same letter is usually placed at each end of the section line. The section is named according to these letters (e.g., Section A-A, Section B-B, and so forth).

A longitudinal section is taken lengthwise while a cross section is usually taken straight across the width of an object. Sometimes, however, a section is not taken along one straight line. It is often taken along a zigzag line to show important parts of the object.

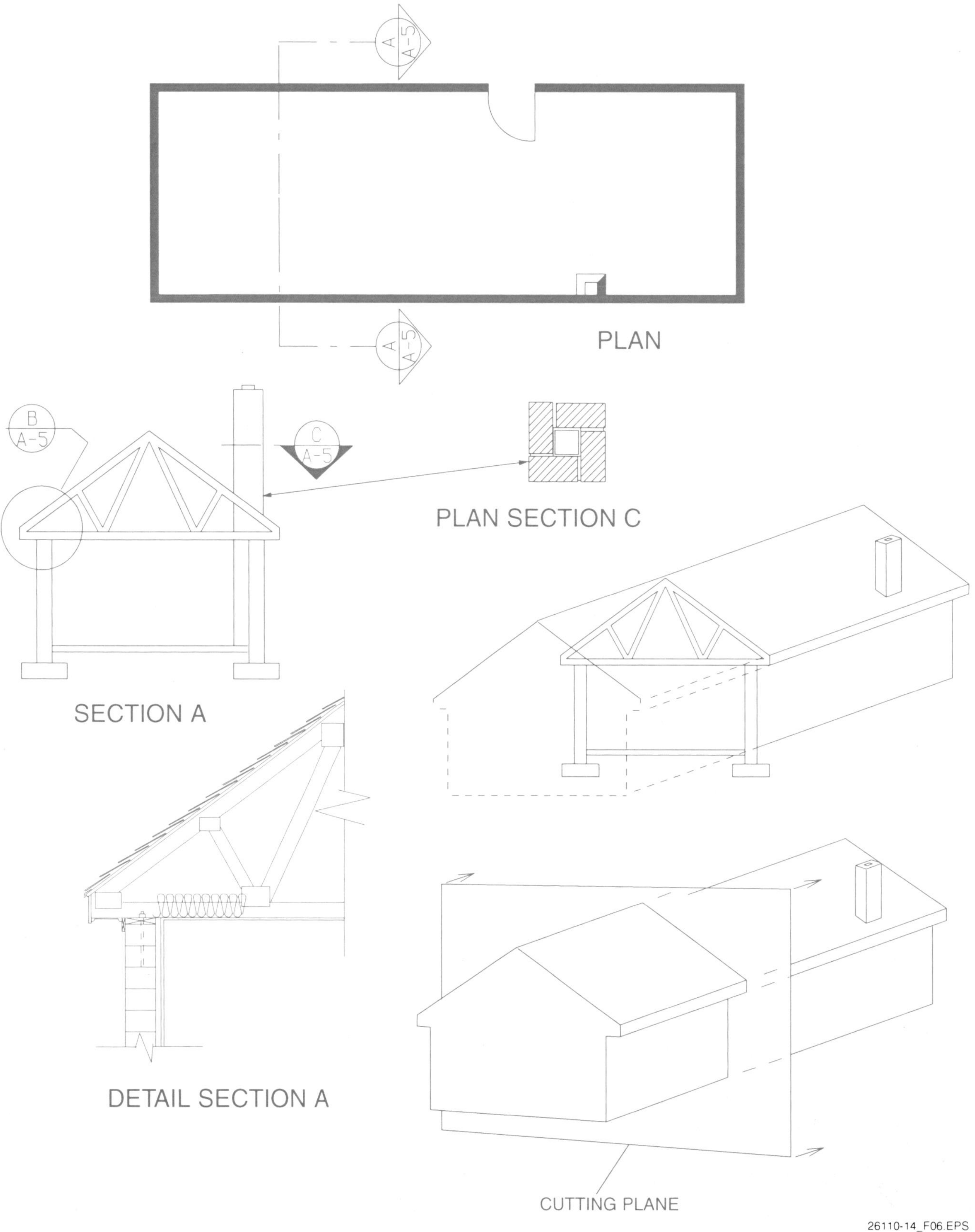

Figure 6 Sectional drawing.

A sectional view, as applied to architectural drawings, is a drawing showing the building, or portion of a building, as though it were cut through on some imaginary line. This line may be either vertical (straight up and down) or horizontal. Wall sections are nearly always made vertically so that the cut edge is exposed from top to bottom. In some ways, the wall section is one of the most important of all the drawings to construction workers, because it answers the questions as to how a structure should be built. The floor plans of a building show how each floor is arranged, but the wall sections tell how each part is constructed and usually indicate the material to be used. The electrician needs to know this information when determining wiring methods that comply with the *NEC*®.

1.5.0 Electrical Drawings

Electrical drawings show in a clear, concise manner exactly what is required of the electricians. The amount of data shown on such drawings should be sufficient, but not overdone. This means that a complete set of electrical drawings could consist of only one 8½" × 11" sheet, or it could consist of several dozen 24" × 36" (or larger) sheets, depending on the size and complexity of a given project. A shop drawing, for example, may contain details of only one piece of equipment, while a set of working drawings for an industrial installation may contain dozens of drawing sheets detailing the electrical system for lighting and power, along with equipment, motor controls, wiring diagrams, schematic diagrams, equipment schedules, and a host of other pertinent data.

In general, the electrical working drawings for a given project serve three distinct functions:

- They provide electrical contractors with an exact description of the project so that materials and labor may be estimated to calculate a total cost of the project for bidding purposes.
- They provide workers on the project with instructions as to how the electrical system is to be installed.
- They provide a map of the electrical system once the job is completed to aid in maintenance and troubleshooting for years to come.

Electrical drawings from consulting engineering firms will vary in quality from sketchy, incomplete drawings to neat, precise drawings that are easy to understand. Few, however, will cover every detail of the electrical system. Therefore, a good knowledge of installation practices must go hand-in-hand with interpreting electrical working drawings.

On Site

Applying Your Skills

Once you learn how to interpret construction drawings, you can apply that knowledge to any type of construction, from simple residential applications to large industrial complexes.

Sometimes electrical contractors will have electrical drafters prepare special supplemental drawings for use by the contractors' employees. On certain projects, these supplemental drawings can save supervision time in the field once the project has begun.

2.0.0 Drawing Layout

Although a strong effort has been made to standardize drawing practices in the building construction industry, the drawings or blueprints prepared by different architectural or engineering firms will rarely be identical. Similarities, however, will exist between most sets of drawings, and with a little experience, you should have no trouble interpreting any set of drawings that might be encountered.

Most drawings used for building construction projects will be drawn on sheets in various sizes. Each drawing sheet has border lines framing the overall drawing and one or more title blocks, as shown in *Figure 7*. The type and size of title blocks varies with each firm preparing the drawings. In addition, some drawing sheets will also contain a revision block near the title block, and perhaps an approval block. This information is normally found on each drawing sheet, regardless of the type of project or the information contained on the sheet.

2.1.0 Title Block

The architect's title block for a drawing is usually boxed in the lower right-hand corner of the drawing sheet; the size of the block varies with the size of the drawing and with the information required. See *Figure 8*.

In general, the title block of an electrical drawing should contain the following information:

- Name of the project
- Address of the project
- Name of the owner or client
- Name of the architectural firm
- Date of completion

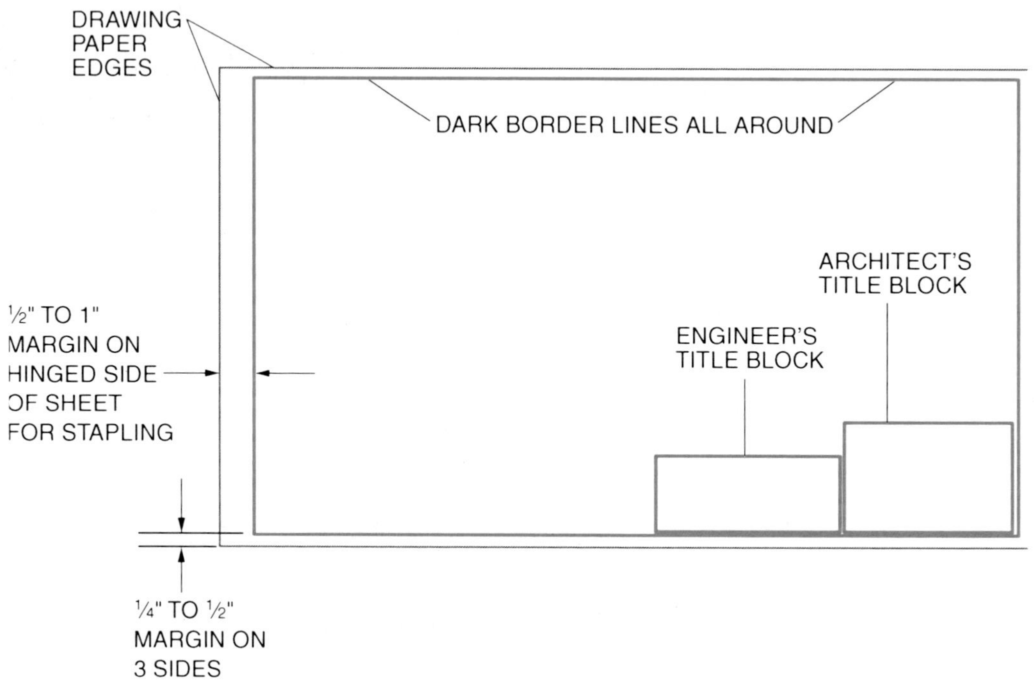

Figure 7 Typical drawing layout.

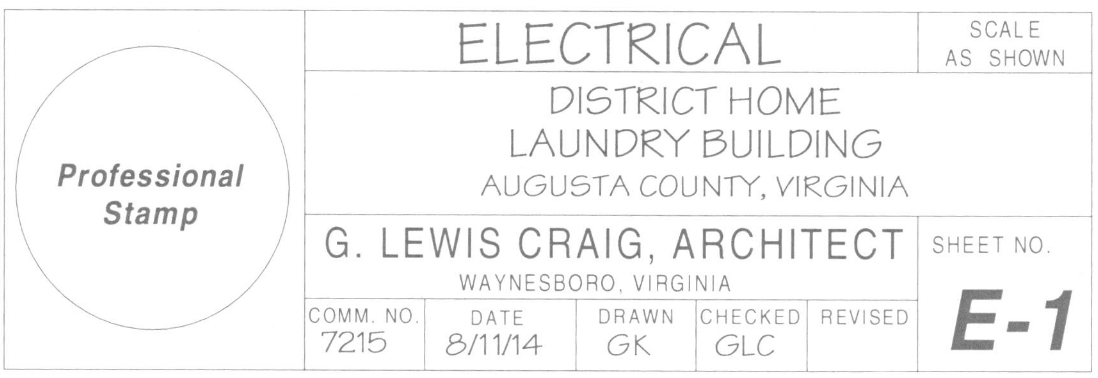

Figure 8 Typical architect's title block.

On Site

Interpreting Electrical Drawings

A good example of when an electrician must interpret the drawings is when wiring a log cabin. The drawings will show the receptacle and switch locations in branch circuits as usual, but the electrician must figure out how to route wires and install boxes where there is no hollow wall and sometimes no ceiling space.

- Scale(s)
- Initials of the drafter, checker, and designer, with dates under each
- Job number
- Sheet number
- General description of the drawing

Often, the consulting engineering firm will also be listed, which means that an additional title block will be applied to the drawing, usually next to the architect's title block. *Figure 9* shows completed architectural and engineering title blocks as they appear on an actual drawing.

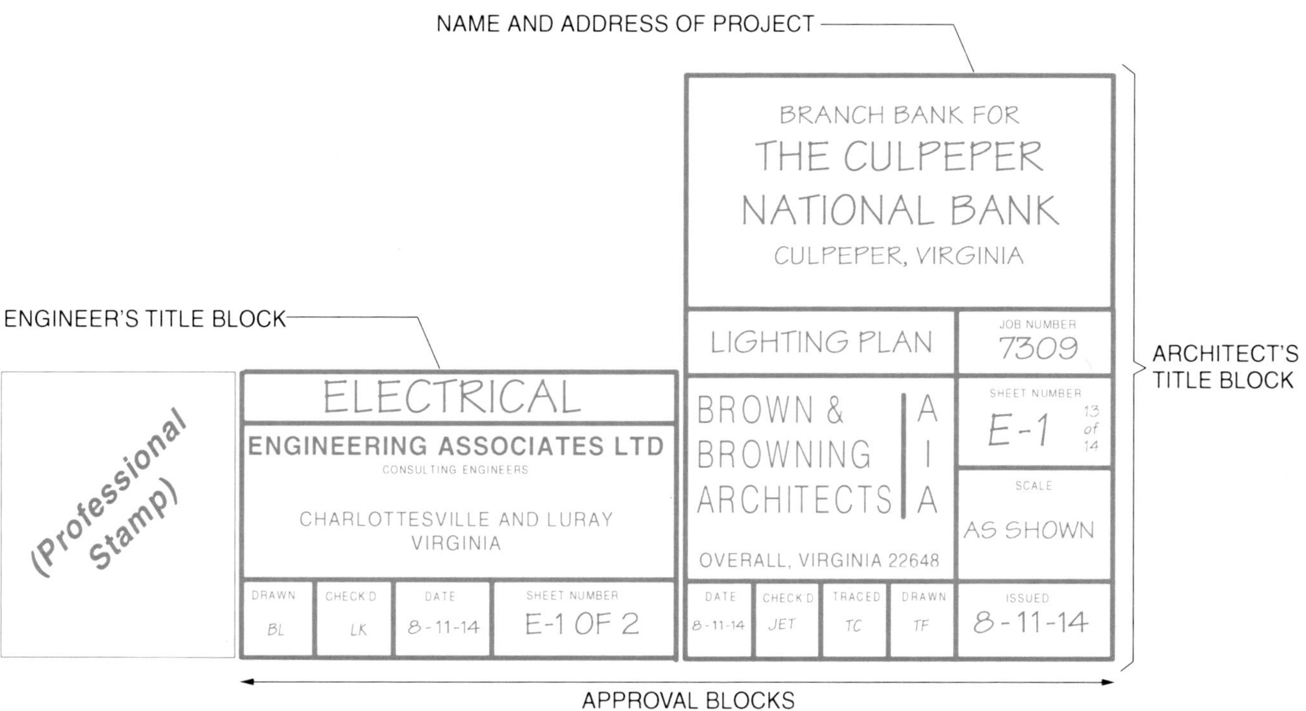

Figure 9 Title blocks.

On Site

Check the Title Block

Always refer to the title block for scale and be aware that it often changes from drawing to drawing within the same set. Also check for the current revision, and when you replace a drawing with a new revision, be sure to remove and file the older version.

2.2.0 Approval Block

The approval block, in most cases, will appear on the drawing sheet as shown in *Figure 10*. The various types of approval blocks (drawn, checked, etc.) will be initialed by the appropriate personnel. This type of approval block is usually part of the title block and appears on each drawing sheet.

On some projects, authorized signatures are required before certain systems may be installed, or even before the project begins. An approval block such as the one shown in *Figure 11* indicates that all required personnel have checked the drawings for accuracy, and that the set meets with everyone's approval. Such an approval block usually appears on the front sheet of the blueprint set and may include:

- *Professional stamp* – Registered seal of approval by the licensed architect or consulting engineer.
- *Design supervisor* – Signature of the person who is overseeing the design.
- *Drawn (by)* – Signature or initials of the person who drafted the drawing and the date it was completed.
- *Checked (by)* – Signature or initials of the person who reviewed the drawing and the date of approval.
- *Approved* – Signature or initials of the architect/engineer and the date of the approval.
- *Owner's approval* – Signature of the project owner or the owner's representative along with the date signed.

COMM. NO.	DATE	DRAWN	CHECKED	REVISED
7215	8/11/14	GK	GLC	

26110-14_F10.EPS

Figure 10 Typical approval block.

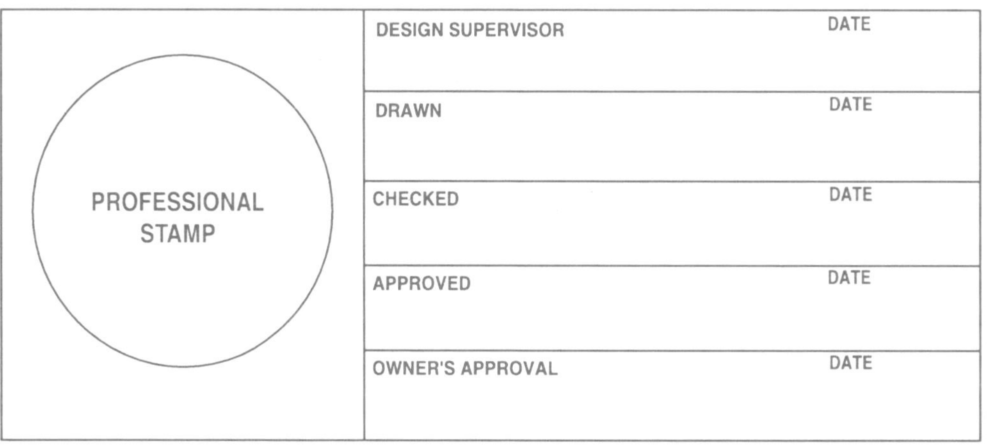

PROFESSIONAL
STAMP
DESIGN SUPERVISOR
DATE
DRAWN
DATE
CHECKED
DATE
APPROVED
DATE
OWNER'S APPROVAL
DATE
26110-14_F11.EPS

Figure 11 Alternate approval block.

On Site

Orient Yourself

When reading a drawing, find the north arrow to orient yourself to the structure. Knowing where north is enables you to accurately describe the locations of walls and other parts of the building.

LEGEND
UGP — UNDERGROUND 13.2 KV POWER DUCTBANK
UGT — UNDERGROUND TELEPHONE/COMMUNICATIONS DUCTBANK
UNDERGROUND LIGHTING CONDUIT AND WIRING
MANHOLE - TYPE AS INDICATED
LIGHT FIXTURE - TYPE/CCT. NO.
HOMERUN TO PANEL AND CIRCUITS AS INDICATED BY ARROWS
PAD-MOUNT TRANSFORMER (NIC)

26110-14_SA01.EPS

Think About It

Using All of the Drawings

Look back over the information on floor plans, elevations, and sections. What kinds of information would an electrician get from each of these drawings? What could a sectional drawing show that a floor plan could not?

2.3.0 Revision Block

Sometimes electrical drawings will have to be partially redrawn or modified during the construction of a project. It is extremely important that such modifications are noted and dated on the drawings to ensure that the workers have an up-to-date set of drawings to work from. In some situations, sufficient space is left near the title block for dates and descriptions of revisions, as shown in *Figure 12*. In other cases, a revision block is provided (again, near the title block), as shown in *Figure 13*. The area on the drawing where the revision has been made will often be circled with a cloud shape.

REVISIONS
9/5/14 - REVISED LIGHTING FIXTURE
NO. 3 IN. LIGHTING FIXTURE SCHEDULE

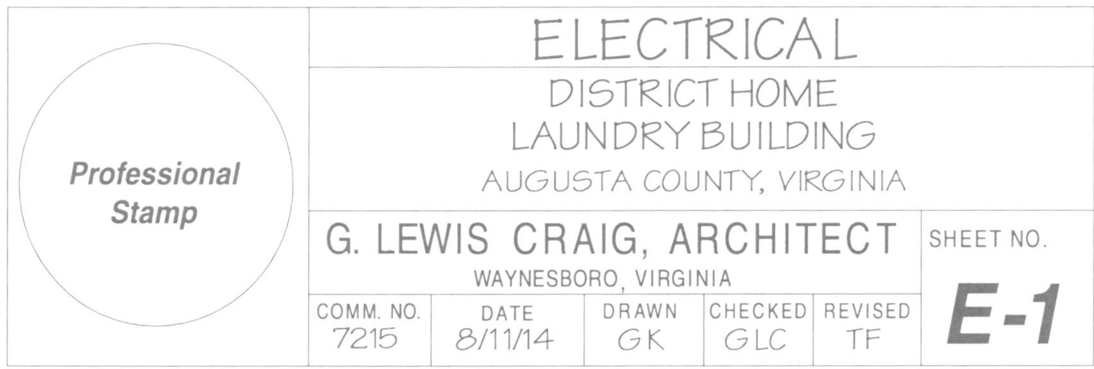

26110-14_F12.EPS

Figure 12 One method of showing revisions on working drawings.

REVISIONS				
REV	DESCRIPTION	DR	APPD	DATE
1	FIXTURE NO. 3 IN. LIGHTING-FIXTURE SCHDL	GK	GLC	9/5/14

Professional
Stamp

ELECTRICAL
DISTRICT HOME
LAUNDRY BUILDING
AUGUSTA COUNTY, VIRGINIA
G. LEWIS CRAIG, ARCHITECT
WAYNESBORO, VIRGINIA

COMM. NO.	DATE	DRAWN	CHECKED	REVISED	SHEET NO.
7215	8/11/14	GK	GLC	TF	E-1

26110-14_F13.EPS

Figure 13 Alternative method of showing revisions on working drawings.

NOTE

Architects, engineers, designers, and drafters have their own methods of showing revisions, so expect to find deviations from those shown here.

CAUTION

When a set of electrical working drawings has been revised, always make certain that the most up-to-date set is used for all future layout work. Either destroy the old, obsolete set of drawings or else clearly mark on the affected sheets, *Obsolete Drawing—Do Not Use.* Also, when working with a set of working drawings and written specifications for the first time, thoroughly check each page to see if any revisions or modifications have been made to the originals. Doing so can save much time and expense to all concerned with the project.

3.0.0 Drafting Lines

You will encounter many types of drafting lines. To specify the meaning of each type of line, contrasting lines can be made by varying the width of the lines or breaking the lines in a uniform way.

Figure 14 shows common lines used on architectural drawings. However, these lines can vary. Architects and engineers have strived for a common standard for the past century, but unfortunately, their goal has yet to be reached. Therefore, you will find variations in lines and symbols from drawing to drawing, so always consult the legend or symbol list when referring to any drawing. Also, carefully inspect each drawing to ensure that line types are used consistently.

The drafting lines shown in *Figure 14* are used as follows:

- *Light full line* – This line is used for section lines, building background (outlines), and similar

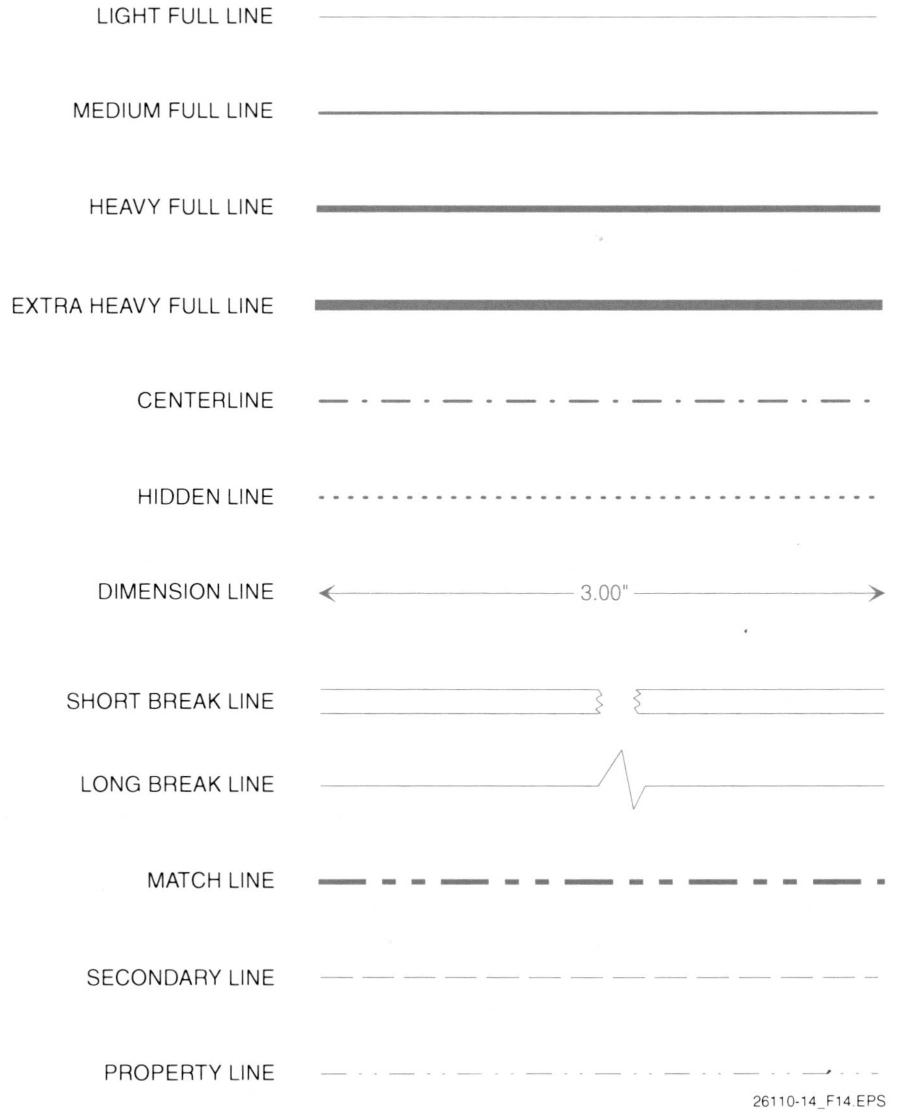

Figure 14 Typical drafting lines.

uses where the object to be drawn is secondary to the system being shown (e.g., HVAC or electrical).

- *Medium full line* – This type of line is frequently used for hand lettering on drawings. It is further used for some drawing symbols, circuit lines, etc.
- *Heavy full line* – This line is used for borders around title blocks, schedules, and for hand lettering drawing titles. Some types of symbols are frequently drawn with a heavy full line.
- *Extra heavy full line* – This line is used for border lines on architectural/engineering drawings.
- *Centerline* – A centerline is a broken line made up of alternately spaced long and short dashes. It indicates the centers of objects such as holes, pillars, or fixtures. Sometimes, the centerline indicates the dimensions of a finished floor.
- *Hidden line* – A hidden line consists of a series of short dashes that are closely and evenly spaced. It shows the edges of objects that are not visible in a particular view. The object outlined by hidden lines in one drawing is often fully pictured in another drawing.
- *Dimension line* – These are thin lines used to show the extent and direction of dimensions. The dimension is usually placed in a break inside the dimension lines. Normal practice is to place the dimension lines outside the object's outline. However, it may sometimes be necessary to draw the dimensions inside the outline.
- *Short break line* – This line is usually drawn freehand and is used for short breaks.
- *Long break line* – This line, which is drawn partly with a straightedge and partly with freehand zigzags, is used for long breaks.
- *Match line* – This line is used to show the position of the cutting plane. Therefore, it is also called the cutting plane line. A match or cutting plane line is a heavy line with long dashes alternating with two short dashes. It is used on drawings of large structures to show where one drawing stops and the next drawing starts.
- *Secondary line* – This line is frequently used to outline pieces of equipment or to indicate reference points of a drawing that are secondary to the drawing's purpose.
- *Property line* – This is a light line made up of one long and two short dashes that are alternately spaced. It indicates land boundaries on the site plan.

Other uses of the lines just mentioned include the following:

- *Extension lines* – Extension lines are lightweight lines that start about ¹⁄₁₆ inch away from the edge of an object and extend out. A common use of extension lines is to create a boundary for dimension lines. Dimension lines meet extension lines with arrowheads, slashes, or dots. Extension lines that point from a note or other reference to a particular feature on a drawing are called leaders. They usually end in either an arrowhead or a dot and may include an explanatory note at the end.
- *Section lines* – These are often referred to as cross-hatch lines. Drawn at a 45° angle, these lines show where an object has been cut away to reveal the inside.
- *Phantom lines* – Phantom lines are solid, light lines that show where an object will be installed. A future door opening or a future piece of equipment can be shown with phantom lines.

3.1.0 Electrical Drafting Lines

Besides the architectural lines shown in *Figure 14* consulting electrical engineers, designers, and drafters use additional lines to represent circuits and their related components. Again, these lines may vary from drawing to drawing, so check the symbol list or legend for the exact meaning of lines on the drawing with which you are working. *Figure 15* shows lines used on some electrical drawings.

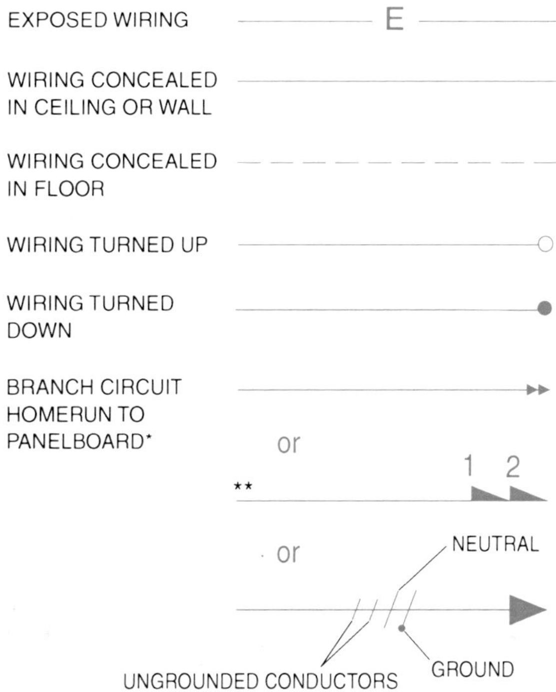

Figure 15 Electrical drafting lines.

On Site

Check the Legend

Be sure to check the legend on every drawing set. Symbols and abbreviations often vary widely from drawing set to drawing set.

4.0.0 Electrical Symbols

The electrician must be able to correctly read and understand electrical working drawings. This includes a thorough knowledge of electrical symbols and their applications.

An electrical symbol is a figure or mark that stands for a component used in the electrical system. *Figure 16* shows a list of electrical symbols that are currently recommended by the American National Standards Institute (ANSI). It is evident from this list of symbols that many have the same basic form, but, because of some slight difference, their meaning changes. For example, the receptacle symbols in *Figure 17* each have the same basic form (a circle), but the addition of a line or an abbreviation gives each an individual meaning. A good procedure to follow in learning symbols is to first learn the basic form and then apply the variations for obtaining different meanings.

It would be much simpler if all architects, engineers, electrical designers, and drafters used the same symbols; however, this is not the case. Although standardization is getting closer to a reality, existing symbols are still modified, and new symbols are created for almost every new project.

The electrical symbols described in the following paragraphs represent those found on actual electrical working drawings throughout the United States and Canada. Many are similar to those recommended by ANSI and the Consulting Engineers Council/US; others are not. Understanding how these symbols were devised will help you to interpret unknown electrical symbols in the future.

Some of the symbols used on electrical drawings are abbreviations, such as WP for weatherproof and AFF for above finished floor. Others are simplified pictographs, such as those shown in *Figure 18*.

In some cases, the symbols are combinations of abbreviations and pictographs, such as in *Figure 18* for a fusible safety switch, a nonfusible safety switch, and a double-throw safety switch. In each example, a pictograph of a switch enclosure has been combined with an abbreviation: F (fusible), DT (double-throw), and NF (nonfusible), respectively.

Lighting outlet symbols have been devised that represent incandescent, fluorescent, and high-intensity discharge lighting; a circle usually represents an incandescent fixture, and a rectangle is used to represent a fluorescent fixture. These symbols are designed to indicate the physical shape of a particular fixture, and while the circles representing incandescent lamps are frequently enlarged somewhat, symbols for fluorescent fixtures are usually drawn as close to scale as possible. The type of mounting used for all lighting fixtures is usually indicated in a lighting fixture schedule, which is shown on the drawings or in the written specifications.

The type of lighting fixture is identified by a numeral placed inside a triangle or other symbol, and placed near the fixture to be identified. A complete description of the fixtures identified by the symbols must be given in the lighting fixture schedule and should include the manufacturer, catalog number, number and type of lamps, voltage, finish, mounting, and any other information needed for proper installation of the fixture.

Switches used to control lighting fixtures are also indicated by symbols (usually the letter S followed by numerals or letters to define the exact type of switch). For example, S_3 indicates a three-way switch; S_4 identifies a four-way switch; and S_P indicates a single-pole switch with a pilot light. A subscript letter is often used to identify the fixtures that are controlled by that switch.

Main distribution centers, panelboards, transformers, safety switches, and other similar electrical components are indicated by electrical symbols on floor plans and by a combination of symbols and semipictorial drawings in riser diagrams.

A detailed description of the service equipment is usually given in the panelboard schedule or in the written specifications. However, on small projects, the service equipment is sometimes indicated only by notes on the drawings.

Circuit and feeder wiring symbols are getting closer to being standardized. Most circuits concealed in the ceiling or wall are indicated by a solid line; a broken line is used for circuits concealed in the floor or ceiling below; and exposed raceways are indicated by short dashes or else the letter *E* placed in the same plane with the circuit line at various intervals. The number of conductors in a conduit or raceway system may be indicated in the panelboard schedule under the appropriate column, or the information may be shown on the floor plan.

Symbols for communication and signal systems, as well as symbols for light and power,

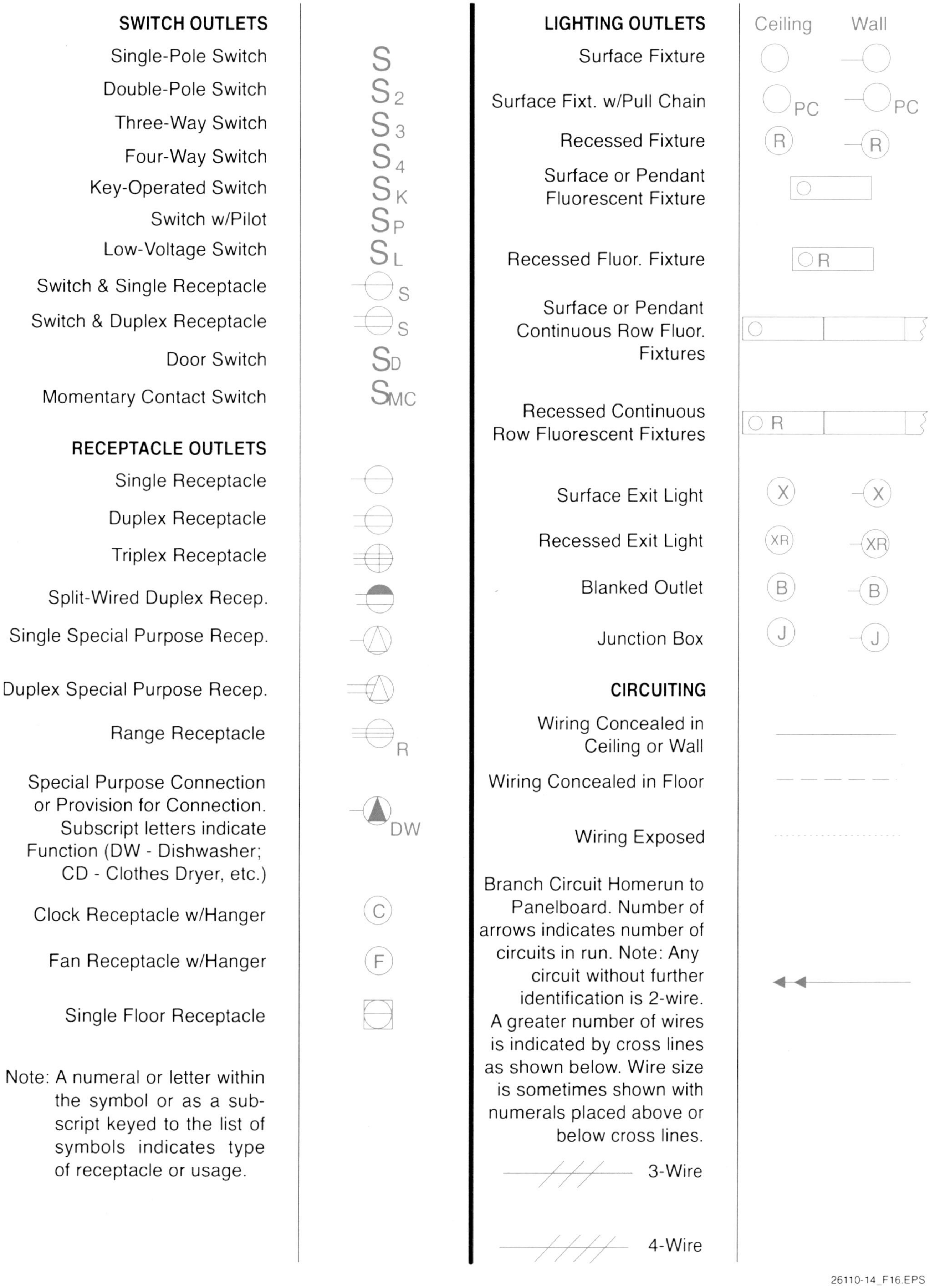

SWITCH OUTLETS	
Single-Pole Switch	S
Double-Pole Switch	S_2
Three-Way Switch	S_3
Four-Way Switch	S_4
Key-Operated Switch	S_K
Switch w/Pilot	S_P
Low-Voltage Switch	S_L
Switch & Single Receptacle	S
Switch & Duplex Receptacle	S
Door Switch	S_D
Momentary Contact Switch	S_{MC}

RECEPTACLE OUTLETS	
Single Receptacle	
Duplex Receptacle	
Triplex Receptacle	
Split-Wired Duplex Recep.	
Single Special Purpose Recep.	
Duplex Special Purpose Recep.	
Range Receptacle	R
Special Purpose Connection or Provision for Connection. Subscript letters indicate Function (DW - Dishwasher; CD - Clothes Dryer, etc.)	DW
Clock Receptacle w/Hanger	C
Fan Receptacle w/Hanger	F
Single Floor Receptacle	

Note: A numeral or letter within the symbol or as a subscript keyed to the list of symbols indicates type of receptacle or usage.

LIGHTING OUTLETS	Ceiling	Wall
Surface Fixture		
Surface Fixt. w/Pull Chain	PC	PC
Recessed Fixture	R	R
Surface or Pendant Fluorescent Fixture		
Recessed Fluor. Fixture	R	
Surface or Pendant Continuous Row Fluor. Fixtures		
Recessed Continuous Row Fluorescent Fixtures	R	
Surface Exit Light	X	X
Recessed Exit Light	XR	XR
Blanked Outlet	B	B
Junction Box	J	J

CIRCUITING

Wiring Concealed in Ceiling or Wall

Wiring Concealed in Floor

Wiring Exposed

Branch Circuit Homerun to Panelboard. Number of arrows indicates number of circuits in run. Note: Any circuit without further identification is 2-wire. A greater number of wires is indicated by cross lines as shown below. Wire size is sometimes shown with numerals placed above or below cross lines.

3-Wire

4-Wire

26110-14_F16.EPS

Figure 16 ANSI electrical symbols.

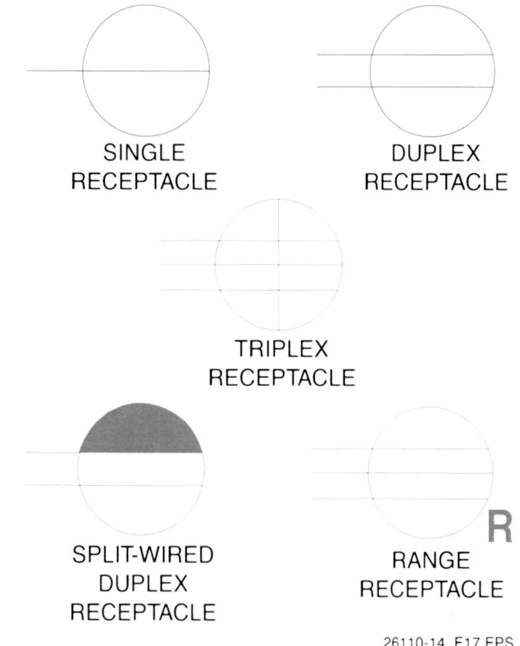

Figure 17 Various receptacle symbols used on electrical drawings.

are drawn to an appropriate scale and accurately located with respect to the building. This reduces the number of references made to the architectural drawings. Where extreme accuracy is required in locating outlets and equipment, exact dimensions are given on larger-scale drawings and shown on the plans.

Each different category in an electrical system is usually represented by a basic distinguishing symbol. To further identify items of equipment or outlets in the category, a numeral or other identifying mark is placed within the open basic symbol. In addition, all such individual symbols used on the drawings should be included in the symbol list or legend. The electrical symbols shown in *Figure 19* were modified by a consulting engineering firm for use on a small industrial electrical installation. The symbols shown in *Figure 20* are those recommended by the Consulting Engineers Council/US. You should become familiar with these symbols.

5.0.0 Scale Drawings

In most electrical drawings, the components are so large that it would be impossible to draw them actual size. Consequently, drawings are made to some reduced scale; that is, all the distances are drawn smaller than the actual dimensions of the object itself, with all dimensions being reduced in the same proportion. For example, if a floor plan of a building is to be drawn to a scale of ¼" = 1'–0", each ¼" on the drawing would equal 1 foot on the building itself; if the scale is ⅛" = 1'–0", each ⅛" on the drawing equals 1 foot on the building, and so forth.

When architectural and engineering drawings are produced, the selected scale is very important. Where dimensions must be held to extreme accuracy, the scale drawings should be made as large as practical with dimension lines added. Where dimensions require only reasonable accuracy, the object may be drawn to a smaller scale (with dimension lines possibly omitted).

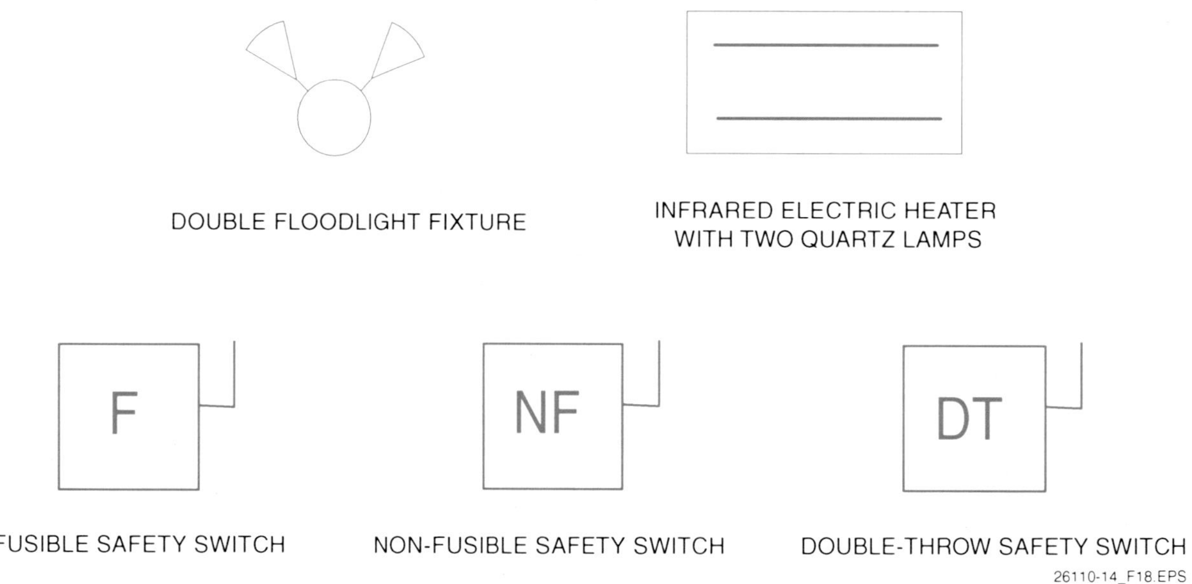

Figure 18 General types of symbols used on electrical drawings.

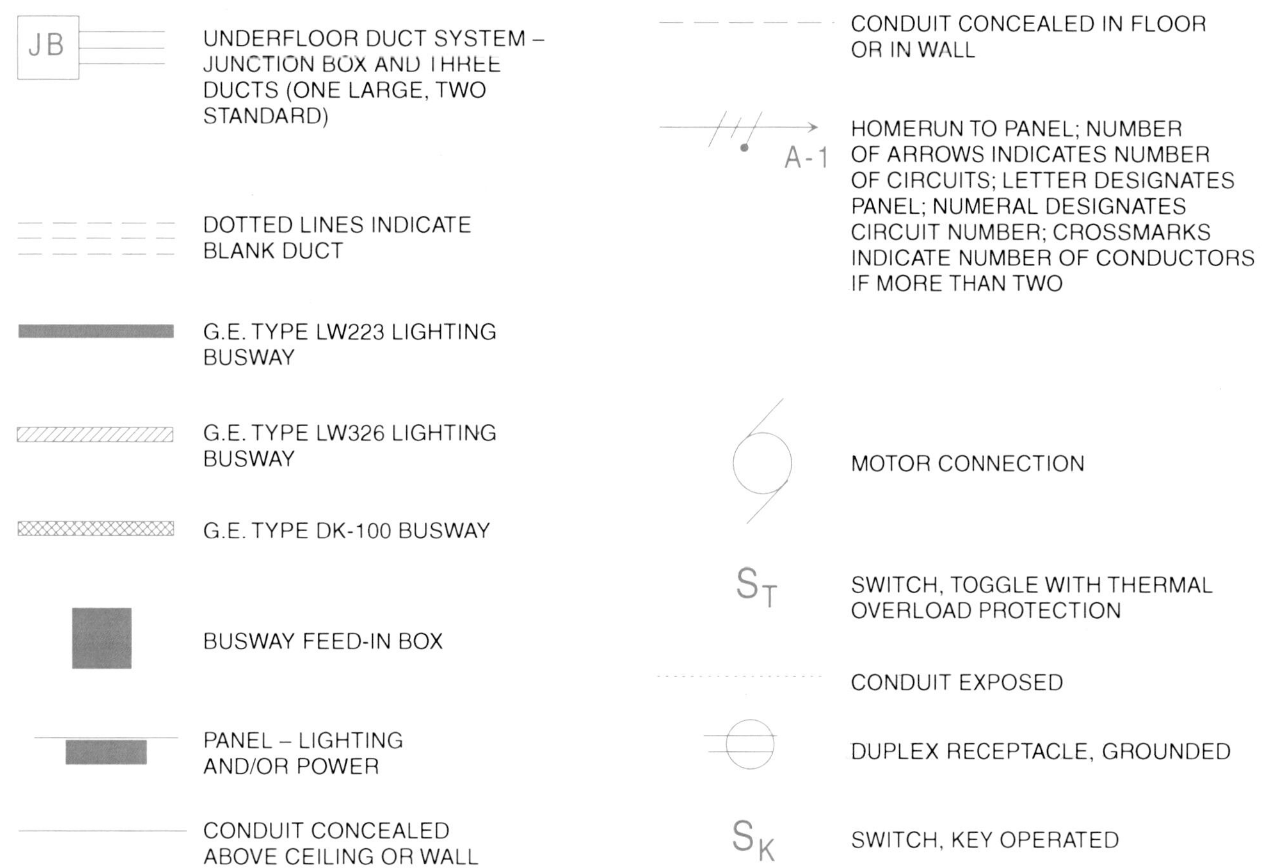

Figure 19 Electrical symbols used by one consulting engineering firm.

In dimensioning drawings, the dimensions written on the drawing are the actual dimensions of the building, not the distances that are measured on the drawing. To further illustrate this point, look at the floor plan in *Figure 21;* it is drawn to a scale of ½" = 1'–0". One of the walls is drawn to an actual length of 3½" on the drawing paper, but since the scale is ½" = 1'–0" and since 3½" contains 7 halves of an inch (7 × ½ = 3½"), the dimension shown on the drawing will therefore be 7'–0" on the actual building.

As shown in the previous example, the most common method of reducing all the dimensions (in feet and inches) in the same proportion is to choose a certain distance and let that distance represent one foot. This distance can then be divided into 12 parts, each of which represents an inch. If half inches are required, these twelfths are further subdivided into halves, etc. Now the scale represents the common foot rule with its subdivisions into inches and fractions, except that the scaled foot is smaller than the distance known as a foot and, likewise, its subdivisions are proportionately smaller.

When a measurement is made on the drawing, it is made with the reduced foot rule or scale; when a measurement is made on the building, it is made with the standard foot rule. The most common reduced foot rules or scales used in electrical drawings are the architect's scale and the engineer's scale. Drawings may sometimes be encountered that use a metric scale, but using this scale is similar to using the architect's or engineer's scales.

5.1.0 Architect's Scale

Figure 22 shows two configurations of architect's scales. The one on the top is designed so that 1" = 1'–0", and the one on the bottom has graduations spaced to represent ⅛" = 1'–0".

Note that on the one-inch scale in *Figure 23,* the longer marks to the right of the zero (with a numeral beneath) represent feet. Therefore, the distance between the zero and the numeral 1 equals one foot. The shorter mark between the zero and 1 represents ½ of a foot, or six inches.

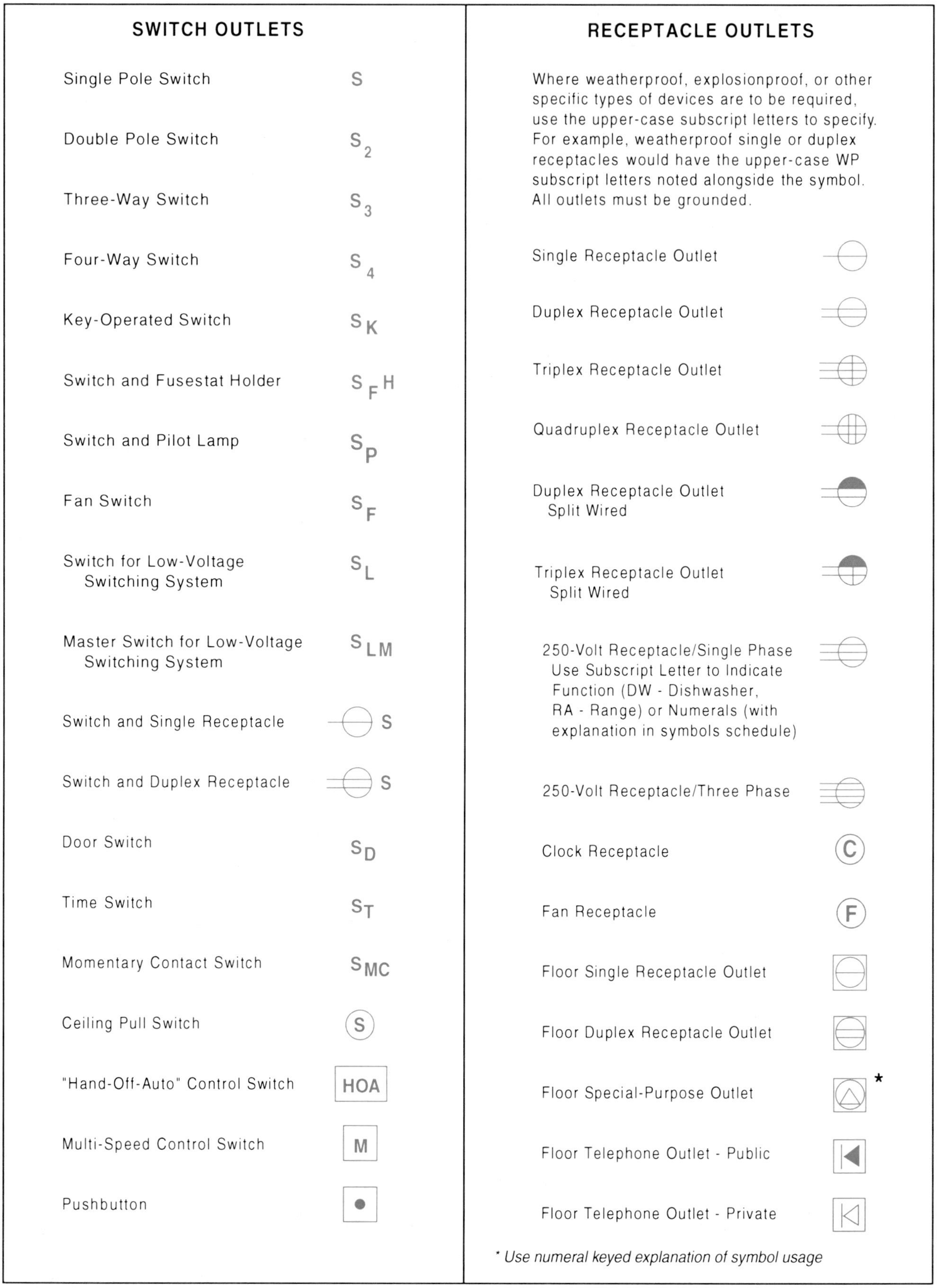

SWITCH OUTLETS	
Single Pole Switch	S
Double Pole Switch	S_2
Three-Way Switch	S_3
Four-Way Switch	S_4
Key-Operated Switch	S_K
Switch and Fusestat Holder	S_{FH}
Switch and Pilot Lamp	S_P
Fan Switch	S_F
Switch for Low-Voltage Switching System	S_L
Master Switch for Low-Voltage Switching System	S_{LM}
Switch and Single Receptacle	S
Switch and Duplex Receptacle	S
Door Switch	S_D
Time Switch	S_T
Momentary Contact Switch	S_{MC}
Ceiling Pull Switch	S
"Hand-Off-Auto" Control Switch	HOA
Multi-Speed Control Switch	M
Pushbutton	

RECEPTACLE OUTLETS

Where weatherproof, explosionproof, or other specific types of devices are to be required, use the upper-case subscript letters to specify. For example, weatherproof single or duplex receptacles would have the upper-case WP subscript letters noted alongside the symbol. All outlets must be grounded.

Single Receptacle Outlet	
Duplex Receptacle Outlet	
Triplex Receptacle Outlet	
Quadruplex Receptacle Outlet	
Duplex Receptacle Outlet Split Wired	
Triplex Receptacle Outlet Split Wired	
250-Volt Receptacle/Single Phase Use Subscript Letter to Indicate Function (DW - Dishwasher, RA - Range) or Numerals (with explanation in symbols schedule)	
250-Volt Receptacle/Three Phase	
Clock Receptacle	C
Fan Receptacle	F
Floor Single Receptacle Outlet	
Floor Duplex Receptacle Outlet	
Floor Special-Purpose Outlet	*
Floor Telephone Outlet - Public	
Floor Telephone Outlet - Private	

** Use numeral keyed explanation of symbol usage*

26110-14_F20A.EPS

Figure 20 Recommended electrical symbols (1 of 7).

Example of the use of several floor outlet symbols to identify a 2, 3, or more gang outlet:

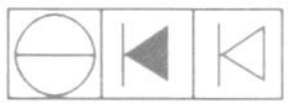

Underfloor duct and junction box for triple, double, or single duct system as indicated by the number of parallel lines

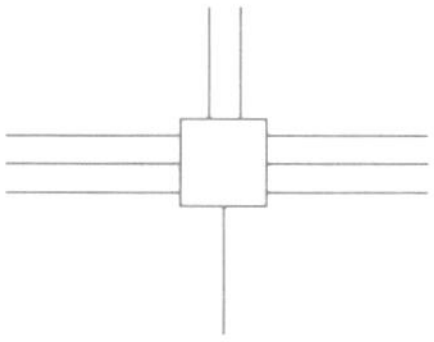

Example of the use of various symbols to identify the location of different types of outlets or connections for underfloor duct or cellular floor systems:

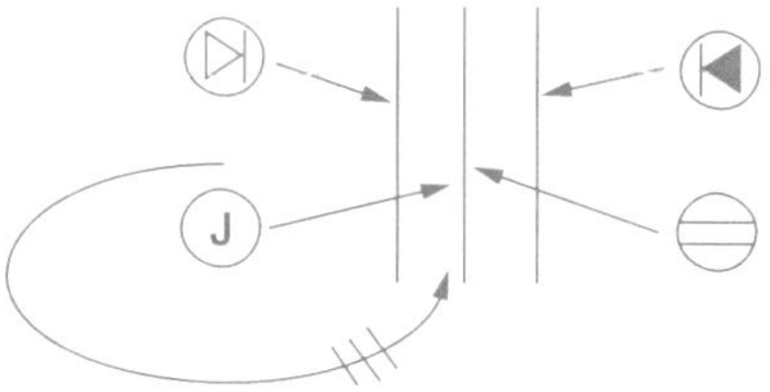

J

Cellular Floor Heater Duct

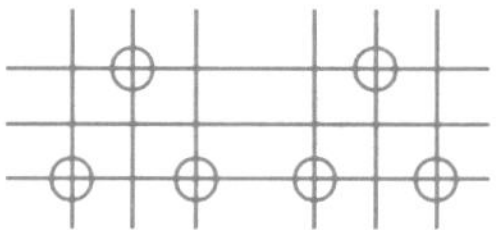

CIRCUITING

Wiring Exposed (not in conduit) — E —

Wiring Concealed in Ceiling or Wall

Wiring Concealed in Floor

Wiring Existing*

Wiring Turned Up

Wiring Turned Down

Branch Circuit Homerun to Panelboard — 2 1

Number of arrows indicates number of circuits. (A number at each arrow may be used to identify the circuit number.)**

BUS DUCTS AND WIREWAYS

Trolley Duct*** — T T

Busway (Service, Feeder or Plug-in)*** — B B

Cable Trough Ladder or Channel*** — C C

Wireway*** — W W

PANELBOARDS, SWITCHBOARDS AND RELATED EQUIPMENT

Flush Mounted Panelboard and Cabinet***

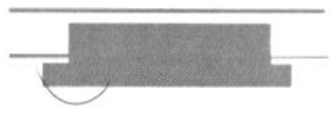

Surface Mounted Panelboard and Cabinet***

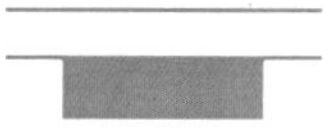

Switchboard, Power Control Center, Unit Substation (Should be drawn to scale)***

Flush Mounted Terminal Cabinet (In small scale drawings the TC may be indicated alongside the symbol)*** — TC

Surface Mounted Terminal Cabinet (In small scale drawings the TC may be indicated alongside the symbol)*** — TC

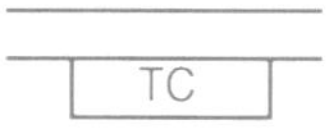

Pull Box (Identify in relation to Wiring System Section and Size)

Motor or Other Power Controller May be a starter or contactor***

Externally Operated Disconnection Switch***

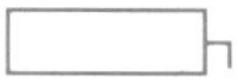

Combination Controller and Disconnection Means***

*Note: Use heavy-weight line to identify service and feeders. Indicate empty conduit by notation CO.

**Note: Any circuit without further identification indicates two-wire circuit. For a greater number of wires, indicate with cross lines, e.g.:

3 wires 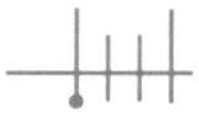 4 wires, etc.

Neutral and ground wires may be shown longer. Unless indicated otherwise, the wire size of the circuit is the minimum size required by the specification. Identify different functions of wiring system (e.g., signaling system) by notation or other means.

***Identify by Notation or Schedule

26110-14_F20B.EPS

Figure 20 Recommended electrical symbols (2 of 7).

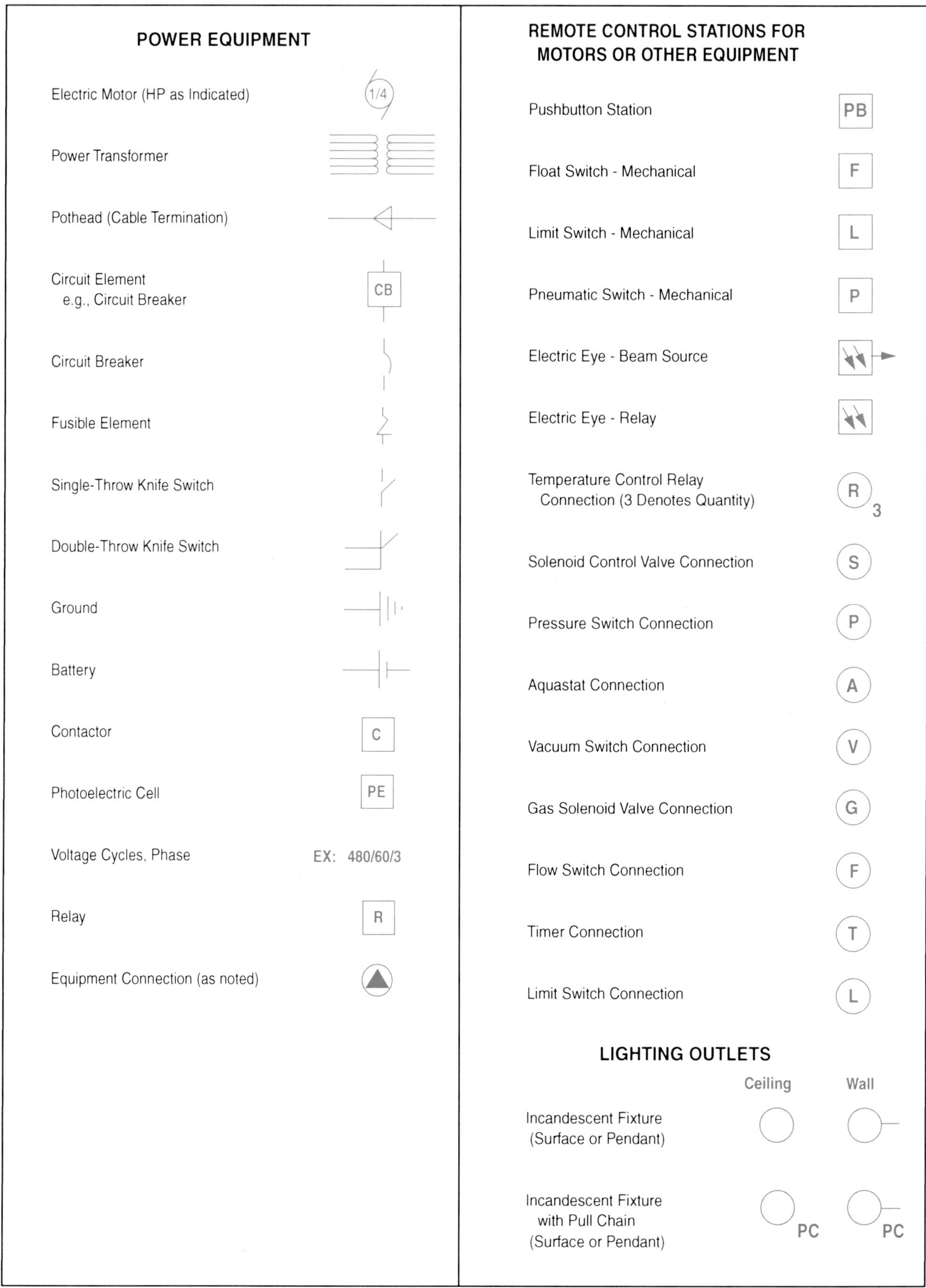
POWER EQUIPMENT
Electric Motor (HP as Indicated)
1/4
Power Transformer
Pothead (Cable Termination)
Circuit Element
e.g., Circuit Breaker
CB
Circuit Breaker
Fusible Element
Single-Throw Knife Switch
Double-Throw Knife Switch
Ground
Battery
Contactor
C
Photoelectric Cell
PE
Voltage Cycles, Phase
EX: 480/60/3
Relay
R
Equipment Connection (as noted)
REMOTE CONTROL STATIONS FOR MOTORS OR OTHER EQUIPMENT
Pushbutton Station
PB
Float Switch - Mechanical
F
Limit Switch - Mechanical
L
Pneumatic Switch - Mechanical
P
Electric Eye - Beam Source
Electric Eye - Relay
Temperature Control Relay Connection (3 Denotes Quantity)
R
3
Solenoid Control Valve Connection
S
Pressure Switch Connection
P
Aquastat Connection
A
Vacuum Switch Connection
V
Gas Solenoid Valve Connection
G
Flow Switch Connection
F
Timer Connection
T
Limit Switch Connection
L
LIGHTING OUTLETS
Ceiling
Wall
Incandescent Fixture (Surface or Pendant)
Incandescent Fixture with Pull Chain (Surface or Pendant)
PC
PC
26110-14_F20C.EPS

Figure 20 Recommended electrical symbols (3 of 7).

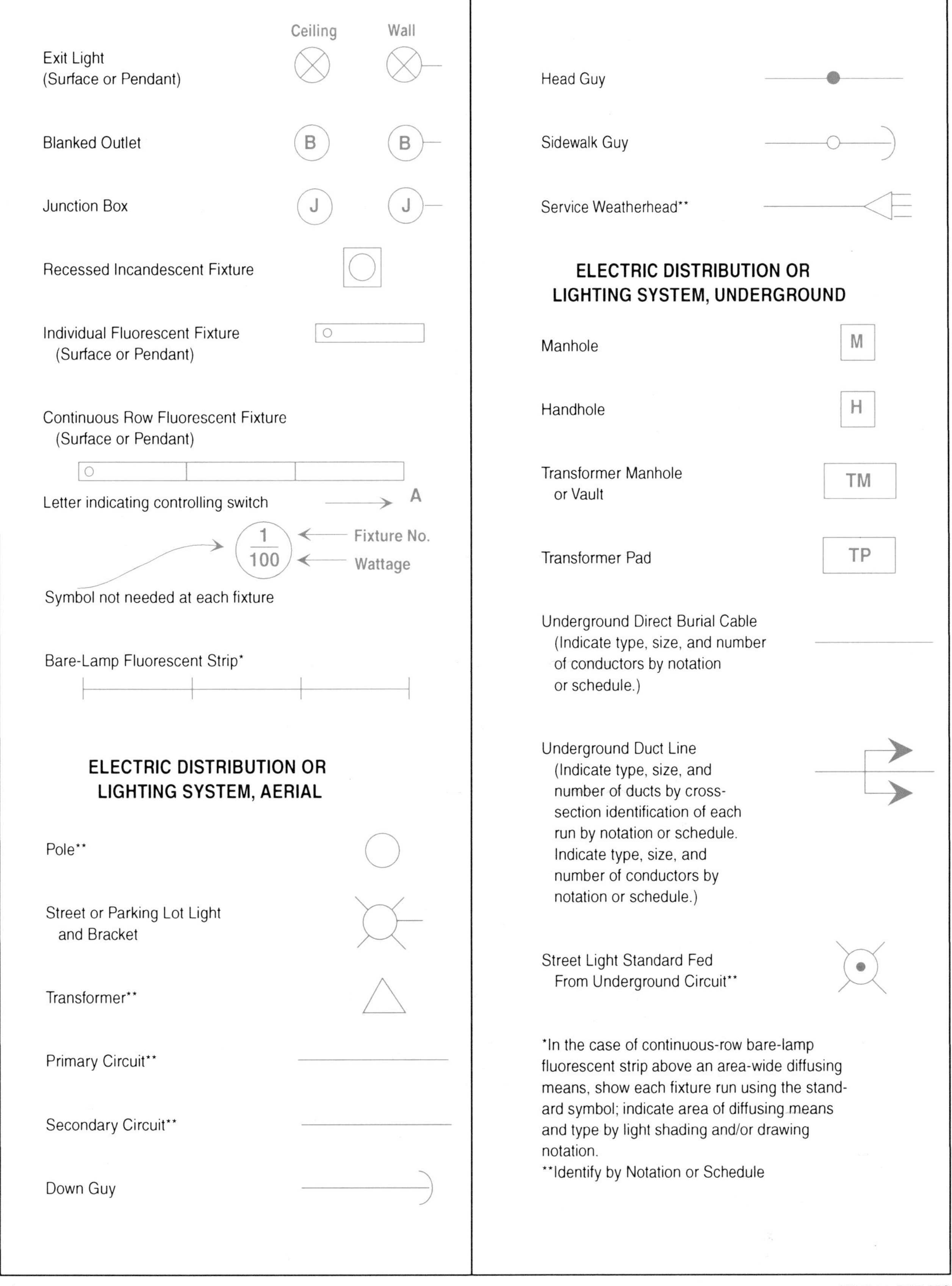

Ceiling
Wall
Exit Light
(Surface or Pendant)
Blanked Outlet
B
B
Junction Box
J
J
Recessed Incandescent Fixture
Individual Fluorescent Fixture
(Surface or Pendant)
Continuous Row Fluorescent Fixture
(Surface or Pendant)
Letter indicating controlling switch
A
1
100
Fixture No.
Wattage
Symbol not needed at each fixture
Bare-Lamp Fluorescent Strip*
ELECTRIC DISTRIBUTION OR
LIGHTING SYSTEM, AERIAL
Pole**
Street or Parking Lot Light
and Bracket
Transformer**
Primary Circuit**
Secondary Circuit**
Down Guy
Head Guy
Sidewalk Guy
Service Weatherhead**
ELECTRIC DISTRIBUTION OR
LIGHTING SYSTEM, UNDERGROUND
Manhole
M
Handhole
H
Transformer Manhole
or Vault
TM
Transformer Pad
TP
Underground Direct Burial Cable
(Indicate type, size, and number
of conductors by notation
or schedule.)
Underground Duct Line
(Indicate type, size, and
number of ducts by cross-
section identification of each
run by notation or schedule.
Indicate type, size, and
number of conductors by
notation or schedule.)
Street Light Standard Fed
From Underground Circuit**
*In the case of continuous-row bare-lamp
fluorescent strip above an area-wide diffusing
means, show each fixture run using the standard symbol; indicate area of diffusing means
and type by light shading and/or drawing
notation.
**Identify by Notation or Schedule
26110-14_F20D.EPS

Figure 20 Recommended electrical symbols (4 of 7).

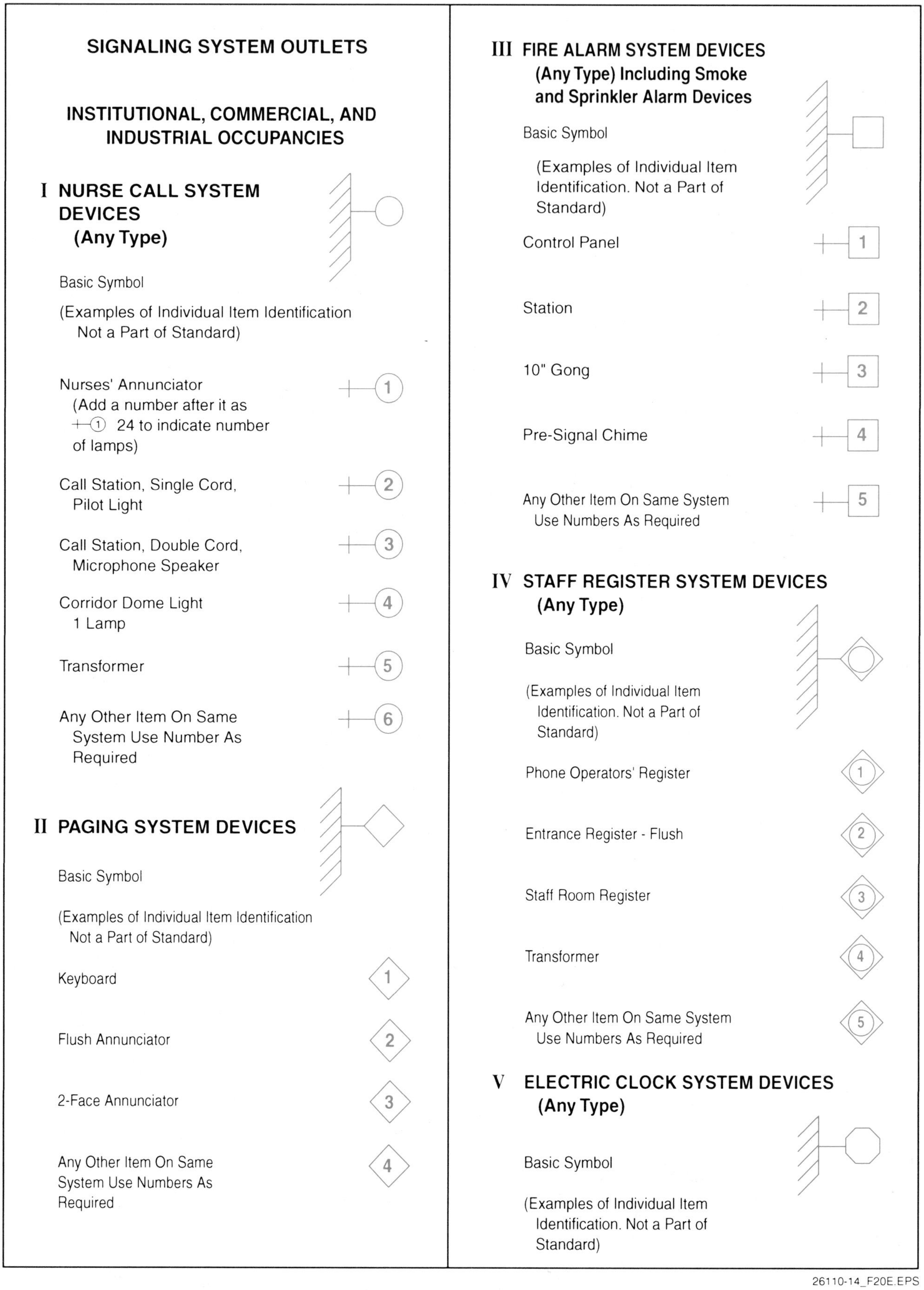

SIGNALING SYSTEM OUTLETS

INSTITUTIONAL, COMMERCIAL, AND INDUSTRIAL OCCUPANCIES

I NURSE CALL SYSTEM DEVICES (Any Type)

Basic Symbol

(Examples of Individual Item Identification Not a Part of Standard)

Nurses' Annunciator (Add a number after it as ⊣① 24 to indicate number of lamps)

Call Station, Single Cord, Pilot Light

Call Station, Double Cord, Microphone Speaker

Corridor Dome Light 1 Lamp

Transformer

Any Other Item On Same System Use Number As Required

II PAGING SYSTEM DEVICES

Basic Symbol

(Examples of Individual Item Identification Not a Part of Standard)

Keyboard

Flush Annunciator

2-Face Annunciator

Any Other Item On Same System Use Numbers As Required

III FIRE ALARM SYSTEM DEVICES (Any Type) Including Smoke and Sprinkler Alarm Devices

Basic Symbol

(Examples of Individual Item Identification. Not a Part of Standard)

Control Panel

Station

10" Gong

Pre-Signal Chime

Any Other Item On Same System Use Numbers As Required

IV STAFF REGISTER SYSTEM DEVICES (Any Type)

Basic Symbol

(Examples of Individual Item Identification. Not a Part of Standard)

Phone Operators' Register

Entrance Register - Flush

Staff Room Register

Transformer

Any Other Item On Same System Use Numbers As Required

V ELECTRIC CLOCK SYSTEM DEVICES (Any Type)

Basic Symbol

(Examples of Individual Item Identification. Not a Part of Standard)

26110-14_F20E.EPS

Figure 20 Recommended electrical symbols (5 of 7).

Master Clock

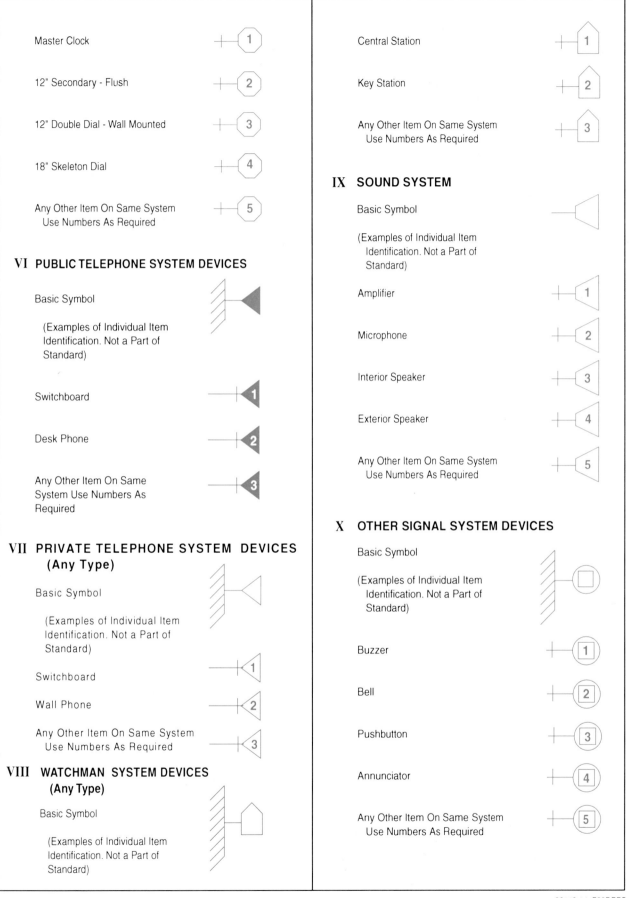

12" Secondary - Flush

12" Double Dial - Wall Mounted

18" Skeleton Dial

Any Other Item On Same System Use Numbers As Required

VI PUBLIC TELEPHONE SYSTEM DEVICES

Basic Symbol

(Examples of Individual Item Identification. Not a Part of Standard)

Switchboard

Desk Phone

Any Other Item On Same System Use Numbers As Required

VII PRIVATE TELEPHONE SYSTEM DEVICES (Any Type)

Basic Symbol

(Examples of Individual Item Identification. Not a Part of Standard)

Switchboard

Wall Phone

Any Other Item On Same System Use Numbers As Required

VIII WATCHMAN SYSTEM DEVICES (Any Type)

Basic Symbol

(Examples of Individual Item Identification. Not a Part of Standard)

Central Station

Key Station

Any Other Item On Same System Use Numbers As Required

IX SOUND SYSTEM

Basic Symbol

(Examples of Individual Item Identification. Not a Part of Standard)

Amplifier

Microphone

Interior Speaker

Exterior Speaker

Any Other Item On Same System Use Numbers As Required

X OTHER SIGNAL SYSTEM DEVICES

Basic Symbol

(Examples of Individual Item Identification. Not a Part of Standard)

Buzzer

Bell

Pushbutton

Annunciator

Any Other Item On Same System Use Numbers As Required

26110-14_F20F.EPS

Figure 20 Recommended electrical symbols (6 of 7).

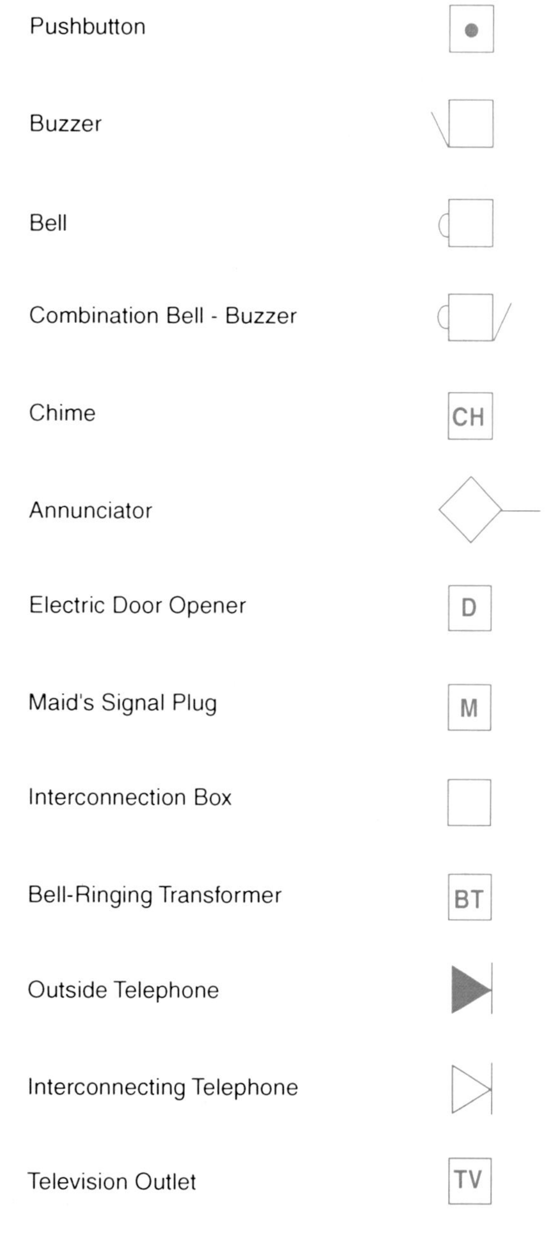

Figure 20 Recommended electrical symbols (7 of 7).

Referring again to *Figure 23*, look at the marks to the left of the zero. The numbered marks are spaced three scaled inches apart and have the numerals 0, 3, 6, and 9 for use as reference points. The other lines of the same length also represent scaled inches, but are not marked with numerals. In use, you can count the number of long marks to the left of the zero to find the number of inches, but after some practice, you will be able to tell the exact measurement at a glance. For example, the measurement A represents five inches because it is the fifth inch mark to the left of the zero; it is also one inch mark short of the six-inch line on the scale.

The lines that are shorter than the inch line are the half-inch lines. On smaller scales, the basic unit is not divided into as many divisions. For example, the smallest subdivision on some scales represents two inches.

5.1.1 Types of Architect's Scales

Architect's scales are available in several types, but the most common include the triangular scale (*Figure 24*) and the flat scale. The quality of architect's scales also varies from cheap plastic scales (costing a dollar or two) to high-quality wooden-laminated tools that are calibrated to precise standards.

The triangular scale is frequently found in drafting and estimating departments or engineering and electrical contracting firms, while the flat scales are more convenient to carry on the job site.

Triangular architect's scales have 12 different scales—two on each edge—as follows:

- Common foot rule (12 inches)
- 1/16" = 1'–0"
- 3/32" = 1'–0"
- 3/16" = 1'–0"
- 1/8" = 1'–0"
- 1/4" = 1'–0"
- 3/8" = 1'–0"
- 3/4" = 1'–0"
- 1" = 1'–0"
- 1/2" = 1'–0"
- 1 1/2" = 1'–0"
- 3" = 1'–0"

Two separate scales on one face may seem confusing at first, but after some experience, reading these scales becomes second nature.

In all but one of the scales on the triangular architect's scale, each face has one of the scales placed opposite to the other. For example, on the one-inch face, the one-inch scale is read from left to right, starting from the zero mark. The half-inch scale is read from right to left, again starting from the zero mark.

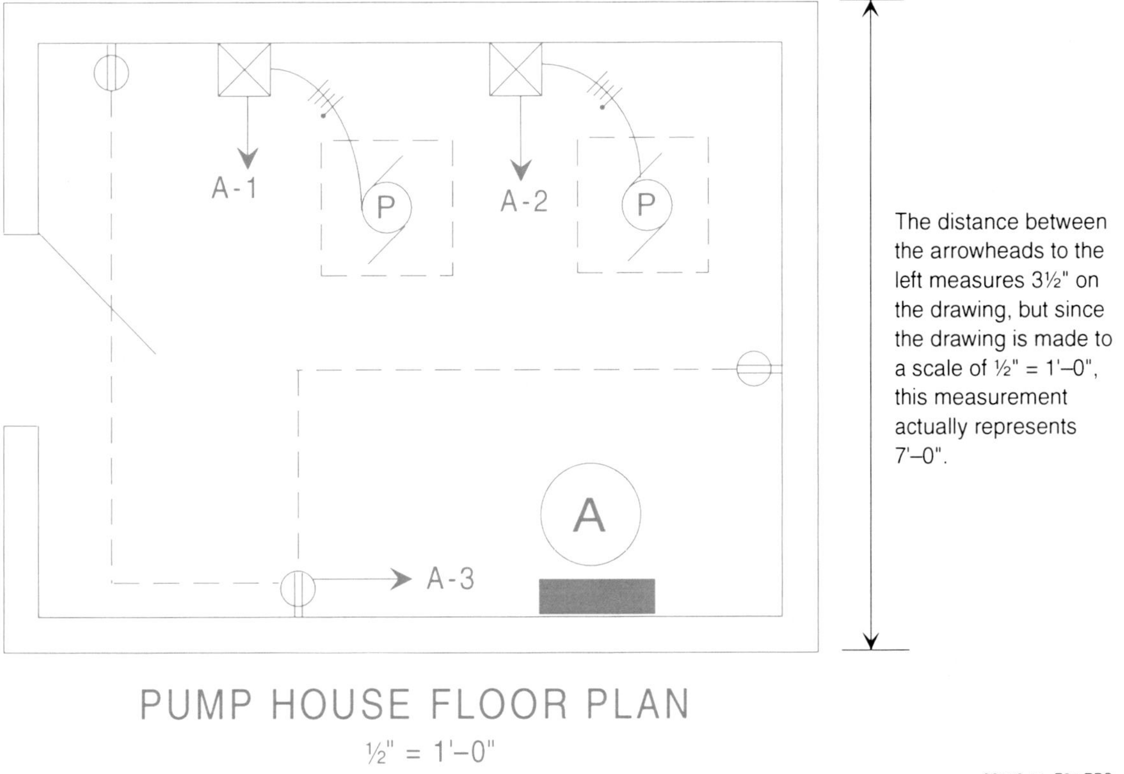

Figure 21 Typical floor plan showing drawing scale.

On the remaining foot-rule scale (1⁄16" = 1'–0") each 1⁄16" mark on the scale represents one foot.

Figure 25 shows all the scales found on the triangular architect's scale.

The flat architect's scale shown in *Figure 26* is ideal for workers on most projects. It is easily and conveniently carried in the shirt pocket, and the four scales (⅛", ¼", ½", and 1") are adequate for the majority of projects that will be encountered.

The partial floor plan shown in *Figure 26* is drawn to a scale of ⅛" = 1'–0". The dimension in question is found by placing the ⅛" architect's scale on the drawing and reading the figures. It can be seen that the dimension reads 24'–6".

Think About It

Using Electrical Symbols

Although there are many electrical symbols, you must be able to read the common ones at a glance. Looking at the simple pump house drawing in *Figure 21,* see how quickly you can explain the symbols and the circuits that they identify.

Every drawing should have the scale to which it is drawn plainly marked on it as part of the drawing title. However, it is not uncommon to have several different drawings on one blueprint sheet—all with different scales. Therefore, always check the scale of each different view found on a drawing sheet.

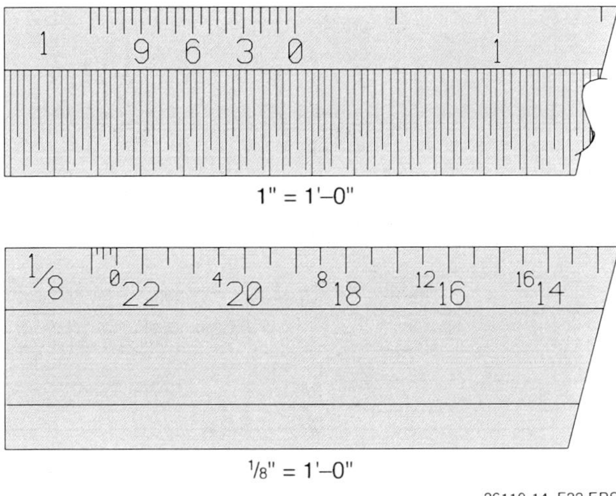

Figure 22 Two different configurations of architect's scales.

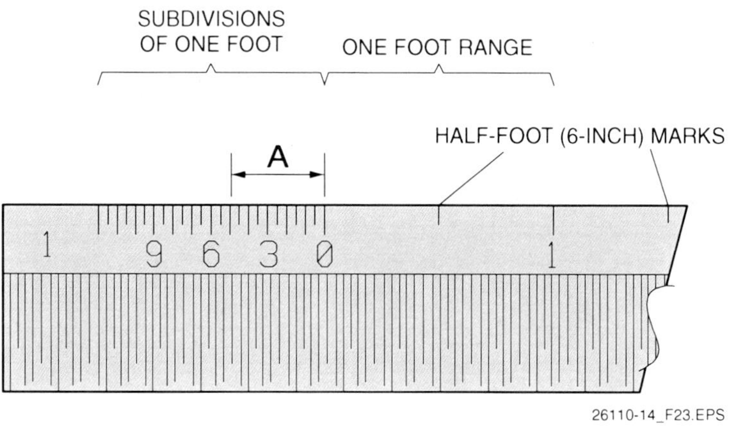

Figure 23 One-inch architect's scale.

On Site

Architect's Scale

Measurements are usually made on architectural drawings using an architect's scale rather than a standard ruler. Architect's scales, like the ones on the left, are divided into feet and inches and usually consist of several scales on one rule. Architect's scales also come in other forms such as tapes or with wheels, like the one shown on the right.

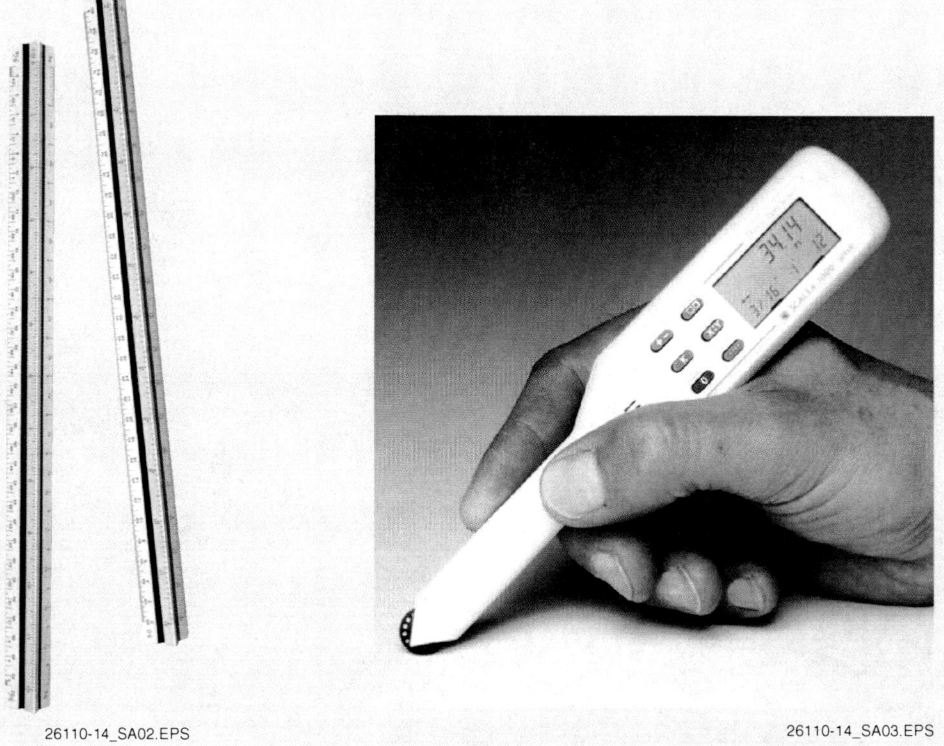

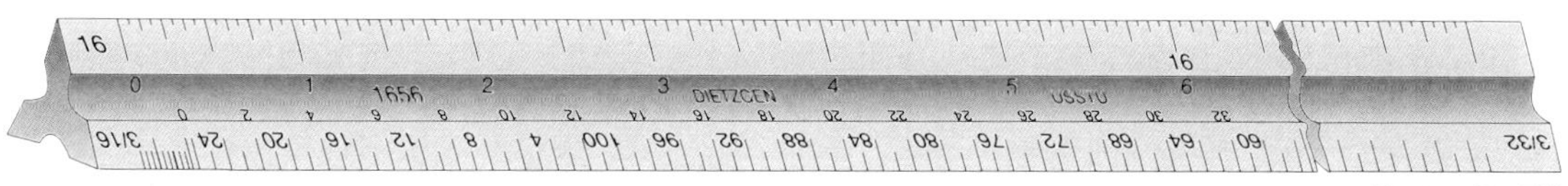

26110-14_F24.EPS

Figure 24 Typical triangular architect's scale.

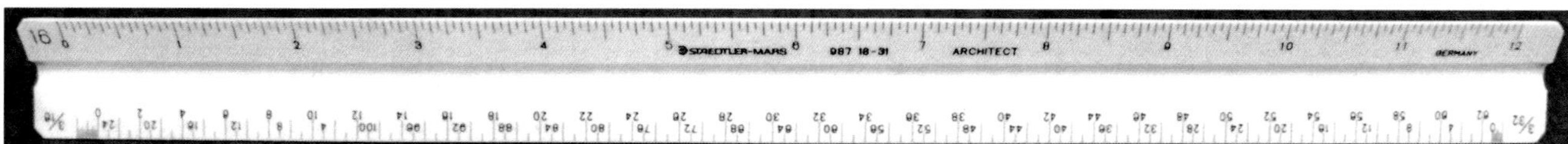

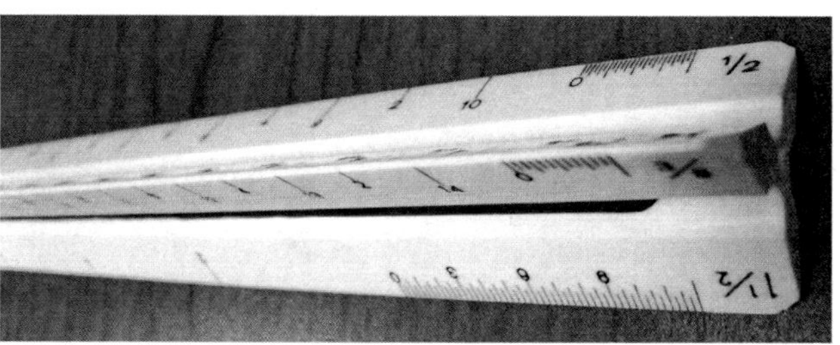

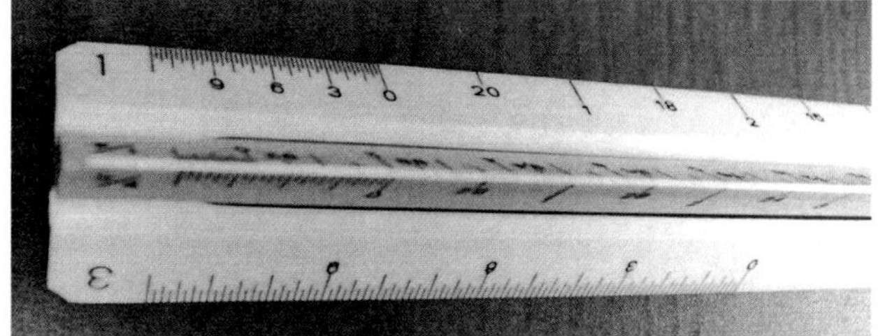

26110-14_F25.EPS

Figure 25 Various scales on a triangular architect's scale.

5.2.0 Engineer's Scale

The civil engineer's scale is used in basically the same manner as the architect's scale, with the principal difference being that the graduations on the engineer's scale are decimal units rather than feet as on the architect's scale.

The engineer's scale is used by placing it on the drawing with the working edge away from the user. The scale is then aligned in the direction of the required measurement. Then, by looking down at the scale, the dimension is read.

Civil engineer's scales commonly show the following graduations:

- 1" = 10 units
- 1" = 20 units
- 1" = 30 units
- 1" = 40 units
- 1" = 60 units
- 1" = 80 units
- 1" = 100 units

The purpose of this scale is to transfer the relative dimensions of an object to the drawing or vice versa. It is used mainly on site plans to determine distances between property lines, manholes, duct runs, direct-burial cable runs, and the like.

Site plans are drawn to scale using the engineer's scale rather than the architect's scale. On small lots, a scale of 1 inch = 10 feet or 1 inch = 20 feet is used. For a 1:10 scale, this means that one inch (the actual measurement on the drawing) is equal to 10 feet on the land itself.

On larger drawings, where a large area must be covered, the scale could be 1 inch = 100 feet or 1 inch = 1,000 feet, or any other integral power of 10. On drawings with the scale in multiples of 10, the engineer's scale marked 10 is used. If the scale is 1 inch = 200 feet, the engineer's scale marked 20 is used, and so on.

Although site plans appear reduced in scale, depending on the size of the object and the size of the drawing sheet to be used, the actual dimensions must be shown on the drawings at all times. When you are reading the drawing plans to scale, think of each dimension in its full size and not in the reduced scale it happens to be on the drawing (*Figure 27*).

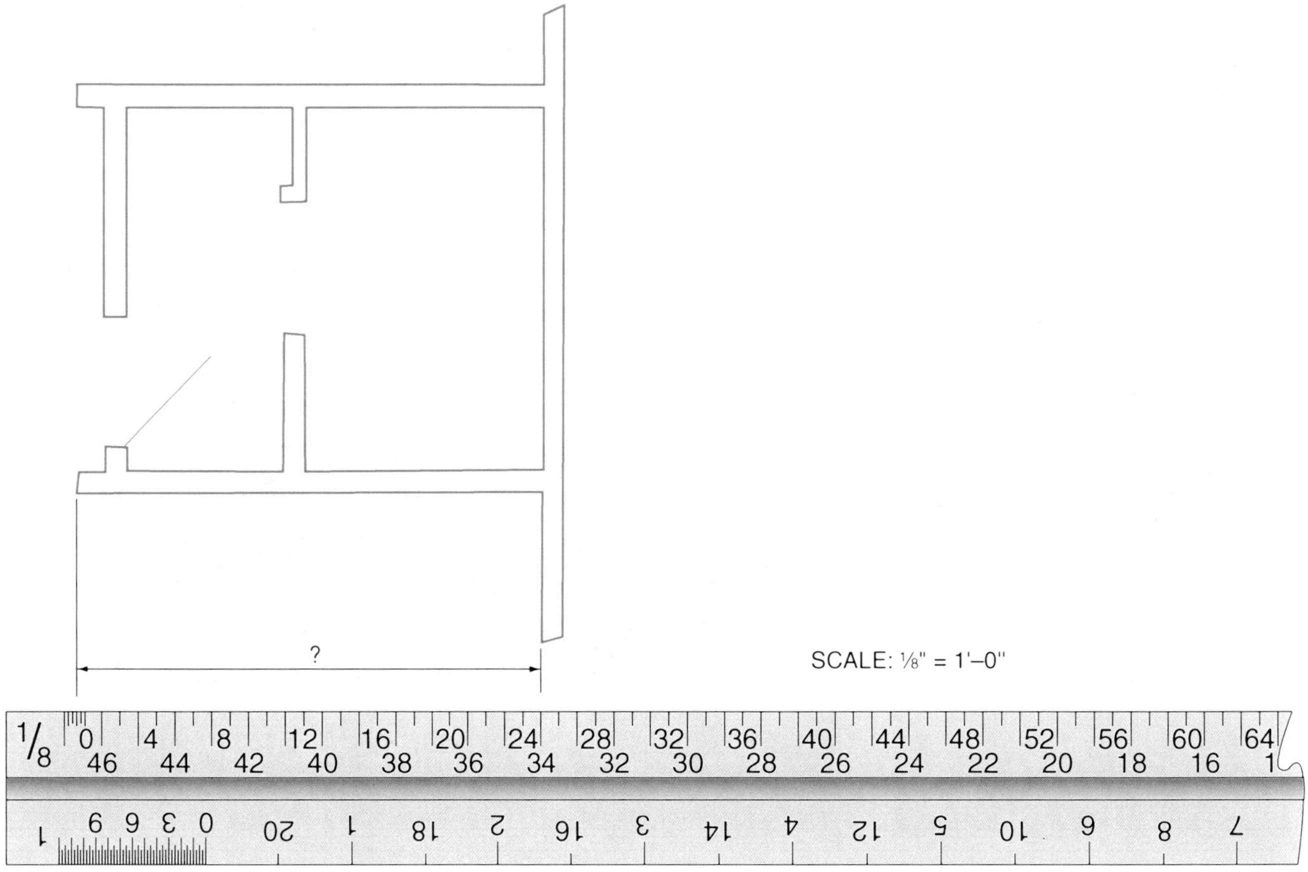

?

SCALE: 1/8" = 1'–0"

26110-14_F26.EPS

Figure 26 Using the 1/8" architect's scale to determine the dimensions on a drawing.

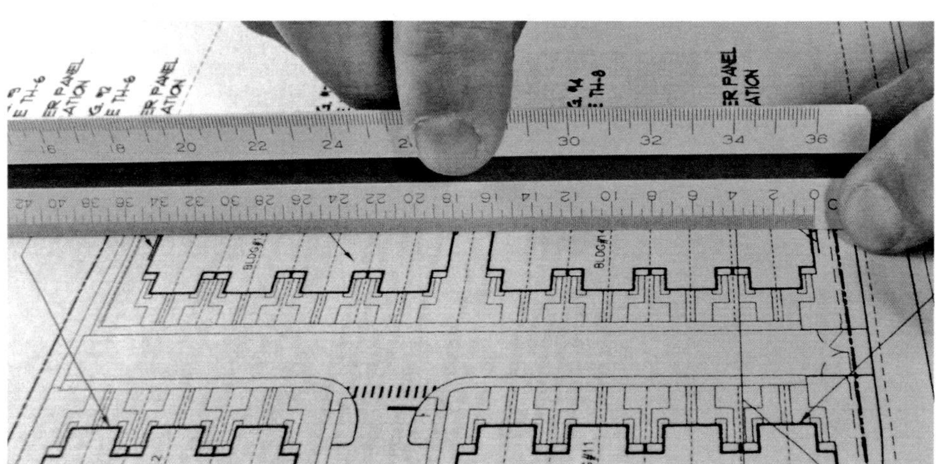

26110-14_F27.EPS

Figure 27 Practical use of the engineer's scale.

5.3.0 Metric Scale

Metric scales are calibrated in units of 10 (*Figure 28*). The two common length measurements used in the metric scale on architectural drawings are the meter and the millimeter, the millimeter being $\frac{1}{1,000}$ of a meter. On drawings drawn to scales between 1:1 and 1:100, the millimeter is typically used. On drawings drawn to scales between 1:200 and 1:2,000, the meter is generally used. Many contracting firms that deal in international trade have adopted a dual-dimensioning system expressed in both metric and English symbols. Drawings prepared for government projects may also require metric dimensions. A metric conversion chart is provided in the Appendix.

6.0.0 Analyzing Electrical Drawings

The most practical way to learn how to read electrical construction documents is to analyze an existing set of drawings prepared by consulting or industrial engineers.

Engineers or electrical designers are responsible for the complete layout of electrical systems for most projects. Electrical drafters then transform the engineer's designs into working drawings, using either manual drafting instruments or computer-aided design (CAD) systems. The following is a brief outline of what usually takes place in the preparation of electrical design and working drawings:

- The engineer meets with the architect and owner to discuss the electrical needs of the building or project and to discuss various recommendations made by all parties.
- After that, an outline of the architect's floor plan is laid out.
- The engineer then calculates the required power and lighting outlets for the project; these are later transferred to the working drawings.
- All communications and alarm systems are located on the floor plan, along with lighting and power panelboards.
- Circuit calculations are made to determine wire size and overcurrent protection.
- The main electric service and related components are determined and shown on the drawings.
- Schedules are then placed on the drawings to identify various pieces of equipment.
- Wiring diagrams are made to show the workers how various electrical components are to be connected.
- A legend or electrical symbol list is drafted and shown on the drawings to identify all symbols used to indicate electrical outlets or equipment.
- Various large-scale electrical details are included, if necessary, to show exactly what is required of the electricians.
- Written specifications are then made to give a description of the materials and installation methods.

6.1.0 Development of Site Plans

In general practice, it is usually the owner's responsibility to furnish the architect/engineer with property and topographic surveys, which are made by a certified land surveyor or civil engineer. These surveys show:

- All property lines
- Existing public utilities and their location on or near the property (e.g., electrical lines, sanitary sewer lines, gas lines, water-supply lines, storm sewers, manholes, telephone lines, etc.)

A land surveyor does the property survey from information obtained from a deed description of the property. A property survey shows only the property lines and their lengths, as if the property were perfectly flat.

The topographic survey shows both the property lines and the physical characteristics of the land by using contour lines, notes, and symbols. The physical characteristics may include:

- The direction of the land slope
- Whether the land is flat, hilly, wooded, swampy, high, or low, and other features of its physical nature

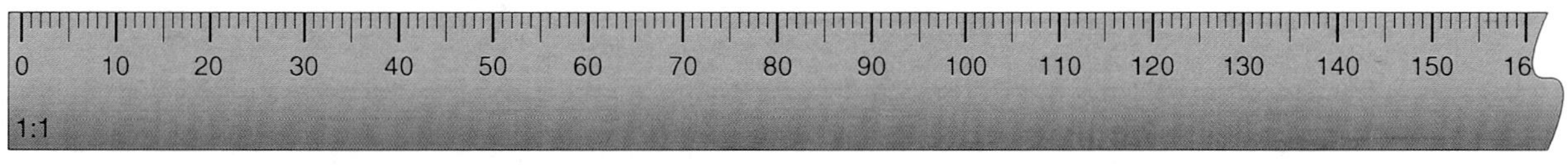

Figure 28 Typical metric scale.

All of this information is necessary so that the architect can properly design a building to fit the property. The electrical engineer also needs this information to locate existing electrical utilities and to route the new service to the building, provide outdoor lighting and circuits, etc.

Electrical site work is sometimes shown on the architect's plot plan. However, when site work involves many trades and several utilities (e.g., gas, telephone, electric, television, water, and sewage), it can become confusing if all details are shown on one drawing sheet. In cases like these, it is best to have a separate drawing devoted entirely to the electrical work, as shown in *Figure 29*. This project is an office/warehouse building for Virginia Electric, Inc. The electrical drawings consist of four 24" × 36" drawing sheets, along with a set of written specifications, which will be discussed later in this module.

The electrical site or plot plan shown in *Figure 29* has the conventional architect's and engineer's title blocks in the lower right-hand corner of the drawing. These blocks identify the project and project owners, the architect, and the engineer. They also show how this drawing sheet relates to the entire set of drawings. Note the engineer's professional stamp of approval to the left of the engineer's title block. Similar blocks appear on all four of the electrical drawing sheets.

When examining a set of electrical drawings for the first time, always look at the area around the title block. This is where most revision blocks or revision notes are placed. If revisions have been made to the drawings, make certain that you have a clear understanding of what has taken place before proceeding with the work.

Refer again to the drawing in *Figure 29* and note the north arrow in the upper left corner. A north arrow shows the direction of true north to help you orient the drawing to the site. Look directly down from the north arrow to the bottom of the page and notice the drawing title, *Plot Utilities*. Directly beneath the drawing title you can see that the drawing scale of 1" = 30' is shown. This means that each inch on the drawing represents 30 feet on the actual job site. This scale holds true for all drawings on the page unless otherwise noted.

An outline of the proposed building is indicated on the drawing along with a callout, *Proposed Bldg. Fin. Flr. Elev. 590.0*. This means that the finished floor level of the building is to be 590 feet above sea level, which in this part of the country will be about two feet above finished grade around the building. This information helps the electrician locate conduit sleeves and stub-ups to the correct height before the finished concrete floor is poured.

On Site

Reading Notes

The notes are crucial elements of the drawing set. Receptacles, for example, are hard to position precisely based on a scaled drawing alone, and yet the designer may call for exact locations. For example, the designer may want receptacles exactly 6" above the kitchen counter backsplash and centered on the sink.

The shaded area represents asphalt paving for the access road, drives, and parking lot. Note that the access road leads into a highway, which is designated Route 35. This information further helps workers to orient the drawing to the building site.

Existing manholes are indicated by a solid circle, while an open circle is used to show the position of the five new pole-mounted lighting fixtures that are to be installed around the new building. Existing power lines are shown with a light solid line with the letter E placed at intervals along the line. The new underground electric service is shown in the same way, except the lines are somewhat wider and darker on the drawing. Note that this new high-voltage cable terminates into a padmount transformer near the proposed building. New telephone lines are similar except the letter T is used to identify the telephone lines.

The direct-burial underground cable supplying the exterior lighting fixtures is indicated with dashed lines on the drawing—shown connecting the open circles. A homerun for this circuit is also shown to a time clock.

The manhole detail shown to the right of the north arrow may seem to serve very little purpose on this drawing since the manholes have already been installed. However, the dimensions and details of their construction will help the electrical contractor or supervisor to better plan the pulling of the high-voltage cable. The same is true of the cross section shown of the duct bank. The electrical contractor knows that three empty ducts are available if it is discovered that one of them is damaged when the work begins.

Although the electrical work will not involve working with gas, the main gas line is shown on the electrical drawing to let the electrical workers know its approximate location while they are installing the direct-burial conductors for the exterior lighting fixtures.

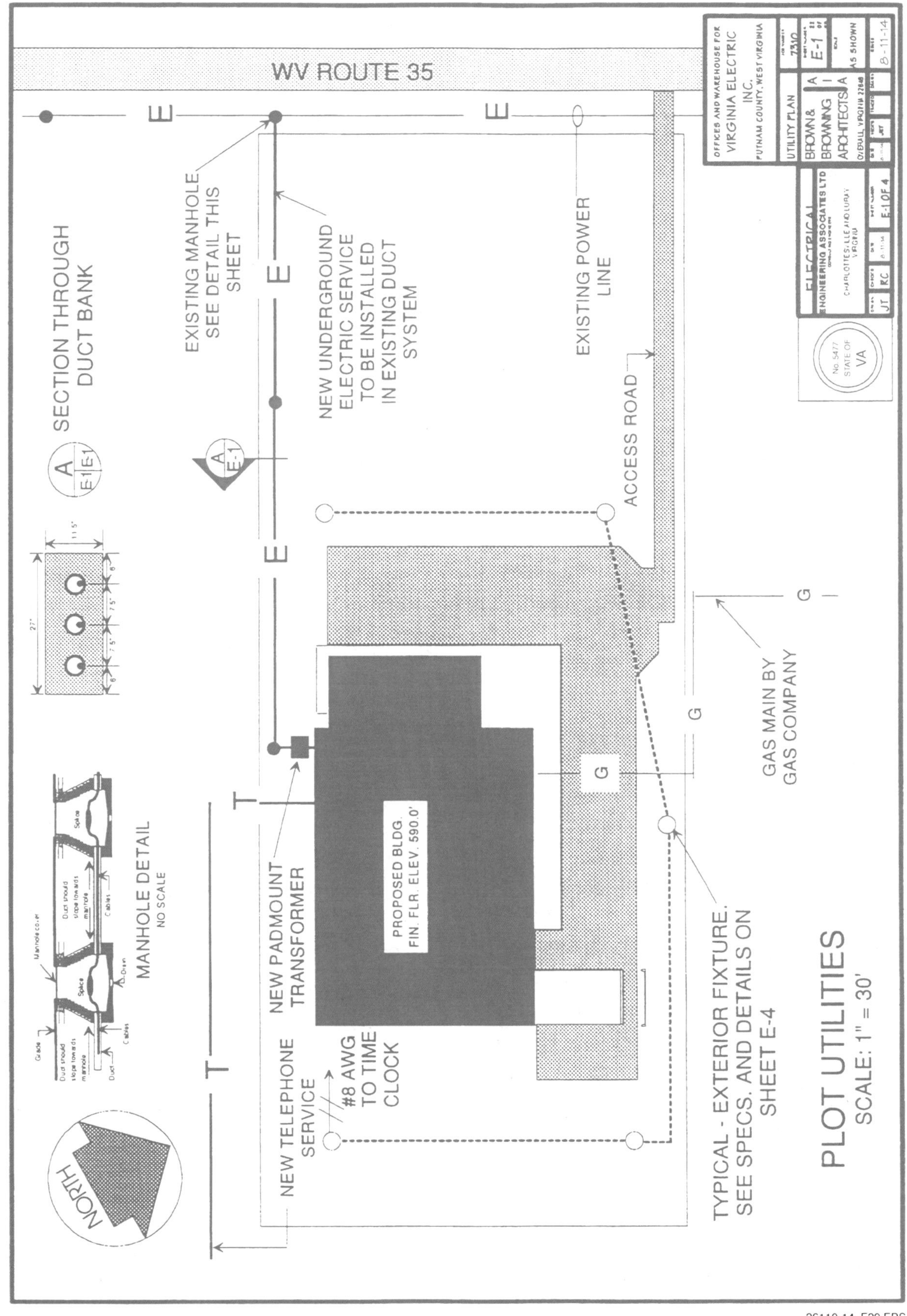

Figure 29 Typical electrical site plan.

7.0.0 Power Plans

The electrical power plan (*Figure 30*) shows the complete floor plan of the office/warehouse building with all interior partitions drawn to scale. Sometimes, the physical locations of all wiring and outlets are shown on one drawing; that is, outlets for lighting, power, signal and communications, special electrical systems, and related equipment are shown on the same plan. However, on complex installations, the drawing would become cluttered if both lighting and power were shown on the same floor plan. Therefore, most projects will have a separate drawing for power and another for lighting. Riser diagrams and details may be shown on yet another drawing sheet, or if room permits, they may be shown on the lighting or power floor plan sheets.

A closer look at this drawing reveals the title blocks in the lower right corner of the drawing sheet. These blocks list both the architectural and engineering firms, along with information to identify the project and drawing sheet. Also note that the floor plan is titled *Floor Plan "B"—Power* and is drawn to a scale of ⅛" = 1'–0". There are no revisions shown on this drawing sheet.

7.1.0 Key Plan

A key plan appears on the drawing sheet immediately above the engineer's title block (*Figure 31*). The purpose of this key plan is to identify that part of the project to which this sheet applies. In this case, the project involves two buildings: Building A and Building B. Since the outline of Building B is cross-hatched in the key plan, this is the building to which this drawing applies. Note that this key plan is not drawn to scale—only its approximate shape.

Although Building A is also shown on this key plan, a note below the key plan title states that there is no electrical work required in Building A.

On Site

Watch Specified Dimensions

When devices are to be located at heights specified above the finished floor (AFF), be sure to find out the actual height of the flooring to be installed. Some materials, such as ceramic tile, can add significantly to the height of the finished floor.

Think About It

Interpreting Site Plans

Study *Figure 29* and explain as many of its features as you can. How much can be understood using common sense? What features require special information?

On some larger installations, the overall project may involve several buildings requiring appropriate key plans on each drawing to help the workers orient the drawings to the appropriate building. In some cases, separate drawing sheets may be used for each room or area in an industrial project—again requiring key plans on each drawing sheet to identify applicable drawings for each room.

7.2.0 Symbol List

A symbol list appears on the electrical power plan (immediately above the architect's title block) to identify the various symbols used for both power and lighting on this project. In most cases, the only symbols listed are those that apply to the particular project. In other cases, however, a standard list of symbols is used for all projects with the following note:

> "These are standard symbols and may not all appear on the project drawings; however, wherever the symbol on the project drawings occurs, the item shall be provided and installed."

Only electrical symbols that are actually used for the office/warehouse drawings are shown in the list on the example electrical power plan. A close-up look at these symbols appears in *Figure 32*.

7.3.0 Floor Plan

A somewhat enlarged view of the electrical floor plan drawing is shown in *Figure 33*. However, due to the size of the drawing in comparison with the size of the pages in this module, it is still difficult to see very much detail. This illustration is meant to show the overall layout of the floor plan and how the symbols and notes are arranged.

In general, this plan shows the service equipment (in plan view), receptacles, underfloor duct system, motor connections, motor controllers, electric heat, busways, and similar details. The electric panels and other service equipment are drawn close to scale. The locations of other electrical outlets and similar components are only

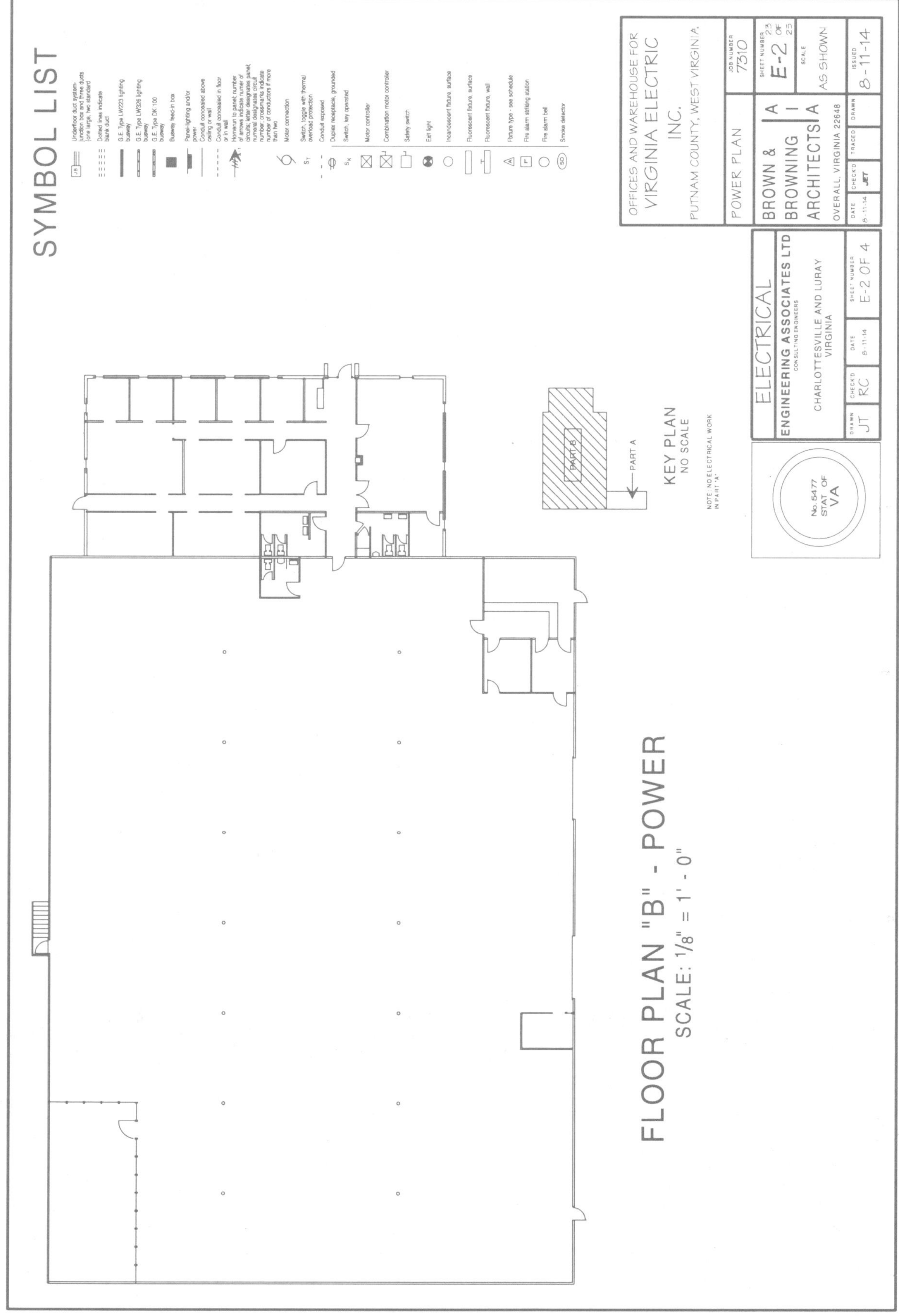

Figure 30 Electrical power plan.

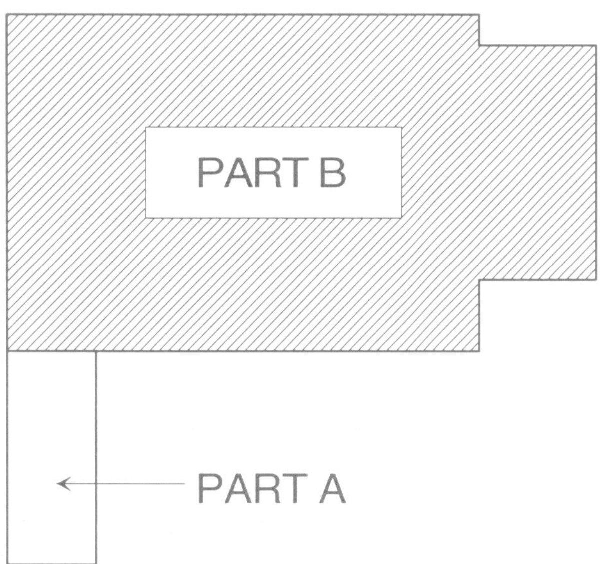

Figure 31 Key plan appearing on electrical power plan.

approximated on the drawings because they have to be exaggerated to show up on the prints. To illustrate, a common duplex receptacle is only about three inches wide. If such a receptacle were to be located on the floor plan of this building (drawn to a scale of ⅛" = 1'–0"), even a small dot on the drawing would be too large to draw the receptacle exactly to scale. Therefore, the receptacle symbol is exaggerated. When such receptacles are scaled on the drawings to determine the proper location, a measurement is usually taken to the center of the symbol to determine the distance between outlets. Junction boxes, switches, and other electrical connections shown on the floor plan will be exaggerated in a similar manner. The partial floor plan drawing in *Figure 34* allows a better view of the drawing details.

7.3.1 Notes and Building Symbols

Referring again to *Figure 33*, you will notice numbers placed inside an oval symbol in each room. These numbered ovals represent the room name or type and correspond to a room schedule in the architectural drawings. For example, room number 112 is designated as the lobby in the room schedule (not shown), room number 113 is designated as office No. 1, etc. On some drawings, these room symbols are omitted and the room names are written out on the drawings.

There are also several notes appearing at various places on the floor plan. These notes offer additional information to clarify certain aspects of the drawing. For example, only one electric heater is to be installed by the electrical contractor; this heater is located in the building's vestibule. Rather than have a symbol in the symbol list for this one heater, a note is used to identify it on the drawing. Other notes on this drawing describe how certain parts of the system are to be installed. For example, in the office area (rooms 112, 113, and 114), you will see the following note: *CONDUIT UP AND STUBBED OUT ABOVE CEILING.* This empty conduit is for telephone/communications cables that will be installed later by the telephone company.

7.3.2 Busways

The office/warehouse project utilizes three types of busways: two types of lighting busways and one power busway. Only the power busway is shown on the floor plan; the lighting busways will appear on the lighting plan.

Figure 33 shows two runs of busways: one running the length of the building on the south end (top wall on drawing), and one running the length of the north wall. The symbol list in *Figure 32* shows this busway to be designated by two parallel lines with a series of X's inside. The symbol

Think About It

Power Plans

Study *Figure 33*. Where does the power enter, and how is it distributed and controlled? What is meant by each of the symbols and lines? Is every electrical connection marked or are some left to the discretion of the electrician?

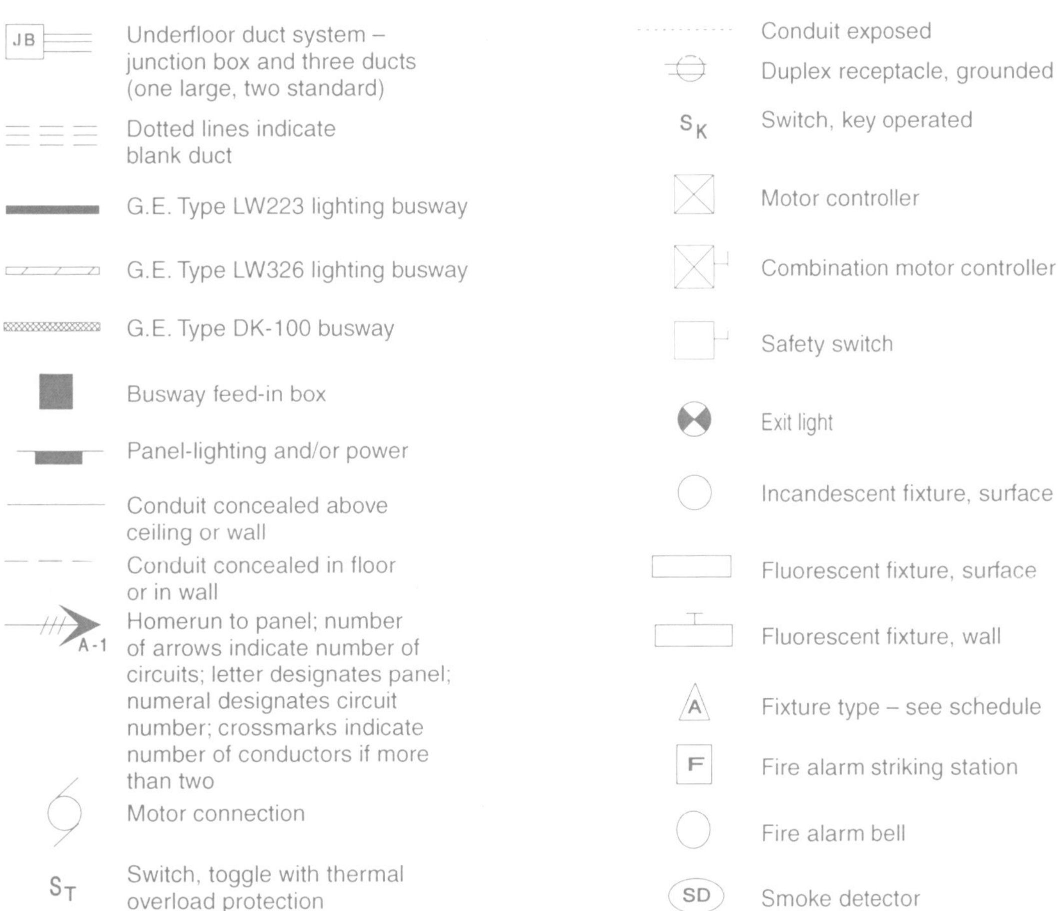

Figure 32 Sample electrical symbols list.

list further describes the busway as General Electric Type DK-100. These busways are fed from the main distribution panel (circuits MDP-1 and MDP-2) through GE No. DHIBBC41 tap boxes.

The *NEC*® defines a busway as a grounded metal enclosure containing factory-mounted, bare or insulated conductors, which are usually copper or aluminum bars, rods, or tubes.

The relationship of the busway and hangers to the building construction should be checked prior to commencing the installation so that any problems due to space conflicts, inadequate or inappropriate supporting structure, openings through walls, etc., are worked out in advance so as not to incur lost time.

For example, the drawings and specifications may call for the busway to be suspended from brackets clamped or welded to steel columns. However, the spacing of the columns may be such that additional supplementary hanger rods suspended from the ceiling or roof structure may be necessary for the adequate support of the busway. To offer more assistance to workers on the office/warehouse project, the engineer may also provide an additional drawing that shows how the busway is to be mounted.

Other details that appear on the floor plan in *Figure 34* include the general arrangement of the underfloor duct system, junction boxes and feeder conduit for the underfloor duct system, and plan views of the service and telephone equipment, along with duplex receptacle outlets. A note on the drawing requires all receptacles in the toilets to be provided with ground fault circuit interrupter (GFCI) protection. The letters EWC next to the receptacle in the vestibule designate this receptacle for use with an electric water cooler.

On Site

Understanding Contact Symbols

When a drawing shows normally open or normally closed contacts, the word *normally* refers to the condition of the contacts in their de-energized or shelf state.

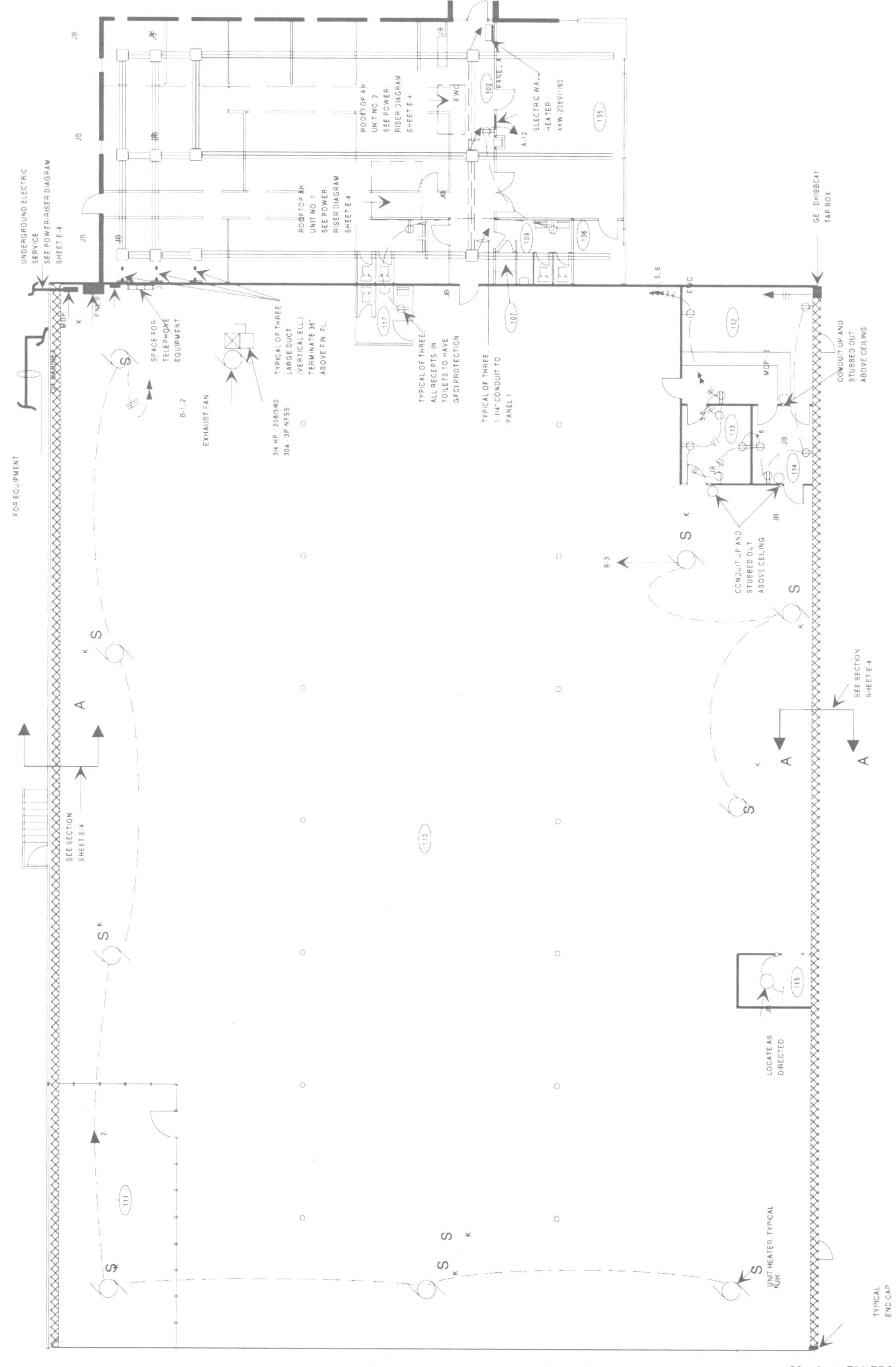

26110-14_F33.EPS

Figure 33 Floor plan for an office/warehouse building.

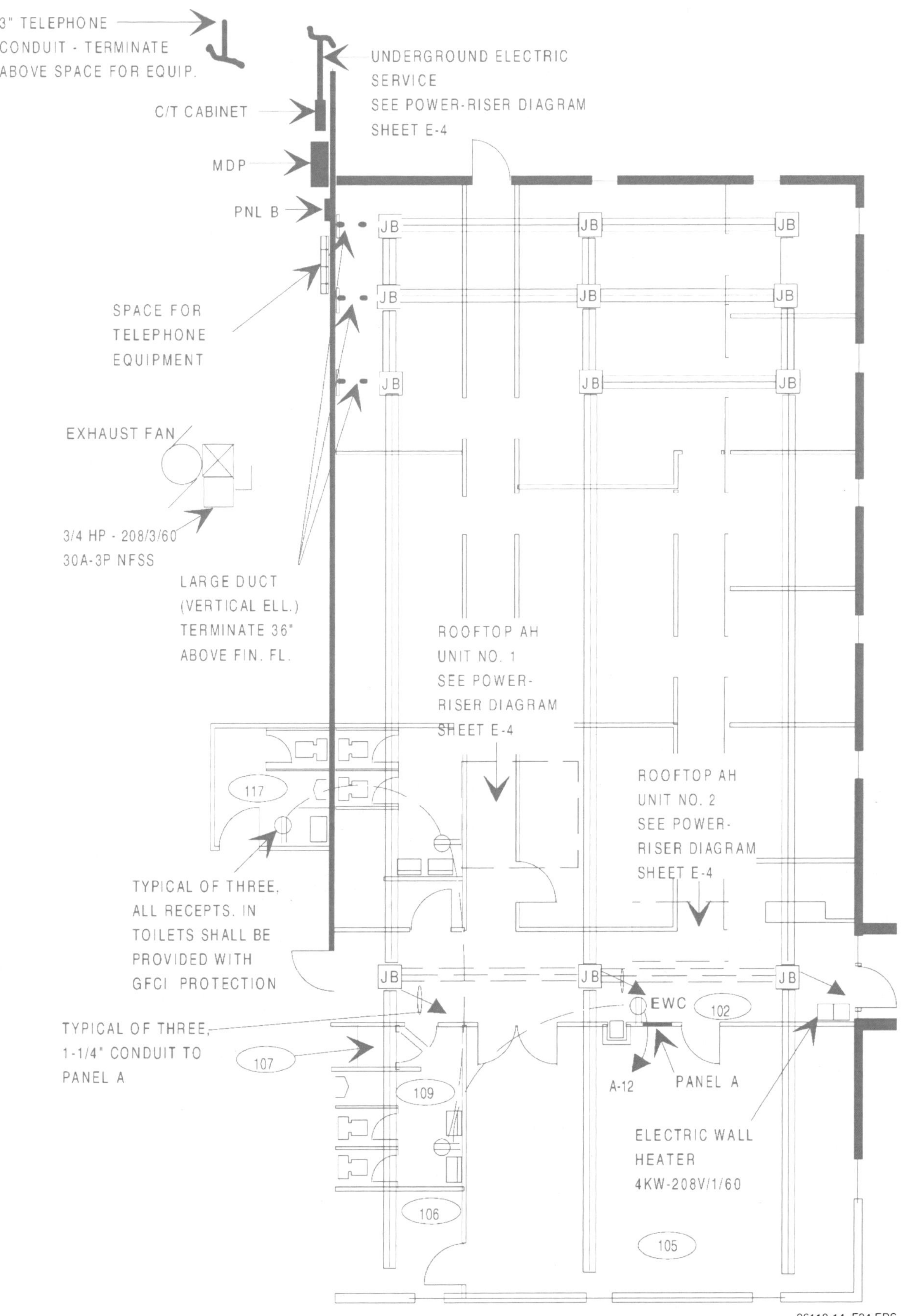
3" TELEPHONE CONDUIT - TERMINATE ABOVE SPACE FOR EQUIP.
UNDERGROUND ELECTRIC SERVICE SEE POWER-RISER DIAGRAM SHEET E-4
C/T CABINET
MDP
PNL B
JB
SPACE FOR TELEPHONE EQUIPMENT
EXHAUST FAN
3/4 HP - 208/3/60 30A-3P NFSS
LARGE DUCT (VERTICAL ELL.) TERMINATE 36" ABOVE FIN. FL.
ROOFTOP AH UNIT NO. 1 SEE POWER-RISER DIAGRAM SHEET E-4
ROOFTOP AH UNIT NO. 2 SEE POWER-RISER DIAGRAM SHEET E-4
117
TYPICAL OF THREE. ALL RECEPTS. IN TOILETS SHALL BE PROVIDED WITH GFCI PROTECTION
TYPICAL OF THREE, 1-1/4" CONDUIT TO PANEL A
107
109
106
EWC
102
A-12
PANEL A
ELECTRIC WALL HEATER 4KW-208V/1/60
105
26110-14_F34.EPS

Figure 34 Partial floor plan for office/warehouse building.

7.4.0 Branch Circuit Layout for Power

The point at which electrical equipment is connected to the wiring system is commonly called an outlet. There are many classifications of outlets: lighting, receptacle, motor, appliance, and so forth. This section, however, deals with the power outlets normally found in residential electrical wiring systems.

When viewing an electrical drawing, outlets are indicated by symbols (usually a small circle with appropriate markings to indicate the type of outlet). The most common symbols for receptacles are shown in *Figure 35.*

7.4.1 Branch Circuit Drawings

In the past, with the exception of very large residences and tract-development houses, the size of the average residential electrical system was not large enough to justify the expense of preparing complete electrical working drawings and specifications. Such electrical systems were either laid out by the architect in the form of a sketchy outlet arrangement, or laid out by the electrician on the job as the work progressed. However, many technical developments in residential electrical use—such as electric heat with sophisticated control wiring, increased use of electrical appliances, various electronic alarm systems, new lighting techniques, and the need for energy conservation techniques—have greatly expanded the demand and extended the complexity of today's residential electrical systems.

Each year, the number of homes with electrical systems designed by consulting engineering firms increases. Such homes are provided with complete electrical working drawings and specifications, similar to those frequently provided for commercial and industrial projects. Still, these are more the exception than the rule. Most residential projects will not have a complete set of drawings.

Circuit layout is provided on the drawings to follow for several reasons:

- They provide a visual layout of house wiring circuitry.
- They provide a sample of electrical residential drawings that are prepared by consulting engineering firms, although the number may still be limited.
- They introduce the method of showing electrical systems on working drawings to provide a foundation for tackling advanced electrical systems.

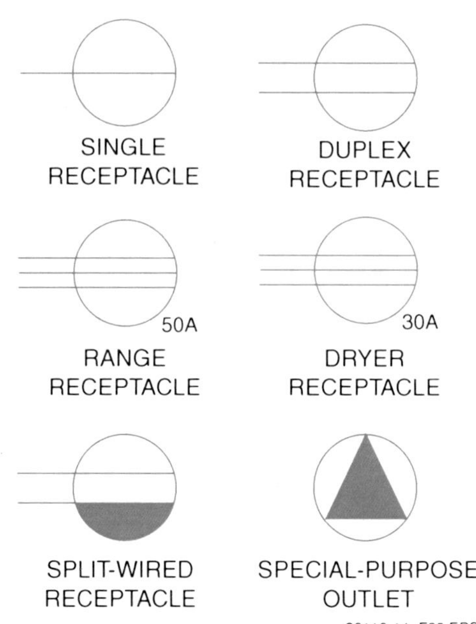

Figure 35 Typical outlet symbols appearing in electrical drawings.

Branch circuits are shown on electrical drawings by means of a single line drawn from the panelboard (or by homerun arrowheads indicating that the circuit goes to the panelboard) to the outlet, or from outlet to outlet where there is more than one outlet on the circuit.

The lines indicating branch circuits can be solid to show that the conductors are to be run concealed in the ceiling or wall; dashed to show that the conductors are to be run in the floor or ceiling below; or dotted to show that the wiring is to be run exposed. *Figure 36* shows examples of these three types of branch circuit lines.

In *Figure 36*, No. 12 indicates the wire size. The slash marks shown through the circuits in *Figure 36* indicate the number of current-carrying conductors in the circuit. Although two slash marks are shown for the current-carrying conductors (along with one slash mark for the ground), in actual practice, a branch circuit containing only two conductors usually contains no slash marks; that is, any circuit with no slash marks is assumed to have two conductors. However, three or more conductors are always indicated on electrical working drawings—either by slash marks for each conductor, or else by a note.

Never assume that you know the meaning of any electrical symbol. Although great efforts have been made in recent years to standardize drawing symbols, architects, consulting engineers, and

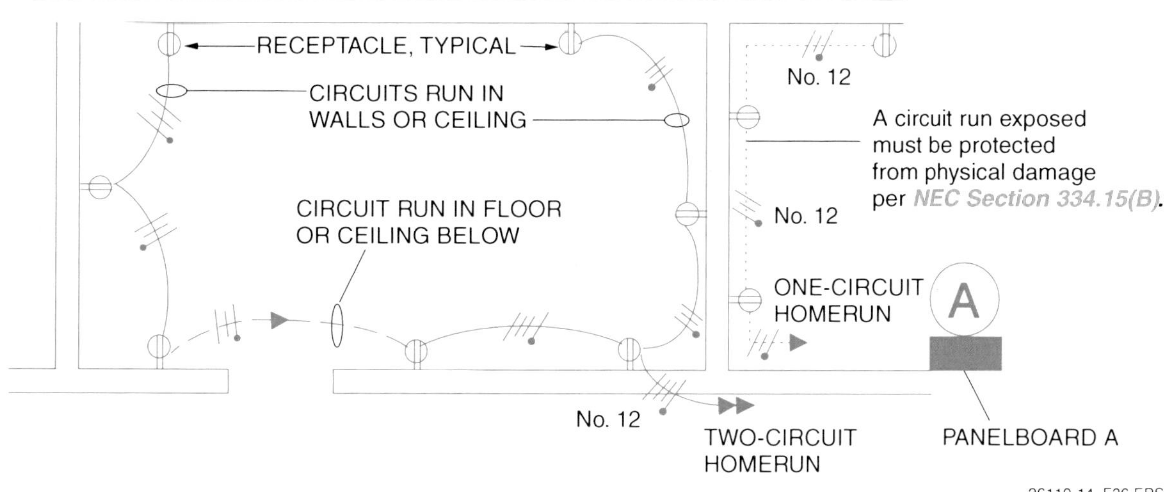

Figure 36 Types of branch circuit lines shown on electrical working drawings.

electrical drafters still modify existing symbols or devise new ones to meet their own needs. Always consult the symbol list or legend on electrical working drawings for an exact interpretation of the symbols used.

7.4.2 Locating Receptacles

NEC Section 210.52(A) states the minimum requirements for the location of receptacles in dwelling units. It specifies that in each kitchen, family room, and dining room, receptacle outlets shall be installed so that no point along the floor line in any wall space is more than 6', measured horizontally, from an outlet in that space, including any wall space 2' or more in width and the wall space occupied by fixed panels in exterior walls, but excluding sliding panels. This means that the outlets will be no more than 12' apart. When spaced in this manner, a 6' extension cord will reach a receptacle at any point along the wall line. Receptacle outlets shall, insofar as practicable, be spaced equal distances apart. Receptacle outlets in floors shall not be counted as part of the required number of receptacle outlets unless located within 18" of the wall.

The *NEC®* defines wall space as a wall that is unbroken along the floor line by doorways, fireplaces, or similar openings. Each wall space that is two feet or more in width must be treated individually and separately from other wall spaces within the room.

The purpose of *NEC Section 210.52(A)* is to minimize the use of cords across doorways, fireplaces, and similar openings.

On Site

Don't Just Check the Electrical Plan

Always review all of the drawings in a drawing set, not just the electrical plan. Several drawings in the set will have information of relevance to the electrician. For example, you should review:

- Site plans for utility lines and elevation information
- Mechanical drawings for routing, clearances, and HVAC equipment and controls
- Architectural drawings for the type of construction (block, wood, metal stud, etc.), fire ratings, and special details.
- Finish drawings (e.g., reflected ceiling plans) for locations of fixtures, fans, and other devices
- Room finish schedules for ceiling heights and floor and wall finishing details
- Plumbing drawings for pumps, water service, and sprinklers

Figure 37 shows the outlets for a sample residence. In laying out these receptacle outlets, the floor line of the wall is measured (also around corners), but not across doorways, fireplaces, passageways, or other spaces where a flexible cord extended across the space would be unsuitable.

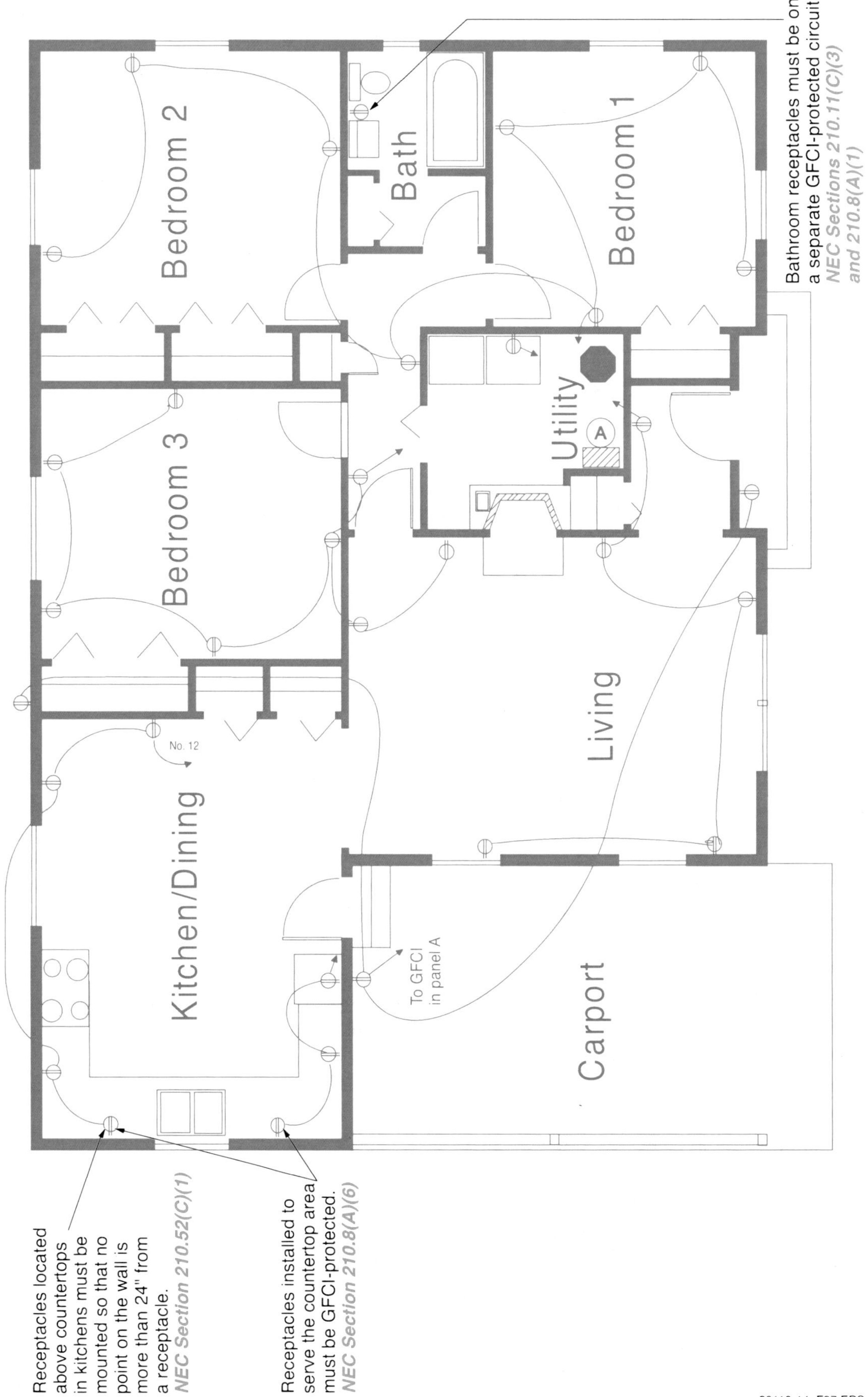
Bathroom receptacles must be on a separate GFCI-protected circuit. NEC Sections 210.11(C)(3) and 210.8(A)(1)
Bedroom 2
Bath
Bedroom 1
Bedroom 3
Utility
A
Living
No. 12
Kitchen/Dining
To GFCI in panel A
Carport
Receptacles located above countertops in kitchens must be mounted so that no point on the wall is more than 24" from a receptacle. NEC Section 210.52(C)(1)
Receptacles installed to serve the countertop area must be GFCI-protected. NEC Section 210.8(A)(6)
26110-14_F37.EPS

Figure 37 Floor plan of a sample residence.

8.0.0 Lighting Floor Plan

A skeleton view of a lighting floor plan is shown in *Figure 38*. Again, the architect's/engineer's title blocks appear in the lower right corner of the drawing. A key plan appears above the engineer's title block. This plan is drawn to the same scale as the power plan; that is, ⅛" = 1'–0". A lighting fixture (luminaire) schedule appears in the upper right corner of the drawing and some installation notes appear below the schedule.

The lighting outlet symbols found on the drawing for the office/warehouse building represent both incandescent and fluorescent types; a circle on most electrical drawings usually represents an incandescent fixture, and a rectangle represents a fluorescent one. All of these symbols are designed to indicate the physical shape of a particular fixture and are usually drawn to scale.

The type of mounting used for all lighting fixtures is usually indicated in a lighting fixture schedule, which in this case is shown on the drawings. On some projects, the schedule may be found only in the written specifications.

The type of lighting fixture is identified by a numeral placed inside a triangle near each lighting fixture. If one type of fixture is used exclusively in one room or area, the triangular indicator need only appear once with the word ALL lettered at the bottom of the triangle.

8.1.0 Drawing Schedules

A schedule is a systematic method of presenting notes or lists of equipment on a drawing in tabular form. When properly organized and thoroughly understood, schedules are powerful timesaving devices for both those preparing the drawings and workers on the job.

For example, the lighting fixture schedule shown in *Figure 39* lists the fixture and identifies each fixture type on the drawing by number. The manufacturer and catalog number of each type are given along with the number, size, and type of lamp for each.

At times, all of the same information found in schedules will be duplicated in the written specifications, but combing through page after page

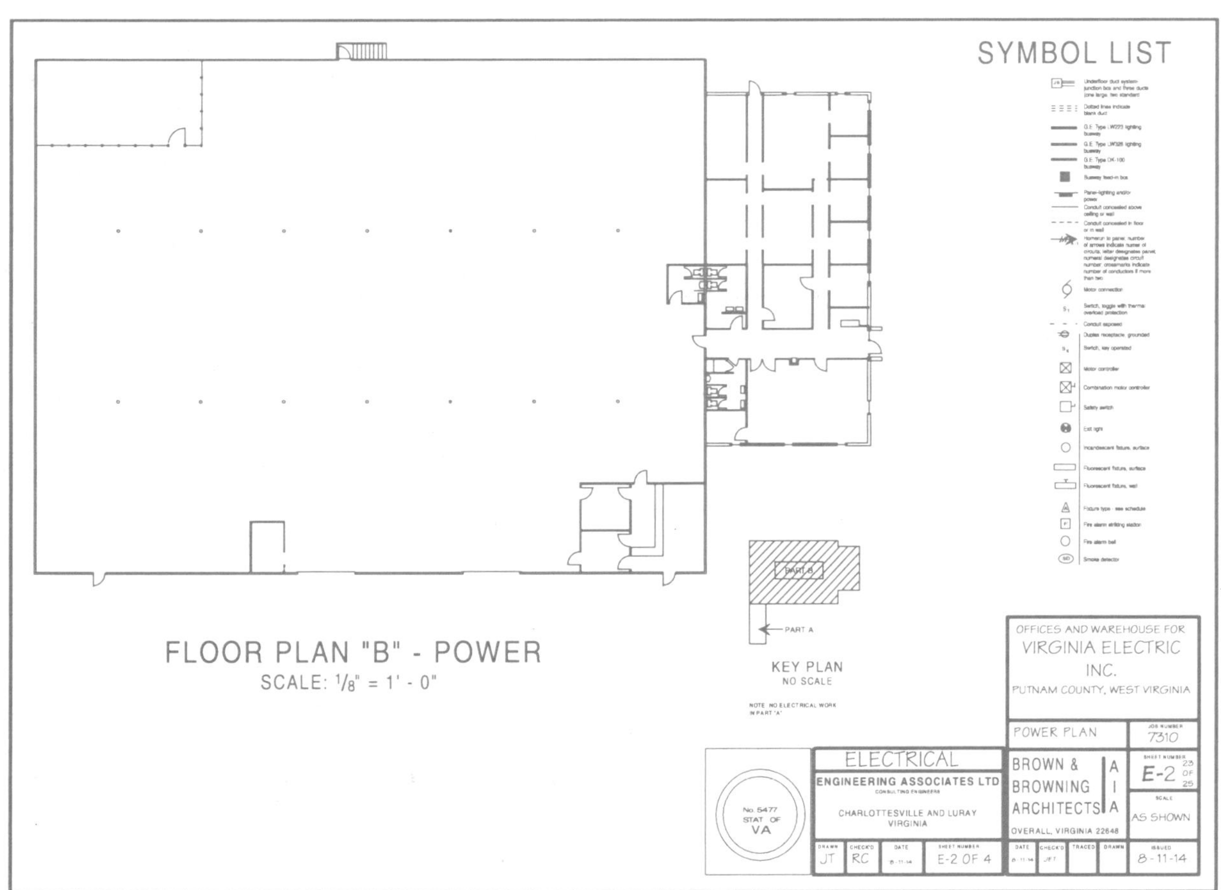

Figure 38 Sample lighting plan.

LIGHTING FIXTURE SCHEDULE				
SYMBOL	TYPE	MANUFACTURER AND CATALOG NUMBER	MOUNTING	LAMPS
	A	LIGHTOLIER 10234	WALL	2-40W T-12WWX
	B	LIGHTOLIER 10420	SURFACE	2-40W T-12 WWX
	C	ALKCO RPC-210-6E	SURFACE	2-8W T-5
	D	P 7 S AL 2936	WALL	1-100W 'A'
	E	P 7 S 110	SURFACE	1-100W 'A'

26110-14_F39.EPS

Figure 39 Lighting fixture (luminaire) schedule.

of written specifications can be time consuming. Workers do not always have access to the specifications while on the job, whereas they usually do have access to the working drawings. Therefore, the schedule is an excellent means of providing essential information in a clear and accurate manner, allowing the workers to carry out their assignments in the least amount of time.

Other schedules that are frequently found on electrical working drawings include:

- Connected load schedule
- Panelboard schedule
- Electric heat schedule
- Kitchen equipment schedule
- Schedule of receptacle types

There are also other schedules found on electrical drawings, depending upon the type of project. However, most will deal with lists of equipment such as motors, motor controllers, and similar items.

8.2.0 Branch Circuit Layout for Lighting

A simple lighting branch circuit requires two conductors to provide a continuous path for current flow. The usual lighting branch circuit operates at either 120V or 277V; the white (grounded) circuit conductor is therefore connected to the neutral bus in the panelboard, while the black (ungrounded) circuit conductor is connected to an overcurrent protection device.

Lighting branch circuits and outlets are shown on electrical drawings by means of lines and symbols; that is, a single line is drawn from outlet to outlet and then terminated with an arrowhead to indicate a homerun to the panelboard. Several methods are used to indicate the number and size of conductors, but the most common is to indicate the number of conductors in the circuit by using slash marks through the circuit lines and then indicate the wire size by a notation adjacent to these slash marks.

The circuits used to feed residential lighting must conform to standards established by the *NEC®* as well as by local and state ordinances. Most of the lighting circuits should be calculated to include the total load, although at times this is not possible because the electrician cannot be certain of the exact wattage that might be used by the homeowner. For example, an electrician may install four porcelain lampholders for the unfinished basement area, each to contain one 100-watt (100W) incandescent lamp. However, the homeowners may eventually replace the original lamps with others rated at 150W or even 200W. Thus, if the electrician initially loads the lighting circuit to full capacity, the circuit will probably become overloaded in the future.

It is recommended that no residential branch circuit be loaded to more than 80% of its rated capacity. Since most circuits used for lighting are rated at 15A, the total ampacity (in volt-amperes) for the circuit is as follows:

$$15A \times 120V = 1{,}800VA$$

Therefore, if the circuit is to be loaded to only 80% of its rated capacity, the maximum initial connected load should be no more than 1,440VA.

Figure 40 shows one possible lighting arrangement for the sample residence discussed earlier. All lighting fixtures are shown in their approximate physical location as they should be installed.

Electrical symbols are used to show the fixture types. Switches and lighting branch circuits are also shown by appropriate lines and symbols. The

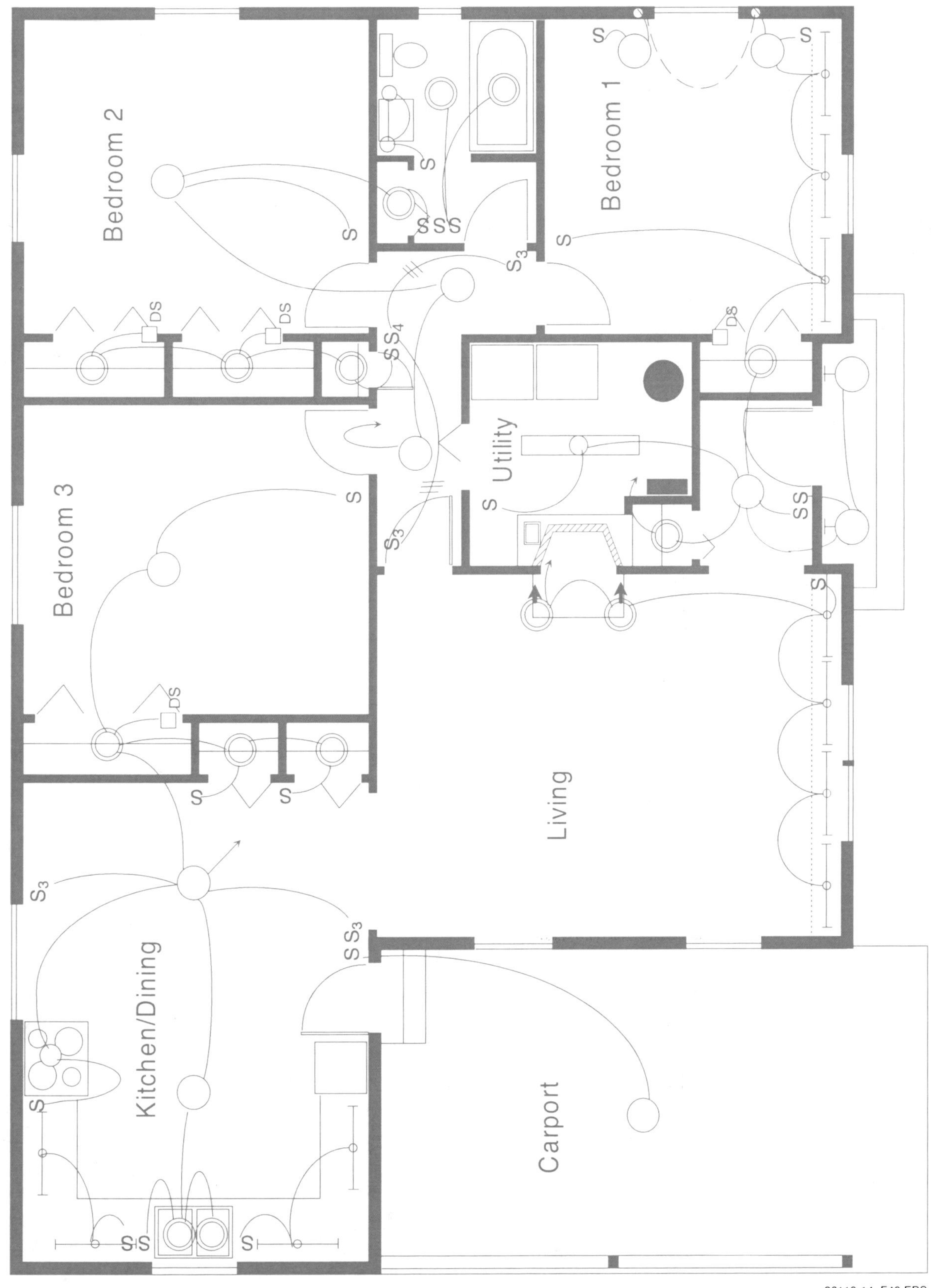

26110-14_F40.EPS

Figure 40 Lighting layout of the sample residence.

meanings of the symbols used on this drawing are explained in the symbol list in *Figure 41*.

In actual practice, the location of lighting fixtures and their related switches will probably be the extent of the information shown on working drawings. The circuits shown in *Figure 40* are meant to illustrate how lighting circuits are routed, not to imply that such drawings are typical for residential construction. If incandescent fixtures are used in a closet, they must meet the requirements of *NEC Section 410.16* and be completely enclosed.

9.0.0 Electrical Details and Diagrams

Electrical diagrams are drawings that are intended to show electrical components and their related connections. They show the electrical association of the different components, but are seldom, if ever, drawn to scale.

9.1.0 Power-Riser Diagrams

One-line (single-line) block diagrams are used extensively to show the arrangement of electric service equipment. Power-riser diagrams (*Figure 42*) are typical of such drawings. These drawings show all pieces of electrical equipment as well as the connecting lines used to indicate service-entrance conductors and feeders. Notes are used to identify the equipment, indicate the size of conduit necessary for each feeder, and show the number, size, and type of conductors in each conduit.

A panelboard schedule (*Figure 43*) is included with the power-riser diagram to indicate the exact components contained in each panelboard. This panelboard schedule is for the main distribution panel. On the actual drawings, schedules would also be shown for the other two panels (PNL A and PNL B).

In general, panelboard schedules usually indicate the panel number, type of cabinet (either flush- or surface-mounted), panel mains (ampere and voltage rating), phase (single- or three-phase), and number of wires. A four-wire panel, for example, indicates that a solid neutral exists in the panel. Branches indicate the type of overcurrent protection; that is, they indicate the number of poles, trip rating, and frame size. The items fed by each overcurrent device are also indicated.

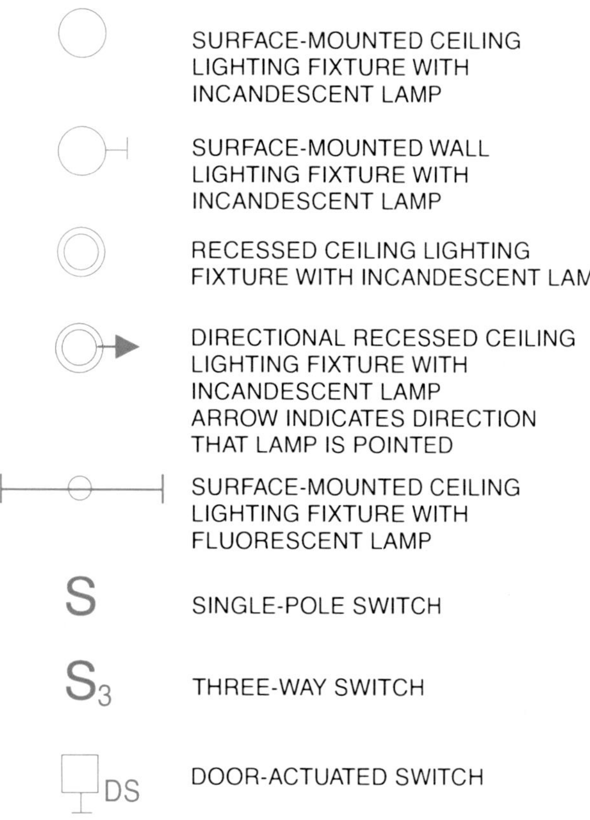

Figure 41 Electrical symbols list.

9.2.0 Schematic Diagrams

Complete schematic wiring diagrams are normally used only in complicated electrical systems, such as control circuits. Components are represented by symbols, and every wire is either shown by itself or included in an assembly of several wires, which appear as one line on the drawing. Each wire should be numbered when it enters an assembly and should keep the same number when it comes out again to be connected to some electrical component in the system. *Figure 44* shows a complete schematic wiring diagram for a three-phase, AC magnetic non-reversing motor starter.

Note that this diagram shows the various devices in symbol form and indicates the actual connections of all wires between the devices. The three-wire supply lines are indicated by L_1, L_2, and L_3; the motor terminals of motor M are indicated by T_1, T_2, and T_3. Lines L_1, L_2, and L_3 each have a thermal overload protection device (OL) connected in series with normally open line contacts C_1 and C_3, respectively, which are both controlled by the magnetic starter coil, C. The control station, consisting of start pushbutton 1 and stop pushbutton 2, is connected across lines L_1 and L_2. Auxiliary contacts (C_4) are connected in series with the stop pushbutton and in parallel with the start pushbutton. The control circuit also has normally closed overload contacts (OC) connected in series with the magnetic starter coil (C).

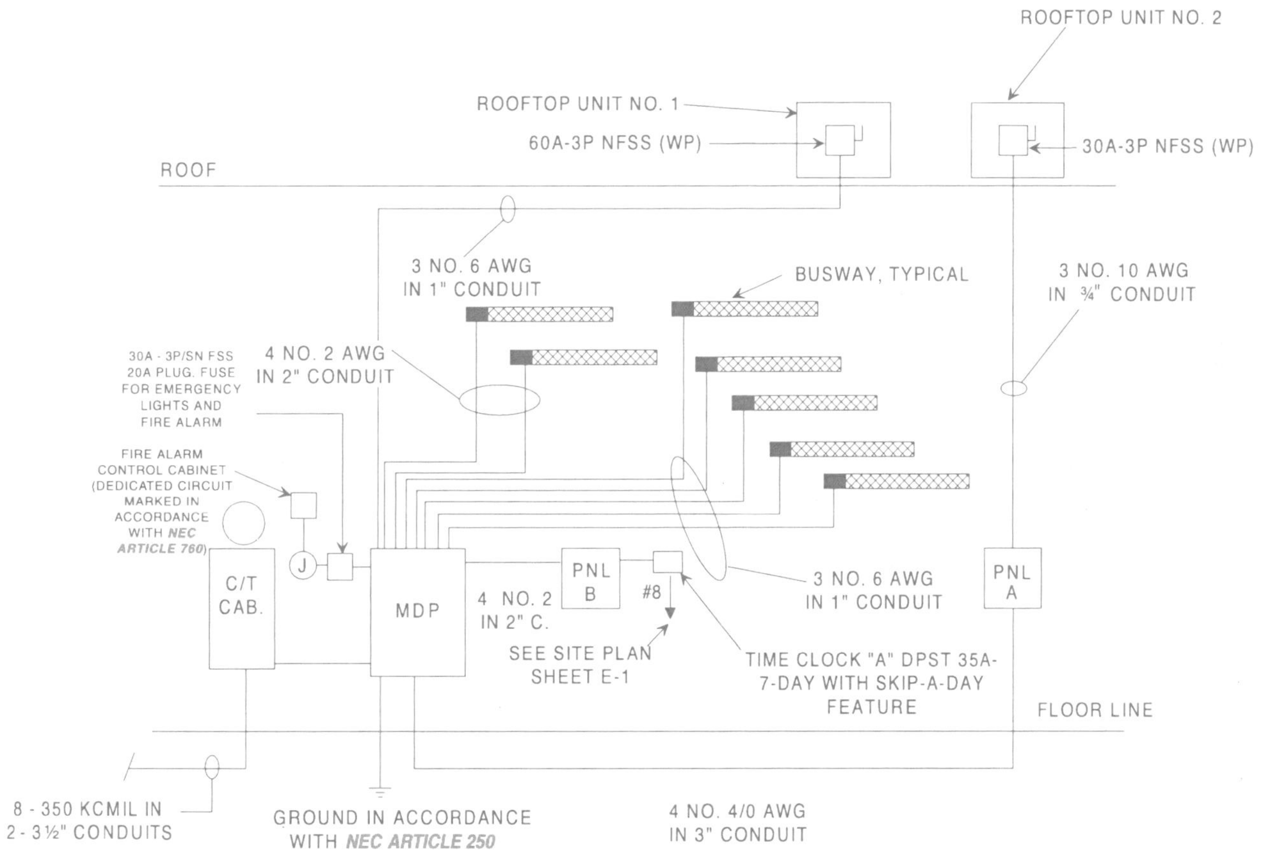
ROOFTOP UNIT NO. 2
ROOFTOP UNIT NO. 1
60A-3P NFSS (WP)
30A-3P NFSS (WP)
ROOF
3 NO. 6 AWG
IN 1" CONDUIT
BUSWAY, TYPICAL
3 NO. 10 AWG
IN ¾" CONDUIT
30A - 3P/SN FSS
20A PLUG. FUSE
FOR EMERGENCY
LIGHTS AND
FIRE ALARM
4 NO. 2 AWG
IN 2" CONDUIT
FIRE ALARM
CONTROL CABINET
(DEDICATED CIRCUIT
MARKED IN
ACCORDANCE
WITH NEC
ARTICLE 760)
J
C/T
CAB.
MDP
4 NO. 2
IN 2" C.
PNL
B
#8
3 NO. 6 AWG
IN 1" CONDUIT
PNL
A
SEE SITE PLAN
SHEET E-1
TIME CLOCK "A" DPST 35A-
7-DAY WITH SKIP-A-DAY
FEATURE
FLOOR LINE
8 - 350 KCMIL IN
2 - 3½" CONDUITS
GROUND IN ACCORDANCE
WITH NEC ARTICLE 250
4 NO. 4/0 AWG
IN 3" CONDUIT
COMMERCIAL

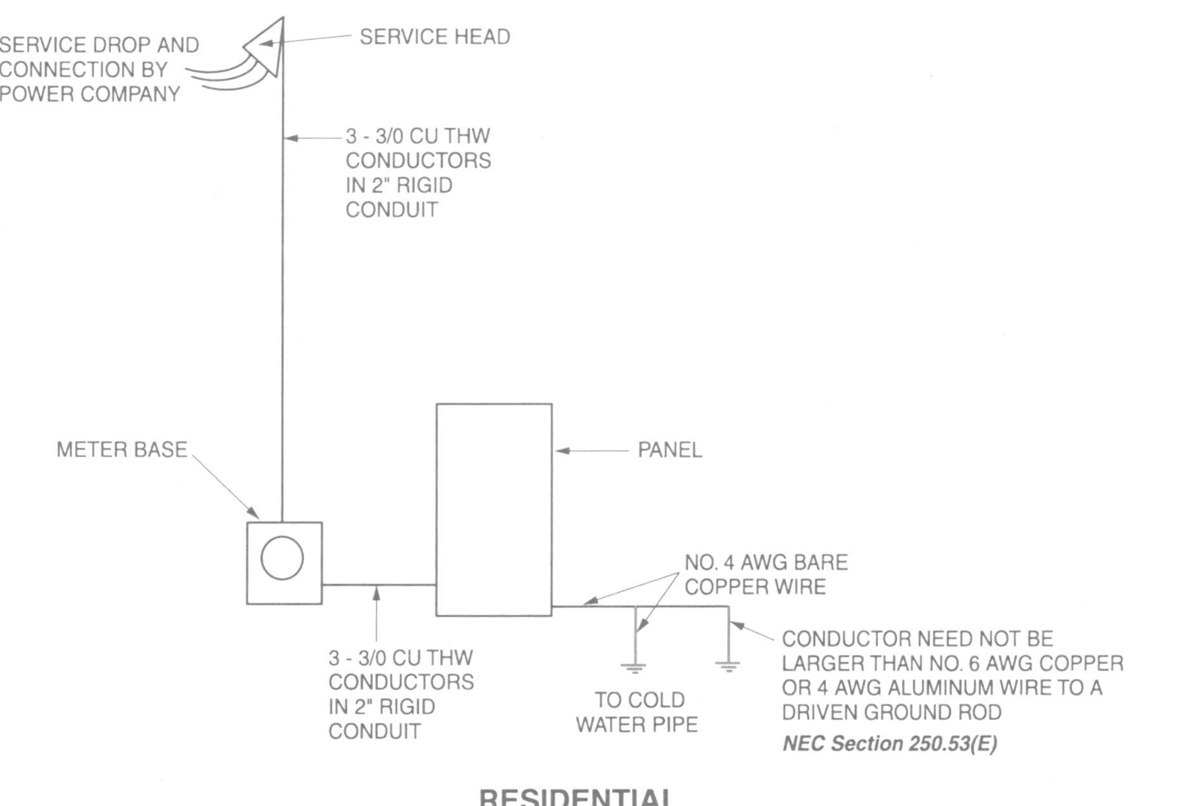
SERVICE DROP AND
CONNECTION BY
POWER COMPANY
SERVICE HEAD
3 - 3/0 CU THW
CONDUCTORS
IN 2" RIGID
CONDUIT
METER BASE
PANEL
NO. 4 AWG BARE
COPPER WIRE
3 - 3/0 CU THW
CONDUCTORS
IN 2" RIGID
CONDUIT
TO COLD
WATER PIPE
CONDUCTOR NEED NOT BE
LARGER THAN NO. 6 AWG COPPER
OR 4 AWG ALUMINUM WIRE TO A
DRIVEN GROUND ROD
NEC Section 250.53(E)
RESIDENTIAL
26110-14_F42.EPS

Figure 42 Typical power-riser diagrams.

PANELBOARD SCHEDULE										
PANEL No.	CABINET TYPE	PANEL MAINS			BRANCHES					ITEMS FED OR REMARKS
		AMPS	VOLTS	PHASE	1P	2P	3P	PROT.	FRAME	
MDP	SURFACE	600A	120/208	3ϕ,4-W	-	-	1	225A	25,000	PANEL "A"
					-	-	1	100A	18,000	PANEL "B"
					-	-	1	100A		POWER BUSWAY
					-	-	1	60A		LIGHTING BUSWAY
					-	-	1	70A		ROOFTOP UNIT #1
					-	-	1	70A	▼	SPARE
					-	-	1	600A	42,000	MAIN CIRCUIT BRKR

2011001OOF03.EP

Figure 43 Typical panelboard schedule.

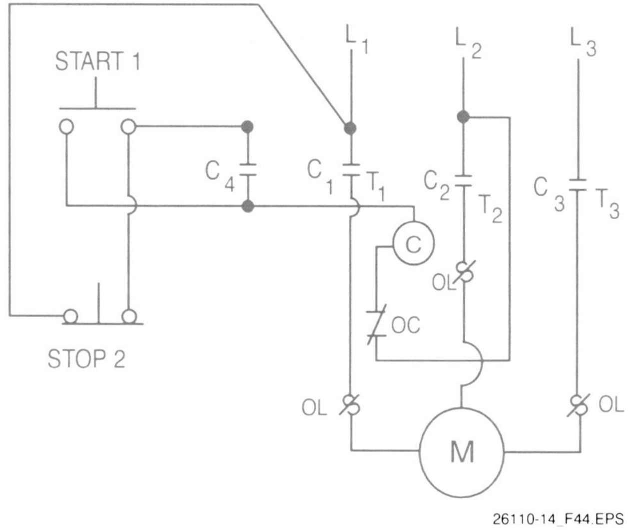

Figure 44 Wiring diagram.

Any number of additional pushbutton stations may be added to this control circuit similarly to the way in which three-way and four-way switches are added to control a lighting circuit. When adding pushbutton stations, the stop buttons are always connected in series and the start buttons are always connected in parallel. *Figure 45* shows the same motor starter circuit in *Figure 44*, but this time it is controlled by two sets of start/stop buttons.

Schematic wiring diagrams have only been touched upon in this module; there are many other details that you will need to know to perform your work in a proficient manner. Later modules cover wiring diagrams in more detail.

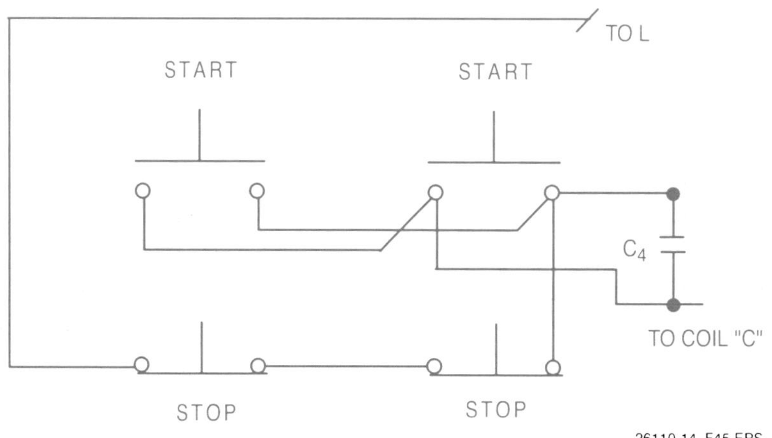

Figure 45 Circuit being controlled by two sets of start/stop buttons.

9.3.0 Drawing Details

A detail drawing is a drawing of a separate item or portion of an electrical system, giving a complete and exact description of its use and all the details needed to show the electrician exactly what is required for its installation. For example, the power plan for the office/warehouse has a sectional cut through the busduct. This is a good example of where an extra, detailed drawing is desirable.

A set of electrical drawings will sometimes require large-scale drawings of certain areas that are not indicated with sufficient clarity on the small-scale drawings. For example, the site plan may show exterior pole-mounted lighting fixtures that are to be installed by the contractor.

10.0.0 Written Specifications

The written specifications for a building or project are the written descriptions of work and duties required of the owner, architect, and consulting engineer. Together with the working drawings, these specifications form the basis of the contract requirements for the construction of the building or project. Those who use the construction drawings and specifications must always be alert to discrepancies between the working drawings and the written specifications. These are some situations where discrepancies may occur:

- Architects or engineers use standard or prototype specifications and attempt to apply them without any modification to specific working drawings.
- Previously prepared standard drawings are changed or amended by reference in the specifications only and the drawings themselves are not changed.
- Items are duplicated in both the drawings and specifications, but an item is subsequently amended in one and overlooked in the other contract document.

In such instances, the person in charge of the project has the responsibility to ascertain whether the drawings or the specifications take precedence. Such questions must be resolved, preferably before the work begins, to avoid added costs to the owner, architect/engineer, or contractor.

10.1.0 How Specifications Are Written

Writing accurate and complete specifications for building construction is a serious responsibility for those who design the buildings because the specifications, combined with the working drawings, govern practically all important decisions that are made during the construction span of every project. Compiling and writing these specifications is not a simple task, even for those who have had considerable experience in preparing such documents. A set of written specifications for a single project will usually contain thousands of products, parts, and components, and the methods of installing them, all of which must be covered in either the drawings and/or specifications. No one can memorize all of the necessary items required to describe accurately the various areas of construction. One must rely upon reference materials such as manufacturer's data, catalogs, checklists, and, most of all, a high-quality master specification.

10.2.0 Format of Specifications

For convenience in writing, speed in estimating, and ease of reference, the most suitable organization of the specifications is a series of sections dealing with the construction requirements, products, and activities that is easily understandable by the different trades. Those people who use the specifications must be able to find all the information they need without spending too much time looking for it.

The most commonly used specification-writing format used in North America is the *MasterFormat*®. This standard was developed jointly by the Construction Specifications Institute (CSI) and Construction Specifications Canada (CSC). For many years prior to 2004, the organization of construction specifications and suppliers catalogs was based on a standard with 16 sections, otherwise known as divisions. The divisions and their subsections were individually identified by a five-digit numbering system. The first two digits represented the division number and the next three individual numbers represented successively lower levels of breakdown. For example, the number 13213 represents division 13, subsection 2, sub-subsection 1, and sub-sub-subsection 3. In this older version of the standard, electrical systems, including any electronic or special electrical systems, were lumped together under Division 16 – *Electrical*. Today, specifications conforming to the 16 division format may still be in use.

In 2004, the *MasterFormat*® standard underwent a major change. What had been 16 divisions was expanded to four major groupings and 49 divisions with some divisions reserved for future expansion. *MasterFormat*® was again updated for 2010 (*Figure 46*). The first 14 divisions are essentially the same as the old format. Subjects under the old Division 15 – *Mechanical*

Applications Guide

MasterFormat GROUPS, SUBGROUPS, AND DIVISIONS

PROCUREMENT AND CONTRACTING REQUIREMENTS GROUP

Division 00 – Procurement and Contracting Requirements
- Introductory Information
- Procurement Requirements
- Contracting Requirements

SPECIFICATIONS GROUP

GENERAL REQUIREMENTS SUBGROUP

Division 01 – General Requirements

FACILITY CONSTRUCTION SUBGROUP

Division 02 – Existing Conditions
Division 03 – Concrete
Division 04 – Masonry
Division 05 – Metals
Division 06 – Wood, Plastics, and Composites
Division 07 – Thermal and Moisture Protection
Division 08 – Openings
Division 09 – Finishes
Division 10 – Specialties
Division 11 – Equipment
Division 12 – Furnishings
Division 13 – Special Construction
Division 14 – Conveying Equipment
Division 15 – Reserved for Future Expansion
Division 16 – Reserved for Future Expansion
Division 17 – Reserved for Future Expansion
Division 18 – Reserved for Future Expansion
Division 19 – Reserved for Future Expansion

FACILITY SERVICES SUBGROUP

Division 20 – Reserved for Future Expansion
Division 21 – Fire Suppression

Division 22 – Plumbing
Division 23 – Heating, Ventilating, and Air-Conditioning (HVAC)
Division 24 – Reserved for Future Expansion
Division 25 – Integrated Automation
Division 26 – Electrical
Division 27 – Communications
Division 28 – Electronic Safety and Security
Division 29 – Reserved for Future Expansion

SITE AND INFRASTRUCTURE SUBGROUP

Division 30 – Reserved for Future Expansion
Division 31 – Earthwork
Division 32 – Exterior Improvements
Division 33 – Utilities
Division 34 – Transportation
Division 35 – Waterway and Marine Construction
Division 36 – Reserved for Future Expansion
Division 37 – Reserved for Future Expansion
Division 38 – Reserved for Future Expansion
Division 39 – Reserved for Future Expansion

PROCESS EQUIPMENT SUBGROUP

Division 40 – Process Integration
Division 41 – Material Processing and Handling Equipment
Division 42 – Process Heating, Cooling, and Drying Equipment
Division 43 – Process Gas and Liquid Handling, Purification, and Storage Equipment
Division 44 – Pollution and Waste Control Equipment
Division 45 – Industry-Specific Manufacturing Equipment
Division 46 – Water and Wastewater Equipment
Division 47 – Reserved for Future Expansion
Division 48 – Electrical Power Generation
Division 49 – Reserved for Future Expansion

26110-14_F46.EPS

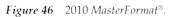

Figure 46 2010 *MasterFormat*®.

On Site

Specifications

Written specifications supplement the related working drawings in that they contain details not shown on the drawings. Specifications define and clarify the scope of the job. They describe the specific types and characteristics of the components that are to be used on the job and the methods for installing some of them. Many components are identified specifically by the manufacturer's model and part numbers. This type of information is used to purchase the various items of hardware needed to accomplish the installation in accordance with the contractual requirements.

have been relocated to new divisions 22 and 23. The basic subjects under old Division 16 – *Electrical* have been relocated to new divisions 26 and 27. In addition, the numbering system was changed to 6 digits to allow for more subsections in each division, which allowed for finer definition. In the new numbering system, the first two digits represent the division number. The next two digits represent subsections of the division and the two remaining digits represent the third level sub-subsection numbers. The fourth level, if required, is a decimal and number added to the end of the last two digits. For example, the number 132013.04 represents division 13, subsection 20, sub-subsection 13, and sub-sub-subsection 04. Under the new standard, the Facility Service Subgroup contains the divisions that are most important to the electrician. These include the following divisions:

- *Division 25 – Integrated Automation*
- *Division 26 – Electrical*
- *Division 27 – Communications*
- *Division 28 – Electronic Safety and Security*

Figure 47 contains a detailed breakdown of the electrical division.

NUMBER	TITLE	EXPLANATION

DIVISION 26 – ELECTRICAL

26 00 00 Electrical

may be used as division level section title.

See: 02 41 19 for selective demolition of existing electrical systems.
03 30 00 for cast-in-place concrete equipment bases.
07 84 00 for firestopping.
07 92 00 for joint sealants.
08 31 00 for access doors and panels.
09 91 00 for field painting.
31 23 33 for trenching and backfilling.

26 01 00 Operation and Maintenance of Electrical Systems

Includes: maintenance, repair, rehabilitation, replacement, restoration, preservation, etc. of electrical systems. medium voltage: 2400 V to 69 kV. low voltage: 600 V and less.

Notes: Definitions medium voltage: 2400 V to 69 kV. low voltage: 600 V and less.

Level 4 Numbering Recommendation: following numbering is recommended for the creation of Level 4 titles:
.51-.59 for maintenance.
.61-.69 for repair.
.71-.79 for rehabilitation.
.81-.89 for replacement.
.91-.99 for restoration.

26 01 10 Operation and Maintenance of Medium-Voltage Electrical Distribution
26 01 20 Operation and Maintenance of Low-Voltage Electrical Distribution
26 01 26 Maintenance Testing of Electrical Systems
26 01 30 Operation and Maintenance of Facility Electrical Power Generating and Storing Equipment
26 01 40 Operation and Maintenance of Electrical and Cathodic Protection Systems
26 01 50 Operation and Maintenance of Lighting
- 26 01 50.51 Luminaire Relamping
- 26 01 50.81 Luminaire Replacement

26 05 00 Common Work Results for Electrical

Includes: subjects common to multiple titles in Division 26. raceway and boxes includes conduit, tubing, surface raceways, and electrical boxes. medium voltage: 2400 V to 69 kV. low voltage: 600 V and less. control voltage: 50 V

311

26110-14_F47A.EPS

Figure 47 Detailed breakdown of the electrical division (1 of 13).

Division **26**

Number	Title		Explanation
			and less. Alternate Terms/Abbreviations: EMT: electrical metallic tubing. Notes: Definitions medium voltage: 2400 V to 69 kV. low voltage: 600 V and less. control voltage: 50 V and less. See 01 80 00 for performance requirements of subjects common to multiple titles. 05 35 00 for raceway decking assemblies. 05 45 16 for electrical metal supports. 13 48 00 for sound, vibration, and seismic control. 25 05 13 for conductors and cables for integrated automation. 25 05 26 for grounding and bonding for integrated automation. 25 05 28 for pathways for integrated automation. 25 05 48 for vibration and seismic control for integrated automation. 25 05 53 for identification for integrated automation. 27 05 28 for pathways for communications systems. 27 05 46 for utility poles for communications systems. 27 05 48 for vibration and seismic controls for communications. 27 05 53 for identification for communications. 28 05 13 for conductors and cables for electronic safety and security. 28 05 26 for grounding and bonding for electronic safety and security. 28 05 28 for pathways for electronic safety and security. 28 05 48 for vibration and seismic controls for electronic safety and security. 28 05 53 for identification for electronic safety and security. 33 71 16 for electrical utility poles. 33 71 19 for electrical utility underground ducts and manholes.
26 05 13	Medium-Voltage Cables		
	26 05 13.13	Medium-Voltage Open Conductors	
	26 05 13.16	Medium-Voltage, Single- and Multi-Conductor Cables	
26 05 19	Low-Voltage Electrical Power Conductors and Cables		
	26 05 19.13	Undercarpet Electrical Power Cables	
	26 05 19.23	Manufactured Wiring Assemblies	
26 05 23	Control-Voltage Electrical Power Cables		
26 05 26	Grounding and Bonding for Electrical Systems		
26 05 29	Hangers and Supports for Electrical Systems		
26 05 33	Raceway and Boxes for Electrical Systems		
	26 05 33.13	Conduit for Electrical Systems	
	26 05 33.16	Boxes for Electrical Systems	
	26 05 33.23	Surface raceways for Electrical Systems	

312

26110-14_F47B.EPS

Figure 47 Detailed breakdown of the electrical division (2 of 13).

Division **26**

Number	Title	Explanation
26 05 36	Cable Trays for Electrical Systems	
26 05 39	Underfloor Raceways for Electrical Systems	
26 05 43	Underground Ducts and Raceways for Electrical Systems	
26 05 46	Utility Poles for Electrical Systems	
26 05 48	Vibration and Seismic Controls for Electrical Systems	
26 05 53	Identification for Electrical Systems	
26 05 73	Overcurrent Protective Device Coordination Study	
26 05 83	Wiring Connections	

26 06 00 Schedules for Electrical

Notes: a schedule may be included on drawings, in the project manual, or a project book.

Definitions: medium voltage: 2400 V to 69 kV. low voltage: 600 V and less.

Includes: schedules of items common to multiple titles in Division 26.

Number	Title
26 06 10	Schedules for Medium-Voltage Electrical Distribution
26 06 20	Schedules for Low-Voltage Electrical Distribution
	26 06 20.13 Electrical Switchboard Schedule
	26 06 20.16 Electrical Panelboard Schedule
	26 06 20.19 Electrical Motor-Control Center Schedule
	26 06 20.23 Electrical Circuit Schedule
	26 06 20.26 Wiring Device Schedule
26 06 30	Schedules for Facility Electrical Power Generating and Storing Equipment
26 06 40	Schedules for Electrical and Cathodic Protection Systems
26 06 50	Schedules for Lighting
	26 06 50.13 Lighting Panelboard Schedule
	26 06 50.16 Lighting Fixture Schedule

26 08 00 Commissioning of Electrical Systems

Includes: commissioning of items common to multiple titles in Division 26.

See: 01 91 00 for commissioning of subjects common to multiple divisions.

26 09 00 Instrumentation and Control for Electrical Systems

Includes: instrumentation and control associated with electrical systems.

See: 13 50 00 for special instrumentation.
25 36 00 for integrated automation instrumentation and terminal devices for electrical systems.
25 56 00 for integrated automation control of electrical systems.

313

26110-14_F47C.EPS

Figure 47 Detailed breakdown of the electrical division (3 of 13).

Division **26**

Number	Title	Explanation
		25 96 00 for integrated automation control sequences for electrical systems. 33 09 70 for instrumentation and control for electrical utilities.
26 09 13	Electrical Power Monitoring	
26 09 15	Peak Load Controllers	
26 09 16	Electrical Controls and Relays	
26 09 17	Programmable Controllers	
26 09 19	Enclosed Contactors	
26 09 23	Lighting Control Devices	
		Includes: clock and calendar, photoelectric switches, occupancy sensors, and light-leveling control devices. control- and low-voltage lighting control devices connected through computers. addressable lighting control devices and lighting components (ballasts) connected through computers. See: 11 61 00 for theater and stage equipment. 26 50 00 for lighting. 26 55 61 for theatrical lighting. See Also: 11 61 00 for theatrical lighting controls.
26 09 26	Lighting Control Panelboards	
26 09 33	Central Dimming Controls	
	26 09 33.13 Multichannel Remote-Controlled Dimmers	
	26 09 33.16 Remote-Controlled Dimming Stations	
26 09 36	Modular Dimming Controls	
	26 09 36.13 Manual Modular Dimming Controls	
	26 09 36.16 Integrated Multipreset Modular Dimming Controls	
26 09 43	Network Lighting Controls	
	26 09 43.13 Digital-Network Lighting Controls	
	26 09 43.16 Addressable Fixture Lighting Control	
26 09 61	Theatrical Lighting Controls	

26 10 00 Medium-Voltage Electrical Distribution

		Includes: substations, transformers, switchgear, and circuit protection devices to distribute medium-voltage electrical power from the facility service point to the point of delivery. Notes: Definitions medium voltage: 2400 V to 69 kV. See 26 05 13 for medium-voltage cables. 26 20 00 for low-voltage electrical distribution. 26 30 00 for facility electrical power generating and storing equipment. 33 71 00 for electrical utility distribution.

314

26110-14_F47D.EPS

Figure 47 Detailed breakdown of the electrical division (4 of 13).

NUMBER	TITLE	EXPLANATION
26 11 00	**Substations**	
		Includes: assembly of switches, circuit breakers, buses, and transformers to switch circuits and convert power from one voltage to another. See: 33 72 00 for utility substations. 34 21 16 for traction power substations.
26 11 13	Primary Unit Substations	
26 11 16	Secondary Unit Substations	
26 12 00	**Medium-Voltage Transformers**	
		Includes: transformers for medium-voltage applications. See: 26 22 00 for low-voltage transformers. 33 73 00 for utility transformers. 34 21 23 for traction power transformer-rectifier units.
26 12 13	Liquid-Filled, Medium-Voltage Transformers	
26 12 16	Dry-Type, Medium-Voltage Transformers	
26 12 19	Pad-Mounted, Liquid-Filled, Medium-Voltage Transformers	
26 13 00	**Medium-Voltage Switchgear**	
		Includes: switchgear for medium-voltage applications. See: 26 23 00 for low-voltage switchgear. 33 77 00 for medium-voltage utility switchgear. 34 21 19 for traction power switchgear.
26 13 13	Medium-Voltage Circuit Breaker Switchgear	
26 13 16	Medium-Voltage Fusible Interrupter Switchgear	
26 13 19	Medium-Voltage Vacuum Interrupter Switchgear	
26 13 23	Medium-Voltage Metal-Enclosed Switchgear	
26 13 26	Medium-Voltage Metal-Clad Switchgear	
26 13 29	Medium-Voltage Compartmentalized Switchgear	
26 16 00	**Medium-Voltage Metering**	
26 18 00	**Medium-Voltage Circuit Protection Devices**	
		Includes: circuit protection devices for medium-voltage applications. See: 26 28 00 for low-voltage circuit protective devices. 26 41 23 for lightning protection surge arresters and suppressors. 33 77 00 for medium-voltage utility circuit protection devices.
26 18 13	Medium-Voltage Cutouts	

315

26110-14_F47E.EPS

Figure 47 Detailed breakdown of the electrical division (5 of 13).

DIVISION **26**

NUMBER	TITLE	EXPLANATION
26 18 16	Medium-Voltage Fuses	
26 18 19	Medium-Voltage Lightning Arresters	
26 18 23	Medium-Voltage Surge Arresters	
26 18 26	Medium-Voltage Reclosers	
26 18 29	Medium-Voltage Enclosed Bus	
26 18 33	Medium-Voltage Enclosed Fuse Cutouts	
26 18 36	Medium-Voltage Enclosed Fuses	
26 18 39	Medium-Voltage Motor Controllers	
26 20 00	**Low-Voltage Electrical Transmission**	Includes: overhead power systems, transformers, switchgear, switchboards, panelboards, enclosed bus assemblies, power distribution units, controllers, wiring devices, and circuit protection devices to distribute low-voltage electrical power from the point of voltage transformation to the point of use. typical voltages: 120, 208, 230, 240, 277, 460, and 480. Notes: Definitions low voltage: 600 V and less. See 26 05 19 for low-voltage electrical power conductors and cables. 26 10 00 for medium-voltage electrical distribution. 26 30 00 for facility electrical power generating and storing equipment.
26 21 00	**Low-Voltage Electrical Service Entrance**	See: 26 05 19 for low-voltage electrical power conductors and cables. 26 05 46 for utility poles for electrical systems. 33 71 13 for site electrical transmission towers. 33 71 16 for electrical utility poles.
26 21 13	Low-Voltage Overhead Electrical Service Entrance	
26 21 16	Low-Voltage Underground Electrical Service Entrance	
26 22 00	**Low-Voltage Transformers**	Includes: transformers for low-voltage applications. See: 26 12 00 for medium-voltage transformers.
26 22 13	Low-Voltage Distribution Transformers	
26 22 16	Low-Voltage Buck-Boost Transformers	
26 22 19	Control and Signal Transformers	
26 23 00	**Low-Voltage Switchgear**	Includes: switchgear for low-voltage applications.

316

26110-14_F47F.EPS

Figure 47 Detailed breakdown of the electrical division (6 of 13).

NUMBER	TITLE	EXPLANATION
		See: 26 13 00 for medium-voltage switchgear.
26 23 13	Paralleling Low-Voltage Switchgear	
26 24 00	**Switchboards and Panelboards**	Includes: switchboards, panelboards, and control centers. See: 26 27 16 for electrical cabinets and enclosures. 26 29 13 for enclosed controllers. 26 29 23 for variable-frequency motor controllers.
26 24 13	Switchboards	
26 24 16	Panelboards	
26 24 19	Motor-Control Centers	
26 25 00	**Enclosed Bus Assemblies**	Includes: busway, step bus, and tap boxes. See: 33 72 26 for utility substation bus assemblies.
26 26 00	**Power Distribution Units**	Includes: distribution units with integral transformers, panelboards, and power conditioning components. See: 26 24 16 for panelboards.
26 27 00	**Low-Voltage Distribution Equipment**	Includes: wiring devices includes receptacles, switches, dimmers, and finish plates. See: 26 24 00 for switchboards and panelboards. 33 71 73 for utility electric meters.
26 27 13	Electricity Metering	
26 27 16	Electrical Cabinets and Enclosures	
26 27 19	Multi-Outlet Assemblies	
26 27 23	Indoor Service Poles	
26 27 26	Wiring Devices	
26 27 73	Door Chimes	
26 28 00	**Low-Voltage Circuit Protective Devices**	Includes: circuit protection devices for low-voltage applications. enclosed switches and transfer switches. See: 26 18 00 for medium-voltage circuit protection devices.

26110-14_F47G.EPS

Figure 47 Detailed breakdown of the electrical division (7 of 13).

DIVISION **26**

NUMBER	TITLE	EXPLANATION
26 28 13	Fuses	
26 28 16	Enclosed Switches and Circuit Breakers	
	26 28 16.13 Enclosed Circuit Breakers	
	26 28 16.16 Enclosed Switches	
26 29 00	**Low-Voltage Controllers**	Includes: contactors and motor controllers. May Include: fuses. Alternate Terms/Abbreviations: enclosed controllers: motor controllers. See: 26 24 19 for motor-control centers. 26 28 13 for fuses.
26 29 13	Enclosed Controllers	
	26 29 13.13 Across-the-Line Motor Controllers	
	26 29 13.16 Reduced-Voltage Motor Controllers	
26 29 23	Variable-Frequency Motor Controllers	
26 29 33	Controllers for Fire Pump Drivers	
	26 29 33.13 Full-Service Controllers for Fire Pump Electric-Motor Drivers	
	26 29 33.16 Limited-Service Controllers for Fire Pump Electric-Motor Drivers	
	26 29 33.19 Controllers for Fire Pump Diesel Engine Drivers	
26 30 00	**Facility Electrical Power Generating and Storing Equipment**	Includes: equipment to generate and store electrical power for a single facility. Notes: 48 10 00 for electrical power generation equipment.
26 31 00	**Photovoltaic Collectors**	Includes: solar cells to convert sunlight to electricity. See: 07 31 00 for solar collector roof shingles. 22 33 30 for residential, collector-to-tank, solar-electric domestic water heaters. 23 56 00 for solar energy heating equipment. 42 12 23 for solar process heaters. 42 13 26 for industrial solar radiation heat exchangers. 48 14 00 for solar energy electrical power generation equipment.
26 32 00	**Packaged Generator Assemblies**	Includes: generators, frequency changers, and rotary converters and uninterruptible power units.

318

26110-14_F47H.EPS

Figure 47 Detailed breakdown of the electrical division (8 of 13).

NUMBER	TITLE	EXPLANATION
		See: 23 11 00 for facility fuel piping. 23 24 00 for internal-combustion engine piping. 48 11 00 for fossil fuel plant electrical power generation equipment. 48 13 00 for hydroelectric plant electrical power generation equipment. 48 15 00 for wind energy electrical power generation equipment.
26 32 13	Engine Generators 26 32 13.13 Diesel-Engine-Driven Generator Sets 26 32 13.16 Gas-Engine-Driven Generator Sets 26 32 13.26 Gas-Turbine Engine-Driven Generators	
		Alternate Terms/Abbreviations: microturbines See: 48 11 23 Fossil Fuel Electrical Power Plant Gas Turbines
26 32 16	Steam-Turbine Generators	
26 32 19	Hydro-Turbine Generators	
26 32 23	Wind Energy Equipment	
26 32 26	Frequency Changers	
26 32 29	Rotary Converters	
26 32 33	Rotary Uninterruptible Power Units	
26 33 00	**Battery Equipment**	
		Includes: batteries, battery racks, battery chargers, static power converters, uninterruptible power supplies, and accessories. May Include: battery-operated emergency light fixtures. See: 25 36 23 for integrated automation battery monitors. 26 31 00 for photovoltaic collectors. 33 72 33 for electrical utility substation. 48 17 13 for electrical power generation batteries. See Also: 26 52 00 for emergency lighting incorporating batteries.
26 33 13	Batteries	
26 33 16	Battery Racks	
26 33 19	Battery Units	
26 33 23	Central Battery Equipment	
26 33 33	Static Power Converters	
26 33 43	Battery Chargers	
26 33 46	Battery Monitoring	

319

26110-14_F47I.EPS

Figure 47 Detailed breakdown of the electrical division (9 of 13).

DIVISION **26**

NUMBER	TITLE	EXPLANATION
26 33 53	Static Uninterruptible Power Supply	
26 35 00	**Power Filters and Conditioners**	Includes: capacitors, chokes and inductors, filters, power factor controllers, and voltage regulators. Alternate Terms/Abbreviations: EMI: electromagnetic interference. RFI: radio frequency interference. power factor correction equipment: power factor controllers. See: 08 34 46 for RFI shielding doors. 08 56 46 for RFI shielding windows. 13 49 00 for radiation protection. 26 18 23 for medium-voltage surge arresters. 28 32 00 for radiation detection and alarm. 40 91 16 for electromagnetic process measurement devices.
26 35 13	Capacitors	
26 35 16	Chokes and Inductors	
26 35 23	Electromagnetic-Interference Filters	
26 35 26	Harmonic Filters	
26 35 33	Power Factor Correction Equipment	
26 35 36	Slip Controllers	
26 35 43	Static-Frequency Converters	
26 35 46	Radio-Frequency-Interference Filters	
26 35 53	Voltage Regulators	
26 36 00	**Transfer Switches**	Includes: switches transfer from one source of electricity to another.
26 36 13	Manual Transfer Switches	
26 36 23	Automatic Transfer Switches	
26 40 00	**Electrical and Cathodic Protection**	
26 41 00	**Facility Lightning Protection**	Includes: wiring and equipment for lightning protection. See: 26 18 19 for medium-voltage lightning arresters. 33 79 00 for site grounding. 33 79 93 for site lightning protection.
26 41 13	Lightning Protection for Structures 26 41 13.13 Lightning Protection for Buildings	
26 41 16	Lightning Prevention and Dissipation	
26 41 19	Early Streamer Emission Lightning Protection	
26 41 23	Lightning Protection Surge Arresters and Suppressors	

320

26110-14_F47J.EPS

Figure 47 Detailed breakdown of the electrical division (10 of 13).

DIVISION **26**

NUMBER	TITLE	EXPLANATION

26 42 00 Cathodic Protection

Includes: equipment, controls, and installation for cathodic protection of structures and underground metal construction and piping.

See: 40 46 42 for cathodic process corrosion protection.

26 42 13 Passive Cathodic Protection for Underground and Submerged Piping
26 42 16 Passive Cathodic Protection for Underground Storage Tank

26 43 00 Transient Voltage Suppression

Includes: devices to protect against voltage surges on electrical distribution systems.

26 43 13 Transient-Voltage Suppression for Low-Voltage Electrical Power Circuits

26 50 00 Lighting

Includes: luminaries, lighting equipment, ballasts, dimming controls, and lighting accessories. fluorescent, high intensity discharge, incandescent, mercury vapor, neon, and sodium vapor lighting.

Alternate Terms/Abbreviations: HID: high intensity discharge.

See: 10 84 00 for Gas Lighting.
25 36 26 for integrated automation lighting relays.
26 09 23 for lighting controls.
26 20 00 for low-voltage electrical transmission.

26 51 00 Interior Lighting

Includes: lighting for interior locations, except for emergency lighting, lighting in hazardous locations, and special purpose lighting. chandeliers, troffers.

See: 09 54 16 for luminous ceilings.
09 58 00 for integrated ceiling assemblies.
10 14 33 for illuminated panel signage.

26 51 13 Interior Lighting Fixtures, Lamps, And Ballasts

26 52 00 Emergency Lighting

Includes: equipment for exitway lighting and other emergency applications, including emergency battery units, fixtures with integral batter power supplies.

See: 26 53 00 for exit signs.

321

26110-14_F47K.EPS

Figure 47 Detailed breakdown of the electrical division (11 of 13).

Division 26		
Number	**Title**	**Explanation**
26 53 00	**Exit Signs**	Includes: electric exit signs. See: 26 52 00 for emergency lighting.
26 54 00	**Classified Location Lighting**	Includes: lighting for application in areas classified as hazardous. See: 26 55 33 for hazard warning lighting.
26 55 00	**Special Purpose Lighting**	Includes: lighting equipment for specialized applications. Alternate Terms/Abbreviations: healthcare lighting: medical lighting. See: 11 13 26 for loading dock lights. 11 18 00 for security equipment. 11 19 00 for detention equipment. 11 59 00 for exhibit and display equipment. 11 61 00 for theater and stage equipment. 11 70 00 for healthcare equipment. 13 10 00 for swimming pools. 13 12 00 for fountains. 13 14 00 for aquatic park structures. 13 17 00 for tubs and pools. 26 54 00 for classified location lighting. 34 40 00 for transportation signals. 35 13 13 for navigation signals. See Also: 11 61 00 for theatrical lighting.
26 55 23	Outline Lighting	
26 55 29	Underwater Lighting	
26 55 33	Hazard Warning Lighting	
26 55 36	Obstruction Lighting	
26 55 39	Helipad Lighting	See: 34 43 00 Airfield Signaling and Control Equipment
26 55 53	Security Lighting	
26 55 59	Display Lighting	
26 55 61	Theatrical Lighting	
26 55 63	Detention Lighting	
26 55 70	Healthcare Lighting	

322

26110-14_F47L.EPS

Figure 47 Detailed breakdown of the electrical division (12 of 13).

Number	Title	Explanation
26 56 00	**Exterior Lighting**	
		Includes: lighting equipment for exterior locations, except for special purpose and signal lighting. airfield general exterior lighting. Alternate Terms/Abbreviations: athletic lighting: sports lighting. See: 10 14 33 for illuminated panel signage. 11 13 26 for loading dock lights. 11 68 23 for exterior court athletic equipment. 32 94 00 for planting accessories. 34 41 13 for traffic signals. 34 42 13 for railway signals. 34 43 13 for airfield signals. 34 43 16 for airfield landing equipment. 34 71 00 for roadway construction. 34 72 00 for railway construction. 34 73 00 for airfield construction. 34 75 00 for roadway equipment.
26 56 13	Lighting Poles and Standards	
26 56 16	Parking Lighting	
26 56 19	Roadway Lighting	
26 56 23	Area Lighting	
26 56 26	Landscape Lighting	
26 56 29	Site Lighting	
26 56 33	Walkway Lighting	
26 56 36	Flood Lighting	
26 56 68	Exterior Athletic Lighting	

26110-14_F47M.EPS

Figure 47 Detailed breakdown of the electrical division (13 of 13).

SUMMARY

In this module, you learned the symbols and conventions used on architectural and engineering drawings. As an electrician, you need to know how to recognize the basic symbols used on electrical drawings and other drawings used in the building construction industry. You should also know where to find the meaning of symbols that you do not immediately recognize. Schedules, diagrams, and specifications often provide detailed information that is not included on the working drawings.

Building projects require detailed specifications. These written specifications are complex and detailed and need a unified format to be easily usable by the trades. The specification format most commonly used is the *MasterFormat*® developed by CSI and CSC. The *MasterFormat*® was updated in 2010 with changes to the division numbering system.

Reading architectural and engineering drawings takes practice and study. Now that you have the basic skills, take the time to master them.

Review Questions

1. A section line on a drawing shows _____.
   a. the north orientation
   b. the location of the section on the plan
   c. where to locate receptacles in that section
   d. the section scale

2. An electrical drafting line with a double arrowhead represents _____.
   a. wiring concealed in the floor
   b. wiring turned down
   c. a branch circuit homerun
   d. wiring concealed in a ceiling or wall

Questions 3 through 9 refer to the seven electrical symbols shown below. In the spaces provided, place the letter corresponding to the correct answer found in the list.

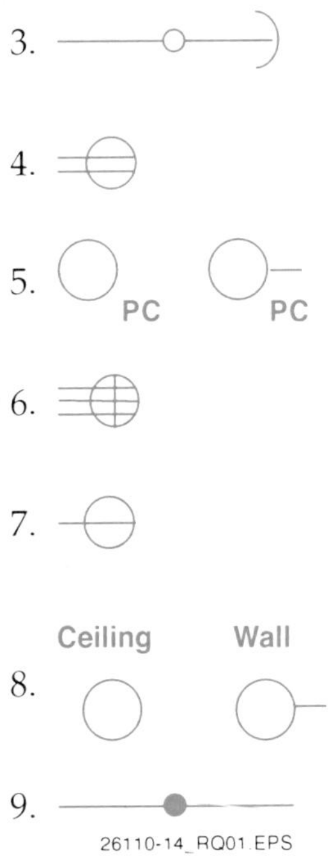

3.

4.

5. PC PC

6.

7.

8. Ceiling Wall

9.

26110-14_RQ01.EPS

_____ a. Single Receptacle Outlet

_____ b. Duplex Receptacle Outlet

_____ c. Triplex Receptacle Outlet

_____ d. Incandescent Fixture (Surface or Pendant)

_____ e. Incandescent Fixture with Pull Chain (Surface or Pendant)

_____ f. Head Guy

_____ g. Sidewalk Guy

10. In dimension drawings, the dimensions written on the drawing are _____.
    a. for reference only
    b. on a larger scale
    c. inaccurate
    d. the actual dimensions

11. The architect's scale is designed so that one inch always equals one foot.
    a. True
    b. False

12. All views on a construction drawing are drawn to the same scale.
    a. True
    b. False

13. The *NEC*® specifies one set of electrical drawing symbols that are used in all cases.
    a. True
    b. False

14. Dotted lines used to represent a branch circuit on a drawing mean that the wiring is to be _____.
    a. concealed in the ceiling or wall
    b. run in the floor or ceiling below
    c. exposed
    d. installed in a future building expansion

15. A branch circuit line or drawing that does *not* have slashes is assumed to have two conductors.
    a. True
    b. False

16. To meet general recommendations, a residential branch circuit rated for 2,400VA should have a connected load of no more than _____.
    a. 1,680VA
    b. 1,920VA
    c. 2,040VA
    d. 2,160VA

17. Power-riser diagrams are used to show the _____.
    a. arrangement of electric service equipment
    b. branch circuit layout for power
    c. branch circuit layout for lighting
    d. panelboard schedule

18. The symbols T_1, T_2, and T_3 in a typical motor starter schematic represent _____.
    a. voltage supply lines
    b. auxiliary contacts
    c. motor terminals
    d. line contacts

19. The updated *MasterFormat*® standard _____.
    a. is specified in the *NEC*®
    b. uses a six-digit code for division content
    c. is required by OSHA
    d. allows for fewer subsections

20. The current *MasterFormat*® standard covering communications systems is under _____.
    a. Division 16
    b. Division 27
    c. Division 37
    d. Division 48

Trade Terms Quiz

Fill in the blank with the correct term that you learned from your study of this module.

1. ___________ typically include the following information: a site plan, floor plans, elevations of all exterior faces of the building, and large-scale detail drawings.
2. A(n) ___________ is an exact copy or reproduction of an original drawing.
3. A simple, single-line diagram used to show electrical equipment and related connections is a(n) ___________ diagram.
4. A(n) ___________ shows the path of an electrical circuit or system of circuits, along with the circuit components.
5. To convey a substantial amount of detailed information to installation electricians, an engineer will use a(n) ___________ drawing.
6. Shown in a separate view, a(n) ___________ view is an enlarged, detailed view taken from an area of a drawing.
7. A cutaway drawing that shows the inside of an object or building is a(n) ___________ drawing.
8. The sizes or measurements that are printed on a drawing are called ___________.
9. The relationship between an object's size in a drawing and the object's actual size is the ___________.
10. The height of the front, rear, or sides of a building is shown in a(n) ___________ drawing.
11. A building's location on the site is shown in a(n) ___________.
12. A drawing that has a top-down view of a building is a(n) ___________ plan.
13. A drawing that has a top-down view of a single object is a(n) ___________ view.
14. A(n) ___________ diagram is a single-line block diagram used to indicate the electric service equipment, service conductors and feeders, and subpanels.
15. Owners, architects, and engineers use ___________ to specify material and workmanship requirements.
16. A(n) ___________ is a systematic way of presenting equipment lists on a drawing in tabular form.
17. Complicated circuits, such as control circuits, are shown in a(n) ___________ diagram.
18. Usually developed by manufacturers, fabricators, or contractors, a(n) ___________ drawing shows specific dimensions and other information about a piece of equipment and its installation methods.

Trade Terms

Architectural drawings
Block diagram
Blueprint
Detail drawing
Dimensions
Electrical drawing
Elevation drawing
Floor plan
One-line diagram
Plan view
Power-riser diagram
Scale
Schedule
Schematic diagram
Sectional view
Shop drawing
Site plan
Written specifications

Module 26110-14
Supplemental Exercises

1. A(n) ____________________ indicates the location of the building on the property.

2. The ____________________ show the walls and partitions for each floor or level.

3. What are the three main functions of electrical drawings?

4. The title block of an electrical drawing should contain the following ten items:

5. Match the following names to their corresponding electrical drafting lines.

____ WIRING TURNED UP

____ BRANCH CIRCUIT HOMERUN TO PANELBOARD

____ WIRING TURNED DOWN

____ EXPOSED WIRING

____ WIRING CONCEALED IN FLOOR

____ WIRING CONCEALED IN CEILING OR WALL

26110-14_WB.EPS

6. What does the letter F stand for in reference to safety switches? ____________________

7. On a floor plan with a scale of ½" = 1'0", what would be the equivalent distance if you measured 3¾" on the drawing?____________________

8. The purpose of a(n) ____________________ is to identify that part of the project to which the sheet applies.

9. One-line block diagrams are also known as ____________________.

10. Divisions ____________________ and ____________________ of the current CSI specifications cover electrical work.

Cornerstone of Craftsmanship

Wayne Stratton

Associated Builders and Contractors

How did you choose a career in the electrical field?
Three events in my childhood created the desire to learn the electrical trade. At age six, the farmhouse we lived in was totally destroyed by fire. The cause was electrical. As a young teen, a local electrician had incorrectly wired a heating element and electrocuted several pigs. In 1973, my father hired this electrician to install a motor starter on a grain conveyor. He could not figure it out. I wanted to learn how to do this type of work and do it safely.

Tell us about your apprenticeship experience.
My education is from a technical school. I have attended several manufacturers' training sessions. I had to gain the hands-on experience after learning the trade. My observation of the apprenticeship programs is this: you get hands-on experience while you learn.

What positions have you held in the industry?
I worked as a plant industrial electrician responsible for motor control, DC motors, co-generation, and medium voltage distribution. Later, I began working for an electrical contractor who wanted to expand his business into the industrial field. I worked as a PLC technician designing and installing control systems. In 1987, I began teaching apprenticeship classes.

What would you say is the primary factor in achieving success?
The desire to learn all that I can learn, the ability to think outside the box, and the opportunities to gain a variety of experiences. All this helps me continue to learn and share with trainees.

What does your current job involve?
I teach electrical apprenticeship levels one through four at two different locations in Iowa. My other responsibilities involve task training for electrical licensing, fire alarm, and code updates.

Do you have any advice for someone just entering the trade?
Continue to learn. Completing an apprenticeship program or acquiring an electrician's license is not the end of learning. With code changes every 3 years, there is always more to learn. If you don't understand something, ask! Observe and learn from experienced individuals.

Appendix

Metric Conversion Chart

METRIC CONVERSION CHART

INCHES Fractional	INCHES Decimal	METRIC mm	INCHES Fractional	INCHES Decimal	METRIC mm	INCHES Fractional	INCHES Decimal	METRIC mm
.	0.0039	0.1000	.	0.5512	14.0000	.	1.8898	48.0000
.	0.0079	0.2000	9/16	0.5625	14.2875	.	1.9291	49.0000
.	0.0118	0.3000	.	0.5709	14.5000	.	1.9685	50.0000
1/64	0.0156	0.3969	37/64	0.5781	14.6844	2	2.0000	50.8000
.	0.0157	0.4000	.	0.5906	15.0000	.	2.0079	51.0000
.	0.0197	0.5000	19/32	0.5938	15.0813	.	2.0472	52.0000
.	0.0236	0.6000	39/64	0.6094	15.4781	.	2.0866	53.0000
.	0.0276	0.7000	.	0.6102	15.5000	.	2.1260	54.0000
1/32	0.0313	0.7938	5/8	0.6250	15.8750	.	2.1654	55.0000
.	0.0315	0.8000	.	0.6299	16.0000	.	2.2047	56.0000
.	0.0354	0.9000	41/64	0.6406	16.2719	.	2.2441	57.0000
.	0.0394	1.0000	.	0.6496	16.5000	2 1/4	2.2500	57.1500
.	0.0433	1.1000	21/32	0.6563	16.6688	.	2.2835	58.0000
3/64	0.0469	1.1906	.	0.6693	17.0000	.	2.3228	59.0000
.	0.0472	1.2000	43/64	0.6719	17.0656	.	2.3622	60.0000
.	0.0512	1.3000	11/16	0.6875	17.4625	.	2.4016	61.0000
.	0.0551	1.4000	.	0.6890	17.5000	.	2.4409	62.0000
.	0.0591	1.5000	45/64	0.7031	17.8594	.	2.4803	63.0000
1/16	0.0625	1.5875	.	0.7087	18.0000	2 1/2	2.5000	63.5000
.	0.0630	1.6000	23/32	0.7188	18.2563	.	2.5197	64.0000
.	0.0669	1.7000	.	0.7283	18.5000	.	2.5591	65.0000
.	0.0709	1.8000	47/64	0.7344	18.6531	.	2.5984	66.0000
.	0.0748	1.9000	.	0.7480	19.0000	.	2.6378	67.0000
5/64	0.0781	1.9844	3/4	0.7500	19.0500	.	2.6772	68.0000
.	0.0787	2.0000	49/64	0.7656	19.4469	.	2.7165	69.0000
.	0.0827	2.1000	.	0.7677	19.5000	2 3/4	2.7500	69.8500
.	0.0866	2.2000	25/32	0.7813	19.8438	.	2.7559	70.0000
.	0.0906	2.3000	.	0.7874	20.0000	.	2.7953	71.0000
3/32	0.0938	2.3813	51/64	0.7969	20.2406	.	2.8346	72.0000
.	0.0945	2.4000	.	0.8071	20.5000	.	2.8740	73.0000
.	0.0984	2.5000	13/16	0.8125	20.6375	.	2.9134	74.0000
7/64	0.1094	2.7781	.	0.8268	21.0000	.	2.9528	75.0000
.	0.1181	3.0000	53/64	0.8281	21.0344	.	2.9921	76.0000
1/8	0.1250	3.1750	27/32	0.8438	21.4313	3	3.0000	76.2000
.	0.1378	3.5000	.	0.8465	21.5000	.	3.0315	77.0000
9/64	0.1406	3.5719	55/64	0.8594	21.8281	.	3.0709	78.0000
5/32	0.1563	3.9688	.	0.8661	22.0000	.	3.1102	79.0000
.	0.1575	4.0000	7/8	0.8750	22.2250	.	3.1496	80.0000
11/64	0.1719	4.3656	.	.8858	22.5000	.	3.1890	81.0000
.	0.1772	4.5000	57/64	.89063	22.6219	.	3.2283	82.0000
3/16	0.1875	4.7625	.	.9055	23.0000	.	3.2677	83.0000
.	0.1969	5.0000	29/32	.90625	23.0188	.	3.3071	84.0000
13/64	0.2031	5.1594	59/64	.92188	23.4156	.	3.3465	85.0000
.	0.2165	5.5000	.	.9252	23.5000	.	3.3858	86.0000
7/32	0.2188	5.5563	15/16	.93750	23.8125	.	3.4252	87.0000
15/64	0.2344	5.9531	.	.9449	24.0000	.	3.4646	88.0000
.	0.2362	6.0000	61/64	.95313	24.2094	3 1/2	3.5000	88.9000
1/4	0.2500	6.3500	.	.9646	24.5000	.	3.5039	89.0000
.	0.2559	6.5000	31/32	.96875	24.6063	.	3.5433	90.0000
17/64	0.2656	6.7469	.	.9843	25.0000	.	3.5827	91.0000
.	0.2756	7.0000	63/64	.98438	25.0031	.	3.6220	92.0000
9/32	0.2813	7.1438	1	1.000	25.40	.	3.6614	93.0000
.	0.2953	7.5000	.	1.0039	25.5000	.	3.7008	94.0000
19/64	0.2969	7.5406	.	1.0236	26.0000	.	3.7402	95.0000
5/16	0.3125	7.9375	.	1.0433	26.5000	.	3.7795	96.0000
.	0.3150	8.0000	.	1.0630	27.0000	.	3.8189	97.0000
21/64	0.3281	8.3344	.	1.0827	27.5000	.	3.8583	98.0000
.	0.3346	8.5000	.	1.1024	28.0000	.	3.8976	99.0000
11/32	0.3438	8.7313	.	1.1220	28.5000	.	3.9370	100.0000
.	0.3543	9.0000	.	1.1417	29.0000	4	4.0000	101.6000
23/64	0.3594	9.1281	.	1.1614	29.5000	.	4.3307	110.0000
.	0.3740	9.5000	.	1.1811	30.0000	4 1/2	4.5000	114.3000
3/8	0.3750	9.5250	.	1.2205	31.0000	.	4.7244	120.0000
25/64	0.3906	9.9219	1 1/4	1.2500	31.7500	5	5.0000	127.0000
.	0.3937	10.0000	.	1.2598	32.0000	.	5.1181	130.0000
13/32	0.4063	10.3188	.	1.2992	33.0000	.	5.5118	140.0000
.	0.4134	10.5000	.	1.3386	34.0000	.	5.9055	150.0000
27/64	0.4219	10.7156	.	1.3780	35.0000	6	6.0000	152.4000
.	0.4331	11.0000	.	1.4173	36.0000	.	6.2992	160.0000
7/16	0.4375	11.1125	.	1.4567	37.0000	.	6.6929	170.0000
.	0.4528	11.5000	.	1.4961	38.0000	.	7.0866	180.0000
29/64	0.4531	11.5094	1 1/2	1.5000	38.1000	.	7.4803	190.0000
15/32	0.4688	11.9063	.	1.5354	39.0000	.	7.8740	200.0000
.	0.4724	12.0000	.	1.5748	40.0000	8	8.0000	203.2000
31/64	0.4844	12.3031	.	1.6142	41.0000	.	9.8425	250.0000
.	0.4921	12.5000	.	1.6535	42.0000	10	10.0000	254.0000
1/2	0.5000	12.7000	.	1.6929	43.0000	20	20.0000	508.0000
.	0.5118	13.0000	.	1.7323	44.0000	30	30.0000	762.0000
33/64	0.5156	13.0969	1 3/4	1.7500	44.4500	40	40.0000	1016.000
17/32	0.5313	13.4938	.	1.7717	45.0000	60	60.0000	1524.000
.	0.5315	13.5000	.	1.8110	46.0000	80	80.0000	2032.000
35/64	0.5469	13.8906	.	1.8504	47.0000	100	100.0000	2540.000

TO CONVERT TO MILLIMETERS, MULTIPLY INCHES X 25.4
TO CONVERT TO INCHES, MULTIPLY MILLIMETERS X 0.03937*
*FOR SLIGHTLY GREATER ACCURACY WHEN CONVERTING TO INCHES, DIVIDE MILLIMETERS BY 25.4

26110-14_A01.EPS

Trade Terms Introduced in This Module

Architectural drawings: Working drawings consisting of plans, elevations, details, and other information necessary for the construction of a building. Architectural drawings usually include:

- A site (plot) plan indicating the location of the building on the property
- Floor plans showing the walls and partitions for each floor or level
- Elevations of all exterior faces of the building
- Several vertical cross sections to indicate clearly the various floor levels and details of the footings, foundations, walls, floors, ceilings, and roof construction
- Large-scale detail drawings showing such construction details as may be required

Block diagram: A single-line diagram used to show electrical equipment and related connections. See *power-riser diagram.*

Blueprint: An exact copy or reproduction of an original drawing.

Detail drawing: An enlarged, detailed view taken from an area of a drawing and shown in a separate view.

Dimensions: Sizes or measurements printed on a drawing.

Electrical drawing: A means of conveying a large amount of exact, detailed information in an abbreviated language. Consists of lines, symbols, dimensions, and notations to accurately convey an engineer's designs to electricians who install the electrical system on a job.

Elevation drawing: An architectural drawing showing height, but not depth; usually the front, rear, and sides of a building or object.

Floor plan: A drawing of a building as if a horizontal cut were made through a building at about window level, and the top portion removed. The floor plan is what would appear if the remaining structure were viewed from above.

One-line diagram: A drawing that shows, by means of lines and symbols, the path of an electrical circuit or system of circuits along with the various circuit components. Also called a single-line diagram.

Plan view: A drawing made as though the viewer were looking straight down (from above) on an object.

Power-riser diagram: A single-line block diagram used to indicate the electric service equipment, service conductors and feeders, and subpanels. Notes are used on power-riser diagrams to identify the equipment; indicate the size of conduit; show the number, size, and type of conductors; and list related materials. A panelboard schedule is usually included with power-riser diagrams to indicate the exact components (panel type and size), along with fuses, circuit breakers, etc., contained in each panelboard.

Scale: On a drawing, the size relationship between an object's actual size and the size it is drawn. Scale also refers to the measuring tool used to determine this relationship.

Schedule: A systematic method of presenting equipment lists on a drawing in tabular form.

Schematic diagram: A detailed diagram showing complicated circuits, such as control circuits.

Sectional view: A cutaway drawing that shows the inside of an object or building.

Shop drawing: A drawing that is usually developed by manufacturers, fabricators, or contractors to show specific dimensions and other pertinent information concerning a particular piece of equipment and its installation methods.

Site plan: A drawing showing the location of a building or buildings on the building site. Such drawings frequently show topographical lines, electrical and communication lines, water and sewer lines, sidewalks, driveways, and similar information.

Written specifications: A written description of what is required by the owner, architect, and engineer in the way of materials and workmanship. Together with working drawings, the specifications form the basis of the contract requirements for construction.

Additional Resources

This module presents thorough resources for task training. The following resource material is suggested for further study.

National Electrical Code® Handbook, Latest Edition. Quincy, MA: National Fire Protection Association.

Figure Credits

AGC of America, Module opener

John Traister, Figures 6–18, 20–23, 29–31, 33–40, 43–45

Mike Powers, Figures 25, 27

MasterFormat® Numbers and Titles used in this book are from MasterFormat®, published by CSI and Construction Specifications Canada (CSC), and are used with permission from CSI. For those interested in a more in-depth explanation of MasterFormat® and its use in the construction industry visit www.masterformat.com or contact:

CSI
110 South Union Street, Suite 100
Alexandria, VA 22314
800-689-2900; 703-684-0300
www.csinet.org, Figures 46, 47

Topaz Publications, Inc., SA01

Staedtler USA, SA02

Scalex Corporation, SA03

NCCER CURRICULA — USER UPDATE

NCCER makes every effort to keep its textbooks up-to-date and free of technical errors. We appreciate your help in this process. If you find an error, a typographical mistake, or an inaccuracy in NCCER's curricula, please fill out this form (or a photocopy), or complete the online form at **www.nccer.org/olf**. Be sure to include the exact module ID number, page number, a detailed description, and your recommended correction. Your input will be brought to the attention of the Authoring Team. Thank you for your assistance.

Instructors – If you have an idea for improving this textbook, or have found that additional materials were necessary to teach this module effectively, please let us know so that we may present your suggestions to the Authoring Team.

NCCER Product Development and Revision
13614 Progress Blvd., Alachua, FL 32615
Email: curriculum@nccer.org
Online: www.nccer.org/olf

❑ Trainee Guide ❑ AIG ❑ Exam ❑ PowerPoints Other ____________________

Craft / Level: Copyright Date:

Module ID Number / Title:

Section Number(s):

Description:

Recommended Correction:

Your Name:

Address:

Email: Phone:

Alternating Current

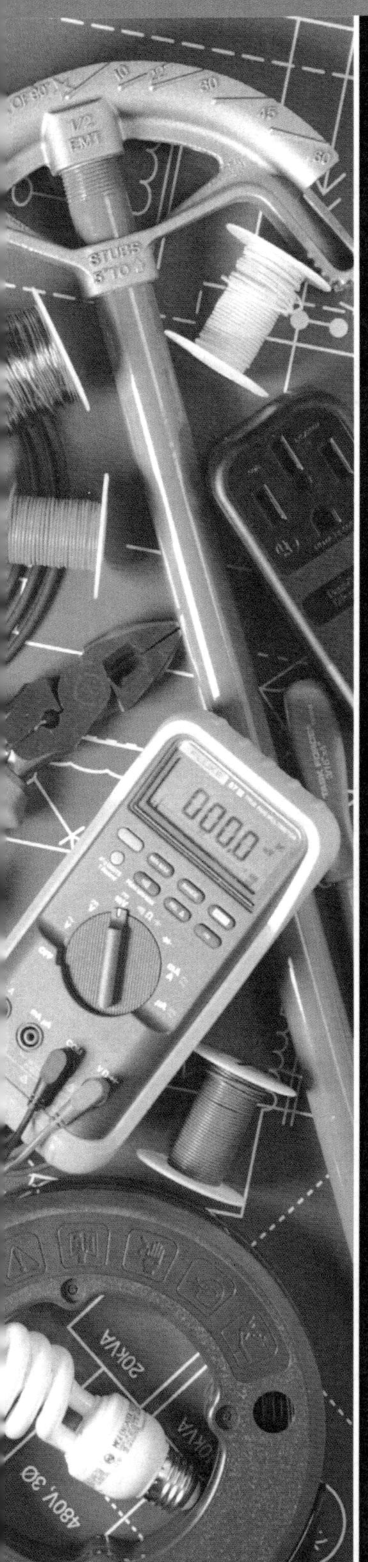

Pawnee Health Center

W. W. Enterprises won an Excellence in Construction award from ABC in the Commercial-Electrical division for its work on the Pawnee Health Center in Pawnee, Oklahoma, which serves the Native American Pawnee Nation.

26201-14

Trainees with successful module completions may be eligible for credentialing through NCCER's National Registry. To learn more, go to **www.nccer.org** or contact us at **1.888.622.3720.** Our website has information on the latest product releases and training, as well as online versions of our *Cornerstone* magazine and Pearson's product catalog.

Your feedback is welcome. You may email your comments to **curriculum@nccer.org,** send general comments and inquiries to **info@nccer.org,** or fill in the User Update form at the back of this module.

This information is general in nature and intended for training purposes only. Actual performance of activities described in this manual requires compliance with all applicable operating, service, maintenance, and safety procedures under the direction of qualified personnel. References in this manual to patented or proprietary devices do not constitute a recommendation of their use.

26201-14

Alternating Current

Objectives

When you have completed this module, you will be able to do the following:

1. Calculate the peak and effective voltage or current values for an AC waveform.
2. Calculate the phase relationship between two AC waveforms.
3. Describe the voltage and current phase relationship in a resistive AC circuit.
4. Describe the voltage and current transients that occur in an inductive circuit.
5. Define inductive reactance and state how it is affected by frequency.
6. Describe the voltage and current transients that occur in a capacitive circuit.
7. Define capacitive reactance and state how it is affected by frequency.
8. Explain the relationship between voltage and current in the following types of AC circuits:
   - RL circuit
   - RC circuit
   - LC circuit
   - RLC circuit
9. Explain the following terms as they relate to AC circuits:
   - True power
   - Apparent power
   - Reactive power
   - Power factor
10. Explain basic transformer action.

Performance Tasks

This is a knowledge-based module. There are no Performance Tasks.

Trade Terms

Capacitance
Frequency
Hertz (Hz)
Impedance
Inductance
Micro
Peak voltage
Radian
Reactance
Root-mean-square (rms)
Self-inductance

Required Trainee Materials

1. Pencil and paper
2. Appropriate personal protective equipment
3. Copy of the latest edition of the *National Electrical Code*®

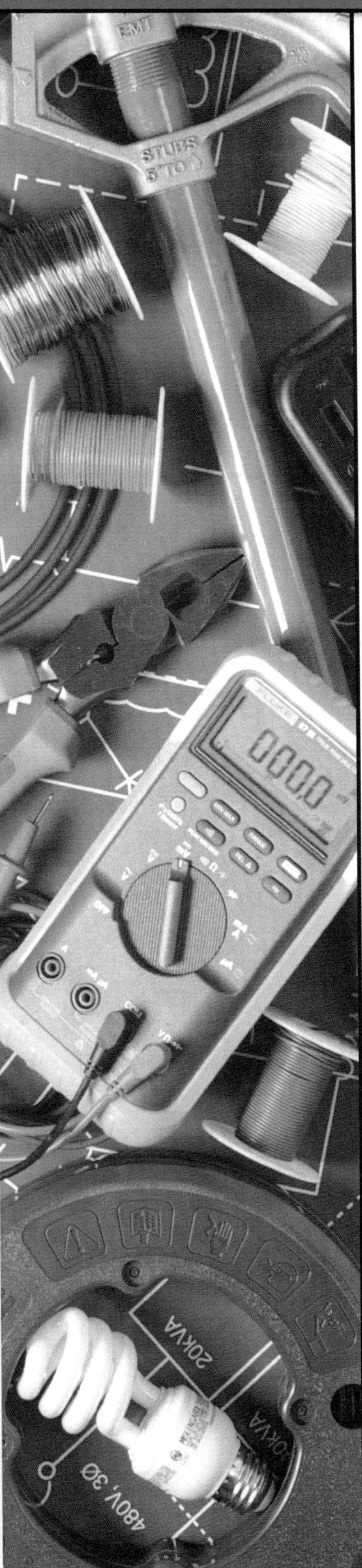

Contents

Topics to be presented in this module include:

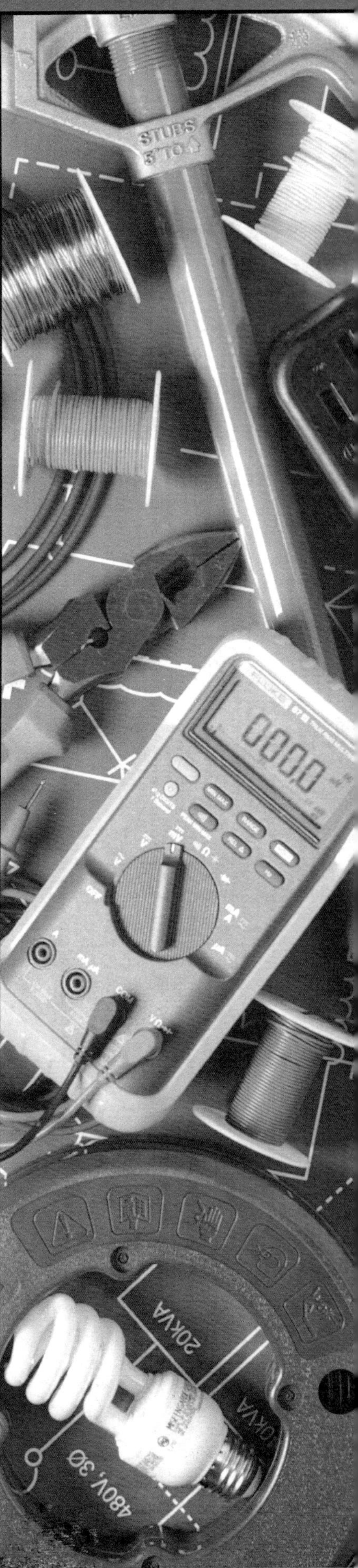
STUBS
5" TO
20KVA
480V, 3Ø

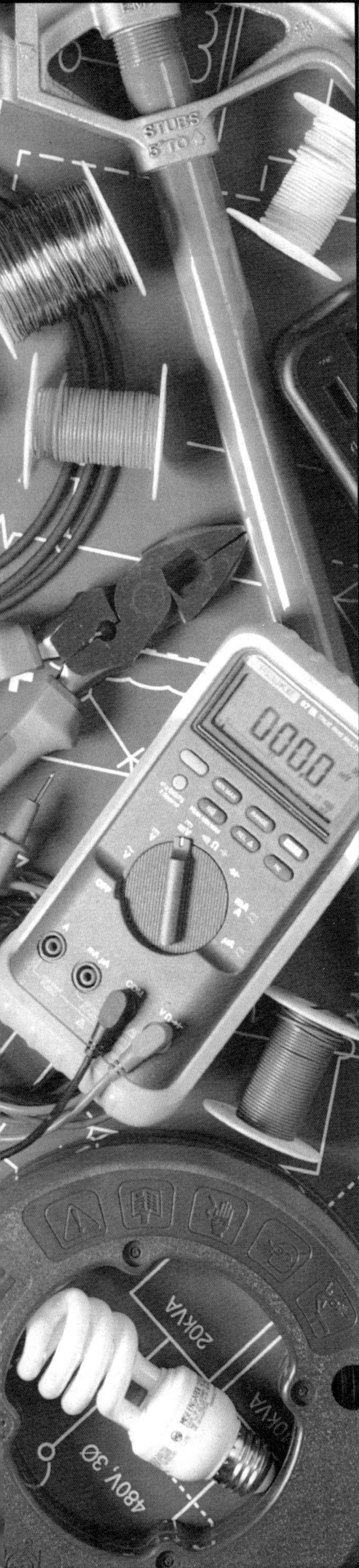

Figures and Tables

1.0.0 Introduction

Alternating current (AC) and its associated voltage reverses between positive and negative polarities and varies in amplitude with time. One complete waveform or cycle includes a complete set of variations, with two alternations in polarity. Many sources of voltage change direction with time and produce a resultant waveform. The most common AC waveform is the sine wave.

2.0.0 Sine Wave Generation

To understand how the alternating current sine wave is generated, some of the basic principles learned in magnetism should be reviewed. Two principles form the basis of all electromagnetic phenomena:

- An electric current in a conductor creates a magnetic field that surrounds the conductor.
- Relative motion between a conductor and a magnetic field, when at least one component of that relative motion is in a direction that is perpendicular to the direction of the field, creates a voltage in the conductor.

Figure 1 shows how these principles are applied to generate an AC waveform in a simple one-loop rotary generator. The conductor loop rotates through the magnetic field to generate the induced AC voltage across its open terminals. The magnetic flux shown here is vertical.

There are three factors affecting the magnitude of voltage developed by a conductor through a magnetic field: the strength of the magnetic field; the length of the conductor; and the rate at which the conductor cuts directly across or perpendicular to the magnetic field.

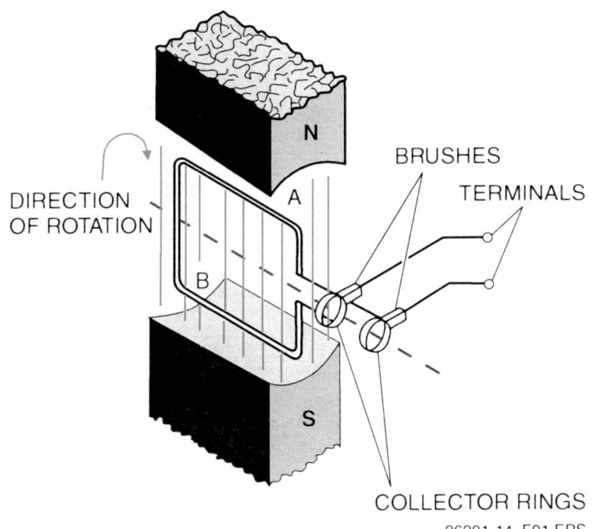

Figure 1 Conductor moving across a magnetic field.

Assuming that the strength of the magnetic field and the length of the conductor making the loop are both constant, the voltage produced will vary depending on the rate at which the loop cuts directly across the magnetic field.

The rate at which the conductor cuts the magnetic field depends on the speed of the generator in revolutions per minute (rpm) and the angle at which the conductor is traveling through the field. If the generator is operated at a constant rpm, the voltage produced at any moment will depend on the angle at which the conductor is cutting the field at that instant.

In *Figure 2*, the magnetic field is shown as parallel lines called lines of flux. These lines always go from the north to south poles in a generator. The motion of the conductor is shown by the large arrow.

Assuming the speed of the conductor is constant, as the angle between the flux and the conductor motion increases, the number of flux

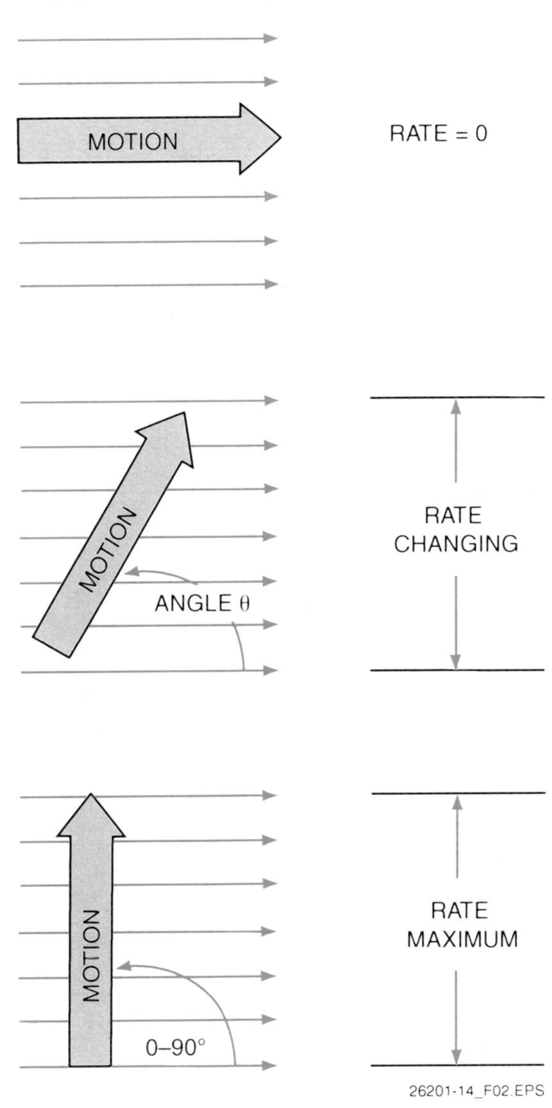

Figure 2 Angle versus rate of cutting lines of flux.

On Site

Why Do Power Companies Generate and Distribute AC Power Instead of DC Power?

The transformer is the key. Power plants generate and distribute AC power because it permits the use of transformers, which makes power delivery more economical. Transformers used at generation plants step the AC voltage up, which decreases the current. Decreased current allows smaller-sized wires to be used for the power transmission lines. Smaller wire is less expensive and easier to support over the long distances that the power must travel from the generation plant to remotely located substations. At the substations, transformers are again used to step AC voltages back down to a level suitable for distribution to homes and businesses.

There is no such thing as a DC transformer. This means DC power would have to be transmitted at low voltages and high currents over very large-sized wires, making the process very uneconomical. When DC is required for special applications, the AC voltage may be converted to DC voltage by using rectifiers, which make the change electrically, or by using AC motor–DC generator sets, which make the change mechanically.

lines cut in a given time (the rate) increases. When the conductor is moving parallel to the lines of flux (angle of 0°), it is not cutting any of them, and the voltage will be zero.

The angle between the lines of flux and the motion of the conductor is called θ (theta). The magnitude of the voltage produced will be proportional to the sine of the angle. Sine is a trigonometric function. Each angle has a sine value that never changes.

The sine of 0° is 0. It increases to a maximum of 1 at 90°. From 90° to 180°, the sine decreases back to 0. From 180° to 270°, the sine decreases to –1. Then from 270° to 360° (back to 0°), the sine increases to its original 0.

Because voltage is proportional to the sine of the angle, as the loop goes 360° around the circle the voltage will increase from 0 to its maximum at 90°, back to 0 at 180°, down to its maximum negative value at 270°, and back up to 0 at 360°, as shown in *Figure 3*.

Notice that at 180° the polarity reverses. This is because the conductor has turned completely around and is now cutting the lines of flux in the opposite direction. This can be shown using the left-hand rule for generators. The curve shown in *Figure 3* is called a sine wave because its shape is generated by the trigonometric function sine. The value of voltage at any point along the sine wave can be calculated if the angle and the maximum obtainable voltage (E_{max}) are known.

The formula used is:

$$E = E_{max} \text{ sine } \theta$$

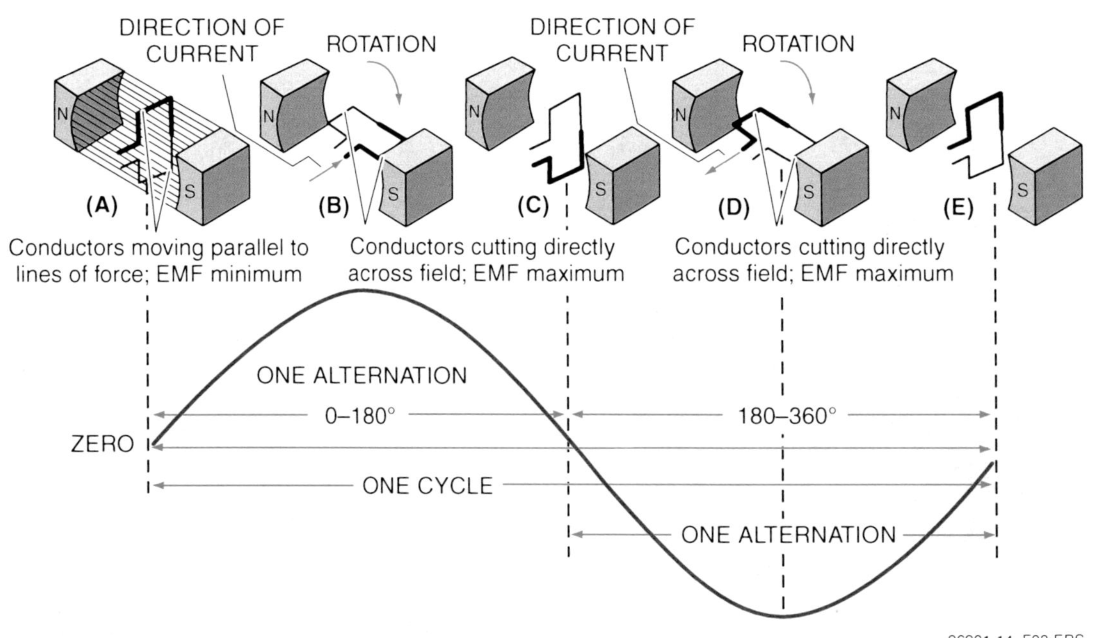

Figure 3 One cycle of alternating voltage.

Where:

E = voltage induced

E_{max} = maximum induced voltage

θ = angle at which the voltage is induced

Using the above formula, the values of voltage anywhere along the sine wave in *Figure 3* can be calculated. Sine values can be found using either a scientific calculator or trigonometric tables. With an E_{max} of 10 volts (V), the following values are calculated as examples:

$\theta = 0°$, sine = 0 $E = E_{max}\text{sine } \theta$ $E = (10V)(0)$ $E = 0V$	$\theta = 45°$, sine = 0.707 $E = E_{max}\text{sine } \theta$ $E = (10V)(0.707)$ $E = 7.07V$
$\theta = 90°$, sine = 1.0 $E = E_{max}\text{sine } \theta$ $E = (10V)(1.0)$ $E = 10V$	$\theta = 135°$, sine = 0.707 $E = E_{max}\text{sine } \theta$ $E = (10V)(0.707)$ $E = 7.07V$
$\theta = 180°$, sine = 0 $E = E_{max}\text{sine } \theta$ $E = (10V)(0)$ $E = 0V$	$\theta = 225°$, sine = −0.707 $E = E_{max}\text{sine } \theta$ $E = (10V)(-0.707)$ $E = -7.07V$
$\theta = 270°$, sine = −1.0 $E = E_{max}\text{sine } \theta$ $E = (10V)(-1.0)$ $E = -10V$	$\theta = 315°$, sine = −0.707 $E = E_{max}\text{sine } \theta$ $E = (10V)(-0.707)$ $E = -7.07V$

3.0.0 Sine Wave Terminology

There are a number of AC voltage terms that are specific to sine waves. The following sections discuss some of these terms, including **frequency**, wavelength, peak value, average value, and effective value.

3.1.0 Frequency

The frequency of a waveform is the number of times per second an identical pattern repeats itself. Each time the waveform changes from zero to a peak value and back to zero is called an alternation. Two alternations form one cycle. The number of cycles per second is the frequency. The unit of frequency is **hertz (Hz)**. One hertz equals one cycle per second (cps).

For example, let us determine the frequency of the waveform shown in *Figure 4*.

In one-half second, the basic sine wave is repeated five times. Therefore, the frequency (f) is:

$$f = \frac{5 \text{ cycles}}{0.5 \text{ second}} = 10 \text{ cycles per second (Hz)}$$

3.1.1 Period

The period of a waveform is the time (t) required to complete one cycle. The period is the inverse of frequency:

$$t = \frac{1}{f}$$

Where:

t = period (seconds)

f = frequency (Hz or cps)

For example, let us determine the period of the waveform in *Figure 4*. If there are five cycles in one-half second, then the frequency for one cycle is 10 cps (5 ÷ 0.5 = 10). Therefore, the period is:

$$t = \frac{1}{\text{cps}}$$

$$t = \frac{1}{10} = 0.1 \text{ second}$$

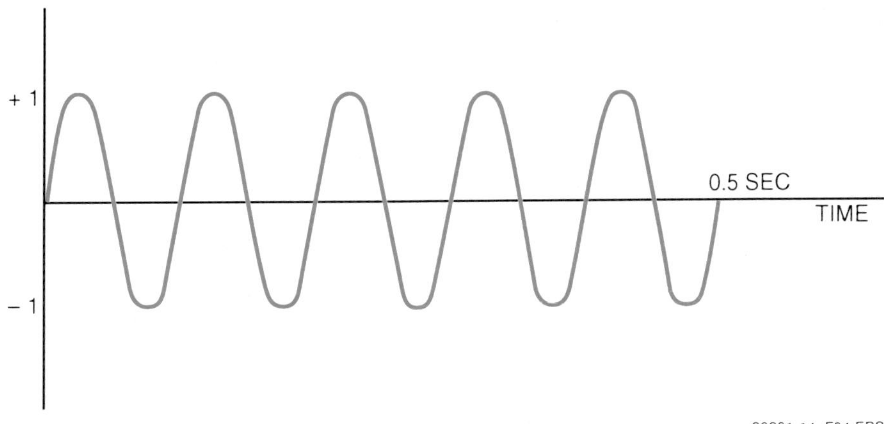

Figure 4 Frequency measurement.

3.2.0 Wavelength

The wavelength or λ (lambda) is the distance traveled by a waveform during one period. Since electromagnetic radiation travels at the speed of light (186,000 miles/second or 300,000 kilometers/second), the wavelength of electrical waveforms equals the product of the period and the speed of light (c):

$$\lambda = tc$$

or:

$$\lambda = \frac{c}{f}$$

Where:

λ = wavelength (meters)
t = period (seconds)
c = speed of light (meters/second)
f = frequency (Hz or cps)

3.3.0 Peak Value

The peak value is the maximum value of voltage (V_M) or current (I_M). For example, specifying that a sine wave has a **peak voltage** of 170V applies to either the positive or the negative peak. To include both peak amplitudes, the peak-to-peak (p–p) value may be specified. In the above example, the peak-to-peak value is 340V, double the peak value of 170V, because the positive and negative peaks are symmetrical. However, the two opposite peak values cannot occur at the same time. Furthermore, in some waveforms the two peaks are not equal. The positive peak value and peak-to-peak value of a sine wave are shown in *Figure 5*.

3.4.0 Average Value

The average value is calculated from all the values in a sine wave for one alternation or half cycle. The half cycle is used for the average because over a full cycle the average value is zero, which is useless for comparison purposes. If the sine values for all angles up to 180° in one alternation are added and then divided by the number of values, this average equals 0.637.

Since the peak value of the sine is 1 and the average equals 0.637, the average value can be calculated as follows:

$$\text{Average value} = 0.637 \times \text{peak value}$$

For example, with a peak of 170V, the average value is 0.637 × 170V, which equals approximately 108V. *Figure 5* shows where the average value would fall on a sine wave.

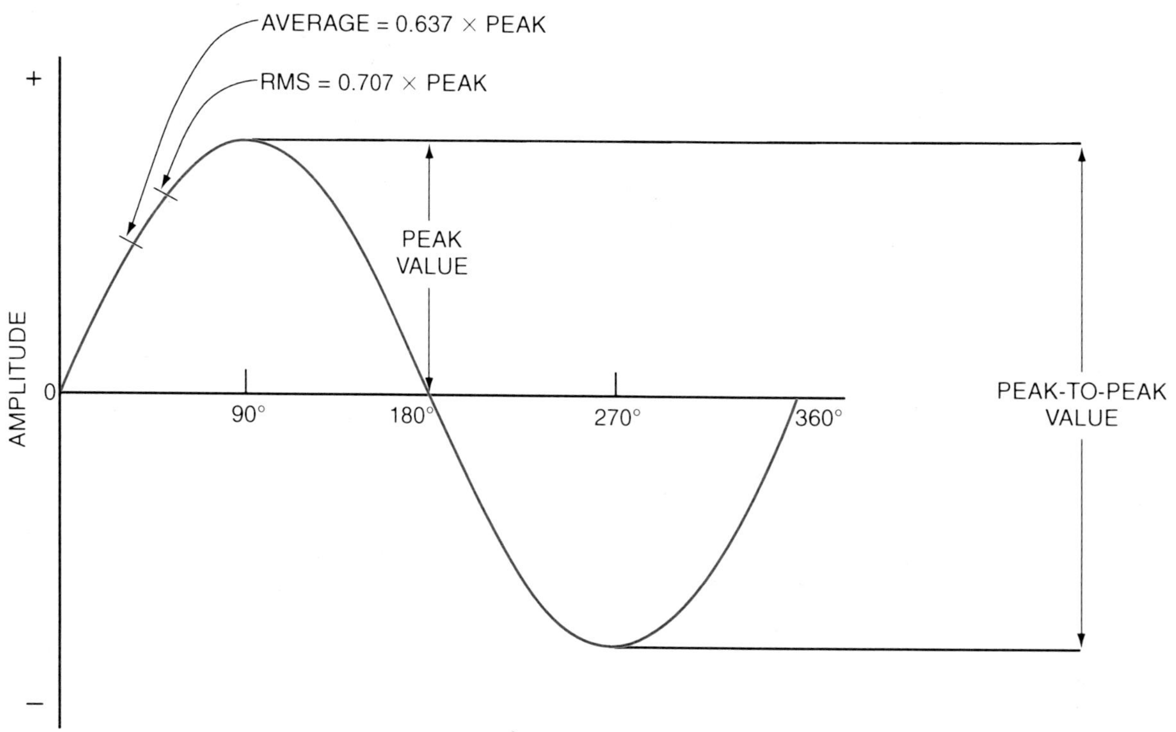

Figure 5 Amplitude values for a sine wave.

Think About It

Frequency

The frequency of the utility power generated in the United States is normally 60Hz. In some European countries and elsewhere, utility power is often generated at a frequency of 50Hz. Which of these frequencies (60Hz or 50Hz) has the shortest period?

3.5.0 Root-Mean-Square or Effective Value

Meters used in AC circuits indicate a value called the effective value. The effective value is the value of the AC current or voltage wave that indicates the same energy transfer as an equivalent direct current (DC) or voltage.

The direct comparison between DC and AC is in the heating effect of the two currents. Heat produced by current is a function of current amplitude only and is independent of current direction. Thus, heat is produced by both alternations of the AC wave, although the current changes direction during each alternation.

In a DC circuit, the current maintains a steady amplitude. Therefore, the heat produced is steady and is equal to I^2R. In an AC circuit, the current is continuously changing; periodically high, periodically low, and periodically zero. To produce the same amount of heat from AC as from an equivalent amount of DC, the instantaneous value of the AC must at times exceed the DC value.

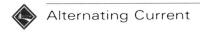

By averaging the heating effects of all the instantaneous values during one cycle of alternating current, it is possible to find the average heat produced by the AC current during the cycle. The amount of DC required to produce that heat will be equal to the effective value of the AC.

The most common method of specifying the amount of a sine wave of voltage or current is by stating its value at 45°, which is 70.7% of the peak. This is its **root-mean-square (rms)** value. Therefore:

$$\text{Value of rms} = 0.707 \times \text{peak value}$$

For example, with a peak of 170V, the rms value is 0.707 × 170, or approximately 120V. This is the voltage of the commercial AC power line, which is always given in rms value.

4.0.0 AC Phase Relationships

In AC systems, phase is involved in two ways: the location of a point on a voltage or current wave with respect to the starting point of the wave, or with respect to some corresponding point on the same wave. In the case of two waves of the same frequency, it is the time at which an event of one takes place with respect to a similar event of the other.

Often, the event is the starting of the waves at zero or the points at which the waves reach their maximum values. When two waves are compared in this manner, there is a phase lead or lag of one with respect to the other unless they are alternating in unison, in which case they are said to be in phase.

4.1.0 Phase Angle

Suppose that a generator started its cycle at 90° where maximum voltage output is produced instead of starting at the point of zero output. The two output voltage waves are shown in *Figure 6*. Each is the same waveform of alternating voltage, but wave B starts at the maximum value while wave A starts at zero. The complete cycle of wave B through 360° takes it back to the maximum value from which it started.

Wave A starts and finishes its cycle at zero. With respect to time, wave B is ahead of wave A in its values of generated voltage. The amount it leads in time equals one quarter revolution, which is 90°. This angular difference is the phase angle between waves B and A. Wave B leads wave A by the phase angle of 90°.

The 90° phase angle between waves B and A is maintained throughout the complete cycle and in all successive cycles as long as they both have the same frequency. At any instant in time, wave B has the value that A will have 90° later. For instance, at 180°, wave A is at zero, but B is already at its negative maximum value, the point where wave A will be later at 270°.

To compare the phase angle between two waves, both waves must have the same frequency. Otherwise, the relative phase keeps changing. Both waves must also have sine wave variations, because this is the only kind of waveform that is measured in angular units of time. The amplitudes can be different for the two waves. The phases of two voltages, two currents, or a current with a voltage can be compared.

4.2.0 Phase Angle Diagrams

To compare AC phases, it is much more convenient to use vector diagrams corresponding to the voltage and current waveforms, as shown in *Figure 6*. V_A and V_B represent the vector quantities corresponding to the generator voltage.

A vector is a quantity that has magnitude and direction. The length of the arrow indicates the magnitude of the alternating voltage in rms, peak, or any AC value as long as the same measure is used for all the vectors. The angle of the arrow with respect to the horizontal axis indicates the phase angle.

In *Figure 6*, the vector V_A represents the voltage wave A, with a phase angle of 0°. This angle can be considered as the plane of the loop in the rotary generator where it starts with zero output voltage. The vector V_B is vertical to show the phase angle of 90° for this voltage wave, corresponding to the vertical generator loop at the start of its cycle. The angle between the two vectors is the phase angle.

The symbol for a phase angle is θ (theta). In *Figure 7*, $\theta = 0°$. *Figure 7* shows the waveforms and vector diagram of two waves that are in phase but have different amplitudes.

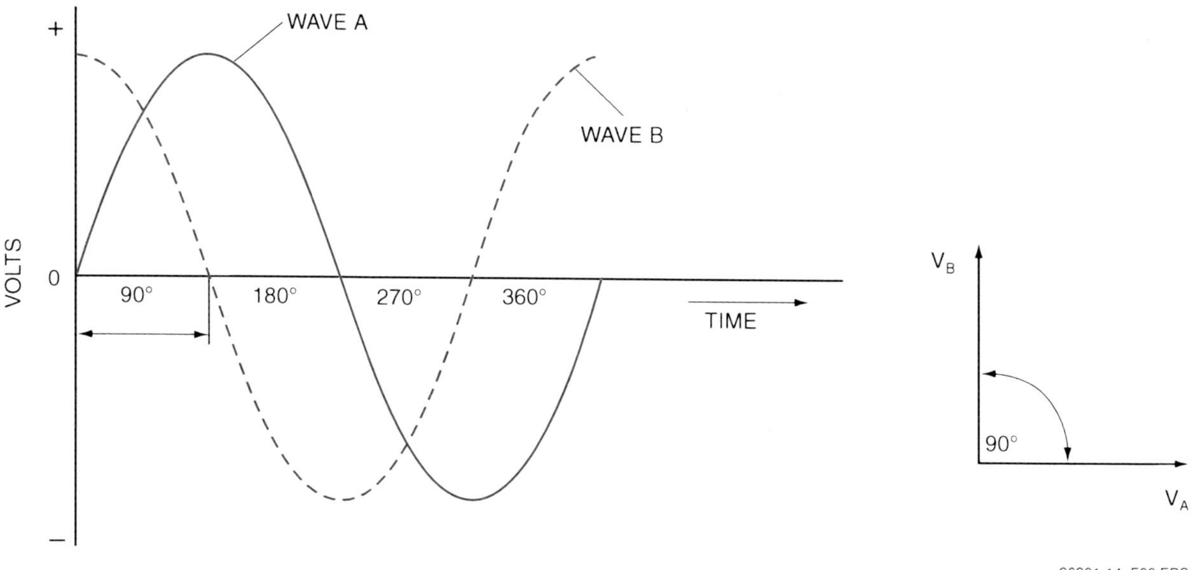

Figure 6 Voltage waveforms 90° out of phase.

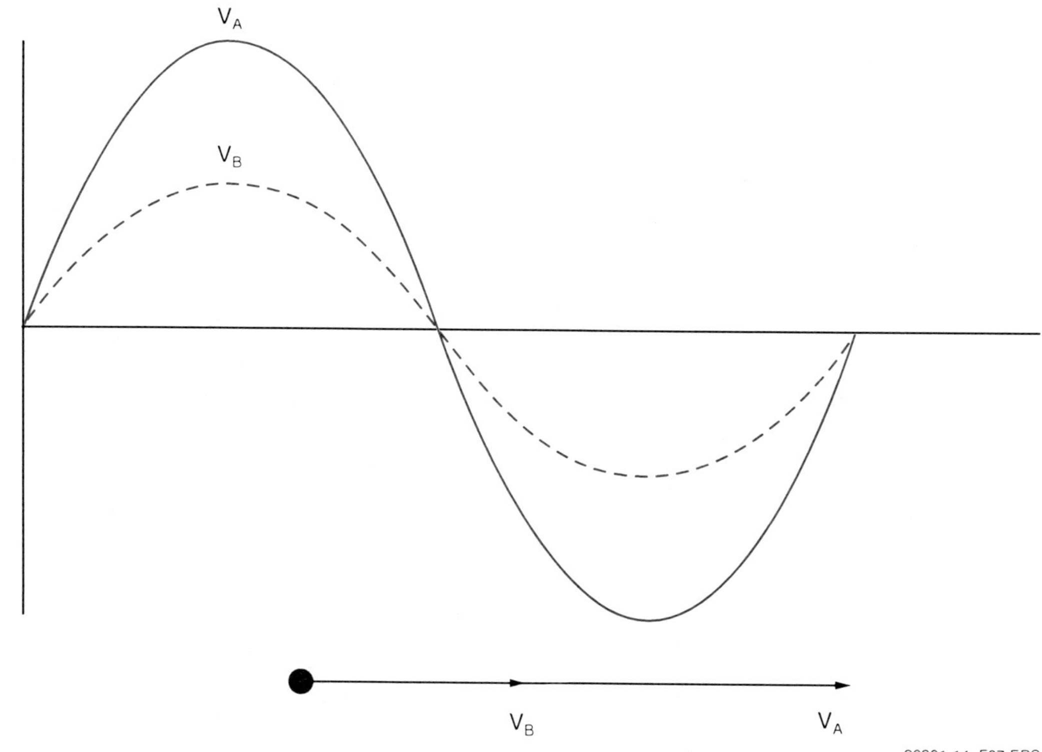

Figure 7 Waves in phase.

On Site

Left-Hand Rule for Generators

Hand rules for generators and motors give direction to the basic principles of induction. For a generator, if you move a conductor through a magnetic field made up of flux lines, you will induce an EMF, which drives current through a conductor. The left-hand rule for generators will help you determine which direction the current will flow in the conductor. It states that if you hold the thumb, first, and middle fingers of the left hand at right angles to one another with the first finger pointing in the flux direction (from the north pole to the south pole), and the thumb pointing in the direction of motion of the conductor, the middle finger will point in the direction of the induced voltage (EMF). The polarity of the EMF determines the direction in which current will flow as a result of this induced EMF. The left-hand rule for generators is also called Fleming's first rule.

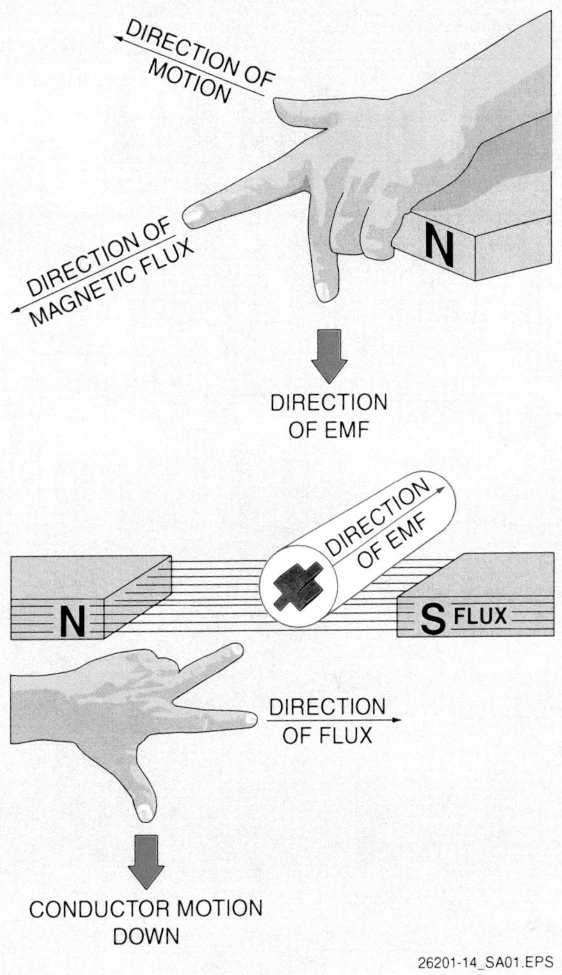

5.0.0 Nonsinusoidal Waveforms

The sine wave is the basic waveform for AC variations for several reasons. This waveform is produced by a rotary generator, as the output is proportional to the angle of rotation. Because of its derivation from circular motion, any sine wave can be analyzed in angular measure, either in degrees from 0° to 360° or in **radians** from 0 to 2π radians.

In many electronic applications, however, other waveshapes are important. Any waveform that is not a sine (or cosine) wave is a nonsinusoidal

On Site

RMS Amplitude

The root-mean-square (rms) value, also called the effective value, is the value assigned to an alternating voltage or current that results in the same power dissipation in a given resistance as DC voltage or current of the same numerical value. This is illustrated below. As shown, 120 (peak) VAC will not produce the same light (350 lumens versus 500 lumens) as 120VDC from a 60W lamp. In order to produce the same light (500 lumens), 120V rms must be applied to the lamp. This requires that the applied sinusoidal AC waveform have a peak voltage of about 170V (170V × 0.707V = 120V).

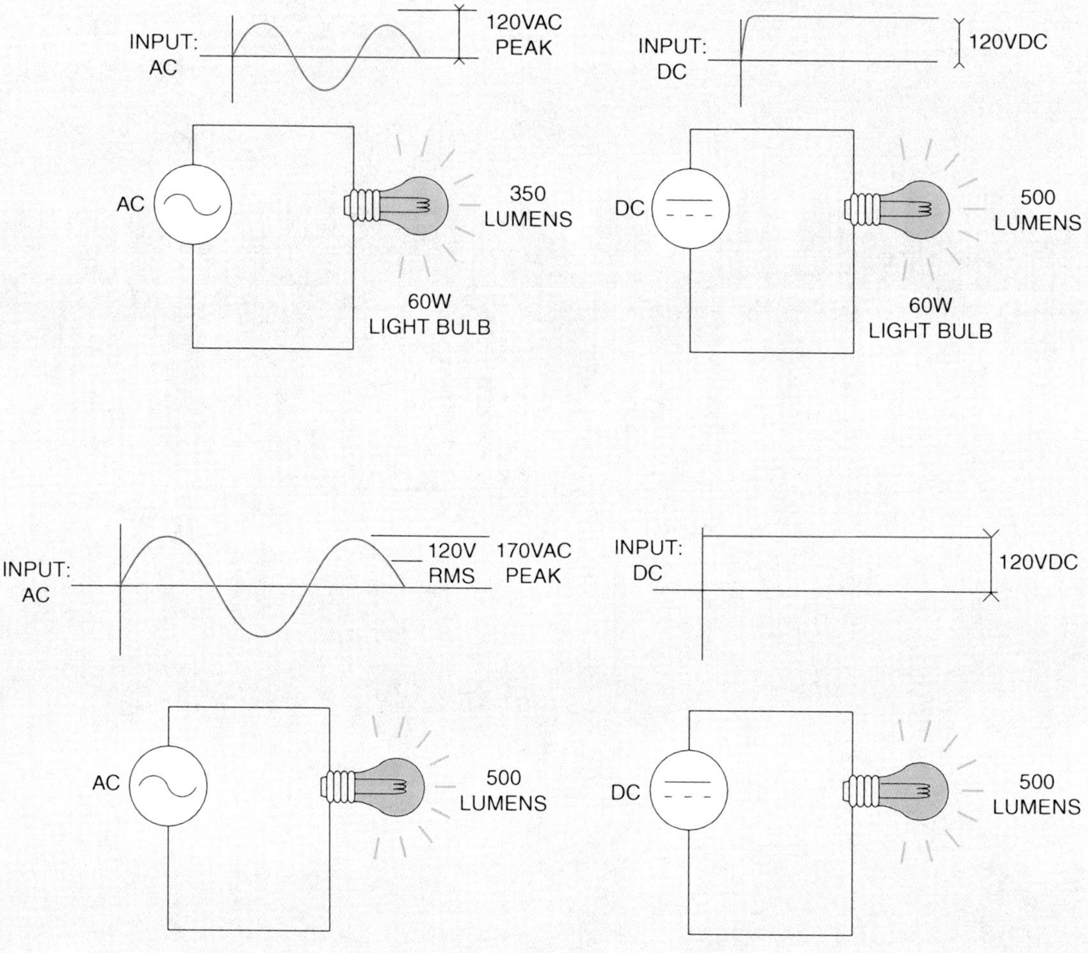

26201-14_SA02.EPS

waveform. Common examples are the square wave and sawtooth wave in *Figure 8*.

With nonsinusoidal waveforms for either voltage or current, there are important differences and similarities to consider. Note the following comparisons with sine waves:

- In all cases, the cycle is measured between two points having the same amplitude and varying in the same direction. The period is the time for one cycle.
- Peak amplitude is measured from the zero axis to the maximum positive or negative value. However, peak-to-peak amplitude is better for measuring nonsinusoidal waveshapes because they can have asymmetrical peaks, as with the rectangular wave in *Figure 8*.
- The rms value 0.707 of peak applies only to sine waves, as this factor is derived from the sine values in the angular measure used only for the sine waveform.
- Phase angles apply only to sine waves, as angular measure is used only for sine waves. Note that the phase angle is indicated only on the sine wave of *Figure 8*.

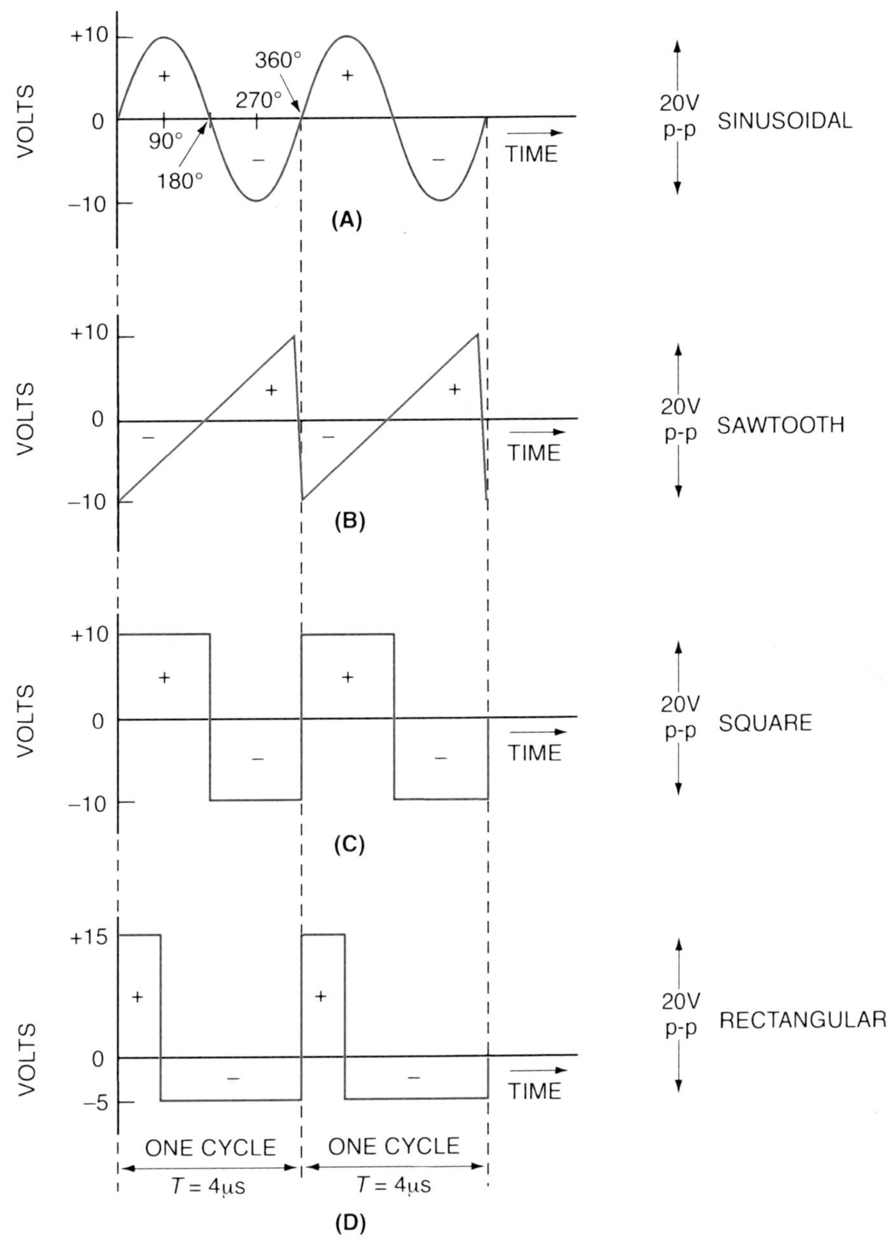

Figure 8 AC waveforms.

Think About It

Phase Angles

Why is the phase angle 90° in *Figure 6* and 0° in *Figure 7?* Why is the vector diagram in *Figure 7* shown as a straight line?

6.0.0 Resistance in AC Circuits

An AC circuit has an AC voltage source. Note the circular symbol with the sine wave inside it shown in *Figure 9*. It is used for any source of sine wave alternating voltage. This voltage connected across an external load resistance produces alternating current of the same waveform, frequency, and phase as the applied voltage.

According to Ohm's law, current (I) equals voltage (E) divided by resistance (R). When E is an rms value, I is also an rms value. For any instantaneous value of E during the cycle, the value of I is for the corresponding instant of time.

In an AC circuit with only resistance, the current variations are in phase with the applied voltage, as shown in *Figure 9*. This in-phase relationship between E and I means that such an AC circuit can be analyzed by the same methods used for DC circuits since there is no phase angle to

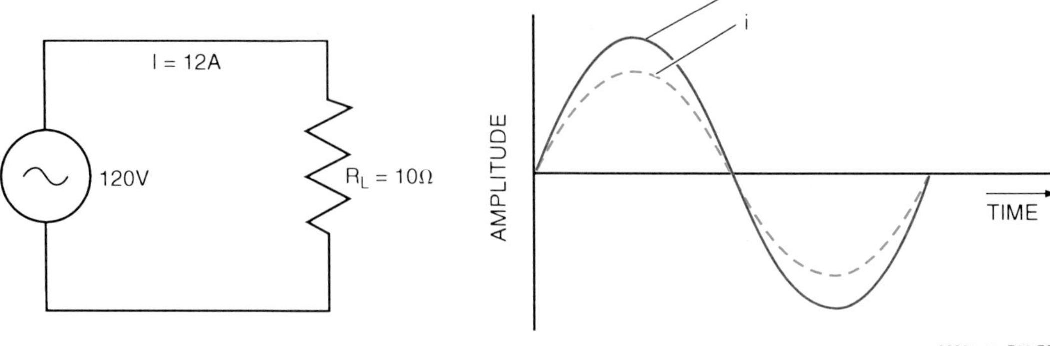

Figure 9 Resistive AC circuit.

consider. Components that have only resistance include resistors, the filaments for incandescent light bulbs, and vacuum tube heaters.

In purely resistive AC circuits, the voltage, current, and resistance are related by Ohm's law because the voltage and current are in phase.

$$I = \frac{E}{R}$$

Unless otherwise noted, the calculations in AC circuits are generally in rms values. For example, in *Figure 9*, the 120V applied across the 10Ω resistance R_L produces an rms current of 12A. This is determined as follows:

$$I = \frac{E}{R_L} = \frac{120V}{10\Omega} = 12A$$

Furthermore, the rms power (true power) dissipation is I^2R or:

$$P = (12A)^2 \times 10\Omega = 1{,}440W$$

Figure 10 shows the relationship between voltage and current in purely resistive AC circuits. The voltage and current are in phase, their cycles begin and end at the same time, and their peaks occur at the same time.

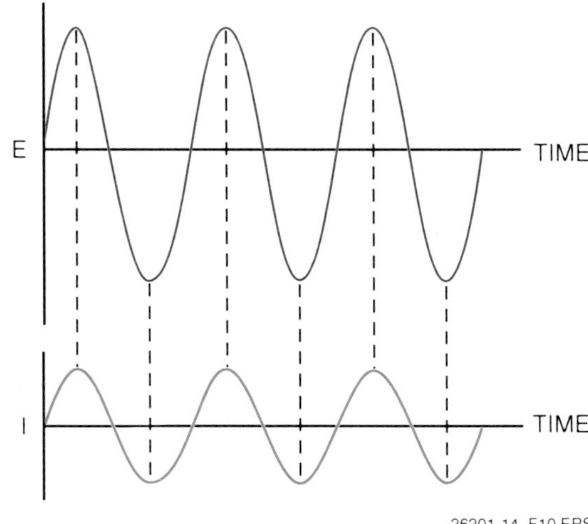

Figure 10 Voltage and current in a resistive AC circuit.

The value of the voltage shown in *Figure 10* depends on the applied voltage to the circuit. The value of the current depends on the applied voltage and the amount of resistance. If resistance is changed, it will affect only the magnitude of the current.

The total resistance in any AC circuit, whether it is a series, parallel, or series-parallel circuit, is calculated using the same rules that were learned and applied to DC circuits with resistance. Power computations are discussed later in this module.

What's wrong with this picture?

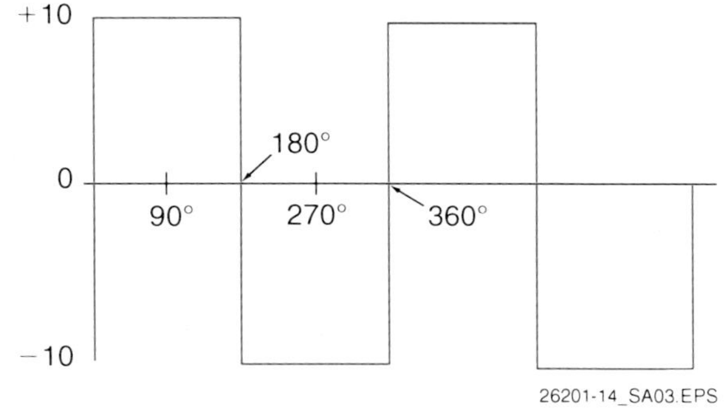

7.0.0 Inductance in AC Circuits

Inductance is the characteristic of an electrical circuit that opposes the change of current flow. It is the result of the expanding and collapsing field caused by the changing current. This moving flux cuts across the conductor that is providing the current, producing induced voltage in the wire itself. Furthermore, any other conductor in the field, whether carrying current or not, is also

cut by the varying flux and has induced voltage. This induced current opposes the current flow that generated it.

In DC circuits, a change must be initiated in the circuit to cause inductance. The current must change to provide motion of the flux. A steady DC of 10A cannot produce any induced voltage as long as the current value is constant. A current of 1A changing to 2A does induce voltage. Also, the faster the current changes, the higher the induced voltage becomes, because when the flux moves at a higher speed it can induce more voltage.

However, in an AC circuit the current is continuously changing and producing induced voltage. Lower frequencies of AC require more inductance to produce the same amount of induced voltage as a higher frequency current. The current can have any waveform as long as the amplitude is changing.

The ability of a conductor to induce voltage in itself when the current changes is its **self-inductance**, or simply inductance. The symbol for inductance is L and its unit is the henry (H). One henry is the amount of inductance that allows one volt to be induced when the current changes at the rate of one ampere per second.

7.1.0 Factors Affecting Inductance

An inductor is a coil of wire that may be wound on a core of metal or paper, or it may be self-supporting. It may consist of turns of wire placed side by side to form a layer of wire over the core or coil form. The inductance of a coil or inductor depends on its physical construction. Some of the factors affecting inductance are:

- *Number of turns* – The greater the number of turns, the greater the inductance. In addition, the spacing of the turns on a coil also affects inductance. A coil that has widely-spaced turns has a lower inductance than one that has the same number of more closely-spaced turns. The reason for this higher inductance is that the closely-wound turns produce a more concentrated magnetic field, causing the coil to exhibit a greater inductance.
- *Coil diameter* – The inductance increases directly as the cross-sectional area of the coil increases.
- *Length of the core* – When the length of the core is decreased, the turn spacing is decreased, increasing the inductance of the coil.
- *Core material* – The core of the coil can be either a magnetic material (such as iron) or a non-magnetic material (such as paper or air). Coils wound on a magnetic core produce a stronger magnetic field than those with non-magnetic cores, giving them higher values of inductance. Air-core coils are used where small values of inductance are required.
- *Winding the coil in layers* – The more layers used to form a coil, the greater the effect the magnetic field has on the conductor. Layering a coil can increase the inductance.

Factors affecting the inductance of a coil can be seen in *Figure 11*.

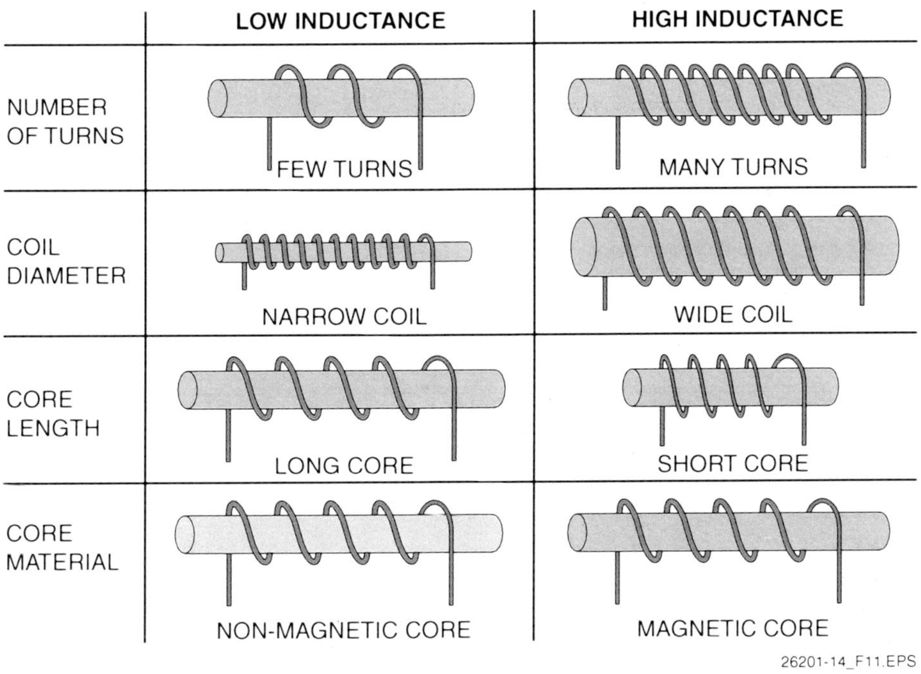

	LOW INDUCTANCE	HIGH INDUCTANCE
NUMBER OF TURNS	FEW TURNS	MANY TURNS
COIL DIAMETER	NARROW COIL	WIDE COIL
CORE LENGTH	LONG CORE	SHORT CORE
CORE MATERIAL	NON-MAGNETIC CORE	MAGNETIC CORE

26201-14_F11.EPS

Figure 11 Factors affecting the inductance of a coil.

Think About It

Inductance in an AC Circuit

Can you name three commonly used electrical devices that insert inductance into an AC circuit?

7.2.0 Voltage and Current in an Inductive AC Circuit

The self-induced voltage across an inductance L is produced by a change in current with respect to time ($\Delta i/\Delta t$) and can be stated as:

$$V_L = L\frac{\Delta i}{\Delta t}$$

Where:

Δ = change
V_L = volts
L = henrys
$\Delta i/\Delta t$ = amperes per second

This gives the voltage in terms of how much magnetic flux is cut per second. When the magnetic flux associated with the current varies the same as I, this formula gives the same results for calculating induced voltage. Remember that the induced voltage across the coil is actually the result of inducing electrons to move in the conductor, so there is also an induced current.

For example, what is the self-induced voltage V_L across a 4h inductance produced by a current change of 12A per second?

$$V_L = L\frac{\Delta i}{\Delta t}$$
$$V_L = 4h \times \frac{12A}{1}$$
$$V_L = 4 \times 12$$
$$V_L = 48V$$

The current through a 200 microhenry (µh) inductor changes from 0 to 200 milliamps (mA) in 2 microseconds (µsec). (The prefix **micro [µ]** means one-millionth.) What is the V_L?

$$V_L = L\frac{\Delta i}{\Delta t}$$
$$V_L = (200 \times 10^{-6})\frac{200 \times 10^{-3}}{2 \times 10^{-6}}$$
$$V_L = 20V$$

The induced voltage is an actual voltage that can be measured, although V_L is produced only while the current is changing. When $\Delta i/\Delta t$ is present for only a short time, V_L is in the form of a voltage pulse. With a sine wave current that is always changing, V_L is a sinusoidal voltage that is 90° out of phase with I_L.

The current that flows in an inductor is induced by the changing magnetic field that surrounds the inductor. This changing magnetic field is produced by an AC voltage source that is applied to the inductor. The magnitude and polarity of the induced current depend on the field strength, direction, and rate at which the field cuts the inductor windings. The overall effect is that the current is out of phase and lags the applied voltage by 90°.

At 270° in *Figure 12*, the applied electromotive force (EMF) is zero, but it is increasing in the positive direction at its greatest rate of change. Likewise, electron flow due to the applied EMF is also increasing at its greatest rate. As the electron flow increases, it produces a magnetic field that is building with it. The lines of flux cut the conductor as they move outward from it with the expanding field.

As the lines of flux cut the conductor, they induce a current into it. The induced current is at its maximum value because the lines of flux are expanding outward through the conductor at their greatest rate. The direction of the induced current is in opposition to the force that generated it. Therefore, at 270° the applied voltage is zero and is increasing to a positive value, while the current is at its maximum negative value.

At 0° in *Figure 12*, the applied voltage is at its maximum positive value, but its rate of change is zero. Therefore, the field it produces is no longer expanding and is not cutting the conductor. Because there is no relative motion between the field and conductor, no current is induced. Therefore, at 0° voltage is at its maximum positive value, while current is zero.

At 90° in *Figure 12*, voltage is once again zero, but this time it is decreasing toward negative at its greatest rate of change. Because the applied voltage is decreasing, the magnetic field is collapsing inward on the conductor. This has the effect of reversing the direction of motion between the field and conductor that existed at 0°.

Therefore, the current will flow in a direction opposite of what it was at 0°. Also, because the applied voltage is decreasing at its greatest rate, the field is collapsing at its greatest rate. This causes the flux to cut the conductor at the greatest rate, causing the induced current magnitude to be maximum. At 90°, the applied voltage is zero

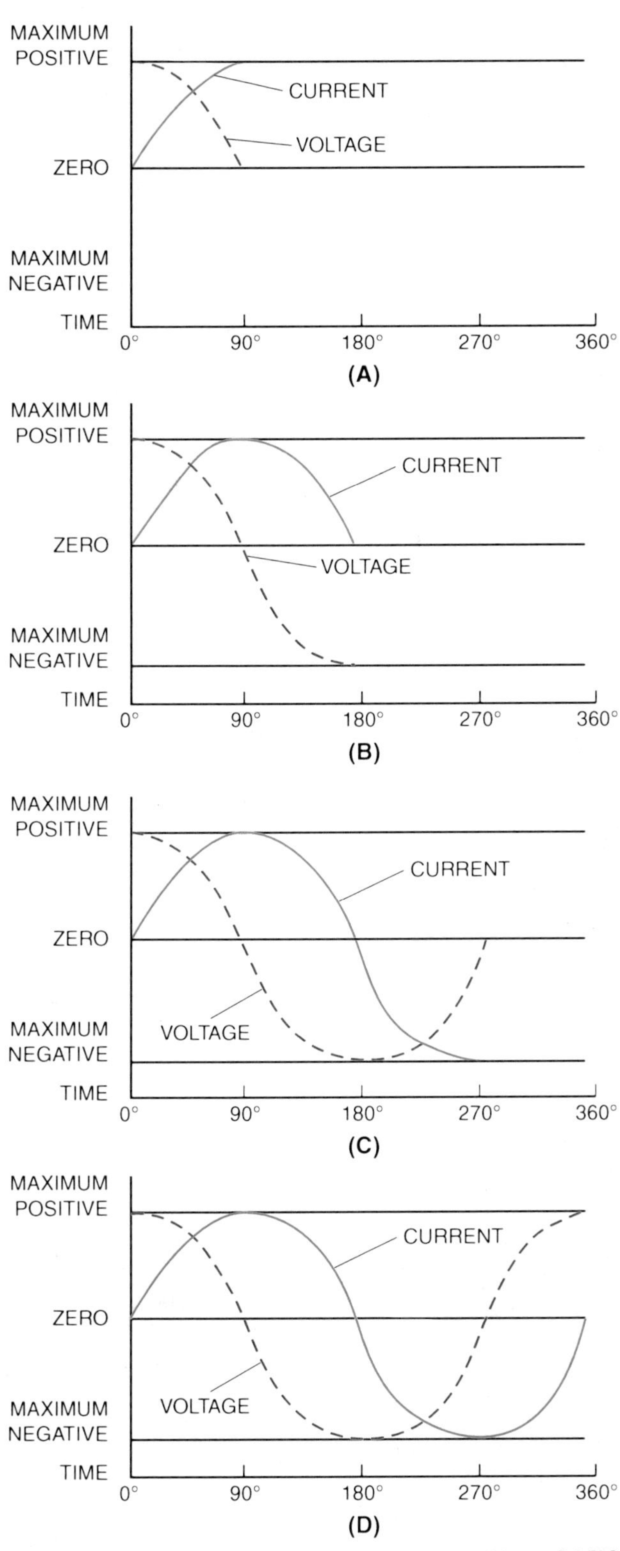

Figure 12 Inductor voltage and current relationship.

decreasing toward negative, while the current is maximum positive.

At 180° in *Figure 12*, the applied voltage is at its maximum negative value, but just as at 0°, its rate of change is zero. At 180°, therefore, current will be zero. This explanation shows that the voltage peaks positive first, then 90° later the current peaks positive. Current thus lags the applied voltage in an inductor by 90°. This can easily be remembered using the phrase "ELI the ICE man." ELI represents voltage (E), inductance (L), and current (I). In an inductor, the voltage leads the current just as the letter E leads or comes before the letter I. The word ICE will be explained in the section on capacitance.

7.3.0 Inductive Reactance

The opposing force that an inductor presents to the flow of alternating current cannot be called resistance since it is not the result of friction within a conductor. The name given to this force is inductive reactance because it is the reaction of the inductor to alternating current. Inductive reactance is measured in ohms and its symbol is X_L.

Remember that the induced voltage in a conductor is proportional to the rate at which magnetic lines of force cut the conductor. The greater the rate or higher the frequency, the greater the counter-electromotive force (CEMF). Also, the induced voltage increases with an increase in inductance; the more turns, the greater the CEMF. Reactance then increases with an increase of frequency and with an increase in inductance. The formula for inductive reactance is as follows:

$$X_L = 2\pi fL$$

Where:

X_L = inductive reactance in ohms

2π = a constant in which the Greek letter pi (π) represents 3.14 and 2 × pi = 6.28

f = frequency of the alternating current in hertz

L = inductance in henrys

On Site

ELI in ELI the ICE Man

Remembering the phrase "ELI" as in "ELI the ICE man" is an easy way to remember the phase relationships that always exist between voltage and current in an inductive circuit. An inductive circuit is a circuit that has more inductive reactance than capacitive reactance. The L in ELI indicates inductance. The E (voltage) is stated before the I (current) in ELI, meaning that the voltage leads the current in an inductive circuit.

For example, if f is equal to 60Hz and L is equal to 20h, find X_L:

$$X_L = 2\pi fL$$
$$X_L = 6.28 \times 60\text{Hz} \times 20\text{h}$$
$$X_L = 7{,}536\Omega$$

Once calculated, the value of X_L is used like resistance in a form of Ohm's law:

$$I = \frac{E}{X_L}$$

Where:

I = effective current (amps)
E = effective voltage (volts)
X_L = inductive reactance (ohms)

Unlike a resistor, there is no power dissipation in an ideal inductor. An inductor limits current, but it uses no net energy since the energy required to build up the field in the inductor is given back to the circuit when the field collapses.

8.0.0 CAPACITANCE

A capacitor is a device that stores an electric charge in a dielectric material. Capacitance is the ability to store a charge. In storing a charge, a capacitor opposes a change in voltage. *Figure 13* shows a simple capacitor in a circuit, schematic representations of two types of capacitors, and a photo of common capacitors.

Figure 14(A) shows a capacitor in a DC circuit. When voltage is applied, the capacitor begins to charge, as shown in *Figure 14(B)*. The charging continues until the potential difference across the capacitor is equal to the applied voltage. This charging current is transient or temporary since it flows only until the capacitor is charged to the applied voltage. Then there is no current in the circuit. *Figure 14(C)* shows this with the voltage across the capacitor equal to the battery voltage or 10V.

The capacitor can be discharged by connecting a conducting path across the dielectric. The stored charge across the dielectric provides the potential difference to produce a discharge current, as shown in *Figure 14(D)*. Once the capacitor is completely discharged, the voltage across it equals zero, and there is no discharge current.

In a capacitive circuit, the charge and discharge current must always be in opposite directions. Current flows in one direction to charge the capacitor and in the opposite direction when the capacitor is allowed to discharge.

Current will flow in a capacitive circuit with AC voltage applied because of the capacitor charge and discharge current. There is no current through the dielectric, which is an insulator. While the capacitor is being charged by increasing applied voltage, the charging current flows in one direction to the plates. While the capacitor is

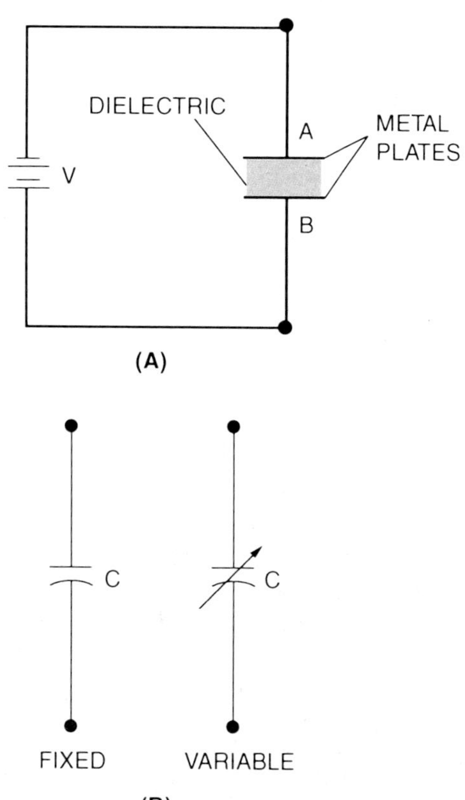

26201-14_F13C.EPS

Figure 13 Capacitors.

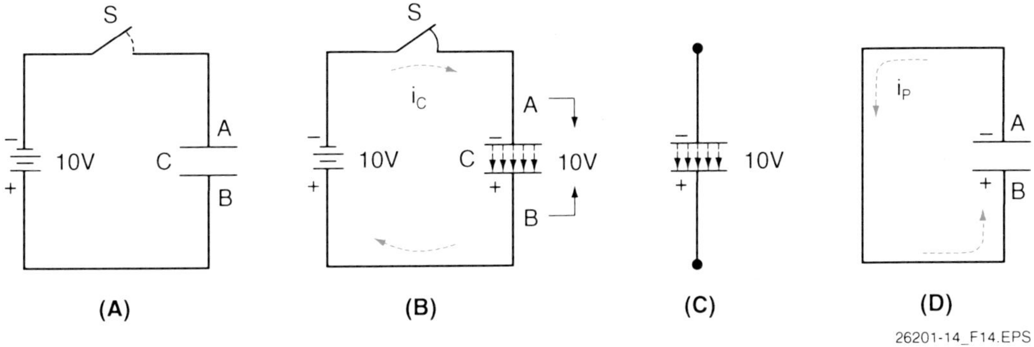

Figure 14 Charging and discharging a capacitor.

discharging as the applied voltage decreases, the discharge current flows in the reverse direction. With alternating voltage applied, the capacitor alternately charges and discharges.

First, the capacitor is charged in one polarity, and then it discharges; next, the capacitor is charged in the opposite polarity, and then it discharges again. The cycles of charge and discharge current provide alternating current in the circuit at the same frequency as the applied voltage. The amount of capacitance in the circuit will determine how much current is allowed to flow.

Capacitance is measured in farads (F), where one farad is the capacitance when one coulomb is stored in the dielectric with a potential difference of one volt. Smaller values are measured in microfarads (μF). A small capacitance will allow less charge and discharge current to flow than a larger capacitance. The smaller capacitor has more opposition to alternating current, because less current flows with the same applied voltage.

In summary, capacitance exhibits the following characteristics:

- DC is blocked by a capacitor. Once charged, no current will flow in the circuit.
- AC flows in a capacitive circuit with AC voltage applied.
- A smaller capacitance allows less current.

8.1.0 Factors Affecting Capacitance

A capacitor consists of two conductors separated by an insulating material called a dielectric. There are many types and sizes of capacitors with different dielectric materials. The capacitance of a capacitor is determined by three factors:

- *Area of the plates* – The initial charge displacement on a set of capacitor plates is related to the number of free electrons in each plate. Larger plates will produce a greater capacitance than smaller ones. Therefore, the capacitance of a capacitor varies directly with the area of the plates. For example, if the area of the plates is doubled, the capacitance is doubled. If the size of the plates is reduced by 50%, the capacitance would also be reduced by 50%.
- *Distance between plates* – As two capacitor plates are brought closer together, more electrons will move away from the positively charged plate and move into the negatively charged plate. This is because the mutual attraction between the opposite charges on the plates increases as the plates move closer together. This added movement of charge is an increase in the capacitance of the capacitor. In a capacitor composed of two plates of equal area, the capacitance varies inversely with the distance between the plates. For example, if the distance between the plates is decreased by one-half, the capacitance will be doubled. If the distance between the plates is doubled, the capacitance would be one-half as great.
- *Dielectric permittivity* – Another factor that determines the value of capacitance is the permittivity of the dielectric. The dielectric is the material between the capacitor plates in which the electric field appears. Relative permittivity expresses the ratio of the electric field strength in a dielectric to that in a vacuum. Permittivity has nothing to do with the dielectric strength of the medium or the breakdown voltage. An insulating material that will withstand a higher applied voltage than some other substance does not always have a higher dielectric permittivity. Many insulating materials have a greater dielectric permittivity than air. For a given applied voltage, a greater attraction exists between the opposite charges on the capacitor plates, and an electric field can be set up more easily than when the dielectric is air. The capacitance of the capacitor is increased when the permittivity of the dielectric is increased if all the other parameters remain unchanged.

On Site

Capacitance

The concept of capacitance, like many electrical quantities, is often hard to visualize or understand. A comparison with a balloon may help to make this concept clearer. Electrical capacitance has a charging effect similar to blowing up a balloon and holding it closed. The expansion capacity of the balloon can be changed by changing the thickness of the balloon walls. A balloon with thick walls will expand less (have less capacity) than one with thin walls. This is like a small 10µF capacitor that has less capacity and will charge less than a larger 100µF capacitor.

8.2.0 Calculating Equivalent Capacitance

Connecting capacitors in parallel is equivalent to adding the plate areas. Therefore, the total capacitance is the sum of the individual capacitances, as illustrated in *Figure 15*.

A 10µF capacitor in parallel with a 5µF capacitor, for example, provides a 15µF capacitance for the parallel combination. The voltage is the same across the parallel capacitors. Note that adding parallel capacitance is opposite to the case of inductances in parallel and resistances in parallel.

Connecting capacitances in series is equivalent to increasing the thickness of the dielectric. Therefore, the combined capacitance is less than the smallest individual value. The combined equivalent capacitance is calculated by the reciprocal formula, as shown in *Figure 16*.

Capacitors connected in series are combined like resistors in parallel. Any of the shortcut calculations for the reciprocal formula apply. For example, the combined capacitance of two equal capacitances of 10µF in series is 5µF.

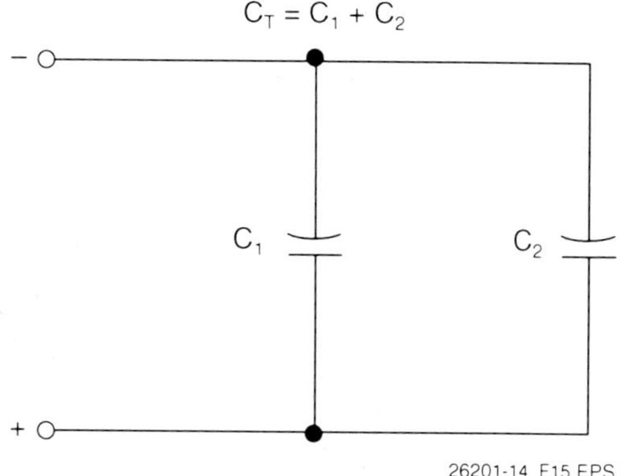

Figure 15 Capacitors in parallel.

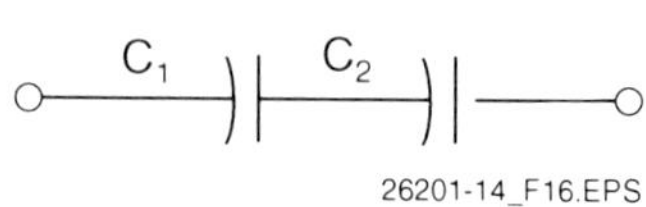

Figure 16 Capacitors in series.

Capacitors are used in series to provide a higher voltage breakdown rating for the combination. For instance, each of three equal capacitances in series has one-third the applied voltage.

In series, the voltage across each capacitor is inversely proportional to its capacitance. The smaller capacitance has the larger proportion of the applied voltage. The reason is that the series capacitances all have the same charge because they are in one current path. With equal charge, a smaller capacitance has a greater potential difference.

8.3.0 Capacitor Specifications

This specifies the maximum potential difference that can be applied across the plates without puncturing the dielectric.

8.3.1 Voltage Rating

Usually, the voltage rating is for temperatures up to about 60°C. High temperatures result in a lower voltage rating. Voltage ratings for general-purpose paper, mica, and ceramic capacitors are typically 200V to 500V. Ceramic capacitors with ratings of 1 to 5kV are also available.

Electrolytic capacitors are commonly used in 25V, 150V, and 450V ratings. In addition, 6V and 10V electrolytic capacitors are often used in transistor circuits. For applications where a lower voltage rating is permissible, more capacitance can be obtained in a smaller physical size.

The potential difference across the capacitor depends on the applied voltage and is not necessarily equal to the voltage rating. A voltage rating higher than the potential difference applied across the capacitor provides a safety factor for long life in service. With electrolytic capacitors, however, the actual capacitor voltage should be close to the rated voltage to produce the oxide film that provides the specified capacitance.

Think About It

Capacitance

Suppose you had a motor with a bad 30μF starting capacitor and no 30μF direct replacement capacitor was available. As a temporary measure, you are authorized to substitute two equal-value capacitors in its place. What size capacitors (μF) should be used if you are connecting them in parallel?

The voltage ratings are for applied DC voltage. The breakdown rating is lower for AC voltage because of the internal heat produced by continuous charge and discharge.

8.3.2 Leak Resistance

Consider a capacitor charged by a DC voltage source. After the charging voltage is removed, a perfect capacitor would keep its charge indefinitely. After a long period of time, however, the charge will be neutralized by a small leakage current through the dielectric and across the insulated case between terminals, because there is no perfect insulator. For paper, ceramic, and mica capacitors, the leakage current is very slight, or inversely, the leakage resistance is very high. For paper, ceramic, or mica capacitors, R_1 is 100MΩ or more. However, electrolytic capacitors may have a leakage resistance of 0.5MΩ or less.

8.4.0 Voltage and Current in a Capacitive AC Circuit

In a capacitive circuit driven by an AC voltage source, the voltage is continuously changing. Thus, the charge on the capacitor is also continuously changing. The four parts of *Figure 17* show the variation of the alternating voltage and current in a capacitive circuit for each quarter of one cycle.

The solid line represents the voltage across the capacitor, and the dotted line represents the current. The line running through the center is the zero or reference point for both the voltage and the current. The bottom line marks off the time of the cycle in terms of electric degrees. Assume that the AC voltage has been acting on the capacitor for some time before the time represented by the starting point of the sine wave.

At the beginning of the first quarter-cycle (0° to 90°), the voltage has just passed through zero and is increasing in the positive direction. Since the zero point is the steepest part of the sine wave, the voltage is changing at its greatest rate.

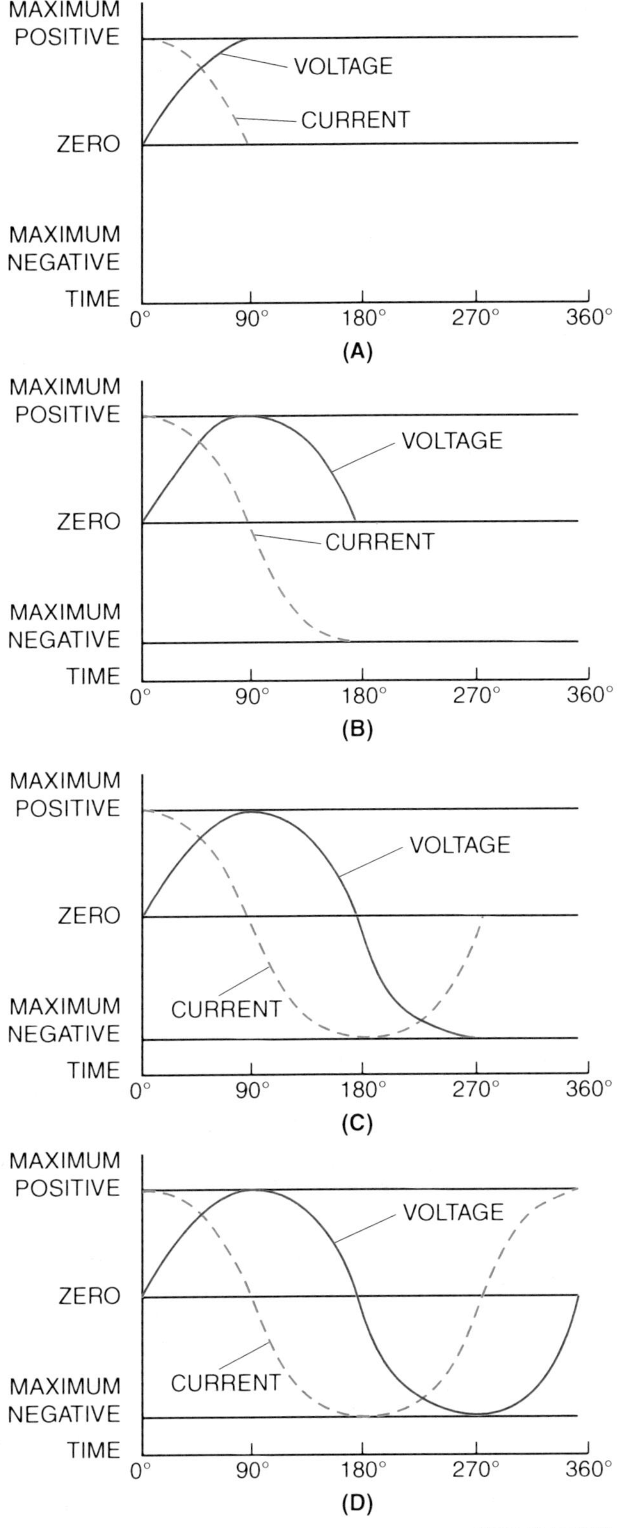

Figure 17 Voltage and current in a capacitive AC circuit.

The charge on a capacitor varies directly with the voltage; therefore, the charge on the capacitor is also changing at its greatest rate at the beginning of the first quarter-cycle. In other words, the greatest number of electrons are moving off one plate and onto the other plate. Thus, the capacitor current is at its maximum value.

As the voltage proceeds toward maximum at 90°, its rate of change becomes lower and lower, making the current decrease toward zero. At 90°, the voltage across the capacitor is maximum, the capacitor is fully charged, and there is no further movement of electrons from plate to plate. That is why the current at 90° is zero.

At the end of the first quarter-cycle, the alternating voltage stops increasing in the positive direction and starts to decrease. It is still a positive voltage; but to the capacitor, the decrease in voltage means that the plate that has just accumulated an excess of electrons must lose some electrons. The current flow must reverse its direction. The second part of the figure shows the current curve to be below the zero line (negative current direction) during the second quarter-cycle (90° to 180°).

At 180°, the voltage has dropped to zero. This means that, for a brief instant, the electrons are equally distributed between the two plates; the current is maximum because the rate of change of voltage is maximum.

Just after 180°, the voltage has reversed polarity and starts building to its maximum negative peak, which is reached at the end of the third quarter-cycle (180° to 270°). During the third quarter-cycle, the rate of voltage change gradually decreases as the charge builds to a maximum at 270°. At this point, the capacitor is fully charged and carries the full impressed voltage. Because the capacitor is fully charged, there is no further exchange of electrons and the current flow is zero at this point. The conditions are exactly the same as at the end of the first quarter-cycle (90°), but the polarity is reversed.

Just after 270°, the impressed voltage once again starts to decrease, and the capacitor must lose electrons from the negative plate. It must discharge, starting at a minimum rate of flow and rising to a maximum. This discharging action continues through the last quarter-cycle (270° to 360°) until the impressed voltage has reached zero. The beginning of the entire cycle is 360°, and everything starts over again.

In *Figure 17*, note that the current always arrives at a certain point in the cycle 90° ahead of the voltage because of the charging and discharging action. This voltage-current phase relationship in a capacitive circuit is exactly opposite to that in an inductive circuit. The current through a capacitor leads the voltage across the capacitor by 90°. A convenient way to remember this is the phrase "ELI the ICE man" (ELI refers to inductors, as previously explained). ICE pertains to capacitors as follows:

I = current
C = capacitor
E = voltage

In capacitors (C), current (I) leads voltage (E) by 90°.

It is important to realize that the current and voltage are both going through their individual cycles at the same time during the period the AC voltage is impressed. The current does not go through part of its cycle (charging or discharging) and then stop and wait for the voltage to catch up. The amplitude and polarity of the voltage and the amplitude and direction of the current are continually changing.

Their positions, with respect to each other and to the zero line at any electrical instant or any degree between 0° and 360°, can be seen by reading upward from the time-degree line. The current swing from the positive peak at 0° to the negative peak at 180° is not a measure of the number of electrons or the charge on the plates. It is a picture of the direction and strength of the current in relation to the polarity and strength of the voltage appearing across the plates.

8.5.0 Capacitive Reactance

Capacitors offer a very real opposition to current flow. This opposition arises from the fact that, at a given voltage and frequency, the number of electrons that go back and forth from plate to plate is limited by the storage ability (capacitance) of the capacitor. As the capacitance is increased, a greater number of electrons changes plates every cycle. Since current is a measure of the number of electrons passing a given point in a given time, the current is increased.

Increasing the frequency will also decrease the opposition offered by a capacitor. This occurs because the number of electrons that the capacitor is capable of handling at a given voltage will change plates more often. As a result, more electrons will pass a given point in a given time (greater current flow). The opposition that a capacitor offers to AC is therefore inversely proportional to frequency and capacitance. This opposition is called capacitive reactance. Capacitive reactance decreases with increasing frequency or, for a given frequency, the capacitive reactance decreases with increasing capacitance. The symbol for capacitive reactance is X_C. The formula is:

$$X_C = \frac{1}{2\pi fC}$$

Where:

X_C = capacitive reactance in ohms
f = frequency in hertz
C = capacitance in farads
$2\pi = 6.28\ (2 \times 3.14)$

For example, what is the capacitive reactance of a 0.05μF capacitor in a circuit whose frequency is 1 megahertz?

$$X_C = \frac{1}{2\pi fC} = \frac{1}{(6.28)(10^6 \text{ hertz } (5 \times 10^{-8} \text{ farads})}$$

$$X_C = \frac{1}{3.14 \times 10^{-1}} = \frac{1}{0.314} = 3.18 \text{ ohms}$$

The capacitive reactance of a 0.05μF capacitor operated at a frequency of 1 megahertz is 3.18 ohms. Suppose this same capacitor is operated at a lower frequency of 1,500 hertz instead of 1 megahertz. What is the capacitive reactance now? Substituting where $1{,}500 = 1.5 \times 10^3$ hertz:

$$X_C = \frac{1}{2\pi fC} = \frac{1}{(6.28)(1.5 \times 10^3 \text{ hertz } (5 \times 10^{-8} \text{ farads})}$$

$$X_C = \frac{1}{4.71 \times 10^{-4}} = 2{,}123 \text{ ohms}$$

On Site

ICE in ELI the ICE Man

Remembering the phrase "ICE" as in "ELI the ICE man" is an easy way to remember the phase relationships that always exist between voltage and current in a capacitive circuit. A capacitive circuit is a circuit in which there is more capacitive reactance than inductive reactance. This is indicated by the C in ICE. The I (current) is stated before the E (voltage) in ICE, meaning that the current leads the voltage in a capacitive circuit.

Think About It

Frequency and Capacitive Reactance

A variable capacitor is used in the tuner of an AM radio to tune the radio to the desired station. Will its capacitive reactance value be higher or lower when it is tuned to the low end of the frequency band (550kHz) than it would be when tuned to the high end of the band (1,440kHz)?

Note a very interesting point from these two examples. As frequency is decreased from 1 megahertz to 1,500 hertz, the capacitive reactance increases from 3.18 ohms to 2,123 ohms. Capacitive reactance increases as the frequency decreases.

9.0.0 LC and RLC Circuits

AC circuits often contain inductors, capacitors, and/or resistors connected in series or parallel combinations. When this is done, it is important to determine the resulting phase relationship between the applied voltage and the current in the circuit. The simplest method of combining factors that have different phase relationships is vector addition with the trigonometric functions. Each quantity is represented as a vector, and the resultant vector and phase angle are then calculated.

In purely resistive circuits, the voltage and current are in phase. In inductive circuits, the voltage leads the current by 90°. In capacitive circuits, the current leads the voltage by 90°. *Figure 18* shows the phase relationships of these components used in AC circuits. Recall that these characteristics are summarized by the phrase "ELI the ICE man."

ELI = *E* Leads *I* (inductive)
ICE = *I* Capacitive (leads) *E*

The impedance Z of a circuit is defined as the total opposition to current flow. The magnitude of the impedance Z is given by the following equation in a series circuit:

$$Z = \sqrt{R^2 + X^2}$$

Where:

Z = impedance (ohms)
R = resistance (ohms)
X = net reactance (ohms)

The current through a resistance is always in phase with the voltage applied to it; thus resistance is shown along the 0° axis. The voltage across an inductor leads the current by 90°; thus inductive reactance is shown along the 90° axis. The voltage across a capacitor lags the current by 90°; thus capacitive reactance is shown along the –90° axis. The net reactance is the difference between the inductive reactance and the capacitive reactance:

X = net reactance (ohms)
X_L = inductive reactance (ohms)
X_C = capacitive reactance (ohms)

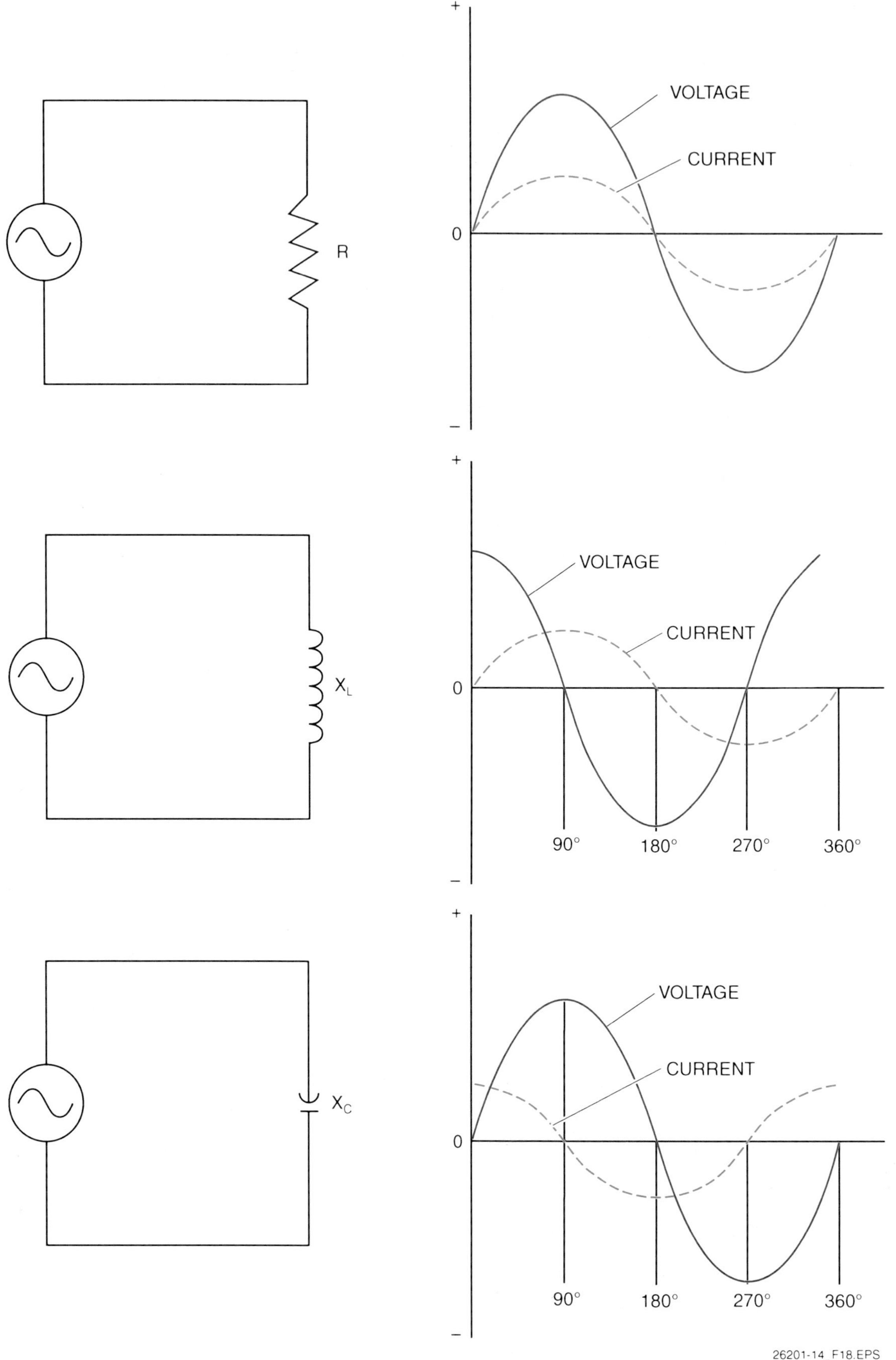

Figure 18 Summary of AC circuit phase relationships.

The impedance Z is the vector sum of the resistance R and the net reactance X. The angle, called the phase angle, gives the phase relationship between the applied voltage and current.

9.1.0 RL Circuits

RL circuits combine resistors and inductors in a series, parallel, or series-parallel configuration. In a pure inductive circuit, the current lags the voltage by an angle of 90°. In a circuit containing both resistance and inductance, the current will lag the voltage by some angle between zero and 90°.

9.1.1 Series RL Circuit

Figure 19 shows a series RL circuit. Since it is a series circuit, the current is the same in all portions of the loop. Using the values shown, the circuit will be analyzed for unknown values such as X_L, Z, I, E_L, and E_R.

The solution would be worked as follows:

Step 1 Compute the value of X_L.

$$X_L = 2\pi fL$$
$$X_L = 6.28 \times 100 \times 4 = 2{,}512 \text{ ohms}$$

Step 2 Draw vectors R and X_L as shown in *Figure 19*. R is drawn horizontally because the circuit current and voltage across R are in phase. It therefore becomes the reference line from which other angles are measured. X_L is drawn upward at 90° from R because voltage across X_L leads circuit current through R.

Step 3 Compute the value of circuit impedance Z, which is equal to the vector sum of X_L and R.

$$\tan = \frac{X_L}{R} = \frac{2{,}512}{1{,}500} = 1.67$$
$$\arctan 1.67 = 59.1°$$
$$\cos 59.1° = 0.5135$$

Find Z using the cosine function:

$$\cos = \frac{R}{Z}$$
$$Z = \frac{R}{\cos}$$
$$Z = \frac{1{,}500}{0.5135} = 2{,}921 \text{ ohms}$$

Step 4 Compute the circuit current using Ohm's law for AC circuits.

$$I = \frac{E}{Z} = \frac{100V}{2{,}921\Omega} = 0.034A$$

Step 5 Compute voltage drops in the circuit.

$$E_L = IX_L = 0.034 \times 2{,}512 = 85 \text{ volts}$$
$$E_R = IR = 0.034 \times 1{,}500 = 51 \text{ volts}$$

Note that the voltage drops across the resistor and inductor do not equal the supply voltage because they must be added vectorially. This would be done as follows (because of rounding, numbers are not exact):

$$\tan = \frac{E_L}{E_R} = \frac{85}{51} = 1.67$$
$$\arctan 1.67 = 59.1°$$
$$\cos = \frac{E_R}{E_Z} \qquad E_Z = \frac{E_R}{\cos}$$
$$E_Z = \frac{51}{0.5135} = \text{approx. } 100V = E_S$$

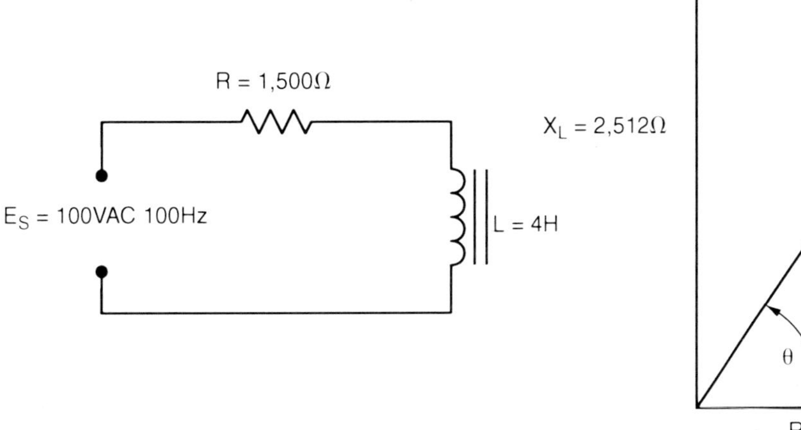

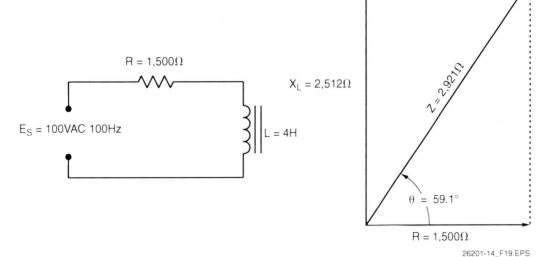

Figure 19 Series RL circuit and vector diagram.

On Site

Vector Analysis

When using vector analysis, the horizontal line is the in-phase value and the vertical line pointing up represents the leading value. The vertical line pointing down represents the lagging value.

In this inductive circuit, the current lags the applied voltage by an angle equal to 59.1°.

NOTE

You could also use the Pythagorean theorem (discussed later) to find this answer.

Figure 20 shows another series RL circuit, its associated waveforms, and vector diagrams. This circuit is used to summarize the characteristics of a series RL circuit:

- The current I flows through all the series components.
- The voltage across X_L, labeled V_L, can be considered an IX_L voltage drop, just as V_R is used for an IR voltage drop.
- The current I through X_L must lag V_L by 90°, as this is the angle between current through an inductance and its self-induced voltage.
- The current I through R and its IR voltage drop have the same phase. There is no reactance to sine wave current in any resistance. Therefore, I and IR have the same phase, or this phase angle is 0°.
- V_T is the vector sum of the two out-of-phase voltages V_R and V_L.
- Circuit current I lags V_T by the phase angle.
- Circuit impedance is the vector sum of R and X_L.

In a series circuit, the higher the value of X_L compared with R, the more inductive the circuit is. This means there is more voltage drop across the inductive reactance, and the phase angle increases toward 90°. The series current lags the applied generator voltage.

Several combinations of X_L and R in series are listed in *Table 1* with their resultant impedance and phase angle. Note that a ratio of 10:1 or more for X_L/R means that the circuit is practically all inductive. The phase angle of 84.3° is only slightly less than 90° for the ratio of 10:1, and the total impedance Z is approximately equal to X_L. The voltage drop across X_L in the series circuit will be equal to the applied voltage, with almost none across R.

Table 1 Series R and X_L Combinations

R (Ω)	X_L (Ω)	Z (Ω) (Approx.)	Phase Angle (θ) (°)
1	10	$\sqrt{101} = 10$	84.3°
10	10	$\sqrt{200} = 14$	45°
10	1	$\sqrt{101} = 10$	5.7°

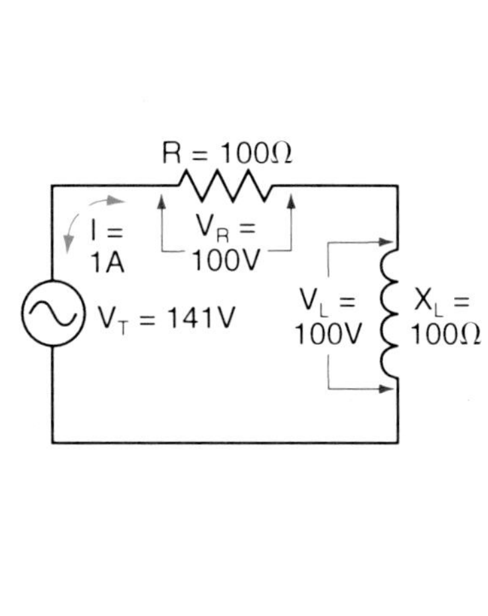

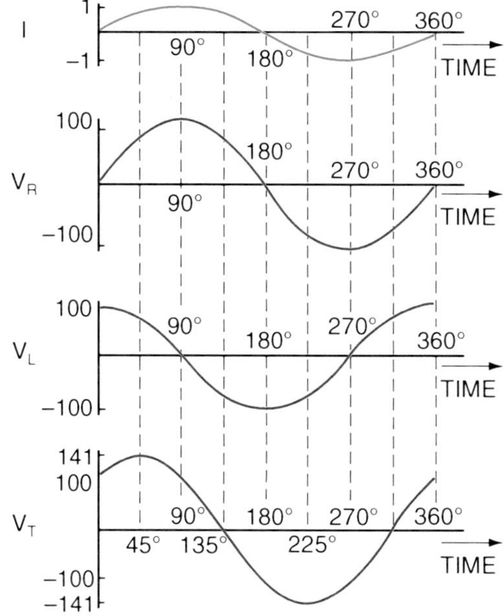

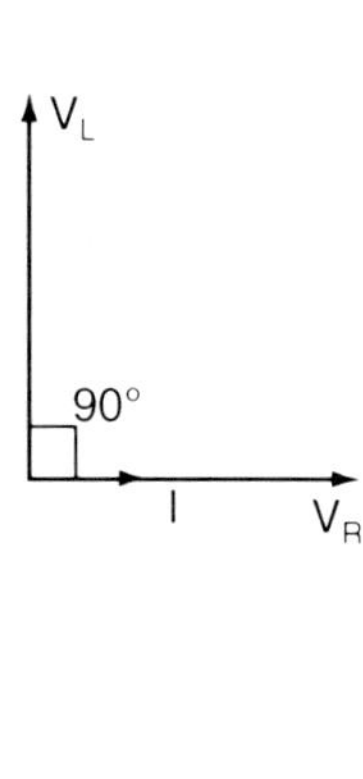

26201-14_F20.EPS

Figure 20 Series RL circuit with waveforms and vector diagram.

At the opposite extreme, when R is 10 times as large as X_L, the series circuit is mainly resistive. The phase angle of 5.7° means the current has almost the same phase as the applied voltage, the total impedance Z is approximately equal to R, and the voltage drop across R is practically equal to the applied voltage, with almost none across X_L.

9.1.2 Parallel RL Circuit

In a parallel RL circuit, the resistance and inductance are connected in parallel across a voltage source. Such a circuit thus has a resistive branch and an inductive branch.

The 90° phase angle must be considered for each of the branch currents, instead of voltage drops in a series circuit. Remember that any series circuit has different voltage drops, but one common current. A parallel circuit has different branch currents, but one common voltage.

In the parallel circuit in *Figure 21*, the applied voltage V_A is the same across X_L, R, and the generator, since they are all in parallel. There cannot be any phase difference between these voltages. Each branch, however, has its individual current. For the resistive branch $I_R = V_A/R$; in the inductive branch $I_L = V_A/X_L$.

The resistive branch current I_R has the same phase as the generator voltage V_A. The inductive branch current I_L lags V_A, however, because the current in an inductance lags the voltage across it by 90°.

The total line current, therefore, consists of I_R and I_L, which are 90° out of phase with each other. The phasor sum of I_R and I_L equals the total line current I_T. These phase relations are shown by the waveforms and vectors in *Figure 21*. I_T will lag V_A by some phase angle that results from the vector addition of I_R and I_L.

The impedance of a parallel RL circuit is the total opposition to current flow by the R of the resistive branch and the X_L of the inductive branch. Since X_L and R are vector quantities, they must be added vectorially.

If the line current and the applied voltage are known, Z can also be calculated by the equation:

$$Z = \frac{V_A}{I_{Line}}$$

The Z of a parallel RL circuit is always less than the R or X_L of any one branch. The branch of a parallel RL circuit that offers the most opposition to current flow has the lesser effect on the phase angle of the current.

Several combinations of X_L and R in parallel are listed in *Table 2*. When X_L is 10 times R, the parallel circuit is practically resistive because there is little inductive current in the line. The small value of I_L results from the high X_L. The total impedance

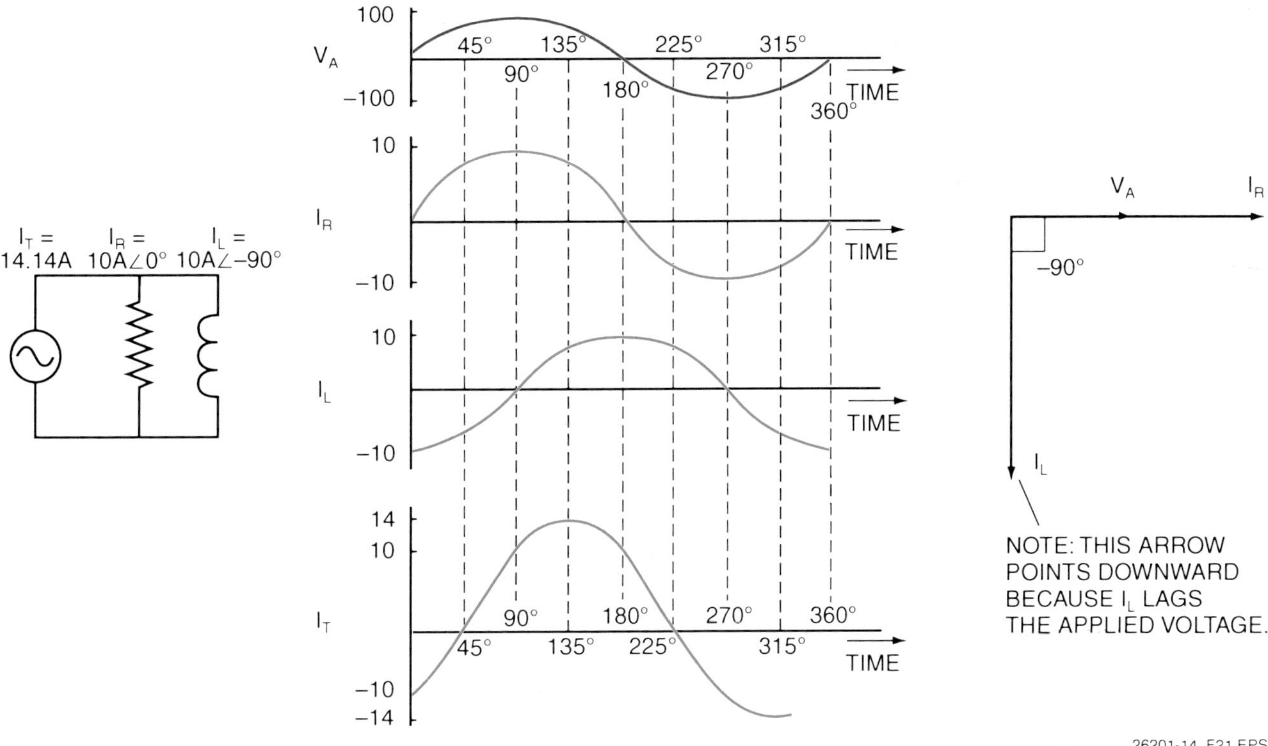

Figure 21 Parallel RL circuit with waveforms and vector diagram.

Table 2 Parallel R and X_L Combinations

R (Ω)	X_L (Ω)	I_R (A)	I_L (A)	I_T (A) (Approx.)	$Z_T = V_A/I_T$ (Ω)	Phase Angle (θ), (°)
1	10	10	1	$\sqrt{101} = 10$	1	−5.7°
10	10	1	1	$\sqrt{2} = 1.4$	7.07	−45°
10	1	1	10	$\sqrt{101} = 10$	1	−84.3°

of the parallel circuit is approximately equal to the resistance then, since the high value of X_L in a parallel branch has little effect. The phase angle of −5.7° is practically 0° because almost all the line current is resistive.

As X_L becomes smaller, it provides more inductive current in the main line. When X_L is $\frac{1}{10}R$, practically all the line current is the I_L component. Then, the parallel circuit is practically all inductive, with a total impedance practically equal to X_L. The phase angle of −84.3° is almost −90° because the line current is mostly inductive. Note that these conditions are opposite from the case of X_L and R in series.

9.2.0 RC Circuits

In a circuit containing resistance only, the current and voltage are in phase. In a circuit of pure capacitance, the current leads the voltage by an angle of 90°. In a circuit that has both resistance and capacitance, the current will lead the voltage by some angle between 0° and 90°.

9.2.1 Series RC Circuit

Figure 22A shows a series RC circuit with resistance R in series with capacitive reactance X_C. Current I is the same in X_C and R since they are in series. Each has its own series voltage drop, equal to IR for the resistance and IX_C for the reactance.

In *Figure 22B*, the phasor is shown horizontal as the reference phase, because I is the same throughout the series circuit. The resistive voltage drop IR has the same phase as I. The capacitor voltage IX_C must be 90° clockwise from I and IR, as the capacitive voltage lags. Note that the IX_C phasor is downward, exactly opposite from an IX_L phasor, because of the opposite phase angle.

If the capacitive reactance alone is considered, its voltage drop lags the series current I by 90°. The IR voltage has the same phase as I, however, because resistance provides no phase shift. Therefore, R and X_C combined in series must be added by vectors because they are 90° out of phase with each other, as shown in *Figure 22C*.

As with inductive reactance, θ (theta) is the phase angle between the generator voltage and its series current. As shown in *Figure 22B* and *Figure 22C*, θ can be calculated from the voltage or impedance triangle.

With series X_C the phase angle is negative, clockwise from the zero reference angle of I because the X_C voltage lags its current. To indicate the negative phase angle, this 90° phasor points downward from the horizontal reference, instead of upward as with the series inductive reactance.

In series, the higher the X_C compared with R, the more capacitive the circuit. There is more voltage drop across the capacitive reactance, and the phase angle increases toward −90°. The series X_C always makes the current lead the applied voltage. With all X_C and no R, the entire applied voltage is across X_C and equals −90°. Several combinations of X_C and R in series are listed in *Table 3*.

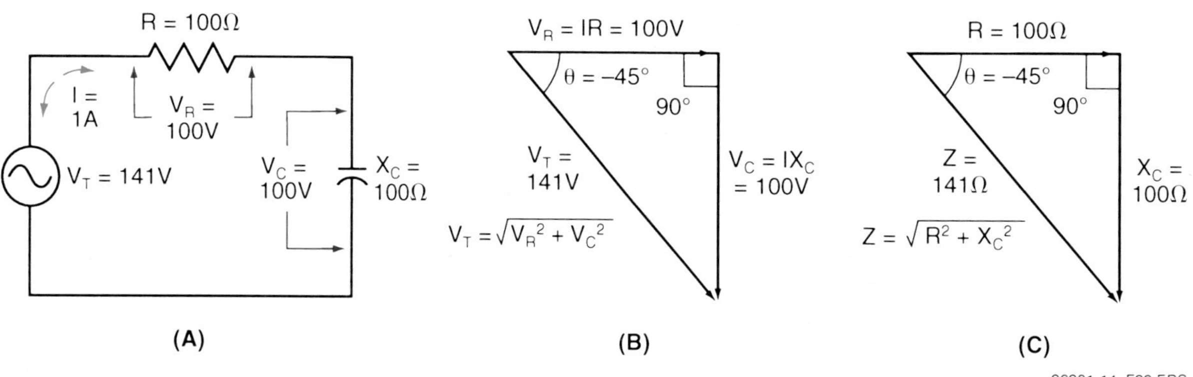

Figure 22 Series RC circuit with vector diagrams.

Table 3 Series R and X_C Combinations

R (Ω)	X_C (Ω)	Z (Ω) (Approx.)	Phase Angle $(\theta)_Z$ (°)
1	10	$\sqrt{101} = 10$	84.3°
10	10	$\sqrt{200} = 14$	45°
10	1	$\sqrt{101} = 10$	5.7°

9.2.2 Parallel RC Circuit

In a parallel RC circuit, as shown in *Figure 23A*, a capacitive branch as well as a resistive branch are connected across a voltage source. The current that leaves the voltage source divides among the branches, so there are different currents in each branch. The current is therefore not a common quantity, as it is in the series RC circuit.

In a parallel RC circuit, the applied voltage is directly across each branch. Therefore, the branch voltages are equal in value to the applied voltage and all voltages are in phase. Since the voltage is common throughout the parallel RC circuit, it serves as the common quantity in any vector representation of parallel RC circuits. This means the reference vector will have the same phase relationship or direction as the circuit voltage. Note in *Figure 23B* that V_A and I_R are both shown as the 0° reference.

Current within an individual branch of an RC parallel circuit is dependent on the voltage across the branch and on the R or X_C contained in the branch. The current in the resistive branch is in phase with the branch voltage, which is the applied voltage. The current in the capacitive branch leads V_A by 90°. Since the branch voltages are the same, I_C leads I_R by 90°, as shown in *Figure 23B*. Since the branch currents are out of phase, they have to be added vectorially to find the line current.

The phase angle, θ, is 45° because R and X_C are equal, resulting in equal branch currents. The phase angle is between the total current I_T and the generator voltage V_A. However, the phase of V_A is the same as the phase of I_R. Therefore, θ is also between I_T and I_R.

The impedance of a parallel RC circuit represents the total opposition to current flow offered by the resistance and capacitive reactance of the circuit. The equation for calculating the impedance of a parallel RC circuit is:

$$Z = \frac{RX_C}{\sqrt{R^2 + X_C^2}} \text{ or } Z = \frac{V_A}{I_T}$$

For the example shown in *Figure 23*, Z is:

$$Z = \frac{V_A}{I_T} = \frac{100}{14.14\text{A}} = 7.07\Omega$$

This is the opposition in ohms across the generator. This Z of 7.07Ω is equal to the resistance of 10Ω in parallel with the reactance of 10Ω. Notice that the impedance of equal values of R and X_C is not one-half, but equals 70.7% of either one.

When X_C is high relative to R, the parallel circuit is practically resistive because there is little leading capacitive current in the main line. The small value of I_C results from the high reactance of shunt X_C. The total impedance of the parallel circuit is approximately equal to the resistance, since the high value of X_C in a parallel branch has little effect.

As X_C becomes smaller, it provides more leading capacitive current in the main line. When X_C is very small relative to R, practically all the line current is the I_C component. The parallel circuit is practically all capacitive, with a total impedance practically equal to X_C.

The characteristics of different circuit arrangements are shown in *Table 4*.

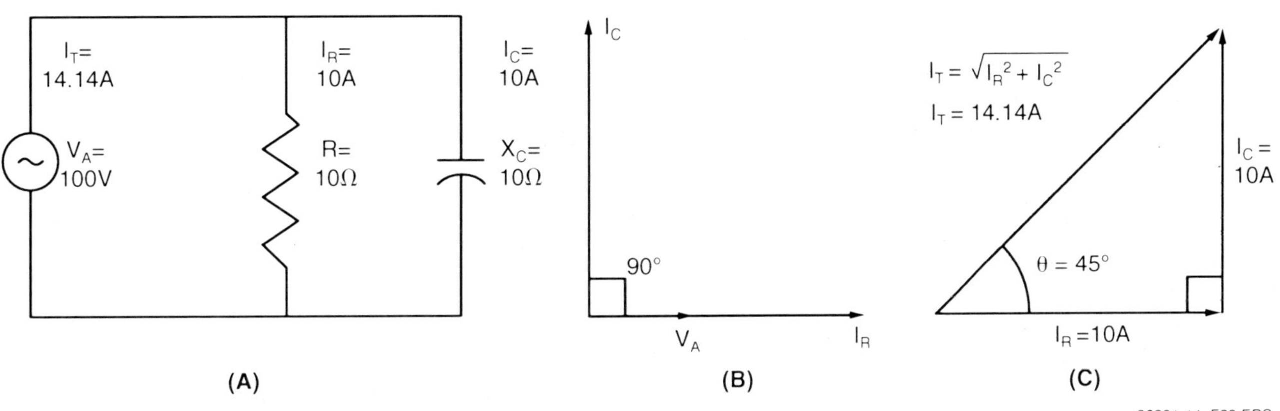

Figure 23 Parallel RC circuit with vector diagrams.

Table 4 Parallel R and X_C Combinations

R (Ω)	X_C (Ω)	I_R (A)	I_C (A)	I_T (A) (Approx.)	Z_T (Ω) (Approx.)	Phase Angle (θ) (°)
1	10	10	1	$\sqrt{101} = 10$	1	5.7°
10	10	1	1	$\sqrt{2} = 1.4$	7.07	45°
10	1	1	10	$\sqrt{101} = 10$	1	84.3°

9.3.0 LC Circuits

An LC circuit consists of an inductance and a capacitance connected in series or in parallel with a voltage source. There is no resistor physically in an LC circuit, but every circuit contains some resistance. Since the circuit resistance of the wiring and voltage source is usually so small, it has little or no effect on circuit operation.

In a circuit with both X_L and X_C, the opposite phase angles enable one to cancel the effect of the other. For X_L and X_C in series, the net reactance is the difference between the two series reactances, resulting in less reactance than either one. In parallel circuits, the I_L and I_C branch currents cancel. The net line current is then the difference between the two branch currents, resulting in less total line current than either branch current.

9.3.1 Series LC Circuit

As in all series circuits, the current in a series LC circuit is the same at all points. Therefore, the current in the inductor is the same as, and in phase with, the current in the capacitor. Because of this, on the vector diagram for a series LC circuit, the direction of the current vector is the reference or in the 0° direction, as shown in *Figure 24*.

When there is current flow in a series LC circuit, the voltage drops across the inductor and capacitor depend on the circuit current and the values of X_L and X_C. The voltage drop across the inductor leads the circuit current by 90°, and the voltage drop across the capacitor lags the circuit current by 90°. Using Kirchhoff's voltage law, the source voltage equals the sum of the voltage drops across the inductor and capacitor, with respect to the polarity of each.

Since the current through both is the same, the voltage across the inductor leads that across the capacitor by 180°. The method used to add the two voltage vectors is to subtract the smaller vector from the larger, and assign the resultant the direction of the larger. When applied to a series LC circuit, this means the applied voltage is equal to the difference between the voltage drops (E_L and E_C), with the phase angle between the applied voltage (E_T) and the circuit current determined by the larger voltage drop.

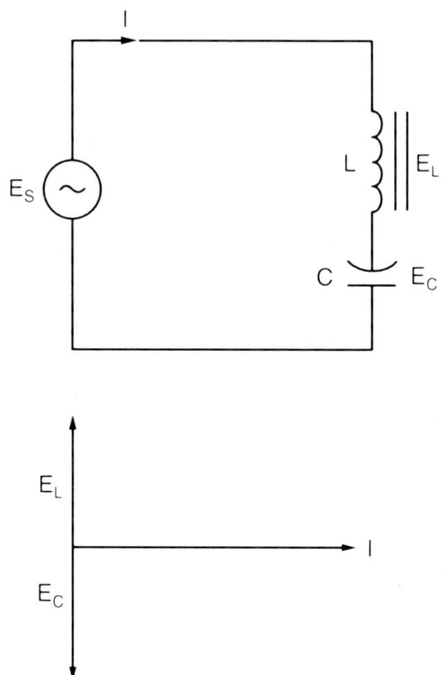

Figure 24 Series LC circuit with vector diagram.

In a series LC circuit, one or both of the voltage drops are always greater than the applied voltage, but remember that they are 180° out of phase. One of them effectively cancels a portion of the other so that the total voltage drop is always equal to the applied voltage.

Recall that X_L is 180° out of phase with X_C. The impedance is then the vector sum of the two reactances. The reactances are 180° apart, so their vector sum is found by subtracting the smaller one from the larger.

Unlike RL and RC circuits, the impedance in an LC circuit is either purely inductive or purely capacitive.

9.3.2 Parallel LC Circuit

In a parallel LC circuit there is an inductance and a capacitance connected in parallel across a voltage source. *Figure 25* shows a parallel LC circuit with its vector diagram.

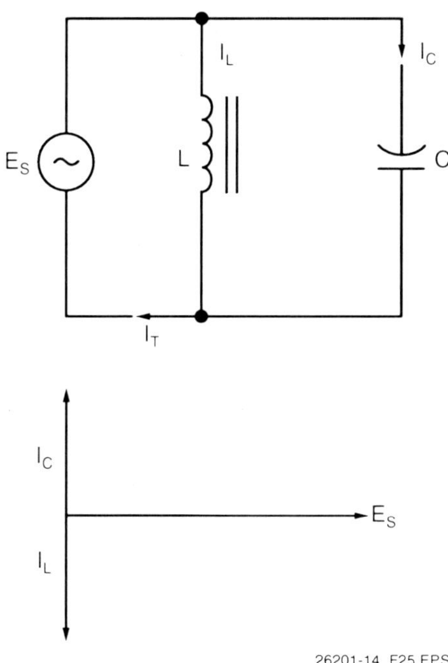

Figure 25 Parallel LC circuit with vector diagram.

As in any parallel circuit, the voltage across the branches is the same as the applied voltage. Since they are actually the same voltage, the branch voltages and applied voltage are in phase. Because of this, the voltage is used as the 0° phase reference and the phases of the other circuit quantities are expressed in relation to the voltage.

The currents in the branches of a parallel LC circuit are both out of phase with the circuit voltage. The current in the inductive branch (I_L) lags the voltage by 90°, while the current in the capacitive branch (I_C) leads the voltage by 90°. Since the voltage is the same for both branches, currents I_L and I_C are therefore 180° out of phase. The amplitudes of the branch currents depend on the value of the reactance in the respective branches.

With the branch currents being 180° out of phase, the line current is equal to their vector sum. This vector addition is done by subtracting the smaller branch current from the larger.

The line current for a parallel LC circuit, therefore, has the phase characteristics of the larger branch current. Thus, if the inductive branch current is the larger, the line current is inductive and lags the applied voltage by 90°; if the capacitive branch current is the larger, the line current is capacitive, and leads the applied voltage by 90°.

The line current in a parallel LC circuit is always less than one of the branch currents and sometimes less than both. The reason that the line current is less than the branch currents is because the two branch currents are 180° out of phase. As a result of the phase difference, some cancellation takes place between the two currents when they combine to produce the line current. The impedance of a parallel LC circuit can be found using the following equations:

$$Z = \frac{X_L \times X_C}{X_L - X_C} \text{ (for } X_L \text{ larger than } X_C\text{)}$$

or:

$$Z = \frac{X_L \times X_C}{X_C - X_L} \text{ (for } X_C \text{ larger than } X_L\text{)}$$

When using these equations, the impedance will have the phase characteristics of the smaller reactance.

9.4.0 RLC Circuits

RLC circuits can be divided into two main categories: series RLC circuits and parallel RLC circuits. These circuits are described in the following sections.

9.4.1 Series RLC Circuit

Circuits in which the inductance, capacitance, and resistance are all connected in series are called series RLC circuits. The fundamental properties of series RLC circuits are similar to those for series LC circuits. The differences are caused by the effects of the resistance. Any practical series LC circuit contains some resistance. When the resistance is very small compared to the circuit reactance, it has almost no effect on the circuit and can be considered as zero. When the resistance is appreciable, though, it has a significant effect on the circuit operation and therefore must be considered in any circuit analysis. In a series RLC circuit, the same current flows through each component. The phase relationships between the voltage drops are the same as they were in series RC, RL, and LC circuits. The voltage drops across the inductance and capacitance are 180° out of phase. With current the same throughout the circuit as a reference, the inductive voltage drop (E_L) leads the resistive voltage drop (E_R) by 90°, and the capacitive voltage drop (E_C) lags the resistive voltage drop by 90°.

Figure 26 shows a series RLC circuit and the vector diagram used to determine the applied voltage. The vector sum of the three voltage drops is equal to the applied voltage. However, to calculate this vector sum, a combination of the methods learned for LC, RL, and RC circuits must be used. First, calculate the combined voltage drop of the two reactances. This value is designated E_X and is found as in pure LC circuits by subtracting the smaller reactive voltage drop from the larger. This is shown in *Figure 26* as E_X. The result of this calculation is the net reactive voltage drop and is either inductive or

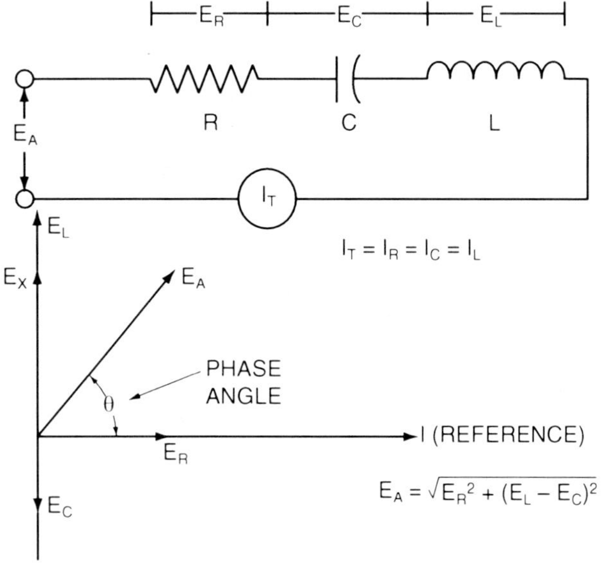

Figure 26 Series RLC circuit and vector diagram.

capacitive, depending on which of the individual voltage drops is larger. In *Figure 26*, the net reactive voltage drop is inductive since $E_L > E_C$. Once the net reactive voltage drop is known, it is added vectorially to the voltage drop across the resistance.

The angle between the applied voltage E_A and the voltage across the resistance E_R is the same as the phase angle between E_A and the circuit current. The reason for this is that E_R and I are in phase.

The impedance of a series RLC circuit is the vector sum of the inductive reactance, the capacitive reactance, and the resistance. This is done using the same method as for voltage drop calculations.

When X_L is greater than X_C, the net reactance is inductive, and the circuit acts essentially as an RL circuit. Similarly, when X_C is greater than X_L, the net reactance is capacitive, and the circuit acts as an RC circuit.

The same current flows in every part of a series RLC circuit. The current always leads the voltage across the capacitance by 90° and is in phase with the voltage across the resistance. The phase relationship between the current and the applied voltage, however, depends on the circuit impedance. If the impedance is inductive (X_L greater than X_C), the current is inductive and lags the applied voltage by some phase angle less than 90°. If the impedance is capacitive (X_C greater than X_L), the current is capacitive, and leads the applied voltage by some phase angle also less than 90°. The angle of the lead or lag is determined by the relative values of the net reactance and the resistance.

The greater the value of X or the smaller the value of R, the larger the phase angle, and the more reactive (or less resistive) the current. Similarly, the smaller the value of X or the larger the value of R, the more resistive (or less reactive) the current. If either R or X is 10 or more times greater than the other, the circuit will essentially act as though it is purely resistive or reactive, as the case may be.

9.4.2 Parallel RLC Circuit

A parallel RLC circuit is basically a parallel LC circuit with an added parallel branch of resistance. The solution of a parallel circuit involves the solution of a parallel LC circuit, and then the solution of either a parallel RL circuit or a parallel RC circuit. The reason for this is that a parallel combination of L and C appears to the source as a pure L or a pure C. So by solving the LC portion of a parallel RLC circuit first, the circuit is reduced to an equivalent RL or RC circuit.

The distribution of the voltage in a parallel RLC circuit is no different from what it is in a parallel LC circuit, or in any parallel circuit. The branch voltages are all equal and in phase, since they are the same as the applied voltage. The resistance is simply another branch across which the applied voltage appears. Because the voltages throughout the circuit are the same, the applied voltage is again used as the θ phase reference.

Figure 27 shows the current relationship in a parallel RLC circuit.

The three branch currents in a parallel RLC circuit are an inductive current I_L, a capacitive current I_C, and a resistive current I_R. Each is independent of the others, and depends only on the applied voltage and the branch resistance or reactance.

The three branch currents all have different phases with respect to the branch voltages. I_L lags the voltage by 90°, I_C leads the voltage by 90°, and I_R is in phase with the voltage. Since the voltages are the same, I_L and I_C are 180° out of phase with each other, and both are 90° out of phase with I_R. Because I_R is in phase with the voltage, it has the same zero-reference direction as the voltage. So I_C leads I_R by 90°, and I_L lags I_R by 90°.

The line current (I_T), or total current, is the vector sum of the three branch currents, and can be calculated by adding I_L, I_C, and I_R vectorially. Whether the line current leads or lags the applied voltage depends on which of the reactive branch currents (I_L or I_C) is the larger. If I_L is larger, I_T lags the applied voltage. If I_C is larger, I_T leads the applied voltage.

To determine the impedance of a parallel RLC circuit, first determine the net reactance X of the inductive and capacitive branches. Then use X to determine the impedance Z, the same as in a parallel RL or RC circuit.

Whenever Z is inductive, the line current will lag the applied voltage. Similarly, when Z is capacitive, the line current will lead the applied voltage.

Think About It

AC Circuits

The photo below shows a simple series circuit comprised of an On/Off switch, small lamp, motor, and capacitor. How would you classify this circuit? When energized, which components insert resistance, inductive reactance, and capacitive reactance into the circuit?

26201-14_SA04.EPS

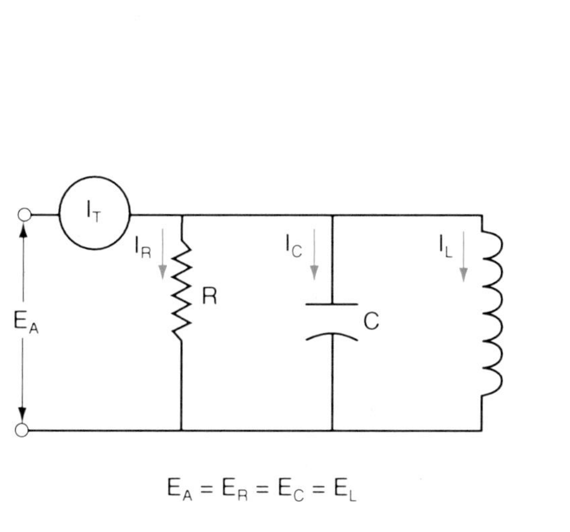

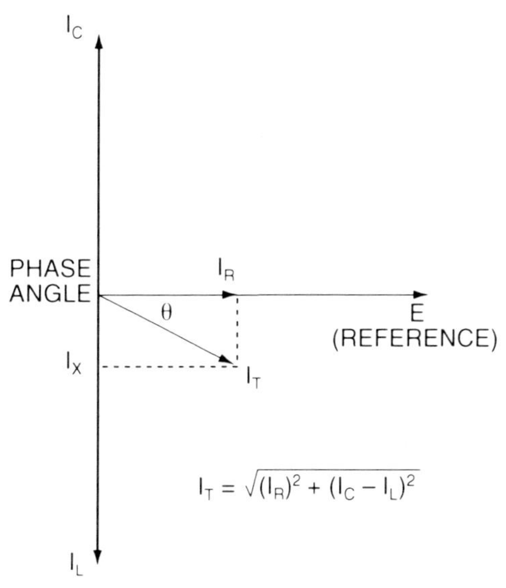

26201-14_F27.EPS

Figure 27 Parallel RLC circuit and vector diagram.

10.0.0 Power in AC Circuits

In DC circuits, the power consumed is the sum of all the I^2R heating in the resistors. It is also equal to the power produced by the source, which is the product of the source voltage and current. In AC circuits containing only resistors, the above relationship also holds true.

10.1.0 True Power

The power consumed by resistance is called true power and is measured in units of watts. True power is the product of the resistor current squared and the resistance:

$$P_T = I^2R$$

This formula applies because current and voltage have the same phase across a resistance. To find the corresponding value of power as a product of voltage and current, this product must be multiplied by the cosine of the phase angle θ:

$$P_T = I^2R \text{ or } P_T = EI\cos\theta$$

Where E and I are in rms values to calculate the true power in watts, multiplying I by the cosine of the phase angle provides the resistive component for true power equal to I^2R.

For example, a series RL circuit has 2A through a 100Ω resistor in series with the X_L of 173Ω. Therefore:

$$P_T = I^2R$$
$$P_T = 4 \times 100$$
$$P_T = 400W$$

Furthermore, in this circuit the phase angle is 60° with a cosine of 0.5. The applied voltage is 400V. Therefore:

$$P_T = EI\cos\theta$$
$$P_T = 400 \times 2 \times 0.5$$
$$P_T = 400W$$

In both cases, the true power is the same (400W) because this is the amount of power supplied by the generator and dissipated in the resistance. Either formula can be used for calculating the true power.

10.2.0 Apparent Power

In ideal AC circuits containing resistors, capacitors, and inductors, the only mechanism for power consumption is $I^2_{eff}R$ heating in the resistors. Inductors and capacitors consume no power. The only function of inductors and capacitors is to store and release energy. However, because of the phase shifts that are introduced by these elements, the power consumed by the resistors is not equal to the product of the source voltage and current. The product of the source voltage and current is called apparent power and has units of volt-amperes (VA).

The apparent power is the product of the source voltage and the total current. Therefore, apparent power is actual power delivered by the source. The formula for apparent power is:

$$P_A = (E_A)(I)$$

Figure 28 shows a series RL circuit and its associated vector diagram.

This circuit is used to calculate the apparent power and compare it to the circuit's true power:

$$P_A = (E_A)(I)$$
$$P_A = (400V)(2A)$$
$$P_A = 800VA$$

$$P_T = EI\cos\theta$$
$$\theta = \frac{R}{Z} = \frac{100}{200} = 0.5 \text{ or } \cos 60°$$
$$P_T = (400V)(2A)(\cos 60°)$$
$$P_T = (400V)(2A)(0.5)$$
$$P_T = 400W$$

Note that the apparent power formula is the product of EI alone without considering the cosine of the phase angle.

10.3.0 Reactive Power

Reactive power is that portion of the apparent power that is caused by inductors and capacitors in the circuit. Inductance and capacitance are always present in real AC circuits. No work is performed by reactive power; the power is stored in the inductors and capacitors, then returned to the circuit. Therefore, reactive power is always 90° out of phase with true power. The units for reactive power are volt-amperes-reactive (VARs).

On Site

Third-Order Harmonics

Harmonics are frequencies that are multiples of the basic frequency. For example, 180Hz is three times the frequency of 60Hz and is therefore known as a third-order harmonic. Harmonics are caused by a variety of devices, such as personal computers, uninterruptible power supplies, adjustable speed drives, and electronic ballasts. Third-order harmonics, also known as triplen harmonics or triplens, may cause transformer overheating and should be a consideration when sizing transformers.

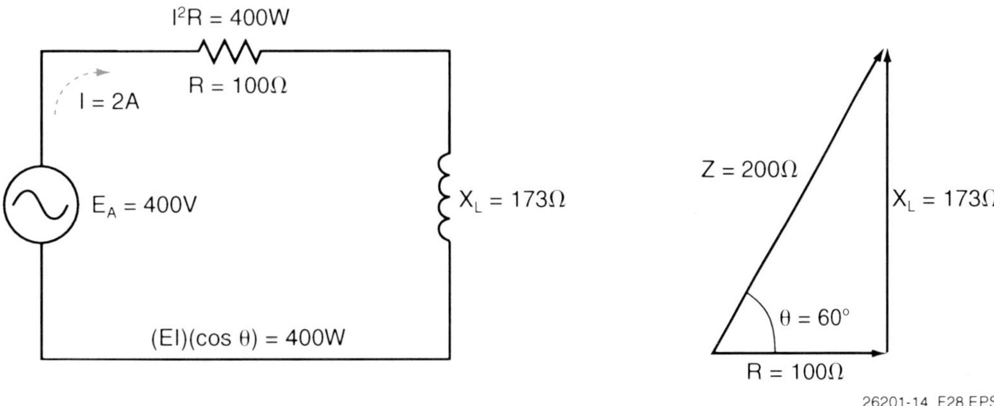

Figure 28 Power calculations in an AC circuit.

In general, for any phase angle θ between E and I, multiplying EI by sine θ gives the vertical component at 90° for the value of the VARs. In *Figure 28*, the value of sine 60° is 800 × 0.866 = 692.8 VARs.

Note that the factor sine θ for the VARs gives the vertical or reactive component of the apparent power EI. However, multiplying EI by cosine θ as the power factor gives the horizontal or resistive component for the real power.

10.4.0 Power Factor

Because it indicates the resistive component, cosine θ is the power factor (pf) of the circuit, converting the EI product to real power. For series circuits, use the formula:

$$pf = \cos\theta = \frac{R}{Z}$$

For parallel circuits, use the formula:

$$pf = \cos\theta = \frac{I_R}{I_T}$$

In *Figure 28* as an example of a series circuit, R and Z are used for the calculations:

$$pf = \cos\theta = \frac{R}{Z} = \frac{100\Omega}{200\Omega} = 0.5$$

The power factor is not an angular measure but a numerical ratio with a value between 0 and 1, equal to the cosine of the phase angle. With all resistance and zero reactance, R and Z are the same for a series circuit of I_R and I_T and are the same for a parallel circuit. The ratio is 1. Therefore, unity power factor means a resistive circuit. At the opposite extreme, all reactance with zero resistance makes the power factor zero, meaning that the circuit is all reactive.

The power factor gives the relationship between apparent power and true power. The power factor can thus be defined as the ratio of true power to apparent power:

$$pf = \frac{P_T}{P_A}$$

For example, calculate the power factor of the circuit shown in *Figure 29*.

The true power is the product of the resistor current squared and the resistance:

$$P_T = I^2R$$
$$P_T = 10A^2 \times 10\Omega$$
$$P_T = 1{,}000W$$

The apparent power is the product of the source voltage and total current:

$$P_A = (I_T)(E)$$
$$P_A = 10.2A \times 100V$$
$$P_A = 1{,}020VA$$

Calculating total current:

$$I_T = \sqrt{I_R^2 + (I_C - I_L)^2} = \sqrt{10A^2 + (4A - 2A)^2}$$
$$I_T = 10.2A$$

The power factor is the ratio of true power to apparent power:

$$pf = \frac{P_T}{P_A}$$
$$pf = \frac{1{,}000}{1{,}020}$$
$$pf = 0.98$$

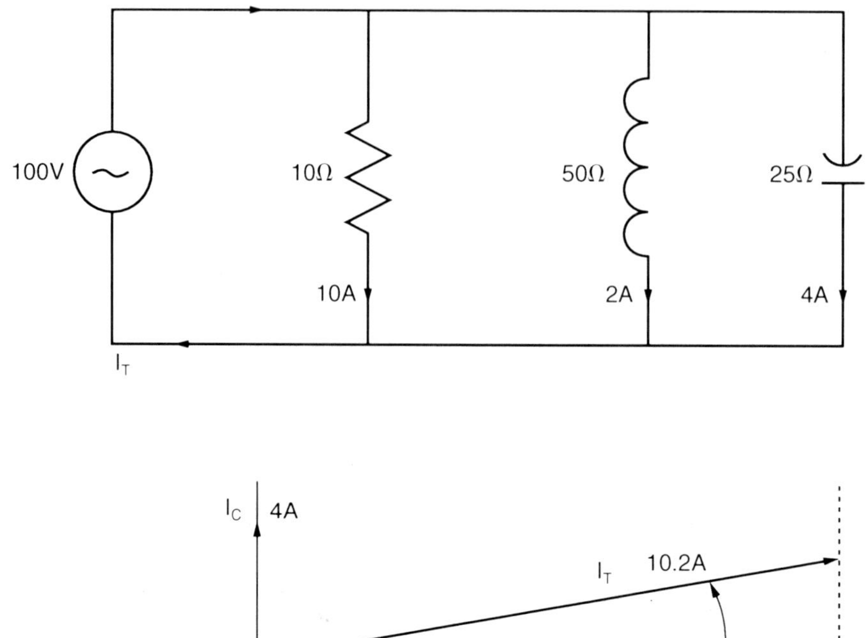

Figure 29 RLC circuit calculation.

As illustrated in the previous example, the power factor is determined by the system load. If the load contained only resistance, the apparent power would equal the true power and the power factor would be at its maximum value of one. Purely resistive circuits have a power factor of unity or one. If the load is more inductive than capacitive, the apparent power will lag the true power and the power factor will be lagging. If the load is more capacitive than inductive, the apparent power will lead the true power and the power factor will be leading. If there is any reactive load on the system, the apparent power will be greater than the true power and the power factor will be less than one.

10.5.0 Power Triangle

The phase relationships among the three types of AC power are easily visualized on the power triangle shown in *Figure 30*. The true power (W) is the horizontal leg, the apparent power (VA) is the hypotenuse, and the cosine of the phase angle between them is the power factor. The vertical leg of the triangle is the reactive power and has units of volt-amperes-reactive (VARs).

As illustrated on the power triangle (*Figure 30*), the apparent power will always be greater than the true power or reactive power. Also, the apparent power is the result of the vector addition of true and reactive power. The power magnitude relationships shown in *Figure 30* can be derived from the Pythagorean theorem for right triangles:

$$c^2 = a^2 + b^2$$

Therefore, c also equals the square root of $a^2 + b^2$, as shown below:

$$c = \sqrt{a^2 + b^2}$$

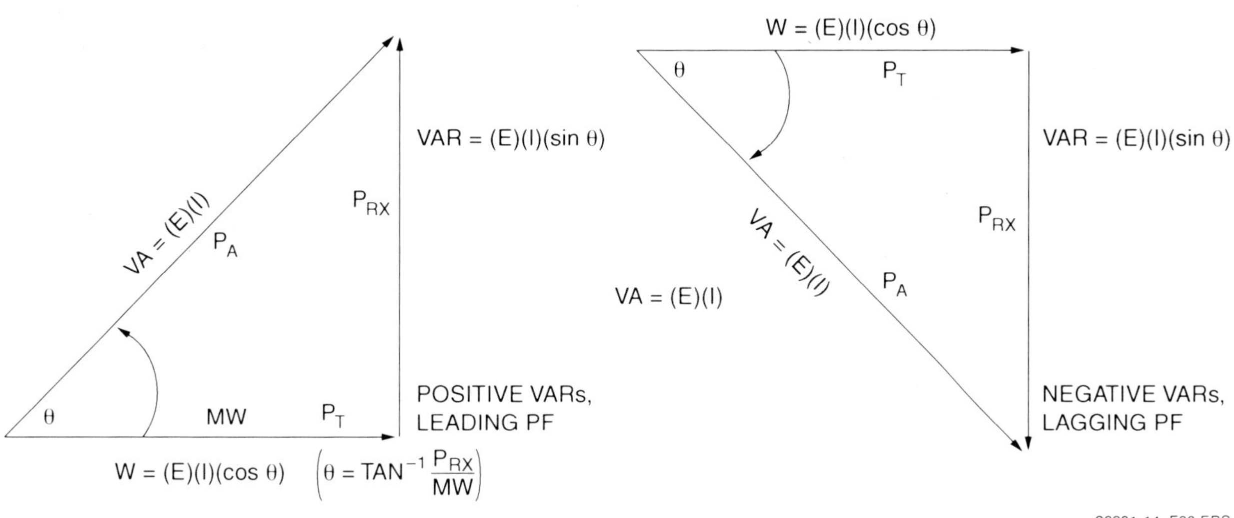

Figure 30 Power triangle.

11.0.0 Transformers

A transformer is a device that transfers electrical energy from one circuit to another by electromagnetic induction (transformer action). The electrical energy is always transferred without a change in frequency, but may involve changes in the magnitudes of voltage and current. Because a transformer works on the principle of electromagnetic induction, it must be used with an input source voltage that varies in amplitude.

11.1.0 Transformer Construction

Figure 31 shows the basic components of a transformer. In its most basic form, a transformer consists of:

- A primary coil or winding
- A secondary coil or winding
- A core that supports the coils or windings

A simple transformer action is shown in *Figure 32*. The primary winding is connected to a 60Hz AC voltage source. The magnetic field or flux builds up (expands) and collapses (contracts) around the primary winding. The expanding and contracting magnetic field around the primary winding cuts the secondary winding and induces an alternating voltage into the winding. This voltage causes AC to flow through the load. The voltage may be stepped up or down depending on the design of the primary and secondary windings.

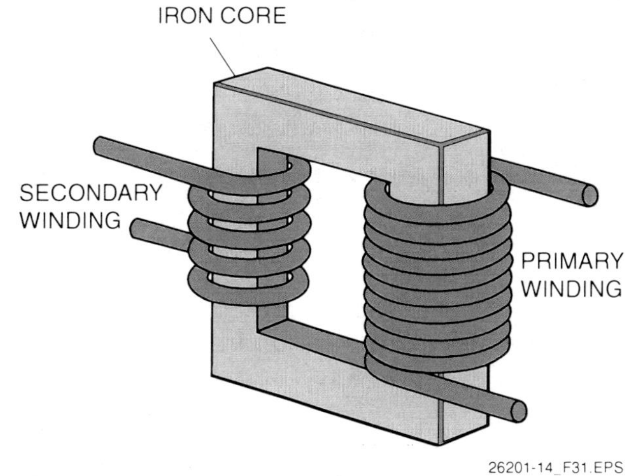

Figure 31 Basic components of a transformer.

Think About It

Power Factor

In power distribution circuits, it is desirable to achieve a power factor approaching a value of 1 in order to obtain the most efficient transfer of power. In AC circuits where there are large inductive loads such as in motors and transformers, the power factor can be considerably less than 1. For example, in a highly inductive motor circuit, if the voltage is 120V, the current is 12A, and the current lags the voltage by 60°, the power factor is 0.5 or 50% (cosine of 60° = 0.5). The apparent power is 1,440VA (120V × 12A), but the true power is only 720W [120V × (0.5 × 12A) = 720W]. This is a very inefficient circuit. What would you do to this circuit in order to achieve a circuit having a power factor as close to 1 as possible?

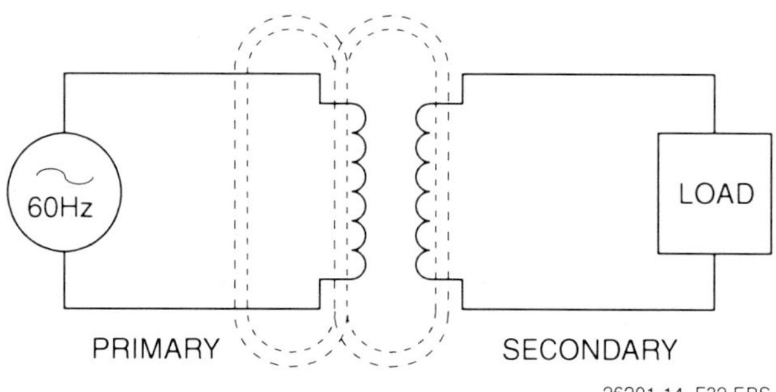

Figure 32 Transformer action.

11.1.1 Core Characteristics

Commonly used core materials are air, soft iron, and steel. Each of these materials is suitable for particular applications and unsuitable for others. Generally, air-core transformers are used when the voltage source has a high frequency (above 20kHz). Iron-core transformers are usually used when the source frequency is low (below 20kHz). A soft-iron transformer is very useful where the transformer must be physically small yet efficient. The iron-core transformer provides better power transfer than the air-core transformer. Laminated sheets of steel are often used in a transformer to reduce one type of power loss known as eddy currents. These are undesirable currents, induced into the core, which circulate around the core. Laminating the core reduces these currents to smaller levels. These steel laminations are insulated with a nonconducting material, such as varnish, and then formed into a core as shown in *Figure 33*. It takes about 50 such laminations to make a core one inch thick. The most efficient transformer core is one that offers the best path for the most lines of flux, with the least loss in magnetic and electrical energy.

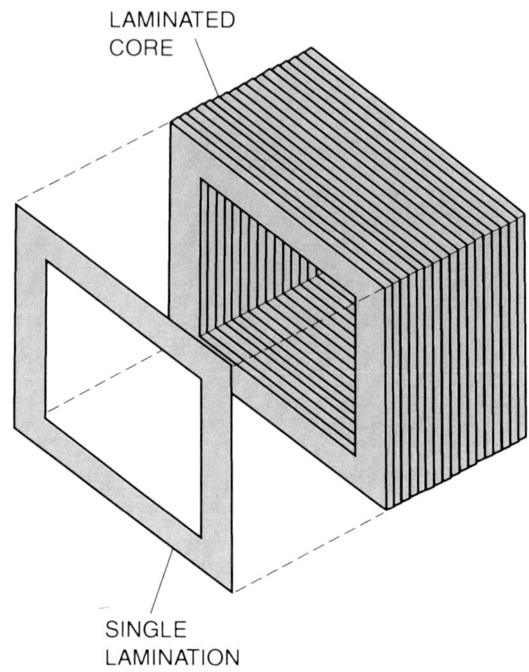

Figure 33 Steel laminated core.

11.1.2 Transformer Windings

A transformer consists of two coils called windings, which are wrapped around a core. The transformer operates when a source of AC voltage is connected to one of the windings and a load device is connected to the other. The winding that is connected to the source is called the primary winding. The winding that is connected to the load is called the secondary winding. *Figure 34* shows a cut-away view of a typical transformer.

The wire is coated with varnish so that each turn of the winding is insulated from every other turn. In a transformer designed for high-voltage applications, sheets of insulating material such as paper are placed between the layers of windings to provide additional insulation.

When the primary winding is completely wound, it is wrapped in insulating paper or cloth. The secondary winding is then wound on top of the primary winding. After the secondary winding is complete, it too is covered with insulating paper. Next, the iron core is inserted into and around the windings as shown.

Sometimes, terminals may be provided on the enclosure for connections to the windings.

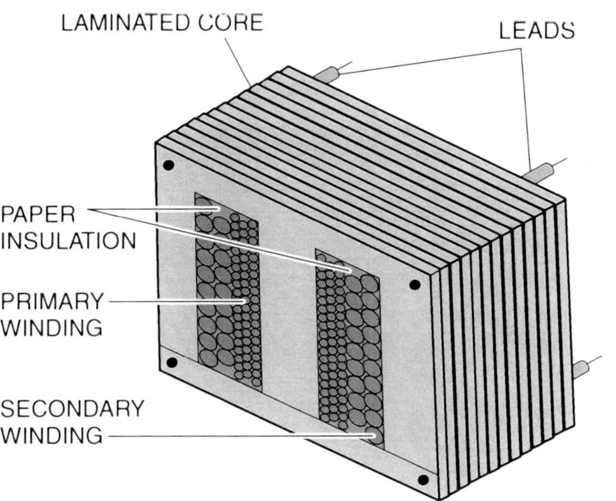

Figure 34 Cut-away view of a transformer core.

On Site

Transformers

Transformers are essential to all electrical systems and all types of electronic equipment. They are especially essential to the operation of AC high-voltage power distribution systems. Transformers are used to both step up voltage and step down voltage throughout the distribution process. For example, a typical power generation plant might generate AC power at 13,800V, step it up to 230,000V for distribution over long transmission lines, step it down to 13,800V again at substations located at different points for local distribution, and finally step it down again to 240V and 120V for lighting and local power use.

The figure shows four leads, two from the primary and two from the secondary. These leads are to be connected to the source and load, respectively.

11.2.0 Operating Characteristics

The operating characteristics of transformers are determined by the applied voltage and the winding design. These affect both the exciting current (no-load condition) and the phase relationship between the windings during transformer operation.

11.2.1 Energized with No Load

A no-load condition is said to exist when a voltage is applied to the primary, but no load is connected to the secondary. Assume the output of the secondary is connected to a load by a switch that is open. Because of the open switch, there is no current flowing in the secondary winding. With the switch open and an AC voltage applied to the primary, there is, however, a very small amount of current, called exciting current, flowing in the primary. Essentially, what this current does is excite the coil of the primary to create a magnetic field. The amount of exciting current is determined by three factors: the amount of voltage applied (E_A); the resistance (R) of the primary coil's wire and core losses; and the X_L, which is dependent on the frequency of the exciting current. These factors are all controlled by transformer design.

This very small amount of exciting current serves two functions:

- Most of the exciting energy is used to support the magnetic field of the primary.
- A small amount of energy is used to overcome the resistance of the wire and core. This is dissipated in the form of heat (power loss).

Exciting current will flow in the primary winding at all times to maintain this magnetic field, but no transfer of energy will take place as long as the secondary circuit is open.

11.2.2 Phase Relationship

The secondary voltage of a simple transformer may be either in phase or out of phase with the primary voltage. This depends on the direction in which the windings are wound and the arrangement of the connection to the external circuit (load). Simply, this means that the two voltages may rise and fall together, or one may rise while the other is falling. Transformers in which the secondary voltage is in phase with the primary are referred to as like-wound transformers, while those in which the voltages are 180° out of phase are called unlike-wound transformers.

Dots are used to indicate points on a transformer schematic symbol that have the same instantaneous polarity (points that are in phase). The use of phase-indicating dots is illustrated in *Figure 35*. In the first part of the figure, both the primary and secondary windings are wound from top to bottom in a clockwise direction, as viewed from above the windings. When constructed in this manner, the top lead of the primary and the top

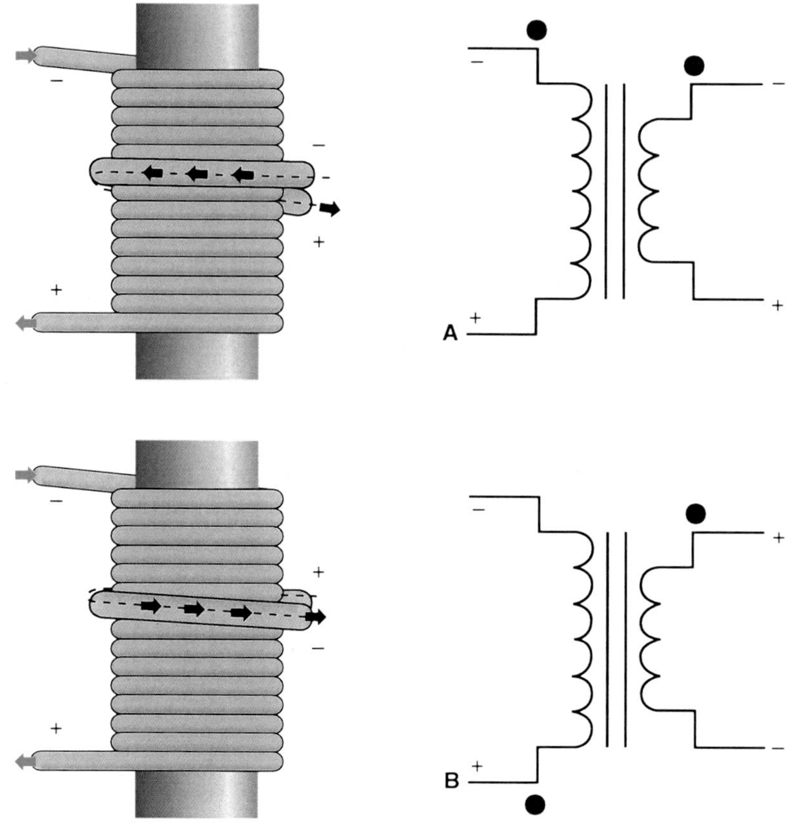

Figure 35 Transformer winding polarity.

lead of the secondary have the same polarity. This is indicated by the dots on the transformer symbol.

The second part of the figure illustrates a transformer in which the primary and secondary are wound in opposite directions. As viewed from above the windings, the primary is wound in a clockwise direction from top to bottom, while the secondary is wound in a counterclockwise direction. Notice that the top leads of the primary and secondary have opposite polarities. This is indicated by the dots being placed on opposite ends of the transformer symbol. Thus, the polarity of voltage at the terminals of the transformer secondary depends on the direction in which the secondary is wound with respect to the primary.

11.3.0 Turns and Voltage Ratios

To understand how a transformer can be used to step up or step down voltage, the term *turns ratio* must be understood. The total voltage induced into the secondary winding of a transformer is determined mainly by the ratio of the number of turns in the primary to the number of turns in the secondary, and by the amount of voltage applied to the primary. Therefore, to set up a formula:

$$\text{Turns ratio} = \frac{\text{Number of turns in the primary}}{\text{Number of turns in the secondary}}$$

The first transformer in *Figure 36* shows a transformer whose primary consists of 10 turns of wire, and whose secondary consists of a single turn of wire. As lines of flux generated by the primary expand and collapse, they cut both the 10 turns of the primary and the single turn of the secondary. Since the length of the wire in the secondary is approximately the same as the length of the wire in each turn of the primary, the EMF induced into the secondary will be the same as the EMF induced into each turn of the primary.

This means that if the voltage applied to the primary winding is 10 volts, the CEMF in the primary is almost 10 volts. Thus, each turn in the primary will have an induced CEMF of approximately $\frac{1}{10}$ of the total applied voltage, or one volt. Since the same flux lines cut the turns in both the secondary and the primary, each turn will have an EMF of one volt induced into it. The first transformer in *Figure 36* has only one turn in the secondary, thus, the EMF across the secondary is one volt.

The second transformer represented in *Figure 36* has a 10-turn primary and a two-turn secondary. Since the flux induces one volt per turn, the

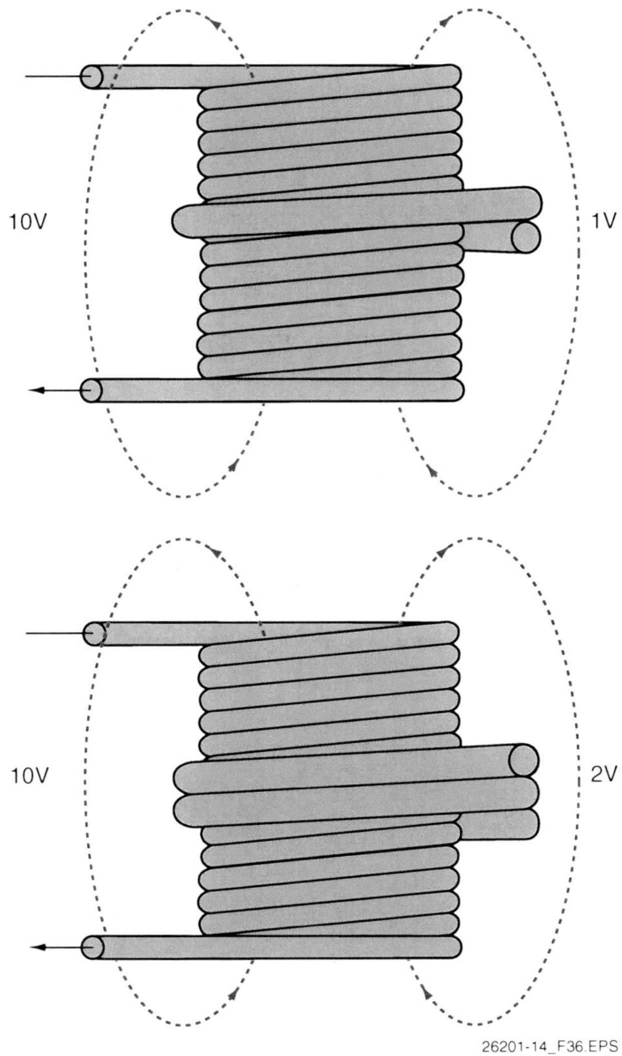

Figure 36 Transformer turns ratio.

total voltage across the secondary is two volts. Notice that the volts per turn are the same for both primary and secondary windings. Since the CEMF in the primary is equal (or almost) to the applied voltage, a proportion may be set up to express the value of the voltage induced in terms of the voltage applied to the primary and the number of turns in each winding. This proportion also shows the relationship between the number of turns in each winding and the voltage across each winding, and is expressed by the equation:

$$\frac{E_S}{E_P} = \frac{N_S}{N_P}$$

Where:

N_P = number of turns in the primary
E_P = voltage applied to the primary
E_S = voltage induced in the secondary
N_S = number of turns in the secondary

The equation shows that the ratio of secondary voltage to primary voltage is equal to the ratio of secondary turns to primary turns. The equation can be written as:

$$E_P N_S = E_S N_P$$

For example, a transformer has 100 turns in the primary, 50 turns in the secondary, and 120VAC applied to the primary (E_P). What is the voltage across the secondary (E_S)?

Think About It

Turns and Voltage Ratios

What is the magnitude of the voltage and current supplied by the secondary of the transformer in the circuit shown below?

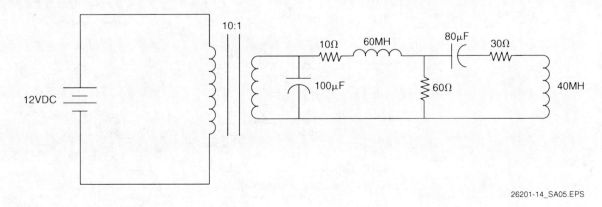

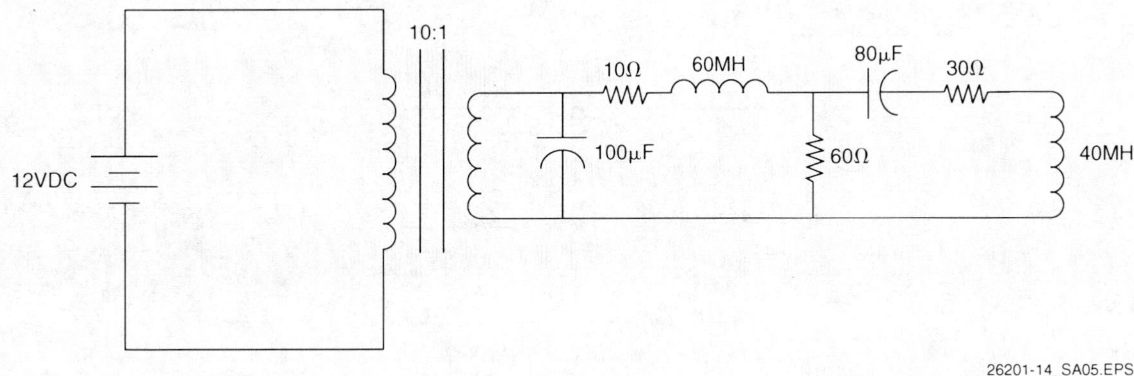

$$N_S = 50 \text{ turns}$$

$$\frac{E_S}{E_P} = \frac{N_S}{N_P} \text{ or } E_S = \frac{E_P N_S}{N_P}$$

$$E_S = \frac{120V \times 50 \text{ turns}}{100 \text{ turns}} = 60VAC$$

The transformers in *Figure 36* have fewer turns in the secondary than in the primary. As a result, there is less voltage across the secondary than across the primary. A transformer in which the voltage across the secondary is less than the voltage across the primary is called a step-down transformer. The ratio of a 10-to-1 step-down transformer is written as 10:1.

A transformer that has fewer turns in the primary than in the secondary will produce a greater voltage across the secondary than the voltage applied to the primary. A transformer in which the voltage across the secondary is greater than the voltage applied to the primary is called a step-up transformer. The ratio of a 1-to-4 step-up transformer should be written 1:4. Notice in the two ratios that the value of the primary winding is always stated first.

11.4.0 Types of Transformers

Transformers are widely used to permit the use of trip coils and instruments of moderate current and voltage capacities and to measure the characteristics of high-voltage and high-current circuits. Since secondary voltage and current are directly related to primary voltage and current, measurements can be made under the low-voltage or low-current conditions of the secondary circuit and still determine primary characteristics. Tripping transformers and instrument transformers are examples of this use of transformers.

The primary or secondary coils of a transformer can be tapped to permit multiple input and output voltages. *Figure 37* shows several tapped transformers. The center-tapped transformer is particularly important because it can be used in conjunction with other components to convert an AC input to a DC output.

11.4.1 Isolation Transformer

Isolation transformers are wound so that their primary and secondary voltages are equal. Their purpose is to electrically isolate a piece of electrical equipment from the power distribution system.

Many pieces of electronic equipment use the metal chassis on which the components are mounted as part of the circuit (*Figure 38*). Personnel working with this equipment may accidentally come in contact with the chassis, completing the circuit to ground, and receive a shock as shown in *Figure 38(A)*. If the resistances of their body and the ground path are low, the shock can be fatal. Placing an isolation transformer in the circuit as shown in *Figure 38(B)* breaks the ground current path that includes the worker. Current can no longer flow from the power supply through the chassis and worker to ground; however, the equipment is still supplied with the normal operating voltage and current.

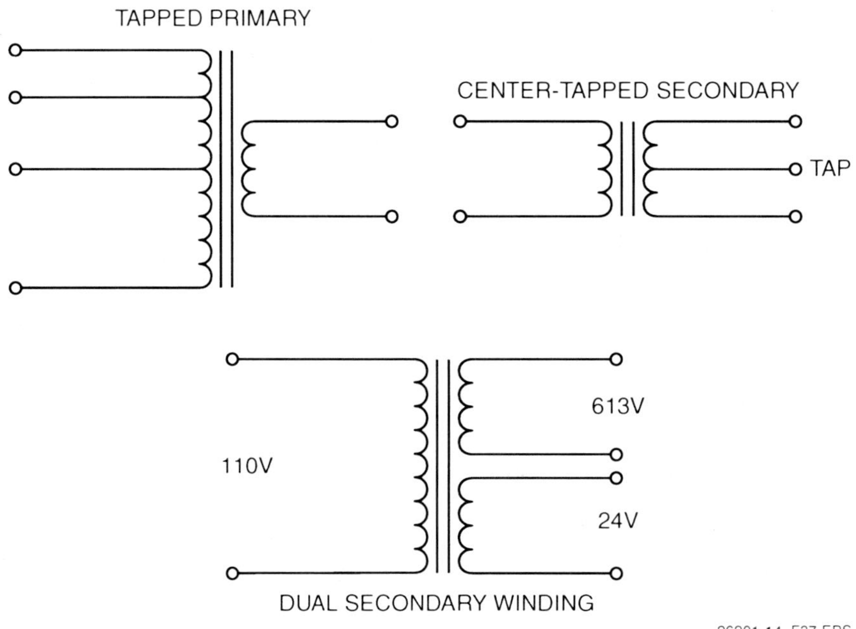

Figure 37 Tapped transformers.

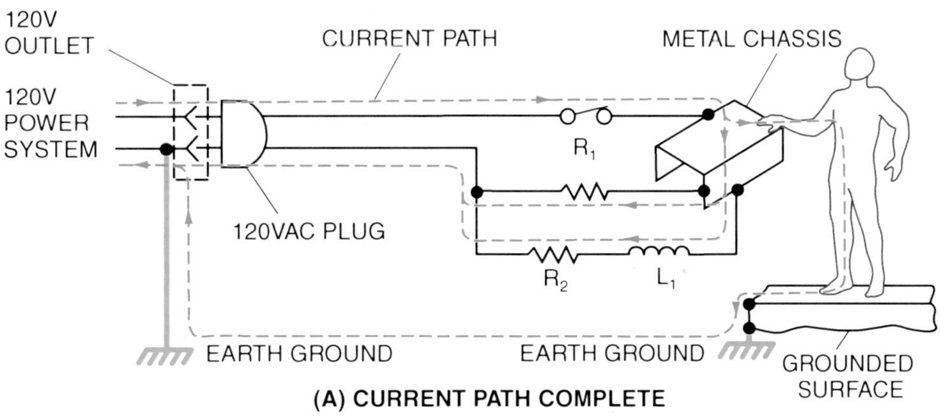

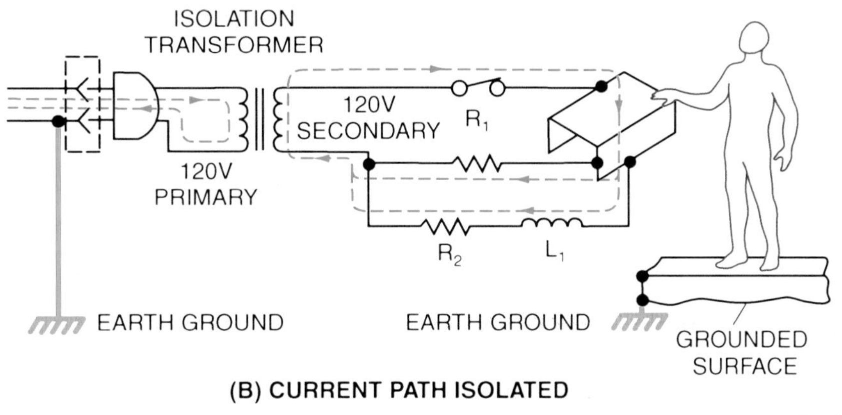

Figure 38 Importance of an isolation transformer.

11.4.2 Autotransformer

In a transformer, it is not necessary for the primary and secondary to be separate and distinct windings. *Figure 39* is a schematic diagram of what is known as an autotransformer. Note that a single coil of wire is tapped to produce what is electrically both a primary and a secondary winding.

The voltage across the secondary winding has the same relationship to the voltage across the primary that it would have if they were two distinct windings. The movable tap in the secondary is used to select a value of output voltage either higher or lower than E_P, within the range of the transformer. When the tap is at Point A, E_S is less than E_P; when the tap is at Point B, E_S is greater than E_P.

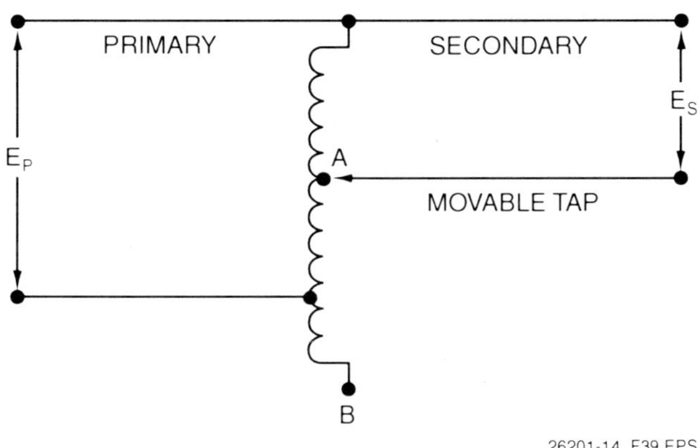

Figure 39 Autotransformer schematic diagram.

Autotransformers rely on self-induction to induce their secondary voltage. The term *autotransformer* can be broken down into two words: auto, meaning self; and transformer, meaning to change potential. The autotransformer is made of one winding that acts as both a primary and a secondary winding. It may be used as either a step-up or step-down transformer. Some common uses of autotransformers are as variable AC voltage supplies and fluorescent light ballast transformers, and to reduce the line voltage for various types of low-voltage motor starters.

11.4.3 Current Transformer

A current transformer differs from other transformers in that the primary is a conductor to the load and the secondary is a coil wrapped around the wire to the load. Just as any ammeter is connected in line with a circuit, the current transformer is connected in series with the current to be measured. *Figure 40* is a diagram of a current transformer.

WARNING!

Do not open circuit a current transformer under load.

Since current transformers are series transformers, the usual voltage and current relationships do not apply. Current transformers vary considerably in rated primary current, but are usually designed with ampere-turn ratios such that the secondary delivers five amperes at full primary load.

Current transformers are generally constructed with only a few turns or no turns in the primary. The voltage in the secondary is induced by the changing magnetic field that exists around a single conductor. The secondary is wound on a circular core, and the large conductor that makes up the primary passes through the hole in its center. Because the primary has few or no turns, the secondary must have many turns (providing a high turns ratio) in order to produce a usable voltage. The advantage of this is that you get an output off the secondary proportional to the current flowing through the primary, without an appreciable voltage drop across the primary. This is because the primary voltage equals the current times the impedance. The impedance is kept near zero by using no or very few primary turns. The disadvantage is that you cannot open the secondary circuit with the primary energized. To do so would cause the secondary current to drop rapidly to zero. This would cause the magnetic field generated by the secondary current to collapse rapidly. The rapid collapse of the secondary

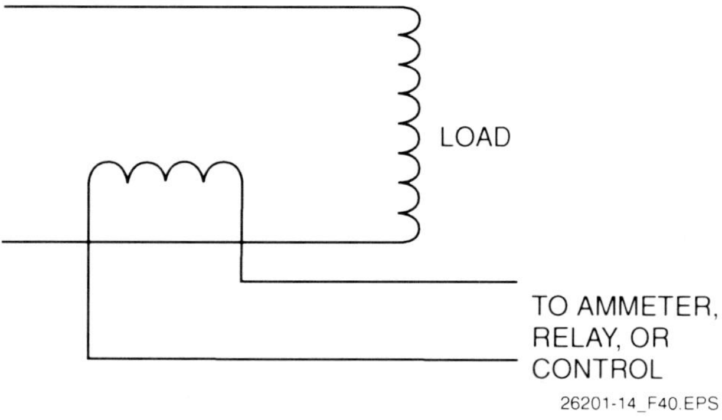

Figure 40 Current transformer schematic diagram.

On Site

Isolation Transformers

In addition to being used to protect personnel from receiving electrical shocks, shielded isolation transformers are widely used to prevent electrical disturbances on power lines from being transmitted into related load circuits. The shielded isolation transformer has a grounded electrostatic shield between the primary and secondary windings that acts to direct unwanted signals to ground.

Case History

AC Power Provides Many Benefits, but Working with It Can Be Dangerous

Working with AC power can be dangerous unless proper safety methods and procedures are followed. The National Institute for Occupational Safety and Health (NIOSH) investigated 224 incidents of electrocutions that resulted in occupational fatalities. One hundred twenty-one of the victims were employed in the construction industry. Two hundred twenty-one of the incidents (99%) involved AC. Of the 221 AC electrocutions, 74 (33%) involved AC voltages less than 600V and 147 (66%) involved 600V or more. Forty of the lower-voltage electrocutions involved 120/240V.

Factors relating to the causes of these electrocutions included the lack of enforcement of existing employer policies including the use of personal protective equipment and the lack of supervisory intervention when existing policies were being violated. Of the 224 victims, 194 (80%) had some type of electrical safety training. Thirty-nine victims had no training at all. It is notable that 100 of the victims had been on the job less than one year.

The Bottom Line: Never assume that you are safe when working at lower voltages. All voltage levels must be considered potentially lethal. Also, safety training does no good if you don't put it into practice every day. Always put safety first.

On Site

Current Transformers

Although the use of a current transformer completely isolates the secondary and the related ammeter from the high-voltage lines, the secondary of a current transformer should never be left open circuited. To do so may result in dangerously high voltage being induced in the secondary.

field through the many turns of the secondary winding would induce a dangerously high voltage in the secondary, creating an equipment and personnel hazard.

Because the output of current transformers is proportional to the current in the primary, they are most often used to power current-sensing meters and relays. This allows the instruments to respond to primary current without having to handle extreme magnitudes of current.

11.4.4 Potential Transformer

The primary of a potential transformer is connected across or in parallel with the voltage to be measured, just as a voltmeter is connected across a circuit. *Figure 41* shows the schematic diagram for a potential transformer.

Potential transformers are basically the same as any other single-phase transformer. Although primary voltage ratings vary widely according to the specific application, secondary voltage ratings are usually 120V, a convenient voltage for meters and relays.

Because the output of potential transformers is proportional to the phase-to-phase voltage of the primary, they are often used to power voltage-sensing meters and relays. This allows the instruments to respond to primary voltage while having to handle only 120V. Also, potential transformers are essentially single-phase step-down transformers. Therefore, power to operate low-voltage auxiliary equipment associated with high-voltage switchgear can be supplied off the high-voltage lines that the equipment serves via potential transformers.

On Site

Potential Transformers

In addition to being used to step down high voltages for the purpose of safe metering, potential transformers are widely used in all kinds of control devices where the condition of high voltages must be monitored. One such example involves the use of a potential transformer-operated contactor in emergency lighting standby generator circuits. Under normal conditions with utility power applied, the contactor is energized and its normally closed contacts are open. If the power fails, the contactor de-energizes, causing its contacts to close and activating the standby generator circuit.

Think About It

Putting It All Together

A power company's distribution system has capacitor banks that are automatically switched into the system by a temperature switch during hot weather. Why?

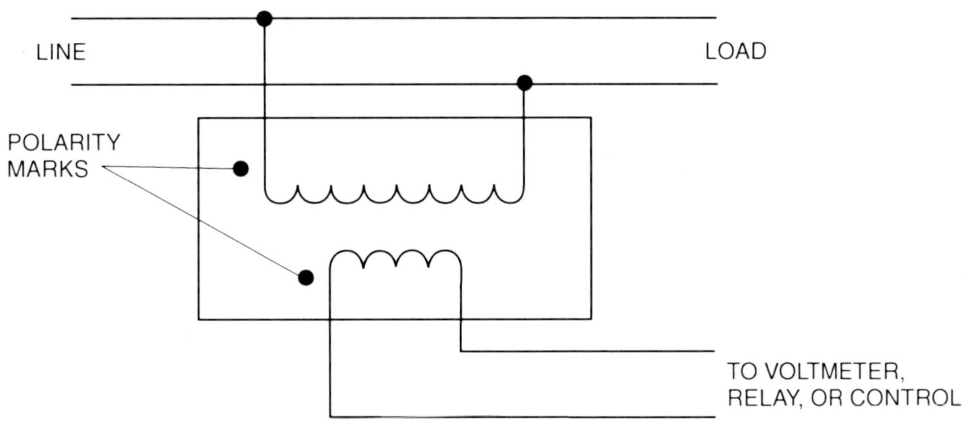

Figure 41 Potential transformer.

SUMMARY

The process by which current is produced electromagnetically is called induction. As the conductor moves across the magnetic field, it cuts the lines of force, and electrons within the conductor flow, creating an electromotive force (EMF). EMF is also known as voltage. There are three conditions that must exist before a current can be produced in this way:

- There must be a magnetic field through which the conductor can pass.
- There must be a conductor in which the voltage will be produced, and the conductor should be perpendicular to the field.
- There must be motion. Either the magnetic field or the conductor must move.

Three factors control the magnitude of the induced current. Voltage will be increased if:

- The speed with which the conductor cuts through the magnetic field is increased (the faster the conductor cuts through the field, the greater the current pulse)
- The strength of the field is increased (the stronger the field, the greater the current pulse)
- The conductor is wound to form a coil (the voltage increases directly with the number of turns of the coil)

A decrease in voltage occurs as the conductor intersects the magnetic field at an angle less than 90°. The greatest current is produced when the conductor intersects the magnetic field at right angles (perpendicular) to the flux lines.

It should be emphasized that a current may be induced by using the magnetic field of a permanent magnet or the magnetic field of another current-carrying conductor (electromagnet).

The magnetic field is among the reasons why phases of current-carrying conductors should not be separated in a raceway; all phase conductors (including the neutral) should be contained in the same raceway. For example, if phase A is separated from phase B and phase C by a metal enclosure, conduit wall, etc., the magnetic field around the conductors will cut across the conduit, causing the conduit to heat up.

Review Questions

1. An electric current always produces _____.
   a. mutual inductance
   b. a magnetic field
   c. capacitive reactance
   d. high voltage
2. The number of cycles an alternating electric current undergoes per second is known as _____.
   a. amperage
   b. frequency
   c. voltage
   d. resistance
3. What is the peak voltage in a circuit with an rms voltage of 120VAC?
   a. 117 volts
   b. 120 volts
   c. 150 volts
   d. 170 volts
4. Which of the following conditions exist in a circuit of pure resistance?
   a. The voltage and current are in phase.
   b. The voltage and current are 90° out of phase.
   c. The voltage and current are 120° out of phase.
   d. The voltage and current are 180° out of phase.
5. In a purely resistive AC circuit where 240V is applied across a 10-ohm resistor, the amperage is _____.
   a. 10A
   b. 24A
   c. 60A
   d. 120A
6. When the current increases in an AC circuit, what role does inductance play?
   a. It increases the current.
   b. It plays no role at all.
   c. It causes the overcurrent protection to open.
   d. It reduces the current.
7. All of the following factors increase the inductance of a coil, *except* a _____.
   a. greater number of turns
   b. longer core
   c. wider coil
   d. magnetic core
8. Which of the following conditions exist in a circuit of pure inductance?
   a. The voltage and current are in phase.
   b. The voltage and current are 90° out of phase.
   c. The voltage and current are 120° out of phase.
   d. The voltage and current are 180° out of phase.
9. True or False? Reactance increases with an increase in inductance.
   a. True
   b. False
10. Capacitance is measured in _____.
    a. farads
    b. joules
    c. henrys
    d. amps
11. The total capacitance of two 15μF capacitors connected in parallel is _____.
    a. 5μF
    b. 10μF
    c. 15μF
    d. 30μF
12. The opposition to current flow offered by the capacitance of a circuit is known as _____.
    a. mutual inductance
    b. pure resistance
    c. inductive reactance
    d. capacitive reactance
13. The total opposition to current flow in an AC circuit is known as _____.
    a. resistance
    b. capacitive reactance
    c. inductive reactance
    d. impedance
14. A power factor is not an angular measure, but a numerical ratio with a value between 0 and 1, equal to the _____.
    a. sine of the phase angle
    b. tangent of the phase angle
    c. cosine of the phase angle
    d. cotangent of the phase angle
15. The two windings of a conventional transformer are known as the _____.
    a. mutual and inductive windings
    b. high and low voltage windings
    c. primary and secondary windings
    d. step-up and step-down windings

Module 26201-14
Supplemental Exercises

1. In a circuit containing resistance only, the voltage and current are ________________ with one another.

2. The power consumed by ________________ is called true power.

3. The power factor is the ratio of ________________ power to ________________ power.

4. LC circuits consist of a(n) ________________ and a(n) ________________ connected in series or in parallel with a voltage source.

5. As in all series circuits, the ________________ in a series LC circuit is the same at all points.

6. On a transformer with 100 volts applied to the primary, 200 turns in the primary, and a secondary with 100 turns, the secondary voltage is ________________ volts.

7. A(n) ________________ can be used to electrically isolate a piece of equipment from the power distribution system.

8. Reactive power is the portion of apparent power that is caused by ________________ and ________________ in the circuit.

9. The primary winding in a transformer is connected to the ________________.

10. Apparent power is the product of the source ________________ and the ________________.

11. The secondary winding in a transformer is connected to the ________________.

12. True power is measured in ________________.

13. VAR is the unit of measurement for ________________ power.

14. The average value is calculated from all the values in a sine wave for only half a cycle. The average value formula is AVG = ________________ × peak value.

15. In purely resistive circuits, the current and voltage are related by Ohm's law, which is E = IR. Define the variables.

    E = ________________

    I = ________________

    R = ________________

Trade Terms Introduced in This Module

Capacitance: The storage of electricity in a capacitor; capacitance produces an opposition to voltage change. The unit of measurement for capacitance is the farad (F) or microfarad (μF).

Frequency: The number of cycles an alternating electric current, sound wave, or vibrating object undergoes per second.

Hertz (Hz): A unit of frequency; one hertz equals one cycle per second.

Impedance: The opposition to current flow in an AC circuit; impedance includes resistance (R), capacitive reactance (X_C), and inductive reactance (X_L). Impedance is measured in ohms (Ω).

Inductance: The creation of a voltage due to a time-varying current; also, the opposition to current change, causing current changes to lag behind voltage changes. The unit of measure for inductance is the henry (H).

Micro (μ): Prefix designating one-millionth of a unit. For example, one microfarad is one-millionth of a farad.

Peak voltage: The peak value of a sinusoidally varying (cyclical) voltage or current is equal to the root-mean-square (rms) value multiplied by the square root of two (1.414). AC voltages are usually expressed as rms values; that is, 120 volts, 208 volts, 240 volts, 277 volts, 480 volts, etc., are all rms values. The peak voltage, however, differs. For example, the peak value of 120 volts (rms) is actually $120 \times 1.414 = 169.71$ volts.

Radian: An angle at the center of a circle, subtending (opposite to) an arc of the circle that is equal in length to the radius.

Reactance: The opposition to alternating current (AC) due to capacitance (X_C) and/or inductance (X_L).

Root-mean-square (rms): The square root of the average of the square of the function taken throughout the period. The rms value of a sinusoidally varying voltage or current is the effective value of the voltage or current.

Self-inductance: A magnetic field induced in the conductor carrying the current.

Additional Resources

This module presents thorough resources for task training. The following resource material is suggested for further study.

Introduction to Electric Circuits, Latest Edition. New York: Prentice Hall.

Principles of Electric Circuits, Latest Edition. New York: Prentice Hall.

Figure Credits

Associated Builders and Contractors, Inc., Module opener

Topaz Publications, Inc., Figure 13C, SA04

NCCER CURRICULA — USER UPDATE

NCCER makes every effort to keep its textbooks up-to-date and free of technical errors. We appreciate your help in this process. If you find an error, a typographical mistake, or an inaccuracy in NCCER's curricula, please fill out this form (or a photocopy), or complete the online form at **www.nccer.org/olf**. Be sure to include the exact module ID number, page number, a detailed description, and your recommended correction. Your input will be brought to the attention of the Authoring Team. Thank you for your assistance.

Instructors – If you have an idea for improving this textbook, or have found that additional materials were necessary to teach this module effectively, please let us know so that we may present your suggestions to the Authoring Team.

NCCER Product Development and Revision

13614 Progress Blvd., Alachua, FL 32615

Email: curriculum@nccer.org
Online: www.nccer.org/olf

❑ Trainee Guide ❑ AIG ❑ Exam ❑ PowerPoints Other ______________________

Craft / Level: Copyright Date:

Module ID Number / Title:

Section Number(s):

Description:

Recommended Correction:

Your Name:

Address:

Email: Phone:

Conductor Installations

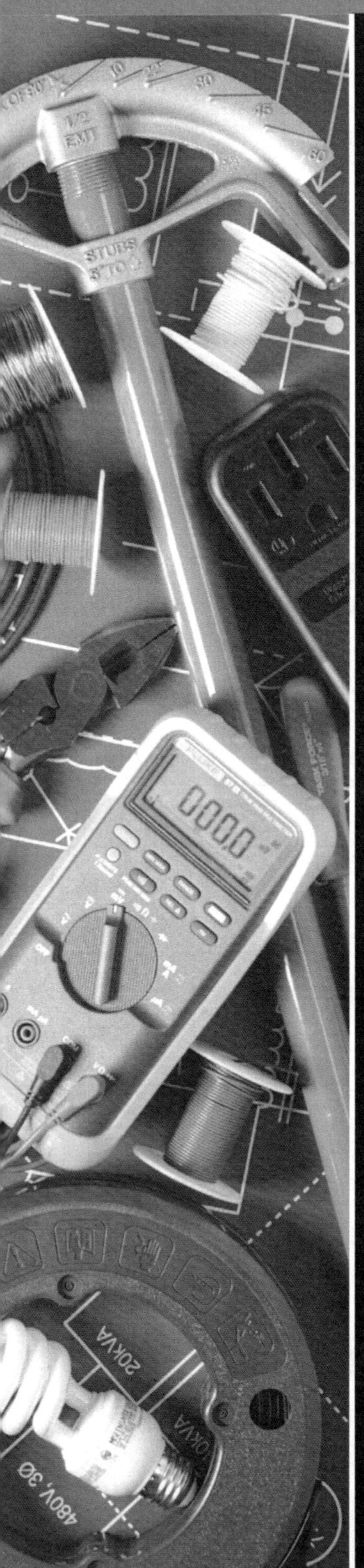

U.S. Department of Transportation Headquarters

Clark Construction Group built the new headquarters for the U.S. Department of Transportation (DOT) in Washington, D.C. on an 11-acre parcel. The 2,000,000-square-foot office complex spans two city blocks.

26206-14

Trainees with successful module completions may be eligible for credentialing through NCCER's National Registry. To learn more, go to **www.nccer.org** or contact us at **1.888.622.3720.** Our website has information on the latest product releases and training, as well as online versions of our *Cornerstone* magazine and Pearson's product catalog.

Your feedback is welcome. You may email your comments to **curriculum@nccer.org,** send general comments and inquiries to **info@nccer.org,** or fill in the User Update form at the back of this module.

This information is general in nature and intended for training purposes only. Actual performance of activities described in this manual requires compliance with all applicable operating, service, maintenance, and safety procedures under the direction of qualified personnel. References in this manual to patented or proprietary devices do not constitute a recommendation of their use.

26206-14

Conductor Installations

Objectives

When you have completed this module, you will be able to do the following:

1. Explain the importance of communication during a cable-pulling operation.
2. Plan and set up for a cable pull.
3. Set up reel stands and spindles for a wire-pulling installation.
4. Explain how mandrels, swabs, and brushes are used to prepare conduit for conductors.
5. Properly install a pull line for a cable-pulling operation.
6. Explain how and when to support conductors in vertical conduit runs.
7. Describe the installation of cables in cable trays.
8. Calculate the probable stress or tension in cable pulls.

Performance Tasks

Under the supervision of the instructor, you should be able to do the following:

1. Prepare multiple conductors for pulling in a raceway system.
2. Prepare multiple conductors for pulling using a wire-pulling basket.

Trade Terms

Basket grip
Cable grip
Capstan
Clevis
Conductor support
Conduit piston
Fish line
Fish tape
Setscrew grip
Sheave
Soap

Required Trainee Materials

1. Paper and pencil
2. Appropriate personal protective equipment
3. Copy of the latest edition of the *National Electrical Code*®

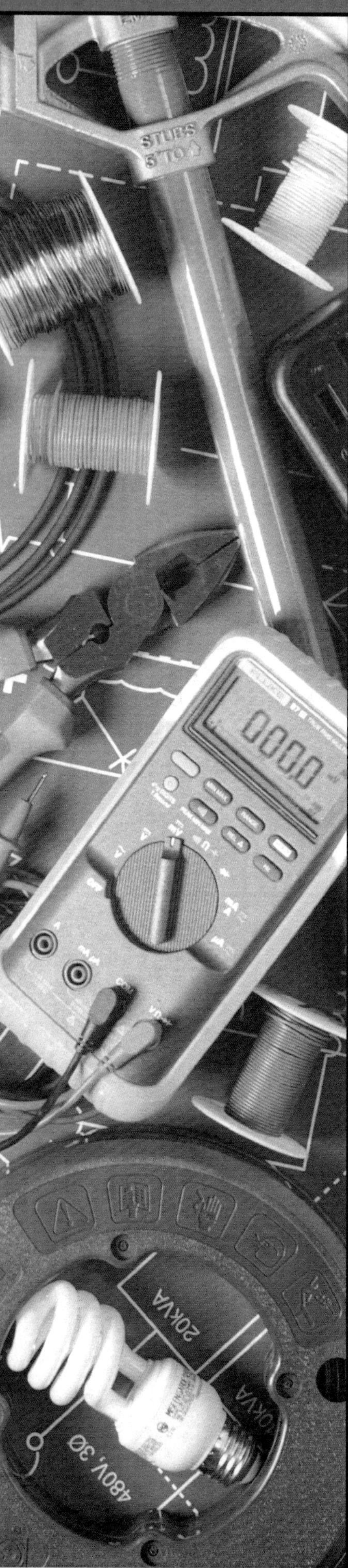

Contents

Topics to be presented in this module include:

Figures and Tables

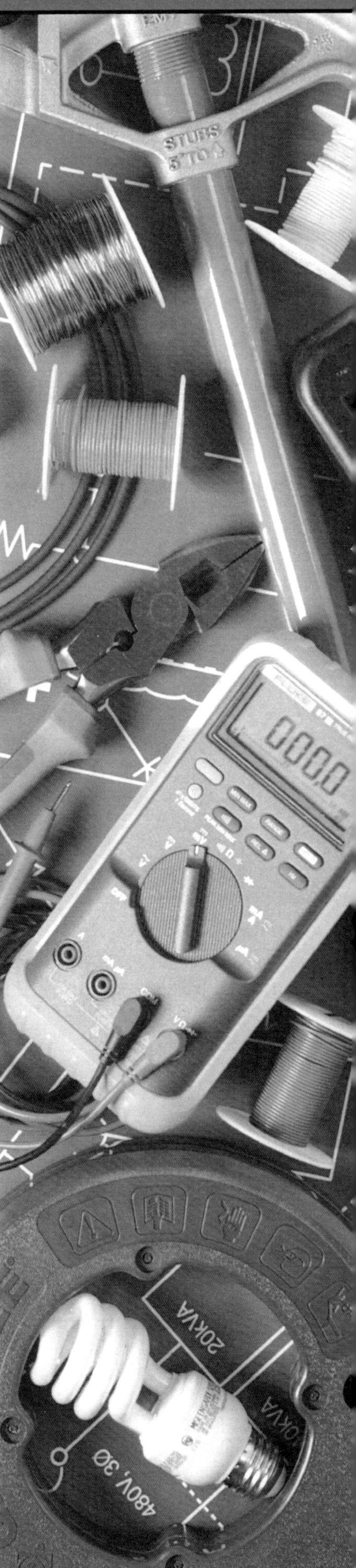

1.0.0 Introduction

In most cases, the installation of conductors in raceway systems is merely routine. However, there are certain practices that can reduce labor and materials and help prevent damage to the conductors. The use of modern equipment, such as vacuum **fish tape** systems, is one way to reduce labor during this phase of the wiring installation.

There are three types of fish tape: steel, nylon, and fiberglass. They also come in different weights for various applications. The proper size and length of the fish tape, as well as the type, should be one of the first considerations. For example, if most of the runs between branch circuit outlets are 20' or less, a short fish tape of 25' will easily handle the job and will not have the weight and bulk of a larger tape. When longer runs are encountered, the required length of the fish tape should be enclosed in one of the metal or plastic fish tape reels. This way, the fish tape can be rewound on the reel as the pull is being made to avoid having an excessive length of tape lying around on the floor or deck.

WARNING!

Never fish a steel tape through or into enclosures or raceways containing an energized conductor.

When several bends are present in the raceway system, the insertion of the fish tape may be made easier by using flexible fish tape leaders on the end of the fish tape.

The combination blower and vacuum fish tape systems are ideal for use on long runs and can save time. Basically, the system consists of a tank and air pump with accessories. An electrician can vacuum or blow a line or tape in any size conduit from ½" through 4", or even up to 6" conduit with optional accessories.

After the fish tape is inserted in the raceway system, the conductors must be firmly attached by some approved means. On short runs, where only a few conductors are involved, all that is necessary is to strip the insulation from the ends of the wires, bend these ends around the hook in the fish tape, and securely tape them in place. Where several wires are to be pulled together, the wires should be staggered and the fish tape securely taped at the point of attachment so that the overall diameter is not increased any more than is absolutely necessary.

Basket grips (*Figure 1*) are available in many sizes for almost any size and combination of conductors. They are designed to hold the conductors firmly to the fish tape and can save time and trouble that would be required when taping wires.

In all but very short runs, the wires should be lubricated with wire lubricant prior to attempting the pull, as well as during the pull. Some of this

On Site

Nonconductive Fish Tape

When fishing conductors in a conduit or raceway that already contains existing energized (live) conductors, the safest method is to turn off and lock out/tag the power sources for all the live conductors. However, in some rare instances, fishing a conductor through a conduit or raceway containing other live conductors may be unavoidable. In this case, always request your supervisor's approval before proceeding and always use a nonconductive fish tape made of nylon or fiberglass.

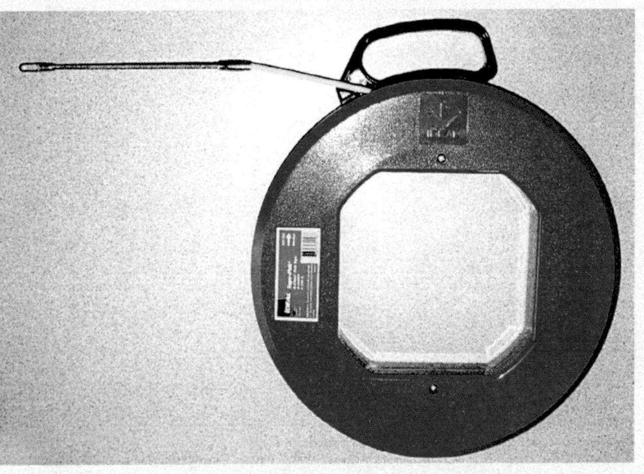

26206-14_SA01.EPS

lubricant should also be applied to the inside of the conduit.

Wire dispensers are great aids in keeping the conductors straight and facilitating the pull. Many different types of wire dispensers are available to handle virtually any size spool of wire or cable. Some dispensers are stationary, while others have casters that make it easy to move heavy spools to the pulling location (*Figure 2*). Wheeled dispensers are sometimes called wire caddies.

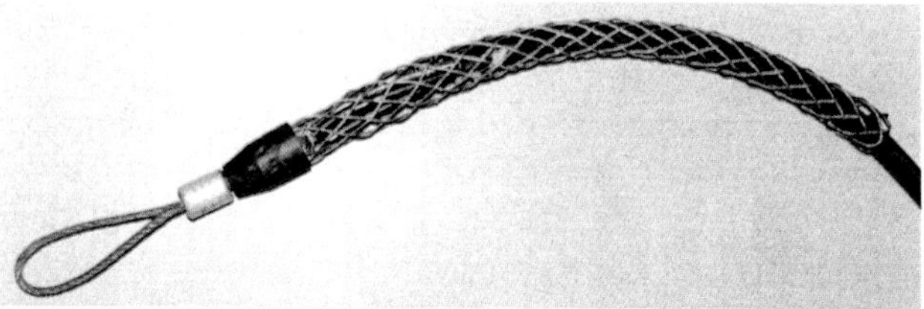

26206-14_F01.EPS

Figure 1 Basket grip.

CABLE DISPENSER

WIRE CADDY

26206-14_F02.EPS

Figure 2 Wire dispensers.

2.0.0 Planning the Installation

The importance of planning any wire-pulling installation cannot be over-stressed. Proper planning will make the work go easier and labor will be saved.

Large sizes of conductors are usually shipped on reels, involving considerable weight and bulk. Consequently, setting up these reels for the pull, measuring cable run lengths, and similar preliminary steps will often involve a relatively large amount of the total cable installation time. Therefore, consideration must be given to reel setup space, proper equipment, and moving the cable reels into place.

Whenever possible, the conductors should be pulled directly from the shipping reels without pre-handling them. This can usually be done through proper coordination of the ordering of the conductors with the job requirements. While doing so requires extremely close checking of the drawings and on-the-job measurements (allowing for adequate lengths of conductors in pull boxes, elbows, troughs, connections, and splices), the extra effort is well worth the time to all involved.

When the lengths of cable have been established, the length of cable per reel can be ordered so that the total length per reel will be equal to the total of a given number of raceway lengths, and the reel so identified.

In most cases, the individual cables of the proper length for a given number of runs are reeled separately onto two or more reels at the factory, depending on the number of conductors in the runs.

When individual conductors are shipped on separate reels, it is necessary to set up for the same number of reels as the number of conductors to be pulled into a given run, as shown in *Figure 3*.

As an extra precaution against error in calculating the lengths of conductors involved, it is a good idea to actually measure all runs with a fish tape before starting the cable pull, adding for makeup to reach the terminations, and accounting for discarding the cable underneath the pulling sleeve or pulling wrap, as it will have been excessively stressed during the pull. Check these totals against the totals indicated on the reels. Under normal cable delivery schedules, when the feeder raceways have been installed at a relatively early stage of the overall building construction, it may not delay the final completion of the electrical installation to delay ordering the cables until the raceways can actually be measured. Several fish tapes with laser foot markings are now available.

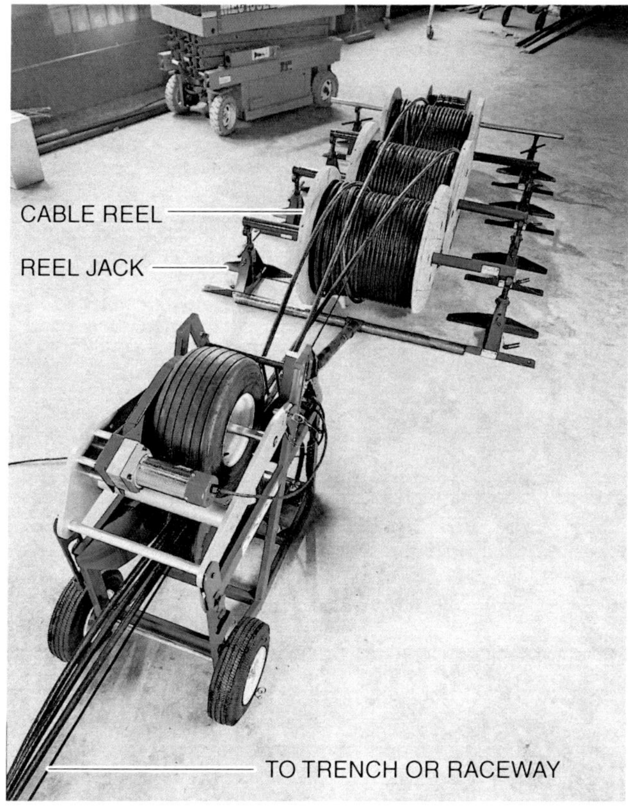

Figure 3 Multi-cable pull.

When pulling conductors directly from the reels, care must be taken that each given run be cut off from the reel so that there is a minimum amount of waste. In other words, preclude the possibility of the final run of cable taken from the reel being too short for that run.

2.1.0 Pulling Location

Each job will have to be judged separately as to the best location of pulling setups; the number of setups should be reduced to a minimum in line with the best direction of the pull. The pulling location for a particular job is determined by the weight of the cable, height of the pull, practicality of moving the equipment to the pulling location, number of setups required, as well as the location of any bends. Also, a separate setup might have to be made at the top of each rise, whereas a single setup might be made at a ground floor pull box location from which several feeders are served with the same size and number of conductors.

Think About It

Multiple Reels

Why are multiple reel pulling setups used?

The location of the pulling equipment determines the number of workers required for the job. A piece of equipment that can be moved in and set up on the first floor by four workers in an hour's time may require six workers working two hours when set up in basements or parking levels of buildings. Therefore, when planning a cable pull, make certain enough workers are on hand to adequately handle the installation.

It is a simple operation for a few workers to roll cable reels from a loading platform to a first floor setup, whereas moving them to upper floors involves more handling and usually requires a crane or other hoists. In addition, the reel jacks have to be moved to the setup point when a downward pull is made, and after the pulling operation is completed, they must be taken back to the first floor.

2.2.0 Cable Pull Operations

These operations are performed to a lesser or greater degree in almost all cable pulls with larger sizes of conductors:

Step 1 Measure or re-check runs and establish communications between both ends of the pull.

Step 2 Provide pulling equipment.

Step 3 Receive and unload pulling equipment.

Step 4 Move pulling equipment to the pulling location.

Step 5 Set up and anchor pulling equipment.

Step 6 Remove to another location or move to a loading platform and load on a truck or forklift.

Step 7 Receive and store cable; may be moved directly to setup location if job conditions permit.

Step 8 Move to setup point.

Step 9 Move reel jacks and mandrel to setup point.

Step 10 Set up reels, then identify and tag the cables.

Step 11 Prepare cable ends.

Step 12 Install fish tape.

Step 13 Install pulling line or cable.

Step 14 Connect pulling line.

Step 15 Lubricate with proper lubricants.

Step 16 Pull cable.

Step 17 Disconnect pulling line.

Step 18 Remove reels.

Step 19 Permanently identify both ends of the cables/conductors.

Step 20 Rack cables in pull boxes and troughs.

Step 21 Splice or connect cables.

Step 22 Check and test.

In some instances, the following additional operations are involved, depending upon the exact details of the project. Other items of importance will be discussed later in this module.

Step 23 Remove lagging or other protective covering from reels.

Step 24 Unreel cable and cut it to length.

Step 25 Re-reel cable for pulling.

Step 26 Replace lagging on reels.

Step 27 Operate such auxiliary equipment as guide-through cabinets or pull boxes and signal systems between reel and pulling setups.

Each of these pulling operations is discussed in detail in this module (also see *Figure 4*).

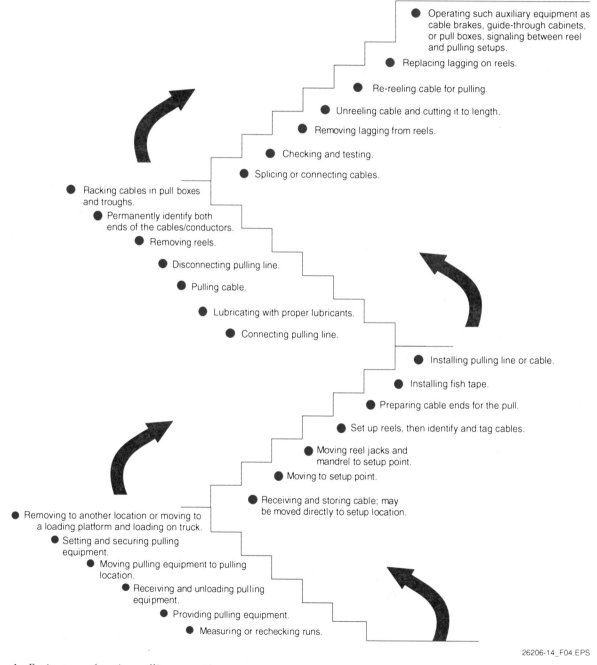

- Operating such auxiliary equipment as cable brakes, guide-through cabinets, or pull boxes, signaling between reel and pulling setups.
- Replacing lagging on reels.
- Re-reeling cable for pulling.
- Unreeling cable and cutting it to length.
- Removing lagging from reels.
- Checking and testing.
- Splicing or connecting cables.
- Racking cables in pull boxes and troughs.
- Permanently identify both ends of the cables/conductors.
- Removing reels.
- Disconnecting pulling line.
- Pulling cable.
- Lubricating with proper lubricants.
- Connecting pulling line.
- Installing pulling line or cable.
- Installing fish tape.
- Preparing cable ends for the pull.
- Set up reels, then identify and tag cables.
- Moving reel jacks and mandrel to setup point.
- Moving to setup point.
- Receiving and storing cable; may be moved directly to setup location.
- Removing to another location or moving to a loading platform and loading on truck.
- Setting and securing pulling equipment.
- Moving pulling equipment to pulling location.
- Receiving and unloading pulling equipment.
- Providing pulling equipment.
- Measuring or rechecking runs.

26206-14_F04.EPS

Figure 4 Basic steps of a wire-pulling operation.

On Site

Measuring Tape

A waterproof polyester tape with permanent markings every foot from 0' to 3,000' is available on reels for use in measuring conduit/raceway runs. It can be fished through the run manually or using a power fishing system.

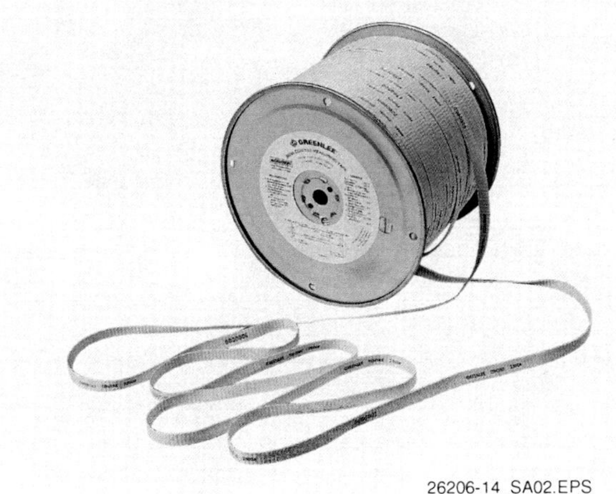

26206-14_SA02.EPS

3.0.0 Setting Up for Wire Pulling

As mentioned previously, much planning is required for pulling the larger sizes of conductors in raceways. There are several preliminary steps required before the actual pull begins.

The proper use of appropriate equipment is crucial to a successful cable installation. The equipment needed for most installations is shown in the checklist in *Figure 5*. Some projects may require all of these items, while others may require only some of them. Each cable-pulling project must be taken on an individual basis and analyzed accordingly. Seldom will two pulls require identical procedures.

NOTE: Think of everything that can go wrong and take every precaution.

3.1.0 Setting Up the Cable Reels

When reels of cable arrive at the job site, it is best to move them directly to the setup location if at all possible. This prevents having to handle the reels more than necessary. However, if this is not practical, arrangements must be made for storage until the cable is needed.

The exact method of handling reels of cable depends on their size and the available tools and equipment. In many cases, the reels may be rolled to the pulling location by one or more workers. For reels up to 24" wide × 40" in diameter, a cable reel transporter can be used to transport the cable reel; it also acts as a dispenser during the pulling operation. When available, a forklift is ideal for lifting and transporting cable reels. See *Figure 6*.

EQUIPMENT CHECKLIST

- ❑ PORTABLE ELECTRIC GENERATOR
- ❑ EXTENSION CORDS AND GFCI
- ❑ PUMP, DIAPHRAGM
- ❑ MAKEUP BLOWER AND HOSE
- ❑ MANHOLE COVER HOOKS
- ❑ WARNING FLAGS, SIGNS
- ❑ ELECTROSTATIC kV TESTER
- ❑ ELECTRIC SAFETY BLANKETS AND CLAMPS
- ❑ RADIOS OR TELEPHONES
- ❑ GLOVES
- ❑ FLOOD LAMPS
- ❑ FISH TAPE OR STRING BLOWER/VACUUM
- ❑ HAND LINE
- ❑ DUCT-CLEANING MANDRELS
- ❑ DUCT-TESTING MANDRELS
- ❑ CAPSTAN-TYPE PULLER
- ❑ SNATCH BLOCKS
- ❑ SHORT ROPES FOR TEMPORARY TIE-OFFS
- ❑ GUIDE-IN FLEXIBLE TUBING (ELEPHANT TRUNKS)
- ❑ SEVERAL WIRE ROPE SLINGS OF VARIOUS LENGTHS
- ❑ SHACKLES/ROPE CLEVIS
- ❑ GANG ROLLERS WITH AT LEAST 4' EFFECTIVE RADIUS
- ❑ HAND WINCHES
- ❑ MANHOLE EDGE SHEAVE
- ❑ PULLING ROPE
- ❑ SWIVELS
- ❑ BASKET GRIP PULLERS
- ❑ 0-1/5/10 KIP DYNAMOMETER
- ❑ REEL ANCHOR
- ❑ REEL JACKS
- ❑ CABLE CUTTERS
- ❑ LINT-FREE RAGS
- ❑ CABLE-PULLING LUBRICANTS
- ❑ PRELUBING DEVICES
- ❑ PLYWOOD SHEETS
- ❑ DIAMETER TAPE
- ❑ 50' MEASURING TAPE
- ❑ SILICONE CAULKING (TO SEAL CABLE ENDS)

26206-14_F05.EPS

Figure 5 Wire-pulling equipment checklist.

Figure 6 Two methods of transporting cable reels.

However, for very large reels (48" or more in diameter), a crane or similar hoisting apparatus is usually necessary for lifting the reels onto reel jacks supported by jack stands to acquire the necessary height. *Figure 7* shows a summary of proper and improper ways to transport reels of wire or cable on the job site.

Figure 8 shows several types of reel jacks, including the spindle. For a complete setup, two stands and a spindle are required for each reel. The reel jacks or stands are available in various sizes from 13" to 54" high to accommodate reel diameters up to 96". Extension stands used in conjunction with reel stands can accommodate larger reels.

Reel-stand spindles are commonly available in diameters from 2⅜" to 3½" and from 59" to 100" in length for carrying reel loads up to 7,500 pounds. However, some heavy-duty spindles are rated for loads up to 15,000 pounds.

3.2.0 Preparing Raceways for Conductors

Another preliminary step prior to pulling conductors in raceway systems is to inspect the raceway itself. Few things are more frustrating than to pull four 1,000 kcmil conductors through a conduit and find out when the pull is almost done that the conduit is blocked or damaged. Such a situation usually requires pulling the conductors back out, repairing the fault, and starting all over again.

These problems are not too serious with exposed banks of conduit, as the conduit can usually be separated at the fault, the fault corrected, and another piece of conduit installed, using unions if necessary. However, in underground conduit runs—especially those encased in concrete—the situation can be both time-consuming and costly.

A test pull will detect any hidden obstructions in the conduit prior to the pull (*Figure 9*). Go and no-go steel and aluminum mandrels are available for pulling through runs of conduit before the cable installation. Mandrels should be approximately 80% of the conduit size (twice the 40% fill factor). If any obstructions are found, they can be corrected before wasting time on an installation that might result in conductor damage and the possibility of having to re-pull the conductors.

Figure 10 shows several devices used to inspect raceway systems, as well as to prepare raceways for easier and safer conductor pulls. The conduit swab in *Figure 10* may be used ahead of the conductors during a pull. Its main purpose is to swab out debris from the raceway and spread a uniform film of pulling compound inside the conduit for easier pulling. The flexible mandrel is also used to clean the conduit and check the run for obstructions. The flexible discs make it easier to pull around tight bends.

The conduit brush in *Figure 10* helps clean and polish the interior of conduit before pulling the cable. Such brushes remove sand and other light obstructions. Note that this brush has a pulling eye on one end and a twisted eye on the opposite end, enabling it to be pushed or pulled through the conduit.

ON THE RIMS OF THE SPOOL (MOVING EQUIPMENT DOES NOT COME INTO CONTACT WITH CABLE)

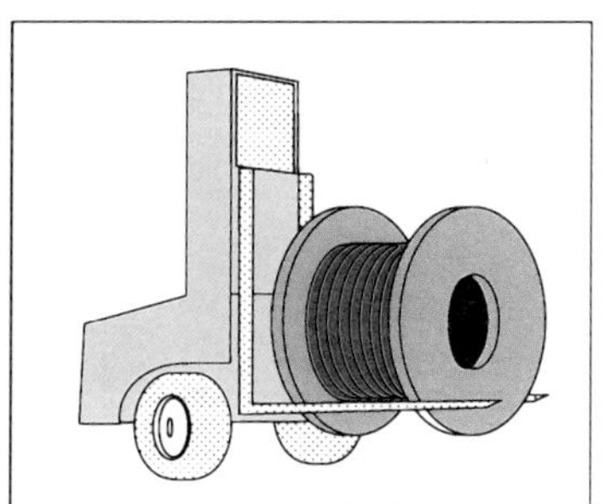

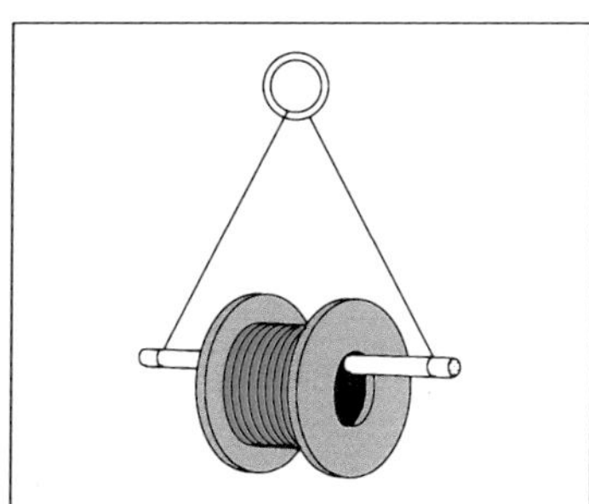

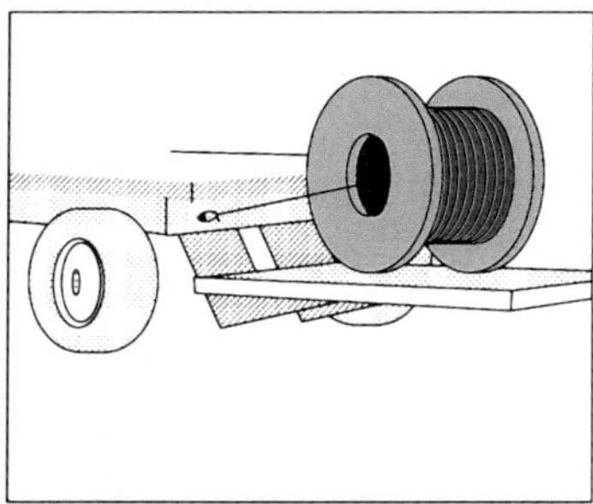

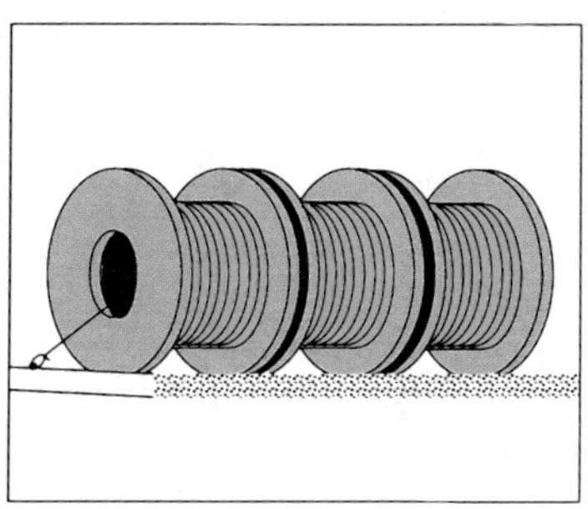

ON THE FLAT SIDE OF THE SPOOL OR ON THE CABLE (MOVING EQUIPMENT COMPRESSES INSULATION AND MAY DAMAGE CABLE)

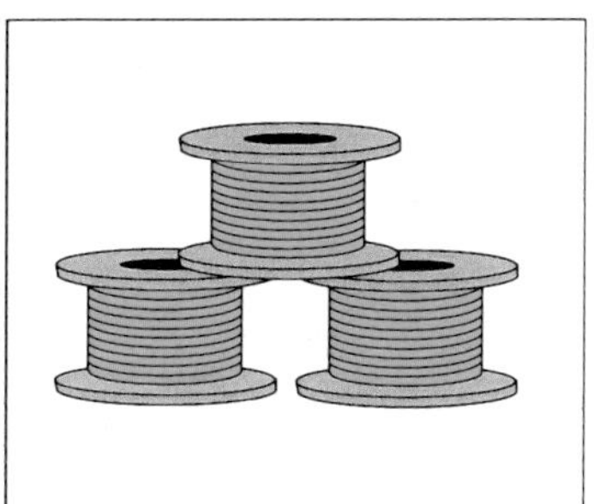

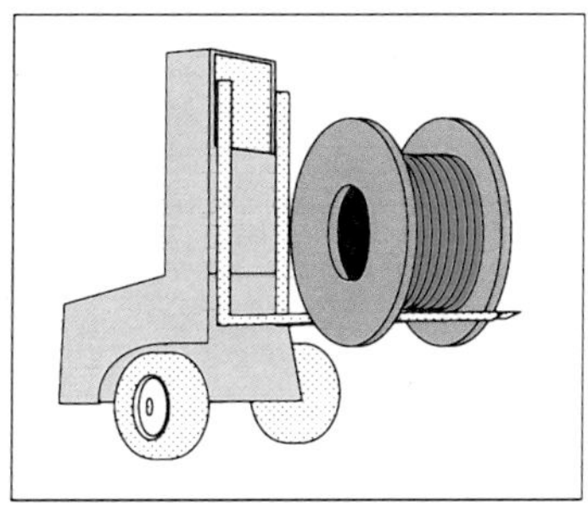

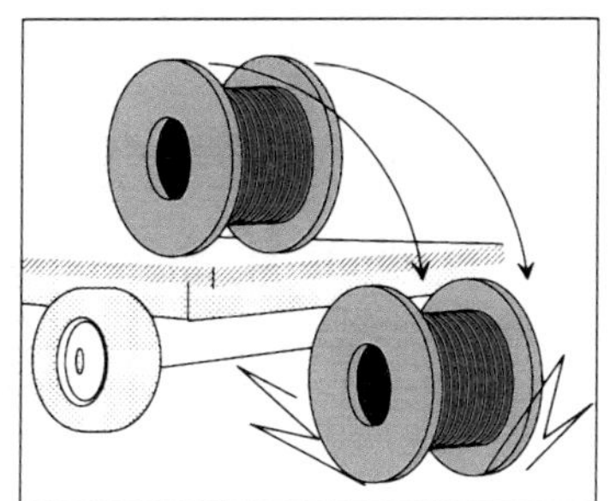

26206-14_F07.EPS

Figure 7 Proper and improper ways of transporting cable reels.

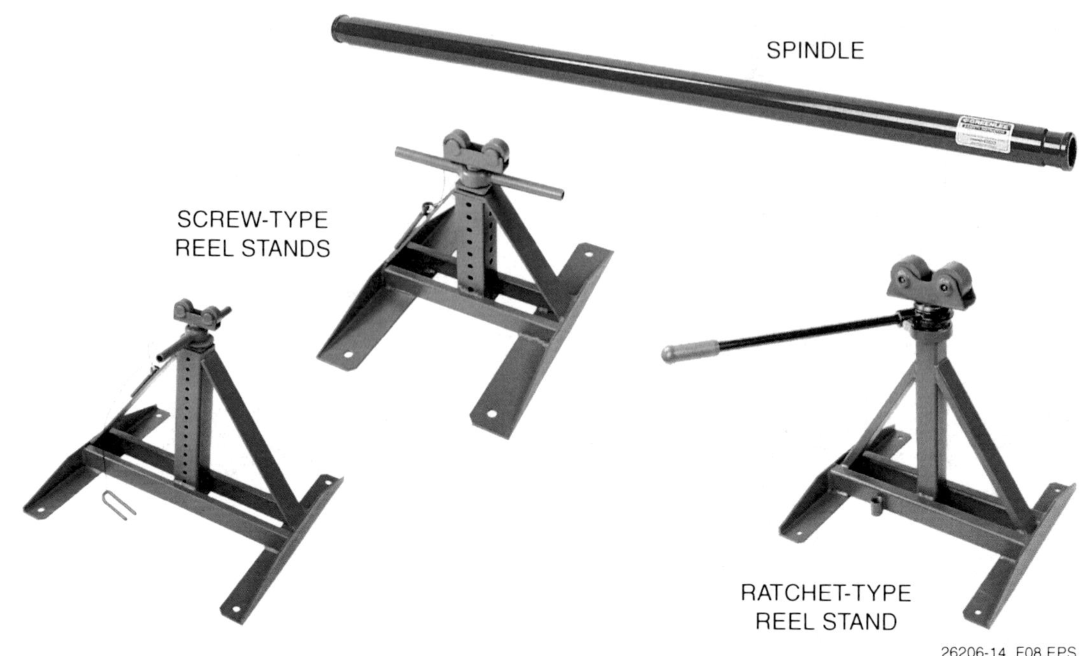

Figure 8 Typical reel stands.

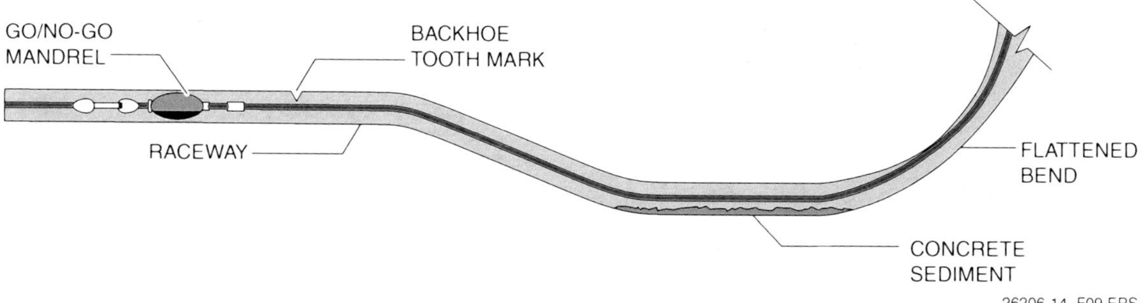

Figure 9 Faults that may be detected with a conduit mandrel.

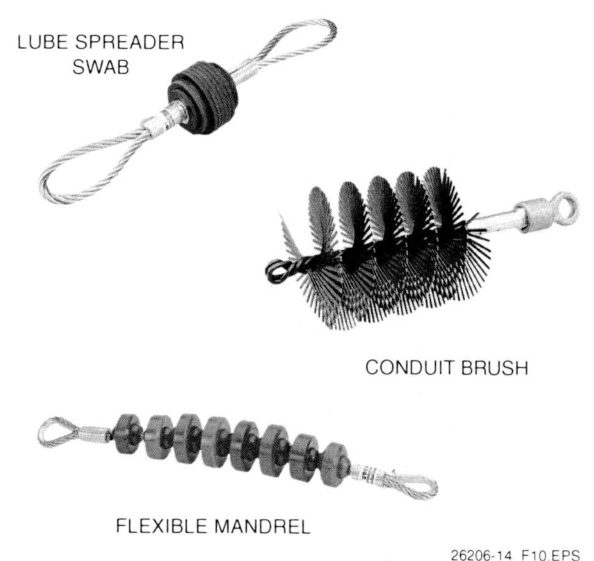

Figure 10 Devices used to inspect, clean, and lubricate raceway systems.

One final step before starting the pull is to measure the length of the raceway, including all turns in junction boxes and the like. A fish tape may be pushed through the raceway system and a piece of tape used to mark the end. When it is pulled back out, a tape measure may be used to measure the exact length. An easier way, however, is to use a power fishing system to push or pull a measuring tape through the conduit run. Details of this operation are explained in the next section.

When measuring the conductor length, be sure to allow sufficient room where measurements are made through a pull box. Conductors should enter and leave pull boxes in such a manner as to allow the greatest possible sweep for the conductors. Large conductors are especially difficult to bend but with proper planning, you can simplify the feeding of these conductors from one conduit to another.

For example, if a conduit run makes a right-angle bend through a pull box, the conduit for a given feeder should come into the box at the lower left-hand corner and leave diagonally opposite at the upper right-hand corner, as shown in *Figure 11*. This gives the conductors the greatest possible sweep with the box, eliminating sharp bends and consequent damage to the conductor insulation.

Runs should also be calculated to allow for splices and terminations in junction boxes, panelboards, motor-control centers, the cable discarded under the sleeve or pulling wrap, etc.

3.3.0 Installing the Pull Line

At one time, pull-in wires were frequently placed in conduit runs as the raceways were installed. However, in recent times, with modern cable-fishing equipment, this practice is seldom used.

Pull lines are sometimes manually fished in with a steel fish tape, but much time can be saved by using a blower/vacuum fish tape system. In general, a conduit piston—sometimes referred to as a mouse or missile—is blown with air pressure or vacuumed through the run. The foam piston is sized to the conduit and has a loop on both ends. In most cases, fish line or measuring tape is attached to the piston as it is blown or vacuumed through the conduit run. The measuring tape serves two purposes: it provides an accurate measurement of the conduit run, and the tape is used to pull the cable-pulling rope into the conduit run. In some cases, if the run is suitable, the pulling rope is attached directly to the piston and vacuumed into the run. *Figure 12* shows a blower/vacuum fish tape system being used to vacuum a pull line in a conduit while *Figure 13* shows the same apparatus blowing the piston through. Most of these units provide enough pressure to clean dirt or water from conduit during the fishing operation. *Figure 14* shows two types of pistons used with this system. The one on the right utilizes air-guide vanes to prevent the piston from tumbling inside the larger sizes of conduit.

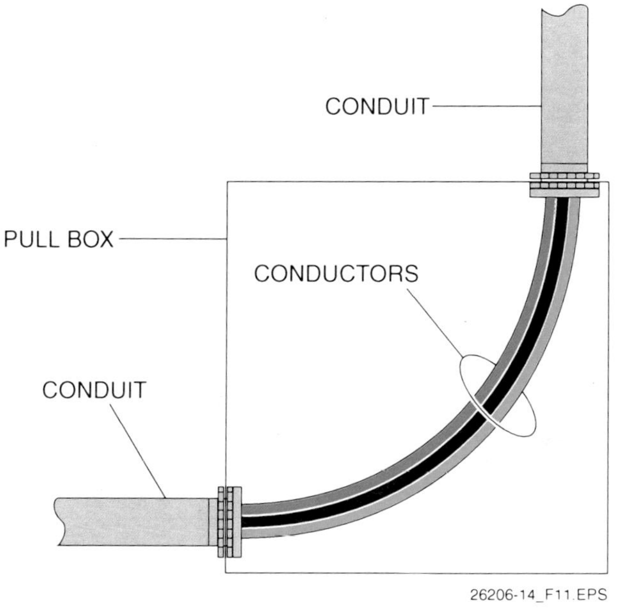

Figure 11 Obtaining the greatest possible conductor sweep in a pull box.

3.4.0 Preparing Cable Ends for Pulling

The pulling-in line or cable must be attached to the cable or conductors in such a manner that it cannot part from the cable during the pull. Two common methods include direct connection with the cable conductors themselves and connection by means of pulling grips or baskets placed over the cable or group of conductors. The use of the proper type of grip or basket will facilitate the pull, but in many cases—especially on long pulls—workers prefer to use three- or four-hole cable grips with setscrews that secure each conductor to the pulling block. *Figure 15* shows several types of pulling grips.

Most pulling blocks have a rope clevis as an integral part of the block. However, when using pulling grips or baskets in 2" or larger conduit, a rope clevis is normally used to facilitate connecting the pulling rope to the wire grip. Two types are currently used: the straight clevis and the swivel clevis.

3.4.1 Stripping the Cable Ends

When the type of grip being used requires that the ends of the cable insulation be stripped from the conductors, conventional methods are used—the same as for terminating conductors for splices or connections to terminal lugs in panelboards, switchgear, etc.

In general, the ends of conductors should first be trimmed. Cable cutters capable of cutting conductors through 1,000 kcmil save workers time over using a hacksaw. There are also cable strippers, adjustable from 1/0 AWG through 1,000 kcmil, that handle midspan and termination stripping of THHN, THWN, XHHW, and similar insulation. These tools are excellent for stripping conductors for use in setscrew clamp-type pulling grips.

On Site

Cable Blowing

Lightweight cables, especially fiber optic cable, can be floated through conduit using a special high-pressure blower unit.

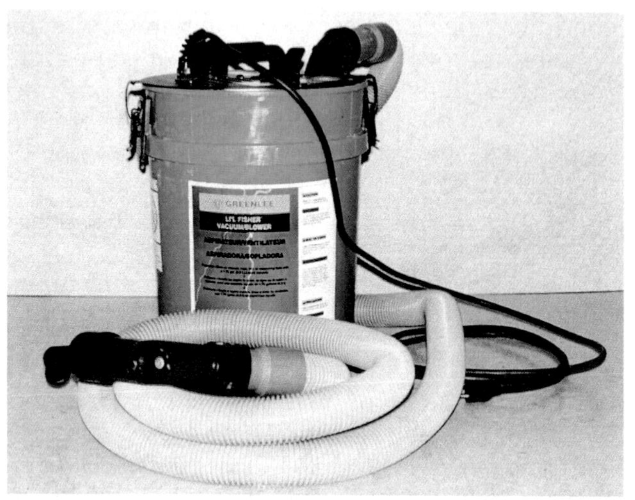

26206-14_F12A.EPS

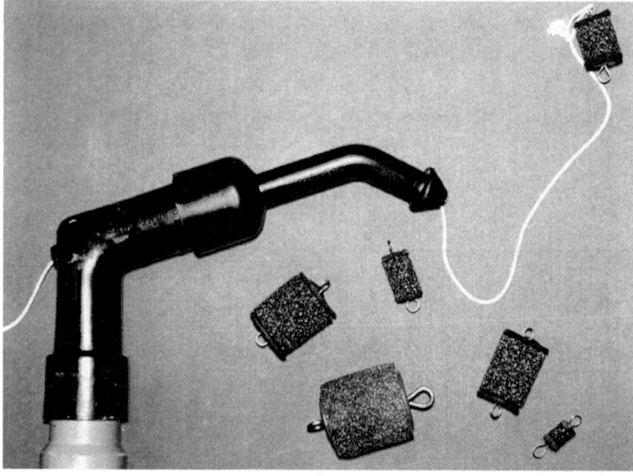

26206-14_F12B.EPS

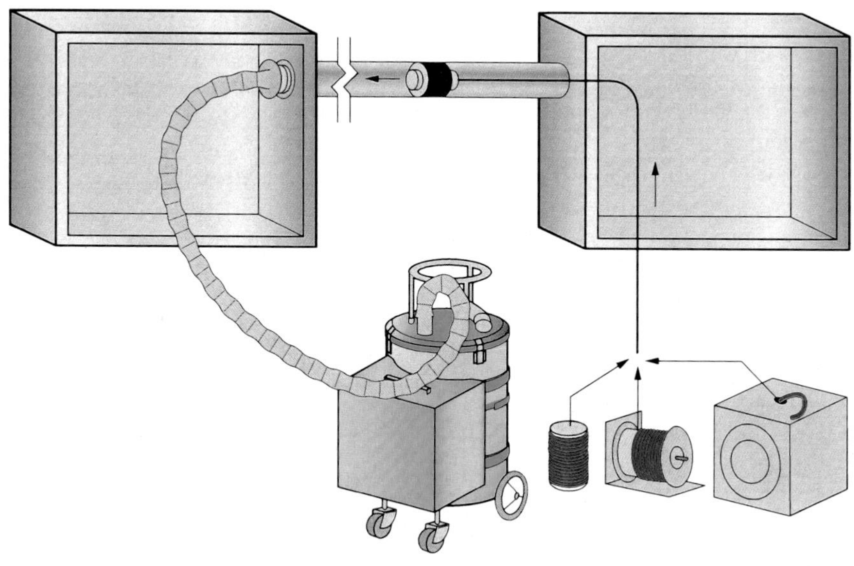

26206-14_F12C.EPS

Figure 12 Power fishing system.

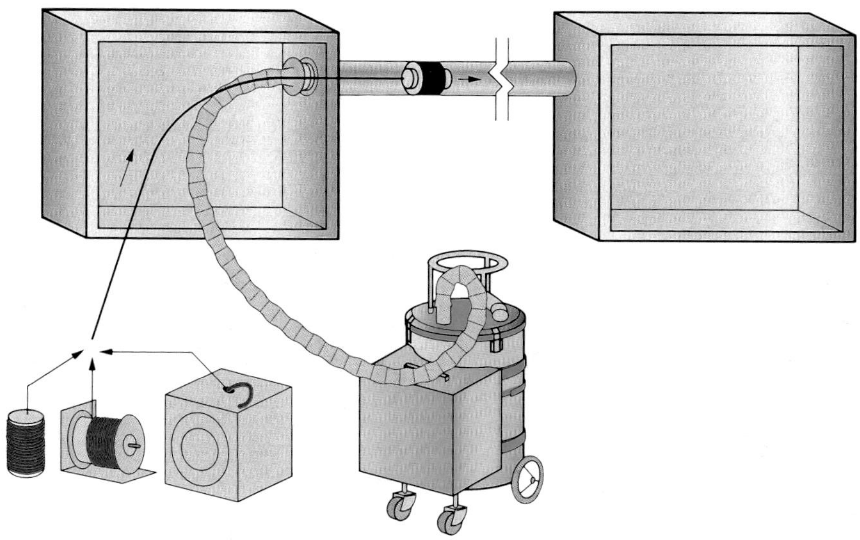

26206-14_F13.EPS

Figure 13 Blower/vacuum fish tape system used to blow a pull line in conduit.

FLEXIBLE FOAM PISTON
FOR AIRTIGHT SEAL
PISTONS ARE AVAILABLE
IN SIZES FROM 1/2" TO 6"

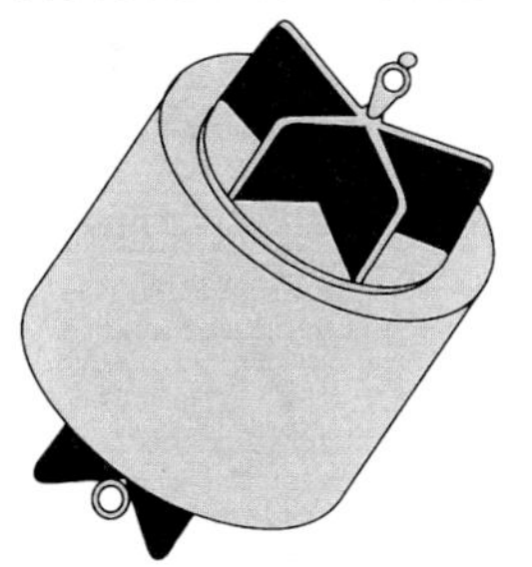
FINS ARE SOMETIMES UTILIZED
ON PISTONS FOR LARGER SIZES
OF CONDUIT TO KEEP THE
PISTONS FROM TUMBLING

26206-14_F14A.EPS

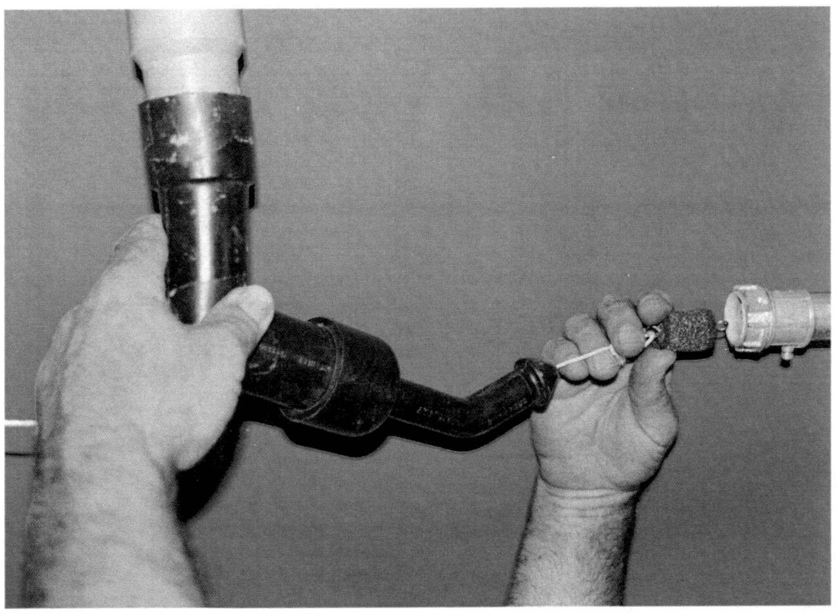

26206-14_F14B.EPS

Figure 14 Types of pistons in common use.

To use a stripping tool, first mark the required distance from the ends of the conductors, using the pulling grip as a gauge. Close the jaws of the stripping tool on the cable and twist. These self-feeding devices ensure positive progression down the cable to any position desired. To stop stripping, apply back pressure to the stripper until a full circle has been completed.

Once the conductor ends have been stripped, insert one conductor at a time into the setscrew grip. Make sure the end of the bare conductor is firmly in place, and then tighten the setscrews with a hex wrench. Continue on to the next conductor, and so on, until all conductors are secured in the pulling grip.

3.4.2 Safety with Cutters

When using a stripping tool for the first time, make sure that you read and understand all instructions and warnings before using the tool. The following should also be observed when working with cable terminators:

- Wear eye protection.
- Inspect tools before using, and replace damaged, missing, or worn parts.
- Be prepared for the unexpected. Make sure your footing and body position are such that you will not lose your balance.
- Use only the type and size material in the stated capacity.
- Do not use the tool on or near live circuits.

3.5.0 Types of Pulling Lines

Wire-pulling ropes have come a long way from the hemp ropes used by electricians a couple of decades ago. The most common wire-pulling ropes on the market include the following:

- Nylon
- Polypropylene

Fish Poles

Rigid fish poles can be used in areas such as over drop-in ceilings where traditional fish tape might get caught up on ductwork or the ceiling grid. Glow-in-the-dark fish poles are also available.

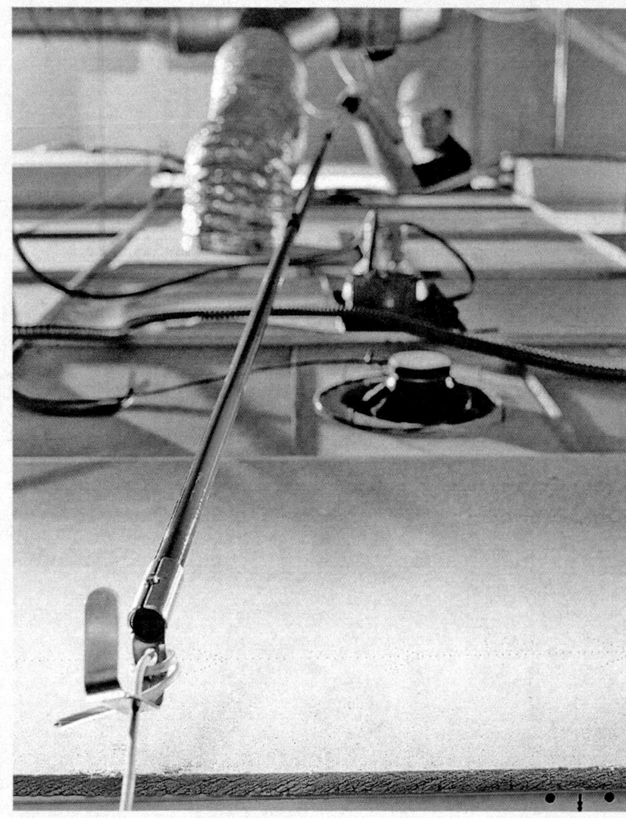

FISH POLE IN USE

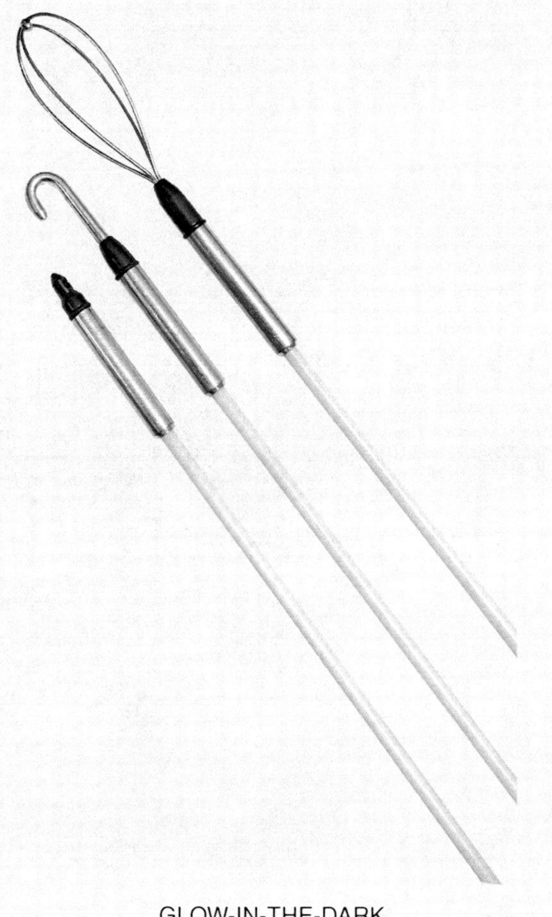

GLOW-IN-THE-DARK FISH POLES

26206-14_SA03.EPS

- Multiplex polyester
- Double-braided polyester composite

The type of rope selected will depend mainly on the pulling load; that is, the weight of the cable, the length of the pull, and the total resistance to the pull. For example, Greenlee's Multiplex cable-pulling rope is designed for low-force cable pullers. It has a low stretch characteristic that makes it suitable for pulls up to 2,000 pounds. Lengths are available from 100 to 1,200 feet. Greenlee's double-braided composite rope for high-force cable pullers is designed for pulls up to 6,500 pounds.

CAUTION

Any equipment associated with the pull must have a working load rating in excess of the force applied during the pull. All equipment must be used and mounted in strict accordance with the manufacturer's instructions.

Care must be used in selecting the proper rope for the pull, and then every precaution must be taken to make sure that the cable-pulling force does not exceed the rope capacity. There are several reasons for this, but the main one is safety. For example, think of a 100' length of nylon rope with a 10,000-pound breaking strength. Such ropes can stretch 40' before breaking, releasing

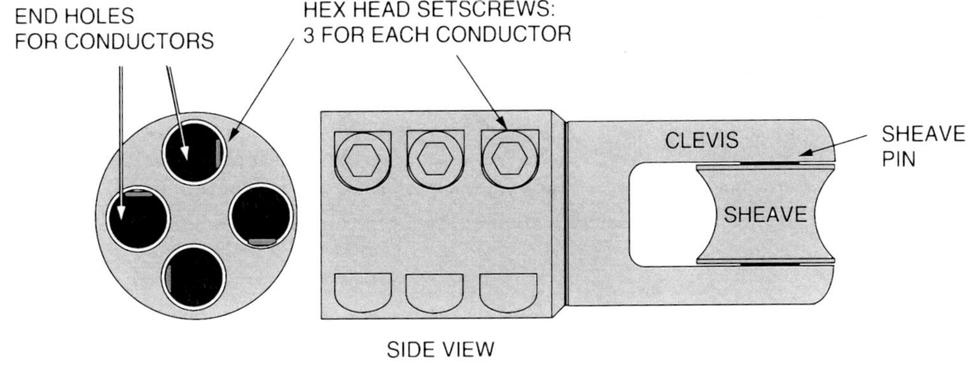

SETSCREW CABLE GRIP

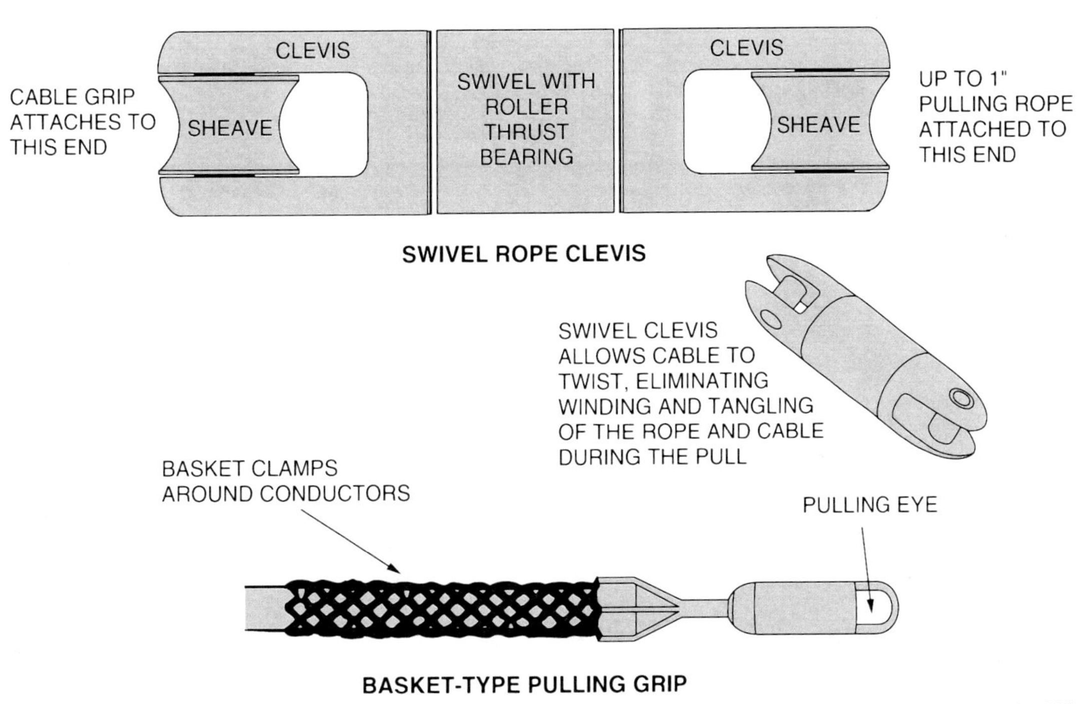

Figure 15 Various types of pulling grips used during conductor installation.

200,000 foot-pounds of energy in the process. Think of the damage this amount of energy could do to a raceway system and to nearby workers if the rope broke under this amount of force.

In some cases, a power blower/vacuum fish tape system is used to vacuum the piston through the raceway with the pulling rope attached. In other cases, a line is first blown or vacuumed

On Site

Pulling Eyes

Smaller conductors may require only a pulling eye attached to the fish tape or pulling line. To attach the pulling eye, the conductors are first stripped, exposing a length of bare wire. These bare wires are inserted through the eye and twisted back onto themselves. The exposed twisted wires of the conductors can then be wrapped with smaller copper wire to prevent them from untwisting. They are then completely taped with three layers of electrical tape, starting from the conductor insulation, to prevent snagging as they are drawn through the conduit run.

On Site

Grips and Swivels

Conductors can be attached to a pulling line using various methods, including setscrew grips or basket grips. No matter what method is used, always insert a swivel of some sort between the pulling line or fish tape and the conductors to alleviate twisting of the conductors. Breakaway swivels are available that release at a specified tension to avoid damage to the conductors if excess force is applied or if the conductors get hung up during the pull.

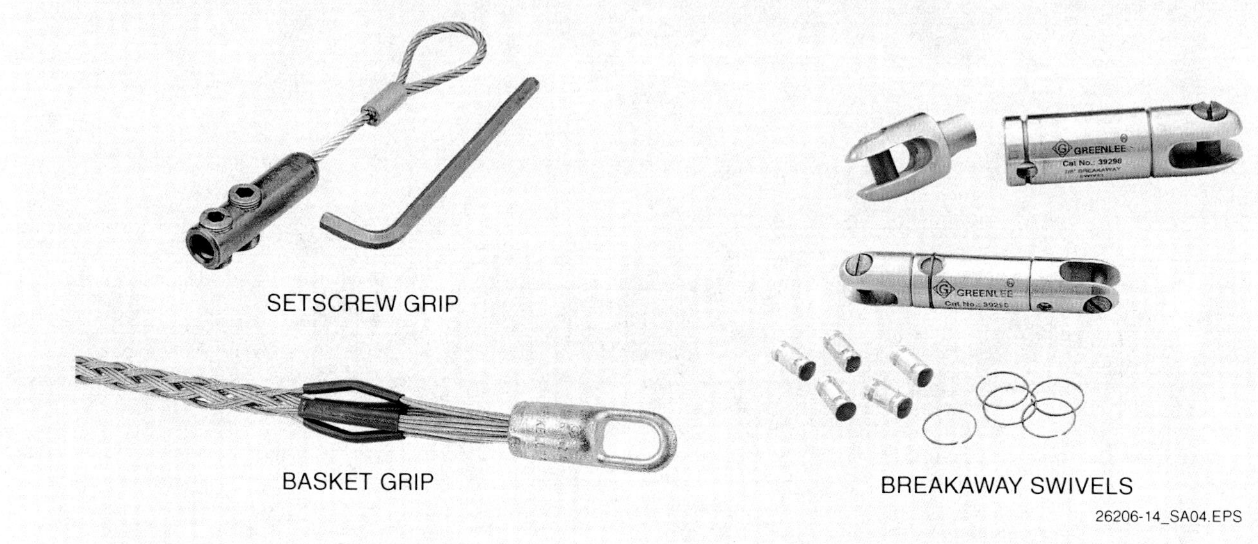

26206-14_SA04.EPS

through the conduit and then the pulling rope is attached to the line for pulling it through the raceway system. In either case, there are certain precautions that should be taken when using a power fish tape system:

- Read and understand all instructions and warnings before using the tool.
- Never fish in runs that might contain live power.
- Be prepared for the unexpected. Make sure your footing and body position are such that you will not lose your balance in any unexpected event.
- Use blower/vacuum systems only for specified light fishing and exploring the raceway system.
- Never use pliers or other devices that are not designed to pull a fish tape. They can kink or nick the tape, creating a weak spot.

4.0.0 Cable-Pulling Equipment

Except for short cable pulls, hand-operated or power-operated cable pullers or winches are used to furnish the pulling power. In general, cable reels are set in place at one end of the raceway system, and the cable puller is set up at the opposite end. One end of the previously-installed pulling rope is attached to a clevis, basket, or other cable grip to which the conductors are attached. The other end of the rope (at the cable puller) is wrapped around the rotating drum **capstan** on the cable puller (*Figure 16*).

Wire-pulling lubricant—sometimes referred to as **soap**—is inserted into the empty conduit as well as wiped thoroughly onto the front of the cable. One or more operators are on hand to feed the cable, while one worker is usually all that is required on the pulling end.

WARNING!

Always use a wire-pulling lubricant that is compatible with the type of cable being pulled. Failure to do so can result in unsafe pulling forces and cable damage. Check with the cable manufacturer for their recommendations, and always contact the lubricant manufacturer about the compatibility of their products with specific cables. Also check the product's MSDS for any applicable safety requirements.

The number of wraps on the puller drum decides the amount of force applied to the pull. For example, the operator needs to apply only 10 pounds of force to the pulling rope in all cases.

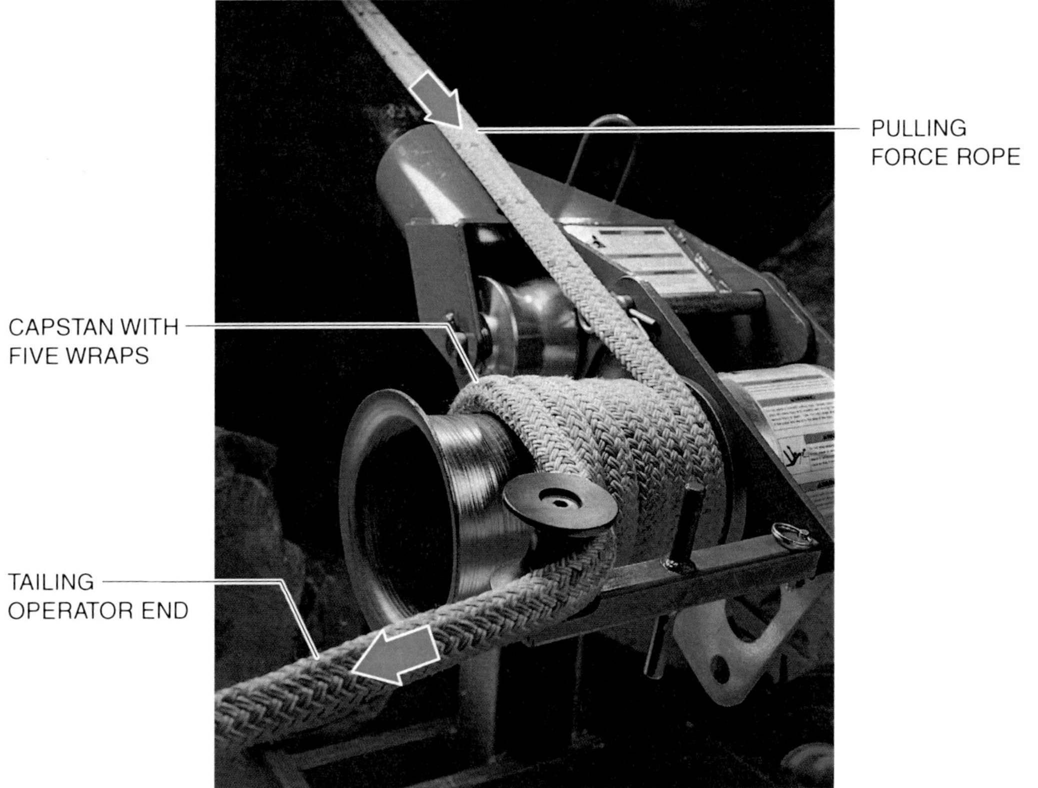

Figure 16 Power cable puller capstan.

With this amount of force applied by the operator, and with one wrap around the rotating drum, 21 pounds of pulling force will be applied to the pulling rope; 2 wraps, 48 pounds; 3 wraps, 106 pounds, etc. This principle is known as the capstan theory and is the same principle applied to block-and-tackle hoists or the lone cowboy who is able to rope and hold a 2,000-pound bronco by wrapping his lariat around the center post in a corral. *Table 1* gives the amount of pulling force with various numbers of wraps when the operator applies only 10 pounds of tailing force for a particular model puller.

NOTE

The strain placed on the wrapped cable during the pull may weaken this part of the cable. Be sure to discard the wrapped cable after making the pull.

4.1.0 Pulling Safety

Adhere to the following precautions when using power cable-pulling equipment:

- Read and understand all instructions and warnings before using the tool.
- Use compatible equipment; that is, use the properly-rated cable puller for the job, along with the proper rope and accessories.
- Always be prepared for the unexpected. Make sure your footing and body position are such that you will not lose your balance. Keep out of the direct line of force.
- Make sure all cable-pulling systems, accessories, and rope have the proper rating for the pull.
- Inspect tools, rope, and accessories before using; replace damaged, missing, or worn parts.

Table 1 Example Pulling Forces for Various Wraps

Number of Wraps	Operator Force (Lbs)	Pulling Force (Lbs)
1	10	21
2	10	48
3	10	106
4	10	233
5	10	512
6	10	1,127
7	10	2,478

- Personally inspect the cable-pulling setup, rope, and accessories before beginning the cable pull. Make sure that all equipment is properly and securely rigged.

On Site

Guiding and Lubricating Conductors

When guiding conductors into a conduit/raceway during a pull, the conductors may tend to twist, overlap, or become crossed during the pulling operation, especially if fed from boxes instead of reels. Excessive twisting, overlaps, crossovers, etc., can cause binding of the conductors in conduit/raceway turns, create bunching obstructions in the conduit/raceway, and can contribute to insulation burns. Operators at the feeding end of the pull must attempt to keep the conductors as straight as possible during the pulling operation and lubricants should be applied liberally during the pull to allow the conductors to slide against each other and the sides of the run.

26206-14_SA05.EPS

- Make sure all electrical connections are properly grounded and adequate for the load.

CAUTION

Make absolutely certain that all communications equipment is in working order prior to the pull. Place personnel at strategic points with operable communications equipment to stop and start the pull as conditions warrant. Anyone involved with the pull has the authority to stop the pull at the first sign of danger to personnel or equipment.

- Use cable-pulling equipment only in uncluttered areas.
- Remind all workers that anyone can stop the pull if it seems unsafe.

4.2.0 Types of Cable Pullers

There are several types of cable pullers on the market. Most, however, operate on the same principle. The self-contained hand-crank wire puller in *Figure 17(A)* is designed to pull up to 1,500 pounds with only 30 pounds of handle force. It is used on projects where only a few cable runs need to be pulled.

Power cable pullers are available in various sizes and pulling capacities, from lightweight units that can be set up and used by a single person to heavy-duty units for high-force cable pulling. *Figure 17(B)* shows two typical units.

WARNING!

Make absolutely certain that all cable-pulling equipment is anchored properly. Follow the manufacturer's recommendations for the type of puller being used.

4.2.1 Setting Up Cable Pullers

Figure 18 shows the basic setup for a down pull using the portable 2,000-pound puller shown in *Figure 17*. To set up for the pull, first adjust the elbow and boom to the correct angle using the attached pins. The elbow attaches to the conduit using the locking knob. This unit has a universal conduit latch so it will attach to all conduit sizes without having to change couplings.

Figure 19 shows a setup for an up pull. The setup is similar to the one described for the down pull except the elbow is attached to the bottom conduit rather than the top conduit.

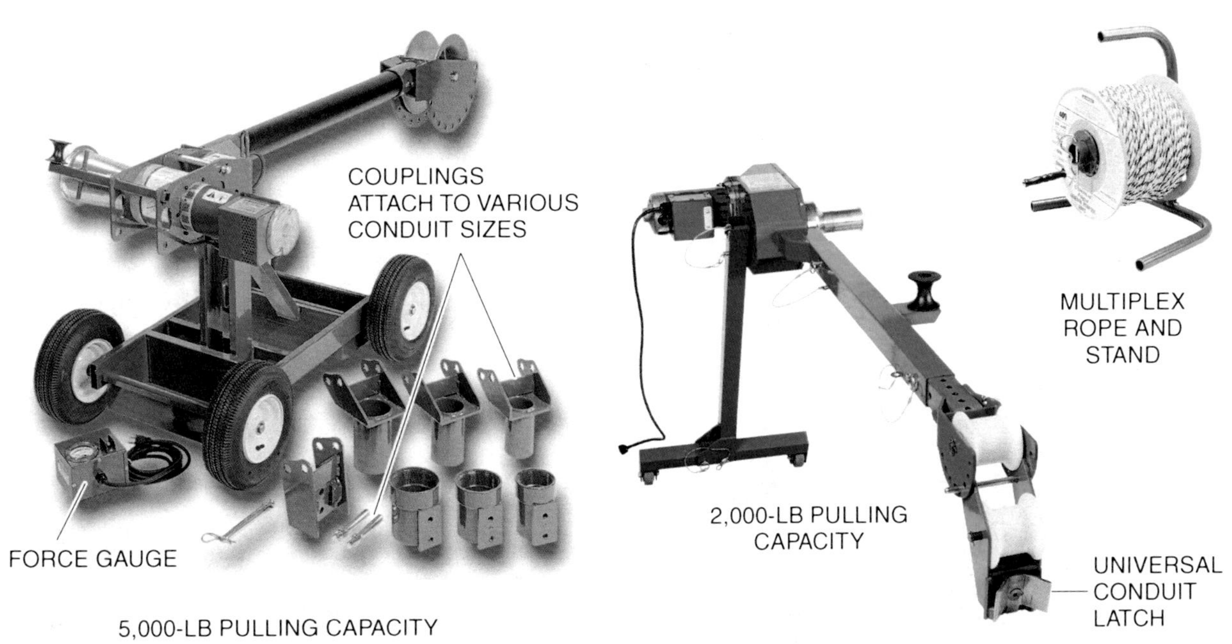

Figure 17 Cable pullers.

On Site

Be Sure to Check the Pulling Rope Rating

Many pulling ropes available today are made of synthetic materials designed for pulling by hand or with a winch-type puller. However, if you are using certain synthetic pulling ropes on friction-type capstan power pullers, make sure the rope is rated by the manufacturer for this use so that it will be able to withstand the heat generated by any extended slippage of the rope on the capstan. During high-force pulling operations, melting damage and possible failure of unrated synthetic rope can occur quickly during periods of capstan slippage.

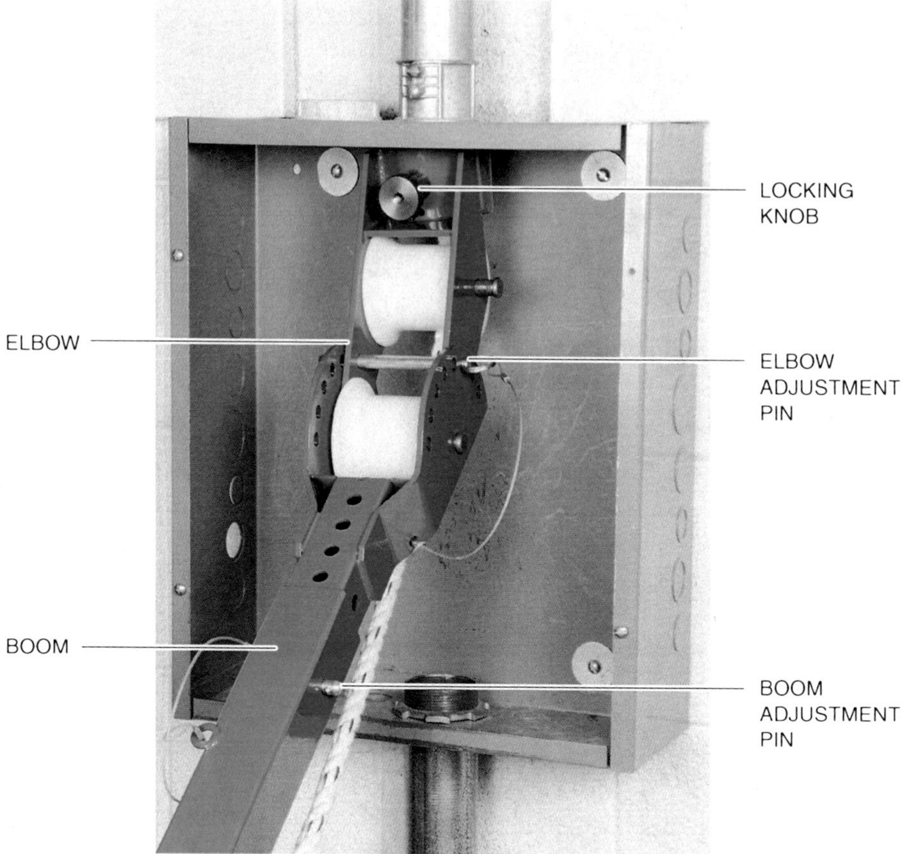

Figure 18 Puller setup for a down pull.

Figure 19 Puller setup for an up pull.

5.0.0 High-Force Cable Pulling

High-force cable pulling is not done every day. It is actually a small part of any electrical raceway installation. Workers may take days, weeks, or even months to install the complete raceway system; the cable-pulling operation typically takes less time.

There are several items to consider during high-force cable pulling:

- The design of the raceway system must be studied by consulting the working drawings and by examining the installed system to ensure that it is properly installed for the type of conductors that will be pulled through the system. Items to consider include conduit sizes, number and size of conductors, number of bends, sufficient pull boxes, and adequate supports.
- The conductors need to be matched to the proper pulling equipment.
- The proper pulling rope must be selected. Choose a rope that has at least four times the strength of the required pulling force; that is, if the estimated pulling force is 1,200 pounds, the rope should be rated for no less than 4,800 pounds. Also check the rope carefully for

Think About It

Communications

What type of communications equipment would most likely be used during cable-pulling operations?

wear or damage prior to the pull. Remember that a rope is only as strong as its weakest point.

- A decision must be made as to the best end of the raceway for pulling. The reel setup must also be carefully placed. In general, conductors that are to be installed downward should be fed off the top of the reel and where conductors are to be fed upward, the best method is to feed from the bottom of the reel. This eliminates sharp kinks or bends in the conductors.
- The appropriate pulling equipment must be used. The equipment must be of the proper capacity for the job. Space consideration for the equipment is also important, as is the particular type of mounting.
- Having enough workers is critical. Never be caught short. This is where experienced workers earn their pay. In high-force wire pulling, experience is the best teacher.
- Safety must be foremost in everyone's mind.

When planning the cable pull, make sure that enough cable is on hand for the run. Cable may be verified while still on the reel by using a cable-length meter. Of course, the conduit run length should have already been checked, as discussed previously. Do not proceed further until everyone is assured that enough cable is on hand for all bends, sweeps in junction boxes, etc. If the cable falls short, take steps to correct the situation before continuing.

Equipment with feeding sheaves will help provide a smooth guide for the cable. Also, have sufficient lubricant on hand and use it both before and during the pull.

Select and install proper cable grips on the cable ends. Gripping must be adequate to handle the imposed force.

When pulling cables in a horizontal run, the worker simply has to reduce the amount of operator pull in order to slow down the cable pull. Releasing all operator pull stops the pulling force entirely. However, when pulling vertical runs, the rope must be tied off after stopping the pull to keep the cable from reversing in the raceway.

The entire operation should be supervised from start to finish. Therefore, communications equipment must be utilized on both ends of the pull at all times.

On Site

Monitored Cable Pullers

Many power cable pullers include force gauges with an automatic over-tension shutoff device. These units prevent you from accidentally exceeding the maximum recommended pulling tension for the conductor(s) being pulled.

26206-14_SA06.EPS

During the pull, make sure that the pulling rope remains free and is not wrapped around any part of the body.

A typical cable-pulling setup is shown in *Figure 20*, including cable reels, reel stands, a power cable puller, conduit system, and other accessories necessary for the pull.

5.1.0 The Feeding End—Sheaves and Rollers

The feed-in setup should unreel the cable along its natural curvature, as shown in *Figure 21(A)*, as opposed to a reverse S curvature, as shown in *Figure 21(B)*. Feed-in setups are shown in *Figure 22*

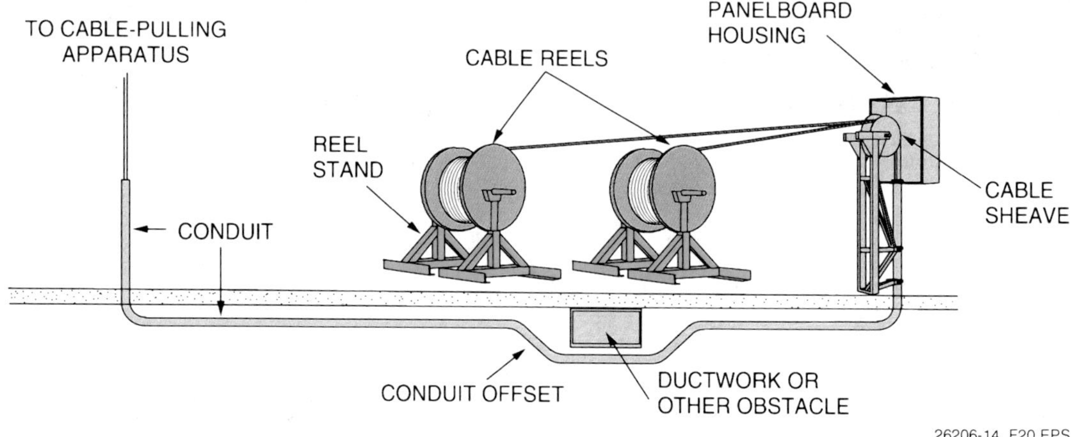

Figure 20 Typical cable-pulling setup.

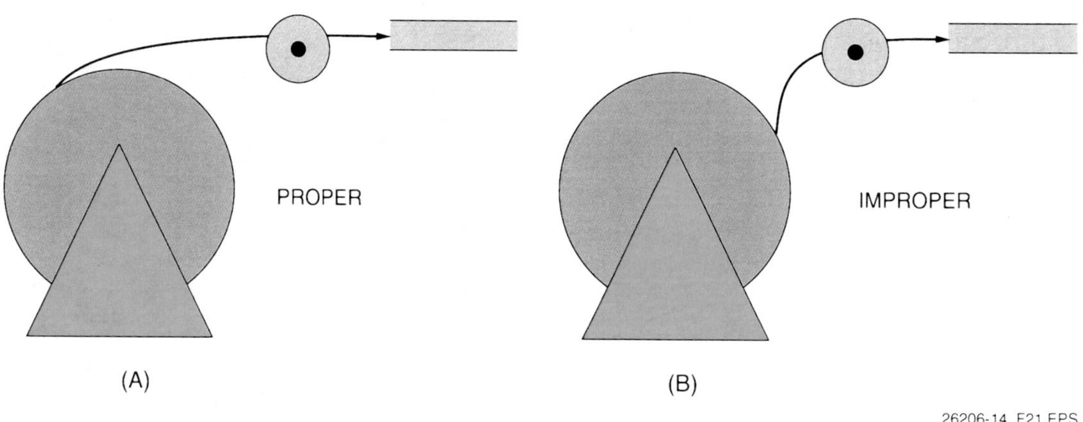

Figure 21 Unreel the cable along its natural curvature.

for manhole, underfloor duct, and overhead cable tray. Note the use of auxiliary equipment in some of these drawings, that is, cable reels, guide-in tubes, sheaves, and rollers.

Single sheaves, such as those shown in *Figure 23(A)*, may be used only for guiding cables. Multiple blocks should be arranged to hold the cable-bending radius wherever the cable is deflected. For pulling around bends, use a conveyor sheave assembly of the appropriate radius series, such as the one shown in *Figure 23(B)*.

Sheaves and pulleys must be positioned to ensure the effective curvature is smooth and deflected evenly at each pulley. Never allow a polygon curvature to occur, as shown in *Figure 24*.

6.0.0 Supporting Conductors

Conductors in vertical raceways must be supported in accordance with *NEC Section 300.19* if the vertical rise exceeds the values in *Table 2*. In general, one **conductor support** must be provided at the top of the vertical raceway or as close to the top as practical. Intermediate supports must also be provided as necessary to limit supported conductor lengths to not greater than those values specified in *NEC Table 300.19(A)*.

The *NEC*® allows several different methods of supporting conductors in vertical raceways; the following are typical:

- Conductors may be supported by clamping devices constructed of or employing insulating wedges inserted in the ends of the conduit, as shown in *Figure 25*. Where clamping of insulation does not adequately support the cable, the conductor itself must also be clamped.
- Conductors may be supported by inserting boxes at the required intervals in which insulating supports are installed and secured in a satisfactory manner to withstand the weight of the conductors attached to them. The boxes must be provided with covers.

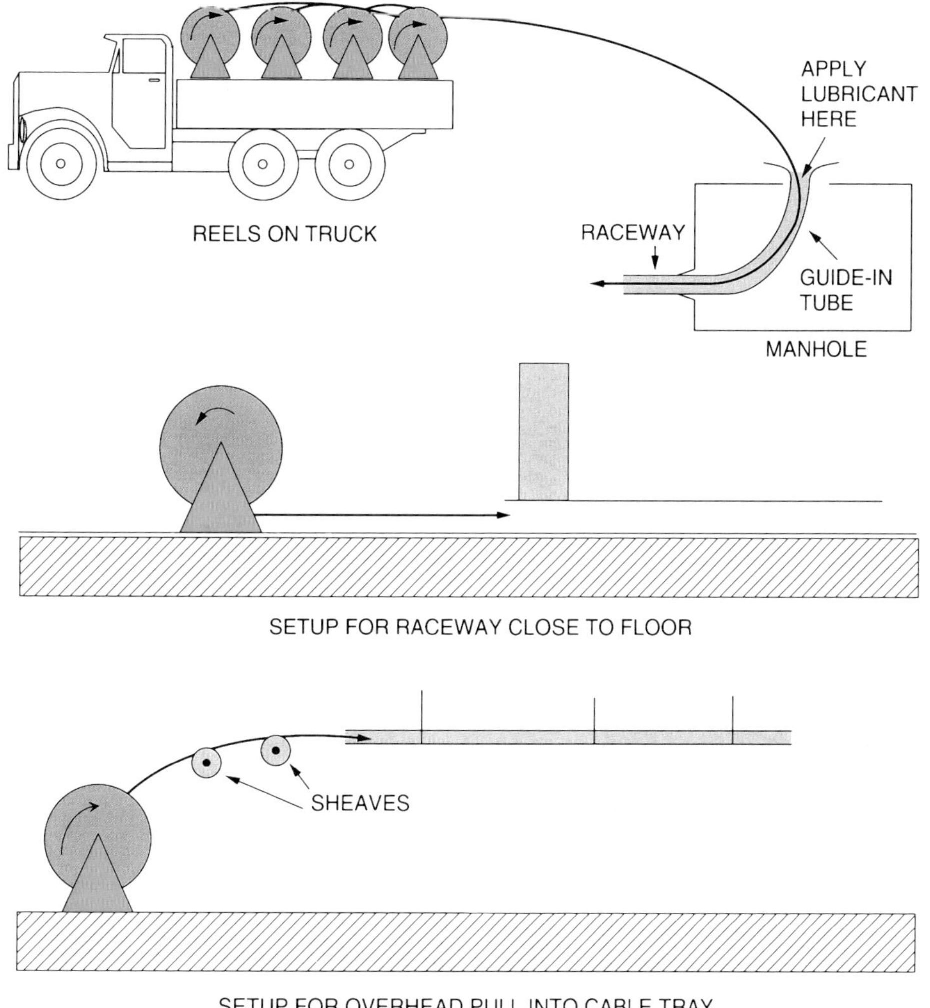

Figure 22 Cable feed-in setups.

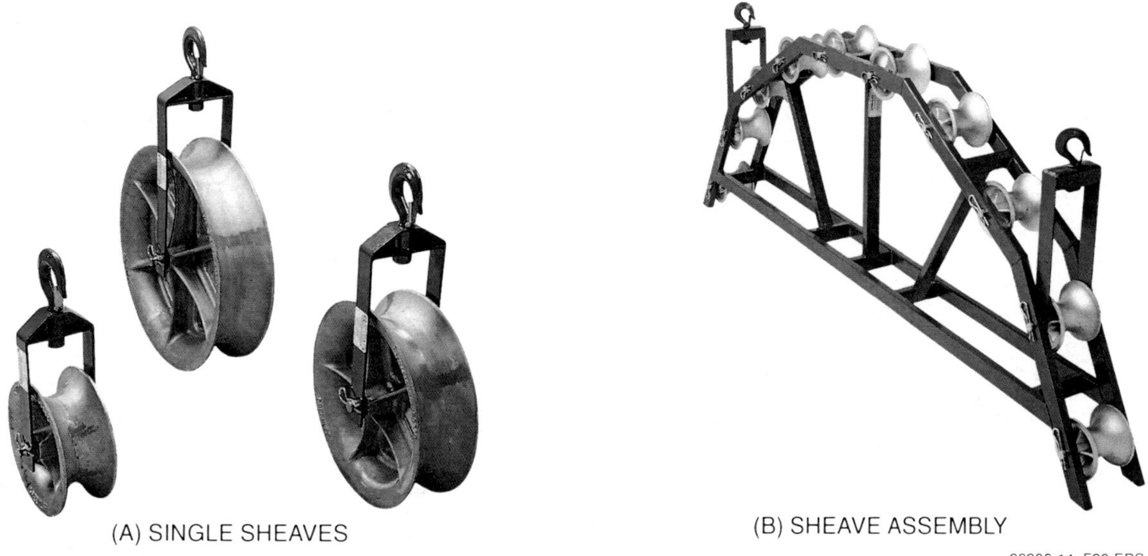

Figure 23 Cable sheaves.

Think About It

Feed-In Setups

Why is an S-curve setup not desirable?

26206-14_F24.EPS

Figure 24 Never allow a polygon curvature to occur in a cable-pulling operation.

26206-14_F25.EPS

Figure 25 Conductors supported with wedges.

Table 2 Spacings for Conductor Supports in Vertical Raceways [Data from *NEC Table 300.19(A)*]

Conductor Size	Support (Aluminum or Copper-Clad Aluminum Conductor)	Support (Copper Conductor)
18 AWG through 8 AWG	≤ 100'	≤ 100'
6 AWG through 1/0 AWG	≤ 200'	≤ 100'
2/0 AWG through 4/0 AWG	≤ 180'	≤ 80'
Over 4/0 through 350 kcmil	≤ 135'	≤ 60'
Over 350 kcmil through 500 kcmil	≤ 120'	≤ 50'
Over 500 kcmil through 750 kcmil	≤ 95'	≤ 40'
Over 750 kcmil	≤ 85'	≤ 35'

CAUTION

Use the radius of the surface over which the cable is bent, not the outside flange diameter of the pulley. For example, a 10" cable sheave typically has an inside (bending) radius of 3".

- Cables may be supported in junction boxes by deflecting the cables not less than 90° and carrying them horizontally to a distance not less than twice the diameter of the cable. The cables are carried on two or more insulating supports and additionally secured to these supports by tie wires, if desired. Where this method is used, cables must be supported at intervals not greater than 20% of those mentioned in *NEC Table 300.19(A)*.
- Cables may be supported by a method of equal effectiveness.

A variety of supports are manufactured specifically for supporting cable in vertical conduit runs, and many ideas can be obtained from the manufacturers' catalogs. Therefore, make an effort to obtain such catalogs from electrical suppliers or manufacturer's representatives. In fact, manufacturers' catalogs of electrical tools and equipment are excellent study guides for any phase of the electrical industry. Manufacturers of electrical equipment want their equipment used, and they have found that one of the best ways to accomplish this is to provide easy-to-understand instructions and examples of practical applications. Most manufacturers go to great expense to provide this information, but it is usually free of charge for those working in the industry.

CAUTION

When installing conductors in vertical raceways, install proper supporting devices to hold the conductors before removing the pulling equipment or cutting the conductors.

There are several precautionary measures that must be taken when pulling cables in vertical runs. The worst danger is runaways; that is, the weight of the cable combined with gravity exceeds the speed of the pull and falls at a rapid rate down the raceway run. Such a situation can cause injury to workers on both ends of the pull. Consequently, braking systems should be used on all long vertical cable pulls. To do otherwise is asking for trouble. Get specific instructions from your supervisor before beginning a vertical pull—either up or down.

WARNING!

Guard against runaways on all vertical pulls. Make certain that proper braking equipment is used to stop a conductor fall should a runaway occur.

7.0.0 Pulling Cable in Cable Trays

When long lengths of cable are to be installed in raceways or cable trays, problems are frequently encountered, particularly when the cable has to be pulled directly into the tray and changes in direction of the tray sections are involved. An entire cable-pulling system has to be planned and set up so that the cable may be pulled into the trays without scuffing or cutting the sheathing and insulation, and also to avoid damaging the cable trays or the tray hangers. To accomplish a successful cable tray pull, a complete line of installation tools is available for pulling lengths of cable up to 1,000 feet or longer. These tools consist mainly of conveyor sheaves and cable rollers. *Figure 26* shows a partial cable tray system with a sheave and roller in place.

Short lengths of cable can be laid in place without tools or pulled with a basket grip. Long lengths of small cable (2" or less in diameter) can also be pulled with a basket grip. Larger cables, however, should be pulled by the conductor and the braid, sheath, or armor. This is done with a pulling eye applied at the cable factory or by tying the conductor to the eye of a basket grip and taping the tail end of the grip to the outside of the cable.

In general, the pull exerted on the cables pulled with a basket grip that is not attached to the conductor should not exceed 1,000 pounds. For heavier pulls, care should be taken not to stretch the insulation, jacket, or armor beyond the end of the conductor nor bend the ladder, trough, or channel out of shape.

The bending radius of the cable should not be less than the values recommended by the cable manufacturer, which range from four times the diameter for a rubber-insulated cable with a 1" maximum outside diameter without lead, shield, or armor, to eight times the diameter for interlocked armor cable. Cables or special construction such as wire armor and high-voltage cables require a larger radius bend.

Best results are obtained in installing long lengths of cable up to 1,000 feet with as many as a dozen bends by pulling the cable in one continuous operation at a speed of 20 to 25 feet per minute. It may be necessary to brake the reel to reduce sagging of the cables between rollers and sheaves.

The pulling line diameter and length will, of course, depend on the pull to be made and the tools and equipment available. Winch and power units must be of adequate size for the job and capable of developing the high pulling speeds required for the best and most economical results.

In general, single or multi-cable rollers are placed in the bottom of trays to protect the cable as it is pulled along. Sheaves are placed at each change of direction—either horizontally or vertically. The bottom rollers may be secured to the tray bottoms except at vertical changes in direction. Extra support is necessary at these locations to prevent damage or movement of the tray system.

NOTE

If single cables are to be installed, always place them on the outside of a bend to allow room on the inside of the bend for pulling other cables.

Sheaves must be supported in the opposite direction of the pull. For example, all right-angle conveyor sheaves should be supported at two locations, as shown in *Figure 26*, to compensate for the pull of the cable.

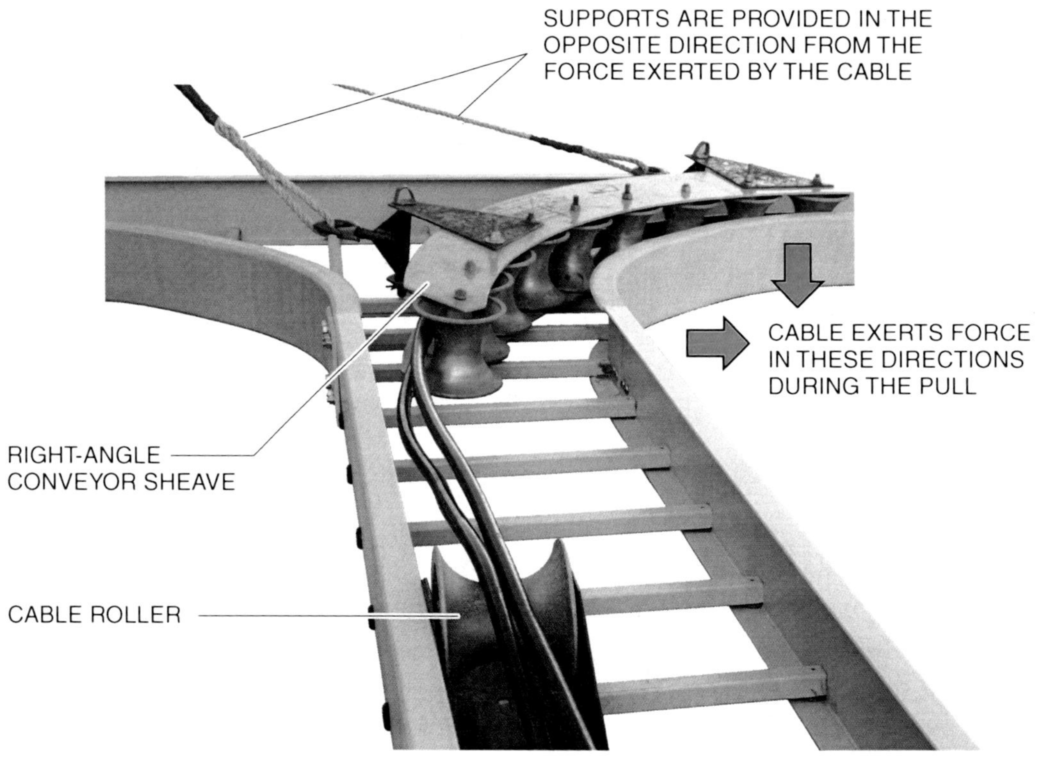
SUPPORTS ARE PROVIDED IN THE OPPOSITE DIRECTION FROM THE FORCE EXERTED BY THE CABLE
CABLE EXERTS FORCE IN THESE DIRECTIONS DURING THE PULL
RIGHT-ANGLE CONVEYOR SHEAVE
CABLE ROLLER
26206-14_F26.EPS

Figure 26 Typical cable tray cable-pulling arrangement.

NOTE

Power cable pulls should not be stopped unless absolutely necessary. However, anyone associated with the pull—upon evidence of danger to either the cable or the workers—may stop a cable-pulling operation. Communication is the most important factor in these cases.

CAUTION

Workers feeding a cable pull must carefully inspect the cable as it is paid off the cable reel. Any visible defects in the cable at the feeding end warrants stopping the pull.

WARNING!

At the first sign of any type of malfunctioning equipment, broken sheaves, or other events that could present a danger to either the workers or the cable, the pull should be stopped. Make certain that all communications equipment is in proper order before starting a pull.

8.0.0 Physical Limitations of Cable

Consideration must be given to the physical limitations of a cable as it is being pulled into position. Pulling subjects cable to extreme stress and, if done improperly, can displace a cable's components. Thus, it is important that the following guidelines be observed:

- While reels are in storage—either before or after a pull—the conductor ends must be sealed to prevent moisture from entering or creeping into the cable ends.
- The minimum ambient working temperatures for cable-pulling operations depend on the cable jackets. In cold weather, cable reels should be stored in a warm area overnight so that the cable jackets will be at the proper temperature for pulling the next day.
- Calculate and stay within the cable's maximum pulling tension, maximum sidewall load, and minimum bending radii.
- Ensure that the raceway joints are aligned and that the wiring space is sufficient.
- Train the cable to avoid dragging on the edge of the raceway; also avoid laying or dragging cable on the ground.
- If using a basket grip, secure it to the cable with steel strapping and cut well behind the areas it covers once the cable is in place. The portion of the cable under the grip should be discarded.
- Ensure that the elongation of the pull rope minimizes jerking.
- Pull with a capstan and no faster than 40 feet per minute.

- Do not stop a pull unless absolutely necessary.
- Never pull the middle of the cable.
- Seal the ends with appropriate putty or silicone caulking and overwrap with tape until the conductors are terminated.

8.1.0 Maximum Pulling Tension

Maximum pulling tension should not exceed the smaller of the following values:

- Allowable tension on pulling device
- Allowable tension on conductor
- Allowable sidewall load

8.1.1 Allowable Tension on Pulling Device

Do not exceed the working load stated by the manufacturer of the pulling devices (pulling eyes, ropes, anchors, basket grips, etc.). If catalog information is not available, work at 10% of the rated braking tensile strength.

The allowable tension with a basket grip must not exceed the lbs/cmil value (as shown in *Table 3*) or 1,000 pounds, whichever is smaller. Exceptions to this rule, however, do occur, but seldom will this figure rise to over 1,250 pounds.

8.1.2 Allowable Tension on Conductors

The metallic phase conductors are the tensile members of the cables and should bear all of the pulling force. Never use shielding drain wires or braids for pulling. *Table 3* provides the allowable pulling tensions of various types of conductors. The listed values should never be exceeded.

Reduce the maximum pulling tension by 20% to 40% if several conductors are being pulled simultaneously since the tension is not always evenly distributed among the conductors.

CAUTION

When smaller conductors are pulled with large conductors, the smaller conductors may be damaged.

Table 3 Physical Limitations of Cable

Material	Cable Type	Temper	Lbs/Cmil
Copper	All	Soft	0.008
Aluminum	Power	Hard	0.008
Aluminum	Power	¾ Hard	0.006
Aluminum	Power	AWM	0.005
Aluminum	URD (solid)	Soft (½ hard)	0.003
All	Thermocouple	—	0.008

8.2.0 Calculating Pulling Tension

Normally, the maximum tension for a specific type of cable can be found using data from the cable manufacturer.

In general, the maximum tension for a single-conductor cable should not exceed 6,000 pounds. The maximum tension for two or more conductors should not exceed 10,000 pounds.

The maximum stress for leaded cables must not exceed 1,500 pounds per square inch of lead sheath area when pulled with a basket grip.

The maximum tension must not exceed 1,000 pounds per square inch of insulation area for non-leaded cables when pulled with a basket grip.

The maximum tension at a bend must not exceed 500 times the radius of curvature of the conduit or duct expressed in feet.

8.2.1 Tension in Horizontal Pulls

The pulling tension in a given horizontal raceway section may be calculated as follows:

For a straight section, the pulling tension is equal to the length of the duct run multiplied by the weight per foot of the cable and the coefficient of friction, which will vary depending on the type and amount of lubrication used. Therefore, the equation is as follows:

$$T = L \times w \times f$$

Where:

T = total pulling tension
L = length of raceway run in feet
w = weight of cable in pounds per foot
f = coefficient of friction

For ducts having curved sections, the following equation applies:

$$T_{OUT} = T_{in} e^{fa}$$

Where:

T_{OUT} = tension of bend
T_{in} = tension into bend
f = coefficient of friction
e = Napierian logarithm base 2.718
a = angle of bends in radians

To aid in solving the above equation, values of e^{fa} for specific angles of bend and coefficients of friction are listed in *Table 4*. For more precise values, tables are available from cable manufacturers.

On Site

Installation Aids

Other tools available to simplify the pulling of cables into cable tray systems include triple pulleys, bull wheels, and both wide and narrow rollers. Be sure to position these pulleys and rollers at the proper locations to prevent damage to the cables during the installation and also to help the installation proceed as quickly as possible. Various rollers are shown here.

SNAP-IN SPINDLE AND CABLE ROLLER

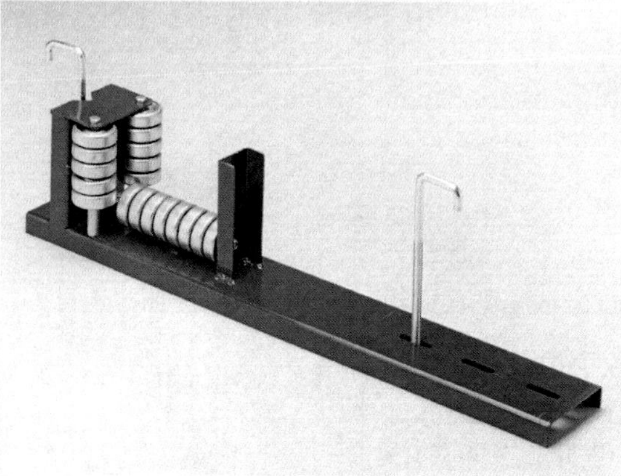

CABLE ROLLER WITH ADJUSTABLE BRACKETS

ELBOW ROLLER

26206-14_SA07.EPS

Table 4 Angle of Bend vs. Coefficients of Friction

Angle of Bend (degrees/ radians)	Values of e^{fa} for Coefficients of Friction		
	f = 0.75	f = 0.50	f = 0.35
15/0.2618	1.22	1.14	1.10
30/0.5236	1.48	1.30	1.20
45/0.7854	1.80	1.48	1.32
60/1.0472	2.19	1.68	1.44
90/1.5708	3.25	2.20	1.73

8.3.0 Sidewall Loading

Before calculating cable-pulling tension, sidewall loading or sidewall bearing pressure must be considered.

The sidewall load is the radial force exerted on a cable being pulled around a conduit bend or sheave. Excessive sidewall loading can crush a cable and is, therefore, one of the most restrictive factors in installations having bends or high tensions. *Figure 27* shows a section taken across a conduit run in a 90° bend. Note that pulling tension

On Site

Software Programs

Software programs are now available to take the math out of calculating pulling tensions. These programs typically calculate pulling tension and sidewall pressures based on conductor size using their own data on friction coefficients. These programs also determine conduit fill, conductor configuration, jam ratios, and the amount of lubricant required for the pull.

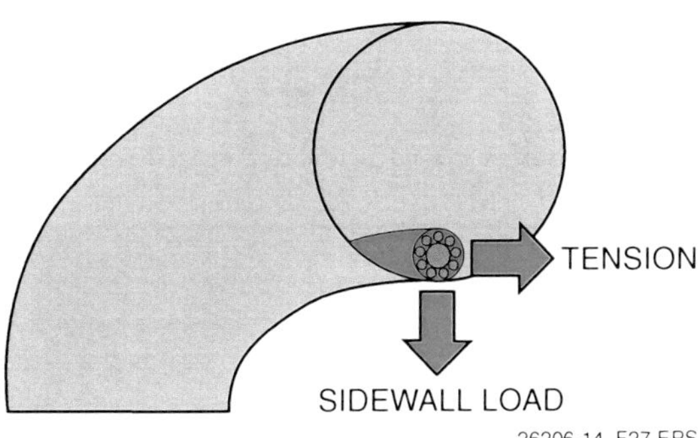

Figure 27 Sidewall loading.

is exerted parallel with the walls of the conduit. However, due to the 90° bend, pressure is also exerted downward against the wall of the conduit. Once again, this is known as the sidewall load. Sidewall loading is reduced by increasing the radius of bends.

In general, the sidewall load on any raceway run should not exceed 500 pounds/foot of bend radius. This pressure, however, must be reduced on some types of cables. For example, *Table 5* shows one manufacturer's recommendations for the maximum sidewall pressures permitted for various types of cables. Always refer to the cable manufacturer's instructions for the type of cable being used.

Table 5 Maximum Sidewall Pressures for Various Types of Cable

Cable Type	Sidewall Pressure in Pounds/Foot of Bend Radius
600V nonshielded control	300
600V and a kV nonshielded EP power	500
5kV and 15kV EP power	500
25kV and 35kV power	300
Interlocked armored cable (all voltages)	300

8.4.0 Practical Applications

Figure 28 shows a typical raceway system containing three 500 kcmil lead sheath copper conductors. Note the straight 300' run from A to B, a 45° kick, and then another 100' straight run from C to D.

To find the calculated pulling tension from D to A, refer to cable data in the manufacturer's catalogs. Suppose this cable weighs 8 pounds per foot and has a 0.141" lead sheath. The outside diameter of the three-conductor cable assembly is 3". Use 0.5 as the coefficient of friction and calculate the pulling tension from A to B (*Figure 28*) as follows:

Step 1 Find the tension between points A and B.

$$\text{Tension at B} = T_1 = L_1 \times w \times f$$

L_1 is the length between points A and B while w is the weight of the cable per foot, and f is the coefficient of friction, which is 0.5. Substituting the known values in the equation gives:

$$T_1 = 300 \times 8 \times 0.5 = 1{,}200 \text{ pounds}$$

Step 2 Find the tension between points B and C.

$$\text{Tension at C} = T_1\, e^{fa}$$

Since the distance between B and C involves an angle, refer to *Table 4* of this module. Looking in the left column of the table, we see that 45° equals 0.7854 radians; this figure multiplied by the coefficient of friction (0.5) equals 0.3927. Radians of angles may also be found with electronic pocket calculators if they have scientific functions. Follow the instructions in the manual accompanying the calculator. The exact key strokes will vary with the brand of calculator, but most require pressing

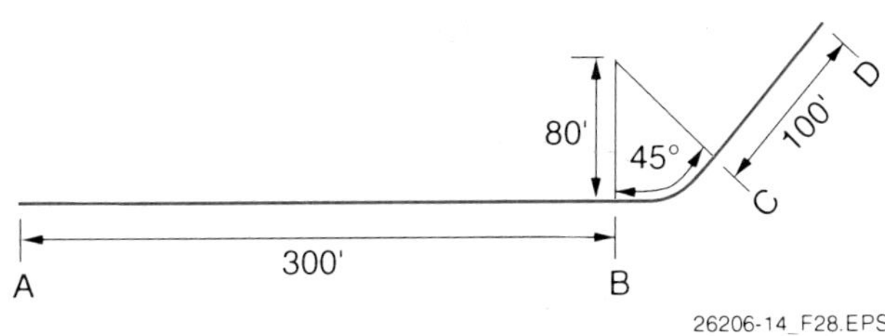

Figure 28 Sample conduit run.

the degree key, entering the numeral for degrees, then pressing the convert key, and finally pressing the radian or RAD key. The radians of the entered angle will be displayed.

Once again, refer to *Table 4*. Find the 45° angle of bend in the left column; read across the row to the column under 0.50—the coefficient of friction figure. The number is 1.48, the value of e^{fa}. Substituting these values in the equation gives the following:

$$A = 45° = 0.7854 \text{ radians}$$

$$fa = 0.7854 \times 0.5 = 0.3927$$

$$e^{fa} = 1.48$$

$$1{,}200 \times 1.48 = 1{,}776 \text{ pounds}$$

Therefore, the tension at C is 1,776 pounds.

Step 3 Find the tension from points C to D.

$$\text{Tension from C to D} = T_2 = L_2 \times w \times f$$

$$T_2 = 100 \times 8 \times 0.5 = 400 \text{ pounds}$$

Step 4 Find the total pulling tension by adding the figures obtained previously.

$$T = T_2 + T_1e^{fa} = 400 + 1{,}776$$
$$= 2{,}176 \text{ pounds}$$

The maximum pulling force using a basket grip for this size cable should not exceed 1,900 pounds. Therefore, if the pull is made from point A to point D, a pulling eye will have to be used since the total pulling tension exceeds 1,900 pounds. However, if the pull is reversed—pulling from point D to point A—the total pulling tension will be reduced since the distance from point D to the 45° angle (point C) is ⅓ the distance from point A to the 45° angle (point B).

$$\text{Tension at C} = 400 \text{ pounds}$$

$$\text{Tension at B} = 400 \times 1.48 = 592 \text{ pounds}$$

$$\text{Total tension at A} = 1{,}200 + 592$$
$$= 1{,}792 \text{ pounds}$$

Therefore, if the cable is pulled from point D to point A, either a pulling eye or basket grip may be used.

NOTE

A lower tension is obtained by feeding the pull from the end nearest the bend.

9.0.0 Cable-Pulling Instruments

There are several instruments used in conjunction with cable-pulling operations. Since details of operation vary with the manufacturer, these instruments will only be briefly discussed in this module. Study the operation manuals for all instruments before using them.

- *Cable length meter* – Cable length meters (*Figure 29*) are available for direct reading in lengths from 2,000' to 20,000'. Most are calibrated for different wire sizes whereas the sizes are selected with a selector switch on the instrument. Controls may also be set for either copper or aluminum conductors. These instruments are ideal for determining the exact length of conductors on reels prior to making a pull.
- *Circuit tester/wire sorter* – This instrument is used to trace conductors on unenergized circuits. See *Figure 30*. One lead of the transmitter is attached to ground while the other lead is attached to the wire being traced. The receiver is then taken to the opposite end of the circuit, where it will show a strong signal on the traced conductor. That wire is marked and other wires are traced in the same way.

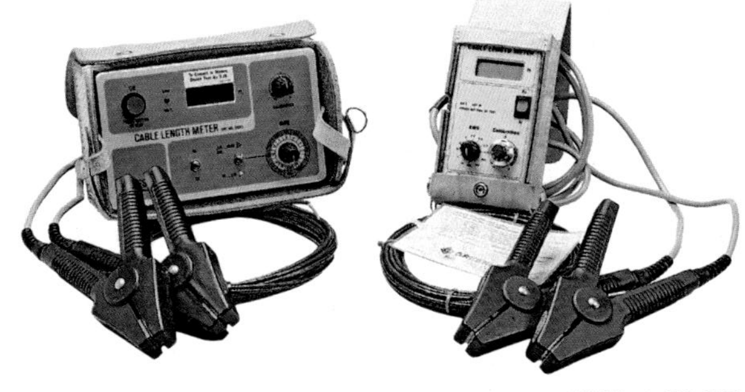

26206-14_F29.EPS

Figure 29 Cable length meters.

Case History

Cable Pulling

At a large commercial job site recently, workers began a complex pull shortly before the end of the day. At 5 PM, they left for the day, having completed only a portion of the pulling operation. The next day, they resumed work promptly at 8 AM, but the pulling lubricant had already dried in the conduit. As a result of the excess friction on the pull, the rope broke, delaying the job and causing extensive rework.

The Bottom Line: Don't stop a pull in the middle of a job.

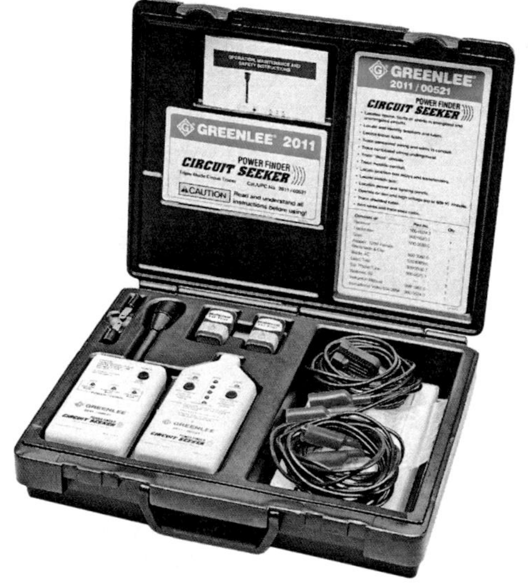

26206-14_F30.EPS

Figure 30 Circuit tester.

Case History

Cable Pulling

In June 2006, an electrician was tagging instrumentation cable on a work platform about 30 feet off the ground. At the same time, a crew was pulling an assembly in an adjacent cable tray but failed to install caution signs or barrier controls. The inexperienced crew did not monitor the tension on the pulling assembly and it failed during the pull, whipping back along the cable tray and picking up a loose cable roller, which propelled into the victim at high speed. It amputated his arm, broke his ribs and femur, and ruptured several internal organs. He died from his injuries.

The Bottom Line: Only qualified individuals may conduct a cable pull. All pulling equipment must be tested and certified for the expected load, and the area must be secured with caution/barrier controls during the pull.

On Site

Complex Installations

Complex cable-pulling installations are best handled by highly experienced contractors. This is one small portion of an award-winning installation that took over 70,000 hours to complete.

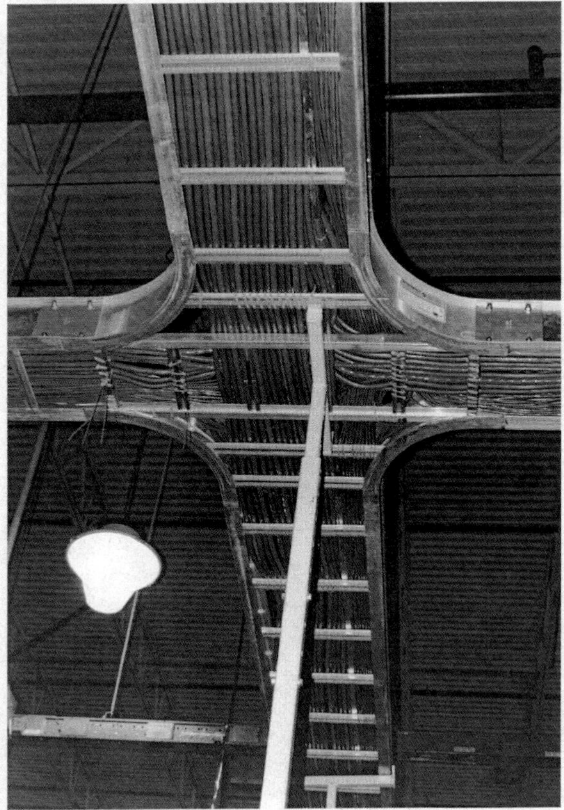

26206-14_SA08.EPS

- *Dynamometer (force gauge)* – This type of meter is designed to read dynamic friction (pulling force) during a cable pull. Many are designed for a specific cable-pulling tool and are shipped as an integral or optional part of the cable puller. For example, one common cable puller electronically displays both actual speed and actual force while running. It automatically shuts down when maximum preset force is reached to prevent damage to the cable being pulled. Others are portable units for use with any type of cable-pulling equipment. Such instruments are invaluable for use during high-force cable pulls to avoid damage to conductors during the pull. When the instrument indicates that the maximum pulling force has been reached, the pull can be stopped before damage occurs to the cable or conductors.

SUMMARY

A cable-pulling operation involves careful planning. Furthermore, the proper use of appropriate equipment is crucial to a successful cable installation. Think of everything that can go wrong, and then plan accordingly.

Communications equipment is another crucial part of a cable installation. Workers on both ends must be in constant contact with each other in case something goes wrong. The workers feeding the cable must carefully inspect the cable as it is paid off the reels and stop the pull immediately if the cable appears damaged. In fact, anyone involved with the pull should be able to stop the pull whenever the safety of the cable or personnel is threatened. Again, good communication is crucial.

Safety precautions must be followed exactly during any cable installation. Use the correct size and type of equipment for the job. Never exceed the maximum force of the weakest component. Do not position yourself in a direct line with a cable pull.

Review Questions

1. Who is allowed to stop the pull at the first sign of danger to the cable, raceway system, or personnel?
   a. Only the project supervisor
   b. Only workers on the feeding end of the run
   c. Only workers on the pulling end of the run
   d. Anyone involved with the pull

2. After some length of conductor has been used from a cable reel, what should be done before placing the reel in storage?
   a. A stress test should be made to see if the cable has been damaged.
   b. An insulation test should be made using a megger.
   c. The ends of the conductors should be sealed.
   d. The conductor jacket should be warmed before storing.

3. Which of the following precautions should be taken when making a cable pull in extremely cold weather?
   a. The cable should be stored in a warm area overnight.
   b. The cable should be stored outside overnight.
   c. Antifreeze should be mixed with the pulling lubricant.
   d. Electric warming blankets should be used during the pull.

4. Which of the following pulling methods should be used when the pulling tension exceeds 1,000 pounds?
   a. A basket grip by itself
   b. A pulling eye
   c. Conductors bent around a hook and taped
   d. Conductors bent around a snake hook and left untaped

5. All the following are acceptable methods of transporting or storing cable reels *except* _____.
   a. reels should be stored in an upright position
   b. reels should be laid flat on their sides
   c. reels should be lifted by a rigged crane with a spindle through the reel
   d. reels should be carried with a forklift so that the forks do not touch the cable

6. Where is the best place to seek information about a wire-pulling lubricant that is compatible with a particular type of cable insulation?
   a. The lubricant manufacturer
   b. The cable manufacturer
   c. Both the cable and lubricant manufacturers
   d. The *NEC*®

7. How should the feed-in setup be handled during a cable installation?
   a. The cable should unreel with a reverse S curvature.
   b. It makes no difference.
   c. Only the pulling end is important when unreeling the cable.
   d. The cable should unreel along its natural curvature.

8. All of the following may be used to guide a cable during a pull *except* _____.
   a. a conveyor sheave
   b. a polygon setup
   c. a guide-in tube
   d. a cable reel

9. Which of the following is the most important consideration when pulling cables in vertical pulls?
   a. Calculate the cable weight before installation.
   b. Install the cable from the bottom up.
   c. Guard against runaways.
   d. Use less wire lubricant than in horizontal applications.

10. Which of the following best describes the location of sheave supports for pulling cable in cable trays?
    a. They should be supported in the opposite direction of the pull.
    b. They should be supported in the same direction as the pull.
    c. They should be supported only by the tray assembly itself.
    d. No support is necessary when sheaves are used in cable trays.

Module 26206-14
Supplemental Exercises

1. Prior to installing conductors in a long conduit run, it is a good idea to use ________ to check for hidden obstructions.

   a. a go/no-go mandrel
   b. ¼" fish tape
   c. a flashlight
   d. a blow gun system

2. If a conduit presently contains energized cables and it must be fished, you should ________.

   a. use fiberglass fish tape
   b. tape the end of the metal fish tape
   c. use a vacuum system
   d. not fish it until the cables are de-energized

3. When installing large cables which require more pulling force, select a rope that is rated for at least ________________ times the strength of the required pulling force.

4. True or False? If commercial wire lubricant is not available, any suitable petroleum-based product may be substituted.

5. When pulling vertical runs, be sure to ________________ the rope after stopping the pull to keep the cable from reversing in the raceway.

6. When installing conductors in long vertical runs, you should install ________________ to help prevent runaways.

7. True or False? When pulling long runs of cable, stopping on a regular basis will allow the cable to cool and will avoid stressing the cable.

8. True or False? Cable length meters may be used to determine the length of conductors on reels prior to making a pull.

9. When applying the capstan theory to a power puller, more wraps on the capstan will result in ______________ pulling force.

10. What type of pulling device uses a flexible steel mesh grip on the ends of cable and attaches to the pulling rope?

    a. Mandrel
    b. Fish tape
    c. Basket grip
    d. Pulling eyes

Trade Terms Introduced in This Module

Basket grip: A flexible steel mesh grip that is used on the ends of cable and conductors for attaching the pulling rope. The more force exerted on the pull, the tighter the grip wraps around the cable.

Cable grip: A device used to secure ends of cables to a pulling rope during cable pulls.

Capstan: The turning drum of a cable puller on which the rope is wrapped and pulled. An increase in the number of wraps increases the pulling force of the cable puller.

Clevis: A device used in cable pulls to facilitate connecting the pulling rope to the cable grip.

Conductor support: The act of providing support in vertical conduit runs to support the cables or conductors. The *NEC®* gives several methods in which cables may be supported, including wedges in the tops of conduits, supports to change the direction of cable in pull boxes, etc.

Conduit piston: A cylinder of foam rubber that fits inside the conduit and is then propelled by compressed air or vacuumed through the conduit run to pull a line, rope, or measuring tape. Also called a mouse.

Fish line: Light cord used in conjunction with vacuum/blower power fishing systems that attaches to the conduit piston to be pushed or pulled through the conduit. Once through, a pulling rope is attached to one end and pulled back through the conduit for use in pulling conductors.

Fish tape: A flat iron wire or fiber cord used to pull conductors or a pulling rope through conduit.

Setscrew grip: A cable grip, usually with built-in clevis, in which the cable ends are inserted in holes and secured with one or more setscrews.

Sheave: A pulley-like device used in cable pulls in both conduit and cable tray systems.

Soap: Slang for wire-pulling lubricant.

Additional Resources

This module presents thorough resources for task training. The following resource material is suggested for further study.

Cable Installation Manual, Latest Edition. New York: Cablec Corp.

National Electrical Code® Handbook, Latest Edition. Quincy, MA: National Fire Protection Association.

Figure Credits

AGC of America, Module opener

Topaz Publications, Inc., Figure 1, SA01, Figures 12A, 12B, 14B, 25, and SA08

Greenlee/A Textron Company, Figures 2, 3, SA02, Figures 8, 10, SA03, Figures 12C, 13, 14A, SA04, Figure 16, SA05, Figures 17–19, SA06, Figures 20, 23, SA07, Figures 29 and 30

National Fire Protection Association, Table 2 Reprinted with permission from *NFPA 70®*-2014, *National Electrical Code®*, Copyright © 2013, National Fire Protection Association, Quincy, MA. This reprinted material is not the complete and official position of the National Fire Protection Association on the referenced subject, which is represented only by the standard in its entirety. *NFPA 70®*, *National Electrical Code®*, and *NEC®* are registered trademarks of the National Fire Protection Association, Inc., Quincy, MA.

Tim Dean, Figure 26

NCCER CURRICULA — USER UPDATE

NCCER makes every effort to keep its textbooks up-to-date and free of technical errors. We appreciate your help in this process. If you find an error, a typographical mistake, or an inaccuracy in NCCER's curricula, please fill out this form (or a photocopy), or complete the online form at **www.nccer.org/olf**. Be sure to include the exact module ID number, page number, a detailed description, and your recommended correction. Your input will be brought to the attention of the Authoring Team. Thank you for your assistance.

Instructors – If you have an idea for improving this textbook, or have found that additional materials were necessary to teach this module effectively, please let us know so that we may present your suggestions to the Authoring Team.

NCCER Product Development and Revision
13614 Progress Blvd., Alachua, FL 32615
Email: curriculum@nccer.org
Online: www.nccer.org/olf

❑ Trainee Guide ❑ AIG ❑ Exam ❑ PowerPoints Other ______________________

Craft / Level: Copyright Date:

Module ID Number / Title:

Section Number(s):

Description:

Recommended Correction:

Your Name:

Address:

Email: Phone:

Conductor Terminations and Splices

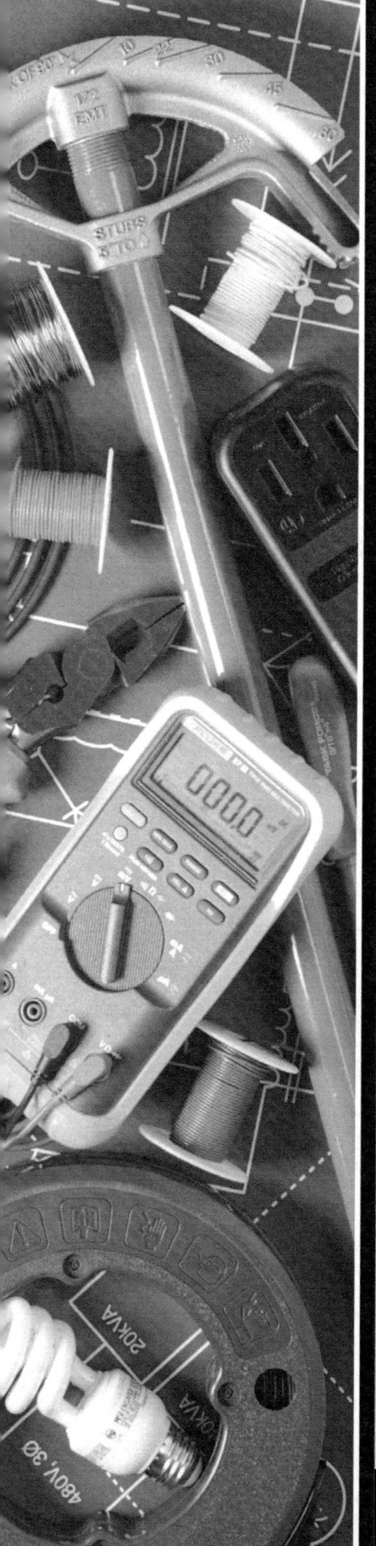

Daytona International Speedway Infield

QuestCom won an ABC Excellence in Construction award for its work on updating Daytona International Speedway's 45-year-old facilities with state-of-the-art telecommunications, fire alarm systems, and concert-quality sound.

26208-14

Trainees with successful module completions may be eligible for credentialing through NCCER's National Registry. To learn more, go to **www.nccer.org** or contact us at **1.888.622.3720.** Our website has information on the latest product releases and training, as well as online versions of our *Cornerstone* magazine and Pearson's product catalog.

Your feedback is welcome. You may email your comments to **curriculum@nccer.org,** send general comments and inquiries to **info@nccer.org,** or fill in the User Update form at the back of this module.

This information is general in nature and intended for training purposes only. Actual performance of activities described in this manual requires compliance with all applicable operating, service, maintenance, and safety procedures under the direction of qualified personnel. References in this manual to patented or proprietary devices do not constitute a recommendation of their use.

26208-14

Conductor Terminations and Splices

Objectives

When you have completed this module, you will be able to do the following:

1. Describe how to make a good conductor termination.
2. Prepare cable ends for terminations and splices and connect using lugs or connectors.
3. Train cable at termination points.
4. Understand the *National Electrical Code®* (*NEC®*) requirements for making cable terminations and splices.
5. Demonstrate crimping techniques.
6. Select the proper lug or connector for the job.

Performance Tasks

Under the supervision of the instructor, you should be able to do the following:

1. Terminate conductors using selected crimp-type and mechanical-type terminals and connectors.
2. Terminate conductors on a terminal strip.
3. Insulate selected types of wire splices and/or install a motor connection kit.

Trade Terms

AL-CU
Amperage capacity
Connection
Connector
Drain wire
Grooming
Insulating tape
Lug
Mechanical advantage (MA)
Pressure connector
Reducing connector
Shielding
Splice
Strand
Terminal
Termination

Required Trainee Materials

1. Pencil and paper
2. Copy of the latest edition of the *National Electrical Code®*
3. Appropriate personal protective equipment

Note:
NFPA 70®, *National Electrical Code®*, and *NEC®* are registered trademarks of the National Fire Protection Association, Inc., Quincy, MA 02269. All *National Electrical Code®* and *NEC®* references in this module refer to the 2014 edition of the *National Electrical Code®*.

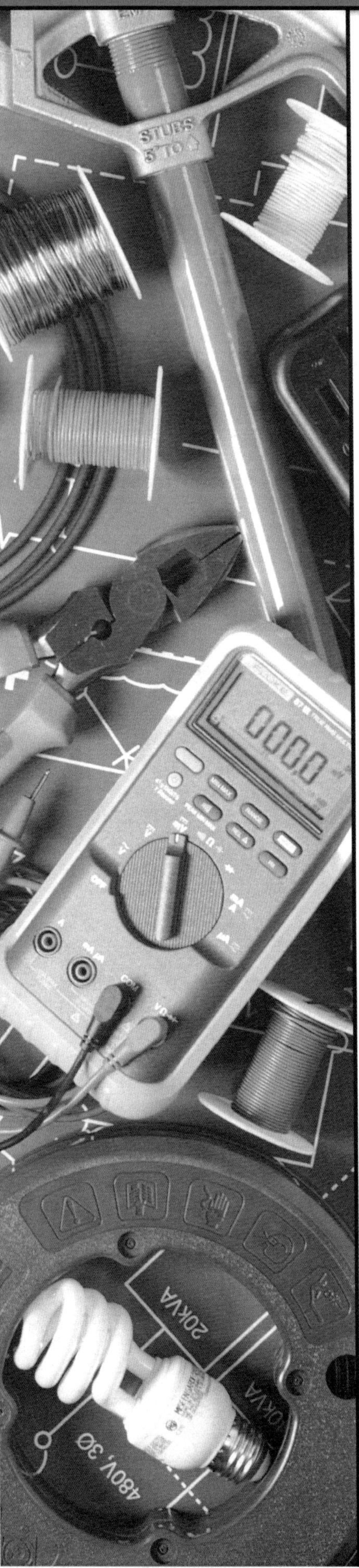

Contents

Topics to be presented in this module include:

Figures and Tables

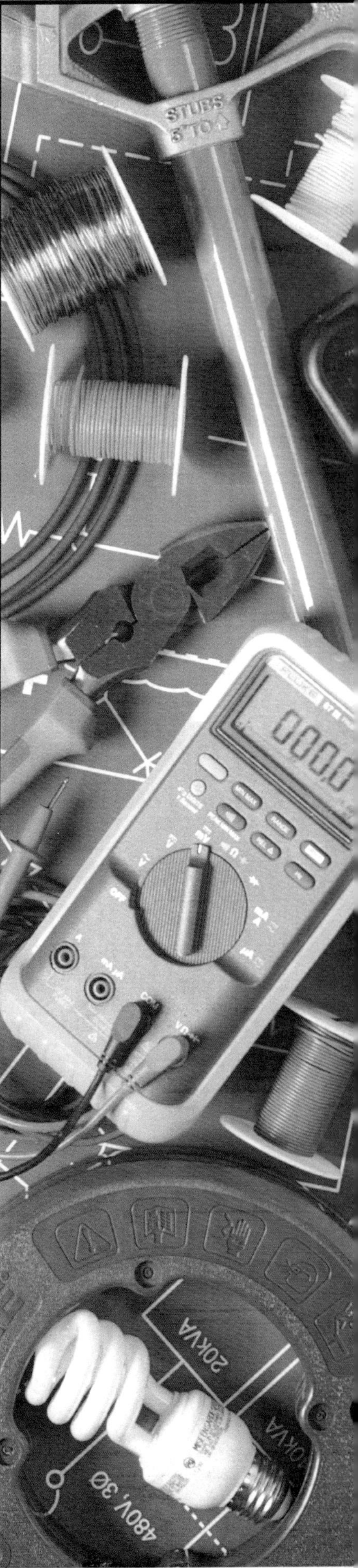

1.0.0 Introduction

Anyone involved with electrical systems of any type must be familiar with wire connectors and splicing, as they are both necessary to make the numerous electrical joints required during the course of an electrical installation. A properly made splice and connection should last as long as the insulation on the wire itself, while a poorly made connection will always be a source of trouble; that is, the joints will overheat under load and eventually fail with the potential for starting a fire. The majority of failures occur at terminations.

The basic requirements for a good electrical connection include the following:

- It must be mechanically and electrically secure.
- It must be insulated as well as or better than the existing insulation on the conductors.
- These characteristics should last as long as the conductor is in service.

> **NOTE**
> Every splice is a point of potential failure. Therefore, splicing should not be used as a solution to providing shorter conductor pulls. In fact, some applications prohibit the use of splices in critical areas.

There are many different types of electrical joints, and the selection of the proper type for a given application often depends on how and where the splice or connection is used. Electrical joints are normally made with a solderless pressure connector or lug to save time.

2.0.0 Stripping and Cleaning Conductors

Before any connection or splice can be made, the ends of the conductors must be properly cleaned and stripped. To ensure a low-resistance connection and avoid contaminating the termination, clean the areas of the cable where it is to be cut and stripped. Remove any pulling compound, dirt, oil, grease, or water to avoid contaminating the exposed conductor.

Stripping is the removal of insulation from the end of the conductor or at the location of the splice. Conductors should only be stripped using the appropriate stripping tool. This will help to prevent cuts and nicks in the wire, which can reduce the conductor area and weaken the conductor.

> **On Site**
>
> **Conductor Terminations and Splices**
>
> Poor electrical connections are responsible for a large percentage of equipment burnouts and fires. Many of these failures are a direct result of improper terminations, poor workmanship, and the use of improper splicing devices.

Poorly stripped conductors can result in nicks, scrapes, or burnishes. Any of these can lead to a stress concentration in the damaged area. Heat, rapid temperature changes, mechanical vibration, and oscillatory motion can aggravate the damage, causing faults in the circuitry or even total failure. Lost strands are a problem in splice or crimp-type terminals, while exposed strands might be a safety hazard.

Faulty stripping can pierce, scuff, or split the insulation. This can cause changes in dielectric strength and lower the conductor's resistance to moisture and abrasion. Insulation particles often get trapped in solder and crimp joints. These form the basis for a defective termination. A variety of factors determine how precisely a conductor can be stripped, including the wire size and type of insulation.

It is a common misconception that a certain gauge of stranded conductor has the same diameter as a solid conductor. This is a very important consideration in selecting the proper blades for strippers. *Table 1* shows the nominal sizes referenced for the different wire gauges.

To eliminate nicking, cutting, and fraying, wires should only be stripped using the appropriate stripping tool. The specific tool used depends on the size and type of wire being stripped.

2.1.0 Stripping Small Conductors

There are many kinds of wire strippers available. *Figure 1* shows a common type of wire stripper for small conductors. It can be used to cut, strip, and crimp wires from No. 22 through No. 10 AWG. To use this tool, insert the conductor into the proper size knife groove, then squeeze the tool handles. The tool cuts the conductor insulation, allowing the conductor to be easily removed

Table 1 Dimensions of Common Wire Sizes

Size (A WG/kcmil)	Area (Circular Mils)	Overall Diameter in Inches	
		Solid	Stranded
18	1,620	0.040	0.046
16	2,580	0.051	0.058
14	4,130	0.064	0.073
12	6,530	0.081	0.092
10	10,380	0.102	0.116
8	16,510	0.128	0.146
6	26,240	—	0.184
4	41,740	—	0.232
3	52,620	—	0.260
2	66,360	—	0.292
1	83,690	—	0.332
1/0	105,600	—	0.373
2/0	133,100	—	0.419
3/0	167,800	—	0.470
4/0	211,600	—	0.528
250	—	—	0.575
300	—	—	0.630
350	—	—	0.681
400	—	—	0.728
500	—	—	0.813
600	—	—	0.893
700	—	—	0.964
750	—	—	0.998
800	—	—	1.03
900	—	—	1.09
1,000	—	—	1.15
1,250	—	—	1.29
1,500	—	—	1.41
1,750	—	—	1.52
2,000	—	—	1.63

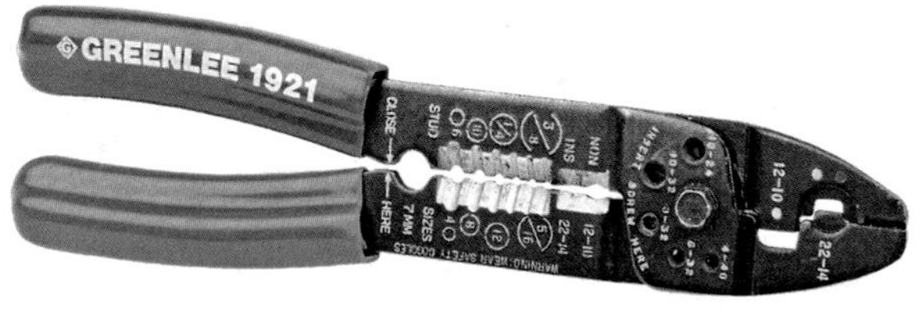

Figure 1 Wire stripper/crimper.

without crushing its stripped end. The length of the strip is regulated by the amount of wire extending beyond the blades when it is inserted in the knife groove.

Figure 2 shows production-grade stripping tools. *Figure 2(A)* can be used to strip conductors from No. 20 to No. 10 AWG, while *Figure 2(B)* strips wires from No. 18 to No. 6 AWG. Note

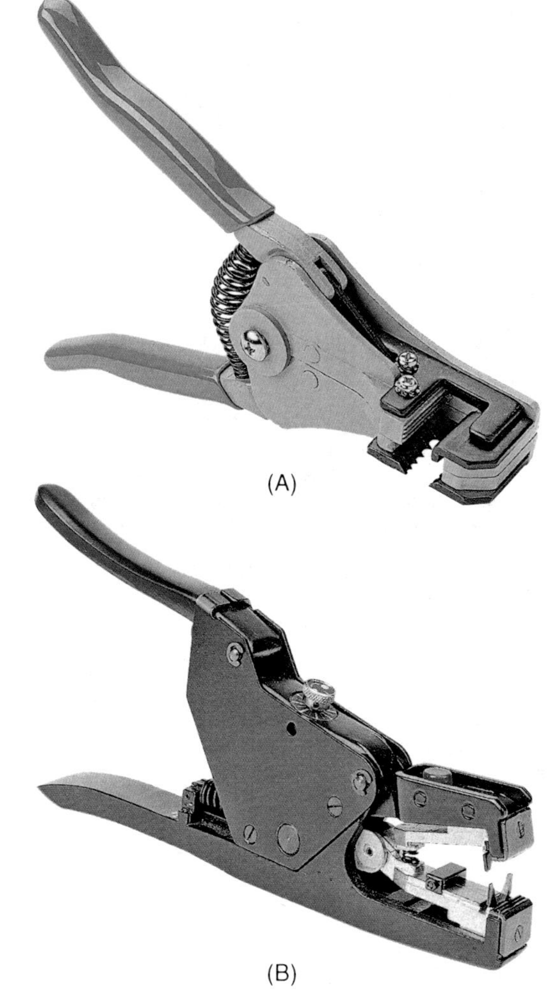

Figure 2 Wire strippers.

that this tool has front entry jaws for use in tight spaces.

2.2.0 Stripping Power Cables and Large Conductors

Larger conductors can be cut using a ratchet-type cable cutter. The cable cutter shown in *Figure 3* can be used to cut cables up to 1,000 kcmil. Heavy-duty strippers are used to strip large power cables. *Figure 4* shows a heavy-duty stripper used to strip power cables with outside diameters ranging from 1/0 through 1,000 kcmil. Strippers can be used to remove insulation from the end of a cable or to make window cuts (*Figure 5*). All stripping tools should be operated according to the manufacturer's instructions. The procedures for using the tool shown in *Figure 4* to strip insulation from the end of a cable and to make a window cut are described here.

Figure 3 Ratchet-type cable cutter.

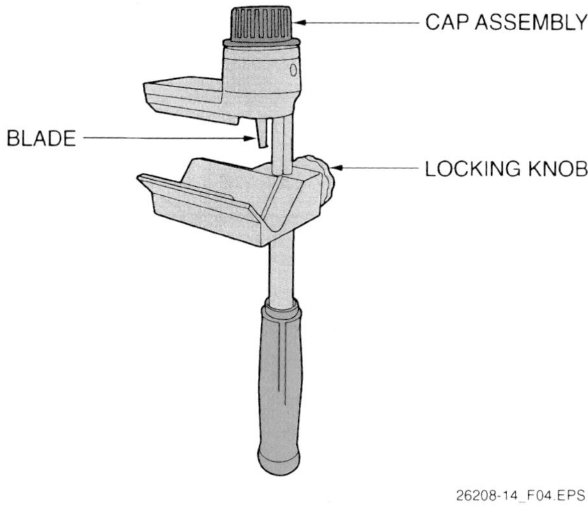

Figure 4 Heavy-duty cable stripper.

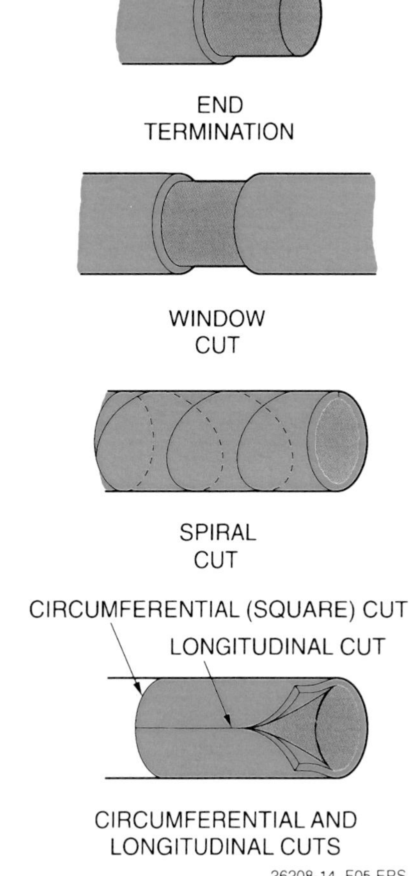

Figure 5 Types of cable stripping.

On Site

Cable Strippers

Open-blade (knife) stripping can damage the conductors and is prohibited on many job sites. Adjustable strippers such as the tool shown here are used instead.

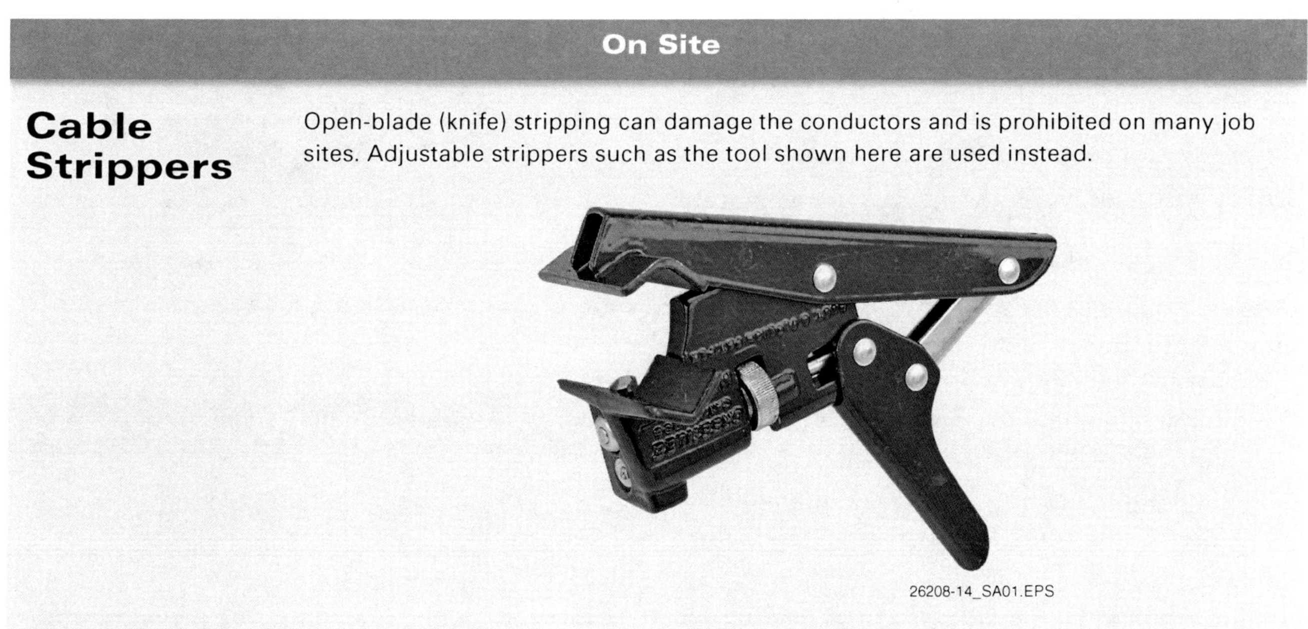

WARNING!

Keep fingers away from the blade when using any stripping tool.

To strip insulation from the end of a cable, proceed as follows:

Step 1 Loosen the locking knob to open the tool to the maximum position. Place the cable in the V-groove and close the tool firmly around the cable. Tighten the locking knob.

Step 2 Turn the cap assembly until the blade reaches the required depth.

CAUTION

Do not allow the blade to contact the conductor because damage to the conductor and/or the blade can result.

Step 3 Rotate the tool around the cable, advancing to the required strip length.

Step 4 Rotate the tool in the reverse direction to produce a square end cut.

Step 5 Loosen the locking knob to release the tool and remove it from the cable.

Step 6 Peel off the insulation.

To make a window cut, proceed as follows:

Step 1 With the tool opened to the maximum position, place the cable in the V-groove and close the tool firmly around the cable. Tighten the locking knob.

Step 2 Turn the cap assembly until the blade reaches the required depth.

Step 3 Rotate the tool to produce the first square cut.

Step 4 Rotate the tool in the reverse direction to cut the required window strip length.

Step 5 Rotate the tool in the original direction to produce the second square cut.

Step 6 Loosen the locking knob assembly to release the tool and remove it from the cable.

Step 7 Peel off the insulation.

Figure 6 shows a round cable slitting and ringing tool that can be used to strip single- or multiconductor cables. This tool can be used to cut around the cable (square cut) or slit the length of the cable jacket (longitudinal cut) for easy removal. The tool blade is adjustable to accommodate different jacket thicknesses.

2.3.0 Stripping Control and Signal Cable/Conductors

A scissor-action type of cutting tool is preferable to cutting tools with jaws that butt against each other. These tools have a tendency to produce a flattened chisel end on the conductor, especially when the cutting edges become dull, as shown in *Figure 7*. This makes it difficult to insert the conductor into the barrel of a terminal.

Observe the following points when stripping conductors:

- Remove the cable jacket using strippers with an adjustable blade or a die designed for the particular wire size (*Figure 8*). The terminal manufacturer will recommend a stripping length. Be careful to avoid nicking or stretching the conductor or insulation in a multi-conductor cable. If this type of damage occurs, it is likely that the wrong groove of the stripping tool was used, the tool was improperly set or damaged, the wrong type of stripping blade was used, or the tool was used incorrectly.

26208-14_F06.EPS

Figure 6 Round cable slitting and ringing tool.

On Site

Stripping Cables

When using any bladed-type cable stripper, make sure to replace the blade whenever it becomes dull. Remember, a dull blade is more dangerous than a sharp one because you are more likely to apply undue pressure when using a dull blade, causing it to slip.

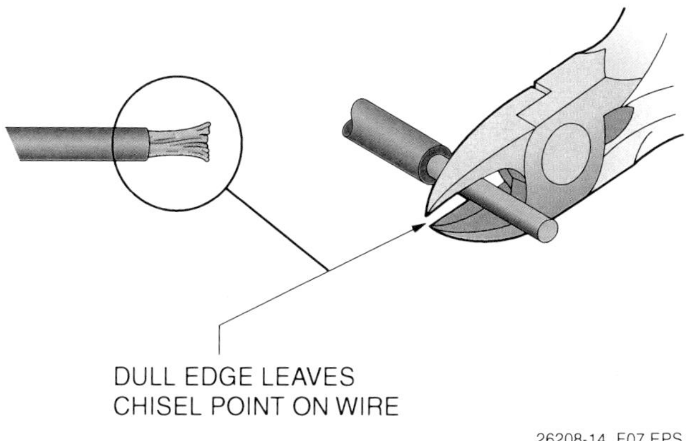

Figure 7 Chisel point on a conductor.

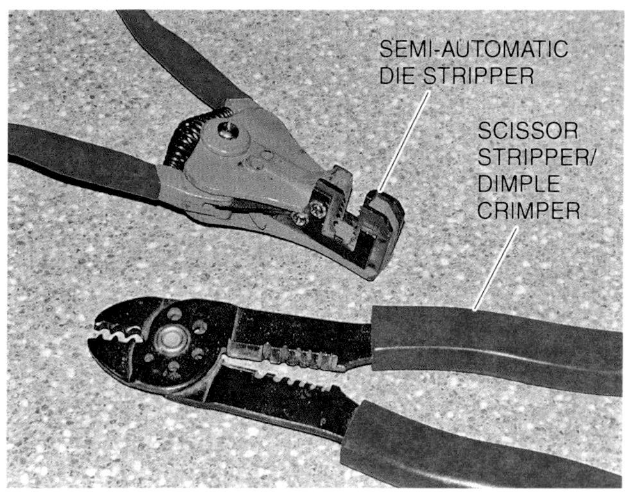

Figure 8 Cable and wire stripping tools.

On Site

Cutting Large Power Cable

When cutting large power cables prior to stripping, you can make the job easier by using a battery-powered cable cutter such as the one shown here. Electric and hydraulic cable cutters are also available.

- Cut the insulation so that no frayed pieces or threads extend past the point of cutoff. Frayed pieces or threads of insulation indicate the use of an improper tool or dull cutter blades.
- If possible, do not twist, spread, or disturb the wire strands from their original position in the cable. Retwisting or tightening the twist of the strands will eventually result in damage.
- Terminate stripped wire as soon as possible. The exposed strands will invariably become bent and spread, making termination difficult. A minimum amount of handling and storage after stripping will result in better terminations.

Figure 9 shows the positioning of the wire in the crimp barrel when stripped to the proper length. The conductor insulation must be in the belled mouth of the terminal. This relieves stress on the strands or wire and increases the strength of the connection. Allowing conductor strands to protrude out of the inspection hole more than 1⁄32" will interfere with the terminal screw. Cutting the strands too short will reduce the contact surface area.

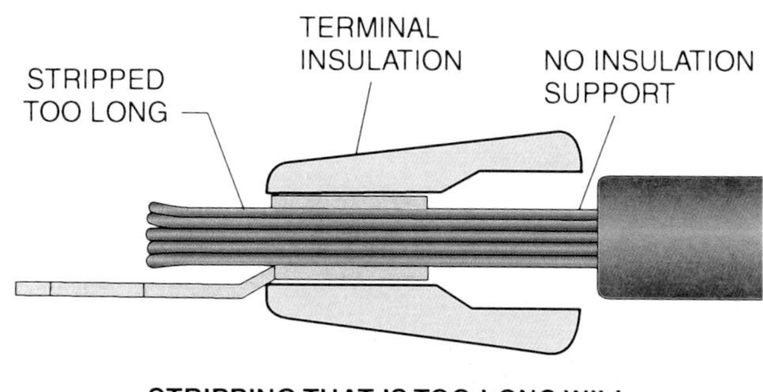

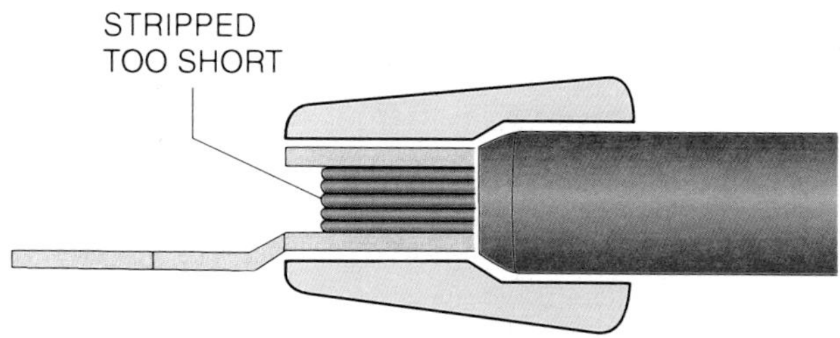

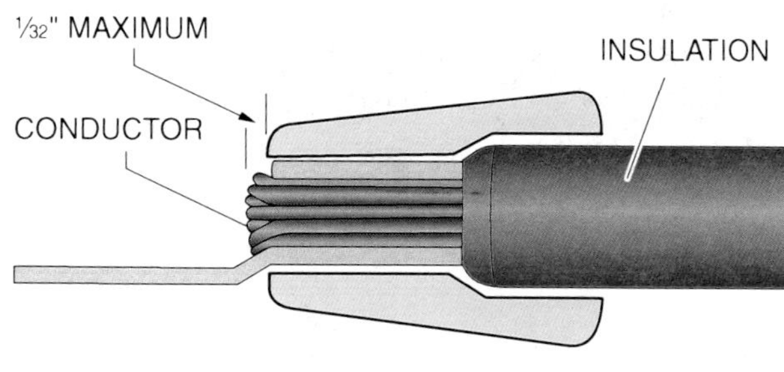

Figure 9 Proper stripping length.

Think About It

Mechanical Compression Connectors

Can you name a use for a compression connector with a two-hole tongue?

3.0.0 Wire Connections

NEC Section 110.14 governs electrical connections, including terminations and splices. Wire connections are used to connect a wire or cable to electrically operated devices such as fan coil units, duct heaters, oil burners, motors, pumps, and control circuits of all types.

A variety of wire connectors for stranded wire are shown in *Figure 10*. These connectors are available in various sizes to accommodate wire sizes No. 22 AWG and larger. They can be installed with crimping tools having a single or double indenter. The range is normally stamped on the tongue of each terminal.

Mechanical compression-type terminators are also available to accommodate wires from No. 8 AWG through 1,000 kcmil. One-hole lugs, two-hole lugs, split-bolt connectors, and other types are shown in *Figure 11*.

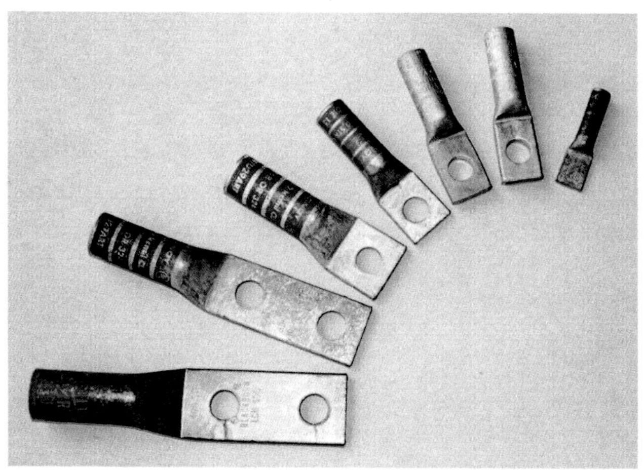

Figure 10 Crimp-on wire lugs.

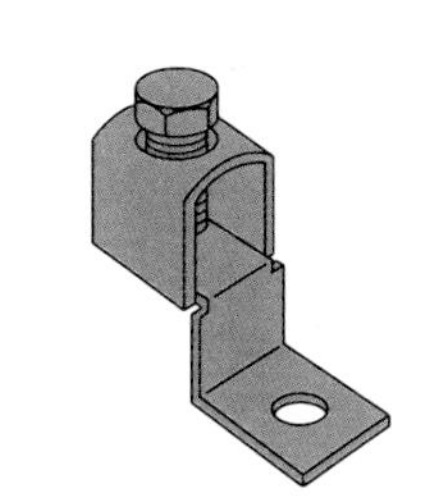
ONE BARREL, OFFSET TONGUE
ONE HOLE
NO. 14 AWG THROUGH 1,000 KCMIL

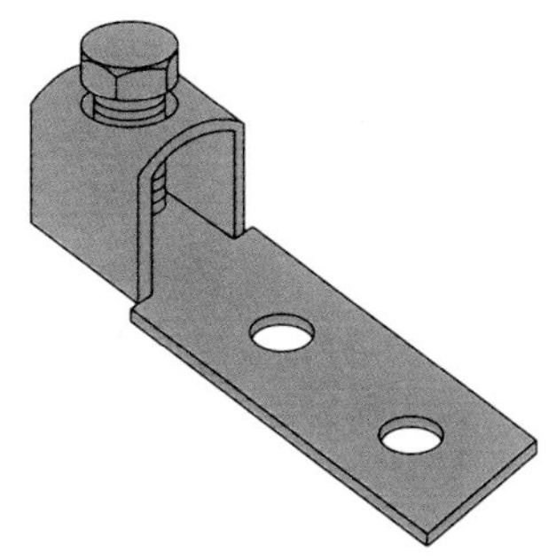
ONE BARREL, STRAIGHT TONGUE
TWO HOLE
NO. 14 AWG THROUGH 1,000 KCMIL

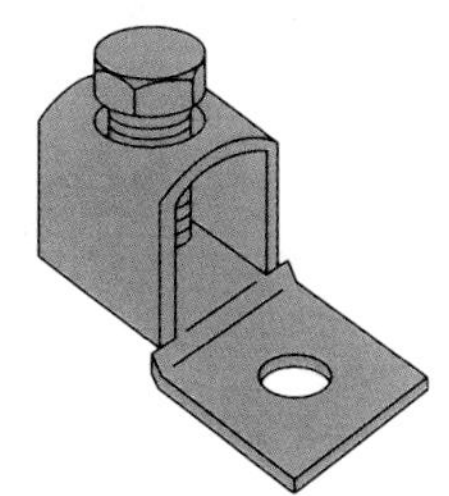
ONE BARREL, FIXED TONGUE
ONE HOLE
NO. 14 AWG THROUGH 500 KCMIL

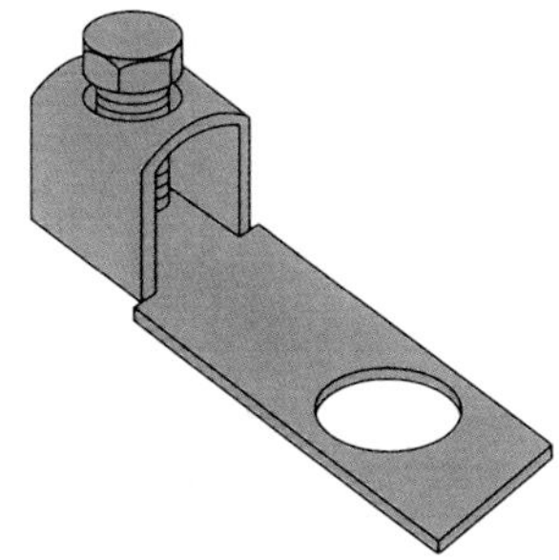
ONE BARREL, STRAIGHT TONGUE
ONE HOLE
NO. 14 AWG THROUGH 1,000 KCMIL

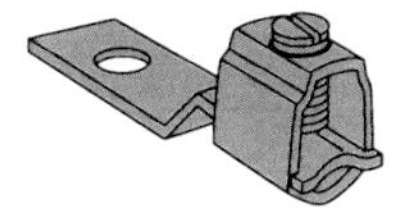
SINGLE HOLE
NO. 14 AWG THROUGH 4/0

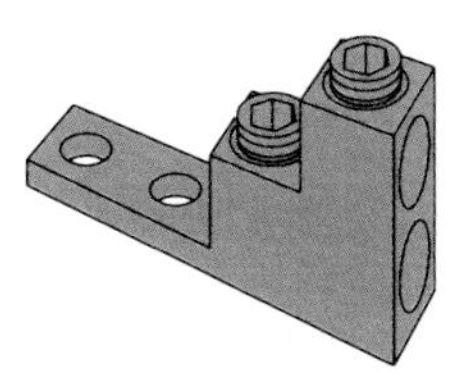
TWO HOLE, PANELBOARD CONNECTOR
NO. 2 AWG THROUGH 750 KCMIL

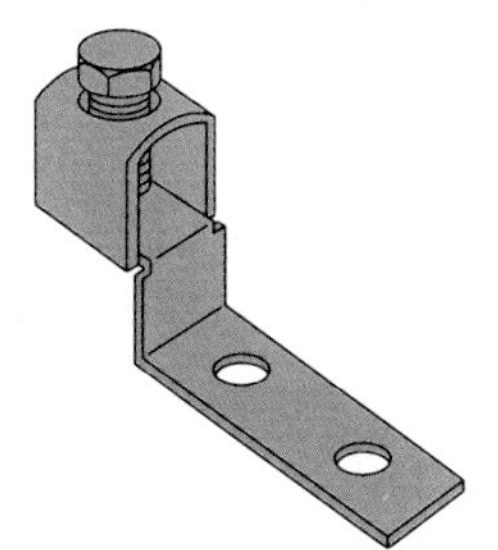
ONE BARREL, OFFSET TONGUE
TWO HOLE
NO. 14 AWG THROUGH 1,000 KCMIL

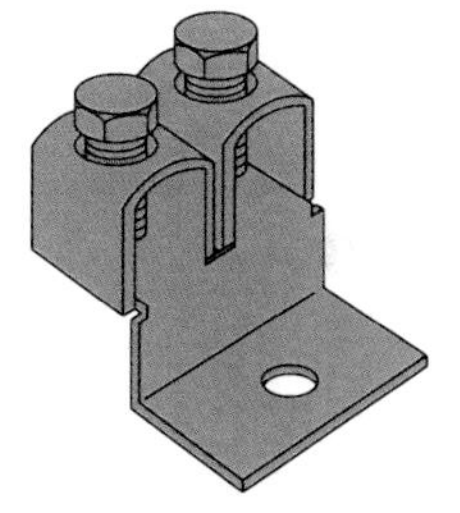
TWO BARRELS, OFFSET TONGUE
ONE HOLE
NO. 6 AWG THROUGH 500 KCMIL

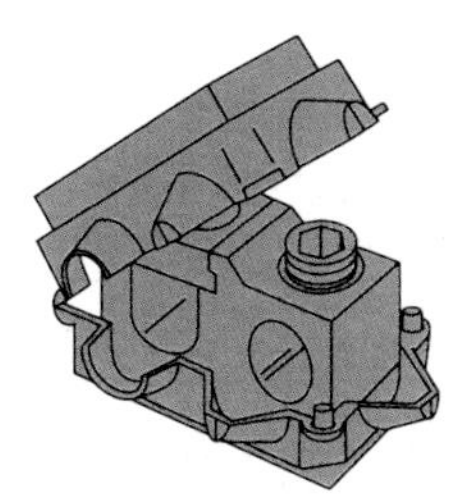
PARALLEL-TAP CONNECTOR
WITH INSULATED COVER
(VARIOUS WIRE SIZE COMBINATIONS)

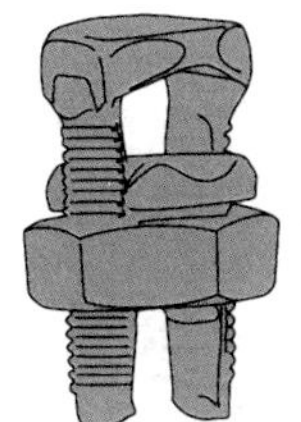
SPLIT BOLT CONNECTOR
(2) NO. 14 AWG THROUGH (2) 1,000 KCMIL
RUN AND TAP COMBINATIONS

26208-14_F11.EPS

Figure 11 Various mechanical compression connectors.

Crimp-type connectors for wires smaller than No. 8 AWG are normally made to accept at least two wire sizes and are often color coded. For example, one manufacturer's color code is red for No. 18 or No. 20 wire, blue for No. 16 or No. 14 wire, and yellow for No. 12 or No. 10 wire. Crimp-type connectors for wire sizes No. 8 and larger, commonly called lugs, are made to accept one specific conductor size. Crimp-type **reducing connectors** are used to connect two different size wires. Mechanical compression-type connectors and lugs are made to accommodate a range of different wire sizes.

The parallel-tap connector with an insulated cover shown in *Figure 11* is one example of a pre-insulated, molded mechanical compression connector. There are several kinds available. They come in setscrew/pressure plate and insulation-piercing configurations made for use in a variety of feeder tap and splice applications. Because they are equipped with an insulating cover, the requirement for taping the joint is eliminated.

On Site

Tightening Compression Connector Screws and Bolts

Mechanical compression connectors must be tightened to a specified torque using a torque screwdriver or torque wrench. Overtightening can cut the wires or break the fitting, while undertightening may lead to loose connections, resulting in overheating and failure.

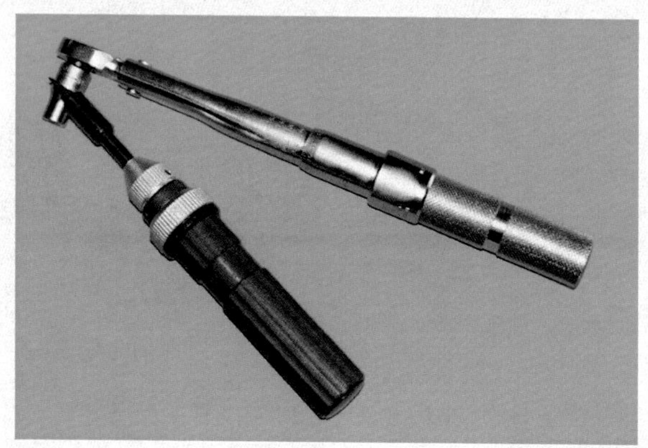

26208-14_SA03.EPS

3.1.0 Aluminum Connections

Aluminum has certain properties that are different from copper and special precautions must be taken to ensure reliable connections. These properties are: cold flow (aluminum does not spring back in the same way as copper and has a tendency to deform), coefficient of thermal expansion, susceptibility to galvanic corrosion, and the formation of oxide film on the surface.

Because of the thermal expansion and cold flow of aluminum, standard copper connectors cannot be safely used on aluminum wire. Most manufacturers design their aluminum connectors with greater contact area to counteract this problem. Tongues and barrels of all aluminum connectors are larger or deeper than comparable copper connectors.

The electrolytic action between aluminum and copper can be controlled by plating the aluminum with a neutral metal (usually tin). The plating prevents electrolysis from taking place, and the joint remains tight. Connectors should also be tin-plated and prefilled with an oxide-inhibiting compound.

The insulating aluminum oxide film must be removed or penetrated before a reliable aluminum joint can be made. Aluminum connectors are designed to bite through this film as they are applied to conductors. The conductor should also be wire brushed and coated with a joint compound to ensure a reliable joint.

CAUTION

Never use connectors designed strictly for use on copper conductors on aluminum conductors. Connectors listed for use on both metals will be marked AL-CU. All connectors must be applied and installed in the manner for which they are listed and labeled.

NEC Section 110.14 prohibits conductors made of dissimilar metals (copper and aluminum, copper and copper-clad aluminum, or aluminum and copper-clad aluminum) from being intermixed in a terminal or splicing connector unless the device is identified for the purpose. As a general rule:

- Connectors marked with only the wire size should only be used with copper conductors.
- Connectors marked with AL and the wire size should only be used with aluminum conductors.
- Connectors marked with AL-CU and the wire size may be safely used with either copper or aluminum.

3.2.0 Heat-Shrink Insulators

Heat-shrink insulators for small connectors provide skintight insulation protection and are fast and easy to use. They are designed to slip over wires, taper pins, connectors, terminals, and splices. When heat is applied, the insulation becomes semi-rigid and provides positive strain relief at the flex point of the conductor. A vaporproof band seals and protects the conductor against abrasion, chemicals, dust, gasoline, oil, and moisture. Extreme temperatures, both hot and cold, will not affect the performance of these insulators. The source of heat can be any number of types, but most manufacturers of these insulators also produce a heat gun especially designed for use on heat-shrink insulators. It is similar to a conventional hair dryer, as shown in *Figure 12*.

In general, a heat-shrink insulator may be thought of as tubing with a memory. After it is initially manufactured, it is heated and expanded to a predetermined diameter and then cooled. Upon a second application of heat, the tubing compound "remembers" its original size and shrinks to that smaller diameter. This property enables it to conform to the contours of any object. Various types of heat-shrink tubing are available, some of which include the following:

- *PVC* – This is a general-purpose, economical tubing widely used in the electronics industry. It provides good electrical and mechanical protection and resists cracking and splitting.
- *Polyolefin* – Polyolefin tubing has a wide range of uses for wire bundling, harnessing, strain relief, and other applications where cables and components require additional insulation. It is flame-retardant, flexible, and comes in a variety of colors.
- *Double wall* – This tubing is designed for outstanding protective characteristics. It is a semirigid tubing with an inner wall that melts and an outer wall that shrinks to conform to the melted area.
- *Teflon®* – This type is considered by many users to be the best overall heat-shrink tubing—physically, electrically, and chemically. Its high temperature rating of 250°C resists brittleness from extended exposure to heat and will not support combustion.
- *Neoprene* – This is a highly durable and flexible tubing that provides superior protection against abrasion.
- *Kynar®* – This is a thin-wall, semi-rigid tubing with outstanding resistance to abrasion. This transparent tubing enables easy inspection of components.

Tubing is available in a wide variety of colors and configurations. The manufacturer's tubing selector guide can help in the selection of the best tubing for any given application. A typical tubing selector guide appears in *Table 2*.

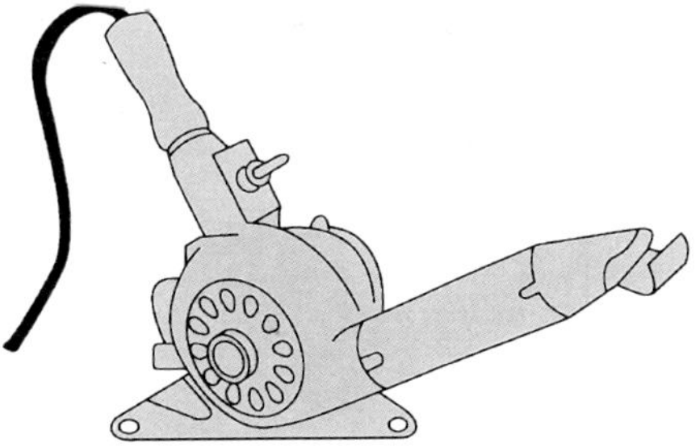

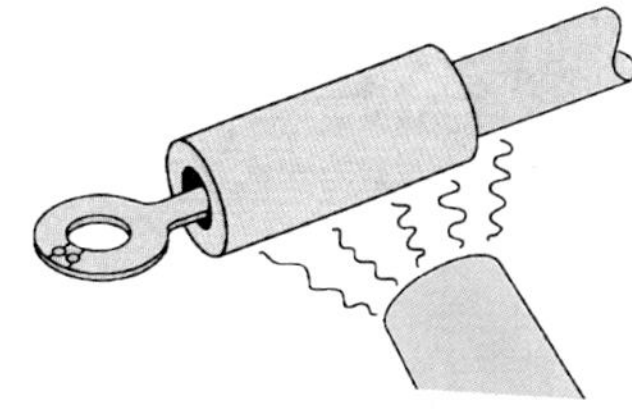

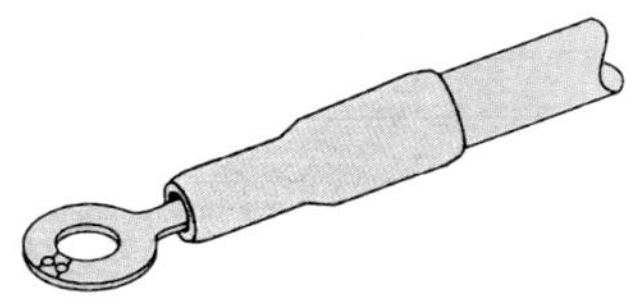

SLIP INSULATOR OVER
OBJECT TO BE INSULATED, THEN
APPLY HEAT FOR A FEW SECONDS

WHEN FINISHED, IT PROVIDES
PERMANENT INSULATION
PROTECTION
26208-14 F12.EPS

Figure 12 Method of installing heat-shrink insulators.

Table 2 Tubing Selector Guide

Type	Material	Temp. Range (°C)	Shrink Ratio	Max. Long. Shrinkage (%)	Tensile Strength (psi)	Colors	Dielectric Strength (V/mil)
Nonshrinkable	PVC	+ 105	—	—	2,700	White, red, clear, black	800
Shrinkable	PVC	– 35 to + 105	2:1	10	2,700	Clear, black	750
Nonshrinkable	Teflon®	– 65 to + 260	—	—	2,700	Clear	1,400
Shrinkable	Flexible polyolefin	– 55 to + 135	2:1	5	2,500	Black, white, red, yellow, blue, clear	1,300
Nonshrinkable	Teflon®	– 65 to + 260	—	—	7,500	Clear	1,400
Shrinkable	Polyolefin double wall	– 55 to + 110	6:1	5	2,500	Black	1,100
Shrinkable	Kynar®	– 55 to + 175	2:1	10	8,000	Clear	1,500
Shrinkable	Teflon®	+ 250	1.2:2	10	6,000	Clear	1,500
Shrinkable	Teflon®	+ 250	1½:1	10	6,000	Clear	1,500
Shrinkable	Neoprene	+ 120	2:1	10	1,500	Black	300

4.0.0 Control and Signal Cable

For the most part, electricians install all the associated power cables and many of the signal cables for the instrumentation systems in industrial facilities. It is necessary to select the proper type and rating of control and signal cables to meet *National Electrical Code®* (*NEC®*) requirements, local codes, and equipment manufacturer requirements for the system being installed. With the exception of optical fiber or communication cables that enter a structure and are terminated in an enclosure within 50' of the entrance, the *NEC®* requires that control and signal cables be listed and marked with an appropriate classification code.

4.1.0 *NEC®* Classifications and Ratings

Control and signal cables are type-classified, rated, and listed for use in various areas of a structure in accordance with the following:

- *NEC Article 725, Remote Control, Signaling, and Power-Limited Circuits (Class 1, 2, and 3 Circuits)*
- *NEC Article 727, Instrumentation Tray Cable*
- *NEC Article 760, Fire Alarm Systems*
- *NEC Article 770, Optical Fiber Cables and Raceways*
- *NEC Article 800, Communications Circuits*

All cable conforming to the requirements of the *NEC®* is normally marked by the cable manufacturer with the appropriate classification code. For more detail, refer to the latest edition of the *NEC®*.

4.2.0 Fire Alarm, Instrumentation, and Control Cable

Fire alarm, instrumentation, and control cable carry low-level signals that require less current than power cable. Conductor sizes range from No. 12 to No. 24 AWG, depending on the circuit requirements. Conductors can be tinned or bare, solid or stranded, and twisted or parallel. Shielding, if used, is usually an aluminum-coated Mylar® film with one or more drain wires (ground wires) inside a jacket. The jacket and conductor insulation are rated for the applicable usage. *Figure 13* shows typical fire alarm and instrumentation cable.

To be effective, the shielding drain wire(s) must be grounded. The installation loop diagrams or instructions for the system equipment will indicate how and where the shields are connected and grounded. Typically, only one end is grounded, and the drain wire at the other end is isolated by folding it back and taping over it. This prevents the electrical noise collected by the shield from recirculating through the system and interfering with the control signals.

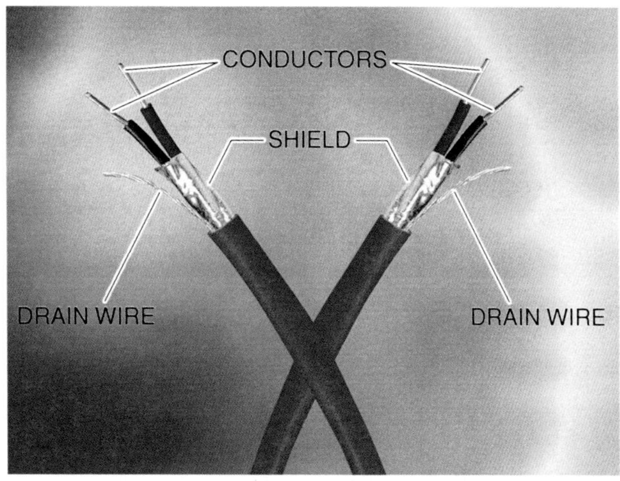

(A) FIRE ALARM CABLE

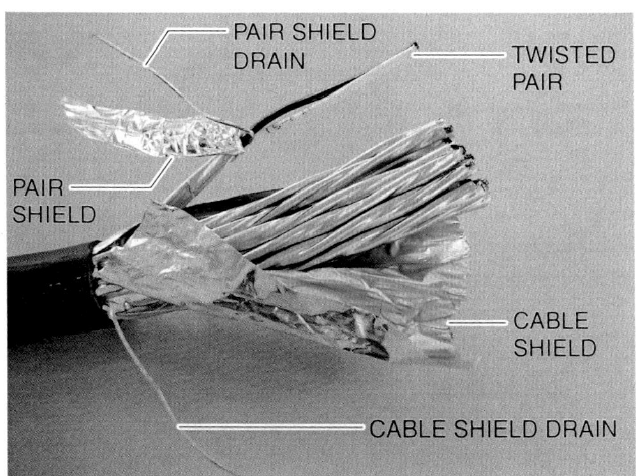

(B) INSTRUMENTATION CABLE

26208-14_F13.EPS

Figure 13 Fire alarm and instrumentation cable.

5.0.0 Low-Voltage and Medium-Voltage Connectors and Terminals

Low-voltage control circuits typically use compression-type crimp connectors. These connectors are often color coded by wire size.

5.1.0 Crimp Connectors for Screw Terminals

Compression-type connectors for connecting conductors to screw terminals for low-voltage circuits include those in which hand tools indent or crimp tube-like sleeves that hold a conductor. Proper crimping action changes the size and shape of the connector and deforms the conductor strands enough to provide good electrical conductivity and mechanical strength.

Figure 14 shows the basic structure of a crimp connector. The crimp barrel receives the wire and is crimped to secure it in place. The V's or dimples inside the barrel improve the wire-to-terminal conductivity and also increase the termination tensile strength. Most crimp connectors have nylon or vinyl insulation covering the barrel to reduce the possibility of shorting to adjacent terminals. The insulation is color coded according to the connector's wire range to reduce the problem of wire-to-connector mismatch. An inspection hole is provided at the end of the barrel to allow visual inspection of the wire position. For the smaller wire sizes, a sleeve is crimped over the conductor insulation in the process of crimping the barrel, providing strain relief for the conductor.

The barrel is connected to the terminal tongue, which physically connects the wire to the termination point, such as a terminal screw. Information about the connector size and conductor range is usually stamped on the tongue by the manufacturer. Tongue styles vary depending on termination requirements. *Figure 15* shows standard tongue styles. The styles most frequently used are the ring tongue and flanged or locking fork. These types are preferred because the terminals will not slip off the terminal screw as the screw is tightened. They are also compatible with most vendor-supplied termination points.

5.2.0 Color Codes

Most manufacturers color code the barrel insulation to provide quick identification for installation and as an aid to inspection. Different colors, or a combination of colors, have special meanings. Although manufacturers vary, common or standard colors have been accepted. *Table 3* lists typical color codes.

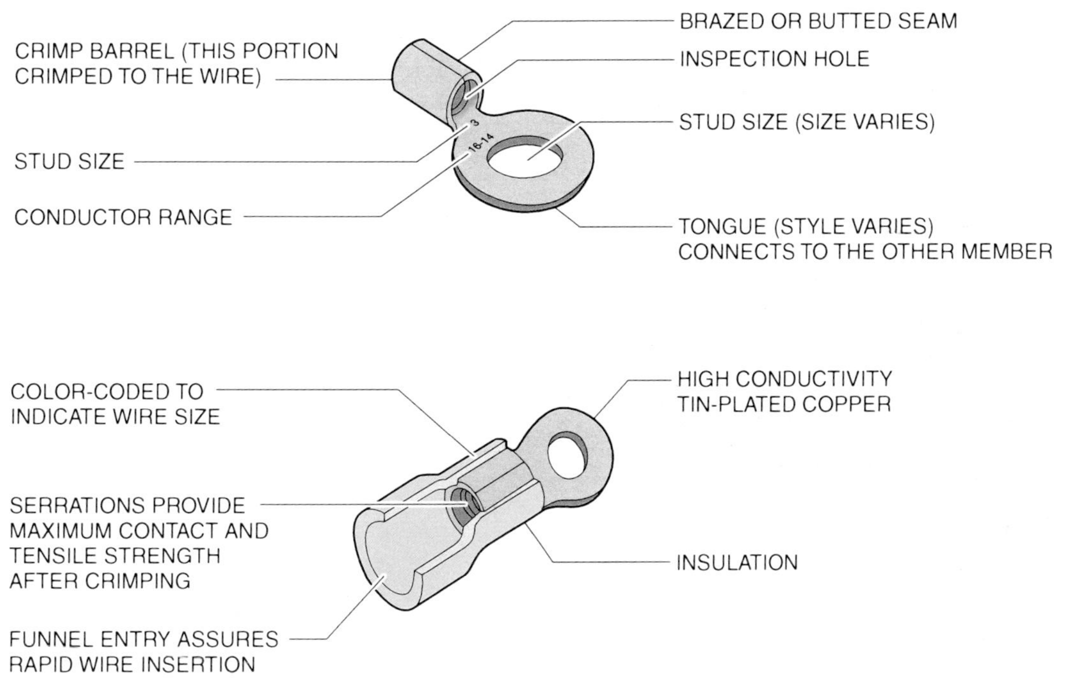

Figure 14 Basic crimp connector structure.

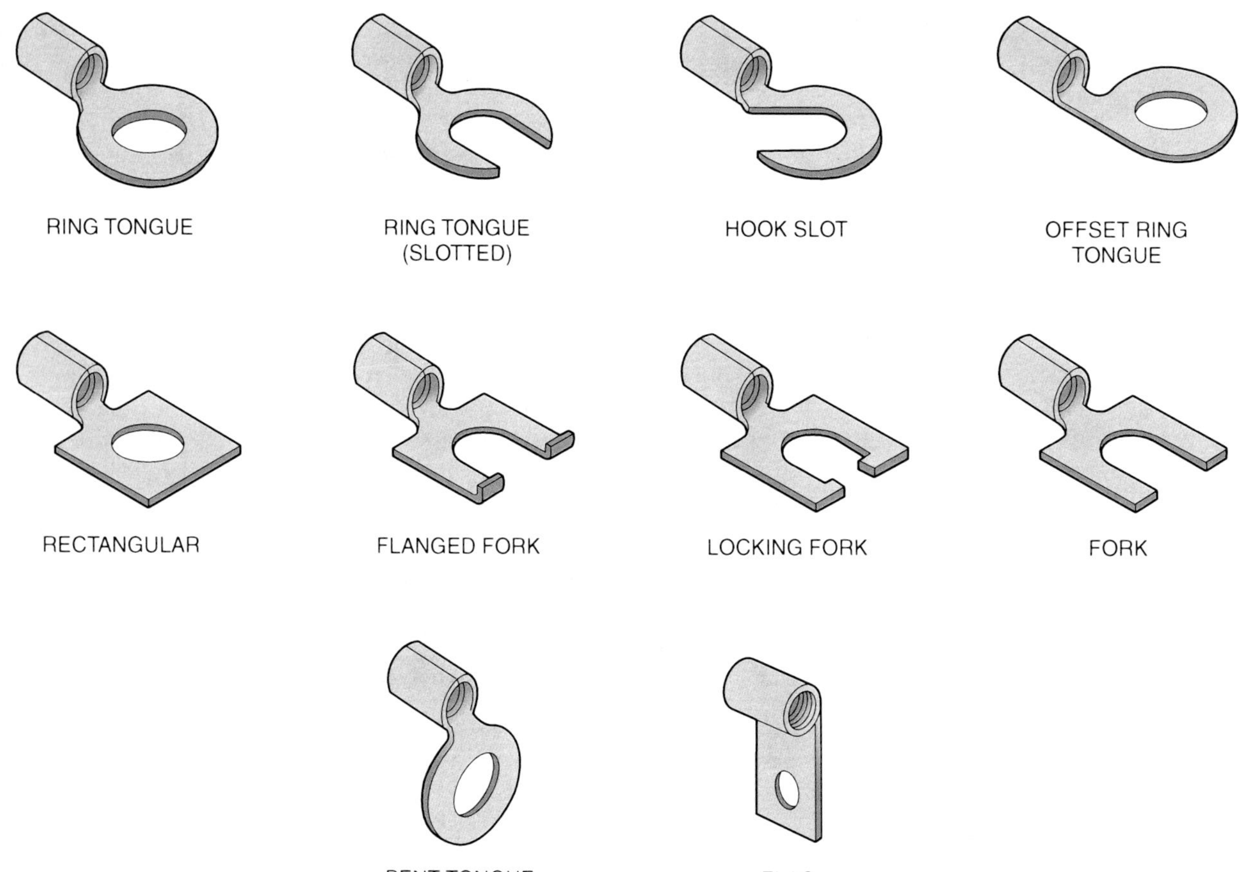

Figure 15 Standard tongue styles of crimped connectors.

Table 3 Typical Color Codes

AWG Wire Size	Color Code
22–16	Red
16–14	Blue
12–10	Yellow

Color combinations are sometimes varied to indicate the class or grade rating of an individual lug or splice. Some manufacturers use a clear plastic or other suitable insulation on the crimp barrel with a colored line to indicate wire size range.

6.0.0 Guidelines for Installing Connectors

Before beginning work on incoming line connections, refer to all drawings and specifications dealing with the project at hand. Details of terminations are usually furnished on larger installations. Guidelines for installing the different types of connectors covered in this module are given in the following sections.

6.1.0 Installing Compression Connectors

The task of fastening a compression connector to a wire requires the use of the proper connector, crimping tool, and installation procedure. Always use the correct tool for the connector and follow the manufacturer's instructions.

6.1.1 Crimping Tools

With a compression connector, an electrical connection between a wire and a terminal can be made by tightly compressing the crimp barrel with an ordinary pair of pliers. However, such a connection would not necessarily be made to the required pressure or in the correct location to ensure a good connection. A crimping tool is required to produce consistently good connections.

Figure 16 shows the relationship between the amount of crimping force and the mechanical and electrical performance. The maximum mechanical strength (A) occurs at a lower crimping force than the maximum electrical performance (B). The point of intersection (C) represents the ideal crimping force. Using a crimping die that is too

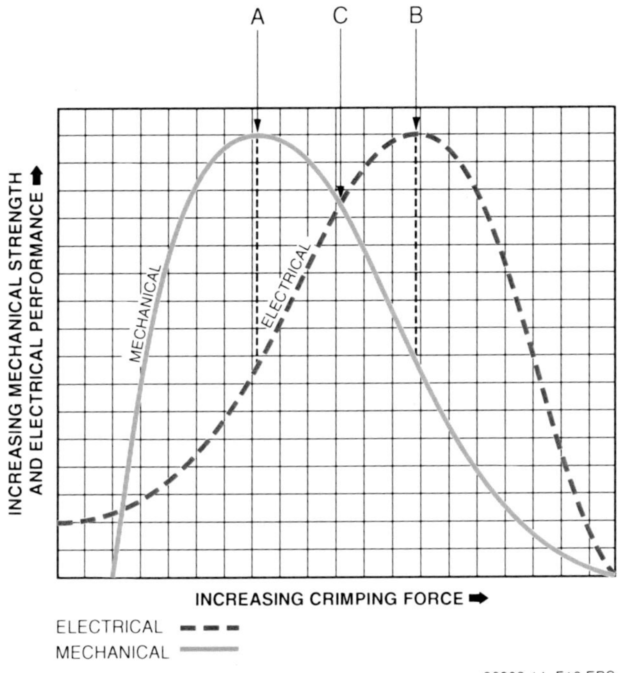

Figure 16 Mechanical strength versus electrical performance of a crimped connector.

large results in poor electrical performance, and using a die that is too small produces a weak mechanical connection.

A simple pliers-type crimping tool was the earliest crimping tool developed and continues to be used for repair operations or where only a few installations are to be made. These tools are similar in construction to ordinary mechanics' pliers except the jaws are specially shaped, as shown in *Figure 17*.

It takes a tremendous amount of force at the lug to make a good crimp. Ratchet tools provide a means of increasing the human output force. The typical force capability of a hand for repetitive operations is 75 pounds for adult men and 50 pounds for adult women. The amount the tool multiplies the hand force is termed the **mechanical advantage (MA)** of the tool.

Simple pliers are basically constant-MA tools; the MA is the same whether the crimp is being started or finished. By adjusting linkage or cam mechanisms connecting the handles to the crimp dies, the MA can be varied so that it is low at the start and high at the finish of the crimp stroke. Thus, when the handles start to close from the open position and little or no crimping is being done, the MA is low. As the handles are closed farther, the crimp dies begin to compress the terminal, and the MA increases. In this manner, the MA is patterned to the crimp force requirements and distributed so that a high MA is achieved over the portion of the cycle where required.

Figure 18 shows a high MA type of tool equipped with a ratchet control. The ratchet mechanism prevents opening the tool and removing the crimped terminal before the handle has been closed all the way and the crimp completed. These provide a consistent, reliable crimp that meets the terminal manufacturer's requirements.

The crimp dies of this tool are interchangeable and may contain two or three positions for crimping different size terminals. These dies may be color coded to be used with a color-coded terminal lug for easy identification and to ensure proper crimping force. The crimp die of the tool determines the completed crimp configuration. There are a variety of configurations in use such as the simple nest and indenter type of die or the more complicated four-indent die.

Figure 19 shows hand-operated and hydraulic crimping tools typical of those used to crimp connectors for stranded wires ranging from No. 8 AWG to 750 kcmil. These tools normally develop about 12 tons of compression force at 10,000 pounds per square inch (psi). Guidelines for the use of these tools are described here. Many other tools operate in a similar manner.

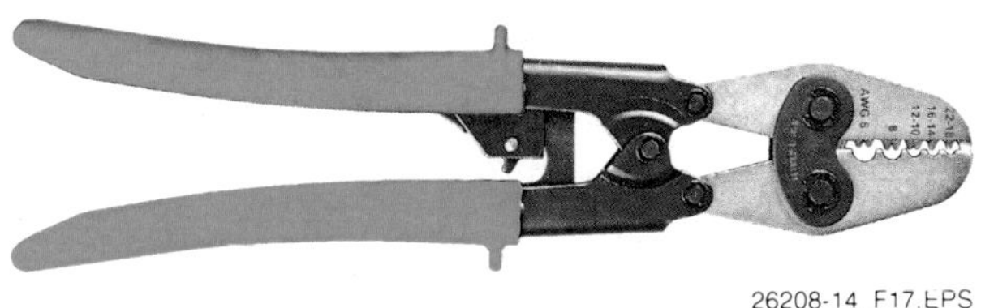

Figure 17 Hand crimpers.

Figure 18 Leveraged crimping tool.

DIE SET

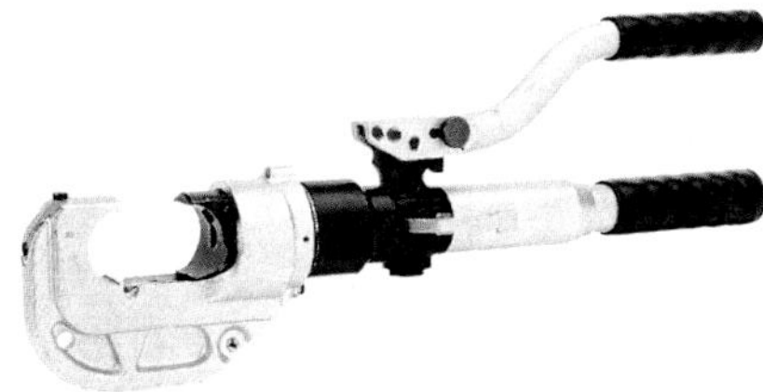

HAND-OPERATED

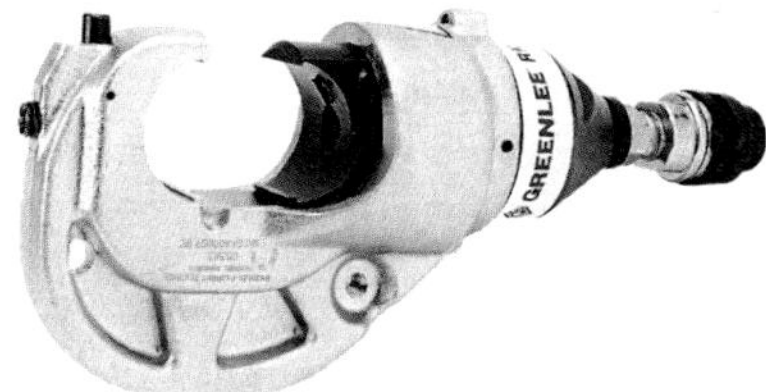

HYDRAULIC

26208-14_F19.EPS

Figure 19 Crimping tools used to crimp large connectors.

> **NOTE**
>
> Some manufacturers design a crimping tool that must be used with their connectors. Use the crimping tool recommended by the manufacturer.

Several different configurations may work equally well for some applications, while for others, a certain shape is superior. Many considerations affect the determination of crimp die configuration, including the type of terminal (size, shape, material, and function), as well as the type and size of wires to be accommodated.

To use a hand-operated crimping tool, proceed as follows:

Step 1 Select the proper die for use with the connector to be crimped. Do not operate the tool without the die.

Step 2 Push the die release button on the C-head and slide one of the die halves into position until the retainer snaps. Insert the other die half in the piston body by pushing the die release button and sliding the die in until the retainer snaps.

Step 3 Place the tool C-head in position over the connector to be crimped. Pump the handle until compression is complete, as indicated by the dies touching at their flat surfaces nearest the throat of the C-head.

Step 4 Retract the ram and remove the connector after completion of the crimp. This is done by raising the pump handle slightly, rotating it clockwise until it stops, and then pushing the handle down in a pumping motion until the pressure release snaps.

> **WARNING!**
>
> Always read and follow the manufacturer's instructions when using power tools.

To operate a hydraulic crimping tool, proceed as follows:

Step 1 Connect the hydraulic pump to the crimping tool using a suitable hydraulic hose.

Step 2 Select the proper dies for use with the connector to be crimped. Do not operate the tool without the dies.

Step 3 Push the die release button on the C-head and slide one of the die halves into position until the retainer pin snaps. In a similar manner, install the other die half in the piston body.

Step 4 Place the tool C-head in position over the connector to be crimped. Operate the remote pump until compression is complete, as indicated by the dies touching on the frame side.

Step 5 Release the pressure at the hydraulic pump to retract the lower die half, and then remove the connector from the tool.

In addition to hand-operated and hydraulic crimpers, battery-operated and corded crimping tools are also available (*Figures 20* and *21*). Battery-operated tools offer the advantage of freedom of movement, while corded tools allow extensive use without worrying about battery changes. Universal crimping tools are also available (*Figure 22*). They operate in the same way as other crimpers but do not require separate dies.

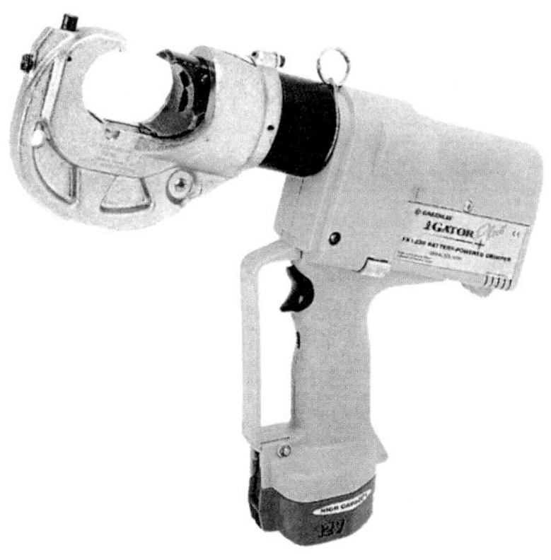

26208-14_F20.EPS

Figure 20 Battery-operated crimping tool.

26208-14_F21.EPS

Figure 21 Corded crimping tool.

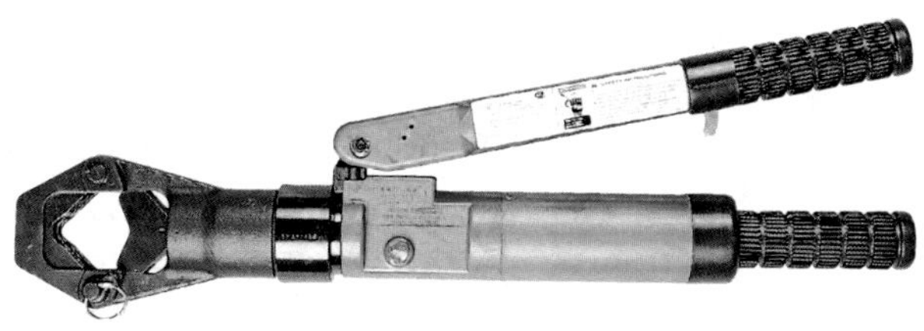

26208-14_F22.EPS

Figure 22 Universal crimping tool.

6.1.2 General Compression (Crimp) Connector Installation Procedure

To make a crimp connection, proceed as follows:

Step 1 Select a crimp connector of proper size and appropriate material for the wire size you are using. Copper connectors should be used with copper wires and aluminum connectors with aluminum wires. Dual-rated connectors may be used with both copper and aluminum wires.

Step 2 Use a suitable wire stripper to remove the insulation from the end of the wire. Be careful not to nick the wire. Strip the insulation back far enough so that the bare conductor will go fully into the connector. Make sure not to strip off too much insulation; it should fit close to the connector when the wire is fully inserted into the connector.

Step 3 Clean the stripped portion of the wire. Use a wire brush for large wire sizes. Also clean the related unplated terminal pad and the surface to which the connector will be attached.

Step 4 Obtain the crimping tool and dies made for the type and size of connector to be crimped.

Step 5 Insert the stripped end of the wire completely into the connector. Position the crimping tool in place over the connector, and then operate the tool to fully crimp the connector, as directed in the tool manufacturer's instructions. Make sure that the crimping tool jaws are fully closed, indicating that a full compression crimp has been made. If multiple crimps are required (*Figure 23*), crimp from the lug back to the barrel base, rotating the crimper as necessary to avoid deforming the connector.

Step 6 Using a bolt or screw and washers (if required), secure the crimped connector and attached wire to the correct terminal in the equipment. Tighten the terminal bolt and torque to the level specified by the equipment manufacturer. Too little or too much torque can adversely affect the performance of the connection.

Table 4 lists some torque values typical of those used for tightening common sizes of steel and aluminum terminal bolts.

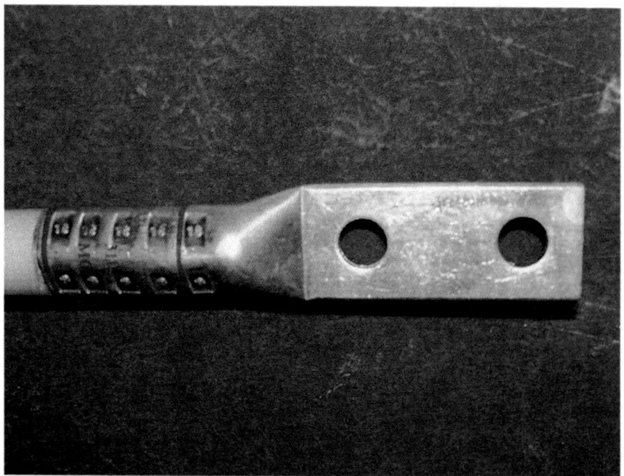

26208-14_F23.EPS

Figure 23 Multiple crimps.

Table 4 Recommended Tightening Torques for Various Bolt Sizes

Steel Hardware		Aluminum Hardware	
Bolt Size	Recommended Torque (Inch-Pounds)	Bolt Size	Recommended Torque (Inch-Pounds)
¼–20	80	½–13	300
5⁄16–18	180	⅝–11	480
⅜–16	240	¾–10	650
½–13	480	—	—
⅝–11	660	—	—
¾–10	1,900	—	—

On Site

Tightening Torques

Many terminations and types of equipment are marked with tightening torque information. For items of equipment, torque information is often marked on the equipment and/or listed in the manufacturer's installation instructions. When specific torque requirements are given, always follow the manufacturer's recommendations.

In cases where no tightening requirements are given, guidelines for tightening screw and bolt-type mechanical compression connectors can be found in the *National Electrical Code® Handbook* comments pertaining to *NEC Section 110.14*. Other good sources of tightening information are manufacturers' catalogs and product literature.

6.2.0 Installing Mechanical Terminals and Connectors

The procedure for installing mechanical connectors is basically the same as that described above for compression connectors, with the following exceptions. Before installing the mechanical connector on the wire, apply an oxide-inhibiting joint compound to the conductor to prevent the formation of surface oxides once the connection is made (also apply the compound to any terminal pad). Following this, install the connector on the wire, and then tighten the connector bolt or screw to the torque level specified by the connector manufacturer. Proper torque is important. Too much torque may sever the wires or break the connector, while too little torque can cause overheating and failure.

6.3.0 Installing Specialized Cable Connectors

There are a wide variety of cables that require specially designed connectors, commonly called terminators, to secure them to equipment enclosures. Normally, these specialized connectors are supplied with installation instructions. This section will introduce you to one type of specialized connector designed for use with metal-clad (Type MC) cable. Its construction and installation are typical of many specialized connectors.

Type MC cable is a factory assembly of one or more insulated circuit conductors with or without optical fiber members. It is enclosed in a metallic sheath of interlocking tape or a smooth or corrugated tube. Throughout the industry, there is increasing use of Type MC cable installed in trays and on racks instead of non-armored cable in conduit. At the appropriate locations, the cables are routed from the trays or racks, then along the structure to the various items of equipment. *NEC Article 330* governs the installation of Type MC cable. There are several types of connectors that can be used with Type MC cable. The specific connector used is determined by the size and type of cable and the application.

For the purpose of an example, the procedure for installing one manufacturer's weatherproof connector designed for use with Type MC cable is given here:

Step 1 Select the correct connector size. This is normally done by comparing the physical dimensions of the cable to a cross-reference table given in the manufacturer's product literature and/or installation instructions.

Step 2 Strip back the jacket and armor of the cable as needed to meet equipment requirements. Expose the cable armoring further by stripping the cable jacket for a specified distance (L), as shown in *Figure 24*. This distance will be found in the manufacturer's installation instructions.

Step 3 Make sure that the jacket seal and retaining spring are in their uncompressed state. If necessary, loosen the connector body and the compression nut. It is not necessary to separate the connector parts.

Step 4 Screw the connector body into the equipment if it has a threaded entry, or secure it with a locknut if it has an unthreaded entry.

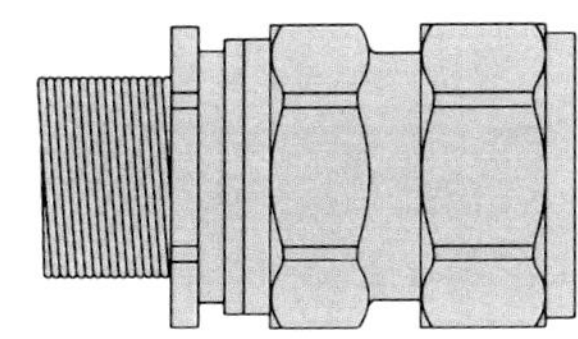

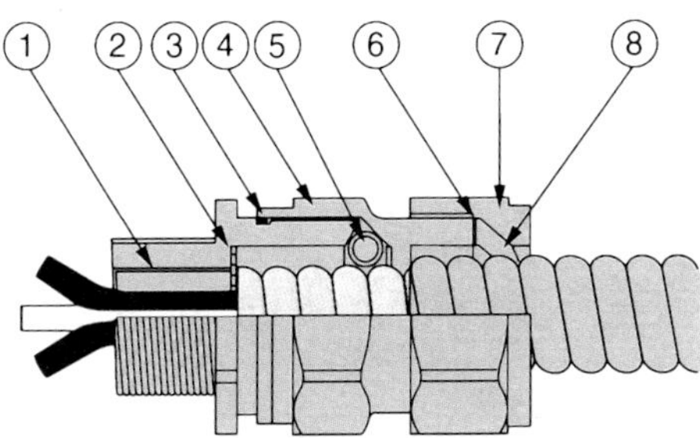

1. ENTRY COMPONENT
2. END STOP
3. O-RING
4. CONNECTOR BODY
5. RETAINING SPRING
6. WASHER
7. JACKET SEAL
8. COMPRESSION NUT

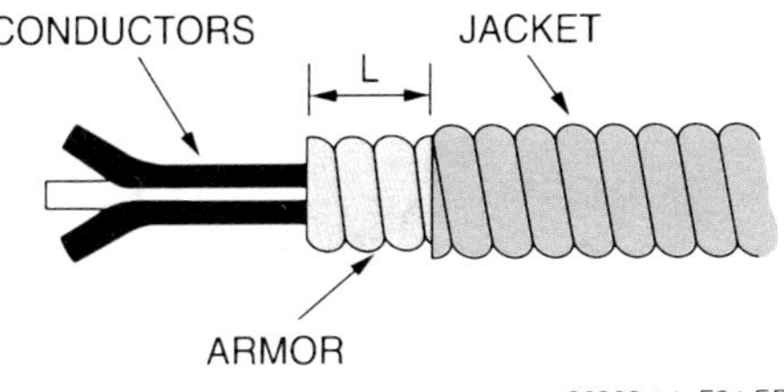

26208-14_F24.EPS

Figure 24 Weatherproof connector used with Type MC cable.

Step 5 Pass the cable through the connector until the armor makes contact with the end stop. If it is not possible for the insulated wires to pass through the end stop, remove the end stop so that the wires can move past it and the armor can make contact with the integral end stop within the entry component.

Step 6 Tighten the connector body to compress the retaining spring and secure the armor. Normally, this is hand-tight plus one and a half full turns.

Step 7 Tighten the outer compression nut to form a seal on the cable jacket. Normally, this is hand-tight plus one full turn.

Step 8 If appropriate, terminate the individual wires contained in the cable using compression or mechanical connectors.

6.4.0 Installing Control and Signal Cables/Conductors

Cable/conductor termination first involves organizing the cables/conductors by destination and mounting or installing the appropriately sized termination panels or devices. Then the cables/conductors must be formed, supported, and dressed to length including appropriate slack. Once this has been accomplished, the cables/conductors are properly labeled and then terminated to an appropriate connection device. See *Figure 25*.

6.4.1 Crimping Procedure

Prior to making a crimped connection, verify the following items:

- The size and type of wire are correct.
- The connector and wire materials are compatible (compare cable and lug designations for material type).

NOTE

Conductors of dissimilar metals should not be intermixed in a terminal lug or splice connector unless the device is listed and labeled for this purpose.

- The correct crimp tool and die for the selected terminal and conductor are being used.
- The tool is in proper working order.

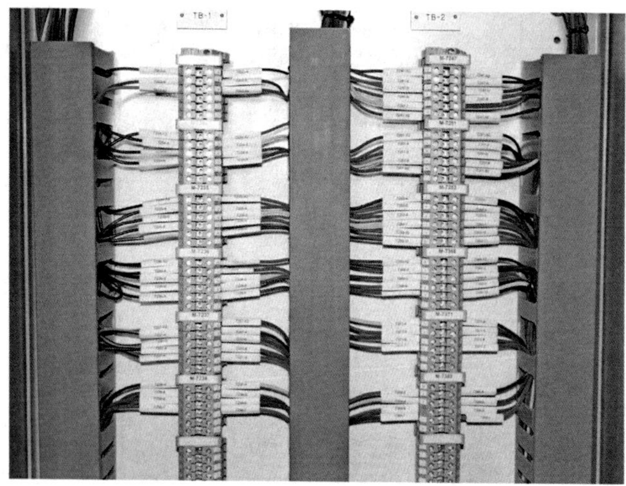

26208-14_F25.EPS

Figure 25 Labeled and terminated control cable.

The installation of a compression terminal should be as follows:

Step 1 Select the proper terminal for the wire size being terminated, as specified by the terminal manufacturer. This ensures the proper fit of the lug and that the amperage capacity of the lug equals that of the conductor.

Step 2 Verify that the terminal stud size matches the terminal screw size.

Step 3 Select the proper crimping tool and die for the terminal being used. This minimizes the possibility of overcrimping or undercrimping the terminal.

Step 4 Train the wire strands if the strands are fanned. Grooming the conductor provides a proper fit in the crimp barrel.

Step 5 Insert the terminal in the proper die nest. Some insulated terminals have increased wire ranges that overlap with other size terminals, such as a terminal covering wire sizes No. 14 through 18 AWG. When crimping this type of terminal, use the middle wire the terminal will accept to determine the correct nest to use. For example, when crimping a No. 18 AWG wire in a 14–18 terminal, use the nest marked 16–14 on the tool. Overcrimping will occur if the terminal is crimped in the nest marked 18–22. When crimping an uninsulated terminal, the top of the crimp barrel should be positioned facing the indenter. This will produce the best crimp and facilitate visual inspection of the crimp after connection to the terminal point. When crimping an insulated terminal, insert the terminal in the color-coded die corresponding to the insulation color.

Step 6 Close the crimp tool handles slightly to secure the terminal while inserting the conductor.

Step 7 Insert the stripped wire into the barrel of the terminal until the insulation butts firmly against the forward stop. Make sure that the insulation is not actually in the barrel. The strands of the conductor should be clearly visible through the inspection opening of the terminal. Make sure all strands of the conductor are inserted into the barrel of the terminal.

Step 8 Complete the crimp by closing the handles until the mechanical cycle has been completed and the ratchet releases.

Step 9 Remove the termination from the tool and examine it for proper crimping.

6.4.2 Termination Inspection

The final step of the crimping procedure is inspecting the termination to ensure that it is electrically and mechanically sound. It must be tight with no loose strands or uninsulated conductor showing. Inspect uninsulated terminals for correct positioning, centering, and size of the crimp indent. Ensure that the terminal wire size stamped on each terminal matches the conductor that was crimped.

Acceptable and unacceptable positioning of a crimp indent is illustrated in *Figure 26*. The crimp barrel is designed to provide the best mechanical strength when the indent is properly placed on

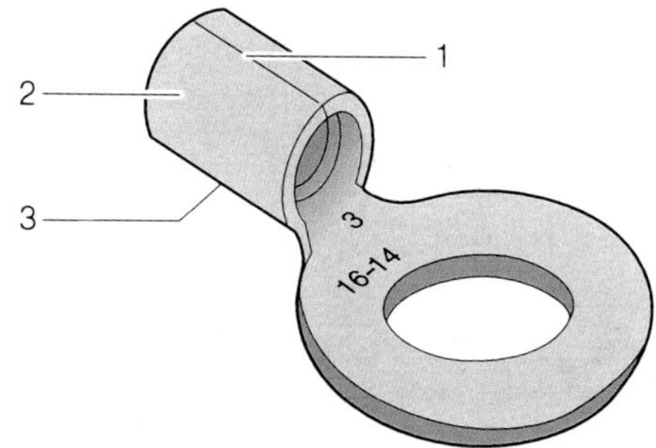

1 – ACCEPTABLE – INDENT ON SEAM (TOP)
2 – UNACCEPTABLE – INDENT ON SIDE
3 – UNACCEPTABLE – INDENT ON BOTTOM

26208-14_F26.EPS

Figure 26 Indent position.

the top (seam) of the barrel. An indent on the side can split the terminal seam, thereby reducing both the electrical and mechanical qualities of the termination.

The centering of a crimp indent is very important. A poor connection will result if a crimp is placed over either the belled mouth or the inspection hole of the terminal, as shown in *Figure 27*. A crimp over the belled mouth will compress the conductor insulation and result in poor or no electrical continuity. Crimping over the inspection hole reduces both electrical continuity and the holding capability of the terminal lug.

Crimping with an incorrect die changes the electrical and mechanical qualities of the termination. The crimp barrel should not be excessively distorted or show any cracks, breaks, or other damage to the base metal.

The position of the conductor is also very important. Tongue terminals should have the end of the conductor flush with and extending beyond the crimp barrel no more than 1⁄32" to ensure proper crimp-to-wire contact area, as shown in *Figure 28*. Conductors extending more than 1⁄32" past the inspection hole may interfere with the terminal screw. If a conductor is too short and does not reach the inspection hole, the connection will not provide enough contact surface area, which increases current density and may cause the lug to slip off the conductor.

Terminal lugs with a belled mouth must have the conductor insulation butted against the tapered edge of the crimp barrel, as shown in *Figure 28*. Terminal lugs without a belled mouth should not have any exposed conductor. The conductor insulation is butted to the terminal. Any exposed conductor reduces the overall strength of the connection.

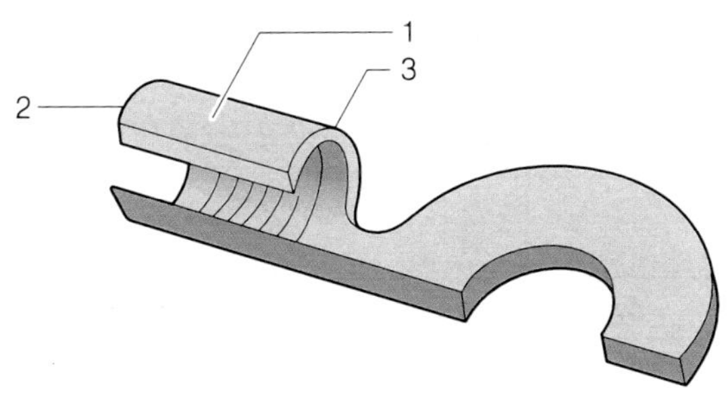

Figure 27 Crimp centering.

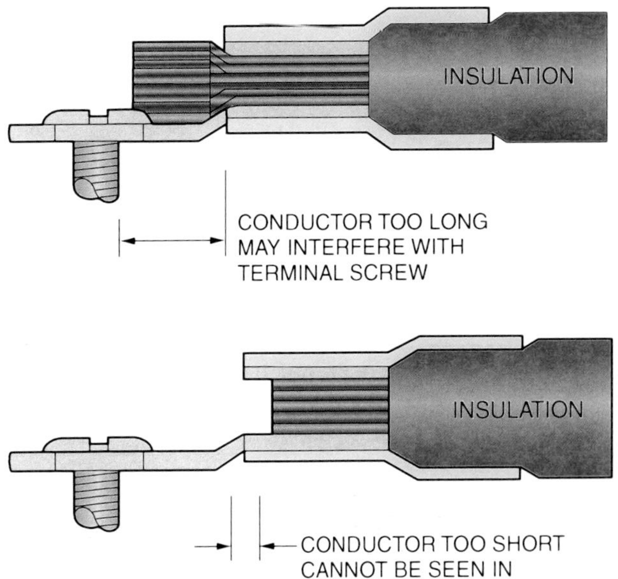

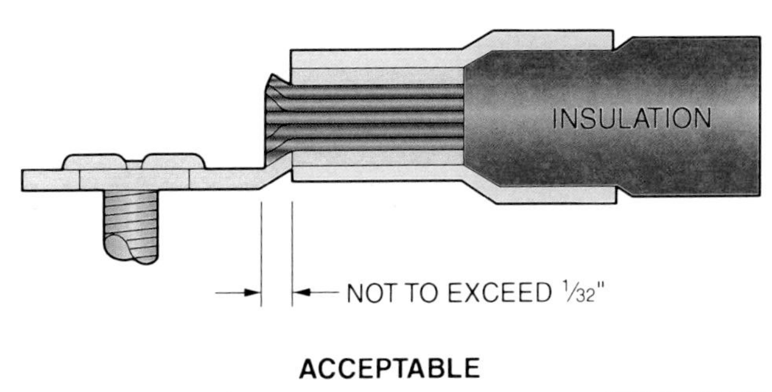

Figure 28 Conductor positioning.

Insulated terminals should be inspected in the same manner as uninsulated terminals: check for proper positioning, centering, and type of crimp. In addition, inspect the terminal insulation for breaks, cracks, holes, or any other damage. Any damage to the insulation is unacceptable. As with uninsulated terminals, inspect insulated terminals to ensure the proper terminal size for each individual conductor. Terminal conductor and stud sizes are usually stamped on the terminal tongue. They can also be checked against the manufacturer's color code.

6.4.3 Terminal Block Connections

A great variety of terminal blocks are available for use, including clamp-type, spring-loaded, and screw-type terminal blocks (*Figure 29*).

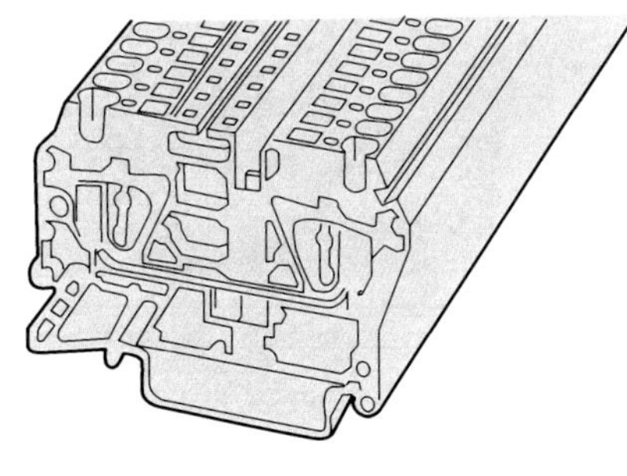

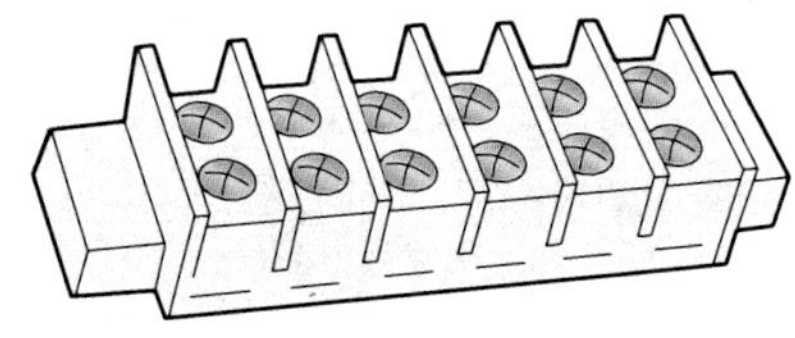

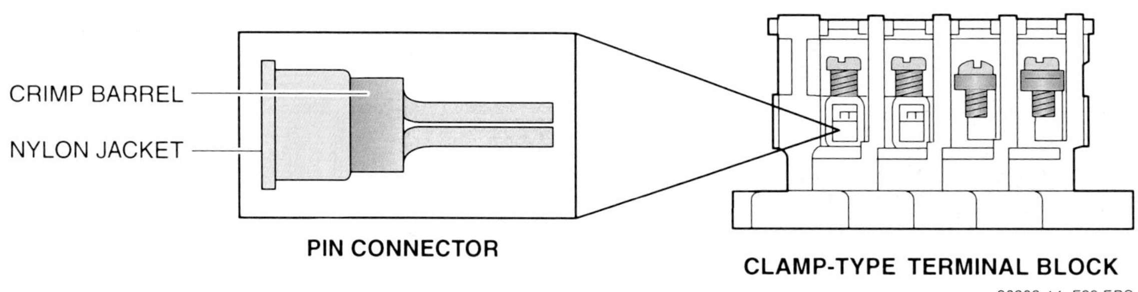

Figure 29 Terminal blocks.

- *Spring-type terminal block* – To install stripped wires in a spring-loaded terminal block, release the spring contact using a flat-blade screwdriver and insert the wire into the hole on top of the block. After the wire is inserted, remove the screwdriver. The wire is clamped in place by the spring contact.
- *Clamp-type terminal block* – To install stripped wires in a clamp-type terminal block, insert the wires into the boxed terminal and tighten the screw to clamp the wire in place.
- *Screw-type terminal block* – To install stripped wires in a common screw-type terminal block, curve the wires around the screw or fit them with a terminal lug that is inserted under the screw. Once the wire or terminal lug is under the head of the screw, tighten the screw to secure the wire.

NOTE

When installing wires in a common screw-type terminal block, only two terminals are permitted at any one terminal point. Also, only one flanged fork terminal may be used. When two types of terminals are located at one point, the bottom terminal should be installed upside down. This will provide easier installation and a neater appearance.

Care should be taken to strip the cable jacket to a point as close as possible to the first termination of the cable, but not to interfere with other terminations originating from that cable, as shown in *Figure 30*. Place the cable identification tag at that point on the cable jacket and make sure it can be read easily.

When multiple cables are installed, tie them neatly to a support without blocking access to the lower terminal blocks or interfering with the connection or disconnection of other wires.

Individual or multi-conductor cables should be routed parallel or at right angles to the frame or wireways. Take care to ensure that wires do not come in contact with sharp edges. Position shielded and coaxial cables on the outer perimeter of a cable bundle whenever possible and keep wire crossover to a minimum.

6.4.4 Cable/Conductor Routing and Inspection Considerations

Cable/conductor routing and inspection considerations include the following:

- *Wire bends* – For all wire and cable routing, use a minimum bend radius of three times the outside diameter of the wire or cable unless otherwise specified by the cable manufacturer.

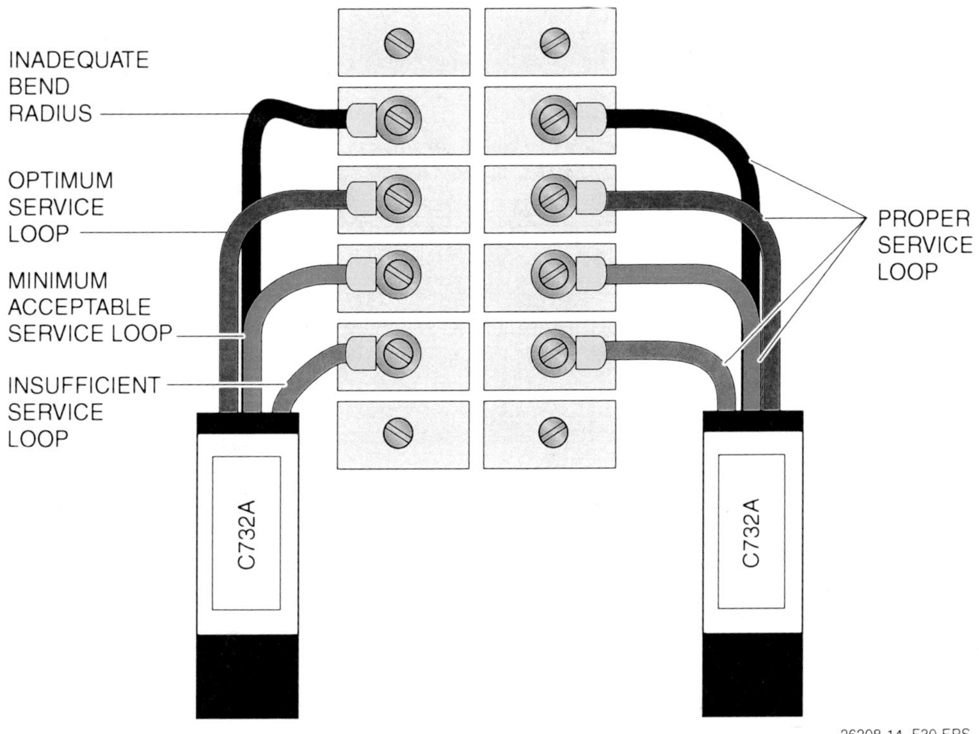

Figure 30 Routing cabling.

- *Neatness of routing* – Provide adequate clearance for movement of mechanical parts. Allow enough slack in the cable for servicing plugs and terminal boards. Support all cables to prevent strain on the conductors or terminals. Strain can cause breaks in the terminations and render the system inoperable. Ensure that cables do not cross maintenance openings or otherwise interfere with normal operation and replacement of components.
- *Protection of wires or cable* – Provide clearance between the conductors and any heat-radiating components to prevent heat-related deterioration of the insulation. Protect all wires against abrasion. Do not route wire over sharp screws, lugs, terminals, or openings. Use grommets, chase nipples, or similar means to protect the insulation when passing wire through a metal partition.
- *Service loops* – Allow sufficient slack at the termination of each wire to permit one repair (such as cutting off a terminal and re-terminating it).
- *Jumper wires* – Bare jumper wires are not permitted. Use only insulated wire for jumpers.
- *Terminal bending limits* – Do not bend terminals more than 30 degrees above or below the termination point, as shown in *Figure 31*.

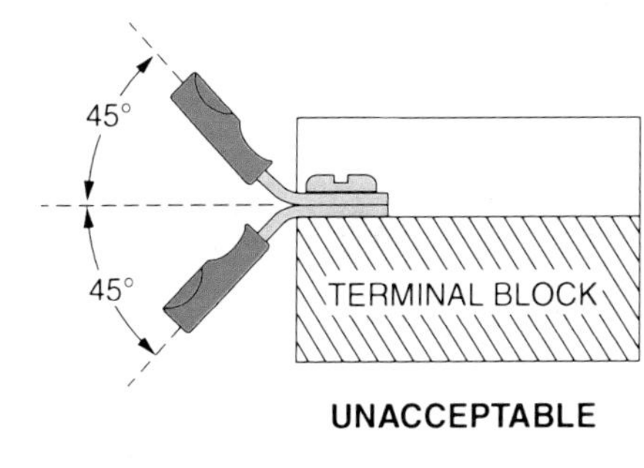

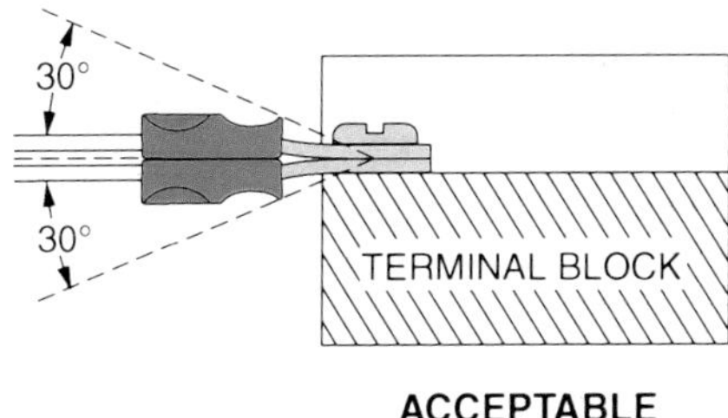

Figure 31 Terminal bend radius.

7.0.0 Bending Cable and Training Conductors

Training is the positioning of cable so that it is not under tension. Bending is the positioning of cable that is under tension. When installing cable or any large conductors, the object is to limit the tension so that the cable's physical and electrical characteristics are maintained for the expected service life. Training conductors, rather than bending them, also reduces the tension on lugs and connectors, extending their service life considerably.

All bends made in cable must comply with the *NEC®*. The minimum bending radius is determined by the cable diameter and, in some instances, by the construction of the cable. For example, *NEC Section 330.24* states that bends in Type MC cable must be made so that the cable is not damaged, and the radius of the curve of the inner edge of any bend shall not be less than the following:

- *Smooth sheath* – Ten times the external diameter of the metallic sheath for cable not more than ¾" in external diameter, twelve times the external diameter of the metallic sheath for cable more than ¾" but not more than 1½" in external diameter, and fifteen times the external diameter of the metallic sheath for cable more than 1½" in external diameter.
- *Interlocked-type armor or corrugated sheath* – Seven times the external diameter of the metal sheath.
- *Shielded conductors* – Twelve times the overall diameter of the individual conductors or seven times the overall diameter of the multiconductor cable, whichever is greater.

26208-14_F32.EPS

Figure 32 Ratchet bender.

GREENLEE

26208-14_F33.EPS

Figure 33 Hydraulic bender.

Two common types of cable bending tools are the ratchet bender and the hydraulic bender. The ratchet cable bender in *Figure 32* bends 600V copper or aluminum conductors up to 500 kcmil, and the hydraulic bender in *Figure 33* is designed for cables from 350 kcmil through 1,000 kcmil. In addition, the hydraulic bender is capable of one-shot bends up to 90° and automatically unloading the cable when the bend is finished. Either type simplifies and speeds cable installation.

Conductors at terminals or conductors entering or leaving cabinets or cutout boxes and the like must comply with certain *NEC®* requirements, many of which are covered in *NEC Article 312*. The bending radii for various sizes of conductors that do not enter or leave an enclosure through the wall opposite its terminal are shown in *Table 5*. When using this table, the bending space at terminals must be measured in a straight line from the end of the lug or wire connector (in the direction that the wire leaves the terminal) to the wall, barrier, or obstruction, as shown in *Figure 34*.

An unshielded cable can tolerate a sharper bend than a shielded cable. This is especially true of cables having helical metal tapes, which, when bent too sharply, can separate or buckle and cut into the insulation. This causes increased electrical stress. The problem is compounded by the fact that most tapes are under jackets that conceal such damage. Damaged cable may initially pass acceptance testing, but often fails prematurely at the shield/insulation interface.

NOTE
Remember that cable offsets are bends.

Table 5 Minimum Wire Bending Space for Conductors Not Entering or Leaving Opposite Wall [Data from NEC Table 312.6(A)]

AWG or Circular-Mil Size of Wire	Wires per Terminal				
	1	2	3	4	5
14–10	Not Specified	—	—	—	—
8–6	1½	—	—	—	—
4–3	2	—	—	—	—
2	2½	—	—	—	—
1	3	—	—	—	—
1/0–2/0	3½	5	7	—	—
3/0–4/0	4	6	8	—	—
250 kcmil	4½	6	8	10	—
300–350 kcmil	5	8	10	12	—
400–500 kcmil	6	8	10	12	14
600–700 kcmil	8	10	12	14	16
750–900 kcmil	8	12	14	16	18
1,000–1,250 kcmil	10	—	—	—	—
1,500–2,000 kcmil	12	—	—	—	—

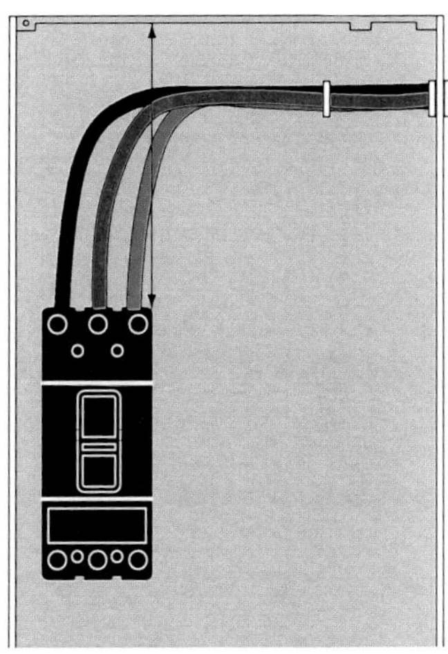

When using NEC Table 312.6(A), bending space at terminals must be measured in a straight line from the end of the lug or wire connector (in the direction that the wire leaves the terminals) to the wall, barrier, or obstruction.

26208-14_F34.EPS

Figure 34 Bending space at terminals is measured in a straight line.

When conductors enter or leave an enclosure through the wall opposite its terminals (*Figure 35*), NEC Table 312.6(B) applies. See *Table 6*. When using this table, the bending space at terminals must be measured in a straight line from the end of the lug or wire connector

Table 6 Minimum Wire Bending Space for Conductors Entering or Leaving Opposite Wall [Data from NEC Table 312.6(B)]

AWG or Circular-Mil Size of Wire	Wires per Terminal			
	1	2	3	4 or More
14–10	Not Specified	—	—	—
8	1½	—	—	—
6	2	—	—	—
4	3	—	—	—
3	3	—	—	—
2	3½	—	—	—
1	4½	—	—	—
1/0	5½	5½	7	—
2/0	6	6	7½	—
3/0	6½ (½)	6½ (½)	8	—
4/0	7 (1)	7½ (1½)	8½ (½)	—
250	8½ (2)	8½ (2)	9 (1)	10
300	10 (3)	10 (2)	11 (1)	12
350	12 (3)	12 (3)	13 (3)	14 (2)
400	13 (3)	13 (3)	14 (3)	15 (3)
500	14 (3)	14 (3)	15 (3)	16 (3)
600	15 (3)	16 (3)	18 (3)	19 (3)
700	16 (3)	18 (3)	20 (3)	22 (3)
750	17 (3)	19 (3)	22 (3)	24 (3)
800	18	20	22	24
900	19	22	24	24
1,000	20	—	—	—
1,250	22	—	—	—
1,500–2,000	24	—	—	—

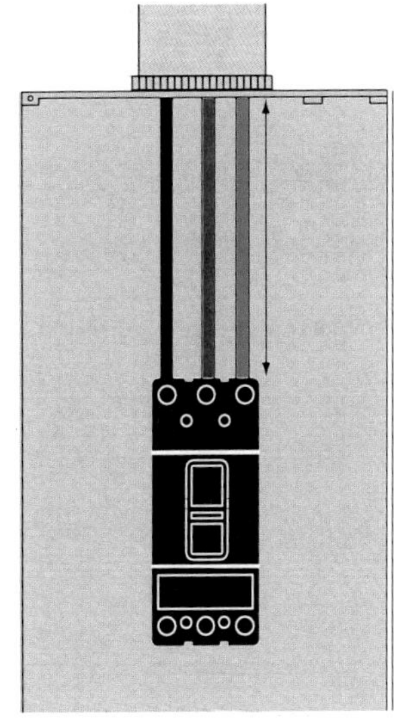

Bending space at terminals must be measured in a straight line from the end of the lug or wire connector in a direction perpendicular to the enclosure wall. Use the values in NEC Table 312.6(B).

26208-14_F35.EPS

Figure 35 Conductors entering an enclosure opposite the conductor terminals.

in a direction perpendicular to the enclosure wall. For removable and lay-in wire terminals intended for only one wire, the bending space in the table may be reduced by the number of inches shown in parentheses.

8.0.0 *NEC*® Termination Requirements

There are many *NEC*® requirements governing the termination of conductors as well as the installation of enclosures containing conductors. *NEC Sections 110.14 and 312.6* cover most installations and terminations. However, other sections, such as *NEC Sections 300.15 and 430.10*, also apply for specific applications.

8.1.0 Overcurrent Protection

In general, all ungrounded conductors from a transformer secondary require overcurrent protection to comply with *NEC Section 240.21*. The conductors from the transformer secondary are the feeder to the service. The secondary conductors are protected by the transformer primary protection (assuming tap rules and other requirements are met) until the first overcurrent device (point of service) in the secondary circuit.

8.1.1 Overcurrent Protection from Upstream Devices

Motor control centers that are fed from protective devices in a switchboard or other switchgear are not required to have a main breaker or disconnect switch in the motor control center (MCC). *Figure 36* shows feeders from a 480V switchboard terminating in the main lugs only (MLO) incoming line compartment of an MCC. This connection is made directly to the horizontal bus system distributing power to the vertical bus in each vertical section of the MCC.

8.1.2 Overcurrent Protection within Equipment

Figure 37 shows a circuit interrupter and fuses serving as the main disconnect and overcurrent protection for an MCC fed directly from a transformer secondary. It also illustrates the *NEC*® requirements for conductors entering enclosures and the use of enclosures for routing or tapping conductors. The load side of the overcurrent protective device is connected to the MCC busbar system. Where the main disconnect is rated at 400A or less, the load connection may be made with stab connections to vertical bus sections connecting to the main horizontal bus.

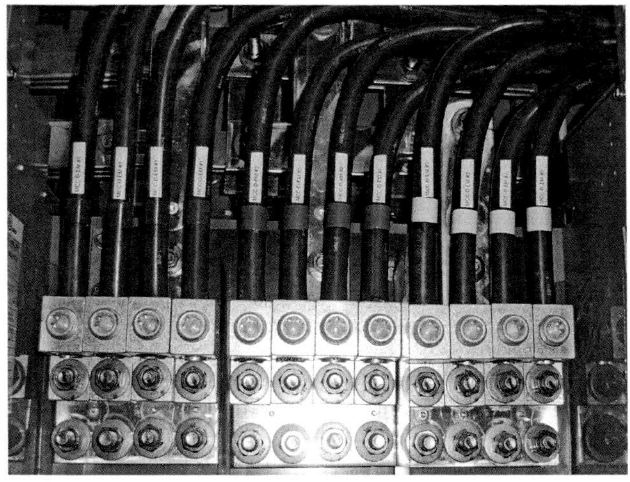

26208-14_F36.EPS

Figure 36 Incoming feeders connected to horizontal bus.

8.1.3 Short Circuit Bracing

All incoming lines to either incoming line lugs or main disconnects must be braced to withstand the mechanical force created by a high fault current. If the cables are not anchored sufficiently or the lugs are not tightened correctly, the connections become the weakest part of a panelboard or motor control center when a fault develops. In most cases, each incoming line compartment is equipped with a two-piece spreader bar located at a certain distance from the conduit entry. This spreader bar should be used along with appropriate lacing material to tie cables together where they can be bundled and to hold them apart where they must be separated. In other words, the incoming line cables should first be positioned and then anchored in place.

Manufacturers of electrical panelboards and motor control centers normally furnish detailed information on recommended methods of short circuit bracing; follow this information exactly.

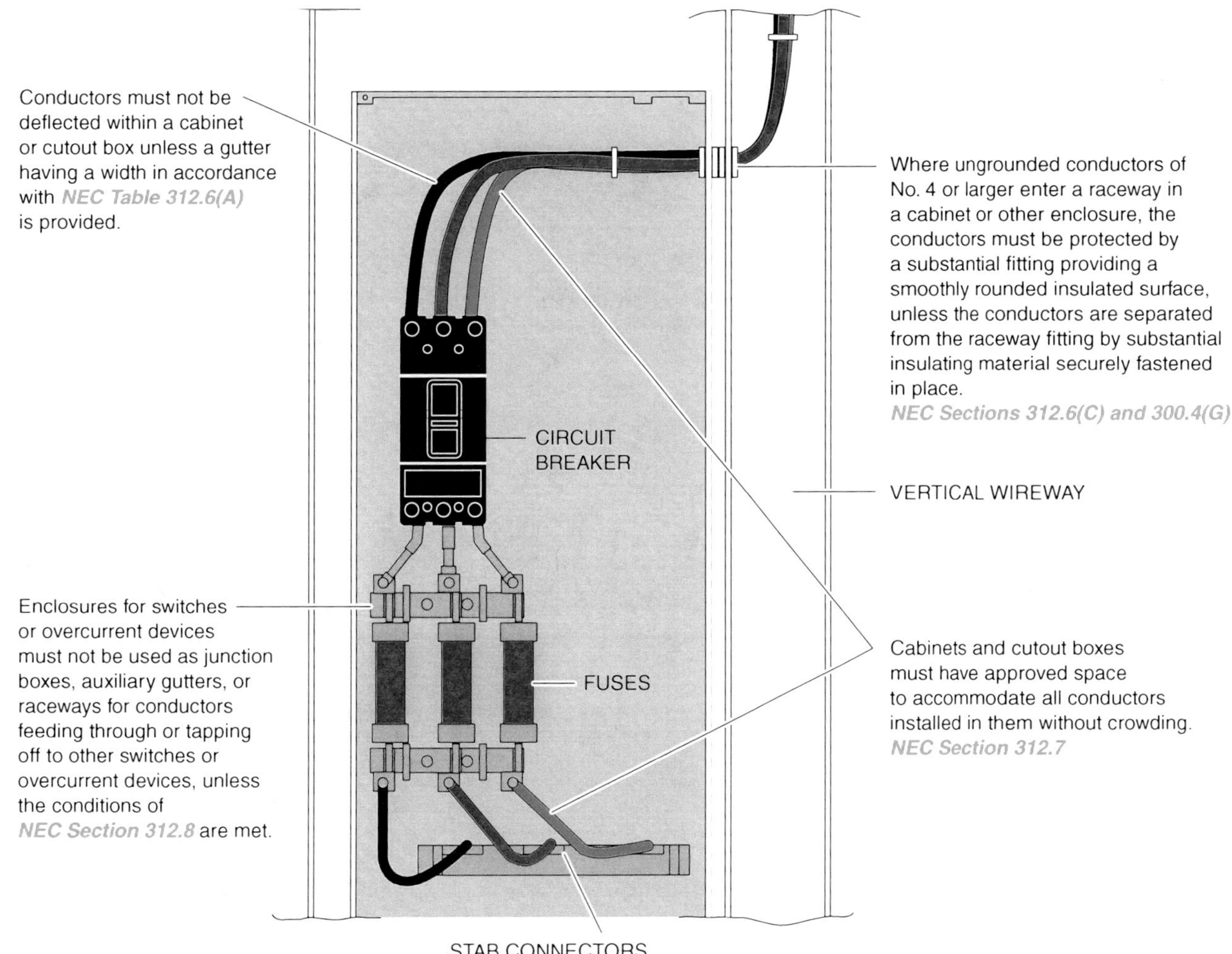

Conductors must not be deflected within a cabinet or cutout box unless a gutter having a width in accordance with NEC Table 312.6(A) is provided.
Where ungrounded conductors of No. 4 or larger enter a raceway in a cabinet or other enclosure, the conductors must be protected by a substantial fitting providing a smoothly rounded insulated surface, unless the conductors are separated from the raceway fitting by substantial insulating material securely fastened in place.
NEC Sections 312.6(C) and 300.4(G)
CIRCUIT BREAKER
VERTICAL WIREWAY
Enclosures for switches or overcurrent devices must not be used as junction boxes, auxiliary gutters, or raceways for conductors feeding through or tapping off to other switches or overcurrent devices, unless the conditions of NEC Section 312.8 are met.
FUSES
Cabinets and cutout boxes must have approved space to accommodate all conductors installed in them without crowding.
NEC Section 312.7
STAB CONNECTORS
26208-14_F37.EPS

Figure 37 MCC fed directly from a transformer secondary.

9.0.0 Taping Electrical Joints

When it is not practical to protect a spliced joint by some other means, electrical tape may be used to insulate the joint. Joints must be taped carefully to provide the same quality of insulation over the splice as over the rest of the conductors.

Various types of electrical **insulating tapes** are available for use in specific applications. Some common types of electrical tape include vinyl plastic tape, linerless rubber tape, high-temperature silicone rubber tape, and glass cloth tape. Electrical tapes made of vinyl plastic are widely used as primary insulation on joints made with thermoplastic-insulated wires. They are used for splices up to 600V and for fixture and wire splices up to 1,000V. Depending on the product, they are made for indoor use, outdoor use, or both.

Linerless rubber splicing tape provides for a tight, void-free, moisture-resistant insulation without loss of electrical characteristics. It is typically used as primary insulation with all solid dielectric cables through 70kV. Other applications include jacketing on high-voltage splices and terminals, moisture-sealing electrical connections, busbar insulations, and end sealing high-voltage cables.

High-temperature silicone rubber tapes are used as a protective overwrap for terminating high-voltage cables. Glass cloth electrical tapes provide a heat-stable insulation for hot-spot applications such as furnace and oven controls, motor leads, and switches. They are also used to reinforce insulation where heavy loads cause high heat and breakdown of insulation, such as in motor control exciter feeds, etc. All-metal braid tapes are also available. These are used to continue electrostatic shielding across a splice. When taping a splice, begin by selecting the correct tape for the job. Always follow the tape manufacturer's recommendations.

A general procedure describing one method of taping a splice or joint, such as encountered when connecting motor lugs, is shown in *Figure 38*. A method for taping a split-bolt connector is shown in *Figure 39*. Prior to taping, make sure the

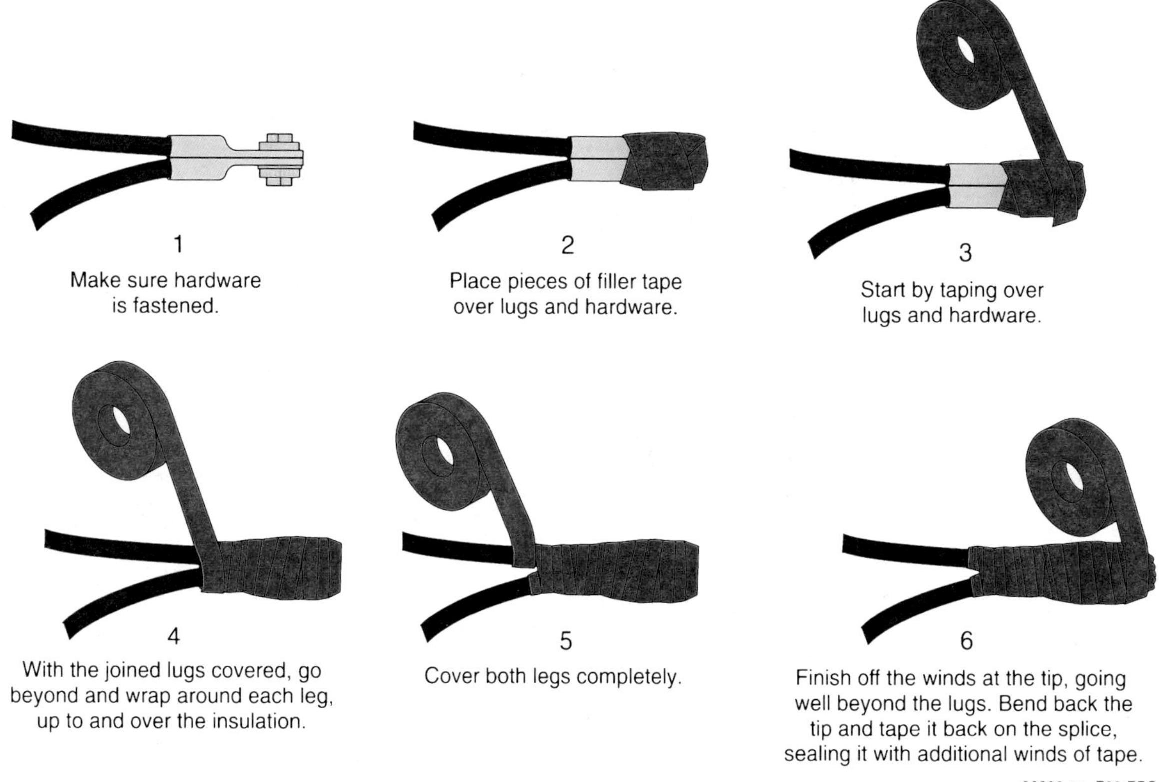

1
Make sure hardware is fastened.
2
Place pieces of filler tape over lugs and hardware.
3
Start by taping over lugs and hardware.
4
With the joined lugs covered, go beyond and wrap around each leg, up to and over the insulation.
5
Cover both legs completely.
6
Finish off the winds at the tip, going well beyond the lugs. Bend back the tip and tape it back on the splice, sealing it with additional winds of tape.
26208-14_F38.EPS

Figure 38 Typical method for taping motor lug connections.

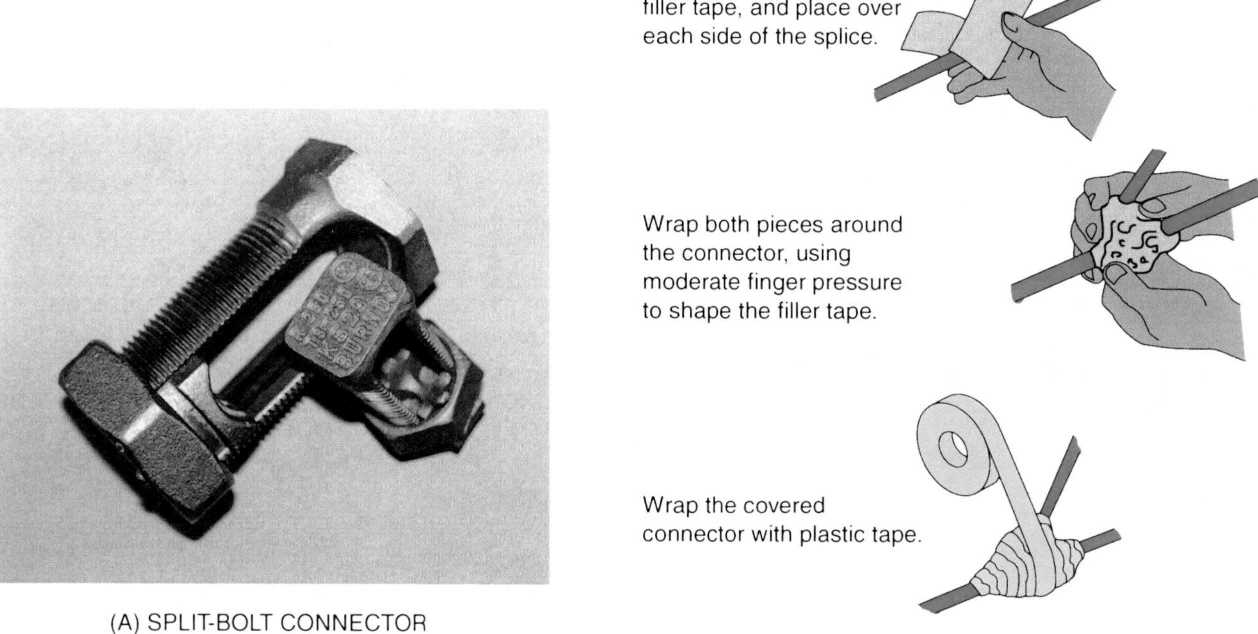

(A) SPLIT-BOLT CONNECTOR
26208-14_F39A.EPS
Once the split-bolt connector has been installed and tightened securely on the conductors, cut pieces of filler tape, and place over each side of the splice.
Wrap both pieces around the connector, using moderate finger pressure to shape the filler tape.
Wrap the covered connector with plastic tape.
(B) TAPING PROCEDURE
26208-14_F39B.EPS

Figure 39 Typical method of taping a split-bolt connector.

On Site

Electrical Tape

Most non-electricians think of electrical tape as only the simple black vinyl variety found in nearly every home toolbox. Electrical tape actually comes in a wide range of colors to be used for labeling various conductors when making terminations.

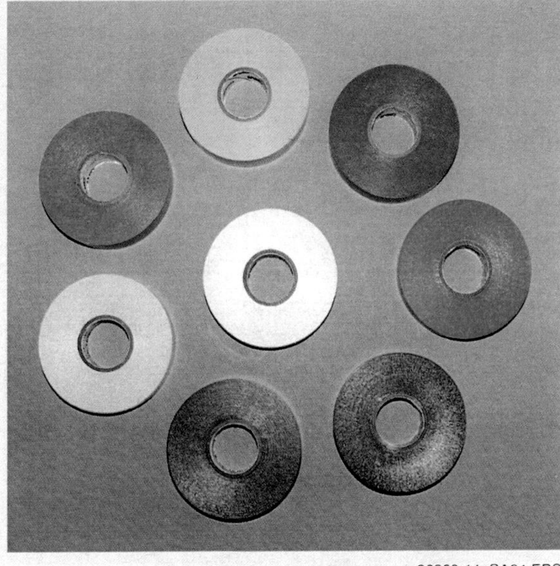

26208-14_SA04.EPS

joined lugs are securely fastened together with the appropriate hardware. Use pieces of a suitable filler tape or putty to fill any voids around the lugs and hardware and eliminate any sharp edges. This also helps to provide a smooth, even surface that makes taping easier.

> **NOTE**
> For all splices and joints where it is likely that the tape will have to be removed at some future date to perform work on the joint, apply an upside down (that is, adhesive side up) wrap of tape to the joint before applying the final layers of insulating tape to the joint in the usual manner. This will keep the area free of tape residue and facilitate the removal of the tape later on, if necessary.

10.0.0 Motor Connection Kits

Motor connection kits are available to insulate bolted splice connections, such as those in motor terminal boxes. These kits eliminate the need for taping and the use of filler tape or putty. To aid in joint reentry during rework, the insulator strips off easily, leaving a clean bolt area and thus eliminating the need to remove old tape and putty. Motor connection kits are available for use with stub (butt splice) connections (*Figure 40*)

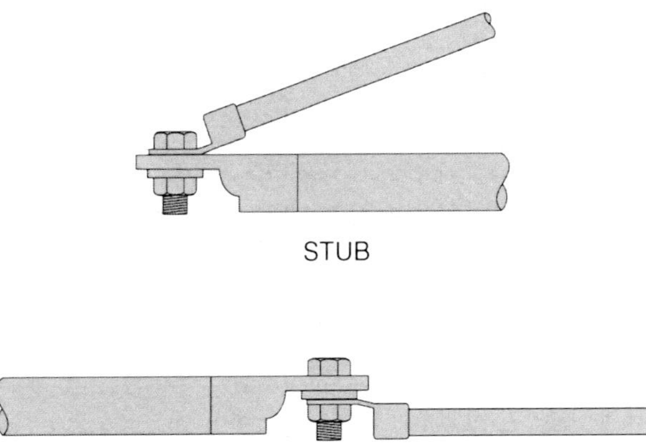

26208-14_F40.EPS

Figure 40 Stub and in-line splice connections.

where there is insufficient room to make in-line connections. They are also made to insulate in-line splice connections where space permits. These insulating kits use a high-voltage mastic that seals the splice against moisture, dirt, and other contaminants.

One type of motor connection kit insulator is heat-shrinkable. It installs easily using heat from a propane torch to shrink the insulator in a manner similar to that of heat-shrink tubing (*Figure 41*). Another type of kit used for insulating stub connections comes in the form of an elastomeric insulating cap that is cold-applied by rolling it over the stub splice. Always follow the kit manufacturer's recommendations when selecting a kit to use for a particular application. Typically, the kit is selected based on the size of the motor feeder cable.

Think About It

Putting It All Together

Examine the wiring connections in your home or workplace. Are they properly made? Can you determine if any connections have the potential for failure?

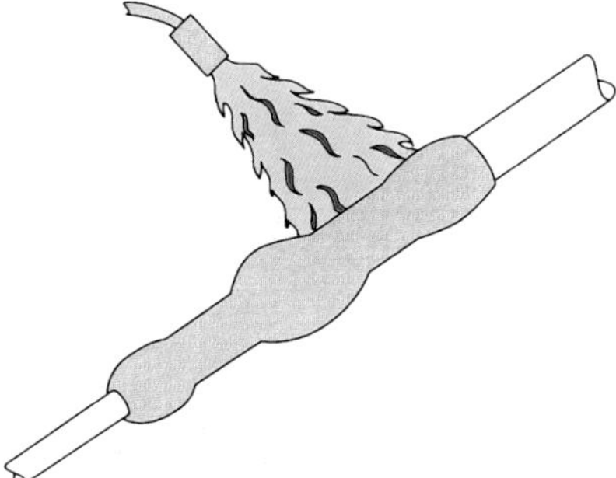

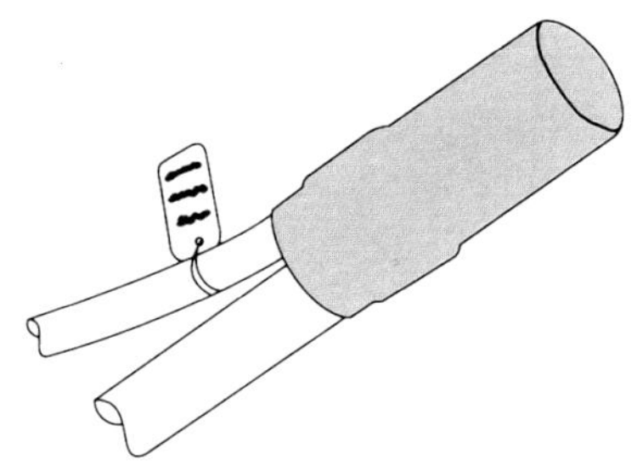

Figure 41 Motor connection kits installed on splices.

Summary

A system is only as good as the weakest link. Poor quality terminations and splices weaken a system and can result in failure or fire. Good terminations and splices are mechanically and electrically secure, well-insulated, and should last as long as the conductor is in service.

Before a connection is made, the conductor must be stripped using the appropriate tool. Even minor damage to the conductor or insulation can affect the strength of the system.

Crimp connectors or terminals are used for many types of wire and cable. They are convenient for terminating conductors at terminal boards, control wiring terminals, and the like.

Lugs are provided for the larger wire sizes on panelboards and motor control centers. It is very important to tighten these lugs properly to provide a sound electrical connection as well as to provide short circuit bracing.

There are a variety of insulating tapes available to seal spliced joints. Always match the tape with the application.

Review Questions

1. A poorly made splice is acceptable as long as it provides a path for current flow.
   a. True
   b. False

2. Which of the following best describes the term *stripping* as it applies to conductor splicing?
   a. Removal of the insulation from conductors
   b. Removal of the packing material from the carton
   c. Removal of any excess strands of wire from a splice
   d. Removal of the pulling ring from lead sheath conductors

3. What is the diameter, in inches, of 2,000 kcmil wire?
   a. 0.89
   b. 0.99
   c. 1.29
   d. 1.63

4. All of the following are types of stripping *except* _____.
   a. end terminations
   b. window cuts
   c. spiral cuts
   d. indent cuts

5. Which of the following best describes the purpose of a reducing connector?
   a. To temporarily connect a circuit
   b. To join two different size conductors
   c. To join conductors of the same size
   d. To make a 90° bend in parallel conductors

6. Information about connector size and conductor range is _____.
   a. stamped on the connector tongue
   b. color coded
   c. printed on the insulation
   d. stamped on the connector barrel

7. The most frequently used tongue styles are _____.
   a. ringed tongue and locking fork
   b. slotted and flanged fork
   c. hook shot and rectangular
   d. fork and flag

8. When using a crimping tool, use _____.
   a. the maximum crimping force possible
   b. a lower mechanical force to achieve maximum electrical performance
   c. the highest force needed for the maximum mechanical strength
   d. an amount of force between optimum mechanical and electrical performance

9. Using a crimp die that is too large will _____.
   a. destroy the crimp barrel
   b. weaken the conductor
   c. provide a weak mechanical connection
   d. provide poor electrical performance

10. The crimp indent is properly placed on the _____.
    a. right side of the barrel
    b. bottom of the barrel
    c. seam of the barrel
    d. left side of the barrel

11. Which of the following tools is best for positioning cable?
    a. Split-bolt connectors
    b. A heat gun
    c. A power connector indenter
    d. Wire-bending tools (either ratchet or hydraulic)

12. The minimum wire bending space for a single 3/0 conductor *not* entering or leaving the wall opposite its terminal is _____.
    a. 2 inches
    b. 3 inches
    c. 4 inches
    d. 5 inches

13. The minimum wire bending space for two 1/0 conductors *not* entering or leaving the wall opposite the terminal is _____.
    a. 2 inches
    b. 3 inches
    c. 4 inches
    d. 5 inches

14. The minimum wire bending space for three 3/0 conductors entering or leaving the wall opposite the terminal is _____.

    a. 7 inches
    b. 8 inches
    c. 9 inches
    d. 10 inches

15. Which of the following types of electrical tape is best for taping most joints for voltages up to 600V?

    a. High-temperature silicone rubber
    b. Rubber
    c. Glass cloth
    d. Vinyl plastic

Module 26208-14
Supplemental Exercises

1. Heavy-duty strippers are used to strip power cables with outside diameters ranging from _______________ to _______________.

2. Properly made splices and connections should last ____
____.

3. Aluminum has certain properties that are different than copper. These properties are:
____
____
____.

4. The electrolytic action between aluminum and copper can be controlled by ___________________
____.

5. Connectors marked AL should only be used with _______________________ wire, while connectors marked AL-CU can be used with either wire.

6. True or False? Poorly stripped conductors can result in changes in the dielectric strength.

7. Nearly all cable installations require the cable to be bent at terminations and other points along the cable route (these bends must comply with the *NEC*®). Minimum bending radii are determined by
____
____.

8. The bending radii for various sizes of conductors entering or leaving cabinets or cutout boxes must comply with certain *NEC*® requirements, many of which are covered in _______________________
____.

9. All incoming lines to either incoming line lugs or main disconnects must be braced to withstand the mechanical force created by a high fault current. Detailed information on the recommended methods of short circuit bracing is normally furnished by _____________________________________
____.

10. All wire joints not protected by some other means should be taped carefully to _________________
____
____.

Trade Terms Introduced in This Module

AL-CU: An abbreviation for aluminum and copper, commonly marked on terminals, lugs, and other electrical connectors to indicate that the device is suitable for use with either aluminum conductors or copper conductors.

Amperage capacity: The maximum amount of current that a lug can safely handle at its rated voltage.

Connection: That part of a circuit that has negligible impedance and joins components or devices.

Connector: A device used to physically and electrically connect two or more conductors.

Drain wire: A wire that is attached to a coaxial connector to allow a path to ground from the outer shield.

Grooming: The act of separating the braid in a coaxial conductor.

Insulating tape: Adhesive tape that has been manufactured from a nonconductive material and is used for covering wire joints and exposed parts.

Lug: A device for terminating a conductor to facilitate the mechanical connection.

Mechanical advantage (MA): The force factor of a crimping tool that is multiplied by the hand force to give the total force.

Pressure connector: A connector applied using pressure to form a cold weld between the conductor and the connector.

Reducing connector: A connector used to join two different sized conductors.

Shielding: The metal covering of a cable that reduces the effects of electromagnetic noise.

Splice: The electrical and mechanical connection between two pieces of cable.

Strand: A group of wires, usually stranded or braided.

Terminal: A device used for connecting cables.

Termination: The connection of a cable.

Additional Resources

This module presents thorough resources for task training. The following resource material is suggested for further study.

National Electrical Code® Handbook, Latest Edition. Quincy, MA: National Fire Protection Association.

Figure Credits

Associated Builders and Contractors, Inc., Module opener

Greenlee/A Textron Company, Figures 1, 2, SA01, Figures 3, 6, SA02, Figures 17–22, 32, and 33

Topaz Publications, Inc., Figures 8, 10, SA03, Figures 13B, 39A, and SA04

Belden Inc., Figure 13A

Jim Mitchem, Figures 23, 25, and 36

National Fire Protection Association, Tables 5 and 6

NCCER CURRICULA — USER UPDATE

NCCER makes every effort to keep its textbooks up-to-date and free of technical errors. We appreciate your help in this process. If you find an error, a typographical mistake, or an inaccuracy in NCCER's curricula, please fill out this form (or a photocopy), or complete the online form at **www.nccer.org/olf**. Be sure to include the exact module ID number, page number, a detailed description, and your recommended correction. Your input will be brought to the attention of the Authoring Team. Thank you for your assistance.

Instructors – If you have an idea for improving this textbook, or have found that additional materials were necessary to teach this module effectively, please let us know so that we may present your suggestions to the Authoring Team.

NCCER Product Development and Revision

13614 Progress Blvd., Alachua, FL 32615

Email: curriculum@nccer.org
Online: www.nccer.org/olf

❑ Trainee Guide ❑ AIG ❑ Exam ❑ PowerPoints Other ______________________

Craft / Level: Copyright Date:

Module ID Number / Title:

Section Number(s):

Description:

Recommended Correction:

Your Name:

Address:

Email: Phone:

Conduits, Raceways, Boxes and Fittings

Modules

26107-14
26108-14
26204-14
26205-14
26207-14

Hand Bending

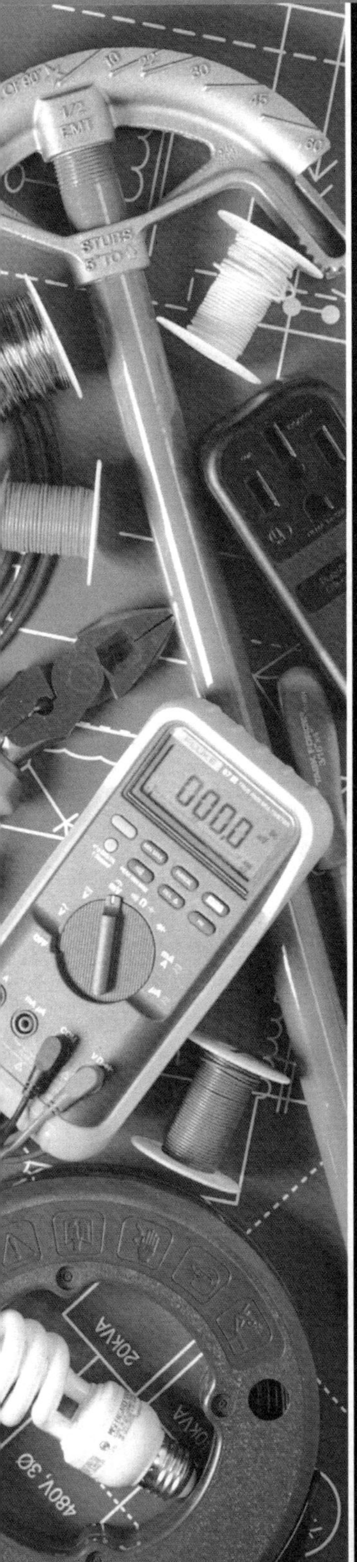

National Air and Space Museum

The Steven F. Udvar-Hazy Center near Washington Dulles International Airport is the companion facility to the Museum on the National Mall. The building opened in December, 2003, and provides enough space for the Smithsonian to display the thousands of aviation and space artifacts that cannot be exhibited on the National Mall.

26107-14

Trainees with successful module completions may be eligible for credentialing through NCCER's National Registry. To learn more, go to **www.nccer.org** or contact us at **1.888.622.3720.** Our website has information on the latest product releases and training, as well as online versions of our *Cornerstone* magazine and Pearson's product catalog.

Your feedback is welcome. You may email your comments to **curriculum@nccer.org,** send general comments and inquiries to **info@nccer.org,** or fill in the User Update form at the back of this module.

This information is general in nature and intended for training purposes only. Actual performance of activities described in this manual requires compliance with all applicable operating, service, maintenance, and safety procedures under the direction of qualified personnel. References in this manual to patented or proprietary devices do not constitute a recommendation of their use.

HAND BENDING

Objectives

When you have completed this module, you will be able to do the following:

1. Identify the methods for hand bending and installing conduit.
2. Determine conduit bends.
3. Make 90-degree bends, back-to-back bends, offsets, kicks, and saddle bends using a hand bender.
4. Cut, ream, and thread conduit.

Performance Tasks

Under the supervision of the instructor, you should be able to do the following:

1. Make 90° bends, back-to-back bends, offsets, kicks, and saddle bends using a hand bender.
2. Cut, ream, and thread conduit.

Trade Terms

90° bend
Back-to-back bend
Concentric bends
Developed length
Gain
Offsets
Rise
Segment bend
Stub-up

Required Trainee Materials

1. Paper and pencil
2. Copy of the latest edition of the *National Electrical Code*®
3. Appropriate personal protective equipment

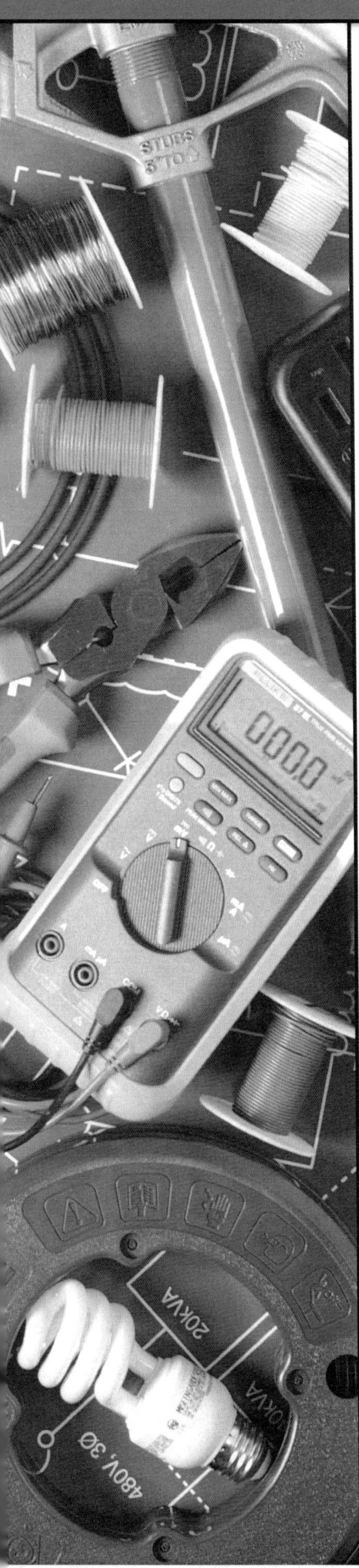

Contents

Topics to be presented in this module include:

Figures and Tables

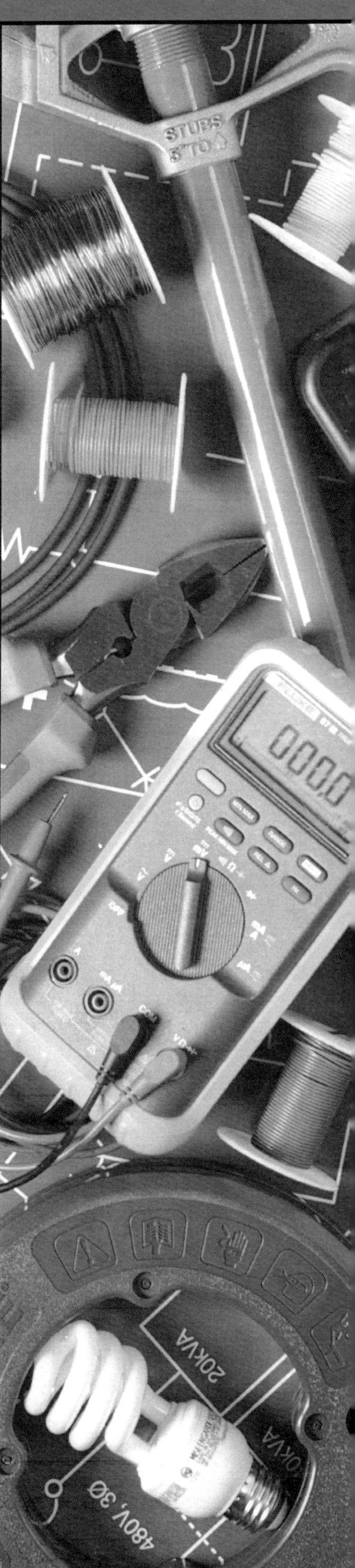

1.0.0 Introduction

The art of conduit bending is dependent upon the skills of the electrician and requires a working knowledge of basic terms and proven procedures. Practice, knowledge, and training will help you gain the skills necessary for proper conduit bending and installation. You will be able to practice conduit bending in the lab and in the field under the supervision of experienced co-workers. In this module, the techniques for using hand-operated and step conduit benders such as the hand bender and the hickey will be covered. The processes of hand bending, cutting, reaming, and threading conduit will also be explained.

2.0.0 Hand Bending Equipment

Figure 1 shows hand benders. Hand benders are convenient to use on the job because they are portable and no electrical power is required. Hand benders have a shape that supports the walls of the conduit being bent.

These benders are used to make various bends in smaller-size conduit (½" to 1¼"). Most hand benders are sized to bend rigid conduit and electrical metallic tubing (EMT) of corresponding sizes. For example, a single hand bender can bend either ¾" EMT or ½" rigid conduit. The next larger size of hand bender will bend either 1" EMT or ¾" rigid conduit. This is because the corresponding sizes of conduit have nearly equal outside diameters.

The first step in making a good bend is familiarizing yourself with the bender. The manufacturer of the bender will typically provide documentation indicating starting points, distance between offsets, gains, and other important values associated with that particular bender. There is no substitute for taking the time to review this information. It will make the job go faster and result in better bends.

On Site

Working with Conduit

Unprotected electrical cable is susceptible to physical damage; therefore, protect the wiring with conduit.

CAUTION

When making bends, be sure you have a firm grip on the handle to avoid slippage and possible injury.

When performing a bend, it is important to keep the conduit on a stable, firm, flat surface for the entire duration of the bend. Hand benders are designed to have force applied using one foot and the hands. See *Figure 2*. It is important to use constant foot pressure as well as force on the handle to achieve uniform bends. Allowing the conduit to rise up or performing the bend on soft ground can result in distorting the conduit outside the bender.

NOTE

Bends should be made in accordance with the guidelines of *NEC Article 342* (intermediate metal conduit or IMC), *Article 344* (rigid metal conduit or RMC), *Article 352* (rigid polyvinyl chloride conduit or PVC), or *Article 358* (electrical metallic tubing or EMT).

A hickey (*Figure 3*) should not be confused with a hand bender. The hickey, which is used for RMC and IMC only, functions quite differently.

When you use a hickey to bend conduit, you are forming the bend as well as the radius. When

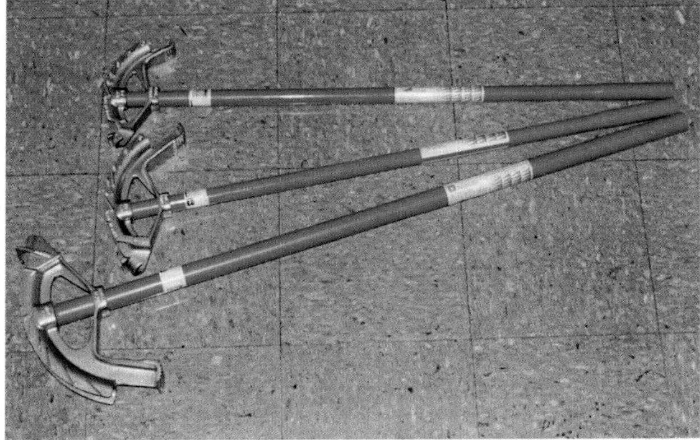

26107-14_F01.EPS

Figure 1 Hand benders.

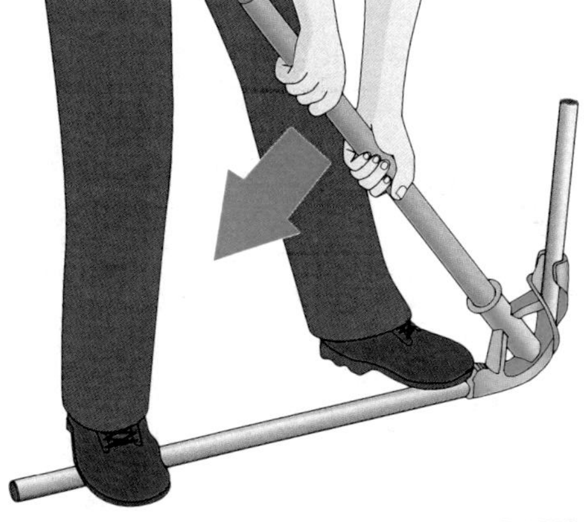

26107-14_F02.EPS

Figure 2 Pushing down on the bender to complete the bend.

On Site

Bending Conduit

A good way to practice bending conduit is to use a piece of No. 10 or No. 12 solid wire and bend it to resemble the bends you need. This gives you some perspective on how to bend the conduit and it will also help you to anticipate any problems with the bends.

using a hickey, be careful not to flatten or kink the conduit. Hickeys should only be used with RMC and IMC because very little support is given to the walls of the conduit being bent.

A hickey is a segment bending device. First, a small bend of about 10° is made. Then, the hickey is moved to a new position and another small bend is made. This process is continued until the bend is completed. A hickey can be used for conduit stub-ups in slabs and decks.

On Site

Proper Bends

Kinks are created by bending too small a radius using a hickey.

26107-14_SA01.EPS

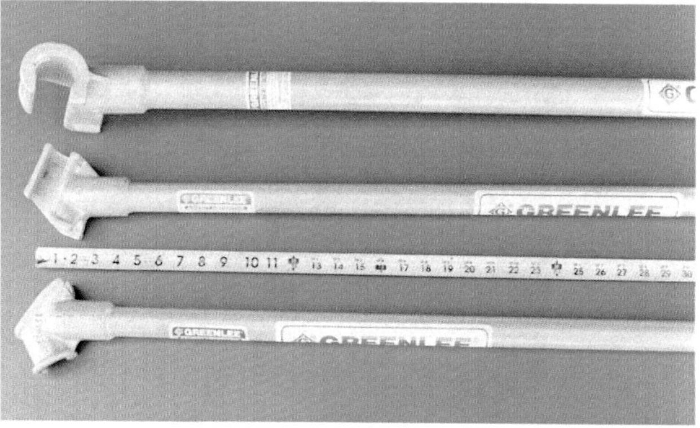

26107-14_F03.EPS

Figure 3 Hickeys.

26107-14_F04.EPS

Figure 4 Typical PVC heating units.

Polyvinyl chloride (PVC) conduit is bent using a heating unit (*Figure 4*). The PVC must be rotated regularly while it is in the heater so that it heats evenly. Once heated, the PVC is removed, and the bending is performed by hand. Some units use an electric heating element, while others use liquid propane (LP). After bending, a damp sponge or cloth is often used so that the PVC sets up faster.

CAUTION

Avoid contact with the case of the heating unit; it can become very hot and cause burns. Also, to avoid a fire hazard, ensure that the unit is cool before storage. If using an LP unit, keep a fire extinguisher nearby.

When bending PVC that is 2" or larger in diameter, there is a risk of wrinkling or flattening the bend. A plug set eliminates this problem (*Figure 5*). A plug is inserted into each end of the piece of PVC being bent. Then, a hand pump is used to pressurize the conduit before bending it. The pressure is about 3 to 5 psi.

NOTE

The plugs must remain in place until the pipe is cooled and set.

2.1.0 Geometry Required to Make a Bend

Bending conduit requires that you use some basic geometry. You may already be familiar with most of the concepts needed; however, here is a review of the concepts directly related to this task.

A right triangle is defined as any triangle with a 90° angle. The side directly opposite the 90° angle is called the hypotenuse, and the side on which the triangle sits is the base. The vertical side is called the height. On the job, you will apply the

What's wrong with this picture?

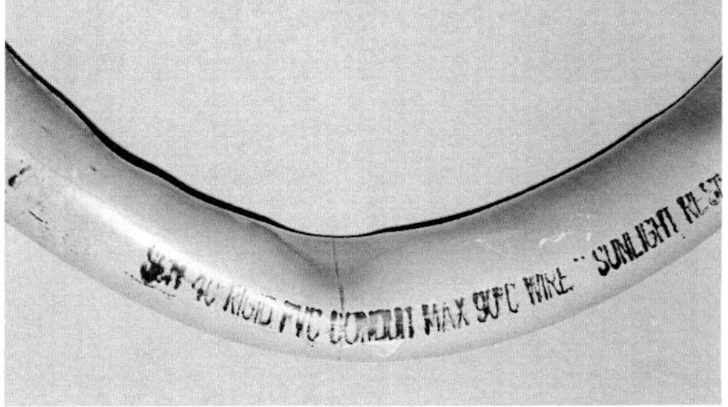

26107-14_SA02.EPS

26107-14_F05.EPS

Figure 5 Typical plug set.

relationships in a right triangle when making an offset bend. The offset forms the hypotenuse of a right triangle (*Figure 6*).

On Site

Practical Bending

When making offset bends of 45° to step conduit up to another level, square floor tiles make a convenient grid to gauge the distance and angles.

> **NOTE** There are reference tables for sizing offset bends based on these relationships (see *Appendix A*).

A circle is defined as a closed curved line whose points are all the same distance from its center. The distance from the center point to the edge of the circle is called the radius. The length from one edge of the circle to the other edge through the center point is the diameter. The distance around the circle is called the circumference. A circle can be divided into four equal quadrants. Each quadrant accounts for 90°, making a total of 360°. When you make a **90° bend**, you will use ¼ of a circle, or one quadrant (see *Figure 7*).

Concentric circles are circles that have a common center but different radii. The concept of concentric circles can be applied to **concentric bends** in conduit. The angle of each bend is 90°. Such bends have the same center point, but the radius of each is different.

To calculate the circumference of a circle, use the following formula:

$$C = \pi \times D \text{ or } C = \pi D$$

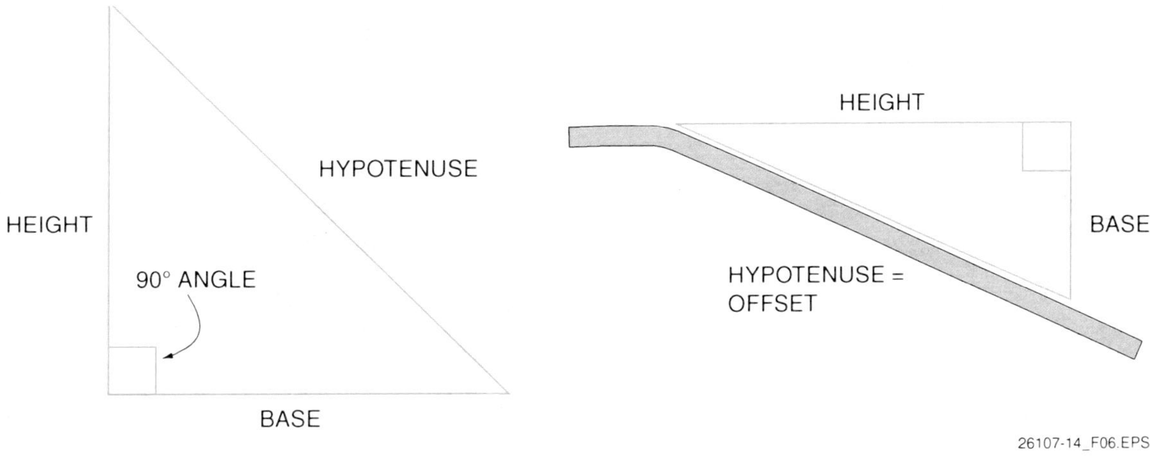

Figure 6 Right triangle and offset bend.

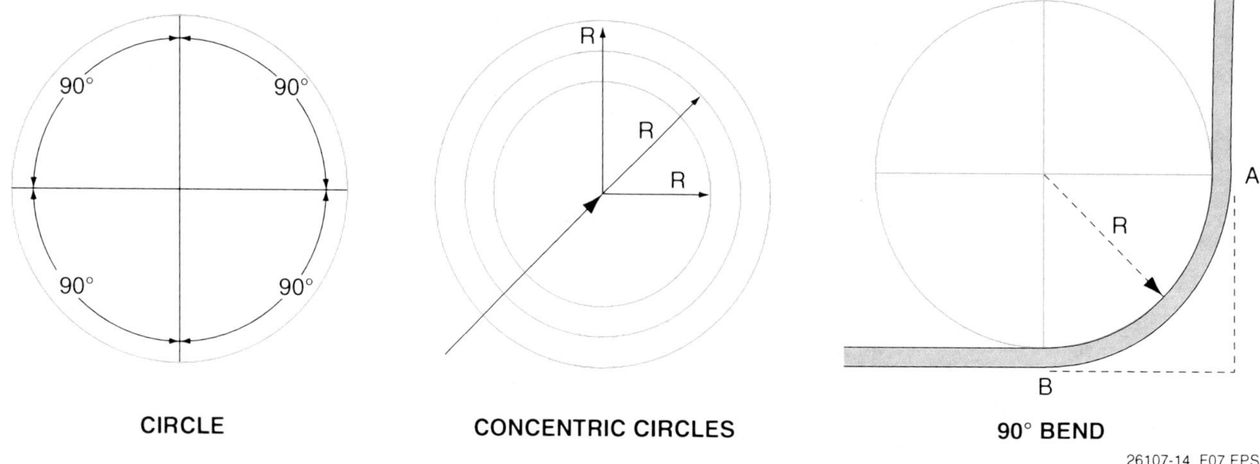

Figure 7 Circles and 90° bends.

In this formula, C = circumference, D = diameter, and π = 3.14. Another way of stating the formula for circumference is $C = 2\pi R$, where R equals the radius or ½ the diameter. To figure the arc of a quadrant use:

$$\text{Length of arc} = (0.25)\ 2\pi R = 1.57R$$

For this formula, the arc of a quadrant equals ¼ the circumference of the circle or 1.57 times the radius.

A bending radius table is included in *Appendix B*.

2.2.0 Making a 90° Bend

The 90° stub bend is probably the most basic bend of all. The stub bend is used much of the time, regardless of the type of conduit being installed. Before beginning to make the bend, you need to know two measurements:

- Desired rise or stub-up
- Take-up distance of the bender

The desired rise is the height of the stub-up. The take-up is the amount of conduit the bender will use to form the bend. Take-up distances are usually listed in the manufacturer's instruction manual. Typical bender take-up distances are shown in *Table 1*.

Table 1 Typical Bender Take-Up Distances

EMT	Rigid/IMC	Take-Up
½"	—	5"
¾"	½"	6"
1"	¾"	8"
1¼"	1"	11"

Once you have determined the take-up, subtract it from the stub-up height. Mark that distance on the conduit (all the way around) at that distance from the end. The mark will indicate the point at which you will begin to bend the conduit. Line up the starting point on the conduit with the starting point on the bender. Most benders have a mark, such as an arrow, to indicate this point. *Figure 8* shows the take-up required to achieve an 18" stub-up on a piece of ½" EMT.

Once you have lined up the bender, use one foot to hold the conduit steady. Keep your heel on the floor for balance. Apply constant pressure on the bender foot pedal with your other foot. Make sure you hold the bender handle perpendicular to the floor, and as far up as possible, to get maximum leverage. Then, bend the conduit in one smooth motion, pulling as steadily as possible. Avoid overstretching.

On Site

Matching Bends in Parallel Runs

Suppose you are running 1" rigid conduit along with a 2" rigid conduit in a rack and you come to a 90° bend. If you used a 1" shoe, the radius would not match that of the 2" conduit bend. To match the 2" 90° bend, take your 1" conduit and put it in the 2" shoe of your bender, then bend as usual. This 1" 90° bend will now have the same radius as the 2" 90° bend. This trick will only work on rigid conduit. If done with EMT, it will flatten the pipe.

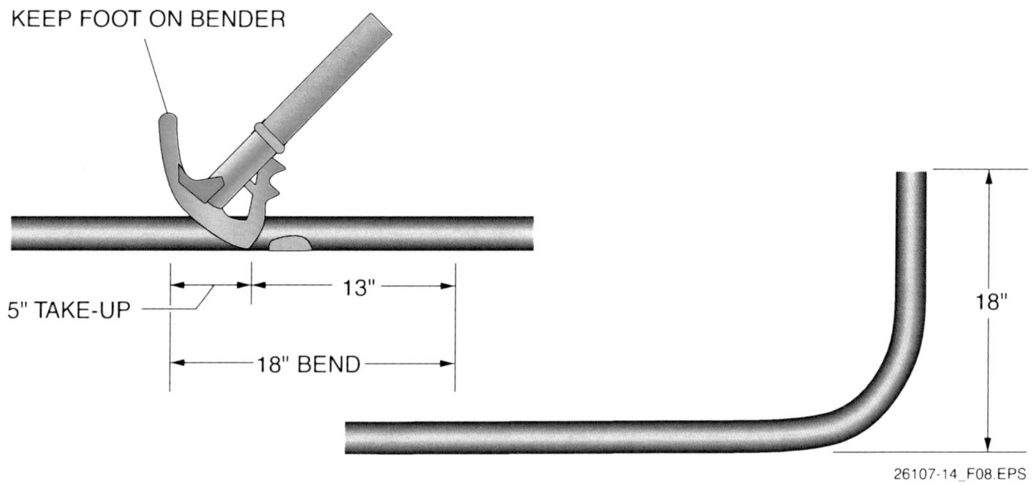

Figure 8 Bending an 18-inch stub-up.

> **NOTE**
> When bending conduit using the take-up method, always place the bender on the conduit and make the bend facing the hook of the conduit from which the measurements were taken.

After finishing the bend, check to make sure you have the correct angle and measurement. Use the following steps to check a 90° bend:

Step 1 With the back of the bend on the floor, measure to the end of the conduit stub-up to make sure it is the right length.

Step 2 Check the 90° angle of the bend with a square or at the angle formed by the floor and a wall. A torpedo level may also be used.

> **NOTE**
> If you overbend a conduit slightly past the desired angle, you can use the bender to bend the conduit back to the correct angle.

The above procedure will produce a 90° one-shot bend. That means that it took a single bend to form the conduit bend. A **segment bend** is any bend that is formed by a series of bends of a few degrees each, rather than a single one-shot bend. A shot is actually one bend in a segment bend. Segment or sweep bends must conform to the provisions of the *NEC®*.

2.3.0 Gain

The gain is the distance saved by the arc of a 90° bend. Knowing the gain can help you to precut, ream, and prethread both ends of the conduit before you bend it. This will make your work go more quickly because it is easier to work with conduit while it is straight. *Figure 9* shows that the overall **developed length** of a piece of conduit with a 90° bend is less than the sum of the horizontal and vertical distances when measured square to the corner. This is shown by the following equation:

$$\text{Developed length} = (A + B) - \text{gain}$$

An example of a manufacturer's gain table is also shown in *Figure 9*. These tables are used to determine the gain for a certain size conduit.

On Site

Take-Up Method

When bending conduit using the take-up method, always place the bender on the conduit and make the bend facing the end of the conduit from which the measurements were taken. It helps to make a narrow mark with a soft lead pencil or marker completely around the conduit. This is called girdling.

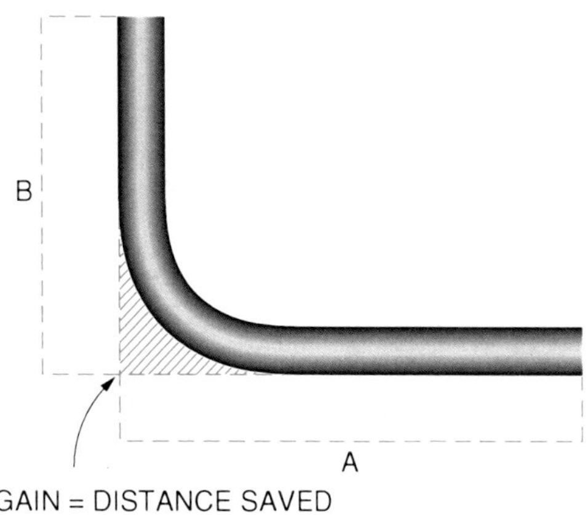

Conduit Size	NEC® Radius	90° Gain
½"	4"	2⅝"
¾"	5"	3¼"
1"	6"	4"
1¼"	8"	5⅝"

TYPICAL GAIN TABLE

26107-14_F09.EPS

Figure 9 Gain.

2.4.0 Back-to-Back 90° Bends

A **back-to-back bend** consists of two 90° bends made on the same piece of conduit and placed back-to-back (*Figure 10*).

To make a back-to-back bend, make the first bend (labeled *X* in *Figure 10*) in the usual manner. To make the second bend, measure the required distance between the bends from the back of the first bend. This distance is labeled *L* in the figure. Reverse the bender on the conduit, as shown in *Figure 10*. Place the bender's back-to-back indicating mark at point *Y* on the conduit. Note that outside measurements from point *X* to point *Y* are used. Holding the bender in the reverse position and properly aligned, apply foot pressure and complete the second bend.

On Site

Checking Vertical Rise

Use a torpedo level to check for plumb on a vertical rise.

26107-14_SA03.EPS

Think About It

Gain

What is the difference between the gain and the take-up of a bend?

2.5.0 Making an Offset

Many situations require that the conduit be bent so that it can pass over objects such as beams and other conduits, or enter meter cabinets and junction boxes. Bends used for this purpose are called offsets (kicks). To produce an offset, two

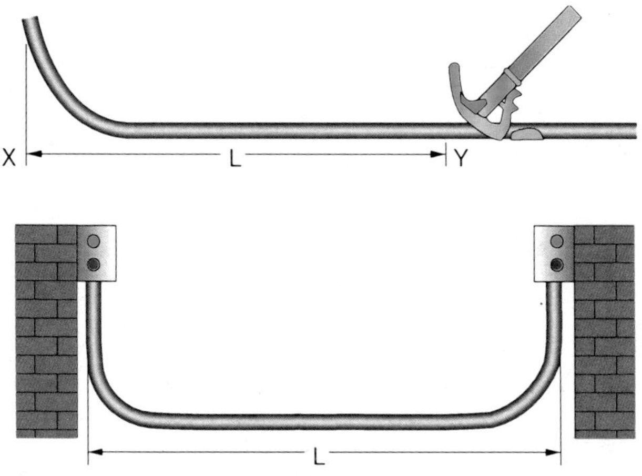

26107-14_F10.EPS

Figure 10 Back-to-back bends.

Think About It

Smooth Bends

Why are smooth bends so important?

equal bends of less than 90° are required, a specified distance apart, as shown in *Figure 11*.

Offsets are a trade-off between space and the effort it will take to pull the wire. The larger the degree of bend, the harder it will be to pull the wire. The smaller the degree of bend, the easier it will be to pull the wire. Use the shallowest degree of bend that will still allow the conduit to bypass the obstruction and fit in the given space.

When conduit is offset, some of the conduit length is used. If the offset is made into the area, an allowance must be made for this shrinkage. If the offset angle is away from the obstruction, the shrinkage can be ignored.

Table 2 shows the amount of shrinkage per inch of rise for common offset angles.

The formula for figuring the distance between bends is as follows:

Distance between bends = depth of offset × multiplier

The distance between the offset bends can generally be found in the manufacturer's documentation for the bender. *Table 3* shows the distance between bends for the most common offset angles.

Calculations related to offsets are derived from the branch of mathematics known as trigonometry, which deals with triangles. The multipliers shown in *Table 2* represent the cosecant (CSC) of the related offset angle. The multiplier is determined by dividing the hypotenuse of the triangle created by the offset by the depth of the offset (*Figure 11*).

On Site

Offset Benders

This offset bender can be used for wall-mounted boxes with exposed conduit. It automatically matches the offset to the box knockout position and is a great timesaver when making multiple offsets.

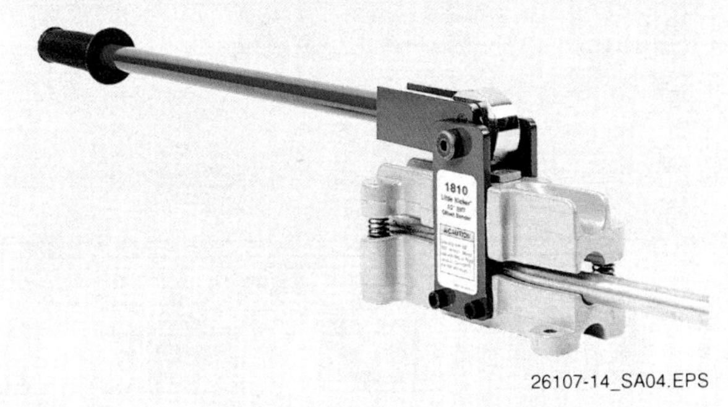

26107-14_SA04.EPS

Table 2 Shrinkage Calculation

Offset Angle	Multiplier	Shrinkage (per inch of rise)
10° × 10°	6.0	1⁄16"
22½° × 22½°	2.6	3⁄16"
30° × 30°	2.0	¼"
45° × 45°	1.4	⅜"
60° × 60°	1.2	½"

Basic trigonometry (trig) functions are briefly covered in *Appendix A*. As you will see in the next section, the tangent (TAN) of the offset angle is also used in calculating parallel offsets. Understanding trig functions will help you understand how offsets are determined. If you have a scientific

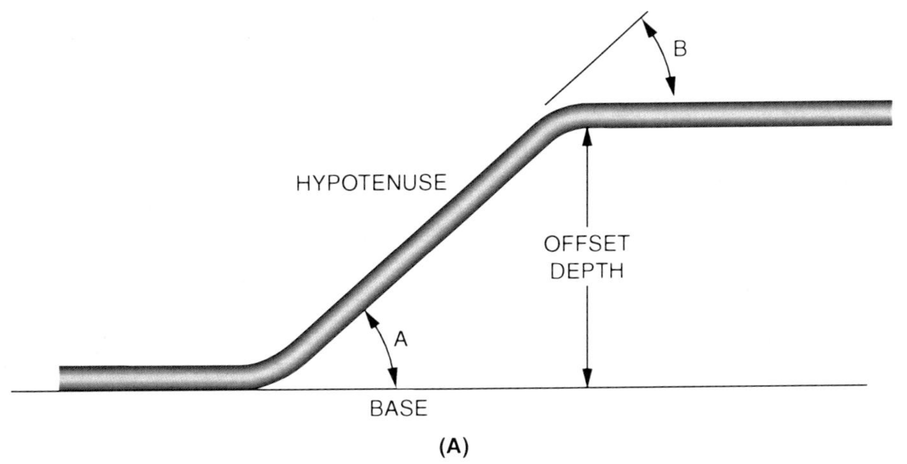

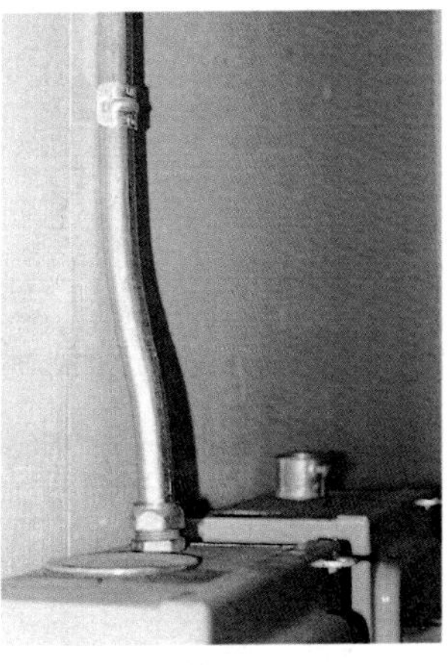

26107-14_F11.EPS

Figure 11 Offsets.

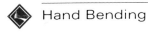

Table 3 Common Offset Factors (in Inches)

Offset Depth	22½° Between Bends	22½° Shrinkage	30° Between Bends	30° Shrinkage	45° Between Bends	45° Shrinkage	60° Between Bends	60° Shrinkage
2	5¼	⅜	—	—	—	—	—	—
3	7¾	9⁄16	6	¾	—	—	—	—
4	10½	¾	8	1	—	—	—	—
5	13	15⁄16	10	1¼	7	1⅞	—	—
6	15½	1⅛	12	1½	8½	2¼	7¼	3
7	18¼	1 5⁄16	14	1¾	9¾	2⅝	8⅜	3½
8	20¾	1½	16	2	11¼	3	9⅝	4
9	23½	1¾	18	2¼	12½	3⅜	10⅞	4½
10	26	1⅞	20	2½	14	3¾	12	5

calculator and understand these functions, you can calculate offset angles when you know the dimensions of the triangle created by the offset and the obstacle.

2.6.0 Parallel Offsets

Often, multiple pieces of conduit must be bent around a common obstruction. In this case, parallel offsets are made. Since the bends are laid out along a common radius, an adjustment must be made to ensure that the ends do not come out uneven, as shown in *Figure 12*.

The center of the first bend of the innermost conduit is found first, as shown in *Figure 13*. Each successive conduit must have its centerline moved farther away from the end of the pipe, as shown in *Figure 14*. The amount to add is calculated as follows:

Amount added = center-to-center spacing × tangent (TAN) of ½ offset angle

Tangents can be found using the trig tables provided in *Appendix A*.

For example, *Figure 15* shows three pipes laid out as parallel and offset. The angle of the offset is 30°. The center-to-center spacing is 3". The start of the innermost pipe's first bend is 12".

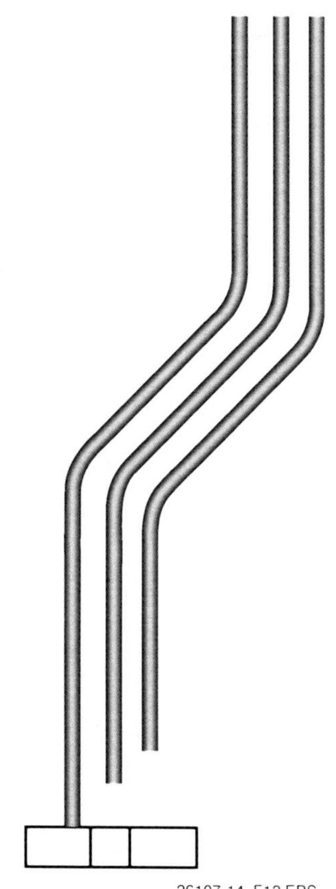

Figure 12 Incorrect parallel offsets.

Think About It

Calculating Shrinkage

You're making a 30° by 30° offset to clear a 6" obstruction. What will be the distance between bends? What will be the developed length shrink? Make the same calculations for a 10" offset with 45° bends.

The starting point of the second pipe will be:

12" + [center-to-center spacing × TAN (½ offset angle)]

12" + (3" × TAN 15°) = 12" + (3" × 0.2679) = 12" + 0.8037"

This is approximately 12 13⁄16".

The starting point for the outermost pipe is:

12 13⁄16" + 13⁄16" = 13⅝"

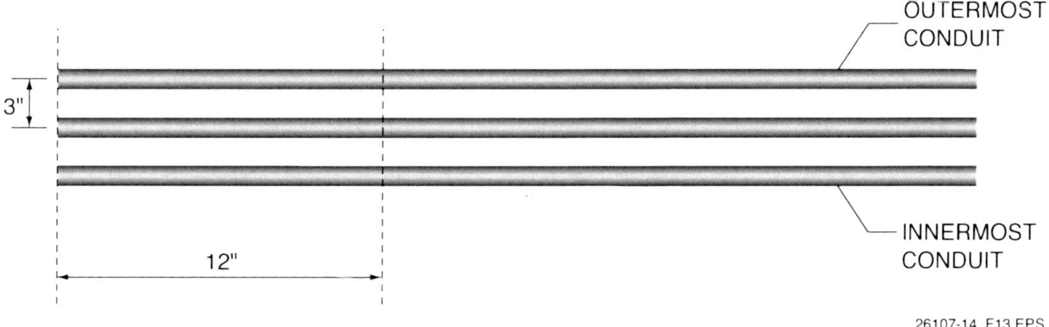

Figure 13 Center of first bend.

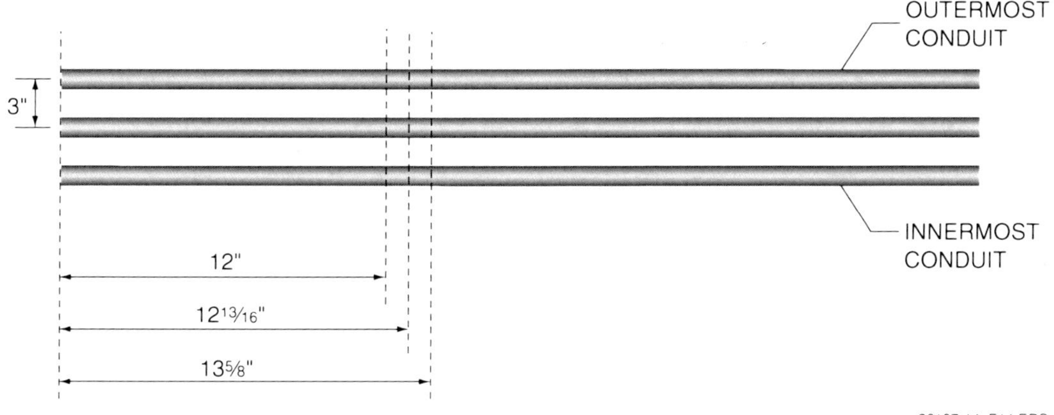

Figure 14 Successive centerlines.

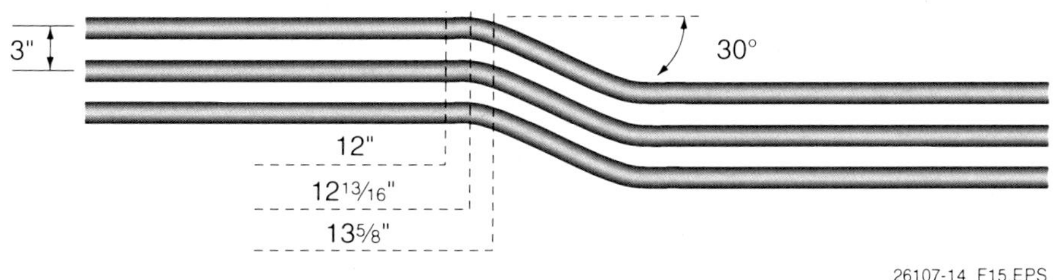

Figure 15 Parallel offset pipes.

Think About It

Equal Angles

Why is it important that the angles be identical when making an offset bend?

2.7.0 Saddle Bends

A saddle bend is used to go around obstructions. *Figure 16* illustrates an example of a saddle bend that is required to clear a pipe obstruction. Making a saddle bend will cause the center of the saddle to shorten 3⁄16" for every inch of saddle depth (see *Table 4*). For example, if the pipe diameter is 2 inches, this would cause a ⅜" shortening of the conduit on each side of the bend. When making saddle bends, the following steps should apply:

Step 1 Locate the center mark A on the conduit by using the size of the obstruction (i.e., pipe diameter) and calculate the shrink rate of the obstruction (for example, if the pipe diameter is 2 inches, ⅜" of conduit will be lost on each side of the bend for a total shrinkage of ¾"). This figure will be added to the measurement from the end of the conduit to the centerline of the obstruction (for example, if the distance measured from the conduit end to the obstruction centerline was 15", the distance to A would be 15⅜").

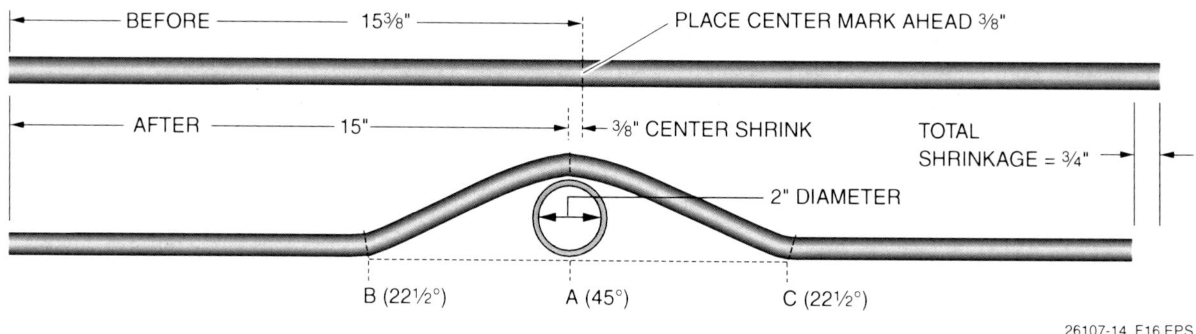

Figure 16 Saddle measurement.

Step 2 Locate marks B and C on the conduit by measuring 2½" for every 1" of saddle depth from the A mark (i.e., for the saddle depth of 2 inches, the B mark would be 5" before the A mark and the C mark would be 5" after the A mark). See *Figure 17*.

Step 3 Refer to *Figure 18* and make a 45° bend at point A, make a 22½° bend at point B, and make a 22½° bend at point C. (Be sure to check the manufacturer's specifications.)

Table 4 Shrinkage Chart for Saddle Bends with a 45° Center Bend and Two 22 ½° Bends

Obstruction Depth	Shrinkage Amount (Move Center Mark Forward)	Make Outside Marks from New Center Mark
1	3/16"	2½"
2	⅜"	5"
3	9/16"	7½"
4	¾"	10"
5	15/16"	12½"
6	1⅛"	15"
For each additional inch, add	3/16"	2½"

Think About It

Calculating Parallel Offsets

You're making parallel offsets of 45° and the lengths of conduit are spaced 4" center to center. If the offset starts 12" down the pipe, what is the starting point for the bend on the second pipe?

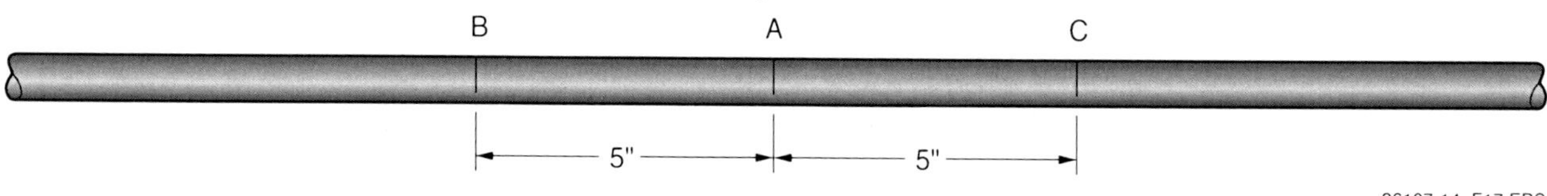

Figure 17 Measurement locations.

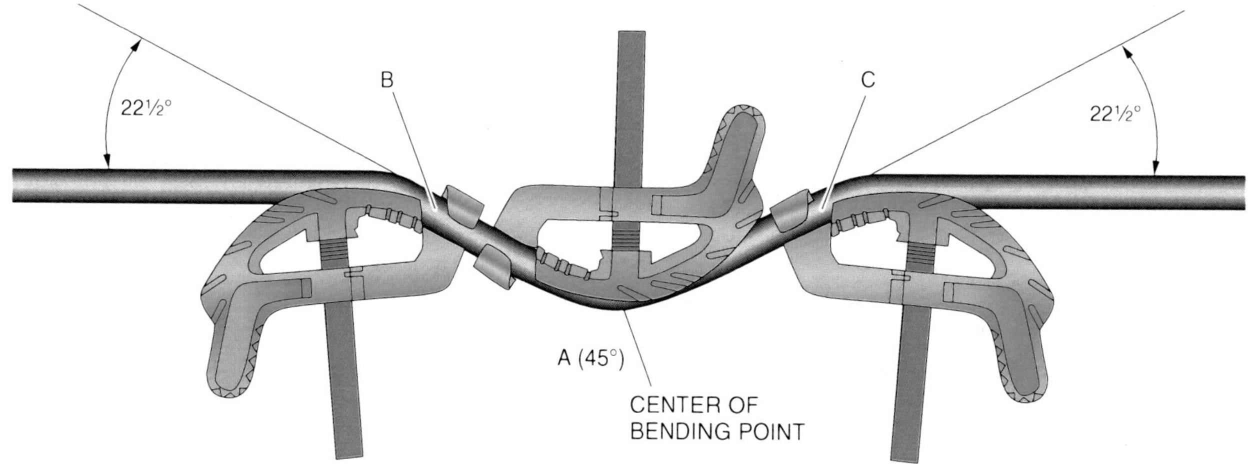

Figure 18 Location of bends.

2.8.0 Four-Bend Saddles

Four-bend saddles can be difficult. The reason is that four bends must be aligned exactly on the same plane. Extra time spent laying it out and performing the bends will pay off in not having to scrap the whole piece and start over.

Figure 19 illustrates that the four-bend saddle is really two offsets formed back-to-back. Working left to right, the procedure for forming this saddle is as follows:

Step 1 Determine the height of the offset.

Step 2 Determine the correct spacing for the first offset and mark the conduit.

Step 3 Bend the first offset.

Step 4 Mark the start point for the second offset at the trailing edge of the obstruction.

Step 5 Mark the spacing for the second offset.

Step 6 Bend the second offset.

Using *Figure 20* as an example, a four-bend saddle using ½" EMT is laid out as follows:

- Height of the box = 6"
- Width of the box = 8"
- Distance to the obstruction = 36"

Two 30° offsets will be used to form the saddle. It is created as follows:

Step 1 See *Figure 21*. Working from left to right, calculate the start point for the first bend. The distance to the obstruction is 36", the offset is 6", and the 30° multiplier from *Table 2* is 2.0:

Distance to the obstruction – (offset × constant for the angle) + shrinkage = distance to the first bend

36" – (6" × 2.0) + 1½" = 25½"

Step 2 Determine where the second bend will end to ensure the conduit clears the obstruction. See *Figure 22*.

Distance to the first bend + distance to second bend + shrinkage = total length of the first offset

25½" + 12" + 1½" = 39"

Step 3 Determine the start point of the second offset. The width of the box is 8"; therefore, the start point of the second offset should be 8" beyond the end of the first offset:

8" + 39" = 47"

Step 4 Determine the spacing for the second offset. Since the first and second offsets have the same rise and angle, the distance between bends will be the same, or 12".

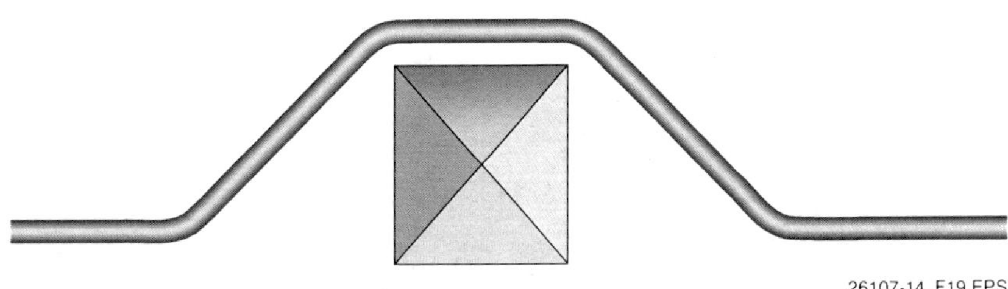

Figure 19 Typical four-bend saddle.

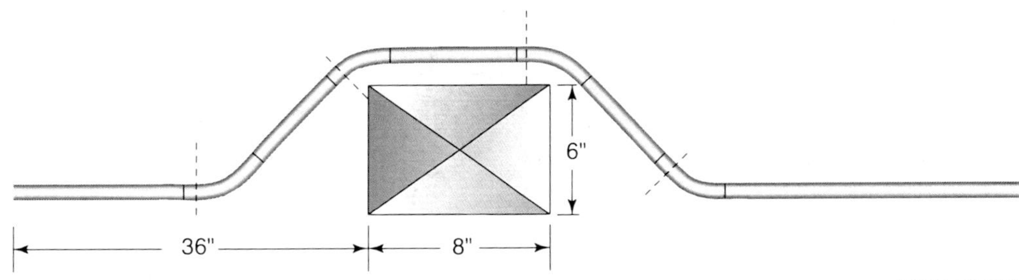

Figure 20 Four-bend saddle.

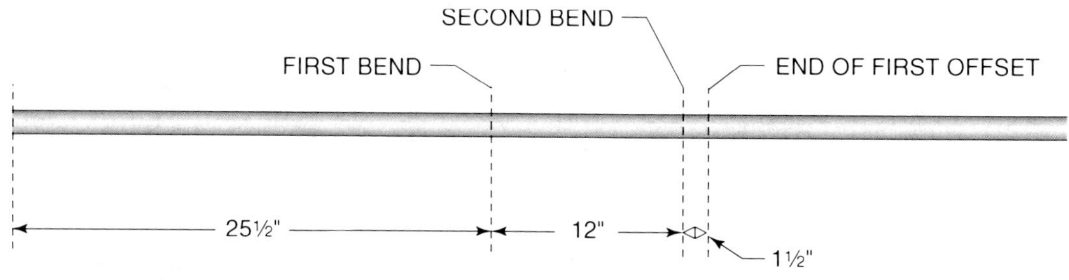

Figure 21 Four-bend saddle measurements.

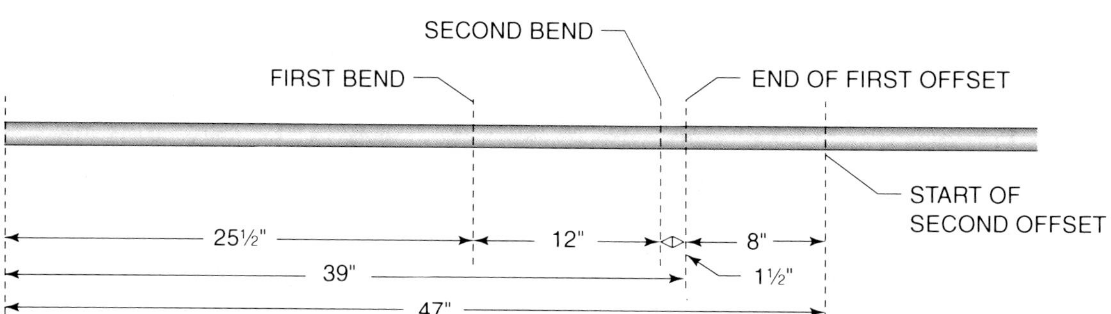

Figure 22 Bend and offset measurements.

On Site

Planning Bends

The more bends you make between pull points, the more difficult it is to pull the wires through the conduit. Therefore, plan your bends in advance, avoid sharp bends, and make as few bends as possible. The *NEC®* allows the bends in a single run of conduit to total 360° between pull points; however, 360° is not as much as you might think. For example, if you bend the conduit 90° for two corners of a room, with two 45° offsets where the conduit connects to a panelboard and junction box, you've used up your 360°.

3.0.0 Cutting, Reaming, and Threading Conduit

RMC, IMC, and EMT are available in standard 10-foot lengths. When installing conduit, it is cut to fit the job requirements.

3.1.0 Hacksaw Method of Cutting Conduit

Conduit is normally cut using a hacksaw. To cut conduit with a hacksaw:

Step 1 Inspect the blade of the hacksaw and replace it, if needed. A blade with 18, 24, or 32 cutting teeth per inch is recommended for conduit. Use a higher tooth count for EMT and a lower tooth count for rigid conduit and IMC. If the blade needs to be replaced, point the teeth toward the front of the saw when installing the new blade.

Step 2 Secure the conduit in a pipe vise.

Step 3 Rest the middle of the hacksaw blade on the conduit where the cut is to be made. Position the saw so the end of the blade is pointing slightly down and the handle is pointing slightly up. Push forward gently until the cut is started. Make even strokes until the cut is finished.

CAUTION

To avoid bruising your knuckles on the newly cut pipe, use gentle strokes for the final cut.

Step 4 Check the cut. The end of the conduit should be straight and smooth. *Figure 23* shows correct and incorrect cuts. Ream the conduit.

Figure 23 Conduit ends after cutting.

On Site

Using Your Bender Head to Secure Conduit

To secure conduit while cutting, insert the conduit into the bender head, brace your foot against the bender to secure it, then proceed to cut the conduit.

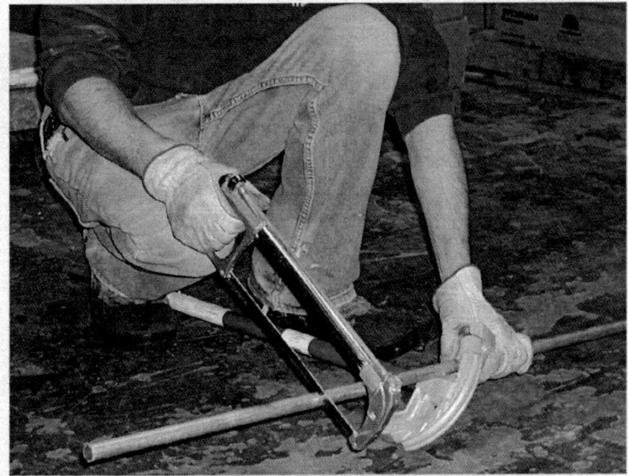

26107-14_SA05.EPS

3.2.0 Pipe Cutter Method

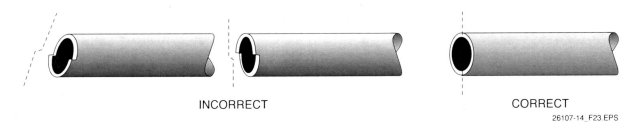

A pipe cutter can also be used to cut RMC and IMC. To use a pipe cutter:

Step 1 Secure the conduit in a pipe vise and mark a place for the cut.

Step 2 Open the cutter and place it over the conduit with the cutter wheel on the mark.

Step 3 Tighten the cutter by rotating the screw handle.

CAUTION

Do not overtighten the cutter. Overtightening can break the cutter wheel and distort the wall of the conduit.

Step 4 Rotate the cutter counterclockwise to start the cut. *Figure 24* shows the proper way to rotate the cutter.

Step 5 Tighten the cutter handle ¼ turn for each full turn around the conduit. Again, make sure that you do not overtighten it.

On Site

EMT Reaming Tools

There are specialty tools available for reaming EMT. One example is shown here. This tool slips over the end of a square-shank screwdriver and is secured in place with setscrews. The tool is inserted into the end of the EMT and rotated back and forth to deburr the conduit.

26107-14_SA06.EPS

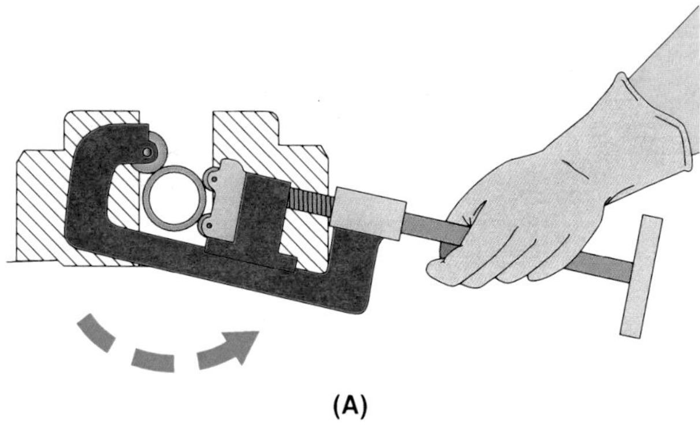
(A)

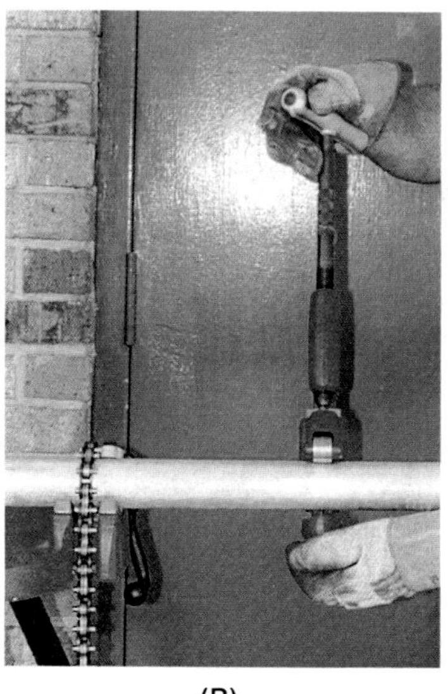
(B)

26107-14_F24.EPS

Figure 24 Cutter rotation.

Step 6 Add a few drops of cutting oil to the groove and continue cutting. Avoid skin contact with the oil.

Step 7 When the cut is almost finished, stop cutting and snap the conduit to finish the cut. This reduces the ridge that can be formed on the inside of the conduit.

Step 8 Clean the conduit and cutter with a shop towel rag.

Step 9 Ream the conduit.

3.3.0 Reaming Conduit

When the conduit is cut, the inside edge is sharp. This edge will damage the insulation of the wire when it is pulled through. To avoid this damage, the inside edge must be smoothed or reamed using a reamer (*Figure 25*).

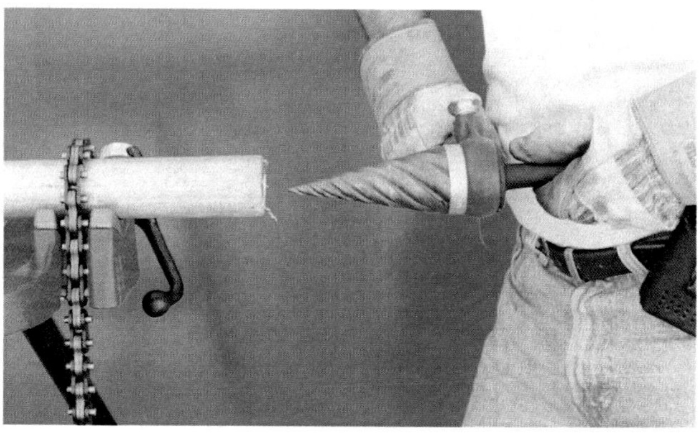
26107-14_F25.EPS

Figure 25 Rigid conduit reamer.

On Site

Using Tape

Use a piece of tape as a guide for marking your cutting lines around the conduit. This ensures a straight cut.

To ream the inside edge of a piece of conduit using a hand reamer, proceed as follows:

Step 1 Place the conduit in a pipe vise.

Step 2 Insert the reamer tip in the conduit.

Step 3 Apply light forward pressure and start rotating the reamer. *Figure 26* shows the proper way to rotate the reamer. It should be rotated using a downward motion. The reamer can be damaged if you rotate it in the wrong direction. The reamer should bite as soon as you apply the proper pressure.

Step 4 Remove the reamer by pulling back on it while continuing to rotate it. Check the progress and then reinsert the reamer. Rotate the reamer until the inside edge is smooth. You should stop when all burrs have been removed.

NOTE

If a conduit reamer is not available, use a half-round file (the tang of the file must have a handle attached). EMT may be reamed using the nose of diagonal cutters or small hand reamers.

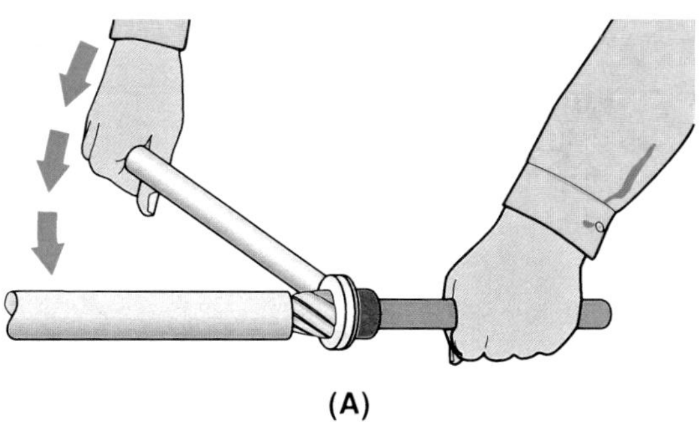
(A)

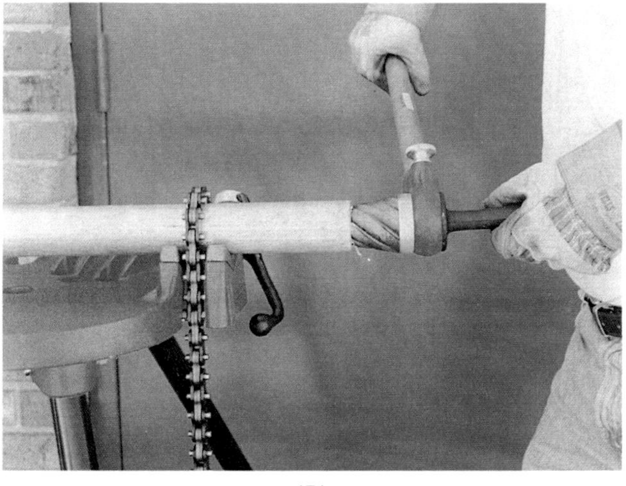
(B)

26102-14_F26.EPS

Figure 26 Reamer rotation.

3.4.0 Threading Conduit

After conduit is cut and reamed, it is usually threaded so it can be properly joined. Only RMC and IMC have walls thick enough for threading.

The tool used to cut threads in conduit is called a die. Conduit dies are made to cut a taper of ¾ inch per foot. The number of threads per inch varies from 8 to 18, depending upon the diameter of the conduit. A thread gauge is used to measure how many threads per inch are cut.

The threading dies are contained in a die head. The die head can be used with a hand-operated ratchet threader (*Figure 27*) or with a portable power drive.

To thread conduit using a hand-operated threader, proceed as follows:

Step 1 Insert the conduit in a pipe vise. Make sure the vise is fastened to a strong surface. Place supports, if necessary, to help secure the conduit.

Step 2 Determine the correct die and head. Inspect the die for damage such as broken teeth. Never use a damaged die.

Step 3 Insert the die securely in the head. Make sure the proper die is in the appropriately numbered slot on the head.

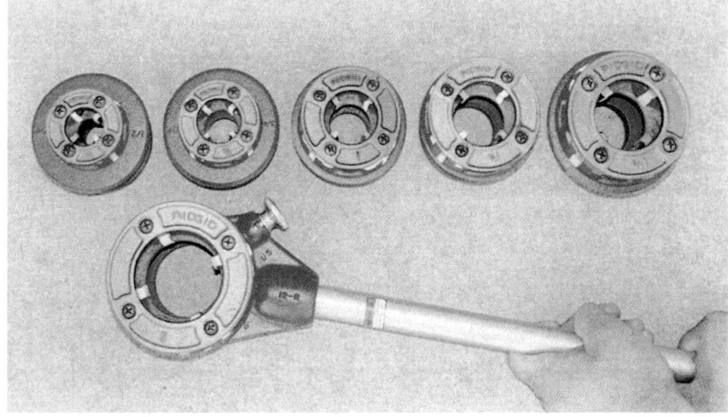
26107-14_F27.EPS

Figure 27 Hand-operated ratchet threader.

Step 4 Determine the correct thread length to cut for the conduit size used (match the manufacturer's thread length).

Step 5 Lubricate the die with cutting oil at the beginning and throughout the threading operation. Avoid skin contact with the oil.

Step 6 Cut threads to the proper length. Make sure that the conduit enters the tapered side of the die. Apply pressure and start turning the head. You should back off the head each quarter-turn to clear away chips.

Step 7 Remove the die when the proper cut is made. Threads should be cut only to the length of the die. Overcutting will leave the threads exposed to corrosion.

Step 8 Inspect the threads to make sure they are clean, sharp, and properly made. Use a thread gauge to measure the threads. The finished end should allow for a wrench-tight fit with one or two threads exposed.

NOTE

The conduit should be reamed again after threading to remove any burrs and edges. Cutting oil must be swabbed from the inside and outside of the conduit. Use a sandbox or drip pan under the threader to collect drips and shavings.

On Site

Threading Conduit

The key to threading conduit is to start with a square cut. If you don't get it right, the conduit won't thread properly.

On Site

Oiling the Threader

For smoother operation, oil the threader often while threading the conduit.

26107-14_SA07.EPS

Die heads can also be used with portable power drives. You will follow the same steps when using a portable power drive. Threading machines are often used on larger conduit and where frequent threading is required. Threading machines hold and rotate the conduit while the die is fed onto the conduit for cutting. When using a threading machine, make sure you secure the legs properly and follow the manufacturer's instructions.

3.5.0 Cutting and Joining PVC Conduit

PVC conduit may be easily cut with a handsaw. To ensure square cuts, a miter box or similar device is recommended for cutting 2" and larger PVC. You can deburr the cut ends using a pocket knife. Smaller diameter PVC conduit, up to 1½", may be cut using a PVC cutter.

Use the following steps to join PVC conduit sections or attachments to plastic boxes:

CAUTION

Solvents and cements used with PVC are hazardous. Wear gloves and eye protection, and always follow the product instructions. Ensure that the area is well ventilated.

Step 1 Wipe all the contacting surfaces clean and dry.

Step 2 Apply a coat of cement (a brush or aerosol can is recommended) on both ends of the conduit.

NOTE

Cementing the PVC must be done quickly. The aerosol spray cans of cement or the cement/brush combination are usually provided by the PVC manufacturer. Make sure you use the recommended cement.

On Site

PVC Cutters

A nylon string can be used to cut PVC in place in awkward locations. However, it is best to use a PVC cutter to cut smaller trade sizes of PVC.

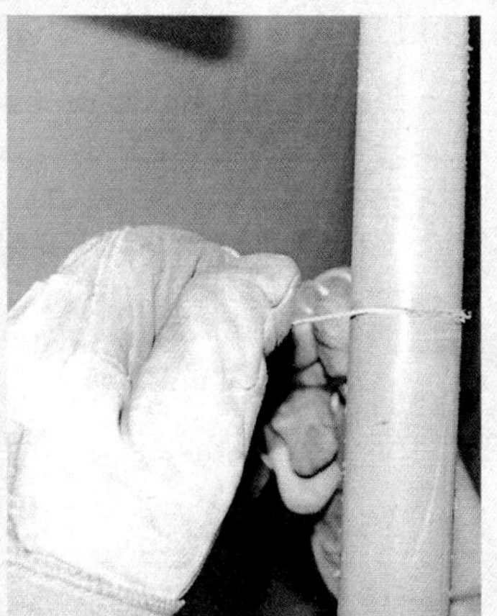

26107-14_SA08.EPS

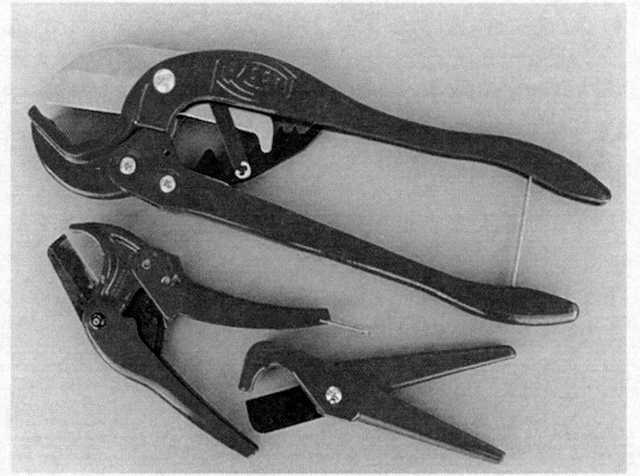

26107-14_SA09.EPS

Step 3 Press the conduit and fitting together and rotate about a half-turn to evenly distribute the cement.

Forming PVC in the field requires a special tool called a hot box or other specialized methods. PVC may not be threaded when it is used for electrical applications.

Think About It

Putting It All Together

This module has stressed the precision necessary for creating accurate and uniform bends. Why is this important? What practical problems can result from sloppy or inaccurate bends?

Summary

You must choose a conduit bender to suit the kind of conduit being installed and the type of bend to be made. Some knowledge of the geometry of right triangles and circles needs to be mastered to make the necessary calculations. You must be able to calculate, lay out, and perform bending operations on a single run of conduit and also on two or more parallel runs of conduit. At times, data tables for the figures may be consulted for the calculations. All work must conform to the requirements of the *NEC*®.

Review Questions

1. The field bending of PVC requires a _____.
   a. hickey
   b. heating unit
   c. segmented bender
   d. one-shot bender

2. A hickey can be used to bend _____.
   a. RMC
   b. EMT
   c. PVC
   d. HDPE

3. What is the key to accurate bending with a hand bender?
   a. Correct size and length of handle
   b. Constant foot pressure on the back piece
   c. Using only the correct brand of bender
   d. Correct inverting of the conduit bender

4. In a right triangle, the side directly opposite the 90° angle is called the _____.
   a. right side
   b. hypotenuse
   c. altitude
   d. base

5. Prior to making a 90° bend, what two measurements must be known?
   a. Length of conduit and size of conduit
   b. Desired rise and length of conduit
   c. Size of bender and size of conduit
   d. Stub-up distance and take-up distance

6. A back-to-back bend is _____.
   a. a two-shot 90° bend
   b. two 90° bends made back-to-back
   c. an offset with four bends back-to-back
   d. a segmented bend

7. To prevent the ends of the conduit from being staggered, what additional information must be used when making parallel offset bends?
   a. Center-to-center spacing and tangent of ½ the offset angle
   b. Length of conduit and size of conduit
   c. Stub-up distance and take-up distance
   d. Offset angle and length of conduit

8. When making a saddle bend, the center of the saddle will cause the conduit to shrink _____ for every inch of saddle depth.
   a. ⅜"
   b. 3⁄16"
   c. ¾"
   d. 3⁄32"

9. When using a pipe cutter, start the cut by rotating the cutter _____.
   a. in a clockwise direction
   b. with the grain
   c. in a counterclockwise direction
   d. against the grain

10. EMT is threaded using a die.
    a. True
    b. False

Trade Terms Quiz

Fill in the blank with the correct term that you learned from your study of this module

1. A right-angle bend is also called a(n) ____________.
2. The rise in a section of conduit is called a(n) ____________.
3. The ____________ length is the actual length of the conduit that will be bent.
4. Also called a kick, a(n) ____________ is two bends placed in a piece of conduit in order to navigate around obstructions.
5. ____________ bends are large bends that are formed by multiple short bends or shots.
6. Two 90° bends with a straight section of conduit between them constitute a(n) ____________ bend.
7. ____________ bends are 90° bends made in two or more parallel sections of conduit, where the radius of each bend in conduit after the inside bend is respectively increased.
8. ____________ is the distance that is saved by the arc of a 90° bend.
9. ____________ is the length of the bent section of conduit measured from the bottom, centerline, or top of the straight section to the end of the bent section.

Trade Terms

90° bend	Developed length	Offsets	Segment bend
Back-to-back bend	Gain	Rise	Stub-up
Concentric bends			

Module 26107-14
Supplemental Exercises

1. The sizes of conduit that can be bent using a hand bender are ________________.
   a. ½ inch through ¾ inch
   b. ½ inch through 1¼ inch
   c. ½ inch through 1½ inch
   d. ½ inch through 2 inch

2. If a bender can be used to bend ¾-inch RMC, then it can also be used to bend ________ EMT.
   a. 1-inch
   b. 2-inch
   c. 2½-inch
   d. 3-inch

3. The take-up on 1-inch EMT is ________________.

4. The take-up on ½-inch RMC is ________________.

5. The typical gain on ½-inch RMC bent at 90° is ________________.

6. On an offset using 30° bends and a depth of 6 inches, the conduit shrink is ________________.
   a. ¹⁄₁₆ inch
   b. 1½ inches
   c. 1 inch
   d. 2¼ inches

7. On an offset using 30° bends and a depth of 6 inches, the distance between bends is ____________.
   a. 6 inches
   b. 7 inches
   c. 10 inches
   d. 12 inches

8. The conduit shrink is ________ per inch of offset when using 30° bends.
   a. ¹⁄₁₆ inch
   b. ⅛ inch
   c. ¼ inch
   d. ½ inch

9. The multiplier for determining the distance between bends is ________ when bending offsets using 30° bends.
   a. 1.4
   b. 2.0
   c. 2.6
   d. 6.0

10. The multiplier for determining the distance between bends is ________ when bending offsets using 45° bends.
    a. 1.2
    b. 1.4
    c. 2.6
    d. 2.8

Cornerstone of Craftsmanship

Timothy Ely

Beacon Electric Company

Tim Ely is a man who believes in giving something back to the industry that nurtured his successful career. Despite working in a demanding executive position, he serves on many industry committees and was instrumental in the development of the NCCER Electrical Program.

What made you decide to become an electrician?
During my last two years of high school, I worked for a do-it-all construction company. We laid concrete, installed roofs, hung drywall, installed plumbing, and did electrical work. I liked the electrical work the best.

How did you learn the trade?
I learned through on-the-job training, hard work, and studying on my own. I had good teachers who were patient with me and took the time to help me succeed.

What kinds of jobs did you hold on the way to your current position?
I started out wiring houses and did that for the first two years. Then I switched over to commercial and industrial work, and worked as an apprentice in that area for two more years before becoming a journeyman. From there, I served as a lead electrician, then foreman, then city superintendent, then finally general superintendent before being promoted to my current job as vice president of construction.

What factor or factors have contributed most to your success?
Hard work helps a lot. I also try to bring a positive attitude to work with me every day. My family and friends have supported me throughout my career.

What does a vice president of construction do in your company?
In my job, I have responsibility for all the job sites, as well as the warehouse and service trucks. I also have responsibility for employee hiring, safety training, job planning and scheduling, quality control, and licensing. I personally hold 28 different state and city licenses, and I firmly believe that getting the training to obtain your licenses and then doing the in-service training to keep your licenses current are important factors in an electrician's success. For example, an electrical contractor can bid on jobs in a wide geographical area. Electricians working for that contractor can work on projects in different cities, even different states. Every place you go will require you to have a valid license.

What advice would you give to someone entering the electrical trade?
Work hard, treat people with respect, and keep an open mind. Be careful how you deal with people. Someone you offend today may wind up being your boss or a potential customer tomorrow.

Trade Terms Introduced in This Module

90° bend: A bend that changes the direction of the conduit by 90°.

Back-to-back bend: Any bend formed by two 90° bends with a straight section of conduit between the bends.

Concentric bends: 90° bends made in two or more parallel runs of conduit with the radius of each bend increasing from the inside of the run toward the outside.

Developed length: The actual length of the conduit that will be bent.

Gain: Because a conduit bends in a radius and not at right angles, the length of conduit needed for a bend will not equal the total determined length. Gain is the distance saved by the arc of a 90° bend.

Offsets: An offset (kick) is two bends placed in a piece of conduit to change elevation to go over or under obstructions or for proper entry into boxes, cabinets, etc.

Rise: The length of the bent section of conduit measured from the bottom, centerline, or top of the straight section to the end of the bent section.

Segment bend: A large bend formed by multiple short bends or shots.

Stub-up: Another name for the rise in a section of conduit. Also, a term used for conduit penetrating a slab or the ground.

Using Trigonometry to Determine Offset Angles and Multipliers

You do not have to be a mathematician to use trigonometry. Understanding the basic trig functions and how to use them can help you calculate unknown distances or angles. Assume that the right triangle below represents a conduit offset. If you know the length of one side and the angle, you can calculate the length of the other sides, or if you know the length of any two of the sides of the triangle, you can then find the offset angle using one or more of these trig functions. You can use a trig table such as that shown on the following pages or a scientific calculator to determine the offset angle. For example, if the cosecant of angle A is 2.6, the trig table tells you that the offset angle is 22½°.

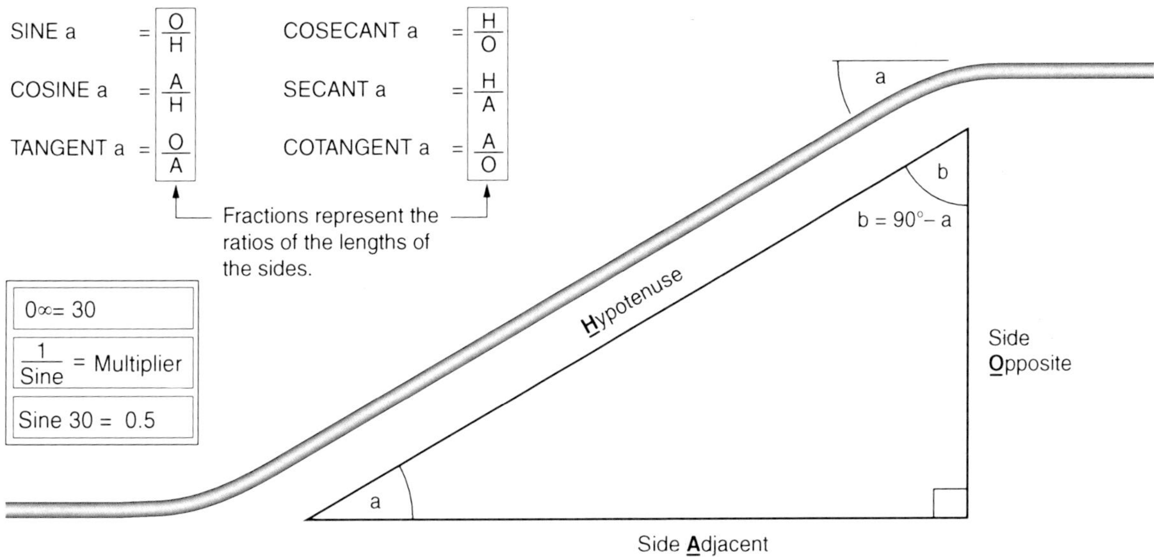

SINE a = O/H
COSINE a = A/H
TANGENT a = O/A
COSECANT a = H/O
SECANT a = H/A
COTANGENT a = A/O
Fractions represent the ratios of the lengths of the sides.
0∝= 30
1/Sine = Multiplier
Sine 30 = 0.5
a
b
b = 90°– a
Hypotenuse
Side Opposite
Side Adjacent

To determine the multiplier for the distance between bends in an offset:

1. Determine the angle of the offset: 30°
2. Find the sine of the angle: 0.5
3. Find the inverse (reciprocal) of the sine: $\frac{1}{0.5} = 2$. This is also listed in trig tables as the cosecant of the angle.
4. This number multiplied by the height of the offset gives the hypotenuse of the triangle, which is equal to the distance between bends.

26107-14_A01.EPS

ANGLE	SINE	COSINE	TANGENT	COTANGENT	COSECANT
1	0.0175	0.9998	0.0175	57.3000	57.3065
2	0.0349	0.9994	0.0349	28.6000	28.6532
3	0.0523	0.9986	0.0524	19.1000	19.1058
4	0.0698	0.9976	0.0699	14.3000	14.3348
5	0.0872	0.9962	0.0875	11.4000	11.4731
6	0.1045	0.9945	0.1051	9.5100	9.5666
7	0.1219	0.9925	0.1228	8.1400	8.2054
8	0.1392	0.9903	0.1405	7.1200	7.1854
9	0.1564	0.9877	0.1584	6.3100	6.3926
10	0.1736	0.9848	0.1763	5.6700	5.7587
11	0.1908	0.9816	0.1944	5.1400	5.2408
12	0.2079	0.9781	0.2126	4.7000	4.8097
13	0.2250	0.9744	0.2309	4.3300	4.4454
14	0.2419	0.9703	0.2493	4.0100	4.1335
15	0.2588	0.9659	0.2679	3.7300	3.8636
16	0.2756	0.9613	0.2867	3.4900	3.5915
17	0.2924	0.9563	0.3057	3.2700	3.4203
18	0.3090	0.9511	0.3249	3.0800	3.2360
19	0.3256	0.9455	0.3443	2.9000	3.0715
20	0.3420	0.9397	0.3640	2.7500	2.9238
21	0.3584	0.9336	0.3839	2.6100	2.7904
22	0.3746	0.9272	0.4040	2.4800	2.6694
23	0.3907	0.9205	0.4245	2.3600	2.5593
24	0.4067	0.9135	0.4452	2.2500	2.4585
25	0.4226	0.9063	0.4663	2.1400	2.3661
26	0.4384	0.8988	0.4877	2.0500	2.2811
27	0.4540	0.8910	0.5095	1.9600	2.2026
28	0.4695	0.8829	0.5317	1.8800	2.1300
29	0.4848	0.8746	0.5543	1.8000	2.0626
30	0.5000	0.8660	0.5774	1.7300	2.0000
31	0.5150	0.8572	0.6009	1.6600	1.9415
32	0.5299	0.8480	0.6249	1.6000	1.8870
33	0.5446	0.8387	0.6494	1.5400	1.8360
34	0.5592	0.8290	0.6745	1.4800	1.7883
35	0.5736	0.8192	0.7002	1.4300	1.7434
36	0.5878	0.8090	0.7265	1.3800	1.7012
37	0.6018	0.7986	0.7536	1.3300	1.6616
38	0.6157	0.7880	0.7813	1.2800	1.6242
39	0.6293	0.7771	0.8098	1.2300	1.5890
40	0.6428	0.7660	0.8391	1.1900	1.5557
41	0.6561	0.7547	0.8693	1.1500	1.5242
42	0.6691	0.7431	0.9004	1.1100	1.4944
43	0.6820	0.7314	0.9325	1.0700	1.4662
44	0.6947	0.7193	0.9657	1.0400	1.4395
45	0.7071	0.7071	1.0000	1.0000	1.4142

26107-14_A02.EPS

ANGLE	SINE	COSINE	TANGENT	COTANGENT	COSECANT
46°	0.7193	0.6947	1.0355	0.9660	1.4395
47°	0.7314	0.6820	1.0724	0.9330	1.3673
48°	0.7431	0.6691	1.1106	0.9000	1.3456
49°	0.7547	0.6561	1.1504	0.8690	1.3250
50°	0.7660	0.6428	1.1918	0.8390	1.3054
51°	0.7771	0.6293	1.2349	0.8100	1.2867
52°	0.7880	0.6157	1.2799	0.7810	1.2690
53°	0.7986	0.6018	1.3270	0.7540	1.2521
54°	0.8090	0.5878	1.3764	0.7270	1.2360
55°	0.8192	0.5736	1.4281	0.7000	1.2207
56°	0.8290	0.5592	1.4826	0.6750	1.2062
57°	0.8387	0.5446	1.5399	0.6490	1.1923
58°	0.8480	0.5299	1.6003	0.6250	1.1791
59°	0.8572	0.5150	1.6643	0.6010	1.1666
60°	0.8660	0.5000	1.7321	0.5770	1.1547
61°	0.8746	0.4848	1.8040	0.5540	1.1433
62°	0.8829	0.4695	1.8807	0.5320	1.1325
63°	0.8910	0.4540	1.9626	0.5100	1.1223
64°	0.8988	0.4384	2.0503	0.4880	1.1126
65°	0.9063	0.4226	2.1445	0.4660	1.1033
66°	0.9135	0.4067	2.2460	0.4450	1.0946
67°	0.9205	0.3907	2.3559	0.4240	1.0863
68°	0.9272	0.3746	2.4751	0.4040	1.0785
69°	0.9336	0.3584	2.6051	0.3840	1.0711
70°	0.9397	0.3420	2.7475	0.3640	1.0641
71°	0.9455	0.3256	2.9042	0.3440	1.0576
72°	0.9511	0.3090	3.0777	0.3250	1.0514
73°	0.9563	0.2924	3.2709	0.3060	1.0456
74°	0.9613	0.2756	3.4874	0.2870	1.0402
75°	0.9659	0.2588	3.7321	0.2680	1.0352
76°	0.9703	0.2419	4.0108	0.2490	1.0306
77°	0.9744	0.2250	4.3315	0.2310	1.0263
78°	0.9781	0.2079	4.7046	0.2130	1.0223
79°	0.9816	0.1908	5.1446	0.1940	1.0187
80°	0.9848	0.1736	5.6713	0.1760	1.0154
81°	0.9877	0.1564	6.3138	0.1580	1.0124
82°	0.9903	0.1392	7.1154	0.1410	1.0098
83°	0.9925	0.1219	8.1443	0.1230	1.0075
84°	0.9945	0.1045	9.5144	0.1050	1.0055
85°	0.9962	0.0872	11.4301	0.0880	1.0038
86°	0.9976	0.0698	14.3007	0.0700	1.0024
87°	0.9986	0.0523	19.0811	0.0520	1.0013
88°	0.9994	0.0349	28.6363	0.0350	1.0006
89°	0.9998	0.0175	57.2900	0.0180	1.0001
90°	1.0000	0.0000	—	0.0000	1.0000

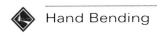

26107-14_A03.EPS

Bending Radius Table

Radius (Inches)	Radius Increments (Inches)									
	0	1	2	3	4	5	6	7	8	9
0	0.00	1.57	3.14	4.71	6.28	7.85	9.42	10.99	12.56	14.13
10	15.70	17.27	18.84	20.41	21.98	23.85	25.12	26.69	28.26	29.83
20	31.40	32.97	34.54	36.11	37.68	39.25	40.82	42.39	43.96	45.83
30	47.10	48.67	50.24	51.81	53.38	54.95	56.52	58.09	59.66	61.23
40	62.80	64.37	65.94	67.50	69.03	70.65	72.22	73.79	75.36	76.93
50	87.50	80.07	81.64	83.21	84.78	86.35	87.92	89.49	91.06	92.63
60	94.20	95.77	97.34	98.91	100.48	102.05	103.62	105.19	106.76	108.33
70	109.90	111.47	113.04	114.61	116.18	117.75	119.32	120.89	122.46	124.03
80	125.60	127.17	128.74	130.31	131.88	133.45	135.02	136.59	138.16	139.73
90	141.30	142.87	144.44	146.01	147.58	149.15	150.72	–	–	–

To find the developed length for the following angles, use a fraction of the 90° chart.

For	15°	22½°	30°	45°	60°	67½°	75°	90°
Take	⅙	¼	⅓	½	⅔	¾	⅚	See Chart

For any other degrees: Developed length = 0.01744 × radius × degrees.

26107-14_A04.EPS

Additional Resources

This module presents thorough resources for task training. The following resource material is suggested for further study.

Benfield Conduit Bending Manual, 2nd Edition. Overland Park, KS: EC&M Books.

National Electrical Code® Handbook, Latest Edition. Quincy, MA: National Fire Protection Association.

Tom Henry's Conduit Bending Package (includes video, book, and bending chart). Winter Park, FL: Code Electrical Classes, Inc.

Figure Credits

Associated Builders and Contractors, Inc., Module opener

Topaz Publications, Inc., Figures 1, 3–5, 11B (photo), 24B (photo), 25, 26B (photo), 27, SA01–SA03, SA07–SA09

John Traister, Table 1, Figures 8–10

Greenlee/A Textron Company, SA04

Tim Ely, SA05

Klein Tools, Inc., SA06

NCCER CURRICULA — USER UPDATE

NCCER makes every effort to keep its textbooks up-to-date and free of technical errors. We appreciate your help in this process. If you find an error, a typographical mistake, or an inaccuracy in NCCER's curricula, please fill out this form (or a photocopy), or complete the online form at **www.nccer.org/olf**. Be sure to include the exact module ID number, page number, a detailed description, and your recommended correction. Your input will be brought to the attention of the Authoring Team. Thank you for your assistance.

Instructors – If you have an idea for improving this textbook, or have found that additional materials were necessary to teach this module effectively, please let us know so that we may present your suggestions to the Authoring Team.

NCCER Product Development and Revision

13614 Progress Blvd., Alachua, FL 32615

Email: curriculum@nccer.org
Online: www.nccer.org/olf

❑ Trainee Guide ❑ AIG ❑ Exam ❑ PowerPoints Other ______________

Craft / Level: Copyright Date:

Module ID Number / Title:

Section Number(s):

Description:

Recommended Correction:

Your Name:

Address:

Email: Phone:

Raceways and Fittings

The Beauvallon

The Beauvallon, a high-end, mixed-use project in Denver's Golden Triangle features two 14-story towers with a total of 210 luxury, for-sale condos. The project's European flavor comes from what designers call its "modified French Baroque style," which features wide balconies, two-story mansard roofs, ornate cornices, urban landscaping, and other Old World architectural elements.

26108-14

Trainees with successful module completions may be eligible for credentialing through NCCER's National Registry. To learn more, go to **www.nccer.org** or contact us at **1.888.622.3720.** Our website has information on the latest product releases and training, as well as online versions of our *Cornerstone* magazine and Pearson's product catalog.

Your feedback is welcome. You may email your comments to **curriculum@nccer.org,** send general comments and inquiries to **info@nccer.org,** or fill in the User Update form at the back of this module.

This information is general in nature and intended for training purposes only. Actual performance of activities described in this manual requires compliance with all applicable operating, service, maintenance, and safety procedures under the direction of qualified personnel. References in this manual to patented or proprietary devices do not constitute a recommendation of their use.

26108-14

Raceways and Fittings

Objectives

When you have completed this module, you will be able to do the following:

1. Identify and select various types and sizes of raceways and fittings for a given application.
2. Identify various methods used to fabricate (join) and install raceway systems.
3. Identify uses permitted for selected raceways.
4. Demonstrate how to install a flexible raceway system.
5. Terminate a selected raceway system.
6. Identify the appropriate conduit body for a given application.

Performance Tasks

Under the supervision of the instructor, you should be able to do the following:

1. Identify and select various types and sizes of raceways, fittings, and fasteners for a given application.
2. Demonstrate how to install a flexible raceway system.
3. Terminate a selected raceway system.
4. Identify the appropriate conduit body for a given application.

Trade Terms

Accessible
Approved
Bonding wire
Cable trays
Conduit
Exposed location
Kick
Raceways
Splice
Tap
Trough
Underwriters Laboratories, Inc. (UL)
Wireways

Required Trainee Materials

1. Paper and pencil
2. Copy of the latest edition of the *National Electrical Code*®
3. Appropriate personal protective equipment

Note:
NFPA 70®, *National Electrical Code*®, and *NEC*® are registered trademarks of the National Fire Protection Association, Inc., Quincy, MA 02269. All *National Electrical Code*® and *NEC*® references in this module refer to the 2014 edition of the *National Electrical Code*®.

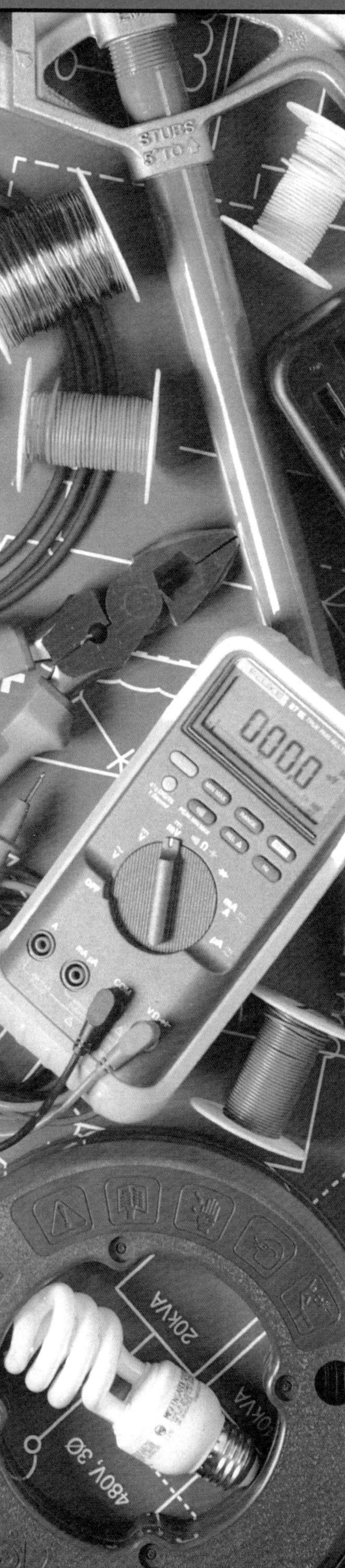

Contents

Topics to be presented in this module include:

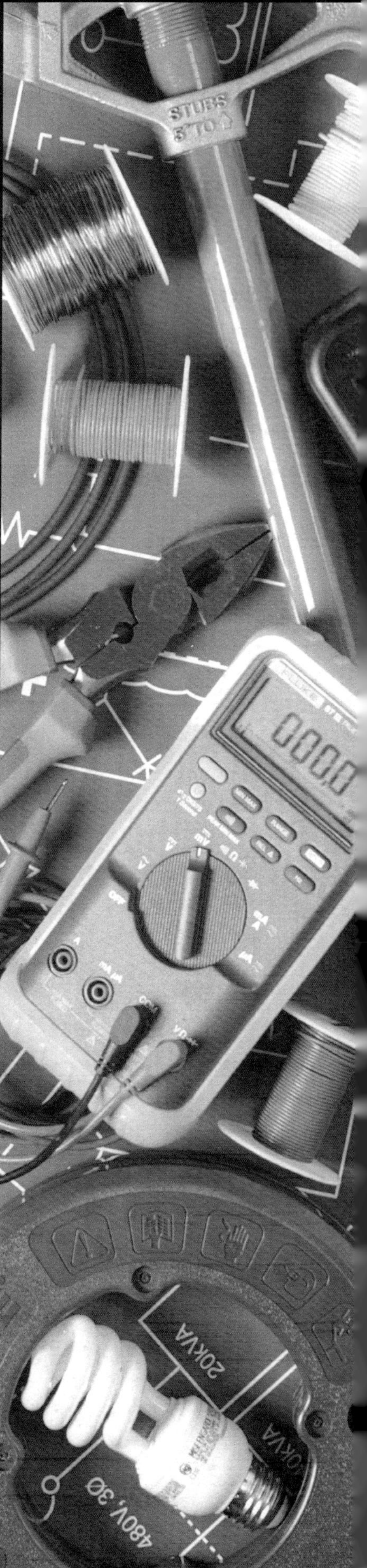
STUBS
20KVA
480V, 3Ø

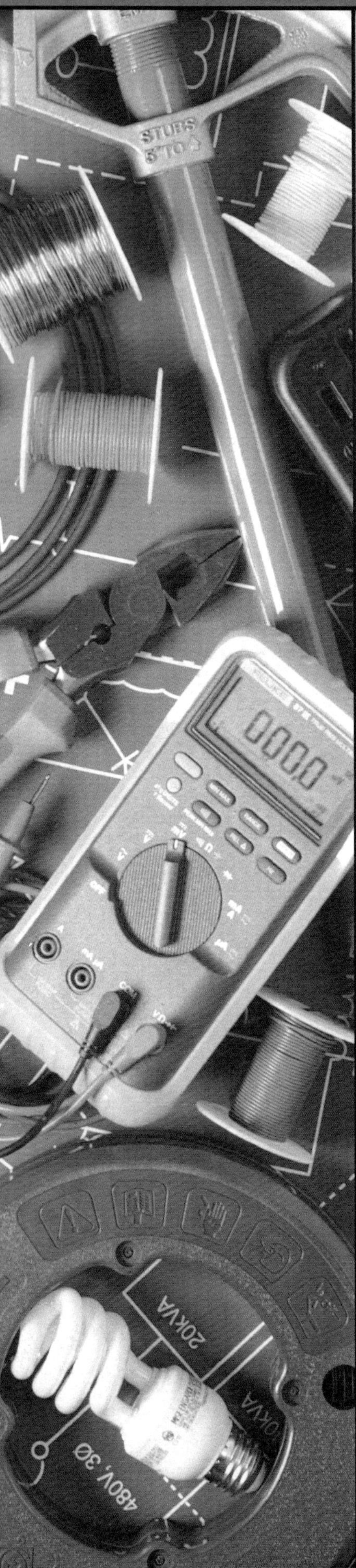

Figures and Tables

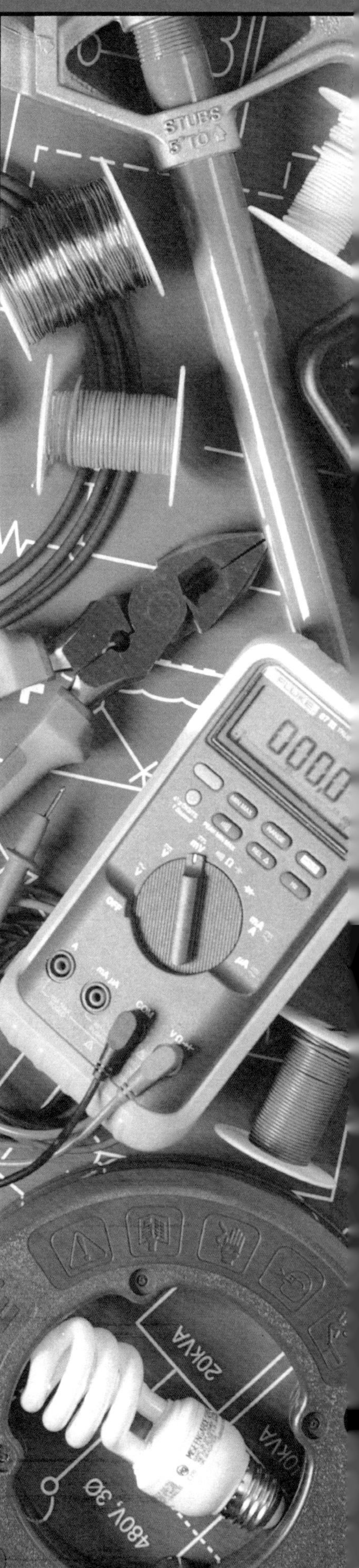
STUBS
3" TO
20KVA
480V, 3Ø

1.0.0 Introduction

Electrical raceways present challenges and requirements involving proper installation techniques, general understanding of raceway systems, and applications of the *NEC®* to raceway systems. Acquiring quality installation skills for raceway systems requires practice, knowledge, and training.

A presentation of the various types of raceway systems and fittings, basic raceway installation skills, and *NEC®* requirements applicable to raceway systems is included in this module. This module also covers raceway supports and environmental considerations for raceway systems, as well as general raceway information.

Along with the study of this module, the following *NEC®* Articles should be referenced:

- *NEC Article 250 – Grounding and Bonding*
- *NEC Article 342 – Intermediate Metal Conduit: Type IMC*
- *NEC Article 344 – Rigid Metal Conduit: Type RMC*
- *NEC Article 348 – Flexible Metal Conduit: Type FMC*
- *NEC Article 350 – Liquidtight Flexible Metal Conduit: Type LFMC*
- *NEC Article 352 – Rigid Polyvinyl Chloride Conduit: Type PVC*
- *NEC Article 353 – High-Density Polyethylene Conduit: Type HDPE*
- *NEC Article 356 – Liquidtight Flexible Nonmetallic Conduit: Type LFNC*
- *NEC Article 358 – Electrical Metallic Tubing: Type EMT*
- *NEC Article 360 – Flexible Metallic Tubing: Type FMT*
- *NEC Article 362 – Electrical Nonmetallic Tubing: Type ENT*
- *NEC Article 376 – Metal Wireways*
- *NEC Article 378 – Nonmetallic Wireways*
- *NEC Article 392 – Cable Trays*

2.0.0 Raceways

Raceway is a general term referring to a wide range of circular and rectangular enclosed channels used to house electrical wiring. Raceways can be metallic or nonmetallic and come in different shapes. Depending on the particular purpose for which they are intended, raceways include enclosures such as underfloor raceways, flexible metal **conduit**, tubing, **wireways**, surface metal raceways, surface nonmetallic raceways, and support systems such as cable trays.

3.0.0 Conduit

Conduit is a raceway with a circular cross section, similar to pipe, that contains wires or cables. Conduit is used to provide protection for conductors and route them from one place to another. Metal conduit also provides a permanent electrical path to ground. This equipment must be listed per the *NEC®*.

3.1.0 Conduit as a Ground Path

For safety reasons, most equipment that receives electrical power and has a metallic frame is bonded. In order to bond the equipment, an electrical connection must be made to connect the metal frame of the electrically powered equipment to the grounding point at the service-entrance equipment. This is usually done in one or both of the following ways:

- The frame of the equipment is connected to a wire (equipment grounding conductor), which is directly connected to the ground point at the grounding terminal.
- The frame of the equipment is connected (bonded) to a metal conduit or other type of raceway system, which provides an uninterrupted and low-impedance circuit to the ground point at the service-entrance equipment. The metal raceway or conduit acts as the equipment grounding conductor.

According to *NEC Section 250.96,* metal raceways, cable trays, cable armor, cable sheath, enclosures, frames, fittings, and other metal noncurrent-carrying parts that are to serve as equipment grounding conductors, with or without the use of supplementary equipment grounding conductors, shall be bonded where necessary to ensure electrical continuity and the capacity to safely conduct any fault current likely to be imposed on them. Any nonconductive paint, enamel, or similar coating shall be removed at threads, contact points, and contact surfaces or be connected by means of fittings designed so as to make such removal unnecessary.

The purpose of the equipment grounding conductor is to provide a low-resistance path to ground for all equipment that receives power. This is done so that if an ungrounded conductor comes in contact with the frame of a piece of equipment, the circuit overcurrent device immediately acts to open the circuit. It also reduces the voltage to ground that would be present on the faulted equipment if a person came in contact with the equipment frame.

3.2.0 Types of Conduit and Tubing

There are many types of conduit used in the construction industry. The size of conduit to be used is determined by engineering specifications, local codes, and the *NEC*®. Refer to *NEC Chapter 9, Tables 1 through 4 and Informative Annex C* for conduit fill with various conductors. There are several common types of conduit to examine.

3.2.1 Electrical Metallic Tubing

Electrical metallic tubing (EMT) is the lightest duty tubing available for enclosing and protecting electrical wiring. EMT is widely used for residential, commercial, and industrial wiring systems. It is lightweight, easily bent and/or cut to shape, and is the least costly type of metallic conduit. Because the wall thickness of EMT is less than that of rigid conduit, it is often referred to as thinwall conduit. A comparison of inside and outside diameters of EMT to rigid metal conduit (RMC) and intermediate metal conduit (IMC) is shown in *Figure 1*.

NEC Section 358.10(A) permits the installation of EMT for either exposed or concealed work. Per *NEC Section 358.10(B)*, ferrous or nonferrous EMT, elbows, couplings, and fittings shall be permitted to be installed in concrete, in direct contact with the earth, or in areas subject to severe corrosive influences where protected by corrosion protection and approved as suitable for the condition. Per *NEC Section 358.10(C)*, supports, bolts, straps, screws, and so forth shall be of corrosion-resistant materials or protected against corrosion by corrosion-resistant materials.

EMT shall not be used (1) where, during installation or afterward, it will be subject to severe physical damage; (2) where protected from corrosion solely by enamel; (3) in cinder concrete or cinder fill where subject to permanent moisture unless protected on all sides by a layer of noncinder concrete at least 2 inches thick or unless the tubing is at least 18 inches under the fill; (4) in any hazardous (classified) locations except as permitted by *NEC Sections 502.10(B)(2), 503.10, and 504.20;* or (5) for the support of fixtures or other equipment.

In a wet area, EMT and other conduit must be installed to prevent water from entering the conduit system. In locations where walls are subject to regular wash-down [see *NEC Section 300.6(D)*], the entire conduit system must be installed to provide a ¼-inch air space between it and the wall or supporting surface. The entire conduit system is considered to include conduit, boxes, and fittings. To ensure resistance to corrosion caused by wet environments, EMT is galvanized. The term *galvanized* is used to describe the procedure in which the interior and exterior of the conduit are coated with a corrosion-resistant zinc compound.

EMT, being a good conductor of electricity, may be used as an equipment grounding conductor. In order to qualify as an equipment grounding conductor [see *NEC Section 250.118(4)*], the conduit system must be tightly connected at each joint and provide a continuous grounding path from each electrical load to the service equipment. The connectors used in an EMT system ensure electrical and mechanical continuity throughout the system (see *NEC Sections 250.96, 300.10, and 358.42*).

NOTE

Support requirements for EMT are also covered in *NEC Section 358.30*. The types of supports will be discussed later in this module.

Because EMT is too thin for threads, fittings listed for EMT must be used. For wet or damp locations, compression fittings such as those shown in *Figure 2* are used. These fittings contain

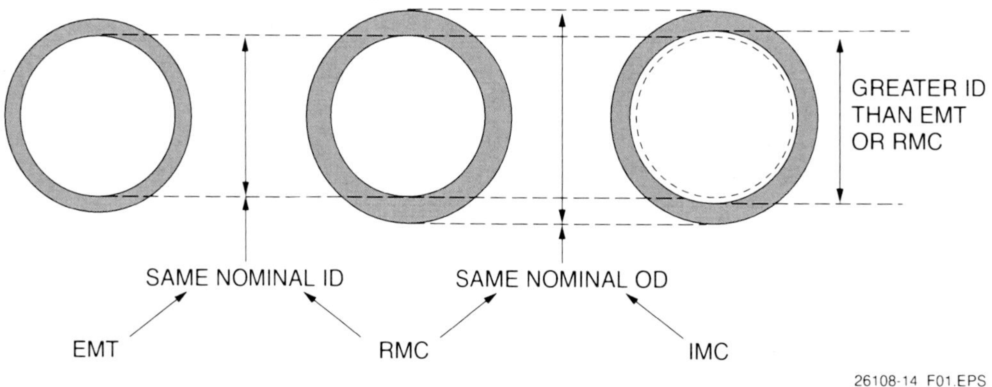

Figure 1 Conduit comparison.

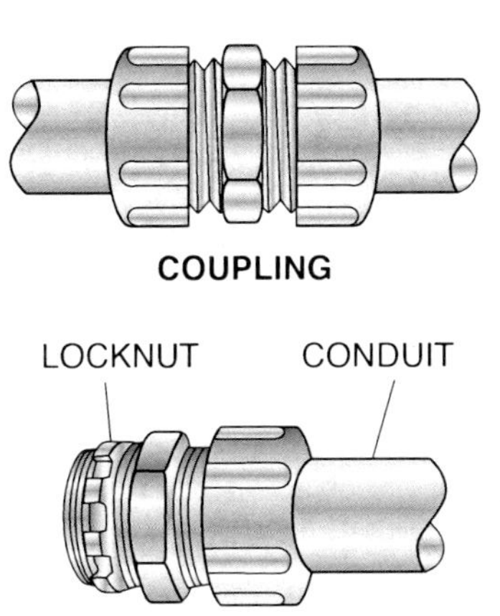

Figure 2 Compression fittings.

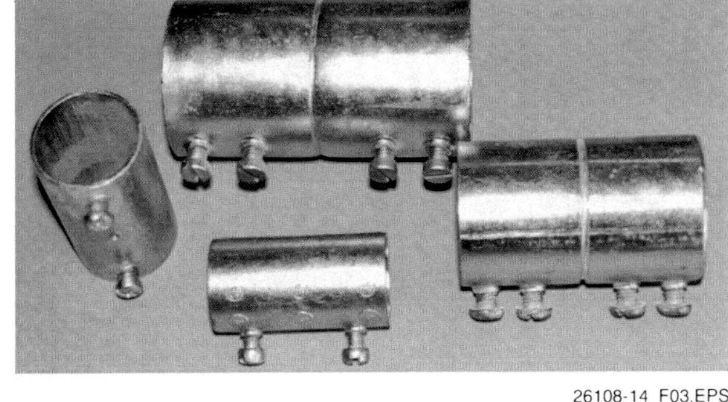

Figure 3 Setscrew fittings.

Think About It

EMT Use

Where would you use EMT? Are there any circumstances where EMT cannot be run through a suspended ceiling? What are some differences between EMT and rigid conduit?

a compression ring made of metal that forms a raintight seal.

When EMT compression couplings are used, they must be securely tightened, and when installed in masonry concrete, they must be of the concrete-tight type. If installed in a wet location, they must be the raintight type. Refer to *NEC Section 358.42.*

EMT fittings for dry locations can be either the setscrew type or the indenting type. To use the setscrew type, the ends of the EMT are inserted into the sleeve and the setscrews are tightened to make the connection. Various types of setscrew fittings are shown in *Figure 3*.

EMT sizes of 2½ inches and larger have the same outside diameter as corresponding sizes of galvanized RMC. RMC threadless connectors may be used to connect EMT.

NOTE

EMT connectors smaller than 2½ inches, although they are the same size as RMC threadless connectors, may not be used to connect RMC.

Both setscrew and compression couplings are available in die-cast or steel construction. Steel couplings are stronger, but may not seal as well.

Support requirements for EMT are presented in *NEC Section 358.30.* As with most other metal conduit, EMT must be supported at least every 10 feet and within 3 feet of each outlet box, junction box, cabinet, fitting, or terminating end of the conduit. An exception to *NEC Section 358.30(A), Exception 1* allows the fastening of unbroken lengths of EMT to be increased to a distance of 5 feet where structural members do not readily permit fastening within 3 feet.

Electrical nonmetallic tubing (ENT) is also available. It provides an economical alternative to EMT, but it can only be used in certain applications. See *NEC Article 362.*

3.2.2 Rigid Metal Conduit

Rigid metal conduit (RMC) is conduit that is constructed of metal of sufficient thickness to permit the cutting of pipe threads at each end. Specific information on RMC may be found in *NEC Article 344*. RMC provides the best physical protection for conductors of any of the various types of conduit. RMC is supplied in 10-foot lengths including a threaded coupling on one end.

RMC may be made from steel or aluminum. Rigid metal steel conduit may be stainless, galvanized, or enamel-coated inside and out. Because of its threaded fittings, RMC provides an excellent equipment grounding conductor as defined in *NEC Section 250.118(2).* A piece of RMC is shown in *Figure 4(A)*. The support requirements for RMC are presented in *NEC Section 344.30(A) and (B)* and *NEC Table 344.30(B)(2).*

(A) RIGID METAL CONDUIT (RMC)

(B) PLASTIC-COATED RMC

26108-14_F04.EPS

Figure 4 Types of rigid metal conduit (RMC).

RMC is mostly used in industrial applications. RMC is heavier than EMT and IMC. It is more difficult to cut and bend, usually requires threading of cut ends, and has a higher purchase price than EMT and IMC. As a result, the cost of installing RMC is generally higher than the cost of installing EMT and IMC.

3.2.3 Plastic-Coated RMC

Plastic-coated RMC has a thin coating of polyvinyl chloride (PVC) over the RMC. See *Figure 4(B)*. This combination is useful when an environment calls for the ruggedness of RMC along with the corrosion resistance of rigid nonmetallic conduit (PVC). Typical installations where plastic-coated RMC may be required are:

- Chemical plants
- Food plants
- Refineries
- Fertilizer plants
- Paper mills
- Wastewater treatment plants

Plastic-coated RMC requires special threading and bending techniques.

3.2.4 Aluminum Conduit

Aluminum conduit has several characteristics that distinguish it from steel conduit. Because it has better resistance to wet environments and some chemical environments, aluminum conduit generally requires less maintenance in installations such as sewage treatment plants.

NEC Section 300.6(B) states that aluminum conduit used in concrete or in direct contact with soil requires supplementary corrosion protection. According to Underwriters Laboratories *Electrical Construction Equipment Directory* (UL Green Book), examples of supplementary protection are paints approved for the purpose (such as bitumastic paint), tape wraps approved for the purpose, or PVC-coated conduit.

NOTE

Caution must be exercised to avoid burial of aluminum conduit in soil or concrete that contains calcium chloride. Calcium chloride may interfere with the corrosion resistance of aluminum conduit. Calcium chloride and similar materials are often added to concrete to speed concrete setting. It is important to determine if chlorides are to be used in the concrete prior to installing aluminum conduit. If chlorides are to be used, aluminum conduit must be avoided. Check with local authorities regarding this type of usage.

3.2.5 Black Enamel Steel Conduit

Rigid black enamel steel conduit (often called black conduit) is steel conduit that is coated with a black enamel. In the past, this type of conduit was used exclusively for indoor wiring. Black enamel steel conduit is no longer manufactured for sale in the United States. It is mentioned only because it may still be found in existing installations.

3.2.6 Intermediate Metal Conduit

Intermediate metal conduit (IMC) has a wall thickness that is less than RMC but greater than that

On Site

RMC Installations

Use RMC in hazardous environments, such as feed mills, or in areas where there is a chance of physical abuse or extreme moisture, such as outdoor environments. The *NEC*® does allow EMT to be buried in the ground or in concrete, but galvanized RMC is more commonly used.

On Site

EMT Installation

When installing EMT, hook your index finger up through the box to check that the conduit is seated in the connector. If you feel a lip between the conduit and the connector, the conduit is not properly seated.

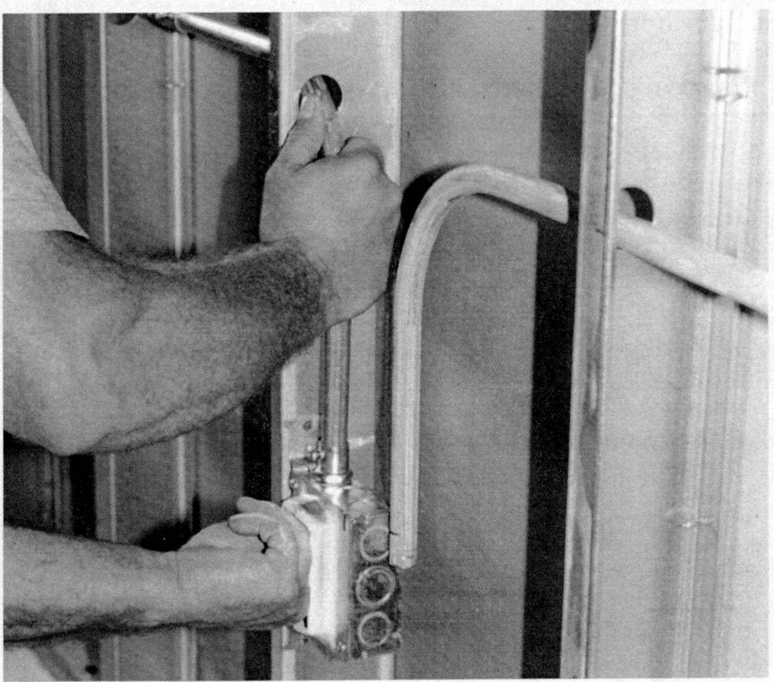

26108-14_SA01.EPS

of EMT. The weight of IMC is approximately ⅔ that of RMC. Because of its lower purchase price, lighter weight, and thinner walls, IMC installations are generally less expensive than comparable RMC installations. However, IMC installations still have high strength ratings.

NOTE

Additional information on IMC may be found in *NEC Article 342*.

The outside diameter of a given size of IMC is the same as that of the comparable size of RMC. Therefore, RMC fittings may be used with IMC. Since the threads on IMC and RMC are the same size, no special threading tools are needed to thread IMC. Some electricians feel that threading IMC is more difficult than threading RMC because IMC is somewhat harder.

The internal diameter of a given size of IMC is somewhat larger than the internal diameter of the same size of RMC because of the difference in wall thickness. Bending IMC is considered easier than bending RMC because of the reduced wall thickness. However, bending is sometimes complicated by kinking, which may be caused by the increased hardness of IMC.

The *NEC®* requires that IMC be identified along its length at 5-foot intervals with the letters IMC. *NEC Sections 110.21 and 342.120* describe this marking requirement.

Like RMC, IMC is permitted to act as an equipment grounding conductor, as defined in *NEC Section 250.118(3)*. The use of IMC may be restricted in some jurisdictions. It is important to

On Site

Use of Aluminum Conduit

Aluminum conduit is used for special purposes such as high-cycle lines (400 cycles or above); around cooling towers, food service areas, and other applications in which corrosion is a factor; or where magnetic induction is a concern, such as near magnetic resonance imaging (MRI) equipment in hospitals.

investigate the requirements of each jurisdiction before selecting any materials.

3.2.7 Rigid Polyvinyl Chloride Conduit

The most common type of rigid nonmetallic conduit is manufactured from polyvinyl chloride (PVC). Because PVC is noncorrosive, chemically inert, and non-aging, it is often used for installation in wet or corrosive environments. Corrosion problems found with steel and aluminum RMC do not occur with PVC. However, PVC may deteriorate under some conditions, such as extreme sunlight, unless marked sunlight resistant.

All PVC is marked according to standards established by the National Electrical Manufacturers Association (NEMA) or **Underwriters Laboratories, Inc. (UL)**. A section of PVC is shown in *Figure 5*.

Since PVC is lighter than steel or aluminum rigid conduit, IMC, or EMT, it is considered easier to handle. PVC can usually be installed much faster than other types of conduit because the joints are made up with cement and require no threading.

PVC contains no metal. This characteristic reduces the voltage drop of conductors carrying alternating current in PVC compared to identical conductors in steel conduit.

Because PVC is nonconducting, it cannot be used as an equipment grounding conductor. An equipment grounding conductor sized in accordance with *NEC Table 250.122* must be pulled in each PVC conductor run (except for underground service-entrance conductors).

PVC is available in lengths up to 20 feet. However, some jurisdictions require it to be cut to 10-foot lengths prior to installation. PVC is subject to expansion and contraction directly related to the difference in temperature, plus any radiating effects on the conduit. In moderate climates, even a 10-foot installation of PVC would require an expansion joint per the *NEC®*. Each straight section of conduit run must be treated independently from other sections when connected by elbows. To avoid damage to PVC caused by temperature changes, expansion couplings are used. See *Figure 6*. The inside of the coupling is sealed with one or more O-rings. This type of coupling may allow up to six inches of movement. Check the requirements of the local jurisdiction prior to installing PVC.

PVC is manufactured in two types:

- *Type EB* – Thin wall for underground use only when encased in concrete. Also referred to as Type I.
- *Type DB* – Thick wall for underground use without encasement in concrete. Also referred to as Type II.

Type DB is available in two wall thicknesses, Schedule 40 and Schedule 80.

- Schedule 40 is heavy wall for direct burial in the earth and aboveground installations.
- Schedule 80 is extra heavy wall for direct burial in the earth, aboveground installations for general applications, and installations where the conduit is subject to physical damage.

PVC is affected by higher-than-usual ambient temperatures. Support requirements for PVC are found in *NEC Section 352.30(B) and Table 352.30.* As with other conduit, it must be supported within three feet of each termination, but the maximum spacing between supports depends upon the size of the conduit. Some of the regulations for the maximum spacing of supports are:

- ½- to 1-inch conduit: every 3 feet
- 1¼- to 2-inch conduit: every 5 feet
- 2½- to 3-inch conduit: every 6 feet
- 3½- to 5-inch conduit: every 7 feet
- 6-inch conduit: every 8 feet

Think About It

Applications of PVC

What installations would be suitable for the use of PVC? For what situations would PVC be a poor choice?

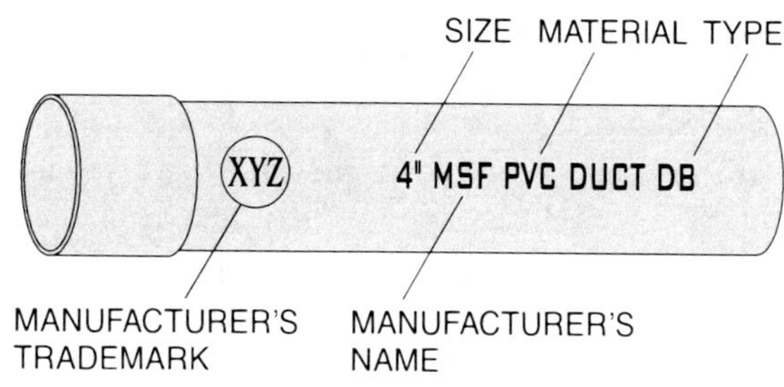

Figure 5 Rigid nonmetallic conduit.

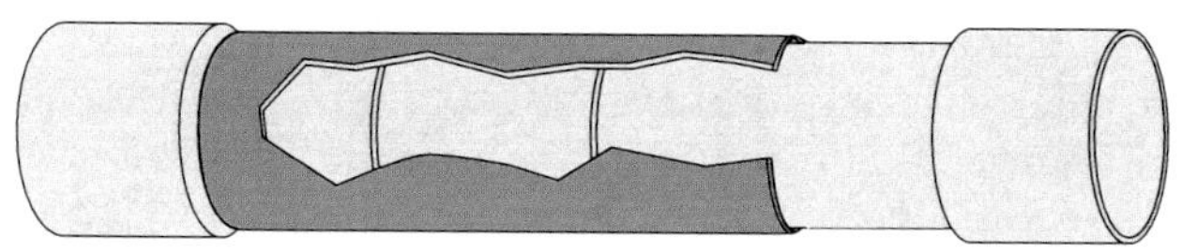

Figure 6 PVC expansion coupling.

3.2.8 *High-Density Polyethylene Conduit*

High-density polyethylene conduit (HDPE) is a rigid nonmetallic conduit listed for underground installations. (It is not listed for aboveground use.) See *NEC Article 353*. It is suitable for direct burial or where encased in concrete. In many signaling and communications applications, it is provided on reels with conductors pre-installed and may be laid in a trench or plowed into the earth.

3.2.9 *Liquidtight Flexible Nonmetallic Conduit*

Liquidtight flexible nonmetallic conduit (LFNC) was developed as a raceway for industrial equipment where flexibility was required and protection of conductors from liquids was also necessary. This is covered by *NEC Article 356*. Usage of LFNC has been expanded from industrial applications to outside and direct burial usage where listed.

Several varieties of LFNC have been introduced. The first product (LFNC-A) is commonly referred to as hose. It consists of an inner and outer layer of neoprene with a nylon reinforcing web between the layers. A second-generation product (LFNC-B), and most widely used, consists of a smooth wall, flexible PVC with a rigid PVC integral reinforcement rod. The third product (LFNC-C) is a nylon corrugated shape without any integral reinforcements. These three permitted LFNC raceway designs must be flame resistant with fittings approved for installation of electrical conductors. Nonmetallic connectors are listed for use and some liquidtight metallic flexible conduit connectors are dual-listed for both metallic and nonmetallic liquidtight flexible conduit.

LFNC is sunlight-resistant and suitable for use at conduit temperatures of 80°C dry and 60°C wet. It is available in ⅜-inch through 4-inch sizes. *NEC Section 356.12* states that LFNC cannot be used where subject to physical damage or in lengths longer than 6 feet, except where properly secured, where flexibility is required, or as permitted by *NEC Section 356.10*. Also, it cannot be used in any hazardous (classified) locations except as specified in other articles of the *NEC®*.

Liquidtight flexible metal conduit is a raceway of circular cross section having an outer liquidtight, nonmetallic, sunlight-resistant jacket over an inner flexible metal core with associated couplings and connectors covered by *NEC Article 350*.

Compression connectors are used to connect liquidtight flexible conduit to boxes or equipment. They are available in straight, 45°, and 90° configurations (*Figure 7*).

On Site

Liquidtight Conduit

Liquidtight conduit protects conductors from vapors, liquids, and solids. Liquidtight conduit that includes an inner metal core is widely used in commercial and industrial construction.

26108-14_SA02.EPS

3.2.10 *Flexible Metal Conduit*

Flexible metal conduit, also called flex, may be used for many kinds of wiring systems. Flexible metal conduit is made from a single strip of steel or aluminum, wound and interlocked. It is typically available in sizes from ⅜ inch to 4 inches in diameter. An illustration of flexible metal conduit is shown in *Figure 8*.

Flexible metal conduit is often used to connect equipment or machines that vibrate or move slightly during operation. Also, final connection to equipment having an electrical connection point that is marginally accessible is often accomplished with flexible metal conduit.

Flexible metal conduit is easily bent, but the minimum bending radius is the same as for other types of conduit. It should not be bent more than the equivalent of four quarter bends (360° total) between pull points (e.g., conduit bodies and boxes). It can be connected to boxes with a flexible conduit connector and to rigid conduit or EMT by using a combination coupling.

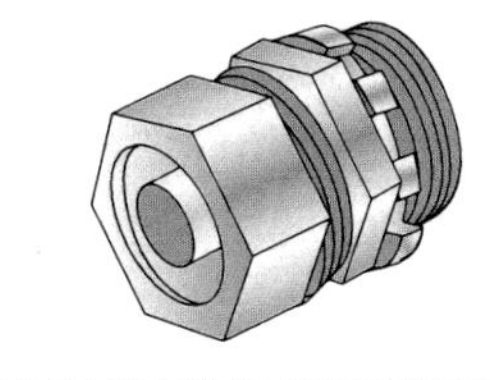

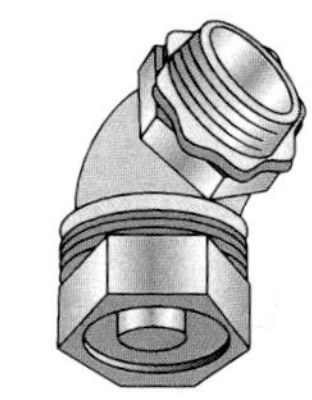

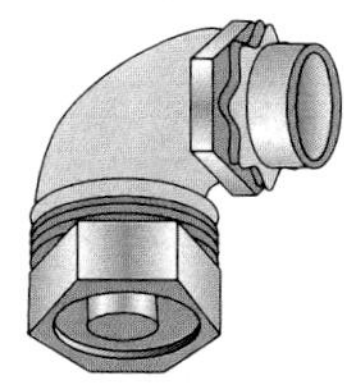

Figure 7 Liquidtight flex connectors.

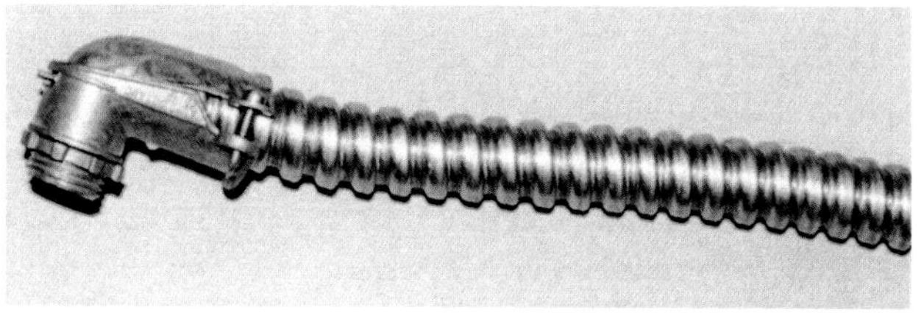

Figure 8 Flexible metal conduit.

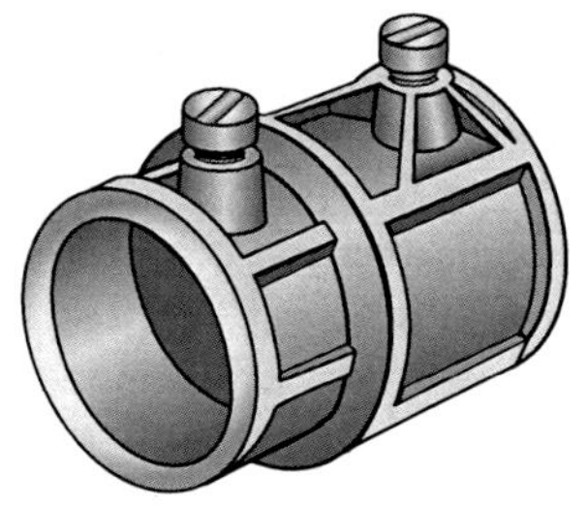

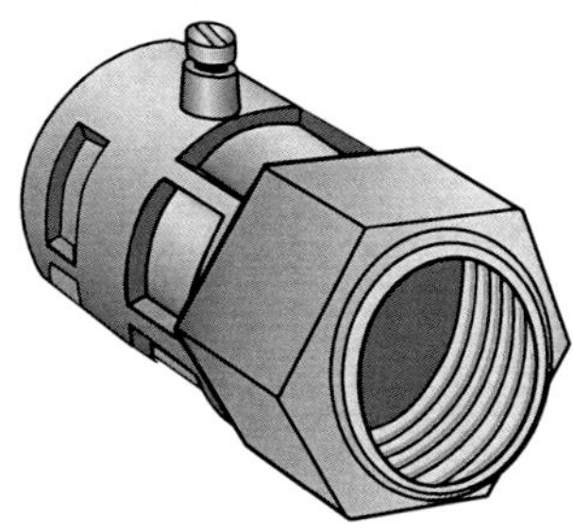

Figure 9 Combination couplings.

Two types of combination couplings are shown in *Figure 9*.

Flexible metal conduit is generally available in two types: nonliquidtight and liquidtight. *NEC Articles 348 and 350* cover the uses of flexible metal conduit.

Liquidtight flexible metal conduit has an outer covering of liquidtight, sunlight-resistant flexible material that acts as a moisture seal. It is intended for use in wet locations. It is used primarily for equipment and motor connections when movement of the equipment is likely to occur. The number of bends, size, and support requirements for liquidtight conduit are the same as for all flexible conduit. Fittings used with liquidtight conduit must also be of the liquidtight type.

Support requirements for flexible metal conduit are found in *NEC Sections 348.30 and 350.30*.

Straps or other means of securing the flexible metal conduit must be spaced every 4½ feet and within 12 inches of each end. (This spacing is closer together than for rigid conduit.) However, at terminals where flexibility is necessary, lengths of up to 36 inches without support are permitted. Failure to provide proper support for flexible conduit can make pulling conductors difficult.

4.0.0 Metal Conduit Fittings

A large variety of conduit fittings are available to do electrical work. Manufacturers design and construct fittings to permit a multitude of applications. The type of conduit fitting used in a particular application depends upon the size and type of conduit, the type of fitting needed for the application, the location of the fitting, and the installation method. The requirements and proper applications of boxes and fittings (conduit bodies) are found in *NEC Section 300.15*. Some of the more common types of fittings are examined in the following sections.

NOTE

When using a combination coupling, be sure the flexible conduit is pushed as far as possible into the coupling. This covers the end and protects the conductors from damage.

4.1.0 Couplings

Couplings are sleeve-like fittings that are typically threaded inside to join two male threaded pieces of rigid conduit or IMC. A piece of conduit with a coupling is shown in *Figure 10.*

Other types of couplings may be used depending upon the location and type of conduit. Several types are shown in *Figure 11*.

4.2.0 Conduit Bodies

Conduit bodies, also called condulets, are a separate portion of a conduit or tubing system that provide access through a removable cover(s) to the interior of the system at a junction of two or more sections of the system, a pull point, or at a terminal point of the system. They are usually cast and are significantly higher in cost than the stamped steel boxes permitted with EMT. However, there are situations in which conduit bodies are preferable, such as in outdoor locations, for appearance's sake in an exposed location, or to change types or sizes of raceways. Also, conduit bodies do not have to be supported, as do stamped steel boxes. They are also used when elbows or bends would not be appropriate.

NEC Section 314.16(C)(2) states that conduit bodies cannot contain splices, taps, or devices unless they are durably and legibly marked by the manufacturer with their cubic inch capacity and wire size. The maximum number of conductors permitted in a conduit body is found using *NEC Table 314.16(B)*. (See *Table 1*.)

4.2.1 Type C Conduit Bodies

Type C conduit bodies may be used to provide a pull point in a long conduit run or a conduit run that has bends totaling more than 360°. A Type C conduit body is shown in *Figure 12*.

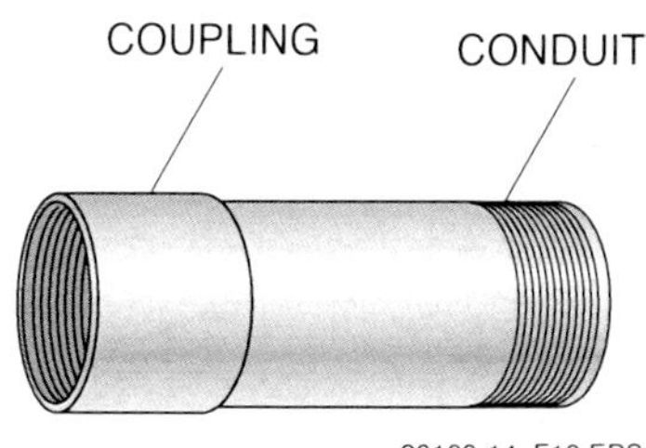

Figure 10 Conduit and coupling.

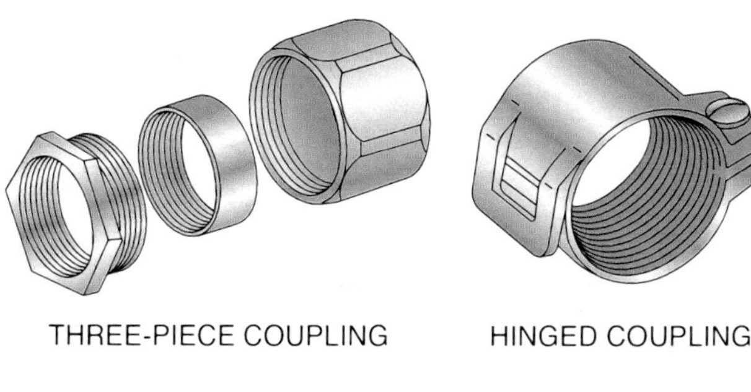

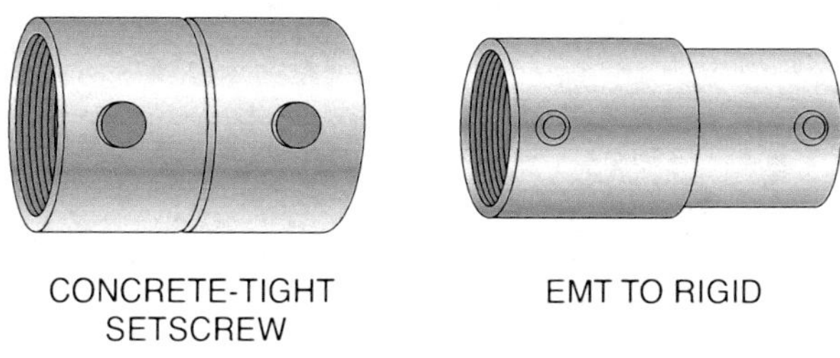

Figure 11 Metal conduit couplings.

Table 1 Volume Required per Conductor [Data from *NEC Table 314.16(B)*]

Size of Conductor	Free Space Within Box for Each Conductor
No. 18	1.5 cubic inches
No. 16	1.75 cubic inches
No. 14	2.0 cubic inches
No. 12	2.25 cubic inches
No. 10	2.5 cubic inches
No. 8	3.0 cubic inches
No. 6	5.0 cubic inches

Figure 12 Type C conduit body.

4.2.2 Type L Conduit Bodies

When referring to conduit bodies, the letter L represents an elbow. A Type L conduit body is used as a pulling point for conduit that requires a 90° change in direction. The cover is removed, then the wire is pulled out, coiled on the ground or floor, reinserted into the other conduit body's opening, and pulled. The cover and its associated gasket are then replaced. Type L conduit bodies are available with the cover on the back (Type LB), on the sides (Type LL or LR), or on both sides (Type LRL). Type L conduit bodies are shown in *Figure 13*.

> **NOTE**
> The cover and gasket must be ordered separately. Do not assume that these parts come with conduit bodies when they are ordered.

To identify Type L conduit bodies, use the following method:

Step 1 Hold the body like a pistol.

Step 2 Locate the opening on the body:
- If the opening is to the left, it is a Type LL.
- If the opening is to the right, it is a Type LR.
- If the opening is on top (back), it is a Type LB.
- If there are openings on both the left and the right, it is a Type LRL.

4.2.3 Type T Conduit Bodies

Type T conduit bodies are used to provide a junction point for three intersecting conduits and are used extensively in conduit systems. A Type T conduit body is shown in *Figure 14*.

4.2.4 Type X Conduit Bodies

Type X conduit bodies are used to provide a junction point for four intersecting conduits. The removable cover provides access to the interior of the X so that wire pulling and splicing may be performed. A Type X conduit body is shown in *Figure 15*.

4.2.5 Threaded Weatherproof Hub

Threaded weatherproof hubs are used for conduit entering a box in a wet location. *Figure 16* shows typical threaded weatherproof hubs.

26108-14_F14.EPS

Figure 14 Type T conduit body.

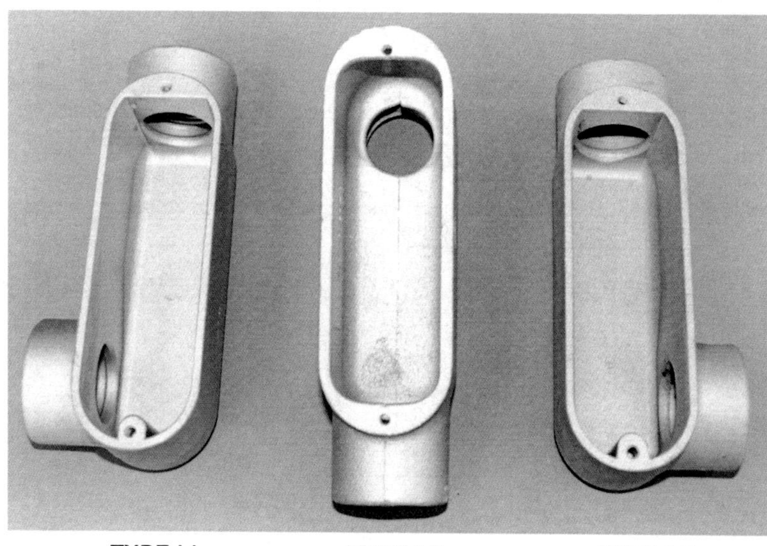

TYPE LL TYPE LB TYPE LR

26108-14_F13A.EPS

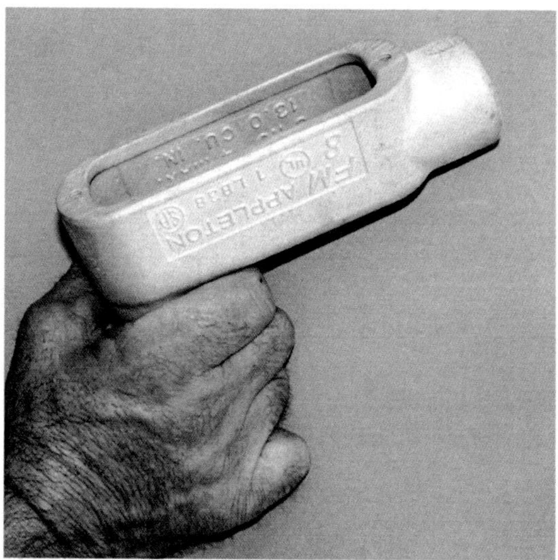

TYPE LB

26108-14_F13B.EPS

Figure 13 Type L conduit bodies and how to identify them.

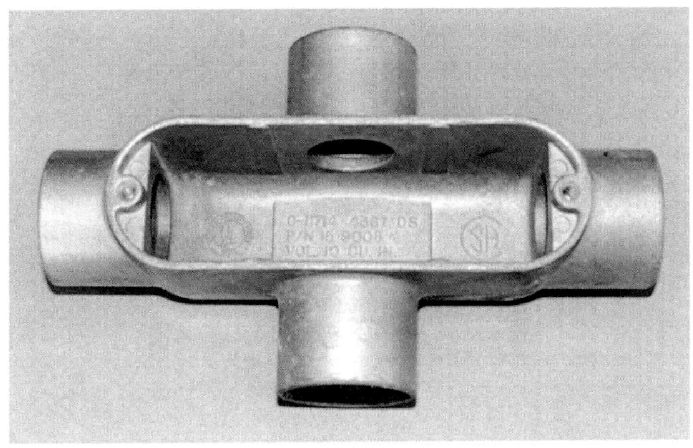
26108-14_F15.EPS

Figure 15 Type X conduit body.

26108-14_F16.EPS

Figure 16 Threaded weatherproof hubs.

4.3.0 Insulating Bushings

An insulating bushing is either nonmetallic or has an insulated throat. Insulating bushings are installed on the threaded end of conduit that enters a sheet metal enclosure.

4.3.1 Nongrounding Insulating Bushings

The purpose of a nongrounding insulating bushing is to protect the conductors from being damaged by the sharp edges of the threaded conduit end. *NEC Section 300.15(C)* states that where a conduit enters a box, fitting, or other enclosure, a fitting must be provided to protect the wire from abrasion unless the design of the box, fitting, or enclosure is such as to afford equivalent protection. *NEC Section 312.6(C)* references *Section 300.4(G),* which states that where ungrounded conductors of No. 4 or larger enter a raceway in a cabinet or box enclosure, the conductors shall be protected by a substantial fitting providing a smoothly rounded insulating surface, unless the conductors are separated from the raceway fitting by substantial insulating material securely fastened in place. An exception is where threaded hubs or bosses that are an integral part of a cabinet, box enclosure, or raceway provide a smoothly rounded or flared entry for conductors. Insulating bushings are shown in *Figure 17*.

4.3.2 Grounding Insulating Bushings

Grounded insulating bushings, usually called grounding bushings, are used to protect conductors and also have provisions for connection of an equipment grounding conductor. The ground wire, once connected to the grounding bushing, may be connected to the enclosure to which the conduit is connected. Grounding insulating bushings are shown in *Figure 18*.

26108-14_F17.EPS

Figure 17 Insulating bushings.

26108-14_F18.EPS

Figure 18 Grounding insulating bushings.

On Site

Installation of Conduit Bodies

It will be much easier to identify conduit bodies once you begin to see them in use. Here you see liquidtight nonmetallic conduit entering a Type T conduit body (A) and a Type LB conduit body in an outdoor commercial application (B).

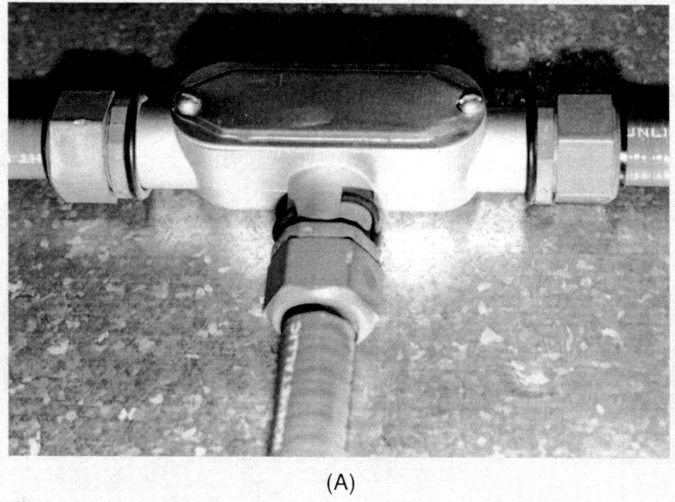

(A)

26108-14_SA03.EPS

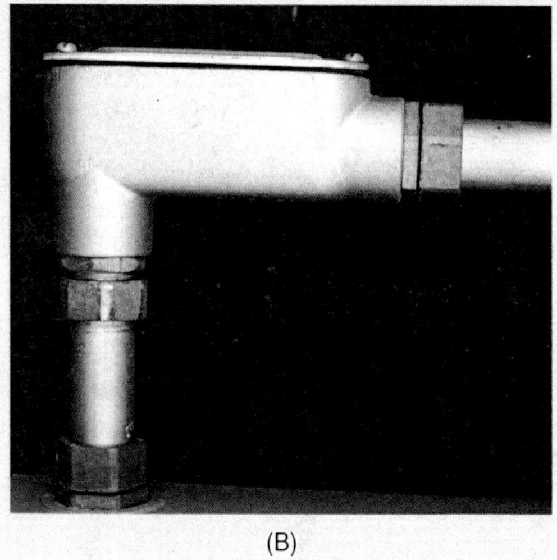

(B)

26108-14_SA04.EPS

4.4.0 Offset Nipples

Offset nipples are used to connect two pieces of electrical equipment in close proximity where a slight offset is required. They come in sizes ranging from ½" to 2" in diameter. See *Figure 19*.

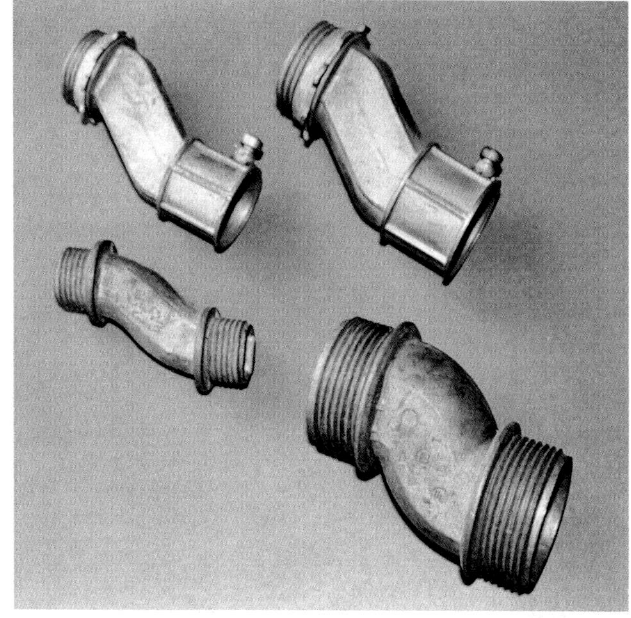

26108-14_F19.EPS

Figure 19 Offset nipples.

5.0.0 Making a Conduit-To-Box Connection

Conduit is joined to boxes by connectors, adapters, threaded hubs, or locknuts.

Bushings protect the wires from the sharp edges of the conduit. As previously discussed, bushings are usually made of plastic or metal. Some metal bushings have a grounding screw to permit a **bonding wire** to be installed.

Locknuts (*Figure 20*) are used on the inside and outside walls of the box to which the conduit is connected. A grounding locknut may be needed

SEALING LOCKNUT

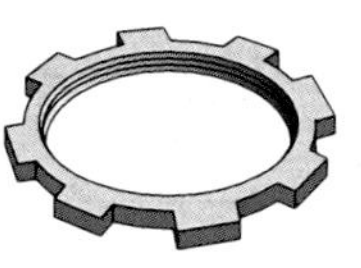

STANDARD LOCKNUT

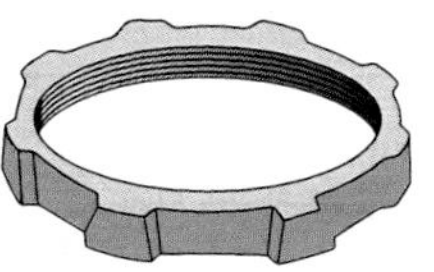

STANDARD LOCKNUT

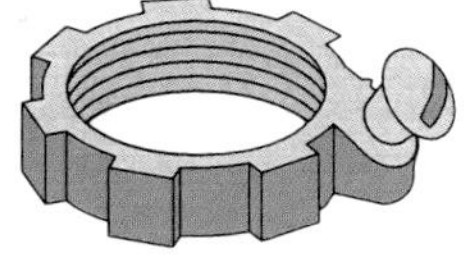

GROUNDING LOCKNUT

26108-14_F20.EPS

Figure 20 Locknuts.

if a bonding wire is to be installed. Special sealing locknuts are also used in wet locations.

When joining metal conduit to metal boxes, a means must be provided in each metal box for the connection of an equipment grounding conductor. The means shall be permitted to be a tapped hole or equivalent per *NEC Section 314.40(D)*.

A proper conduit-to-box connection is shown in *Figure 21*.

In order to make a good connection, use the following procedure:

Step 1 Thread the external locknut onto the conduit. Run the locknut to the bottom of the threads.

Step 2 Insert the conduit into the box opening.

Step 3 If an inside locknut or grounding locknut is required, screw it onto the conduit inside the box opening.

Step 4 Screw the bushing onto the threads projecting into the box opening. Make sure the bushing is tightened as much as possible.

Step 5 Tighten the external locknut to secure the conduit to the box.

It is important that the bushings and locknuts fit tightly. For this reason, the conduit must enter straight into the box. This may require that a box offset or **kick** be made in the conduit.

6.0.0 Sealing Fittings

Hazardous locations in manufacturing plants and other industrial facilities involve a wide variety of flammable gases and vapors and ignitable dusts. These hazardous substances have widely different flash points, ignition temperatures, and flammable limits requiring fittings that can be sealed. Sealing fittings are installed in conduit runs to minimize the passage of gases, vapors, or flames through the conduit and reduce the accumulation of moisture. They are required by *NEC Article 500* in hazardous locations where explosions may occur. They are also required where conduit passes from a hazardous location of one classification to another or to an unclassified location. Several types of sealing fittings are shown in *Figure 22*.

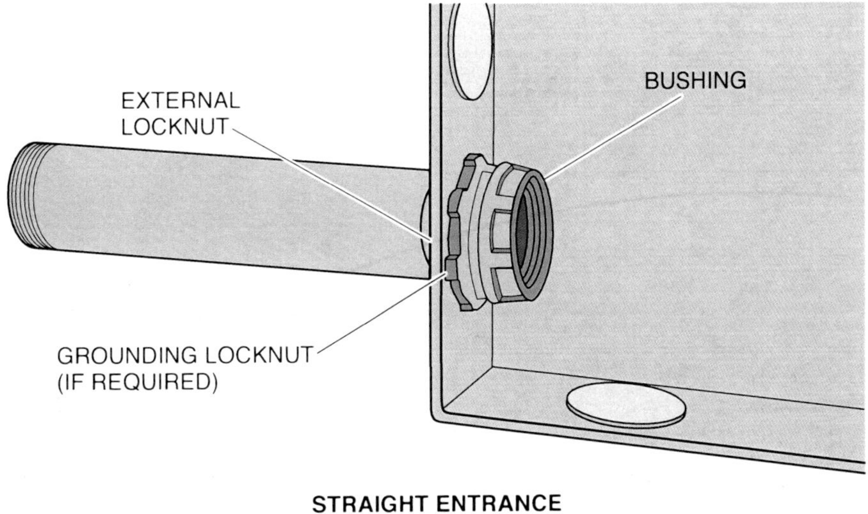

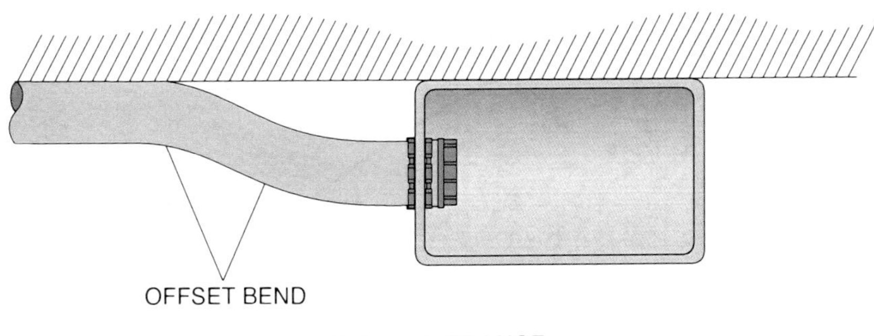

Figure 21 Conduit-to-box connections.

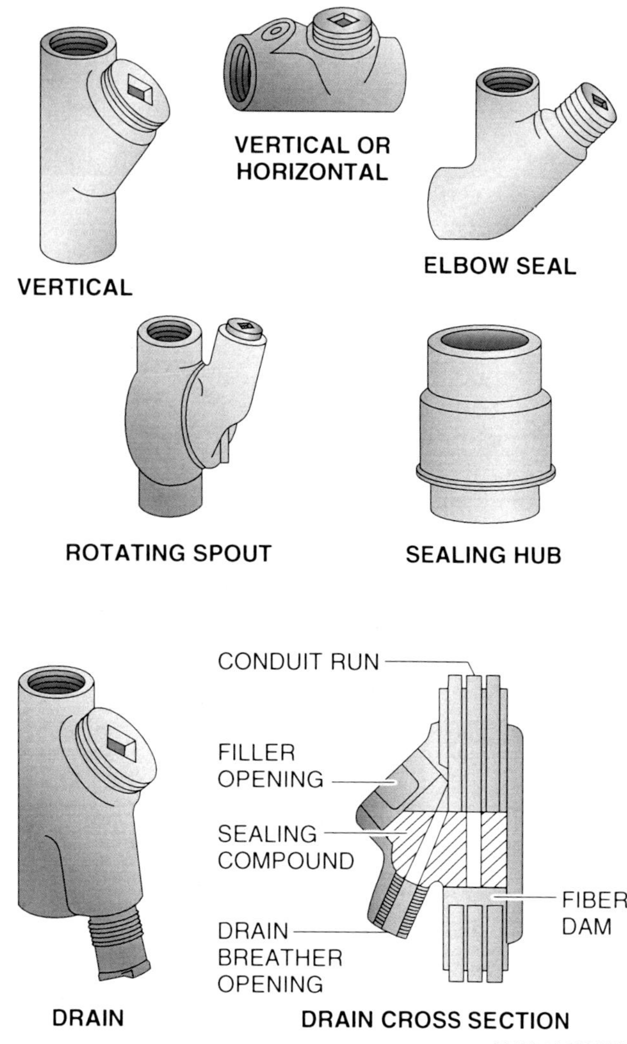

Figure 22 Sealing fittings.

7.0.0 Fasteners and Anchors

Conduit and other types of raceways used to carry wiring and cables must be properly supported. This generally means attaching the raceway to the building structure. Depending on the type of construction, the raceways may have to be attached to wood, concrete, or metal. Each of these materials requires the use of fasteners designed for the specific use. Using the wrong fastener, or installing the right fastener incorrectly, can lead to a failure of the raceway support.

The project specifications and manufacturer's installation instructions may specify the type and size of fasteners to use and how to install them. In other instances, the electrician will be expected to select the right type of fastener for a given application. It is therefore important that every electrician be familiar with the different types of fasteners, their uses, and their limitations.

7.1.0 Tie Wraps

A tie wrap is a one-piece, self-locking cable tie, usually made of nylon, that is used to fasten a bundle of wires and cables together. Tie wraps can be quickly installed either manually or using a special installation tool. Black tie wraps resist ultraviolet light and are recommended for outdoor use.

Tie wraps are made in standard, cable strap and clamp, and identification configurations (*Figure 23*). All types function to clamp bundled

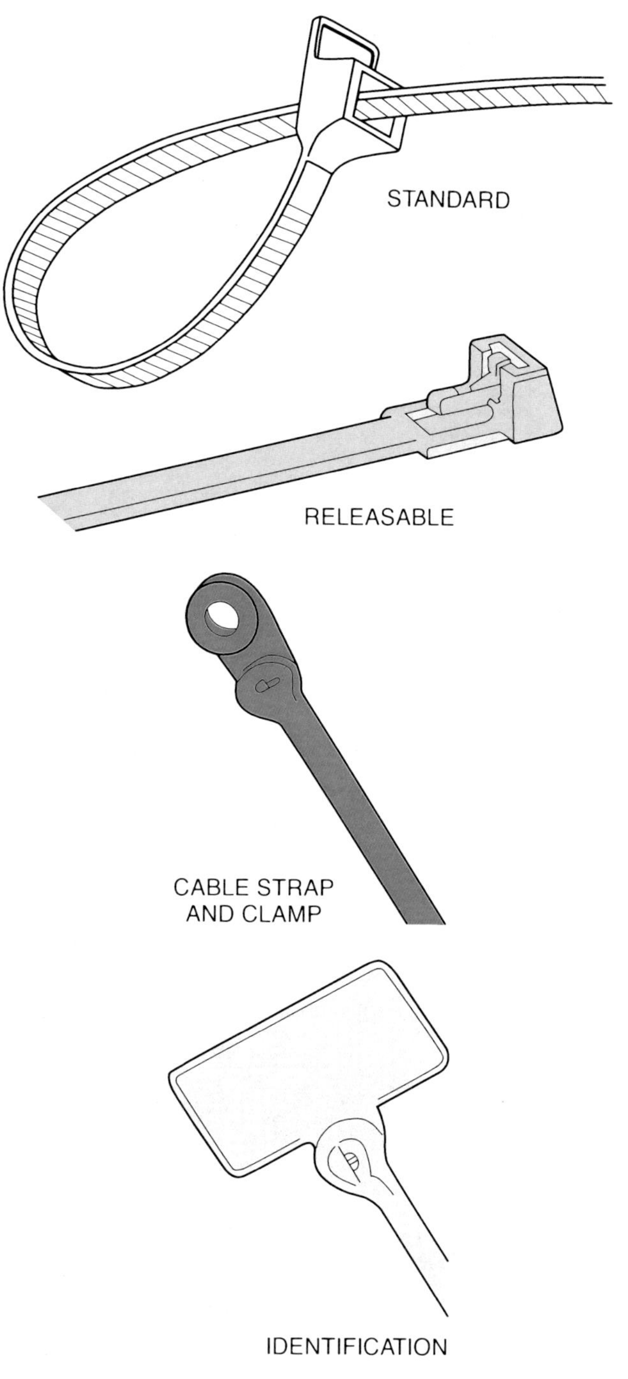

Figure 23 Tie wraps.

On Site

Installing Sealing Fittings

These fittings must be sealed after the wires are pulled. A fiber dam is first packed into the base of the fitting between and around the conductors, then the liquid sealing compound is poured into the fitting.

26108-14_SA05.EPS

wires or cables together. In addition, the cable strap and clamp has a molded mounting hole in the head used to secure the tie with a rivet, screw, or bolt after the tie wrap has been installed around the wires or cable. Identification tie wraps have a large flat area provided for imprinting or writing cable identification information. There is also a releasable version available. It is a non-permanent tie used for bundling wires or cables that may require frequent additions or deletions. Cable ties are made in various lengths ranging from about 3" to 30", allowing them to be used for fastening wires and cables into bundles with diameters ranging from about ½" to 9", respectively. Tie wraps can also be attached to a variety of adhesive mounting bases made for that purpose.

7.2.0 Screws

Screws are made in a variety of shapes and sizes for different fastening jobs. The finish or coating used on a screw determines whether it is for interior or exterior use, corrosion resistant, etc. Screws of all types have heads with different shapes and slots. Some have machine threads and are self-drilling. The size or diameter of a screw body or shank is given in gauge numbers ranging from No. 0 to No. 24, and in fractions of an inch for screws with diameters larger than ¼". The higher the gauge number, the larger the diameter of the shank. Screw lengths range from ¼" to 6", measured from the tip to the part of the head that is flush to the surface when driven in. When choosing a screw for an application, you must consider the type and thickness of the materials to be fastened, the size of the screw, the material it is made of, the shape of its head, and the type of driver. Because of the wide diversity in the types of screws and their application, always follow the manufacturer's recommendation to select the right screw for the job. To prevent damage to the screw head or the material being fastened, always use a screwdriver or power driver bit with the proper size and shape tip to fit the screw.

Some of the more common types of screws are:

- Wood screws
- Lag screws
- Masonry/concrete screws
- Thread-forming and thread-cutting screws
- Deck screws
- Drywall screws
- Drive screws

On Site

Tie Wraps

Tie wraps are available in a wide variety of colors that can be used to color code different cable bundles.

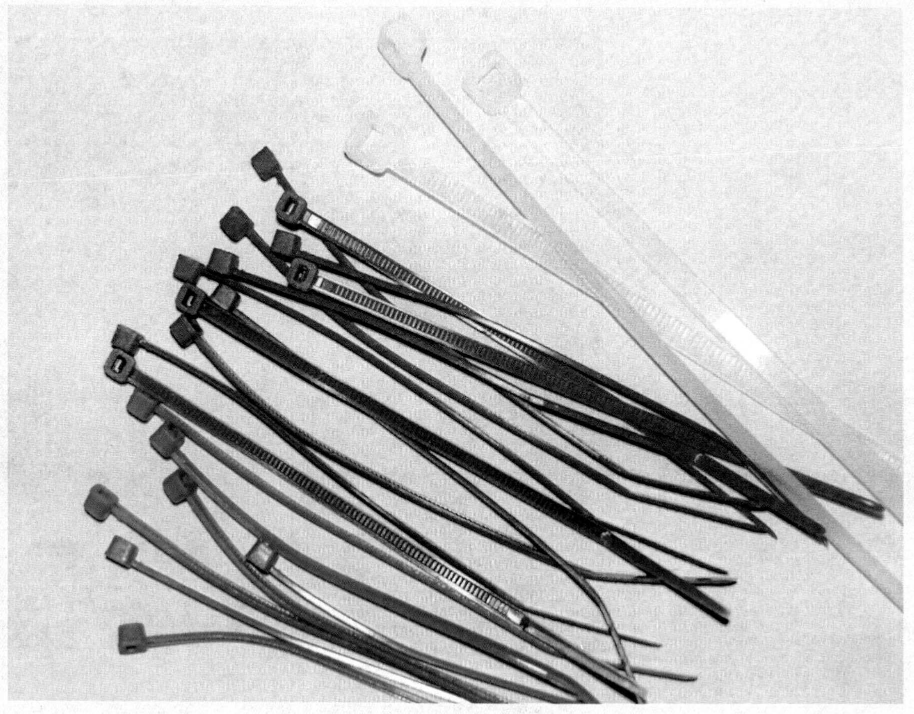

26108-14_SA06.EPS

7.2.1 Wood Screws

Wood screws (*Figure 24*) are typically used to fasten boxes, panel enclosures, etc. to wood framing or structures where greater holding power is needed than can be provided by nails. They are also used to fasten equipment to wood in applications where it may occasionally need to be unfastened and removed. Wood screws are commonly made in lengths from ¼" to 4", with shank gauge sizes ranging from 0 to 24. The shank size used is normally determined by the size hole provided in the box, panel, etc. to be fastened. When determining the length of a wood screw to use, a good rule of thumb is to select screws long enough to allow about ⅔ of the screw length to enter the piece of wood that is being gripped.

On Site

Screws

In most applications, either threaded or non-threaded fasteners such as nails could be used. However, threaded fasteners are sometimes preferred because they can usually be tightened and removed without damaging the surrounding material.

7.2.2 Lag Screws and Shields

Lag screws (*Figure 25*) or lag bolts are heavy-duty wood screws with square- or hex-shaped heads that provide greater holding power. Lag screws with diameters ranging between ¼" and ½" and lengths ranging from 1" to 6" are common. They are typically used to fasten heavy equipment to wood, but can also be used to fasten equipment to concrete when a lag shield is used.

A lag shield is a tube that is split lengthwise but remains joined at one end. It is placed in a predrilled hole in the concrete. When a lag screw is screwed into the lag shield, the shield expands in the hole, firmly securing the lag screw. In hard masonry, short lag shields (typically 1" to 2" long) may be used to minimize drilling time. In soft or weak masonry, long lag shields (typically 1½" to 3" long) should be used to achieve maximum holding strength.

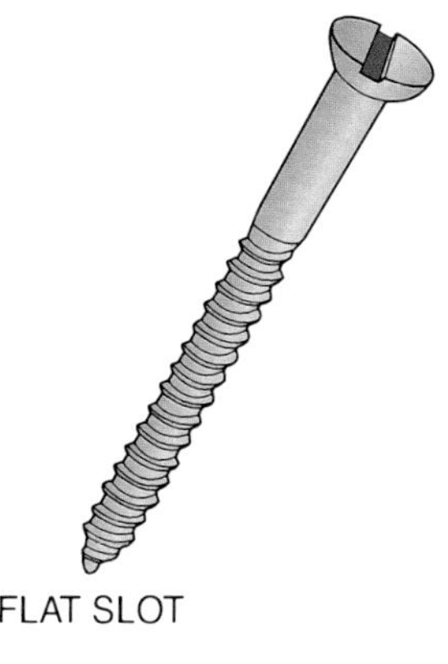

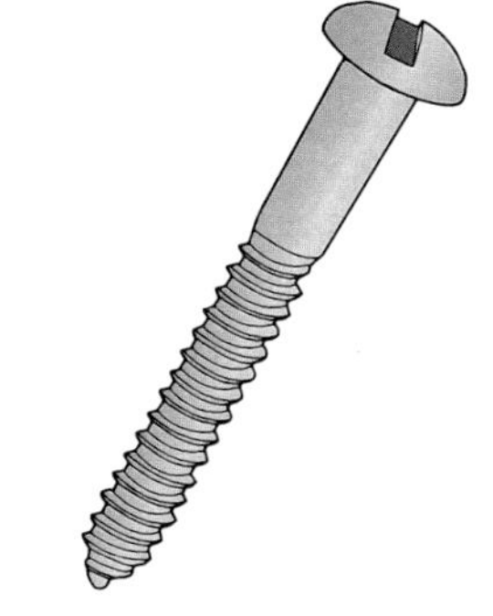

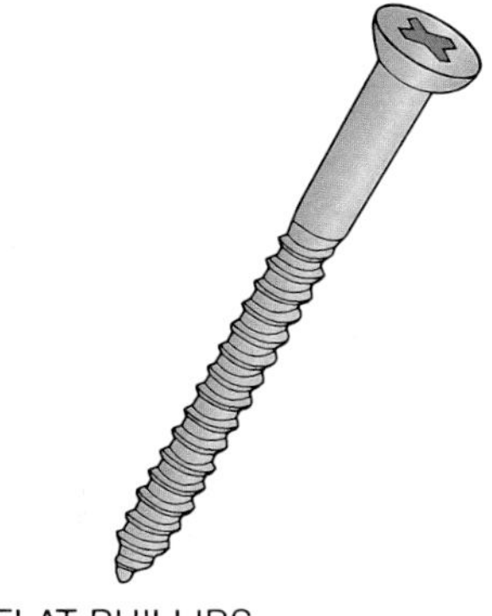

26108-14_F24.EPS

Figure 24 Wood screws.

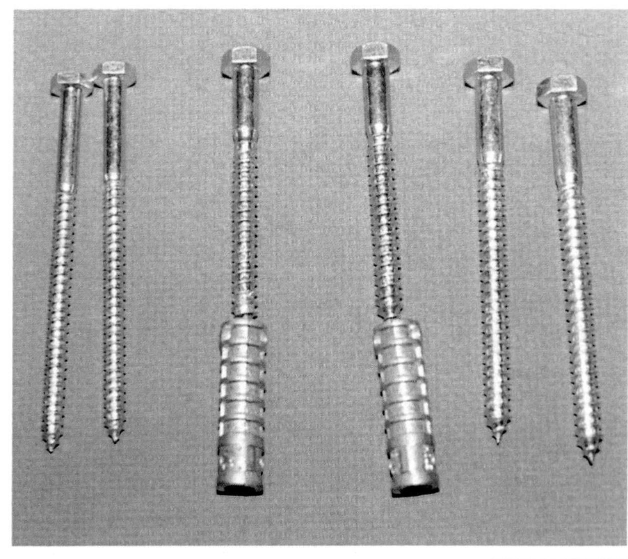

26108-14_F25.EPS

Figure 25 Lag screws and shields.

Make sure to use the proper length lag screw to achieve proper expansion. The length of the lag screw used should be equal to the thickness of the component being fastened plus the length of the lag shield. Also, drill the hole in the masonry to a depth approximately ½" longer than the shield being used. If the head of a lag screw rests directly on wood when installed, a flat washer should be placed under the head to prevent the head from digging into the wood as the lag screw is tightened down. Be sure to take the thickness of any washers used into account when selecting the length of the screw.

7.2.3 Concrete/Masonry Screws

Concrete/masonry screws (*Figure 26*), commonly called self-threading anchors, are used to fasten a device or fixture to concrete, block, or brick. No anchor is needed. To provide a matched tolerance anchoring system, the screws are installed using specially designed carbide drill bits and

On Site

Installing Wood Screws

To maintain holding power, be careful not to drill your pilot hole too large. It's wise to drill a pilot hole deep enough to equal about two-thirds of the length of the threaded portion of the screw. Additionally, to lubricate screw threads, use soap, which makes the screw easier to drive.

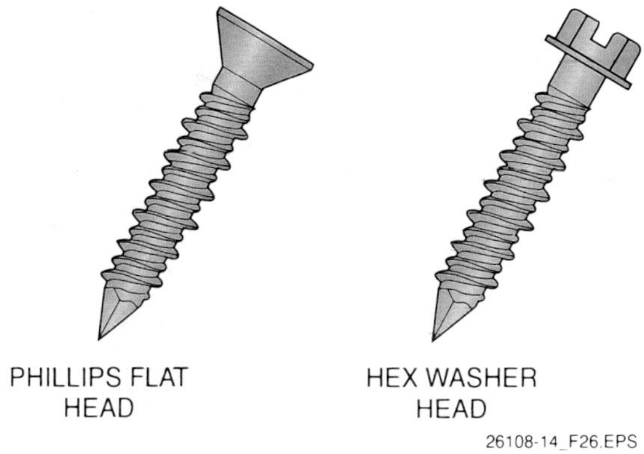

26108-14_F26.EPS

Figure 26 Concrete screws.

installation tools made for use with the screws. These tools are typically used with a standard rotary drill hammer. The installation tool, along with an appropriate drive socket or bit, is used to drive the screws directly into predrilled holes that have a diameter and depth specified by the screw manufacturer. When being driven into the concrete, the widely spaced threads on the screws cut into the walls of the hole to provide a tight friction fit. Most types of concrete/masonry screws can be removed and reinstalled to allow for shimming and leveling of the fastened device.

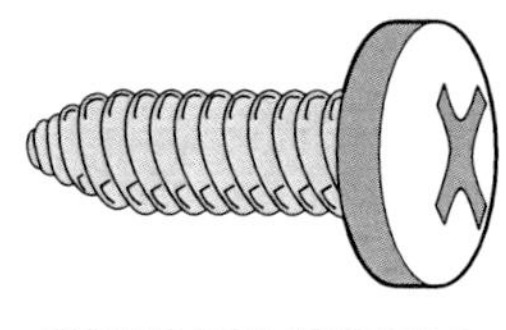

Figure 27 Thread-forming screws.

7.2.4 Thread-Forming and Thread-Cutting Screws

Thread-forming screws (*Figure 27*), commonly called sheet metal screws, are made of hard metal. They form a thread as they are driven into the work. This thread-forming action eliminates the need to tap a hole before installing the screw. To achieve proper holding, it is important to make sure to use the proper size bit when drilling pilot holes for thread-forming screws. The correct drill bit size used for a specific size screw is usually marked on the box containing the screws. Some types of thread-forming screws also drill their own holes, eliminating drilling, punching, and aligning parts. Thread-forming screws are primarily used to fasten light-gauge metal parts together. They are made in the same diameters and lengths as wood screws.

Hardened steel thread-cutting metal screws with blunt points and fine threads (*Figure 28*) are used to join heavy-gauge metals, metals of different gauges, and nonferrous metals. They are also used to fasten sheet metal to building structural members. These screws are made of hardened steel that is harder than the metal being tapped. They cut threads by removing and cutting a portion of the metal as they are driven into a pilot hole and through the material.

Think About It

Self-Drilling Screws

Can you name an electrical application for self-drilling screws?

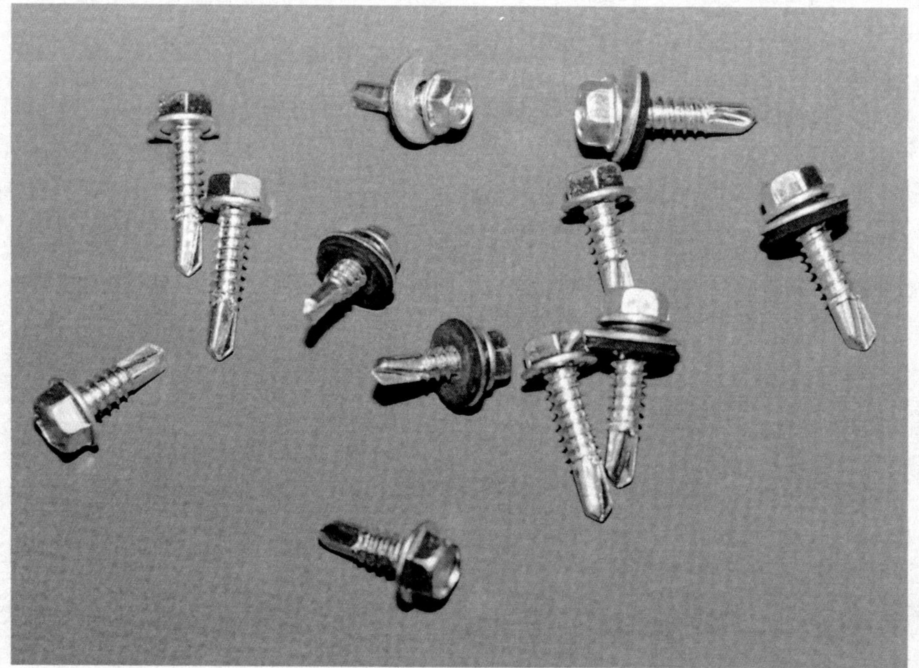

26108-14_SA07.EPS

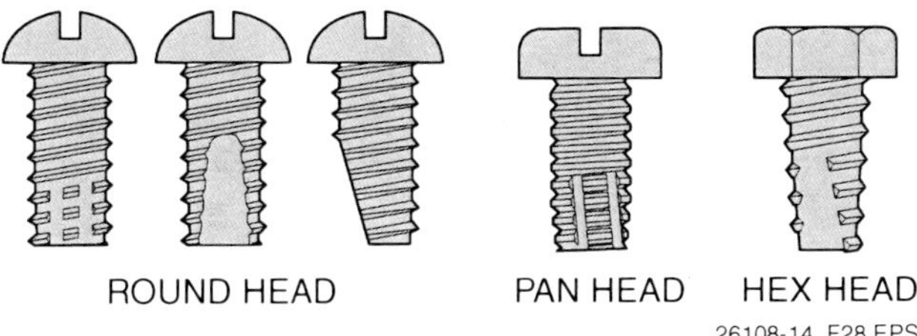

Figure 28 Thread-cutting screws.

7.2.5 Drywall Screws

Drywall screws (*Figure 29*) are thin, self-drilling screws with bugle-shaped heads. Depending on the type of screw, it cuts through the wallboard and anchors itself into wood and/or metal studs, holding the wallboard tight to the stud. Coarse thread screws are normally used to fasten wallboard to wood studs. Fine thread and high-and-low thread types are generally used for fastening to metal studs. Some screws are made for use in either wood or metal. A Phillips or Robertson drive head allows the drywall screw to be countersunk without tearing the surface of the wallboard.

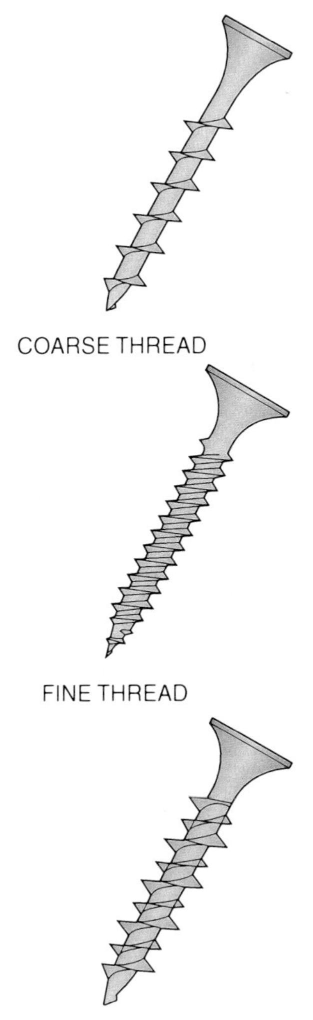

Figure 29 Drywall screws.

7.2.6 Drive Screws

Drive screws do not require that the hole be tapped. They are installed by hammering the screw into a drilled or punched hole of the proper size. Drive screws are mostly used to fasten parts that will not be exposed to much pressure. A typical use of drive screws is to attach permanent name plates on electric motors and other types of equipment. *Figure 30* shows typical drive screws.

7.3.0 Hammer-Driven Pins and Studs

Hammer-driven pins or threaded studs (*Figure 31*) can be used to fasten wood or steel to concrete or block without the need to predrill holes. The pin or threaded stud is inserted into a hammer-driven tool designed for its use. The pin or stud is inserted in the tool point end out with the washer seated in the recess. The pin or stud is then positioned against the base material where it is to be fastened and the drive rod of the tool tapped lightly until the striker pin contacts the pin or stud. Following this, the tool's drive rod is struck using heavy blows with about a two-pound engineer's hammer. The force of the hammer blows is transmitted through the tool directly to the head of the fastener, causing it to be driven into the concrete or block. For best results, the drive pin or stud should be embedded a minimum of ½" in hard concrete to 1¼" in softer concrete block.

7.4.0 Powder-Actuated Tools and Fasteners

Powder-actuated tools (*Figure 32*) can be used to drive a wide variety of specially designed pin and threaded stud-type fasteners into masonry and steel. These tools look and fire like a gun and use

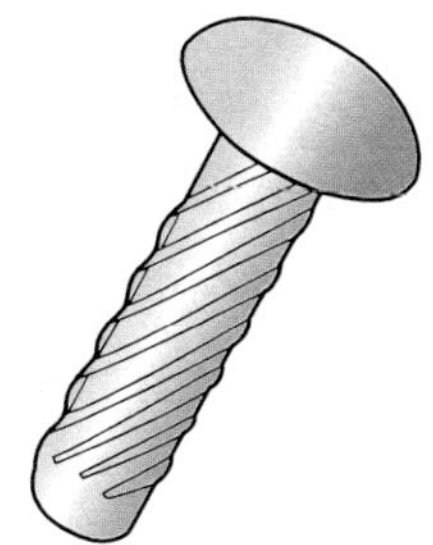

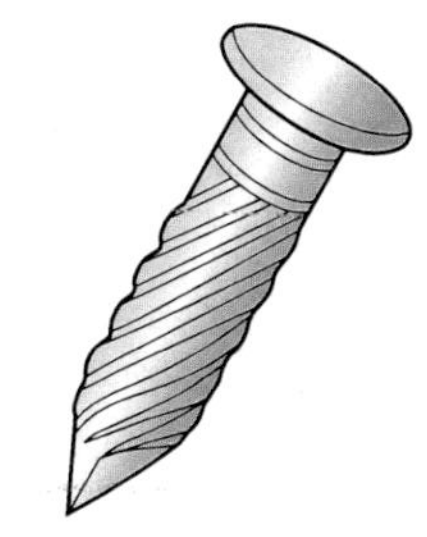

Figure 30 Drive screws.

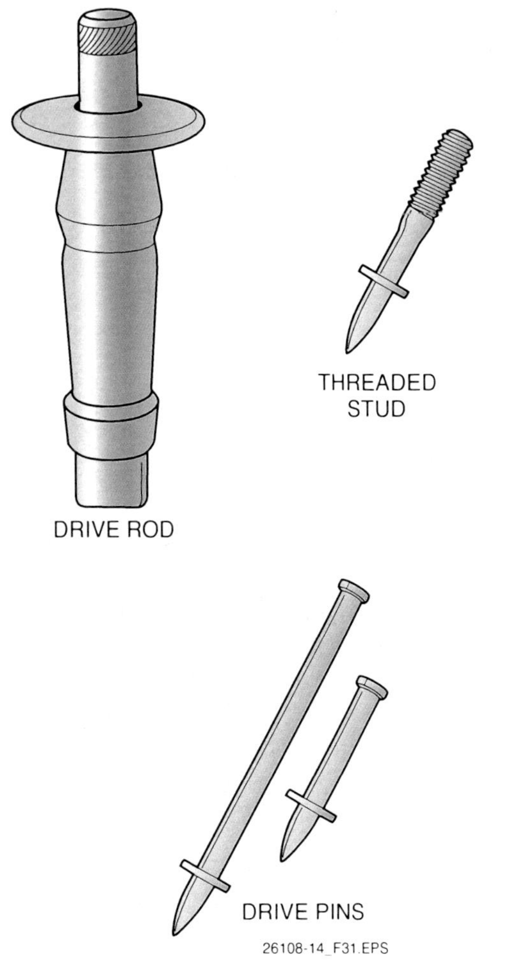

Figure 31 Hammer-driven pins and installation tool.

the force of a detonated gunpowder load (typically .22, .25, or .27 caliber) to drive the fastener into the material. The depth to which the pin or stud is driven is controlled by the density of the base material in which the pin or stud is being installed and by the power level or strength of the cased powder load.

Powder loads and their cases are designed for use with specific types and/or models of powder-actuated tools and are not interchangeable. Typically, powder loads are made in 12 increasing power or load levels used to achieve the proper penetration. The different power levels are identified by a color-code system and load case types. Note that different manufacturers may use different color codes to identify load strength. Power level 1 is the lowest power level while 12 is the highest. Higher number power levels are used when driving into hard materials or when a deeper penetration is needed. Powder loads are available as single-shot units for use with single-shot tools. They are also made in multi-shot strips or disks for semiautomatic tools.

WARNING!

Powder-actuated fastening tools are to be used only by trained and licensed operators and in accordance with the tool operator's manual. You must carry your license with you whenever you are using a powder-actuated tool.

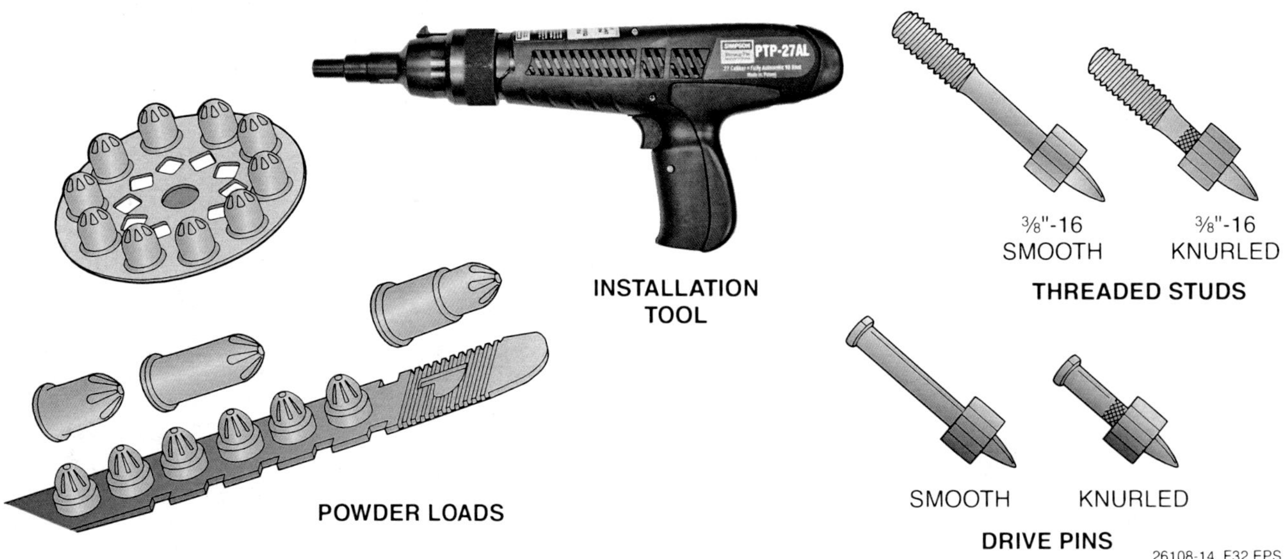

Figure 32 Powder-actuated installation tools and fasteners.

OSHA Standard 29 CFR 1926.302(e) governs the use of powder-actuated tools and states that only those individuals who have been trained in the operation of the particular powder-actuated tool in use be allowed to operate it. Authorized instructors available from the various powder-actuated tool manufacturers generally provide such training and licensing. Trained operators must take precautions to protect both themselves and others in the area when using a powder-actuated driver tool:

- Always use the tool in accordance with the published tool operation instructions. The instructions should be kept with the tool. Never attempt to override the safety features of the tool.
- Never place your hand or other body parts over the front muzzle end of the tool.
- Use only fasteners, powder loads, and tool parts specifically made for use with the tool. Use of other materials can cause improper and unsafe functioning of the tool.
- Operators and bystanders must wear eye and hearing protection along with hard hats. Other personal safety gear, as required, must also be used.
- Always post warning signs that state Powder-Actuated Tool in Use within 50 feet of the area where tools are used.

Case History

Powder-Actuated Tools

A 22-year-old apprentice was killed when he was struck in the head by a nail fired from a powder-actuated tool in an adjacent room. The tool operator was attempting to anchor plywood to a hollow wall and fired the gun, causing the nail to pass through the wall, where it traveled nearly thirty feet before striking the victim. The tool operator had never received training in the proper use of the tool, and none of the employees in the area were wearing personal protective equipment.

The Bottom Line: Never use a powder-actuated tool to secure fasteners into easily penetrated materials; these tools are designed primarily for installing fasteners into masonry. The use of powder-actuated tools requires special training and certification. In addition, all personnel in the area must be aware that the tool is in use and should be wearing appropriate personal protective equipment.

- Before using a tool, make sure it is unloaded and perform a proper function test. Check the functioning of the unloaded tool as described in the published tool operation instructions.
- Do not guess before fastening into any base material; always perform a center punch test.
- Always make a test firing into a suitable base material with the lowest power level recommended for the tool being used. If this does not set the fastener, try the next higher power level. Continue this procedure until the proper fastener penetration is obtained.
- Always point the tool away from operators or bystanders.
- Never use the tool in an explosive or flammable area.
- Never leave a loaded tool unattended. Do not load the tool until you are prepared to complete the fastening. Should you decide not to make a fastening after the tool has been loaded, always remove the powder load first, then the fastener. Always unload the tool before cleaning or servicing, when changing parts, prior to work breaks, and when storing the tool.
- Always hold the tool perpendicular to the work surface and use the spall (chip or fragment) guard or stop spall whenever possible.
- Always follow the required spacing, edge distance, and base material thickness requirements.
- Never fire through an existing hole or into a weld area.
- In the event of a misfire, always hold the tool depressed against the work surface for at least 30 seconds. If the tool still does not fire, follow the published tool instructions. Never carelessly discard or throw unfired powder loads into a trash receptacle.
- Always store the powder loads and unloaded tool under lock and key.

7.5.0 Mechanical Anchors

Mechanical anchors are devices used to give fasteners a firm grip in a variety of materials, where the fasteners by themselves would otherwise have a tendency to pull out. Anchors can be classified in many ways by different manufacturers. In this module, anchors have been divided into five broad categories:

- One-step anchors
- Bolt anchors
- Screw anchors
- Self-drilling anchors
- Hollow-wall anchors

7.5.1 One-Step Anchors

One-step anchors are designed so that they can be installed through the mounting holes in the component to be fastened. This is because the anchor and the drilled hole into which it is installed have the same size diameter. They come in various diameters ranging from ¼" to 1¼" with lengths ranging from 1¾ to 12". Wedge, stud, sleeve, one-piece, screw, and nail anchors (*Figure 33*) are common types of one-step anchors.

- *Wedge anchors* – Wedge anchors are heavy-duty anchors supplied with nuts and washers. The drill bit size used to drill the hole is the same diameter as the anchor. The depth of the hole is not critical as long as the minimum length recommended by the manufacturer is drilled. After the hole is blown clean of dust and other material, the anchor is inserted into the hole and driven with a hammer far enough so that at least six threads are below the top surface of the component. Then, the component is fastened by tightening the anchor nut to expand the anchor and tighten it in the hole.
- *Stud bolt anchors* – Stud bolt anchors are heavy-duty threaded anchors. Because this type of anchor is made to bottom in its mounting hole, it is a good choice to use when jacking or leveling of the fastened component is needed. The depth of the hole drilled in the masonry must be as specified by the manufacturer in order to achieve proper expansion. After the hole is blown clean of dust and other material, the anchor is inserted in the hole with the expander plug end down. Following this, the anchor is driven into the hole with a hammer (or setting tool) to expand the anchor and tighten it in the hole. The anchor is fully set when it can no longer be driven into the hole. The component is fastened using the correct size and thread bolt for use with the anchor stud.
- *Sleeve anchors* – Sleeve anchors are multi-purpose anchors. The depth of the anchor hole is not critical as long as the minimum length recommended by the manufacturer is drilled. After the hole is blown clean of dust and other material, the anchor is inserted into the hole and tapped until flush with the component. Then, the anchor nut or screw is tightened to expand the anchor and tighten it in the hole.
- *One-piece anchors* – One-piece anchors are multi-purpose anchors. They work on the principle that as the anchor is driven into the hole, the spring force of the expansion mechanism is compressed and flexes to fit the size of the hole. Once set, it tries to regain its original shape. The depth of the hole drilled in the masonry must be at least ½" deeper than the required embedment. The proper depth is crucial. Overdrilling is as bad as underdrilling. After the hole is blown clean of dust and other material, the anchor is inserted through the component and driven with a hammer into the hole until the head is firmly seated against the component. It is important to make sure that the anchor is driven to the proper embedment depth. Note that manufacturers also make specially designed drivers and manual tools that are used instead of a hammer to drive one-piece anchors. These tools allow the anchors to be installed in confined spaces and help prevent damage to the component from stray hammer blows.
- *Hammer-set anchors* – Hammer-set anchors are made for use in concrete and masonry. There are two types: nail and screw. An advantage of the screw-type anchors is that they are removable. Both types have a diameter the same size as the anchoring hole. For both types, the anchor hole must be drilled to the diameter of

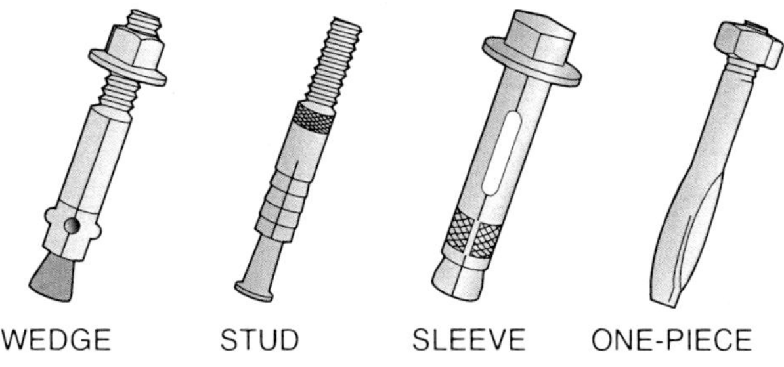

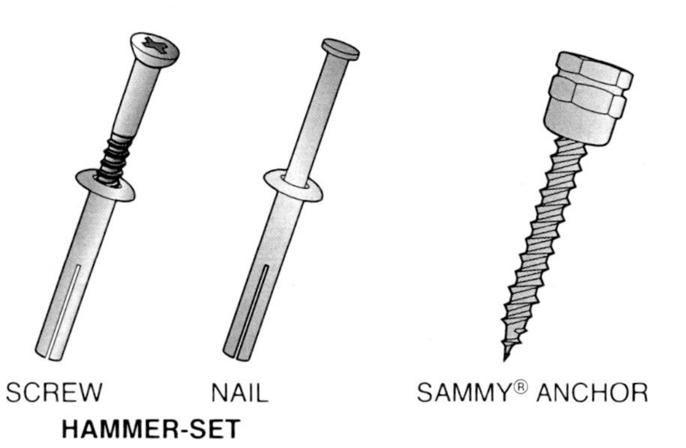

Figure 33 One-step anchors.

the anchor and to a depth of at least ¼" deeper than that required for embedment. After the hole is blown clean of dust and other material, the anchor is inserted into the hole through the mounting holes in the component to be fastened; then the screw or nail is driven into the anchor body to expand it. It is important to make sure that the head is seated firmly against the component and is at the proper embedment.

- *Threaded-rod anchors* – Threaded-rod anchors, such as the Sammy® anchor, are available for installation in concrete, steel, or wood. The anchor is designed to support a threaded rod, which is screwed into the head of the anchor after the anchor is installed. A special nut driver is available for installing the screws.

7.5.2 Bolt Anchors

Bolt anchors are designed to be installed flush with the surface of the base material. They are used in conjunction with threaded machine bolts or screws. In some types, they can be used with threaded rod. Drop-in, single and double expansion, and caulk-in anchors (*Figure 34*) are commonly used types of bolt anchors.

- *Drop-in anchors* – Drop-in anchors are typically used as heavy-duty anchors. There are two types of drop-in anchors. The first type, made for use in solid concrete and masonry, has an internally threaded expansion anchor with a preassembled internal expander plug. The anchor hole must be drilled to the specific diameter and depth specified by the manufacturer. After the hole is blown clean of dust and other material, the anchor is inserted into the hole and tapped until it is flush with the surface. Following this, a setting tool supplied with the anchor is driven into the anchor to expand it. The component to be fastened is positioned in place and fastened by threading and tightening the correct size machine bolt or screw into the anchor.

  The second type, called a hollow set drop-in anchor, is made for use in hollow concrete and masonry base materials. Hollow set drop-in anchors have a slotted, tapered expansion sleeve and a serrated expansion cone. They come in various lengths compatible with the outer wall thickness of most hollow base materials. They can also be used in solid concrete and masonry. The anchor hole must be drilled to the specific diameter specified by the manufacturer. When installed in hollow base materials, the hole is drilled into the cell or void. After the hole is blown clean of dust and other material, the anchor is inserted into the hole and tapped until it is flush with the surface. Following this, the component to be fastened is positioned in place; then the proper size machine bolt or screw is threaded into the anchor and tightened to expand the anchor in the hole.
- *Single- and double-expansion anchors* – Single- and double-expansion anchors are both made for use in concrete and other masonry. The double-expansion anchor is used mainly when fastening into concrete or masonry of questionable strength. For both types, the anchor hole must be drilled to the specific diameter and depth specified by the manufacturer. After the hole is blown clean of dust and other material, the anchor is inserted into the hole, threaded cone end first. It is then tapped until it is flush with the surface. Following this, the component to be fastened is positioned in place; then the proper size machine bolt or screw is threaded into the anchor and tightened to expand the anchor in the hole.

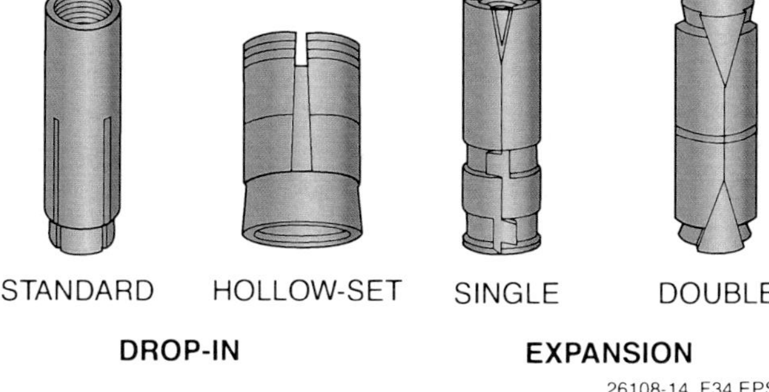

Figure 34 Bolt anchors.

7.5.3 Screw Anchors

Screw anchors are lighter-duty anchors made to be installed flush with the surface of the base material. They are used in conjunction with sheet metal, wood, or lag screws depending on the anchor type. Fiber and plastic anchors are common types of screw anchors (*Figure 35*). The lag shield anchor used with lag screws was described earlier in this module.

Fiber and plastic anchors are typically used in concrete and masonry. Plastic anchors are also

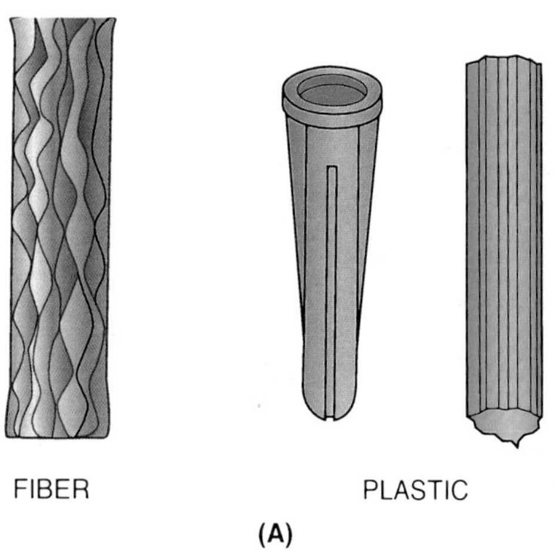

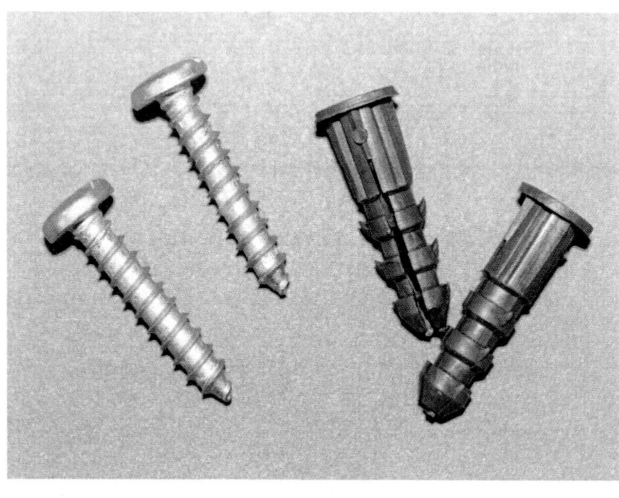

26108-14_F35.EPS

Figure 35 Screw anchors and screws.

commonly used in wallboard and similar base materials. The installation of all types is simple. The anchor hole must be drilled to the diameter specified by the manufacturer. The minimum depth of the hole must equal the anchor length. After the hole is blown clean of dust and other material, the anchor is inserted into the hole and tapped until it is flush with the surface. Following this, the component to be fastened is positioned in place; then the proper type and size screw is driven through the component mounting hole and into the anchor to expand the anchor in the hole.

7.5.4 Self-Drilling Anchors

Some anchors made for use in masonry are self-drilling anchors. *Figure 36* is typical of those in common use. This fastener has a cutting sleeve that is first used as a drill bit and later becomes the expandable fastener itself. A rotary

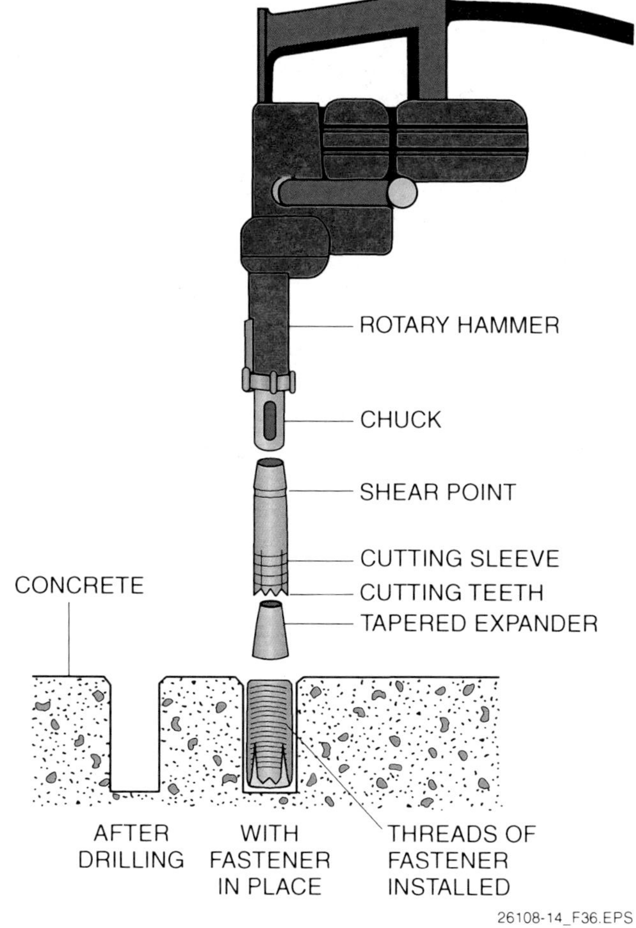

Figure 36 Self-drilling anchor.

hammer is used to drill the hole in the concrete using the anchor sleeve as the drill bit. After the hole is drilled, the anchor is pulled out and the hole cleaned. This is followed by inserting the anchor's expander plug into the cutting end of the sleeve. The anchor sleeve and expander plug are driven back into the hole with the rotary hammer until they are flush with the surface of the concrete. As the fastener is hammered down, it hits the bottom, where the tapered expander causes the fastener to expand and lock into the hole. The anchor is then snapped off at the shear point with a quick lateral movement of the hammer. The component to be fastened can then be attached to the anchor using the proper size bolt.

7.6.0 Guidelines for Drilling Anchor Holes in Hardened Concrete or Masonry

When selecting masonry anchors, regardless of the type, always take into consideration and follow the manufacturer's recommendations pertaining to hole diameter and depth, minimum embedment in concrete, maximum thickness of material to be fastened, and the pullout and shear load capacities.

When installing anchors and/or anchor bolts in hardened concrete, make sure the area where the equipment or component is to be fastened is smooth so that it will have solid footing. Uneven footing might cause the equipment to twist, warp, not tighten properly, or vibrate when in operation. Before starting, carefully inspect the rotary hammer or hammer drill and the drill bit(s) to ensure they are in good operating condition. Be sure to use the type of carbide-tipped masonry or percussion drill bits recommended by the drill/hammer or anchor manufacturer because these bits are made to take the higher impact of the masonry materials. Also, it is recommended that the drill or hammer tool depth gauge be set to the depth of the hole needed. The trick to using masonry drill bits is not to force them into the material by pushing down hard on the drill. Use a little pressure and let the drill do the work. For large holes, start with a smaller bit, then change to a larger bit.

The methods for installing the different types of anchors in hardened concrete or masonry have been briefly described. Always install the selected anchors according to the manufacturer's directions. Here is an example of a typical procedure used to install many types of expansion anchors in hardened concrete or masonry.

On Site

Safety

Be sure to wear safety goggles whenever you tackle any fastening project, regardless of how small the job may seem. Remember, you can never replace lost eyesight.

Refer to *Figure 37* as you study the procedure.

WARNING!

Drilling in concrete generates noise, dust, and flying particles. Always wear safety goggles, ear protectors, and gloves. Make sure other workers in the area also wear protective equipment.

Step 1 Drill the anchor bolt hole the same size as the anchor bolt. The hole must be deep enough for six threads of the bolt to be below the surface of the concrete (see *Figure 37, Step 1*). Clean out the hole using a squeeze bulb.

Step 2 Drive the anchor bolt into the hole using a hammer (*Figure 37, Step 2*). Protect the threads of the bolt with a nut that does not allow any threads to be exposed.

Step 3 Put a washer and nut on the bolt, and tighten the nut with a wrench until the anchor is secure in the concrete (*Figure 37, Step 3*).

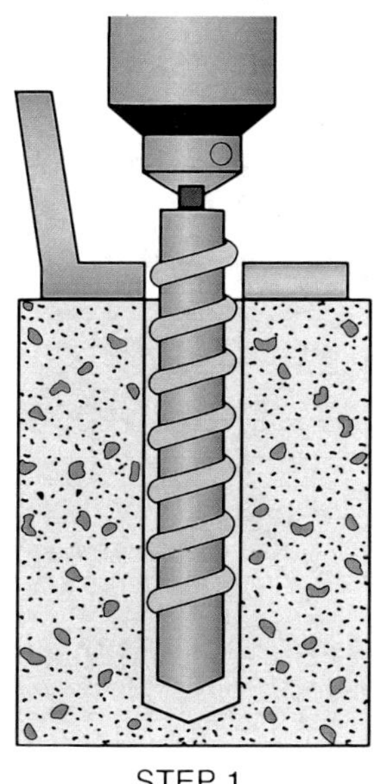

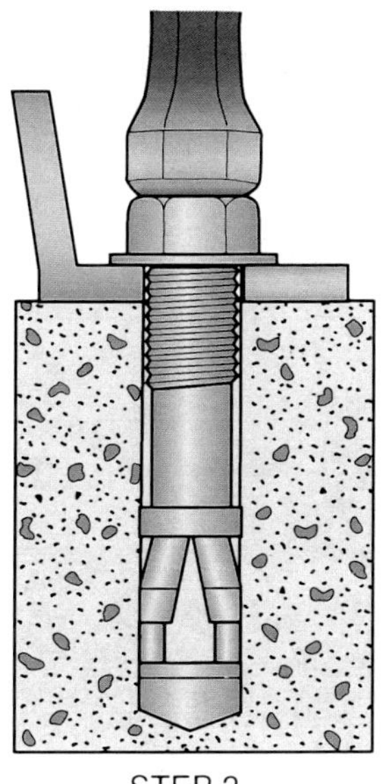

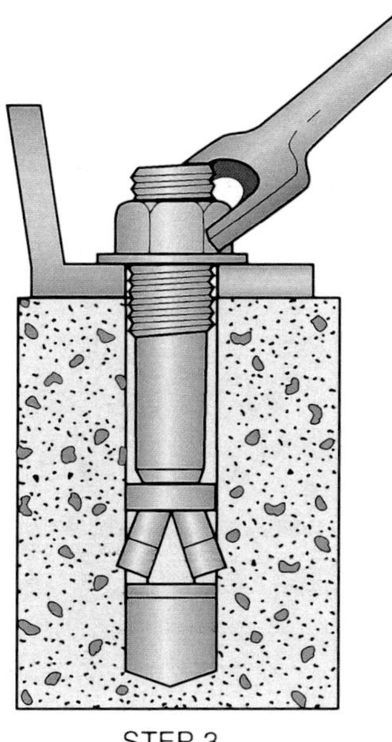

Figure 37 Installing an anchor bolt in hardened concrete.

7.7.0 Hollow-Wall Anchors

Hollow-wall anchors are used in hollow materials such as concrete plank, block, structural steel, wallboard, and plaster. Some types can also be used in solid materials. Toggle bolts, sleeve-type wall anchors, wallboard anchors, and metal drive-in anchors are common anchors used when fastening to hollow materials.

When installing anchors in hollow walls or ceilings, regardless of the type, always follow the manufacturer's recommendations pertaining to use, hole diameter, wall thickness, grip range (thickness of the anchoring material), and the pullout and shear load capacities.

7.7.1 Toggle Bolts

Toggle bolts (*Figure 38*) are used to fasten equipment, hangers, supports, and similar items into hollow surfaces such as walls and ceilings. They consist of a slotted bolt or screw and spring-loaded wings. When the bolt is inserted through the item to be fastened, then through a predrilled hole in the wall or ceiling, the wings spring apart and provide a firm hold on the inside of the hollow wall or ceiling as the bolt is tightened. Note that the hole drilled in the wall or ceiling should be just large enough for the compressed wing-head to pass through. Once the toggle bolt is installed, be careful not to completely unscrew the bolt because the wings will fall off, making the fastener useless. Screw-actuated plastic toggle bolts are also made. These are similar to metal toggle bolts, but they come with a pointed screw and do not require as large a hole. Unlike the metal version, the plastic wings remain in place if the screw is removed.

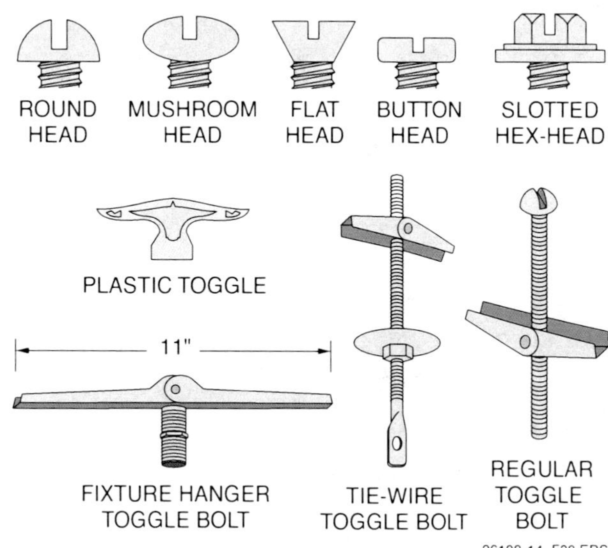

Figure 38 Toggle bolts.

Think About It

Toggle Bolts

What will happen if you fasten a toggle bolt too tightly?

Toggle bolts are used to fasten a part to hollow block, wallboard, plaster, panel, or tile. The following general procedure can be used to install toggle bolts.

WARNING!

Follow all safety precautions when using an electric drill.

Step 1 Select the proper size drill bit or punch and toggle bolt for the job.

Step 2 Check the toggle bolt for damaged or dirty threads or a malfunctioning wing mechanism.

Step 3 Drill a hole completely through the surface to which the part is to be fastened.

Step 4 Insert the toggle bolt through the opening in the item to be fastened.

Step 5 Screw the toggle wing onto the end of the toggle bolt, ensuring that the flat side of the toggle wing is facing the bolt head.

Step 6 Fold the wings completely back and push them through the drilled hole until the wings spring open.

Step 7 Pull back on the item to be fastened in order to hold the wings firmly against the inside surface to which the item is being attached.

Step 8 Tighten the toggle bolt with a screwdriver until it is snug.

7.7.2 Sleeve-Type Wall Anchors

Sleeve-type wall anchors (*Figure 39*) are suitable for use in concrete, block, plywood, wallboard, hollow tile, and similar materials. The two types made are standard and drive. The standard type is commonly used in walls and ceilings and is installed by drilling a mounting hole to the

Case History

Installation Requirements

In a college dormitory, battery-powered emergency lights were anchored to sheetrock hallway ceilings with sheetrock screws, with no additional support. These fixtures weigh 8-10 pounds each and might easily have fallen out of the ceiling, causing severe injury. When the situation was discovered, the contractor had to remove and replace dozens of fixtures.

The Bottom Line: Incorrect anchoring methods can be both costly and dangerous.

Think About It

Sleeve-Type Drive Anchors

What happens when you remove the screw when a sleeve-type drive anchor is in place?

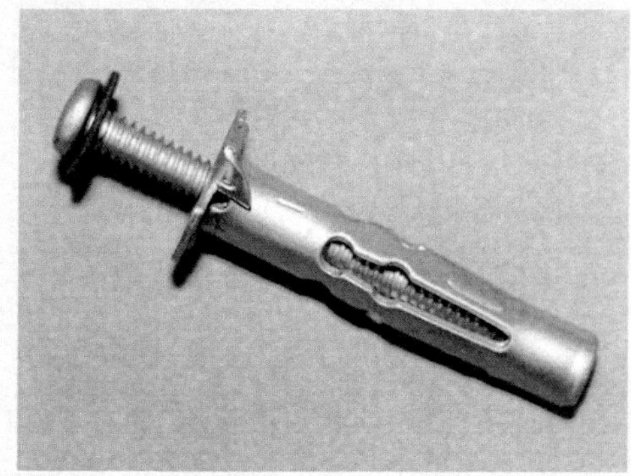

26108-14_SA08.EPS

required diameter. The anchor is inserted into the hole and tapped until the gripper prongs embed in the base material. Following this, the anchor's screw is tightened to draw the anchor tight against the inside of the wall or ceiling. Note that the drive-type anchor is hammered into the material without the need for drilling a mounting hole. After the anchor is installed, the anchor screw is removed, the component being fastened is positioned in place, then the screw is reinstalled through the mounting hole in the component and into the anchor. The screw is tightened into the anchor to secure the component.

7.7.3 Wallboard Anchors

Wallboard anchors (*Figure 39*) are self-drilling medium- and light-duty anchors used for fastening in wallboard. The anchor is driven into the wall with a Phillips head manual or cordless screwdriver until the head of the anchor is flush with the wall or ceiling surface. Following this, the component being fastened is positioned over the anchor, then secured with the proper size sheet metal screw driven into the anchor.

7.7.4 Metal Drive-In Anchors

Metal drive-in anchors (*Figure 39*) are used to fasten light to medium loads to wallboard. They have two pointed legs that stay together when the anchor is hammered into a wall and spread out against the inside of the wall when a No. 6 or 8 sheet metal screw is driven in.

7.8.0 Epoxy Anchoring Systems

Epoxy resin compounds can be used to anchor threaded rods, dowels, and similar fasteners in solid concrete, hollow wall, and brick. For one manufacturer's product, a two-part epoxy is packaged in a two-chamber cartridge that keeps the resin and hardener ingredients separated until use. This cartridge is placed into a special tool

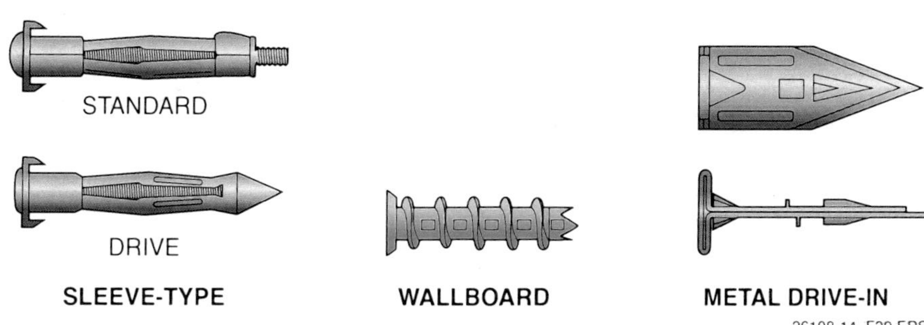

Figure 39 Sleeve-type, wallboard, and metal drive-in anchors.

Think About It

Ceiling Installations

In the dormitory problem discussed earlier, which of the following fasteners could have been used to safely secure the emergency lights?

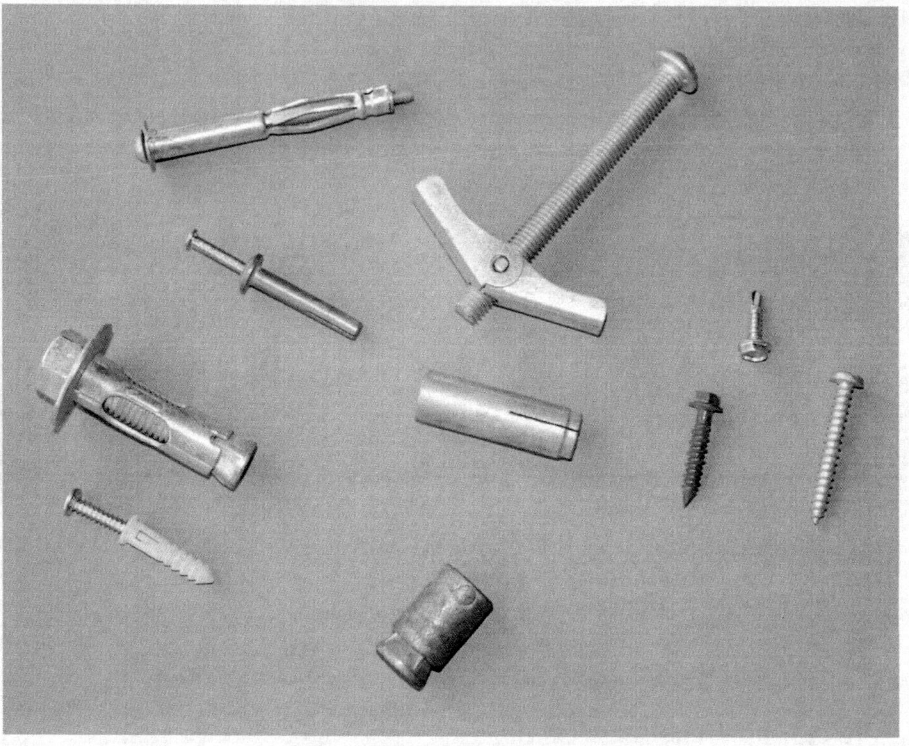

26108-14_SA09.EPS

similar to a caulking gun. When the gun handle is pumped, the epoxy resin and hardener components are mixed within the gun; then the epoxy is ejected from the gun nozzle.

To use the epoxy to install an anchor in solid concrete (*Figure 40*), a hole of the proper size is drilled in the concrete and cleaned using a nylon (not metal) brush. Following this, a small amount of epoxy is dispensed from the gun to make sure that the resin and hardener have mixed properly. This is indicated by the epoxy being of a uniform color. The gun nozzle is then placed into the hole, and the epoxy is injected into the hole until half the depth of the hole is filled. Following this, the selected fastener is pushed into the hole with a slow twisting motion to make sure that the epoxy fills all voids and crevices, then is set to the required plumb (or level) position. After the recommended cure time for the epoxy has elapsed, the fastener nut can be tightened to secure the component or fixture in place.

The procedure for installing a fastener in a hollow wall or brick using epoxy is basically the same as described above. The difference is that the epoxy is first injected into an anchor screen to fill the screen, then the anchor screen is installed into the drilled hole. Use of the anchor screen is necessary to hold the epoxy intact in the hole until the anchor is inserted into the epoxy.

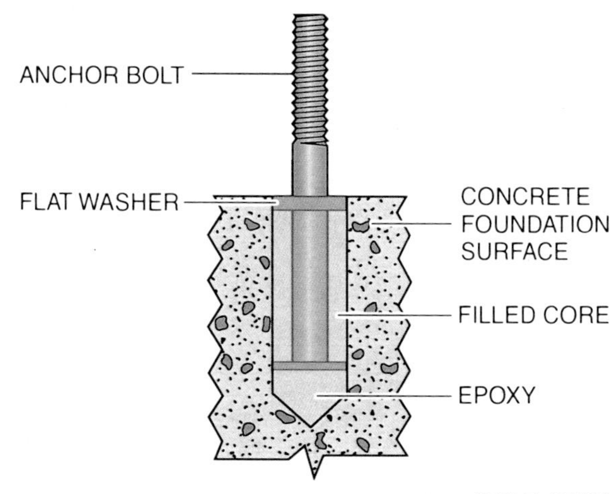

Figure 40 Fastener anchored in epoxy.

On Site

Using Epoxy

Once mixed, epoxy has a limited working time. Therefore, mix exactly what you need and work quickly. After the working time is up, epoxy requires a specific curing time. Always give epoxy its recommended curing time; since epoxy is so strong and sets so quickly, you'll be tempted to stress the bond before it's fully cured.

On Site

Wall-Mounted Supports

This wall-mounted support has been fabricated to hold the conduit away from the metal building. While it is shown with only one raceway, additional raceways can be added to the framing channel.

26108-14_SA10.EPS

8.0.0 Raceway Supports

Raceway supports are available in many types and configurations. This section discusses the most common conduit supports found in electrical installations. *NEC Section 300.11* discusses the requirements for branch circuit wiring that is supported from above suspended ceilings. Electrical equipment and raceways must have their own supporting methods and may not be supported by the supporting hardware of a fire-rated roof/ceiling assembly.

8.1.0 Straps

Straps are used to support conduit to a surface (see *Figure 41*). The spacing of these supports must conform to the minimum support spacing requirements for each type of conduit. One- and two-hole straps are used for all types of conduit: EMT, RMC, IMC, PVC, and flex. The straps can be flexible or rigid. Two-part straps are used to secure conduit to electrical framing channels (struts). Parallel and right angle beam clamps are also used to support conduit from structural members.

Clamp back straps can also be used with a backplate to maintain the ¼-inch spacing from the surface required for installations in wet locations.

On Site

Use the Proper Tool for the Application

To avoid damaging fasteners, use the correct tool for the job. For example, don't use pliers to install bolts, and don't use a screwdriver that is too large or too small.

8.2.0 Standoff Supports

The standoff support, often referred to as a Minerallac® (the name of a manufacturer of this type of support), is used to support conduit away from the supporting structure. In the case of the one-hole and two-hole straps, the conduit must be offset wherever a fitting occurs. If standoff supports are used, the conduit is held away from the supporting surface, and no offsets are required in the conduit at the fittings. Standoff supports may be used to support all types of conduit including RMC, IMC, EMT, PVC, and flex, as well as tubing installations. A standoff support is shown in *Figure 42*.

8.3.0 Electrical Framing Channels

Electrical framing channels or other similar framing materials are used together with Unistrut®-type conduit clamps to support conduit (see *Figure 43*). They may be attached to a ceiling, wall, or other surface or be supported from a trapeze hanger.

8.4.0 Beam Clamps

Beam clamps are used with suspended hangers. The raceway is attached to or laid in the hanger.

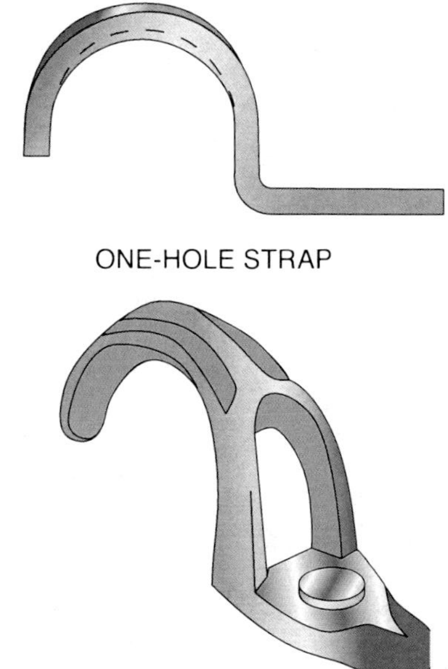

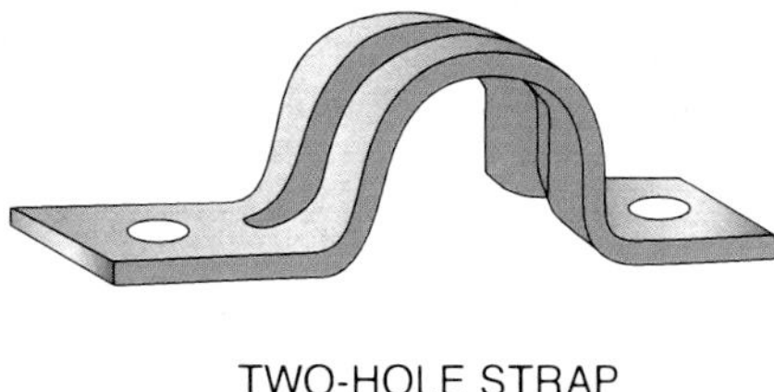

Figure 41 Straps.

The hanger is suspended by a threaded rod. One end of the threaded rod is attached to the hanger and the other end is attached to a beam clamp. The beam clamp is then attached to a beam. A beam clamp with wireway support assembly is shown in *Figure 44*.

On Site

Bundling Conductors

When conductors are bundled together in a wireway their magnetic fields tend to cancel, thus minimizing inductive heating in the conductors.

Figure 42 Standoff support.

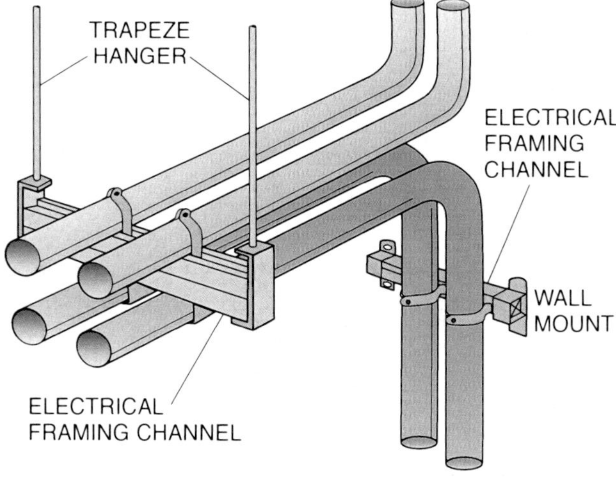

Figure 43 Electrical framing channels.

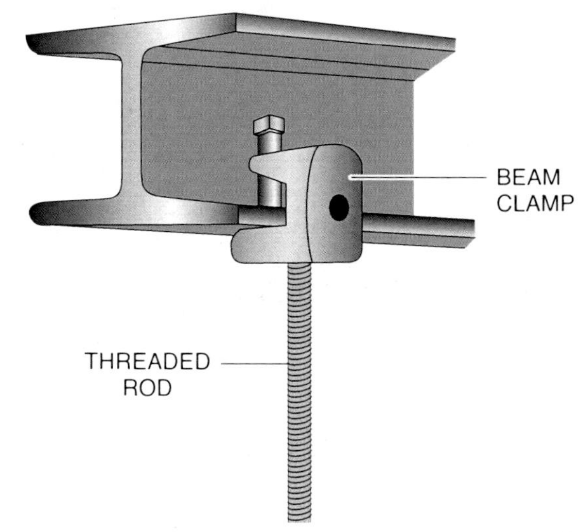

Figure 44 Beam clamp.

9.0.0 Wireways

Wireways are sheet metal troughs provided with hinged or screw-on removable covers. Like other types of raceways, wireways are used for housing electric wires and cables. Wireways are available in various lengths, including 1, 2, 3, 4, 5, and 10 feet. The availability of various lengths allows runs of any exact number of feet to be made without cutting the wireway ducts. Wireways are dealt with specifically in *NEC Article 376.*

As listed in *NEC Section 376.22(A),* the sum of the cross-sectional areas of all contained conductors at any cross section of a wireway shall not exceed 20% of the interior cross-sectional area of the wireway. The derating factors in *NEC Table 310.15(B)(3)(a)* shall be applied only where the number of current-carrying conductors exceeds 3, including neutral conductors classified as current-carrying under the provisions of *NEC Section 310.15(B)(5).* Conductors for signaling or controller conductors between a motor and its starter used only for starting duty shall not be considered current-carrying conductors.

It is also noted in *NEC Section 376.56(A)* that conductors, together with splices and taps, must not fill the wireway to more than 75% of its cross-sectional area. No conductor larger than that for which the wireway is designed shall be installed in any wireway. Be sure to check *NEC Article 378* for the requirements of nonmetallic wireways.

NEC Section 376.23(A) requires that the dimensions of *NEC Table 312.6(A)* be applied where insulated conductors are deflected in a wireway. *NEC Section 376.23(B)* requires that the provisions of *NEC Section 314.28* apply where wireways are used as pull boxes.

9.1.0 Auxiliary Gutters

Strictly speaking, an auxiliary gutter is a wireway that is intended to add to wiring space at switchboards, meters, and other distribution locations. Auxiliary gutters are dealt with specifically in *NEC Article 366.* Even though the component parts of wireways and auxiliary gutters are identical, you should be familiar with the differences in their use. Auxiliary gutters are used as parts of complete assemblies of apparatus such as switchboards, distribution centers, and control equipment. However, an auxiliary gutter may only contain conductors or busbars, even though it looks like a surface metal raceway that may contain devices and equipment. Unlike auxiliary gutters, wireways represent a type of wiring because they are used to carry conductors between points located considerable distances apart.

The allowable ampacities for insulated conductors in wireways and gutters are given in *NEC Tables 310.15(B)(16) and 310.15(B)(18).* It should be noted that these tables are used for raceways in general. These *NEC®* tables and the notes are often used to determine if the correct materials are on hand for an installation. They are also used to determine if it is possible to add conductors in an existing wireway or gutter.

In many situations, it is necessary to make extensions from the wireways to wall receptacles and control devices. In these cases, *NEC Section 376.70* specifies that these extensions be made using any wiring method presented in *NEC Chapter 3* that includes a means for equipment grounding. Finally, as required in *NEC Section 376.120,* wireways must be marked in such a way that their manufacturer's name or trademark will be visible.

As you can see in *Figure 45*, a wide range of fittings is required for connecting wireways to one another and to fixtures such as switchboards, power panels, and conduit.

9.2.0 Types of Wireways

Rectangular duct-type wireways come as either hinged-cover or screw-cover troughs. Typical lengths are 1, 2, 3, 4, 5, and 10 feet. Shorter lengths are also available. Raintight troughs are permitted to be used in environments where moisture is not permitted within the raceway. However, the raintight trough should not be confused with the raintight lay-in wireway, which has a hinged cover. *Figure 46* shows a raintight trough with a removable side cover.

Wireway troughs are exposed when first installed. Whenever possible, they are mounted on the ceilings or walls, although they may sometimes be suspended from the ceiling. Note that in *Figure 47*, the trough has knockouts similar to those found on junction boxes. After the wireway system has been installed, branch circuits are brought from the distribution panels using conduit. The conduit is joined to the wireway at the most convenient knockout possible.

Wireway components such as trough crosses, 90° internal elbows, and tee connectors serve the same function as fittings on other types of

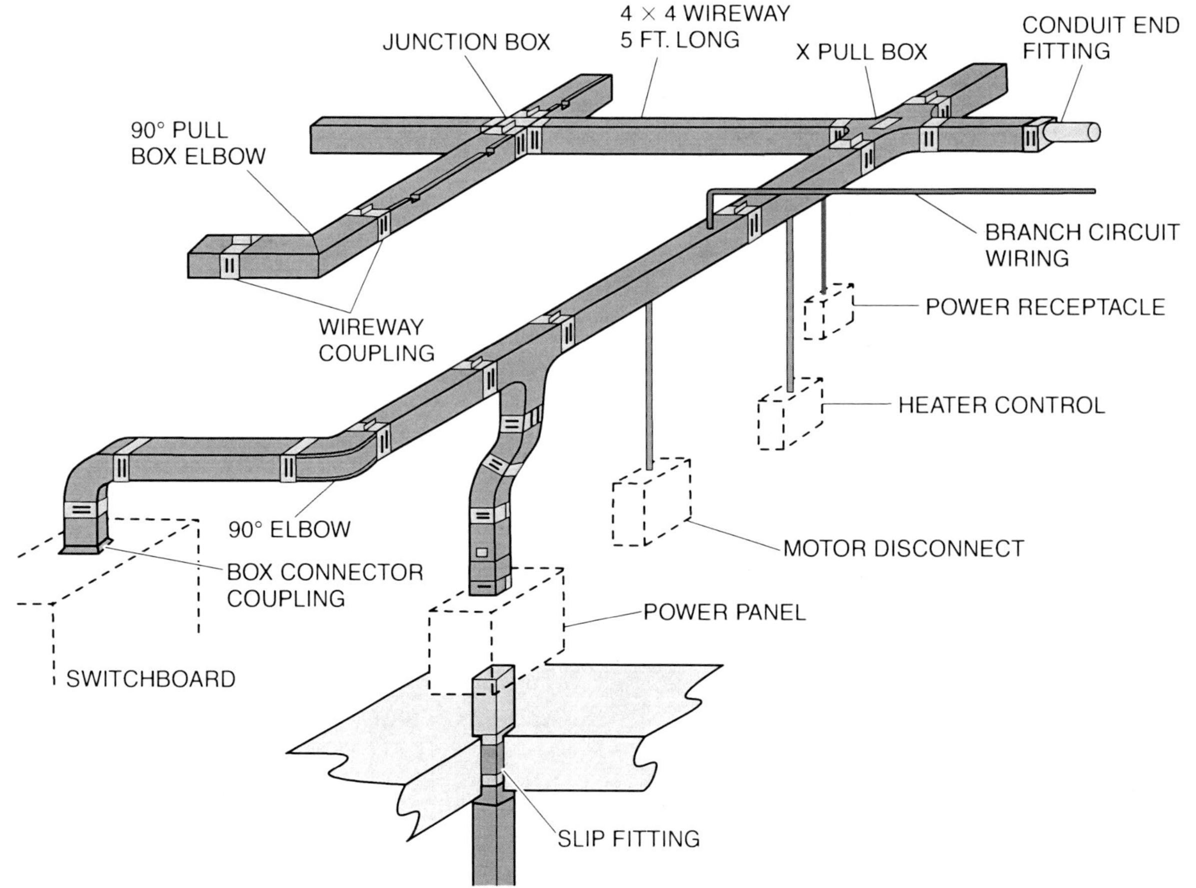

Figure 45 Wireway system layout.

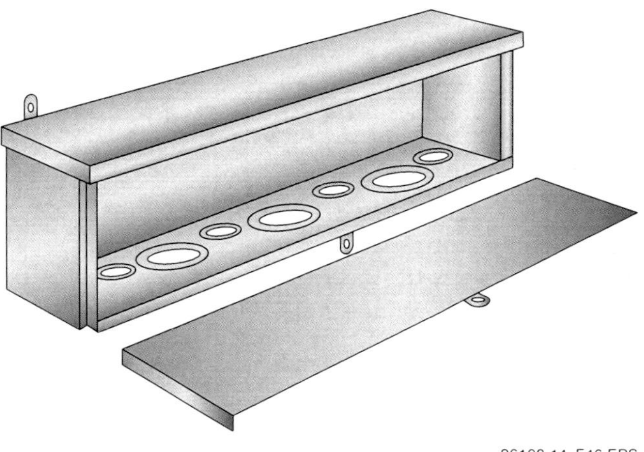

Figure 46 Raintight trough.

raceways. The fittings are attached to the duct using slip-on connectors. All attachments are made with nuts and bolts or screws. When assembling wireways, always place the head of the bolt on the inside and the nut on the outside so that the conductors will not be resting against a sharp edge. It is usually best to assemble sections of the wireway system on the floor, and then raise the sections into position. An exploded view of a section of wireway is shown in *Figure 48*. Both the wireway fittings and the duct come with screw-on, hinged, or snap-on covers to permit conductors to be laid in or pulled through.

The *NEC*® specifies that wireways may be used only for exposed work. Therefore, they cannot be used in underfloor installations. If they are used for outdoor work, they must be of an approved raintight construction. It is important to note that wireways must not be installed where they are subject to severe physical damage, corrosive vapors, or hazardous locations.

Wireway troughs must be installed so that they are supported at distances not exceeding 5 feet. When specially approved supports are used, the distance between supports must not exceed 10 feet.

9.2.1 Wireway Fittings

Many different types of fittings are available for wireways, especially for use in exposed, dry locations. The following sections explain fittings commonly used in the electrical craft.

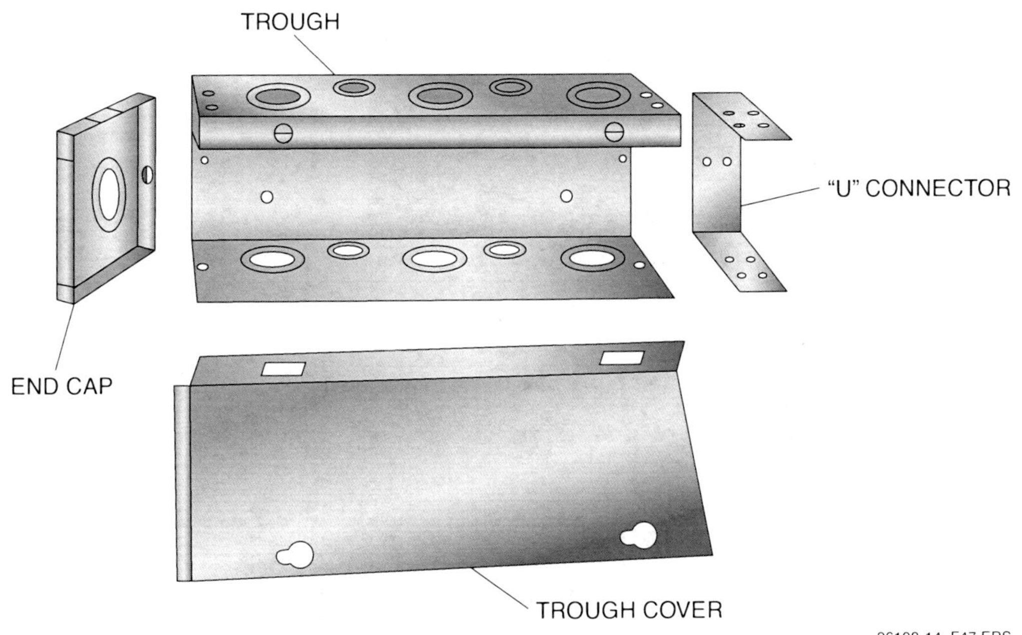

Figure 47 Trough.

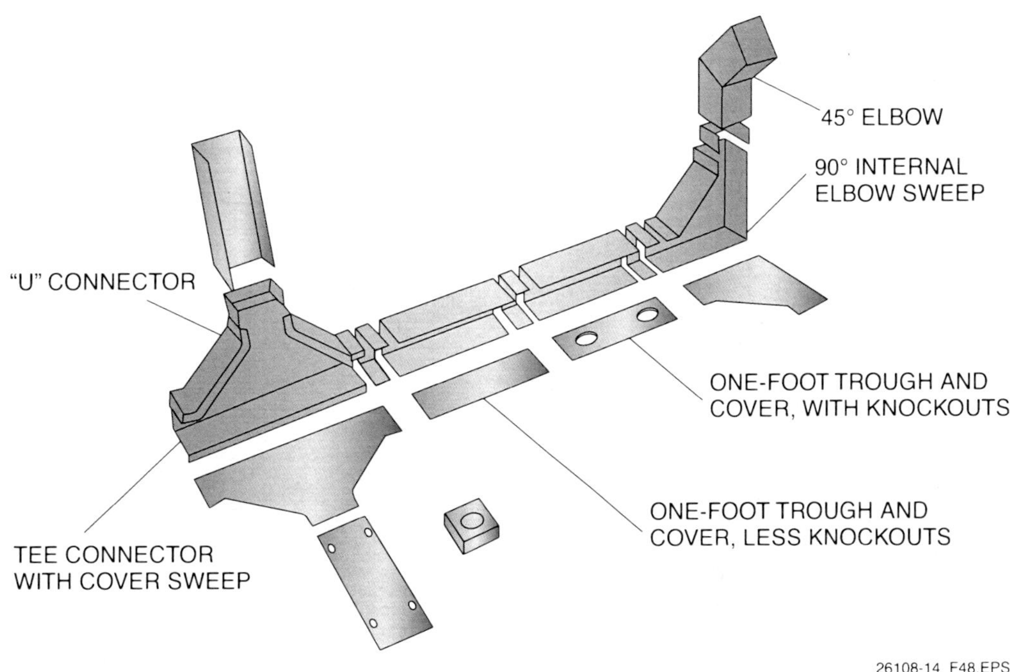

Figure 48 Wireway sections.

9.2.2 Connectors

Connectors (*Figure 49*) are used to join wireway sections and fittings. Connectors are slipped inside the end of a wireway section and are held in place by small bolts and nuts. Alignment slots allow the connector to be moved until it is flush with the inside surface of the wireway. After the connector is in position, it can be bolted to the wireway. This helps to ensure a strong rigid connection. Connectors have a friction hinge that helps hold the wireway cover open when needed.

On Site

Wireway or Trough?

A raintight lay-in wireway has a hinged cover, as shown here. A raintight trough simply has a removable cover.

26108-14_SA11.EPS

9.2.3 End Plates

End plates, or closing plates (*Figure 50*), are used to seal the ends of wireways. They are inserted into the end of the wireway and fastened by screws and bolts. End plates contain knockouts so that conduit or cable may be extended from the wireway.

9.2.4 Tees

Tee fittings (*Figure 51*) are used when a tee connection is needed in a wireway system. A tee connection is used where circuit conductors may branch in different directions. The tee fitting's covers and

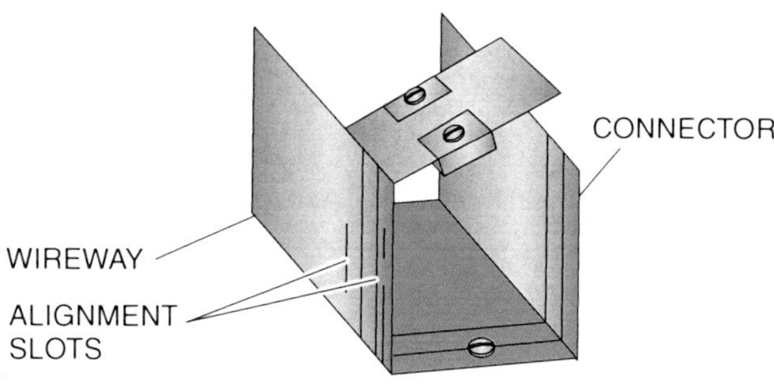

26108-14_F49.EPS

Figure 49 Connector.

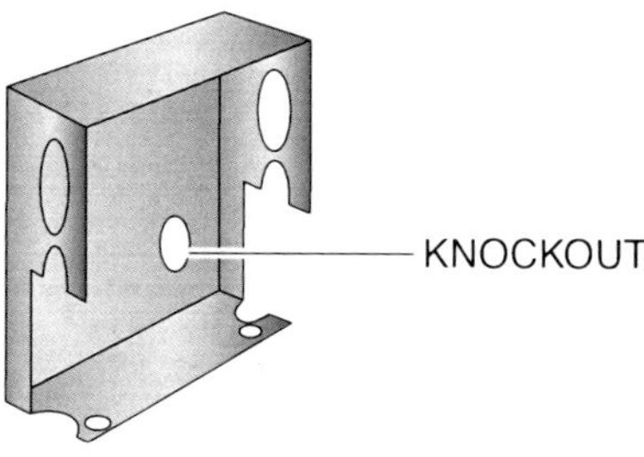

26108-14_F50.EPS

Figure 50 End plate.

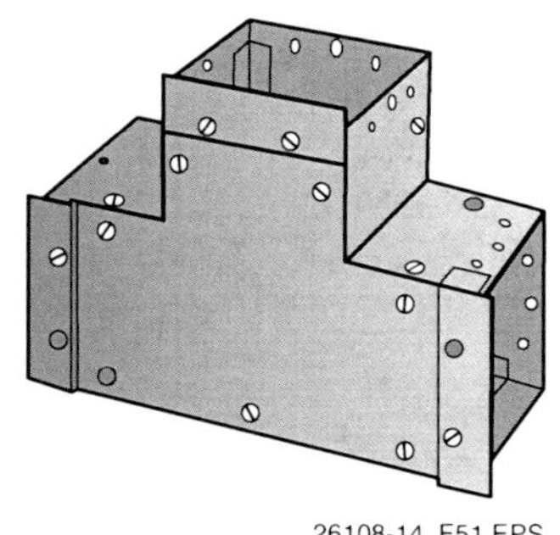

26108-14_F51.EPS

Figure 51 Tee.

sides can be removed for access to splices and taps. Tee fittings are attached to other wireway sections using standard connectors.

9.2.5 Crosses

Crosses (*Figure 52*) have four openings and are attached to other wireway sections with standard connectors. The cover is held in place by screws and can be easily removed for laying in wires or for making connections.

9.2.6 Elbows

Elbows are used to make a bend in the wireway. They are available in angles of 22½°, 45°, or 90°, and are either internal or external. They are attached to wireway sections with standard connectors. Covers and sides can be removed for wire installation. The inside corners of elbows are rounded to prevent damage to conductor insulation. An inside elbow is shown in *Figure 53*.

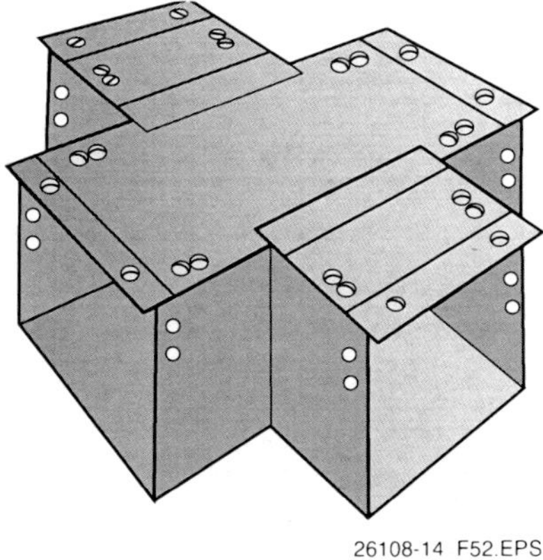

Figure 52 Cross.

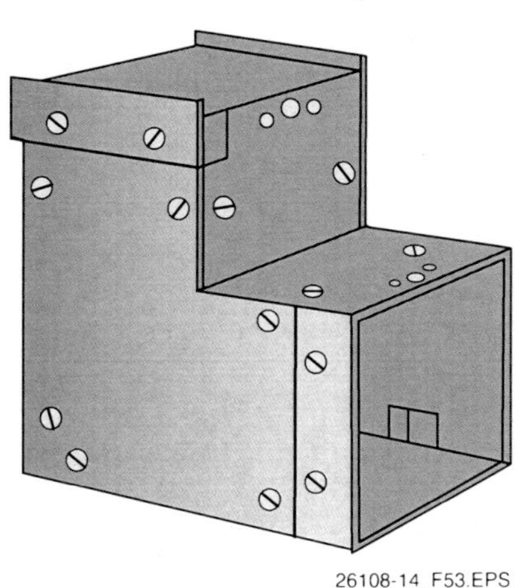

Figure 53 90° inside elbow.

9.2.7 Telescopic Fittings

Telescopic or slip fittings may be used between lengths of wireway. Slip fittings are attached to standard lengths by setscrews and usually adjust from ½ inch to 11½ inches. Slip fittings have a removable cover for installing wires and are similar in appearance to a nipple.

9.3.0 Wireway Supports

Horizontal wireway runs must be securely supported at each end and at intervals of no more than 5 feet or for individual lengths greater than 5 feet at each end or joint, unless listed for other support intervals. In no case shall the support distance be greater than 10 feet, in accordance with *NEC Section 376.30(A)*. If possible, wireways can be mounted directly to a surface. Otherwise, wireways are supported by hangers or brackets.

9.3.1 Suspended Hangers

In many cases, the wireway is supported from a ceiling, beam, or other structural member. In such installations, a suspended hanger (*Figure 54*) may be used to support the wireway.

The wireway is attached to or laid in the hanger. The hanger is suspended by a threaded rod. One end of the rod is attached to the hanger with hex nuts. The other end of the rod is attached to a beam clamp or anchor.

9.3.2 Gusset Brackets

Another type of support used to mount wireways is a gusset bracket (*Figure 55*). This is an L-type bracket that is mounted to a wall. The wireway rests on the bracket and is attached by screws or bolts.

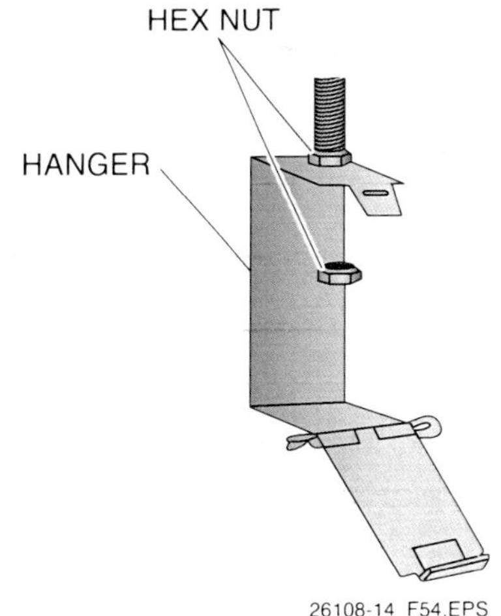

Figure 54 Suspended hanger.

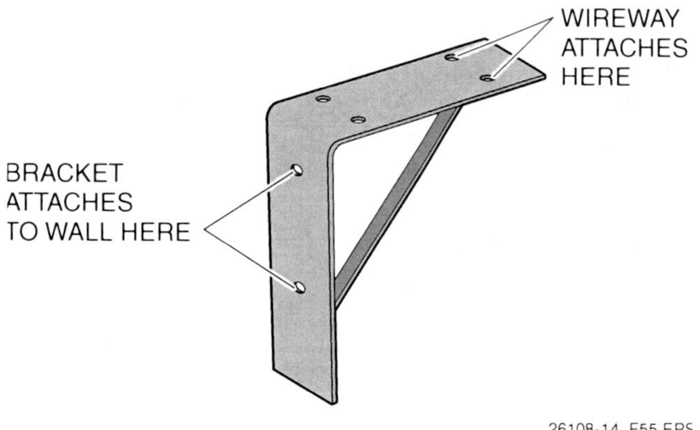

Figure 55 Gusset bracket.

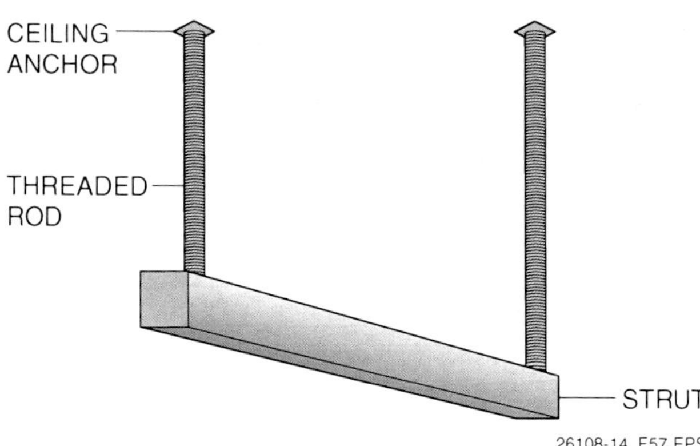

Figure 57 Wireway hanger.

9.3.3 Standard Hangers

Standard hangers (*Figure 56*) are made in two pieces. The two pieces are combined in different ways for different installation requirements. The wireway is attached to the hanger by bolts and nuts.

9.3.4 Wireway Hangers

When a larger wireway must be suspended, a wireway hanger may be used. A wireway hanger is made by suspending a piece of strut from a ceiling, beam, or other structural member. The strut is suspended by threaded rods attached to beam clamps or other ceiling anchors, as shown in *Figure 57*.

9.4.0 Other Types of Raceways

In this section, other types of raceways will be discussed. Depending on the particular purpose for which they are intended, raceways include enclosures such as surface metal and nonmetallic raceways, and underfloor raceways.

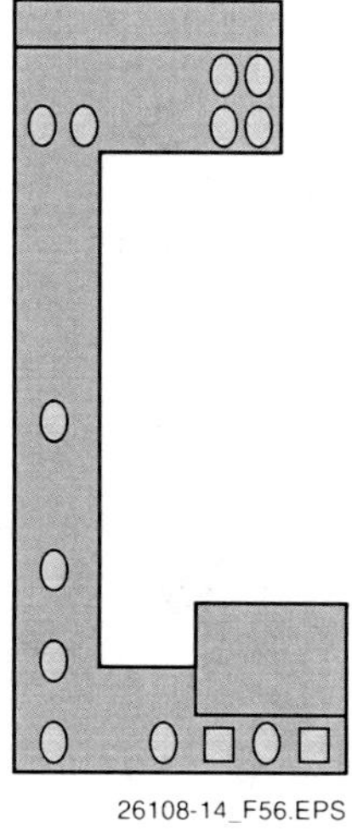

Figure 56 Standard hanger.

9.4.1 Surface Metal and Nonmetallic Raceways

Surface metal raceways consist of a wide variety of special raceways designed primarily to carry power and communications wiring to locations on the surface of ceilings or walls of building interiors.

Installation specifications of both surface metal raceways and surface nonmetallic raceways are listed in detail in *NEC Articles 386 and 388*, respectively. All these raceways must be installed in dry, interior locations. The number of conductors, their amperage, and the allowable cross-sectional area of the conductors, as well as regulations for combination raceways, are specified in *NEC Tables 310.15(B)(16) and 310.15(B)(18)* and *NEC Articles 386 and 388.*

One use of surface metal raceways is to protect conductors that run to non-accessible outlets.

Surface metal and nonmetallic raceways are divided into subgroups based on the specific purpose for which they are intended. There are three small surface raceways that are primarily used for extending power circuits from one point to another. In addition, there are six larger surface raceways that have a much wider range of applications. Typical cross sections of the first three smaller raceways are shown in *Figure 58*.

Additional surface metal raceway designs are referred to as pancake raceways, because their flat cross sections resemble pancakes. Their primary use is to extend power, lighting, telephone, or signal wire across a floor to locations away from the walls of a room without embedding them under the floor. A pancake raceway is shown in *Figure 59*.

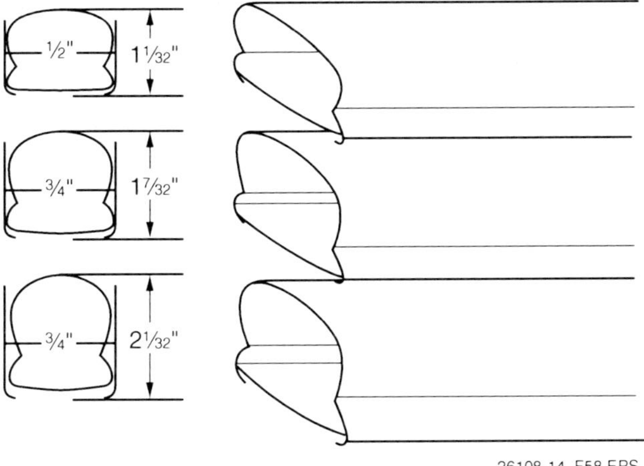

Figure 58 Smaller surface raceways.

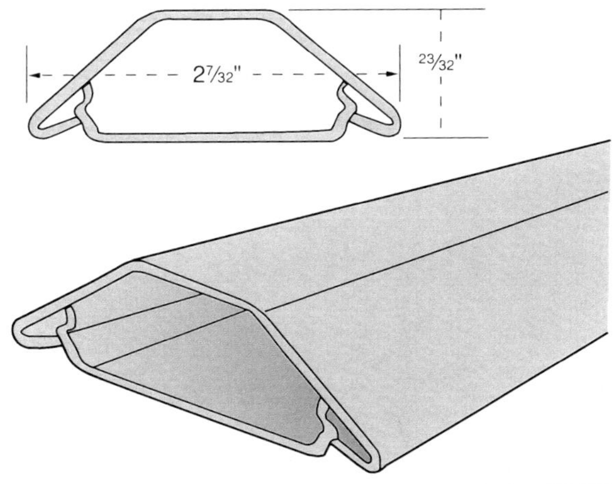

Figure 59 Pancake raceway.

There are also surface metal raceways available that house two or three different conductor raceways. These are referred to as twinduct or tripleduct. These raceways permit different circuits, such as power and signal, to be placed within the same raceway.

Nonmetallic raceways come in a variety of styles. The perimeter raceways shown in *Figure 60* are available in sizes ranging from ¾ to more than 7" wide. Many of these raceways contain barriers that allow them to carry both low voltage and power wiring.

The number and types of conductors permitted to be installed and the capacity of a particular surface raceway must be calculated and matched with *NEC*® requirements, as discussed previously. *NEC Tables 310.15(B)(16) through 310.15(B)(18)* are used for surface raceways in the same manner in which they are used for wireways. For surface raceway installations with more than three conductors in each raceway, particular reference must be made to *NEC Table 310.15(B)(3)(a).*

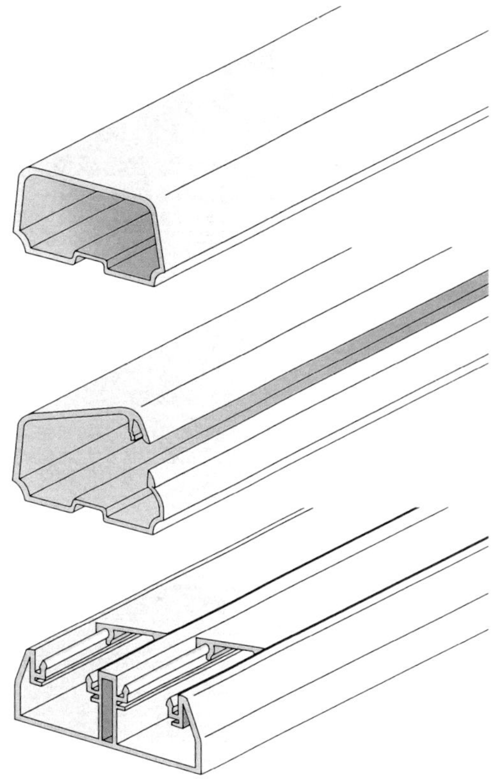

Figure 60 Examples of surface raceway.

9.4.2 Multi-Outlet Assemblies

Manufacturers offer a wide variety of multi-outlet surface raceways. Their function is to hold receptacles and other devices within the raceway. When surface raceways are used in this manner, the assembly is referred to as a multi-outlet assembly. Multi-outlet assemblies (*Figure 61*) are covered in *NEC Article 380.* Multi-outlet systems are either wired in the field or come pre-wired from the factory.

Figure 61 Multi-outlet assembly.

On Site

Surface Raceways

Surface raceways with multiple channels are commonly used in computer networking applications to provide conductors for AC power to the computers, as well as telephone and other low-voltage wiring.

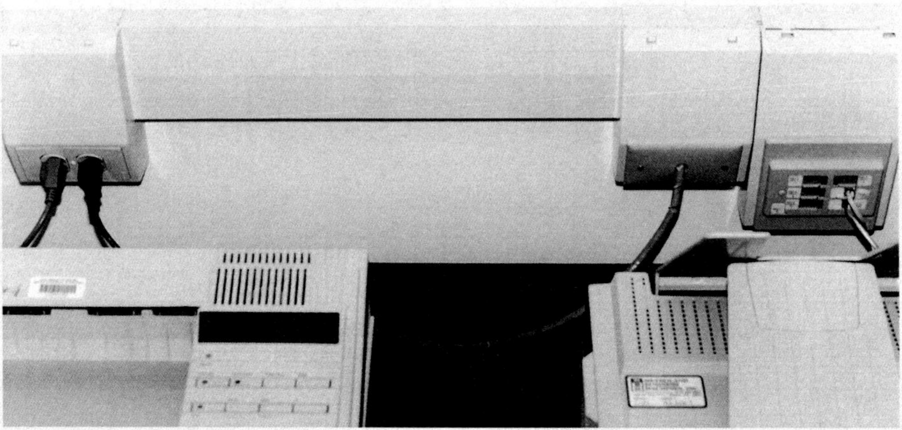

26108-14_SA12.EPS

9.4.3 Pole Systems

There are many situations in which power and other electric circuits have to be carried from overhead wiring systems to devices that are not located near existing wall outlets or control circuits. This type of wiring is typically used in open office spaces where cubicles are provided by temporary dividers. Poles are used to accomplish this. The poles usually come in lengths suitable for 10-, 12-, or 15-foot ceilings. *Figure 62* shows a typical pole base.

9.4.4 Underfloor Systems

Underfloor raceway systems were developed to provide a practical means of bringing conductors for lighting, power, and signaling to cabinets and consoles. Underfloor raceways are available in 10-foot lengths and widths of 4 and 8 inches. The sections are made with inserts spaced every 24 inches. The inserts can be removed for outlet installation. These are explained in *NEC Article 390.*

NOTE

Inserts must be installed so that they are flush with the finished grade of the floor.

Junction boxes are used to join sections of underfloor raceways. Conduit is also used with underfloor raceways by using a raceway-to-conduit connector (conduit adapter). A typical

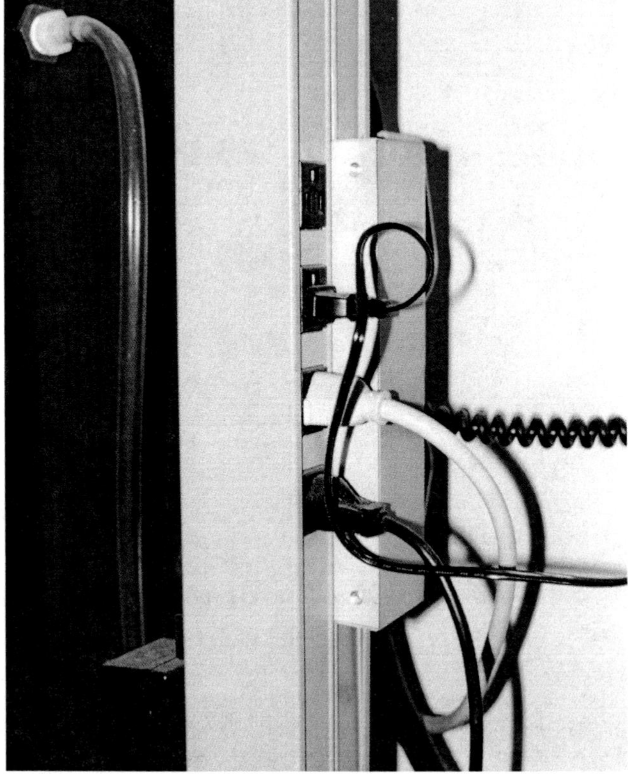

26108-14_F62.EPS

Figure 62 Power pole.

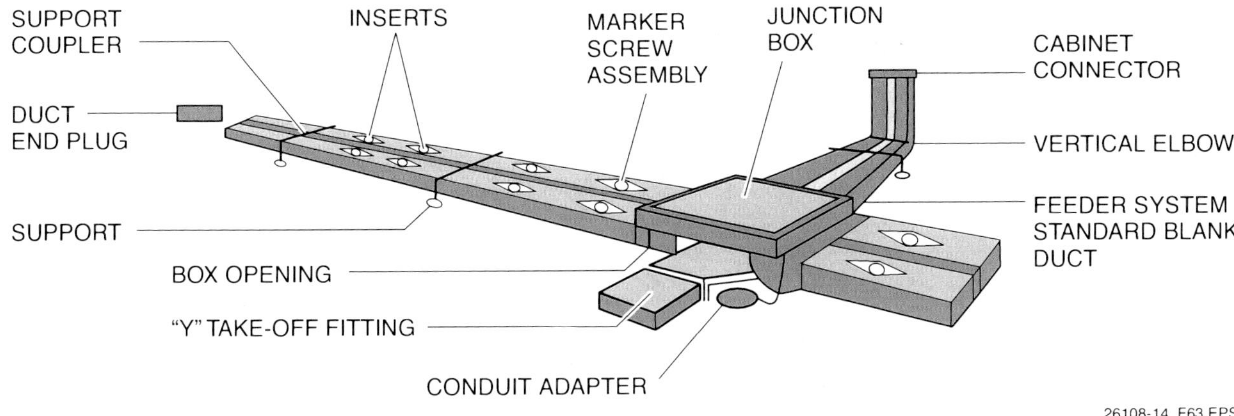

Figure 63 Underfloor raceway duct.

underfloor raceway duct with fittings is shown in *Figure 63*.

This wiring method makes it possible to place a desk or table in any location where it will always be over, or very near to, a duct line. The wiring method for lighting and power between cabinets and the raceway junction boxes may be conduit, underfloor raceway, wall elbows, and cabinet connectors. *NEC Article 390* covers the installation of underfloor raceways.

9.4.5 Cellular Metal Floor Raceways

A cellular metal floor raceway is a type of floor construction designed for use in steel-frame buildings. In these buildings, the members supporting the floor between the beams consist of sheet steel rolled into shapes. These shapes are combined to form cells, or closed passageways, which extend across the building. The cells are of various shapes and sizes, depending upon the structural strength required. The cells of this type of floor construction form the raceways, as shown in *Figure 64*.

Connections to the cells are made using headers that extend across the cells. A header connects only to those cells to be used as raceways for conductors. A junction box or access fitting is necessary at each joint where a header connects to a cell. Two or three separate headers, connecting to different sets of cells, may be used for different systems. For example, light and power, signaling systems, and public telephones would each have a separate header. A special elbow fitting is used to extend the headers up to the distribution equipment on a wall or column. *NEC Article 374* covers the installation of cellular metal floor raceways.

9.4.6 Cellular Concrete Floor Raceways

The term *precast cellular concrete floor* refers to a type of floor used in steel-frame, concrete-frame, and wall-bearing construction. In this type of system, the floor members are precast with hollow voids that form smooth, round cells. The cells form raceways, which can be adapted, using fittings, for use as underfloor raceways. A precast cellular concrete floor is fire-resistant and requires

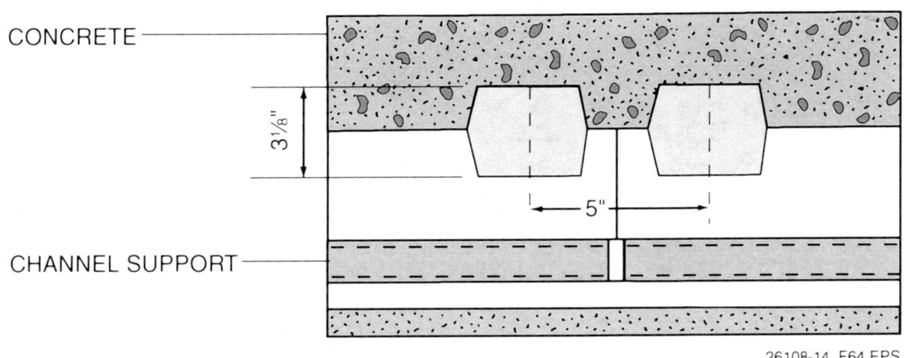

Figure 64 Cross section of a cellular floor.

no further fireproofing. The precast reinforced concrete floor members form the structural floor and are supported by beams or bearing walls. Connections to the cells are made with headers that are secured to the precast concrete floor. *NEC Article 372* covers the installation of cellular concrete floor raceways.

10.0.0 Cable Trays

Cable trays function as a support for conductors and tubing (see *NEC Article 392*). A cable tray has the advantage of easy access to conductors, and thus lends itself to installations where the addition or removal of conductors is a common practice. Cable trays are fabricated from aluminum, steel, and fiberglass. Cable trays are available in two basic forms: ladder and trough. Ladder tray, as the name implies, consists of two parallel channels connected by rungs. Trough consists of two parallel channels (side rails) having a corrugated, ventilated bottom, or a corrugated, solid bottom. There is also a special center rail cable tray available for use in light-duty applications such as telephone and sound wiring.

Cable trays are commonly available in 12- and 24-foot lengths. They are usually available in widths of 6, 9, 12, 18, 24, 30, and 36 inches, and load depths of 4, 6, and 8 inches.

Cable trays may be used in most electrical installations. Cable trays may be used in air handling ceiling space, but only to support the wiring methods permitted in such spaces by *NEC Section 300.22(C)(1)*. Also, cable trays may be used in Class 1, Division 2 locations according to *NEC Section 501.10(B)*. Cable trays may also be used above a suspended ceiling that is not used as an air handling space. Some manufacturers offer an aluminum cable tray that is coated with PVC for installation in caustic environments. A typical cable tray system with fittings is shown in *Figure 65*.

Wire and cable installation in cable trays is defined by the *NEC®*. Read *NEC Article 392* to become familiar with the requirements and restrictions made by the *NEC®* for safe installation of wire and cable in a cable tray.

Metallic cable trays that support electrical conductors must be grounded as required by *NEC Article 250*. Where steel and aluminum cable tray systems are used as an equipment grounding conductor, all of the provisions of *NEC Section 392.60* must be complied with.

WARNING!

Do not stand on, climb in, or walk on a cable tray.

10.1.0 Cable Tray Fittings

Cable tray fittings are part of the cable tray system and provide a means of changing the direction or dimension of the different trays. Some of the uses of horizontal and vertical tees, horizontal and vertical bends, horizontal crosses, reducers, barrier strips, covers, and box connectors are shown in *Figure 65*.

Think About It

Cable Trays and Wireways

What is the difference between a wireway and a cable tray? What kinds of conductors would you expect to find in a cable tray as compared to a wireway?

10.2.0 Cable Tray Supports

Cable trays are usually supported in one of five ways: direct rod suspension, trapeze mounting, center hung, wall mounting, and pipe rack mounting.

10.2.1 Direct Rod Suspension

The direct rod suspension method of supporting cable tray uses threaded rods and hanger clamps. One end of the threaded rod is connected to the ceiling or other overhead structure. The other end is connected to hanger clamps that are attached to the cable tray side rails. A direct rod suspension assembly is shown in *Figure 66*.

10.2.2 Trapeze Mounting and Center Hung Support

Trapeze mounting of cable tray is similar to direct rod suspension mounting. The difference is in the method of attaching the cable tray to the

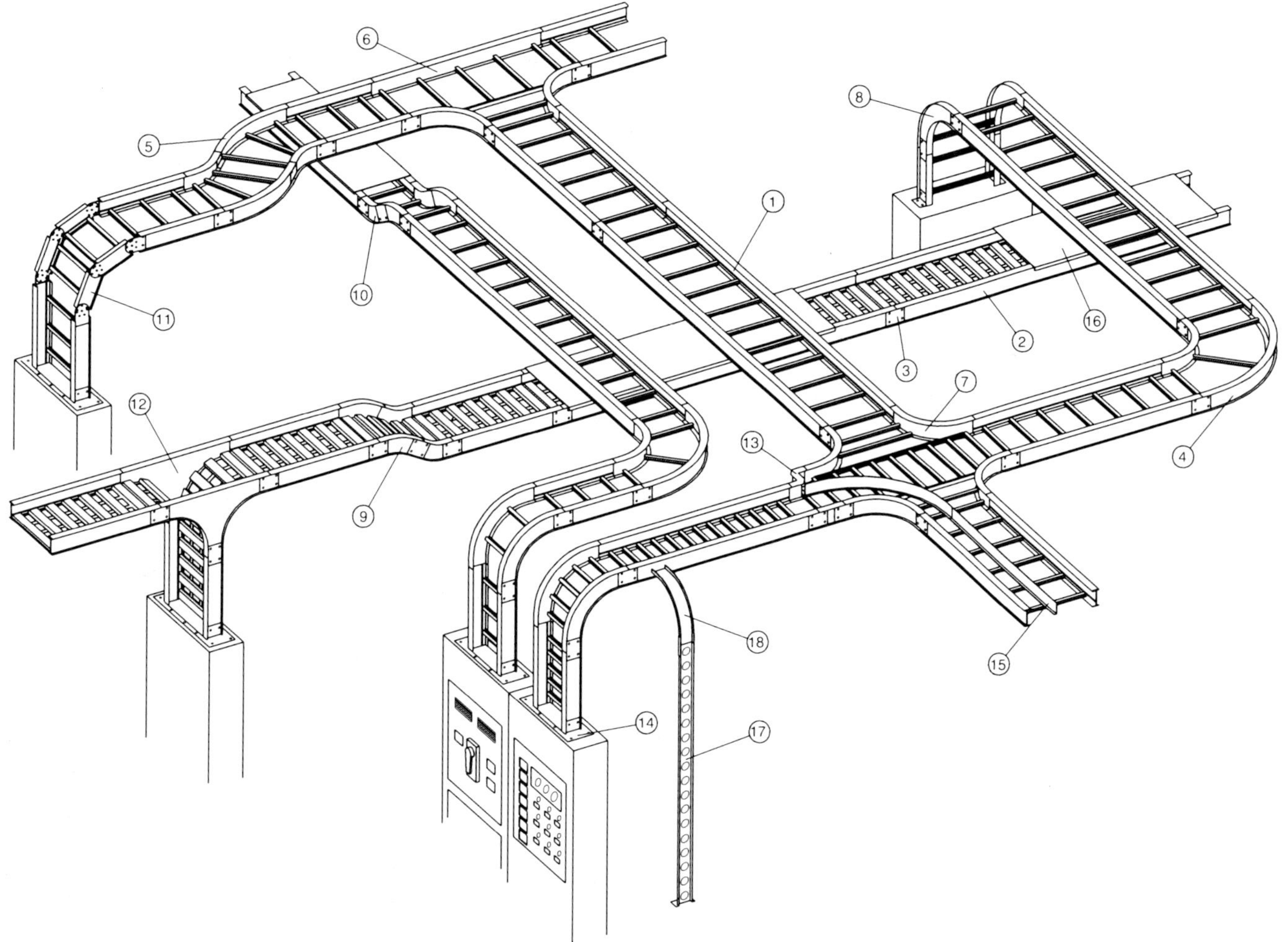

Legend

1. LADDER TYPE CABLE TRAY
2. VENTILATED TROUGH TYPE CABLE TRAY
3. STRAIGHT SPLICE PLATE
4. 90° HORIZONTAL BEND, LADDER TYPE CABLE TRAY
5. 45° HORIZONTAL BEND, LADDER TYPE CABLE TRAY
6. HORIZONTAL TEE, LADDER TYPE CABLE TRAY
7. HORIZONTAL CROSS, LADDER TYPE CABLE TRAY
8. 90° VERTICAL OUTSIDE BEND, LADDER TYPE CABLE TRAY
9. 45° VERTICAL OUTSIDE BEND, VENTILATED TYPE CABLE TRAY
10. 30° VERTICAL INSIDE BEND, LADDER TYPE CABLE TRAY
11. VERTICAL BEND SEGMENT (VBS)
12. VERTICAL TEE DOWN, VENTILATED TROUGH TYPE CABLE TRAY
13. LEFT HAND REDUCER, LADDER TYPE CABLE TRAY
14. FRAME TYPE BOX CONNECTOR
15. BARRIER STRIP STRAIGHT SECTION
16. SOLID FLANGED TRAY COVER
17. VENTILATED CHANNEL STRAIGHT SECTION
18. CHANNEL CABLE TRAY, 90° VERTICAL OUTSIDE BEND

26108-14_F65.EPS

Figure 65 Cable tray system.

threaded rods. A structural member, usually a steel channel or strut, is connected to the vertical supports to provide an appearance similar to a swing or trapeze. The cable tray is mounted to the structural member. Often, the underside of the channel or strut is used to support conduit. A trapeze mounting assembly is shown in *Figure 67*.

A method that is similar to trapeze mounting is a center hung tray support. In this case, only one rod is used and it is centered between the cable tray side rails.

On Site

Cable Tray Systems

Cable tray systems must be continuous and grounded. One of the advantages of using a cable tray system is that it makes it easy to expand or modify the wiring system following installation. Unlike conduit systems, wires can be added or changed by simply laying them into (or lifting them out of) the tray.

26108-14_SA13.EPS

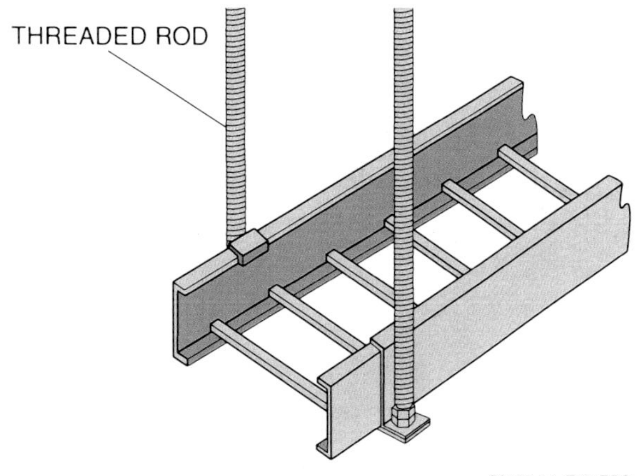

26108-14_F66.EPS

Figure 66 Direct rod suspension.

10.2.3 Wall Mounting

Wall mounting is accomplished by supporting the cable tray with structural members attached to the wall (*Figure 68*). This method of support is often used in tunnels and other underground or sheltered installations where large numbers of conductors interconnect equipment that is separated by long distances.

10.2.4 Pipe Rack Mounting

Pipe racks are structural frames used to support piping that interconnects equipment in outdoor industrial facilities. Usually, some space on the rack is reserved for conduit and cable tray. Pipe

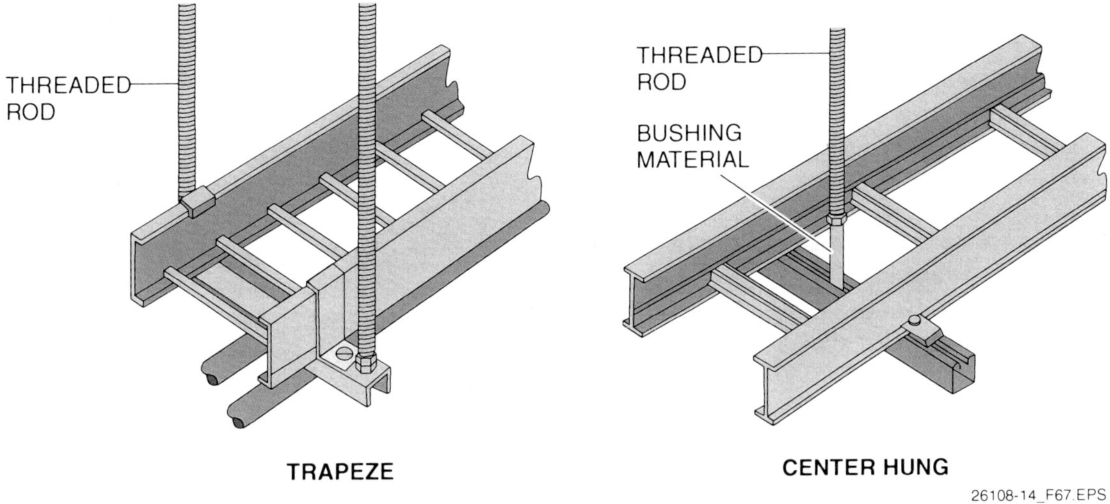

Figure 67 Trapeze mounting and center hung support.

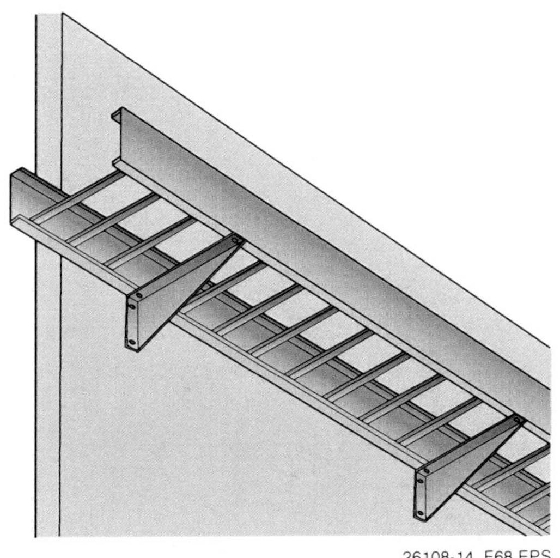

Figure 68 Wall mounting.

rack mounting of cable tray is often used when power distribution and electrical wiring is routed over a large area.

11.0.0 Storing Raceways

Proper and safe methods of storing conduit, wireways, raceways, and cable trays may sound like a simple task, but improper storage techniques can result in wasted time and damage to the raceways, as well as personal injury. There are correct ways to store raceways that will help avoid costly damage, save time in identifying stored raceways, and reduce the chance of personal injury.

Pipe racks are commonly used for storing conduit. The racks provide support to prevent bending, sagging, distorting, scratching, or marring of conduit surfaces. Most racks have compartments where different types and sizes of conduit can be separated for ease of identification and selection. The storage compartments in racks are usually elevated to help avoid damage that might occur at floor level. Conduit that is stored at floor level is easily damaged by people and other materials or equipment in the area.

The ends of stored conduit should be sealed to help prevent contamination and damage. Conduit ends can be capped, taped, or plugged.

Always inspect raceway before storing it to make sure that it is clean and not damaged. It is discouraging to get raceway for a job and find that it is dirty or damaged. Also, make sure that the raceway is stored securely so that when someone comes to get it for a job, it will not fall in any way that could cause injury.

To prevent contamination and corrosion of stored raceway, it should be covered with a tarpaulin or other suitable covering. It should also be separated from noncompatible materials such as hazardous chemicals.

Wireways, surface metal raceways, and cable trays should always be stored off the ground on boards in an area where people will not step on it and equipment will not run over it. Stepping on or running over raceway bends the metal and makes it unusable.

12.0.0 Handling Raceways

Raceway is made to strict specifications. It can be easily damaged by careless handling. From the time raceway is delivered to a job site until the installation is complete, use proper and safe handling techniques. These are a few basic guidelines for handling raceway that will help avoid damaging or contaminating it:

- Never drag raceway off a delivery truck or off other lengths of raceway.
- Never drag raceway on the ground or floor. Dragging raceway can cause damage to the ends.
- Keep the thread protection caps on when handling or transporting conduit raceway.
- Keep raceway away from any material that might contaminate it during handling.
- Flag the ends of long lengths of raceway when transporting it to the job site.
- Never drop or throw raceway when handling it.
- Never hit raceway against other objects when transporting it.
- Always use two people when carrying long pieces of raceway. Make sure that you both stay on the same side and that the load is balanced. Each person should be about one-quarter of the length of the raceway from the end. Lift and put down the raceway at the same time.

13.0.0 Ducting

In the common vocabulary of the electrical trade, a duct is a single enclosed raceway, or runway, through which conductors or cables can be led. Basically, ducting is a system of ducts. However, underground duct systems include manholes, transformer vaults, and risers.

There are several reasons for running power lines underground rather than overhead. In some situations, an overhead high-voltage line would be dangerous, or the space may not be adequate. For aesthetic reasons, architectural plans may require buried lines throughout a subdivision or a planned community. Tunnels may already exist, or be planned, for carrying steam or water lines. In any of these situations, underground installations are appropriate. Underground cables may be buried directly in the ground or run through tunnels or raceways, including conduit and recognized ducts.

In underground construction, a duct system provides a safe passageway for power lines, communication cables, or both. In buildings, underfloor raceways and cellular floor raceways are built to provide ducting so that electricity will be available throughout a large area. As an electrician, you need to know the approved methods of constructing underground ducting. You also need to know how to avoid potential electrical hazards in both original construction and maintenance. It is essential to understand the requirements and limitations imposed on running wires through underfloor and cellular floor raceways and ducts.

13.1.0 Underground Ducts

A duct consists of conduit or an approved duct system (such as HDPE) placed in a trench and covered with earth or concrete. The minimum depth at which the duct will be placed is determined using *NEC Table 300.5*. Encasing the duct in concrete or other materials provides mechanical strength and helps dissipate heat. *Figure 69* shows a duct bank in place and ready for backfill. In this case, it will be covered in concrete.

Manholes are set at intervals in an underground duct run. *Figure 70* shows a manhole with pull strings installed and tied off in preparation for the conductor installation. Manholes provide access through throats (sometimes called chimneys). At ground level, or street surface level, a manhole

26108-14_F69.EPS

Figure 69 Duct bank.

26108-14_F70.EPS

Figure 70 Manhole.

cover closes off the manhole area tightly. A duct line may consist of a single conduit or several, each carrying a cable length from one manhole to the next.

Manholes provide room for conductor installation and maintenance. Workers enter a manhole from above. In a two-way manhole, cables enter and leave in only two directions. There are also three-way and four-way manholes. Often manholes are located at the intersection of two streets so that they can be used for cables leaving in four directions. Manholes are usually constructed of brick or concrete. Their design must provide room for drainage and for workers to move around inside them. A similar opening known as a handhole is sometimes provided for splicing on lateral two-way duct lines.

Transformer vaults house power transformers, voltage regulators, network protectors, meters, and circuit breakers. A cable may end at a transformer vault. Other cables end at a customer's substation or terminate as risers that connect with overhead lines.

13.2.0 Duct Materials

Underground duct lines can be made of fiber, vitrified tile, rigid metal or nonmetallic conduit, or poured concrete. The inside diameter of the ducting for a specific job is determined by the size of the cable that will be drawn into the duct. Sizes from two to six inches (inside diameter) are available for most types of ducting.

> **WARNING!**
>
> Be careful when working with unfamiliar duct materials. In older installations, asbestos/cement duct may have been used. You must be certified to remove or disturb asbestos.

Rigid nonmetallic conduit may be made of PVC (polyvinyl chloride), PE (polyethylene), or styrene. Since this type of conduit is available in lengths up to 20 feet, fewer couplings are needed than with other types of ducting. PVC is popular because it is easy to install, requires less labor than other types of conduit, and is low in cost.

13.3.0 Monolithic Concrete Duct

Monolithic concrete duct is poured at the job site. Multiple duct lines can be formed using rubber tubing cores on spacers. The cores may be removed after the concrete has set. A die containing steel tubes, known as a boat, can also be used to form ducts. It is pulled slowly through the trench on a track as concrete is poured from the top. Poured concrete ducting made by either method is relatively expensive, but offers the advantage of creating a very clean duct interior with no residue that can decay. The rubber core method is especially useful for curving or turning part of a duct system.

13.4.0 Cable-in-Duct

One of the most popular duct types is the cable-in-duct. This type of duct comes from the manufacturer with cables already installed. The duct comes in a reel and can be laid in the trench with ease. The installed cables can be withdrawn in the future, if necessary. This type of duct, because of the form in which it comes, reduces the need for fittings and couplings. It is most frequently used for street lighting systems.

14.0.0 Construction Methods

Conduit and box installation varies with the type of construction. This section discusses some special requirements for masonry and concrete, metal framing, wood, and structural steel construction.

14.1.0 Masonry and Concrete Flush-Mount Construction

In a reinforced concrete construction environment, the conduit and boxes must be embedded in the concrete to achieve a flush surface. Ordinary boxes may be used, but special concrete boxes are preferred and are available in depths up to six inches. These boxes have special ears by which they are nailed to the wooden forms for the concrete. When installing them, stuff the boxes tightly with paper to prevent concrete from seeping in. *Figure 71* shows an installed box.

Flush construction can also be done on existing concrete walls, but this requires chiseling a channel and box opening, anchoring the box and conduit, and then resealing the wall.

To achieve flush construction with masonry walls, the most acceptable method is for the electrician to work closely with the mason laying the blocks. When the construction blocks reach the convenience outlet elevation, boxes are made up as shown in *Figure 72*. The figure shows a raised tile ring or box device cover.

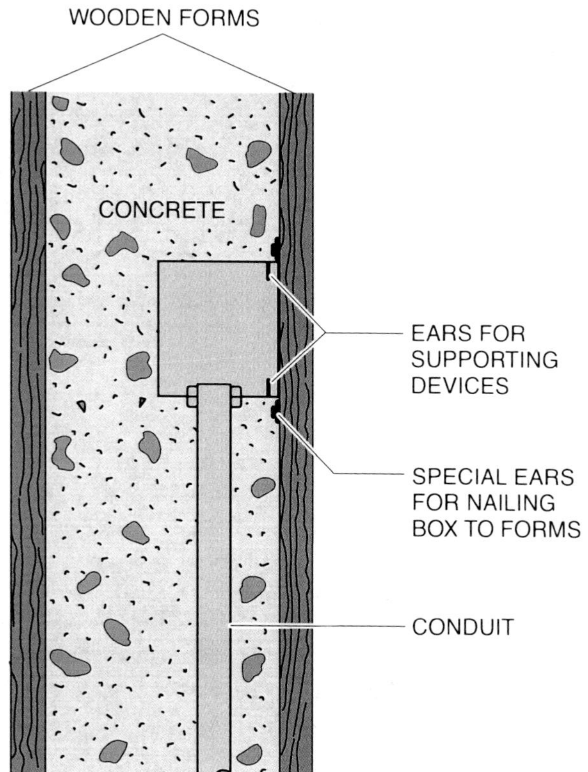

Figure 71 Concrete flush-mount installation.

Figure 72 Box with raised ring.

Figure 73 shows a masonry box that needs no extension or deep plaster ring to bring it to the surface.

NOTE

The electrician must work with the mason to ensure the box is properly grouted and sealed.

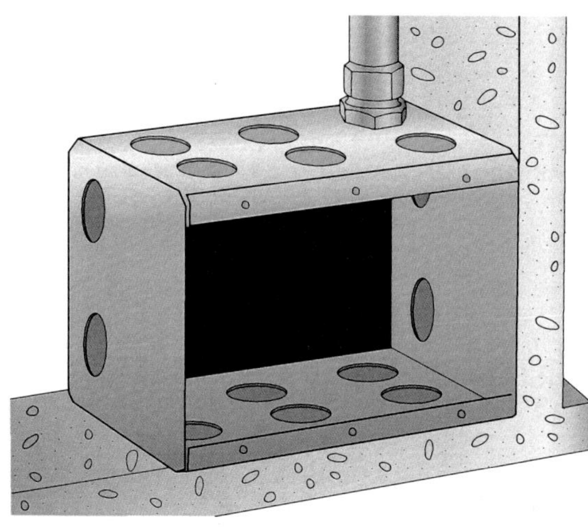

Figure 73 Three-gang concrete box.

Sections of conduit are then coupled in short (4- or 5-foot) lengths. This is done because it is impractical for the mason to maneuver blocks over 10-foot sections of conduit.

14.2.0 Metal Stud Environment

Metal stud walls are a popular method of construction for the interior walls of commercial buildings. Metal stud framing consists of relatively thin metal channel studs, usually constructed of galvanized steel and with an overall dimension the same as standard 2 × 4 wooden studs. Wiring in this type of construction is relatively easy when compared to masonry.

EMT conduit and MC cable are the most common type of wiring methods for metal stud environments. Metal studs usually have some number of pre-punched holes that can be used to route the conduit. If a pre-punched hole is not located where it needs to be, holes can be easily punched in the metal stud with a hole cutter or knockout punch (*Figure 74*).

WARNING!

Cutting or punching metal studs can create sharp edges. Avoid contact that can result in cuts.

Boxes can be secured to the metal stud using self-tapping screws or one of the many types of box supports available. EMT conduit is supported by the metal studs using conduit straps or other approved

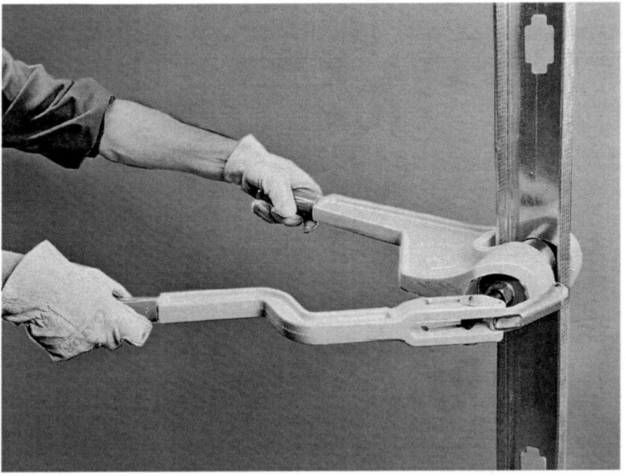

26108-14_F74.EPS

Figure 74 Metal stud punch.

26108-14_F75.EPS

Figure 75 NM cable protected by grommets.

methods. It is important that the conduit be properly supported to facilitate pulling the conductors through the tubing. Boxes are mounted on the metal studs so that the box will be flush with the finished walls. You must know what the finished wall thickness is going to be to properly secure the boxes to the metal studs. For example, if the finished wall will be ⅝-inch drywall, then the box must be fastened so that it protrudes ⅝ of an inch from the metal stud.

WARNING!

When using a screw gun or cordless drill to mount boxes to studs, keep the hand holding the box away from the gun/drill to avoid injury.

Per *NEC Section 300.4(B)(1),* NM cable run through metal studs must be protected by listed bushings or listed grommets (*Figure 75*). This protects the cables from the friction of pulling during installation and from the weight of the cable and vibrations following the installation.

14.3.0 Wood Frame Environment

At one time, the use of rigid conduit in partitions and ceilings was a time-consuming operation. Thinwall conduit makes an easier and quicker job, largely because of the types of fittings that are specially adapted to it.

Figure 76 shows two methods of running thinwall conduit in these locations: boring timbers and notching them. When boring, holes must be drilled large enough for the tubing to be inserted between the studs. The tubing is cut rather short, calling for multiple couplings. EMT can be bowed quite a bit while threading through holes in studs. Boring is the preferred method.

WARNING!

Always wear safety goggles when boring wood.

NEC Section 300.4 addresses the requirements to prevent physical damage to conductors and cabling in wood members. By keeping the edge of the drilled hole 1¼" from the closest edge of the stud, nails are not likely to penetrate the stud far enough to damage the cables. The building codes provide maximum requirements for bored or notched holes in studs.

NEC Section 300.4(A)(1) requires the use of a steel plate or bushing at least 1⁄16" thick or a listed steel nail plate where wiring is installed through bored wooden members less than 1¼" from the nearest edge. See *Figure 77*. Nail plates are also required to protect the conductors in all notched wooden members per *NEC Section 300.4(A)(2)*.

The exception in the *NEC®* permits IMC, RMC, PVC, and EMT to be installed through bored holes

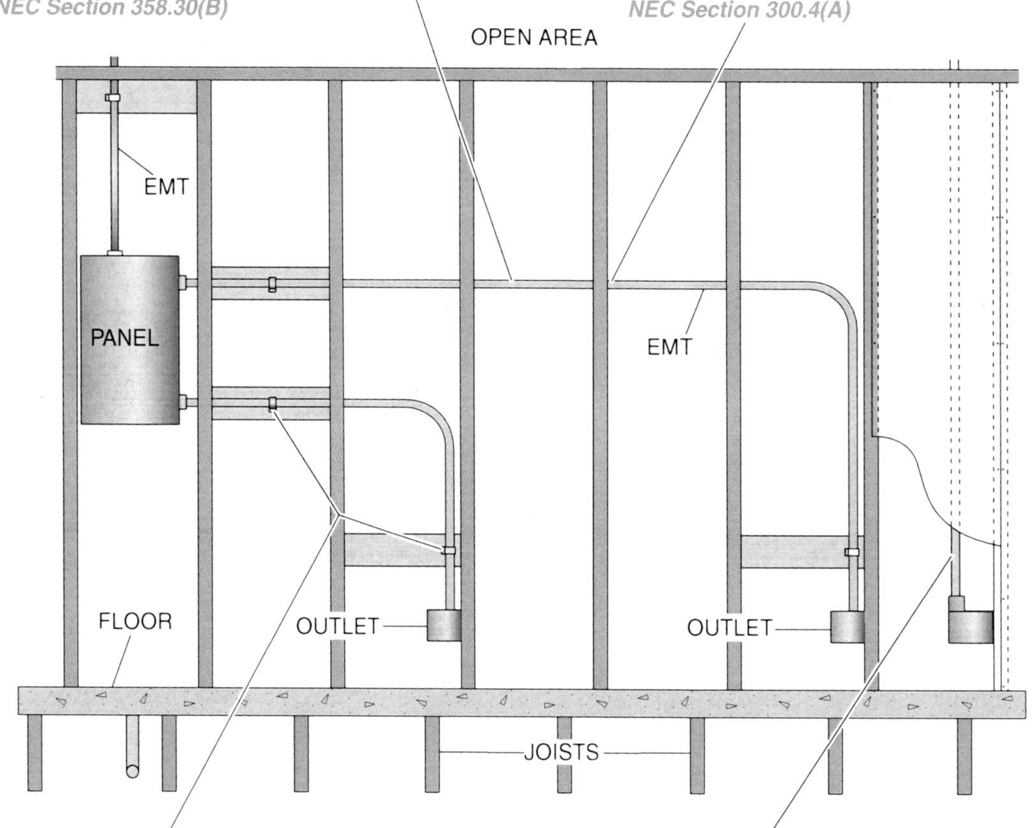
Horizontal runs of EMT may be supported by openings in framing members at intervals not greater than 10 feet when securely fastened within a distance of 3 feet at each of its termination points.
NEC Section 358.30(B)
EMT may be run through wood joists where the edges of the bored holes are less than 1 1/4" from the nearest edge of the stud, or where the studs are notched without the need for a steel plate.
NEC Section 300.4(A)
OPEN AREA
EMT
PANEL
EMT
FLOOR
OUTLET
OUTLET
JOISTS
EMT must be securely fastened in place every 10 feet and within 3 feet of each outlet box, device box, cabinet, conduit body, or other termination.
NEC Section 358.30(A) and (B)
Unbroken lengths of EMT can be fastened at a distance of up to 5 feet from a termination point when structural members do not readily permit fastening within 3 feet.
NEC Section 358.30(A), Exception 1
Where fastening of EMT is impractical in finished buildings or prefinished walls, unbroken lengths of EMT may be fished.
NEC Section 358.30(A), Exception 2
26108-14_F76.EPS

Figure 76 Installing wire or conduit in a wood-frame building.

or laid in notches less than 1¼" from the nearest edge without a steel plate or bushing.

Because of its weakening effect upon the structure, notching should be resorted to only where absolutely necessary. Notches should be as narrow as possible and in no case deeper than ⅟₁₆ the stock of a bearing timber. A bearing timber supports floor joists or other weight.

> **NOTE**
> Always check with the architect before notching or drilling.

Some wood I-beams are manufactured with perforated knockouts in their web, approximately 12" apart. Never notch or drill through the beam flange or cut other openings in the web without checking the manufacturer's specification sheet.

Also, do not drill or notch other types of engineered lumber without first checking the specification sheets.

14.4.0 Metal Buildings

Many commercial and industrial buildings are prefabricated structures with steel structural supports, and roofing and siding made of light-gauge metal sheets (*Figure 78*). Conduit can be

Figure 77 Steel nail plate.

Figure 78 Metal building.

routed across the structural members that support the roof. *NEC Section 300.4(E)* states that a cable, raceway, or box in exposed or concealed locations under metal-corrugated sheet roof decking must be installed and supported so the nearest outside surface of the cable or raceway is not less than 1½" from the nearest surface of the roof decking. The roof structure can consist of beams and purlins (*Figure 79*) or open-web steel joists (*Figure 80*).

Beams and purlins should not be drilled through; consequently, the conduit is supported

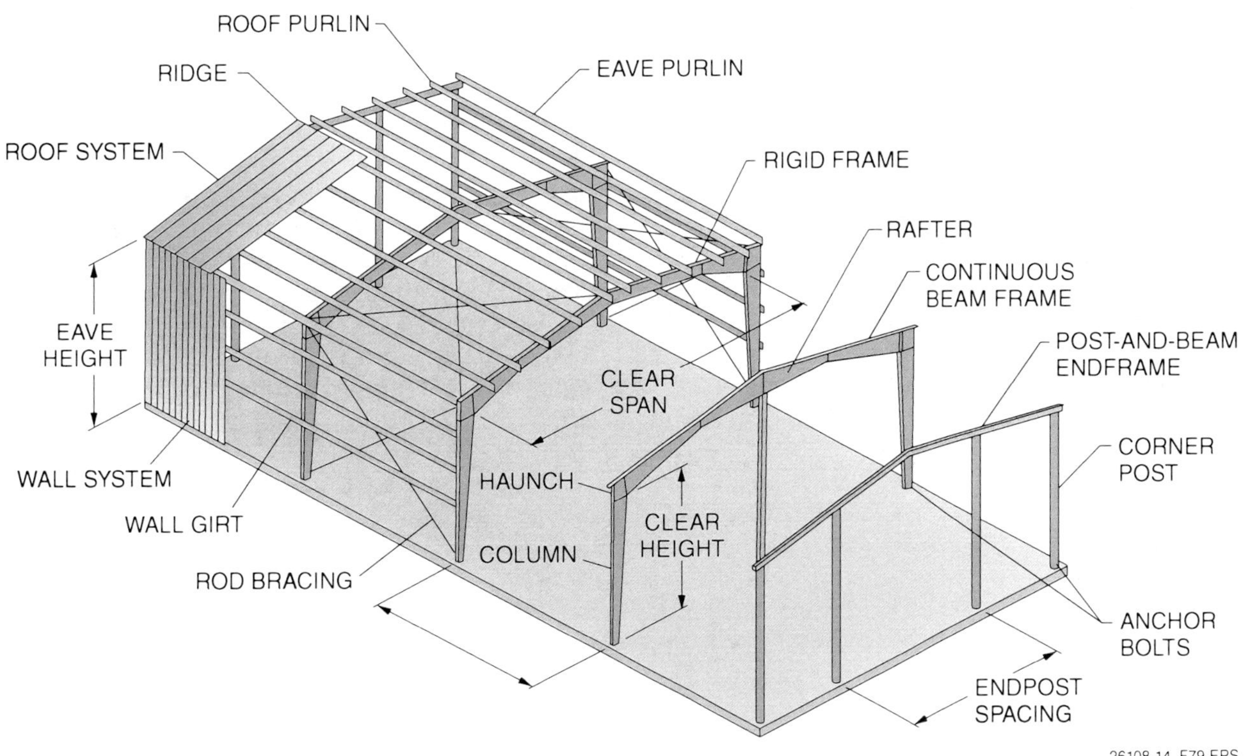

Figure 79 Beam and purlin roof system.

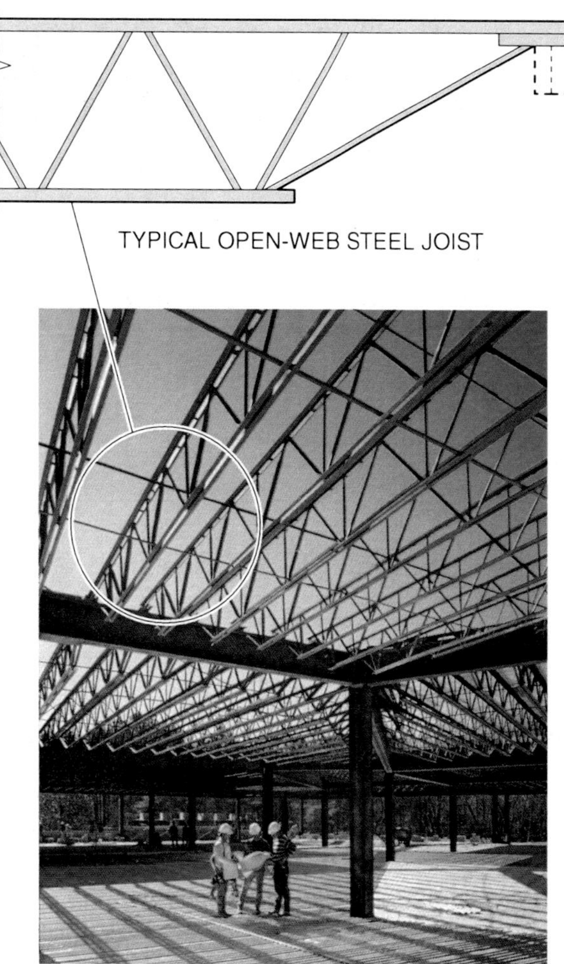

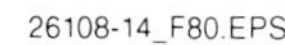
26108-14_F80.EPS

Figure 80 Open-web steel joist roof supports.

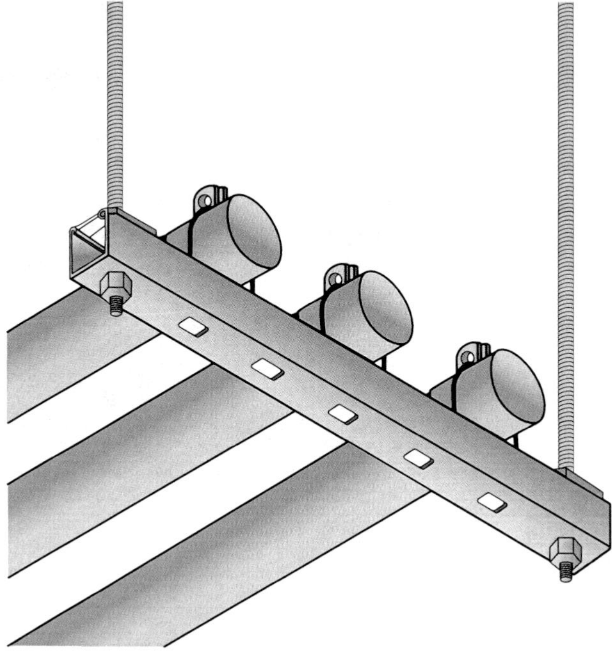
26108-14_F81.EPS

Figure 81 Steel strut system.

from the metal beams by anchoring devices designed especially for that purpose. The supports attach to the beams or supports and have clamps to secure the conduit to the structure. All conduit runs should be plumb since they are exposed. Bends should be correct and have a neat and orderly appearance.

Rigid metal conduit is often required in metal buildings. If a large number of conduits are run along the same path, strut-type systems are used. These systems are sometimes referred to as Unistrut® systems (Unistrut® is a manufacturer of these systems). Another manufacturer of strut systems is B-Line systems. Both are very similar. These systems use a channel-type member that can support conduits from the ceiling by using threaded rod supports for the channel, as shown in *Figure 81*. Strut channel can also be secured to masonry walls to support vertical runs of conduit, wireways, and various types of boxes.

What's wrong with this picture?

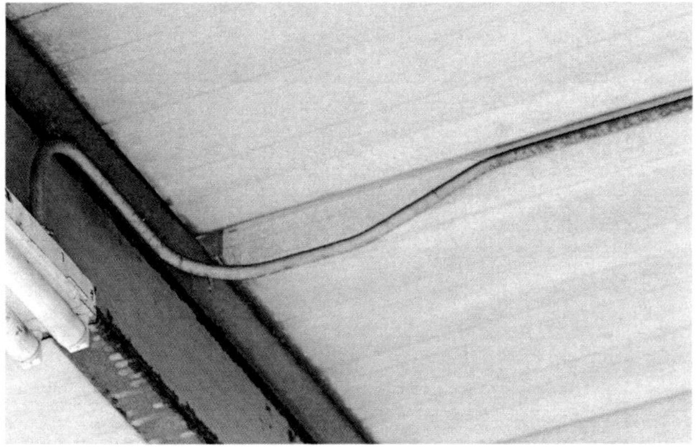

26108-14_SA14.EPS

Think About It

Putting It All Together

Think about the effort that goes into the design of a large industrial installation. If you were to design a large complex, such as the one shown here, where would you start and why?

26108-14_SA15.EPS

SUMMARY

This module discussed the various types of raceways, boxes, and fittings, including their uses and procedures for installation. The primary purpose of raceways is to house electric wire used for power distribution, communication, or electronic signal transmission. Raceways provide protection to the wiring and even a means of identifying one type of wire from another when run adjacent to each other. This process requires proper planning to allow for current needs, future expansion, and a neat and orderly appearance.

Review Questions

1. The lightest duty and most widely used non-flexible metal conduit is _____.
   a. electrical metallic tubing
   b. rigid metal conduit
   c. aluminum conduit
   d. plastic-coated RMC

2. EMT and RMC connectors are interchangeable.
   a. True
   b. False

3. Which of the following is often referred to as thinwall conduit?
   a. IMC
   b. EMT
   c. RMC
   d. Galvanized rigid steel conduit

4. RMC is made of _____.
   a. cast iron
   b. steel or aluminum
   c. copper or aluminum
   d. PVC

5. A Type LB conduit body has a cover on _____.
   a. the left
   b. the right
   c. the back
   d. both sides

6. The fitting used to protect conductors from the sharp edges of conduit where it enters a box is called a _____.
   a. bushing
   b. locknut
   c. coupling
   d. nipple

7. Hammer-set anchors are designed for use in _____.
   a. wood
   b. metal studs
   c. concrete
   d. structural steel

8. *NEC Section 376.56(A)* limits wireway fill to no more than _____ of the cross-sectional area of the wireway.
   a. 40%
   b. 60%
   c. 75%
   d. 90%

9. Raceways designed to extend conductors across a floor without embedding it in the floor are called _____.
   a. cellular raceways
   b. raceway ducts
   c. cellular ductways
   d. pancake raceways

10. Which of the following regulations applies to drilling of wood joists and girders?
    a. A joist cannot be drilled unless approved by the manufacturer.
    b. They can only be drilled in the center third.
    c. The hole must be at least 1 inch from an edge.
    d. The hole diameter must not exceed one-half of the depth of the girder or joist.

Trade Terms Quiz

Fill in the blank with the correct term that you learned from your study of this module.

1. A(n) ____________ area is one that can be reached for service or repair.
2. When something is in a(n) ____________, it is not permanently closed in by the structure or finish of a building.
3. When materials meet a regulatory agency's requirements, the material is then said to be ____________.
4. ____________ is a regulatory agency that evaluates and approves electrical components and equipment.
5. A(n) ____________ is used to make a continuous grounding path between equipment and ground.
6. ____________ are rigid structures, either suspended or mounted, that are used to support electrical conductors.
7. Similar to pipe, ____________ is a round raceway that houses conductors.
8. A(n)____________ is a bend made in a piece of conduit to alter its course.
9. ____________ are enclosed channels that are used to house wires and cables.
10. ____________ are steel troughs designed to carry electrical wire and cable.
11. A(n) ____________ is the connection of two or more conductors.
12. An intermediate point on a main circuit where another wire is connected to supply electrical current to another circuit is called a(n) ____________.
13. Electrical connectors that could be exposed to the environment are housed in long, narrow boxes, or ____________.

Trade Terms

Accessible
Approved
Bonding wire
Cable trays
Conduit
Exposed location
Kick
Raceways
Splice
Tap
Trough
Underwriters Laboratories, Inc. (UL)
Wireways

Module 26108-14
Supplemental Exercises

1. Most electrical equipment that has a metal frame must be ______________.

2. When installing EMT in a wet location, what type of fittings must be used?
   a. Setscrew
   b. Compression
   c. Raintight
   d. Steel

3. Conductors, along with splices and taps, must not fill a wireway to more than ______________ of its cross-sectional area.
   a. 20%
   b. 30%
   c. 75%
   d. 90%

4. Which of the following covers the installation requirements for cable tray?
   a. *NEC Article 333*
   b. *NEC Article 338*
   c. *NEC Article 392*
   d. *NEC Article 394*

5. True or False? Two-inch IMC conduit has the same internal diameter as two-inch RMC.

6. Which of the following cannot be used as an equipment grounding conductor?
   a. Rigid metal conduit
   b. Rigid nonmetallic conduit
   c. Electrical metallic tubing
   d. Intermediate metal conduit

7. Flexible metal conduit can be connected to rigid metal conduit using a(n) ______________ coupling.

8. Which of the following covers grounding provisions for metal boxes?
   a. *NEC Section 500.8(A)*
   b. *NEC Section 250.30(A)*
   c. *NEC Section 250.53(C)*
   d. *NEC Section 314.40(D)*

9. What type of rigid nonmetallic conduit may be installed where exposed to physical damage?
   a. Type DB Schedule 80
   b. Type DB Schedule 40
   c. Type EB
   d. Type 1

10. RMC is commonly used in ______________ locations.

11. What type of conduit body is used to provide a junction point for three intersecting conduits?

    a. Type LL
    b. Type LR
    c. Type C
    d. Type T

12. When installing conduit in a wet area, a(n) ____________ air space must be provided between it and the supporting surface.

13. Conductors installed in PVC are subject to a(n) ____________.

    a. increase in operating temperature
    b. decrease in operating temperature
    c. increase in ampacity
    d. reduced voltage drop

14. Flexible metal conduit must be supported within ____________ inches of each end.

    a. 8
    b. 10
    c. 12
    d. 18

15. When installing a cable system near a metal corrugated sheet roofing deck, a spacing of ____________ must be maintained from any point of the roof system.

    a. 1¼"
    b. 1⅜"
    c. 1½"
    d. 1¾"

Cornerstone of Craftsmanship

Leonard "Skip" Layne

Rust Constructors Inc.

How did you choose a career in the electrical field?
I think the electrical field chose me. My father was a contractor for several years before closing shop and accepting a job as an electrical superintendent with the Rust Engineering Company. That happened when I was nine years old. After being moved around the country for the next several years and working as an apprentice on Dad's projects during my college summers, I couldn't think of anything that I would rather do.

Tell us about your apprenticeship experience.
I've never attended a formal apprenticeship school. There are probably several in our group who might say that they suspected this. My electrical education came from field work exposure and several electrical and engineering courses and seminars I've attended over the years.

I'm happy to say that I'm still learning and I've learned a great deal while working on the NCCER Electrical Committee and from my association with the other subject matter experts.

What positions have you held in the industry?
I started as a field apprentice on a tire plant in Madison, Tennessee, in 1959. I've held field positions as an apprentice, journeyman, field engineer, start-up manager, and superintendent. I spent a number of years estimating work, and I established the material control department for another major open-shop contractor several years ago. I managed the project controls group on a nuclear project for another open-shop contractor. I even spent a few years as vice president with an underground utility/treatment plant contractor.

What would you say is the primary factor in achieving success?
Keep learning. Work hard. I've had to work sixteen-hour days on the job site and in the office in order to meet the schedule and incorporate changes. Do what is asked of you and do it well.

What does your current job involve?
My job title says that I'm the Construction Engineering Manager for Rust, but the lack of a definitive job title means that I do whatever the company needs me to do at the time. I qualify the company's electrical licenses in seventeen states where we work.

Recently, Rust volunteered my services to the Gulf Coast Workforce Initiative, a business roundtable initiative to train 20,000 new construction workers for the Gulf Coast area devastated by hurricanes Katrina and Rita.

Do you have any advice for someone just entering the trade?
Get all of the classroom learning you can. Go through all four levels of the Electrical program while working in the field. Ask questions and try to get assigned to as many new and different tasks as you can. All of our larger ABC contractors have excellent supervisory training programs and you need to get into those after your craft training. Be adaptable and keep learning.

Cornerstone of Craftsmanship

Al Hamilton

Willmar Electric Service

How did you become an electrician?

I was in college and met Ed, an electrician who told me about wiring buildings. I went to work for him part time at first and liked it which led to my becoming his apprentice. He was tough taskmaster who cared about his apprentices and he was an excellent communicator and teacher.

How did you get your training?

My training was 100% on the job. Everything was learned "hands on."

I was very fortunate to work for Ed and other experienced electricians who were true craftsmen.

What factor or factors have contributed to your success?

Work ethic, relationships, and reading. A good work ethic has allowed me to overcome mistakes and keep working to learn our craft. I was able to learn about electrical work, business, and life through relationships. I have always looked for successful people to listen and learn from. I discovered that many successful people are happy to share their ideas and that proved to be the key to personal growth. I was told long ago that if I could force myself to read just 10 pages a day that I could read a book a month because the average book is 300 pages. I have done this for many years and I read books on many subjects including the Bible, business, history, biographies, and money and, of course, the *National Electrical Code*. Through reading you can educate yourself and become a more knowledgeable and interesting person who others will look to for advice.

What does your current job entail?

I work for a leading electrical company, Willmar Electric Service Corp. and my responsibilities are business development and estimating. This includes maintaining relationships with our existing customers and finding new customers to work for. Our estimating team uses estimating software to bid jobs. We do competitive bidding to win jobs and we also estimate for design/build projects and projects that are negotiated with customers.

Any advice for apprentices just beginning their careers?

Work for an organization that shares your values and will recognize and reward your efforts. Don't ever give up! Who you become will depend largely on the people you meet and the books that you read. Find honest, ethical people who have demonstrated success and get to know them. If you have not been reading, start today—make yourself do it. Get involved in helping others by becoming a leader in your company, helping out at church, and passing on what you have learned.

Trade Terms Introduced in This Module

Accessible: Able to be reached, as for service or repair.

Approved: Meeting the requirements of an appropriate regulatory agency.

Bonding wire: A wire used to make a continuous grounding path between equipment and ground.

Cable trays: Rigid structures used to support electrical conductors.

Conduit: A round raceway, similar to pipe, that houses conductors.

Exposed location: Not permanently closed in by the structure or finish of a building; able to be installed or removed without damage to the structure.

Kick: A bend in a piece of conduit, usually less than 45°, made to change the direction of the conduit.

Raceways: Enclosed channels designed expressly for holding wires, cables, or busbars, with additional functions as permitted in the *NEC*®.

Splice: Connection of two or more conductors.

Tap: Intermediate point on a main circuit where another wire is connected to supply electrical current to another circuit.

Trough: A long, narrow box used to house electrical connections that could be exposed to the environment.

Underwriters Laboratories, Inc. (UL): An agency that evaluates and approves electrical components and equipment.

Wireways: Steel troughs designed to carry electrical wire and cable.

Additional Resources

This module presents thorough resources for task training. The following resource material is suggested for further study.

Benfield Conduit Bending Manual, 2nd Edition. Overland Park, KS: EC&M Books.

National Electrical Code® Handbook, Latest Edition. Quincy, MA: National Fire Protection Association.

Figure Credits

Associated Builders and Contractors, Inc., Module opener

Topaz Publications, Inc., Figures 3, 4A, 8, 12–19, 25, 35B (photo), 42, 62, 78, SA01–SA09, SA11, SA12, SA15

Tim Dean, Figures 4B, 61, 77, SA10, SA14

Photo courtesy of Simpson Strong-Tie Company, Inc., Figure 32 (photo)

Wiremold/Legrand, Figures 58, 59

Panduit Corp., Figure 60

Cooper B-Line, Figure 65

Jim Mitchem, Figures 69, 70, SA13

Greenlee/A Textron Company, Figures 74, 75

VP Buildings, Figure 79

Nucor Corporation - Vulcraft Group, Figure 80 (photo)

Reprinted with permission from NFPA 70-2014, *National Electrical Code®*, Copyright © 2013, National Fire Protection Association, Quincy, MA. This reprinted material is not the complete and official position of the NFPA on the referenced subject, which is represented only by the standard in its entirety., Table 1

NCCER CURRICULA — USER UPDATE

NCCER makes every effort to keep its textbooks up-to-date and free of technical errors. We appreciate your help in this process. If you find an error, a typographical mistake, or an inaccuracy in NCCER's curricula, please fill out this form (or a photocopy), or complete the online form at **www.nccer.org/olf**. Be sure to include the exact module ID number, page number, a detailed description, and your recommended correction. Your input will be brought to the attention of the Authoring Team. Thank you for your assistance.

Instructors – If you have an idea for improving this textbook, or have found that additional materials were necessary to teach this module effectively, please let us know so that we may present your suggestions to the Authoring Team.

NCCER Product Development and Revision

13614 Progress Blvd., Alachua, FL 32615

Email: curriculum@nccer.org
Online: www.nccer.org/olf

❑ Trainee Guide ❑ AIG ❑ Exam ❑ PowerPoints Other ______________________

Craft / Level: Copyright Date:

Module ID Number / Title:

Section Number(s):

Description:

Recommended Correction:

Your Name:

Address:

Email: Phone:

Conduit Bending

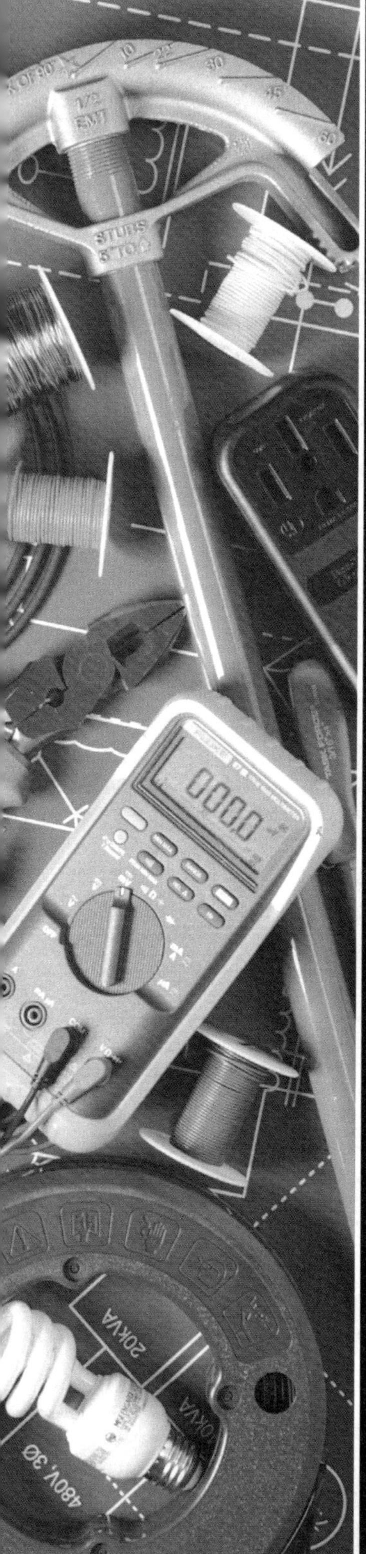

John Paul Jones Arena

The Barton Malow Company won an Aon Build America Award for New Construction Management for its work with the University of Virginia's sports and entertainment complex in Charlottesville, Va.

26204-14

Trainees with successful module completions may be eligible for credentialing through NCCER's National Registry. To learn more, go to **www.nccer.org** or contact us at **1.888.622.3720.** Our website has information on the latest product releases and training, as well as online versions of our *Cornerstone* magazine and Pearson's product catalog.

Your feedback is welcome. You may email your comments to **curriculum@nccer.org,** send general comments and inquiries to **info@nccer.org,** or fill in the User Update form at the back of this module.

This information is general in nature and intended for training purposes only. Actual performance of activities described in this manual requires compliance with all applicable operating, service, maintenance, and safety procedures under the direction of qualified personnel. References in this manual to patented or proprietary devices do not constitute a recommendation of their use.

26204-14
Conduit Bending

Objectives

When you have completed this module, you will be able to do the following:

1. Describe the process of conduit bending using power tools.
2. Identify all parts of electric and hydraulic benders.
3. Bend offsets, kicks, saddles, segmented, and parallel bends.
4. Explain the requirements of the *National Electrical Code®* (*NEC®*) for bending conduit.
5. Compute the radius, degrees in bend, developed length, and gain for conduit up to six inches.

Performance Tasks

Under the supervision of the instructor, you should be able to do the following:

1. Use an electric or hydraulic bender to bend a 1"conduit stub-up to an exact distance of 15¼" above the deck.
2. Make an offset in a length of conduit to miss a 10" high obstruction with a clearance between the obstruction and the conduit of not less than 1" nor more than 1½".
3. Make a saddle in a length of conduit to cross an 8" pipe with 1" clearance between the pipe and the conduit.

Trade Terms

Approximate ram travel
Back-to-back bend
Bending protractor
Bending shot
Concentric bending
Conduit
Degree indicator
Developed length
Elbow
Gain
Inside diameter (ID)
Kicks
Leg length
Ninety-degree bend
Offsets
One-shot shoe
Outside diameter (OD)
Radius
Rise
Segment bend
Segmented bending shoe
Springback
Stub-up
Sweep bend
Take-up (comeback)

Required Trainee Materials

1. Pencil and paper
2. Appropriate personal protective equipment
3. Copy of the latest edition of the *National Electrical Code®*

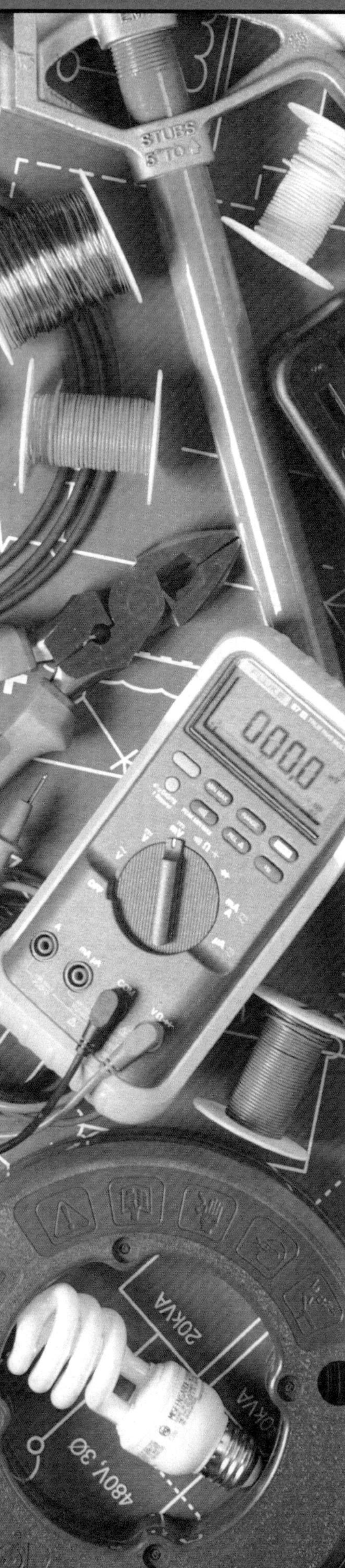

Contents

Topics to be presented in this module include:

Figures and Tables

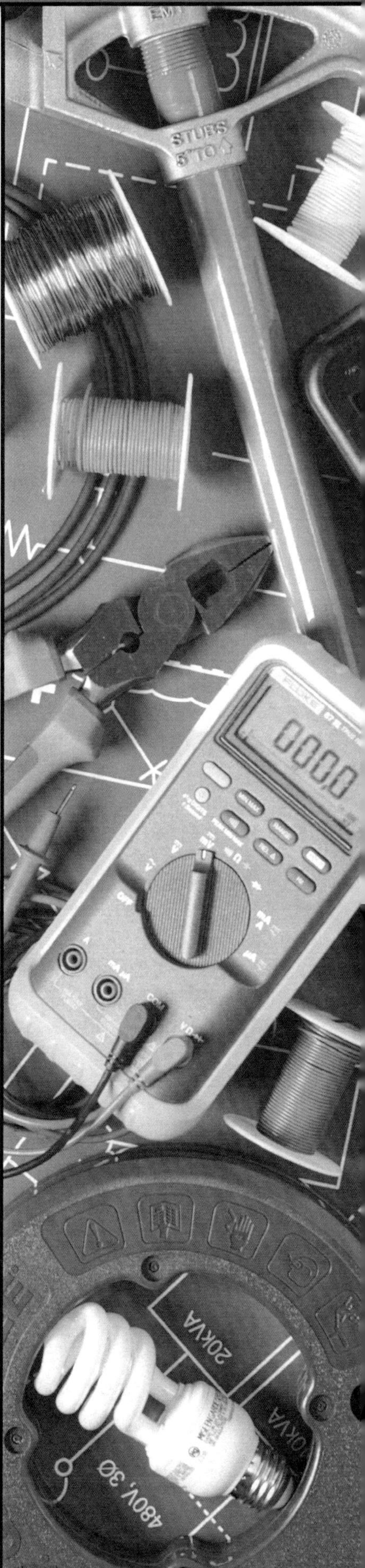

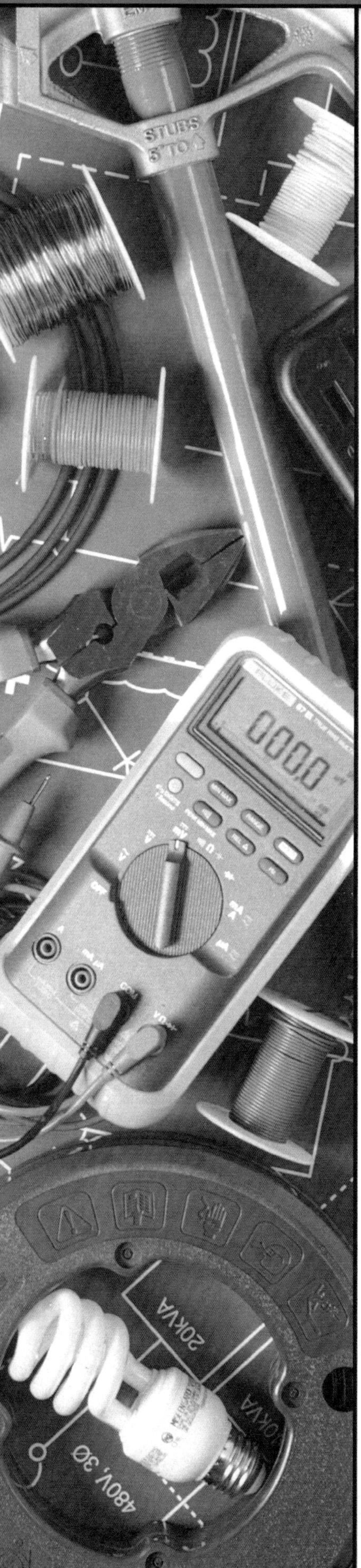

Figures and Tables (*continued*)

1.0.0 Introduction

The normal installation of intermediate metal conduit (IMC), rigid metal conduit (RMC), and electrical metallic tubing (EMT) requires many changes of direction in the conduit runs, ranging from simple offsets at the point of termination at outlet boxes and cabinets to complicated angular offsets at columns, beams, cornices, and so forth. This module explains how to use conduit bending machines for these tasks.

Unless the contract specifications dictate otherwise, such changes in direction, particularly in the case of smaller sizes, are made by bending the conduit or tubing as is required. In the case of 1¼" and larger sizes, right angle changes of direction are sometimes accomplished with the use of factory elbows or conduit bodies. In most cases, however, it is more economical to make these conduit bends in the field.

On-the-job conduit bends are also performed when multiple runs of the larger conduit sizes are installed. Truer parallel alignment of multiple runs is maintained by using on-the-job conduit bends rather than factory elbows. Such bends can all be made from the same center, using the bends of the largest conduit in the run as the pattern for all other bends. This is just one of the useful techniques covered in this module.

Exposed conduit work is one area of electricians' work that puts their skills on display. Exposed conduit directly reflects on the ability of the installer. With these thoughts in mind, it will benefit you to learn several methods of bending conduit that will ensure accurate and precisely bent conduit—conduit that you can step back and look at with pride because it was bent right the first time.

On Site

Take Pride in Your Work

Even though the conduit in this installation will be hidden by the flooring and the final wall finish, notice how the installing electrician made a special effort to keep the bends perfectly spaced and aligned. Doing a good job even when it might never be seen or admired is the mark of a true professional.

26204-14_SA01.EPS

1.1.0 Safety Considerations

Always keep the following safety guidelines in mind when bending conduit:

- Read and understand the operating instructions before using any tool. Always use the right tool for the job; never use bending tools for any other purpose.
- Never operate tools with damaged or missing parts.
- Watch for pinch points on power bending tools.
- Use tools in a well-lit, uncluttered area, with enough space for the conduit to move while bending.
- Be prepared for the unexpected.
- Make sure all hydraulic connections are clean and tight. Replace damaged or worn hoses before using.
- Make sure tools are complete and properly assembled before operating.
- Bending shoes and follow bars should be treated as precision instruments. Never toss them into a tool chest or allow them to become damaged or bent out of shape. The quality of the final job will depend on using the proper shoes and follow bars in good condition.
- When working with PVC conduit, make sure adequate ventilation is provided to carry off fumes from joint cement or glue.

2.0.0 *NEC*® Requirements

NEC Chapter 3 contains the installation requirements for various types of conduit. *NEC Section 344.24* requires that all rigid metal conduit bends be made so that the conduit will not be damaged and the internal diameter of the conduit will not be effectively reduced. To accomplish this, the *NEC*® further specifies that the minimum radius (*Figure 1*) to the centerline of the conduit shall not be less than that listed in *Table 1*. There is a good reason for this rule. When bends are too tight, pulling becomes extremely difficult and the insulation on the conductors may be damaged.

The *NEC*® requirements for other bends are shown in *Table 2*.

2.1.0 Number of Bends per Run

Every change of direction in a conduit run adds to the difficulty of the pull. The *NEC*® specifically states that no more than four quarter bends (360° total) may be made in any one conduit run between outlet boxes, cabinets, panels, or junction boxes; that is, between pull points.

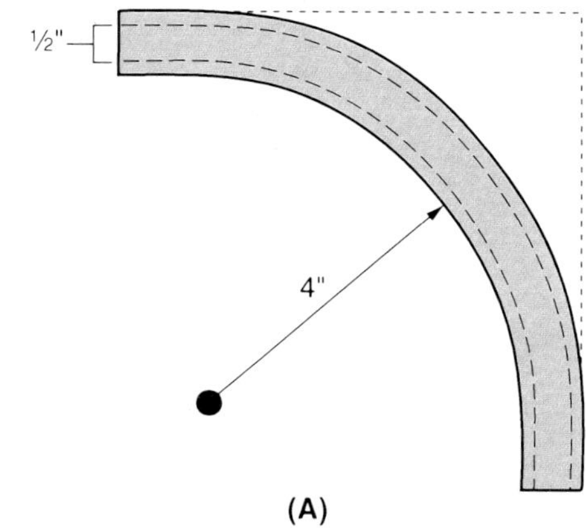

(A)

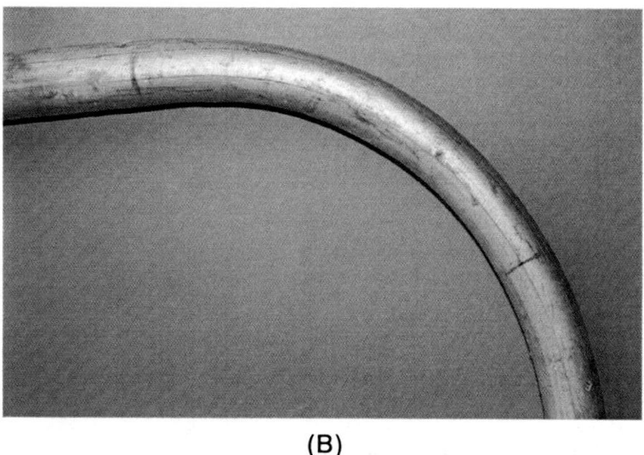

(B)

26204-14_F01.EPS

Figure 1 Inside radius requirements.

On Site

International Differences

Everywhere except in the United States, steel conduit is measured using the metric system, so it might be helpful to familiarize yourself with common metric conversion calculations, especially if you live near the Canadian or Mexican border. For example, to convert inches to centimeters (cm), multiply inches by 2.54; to convert yards to meters (m), multiply yards by 0.9.

Some electricians believe that offsets, kicks, and saddles are not bends, especially in areas where the electrical inspectors are lax. These electricians count only those bends that are actually a quarter circle (90°). The misconception of this is quickly apparent when wires are pulled. Offsets and saddles add just as much resistance to pulling conductors as any 90° elbow. A 45° offset, for example, takes two 45° bends, which equal one 90° bend. A saddle may be as low as 60° or as high as 180°, depending on the types of bends used.

A 15° kick in a conduit run may seem insignificant, but after several of these are incorporated into the run, the difficulty of pulling wire becomes apparent. The number of degrees in each kick should be included in the total count, and in no case should the total number (number of bends × number of degrees in each bend) exceed 360°. This is the maximum number of degrees allowed. For example, you could have one 45° offset, a 90° saddle, and two elbows. Many electricians prefer to install pull boxes at closer intervals to reduce the number of bends, especially when the larger conductor sizes are being pulled. The additional cost of the pull boxes and the labor to install them is often offset by the labor saved in pulling the conductors.

On Site

Don't Ignore the Outside Diameter

Although conduit measurements are based on the inside diameter, don't forget that the outside diameter determines the size of the opening that the conduit must penetrate.

Table 1 *NEC*® Minimum Requirements for Radius of Conduit Bends – One-Shot and Full-Shoe Benders (Data from *NEC Chapter 9, Table 2*)

Trade Size (Inches)	Radius to Center of Conduit (Inches)
½	4
¾	4½
1	5¾
1¼	7¼
1½	8¼
2	9½
2½	10½
3	13
3½	15
4	16
5	24
6	30

Table 2 *NEC*® Minimum Requirements for Radius of Other Conduit Bends (Data from *NEC Chapter 9, Table 2*)

Trade Size (Inches)	Other Bends (Inches)
½	4
¾	5
1	6
1¼	8
1½	10
2	12
2½	15
3	18
3½	21
4	24
5	30
6	36

Reprinted with permission from *NFPA 70*®-2014, the *National Electrical Code*®. Copyright © 2013, National Fire Protection Association, Quincy, MA. This reprinted material is not the complete and official position of the NFPA on the referenced subject, which is represented only by the standard in its entirety.

3.0.0 Types of Bends

There are various types of conduit bends: elbows, offset bends, back-to-back bends, saddles, etc. A brief review of each follows:

- *Elbow* – An elbow, or ell, is a 90° bend that is used when a conduit must turn at a 90° angle. In single conduit runs when the larger sizes of conduit are being installed, factory elbows are frequently used to save labor on setting up a power bending machine, calculating and marking the conduit for bending, and finally, making the bend. However, in multiple conduit runs, a neater job will result if on-the-job sweep bends or concentric bends are properly calculated and installed. See *Figure 2*.
- *Offset* – An offset consists of two equal bends and is used when the conduit run must go over, under, or around an obstacle. An offset is also used at outlet boxes, cabinets, panelboards, and pull boxes. See *Figure 3*.

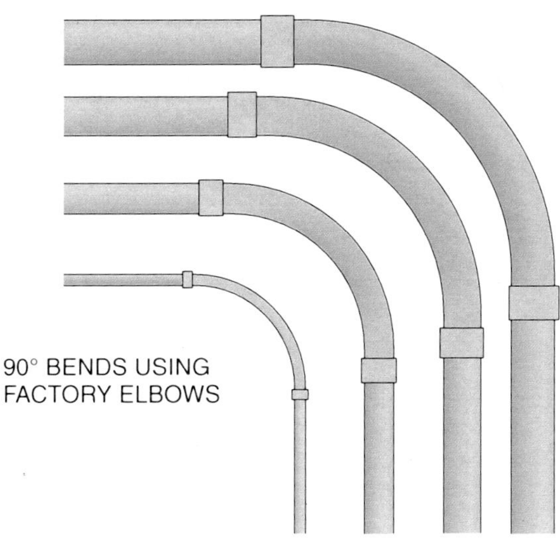

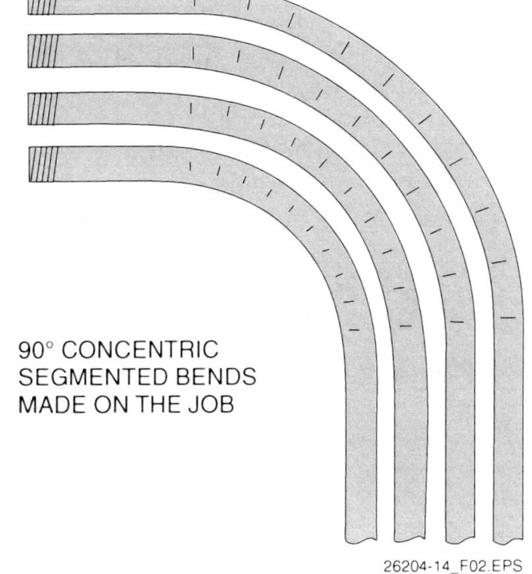

Figure 2 Typical 90° bends.

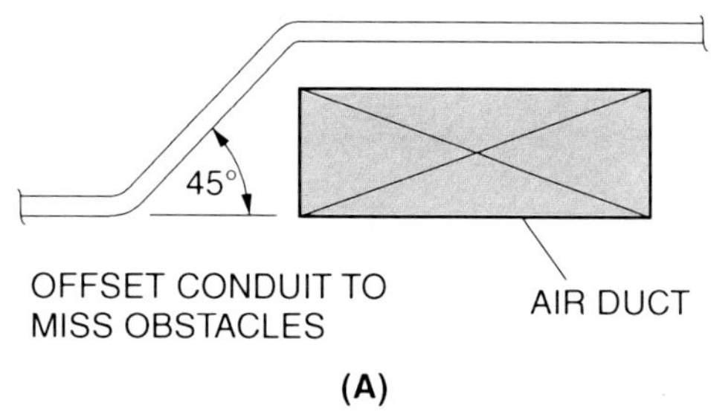

Figure 3 Applications of conduit offsets.

- *Saddle* – A saddle is used to cross a small obstruction or other runs of conduit. A saddle is made by marking the conduit at a point where the saddle is required and placing a bender a few inches ahead of this point. Bends are made as shown in *Figure 4*. Both three-bend and four-bend saddles can be used, depending on the type of obstruction.

On Site

Check It Out

When making complex bends, it is a good idea to test your bends using a piece of wire first, then use the bent wire as a template for your bend. This will give you an idea of whether or not the bend will do the job before wasting expensive conduit.

- *Kick* – A kick is a single change in direction of a conduit run of less than 90°. It is used mostly where the conduit run will be concealed in deck work. The first bend in an offset, for example, is really a kick, as shown in *Figure 5*; another kick in the opposite direction transforms the bend into an offset.

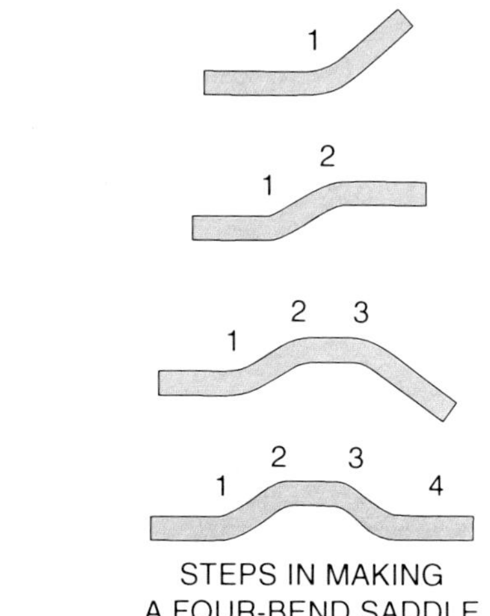

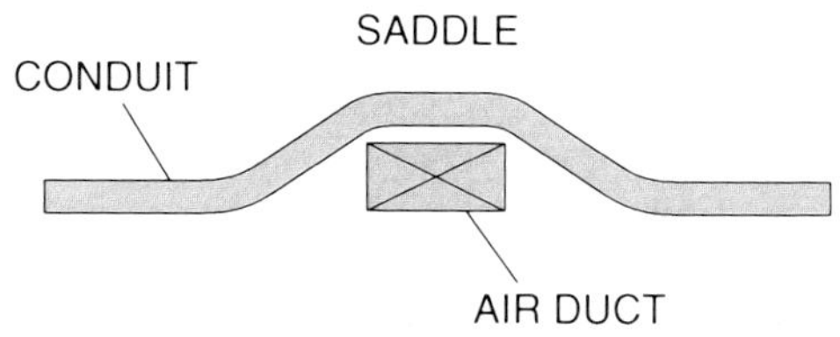

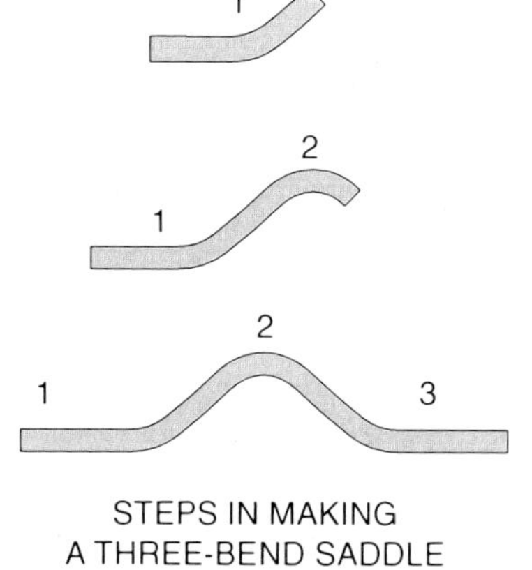

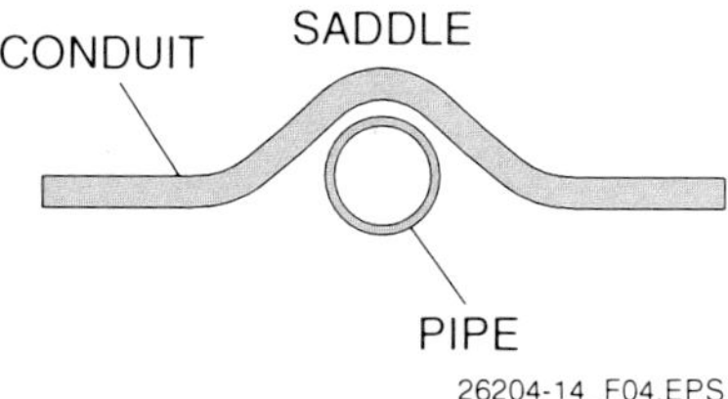

Figure 4 Practical application of a saddle bend.

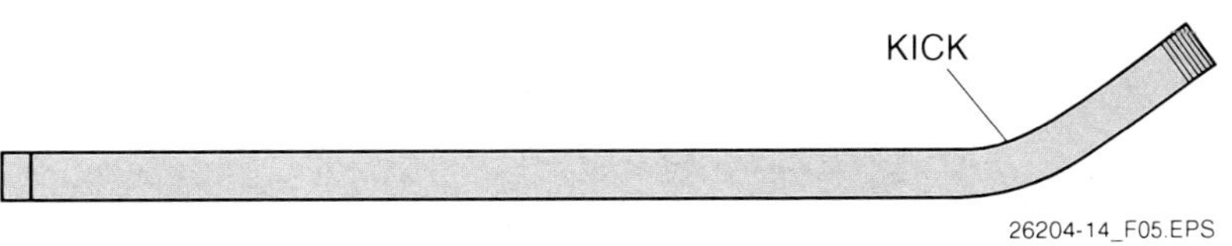

Figure 5 Kick.

4.0.0 The Geometry of Bending Conduit

Learning to bend conduit involves a thorough knowledge of some basic geometry (the science that deals with the properties of lines, angles, surfaces, and solids). The basic bends discussed previously will handle the majority of the electrician's needs, as these simple bends are merely combined to form more complex bends. When these basic skills are mastered, you will be able to calculate and bend conduit to fit most situations.

The 90° or right angle bend is probably the most basic of all and is used much of the time, regardless of the type of conduit being installed. All other bends are typically made with angles less than 90°.

4.1.0 Right Triangle

A right triangle, as shown in *Figure 6(A)*, is defined as any triangle with one 90° angle. The side directly opposite the 90° angle is called the hypotenuse and the side on which the triangle sits is the base. The vertical side is called the height or altitude. For offset bends, right triangle characteristics can also be applied because the offset forms the hypotenuse of a right triangle, as shown in *Figure 6(B)*. There are reference tables available for sizing offset bends based on these characteristics.

4.1.1 Trigonometry Fundamentals

Right triangles are used to develop trigonometric equations (*Figure 7*). These equations can be used to determine the **rise** or **stub-up** distance between bend points, the distance between bend joints, the distance a kick needs to be above the surface, or the amount of additional conduit required. There are six basic trigonometric functions that will be required:

- Sine
- Cosine
- Tangent
- Cotangent
- Secant
- Cosecant

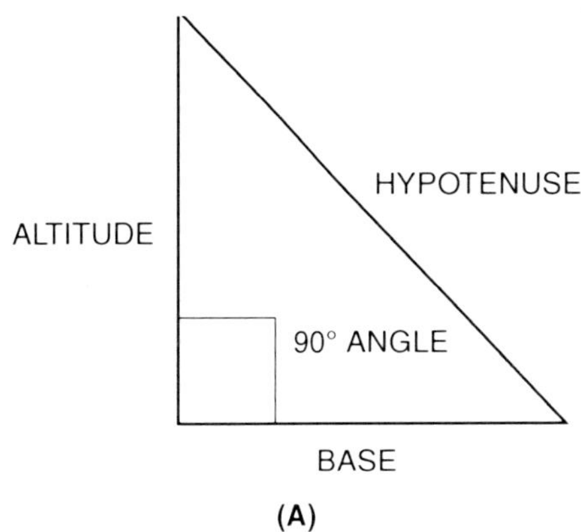

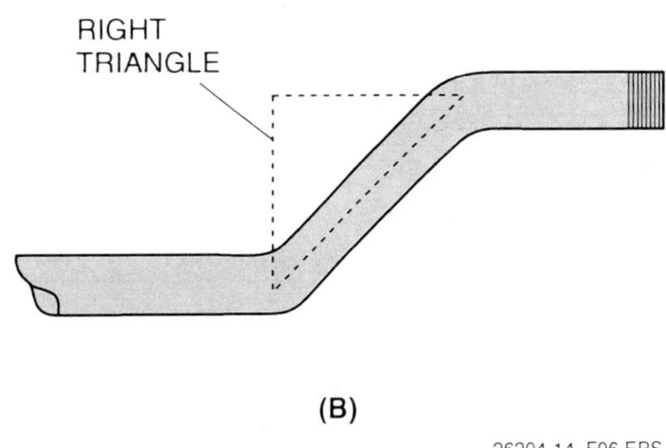

Figure 6 A right triangle and its relationship to a conduit offset.

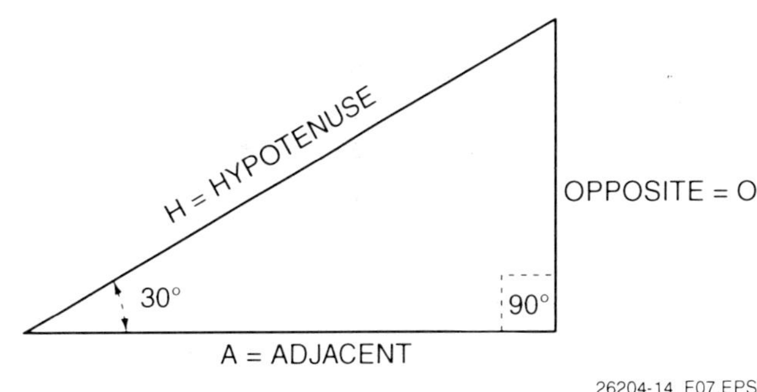

Figure 7 Trigonometry fundamentals of a right triangle.

The sine function can be computed by dividing the hypotenuse by the side opposite the angle being considered. This function can be represented by the following equation:

$$\text{Sine} = \frac{\text{opposite}}{\text{hypotenuse}} = \frac{O}{H}$$

The equations for the other functions are as follows:

$$\text{Cosine} = \frac{\text{adjacent}}{\text{hypotenuse}} = \frac{A}{H}$$

$$\text{Tangent} = \frac{\text{opposite}}{\text{adjacent}} = \frac{O}{A}$$

$$\text{Cotangent} = \frac{\text{adjacent}}{\text{opposite}} = \frac{A}{O}$$

$$\text{Secant} = \frac{\text{hypotenuse}}{\text{adjacent}} = \frac{H}{A}$$

$$\text{Cosecant} = \frac{\text{hypotenuse}}{\text{opposite}} = \frac{H}{O}$$

Where:

H = hypotenuse, side facing the right (90°) angle

O = side opposite the angle you are working with

A = side adjacent to the angle you are working with, but not the hypotenuse

Therefore, in *Figure 6(B)*, the hypotenuse or distance between bends could be computed by using the following cosecant trigonometric function:

$$\text{Cosecant} = \frac{\text{hypotenuse}}{\text{opposite}} = \frac{H}{O}$$

Let's say that the angle of the first bend is 30° and the rise or side opposite is 12". Therefore:

$$\text{Cosecant } 30° = \frac{H}{12''}$$

The cosecant of 30° is 2 (check using your calculator).

$$2 = \frac{H}{12''}$$

Cross multiply:

$$H = 2 \times 12''$$
$$H = 24''$$

Therefore, the hypotenuse or distance between bends would be 24".

Here is another example. In this case, a kick is to be made on the end of a piece of conduit (*Figure 8*). The angle of the kick is to be 30°. The hypotenuse of the kick is 20". Determine how far off the surface the end of the kick needs to be.

When calculating the hypotenuse of a bend, the cosecant of the angle is multiplied by the side opposite. If the angle and the hypotenuse are known, then the inverse can be used to determine the side opposite. Therefore, divide 20" by the cosecant of 30°, or:

$$20'' \div 2 = 10''$$

The end of the conduit needs to be brought 10" off the surface to acquire a 30° bend. This process eliminates the need for a protractor level.

4.2.0 Circle

A circle is defined as a closed curved line whose points are all the same distance from its center, as shown in *Figure 9(A)*. The distance from the center point to the edge of the circle is called the radius and the length of a straight line from one edge through the center to the other edge is called the diameter. The distance around the circle is called the circumference. A circle can be divided into four equal quadrants, as shown in *Figure 9(B)*. Each quadrant accounts for 90°, making a total of 360°. A 90° bend is based on ¼ of a circle, or one quadrant.

Concentric circles, shown in *Figure 9(C)*, are several circles that have a common center but different radii. The concept of concentric circles can be applied to concentric 90° bends in conduit.

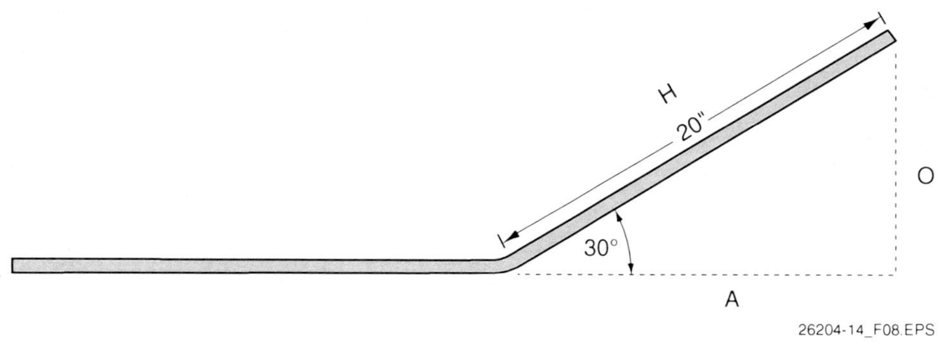

Figure 8 Kick example.

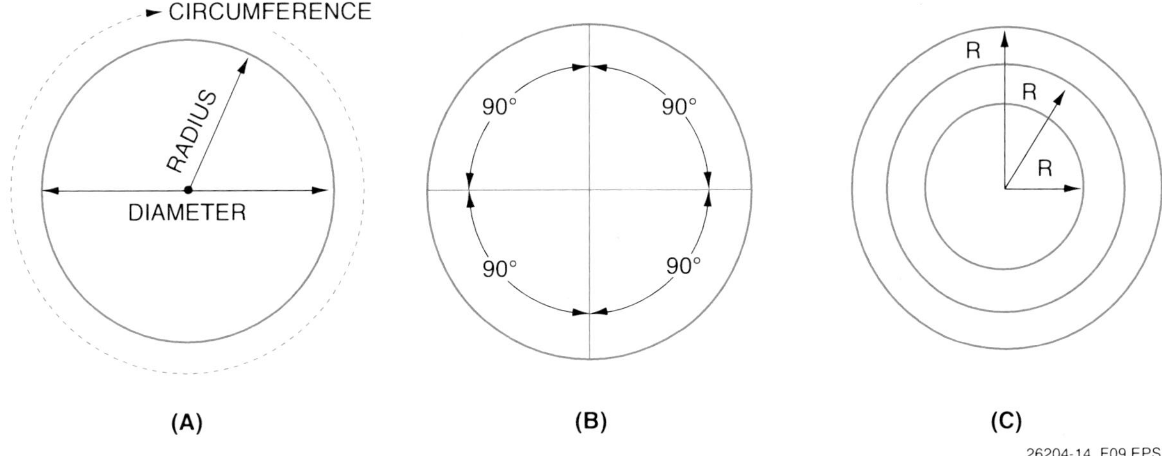

Figure 9 Characteristics of a circle.

Such bends have the same center point, but the radius of each is different. *Figure 10* shows how parts of a circle relate to a 90° conduit bend.

For bending conduit, it is necessary to understand the dynamics of the unit circle (*Figure 11*). The unit circle is a circle with a given radius of 1.

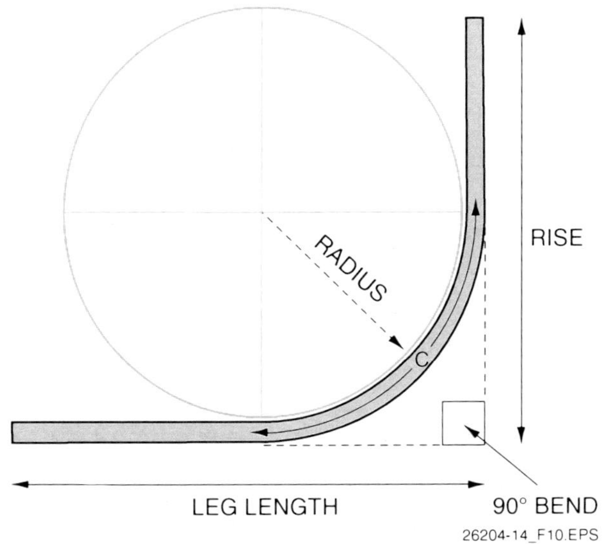

Figure 10 Parts of a circle related to conduit bending.

In calculating the circumference of a circle, the following formula is used:

$$C = 2\pi R$$

Where:

C = circumference
π = 3.14 (pi)
R = radius

By taking the radius of the unit circle and substituting it into the formula, the result is:

$$C = 2\pi \times 1$$

Any number multiplied by the number 1 is equal to that number, or:

$$1 \times 2 = 2$$

Therefore, $2\pi \times 1 = 2\pi$. This means that in terms of pi, the circumference of the circle is 2π; 360° is 2π and 180° = π. See *Figure 12*.

If you look at 90° in terms of π, 90° is half of 180° or half of π, so 90° is equal to ½ π or $\pi \div 2$. Again, π is a symbol for the numerical value 3.14 (rounded). $\pi \div 2$ is $3.14 \div 2$ or 1.57. Therefore, 90° is represented by the numerical value 1.57. Looking

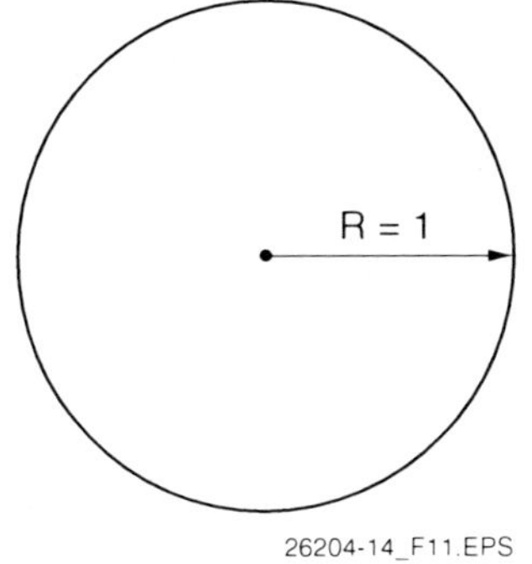

Figure 11 Unit circle.

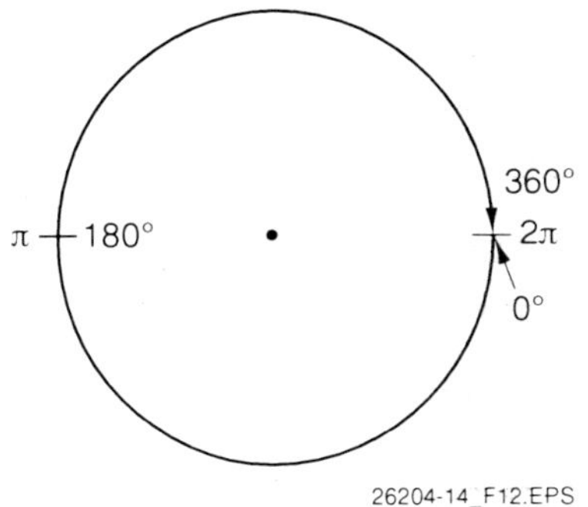

Figure 12 π and 2π.

back at the circumference formula shows that multiplying 2 × π or 6.28 times the given radius of the circle gives the linear distance around the circle. With that in mind, if you multiply 1.57 times the given radius, it will provide the linear distance from 0° to 90° on the circle. This linear distance is known as the **developed length** in regard to the amount of conduit that is required to make a 90° sweep.

4.2.1 Types of Angular Representations

There are three basic ways that angles can be represented or specified. Angles can be stated in degrees, as already mentioned; radians; or gradients.

Angles are measured in degrees from 0° to 360°. They may also be measured in radians from 0 to 6.28 or 0 to 2π. The third way is to specify angles in gradients, from 0 to 400 gradients (grads). These measurements can be equated as follows:

$$90° = \pi \div 2 = 1.57 \text{ radians} = 100 \text{ grads}$$
$$180° = \pi = 3.14 \text{ radians} = 200 \text{ grads}$$
$$270° = 3\pi \div 2 = 4.71 \text{ radians} = 300 \text{ grads}$$
$$360° = 2\pi = 6.28 \text{ radians} = 400 \text{ grads}$$

4.3.0 Equations

To calculate conduit bends accurately, you need to use some basic equations. The equations given here are the most relevant ones for the electrician. Examples are provided for clarification. To calculate the circumference of a circle, use the following equation:

$$C = \pi D$$

Where:

C = circumference
D = diameter
π = 3.14

As discussed earlier, another equation for finding the circumference of a circle is as follows:

$$C = 2\pi R$$

Where:

C = circumference
R = radius (½ the diameter)
π = 3.14

If the radius in a circle (and conduit bend) measures two feet, the circumference of the circle may be found as follows:

$$C = 2\pi R$$
$$C = 2 \times 3.14 \times 2' = 12.56'$$

The arc of a quadrant equals ¼ the circumference of the circle, and its length is found as follows:

$$\text{Length of arc} = (0.25)(2\pi R)$$
$$\text{Length of arc} = (0.25)(2 \times 3.14 \times R)$$
$$\text{Length of arc} = 1.57R$$

Therefore, the length of the arc in the quadrant, if the radius is 2', may be found as follows:

$$\text{Length of arc} = 1.57R$$
$$\text{Length of arc} = 1.57 \times 2' = 3.14'$$

If the radius of the bend and the outside diameter of the conduit are known, then the distance C (the length of the arc) can be calculated. This length, as related to conduit bending, is known as the developed length; it is the actual length of the bend.

Conduit bends with the circumference of the circle (*Figure 13*) and not at right angles. Therefore, the length of the conduit needed for a bend will not equal the right angle distances A and B. **Gain** is the difference between the right angle distances A and B and the shorter distance C, the length of conduit actually needed for the bend.

The gain for a 90° bend is found by multiplying the radius of the bend × 0.43 (rounded up from the value of 0.4292 in *Table 3*). Therefore, if the radius of the bend in *Figure 13* is 2', the gain may be found as follows:

$$\text{Gain} = 2' \times 0.43 = 0.86' = 10.32''$$

4.3.1 Making a 90° Bend

The 90° stub bend is probably the most basic bend of all. The stub bend is used much of the time, regardless of the type of conduit being installed.

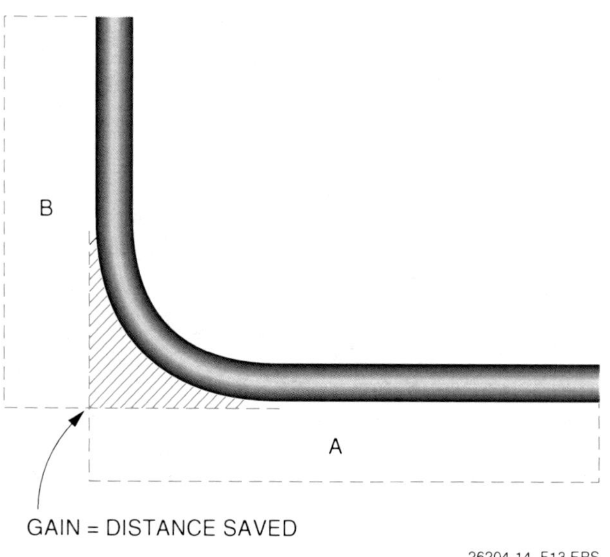

Figure 13 Gain.

Table 3 Gain Factors

	—	1°	2°	3°	4°	5°	6°	7°	8°	9°
0°	0	0	0	0	0	0	0.0001	0.0001	0.0003	0.0003
10°	0.0005	0.0006	0.0008	0.001	0.0013	0.0015	0.0018	0.0022	0.0026	0.0031
20°	0.0036	0.0042	0.0048	0.0055	0.0062	0.0071	0.0079	0.009	0.01	0.0111
30°	0.0126	0.0136	0.015	0.0165	0.0181	0.0197	0.0215	0.0234	0.0254	0.0276
40°	0.0298	0.0322	0.0347	0.0373	0.04	0.043	0.0461	0.0493	0.0527	0.0562
50°	0.06	0.0637	0.0679	0.0721	0.0766	0.0812	0.086	0.0911	0.0963	0.1018
60°	0.1075	0.1134	0.1196	0.126	0.1327	0.1397	0.1469	0.1544	0.1622	0.1703
70°	0.1787	0.1874	0.1964	0.2058	0.2156	0.2257	0.2361	0.247	0.2582	0.2699
80°	0.2819	0.2944	0.3074	0.3208	0.3347	0.3491	0.364	0.3795	0.3955	0.4121
90°	0.4292	—	—	—	—	—	—	—	—	—

Before beginning to make the bend, you need to know two measurements:

- The desired rise or stub-up
- The **take-up (comeback)** distance of the bender

The desired rise is the height of the stub-up. The take-up is the amount of conduit the bender will use to form the bend. Take-up distances are usually listed in the manufacturer's instruction manual. Once the take-up has been determined, subtract it from the stub-up height. Mark that distance on the conduit (all the way around) at that distance from the end. The mark will indicate the point at which you will begin to bend the conduit. Line up the starting point on the conduit with the starting point on the bender. Most benders have a mark, such as an arrow, to indicate the starting point.

> **NOTE**
> When bending conduit, the conduit is placed in the bender and the bend is made facing the end of the conduit from which the measurements were taken.

As discussed above, if the radius of the bend in *Figure 13* is 2', the gain is 10.32".

Table 4 shows the equivalent fractions for many decimals. For 10.32", search the decimal column for 0.32. The closest decimal in the table is 0.3125, equivalent to $\frac{5}{16}$. Therefore, the number in question becomes $10\frac{5}{16}$".

A decimal may also be mathematically converted to a fraction. A decimal whose denominator is contained in the numerator without a remainder can easily be converted to a fraction by removing the decimal point from the numeral, which then becomes the numerator (the top numeral of the fraction). The denominator is always one plus as many zeros as there are decimal places in the decimal. For example:

$$0.75 = \frac{75}{100} = \frac{3}{4}$$

or:

$$0.375 = \frac{375}{1000} = \frac{3}{8}$$

> **NOTE**
> Decimals may also be converted to fractions by using a calculator, provided the calculator has a fraction key. The exact procedure will vary with the different models of calculators.

Gain factors for 0° to 90° bends are shown in *Table 3*. To demonstrate the use of this table, assume that it is desired to find the gain on a 45° conduit bend with a 15" centerline radius. Referring to *Table 3*, look in the left-hand column; glance down the column until the number 40° is found. Since the bend is 45°, read to the right in this row until the column titled 5° is found; note the figure, 0.043. Therefore, the gain factor for a 45° bend is 0.043.

Multiply the gain factor by the centerline radius (15") to obtain the full gain of a 45° bend.

$$0.043 \times 15" = 0.645"$$

To convert this figure to a readable figure on the foot rule, convert the decimal to a common fraction: $\frac{645}{1000}$ = approximately $\frac{5}{8}$. Thus, the full gain of the 45° bend is $\frac{5}{8}$".

For example, the gain for a given bend is $2\frac{1}{2}$". In *Figure 14*, there are two back-to-back 90° bends. The rise for the first 90° bend is 2' and the rise for the second 90° bend is 3'. The back-to-back measurement for these bends is 4'. You need to

Table 4 Decimal Equivalents of Some Common Fractions

Fraction	Decimal	MM	Fraction	Decimal	MM
1/64	0.015625	0.397	33/64	0.515625	13.097
1/32	0.03125	0.794	17/32	0.53125	13.494
3/64	0.046875	1.191	35/64	0.546875	13.891
1/16	0.0625	1.588	9/16	0.5625	14.288
5/64	0.078125	1.984	37/64	0.578125	14.684
3/32	0.09375	2.381	19/32	0.59375	15.081
7/64	0.109375	2.778	39/64	0.609375	15.478
1/8	0.125	3.175	5/8	0.625	15.875
9/64	0.140625	3.572	41/64	0.640625	16.272
5/32	0.15625	3.969	21/32	0.65625	16.669
11/64	0.171875	4.366	43/64	0.671875	17.066
3/16	0.1875	4.763	11/16	0.6875	17.463
13/64	0.203125	5.159	45/64	0.703125	17.859
7/32	0.21875	5.556	23/32	0.71875	18.256
15/64	0.234375	5.953	47/64	0.734375	18.653
¼	0.25	6.35	¾	0.75	19.05
17/64	0.265625	6.747	49/64	0.765625	19.447
9/32	0.28125	7.144	25/32	0.78125	19.844
19/64	0.296875	7.54	51/64	0.796875	20.241
5/16	0.3125	7.938	13/16	0.8125	20.638
21/64	0.32812	8.334	53/64	0.828125	21.034
11/32	0.34375	8.731	27/32	0.84375	21.431
23/64	0.359375	9.128	55/64	0.859375	21.828
3/8	0.375	9.525	7/8	0.875	22.225
25/64	0.390625	9.922	57/64	0.890625	22.622
13/32	0.40625	10.319	29/32	0.90625	23.019
27/64	0.421875	10.716	59/64	0.921875	23.416
7/16	0.4375	11.113	15/16	0.9375	23.813
29/64	0.453125	11.509	61/64	0.953125	24.209
15/32	0.46875	11.906	31/32	0.96875	24.606
31/64	0.484375	12.303	63/64	0.984375	25.003
½	0.5	12.7	1	1	25.400

determine the length of straight conduit required to accomplish this task. The conduit is to be cut to length and threaded before bending.

The gain is the amount of conduit that is saved by the radius of the bend. The amount of conduit saved is 2½" per 90° bend. In this situation, there are two 90° bends, or a savings of 5". The total straight lengths add up to 9' of conduit. Therefore:

9' – 5" = 8'-7"

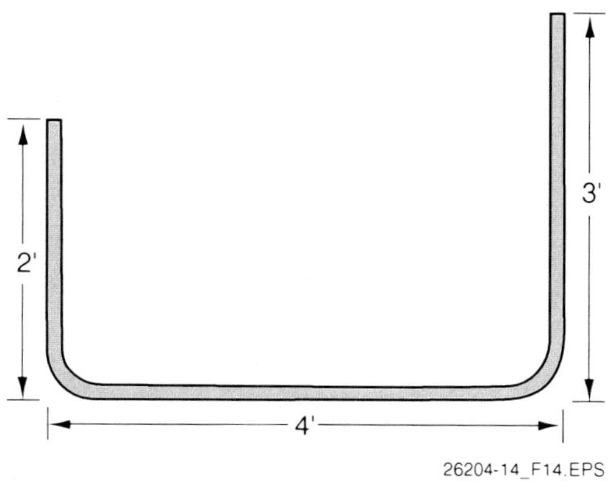

Figure 14 Back-to-back 90° bends.

5.0.0 Mechanical Benders

Conduit bends are normally made in the smaller sizes of conduit and tubing by hand with the use of hickeys or EMT bending tools. However, on many projects, an advantage can be gained by the use of mechanical bending equipment with suitable adjustable stops and guides. With the use of such equipment, the exact bend can be duplicated in quantity with a minimum of effort. The angle of the bend and the location of the bend in relation to the end of the length of conduit are preset.

A popular mechanical bender is shown in *Figure 15*. This type of bender was originally called the Chicago bender, as it was made by the Chicago Equipment and Manufacturing

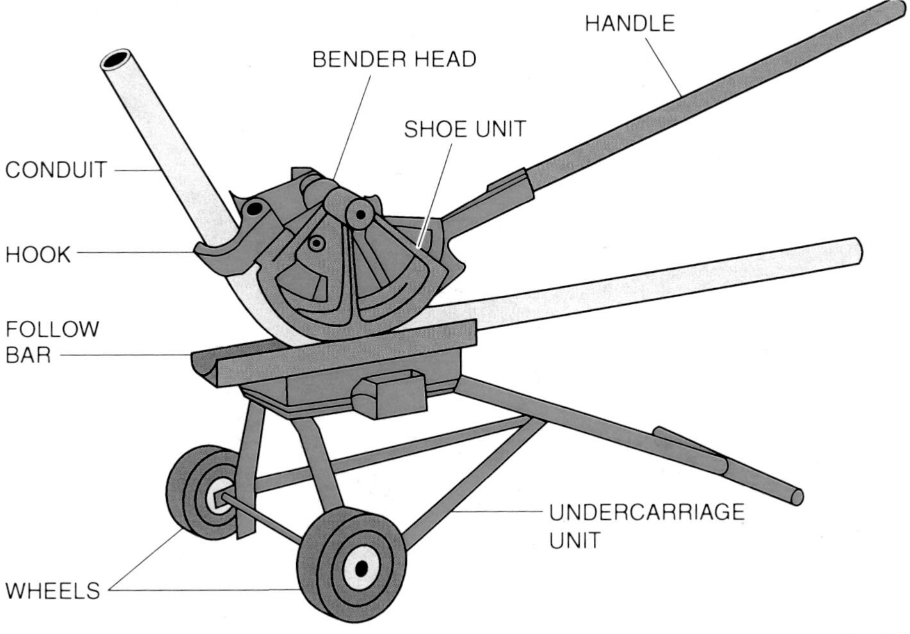

Figure 15 Typical mechanical bender.

Company. Today, however, this type of bender is manufactured by several different companies and the correct name is *portable mechanical conduit bender*. In any event, you may still hear the term *Chicago bender* on many jobs.

This type of mechanical bender is very popular with many electrical contractors. To use it, a length of conduit is placed in position and secured in place; a long bending handle is then pulled around and the bend completed. This type of bender may be used as a one-shot bender for the smaller sizes of conduit (bypassing the ratchet mechanism). The ratchet mechanism, however, is usually activated when bending the larger sizes of conduit to make the work easier. It is suitable for making bends in conduit sizes up to 2" EMT, 1¼" IMC, and 1½" rigid steel conduit, provided the proper bending accessories are used (e.g., bending shoes, follow bars, etc.).

Bending shoes and follow bars are designed to form a particular radius bend for a certain type and size of conduit, that is, EMT, IMC, or rigid conduit. These accessories should be treated as precision instruments; any damage will result in inaccurate bends, kinks, and so on. The first consideration is to use only the proper shoe and follow bar for the type and size of conduit being bent. For example, never use an EMT shoe for bending rigid conduit or a 3" shoe for bending 2½" conduit. In general, make certain that the bending shoes and follow bar are compatible with the type and size of conduit to be bent; to do otherwise may damage the tool and result in inaccurate bends.

The ratchet feature is normally engaged for the larger sizes of conduit, whereas a spring-loaded pawl engages the ratchet for easier bending in segments. For the smaller sizes of conduit, however, the ratchet may be bypassed so that the bend can be made in one shot.

A bending gauge with an adjustable pointer on the bender is helpful when making multiple bends at the same angle. This pointer is set at the desired angle and then the setscrew is tightened. As the bend is being made, the handle is operated until the pointer reaches the index mark. To ensure the correct angle of bend, the first bend should be checked with a **bending protractor** (*Figure 16*) and any necessary adjustments made to the bending gauge pointer before continuing. All successive bends will be exactly the same as the first.

For example, follow this process for charting a bender. This chart will contain minimum size, gain, and centerline distances from the arrow on the bender to the center of the bend for 15°, 30°, 45°, and 60° bends. This is to be accomplished with one scrap piece of conduit.

For this discussion, the scrap piece will be ½" conduit and will be 3' in length (*Figure 17*).

Place a mark on the conduit at a given distance from the end of the conduit. For this discussion, the mark will be 10" in from the end of the conduit (*Figure 18*).

Take a ½" conduit bender and place the arrow, which represents the take-up or minimum rise of the bender, on the mark 10" in from the end of the bender.

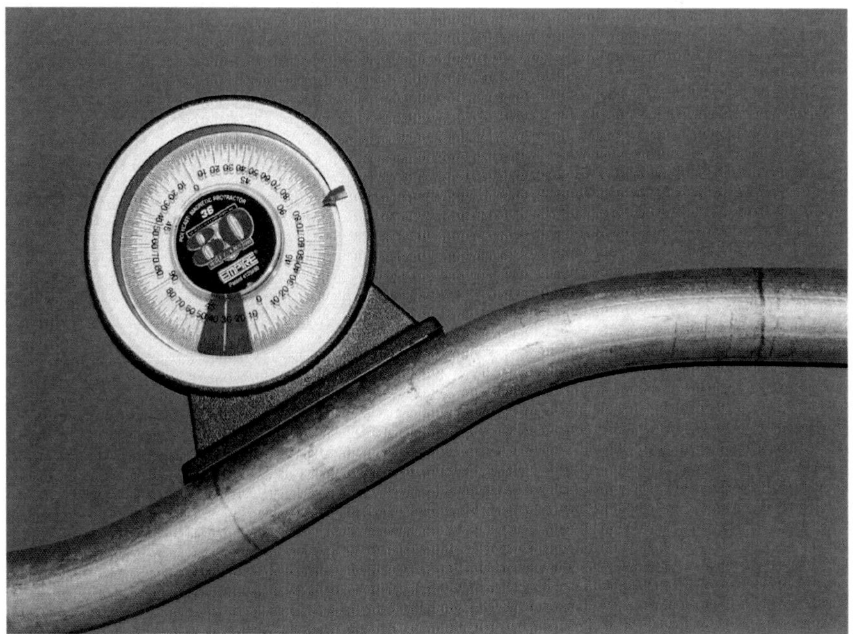

26204-14_F16.EPS

Figure 16 Bending protractor.

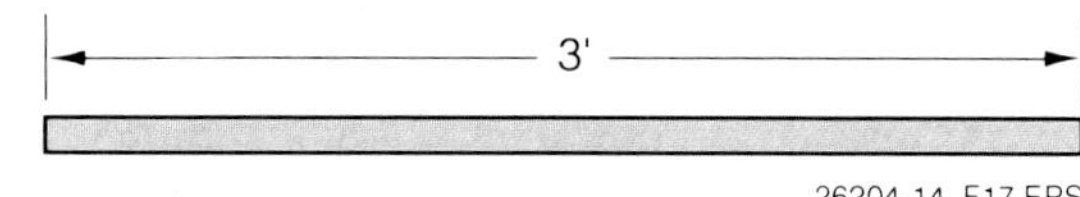

Figure 17 Conduit.

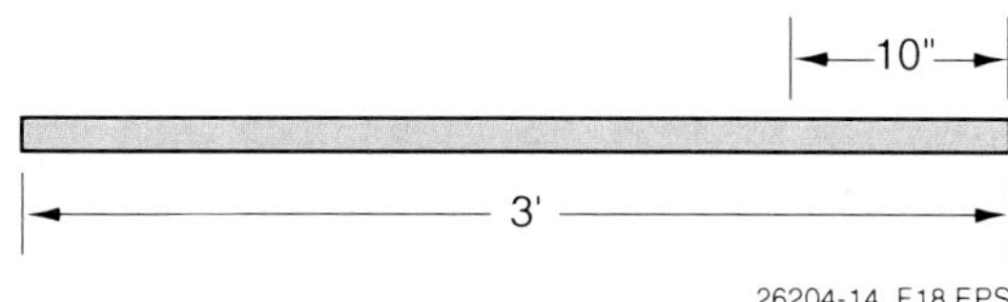

Figure 18 Conduit with 10" mark.

Place a protractor level on the conduit in front of the bender. This will be on the piece of conduit marked for 10" back from the end. Bend the 10" portion until the protractor level reads 15°. Remove the bender from the conduit (*Figure 19*).

Now take a straightedge, such as a ruler or torpedo level, and lay it on the inside of the bend so the straightedge lies across the bend and rests against the straight portion of the conduit (*Figure 20*).

With a sharp pencil, scribe a line across the bend of the conduit.

Now take the straightedge and lay it across the conduit so the straightedge is against the side adjacent to the previous position. It should extend across the bend once again (*Figure 21*).

Now scribe a line across the bend of the conduit. The two pencil lines should cross to form an X on the conduit. This represents the center of the bend (*Figure 22*).

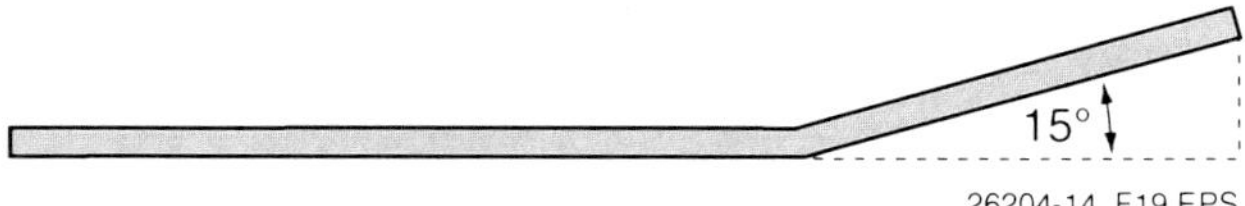

Figure 19 Kick of 15°.

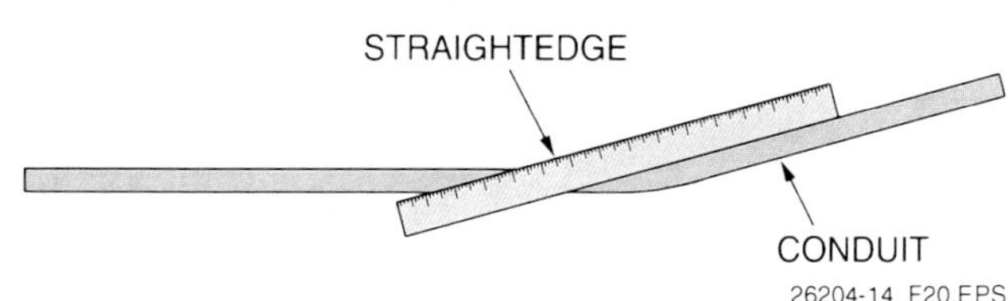

Figure 20 Conduit and straightedge.

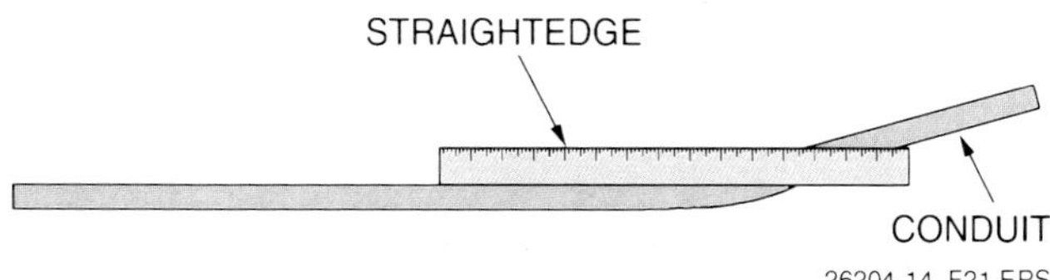

Figure 21 Conduit and horizontal straightedge.

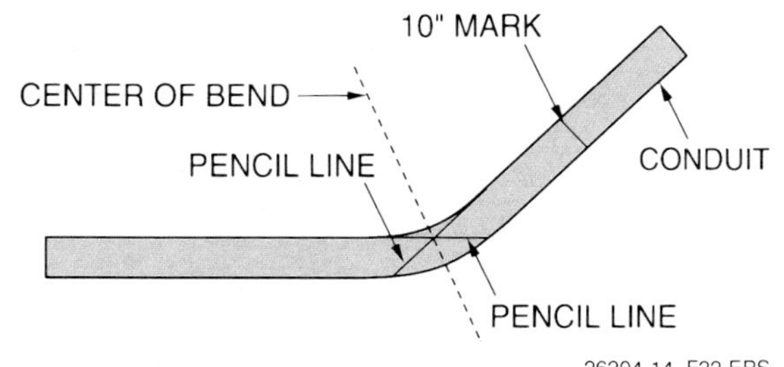

Figure 22 Center of bend.

Now take a tape measure and measure from the 10" mark to the centerline of the bend. Record this distance as follows:

15° – 1" (assuming 1" is the measured distance)

Now place the bender back on the conduit so that the take-up arrow is on the 10" mark on the conduit. Place the protractor level back on the conduit. Bend the conduit until the protractor level reads 30°. Take the bender off the conduit and repeat the line crossing process that was discussed for 15°, using the same straightedge. Once again, measure from the 10" mark to the point where the pencil lines cross in the center of the bend. Record this measurement.

15° – 1"
30° – 1½" (assuming this is the measured distance)

Repeat the previous process for 45°. Record this measurement.

15° – 1"
30° – 1½"
45° – 2" (assuming this is the measured distance)

Repeat the previous process for 60°. Record this measurement.

15° – 1"
30° – 1½"
45° – 2"
60° – 2¼" (assuming this is the measured distance)

The centerline distances for the different bends from the take-up mark of the bend have now been recorded. This portion of the chart is now completed.

The next step is to determine the minimum rise of the bender. Place the bender back on the conduit so the take-up mark of the bender is on the 10" mark on the conduit. Place the protractor level back on the conduit and bend the conduit until the protractor level reads 90°. Take the bender off the conduit. Measure from the back of the conduit to the 10" mark. The reading on the tape is 5". This is the minimum 90° stub length (*Figure 23*). Record this measurement.

15° – 1"
30° – 1½"
45° – 2"
60° – 2½"
Minimum rise – 5" (assuming this is the measured distance)

The next step is to determine the gain of the bender for 90°. Measure the length of both sides of the scrap piece of conduit (*Figure 24*).

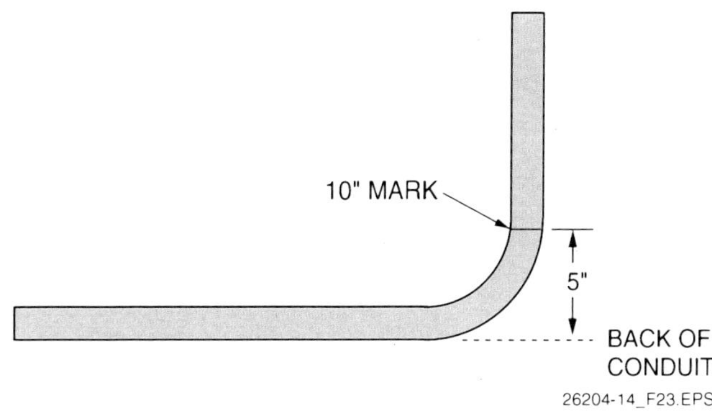

Figure 23 90° stub-up.

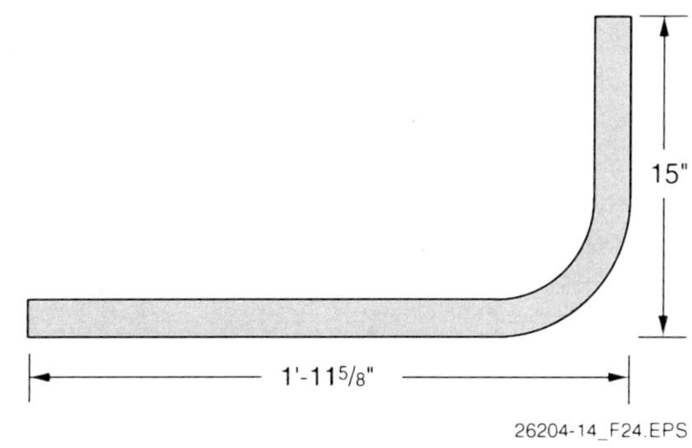

Figure 24 90° elbow.

Add the two measured stub lengths together.

15" + 1'-11⅝" = 3'-2⅝"

Subtract the original length of the conduit, which was 3', from 3'-2⅝".

3'-2⅝" – 3' = 2⅝"

This is the gain for this particular ½" conduit bender. Record this information.

15° – 1"
30° – 1½"
45° – 2"
60° – 2½"
Minimum rise – 5"
Gain – 2⅝" (assuming this is the measured distance)

The ½" bender has now been charted. This same process would need to be repeated for a ¾" bender, 1" bender, 1¼" bender, 1½" bender, etc.

This charting process should help you to understand how the manufacturer of a bender comes up with the marks that determine the ability to bend exact 90° bends of any length, which is the minimum rise mark. The star mark seen on many benders is used for back-to-back bends. The star mark is 2⅝" back from the minimum rise mark (take-up). In other words, it is the measured gain distance back from the minimum rise mark. The centerline marks are used in lining up the centers of bends for various sizes of conduit. The centerline marks can also be used in lining up saddles on the centerlines of I-beams and process piping. This information is good for charting any type of wrap-around bender.

6.0.0 Mechanical Stub-Ups

Stub-ups are quickly and easily made with mechanical benders. A deduct decal is provided on many benders, but sometimes these decals become damaged, making them difficult to read. Therefore, backup charts should be provided on all jobs. With this deduct chart on hand, the following is an example of making a 90° stub-up to a given height.

Assume that you are working on a deck job and need a number of 1" rigid stub-ups with a rise of 15" each. When you check the deduct chart on the bender for a 15" stub-up using 1" rigid conduit, you note that 11" should be deducted from the total rise of 15". Since 15" – 11" = 4", measure back from the end of the conduit by 4" and make a mark. Encircle the entire conduit at this point so you will not lose the mark once the conduit is placed in the bender. Many electricians like to use a black felt-tip marker for marking conduit.

Load the conduit into the bender with the mark lined up with the front of the bender hook. Engage the ratchet and start pumping the bender handle until the bender pointer reaches the preset index mark for 90°. Move the bender handle forward, then remove the conduit from the bender and check its height. It should be exactly 15". If the height of the bend is slightly off, make the necessary adjustments before continuing. Once the correct height is reached, the remaining bends will also be correct.

7.0.0 Mechanical Offsets

The decal chart on the bender that provides deduct information for the stub-ups also contains data for making offsets that require 20°, 30°, and 45° bends. This chart is necessary to make perfect offsets every time using the mechanical bender.

Assume that you are running a raceway system with ½" rigid conduit and an air duct must be bypassed, requiring the conduit run to be offset. After taking measurements on the job, you find that an offset of 12" is needed to clear the air duct.

Measure the distance from the end of the conduit to the start of the first bend; mark the conduit as before. Referring to the chart on the bender with offset information, you decide to make the offset with two 45° bends. The chart indicates that the distance between bends is 16⁵⁄₁₆". Therefore, measure and mark this distance back from the first mark.

Insert the conduit into the bender and line up the first mark with the front of the bender hook. The ratchet may be used, but for ½" conduit, the ratchet override on the front of the bender shoe is normally employed. Make the first 45° bend. Move the bender handle forward to release the conduit. Now slide the conduit forward through the bender hook until the second mark lines up with the front of the bender hook, and then turn the bend over so the end of the conduit is pointing downward toward the deck. Also, make sure that the first bend lines up with the next bend to be made to prevent a crooked bend (commonly referred to as a dog leg) in the conduit. Once everything is aligned, engage the bender handle and make another 45° bend. The height of the offset should be exactly 12" (see *Figure 25*).

On Site

Making Accurate Offsets

Be sure to use the same angle for both bends of an offset. To avoid dog legs, make sure your first bend lines up evenly with the rest of the conduit, the handle, and the bender. Take your time, and be sure of proper alignment before making the second bend. A No-Dog® is a simple, pocket-sized device that may be used to prevent crooked bends. It is screwed onto the end of the conduit and has a built-in level to ensure straight bends.

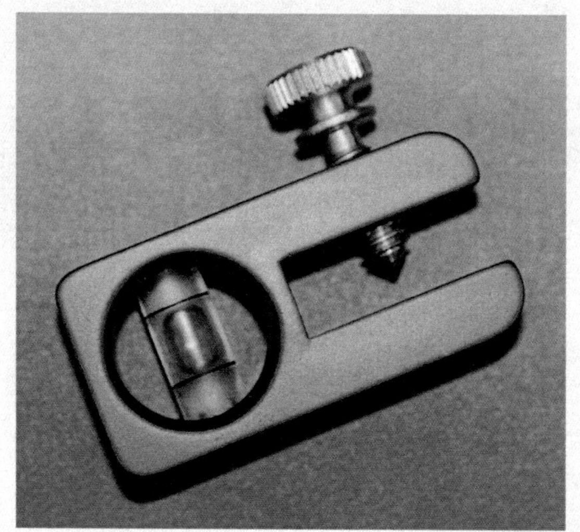

26204-14_SA02.EPS

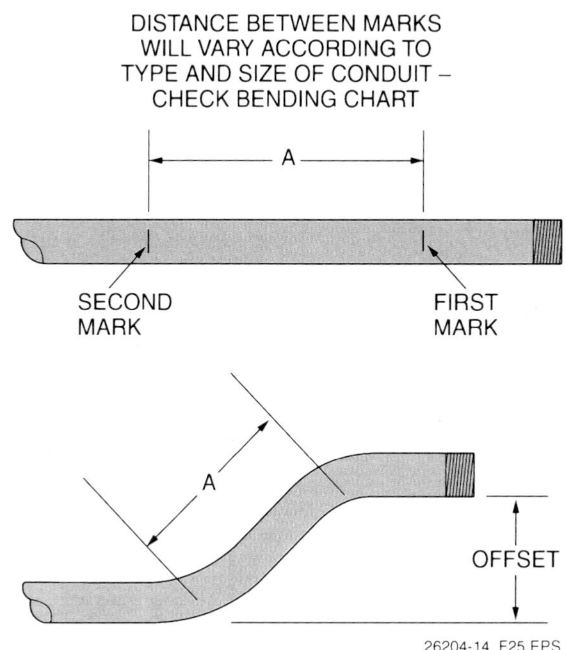
DISTANCE BETWEEN MARKS WILL VARY ACCORDING TO TYPE AND SIZE OF CONDUIT – CHECK BENDING CHART
A
SECOND MARK
FIRST MARK
A
OFFSET
26204-14_F25.EPS

Figure 25 Bending offsets in conduit.

The distances between marks for offset bends will vary depending upon the size and type of conduit being bent, so always check the offset information on the bender.

7.1.0 General Tips for Bending with the Chicago Bender

The following are some general tips to keep in mind when bending with the portable mechanical conduit bender:

- An engineer's rule marked in hundredths will simplify formula bending by eliminating the need to convert to fractions.
- When minimum length stubs are being bent, the shoe tends to creep and deforms the end of the conduit and threads. Screwing a coupling onto the pipe stops the shoe from creeping forward and protects the threads.
- When bending offsets, the front of the bender can be temporarily elevated for clearance requirements.
- Most bender shoes are made of cast aluminum and are easily pitted and gouged if foreign material gets between the shoe and the pipe. For longer shoe life, keep the pipe clean and the shoes wiped down.
- When the remaining pipe length is not long enough to reach the roller or pipe support, a larger diameter conduit can be slid over the pipe being bent to complete the bend; or, if the pipe has threads, screw on a coupling and a short piece of scrap pipe.
- Segment and concentric bending of smaller sizes of pipe can be performed with this bender. Bend a scrap piece of pipe and measure from the center of the bend to the front of the bending shoe. Use this measurement to adjust the start mark using the segment and concentric bending procedures.
- To make matching bends in two different sizes of conduit when using a mechanical bender, make both bends using the larger shoe.

> **NOTE**
> For matching bends in sizes ½", ¾", and 1" rigid conduit and IMC, bend all pipes with the 1" shoe.

8.0.0 Electric and Hydraulic Conduit Benders

Bends in larger sizes of conduit (over 2" EMT, 1¼" IMC, or 1½" rigid conduit) are normally made using hydraulic benders. In some instances, bending tables have been developed for use with bending tools or hydraulic benders to simplify making bends to certain dimensions. Various adaptations of benders have been developed to serve certain specific purposes. For example, one type of hydraulic bender is designed for making bends in a section of conduit that has been installed in a raceway system.

8.1.0 Electric Conduit Benders

Electric conduit benders operate on the same basic principle as the mechanical benders described previously except that the bending is accomplished by a gear motor rather than manual power. There are several types of electric benders on the market. A typical electric unit is shown in *Figure 26*. This bender will make stub-ups, offsets, and saddles quickly and easily at any location where a 120V receptacle is available. Furthermore, this bender will make 90° one-shot bends in ½" through 2" EMT, IMC, or rigid conduit.

Bending charts are often included in the form of decals attached to the bender for quick reference on the job. These include deduct and springback figures along with information for making offsets. Springback is when the conduit relaxes to a slightly looser bend angle when the bender is released.

Many electric benders are sold as a power unit and the bending shoes for various types of conduit are sold as accessories. These shoes quickly

Figure 26 Typical electric bender.

snap into place on the power unit, ready for use in seconds.

To describe the operation of the example bender, assume that you need a 16" stub-up in a piece of 1¼" rigid conduit. Measure and mark a piece of conduit 16" from one end. When you check the deduct chart on the bender for this size conduit, the figure is 12¾". Therefore, 12¾" must be deducted from 16", which leaves 3¼". So a mark is made at this distance from the end of the conduit. Encircle the conduit with this mark so it will be plainly visible during the bend.

Insert the conduit in the bender with the mark lined up with the front of the bender hook. For this particular bend, the mark is 3¼" from the end of the conduit.

The three-position operating switch on the example bender is attached to a flexible cord. The center position de-energizes the machine, the Up position (forward) is for bending, and the Down position (reverse) is for unloading the conduit after the bend has been made. When released, the switch automatically springs to the center or Off position. A pointer on the shoe indicates the degree of bend as the bend is being made.

The machine is jogged or inched up until the shoe pointer lines up with the zero mark on the degree scale. The switch is then pressed upward and held in this position to start the bend. As the pointer approaches the 90° mark, refer to the springback chart for the size and type of conduit being bent. In this case, 1¼" rigid conduit, the chart indicates 95°. Therefore, the pointer should pass the 90° mark and stop at 95° to allow for springback when the conduit is removed from the bender; the stub-up is ready for installation.

An offset is made in the electric bender similar to the method described for the mechanical bender; that is, the first mark is located on the conduit and then offset information is obtained from the bender chart. In the case of a 16" offset in a length of 1¼" rigid conduit, the chart indicates a distance of 22⅝" between marks for a 16" offset using 45° bends.

Mark the conduit and insert the conduit into the bending shoe, positioning the mark so that it is even with the front of the bender hook. Start the bend as discussed previously until the pointer reaches the 45° mark on the scale; allow for any springback as indicated in the chart. Reverse the motor until the conduit is loose, then turn the conduit upside down. Position the second mark at the front of the bender hook, making certain the conduit is aligned to prevent a dog leg in the bend. Start the second bend until the pointer reaches the 45° mark, reverse the bender, and unload the conduit. A magnetic torpedo level placed on the side of the conduit will help align bends for offsets. An anti-dog device can also be used for this.

Finally, check the bends for accuracy. Although rebending is possible, it is not a good practice. Rebending puts considerable strain on the conduit, and while it may not break, the coating may crack and cause corrosion.

8.1.1 Speed Benders

A speed bender operates basically the same as the standard bender except the speed bender utilizes remote digital control with easy-to-use bending charts and instructions to ensure fast, accurate, and consistent bends in conduit sizes from ½" to 2".

This bender can be operated upright or laid on its back for large offsets and saddles. In operation, rather than holding the switch up in the bend position as with the standard bender, the operator sets the desired bend via digital controls. The bender automatically bends to that degree once the conduit is placed in the bending shoe and the start control is activated. Otherwise, the conduit is marked and bent in the same way as described for the standard bender.

8.2.0 Hydraulic Conduit Benders

The hydraulic bender is indispensable for bending large conduit. Only by the addition of the hydraulic pump and cylinder to a bender frame is the necessary power available for bending rigid conduit up to 6" trade size.

The typical hydraulic bender (*Figure 27*) provides extended bending capability, but also requires additional responsibility. Hydraulic bending equipment requires a large initial investment, and the bender must be properly cared for if it is to last and give the service necessary to justify the cost.

> **WARNING!**
>
> Dangerous pressures are used in hydraulic benders. Exercise care when working with or around hydraulic benders.

The bender frame, shoes, follow bars, and saddles will require little more than occasional wiping down to remove the dirt and oil film. The pump, cylinder, and hydraulic hoses, however, will demand more attention.

The pump should have its fluid level checked periodically. Low fluid pressure will keep the pump from developing its rated hydraulic pressure. When the level is low and fluid must be added, use only approved hydraulic oil. Ordinary oil will cause damage to the pump assembly.

Hydraulic benders have two types of bending shoes, one-shot and segment.

The **one-shot shoe** has a full 90° radius. The conduit can be formed around the shoe to a full 90° bend without collapsing the walls of the pipe. One-shot benders require no new bending techniques. The take-up is figured to the center of the bend and the bender shoe will have an indicating mark at its center. If take-up values are not listed on the bender frame or bender storage case, scrap pipe can be bent and take-up figures found. All the methods and layout techniques discussed for EMT and rigid metal conduit can be used with a hydraulic bender and one-shot shoes. Offsets will have to be adjusted (less angle of bend) so the spacing between the bend marks is far enough apart to allow the first bend to be rolled 180° and advanced enough to clear the shoe.

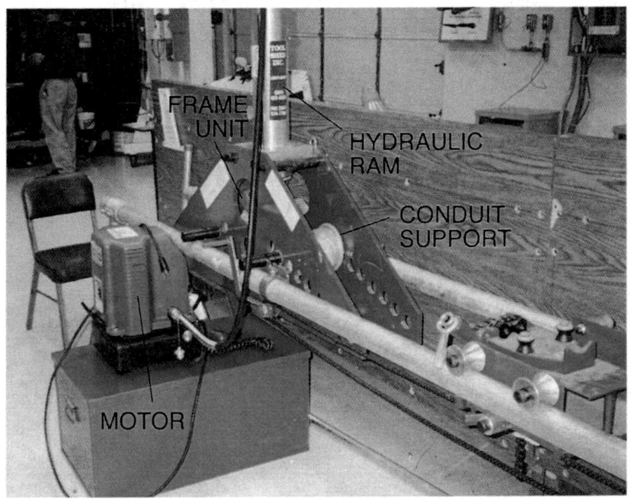

26204-14_F27.EPS

Figure 27 Hydraulic conduit bender.

Segment shoes are shorter and have a radius that is far less than 90°. A **ninety-degree bend** cannot be made in one operation, as the conduit walls would collapse. Bends, then, must be made in several steps (as few as four and as many as 30) to form a smooth radius. The **segmented bending shoe** allows pipe to be bent to larger size radii.

Segmented shoes are used for concentric bending (bending several conduits with increasing or decreasing radii). One-shot shoes can be used for a **segment bend**, but are not as convenient. Concentric bending is covered in detail later in this module.

Accurate bending of large conduit is possible but requires practice, patience, and ability. With few exceptions, all formulas and bending techniques discussed to this point will apply.

8.2.1 Bending Tips for Rigid Aluminum

Rigid aluminum conduit is available in all trade sizes from ½" through 6". It is lightweight, corrosion resistant, and has low ground impedance. It is, however, difficult to bend consistently and accurately. Two pipes out of the same bundle will act differently when bent. Even if two pipes are bent using the same layout, they do not always come out the same. Do not be discouraged by this; it is the nature of the metal and it cannot be helped.

Another disadvantage of aluminum is that a one-shot bending shoe will dig in and score the pipe. Also, where the pipe rides on the shoe, it is prone to wrinkling and scoring. Applying petroleum jelly or a lubricant such as WD-40® to the

> **On Site**
>
> ## Hydraulic Bender Safety
>
> A hydraulic bender generates a tremendous amount of power and operates under dangerous pressures. Do not attempt to use a hydraulic bender unless you have been properly trained and are thoroughly familiar with the unit's operating and safety instructions. Even then, exercise extreme caution and always work in conjunction with a bending partner.

shoe will allow the pipe to slide without the shoe digging in. Petroleum jelly will also make it easier to remove the conduit when the bend is complete.

8.2.2 One-Shot Bending

Accurate one-shot stub-ups are easily made on hydraulic benders by applying a little basic geometry in making calculations, and then knowing the operating principles of the bender. *Figure 28* shows the reference points of a common 90° bend. To make one-shot 90° bends, first determine the leg length and rise, the gain, the radius of the bend, and the half-gain.

Use the following procedure for laying out accurate stub-ups:

Step 1 Determine lengths A and B.

Step 2 Add lengths A and B. Subtract X for the length of pipe required.

Step 3 Subtract Y from length A or B to get the center of the bend.

Step 4 Calculate the developed length and the length of conduit required.

Step 5 Determine the center of the bend. This can be done by taking the half-gain value from the distance A or B. See *Table 5*.

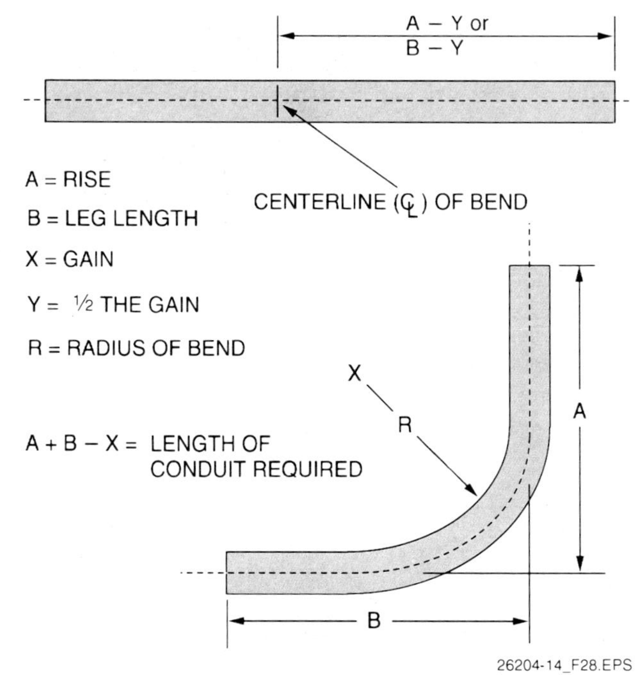

Figure 28 Laying out stub-ups.

Table 5 Dimensions of Stub-Ups for Various Sizes of Conduit

Pipe and Conduit Size	Radius of Bend R	Minimum Developed Length 90°	Gain X	½ Gain Y
½"	4"	6⁵⁄₁₆"	1¹¹⁄₁₆"	²⁷⁄₃₂"
¾"	4½"	7¹⁄₁₆"	1¹⁵⁄₁₆"	³¹⁄₃₂"
1"	5¾"	9"	2½"	1¼"
1¼"	7¼"	11⅜"	3⅛"	1⁹⁄₁₆"
1½"	8¼"	13"	3½"	1¾"
2"	9½"	14¹⁵⁄₁₆"	4¹⁄₁₆"	2¹⁄₃₂"

8.2.3 90° Segment Bends

When bending conduit in segments with a hydraulic bender, the following factors must be determined:

- The size of conduit to be bent
- The radius of the bend
- The total number of degrees in the bend
- The developed length
- The gain of the bend

To determine the developed length for a 90° bend, multiply the radius by 1.57. The next step is to locate the center of the bend. Most benders have the center mark indicated on the bending shoes. Once the center mark on the conduit is found, it is easy to locate the other bend marks (see *Figure 29*).

Think About It

Developed Length

Why is the radius multiplied by a factor of 1.57 to determine the developed length for a 90° bend?

You must now determine the number of bending shots that will make the bend to suit the requirements, preferably an odd number so that there are an equal number of bends on each side of the center mark. Next, calculate the width of the spaces for each segment bend and make the layout on the conduit. Make an equal number of spaces on each side of the center mark. The gain need only be determined if the bend is being fitted between two existing conduit runs or junction boxes.

To determine the bending data for a 90° bend using 3" conduit with a rise of 48", a leg length of 46", and a centerline radius of 30", proceed as follows (see *Figure 30*).

Step 1 Multiply the radius by 1.57 to determine the developed length.

30" × 1.57 = 47.10" (47⅛") developed length

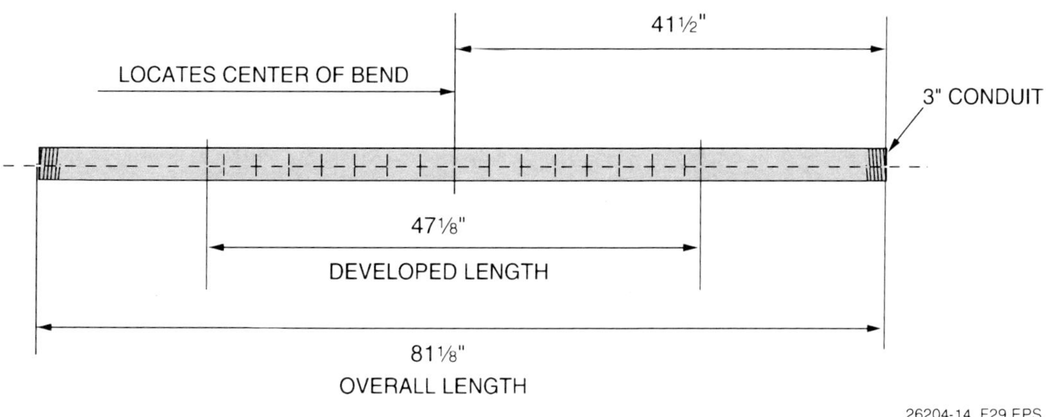

Figure 29 Laying out segment bends.

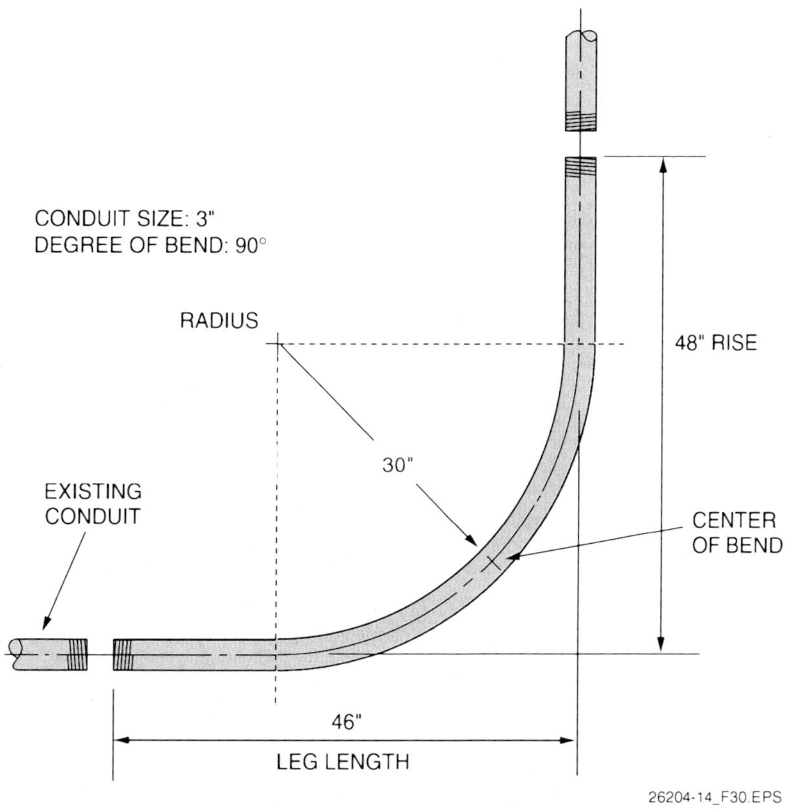

Figure 30 Specifications for sample bend.

Step 2 Determine the gain for a 90° bend.

Gain = (2 × R) – developed length

Gain = (2 × 30") – 47⅛" = 12⅞"

Step 3 To calculate the overall length (OL) of the conduit, add the leg and stub-up lengths and subtract the gain. See *Figure 30.*

OL = leg length + rise – gain

OL = 46" + 48" – 12⅞"

OL = 81⅛"

Step 4 Now locate the center of the required bend. First, determine one-half of the developed length:

½ (47⅛") = 23.56" = 23½"

Use the rise or stub-up dimension of 48". Subtract the radius (30") and add one-half of the developed length:

48" – 30" + 23½" = 41½"

Step 5 As a rule, 6° or less per bend will produce a good bend for a 30" radius. In this case, 6° per bend will be used, making 15 segment bends (90 ÷ 6 = 15). An odd number of segment bends is easy to lay out after finding the center mark because there will be an equal number of spaces on each side of the center mark.

Step 6 To determine the space between the segment marks, divide the developed length by the total number of segments:

$$47\frac{1}{8}" = 47.125"$$
$$47.125" \div 15 = 3.14"$$
$$3.14" = 3\frac{1}{8}"$$

Step 7 Position the conduit in the pipe holders, making sure to clamp them securely.

Step 8 Place the center mark 41½" from one end of the conduit. Next, mark seven points on each side of the center point, 3⅛" apart, for a total of 15 marks. These are the centers of the segment bends.

Step 9 It is a good idea to check the distance between the first and last bend marks to be sure the layout is correct before starting the first bend. The distance from the first mark to the last is the developed length minus the length of one bend. (Actually, you are subtracting one-half of a segment bend from each end of the conduit.)

$$47\frac{1}{8}" - 3\frac{1}{8}" = 44"$$

Step 10 After positioning the conduit in the bender (*Figure 31*), attach the pipe bending **degree indicator** in a convenient location.

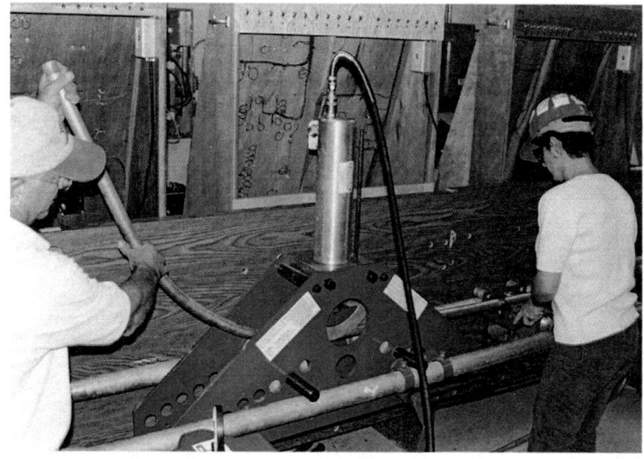

26204-14_F31.EPS

Figure 31 Conduit placed in hydraulic bender for segment bends.

Step 11 Attach the pipe supports with the proper face toward the conduit and insert the pipe support pins. Lock them in position by turning the small lock pin. Now, proceed to make the series of bends.

Step 12 Begin by bending 6° on the first mark. When this is done, the indicator will read 6°. Release the pressure and check the springback; if any is found, overbend by the same amount.

Step 13 When using a bender with a rigid frame, move the pipe support one hole position in (toward the ram) on the side that you have bent the conduit.

Step 14 Continue to bend to 12° on the second mark. Check for springback. When the first bend in the conduit is moved past the one pipe support, the **approximate ram travel** for the remaining bends will be exactly the same.

Step 15 Follow this procedure until you get to the last mark, where you will be bending to 90°. Stop at exactly 90°, release the pressure, and check for springback, correcting if necessary. The result will be a 90° bend without any bows or twists.

For example, suppose the task is to bend a 90° sweep with a given radius of 25". This particular sweep has no definite height. This is to be done on a hydraulic bender using a segmented bending process.

The first step is to determine the linear length or developed length of the conduit required to be used for the bend. This can be done by multiplying the radius of 25" by $\pi \div 2$ or $3.14 \div 2 = 1.57$. The answer is 39.25, as shown below:

$$1.57 \times 25" = 39.25"$$

Therefore, it takes 39.25" of conduit to accomplish a 90° bend with a 25" radius.

The next step is to decide how to lay out the number of segments to be bent to attain the 90° sweep. A rule of thumb is that there will be 20 segments or 21 shots. A shot is the actual bending process. There are 21 shots because the sweep is always laid out from the center of the developed length (*Figure 32*).

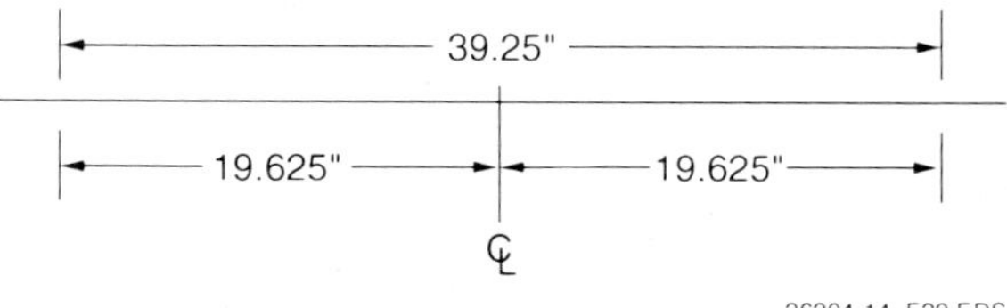

26204-14_F32.EPS

Figure 32 Conduit center.

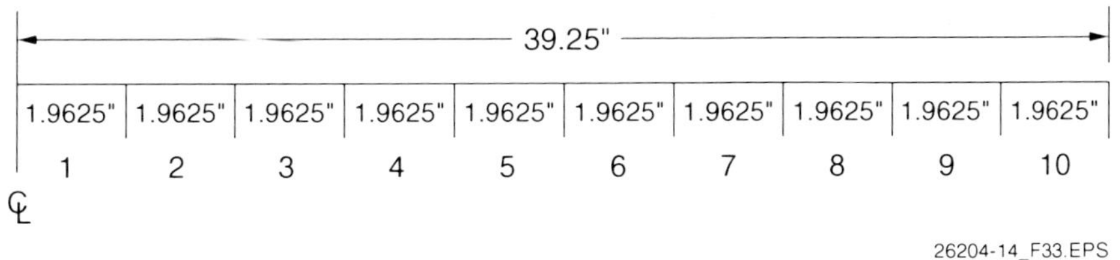

Figure 33 Conduit segments.

Once the center of the developed length is established, half of the developed length is measured out in each direction from the centerline.

To establish the linear distance between segments, divide the developed length by the number of shots (39.25 ÷ 20) or 1.9625" between segments (*Figure 33*).

Once the 20 segments are laid out, the number of degrees per shot (bend) needs to be determined. There are 21 shots, so dividing 90° by 21 will give you the number of degrees per shot:

$$90° \div 21 = 4.29°$$

You are now ready to do the bending. Starting at one end of the developed length, place the centerline of the bending shoe on the first shot mark and bend to 4.29°. Repeat the process for the remaining 20 bend marks. If the bend is not quite 90°, make the final adjustment in the last bend.

There is another way to lay out the segment marks for the developed length of a bend. Cut a piece of white elastic band to the length of the outside radius of the innermost bend and lay it out on a table. Make sure that it is not stretched. From one end of the elastic, measure 15 marks spaced evenly apart and mark these points with a fine-tip ink pen. Now place the end of the elastic tape on the centerline of the developed bend length. Stretch out the elastic until the 15th mark is on the end of the developed length. Place a mark on the conduit beside each mark on the elastic tape. Repeat this process on the other half of the developed length. You are now ready to do the segmented bends.

9.0.0 Segment Bending Techniques

Now that the procedure for laying out the conduit with bending marks is understood, the next step is bending. Because segment bending requires several small angle bends to complete a 90° stub, some method to measure the amount of bend will be required. This can be done in four ways:

- Bend degree protractor
- Magnetic angle finder
- Amount of travel method
- Number of pumps method

Bend degree protractor – This is a device that hooks onto the pipe being bent. The circular face is divided into four sections (18, 20, 21, and 30 shots) and is capable of being rotated to whichever scale is to be used. The indicating pointer is weighted and swings free. To use this device, proceed as follows:

Step 1 Level the conduit and secure it using a pipe vise or other means.

Step 2 Rotate the face to the desired scale that corresponds to the number of shots being used.

Step 3 Adjust the scale so the pointer is on 0.

Step 4 Bend the pipe until the pointer reaches the first mark. (Bend a little past to compensate for springback, release the pressure, and then check the pointer. Only a few bends will be needed to find out how much you must bend past the mark to account for springback.)

Step 5 Move the pipe forward in the bender to the second bend mark, and bend until the pointer reaches the second mark on the protractor face. (Again, bend past for springback.)

Step 6 Move the conduit to the third mark and bend the pipe so the pointer is at the third mark (after allowing for springback). Follow this procedure at each bend mark until the 90° stub is achieved, the pipe is level, and the bender is in a vertical position.

NOTE

It is a good idea to check the developing stub length before the last few bends are made. Make spacing corrections as required (e.g., shorten the spacing if the stub is coming up short). If the stub length is reached before the stub is plumb, do not bend at any of the remaining marks. Instead, move the pipe in the bender and bend at the start mark. This will make the stub plumb without adding to the stub length.

Magnetic angle finder – With the magnetic angle finder, the pipe must be kept level and bent vertically (the bender is in vertical position). When a magnetic angle finder is used, care must be taken with each bend as a very small error may become multiplied by 15 to 30 times, becoming a large error. To use the angle finder:

Step 1 Level the conduit and place the angle finder on the stub end. The angle finder will indicate the number of degrees in each bend as determined by the number of shots (e.g., for 20 shots, each bend is about 4.5°).

Step 2 Bend the pipe until the angle finder indicates that the bend is just past the desired degree of bend. This allows for springback. Release hydraulic pressure. If the right amount of overbend was made to allow for springback, the angle finder should read the desired angle of bend. If you bent too much or too little, make the adjustment on the next bend. In two or three bends, you will find the right amount to overbend at each mark to allow for springback.

Step 3 Move the pipe to the second bend mark. Bend at this mark until the next setting on the angle finder (allowing for springback) is indicated by the angle finder pointer. (For example, first bend 4½°, second bend 9°, third bend 13½°, etc.)

Step 4 Bend the pipe at each successive bend mark using the angle finder to indicate the proper degree of bend.

NOTE

Again, check the developing stub length before bending the last few bends. Adjust the spacing or amount of bend as required.

Amount of travel method – The pipe may be bent in any position. To find the amount of theoretical travel for a 90° bend, proceed as follows:

Step 1 Set up the bender with the pivot shoes in the proper holes for the conduit to be bent.

Step 2 Measure the distance (D) center-to-center between the pivot shoe pins (i.e., from center of pin A to center of pin B). The plunger (also called the ram) will have to travel half this distance to bend a full 90° stub.

Step 3 The travel per shot is one-half the distance from pin to pin divided by the number of shots. For example, the distance from the center of the pins is 24" and the pipe is to be bent in 18 shots. The travel per shot equals one-half the distance from the center of the pins (12") divided by the number of shots (18), which equals 0.666 or approximately ⅔" travel per shot.

Step 4 Bending with this method will follow a slightly different procedure.

Place the center of the bending shoe on the first bending mark (not the start mark) and activate the pump until ⅔" of ram travel is measured. Do not allow for springback with this method.

Move the pipe to the next mark and activate the pump until another ⅔" of ram travel has been measured. Continue to move the pipe and measure ram travel.

As you approach the last few marks (4 or 5), check both the developing stub length and the angle of the bend. The spacing and/or amount of travel can be adjusted on these last marks, as required.

NOTE

Once you have found the amount of travel for 90°, you can also find the amount of travel for any other angle for offsets, kicks, etc.

Number of pumps method – The pipe may be bent in any position. This method depends on the fact that a given hydraulic pump will produce the same amount of bend for a given number of pumps of the handle; however, it does not take into account that the number of pumps will change with a change in fluid level, the condition of the pump, and the condition of the O-rings.

For example, if it takes 40 pumps to bend a 90° stub, it should only take 20 pumps to achieve 45°, 10 pumps for 22½°, 2 pumps for 4½°, etc. As you can see, this method should work very well, but it will require additional time to determine pump/degree values. However, this can be offset by not having to measure ram travel at each bend as required by the amount of travel method.

Use the same procedure for bending as outlined in the amount of travel method. Check the developing stub length and degree of bend prior to bending the last few shots. Use these remaining shots for final adjustments in stub length and for checking the 90° bend.

Using a bending table – To make hydraulic bending easier, a bending table, either a commercial model or one constructed on the job, is a necessity. The table will hold the conduit and the bender, make leveling and plumbing easier, and produce more accurate bends. The table will also eliminate the need to continually wrestle with the conduit and bender.

> **NOTE**
>
> Use whichever one of the four methods is the most convenient, but bear in mind that extreme care and attention to detail are required in all methods. A small amount of error at each bend will compound itself, and accuracy in bending will be impossible to achieve.

Hydraulic bending example – For example, suppose that the task is to bend an offset containing two sweeping bends. The radius for the two sweeping bends is 30". This is to be done on a hydraulic bender using a segmented bending process. The angles of the sweeping bends are to be 30° each. The height of the offset is to be 30" (*Figure 34*).

This problem incorporates the concept of the unit circle, along with the cosecant trigonometric function.

In continuing with the concept of the unit circle and the linear distance on the circumference of the circle in terms of pi, it is necessary to understand the development of the pi relationship from 0° to 90°. All of these relationships from 0° to 90° and other interval angles in the circle are always in reference to 180°. For example: $360° = 2\pi$ or $2 \times 180°$; $180° = \pi$ or $1 \times 180°$; and $90° = \pi \div 2$ or $\frac{1}{2} \times 180°$.

The same process holds true for any angle from 0° through 90°. For example: $45° = \pi \div 4$ or $\frac{1}{4} \times 180°$; $60° = \frac{1}{3}\pi$ or $\frac{1}{3} \times 180°$; $30° = \frac{1}{6}\pi$ or $\frac{1}{6} \times 180°$; and $15° = \frac{1}{12}\pi$ or $\frac{1}{12} \times 180°$ (*Figure 35*).

To figure the developed length of the conduit to be used by one swing in the 30" radius, simply multiply $\pi \div 6$, which represents pi at 30°, times the 30" radius. It is nothing more than a converted circumference formula.

$C = 2\pi R$ (linear distance around a complete circle)

$C = \frac{\pi}{6} R$ (linear distance from 0° to 30°)

$C = \frac{\pi}{6} R$ or $C = 0.523 \times R$ or $C = 0.523 \times 30'' = 15.7''$

The developed length for the first radius is 15.7". That means that the developed length for the second sweeping radius is also 15.7". The total amount of conduit used to develop the two sweeps is 31.4".

The next step is to figure out the distance between the centerline of each of these bends on the hypotenuse of the imaginary triangle. To do this, simply use the cosecant of the angle trigonometric function or Cosecant = H ÷ O. Converting the formula gives H = O × Cosecant or H = 30" × 2 or 60". The layout of these measurements is shown in *Figure 36*.

Again, laying out the segments for the bending process is done from the centerline of the developed length of each sweeping bend (*Figure 37*). Therefore:

$$15.7'' \div 2 = 7.85''$$

When building a 90° sweep, the rule of thumb is 21 shots or 20 segments. This gives the conduit the appearance of being a natural sweep and not

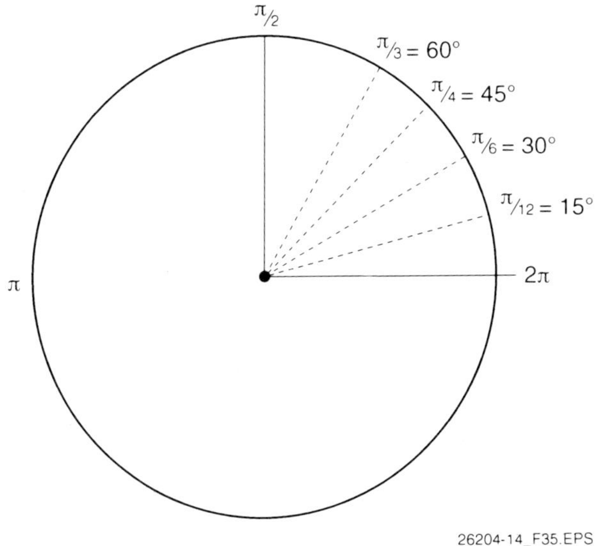

Figure 35 Radians and degrees.

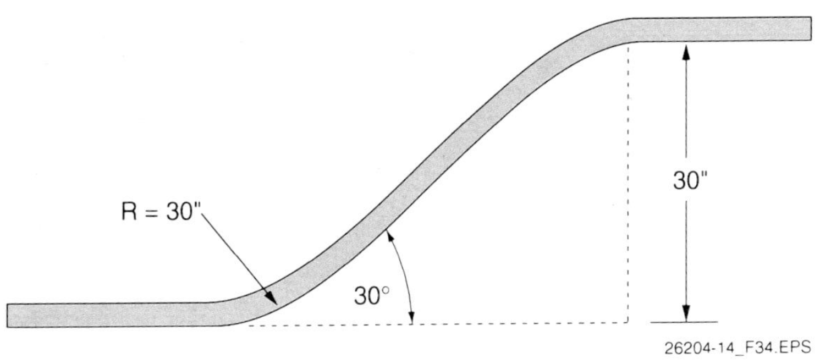

Figure 34 Two 30° sweeping bends.

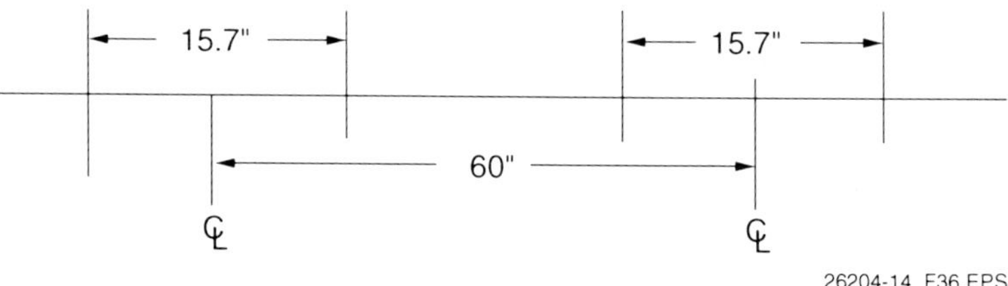

26204-14_F36.EPS

Figure 36 Bend centerline distance.

26204-14_F37.EPS

Figure 37 Bend centerline.

26204-14_F38.EPS

Figure 38 Bend segments.

a line of straight segments. (The same odd shot/even segment process will appear again.) If you choose to have seven shots or six segments within the 15.7" of developed length, each segment will be 15.7" ÷ 6 or 2.62" long. Because there are seven shots (bends), each shot will be 30 ÷ 7 or 4.29°. The layout of the bend is shown in *Figure 38*.

Once you have both sweeps laid out as described previously and the centerlines of these sweeps are 60" apart, you are ready to start the bending process. Again, start at one end of the offset and swing the bender segmented shoe down on the conduit. Because you are working an offset, an anti-dog device should be attached to one end of the conduit. This device maintains the centerline for each bend. Begin bending the first sweep, and once this is accomplished, roll the conduit in the bender and re-level the anti-dog device.

On Site

Magnetic Angle Finders

A magnetic angle finder is an invaluable tool when making segmented bends.

26204-14_SA03.EPS

Bend the second sweep and your offset is built. The final measurements should be as follows:

Developed length of each sweep = 15.7"

Distance between centerline of each sweep = 60"

Distance between shot marks in each sweep = 2.62"

Degrees per shot in each sweep = 4.29°

9.1.0 Concentric Bending

If two or more parallel runs of conduit must be bent in the same direction, as shown in *Figure 39*, the best results will be obtained by using concentric bends. When laying out concentric bends, the bend for the innermost conduit is calculated first. In the example in *Figure 39*, the first bend has a radius of 20". If this dimension is multiplied by 1.57, it yields a value of 31¹³⁄₃₂". This is the developed length of the shortest radius bend.

The second radius is found by adding the **outside diameter (OD)** size of the first pipe to the radius of the first pipe and the desired spacing between pipes. In this example, the radius of the second bend would be equal to 24⅜" (see *Figure 39*).

Radius of first pipe = 20"

OD size of first pipe = 2⅜"

Spacing between pipes = 2"

Radius of second pipe:

20" + 2⅜" + 2" = 24⅜" or 24.375"

Once the developed length of the second radius is found, the spacing between marks can be determined. The start mark must be the same distance from the end of the second pipe as it was for the first pipe (*Figure 39*). This will be true for each additional pipe as well. The spacing will increase

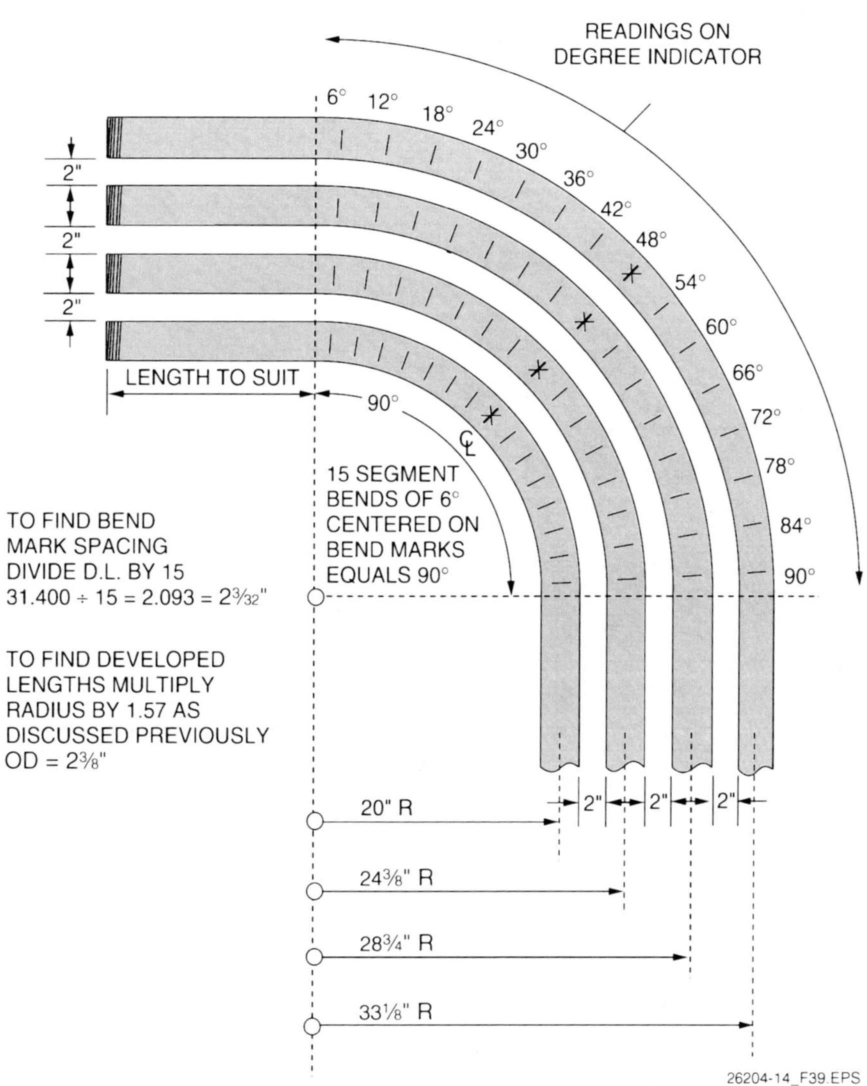

Figure 39 Principles of concentric bending.

between marks as the radius of the pipes increases. This is due to increasing developed length. The pipes in *Figure 39* are all laid out for 15 shots.

The equation for the developed length (DL) is 1.57 × R (radius). The developed length for the second bend is found by multiplying 1.57 × 24.375" = 38.27".

The radius and developed length of each successive bend are found in a similar manner. After determining the developed length, you must establish the number of segment bends needed to form each 90° bend. In concentric bending, every bend must receive the same number of segment bends to maintain concentricity. As illustrated, 15 segment bends of 6° each will total 90°.

> **NOTE**
> The radius change from one bend to another affects the spacing of segment bends. To find the segment bend spacing, divide the developed length of each bend by 15. For the first bend illustrated, the spacing for each segment bend is $2\frac{3}{32}$"; for the second bend, it is $2\frac{9}{16}$", and so on, as shown in *Figure 39*.

If the legs of the bends have to be a certain length, the gain must be considered just as in any segment bending procedure. When the runs of conduit are not the same size, the radius of each successive bend can be found as follows:

Step 1 Determine the radius of the innermost bend.

Step 2 Calculate one-half the outside diameter of the innermost conduit and of the next adjacent conduit.

Step 3 Note the distance between the two runs of conduit.

Step 4 Add these quantities.

9.2.0 Offset Bends

Many situations require a conduit to be bent so that it can pass by or over objects such as beams and other conduit or to enter panelboards and junction boxes. The bends used for this purpose are called offsets. To produce an offset, two equal bends of less than 90° are required at a specified distance apart. This distance is determined by the angle of the two bends and can be calculated by using the following procedure and the table in *Figure 40*.

First, determine the offset needed, then find the degree of bend. Next, multiply the offset measurements by the figure directly under the degree of bend (see *Figure 40*). This applies to all sizes of

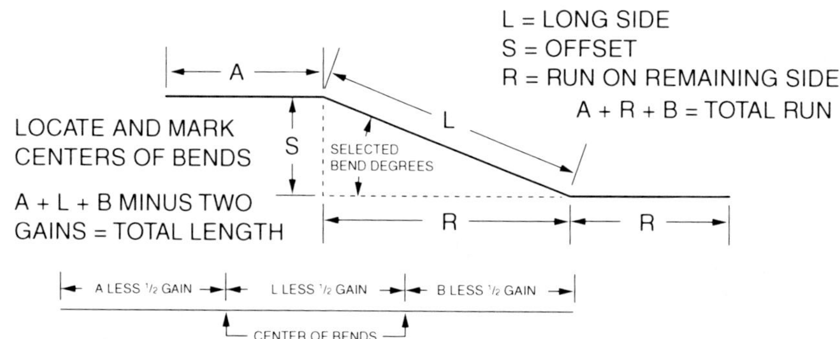

TO FIND UNKNOWN	KNOWN	TIMES CORRESPONDING MULTIPLIER EQUALS — TABLE OF MULTIPLIER FOR SELECTED DEGREES OF BEND								UNKNOWN
		5⅝°	11¼°	15°	22½°	30°	37½°	45°	60°	
L	S	10.207	5.126	3.864	2.613	2.00	1.643	1.414	1.155	L
S	L	0.098	0.195	0.259	0.383	0.50	0.609	0.707	0.866	S
R	S	10.158	5.027	3.732	2.414	1.732	1.303	1.00	0.577	R
S	R	0.098	0.199	0.268	0.414	0.577	0.767	1.00	1.732	S
L	R	1.005	1.02	1.035	1.082	1.155	1.260	1.414	2.00	L
R	L	0.995	0.981	0.966	0.933	0.866	0.793	0.707	0.50	R
GAIN PER BEND	RADIUS OR SHOE	0.0002	0.0006	0.0015	0.0051	0.0124	0.0212	0.0430	0.1076	GAIN PER BEND

26204-14_F40.EPS

Figure 40 Conduit offset bending table.

On Site

Leave Room for System Expansion

It's a good idea to make your first concentric bend large enough to fit another bend or two inside it in case you have to add additional conduit runs later on. Another method is to add any additional conduit runs on the outside of the original bend. Both methods produce a neat and professional installation.

conduit. For example, to form an 18" offset with two 45° bends, first make the following calculation to determine the distance between bends:

$$18" \times 1.414 = 25\frac{1}{2}"$$

This is the distance between bends and is labeled side *L* (see *Figure 40*). To connect the two ends of an offset to two pieces of conduit that are already in place, it is necessary to know the total or overall length (OL) of the offset from end to end before bending.

Note the following equation:

$$OL = (A + L + B) - (2 \times gain)$$

Where:

$$A = 36"$$
$$L = 25\frac{1}{2}"$$
$$B = 48"$$
$$2 \times gain = 1\frac{9}{32}"$$

The gain is calculated by multiplying the shoe radius by the decimal figures shown on the last line under Degrees of Bend in *Figure 40*. For example, to calculate how an offset might be made in a length of 3" conduit using 45° bends:

$$OL = (A + L + B) - (2 \times gain)$$

NOTE

This offset uses a 15" radius.

$$OL = 109\frac{1}{2}" - 1\frac{9}{32}" = 108\frac{7}{32}"$$

15" × 0.0430 (from the table in *Figure 40*) = 0.645°

For two gains, you have:

$$1.290 = 1\frac{9}{32}$$

Since you already know the long dimension of the offset (25"), to find the amount of offset, refer to the table in *Figure 40*, second line down

Think About It

Concentric Bends

What does concentric mean? Why can't you just bend all your conduit sections to the same radius and lay them side by side?

26204-14_SA04.EPS

(to find S), then move across the row until you come to the 45° column. Note that the multiplier is 0.707.

Therefore:

$$25" \times 0.707 = 17.675"$$

This is the height of the offset. To make the offset, the conduit is positioned in the hydraulic bender, as shown in *Figure 41*. The bending shoe makes one 45° bend on the first center mark, the conduit is reversed in the bender, and the next 45° bend is made at the second mark. When making bends, always refer to the bending charts that accompany the bender being used for the operation.

For example, an offset is to be built to go over an I-beam that is 24" in height. The distance from the end of the conduit run to the J box on the opposite side of the I-beam is 8' (see *Figure 42*).

The task is to determine the distance between bend points where a 45° bend is being used. Determine the exact length of conduit needed so threading can occur before bending. The conduit will have no clearance over the top of the I-beam.

To find the distance between bend points, multiply the amount of offset required by the cosecant of the bending angle (in this case, 45°):

$$24" \times 1.41 = 33.84"$$

The straight distance from the end of the conduit run to the J box is 8'. To find the amount of conduit to add to this because of the 45° bend, use the cosine formula (C = A ÷ H). The hypotenuse

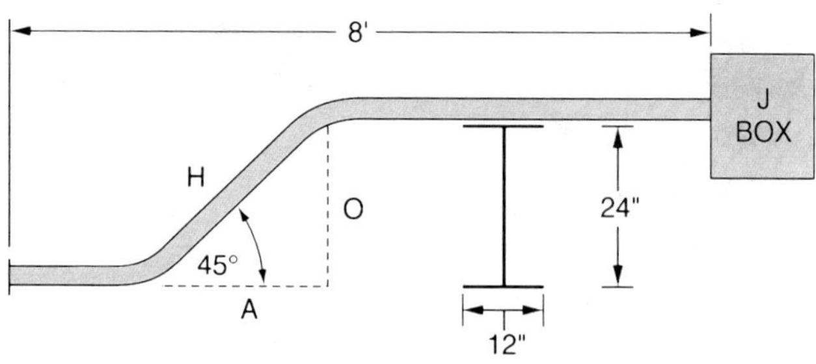

Figure 42 24" offset.

or the distance between bend points is 33.84". The side adjacent is found by converting C = A ÷ H to A = C × H, or:

$$A = 0.707 \times 33.84" = 23.92"$$

Subtract 23.92" from 33.84" and this gives the amount of extra conduit needed when making this 45° bend:

$$33.84" - 23.92" = 9.92" \text{ or } 9^{92}/_{100}"$$

Add the 9.92" to 8' and the amount of straight conduit required has been determined:

$$8' + 9.92" = 8'\text{-}9.92" \text{ of straight conduit}$$

The final measurements should be as follows:

Distance between bend points = $33^{21}/_{25}$" or 33.84"

Length of straight conduit = 8'-9.92" or 8'-$9^{92}/_{100}$"

Now let us complete another example. In this case, an offset is to be made without the use of a

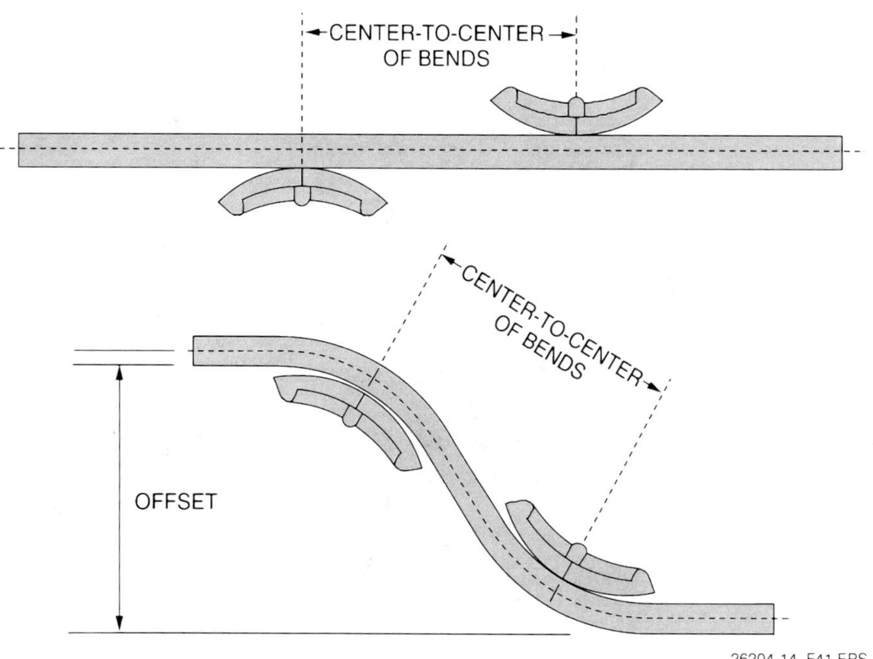

Figure 41 Position of conduit in bender for making offsets.

protractor level. The offset is to be 20" in height (*Figure 43*). The bend angle is 45°. Explain the process required to accomplish this.

The cosecant for 45° is 1.41. The distance between bend points is 1.41 × 20". Therefore:

$$1.41 \times 20" = 28.2"$$

The first mark on the conduit is placed 14.1" back from the end of the conduit. The end of the conduit needs to be brought up 10" to accomplish a 45° bend. The second mark on the conduit is placed 28.2" down the conduit from the first mark. The bender is placed on the second mark. The conduit is bent until the two surfaces are parallel. At this point, a 20" offset has been created.

9.3.0 Concentric Offsets

To make concentric offsets, use the same procedure as for 90° stubs. Increase the radius of the second pipe by an amount equal to the radius of the first pipe plus the OD size of the first pipe plus the spacing desired between pipes. Although the examples used to explain offset bending had several shots per bend, fewer shots can be used. Successful offsets can be made with only two or three shots per bend. However, with offsets, 90° bends, or any other segment bends, the extra time spent bending smoother radius bends (more shots) is returned when the conductors are pulled into the completed raceway.

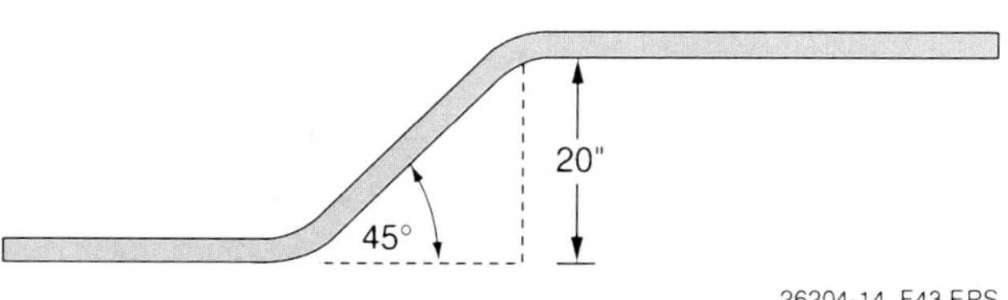

Figure 43 20" offset.

9.3.1 Saddle Bends

As mentioned previously, saddle bends are used to cross small obstructions or other runs of conduit. Saddle bends in conduit up to four inches inside diameter (ID) may be made in hydraulic conduit benders. Always refer to the charts that accompany the bender. For example, to make a saddle bend on a length of 2" rigid conduit so that it can pass over a 3" water pipe with ¼" clearance, three bending operations are required, as shown in *Figure 44*.

The bend is calculated by referring to appropriate bending charts. The one shown in *Table 6* gives measurements for 2" conduit with ¼" clearance. Therefore, look in the left column under straight-run conduit and go down the column until the 3" row is reached. Moving to the right in this row, it can be seen that the spacing between bends is 15⅝" on center, and bends No. 1 and No. 2 will be 15°, while the third bend is 30°.

Using the information found in the bending table, mark the conduit accordingly. Insert the conduit in the bender and make bends No. 1 and No. 2 first, both at 15°. Back off the pump pressure, reverse the conduit in the bender, and then make the third bend at 30°. Release the pump pressure, remove the conduit from the bender, and check the saddle for accuracy.

For another example, suppose a saddle is to be built to go over an I-beam that is 36" in height (*Figure 45*). The distance from the end of the conduit to the center of the I-beam is 5'.

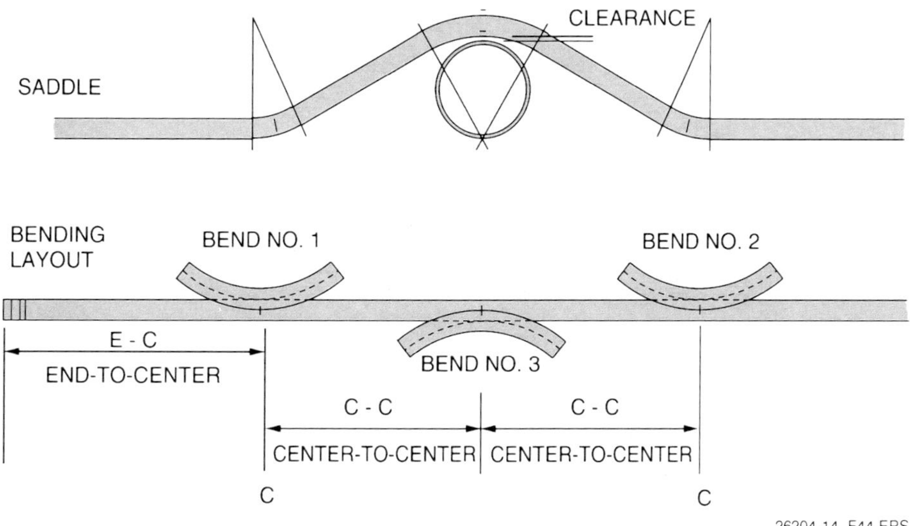

Figure 44 Principles of saddle bending.

Table 6 Saddle Table

Straight-Run Conduit	Minimum Length	Bend Spacing	Bend Degrees	Bend Degrees	Bend Degrees
—	E-C	C-C	No. 1	No. 2	No. 3
1"	20"	16"	6	6	12
1¼"	20"	16"	7	7	14
1½"	20"	16"	8	8	16
2"	20"	15⅞"	10	10	20
2½"	20"	15¾"	12½	12½	25
3"	20"	15⅝"	15	15	30
3½"	20"	15½"	18	18	36
4"	20"	15½"	20	20	40

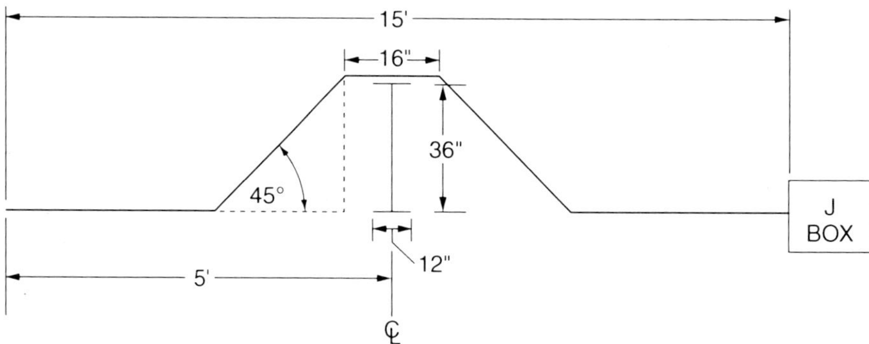

Figure 45 36" saddle.

The task is to determine the distance between bend points when a 45° bend is being used. Determine the exact length of conduit needed so threading can be completed before bending. The conduit is to clear the top of the I-beam by 1". Determine the centerline layout of the saddle (*Figure 46*).

The 16" between bend points in this problem is an arbitrary measurement. It is determined by the person doing the bending. Enough conduit should be used to extend past the outside dimensions of the 12" I-beam so the radius of each bend does not run into the I-beam.

The distance between bend points on the hypotenuse of the imaginary triangle is calculated by multiplying the total height of the I-beam (36" + 1" clearance = 37") by the cosecant of the 45° angle of the bend or 1.41 × 37":

$$1.41 \times 37" = 52^{17}/_{100}" \text{ or } 52.17"$$

The centerline layout mark for the saddle would be 5' if the conduit were to be installed on a straight line from the end of the existing conduit run to the center of the I-beam. However, the conduit is not being installed on a straight line. Therefore, the measurement in question is the amount of additional conduit needed because of the 45° angle of deviation (*Figure 47*). The amount of additional conduit is equal to the side adjacent subtracted from the hypotenuse.

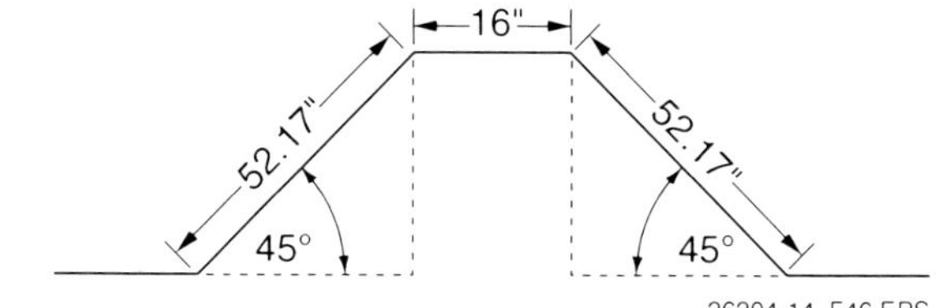

Figure 46 Saddle.

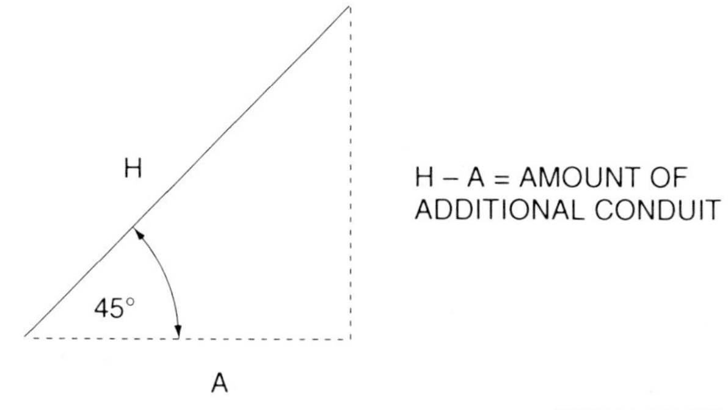

Figure 47 Cosine function.

The side adjacent (A) first needs to be calculated, then that measurement can be subtracted from the hypotenuse (52.17"). To calculate the side adjacent, use the cosine formula (C = A ÷ H).

On Site

Saddle Bends

Whenever possible, a three-bend saddle should not be sharper than 30°. If the object you are trying to saddle is more than 6" in diameter, use a four-bend saddle rather than a three-bend saddle. In this installation, two three-bend saddles were required.

26204-14_SA05.EPS

Because you are looking for A, convert the formula to A = C × H, or:

$$A = 0.707 \times 52.17"$$
$$A = 36.88"$$

Subtract 36.88 from 57.17, or:

$$52.17" - 36.88" = 15.29"$$

That is how much extra conduit is needed to get the center of the saddle to the center of the I-beam. Therefore, the layout mark for the saddle is:

$$5' + 15.29" = 6'\text{-}3.29"$$

The layout of the conduit is shown in *Figure 48*.

To find the total amount of conduit to be used from the end of the existing conduit to the J box, simply take the straight line distance of 15' and add the difference between the hypotenuse and side adjacent to 15' two times, or:

$$15' + 15.29" + 15.29" = 15' + 30.58" = 17'\text{-}6.58"$$

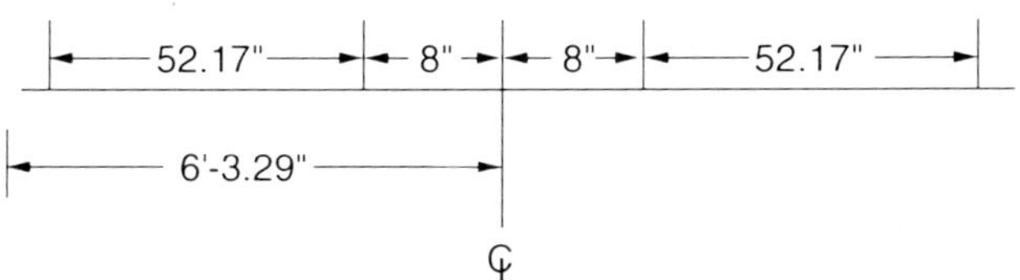

26204-14_F48.EPS

Figure 48 Conduit layout.

The final measurements should be as follows:

Distance between bend points on the top portion of the saddle = 16"

Distance between bend points that form each hypotenuse = $52\frac{17}{100}$" or 52.17"

Distance from the end of the conduit to the centerline layout mark of the saddle = 6'-3.29" or 6'-$3\frac{29}{100}$"

Overall length of the conduit required to reach the J box = 17'-$6\frac{58}{100}$" or 17'-6.58"

10.0.0 Tricks of the Trade

There are many tricks of the trade that you will learn during your career as an electrician. Some of these will be handed down to you by experienced workers; others will be learned through experience. Most professionals are constantly seeking new methods to improve their efficiency and to make the work go smoother and faster without sacrificing workmanship.

One of the handiest personal tools for bending conduit is the small, magnetic torpedo level with a 30° and 45° bubble. This tool should be in the tool pouch of every electrician. In many cases, it can make the difference between a good job and a poor job; that is, obtaining level and plumb conduit runs or not.

Workers have also designed their own custom tools to help in conduit installations. One tip is to take a pair of vice grips and weld a small, flat piece of iron on the top of the jaws for use with the magnetic level. During multiple bends, the vice grips are positioned at the desired point on the end of a piece of conduit, locked in place, and then the magnetic level is placed on the flat plate so the bubble may be watched during the bend. There are also some new commercial tools that are designed for leveling conduit bends; keep up with these developments by reading trade journals.

10.1.0 Eliminating Dog Legs

One of the problems that exists when bending an offset or saddle is the creation of a dog leg. A dog leg occurs when the centerline that runs the length of the conduit is not maintained for both bends of an offset and for the four bends of a saddle. Dog legs can be eliminated using an anti-dog device, as discussed earlier, or by following the procedure described here.

See *Figure 49*. When the conduit is snugged up by the bender, take a piece of Unistrut® and clamp it to the end of the conduit farthest from the bending shoe. Before tightening the conduit strap, level the Unistrut®. Once this is done, make your first bend. Release the conduit from the bending shoe and move the conduit forward to the next bending mark. Roll the conduit 180° and re-level the Unistrut®. Tighten the conduit in the bender and again make sure that the Unistrut® is level. Bend the second bend and you will have an offset with no dog leg.

10.2.0 Using a Table Corner or Plywood Sheet for Calculating Added Length

The task is to use a table corner or the corner of a sheet of plywood and demonstrate how to come up with the amount of additional conduit needed to go from one point to another once a bend has been made. The distance between points is 8'. The amount of offset to be made is 25" (*Figure 50*). The degree of bend is 30°.

On Site

Trapeze Hangers

Trapeze hangers are often used to support multiple overhead conduit runs. This reduces the number of individual supports and also reduces the number of bends, as the conduit can be run below obstacles as shown here.

26204-14_SA06.EPS

See *Figure 51*. Measure 25" up one side of the sheet of plywood or the corner of a table. The hypotenuse of the triangle will be 2 × 25" or 50"

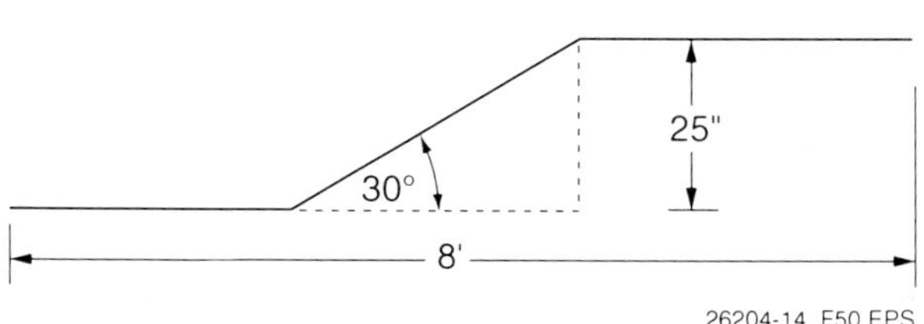

Figure 50 25" offset.

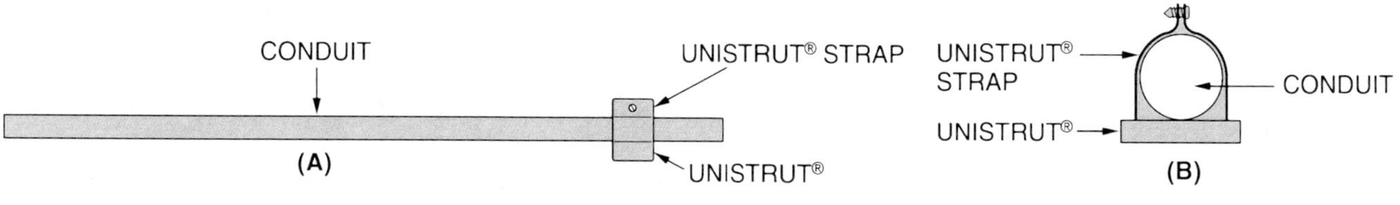

Figure 49 Dog leg elimination.

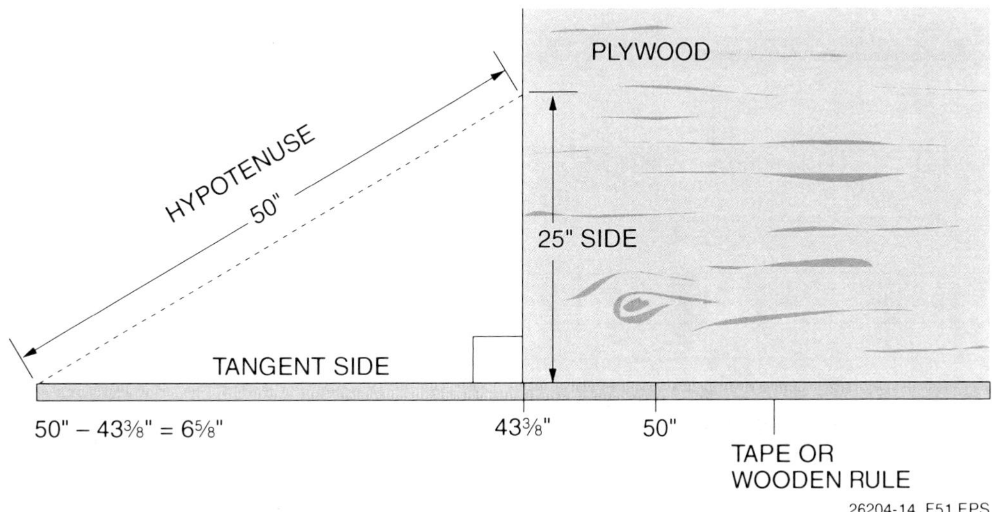

Figure 51 Extra conduit.

(2 is the cosecant for 30°). Measure from the 25" mark to the surface that is tangent to the side that is 25" long, until the 50" mark on the tape measure crosses the tangent side. Mark this 50" point. Then, place the end of the ruler on the 50" mark and let the 50" point on the ruler extend beyond the end of the plywood or table. The amount of tape that extends beyond the plywood or table edge is the amount of extra conduit that is needed to accomplish this bend. This is 6⅝" more conduit than if going on a straight line for 8' or 8'-6⅝" of conduit required to accomplish the task.

11.0.0 PVC Conduit Installations

Rigid nonmetallic conduit and fittings (PVC electric conduit) may be used in direct earth burial; in walls, floors, and ceilings of buildings; in cinder fill; and in damp and dry locations. Its use is prohibited by the *NEC®* in certain hazardous locations, for support of fixtures or other equipment, where subject to physical damage, and under certain other conditions. See *NEC Article 352*.

PVC conduit can be cut easily at the job site without special tools, although PVC cutters help in cutting square ends. Sizes from ½" through 1½" can be cut with a fine-tooth saw. For sizes 2" through 6", a miter box or similar saw guide should be used to keep the conduit steady and ensure a square cut. To ensure satisfactory joining, care should be taken not to distort the end of the conduit when cutting.

After cutting, deburr the pipe ends and wipe clean of dust, dirt, and plastic shavings. Deburring is accomplished easily using a pocket knife or file.

One of the important advantages of PVC conduit, in comparison with other rigid conduit materials, is the ease and speed with which solvent-cemented joints can be made. The following steps are required for a proper joint:

Step 1 The conduit should be wiped clean and dry.

WARNING!

The cement used with PVC can be hazardous. Provide adequate ventilation, avoid skin contact, and always refer to the MSDS and follow the manufacturer's usage and safety instructions.

Step 2 Apply a full, even coat of PVC cement to the end of the conduit and the fitting. The cement should cover the area that will be inserted in the fitting.

Step 3 Push the conduit and fitting firmly together with a slight twisting action until it bottoms and then rotate the conduit in the fitting (about a half turn) to distribute the cement evenly. Avoid cement buildup inside the conduit. The cementing and joining operation should not exceed more than 20 seconds.

Step 4 When the proper amount of cement has been applied, a bead of cement will form at the joint. Wipe the joint with a brush to remove any excess cement. The joint should not be disturbed for 10 minutes.

On Site

Magnetic Level

A magnetic torpedo level can be attached directly to the conduit. It will remain where you put it, even if the conduit is turned over.

26204-14_SA07.EPS

12.0.0 Bending PVC Conduit

Most manufacturers of PVC conduit offer various radius bends in a number of segments. Where special bends are required, PVC conduit is easy to bend on the job. Stub-ups, saddles, concentric bends, offsets, and kicks are all possible with PVC conduit, just as with metallic conduit.

PVC conduit is bent with the aid of a heating unit. The PVC must be heated evenly over the entire length of the curve. Heating units are available from various sources that are designed specifically for the purpose in sizes to accommodate all conduit diameters (*Figure 52*). While some heaters use gas for the heat source, most employ infrared heat energy, which is more quickly absorbed in the conduit. Small sizes are ready to bend after a few seconds in the hotbox. Larger diameters require two or three minutes, depending on the conditions. Other methods of heating PVC conduit for bending include heating blankets and hot air blowers. The use of torches or other flame-type devices is not recommended. PVC conduit exposed to excessively high temperatures may take on a brownish color. Sections showing evidence of such scorching should be discarded.

26204-14_F52.EPS

Figure 52 PVC heating units.

WARNING!

Always wear gloves when working with heat.

If a number of identical bends are required, a template can be helpful (*Figure 53*). A simple template can be made by sawing a sheet of plywood to match the desired bend. Nail to a second sheet of plywood. The heated conduit section is placed in the template, sponged with water to cool, and is then ready to install. Care should be taken to fully maintain the ID of the conduit when bending.

If only a few bends are needed, scribe a chalk line on the floor or workbench. Then, match the heated conduit to the chalk line and cool. The conduit must be held in the desired position until it is relatively cool since the PVC material will tend to revert to its original shape. Templates are also available for many bends.

Another method is to take the heated conduit section to the point of installation and form it to fit the actual installation (*Figure 54*). This method is especially effective for making blind bends or compound bends using smaller sizes of PVC. After bending, wipe a wet rag over the bend (*Figure 55*) to cool it.

Bends in small-diameter PVC conduit (½" to 1½") require no filling for code-approved radii. When bending PVC of 2" or larger diameter, there is a risk of wrinkling or flattening the bend. To help eliminate this problem, a plug set is used. A plug is inserted in each end of the piece of PVC being bent, and then the conduit is pressurized using either a hand pump or the heat of the bender, depending on the type of plug used.

Place airtight plugs (*Figure 56*) in each end of the conduit section before heating. The retained air will expand during the heating process and hold the conduit open during bending. Do not remove the plugs until the conduit has cooled.

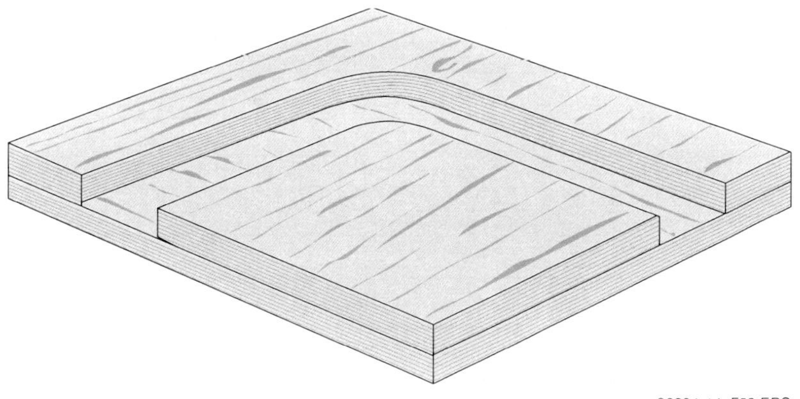

26204-14_F53.EPS

Figure 53 Plywood template.

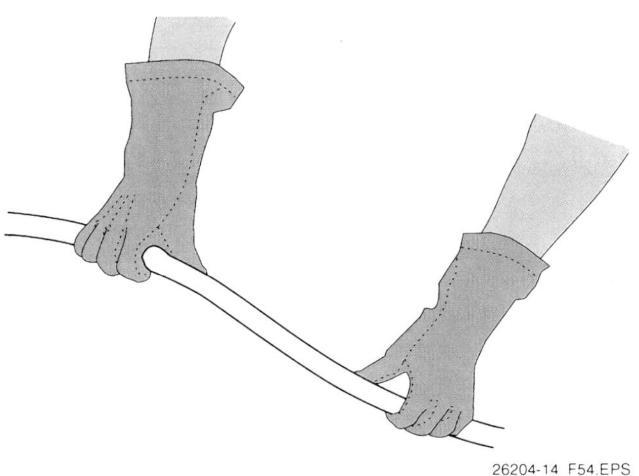

26204-14_F54.EPS

Figure 54 Some PVC bends may be formed by hand.

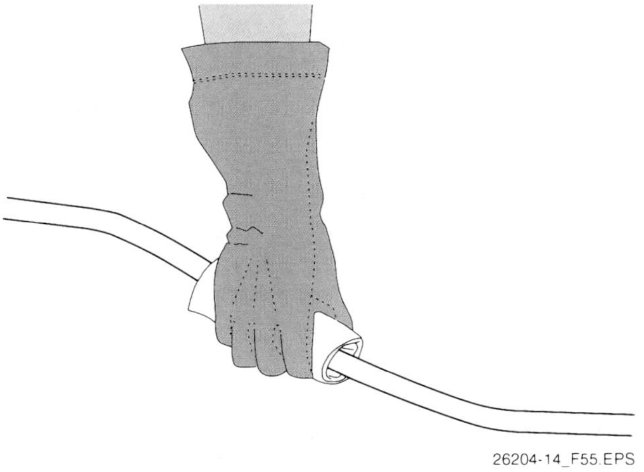

26204-14_F55.EPS

Figure 55 After the bend is formed, wipe a wet rag over the bend to cool it.

In applications where the conduit installation is subject to constantly changing temperatures and the runs are long, precautions should be taken to allow for expansion and contraction of PVC conduit. When expansion and contraction

26204-14_F56.EPS

Figure 56 Typical plug set.

are factors, an O-ring expansion coupling should be installed near the fixed end of the run, or fixture, to take up any expansion or contraction that may occur. Confirm the expansion and contraction lengths available in these fittings as they may vary by manufacturer. Charts are available that indicate what expansion can be expected at various temperature levels. The coefficient of linear expansion of PVC conduit is 0.0034" per 10' per °F. *Table 7* lists the expansion rates for various temperatures.

Expansion couplings are seldom required in underground or slab applications. Expansion

On Site

PVC Conduit Bending

PVC conduit has a memory. As soon as you have finished bending the PVC, cool it down with cold, wet towels or hose it down with cold water. Otherwise, it will begin to return to its original position.

Table 7 PVC Expansion Rates

Temperature Change in °F	Length Change in Inches per 100 Ft of PVC Conduit	Temperature Change in °F	Length Change in Inches per 100 Ft of PVC Conduit
5	0.2	105	4.2
10	0.4	110	4.5
15	0.6	115	4.7
20	0.8	120	4.9
25	1.0	125	5.1
30	1.2	130	5.3
35	1.4	135	5.5
40	1.6	140	5.7
45	1.8	145	5.9
50	2.0	150	6.1
55	2.2	155	6.3
60	2.4	160	6.5
65	2.6	165	6.7
70	2.8	170	6.9
75	3.0	175	7.1
80	3.2	180	7.3
85	3.4	185	7.5
90	3.6	190	7.7
95	3.8	195	7.9
100	4.1	200	8.1

and contraction may generally be controlled by bowing the conduit slightly or burying the conduit immediately. After the conduit is buried, expansion and contraction cease to be factors. Care should be taken, however, in constructing a buried installation. If the conduit should be left exposed for an extended period of time during widely-variable temperature conditions, an allowance should be made for expansion and contraction.

In above-ground installations, care should be taken to provide proper support of PVC conduit because of its semi-rigidity. This is particularly important at high temperatures. The distance between supports should be based on temperatures encountered at the specific installation. Charts are available that clearly outline at what intervals support is required for PVC conduit at various temperature levels.

Think About It

Putting It All Together

Examine the visible conduit bends in your home or workplace. Are they neat and professionally made? If not, what might you have done differently to improve the installation?

Summary

Many conduit installations are visible; that is, they run exposed. Consequently, electricians must take special care to ensure that all exposed conduit runs are parallel, level, and plumb. Nothing else will do. This is one phase of the electrical construction industry where electricians have an opportunity to show off. In fact, an expert installation of a conduit system is similar to a work of art.

Learn the basics of conduit bending and installations, put your knowledge to practical use, and take pride in your abilities to perform a professional conduit installation. Make your work second to none. Of course, contractors and clients want speed, but if you have a good basic knowledge of conduit bending and then put this knowledge to use, your craftsmanship will let you bend conduit smarter and faster, giving a good-looking installation along with speed to satisfy your employer, the building owners, and all concerned.

Review Questions

1. The minimum bending radius for 3" rigid conduit is _____.
   a. 8"
   b. 10"
   c. 11"
   d. 13"

2. The minimum bending radius for ½" rigid conduit is _____.
   a. 4"
   b. 6"
   c. 8"
   d. 10"

3. The maximum number of 90° bends allowed between pull points in a conduit system is _____.
   a. one
   b. two
   c. three
   d. four

4. A saddle bend is counted as _____.
   a. 90°
   b. 120°
   c. 180°
   d. It depends on the type of bends used.

5. When referring to the two bends required to make an offset in a length of conduit, which of the following is always true?
   a. The degree of bend for each must be exactly 45°.
   b. The degree of bend for each must be exactly 30°.
   c. The degree of bend for each must be equal.
   d. The degree of bend for each must be unequal.

6. The reason for making a saddle bend in a run of conduit is to _____.
   a. change direction in the height of a conduit run
   b. make a 90° bend
   c. cross a small obstacle
   d. make a conduit termination in an outlet box

7. The equation used to calculate the circumference of a circle is _____.
   a. $C = \pi D$
   b. $C = 1\pi R$
   c. $C = \pi R^2$
   d. $C = \pi^2$

8. The fractional equivalent of the decimal 0.015625 is _____.
   a. 1⁄64
   b. 1⁄32
   c. 3⁄64
   d. 1⁄16

9. The rise in a conduit bend is best described as the _____.
   a. horizontal distance that runs from the point of bend and parallel with the deck
   b. leg length
   c. radius
   d. height of the stub-up

10. The best type of bending shoe for making concentric bends is the _____.
    a. concentric shoe
    b. one-shot shoe
    c. segmented shoe
    d. long shoe

11. Rigid aluminum conduit is available in standard sizes from _____.
    a. ½" to 4"
    b. ½" to 6"
    c. ¾" to 6"
    d. ¾" to 4"

12. Two or more parallel bends that are bent in the same direction are known as _____.
    a. stubs
    b. perpendicular bends
    c. concentric bends
    d. axial bends

13. Which of the following formulas should be used to find the side adjacent?
    a. $S = O \times H$
    b. $S = O \div H$
    c. $C = A \div H$
    d. $C = A \times H$

14. An important safety precaution to use when working with PVC conduit is to _____.
    a. provide proper ventilation to carry off fumes from the joint cement
    b. use lengths of PVC of not more than 8'
    c. use inside diameters of 4" or less
    d. never wear gloves that may adhere to the joint cement

15. To prevent flattening when bending larger diameter PVC pipe, use _____.
    a. plugs and air pressure
    b. sand fill
    c. water fill
    d. a higher temperature

Module 26204-14

Supplemental Exercises

1. In what chapter of the *NEC*® will you find the installation requirements for conduit?
   a. Two
   b. Three
   c. Four
   d. Five

2. The maximum number of degrees allowed between pull points in a conduit run is ________.

3. Offsets and saddles ____________________.
   a. do not need to be counted if less than 15°
   b. must be included when calculating total degrees between pull points
   c. add no resistance
   d. all count as 30°

4. A conduit run with ____________________ is acceptable to pull wire.
   a. two 90° bends, four 45° bends, and one box offset
   b. two 90° bends, three 45° bends, and one saddle
   c. two 90° bends, two 45° bends, and two 30° bends
   d. four 90° bends and two box offsets

5. The maximum size rigid steel conduit that can be bent using a portable mechanical bender is ____________________.

6. The maximum size IMC that can be bent using a portable mechanical conduit bender is ____________________.

7. All of the following may be bent using a mechanical bender *except* ____________________.
   a. EMT
   b. IMC
   c. PVC
   d. rigid conduit

8. The maximum size rigid conduit that can be bent with a hydraulic bender is ______________.

9. When making segment bends, ____________________ must be determined.
   a. the radius of the bend
   b. the total number of degrees in the bend
   c. the developed length
   d. All of the above.

10. When making a saddle bend using 4" conduit with a minimum length (E-C) of 20" and bend spacing (C-C) of 15½", the angle of the third bend will be ____________________.
    a. 36°
    b. 20°
    c. 40°
    d. 30°

11. The code requires a minimum radius for rigid conduit bends because ____________________

    ____

12. A bend used for a change in direction of less than 90° is called a(n) ___________________.
   a. kick
   b. saddle
   c. stub-up
   d. offset

13. A mechanical bender may be used to make bends in ___________________.
   a. 2" EMT
   b. 4" rigid conduit
   c. 1½" PVC
   d. IMC conduit only

14. To make matching bends in both ½" and 1" IMC when using a mechanical bender, ________.
   a. adjust the deduct length for the ½" conduit
   b. use the ½" shoe for the ½" conduit and the 1" shoe for the 1" conduit
   c. use the 1" shoe for both conduits
   d. get matched pairs of conduit shoes from the manufacturer

15. Speed benders can bend conduit up to ___________________.

16. True or False? The one-shot shoes used with hydraulic benders can make 90° bends in a single operation.

17. One method of bending segment is to use ___________________.
   a. an elapsed time method to keep track of each bend
   b. a stress meter to monitor each bend
   c. a level to monitor each bend
   d. the amount of travel method to monitor each bend

18. To make a 20" offset using 45° angles, a multiplier of 1.414 is used. If the first bend is marked at 12" from the end of the conduit, the second bend would be marked at _________________ from the end.
   a. 16.96"
   b. 28.28"
   c. 40.28"
   d. 32"

19. Airtight plugs are installed in the ends of large sizes of PVC conduit during bending to ___________________.
   a. prevent the conduit from wrinkling or flattening the bend
   b. hold the heat inside the conduit to keep it flexible
   c. prevent condensation within the conduit
   d. prevent deadly PVC gases from escaping

20. One of the disadvantages of aluminum conduit is that ___________________.
   a. it cannot be bent with one-shot benders
   b. it is difficult to bend consistently and accurately
   c. special bending shoes must be used
   d. aluminum kinks when bent

Trade Terms Introduced in This Module

Approximate ram travel: The distance the ram of a hydraulic bender travels to make a bend. To simplify and speed bending operations, many benders are equipped with a scale that shows ram travel. Using a simple table (supplied with many benders), the degree of bend can easily be converted to inches of ram travel. This measurement, however, can only be approximated because of the variation in springback of the conduit being bent.

Back-to-back bend: Any bend formed by two 90° bends with a straight section of conduit between the bends.

Bending protractor: Made for use with benders mounted on a bending table and used to measure degrees; also has a scale for 18, 20, 21, and 22 shots when using it to make a large sweep bend.

Bending shot: The number of shots needed to produce a specific bend.

Concentric bending: The process of making 90° bends in parallel runs of conduit. This requires increasing the radius of each conduit from the inside of the bend toward the outside.

Conduit: Piping designed especially for pulling electrical conductors. Types include rigid, IMC, EMT, PVC, aluminum, and other materials.

Degree indicator: An instrument designed to indicate the exact degree of bend while it is being made.

Developed length: The amount of straight pipe needed to bend a given radius. Also, the actual length of the conduit that will be bent.

Elbow: A 90° bend.

Gain: The amount of pipe saved by bending on a radius as opposed to right angles. Because conduit bends in a radius and not at right angles, the length of conduit needed for a bend will not equal the total determined length. Gain is the difference between the right angle distances A and B and the shorter distance C—the length of conduit actually needed for the bend.

Inside diameter (ID): The inside diameter of conduit. All electrical conduit is measured in this manner. The outside dimensions, however, will vary with the type of conduit used.

Kicks: Bends in a piece of conduit, usually less than 90°, made to change the direction of the conduit.

Leg length: The distance from the end of the straight section of conduit to the bend, measured to the centerline or to the inside or outside of the bend or rise.

Ninety-degree bend: A bend in a piece of conduit that changes its direction by 90°.

Offsets: Two equal bends made to avoid an obstruction blocking the run of the conduit.

One-shot shoe: A large bending shoe that is designed to make 90° bends in conduit.

Outside diameter (OD): The size of any piece of conduit measured on the outside diameter.

Radius: The relative size of the bent portion of a pipe.

Rise: The length of the bent section of conduit measured from the bottom, centerline, or top of the straight section to the end of the bent section.

Segment bend: Any bend formed by a series of bends of a few degrees each, rather than a single one-shot bend.

Segmented bending shoe: A smaller type of shoe designed for bending segmented bends only (always less than 15°).

Springback: The amount, measured in degrees, that a bent conduit tends to straighten after pressure is released on the bender ram. For example, a 90° bend, after pressure is released, will pull back about 2° to 88°.

Stub-up: Another name for the rise in a section of conduit.

Sweep bend: A 90° bend with a radius larger than that produced by a standard one-shot shoe.

Take-up (comeback): The amount that must be subtracted from the desired stub length to make the bend come out correctly using a point of reference on the bender or bending shoe.

Additional Resources

This module presents thorough resources for task training. The following resource material is suggested for further study.

Benfield Conduit Bending Manual, 2nd Edition. KS: EC&M Books.

National Electrical Code® Handbook, Latest Edition. Quincy, MA: National Fire Protection Association.

Tom Henry's Conduit Bending Package (includes video, book, and bending chart). Winter Park, FL: Code Electrical Classes, Inc.

Figure Credits

AGC of America, Module opener

Topaz Publications, Inc., SA01, Figures 1B (photo), 16, SA02, Figures 26, 31, SA05, SA07, Figures 52 and 56

National Fire Protection Association, Tables 1 and 2

Reprinted with permission from *NFPA 70®* -2014, *National Electrical Code®*, Copyright © 2013, National Fire Protection Association, Quincy, MA. This reprinted material is not the complete and official position of the National Fire Protection Association on the referenced subject, which is represented only by the standard in its entirety. *NFPA 70®*, *National Electrical Code®*, and *NEC®* are registered trademarks of the National Fire Protection Association, Inc., Quincy, MA.

John Traister, Figures 2, 9, and 10

Tim Ely, Figures 3B (photo) and 27

Greenlee / A Textron Company, Figures 15, 25, 28, 39–42, and 44

Mike Powers, SA03

Tim Dean, SA04 and SA06

NCCER CURRICULA — USER UPDATE

NCCER makes every effort to keep its textbooks up-to-date and free of technical errors. We appreciate your help in this process. If you find an error, a typographical mistake, or an inaccuracy in NCCER's curricula, please fill out this form (or a photocopy), or complete the online form at **www.nccer.org/olf**. Be sure to include the exact module ID number, page number, a detailed description, and your recommended correction. Your input will be brought to the attention of the Authoring Team. Thank you for your assistance.

Instructors – If you have an idea for improving this textbook, or have found that additional materials were necessary to teach this module effectively, please let us know so that we may present your suggestions to the Authoring Team.

NCCER Product Development and Revision

13614 Progress Blvd., Alachua, FL 32615

Email: curriculum@nccer.org
Online: www.nccer.org/olf

❑ Trainee Guide ❑ AIG ❑ Exam ❑ PowerPoints Other ____________________

Craft / Level: Copyright Date:

Module ID Number / Title:

Section Number(s):

Description:

Recommended Correction:

Your Name:

Address:

Email: Phone:

Pull and Junction Boxes

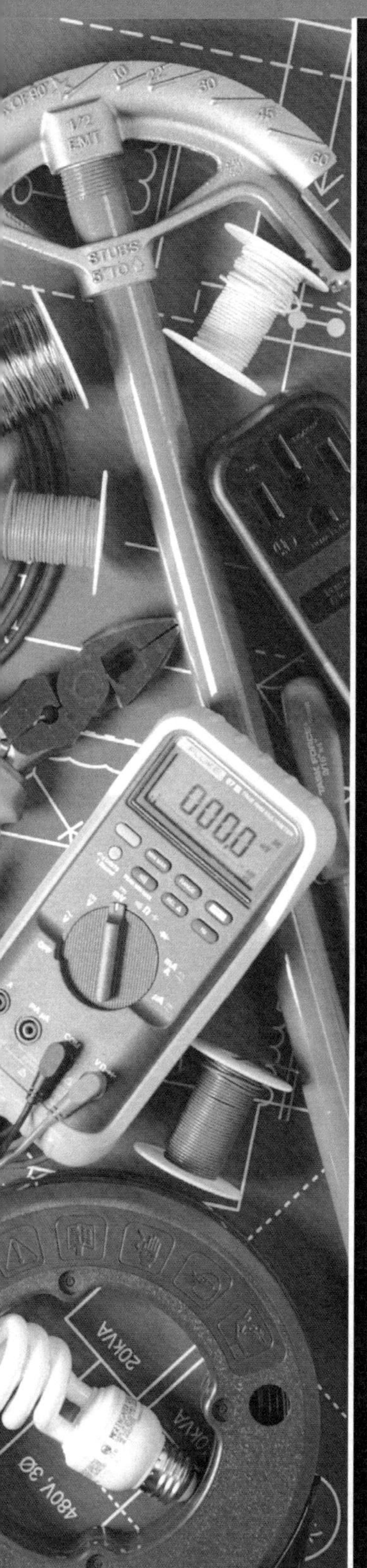

Zachry Corporate Headquarters

Zachry Construction Corporation won the Aon Build America Award for its work on its own Corporate Headquarters in San Antonio, Texas. Zachary constructed a new conference and employment center using the U.S. Green Building Council (USGBC) Leadership in Energy and Environmental Design (LEED) Programs.

26205-14

Trainees with successful module completions may be eligible for credentialing through NCCER's National Registry. To learn more, go to **www.nccer.org** or contact us at **1.888.622.3720.** Our website has information on the latest product releases and training, as well as online versions of our *Cornerstone* magazine and Pearson's product catalog.

Your feedback is welcome. You may email your comments to **curriculum@nccer.org,** send general comments and inquiries to **info@nccer.org,** or fill in the User Update form at the back of this module.

This information is general in nature and intended for training purposes only. Actual performance of activities described in this manual requires compliance with all applicable operating, service, maintenance, and safety procedures under the direction of qualified personnel. References in this manual to patented or proprietary devices do not constitute a recommendation of their use.

26205-14

Pull and Junction Boxes

Objectives

When you have completed this module, you will be able to do the following:

1. Describe the different types of nonmetallic and metallic pull and junction boxes.
2. Properly select, install, and support pull and junction boxes and their associated fittings.
3. Describe the *National Electrical Code® (NEC®)* regulations governing pull and junction boxes.
4. Size pull and junction boxes for various applications.
5. Understand the NEMA and IP classifications for pull and junction boxes.
6. Describe the purpose of conduit bodies and Type FS boxes.

Performance Tasks

Under the supervision of the instructor, you should be able to do the following:

1. Identify various NEMA boxes.
2. Properly select, install, and support pull and junction boxes over 100 cubic inches in size.
3. Identify various conduit bodies and fittings.

Trade Terms

Conduit body
Explosion-proof
Handhole
Junction box
Mogul
Pull box
Raintight
Waterproof
Watertight
Weatherproof

Required Trainee Materials

1. Pencil and paper
2. Copy of the latest edition of the *National Electrical Code®*
3. Appropriate personal protective equipment

Note:
NFPA 70®, *National Electrical Code®*, and *NEC®* are registered trademarks of the National Fire Protection Association, Inc., Quincy, MA 02269. All *National Electrical Code®* and *NEC®* references in this module refer to the 2014 edition of the *National Electrical Code®*.

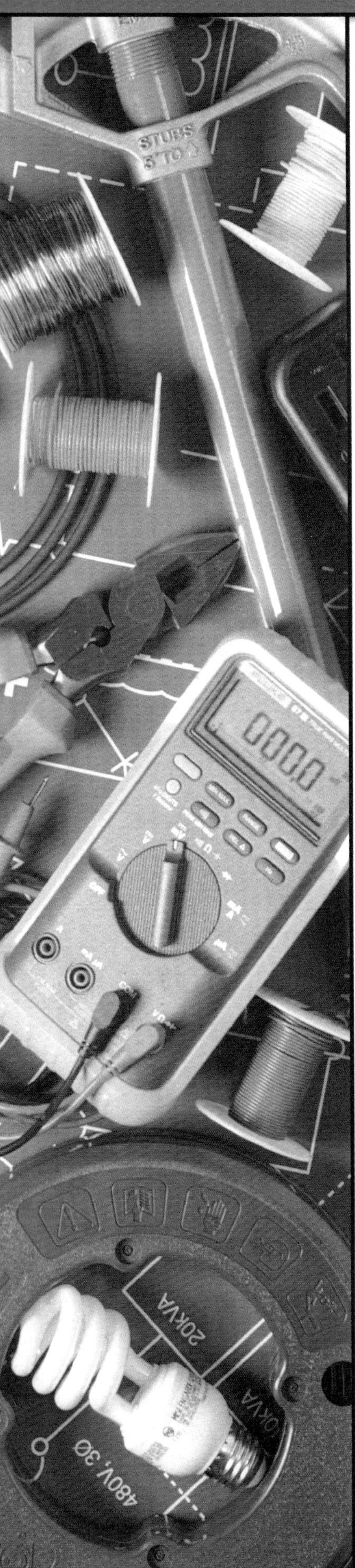

Contents

Topics to be presented in this module include:

Figures and Tables

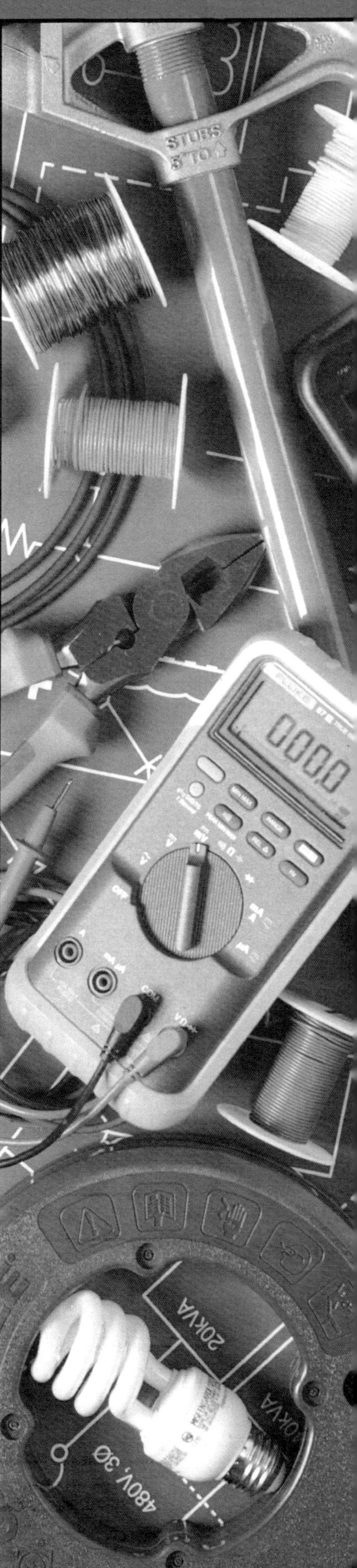

1.0.0 Introduction

Pull boxes and junction boxes (*Figure 1*) are provided in an electrical installation to facilitate the installation of conductors, or to provide a junction point for the connection of conductors, or both. In some instances, the location and size of pull boxes are designated on the drawings. In most cases, however, the electricians on the job will have to determine the proper number, location, and sizes of pull or junction boxes to facilitate conductor installation.

NOTE

Smaller conductors may use a regular octagon or square device box with a blank cover as a junction box.

Pull and junction boxes must be sized, installed, and supported to meet the requirements of *NEC Article 314*. Since the *NEC®* limits the number of conductors allowed in each box according to its volume, you must install boxes that are large enough to accommodate the number of conductors that must be spliced in the box or fed through it. Therefore, a knowledge of the various types of boxes and their volumes is essential.

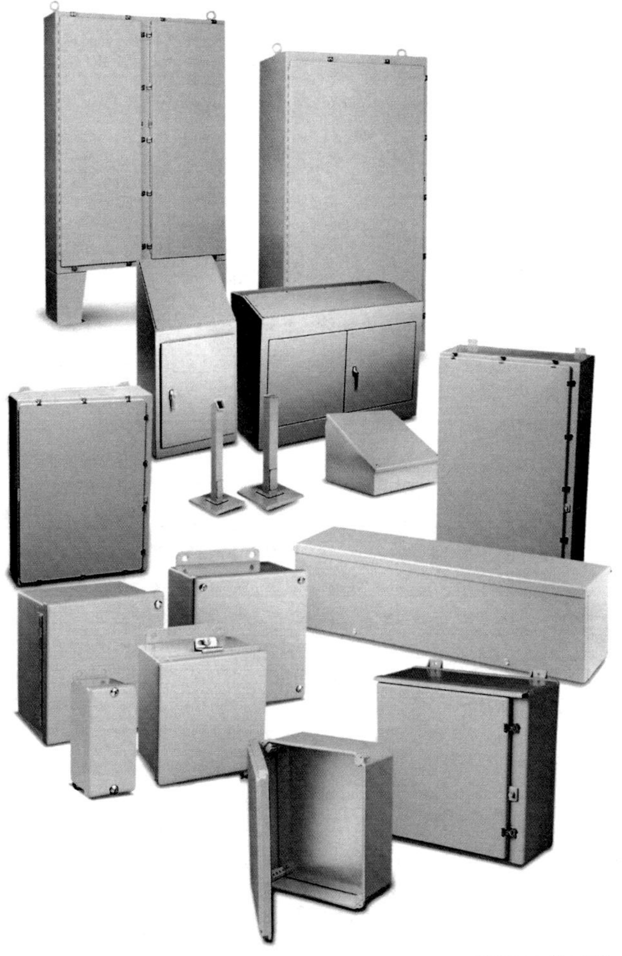

26205-14_F01.EPS

Figure 1 Pull and junction boxes.

On Site

Floor Boxes

A floor box that is listed specifically for installation in a floor is required when junction boxes are installed in a floor. Listed floor boxes are provided with covers and gaskets to exclude surface water and cleaning compounds.

Besides being able to calculate the required box sizes, you must also know how to select the proper type of box for any given application. For example, metallic boxes used in concrete deck pours are different from those used as pull and junction boxes in residential or commercial buildings. Boxes for use in hazardous locations must be rated as explosion-proof.

You must also know what fittings are available for terminating the various wiring methods in these boxes.

1.1.0 Boxes for Damp and Wet Locations

In damp or wet locations, boxes and fittings must be placed or equipped to prevent moisture or water from entering and accumulating within the box or fitting. It is recommended that approved boxes of nonconductive material be used with nonmetallic sheathed cable or approved nonmetallic conduit when the cable or conduit is used in moisture-prone locations. Boxes installed in wet locations must be approved for the purpose per *NEC Section 314.15*.

A wet location is any location subject to saturation with water or other liquids, such as locations exposed to weather or water, washrooms, garages, and interiors that might be hosed down. Underground installations or those in concrete slabs or masonry in direct contact with the earth must be considered to be wet locations. Raintight, waterproof, or watertight equipment (including fittings) may satisfy the requirements for weatherproof equipment. Boxes with threaded conduit hubs and gasketed covers will normally prevent water from entering the box except for condensation within the box.

A damp location is a location subject to some degree of moisture. Such locations include partially protected outdoor locations—such as under canopies, marquees, and roofed open porches.

On Site

Outdoor Boxes

Outdoor wiring must be able to resist the entry of water. Outdoor boxes are either driptight, which means sealed against falling water from above, or watertight, which means sealed against water from any direction. Driptight boxes simply have lids that deflect rain; they are not waterproof. Watertight boxes are sealed with gaskets to prevent the entry of water from any angle.

It also includes interior locations subject to moderate degrees of moisture—such as some basements, some barns, and cold storage warehouses.

1.2.0 NEMA and IP Enclosure Classifications

Like switch enclosures, pull and junction boxes are also classified according to the degree of protection they provide from the elements. The National Electrical Manufacturers Association (NEMA) classifications for enclosures are as follows:

- *NEMA Type 1: General Purpose* – This enclosure is primarily intended to prevent accidental contact with the enclosed apparatus. It is suitable for general-purpose applications indoors where it is not exposed to unusual service conditions. A NEMA Type 1 enclosure serves as protection against dust and light and indirect splashing, but is not dust-tight.
- *NEMA Type 3: Dust-Tight, Raintight* – This enclosure is intended to provide suitable protection against specified weather hazards. A NEMA Type 3 enclosure is suitable for outdoor applications, such as construction work. It is also sleet-resistant.
- *NEMA Type 3R: Rainproof, Sleet Resistant* – This enclosure protects against interference in operation of the contained equipment due to rain and resists damage from exposure to sleet. It is designed with conduit hubs and external mounting as well as drainage provisions.
- *NEMA Type 4: Watertight* – A watertight enclosure is designed to meet a hose test, which consists of a stream of water from a hose with a 1" nozzle, delivering at least 65 gallons per minute. The water is directed on the enclosure from a distance of not less than 10' for a period of five minutes. During this period, it may be pointed in one or more directions, as desired. There should be no leakage of water into the enclosure under these conditions.
- *NEMA Type 4X: Watertight, Corrosion-Resistant* – These enclosures are generally constructed along the lines of NEMA Type 4 enclosures except that they are made of a material that is highly resistant to corrosion. For this reason, they are ideal in applications such as meat packing and chemical plants, where contaminants would ordinarily destroy a steel enclosure over a period of time.
- *NEMA Type 7: Hazardous Locations, Class I* – These enclosures are designed to meet the application requirements of the *NEC®* for Class I hazardous locations. Class I locations are those in which flammable gases or vapors are or may be present in the air in sufficient quantities to produce explosive or ignitable mixtures. In this type of equipment, the circuit interruption occurs in the air.
- *NEMA Type 9: Hazardous Locations, Class II* – These enclosures are designed to meet the application requirements of the *NEC®* for Class II hazardous locations. Class II locations are those that are hazardous because of the presence of combustible dust. The letter or letters following the type number indicate the particular group or groups of hazardous locations (as defined in the *NEC®*) for which the enclosure is designed. The designation is incomplete without a suffix letter or letters.
- *NEMA Type 12: Industrial Use* – This type of enclosure is designed for use in those industries where it is desired to exclude such materials as dust, lint, fibers and flyings, oil seepage, or coolant seepage. There are no conduit openings or knockouts in the enclosure, and mounting is by means of flanges or mounting feet.
- *NEMA Type 13: Oil-Tight, Dust-Tight* – NEMA Type 13 enclosures are generally made of cast iron, gasketed, or permit use in the same environments as NEMA Type 12 devices. The essential difference is that due to its cast housing, a conduit entry is provided as an integral part of the NEMA Type 13 enclosure, and mounting is by means of blind holes rather than mounting brackets.

Table 1 provides an explanation of the ingress protection (IP) classification system. Each enclosure is designated IP followed by a two-digit number. For example, a dust-tight enclosure that is suitable for continuous immersion would be an IP68. *Table 2* is a cross reference of NEMA and IP enclosure classifications.

Table 1 IP Classification System

First Number Degree of Protection against Solid Objects	Second Number Degree of Protection against Water
0 Not protected.	0 Not protected.
1 Protected against a solid object greater than 50 mm, such as a hand.	1 Protected against water dripping vertically such as condensation.
2 Protected against a solid object greater than 12 mm, such as a finger.	2 Protected against dripping water when tilted up to a 15°.
3 Protected against a solid object greater than 2.5 mm, such as a wire or tool.	3 Protected against water when spraying at an angle of up to 60°.
4 Protected against a solid object greater than 1.0 mm, such as wire or thin strips of metal.	4 Protected against water splashing from any direction.
5 Dust-protected. Prevents ingress of dust sufficient to cause harm.	5 Protected against jets of water from any direction.
6 Dust-tight. No dust ingress.	6 Protected against heavy seas or powerful jets of water. Prevents ingress sufficient to cause harm.
	7 Protected against harmful ingress of water when immersed between a depth of 150 mm to 1 m.
	8 Protected against submersion. Suitable for continuous immersion in water.

Table 2 NEMA and IP Enclosures

NEMA Enclosure Type	IP Classification
1	IP20
2	IP21
3	IP54
3R	IP24
3S	IP54
4,4X	IP56
5	IP52
6,6P	IP67
12,12K	IP52
13	IP54

2.0.0 Sizing Pull and Junction Boxes

Pull boxes should be as large as possible. Workers need space within the box for both hands and in the case of the larger wire sizes, workers will need room for their arms to feed the wire. *NEC Section 314.16* specifies that pull and junction boxes must provide adequate space and dimensions for the installation of conductors.

Long runs of conductors should not be made in one pull. Pull boxes, installed at convenient intervals, will relieve much of the strain on the conductors. The length of the pull, in many cases, is left to the judgment of the workers or their supervisor, and the conditions under which the work is installed.

The installation of pull boxes may seem to cause a great deal of extra work and trouble, but they save a considerable amount of time and hard work when pulling conductors. Properly placed, they eliminate many bends and elbows and do away with the necessity of fishing from both ends of a conduit run.

If possible, pull boxes should be installed in a location that allows electricians to work easily and conveniently. For example, in an installation where the conduit comes up a corner of a wall and changes direction at the ceiling, a pull box that is installed too high will force the electrician to stand on a ladder when feeding conductors, and will allow no room for supporting the weight of the wire loop or for the cable-pulling tools.

Unless the contract drawings or project engineer state otherwise, it is just as easy for the pull boxes to be placed at a convenient height that allows workers to stand on the floor with sufficient room for both wire loop and tools.

In some electrical installations, a number of junction boxes must be installed to route the conduit in the shortest, most economical way. The *NEC®* requires all junction boxes to be accessible. This means that a person must be able to get to the conductors inside the box without removing plaster, wall covering, or any other part of the building.

Junction boxes detract from the decorative scheme of a building. Therefore, where such boxes will be used in areas open to the public or in other areas where the boxes will be unattractive, they should be installed above suspended ceilings, in closets, or at least in corners of the room or area.

Junction boxes or pull boxes must be securely fastened in place on walls or ceilings or adequately suspended.

While certain sizes of factory-constructed boxes are available with knockouts, it may be necessary to have them custom built to meet the job requirements. When it is not possible to accurately anticipate the raceway entrance requirements, it will be necessary to cut the required knockouts on the job. In the case of large pull boxes and troughs, shop drawings should be prepared prior to the construction of these items with all required knockouts accurately indicated in relation to the conduit run requirements.

2.1.0 Sizing Pull and Junction Boxes for Systems Under 1,000V

For raceways containing conductors of No. 4 or larger, and for cables containing conductors of No. 4 or larger but carrying less than 1,000V, the minimum dimensions of pull boxes, junction boxes, and conduit bodies must meet the following requirements:

- In straight pulls, the length of the box or conduit body shall not be less than eight times the trade diameter of the largest raceway.
- Where angle or U pulls are made, the distance between each raceway entry inside the box or conduit body and the opposite wall of the box or conduit body shall not be less than six times the trade diameter of the largest raceway in a row. This distance shall be increased for additional entries by the amount of the sum of the diameter of all other raceway entries in the same row on the same wall of the box. Each row shall be calculated individually, and the single row that provides the maximum distance shall be used.
- The distance between raceway entries enclosing the same conductor shall not be less than six times the trade diameter of the larger raceway.
- When transposing cable size into raceway size, the minimum trade size raceway required for the number and size of conductors in the cable shall be used.

Figure 2 shows a junction box with several runs of conduit. Since this is a straight pull, and 4" conduit is the largest size in the group, the minimum length required for the box can be determined by the following calculation:

Trade size of largest conduit × 8 [per *NEC Section 314.28(A)(1)*] = minimum length of box

or:

$$4" \times 8 = 32"$$

Therefore, this particular pull box must be at least 32" in length. The width of the box, however, need only be of sufficient size to enable locknuts and bushings to be installed on all the conduits or connectors entering the enclosure.

Junction or pull boxes in which the conductors are pulled at an angle (*Figure 3*) must have a distance of not less than six times the trade diameter of the largest conduit [*NEC Section 314.28(A)(2)*]. The distance must be increased for additional conduit entries by the amount of the sum of the diameters of all other conduits entering the box on the same

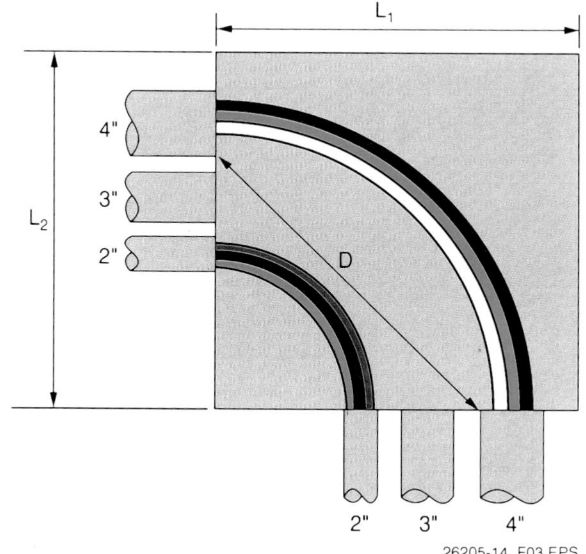

Figure 3 Pull box with conduit runs entering at right angles.

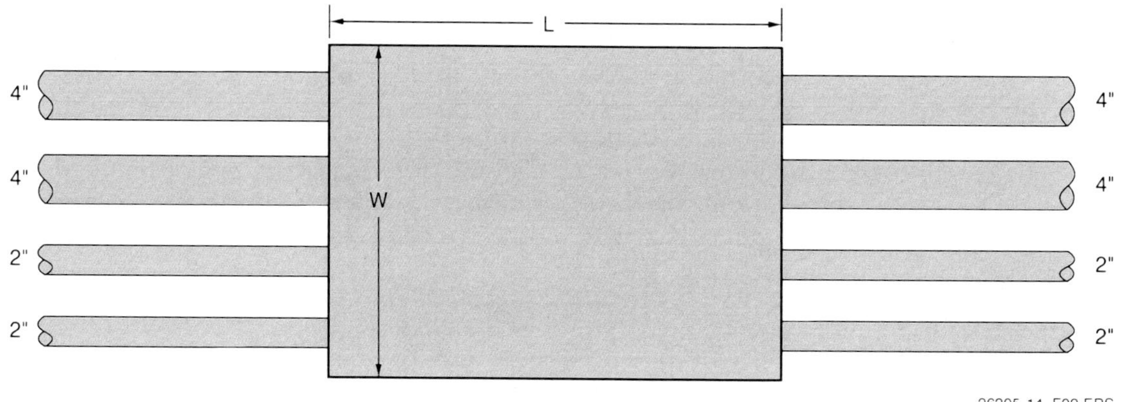

Figure 2 Pull box with two 4" and two 2" conduit runs.

On Site

Using Pull Boxes

Pull boxes make it easier to install conductors. They can also be installed to avoid having more than 360° worth of bends in a single run. (Remember, if a pull box is used, it is considered the end of the run for the purposes of the *NEC*® 360° rule.)

side. The distance between raceway entries enclosing the same conductors must not be less than six times the trade diameter of the largest conduit.

Since the 4" conduit is the largest size in this case:

$$L_1 = 6 \times 4" + (3 + 2) = 29"$$

Since the same conduit runs are located on the adjacent wall of the box, L_2 is calculated in the same way; therefore, $L_2 = 29"$.

The distance (D) = 6 × 4" or 24". This is the minimum distance permitted between conduit entries enclosing the same conductor.

The depth of the box need only be of sufficient size to permit locknuts and bushings to be properly installed. In this case, a 6"-deep box would suffice.

Power distribution blocks are permitted to be installed into pull and junction boxes rated over 100 in^3. These blocks must be listed, and the installation must comply with *NEC Section 314.28(E)*. This requires proper bending space and protection from live parts. In addition, the terminals must be unobstructed.

2.2.0 Sizing Pull and Junction Boxes for Systems over 1,000V

NEC Article 314, Part IV covers requirements for pull and junction boxes, conduit bodies, and handholes used on systems over 1,000V. Because the conductors used with these systems are larger and heavier than those used on lower-voltage systems, the *NEC*® requires additional pulling and bending space. The *NEC*® requirements for these systems include the following:

- For straight pulls, the length of the box must be at least 48 times the outside diameter of the largest shielded or lead-covered conductor entering the box. See *NEC Section 314.71(A)*. When the cable is unshielded, the length may be reduced to 32 times the outside diameter of the largest nonshielded conductor entering the box.
- For angle or U pulls, the distance between each cable or conductor entry inside the box and the opposite wall of the box must be at least 36 times the diameter, over sheath, of the largest cable or conductor. See *NEC Section 314.71(B)(1)*. The distance must be increased by the sum of the outside diameters, over sheath, of all other cables or conductors entering through the same wall of the box. When the cable is unshielded and not lead covered, the length may be reduced to 24 times the outside diameter of the largest nonshielded conductor entering the box.
- The distance between a cable or conductor entry and its exit must be at least 36 times the outside diameter, over sheath, of that cable or conductor. See *NEC Section 314.71(B)(2)*. When the cable is both unshielded and not lead covered, the distance may be reduced to 24 times the outside diameter.
- In addition to a suitable cover, pull boxes containing conductors over 1,000V must be provided with at least one removable side.
- Per *NEC Section 314.72(E)*, boxes housing conductors over 1,000V must be completely enclosed and permanently marked DANGER – HIGH VOLTAGE – KEEP OUT.

On Site

Label Junction Boxes

It's a good idea to label every junction box plate with the circuit number, the panel it came from, and its destination. The next person to service the installation will be grateful for this extra help.

3.0.0 Conduit Bodies

Conduit bodies, also called condulets, are defined in *NEC Article 100* as a separate portion of a conduit or tubing system that provides access through a removable cover to the interior of the system at a junction of two or more sections of the system or at a terminal point of the system. Conduit bodies are usually used with RMC and IMC. The cost of conduit bodies, because they are cast, is significantly higher than the stamped steel boxes. Splicing in conduit bodies is typically not recommended; however, it is permitted under certain conditions as specified in *NEC Section 314.16(C)(2)*.

As an electrical trainee, you will hear such terms as LL, LR, as well as other letters to distinguish between the various types of conduit bodies. To identify certain conduit bodies, an old trick of the trade is to hold the **conduit body** like a pistol (*Figure 4*). When doing so, if the oval-shaped

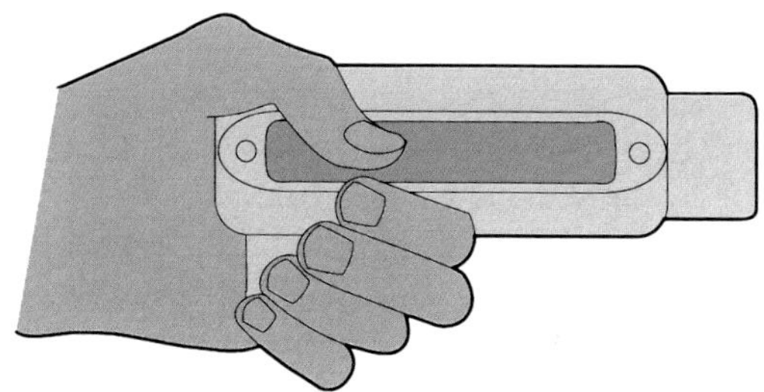

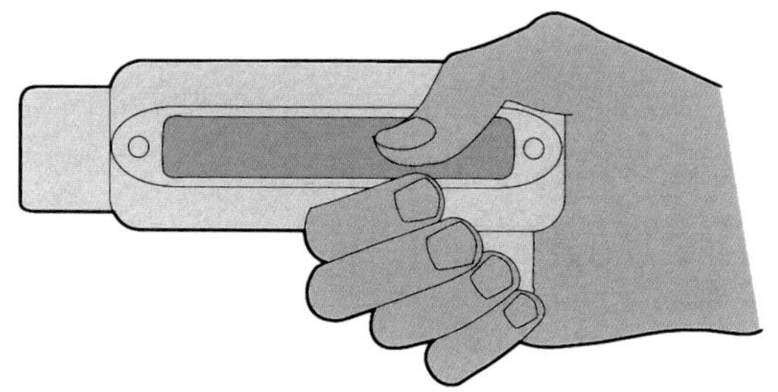

Figure 4 Identifying conduit bodies.

opening of the conduit body is to your left, it is called an LL—the first L stands for elbow and the second L stands for left. If the opening is on your right, it is called an LR—the R stands for right. If the opening is facing upward, this type of conduit body is called an LB—the B stands for back. If there is an opening on both sides, it is called an LRL—for both left and right. The other popular shapes are named for their letter look-alikes, that is, T and X. The only exception is the C conduit body. Let us take a closer look at each of these.

3.1.0 Type C Conduit Body

A Type C conduit body (*Figure 5*) may be used to provide a pull point in a long conduit run or a conduit run that has bends totaling more than 360° (see *NEC Sections 342.26, 344.26, and 358.26*). In this application, the Type C conduit body is used as a pull point.

3.2.0 Type L Conduit Bodies

A Type L conduit body (*Figure 6*) is used as a pulling point for conduit that requires a 90° change in direction. (Again, the letter L is short for elbow.) To use a Type L conduit body, the cover is removed, the wire is pulled out and coiled on the ground (or floor), and then it is reinserted into the other opening and pulled. Type L conduit bodies are available with the cover on the back (Type LB), on the sides (Type LL and Type LR), or on both sides (Type LRL). The cover and gasket for conduit body fittings must be ordered separately; do not assume that these parts come with the conduit body when it is ordered.

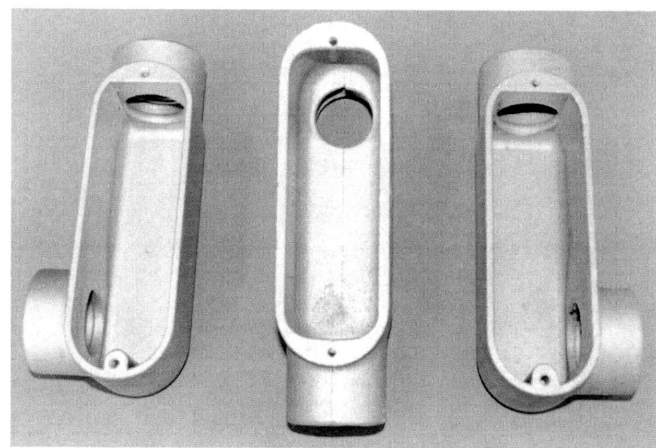

Figure 6 Type L conduit bodies.

3.3.0 Type T Conduit Body

A Type T conduit body, also known as a tee, is used to provide a junction point for three intersecting conduits and low point drains (*Figure 7*). Tees are used extensively in rigid conduit systems. The cost of a tee conduit body is more than twice that of a standard 4" square box with a cover. Therefore, the use of Type T conduit bodies with EMT is limited.

Figure 5 Type C conduit body.

Figure 7 Type T conduit body.

3.4.0 Type X Conduit Body

A Type X conduit body is used to provide a junction point for four intersecting conduits. The removable cover provides access to the interior of the X so that wire pulling and splicing may be performed (see *Figure 8*).

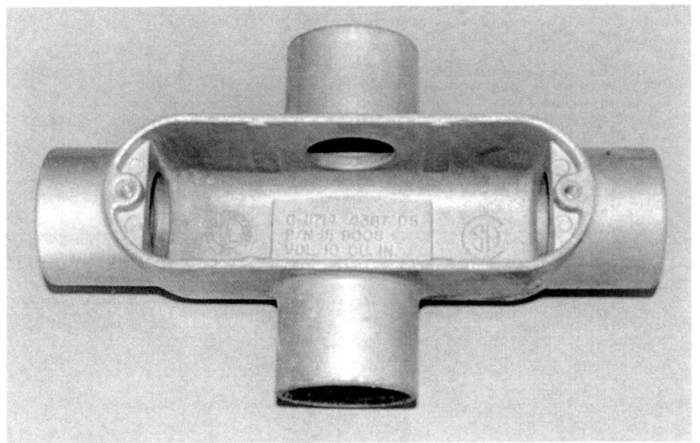

26205-14_F08.EPS

Figure 8 Type X conduit body.

On Site

All-in-One Conduit Bodies

All-in-one conduit bodies are also available. The conduit body shown here easily converts between LB, LL, LR, T, and C types by removing the appropriate covers. It is threaded for use with rigid conduit but also includes setscrews for use with EMT.

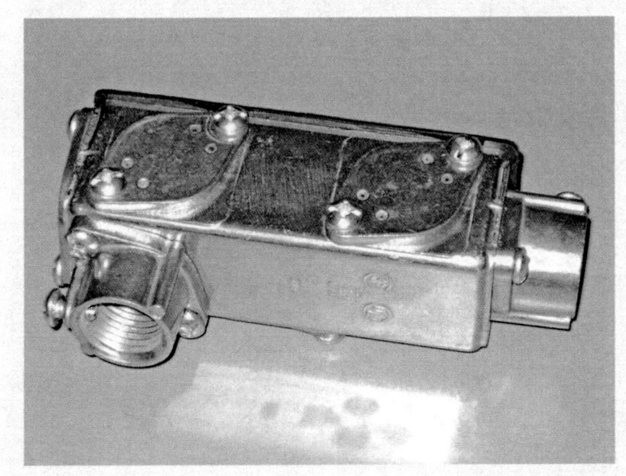

26205-14_SA01.EPS

On Site

FS and FD Boxes

FS and FD boxes are precision-molded boxes with a cover and gasket designed to provide a tight seal. Because they cost significantly more than standard boxes, they are typically used only in industrial environments where the boxes are subjected to moisture, dirt, dust, and corrosion.

3.5.0 FS and FD Boxes

FS boxes are cast boxes available in single-gang, two-gang, and three-gang configurations. They are sized to permit the installation of switches and receptacles. Covers for switches and receptacles are available for FS boxes that have formed openings much like switch and receptacle plates. FD boxes are similar to FS boxes. The letter D in the FD box indicates it is a deeper box (2½" deep versus 1⅝" deep for an FS box). Neither FS nor FD boxes are considered by the *NEC®* to be conduit bodies. FS and FD boxes may be used in environments defined by NEMA 1 (dry, clean environments); NEMA 3R (outdoor, wet environments); and NEMA 12 (dusty, oily environments).

Engineers specify and electricians install FS and FD boxes for a reason. Never alter these boxes by drilling mounting holes in them. Most are provided with cast-in mounting eyes for this purpose. Mount these boxes only as recommended by the manufacturer.

3.6.0 Pulling Elbows

Pulling elbows are used exclusively for pulling wire at a corner point of a conduit run. The volume of a pulling elbow is too low to permit splicing wire. See *Figure 9(A)*.

3.7.0 Entrance Ells (SLBs)

An entrance ell, or SLB, is built with an offset so that it may be attached directly to the surface that is to have a conduit penetration. A cover on the back of the SLB permits wire to be pulled out and reinserted into the conduit that penetrates the support surface. See *Figure 9(B)*.

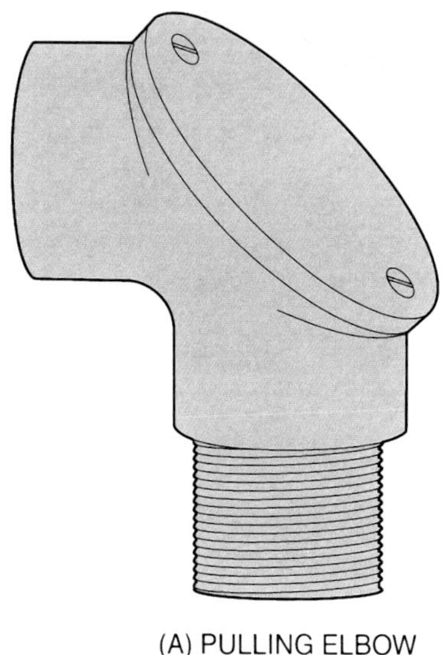

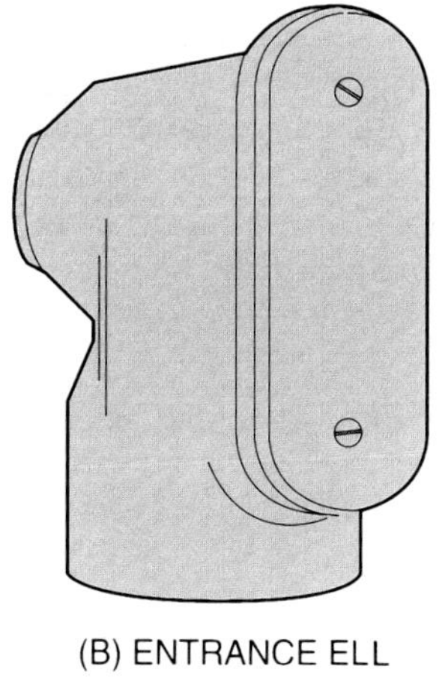

26205-14_F09.EPS

Figure 9 Elbows.

CAUTION

Never make splices in an entrance ell (SLB). Splices can be made in a conduit body that has the cubic inches marked, but never in an SLB.

3.8.0 Moguls

Mogul conduit bodies (*Figure 10*) are available in the same types as standard conduit bodies (Type L, Type T, and so on). They have raised covers to provide better access to large conductors during conductor installation or maintenance. Moguls also allow right angle bends where splices, pulls, and taps are needed in a weatherproof chamber. Like regular boxes, they must comply with the bending space requirements of *NEC Section 314.28*. Larger moguls may contain built-in cable-pulling rollers to facilitate installation.

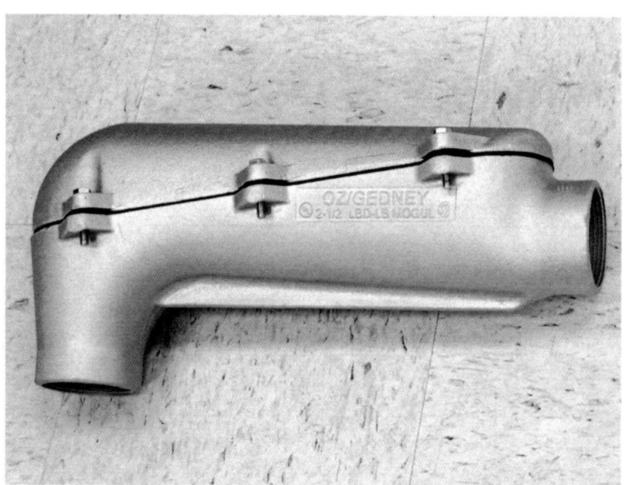

26205-14_F10.EPS

Figure 10 Mogul.

NOTE

When installing conduit bodies, remember that just because the body matches the conduit size does not mean it matches the conductor size. For example, if the conductor fill is near the limit for a four-inch conduit, it may not be acceptable for a four-inch conduit body per *NEC Section 314.28*. If this is the case, a six-inch conduit body would be installed, along with the appropriate reducing fitting.

4.0.0 Handholes

According to *NEC Article 100*, a **handhole** (*Figure 11*) is "an enclosure identified for use in underground systems, provided with an open or closed bottom, and sized to allow personnel to reach into, but not enter, for the purpose of installing, operating, or maintaining equipment or wiring or both." Handholes are often used with underground PVC conduit for the installation of landscape lighting, light poles, traffic lights, and other applications. Because handholes are exposed to various levels of foot traffic and/or vehicular loading, it is critical to select the correct enclosure for the application. *NEC Section 314.30,*

Informational Note refers to *ANSI/SCTE 77-2002, Specification for Underground Enclosure Integrity,* for additional information on loading for underground enclosures. Some of the *NEC*® requirements for handholes are as follows:

- Like boxes and conduit bodies, handholes must be installed in such a way that the enclosed wiring remains accessible without removing any portion of the building, such as wall coverings, or without requiring excavation, such as for enclosures serving underground wiring installations. See *NEC Section 314.29*.
- Per *NEC Section 314.30(A)*, handhole enclosures must be sized in accordance with *NEC Section 314.28(A)* for conductors operating at 1,000 volts or below, and in accordance with *NEC Section 314.71* for conductors operating at over 1,000 volts.
- Underground raceways and cable assemblies entering a handhole enclosure must extend into the enclosure, but they are not required to be mechanically connected to the enclosure per *NEC Section 314.30(B)*.
- Where handhole enclosures without bottoms are installed, all enclosed conductors and any splices or terminations, if present, must be listed as suitable for wet locations per *NEC Section 314.30(C)*.
- Handhole enclosure covers shall have an identifying mark or logo that prominently identifies the function of the enclosure, such as ELECTRIC (*Figure 11*) or TRAFFIC SIGNALS (*Figure 12*). To discourage unauthorized entry, handhole enclosure covers must either weigh over 100 pounds or require the use of tools to open.
- Per *NEC Section 314.30(D)*, metal covers and other exposed conductive surfaces must be bonded in accordance with *NEC Sections 250.92 and 250.96(A)*.

4.1.0 Handhole Construction

Handhole enclosures may be constructed of a variety of materials, including precast portland cement concrete, precast polymer concrete, thermoplastic, fiberglass-reinforced resin, steel, and aluminum. The type of material selected depends on the environment and the expected load.

> **CAUTION**
>
> Some enclosures use dissimilar materials for the body and cover of the enclosure. Dissimilar materials are likely to have different responses to temperature and pressure variations, which may result in cracking or other performance failures.

26205-14_F11.EPS

Figure 11 Handhole.

4.2.0 ANSI/SCTE Requirements

According to *ANSI/SCTE 77-2002*, handhole enclosures must be constructed in such a way that they withstand all loads likely to be imposed and remain safe and reliable for the intended

26205-14_F12.EPS

Figure 12 Handhole containing traffic signal wiring.

application. To meet the ANSI standard, enclosures must pass various physical, environmental, and internal equipment protection tests. The ANSI standard defines loading requirements for enclosures based upon anticipated loads and separates these requirements into various tiers defined by the application. Some manufacturers mark tier designations on the enclosure cover.

While the *NEC*® does not explicitly require third party listing, some enclosure manufacturers have submitted products to UL for testing and enclosures that meet the testing requirements may now be UL Listed to the ANSI standard.

On Site

Lighting Poles

While the *NEC*® states that handholes are used in underground systems, the access holes on lighting poles are also typically referred to as handholes.

26205-14_SA02.EPS

Case History

Handhole Failure

In July 2003, an eight-year-old girl was electrocuted when she stepped on the cover of an in-ground pull box (handhole) in a ballpark in Ohio. Over the years, the unsupported box sank, bringing the lid in contact with the conductors, one of which contained a damaged splice. The exposed conductor energized the lid of the handhole. When the box was installed, there were no performance standards for the construction of underground enclosures and the *NEC*® did not require bonding.

The Bottom Line: Because of this and similar incidents involving foot traffic over energized handholes, the *NEC*® now requires that handholes be effectively bonded and designed to support the expected load.

WARNING!

Without a solid footing, a handhole can sink and result in structural failure. A solid footing is essential and must be designed by a qualified individual in accordance with good engineering practices. Refer to the manufacturer's instructions for the proper installation of underground enclosures.

5.0.0 Fittings

Certain fittings are required in every raceway system for joining runs of conduit and also when the raceway terminates in an outlet box or other enclosure. Most metallic raceways qualify as an equipment grounding conductor provided they are tightly connected at each joint and termination point to provide a continuous grounding path.

5.1.0 EMT Fittings

Because EMT or thinwall is too thin for threads, special fittings must be used. For wet or damp locations, compression fittings such as those shown in *Figure 13* are used. This type of fitting contains compression rings made of plastic or other soft material that forms a watertight seal.

NOTE

To be used outdoors, an EMT compression fitting must be listed as raintight.

EMT fittings for dry locations can be either the setscrew type or the compression type. To use the setscrew type, the reamed ends of the EMT are inserted into the sleeve and the setscrews are tightened with a screwdriver to secure them and the conduit in place. Various types of setscrew couplings are shown in *Figure 14*.

EMT also requires connectors at each termination point, and EMT connectors are available to match the couplings described previously, that is, compression and setscrew types. They are similar to the couplings except that one end of the connector is threaded to accept a locknut and bushing.

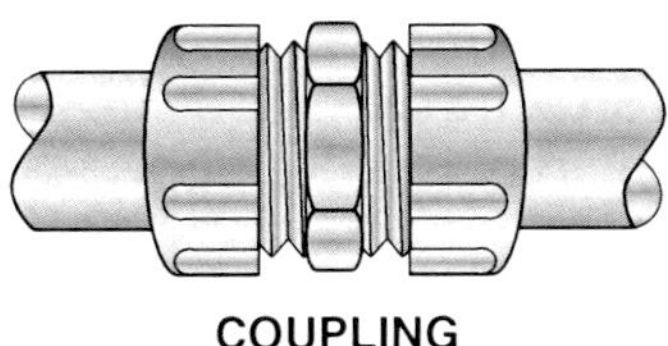

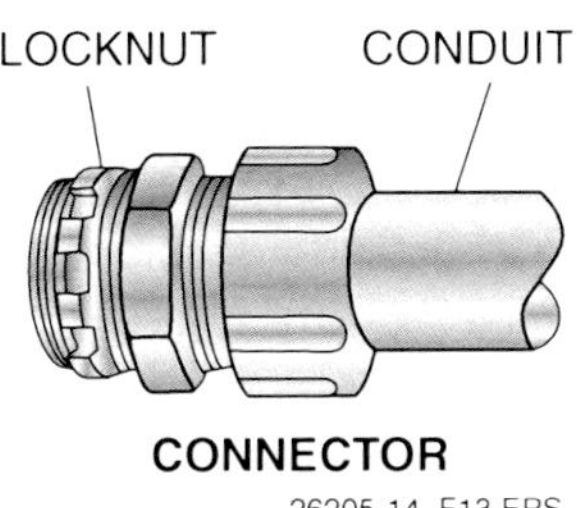

Figure 13 EMT compression fittings.

Figure 14 Setscrew fittings.

5.2.0 Rigid, Aluminum, and IMC Fittings

Rigid metal conduit, aluminum conduit, and intermediate metal conduit all have sufficient wall thicknesses to permit threading. Consequently, all three types may be joined with threaded couplings (*Figure 15*) and when any of these types terminate into an outlet box or other enclosure, double locknuts are used to secure the conduit to the box opening. Running threads are not permitted for connection at couplings.

Sometimes rigid conduit or tubing must be connected to flexible metal conduit for connection to electric motors and other machinery that may vibrate during operation. Combination couplings (*Figure 16*) are used to make the transition. When using combination couplings, be sure the flexible conduit is pushed as far as possible into the coupling. This covers the sharp edges of the conduit to protect the conductors from damage.

Think About It

Setscrew and Compression Fittings

This picture shows both setscrew and compression fittings. Which type provides a better connection? Why?

Figure 15 Rigid metal conduit with coupling.

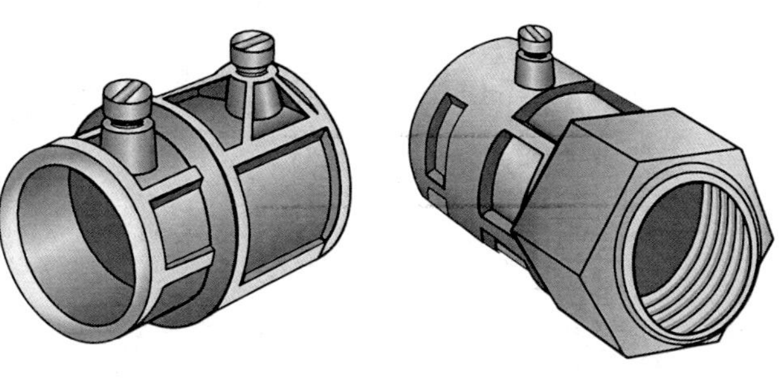

Figure 16 Combination couplings.

Threadless couplings and connectors may also be used under certain conditions with rigid, IMC, and aluminum conduit. When used, they must be made up wrench-tight and where buried in masonry or concrete, they must be concrete-tight. Where installed in wet locations, they must be rainproof. This type of coupling is not permitted in most hazardous locations.

Other types of fittings used with raceway systems are shown in *Figure 17*.

5.3.0 Locknuts and Bushings

In general, locknuts are used on the inside and outside walls of outlet boxes or other enclosures to which threaded conduit is connected. When conduit connectors are used, such as EMT connectors, only one locknut is required on the threads that protrude inside the box. A grounding locknut may be needed if bonding jumpers are used inside the box or enclosure. Special sealing locknuts are also available for use in wet locations. Locknuts are shown in *Figure 18*.

Bushings protect the wires from the sharp edges of the conduit or connector. Bushings are usually made of plastic, fiber, or metal. Some metal bushings have a grounding screw to permit an equipment or bonding jumper wire to be installed. Several types of bushings are shown in *Figure 19*.

An insulating bushing is installed on the threaded end of conduit that enters a sheet metal enclosure. The purpose of the bushing is to protect the conductors from being damaged by the sharp edges of the threaded conduit end. Any ungrounded conductor, No. 4 AWG or larger, that enters a raceway, box, or enclosure must be protected with an insulating bushing, as required in *NEC Sections 300.4(G), 312.6(C), and 314.17(D)*.

A grounding insulated bushing has provisions for protecting conductors and also has provisions for the connection of a ground wire. The ground wire, once connected to the grounding bushing, may be connected to the box to which the conduit is connected. See *Figure 20*.

According to *NEC Section 314.15*, boxes, conduit bodies, and fittings installed in damp or wet locations must be listed for and provide protection against the entry of moisture. This can be accomplished using either a sealing locknut or a gasketed fitting. Myers hubs are gasketed fittings with an integral O-ring to provide a watertight seal for enclosures installed in wet locations *(Figure 21)*. They are often used in place of sealing locknuts because they provide a more reliable seal in areas where water tends to accumulate. For example, in wet locations where the knockout entry is at the side of the box, a sealing locknut might be used because the water tends to shed itself. However, if there is a knockout on top of the box where the water tends to settle, a

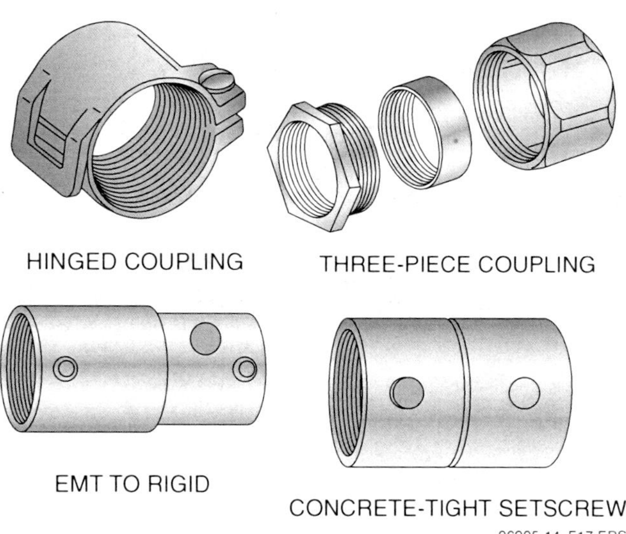

Figure 17 Metal conduit couplings.

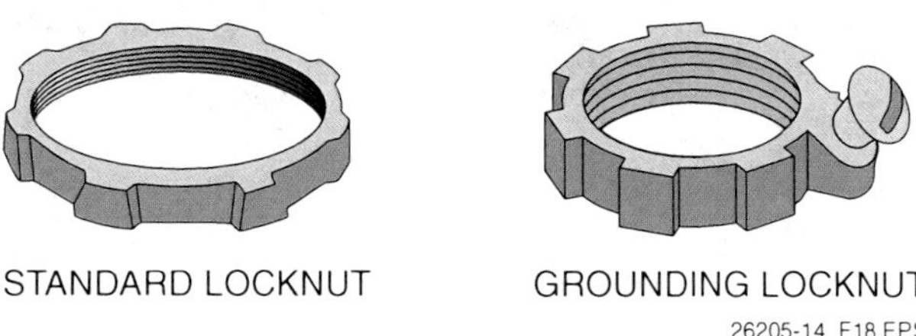

Figure 18 Common types of locknuts.

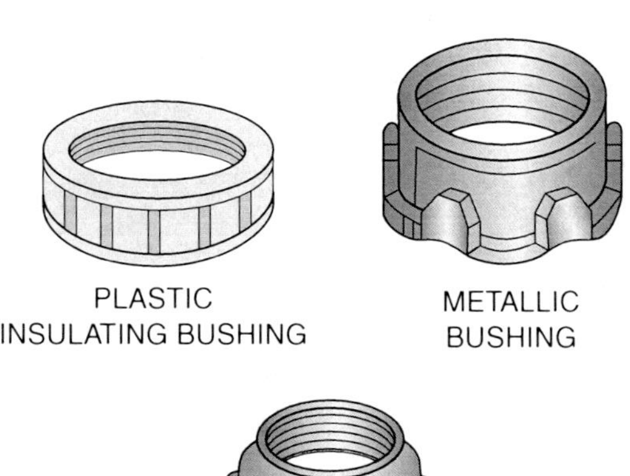

Figure 19 Typical bushings used at termination points.

(A)

(B)

26205-14_F20.EPS

Figure 20 (A) Regular insulating bushings and (B) grounding insulating bushings.

Myers hub should be used because it provides a better seal. Myers hubs are also listed for use in certain hazardous locations.

> **NOTE**
>
> Many manufacturers will void the warranty on a watertight enclosure if a Myers hub or other gasketed fitting is not used. Always read and follow the manufacturer's instructions for any product you are installing.

An opening must be provided in the outlet box or enclosure for the entrance of conduit and connectors when raceway systems terminate. Most boxes and enclosures are provided with

On Site

Stainless Steel Gasketed Hubs

Stainless steel gasketed hubs are available for use with stainless steel conduit systems. Stainless steel is commonly used in the food industry.

26205-14_SA04.EPS

26205-14_F21.EPS

Figure 21 Myers-type (gasketed) hub.

an adequate number of concentric knockouts. However, some may not have precut knockouts or the ones that are available may not be in the required location. In these cases, a knockout punch must be used to make a hole for the conduit connection. A hand-operated knockout punch is shown in *Figure 22*.

To use the knockout punch, the center of the hole is located in the box or enclosure and marked with a center punch. A pilot hole is then drilled to accept the threaded drive bolt of the knockout punch. The punch is separated from the drive screw, the screw is then placed through the pilot hole with the die on one side of the box wall, and the punch is screwed onto the drive screw on the opposite side of the wall. The punch is then aligned and screwed onto the drive screw hand-tight, in which case the punch should lightly bite into the wall of the enclosure. Finally, a wrench is then used to tighten the drive nut until the punch is drawn through the enclosure wall, making a neat circular opening.

Where many such openings must be made, or when holes for the larger sizes of conduit must be cut, power knockout tools are often used to speed up the process. The battery-powered knockout kit shown in *Figure 23* can be used to punch up to 2" conduit, while the hydraulic kit in *Figure 24* can be used to punch up to 4" conduit.

26205-14_F22.EPS

Figure 22 Knockout punch kit.

On Site

Step Bits

Step bits can be used to quickly create holes for smaller size conduit.

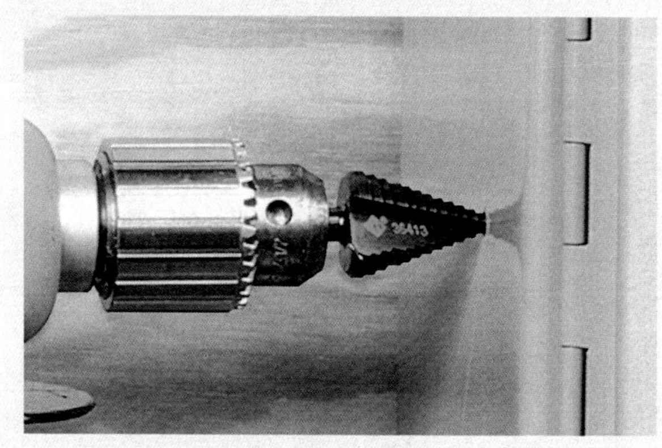

26205-14_SA05.EPS

26205-14_F23.EPS

Figure 23 Battery-powered knockout kit.

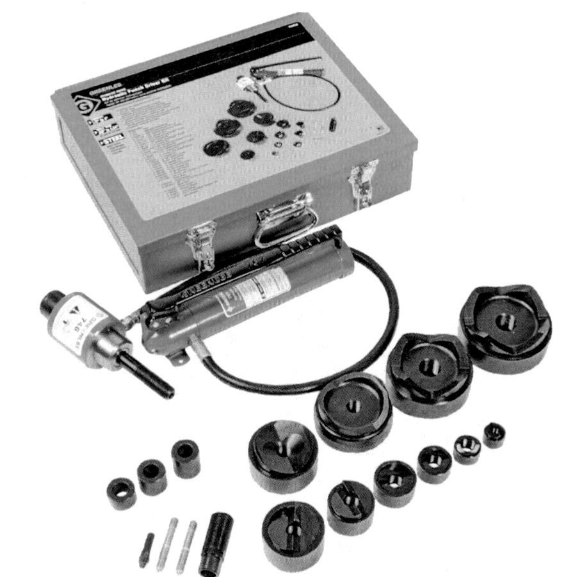

26205-14_F24.EPS

Figure 24 Hydraulic knockout kit.

Summary

Pull and junction boxes play an important role in conductor installation and maintenance. They are installed at various locations in a conduit run to provide additional pull points to facilitate conductor installation or to provide access for system service and maintenance. *NEC Article 314* provides details on the proper sizing and selection of pull and junction boxes. The rules for systems carrying over 1,000V are much more stringent than those for systems operating at lower voltages. Always refer to the latest edition of the *NEC®* as well as the manufacturer's instructions for the proper application and installation of pull and junction boxes.

Conduit bodies provide access to the electrical system at junction and termination points. Moguls are a special type of conduit body with a raised cover to provide extra space when using larger conductors.

Handholes are underground enclosures that typically serve outdoor lighting systems and traffic signal wiring. Because they are subject to varying load conditions and may become energized if they fail, it is essential to select and install them for the specific environment to which they will be exposed.

Fittings are required to connect a raceway to a pull or junction box. The type of fitting selected depends on the type of conduit used and the application.

Review Questions

1. Where in the *NEC®* will you find the most information on pull and junction boxes?
   a. *NEC Article 240*
   b. *NEC Article 250*
   c. *NEC Article 314*
   d. *NEC Article 320*

2. When calculating the pull box size for straight pulls on systems operating at less than 1,000V, the length of the box must not be less than _____ times the trade diameter of the largest raceway.
   a. two
   b. four
   c. six
   d. eight

3. If the largest trade diameter of a raceway entering a pull box is 3", and it is a straight pull for a system operating at less than 1,000V, the minimum size box allowed is _____.
   a. 20"
   b. 24"
   c. 30"
   d. 36"

4. For a straight pull, the length of a pull box housing unshielded conductors carrying over 1,000V must be _____ times the outside diameter of the largest unshielded conductor entering the box.
   a. 24
   b. 32
   c. 48
   d. 60

5. For a straight pull, the length of a pull box housing shielded conductors carrying over 1,000V must be _____ times the outside diameter of the largest shielded conductor entering the box.
   a. 24
   b. 32
   c. 48
   d. 60

6. True or False? In addition to a suitable cover, pull boxes containing conductors over 1,000V must be provided with at least one removable side.
   a. True
   b. False

7. A conduit body that has openings on four different sides plus an access opening is called a _____.
   a. Type X
   b. Type C
   c. Type T
   d. Type LL

8. Which of the following best describes how Type FS boxes should be installed?
   a. Holes should be drilled in back of the box for mounting screws.
   b. Holes should be drilled on the sides of the box only for mounting screws.
   c. No holes should be drilled in the box for mounting.
   d. Holes may be drilled only in existing installations.

9. Which of the following enclosures is best suited for splicing conductors?
   a. Pulling ell
   b. SLB
   c. Conduit body
   d. Mogul

10. The combination coupling in *Figure 1* is used to connect _____.
   a. two sections of flexible conduit
   b. flexible conduit to EMT
   c. EMT to rigid conduit
   d. flexible conduit to rigid conduit

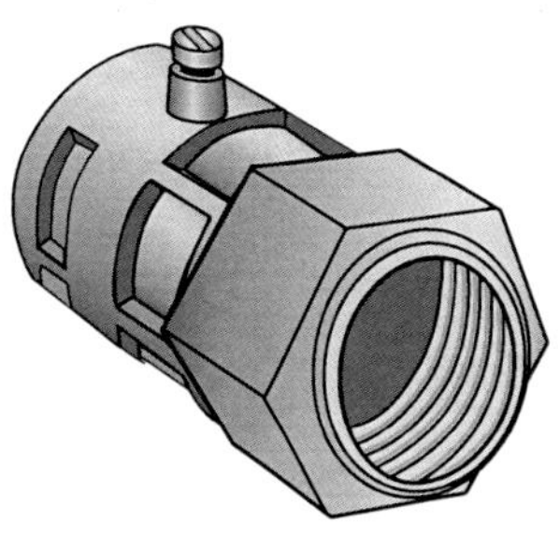

Figure 1

Module 26205-14
Supplemental Exercises

1. A Type T conduit body is used to provide a junction point for _______________ intersecting conduits.

2. All boxes must be sized, installed, and supported to meet the current _______________ requirements.

3. Class 1 locations contain flammable _______________ or _______________.

4. Conduit bodies, also called _______________, provide access through a removable cover or covers to the interior of the system.

5. To distinguish between Type LL and Type LR conduit bodies, hold the fitting as if it were a(n) _______________ and see where the cover is situated.

6. For a straight pull, the minimum length of the box must be at least _______________ times the trade diameter of the largest raceway.

7. The minimum length for a junction box in which the conductors are pulled at an angle and that contains two 3" conduits and one 4" conduit entering each side is _______________.

8. A(n) _______________ locknut may be required if bonding jumpers are used inside of the box or enclosure.

9. The minimum length for a junction box with one 4" conduit on each side in which the conductors are pulled straight through the box is _______________.

10. When sizing pull and/or junction boxes for systems over 1,000V, you need to know the outside diameter of the _______________.

Trade Terms Introduced in This Module

Conduit body: A separate portion of a conduit or tubing system that provides access through a removable cover (or covers) to the interior of the system at a junction of two or more sections of the system or at a terminal point of the system. Boxes such as FS and FD or larger cast or sheet metal boxes are not classified as conduit bodies.

Explosion-proof: Designed and constructed to withstand an internal explosion without creating an external explosion or fire.

Handhole: An enclosure used with underground systems to provide access for installation and maintenance.

Junction box: An enclosure where one or more raceways or cables enter, and in which electrical conductors can be, or are, spliced.

Mogul: A type of conduit body with a raised cover to provide additional space for large conductors.

Pull box: A sheet metal box-like enclosure used in conduit runs to facilitate the pulling of cables from point to point in long runs, or to provide for the installation of conduit support bushings needed to support the weight of long riser cables, or to provide for turns in multiple-conduit runs.

Raintight: Constructed or protected so that exposure to a beating rain will not result in the entrance of water under specified test conditions.

Waterproof: Constructed so that moisture will not interfere with successful operation.

Watertight: Constructed so that water will not enter the enclosure under specified test conditions.

Weatherproof: Constructed or protected so that exposure to the weather will not interfere with successful operation.

Additional Resources

This module presents thorough resources for task training. The following resource material is suggested for further study.

National Electrical Code® Handbook, Latest Edition. Quincy, MA: National Fire Protection Association.

Figure Credits

AGC of America, Module opener

Hubbell Wiegmann, Figure 1

John Traister, Figures 2 and 18

Topaz Publications, Inc., Figures 5–8, 12, SA02, SA03, Figures 15, 20, and 22

Tim Ely, SA01, Figures 10, 11, 14, and 21

Photo courtesy of Cooper Crouse-Hinds, SA04

Greenlee/A Textron Company, SA05, Figures 23 and 24

NCCER CURRICULA — USER UPDATE

NCCER makes every effort to keep its textbooks up-to-date and free of technical errors. We appreciate your help in this process. If you find an error, a typographical mistake, or an inaccuracy in NCCER's curricula, please fill out this form (or a photocopy), or complete the online form at **www.nccer.org/olf**. Be sure to include the exact module ID number, page number, a detailed description, and your recommended correction. Your input will be brought to the attention of the Authoring Team. Thank you for your assistance.

Instructors – If you have an idea for improving this textbook, or have found that additional materials were necessary to teach this module effectively, please let us know so that we may present your suggestions to the Authoring Team.

NCCER Product Development and Revision

13614 Progress Blvd., Alachua, FL 32615

Email: curriculum@nccer.org
Online: www.nccer.org/olf

❑ Trainee Guide ❑ AIG ❑ Exam ❑ PowerPoints Other ____________________

Craft / Level: Copyright Date:

Module ID Number / Title:

Section Number(s):

Description:

Recommended Correction:

Your Name:

Address:

Email: Phone:

Cable Tray

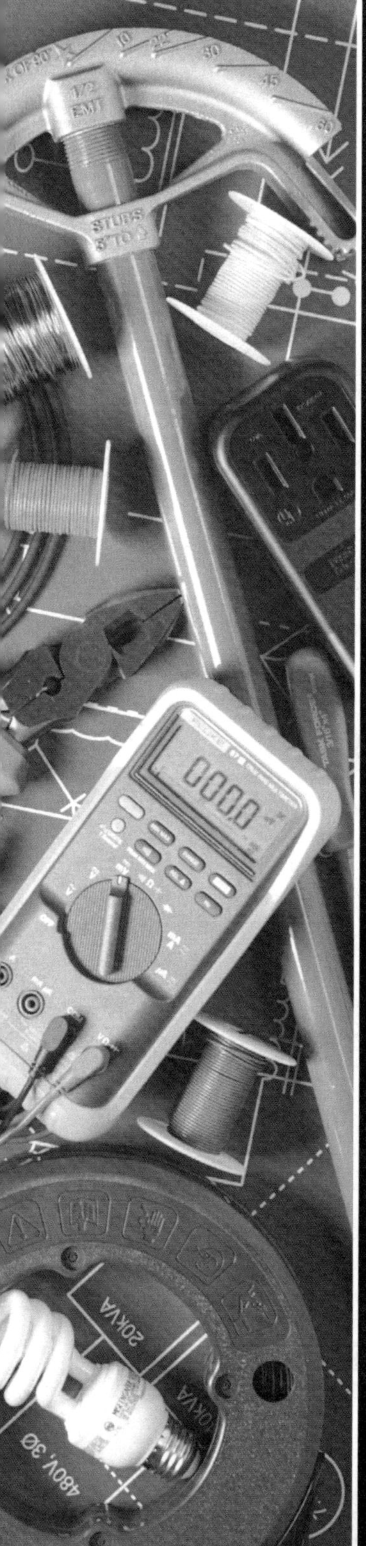

Dallas/Fort Worth International Airport

Hensel Phelps Construction Co. won an ABC Excellence in Construction award in the mega-projects division for its work on the automated people mover stations at Dallas/Fort Worth International Airport.

26207-14

Trainees with successful module completions may be eligible for credentialing through NCCER's National Registry. To learn more, go to **www.nccer.org** or contact us at **1.888.622.3720.** Our website has information on the latest product releases and training, as well as online versions of our *Cornerstone* magazine and Pearson's product catalog.

Your feedback is welcome. You may email your comments to **curriculum@nccer.org,** send general comments and inquiries to **info@nccer.org,** or fill in the User Update form at the back of this module.

This information is general in nature and intended for training purposes only. Actual performance of activities described in this manual requires compliance with all applicable operating, service, maintenance, and safety procedures under the direction of qualified personnel. References in this manual to patented or proprietary devices do not constitute a recommendation of their use.

26207-14

Cable Tray

Objectives

When you have completed this module, you will be able to do the following:

1. Describe the components that make up a cable tray assembly.
2. Explain the methods used to hang and secure cable tray.
3. Describe how cable enters and exits cable tray.
4. Select the proper cable tray fitting for the situation.
5. Explain the *National Electrical Code*® (*NEC*®) requirements for cable tray installations.
6. Select the required fittings to ensure equipment grounding continuity in cable tray systems.
7. Interpret electrical working drawings showing cable tray fittings.
8. Size cable tray for the number and type of conductors contained in the system.

Performance Tasks

Under the supervision of the instructor, you should be able to do the following:

1. Generate a list of materials for a cable tray layout. List all the components required, including the fasteners required to complete the system.
2. Join two straight, ladder-type cable tray sections together.

Trade Terms

Barrier strip
Cable pulley
Cross
Direct rod suspension
Dropout
Dropout plate
Elbow
Expansion joints
Fittings
Interlocked armor cable
Ladder tray
Pipe racks
Swivel plates
Tee
Trapeze mounting
Tray cover
Trough
Unistrut®
Wall mounting
Wye

Required Trainee Materials

1. Paper and pencil
2. Appropriate personal protective equipment
3. Copy of the latest edition of the *National Electrical Code*®

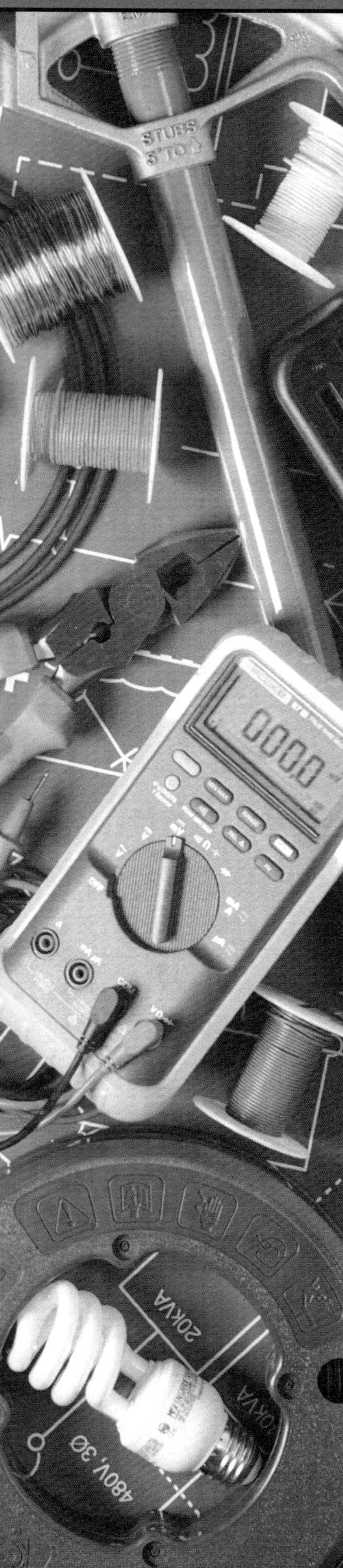

Contents

Topics to be presented in this module include:

Figures

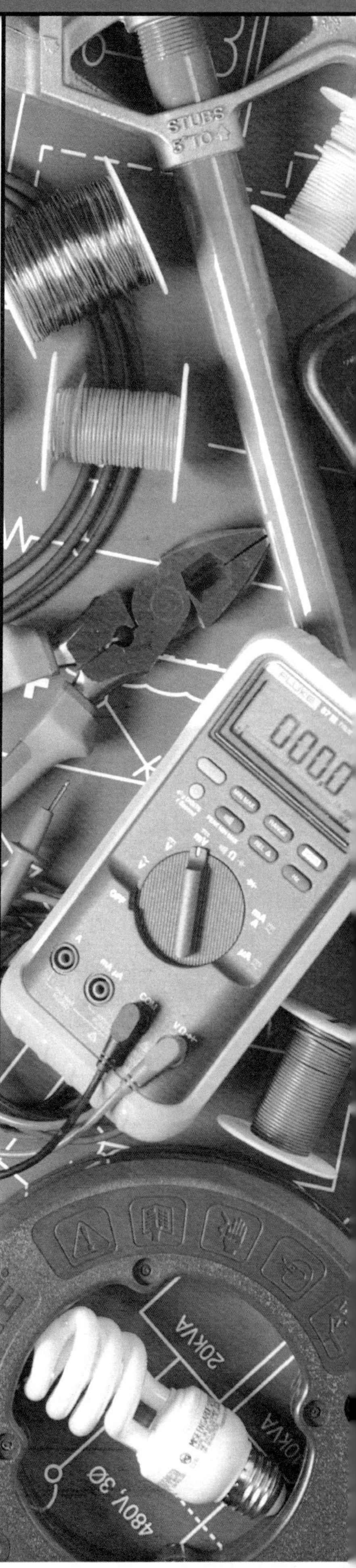

1.0.0 Introduction

NEC Section 392.2 defines a cable tray system as a unit or assembly of units or sections and associated fittings forming a structural system used to securely fasten or support cables and raceways. *NEC Article 392* covers cable tray installations, along with the types of conductors to be used in various systems. Whenever a question arises concerning cable tray installations, this is the *NEC®* article to use.

Cable trays are the usual means of supporting cable systems in industrial applications. The trays themselves are usually made up into a system of assembled, interconnected sections and associated fittings, all of which are made of metal or noncombustible units. The finished system forms into a continuous rigid assembly for supporting and carrying single, multiconductor, or other electrical cables and raceways from their origin to their point of termination, frequently over considerable distances.

Cable tray is fabricated from both aluminum and steel. Some manufacturers provide an aluminum cable tray that is coated with PVC for installation in caustic environments. Nonmetallic trays are also available; this type of tray is ideally suited for use in corrosive areas and in areas requiring voltage isolation. Cable tray is available in various forms, including ladder, trough, center rail, and solid bottom, and can be supported by either side mounts or center mounts.

Ladder tray, as the name implies, consists of two parallel channels connected by rungs, similar in appearance to a conventional straight or extension ladder. Trough types consist of two parallel channels (side rails) having a corrugated, ventilated bottom. The solid bottom cable tray is similar to the trough. All of these types are shown in *Figure 1*. Ladder, trough, and solid bottom trays are completely interchangeable; that is, all three types can be used in the same run when needed.

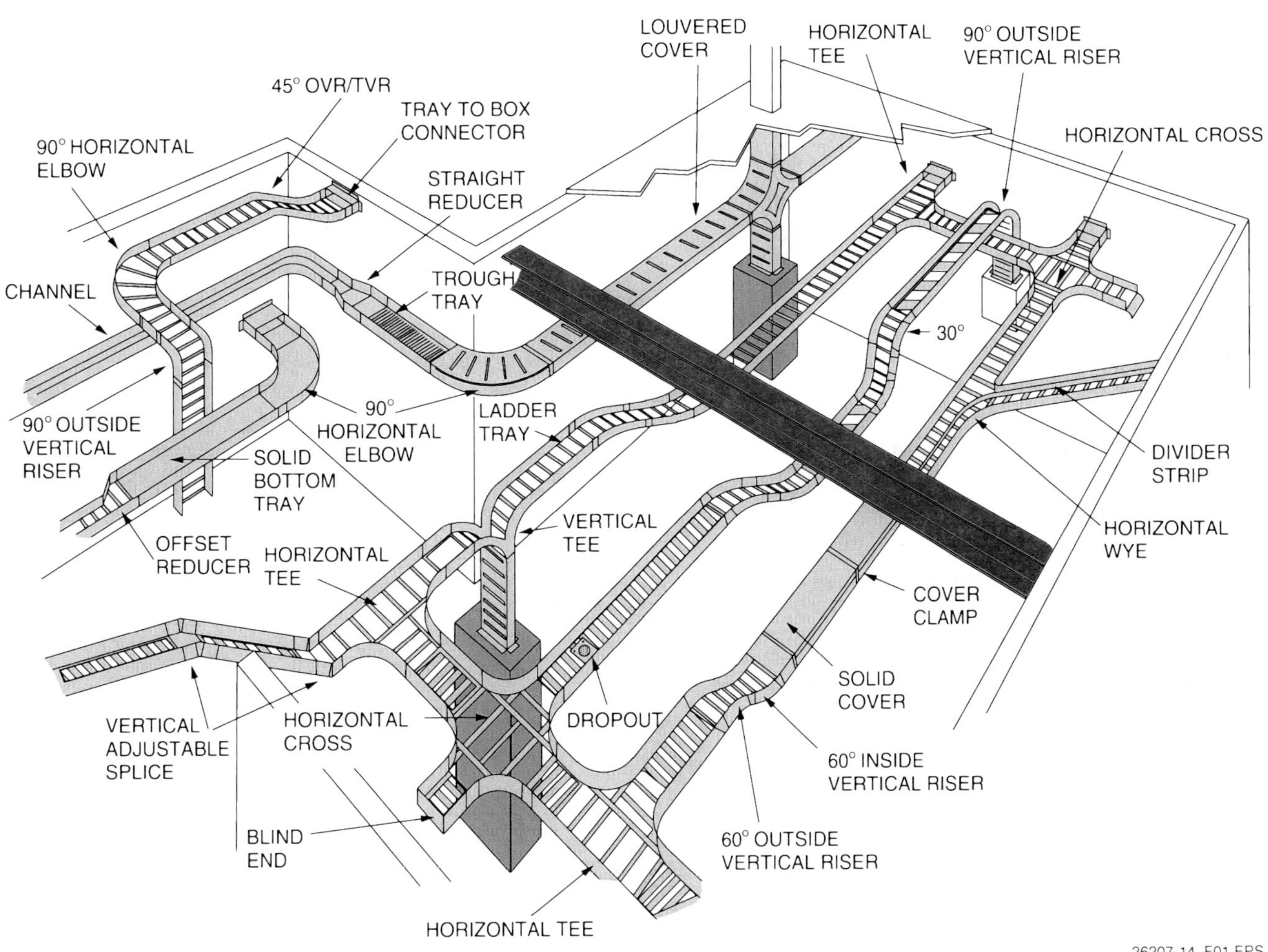

Figure 1 Typical cable tray system.

Cable Tray Installation

Cable trays are widely used in many commercial and industrial installations.

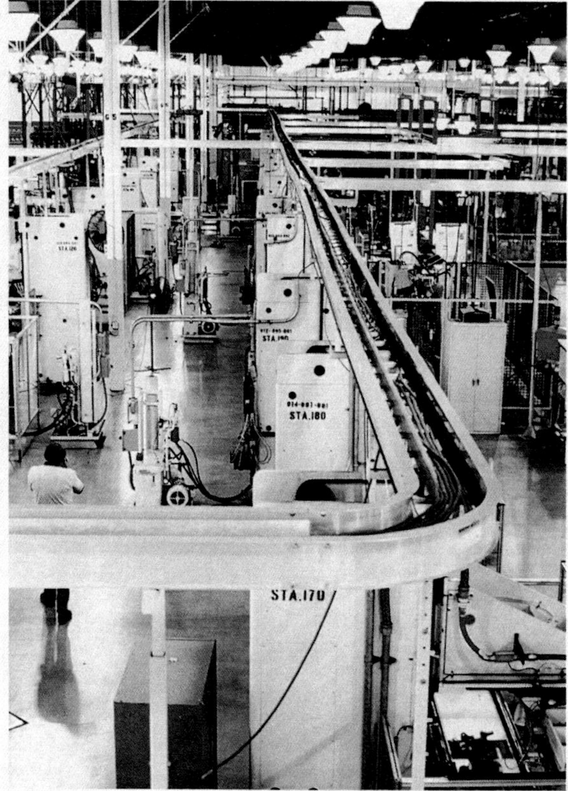

26207-14_SA01.EPS

Cable tray is manufactured in 12' and 24' lengths. Common widths range from 6" to 36". All sizes are provided in either 3", 4", 5", or 6" depths.

Cable tray sections are interconnected with various types of fittings. Fittings are also used to provide a means of changing the direction or dimension of the cable tray system. Some of the more common fittings include:

- Horizontal and vertical tees
- Wyes
- Horizontal and vertical bends
- Horizontal crosses
- Reducers
- Barrier strips
- Covers
- Splice plates
- Box connectors

The area of a cable tray cross section that is usable for cables is defined by width (W) × depth (D), as shown in *Figure 2*. The overall dimensions of a cable tray, however, are greater than W times D because of the side flanges and seams. Therefore, overall dimensions vary according to the tray design. Cables rest on the bottom of the tray and are held within the tray area by two longitudinal side rails, as shown in *Figure 3*.

A channel is used to carry one or more cables from the main tray system to the vicinity of the cable termination (see *Figure 4*). Conduit is then used to finish the run from the channel to the actual termination.

Certain *NEC*® regulations and National Electrical Manufacturers Association (NEMA) standards should be followed when designing or installing cable tray. Consequently, practically all projects of any great size will have detailed drawings and specifications for the workers to follow. Shop drawings may also be provided.

On Site

Special-Application Cable Management Systems

This lightweight, flexible nonmetallic cable management system is used to route wiring to the large motors in a manufacturing facility.

26207-14_SA02.EPS

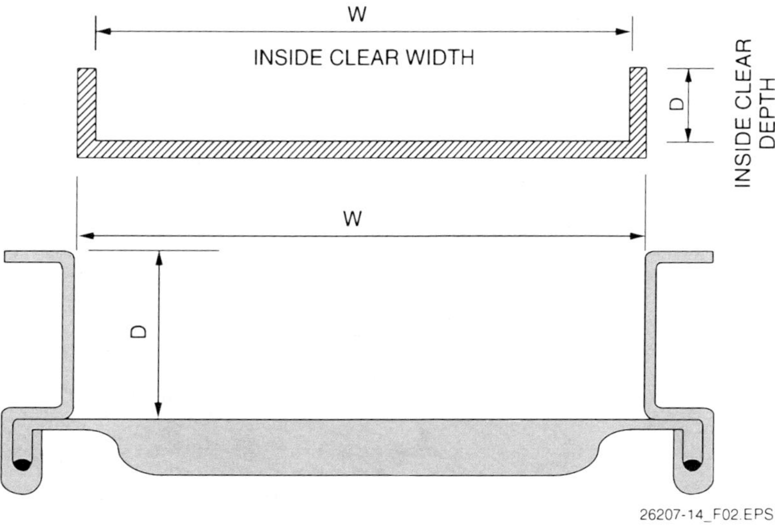

26207-14_F02.EPS

Figure 2 Cross section of cable tray comparing usable dimensions to overall dimensions.

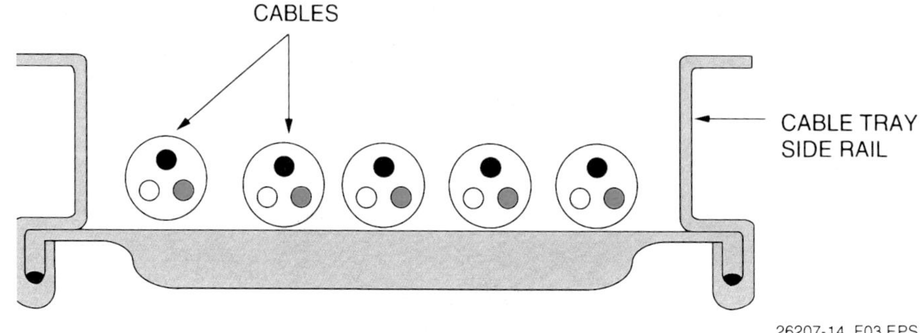

Figure 3 Cables rest on the bottom of the tray and are held in place by the longitudinal side rails.

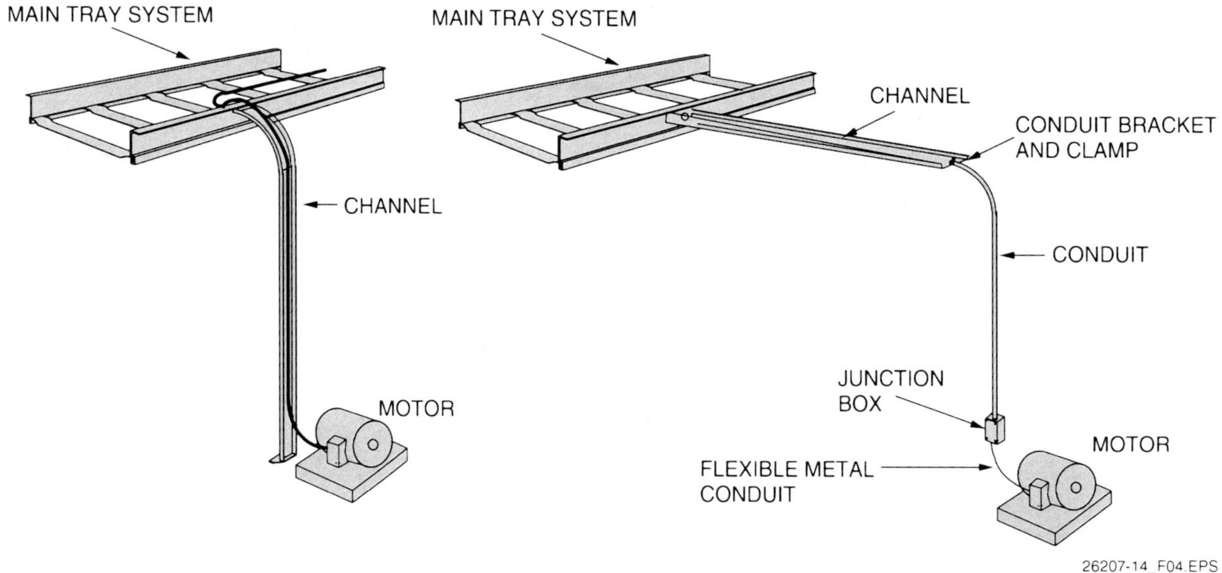

Figure 4 Two applications of cable tray channel.

On Site

Ladder Tray

Ladder tray is currently used for a majority of today's installations. It offers numerous advantages:

- Ladder tray has greater air circulation than other trays, which helps to dissipate heat.
- The ladder rungs are convenient for tying down conductors.
- Ladder tray does not collect moisture.
- Conductors can be dropped through the bottom of the tray at any point.

On Site

Basket Tray

Basket tray offers many of the same advantages as ladder tray. It is lightweight and easy to install using special clips that attach to threaded rods.

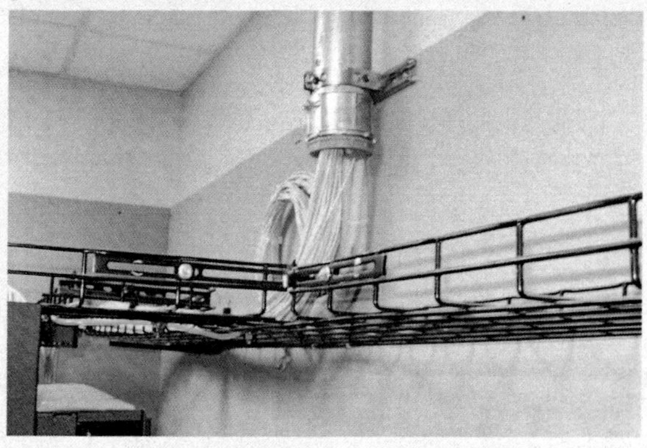

26207-14_SA04.EPS

Basket tray can be easily cut using bolt cutters or a basket tray cutter, such as that shown here.

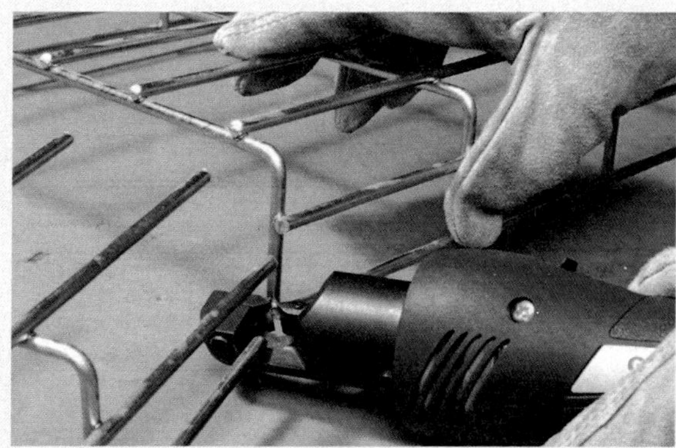

26207-14_SA05.EPS

One additional advantage of basket tray is that it can be cut, bent, and connected to create tees, crosses, and elbows without the need for separate fittings.

26207-14_SA06.EPS

2.0.0 Cable Tray Loading

The *NEC*® requires that cable trays have sufficient strength to support all contained wiring, and that they be supported at the intervals provided in the manufacturer's installation instructions. The following sections describe some additional load considerations in the design of a cable tray system.

2.1.0 Load Factors

The load capacity of cable tray varies with each manufacturer and depends on the shape and thickness of the side rails, the shape and thickness of the bottom members, spacing of rungs (if any), material used, safety factor used, method used to determine the allowable load, method of supporting the tray, and volume capacity. Consequently, each manufacturer publishes load data.

2.2.0 Determining Fill

The density of fill can only be determined by personnel laying out the system. In doing so, however, be aware that cables packed closely together can impair each other's efficiency (see *Figure 5*).

2.3.0 Determining the Load on Supports

Each support should be capable of safely supporting approximately 1.25 times the full weight of the cable and tray on a typical span, as shown in *Figure 6*.

2.4.0 Deflection Under Load

Consider the case of a cable tray spanning only two supports (simple span). As the tray is loaded, the side rails take the deflected form. Simultaneously, in cross section, the side rails rotate inward and the tray bottom deflects. The amount of inward or outward movement of the side rails is a critical factor in the ability of the tray to carry a load.

2.5.0 Failure Under Load

There are two types of failures that can occur with a loaded cable tray. These are longitudinal (side rail) failures and transverse (rung) failures.

> **Think About It**
>
> **Cable Fill**
>
> In what way can cables installed too closely together impair each other's efficiency?

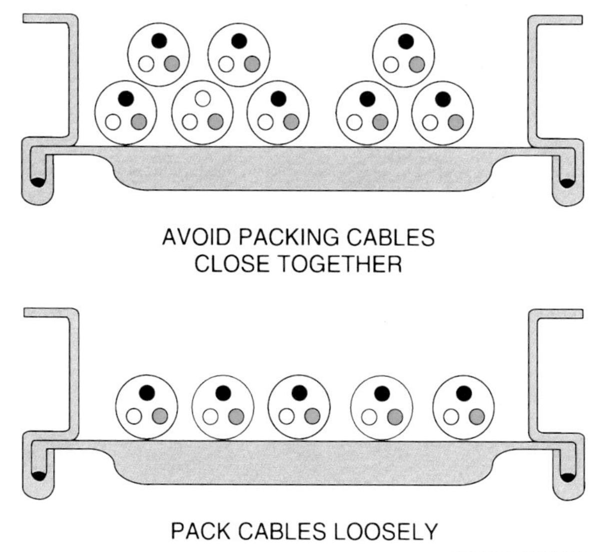

Figure 5 Cables packed closely together can impair efficiency.

Transverse (rung) failures occur when the load applied causes the fibers on the tension side (bottom edge) of the rung to stretch and permanently deform. Simultaneously, fibers on the compression side (top edge) are permanently crushed. Longitudinal (side rail) failures occur either as bending failures when the tray is supported on a larger span, or, on longer spans, buckling failures may occur because the side rails of the tray have little resistance to inward or outward movement. As the tray deflects, the side rails rotate and the top (compression) flanges of the tray buckle. Bending failures occur on short spans because the side rails of the tray have greater resistance to rotation and remain reasonably upright. The tray does not fail until the load is such that it causes the fibers on the tension side (bottom edge) of the side rail to stretch and permanently deform. Simultaneously, fibers on the compression side (top edge) are permanently crushed. For any tray on an intermediate span, it is difficult to anticipate whether a bending or buckling failure would occur (see *Figure 7*).

2.6.0 Splicing Straight Sections

In *Figure 8*, the load on the cable tray creates bending moments along the spans. The stress in the side rails of the tray is directly related to the bending moments at all points along the tray. The magnitude of the bending moment at any point is determined by measuring the vertical height of the shaded portion. In any cable tray system, a splice is a point of weakness. Consequently, splices should be located at the points of least stress. Ideally, splices would be located at the points of zero bending moment, and the strength

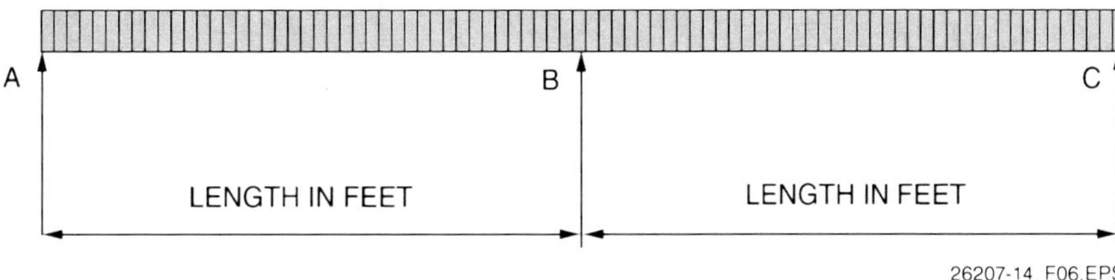

Figure 6 Each tray support should be capable of safely supporting 1.25 times the weight of the entire tray and cable assembly span.

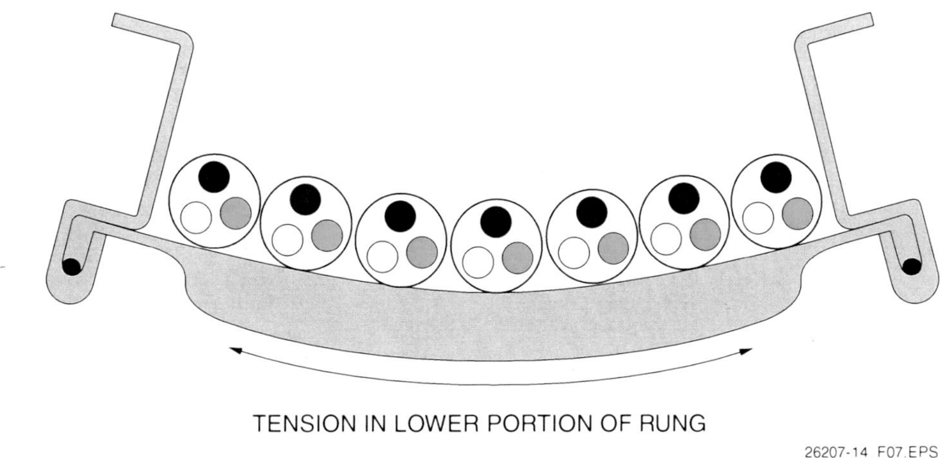

Figure 7 Bending of loaded tray.

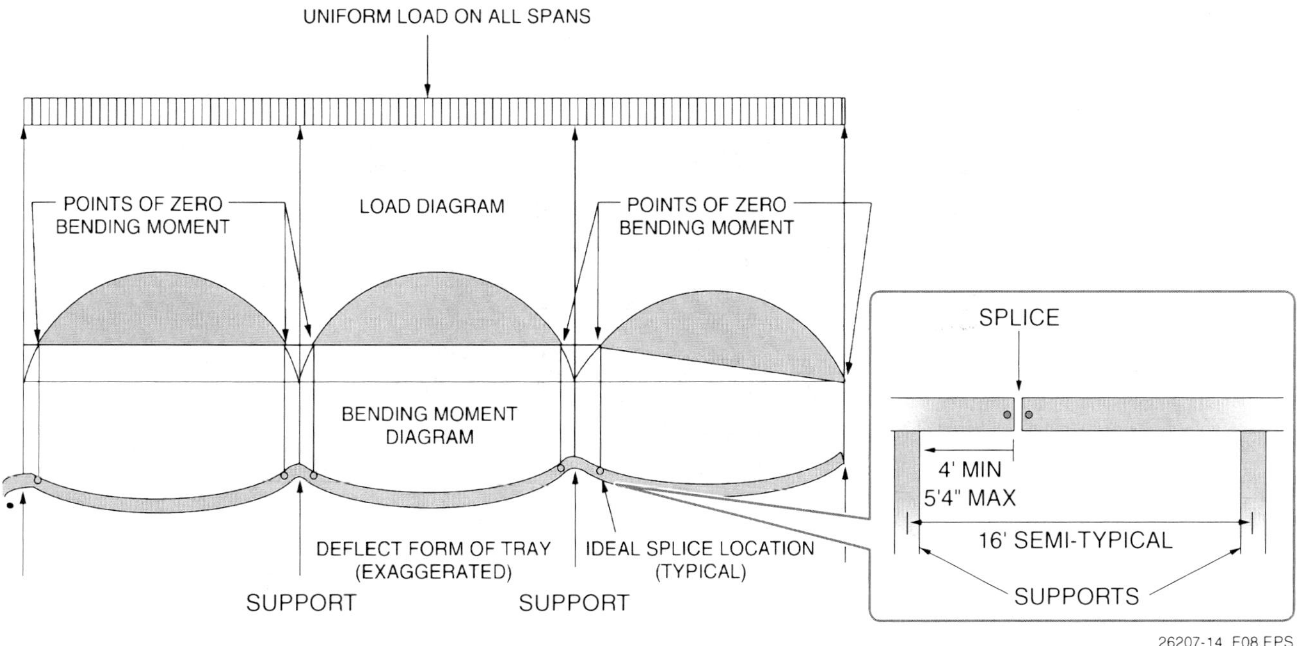

Figure 8 Load of cable creates bending moments along the span.

of the tray system would be at a maximum. In actual practice, if the splice is located within one-fourth of the span's distance from the support, the result will be close to ideal.

Locating the splice within the one-fourth points of the span requires extra labor on the part of the installer. When a splice occurs within the central length of a span between the one-fourth points, the tray will support the load for which it was designed, but the safety factor will be greatly reduced.

2.7.0 Cable Placement in Tray

Cables are placed in the tray either by being pulled along the tray or by being laid in over the side. *Figure 9* shows a cable pulley being used to facilitate a cable pull in a tray.

2.8.0 Cable Tray Cover

A cable tray cover is used primarily for two reasons:

- To protect the insulation of the cables against damage that might be caused if an object were to fall into the tray. Prime hazards are tools, discarded cigarettes, and weld splatter.
- To protect certain types of cable insulation against the damaging effects of direct sunlight.

2.8.1 Cover Selection

When maximum protection is desired, solid covers should be used. However, if accumulation of heat from the cables is expected, caution should be used. Ventilated covers should be used if some protection of the cable is desired and provisions must be made to allow the escape of heat developed by the cables.

2.9.0 Cable Exit from Tray

Several different ways in which cables may exit from a cable tray are shown in *Figure 10*. While all of these methods are *NEC*®-approved and endorsed by most cable tray manufacturers, the engineering specifications on some projects may prohibit the use of some of these methods. Most notable are the dropout between rungs method and the dropout from the end of the tray method. The cable radius may be too short with either of these methods. Also, since no dropout plates are used, the cable or conductors are not protected. Although *NEC Section 392.100(B)* specifically requires that cable trays have smooth edges to ensure that cable will not be damaged, accidents do occur. For example, a tool might be dropped on a cable tray rung during the installation, which may cause a burr or other sharp edge on the rung. Then, after the cable is installed and the system is in use, vibrating machinery may cause this burr to cut into the cable insulation, resulting in a ground fault and possible power outage. Always review the project specifications carefully and/or check with the project supervisor before using either of these methods.

2.9.1 Dropout Plates

A dropout plate provides a curved surface for the cable to follow as it passes from the tray, as shown in *Figure 11(A)*. Without a dropout plate, cables can be bent sharply, causing damage to the insulation. See *Figure 11(B)*.

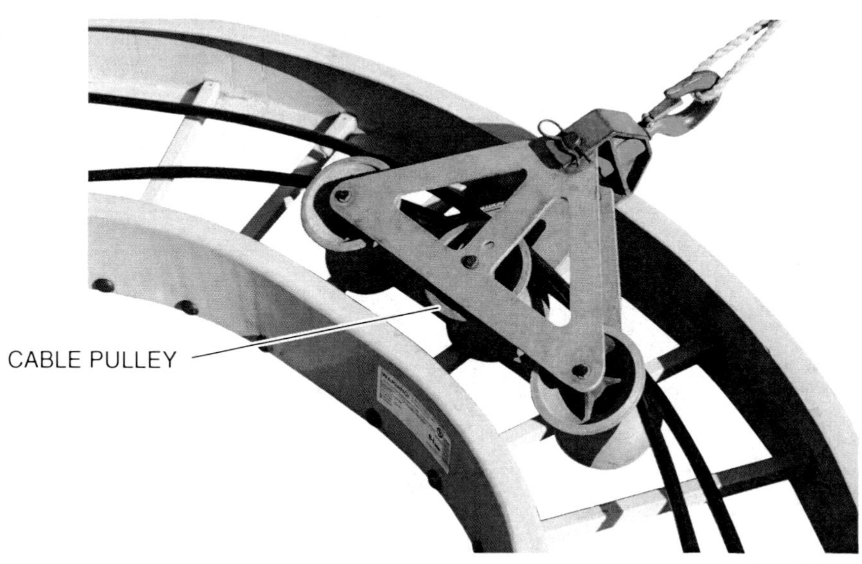

Figure 9 Cable pulley used to facilitate a cable pull in a tray.

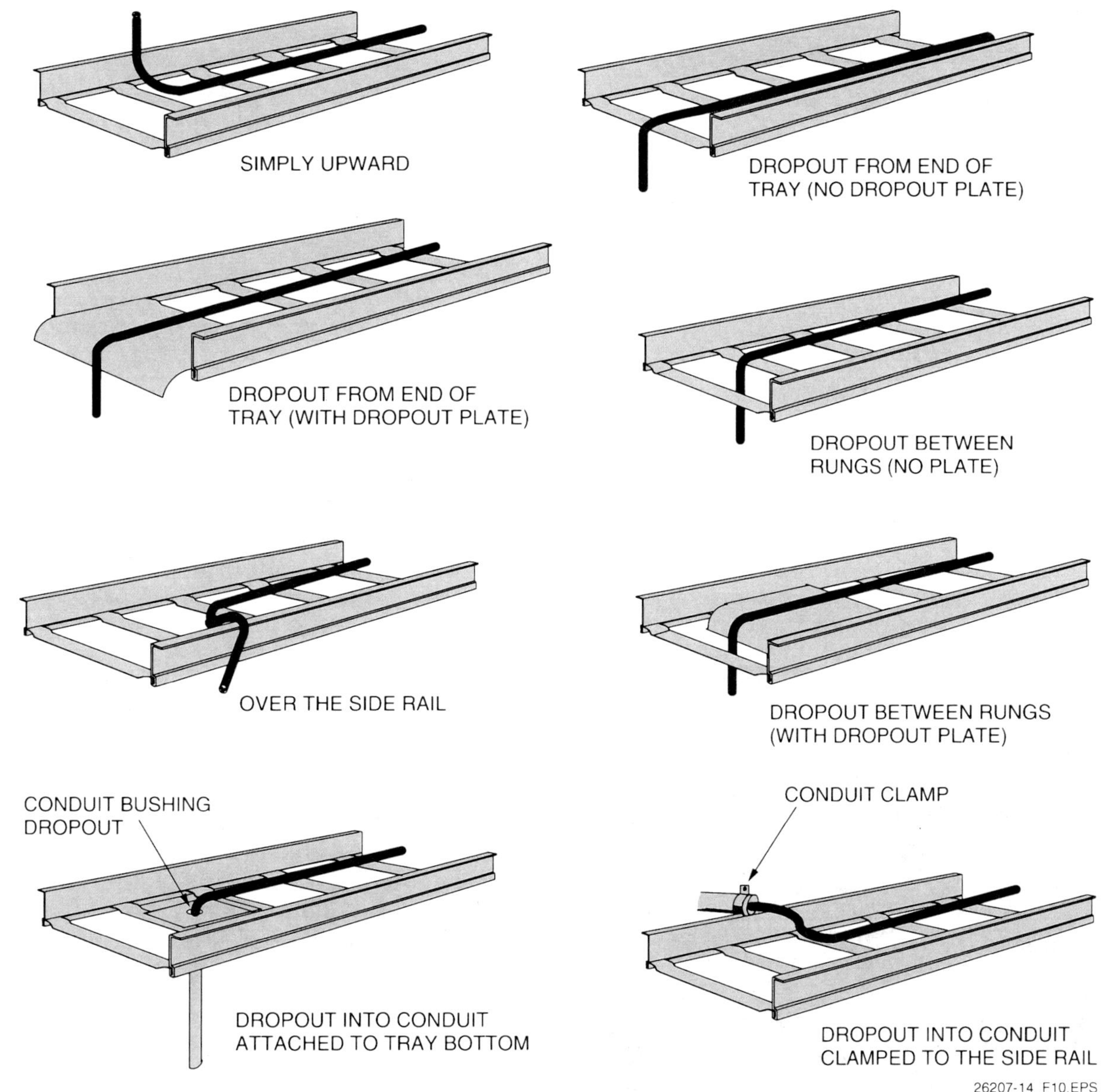

Figure 10 Several ways in which cables may exit from a cable tray.

2.10.0 Cable Supports in Vertical Trays

A cable hanger elbow is used to suspend cables in long vertical runs. Care should be taken to ensure that the weight of the suspended length of cable does not exceed the cable manufacturer's recommendation for the maximum allowable tension in the cable.

In short vertical runs, the weight of cables can be supported either by the outside vertical riser elbow or by the vertical straight section when the cables are tied to it. *Figure 12* shows a typical application of a cable hanger elbow in a vertical run.

2.11.0 Cable Edge Protection

The bottom of the solid bottom tray might be convex, concave, or flat. When two pieces of tray are butted together, the bottoms may be out of alignment. An alignment strip, also known as an H bar, is placed between the tray bottoms.

2.12.0 Splice Plates

There are several types of splice plates available, including vertical, horizontal, and expansion plates.

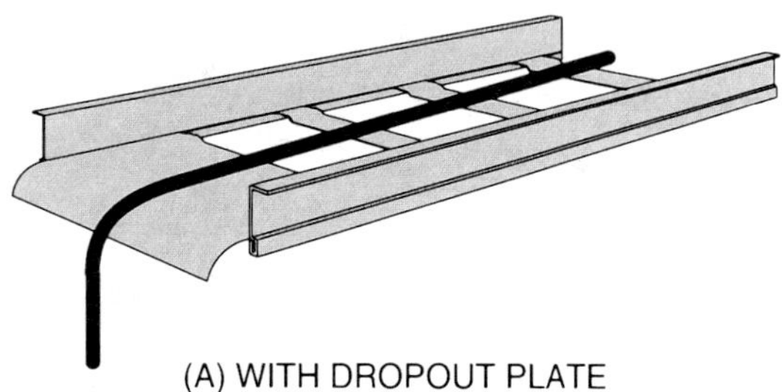

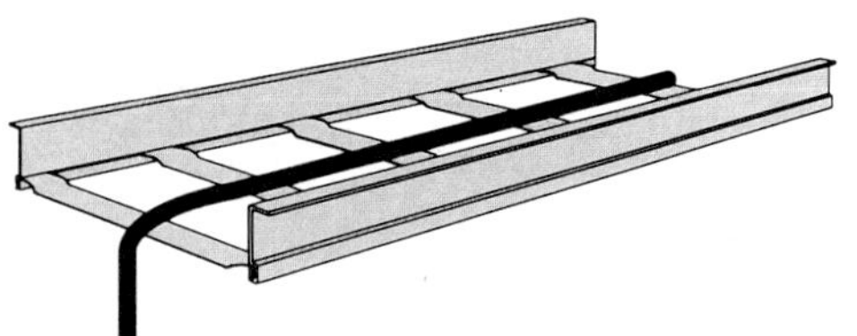

Figure 11 A dropout plate provides a curved surface for the cable to follow as it leaves the tray.

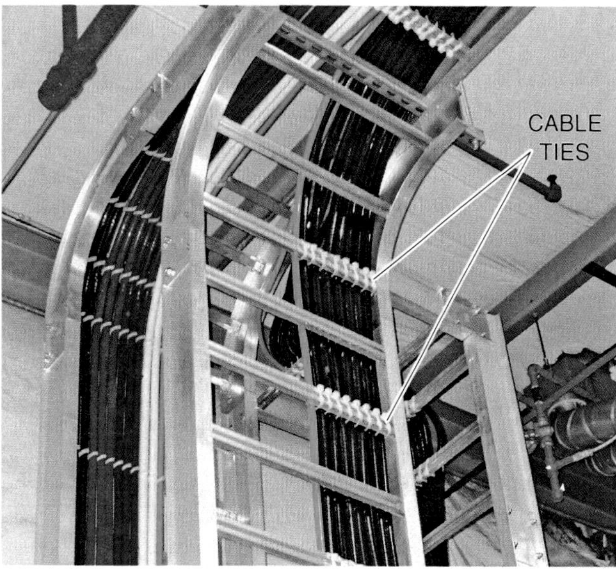

Figure 12 Typical application of supports in a vertical run.

2.12.1 Vertical Adjustment Splice Plates

Vertical adjustment splice plates are used to change the elevation in a run of cable tray. They should not be used when it is important to maintain a cable bending radius. Vertical adjustment splice plates are useful when the change in elevation is so slight or the angle so unusual that it would not be possible to install a standard outside vertical riser elbow and an inside vertical riser elbow in the space available.

In general, four **swivel plates** are used to build an offset in a cable tray system. Once the proper angles have been calculated, proceed as follows:

Step 1 Bolt four swivel plates together at the proper angles, using the inner holes as the center or pivot hole (see *Figure 13*).

Step 2 Using a flat surface such as a bench or concrete deck, space two swivel plates at the proper center-to-center distance apart (refer to *Figure 13*).

Step 3 Measure and cut the amount of tray needed to complete the offset.

2.12.2 Horizontal Adjustment Splice Plates

These plates are sometimes used in place of horizontal elbows to change the direction in a run of cable tray. They are used primarily where there is insufficient space or an unusual angle that prevents the use of a standard elbow.

2.12.3 Expansion Splice Plates

These plates are used at intervals along a straight run of cable tray to allow space for thermal expansion or contraction of the tray to occur, or where offsets or **expansion joints** occur in the supporting structure.

To enable the expansion joint to function properly, the cable tray must be allowed to slide freely on its supports. Any cable tray hold-down device used in an installation subject to expansion or contraction must give clearance to the tray. An expansion joint and splice plates are shown in *Figure 14*.

2.13.0 Barrier Strips

Barrier (divider) strips are used to separate certain types of cable as a result of the nature of the installation, types of circuits used, type of equipment used, local codes, or the *NEC®*. Some reasons for using divider strips are to:

- Separate or isolate electrical circuits
- Separate or isolate cables of different voltages
- Separate cable or wire runs from each other to prevent fire or ground fault damage from spreading to other cables or wires in the same tray
- Aid neatness in the arrangement of the cables
- Warn electricians of the difference between cables on each side of the divider strip

2.13.1 Barrier Strip Cable Protectors

Barrier strip cable protectors are used to bind any raw metallic edge over which a cable is to pass. Their purpose is to protect the cable insulation against damage.

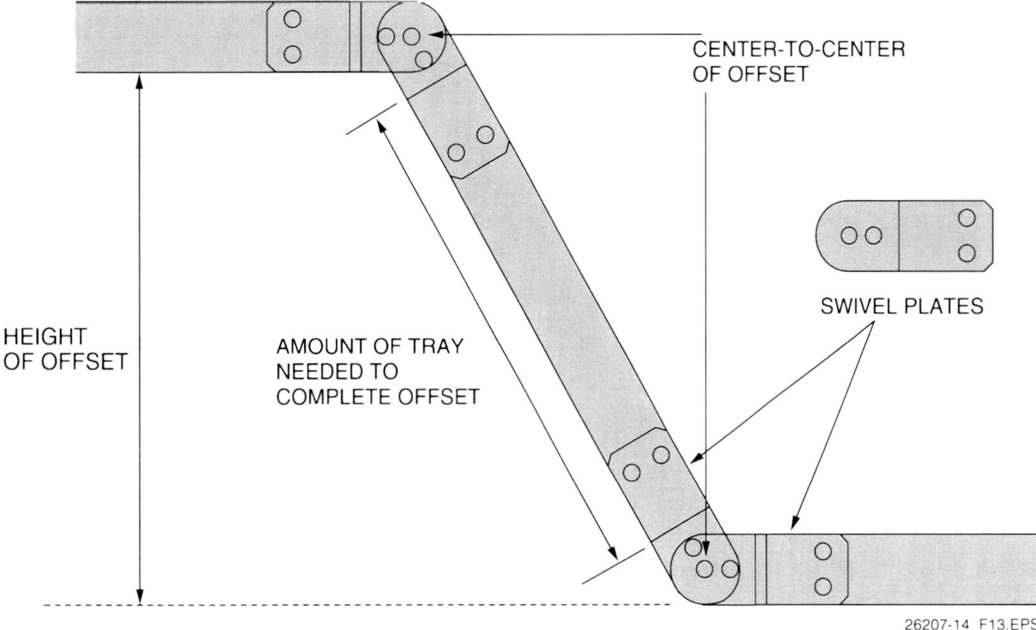

Figure 13 Fabricating a cable tray offset with swivel plates.

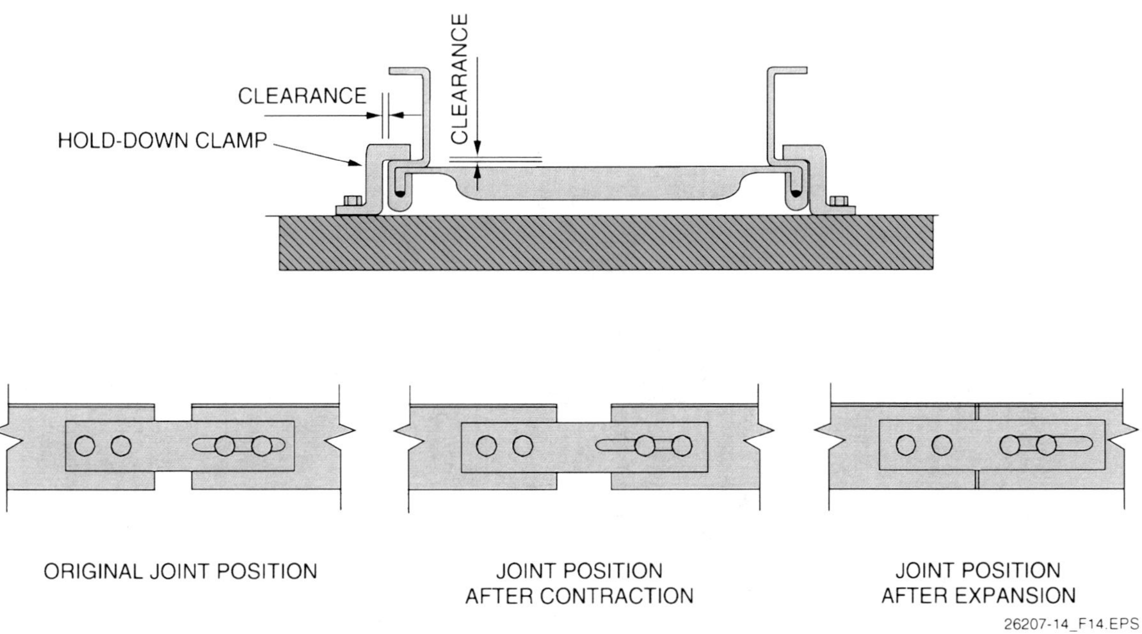

Figure 14 Expansion joint and splice plates.

On Site

Contraction and Expansion of Cable Tray

Structural expansion joints do not normally provide a solution to the thermal contraction and expansion of cable trays, because the materials of the structures and trays are different. For example, for a 100°F variance in temperature, a steel tray will require an expansion joint every 128' and an aluminum tray will require a joint every 65'. You must determine the gap setting for the joint according to the temperature at the time of installation. Tables for setting up the gap distances are available from cable tray manufacturers.

3.0.0 Cable Tray Support

Proper supports for cable tray installations are very important in obtaining a good overall layout. Cable is usually supported in one or more of the following ways:

- Trapeze mounting
- Direct rod suspension
- Wall mounting
- Center hung support
- Pipe rack mounting

3.1.0 Trapeze Mounting

When trapeze mounting is used, a structural member—usually a steel channel or Unistrut®—is connected to the vertical supports to provide an appearance similar to a swing or trapeze (*Figure 15*). The cable tray is mounted to the structural member using bolts, anchor clips, or J-clamps. The underside of the channel or Unistrut® may also be used to support conduit.

3.2.0 Direct Rod Suspension

The direct rod suspension method of supporting cable tray uses threaded rods and hanger clamps. The threaded rod is connected to the ceiling or other overhead structure and is connected to the hanger clamps that are attached to the cable tray side rails, as shown in *Figure 16(A)*.

3.3.0 Wall Mounting

Wall mounting is accomplished by supporting the tray with structural members attached to the wall, as shown in *Figure 16(B)*. This method of support is often used in tunnels (mining operations) and other underground or sheltered installations where large numbers of conductors interconnect equipment that is separated by long distances. When using this or any other method of supporting cable tray, always examine the structure to which the hangers are attached, and make absolutely certain that the structure is of adequate strength to support the tray system.

Figure 15 Channel support.

3.4.0 Trapeze Mounting and Center Hung Support

Trapeze mounting of cable tray is similar to direct rod suspension mounting. The difference is in the method of attaching the cable tray to the threaded rods. A structural member, usually a steel channel or strut, is connected to the vertical supports to provide an appearance similar to a swing or trapeze. The cable tray is mounted to the structural member. Often, the underside of the channel or strut is used to support conduit. A trapeze mounting assembly is shown in *Figure 16(C)*.

A method that is similar to trapeze mounting is a center hung tray support, as shown in *Figure 16(D)*. In this case, only one rod is used and it is centered between the cable tray side rails. A bushing sleeve, such as a short piece of small-diameter PVC, may be used over the center rod to protect the conductors.

3.5.0 Pipe Rack Mounting

Pipe racks are structural frames used to support the piping that interconnects equipment in outdoor industrial facilities. Usually, some space on the rack is reserved for conduit and cable tray. Pipe rack mounting of cable tray is often seen in petrochemical plants where power distribution and instrumentation wiring is routed over a large area and for long distances.

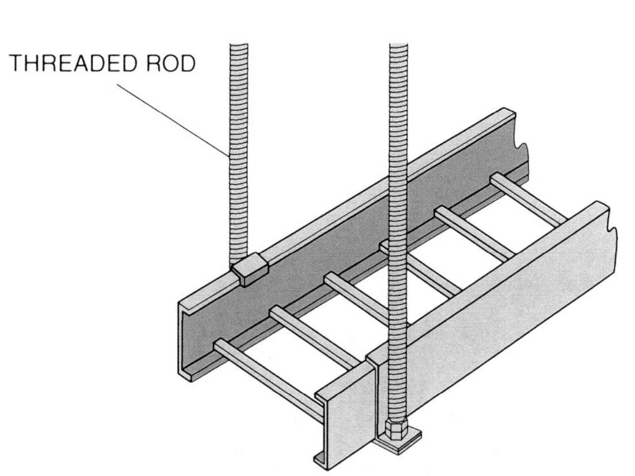

(A) DIRECT ROD SUSPENSION

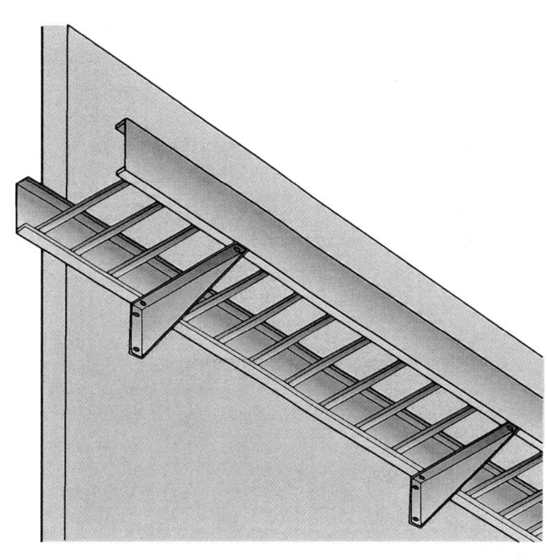

(B) WALL MOUNTING

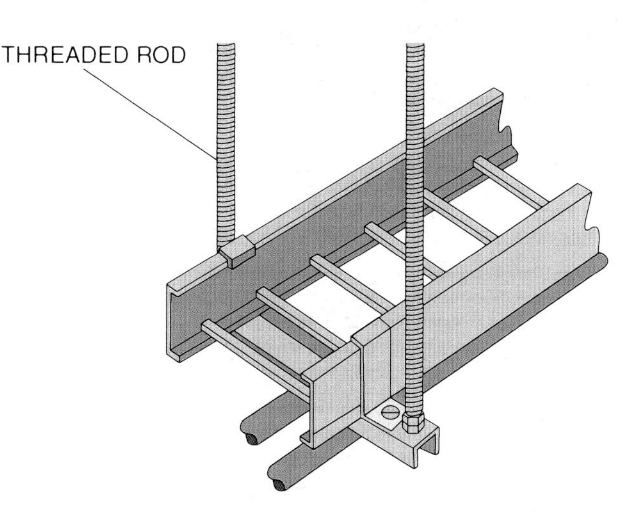

(C) TRAPEZE MOUNTING

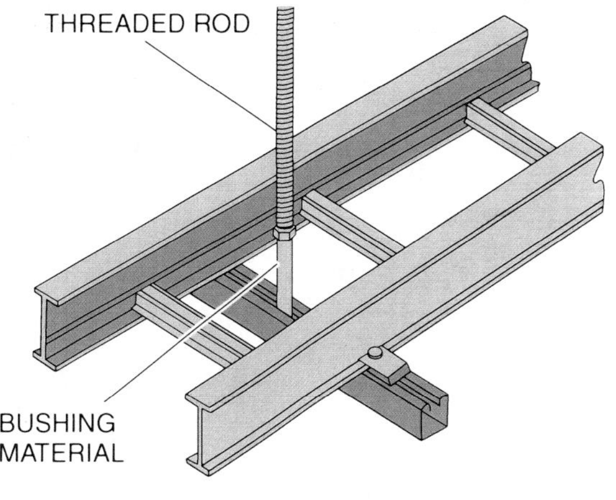

(D) CENTER HUNG SUPPORT

26207-14_F16.EPS

Figure 16 Alternate ways to hang cable tray.

On Site

Center Hung Tray

With center hung tray, care must be taken to balance the weight of the cable on either side of the tray to prevent tipping. In addition, extra support may be required for a long drop, such as that shown here.

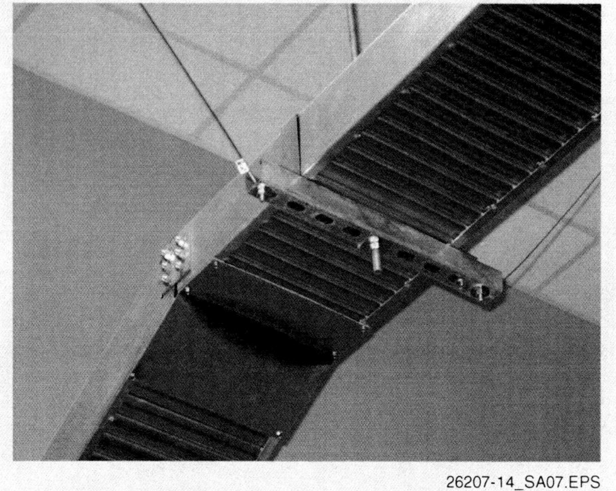

26207-14_SA07.EPS

4.0.0 Center Rail Cable Tray Systems

Center rail or monorail cable tray systems (*Figure 17*) are light, easy to install, and provide open sides for ready access when changing or adding cables. Center rail cable tray is used in light-duty applications such as sound, telephone, and other communications systems. In addition to its weight limitations, it cannot be used with dividers so its use is restricted to systems where dividers are not necessary.

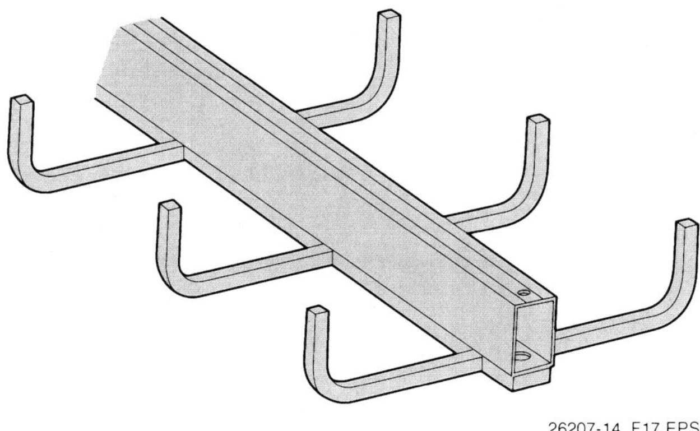

26207-14_F17.EPS

Figure 17 Center rail cable tray.

On Site

Cable Tray in Raised-Floor Systems

Cable tray can also be located beneath raised floors as shown here. This provides design flexibility because outlets can be located anywhere on the raised floor and conductors routed to the outlet. These systems are used in many office areas, libraries, and data rooms.

26207-14_SA08.EPS

5.0.0 *NEC*® Requirements

NEC Article 392 deals with cable tray systems along with related wire, cable, and raceway installations.

Figures 18, 19, and *20* summarize the *NEC*® requirements for cable tray installations. For in-depth coverage, always refer to the *NEC*®. Cable tray manufacturers also have some excellent reference material available that details the installation of their products. Consult your local dealer for more information.

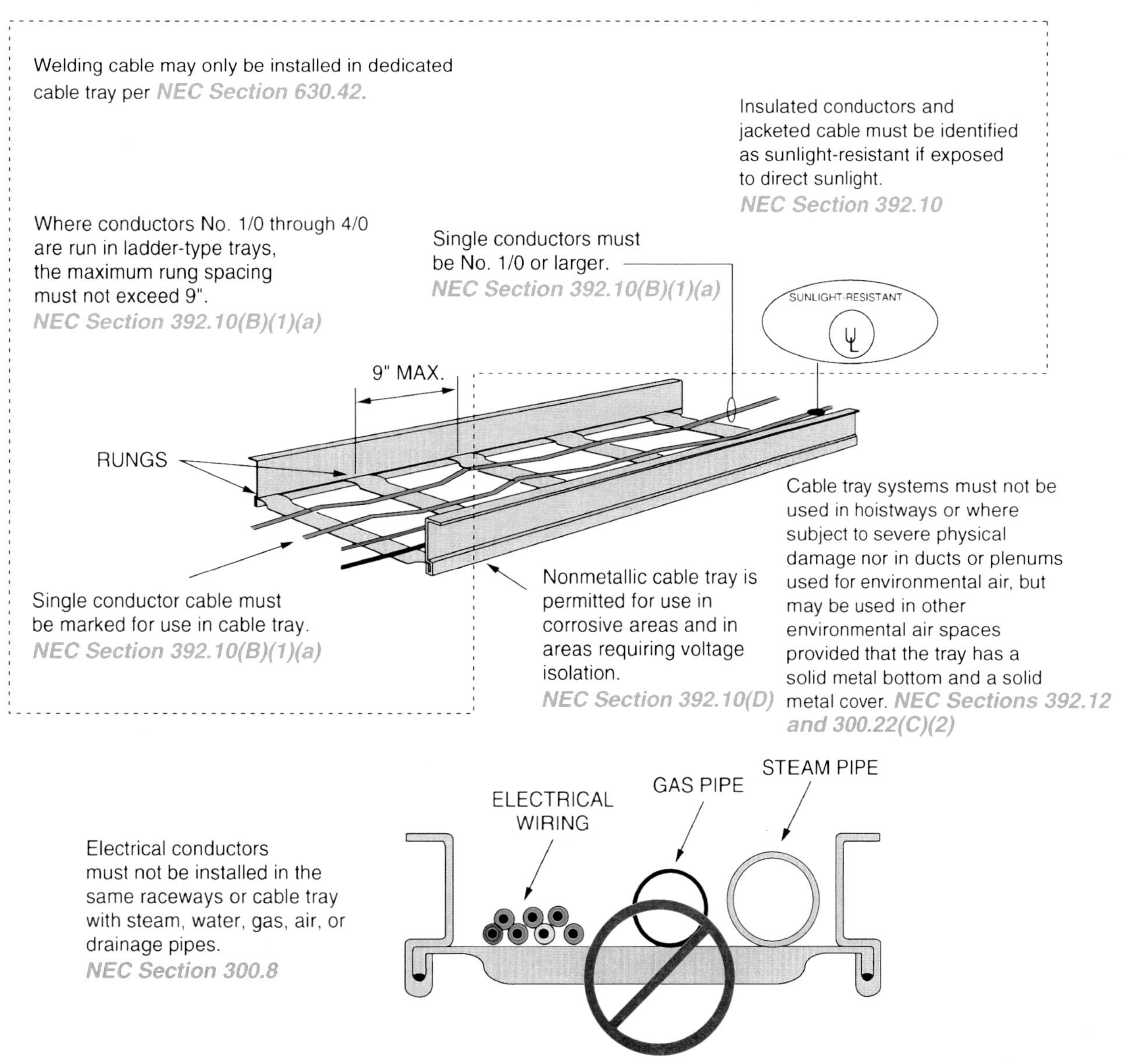

Welding cable may only be installed in dedicated cable tray per NEC Section 630.42.
Insulated conductors and jacketed cable must be identified as sunlight-resistant if exposed to direct sunlight. NEC Section 392.10
Where conductors No. 1/0 through 4/0 are run in ladder-type trays, the maximum rung spacing must not exceed 9". NEC Section 392.10(B)(1)(a)
Single conductors must be No. 1/0 or larger. NEC Section 392.10(B)(1)(a)
SUNLIGHT-RESISTANT
9" MAX.
RUNGS
Cable tray systems must not be used in hoistways or where subject to severe physical damage nor in ducts or plenums used for environmental air, but may be used in other environmental air spaces provided that the tray has a solid metal bottom and a solid metal cover. NEC Sections 392.12 and 300.22(C)(2)
Nonmetallic cable tray is permitted for use in corrosive areas and in areas requiring voltage isolation. NEC Section 392.10(D)
Single conductor cable must be marked for use in cable tray. NEC Section 392.10(B)(1)(a)
STEAM PIPE
GAS PIPE
ELECTRICAL WIRING
Electrical conductors must not be installed in the same raceways or cable tray with steam, water, gas, air, or drainage pipes. NEC Section 300.8
26207-14_F18.EPS

Figure 18 *NEC*® regulations governing the use of cable tray.

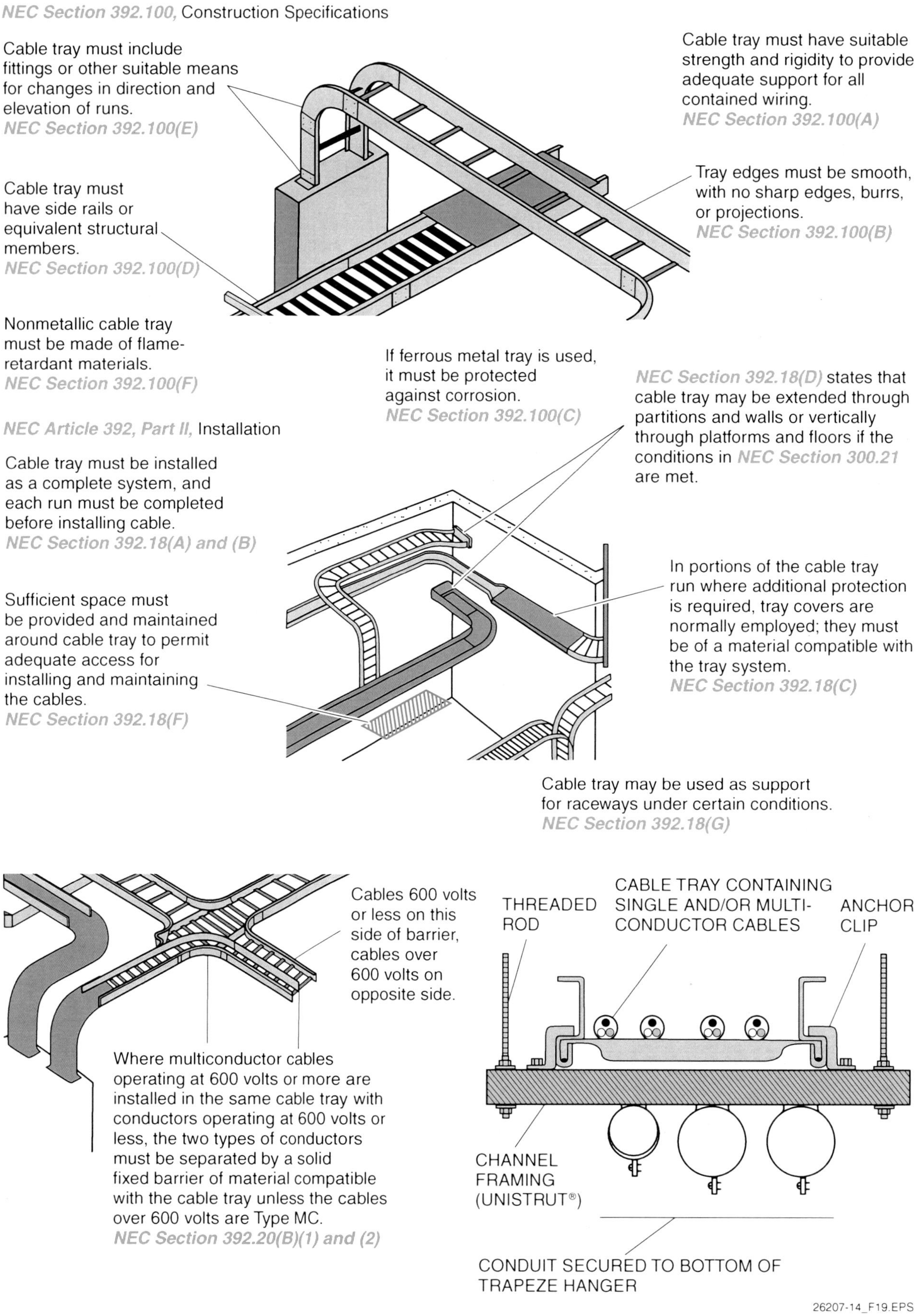

NEC Section 392.100, Construction Specifications

Cable tray must include fittings or other suitable means for changes in direction and elevation of runs. *NEC Section 392.100(E)*

Cable tray must have suitable strength and rigidity to provide adequate support for all contained wiring. *NEC Section 392.100(A)*

Cable tray must have side rails or equivalent structural members. *NEC Section 392.100(D)*

Tray edges must be smooth, with no sharp edges, burrs, or projections. *NEC Section 392.100(B)*

Nonmetallic cable tray must be made of flame-retardant materials. *NEC Section 392.100(F)*

If ferrous metal tray is used, it must be protected against corrosion. *NEC Section 392.100(C)*

NEC Article 392, Part II, Installation

NEC Section 392.18(D) states that cable tray may be extended through partitions and walls or vertically through platforms and floors if the conditions in *NEC Section 300.21* are met.

Cable tray must be installed as a complete system, and each run must be completed before installing cable. *NEC Section 392.18(A) and (B)*

In portions of the cable tray run where additional protection is required, tray covers are normally employed; they must be of a material compatible with the tray system. *NEC Section 392.18(C)*

Sufficient space must be provided and maintained around cable tray to permit adequate access for installing and maintaining the cables. *NEC Section 392.18(F)*

Cable tray may be used as support for raceways under certain conditions. *NEC Section 392.18(G)*

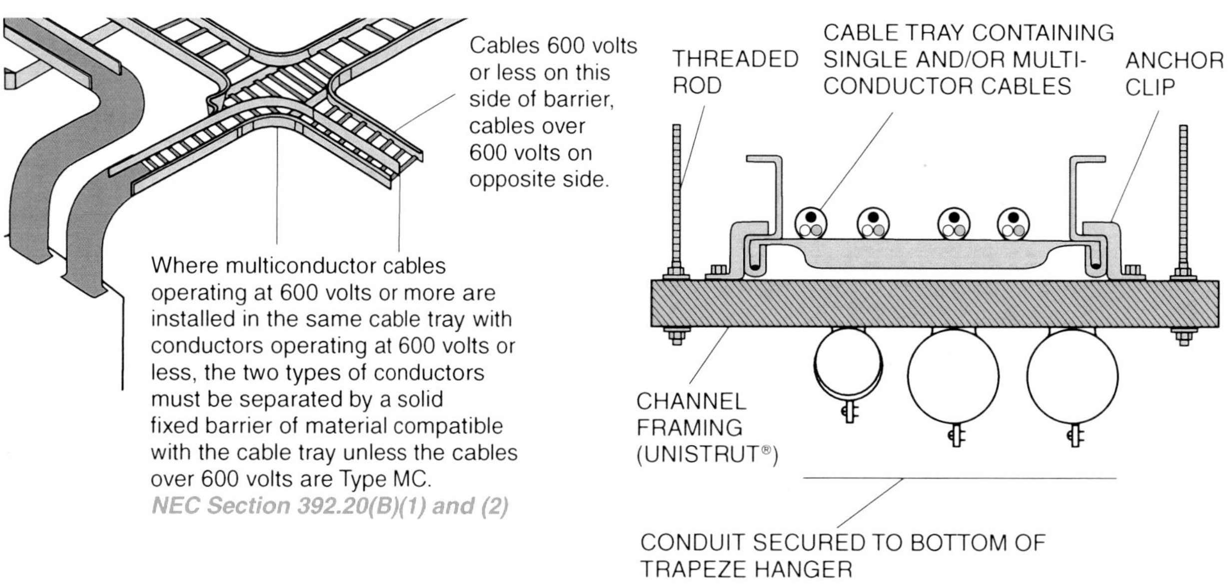

Cables 600 volts or less on this side of barrier, cables over 600 volts on opposite side.
Where multiconductor cables operating at 600 volts or more are installed in the same cable tray with conductors operating at 600 volts or less, the two types of conductors must be separated by a solid fixed barrier of material compatible with the cable tray unless the cables over 600 volts are Type MC.
NEC Section 392.20(B)(1) and (2)
THREADED ROD
CABLE TRAY CONTAINING SINGLE AND/OR MULTI-CONDUCTOR CABLES
ANCHOR CLIP
CHANNEL FRAMING (UNISTRUT®)
CONDUIT SECURED TO BOTTOM OF TRAPEZE HANGER

26207-14_F19.EPS

Figure 19 NEC® regulations governing cable tray construction and installation.

NEC Section 392.60, Grounding and Bonding

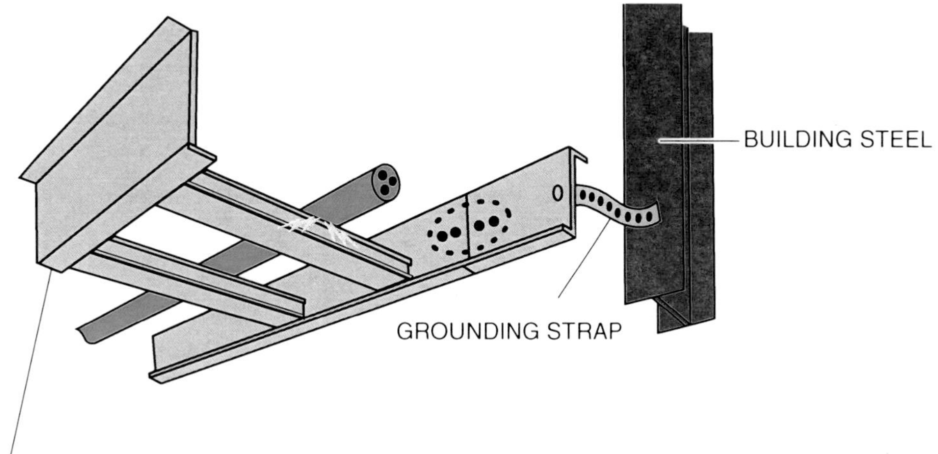

Steel or aluminum cable tray systems are permitted to be used as equipment grounding conductors if they meet all of the requirements in *NEC Section 392.60(B)*.

Proper grounding lessens hazards due to ground faults. Therefore, the *NEC*® requires all metallic cable tray to be grounded as required for conductor enclosures in accordance with *NEC Section 250.96*.

Per *NEC Section 392.60(B)(2)*, the minimum cross-sectional area of cable tray must conform to the requirements in *NEC Table 392.60(A)*.

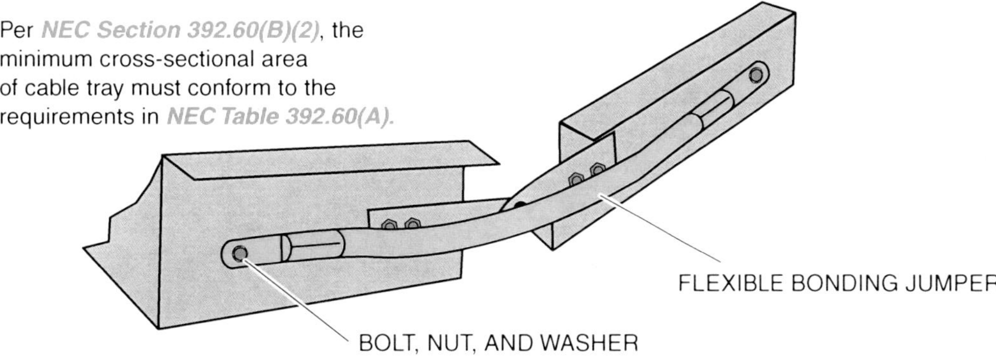

Where supervised by qualified personnel, grounded metallic cable tray may also be used as an equipment grounding conductor. *NEC Section 392.60(A)*.

Cable tray sections and fittings must be bonded in accordance with *NEC Section 250.96*.

26207-14_F20.EPS

Figure 20 *NEC*® regulations governing cable tray grounding.

6.0.0 Cable Installation

NEC Section 392.20 covers the general installation requirements for all conductors used in cable tray systems; that is, splicing, securing, and running conductors in parallel. For example, cable splices are permitted in cable trays provided they are made and insulated by *NEC*®-approved methods. Furthermore, any splices must be readily accessible and must not project above the side rails of the tray.

In most horizontal runs, the cables may be laid in the tray without securing them in place. However, on vertical runs or any runs other than horizontal, the cables must be secured to transverse members of the cable tray.

Cables may enter and leave a cable tray system in a number of different ways, as discussed previously. In general, no junction box is required where such cables are installed in bushed conduit or tubing. Where conduit or tubing is used, it must be secured to the tray with the proper fittings. Further precautions must be taken to ensure that the cable is not bent sharply as it enters or leaves the conduit or tubing.

6.1.0 Conductors Connected in Parallel

Where single-conductor cables comprising each phase, neutral, or grounded conductor of a circuit are connected in parallel as permitted in *NEC Section 310.10(H)*, the conductors must be installed in groups consisting of not more than one conductor per phase, neutral, or grounded conductor to prevent a current imbalance in the paralleled conductors due to inductive reactance. This also prevents excessive movement due to fault current magnetic forces.

6.2.0 Number of Cables Allowed in Cable Tray (2,000V or Less)

The number of multiconductor cables rated at 2,000V or less that are permitted in a single cable tray must not exceed the requirements of *NEC Section 392.22(A)*. This section applies to both copper and aluminum conductors.

6.2.1 All Conductors Size 4/0 or Larger

Per *NEC Section 392.22(A)(1)(a)*, where all of the cables installed in ladder or ventilated trough tray are 4/0 or larger, the sum of the diameters of all cables shall not exceed the cable tray width, and the cables must be installed in a single layer. For example, if a cable tray installation is to contain three 4/0 multiconductor cables (1.5" in diameter), two 250 kcmil multiconductor cables (1.85"), and two 350 kcmil multiconductor cables (2.5"), the minimum width of the cable tray is determined as follows:

$$3(1.5) + 2(1.85) + 2(2.5) = 13.2"$$

The closest standard cable tray size that meets or exceeds 13.2" is 18". Therefore, this is the size to use.

6.2.2 All Conductors Smaller Than 4/0

Per *NEC Section 392.22(A)(1)(b)*, where all of the cables are smaller than 4/0, the sum of the cross-sectional area of all cables smaller than 4/0 must not exceed the maximum allowable cable fill area as specified in Column 1 of *NEC Table 392.22(A);* this gives the appropriate cable tray width. To use this table, however, you must have the manufacturer's data for the cables being used. This will give the cross-sectional area of the cables.

The steps involved in determining the size of cable tray for multiconductors smaller than 4/0 AWG are as follows:

Step 1 Calculate the total cross-sectional area of all cables used in the tray. Obtain the area of each from the manufacturer's data.

Step 2 Look in Column 1 of *NEC Table 392.22(A)* and find the smallest number that is at least as large as the calculated number.

Step 3 Look at the number to the left of the row selected in Step 2. This is the minimum width of cable tray that may be used.

For example, determine the minimum cable tray width required for the following multiple conductor cables—all less than 4/0 AWG:

- Four at 1.5" diameter
- Five at 1.75" diameter
- Three at 2.15" diameter

Step 1 Determine the cross-sectional area of the cables from the equation:

$$A = \frac{\pi \times D^2}{4}$$

Where:

A = area

D = diameter

The area of a 1.5"-diameter cable is:

$$\frac{(3.14159)(1.5^2)}{4} = 1.7671 \text{ square inches}$$

The area of the four 1.5" cables is:

$$4 \times 1.7662 \text{ square inches} = 7.0648 \text{ square inches}$$

The area of 1.75"-diameter cable is:

$$\frac{(3.14159)(1.75^2)}{4} = 2.4053 \text{ square inches}$$

The area of the five 1.75" cables is:

$$5 \times 2.4041 \text{ square inches} = 12.0205 \text{ square inches}$$

The area of the three 2.15" cables is:

$$\frac{(3.14159)(2.15^2)}{4} = 3.6305 \text{ square inches}$$

Therefore, the total area of the three cables is:

$$3 \times 3.6287 \text{ square inches} = 10.8861 \text{ square inches}$$

The total cross-sectional area is found by adding the above three totals to obtain:

$$7.0648 + 12.0205 + 10.8861 = 29.9714 \text{ square inches}$$

Step 2 Look in Column 1 of *NEC Table 392.22(A)* and find the smallest number that is at least as large as 29.9714 square inches. The number is 35.

Step 3 Look to the left of 35 and you will see the inside tray width of 30". Therefore, the minimum tray width that can be used for the given group of conductors is 30".

On Site

Low-Voltage Cable

Increasingly, cable trays are being used to carry many low-voltage conductors in communication centers. In a large commercial building, thousands of telecommunications cables are distributed in bundles from the equipment room to the telecommunications closets on each floor. Cable trays offer a convenient means of running these cables through the building as well as a much easier method of allowing for system expansion. Instead of having to access conduit buried within the building walls, a new communication cable can simply be added to the cable tray system, which is normally accessible through a dropped ceiling.

26207-14_SA09.EPS

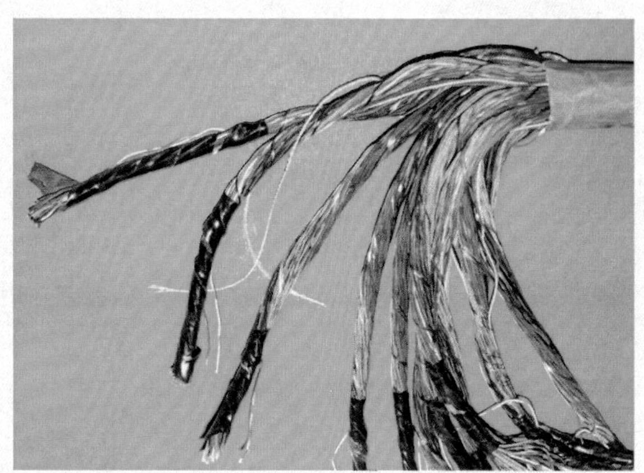

26207-14_SA10.EPS

6.2.3 Combination Cables

Per *NEC Section 392.22(A)(1)(c)*, where 4/0 or larger cables are installed in the same ladder or ventilated trough cable tray with cables smaller than 4/0, the sum of the cross-sectional area of all cables smaller than 4/0 must not exceed the maximum allowable fill area from Column 2 of *NEC Table 392.22(A)* for the appropriate cable tray width. The 4/0 and larger cables must be installed in a single layer, and no other cables can be placed on them.

To determine the tray size for a combination of cables as discussed in the above paragraph, proceed as follows:

Step 1 Repeat the steps from the procedure used previously to determine the minimum tray width required for the multiconductor cables having conductors sized 4/0 and larger.

Step 2 Repeat the steps from the procedure used previously to determine the cross-sectional area of all multiconductor cables having conductors smaller than 4/0 AWG.

Step 3 Multiply the result of Step 1 by the constant 1.2 and add this product to the result of Step 2. Call this sum A. Search Column 2 of *NEC Table 392.22(A)* for the smallest number that is at least as large as A. Look to the left in that row to determine the minimum size cable tray required.

To illustrate these steps, assume that you need to find the minimum cable tray width of two multiconductor cables, each with a diameter of 2.54" (conductors size 4/0 or larger); three cables with a diameter of 3.30" (conductors size 4/0 or larger), plus eight cables with a diameter of 1.92" (conductors less than 4/0).

Step 1 The sum of all the diameters of cable having conductors 4/0 or larger is:

$$2(2.54) + 3(3.30) = 14.98''$$

Step 2 The sum of the cross-sectional areas of all cables having conductors smaller than 4/0 is:

$$\frac{(8)(3.14159)(1.92^2)}{4} = 23.1623 \text{ square inches}$$

Step 3 Multiply the result of Step 1 by 1.2 and add this product to the result of Step 2:

$$(1.2 \times 14.98) + 23.1506$$
$$= 41.1266 \text{ square inches}$$

Refer to Column 2 of *NEC Table 392.22(A)* and find the closest number to 41.1383. It is 42. The tray width that corresponds to 42 is 36". Therefore, select a cable tray width of 36".

6.2.4 Solid Bottom Tray

Per *NEC Section 392.22(A)(3)*, where solid bottom cable trays contain multiconductor power or lighting cables, or any mixture of multiconductor power, lighting, control, and signal cables, the maximum number of cables must conform to the following:

- Where all of the cables are 4/0 or larger, the sum of the diameters of all cables must not exceed 90% of the cable tray width, and the cables must be installed in a single layer.
- Where all of the cables are smaller than 4/0, the sum of the cross-sectional areas of all cables must not exceed the maximum allowable cable fill area in Column 3 of *NEC Table 392.22(A)* for the appropriate cable tray width.
- Where 4/0 or larger cables are installed in the same cable tray with cables smaller than 4/0, the sum of the cross-sectional areas of all of the smaller cables must not exceed the maximum allowable fill area resulting from the computation in Column 4, *NEC Table 392.22(A)* for the appropriate cable tray width. The 4/0 and larger cables must be installed in a single layer, and no other cables can be placed on them.

Where a solid bottom cable tray with a usable inside depth of 6" or less contains multiconductor control and/or signal cables only, the sum of the cross-sectional areas of all cables at any cross section must not exceed 40% of the interior cross-sectional area of the cable tray. A depth of 6" must be used to compute the allowable interior cross-sectional area of any cable tray that has a usable inside depth of more than 6".

In a previous example, it was determined that the minimum tray size for multiconductor cables with all conductors size 4/0 or larger was 18". The sum of all cable diameters for this example was 13.2". To see if an 18" solid bottom tray can be used, multiply the tray width by 0.90 (90%):

$$18" \times 0.9 = 16.2"$$

Therefore, 16.2" is the minimum width allowed for solid bottom tray. Since we are using 18" tray, this meets the requirements of *NEC Section 392.22(A)(3)(a)*.

When dealing with solid bottom trays and using *NEC Table 392.22(A)*, use Columns 3 and 4 instead of Columns 1 and 2, as used for ladder and trough-type cable trays.

6.2.5 Single-Conductor Cables

Calculating cable tray widths for single-conductor cables (2,000V or under) is similar to the calculations used for multiconductor cables, with the following exceptions:

- Conductors that are 1,000 kcmil and larger are treated the same as multiconductor cables having conductors size 4/0 or larger.
- Conductors that are smaller than 1,000 kcmil are treated the same as multiconductor cables having conductors smaller than size 4/0.

NEC Section 392.22(B) covers the details of installing single-conductor cables with rated voltages of less than 2,000V in cable tray systems.

6.3.0 Ampacity of Cable Tray Conductors

NEC Section 392.80 gives the requirements for cables used in tray systems with rated voltages of 2,000 volts or less. Cables in cable tray use the same ampacity tables as other cable (see *NEC Section 310.15*), with additional derating applied for the following conditions:

- Cable tray construction
  - Open or covered
  - Solid or ventilated/ladder
- Type(s) of cable
  - Ampacity (less than 2,000V or over 2,001V)
  - Single conductor or multiconductor
- Number of cables and cable configuration in the tray

NEC Section 392.80(B) covers the installation and ampacity of cables with voltages of 2,001 and over.

What's wrong with this picture?

26207-14_SA11.EPS

7.0.0 Cable Tray Drawings

For an economical and satisfactory installation, working out the details of supports and hangers for a cable tray system is usually done beforehand by the engineering department or project engineer and is seldom left to the judgment of a field force that is not acquainted with the loads and forces to be encountered. As a result, drawings and specifications will usually be furnished to the work crew to provide details about the cable tray system. All workers involved with the installation should know how to interpret these drawings.

The exact method of showing cable tray systems on working drawings will vary, so always consult the symbol list or legend before beginning the installation. Also, study any shop or detail drawings that might accompany the construction documents.

If space permits, many engineers prefer to draw the cable tray system as close to scale as possible, using various symbols to show the different types of cable tray to be installed.

Look at the floor plan drawing in *Figure 21*. The cable tray system in this project originates at several power panels and motor control centers to feed and control motors in other parts of the building. The trays run from the motor control centers, are offset to miss beams and other runs of cable tray, and then branch off to various parts of the building.

Although experienced workers in the industrial electrical trade will have little trouble reading the information in this drawing, new electricians may have some difficulty in visualizing the system. However, if a supplemental drawing were provided with the floor plan drawing in *Figure 21*, it would provide a clearer picture of the system and leave little doubt as to how the cable tray system is to be installed. Even new workers in the

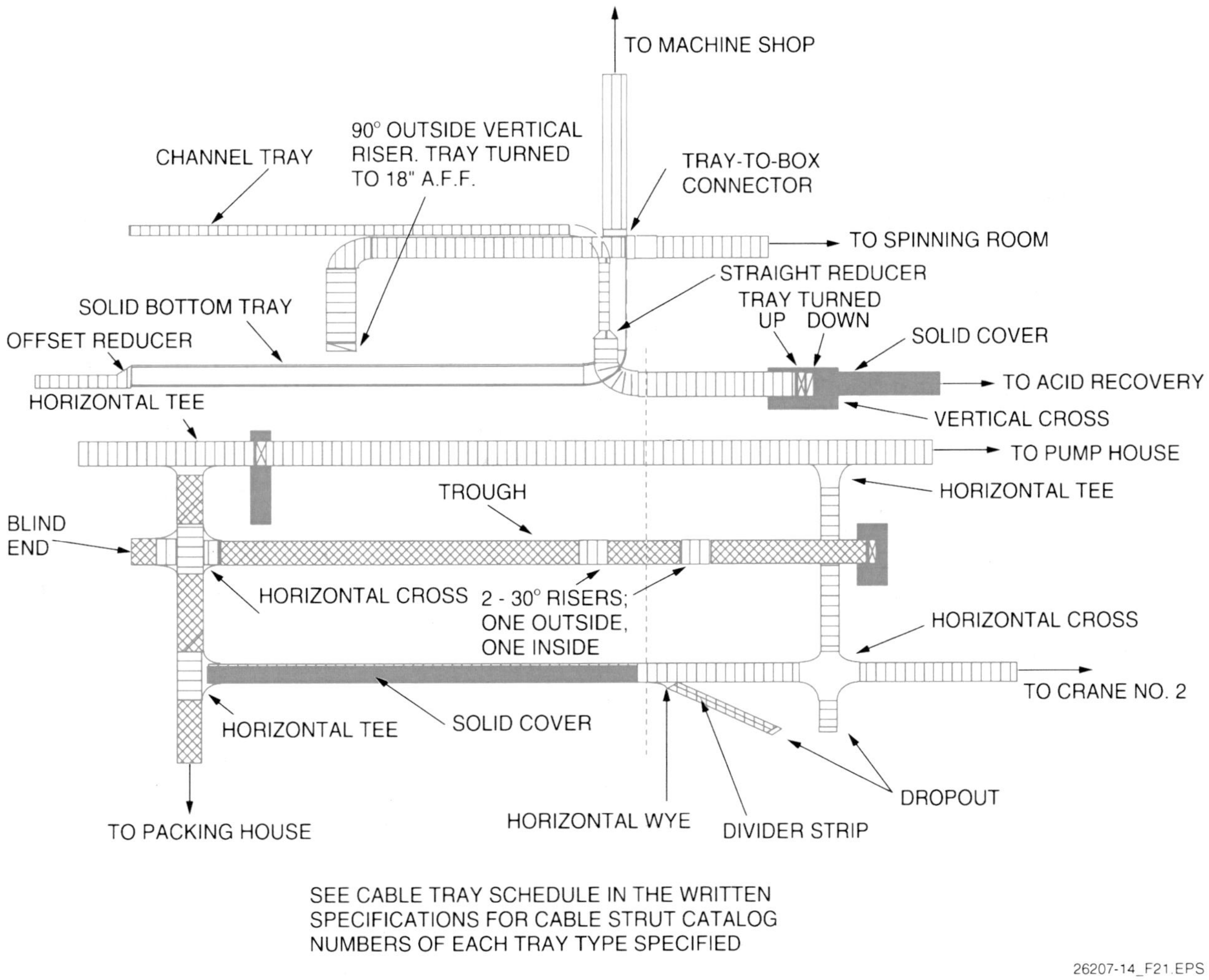

Figure 21 Sample floor plan of a cable tray system.

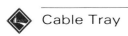

trade would be able to see how the system should be installed, and this would take some of the load off experienced workers and give them more time to accomplish other tasks.

In actual practice, however, consulting engineering firms seldom furnish the isometric drawing; they merely show the layout in plan view. Consequently, plan views involving the construction details of cable tray systems must be studied carefully during the planning stage—before the work is begun.

NOTE

In some areas, cable tray components are ordered in metric units. A metric conversion chart is included at the back of this module.

8.0.0 Pulling Cable in Tray Systems

When installing cables in tray systems, proper precautions must be taken to avoid damaging the cables. A complete line of installation tools is available for pulling long lengths of cable up to 1,000' or longer. These tools save considerable installation time.

Short lengths of cable can be laid in place without power pulling tools, or the cable can be pulled manually using a basket grip and pulling rope. Long lengths of small cable, 2" or less in diameter, can also be pulled with a basket grip and pulling rope. Larger cables, however, should be pulled by the conductor and the braid, sheath, or armor. This is usually done with a pulling eye applied to the cable at the factory, or by tying the conductor to the eye of a basket grip and taping the tail end of the grip to the outside of the cable.

Case History

Pulling Cable in a Tray

At a clothing manufacturing plant in New York, an electrician attempted to pull cable in a tray already partly filled with energized cables. He used plenty of cable-pulling lubricant, but did not use sheaves and rollers to isolate the new cables from the existing ones. During the pull, the new cables wedged against the live ones, yanking one hot wire apart at a splice. The wire grounded itself on the tray and arced for 30' down the tray, fatally shocking the electrician.

The Bottom Line: Use sheaves and rollers when pulling cables, especially when pulling them between existing live cables.

On Site

Big Pulls

For very long pulls, some contractors use an auxiliary winch. Power winches may exceed their preset tension limits and abort the pull, so a second winch is installed in a high-tension area of the pull in a straight section of tray. The second winch is used to pull a loop of slack cable and reduce the tension on the main winch, which now pulls only the length of slack cable between itself and the auxiliary winch.

In general, the pull exerted on the cables pulled with a basket grip that is not attached to the conductor should not exceed 1,000 pounds. For heavier pulls, care should be taken not to stretch the insulation, jacket, or armor beyond the end of the conductor nor bend the ladder, trough, or channel out of shape.

The bending radius of the cable should not be less than the values recommended by the cable manufacturer, which range from four times the diameter for a rubber-insulated cable that has a 1" maximum outside diameter without lead, shield, or armor, to eight times the diameter for **interlocked armor cable**. Cables of special construction such as wire armor and high-voltage cables require a larger radius bend.

When installing long lengths of cable up to 1,000' with as many as a dozen bends, best results are obtained by pulling the cable in one continuous operation at a speed of 20' to 25' per minute. The pulling line diameter and length will depend on the pull to be made and construction equipment available. The winch and power unit must be of an adequate size for the job and capable of developing the high pulling speed required for the best and most economical results. A complete description of pulling equipment was covered in the *Conductor Installations* module.

9.0.0 Safety

Installing cable tray means working at heights above the floor. Consequently, workers must take the necessary precautions. In general, workers installing cable tray will use ladders, scaffolds, lifts, work from the tray assembly itself, or a combination of all these.

Keep the tray assembly uncluttered during installation. Tools, tray fittings, and the like are ideal obstacles for tripping workers. They may also fall off the tray and injure workers below.

To help prevent the latter, set up work barriers beneath the section of tray assembly being worked on. If you are working on the ground, never penetrate or move these barriers until the work above is complete.

Learn to secure your lifeline properly, and also make sure your full body harness is a proper fit. A harness that is too large may slip, resulting in a serious injury or even death.

Think About It

Putting It All Together

If possible, examine the conduit system at your workplace or school. Did the installers make use of cable tray? If not, is the system large enough to warrant the use of it?

SUMMARY

A cable tray system includes the assembly of units or sections and associated fittings that form a rigid structural system used to support cables and raceways. Cable tray systems are commonly used in industrial applications and are normally constructed of either aluminum or steel, although PVC-coated and all-nonmetallic trays are also available.

Cable tray is available in various forms, including ladder, trough, center rail, and solid bottom, and can be supported by either side mounts or center mounts. *NEC Article 392* covers cable tray installations, along with the types of conductors to be used in various cable tray systems.

Review Questions

1. When a cable tray section branches off from a main section in two 90° turns, the section is called a(n) _____.
   a. wye
   b. tee
   c. divider strip
   d. ell

2. A section of cable tray that makes a single horizontal 90° turn is known as a(n) _____.
   a. tee
   b. wye
   c. elbow
   d. cross

3. Which of the following best describes the type of fitting that will be used with a solid cover cable tray?
   a. An Ericson coupling
   b. Vertical splices
   c. A horizontal cross
   d. A cover clamp

4. Which of the following branches in four different directions?
   a. A horizontal wye
   b. A horizontal cross
   c. An inside vertical riser
   d. A dropout

5. Which of the following best describes how closely packed cables will be affected when energized?
   a. Their efficiency will be increased.
   b. Their efficiency will be decreased.
   c. No change will be encountered.
   d. The operating temperature of each cable will be lower.

6. When a cable tray system must be protected from dropping objects that may damage the cable, a _____.
   a. solid bottom tray is used
   b. trough-type tray is used
   c. tray cover is used
   d. blind end is used

7. When cable exits downward from a tray without a dropout plate, which of the following could occur?
   a. Current surges
   b. Reduced amperage
   c. Voltage surges
   d. Insulation damage

8. The main purpose of vertical adjustment splice plates is to _____.
   a. increase the strength of a cable tray section
   b. support the cable tray system
   c. change the elevation in a run of cable tray
   d. secure the cable within the tray

9. A barrier strip is a _____.
   a. division strip installed in a raceway to separate certain types of cables
   b. strip used to provide the tray with added support
   c. glass strip used as a cable tray insulator
   d. metal strip used solely for grounding purposes

10. Which of the following is a violation of *NEC Section 300.8*?
    a. Placing an instrumentation air line in the same tray with electrical conductors
    b. Spacing tray rungs 9" or less apart
    c. Running single conductors in trays that are larger than size 1/0
    d. Using nonmetallic tray systems in corrosive areas

Module 26207-14

Supplemental Exercises

1. Cable supports should be capable of supporting ________________ times the full weight of the cable and tray.

2. Where solid bottom cable trays contain multiconductor power or lighting cables, and all cables are larger than 4/0, the sum of the diameters of all cables must not exceed ________________ of the cable tray width.

3. The two types of cable tray failure under load are ________________________ and ________________________.

4. Cable tray is commonly manufactured in ________________ and ________________ lengths.

5. List the five reasons for using divider strip in cable:

   ____

   ____

   ____

   ____

   ____

6. Locate splices within ________________ of the span's distance from the nearest support.

7. True or False? When installing long lengths of cable, it is best to pull the cable in one continuous operation.

8. List five types of cable tray supports:

   ____

   ____

   ____

   ____

   ____

9. True or False? Long runs of instrumentation wiring are typically supported by pipe rack mounting.

10. Cable tray is covered in ________________.
    a. *NEC Article 300*
    b. *NEC Article 392*
    c. *NEC Article 517*
    d. *NEC Article 550*

11. Cable tray must be bonded in accordance with ______.

a. *NEC Section 250.96*
b. *NEC Section 300.96*
c. *NEC Section 300.21*
d. *NEC Section 392.6(J)*

12. True or False? Water piping may be run in cable tray with electrical conductors.

13. When conductors 1/0 through 4/0 are run in ladder-type trays, the maximum rung spacing must not exceed ______.

a. 9"
b. 8"
c. 7"
d. 6"

14. All of the following are basic forms of cable tray *except* ______.

a. ladder
b. ratchet
c. trough
d. solid bottom

15. Cable in vertical trays should be supported ______.

a. per the manufacturer's recommendations
b. every 6" or 8"
c. every 12"
d. every 24"

Trade Terms Introduced in This Module

Barrier strip: A metal strip constructed to divide a section of cable tray so that certain kinds of cable may be separated from each other.

Cable pulley: A device used to facilitate pulling conductor in cable tray where the tray changes direction. Several types are available (single, triple, etc.) to accommodate almost all pulling situations.

Cross: A four-way section of cable tray used when the tray assembly must branch off in four different directions.

Direct rod suspension: A method used to support cable tray by means of threaded rods and hanger clamps. One end of the threaded rod is secured to an overhead structure, while the other end is connected to hanger clamps that are attached to the cable tray side rails.

Dropout: Cable leaving the tray assembly and travelling directly downward; that is, the cable is not routed into a conduit or channel.

Dropout plate: A metal plate used at the end of a cable tray section to ensure a greater cable bending radius as the cable leaves the tray assembly.

Elbow: A section of cable tray used to change the direction of the tray assembly a full quarter turn (90°). Both vertical and horizontal elbows are common.

Expansion joints: Plates used at intervals along a straight run of cable tray to allow space for thermal expansion or contraction of the tray.

Fittings: Devices used to assemble and/or change the direction of cable tray systems.

Interlocked armor cable: Mechanically protected cable; usually a helical winding of metal tape formed so that each convolution locks mechanically upon the previous one (armor interlock).

Ladder tray: A type of cable tray that consists of two parallel channels connected by rungs, similar in appearance to the common straight ladder.

Pipe racks: Structural frames used to support the piping that interconnects equipment in outdoor industrial facilities.

Swivel plates: Devices used to make vertical offsets in cable tray.

Tee: A section of cable tray that branches off the main section in two other directions.

Trapeze mounting: A method of supporting cable tray using metal channel, such as Unistrut®, Kindorf®, etc., supported by two threaded rods, and giving the appearance of a swing or trapeze.

Tray cover: A flat piece of metal, fiberglass, or plastic designed to provide a solid covering that is needed in some locations where conductors in the tray system may be damaged.

Trough: A type of cable tray consisting of two parallel channels (side rails) having a corrugated, ventilated bottom or a corrugated, solid bottom.

Unistrut®: A brand of metal channel used as the bottom bracket for hanging cable trays. Double Unistrut® adds strength and stability to the trays and also provides a means of securing future runs of conduit.

Wall mounting: A method of supporting cable tray systems using supports secured directly to the wall.

Wye: A section of cable tray that branches off the main section in one direction.

Appendix

METRIC CONVERSION CHART

METRIC CONVERSION CHART

INCHES		METRIC	INCHES		METRIC	INCHES		METRIC
Fractional	Decimal	mm	Fractional	Decimal	mm	Fractional	Decimal	mm
.	0.0039	0.1000	.	0.5512	14.0000	.	1.8898	48.0000
.	0.0079	0.2000	9/16	0.5625	14.2875	.	1.9291	49.0000
.	0.0118	0.3000	.	0.5709	14.5000	.	1.9685	50.0000
1/64	0.0156	0.3969	37/64	0.5781	14.6844	2	2.0000	50.8000
.	0.0157	0.4000	.	0.5906	15.0000	.	2.0079	51.0000
.	0.0197	0.5000	19/32	0.5938	15.0813	.	2.0472	52.0000
.	0.0236	0.6000	39/64	0.6094	15.4781	.	2.0866	53.0000
.	0.0276	0.7000	.	0.6102	15.5000	.	2.1260	54.0000
1/32	0.0313	0.7938	5/8	0.6250	15.8750	.	2.1654	55.0000
.	0.0315	0.8000	.	0.6299	16.0000	.	2.2047	56.0000
.	0.0354	0.9000	41/64	0.6406	16.2719	.	2.2441	57.0000
.	0.0394	1.0000	.	0.6496	16.5000	2 1/4	2.2500	57.1500
.	0.0433	1.1000	21/32	0.6563	16.6688	.	2.2835	58.0000
3/64	0.0469	1.1906	.	0.6693	17.0000	.	2.3228	59.0000
.	0.0472	1.2000	43/64	0.6719	17.0656	.	2.3622	60.0000
.	0.0512	1.3000	11/16	0.6875	17.4625	.	2.4016	61.0000
.	0.0551	1.4000	.	0.6890	17.5000	.	2.4409	62.0000
.	0.0591	1.5000	45/64	0.7031	17.8594	.	2.4803	63.0000
1/16	0.0625	1.5875	.	0.7087	18.0000	2 1/2	2.5000	63.5000
.	0.0630	1.6000	23/32	0.7188	18.2563	.	2.5197	64.0000
.	0.0669	1.7000	.	0.7283	18.5000	.	2.5591	65.0000
.	0.0709	1.8000	47/64	0.7344	18.6531	.	2.5984	66.0000
.	0.0748	1.9000	.	0.7480	19.0000	.	2.6378	67.0000
5/64	0.0781	1.9844	3/4	0.7500	19.0500	.	2.6772	68.0000
.	0.0787	2.0000	49/64	0.7656	19.4469	.	2.7165	69.0000
.	0.0827	2.1000	.	0.7677	19.5000	2 3/4	2.7500	69.8500
.	0.0866	2.2000	25/32	0.7813	19.8438	.	2.7559	70.0000
.	0.0906	2.3000	.	0.7874	20.0000	.	2.7953	71.0000
3/32	0.0938	2.3813	51/64	0.7969	20.2406	.	2.8346	72.0000
.	0.0945	2.4000	.	0.8071	20.5000	.	2.8740	73.0000
.	0.0984	2.5000	13/16	0.8125	20.6375	.	2.9134	74.0000
7/64	0.1094	2.7781	.	0.8268	21.0000	.	2.9528	75.0000
.	0.1181	3.0000	53/64	0.8281	21.0344	.	2.9921	76.0000
1/8	0.1250	3.1750	27/32	0.8438	21.4313	3	3.0000	76.2000
.	0.1378	3.5000	.	0.8465	21.5000	.	3.0315	77.0000
9/64	0.1406	3.5719	55/64	0.8594	21.8281	.	3.0709	78.0000
5/32	0.1563	3.9688	.	0.8661	22.0000	.	3.1102	79.0000
.	0.1575	4.0000	7/8	0.8750	22.2250	.	3.1496	80.0000
11/64	0.1719	4.3656	.	.8858	22.5000	.	3.1890	81.0000
.	0.1772	4.5000	57/64	.89063	22.6219	.	3.2283	82.0000
3/16	0.1875	4.7625	.	.9055	23.0000	.	3.2677	83.0000
.	0.1969	5.0000	29/32	.90625	23.0188	.	3.3071	84.0000
13/64	0.2031	5.1594	59/64	.92188	23.4156	.	3.3465	85.0000
.	0.2165	5.5000	.	.9252	23.5000	.	3.3858	86.0000
7/32	0.2188	5.5563	15/16	.93750	23.8125	.	3.4252	87.0000
15/64	0.2344	5.9531	.	.9449	24.0000	.	3.4646	88.0000
.	0.2362	6.0000	61/64	.95313	24.2094	3 1/2	3.5000	88.9000
1/4	0.2500	6.3500	.	.9646	24.5000	.	3.5039	89.0000
.	0.2559	6.5000	31/32	.96875	24.6063	.	3.5433	90.0000
17/64	0.2656	6.7469	.	.9843	25.0000	.	3.5827	91.0000
.	0.2756	7.0000	63/64	.98438	25.0031	.	3.6220	92.0000
9/32	0.2813	7.1438	1	1.000	25.40	.	3.6614	93.0000
.	0.2953	7.5000	.	1.0039	25.5000	.	3.7008	94.0000
19/64	0.2969	7.5406	.	1.0236	26.0000	.	3.7402	95.0000
5/16	0.3125	7.9375	.	1.0433	26.5000	.	3.7795	96.0000
.	0.3150	8.0000	.	1.0630	27.0000	.	3.8189	97.0000
21/64	0.3281	8.3344	.	1.0827	27.5000	.	3.8583	98.0000
.	0.3346	8.5000	.	1.1024	28.0000	.	3.8976	99.0000
11/32	0.3438	8.7313	.	1.1220	28.5000	.	3.9370	100.0000
.	0.3543	9.0000	.	1.1417	29.0000	4	4.0000	101.6000
23/64	0.3594	9.1281	.	1.1614	29.5000	.	4.3307	110.0000
.	0.3740	9.5000	.	1.1811	30.0000	4 1/2	4.5000	114.3000
3/8	0.3750	9.5250	.	1.2205	31.0000	.	4.7244	120.0000
25/64	0.3906	9.9219	1 1/4	1.2500	31.7500	5	5.0000	127.0000
.	0.3937	10.0000	.	1.2598	32.0000	.	5.1181	130.0000
13/32	0.4063	10.3188	.	1.2992	33.0000	.	5.5118	140.0000
.	0.4134	10.5000	.	1.3386	34.0000	.	5.9055	150.0000
27/64	0.4219	10.7156	.	1.3780	35.0000	6	6.0000	152.4000
.	0.4331	11.0000	.	1.4173	36.0000	.	6.2992	160.0000
7/16	0.4375	11.1125	.	1.4567	37.0000	.	6.6929	170.0000
.	0.4528	11.5000	.	1.4961	38.0000	.	7.0866	180.0000
29/64	0.4531	11.5094	1 1/2	1.5000	38.1000	.	7.4803	190.0000
15/32	0.4688	11.9063	.	1.5354	39.0000	.	7.8740	200.0000
.	0.4724	12.0000	.	1.5748	40.0000	8	8.0000	203.2000
31/64	0.4844	12.3031	.	1.6142	41.0000	.	9.8425	250.0000
.	0.4921	12.5000	.	1.6535	42.0000	10	10.0000	254.0000
1/2	0.5000	12.7000	.	1.6929	43.0000	20	20.0000	508.0000
.	0.5118	13.0000	.	1.7323	44.0000	30	30.0000	762.0000
33/64	0.5156	13.0969	1 3/4	1.7500	44.4500	40	40.0000	1016.000
17/32	0.5313	13.4938	.	1.7717	45.0000	60	60.0000	1524.000
.	0.5315	13.5000	.	1.8110	46.0000	80	80.0000	2032.000
35/64	0.5469	13.8906	.	1.8504	47.0000	100	100.0000	2540.000

TO CONVERT TO MILLIMETERS; MULTIPLY INCHES X 25.4
TO CONVERT TO INCHES; MULTIPLY MILLIMETERS X 0.03937*
*FOR SLIGHTLY GREATER ACCURACY WHEN CONVERTING TO INCHES; DIVIDE MILLIMETERS BY 25.4

26207-14_A01.EPS

Additional Resources

This module presents thorough resources for task training. The following resource material is suggested for further study.

National Electrical Code® Handbook, Latest Edition. Quincy, MA: National Fire Protection Association.

Figure Credits

Associated Builders and Contractors, Inc., Module opener

Topaz Publications, Inc., SA01, SA02, SA09, and SA10

John Traister, Figures 1–3 and 18

Tim Dean, SA03, SA04, Figures 9, 12, 15, SA07, and SA08

Greenlee/A Textron Company, SA05

Jim Mitchem, SA06

Tim Ely, SA11

NCCER CURRICULA — USER UPDATE

NCCER makes every effort to keep its textbooks up-to-date and free of technical errors. We appreciate your help in this process. If you find an error, a typographical mistake, or an inaccuracy in NCCER's curricula, please fill out this form (or a photocopy), or complete the online form at **www.nccer.org/olf**. Be sure to include the exact module ID number, page number, a detailed description, and your recommended correction. Your input will be brought to the attention of the Authoring Team. Thank you for your assistance.

Instructors – If you have an idea for improving this textbook, or have found that additional materials were necessary to teach this module effectively, please let us know so that we may present your suggestions to the Authoring Team.

NCCER Product Development and Revision

13614 Progress Blvd., Alachua, FL 32615

Email: curriculum@nccer.org

Online: www.nccer.org/olf

❑ Trainee Guide ❑ AIG ❑ Exam ❑ PowerPoints Other ______________________________

Craft / Level: Copyright Date:

Module ID Number / Title:

Section Number(s):

Description:

Recommended Correction:

Your Name:

Address:

Email: Phone:

Residential & Commercial Wiring and Services

Modules

26111-14

26306-14

26308-14

Residential Electrical Services

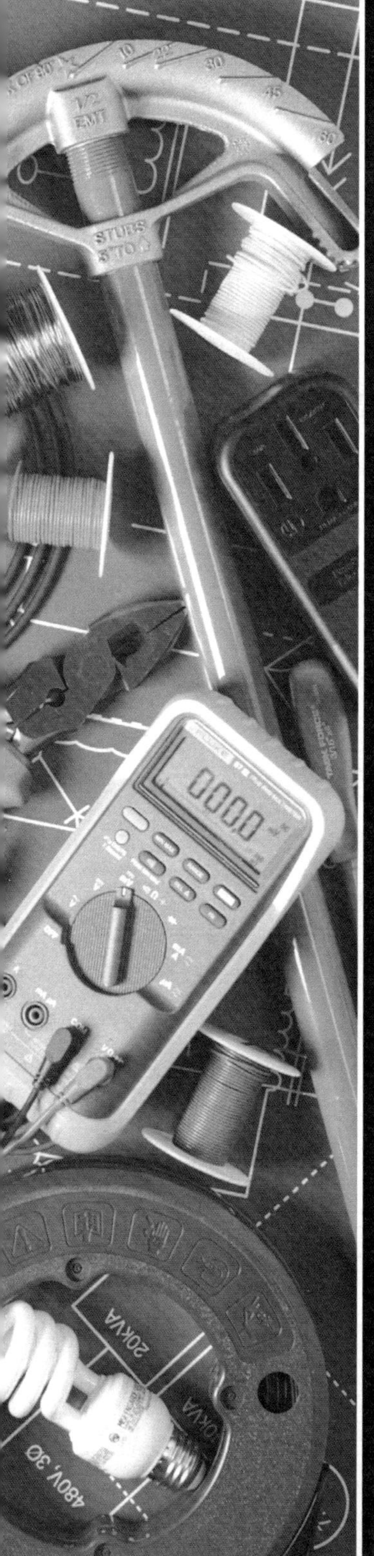

Phoenix Fire Station No. 50

Phoenix's Fire Station No. 50 sports many environmentally protective measures in its construction, such as a roof made of recycled aluminum cans and terra-cotta colored terrazzo flooring made by grinding down the concrete structural slab. Recycled countertops are used in the kitchen and more than 80 percent of the lighting takes advantage of natural sources to save energy. The landscape is a xeriscape design that will require no irrigation after two years.

26111-14

Trainees with successful module completions may be eligible for credentialing through NCCER's National Registry. To learn more, go to **www.nccer.org** or contact us at **1.888.622.3720.** Our website has information on the latest product releases and training, as well as online versions of our *Cornerstone* magazine and Pearson's product catalog.

Your feedback is welcome. You may email your comments to **curriculum@nccer.org,** send general comments and inquiries to **info@nccer.org,** or fill in the User Update form at the back of this module.

This information is general in nature and intended for training purposes only. Actual performance of activities described in this manual requires compliance with all applicable operating, service, maintenance, and safety procedures under the direction of qualified personnel. References in this manual to patented or proprietary devices do not constitute a recommendation of their use.

Residential Electrical Services

Objectives

When you have completed this module, you will be able to do the following:

1. Explain the role of the *National Electrical Code*® in residential wiring and describe how to determine electric service requirements for dwellings.
2. Explain the grounding requirements of a residential electric service.
3. Calculate and select service-entrance equipment.
4. Select the proper wiring methods for various types of residences.
5. Compute branch circuit loads and explain their installation requirements.
6. Explain the types and purposes of equipment grounding conductors.
7. Explain the purpose of ground fault circuit interrupters and tell where they must be installed.
8. Size outlet boxes and select the proper type for different wiring methods.
9. Describe rules for installing electric space heating and HVAC equipment.
10. Describe the installation rules for electrical systems around swimming pools, spas, and hot tubs.
11. Explain how wiring devices are selected and installed.
12. Describe the installation and control of lighting fixtures.

Performance Tasks

Under the supervision of the instructor, you should be able to do the following:

1. For a residential dwelling of a given size, and equipped with a given list of major appliances, demonstrate or explain how to:
   - Compute lighting, small appliance, and laundry loads.
   - Compute the loads for large appliances.
   - Determine the number of branch circuits required.
   - Size and select the service-entrance equipment (conductors, panelboard, and protective devices).
2. Using an unlabeled diagram of a panelboard (Performance Profile Sheet 3), label the lettered components.
3. Select the proper type and size outlet box needed for a given set of wiring conditions.

Trade Terms

Appliance
Bonding bushing
Bonding jumper
Branch circuit
Feeder
Load center
Metal-clad (MC) cable
Nonmetallic-sheathed (Type NM, NMC, NMS) cable
Romex®
Roughing in
Service drop
Service entrance
Service-entrance conductors
Service-entrance equipment
Service lateral
Switch
Switch leg

Required Trainee Materials

1. Paper and pencil
2. Copy of the latest edition of the *National Electrical Code*®
3. Appropriate personal protective equipment

Note:
NFPA 70®, *National Electrical Code*®, and *NEC*® are registered trademarks of the National Fire Protection Association, Inc., Quincy, MA 02269. All *National Electrical Code*® and *NEC*® references in this module refer to the 2011 edition of the *National Electrical Code*®.

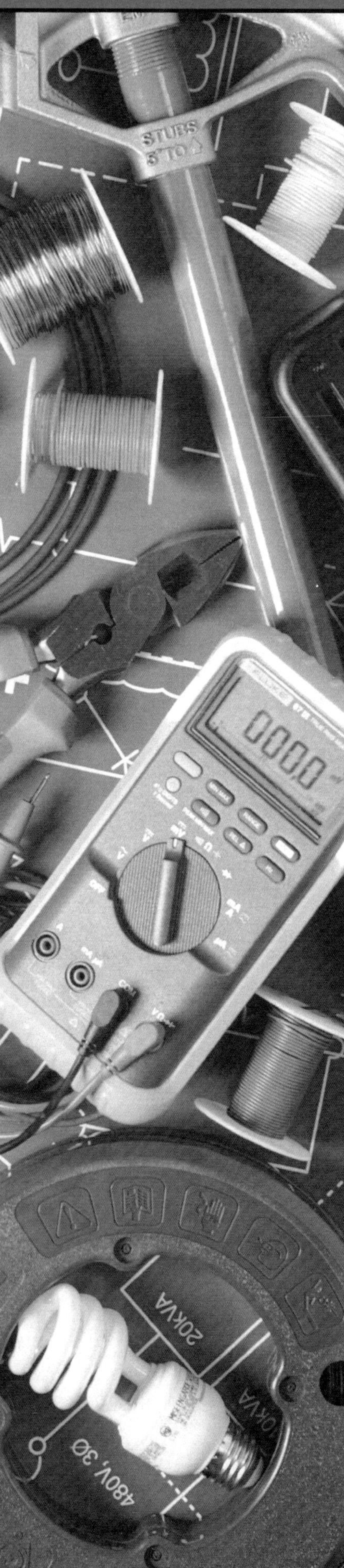

Contents

Topics to be presented in this module include:

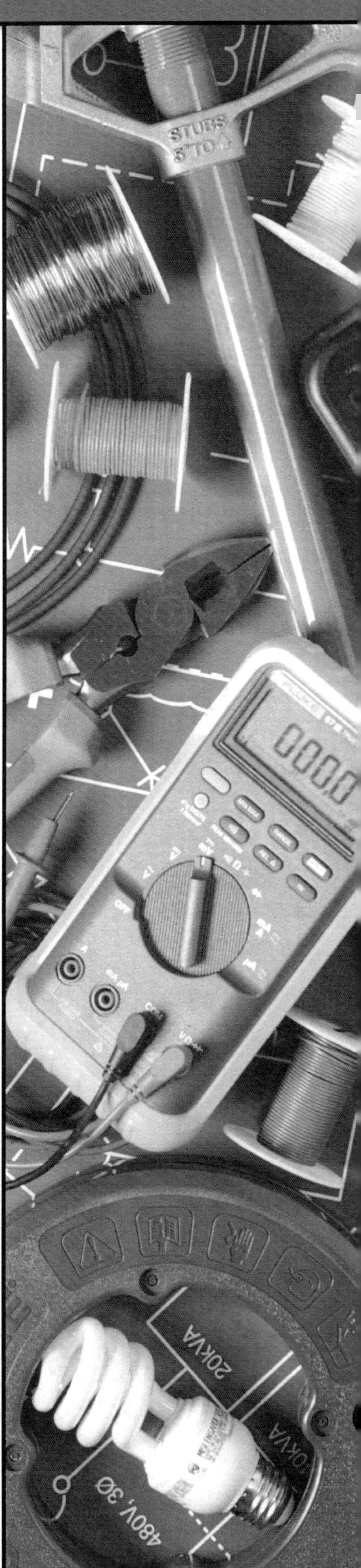

STUBS
5"TO
20KVA
480V, 3Ø

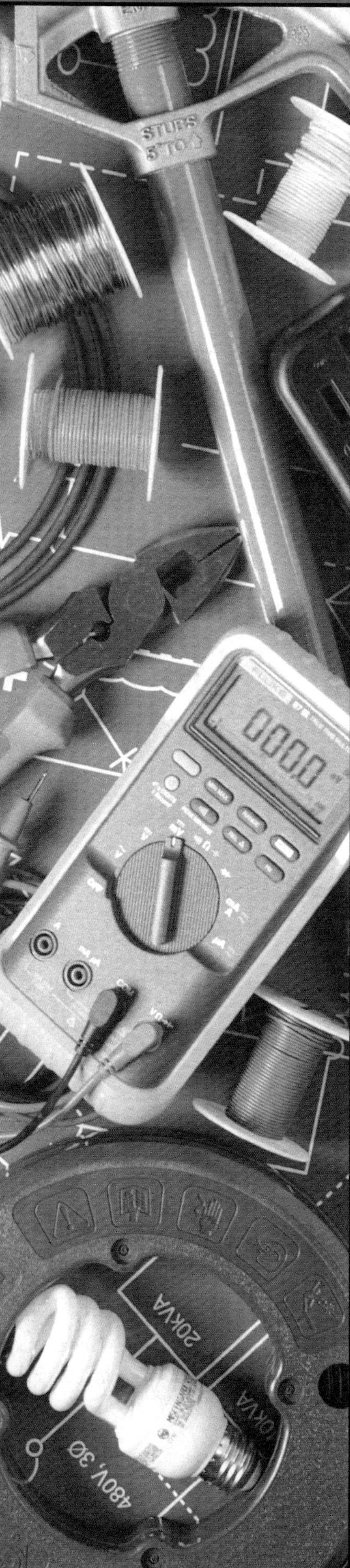

Figures

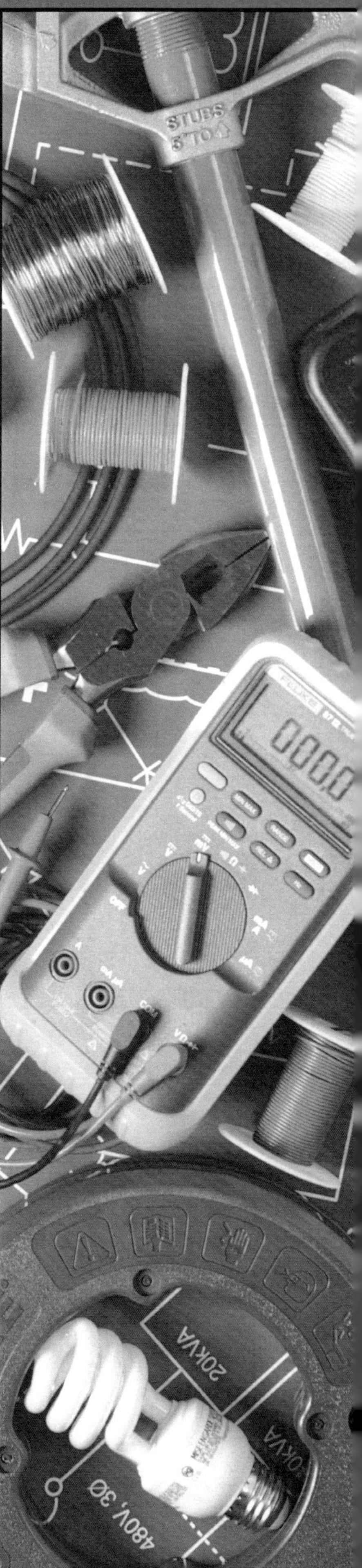

STUBS
5"TO
FLUKE
20KVA
480V, 3Ø

1.0.0 INTRODUCTION

The use of electricity in houses began shortly after the opening of the California Electric Light Company in 1879 and Thomas Edison's Pearl Street Station in New York City in 1882. These two companies were the first to enter the business of producing and selling electric service to the public. In 1886, the Westinghouse Electric Company secured patents that resulted in the development and introduction of alternating current; this paved the way for rapid acceleration in the use of electricity.

The primary use of early home electrical systems was to provide interior lighting, but today's uses of electricity include:

- Heating and air conditioning
- Electrical appliances
- Interior and exterior lighting
- Communications systems
- Alarm systems

When planning any electrical system, there are certain general steps to be followed, regardless of the type of construction. In planning a residential electrical system, the electrician must take certain factors into consideration. These include:

- Wiring method
- Overhead or underground electrical service
- Type of building construction
- Type of service entrance and equipment
- Grade of wiring devices and lighting fixtures
- Selection of lighting fixtures
- Type of heating and cooling system
- Control wiring for the heating and cooling system
- Signal and alarm systems
- Presence of alternative electrical systems, if any

The experienced electrician readily recognizes, within certain limits, the type of system that will be required. However, always check the local code requirements when selecting a wiring method. The *NEC®* provides minimum requirements for the practical safeguarding of persons and property from hazards arising from the use of electricity. These minimum requirements are not necessarily efficient, convenient, or adequate for good service or future expansion of electrical use. Some local building codes require electrical installations that surpass the requirements of the *NEC®*. For example, *NEC Section 230.51(A)* requires that service cable be secured by means of cable straps placed every 30 inches and within 12 inches of every service head, gooseneck, or connection to a raceway or enclosure. The electrical inspection department in one area requires these cable straps to be placed at a minimum distance of 18 inches.

If more than one wiring method may be practical, a decision as to which type to use should be made prior to beginning the installation.

NOTE

See the *Appendix* for other codes and electrical standards that apply to residential electrical installations.

In a residential occupancy, the electrician should know that a 120/240-volt (V), single-phase service entrance will invariably be provided by the utility company. The electrician knows that the service and feeders will be three-wire, that the branch circuits will be either two- or three-wire, and that the safety switches, service equipment, and panelboards will be three-wire, solid neutral. On each project, however, the electrician must consult with the local utility to determine the point of attachment for overhead connections and the location of the metering equipment.

2.0.0 SIZING THE ELECTRICAL SERVICE

It may be difficult to decide at times which comes first, the layout of the outlets or the sizing of the electric service. In many cases, the service (main disconnect, panelboard, service conductors, etc.) can be sized using the *NEC®* before the outlets are actually located. In other cases, the outlets will have to be laid out first. However, in either case, the service entrance and panelboard locations will have to be determined before the circuits can be installed—so the electrician will know in which direction (and to what points) the circuit homeruns will terminate. In this module, a typical residence will be used as a model to size the electric service according to the latest edition of the *NEC®*.

2.1.0 Floor Plans

A floor plan is a drawing that shows the length and width of a building and the rooms that it contains. A separate plan is made for each floor.

Figure 1 shows how a floor plan is developed. An imaginary cut is made through the building as shown in the view on the left. The top half of this cut is removed (top right), and the resulting floor plan (bottom) is what the remaining structure looks like when viewed directly from above.

The floor plan for a small residence is shown in *Figure 2*. This building is constructed on a concrete slab with no basement or crawl space. There is an unfinished attic above the living area and an open carport just outside the kitchen entrance.

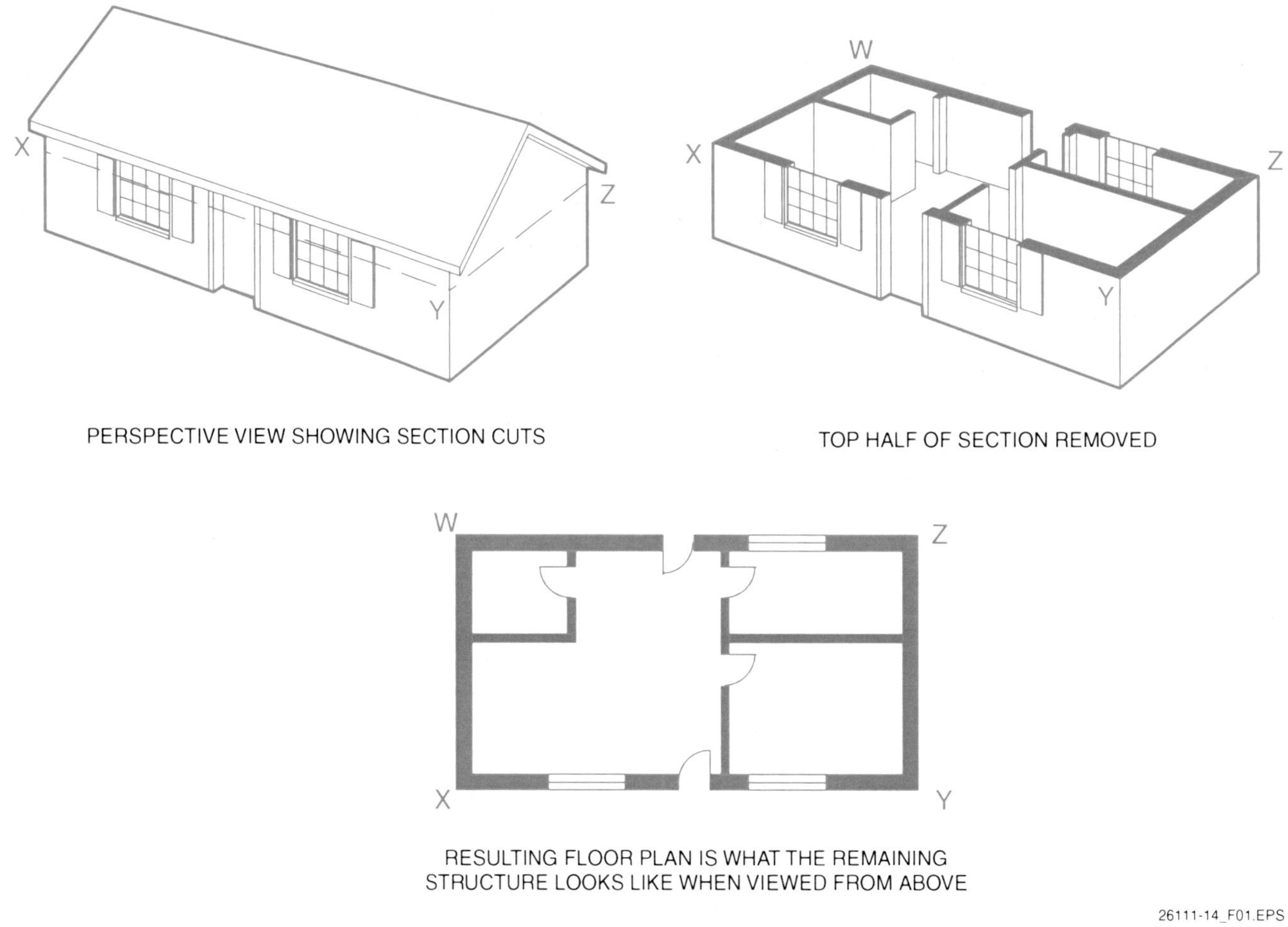

W X Z Y

PERSPECTIVE VIEW SHOWING SECTION CUTS

TOP HALF OF SECTION REMOVED

RESULTING FLOOR PLAN IS WHAT THE REMAINING STRUCTURE LOOKS LIKE WHEN VIEWED FROM ABOVE

26111-14_F01.EPS

Figure 1 Principles of floor plan layout.

Appliances include a 12 kilovolt-ampere (kVA) electric range, a 4.5kVA water heater, a ½hp 120V disposal, and a 1.5kVA dishwasher.

There is also a washer/dryer (rated at 5.5kVA) in the utility room. A gas furnace with a ⅓hp 120V blower supplies the heating. In this module, the electrical requirements of this example building will be computed.

2.2.0 General Lighting Loads

General lighting loads are calculated on the basis of *NEC Table 220.12.* For residential occupancies, three volt-amperes (watts) per square foot of living space is the figure to use. This includes non-appliance duplex receptacles into which lamps, televisions, etc., may be connected. Therefore, the area of the building must be calculated first. If the building is under construction, the dimensions can be determined by scaling the working drawings used by the builder. If the residence is an existing building with no drawings, actual measurements will have to be made on the site.

Using the floor plan of the residence in *Figure 2* as a guide, an architect's scale is used to measure the longest width of the building (using outside dimensions). It is determined to be 33 feet. The longest length of the building is 48 feet. These two measurements multiplied together give 33 × 48 = 1,584 square feet of living area. However, there is an open carport on the lower left of the drawing. This carport area will have to be calculated and then deducted from 1,584 to give the true amount of living space. This open area (carport) is 12 feet wide by 19.5 feet long: 12 × 19.5 = 234 square feet. Subtract the carport area from 1,584 square feet: 1,584 – 234 = 1,350 square feet of living area.

When using the square-foot method to determine lighting loads for buildings, *NEC Section 220.12* requires the floor area for each floor to be computed from the outside dimensions. When calculating lighting loads for residences, the computed floor area must not include open porches, carports, garages, or unused or unfinished spaces that are not adaptable to future use.

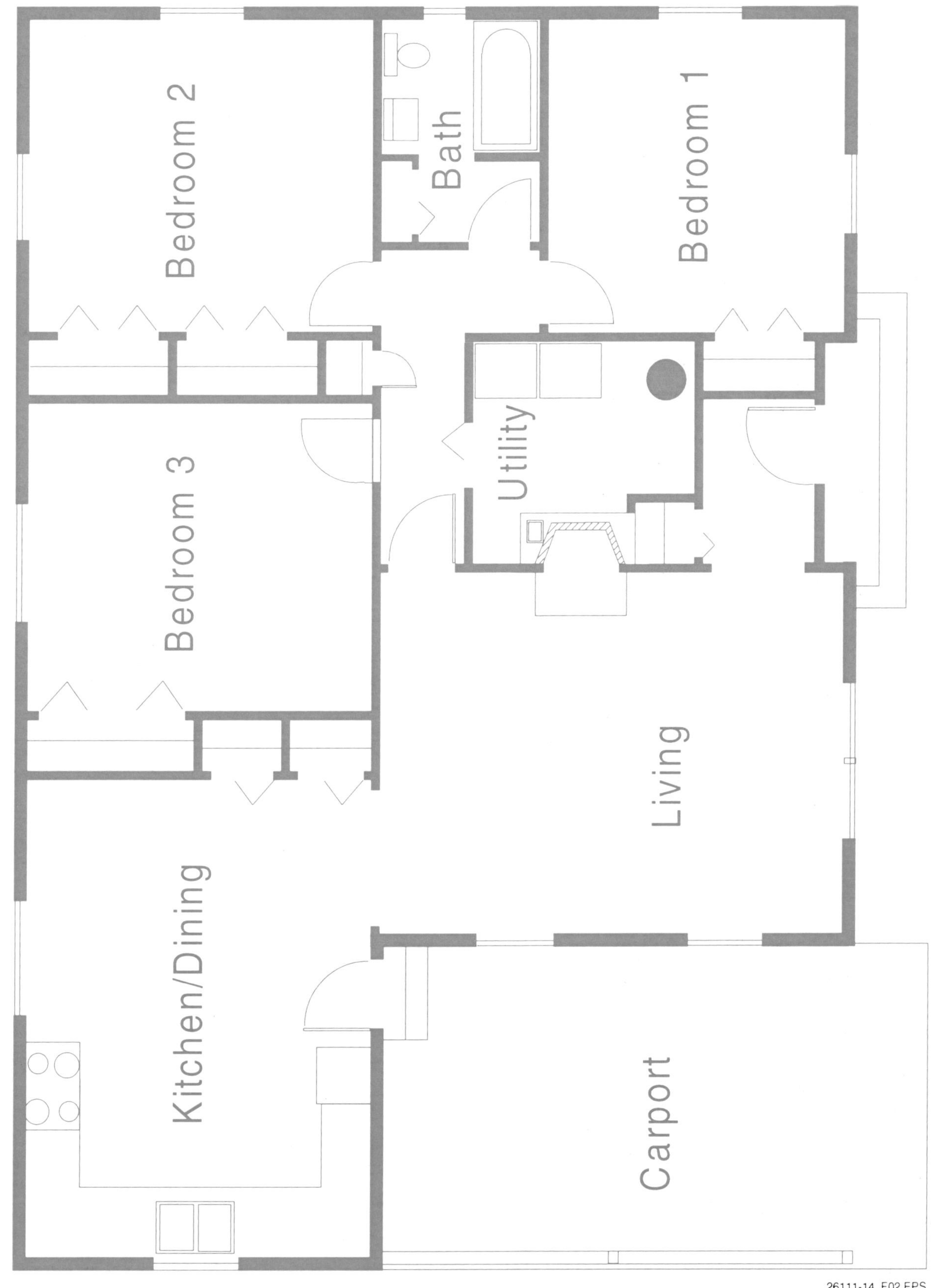

Figure 2 Floor plan of a typical residence.

2.3.0 Calculating the Electric Service Load

Figure 3 shows a standard calculation worksheet for a single-family dwelling. This form contains numbered blank spaces to be filled in while making the service calculation.

The total area of our sample dwelling has been determined to be 1,350 square feet of living space. This figure is entered in the appropriate space (Box 1) on the form and multiplied by 3 volt-amperes (VA) for a total general lighting load of 4,050VA (Box 2).

2.3.1 Small Appliance Loads

NEC Section 210.11(C)(1) requires at least two 120V, 20A small appliance branch circuits to be installed for the small appliance loads in each kitchen area of a dwelling. Kitchen areas include the dining area, breakfast nook, pantry, and similar areas where small appliances will be used.

NEC Section 220.52(A) gives further requirements for residential small appliance circuits; that is, the load for those circuits is to be computed at 1,500VA each. Since our example dwelling has only one kitchen area, the number 2 is entered in Box 3 for the number of required kitchen small appliance branch circuits. Multiply the number of these circuits by 1,500 and enter the result in Box 4.

2.3.2 Laundry Circuit

NEC Section 210.11(C)(2) requires an additional 20A branch circuit to be provided for the exclusive use of the laundry area (Box 5). This circuit must not have any other outlets connected except for the laundry receptacle(s). Therefore, enter 1,500VA in Box 6 on the form.

So far, there is enough information to complete the first portion of the service calculation form:

- General lighting 4,050VA (Box 2)
- Small appliance load 3,000VA (Box 4)

General Lighting Load					**Phase**	**Neutral**
Square footage of the dwelling	[1] 1350	× 3VA =	[2] 4050	*NEC Table 220.12*		
Kitchen small appliance circuits	[3] 2	× 1500 =	[4] 3000	*NEC Section 220.52(A)*		
Laundry branch circuit	[5] 1	× 1500 =	[6] 1500	*NEC Section 220.52(B)*		
	Subtotal of gen. lighting loads		[7] 8550			
	Subtract 1st 3000VA per *NEC Table 220.42*		[8] 3000	× 100% =	[9] 3000	
	Remaining VA times 35% per *NEC Table 220.42*		[10] 5550	× 35% =	[11] 1943	
			Total demand for general lighting loads =		[12] 4943	[13]
Fixed Appliance Loads (Nameplate or NEC FLA of motors) per *NEC Section 220.14*						
Hot water tank, 4.5kVA, 240V			[14] 4500			
Dishwasher 1.5kVA, 120V			[15] 1500			
Disposal 1/2HP, 120V per *NEC Table 430.248* = 9.8A			[16] 1176			
Blower 1/3HP, 120V per *NEC Table 430.248* = 7.2A			[17] 864			
			[18]			
			[19]			
	Subtotal of fixed appliances		[20] 8040			
	NEC Section 220.53	If 3 or less fixed appliances take @ 100% =			[21]	[22]
		If 4 or more fixed appliances take @ 75% =			[23] 6030	[24]
Other Loads per *NEC Section 220.14*						
Electric Range per *NEC Section 220.55* [neutral @ 70% per *NEC Section 220.61(B)*]					[25] 8000	[26]
Electric Dryer per *NEC Section 220.54* [neutral @ 70% per *NEC Section 220.61(B)*]					[27] 5500	[28]
Electric Heat per *NEC Section 220.51*						
Air Conditioning *NEC Section 220.82(C)*		omit smaller load per *NEC Section 220.60*			[29]	[30]
Largest Motor = 1176		× 25% (per *NEC Section 430.24*) =			[31] 294	[32]
			Total VA Demand =		[33] 24767	[34]
			(VA divided by 240 volts) **Amps** =		[35] **103**	[36]
			Service OCD and minimum size grounding electrode conductor		[37] 125	[38]
			AWG per *NEC Section 310.15(B)(7); NEC Section 220.61 and Table 310.15(B)(16)* for neutral		[39]	[40]

26111-14_F03.EPS

Figure 3 Calculation worksheet for residential requirements.

- Laundry load 1,500VA (Box 6)
- Total general lighting and appliance loads 8,550VA (Box 7)

2.3.3 Lighting Demand Factors

All residential electrical outlets are never used at one time. There may be a rare instance when all the lighting may be on for a short time every night, but even so, all the small appliances and receptacles throughout the house will never be used simultaneously. Knowing this, *NEC Section 220.42* allows a diversity or demand factor to be used when computing the general lighting load for services. Our calculation continues as follows:

- The first 3,000VA is rated at 100% 3,000VA (Box 8)
- The remaining 5,550VA (Box 10) may be rated at 35% (the allowable demand factor) Therefore, 5,550 × 0.35 = 1,943VA (Box 11)
- Net general lighting and small appliance load (rounded off) 4,943VA (Box 12)

2.3.4 Fixed Appliances

NEC Section 220.53 permits the loads for four fixed appliances in a single-family dwelling only to be computed at 75% as long as they are not electric heating, air conditioning, electric cooking, or electric clothes dryer loads. To compute the load of the fixed appliances in this dwelling, list all the fixed appliances that meet *NEC Section 220.53.* Enter the nameplate rating of the appliance or VA for motors by using *NEC Table 430.248* to find the FLA of each motor. *NEC Section 220.5(A)* tells us to use 120V (not 115V) for calculation purposes. The fixed appliances would be as follows:

- Hot water tank 4,500VA (Box 14)
- Dishwasher 1,500VA (Box 15)
- ½hp 120V disposal (9.8A × 120V) 1,176VA (Box 16)
- Gas furnace blower (7.2A × 120V) 864VA (Box 17)
- Add the loads for the fixed appliances 8,040VA (Box 20)
- Since there are four or more fixed appliances, multiply the total in Box 20 by 75% 6,030VA (Box 23)

2.3.5 Other Loads

The remaining loads of the dwelling are now computed in the Other Loads section in *Figure 3. NEC Section 220.14(B)* allows electric dryers to be computed as permitted in *NEC Table 220.54* and electric cooking appliances to be computed per *NEC Table 220.55.* For a single range rated over 8.75kVA, but not over 12kVA, Column C of *NEC Table 220.55* permits a demand of 8kVA for the range in this dwelling. Enter 8,000VA in Box 25.

The electric dryer must be computed at 5,000VA or the nameplate, whichever is greater, according to *NEC Section 220.54.* Up to four electric dryers must be taken at 100%. Enter 5,500VA in Box 27.

If this dwelling had electric space heating and/or air conditioning, it would be computed in this section using the larger of the two loads. Since they are typical noncoincidental loads, *NEC Section 220.60* permits the smaller of those loads to be omitted. There are no demand factors for either electric heating or air conditioning; therefore, the larger of the two loads would be computed at 100%.

The final step in this calculation is to add in 25% of the largest motor in the dwelling. This dwelling unit has two motors: the disposal at 9.8A and the blower at 7.2A. (See *NEC Section 430.17.*) In this case, the larger motor is the disposal; therefore, we must add 25% of the rating to meet the requirements of *NEC Section 430.24.* Enter 294VA (1,176 × 25%) in Box 31. Adding together the individual loads as computed, we have a minimum demand of 24,767VA (Box 33) for the phase conductors.

2.3.6 Required Service Size

The conventional electric service for residential use is 120/240V, three-wire, single-phase. Services are sized in amperes, and when the volt-amperes are known on single-phase services, amperes may be found by dividing the highest voltage into the total volt-amperes. For example:

24,767VA ÷ 240V = 103A (Box 35)

The **service-entrance conductors** have now been calculated and must be rated at a minimum of 110A, which is a standard rating for overcurrent protection. However, this is not a typical trade size; therefore, we will use the more common rating of 125A as the size of our service.

If the demand for our dwelling unit had resulted in a load of less than 100A, *NEC Section 230.79(C)* would have required that the minimum rating of the service disconnect be 100A. *NEC Section 230.42(B)* would have required the ampacity of the service conductors to be equal to the rating of the 100A disconnect as well.

2.4.0 Demand Factors

NEC Article 220, Part III provides the rules regarding the application of demand factors to certain types of loads. Recall that a demand factor is the maximum amount of volt-amp load expected at any given time compared to the total connected load of the circuit. The maximum demand of a feeder circuit is equal to the connected load times the demand factor. The loads to which demand factors apply can be found in the *NEC*® as follows:

- Receptacle loads — *NEC Table 220.14*
- Lighting loads — *NEC Table 220.42*
- Dryer loads — *NEC Table 220.54*
- Range loads — *NEC Table 220.55*

In addition to those demand factors listed in *NEC Article 220, Part III,* alternative (optional) methods for computing loads can be found in *NEC Article 220, Part IV.* They include the following:

- Dwelling unit loads — *NEC Section 220.82*
- Existing dwelling unit loads — *NEC Section 220.83*
- Multi-family dwelling unit loads — *NEC Section 220.84*

2.5.0 General Lighting and Receptacle Load Demand Factors

NEC Table 220.42 provides the demand factors allowed for dwelling units and apartment houses without provisions for tenant cooking.

2.6.0 Appliance Loads

NEC Section 210.11(C) provides the number of branch circuits required for small appliances and laundry loads. Demand factors for dryers and ranges are found in *NEC Tables 220.54 and 220.55*.

2.6.1 Small Appliance Loads

The small appliance branch circuits required by *NEC Section 210.11(C)(1)* for small appliances supplied by 15A or 20A receptacles on 20A branch circuits for each kitchen area served are calculated at 1,500VA. If a dwelling has more than one kitchen area, the *NEC*® will require two small appliance branch circuits computed at 1,500VA for each kitchen area served. Where a dwelling with only one kitchen area has more than the required two small appliance branch circuits installed to serve a single kitchen area, only the first two required circuits need be computed. Additional circuits for countertops or refrigeration provide a separation of load, not additional loads. If a dwelling has two kitchen areas, then the total small appliance branch circuits required would be four at 1,500VA each. These loads are permitted to be included with the general lighting load and subjected to the demand factors of *NEC Table 220.42.*

2.6.2 Laundry Circuit Load

A 1,500VA feeder load is added to load calculations for each two-wire laundry branch circuit installed in a home. The branch circuit is required by *NEC Section 210.11(C)(2).* This load may also be added to the general lighting load and subjected to the same demand factors provided in *NEC Section 220.42.*

2.6.3 Dryer Load

The dryer load for each electric clothes dryer is 5,000VA or the actual nameplate value of the dryer, whichever is larger. Demand factors listed in *NEC Table 220.54* may be applied for more than one dryer in the same dwelling. If two or more single-phase dryers are supplied by a three-phase, four-wire feeder, the total load is computed by using twice the maximum number connected between any two phases.

2.6.4 Range Load

Range loads and other cooking appliances are covered under *NEC Section 220.55.* The feeder demand loads for household electric ranges, wall-mounted ovens, countertop cooking units, and other similar household appliances individually rated over 1¾kW are permitted to be computed in accordance with *NEC Table 220.55.* If two or more single-phase ranges are supplied by a three-phase, four-wire feeder, the total load is computed by using twice the maximum number connected between any two phases.

Think About It

Demand Factors

Examine *NEC Table 220.55.* Why does the demand factor decrease as the number of appliances increases? Why does the demand factor decrease more for larger ranges than it does for smaller ones?

2.6.5 Demand Factors for Electric Ranges

Ranges can be computed in various ways that depend on which part of *NEC Article 220* you are using and the occupancy type for the ranges involved. Note the demand factors permitted for the following occupancy types:

- Dwelling units per Part III — *NEC Section 220.55*
- Dwelling units per Part IV — *NEC Section 220.82*
- Additions to existing dwellings per Part IV — *NEC Section 220.83*
- Multi-family dwellings per Part III — *NEC Section 220.55*
- Multi-family dwellings per Part IV — *NEC Section 220.84*

2.7.0 Demand Factors for Neutral Conductors

The neutral conductor of electrical systems generally carries only the maximum current imbalance of the phase conductors. For example, in a single-phase feeder circuit with one phase conductor carrying 50A and the other carrying 40A, the neutral conductor would carry 10A. Since the neutral in many cases will never be required to carry as much current as the phase conductors, the *NEC®* allows us to apply a demand factor. (See *NEC Section 220.61.*) Note that in certain circumstances such as electrical discharge lighting, data processing equipment, and other similar equipment, a demand factor cannot be applied to the neutral conductors because these types of equipment produce harmonic currents that increase the heating effect in the neutral conductor.

Think About It

Balanced Phase Conductors

The word *phase* is used in these modules to refer to a hot wire rather than a neutral one. Some electricians call these legs rather than phases. Why must the two phase conductors be balanced?

3.0.0 Sizing Residential Neutral Conductors

The neutral conductor in a three-wire, single-phase service carries only the unbalanced load between the two ungrounded (hot) wires or legs. Since there are several 240V loads in the above calculations, these 240V loads will be balanced and therefore reduce the load on the service neutral conductor. Consequently, in most cases, the service neutral does not have to be as large as the ungrounded (hot) conductors.

In the previous example, the water heater does not have to be included in the neutral conductor calculation, since it is strictly 240V with no 120V loads. This takes the total number of fixed appliances on the neutral conductor down to three appliances. Therefore, each of the fixed appliance loads on the neutral must be computed at 100% (dishwasher at 1,500VA, plus disposal at 1,176VA, plus the blower at 864VA). The neutral loads of the electric range and clothes dryer are permitted by *NEC Section 220.61* to be computed at 70% of the demand for the phase conductors since these appliances have both 120V and 240V loads. In this case, the largest motor is the same for the neutral conductors as it is for the phase conductors; therefore, it is computed in the same manner. Using this information, the neutral conductor may be sized accordingly:

- Net general lighting and small appliance load — 4,943VA (Box 13)
- Fixed appliance loads — 3,540VA (Box 22)
- Electric range (8,000VA × 0.70) — 5,600VA (Box 26)
- Clothes dryer (5,500VA × 0.70) — 3,850VA (Box 28)
- Largest motor — 294VA (Box 32)
- Total — 18,227VA (Box 34)

To find the total phase-to-phase amperes, divide the total volt-amperes by the voltage between phases:

$$18{,}227\text{VA} \div 240\text{V} = 75.9\text{A or } 76\text{A}$$

The service-entrance conductors have now been calculated and are rated at 125A with a neutral conductor rated for at least 76A. See *Figure 4* for a completed calculation form for the example residence.

In *NEC Section 310.15(B)(7),* special consideration is given to 120/240V, single-phase residential services and feeders. Conductor sizes are

General Lighting Load					Phase	Neutral
Square footage of the dwelling	[1] 1350	× 3VA =	[2] 4050	NEC Table 220.12		
Kitchen small appliance circuits	[3] 2	× 1500 =	[4] 3000	NEC Section 220.52(A)		
Laundry branch circuit	[5] 1	× 1500 =	[6] 1500	NEC Section 220.52(B)		
Subtotal of gen. lighting loads			[7] 8550			
Subtract 1st 3000VA per NEC Table 220.42			[8] 3000	× 100% =	[9] 3000	
Remaining VA times 35% per NEC Table 220.42			[10] 5550	× 35% =	[11] 1943	
Total demand for general lighting loads =					[12] 4943	[13] 4943
Fixed Appliance Loads (Nameplate or NEC FLA of motors) per NEC Section 220.14						
Hot water tank, 4.5kVA, 240V			[14] 4500			
Dishwasher 1.5kVA, 120V			[15] 1500			
Disposal 1/2HP, 120V per NEC Table 430.248 = 9.8A			[16] 1176			
Blower 1/3HP, 120V per NEC Table 430.248 = 7.2A			[17] 864			
			[18]			
			[19]			
Subtotal of fixed appliances			[20] 8040			
NEC Section 220.53 — If 3 or less fixed appliances take @ 100% =					[21]	[22] 3540
NEC Section 220.53 — If 4 or more fixed appliances take @ 75% =					[23] 6030	[24]
Other Loads per NEC Section 220.14						
Electric Range per NEC Section 220.55 [neutral @ 70% per NEC Section 220.61(B)]					[25] 8000	[26] 5600
Electric Dryer per NEC Section 220.5 [neutral @ 70% per NEC Section 220.61(B)]					[27] 5500	[28] 3850
Electric Heat per NEC Section 220.51				omit smaller load per NEC Section 220.60	[29]	[30]
Air Conditioning NEC Section 220.82(C)						
Largest Motor =	1176	× 25% (per NEC Section 430.24) =			[31] 294	[32] 294
Total VA Demand =					[33] 24767	[34] 18227
(VA divided by 240 volts) **Amps** =					[35] **103**	[36] **76**
Service OCD and minimum size grounding electrode conductor					[37] 125	[38] 8 AWG
AWG per NEC Section 310.15(B)(7); NEC Section 220.61 and Table 310.15(B)(16) for neutral					[39] 2 AWG	[40] 4 AWG

26111-14_F04.EPS

Figure 4 Completed calculation form.

shown in *NEC Table 310.15(B)(7)*. Reference to this table shows that the *NEC*® allows a No. 2 AWG copper or a 1/0 AWG aluminum conductor for a 125A service. The neutral conductor is sized per *NEC Tables 310.15(B)(7) or 310.15(B)(16)* using the appropriate column for the markings on the service equipment per *NEC Section 110.14(C)*. Assuming our service panel is marked as suitable for use with 75°C-rated conductors, the minimum size of the neutral would be a No. 4 AWG copper or No. 2 AWG aluminum.

When sizing the grounded conductor for services, the provisions stated in *NEC Sections 215.2, 220.61, and 230.42* must be met, along with other applicable sections.

4.0.0 Sizing the Load Center

Each ungrounded conductor in all circuits must be provided with overcurrent protection in the form of either fuses or circuit breakers. If more than six such devices are used, a means of disconnecting the entire service must be provided using either a main disconnect switch or a main circuit breaker.

To calculate the number of fuse holders or circuit breakers required in the sample residence, look at the general lighting load first. The total general lighting load of 4,050VA can be divided by 120V to find the amperage:

$$4{,}050\text{VA} \div 120\text{V} = 33.75\text{A}$$

Either 15A or 20A circuits may be used for the lighting load. Two 20A circuits (2 × 20) equal 40A, so two 20A circuits would be adequate for the lighting. However, two 15A circuits totalling only 30A and 33.75A are needed. Therefore, if 15A circuits are used, three will be required for the total lighting load. In this example, three 15A circuits will be used.

In addition to the lighting circuits, the sample residence will require a minimum of two 20A circuits

Think About It

Common Loads

Which of the following devices uses the most power?

- Giant-screen television
- Typical hair dryer
- Curling iron
- Crockpot

for the small appliance load and one 20A circuit for the laundry. So far, the following branch circuits can be counted:

• General lighting load	Three 15A circuits
• Small appliance load	Two 20A circuits
• Laundry load	One 20A circuit
• Total	Six branch circuits

Most load centers and panelboards are provided with an even number of circuit breaker spaces or fuse holders (for example, four, six, eight, or ten). But before the panelboard can be selected, space must be provided for the remaining loads. Each 240V load will require two spaces. In some existing installations, you might find a two-pole fuse block containing two cartridge fuses being used to feed a residential electric range. Each 120V load will require one space each. Thus, the remaining number of circuits for this example is as follows:

• Hot water heater	One two-pole breaker
• Dishwasher	One single-pole breaker
• Disposal	One single-pole breaker
• Blower	One single-pole breaker
• Electric range	One two-pole breaker
• Electric dryer	One two-pole breaker

These additional appliances will therefore require an additional nine spaces in the load center or panelboard. *NEC Section 210.11(C)(3)* requires that a separate 20A branch circuit be provided for the bathroom receptacles. While this circuit requires extra space within a load center, it does not add to the demand on the service for a dwelling unit. Adding the nine spaces for the other loads in the dwelling, plus one for a bathroom circuit, to the six required for the general lighting and small appliance loads requires at least a 16-space load center to handle the circuits.

4.1.0 Ground Fault Circuit Interrupters

Under certain conditions, the amount of current it takes to open an overcurrent protective device can be critical. You should remember from the *Electrical Safety* module that when persons are subject to very low current values (less than one full ampere), it can be fatal. The overcurrent protection installed on services, feeders, and branch circuits protects only the conductors and equipment.

Because of this fact, the *NEC®* requires ground fault circuit interrupter (GFCI) protection for receptacle outlets and/or equipment in many locations and occupancies. The *NEC®* defines a GFCI as "a device intended for the protection of personnel that functions to de-energize a circuit or portion thereof within an established period of time when a current to ground exceeds the values established for a Class A device." Class A GFCIs trip when the current to ground has a value in the range of 4mA to 6mA.

For dwelling units, the majority of requirements to provide protection for 15A or 20A, 125V-rated receptacles can be found in *NEC Section 210.8(A).* Further requirements for GFCI protection at dwelling units can be found in other *NEC®* articles such as *NEC Article 590* for temporary construction sites; *NEC Article 620* for special equipment such as elevators; or in *NEC Article 680* for special equipment such as swimming pools, hot tubs, and hydromassage tubs. These articles may also expand the requirements for GFCI protection to include circuits rated at more than 20A or operating at 240V.

According to *NEC Section 210.8(A),* the 15A and 20A, 125V-rated receptacles in a dwelling that require GFCI protection must be readily accessible and include the following:

- Bathrooms
- Outdoor receptacles (except those provided on dedicated circuits for snow melting and deicing equipment)
- Receptacles that serve the countertops in kitchens

Further requirements for GFCI protection at dwelling units are as follows:

- Receptacles within garages and accessory buildings, such as storage sheds or workshops, or similar uses that have a floor located at or below grade level
- Receptacles in unfinished basements
- Crawl spaces at or below grade level
- Receptacles that serve countertops and are within 6' of wet bar sinks, utility, or laundry sinks
- Boathouses and boat hoists

One way to provide this GFCI protection is through the use of a GFCI circuit breaker. GFCI circuit breakers require the same mounting space as standard single-pole circuit breakers and provide the same branch circuit wiring protection as standard circuit breakers. They also provide Class A ground fault protection.

Listed GFCI circuit breakers are available in single- and two-pole construction; 15A, 20A, 25A, and 30A, 50A, and 60A ratings; and have a 10,000A interrupting capacity. Single-pole units are rated at 120VAC; two-pole units are rated at 120/240VAC.

GFCI breakers can be used not only in load centers and panelboards, but they are also available factory-installed in meter pedestals and power outlet panels for recreational vehicle (RV) parks and construction sites.

The GFCI sensor continuously monitors the current balance in the ungrounded or energized (hot) load conductor and the neutral load conductor. If the current in the neutral load wire becomes less than the current in the hot load wire, then a ground fault exists, since a portion of the current is returning to the source by some means other than the neutral load wire. When a current imbalance occurs, the sensor, which is a differential current transformer, sends a signal to the solid-state circuit, which activates the ground trip solenoid mechanism and breaks the hot load connection (*Figure 5*). A current imbalance as low as four milliamps (4mA) will cause the circuit breaker to interrupt the circuit. This is indicated by the trip indicator on the front of the device.

The two-pole GFCI breaker (*Figure 6*) continuously monitors the current balance between the two hot conductors and the neutral conductor. As long as the sum of these three currents is zero, the device will not trip; that is, if the A load wire is carrying 10A of current, the neutral is carrying 5A, and the B load wire is carrying 5A, then the sensor is balanced and will not produce a signal. A current imbalance from a ground fault condition as low as 4mA will cause the sensor to produce a signal of sufficient magnitude to trip the device.

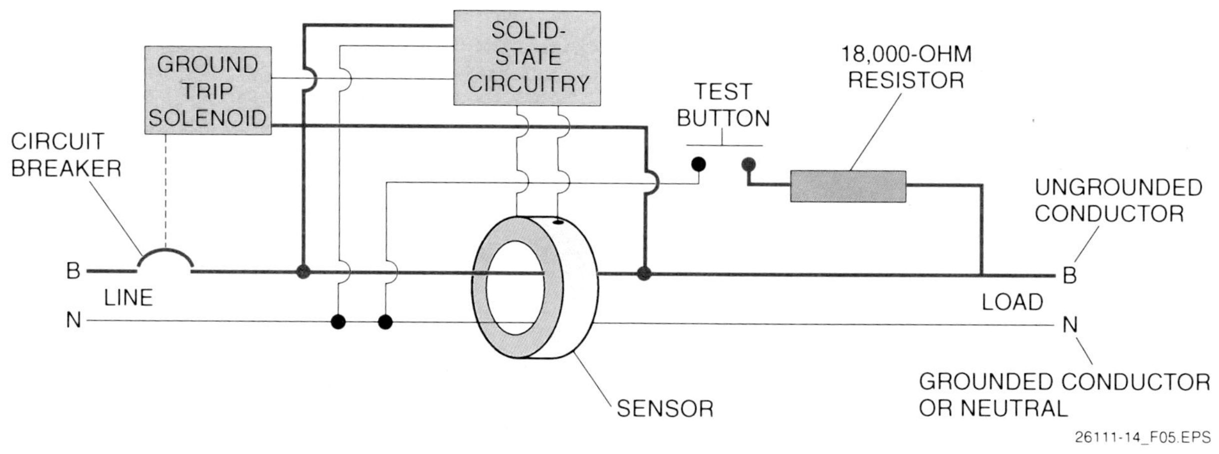

Figure 5 Operating circuitry of a typical GFCI.

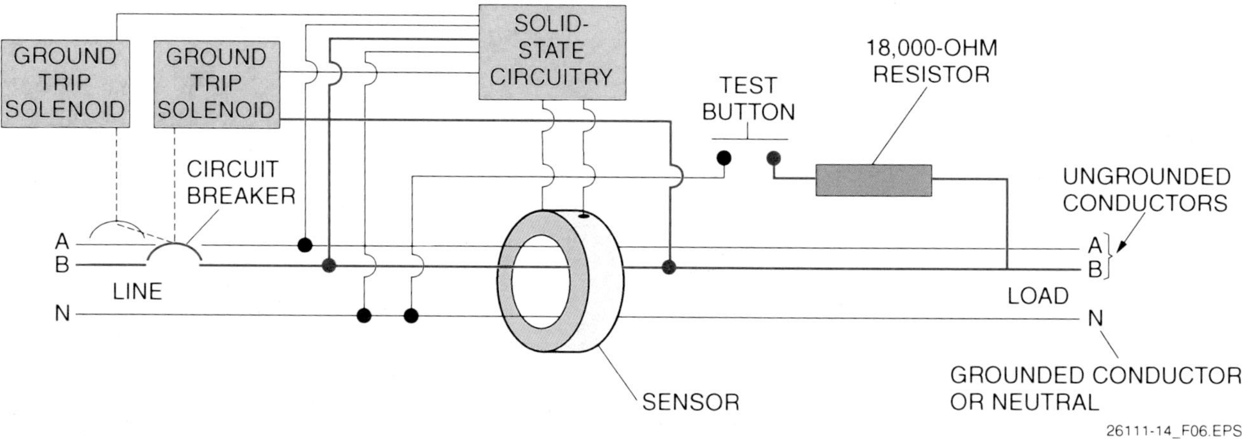

Figure 6 Operating characteristics of a two-pole GFCI.

4.1.1 Single-Pole GFCI Circuit Breakers

The single-pole GFCI breaker has two load lugs and a white wire pigtail in addition to the line side plug-on or bolt-on connector. The line side hot connection is made by installing the GFCI breaker in the panel just as any other circuit breaker is installed. The white wire pigtail is attached to the panel neutral (S/N) assembly. Both the neutral and hot wires of the branch circuit being protected are terminated in the GFCI breaker. These two load lugs are clearly marked Load Power and Load Neutral in the breaker case. Also in the case is the identifying marking for the pigtail, Panel Neutral.

> **NOTE**
> Single-pole GFCI circuit breakers cannot be used on multi-wire circuits.

Care should be exercised when installing GFCI breakers in existing panels. Be sure that the neutral wire for the branch circuit corresponds with the hot wire of the same circuit. Always remember that unless the current in the neutral wire is equal to that in the hot wire (within 4mA), the GFCI breaker senses this as being a possible ground fault (see *Figure 7*).

4.1.2 Two-Pole GFCI Circuit Breakers

A two-pole GFCI circuit breaker can be installed on a 120/240VAC single-phase, three-wire system; the 120/240VAC portion of a 120/240VAC three-phase, four-wire system; or the two phases and neutral of a 120/208VAC three-phase, four-wire system. Regardless of the application, the installation of the breaker is the same—connections are made to two hot buses and the panel neutral assembly. When installed on these systems, protection is provided for two-wire 240VAC or 208VAC circuits, three-wire 120/240VAC or 120/208VAC circuits, and 120VAC multiwire circuits.

The circuit in *Figure 8* illustrates the problems that are encountered when a common load neutral is used for two single-pole GFCI breakers. Either or both breakers will trip when a load is applied at the #2 duplex receptacle. The neutral current from the #2 duplex receptacle flows through breaker #1; this increase in neutral current through breaker #1 causes an imbalance in its sensor, thus causing it to produce a fault signal. At the same time, there is no neutral current flowing through breaker #2; therefore, it also senses a current imbalance. If a load is applied at the #1 duplex receptacle, and there is no load at the #2 duplex receptacle, then neither breaker will trip because neither breaker will sense a current imbalance.

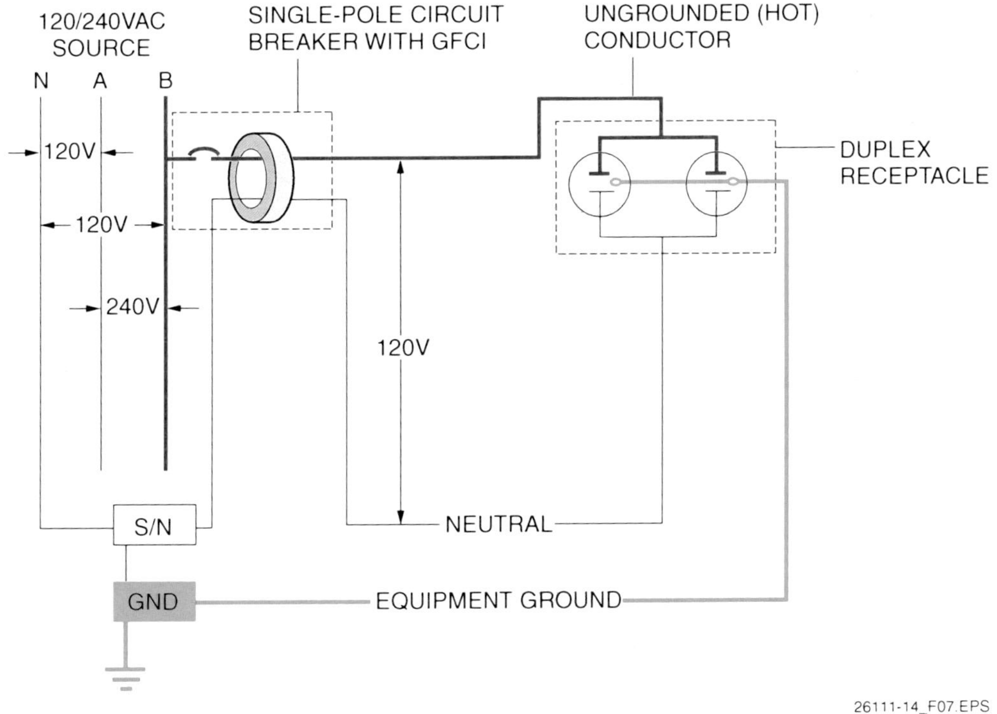

Figure 7 Operating characteristics of a single-pole circuit breaker with a GFCI.

On Site

GFCI and AFCI Circuit Breakers

GFCI breakers protect against ground faults, while AFCI breakers protect against arc faults.

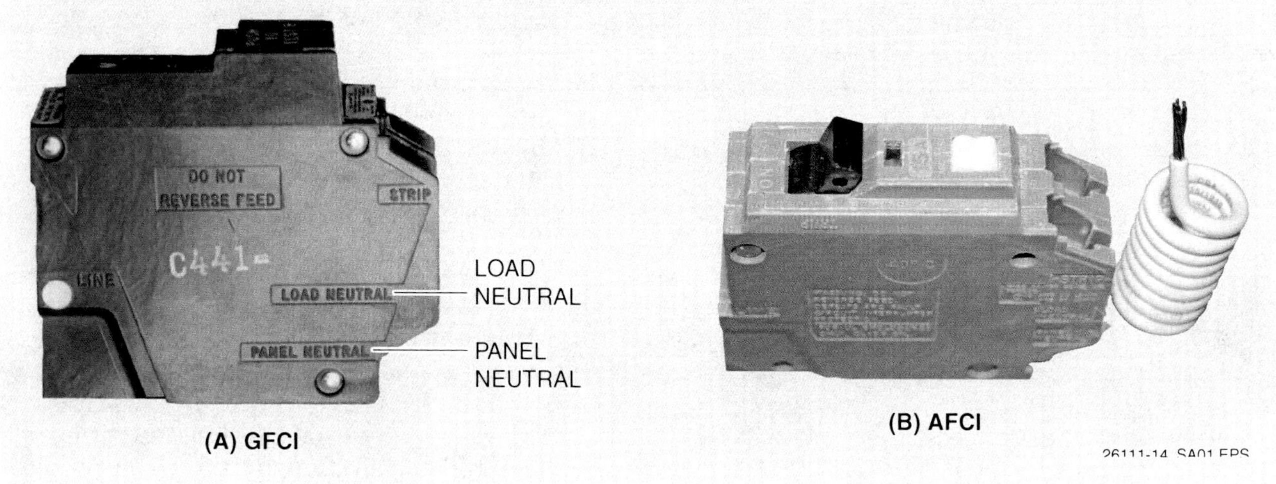

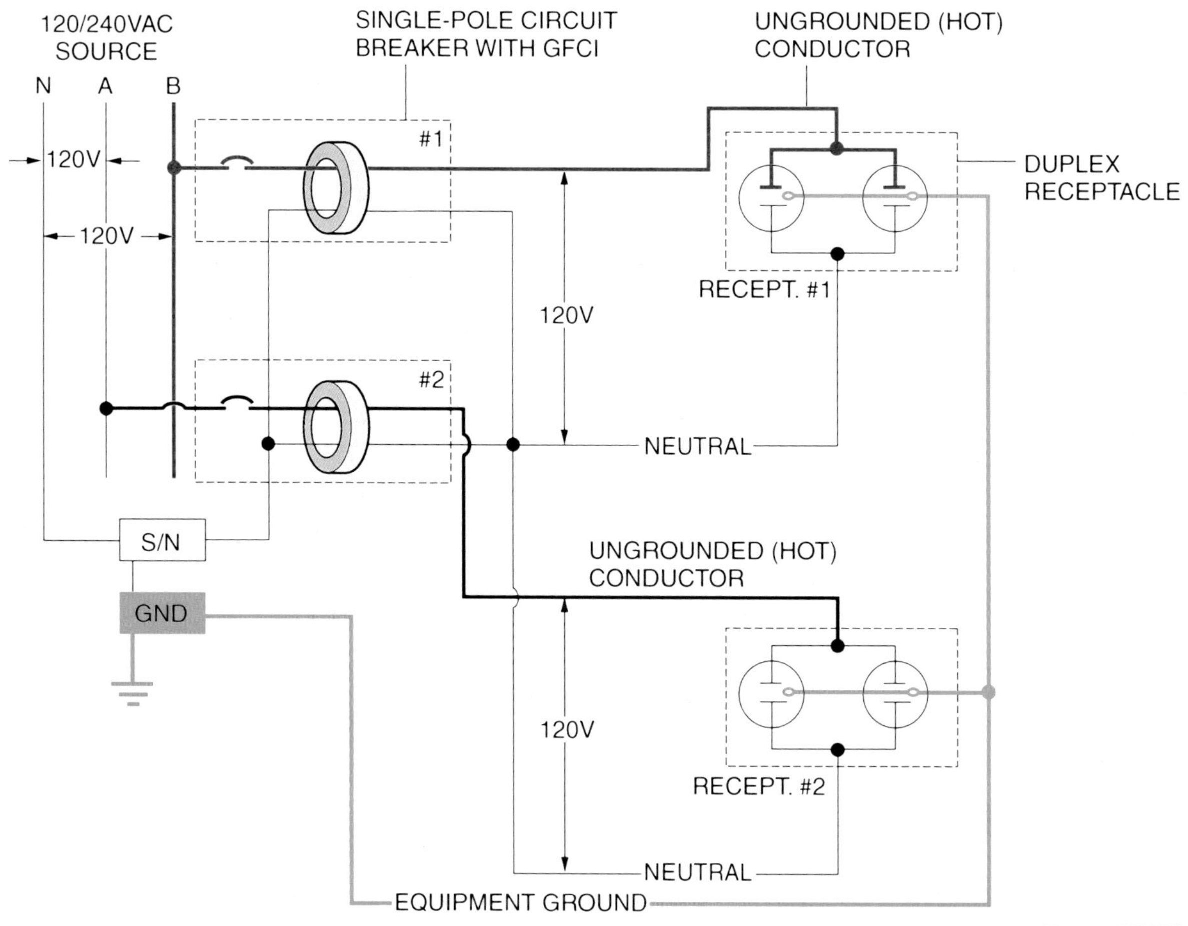

Figure 8 Circuit depicting the common load neutral.

Junction boxes can also present problems when they are used to provide taps for more than one branch circuit. Even though the circuits are not wired using a common neutral, sometimes all neutral conductors are connected together. Thus, parallel neutral paths are established, producing an imbalance in each GFCI breaker sensor, causing them to trip.

The two-pole GFCI breaker eliminates the problems encountered when trying to use two single-pole GFCI breakers with a common neutral. Because both hot currents and the neutral current pass through the same sensor, no imbalance occurs between the three currents, and the breaker will not trip.

4.1.3 Direct-Wired GFCI Receptacles

Direct-wired GFCI receptacles provide Class A ground fault protection on 120VAC circuits. They are available in both 15A and 20A arrangements. The 15A unit has a NEMA 5-15R receptacle configuration for use with 15A plugs only. The 20A device has a NEMA 5-20R receptacle configuration for use with 15A or 20A plugs. Both 15A and 20A units have a 120VAC, 20A circuit rating. This is to comply with *NEC Table 210.24,* which requires that 15A circuits use 15A receptacles but permits the use of either 15A or 20A receptacles on 20A circuits. Therefore, GFCI receptacle units that contain a 15A receptacle may be used on 20A circuits.

These receptacles have line terminals for the hot, neutral, and ground wires. In addition, they have load terminals that can be used to provide ground fault protection for other receptacles electrically downstream on the same branch circuit (*Figure 9*). All terminals will accept No. 14 to No. 10 AWG copper wire.

GFCI receptacles have a two-pole tripping mechanism that breaks both the hot and the neutral load connections.

When tripped, the RESET button pops out. The unit is reset by pushing the button back in.

GFCI receptacles have the additional benefit of noise suppression. Noise suppression minimizes false tripping due to spurious line voltages or radio frequency (RF) signals between 10 and 500 megahertz (MHz).

GFCI receptacles can be mounted without adapters in wall outlet boxes that are at least 1.5 inches deep.

Think About It

GFCIs

Explain the difference(s) in the operation of single-pole and double-pole GFCIs.

4.2.0 Arc Fault Circuit Interrupters

All branch circuits that supply the lighting and general-purpose receptacles in dwelling unit family rooms, dining rooms, living rooms, parlors, libraries, dens, bedrooms, sunrooms, recreation rooms, closets, hallways, or similar rooms or areas, as well as all circuit extensions or modifications, must have arc fault circuit interrupter protection to comply with *NEC Section 210.12.*

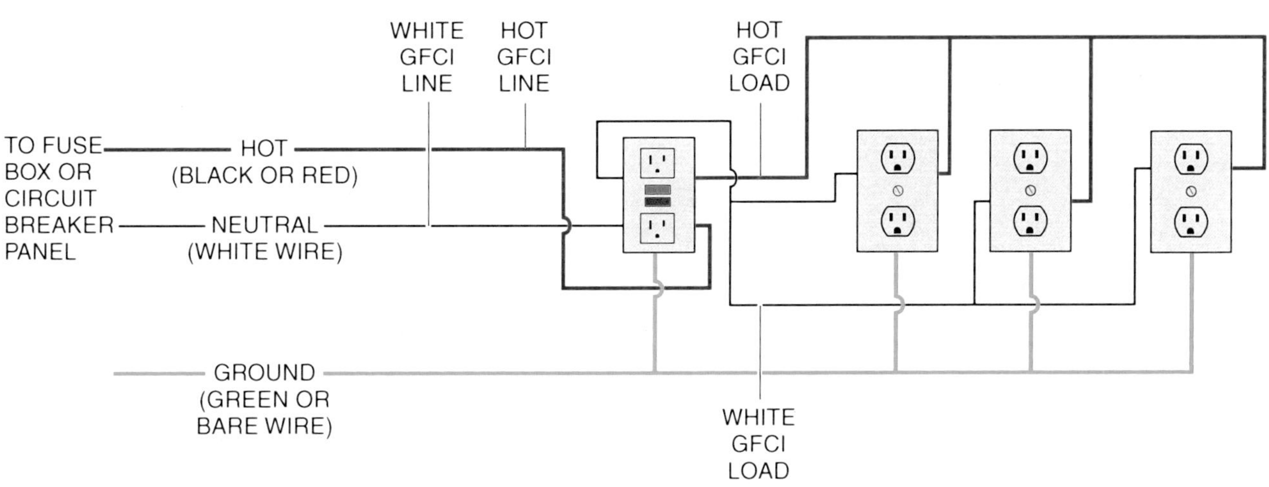

Figure 9 GFCI receptacle used to protect other outlets on the same circuit.

5.0.0 Grounding

NEC Section 250.4(A) provides the general requirements for grounding and bonding of grounded electrical systems. In order to ensure systems are properly grounded and bonded, the prescriptive requirements of *NEC Article 250* must be followed.

The grounding system is a major part of the electrical system. Its purpose is to protect people and equipment against the various electrical faults that can occur. It is sometimes possible for higher-than-normal voltages to appear at certain points in an electrical system or in the electrical equipment connected to the system. Proper grounding ensures that the electrical charges that cause these higher voltages are channeled to the earth or ground and that an effective ground fault path is provided throughout the system so that overcurrent devices will open before people are endangered or equipment is damaged.

The word *ground* refers to ground potential or earth ground. If a conductor is connected to the earth or some conducting body that serves in place of the earth, such as a driven ground rod (electrode), the conductor is said to be grounded. The neutral conductor in a three- or four-wire service, for example, is intentionally grounded, and therefore becomes a grounded conductor. This is the path back to the source of supply for all ground faults in an electrical system. This conductor is intended not only to carry the unbalanced loads of an installation, but also to provide the low-impedance path back to the source so that enough current will flow in the system to open the overcurrent devices. A wire that is used to connect this neutral conductor to a grounding electrode or electrodes is referred to as a grounding electrode conductor (GEC). Note the difference in the two meanings: one is grounded, while the other provides a means for grounding.

There are two general classifications of protective grounding:

- System grounding
- Equipment grounding

The system ground relates to the **service-entrance equipment** and its interrelated and bonded components; that is, the system and circuit conductors are grounded to limit voltages due to lightning, line surges, or unintentional contact with higher voltage and to stabilize the voltage to ground during normal operation per *NEC Sections 250.4(A)(1) and (2)*.

The noncurrent-carrying conductive parts of materials enclosing electrical conductors or equipment, or forming a part of such equipment, and electrically conductive materials that are likely to become energized are all connected together to the supply source in a manner that establishes an effective ground fault path per *NEC Sections 250.4(A)(3) and (4)*.

NEC Section 250.4(A)(5) defines the requirements for an effective ground path. It requires that electrical equipment and wiring and other electrically conductive materials likely to become energized shall be installed in a manner that creates a permanent, low-impedance circuit capable of safely carrying the maximum ground fault current likely to be imposed on it from any point on the wiring system where a ground fault may occur to the electrical supply source. The earth shall not be used as the sole equipment grounding conductor or effective ground fault current path.

To better understand a complete grounding system, a conventional residential system will be examined, beginning at the power company's high-voltage lines and transformer, as shown in *Figure 10*. The pole-mounted transformer is fed with a two-wire, single-phase 7,200V system, which is transformed and stepped down to a three-wired, 120/240V, single-phase electric service suitable for residential use. Note that the voltage between line A and line B is 240V. However, by connecting a third (neutral) wire on the secondary winding of the transformer—between the other two—the 240V is split in half, providing 120V between either line A or line B and the neutral conductor. Consequently, 240V is available for household appliances such as ranges, hot water heaters, and clothes dryers, while 120V is available for lights and small appliances.

Referring again to *Figure 10*, conductors A and B are ungrounded conductors, while the neutral is a grounded conductor. If only 240V loads were connected, the neutral (grounded conductor)

On Site

Grounding

Systematic grounding wasn't required by the *NEC*® until the mid-1950s; even then, electricians commonly grounded an outlet by wrapping an uninsulated wire around a cold-water pipe and taping it. Three-hole receptacles with grounding terminals became common in the 1960s, but in many older houses, you cannot assume that receptacles are grounded, even when you see a three-hole receptacle. Sometimes, new receptacles have simply been screwed onto old boxes where there is no equipment grounding conductor.

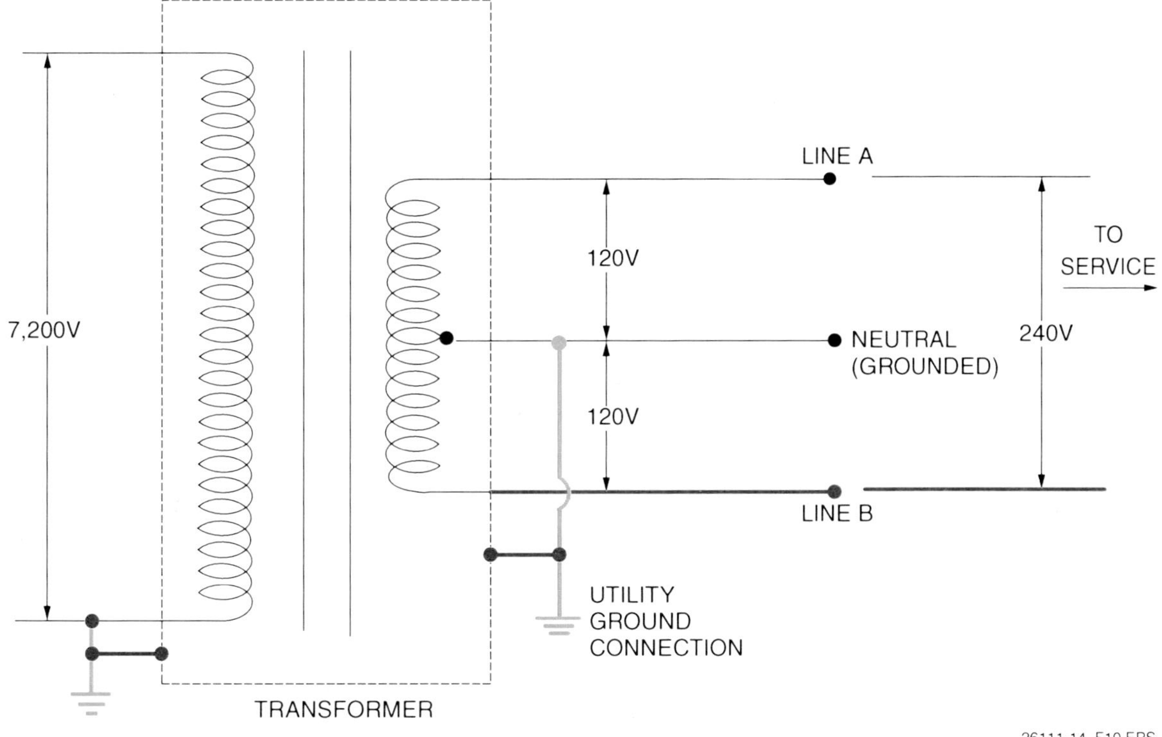

Figure 10 Wiring diagram of a 7,200V to 120/240V, single-phase transformer connection.

would carry no current. In this instance, the neutral would be used to carry any ground fault currents from the load side of the service back to the utility instead of depending on the earth as the path back to the source. However, since 120V loads are present, the neutral will carry the unbalanced load and become a current-carrying conductor. For example, if line A carries 60A and line B carries 50A, the neutral would carry only 10A (60A – 50A = 10A). This is why the *NEC®* allows the neutral conductor in an electric service to be smaller than the ungrounded conductors. However, *NEC Section 250.24(C)(1)* requires that it must be sufficient to carry fault currents back to the source and, therefore, must not be less than the required grounding electrode conductor using *NEC Table 250.66* for service conductors up to 1,100 kcmil and not less than 12.5% of the area of the service-entrance conductors (or equivalent) larger than 1,100 kcmil. The typical pole-mounted service drop conductors are normally routed by a messenger cable from a point on the pole to a point on the building being served, terminating at the point where service-entrance conductors exit a weatherhead. Service-entrance conductors are then typically routed through metering equipment into the service disconnecting means. This is the point where most services are grounded. See *Figure 11*. *NEC Section 250.24(A)(1)* requires that the grounding electrode for the structure connection to the neutral (grounded conductor) be at any accessible point from the load end of the service drop or **service lateral** to and including the terminal or bus to which the neutral (grounded service conductor) is connected to the service disconnecting means.

> **NOTE**
>
> Effectively grounded means intentionally connected to earth through one or more ground connection(s) of sufficiently low impedance and having sufficient current-carrying capacity to prevent the buildup of voltages that may result in a hazard to people or connected equipment.

5.1.0 Grounding Electrodes

NEC Article 250, Part III provides the requirements for connecting an electric service to the grounding electrode system of a building or structure. *NEC Section 250.50* requires, in general, that all of the electrodes described in *NEC Section 250.52(A)* be used (if present), and they must be bonded together to form the grounding electrode system. The electrodes listed in *NEC Section 250.52(A)* are as follows:

- Metal underground water pipe in direct contact with the earth for 10' or more and electrically continuous (or made electrically continuous

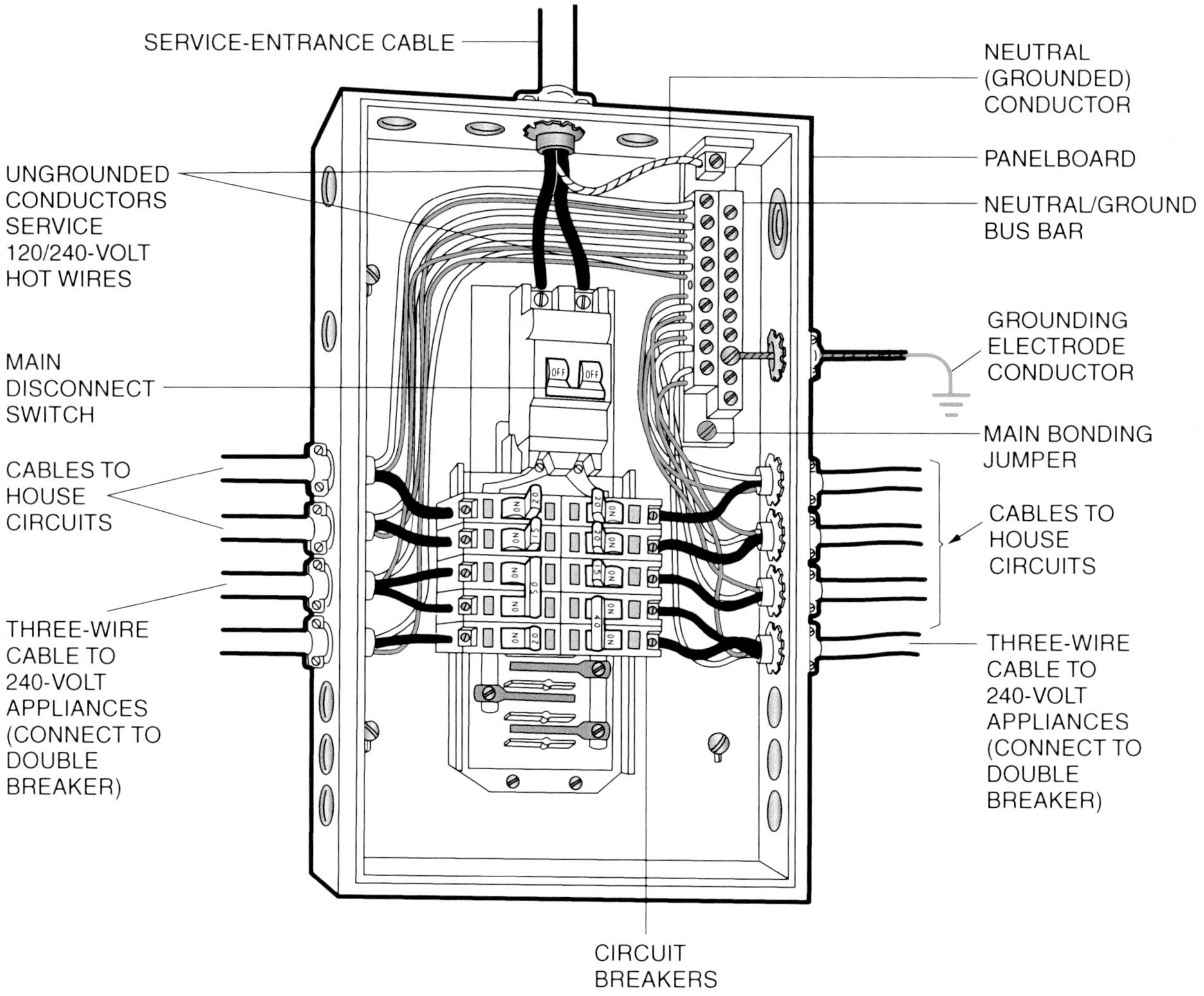

Figure 11 Interior view of panelboard showing connections.

by bonding around insulating joints or insulating pipe) to the points of connection of the grounding electrode conductor and the bonding conductors. Interior metal water piping located more than 5' from the point of entrance to the building shall not be used as part of the grounding electrode system or as a conductor to interconnect electrodes that are part of the grounding electrode system.

- Metal frame of the building or structure that complies with *NEC Section 250.52(A)(2).*
- An electrode encased by at least 2" of concrete may be used if it is located within and near the bottom of a concrete foundation or footing that is in direct contact with the earth. The electrode must be at least 20' long and must be made of electrically conductive coated steel reinforcing bars or rods of not less than ½" in diameter, or consisting of at least 20' of bare copper conductor not smaller than No. 4 AWG wire size.
- A ground ring encircling the building or structure, in direct contact with the earth, consisting of at least 20' of bare copper conductor not smaller than No. 2 AWG.
- Rod and pipe electrodes shall not be less than 8' in length and consist of either:
  - Pipe or conduit not smaller than trade size ¾ and, where of iron or steel, shall have the outer surface galvanized or otherwise metal-coated for corrosion protection.
  - Rods of iron or steel not smaller than ⅝" in diameter. Stainless steel rods less than ⅝" in diameter, nonferrous rods, or their equivalent shall be listed and not less than ½" in diameter.
- Plate electrodes shall expose less than two square feet of surface to exterior soil. Plates made of iron or steel shall be at least ¼" thick. Nonferrous metal plates shall be at least 0.06" thick.

- Other local metal underground systems or structures such as piping systems and underground tanks.

Often in residential construction, the only grounding electrode that is available is the metal underground water piping system. *NEC Section 250.53(D)(2)* requires that whenever water piping is used as an electrode, it must be supplemented. Any of the electrodes listed above can be used to supplement the water pipe electrode. *Figure 12* shows a typical residential electric service and the available grounding electrodes for this structure using a ground rod to supplement the water pipe electrode.

This house also has a metal underground gas piping system, but this may not be used as an electrode per *NEC Section 250.52(B)*. In some cases, a water pipe electrode, building steel, and a concrete-encased electrode are not available to be used as a part of the grounding electrode system. For example, a building may be fed by plastic water piping, be constructed of wood, and an electrician may not be present at the site when the foundation for the structure is poured. When that happens, *NEC Section 250.50* requires that rod, pipe, plate, or other local metal underground structures be used.

WARNING!

A metal underground gas piping system must never be used as a grounding electrode.

Some local jurisdictions do not recognize water piping as an electrode due to the rise in the use of nonmetallic piping for both new and replacement water systems. They do not want to rely on the maintained viability of an existing metallic water service and therefore require the use of other electrodes such as the concrete-encased or rod electrodes. This means electricians must be involved with the construction prior to the foundation being poured in order to utilize concrete-encased electrodes.

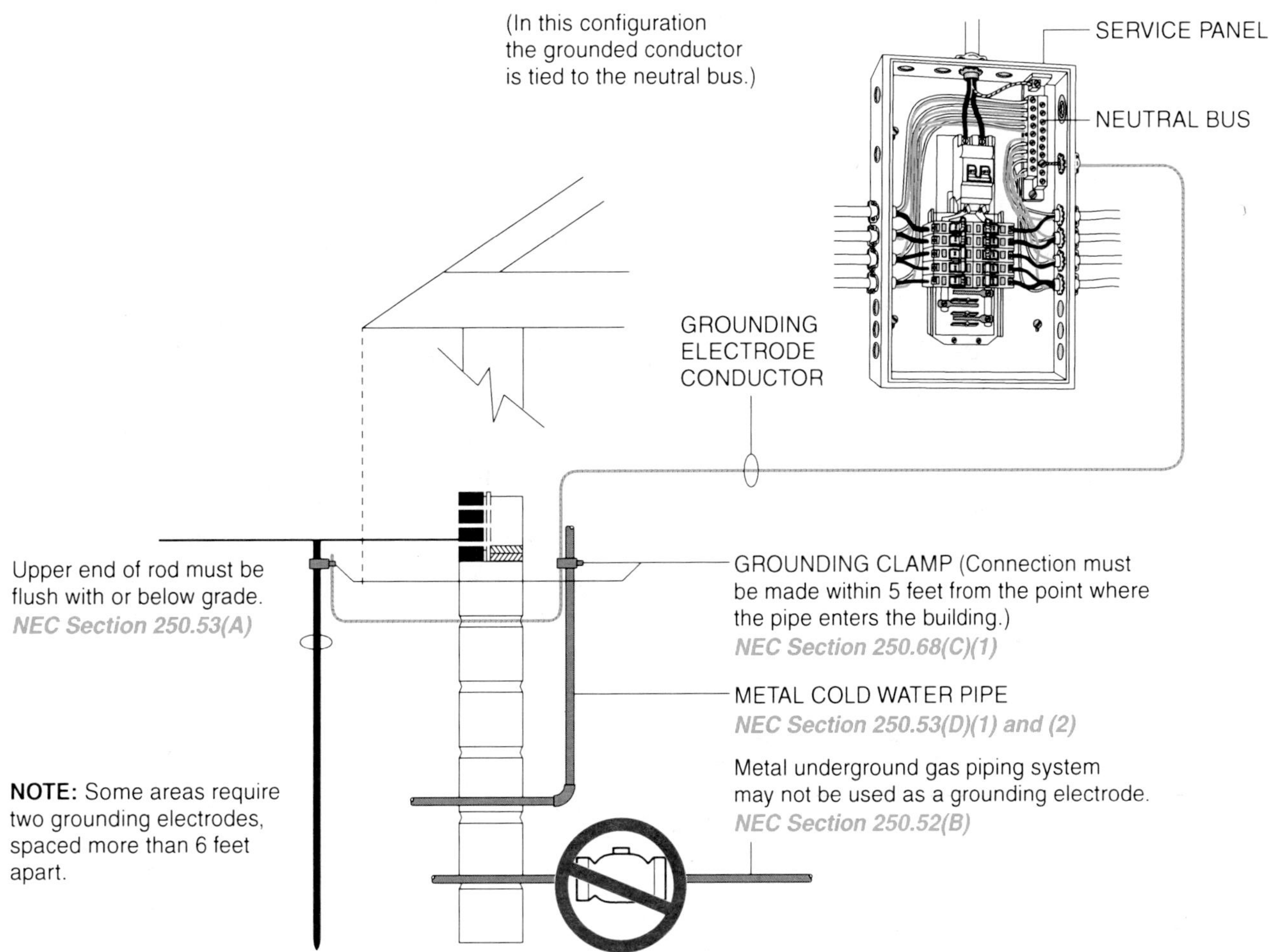
(In this configuration
the grounded conductor
is tied to the neutral bus.)
SERVICE PANEL
NEUTRAL BUS
GROUNDING
ELECTRODE
CONDUCTOR
Upper end of rod must be
flush with or below grade.
NEC Section 250.53(A)
GROUNDING CLAMP (Connection must
be made within 5 feet from the point where
the pipe enters the building.)
NEC Section 250.68(C)(1)
METAL COLD WATER PIPE
NEC Section 250.53(D)(1) and (2)
Metal underground gas piping system
may not be used as a grounding electrode.
NEC Section 250.52(B)
NOTE: Some areas require
two grounding electrodes,
spaced more than 6 feet
apart.
26111-14_F12.EPS

Figure 12 Components of a residential grounding system.

In most cases, the supplemental electrode used for a water pipe electrode will consist of either a driven rod or pipe electrode, the specifications for which are shown in *Figure 13*.

5.1.1 Grounding Electrode Installations

NEC Section 250.53(A)(1) requires that rod, pipe, and plate electrodes, where practical, be buried below the permanent moisture level and that they are free from any nonconductive coatings, such as paint or enamel. This section also requires that each electrode system used for a structure be at least 6' from other electrode systems, such as those for lightning protection.

NEC Section 250.53(G) permits a rod or pipe electrode to be driven at a 45-degree angle if rock bottom is encountered and prevents the rod or pipe from being driven vertically for at least 8'. Where driving a rod or pipe electrode at a 45-degree angle will not work, it is permitted to lay a rod or pipe horizontally in a trench that is at least 30" deep. For rod or pipe electrodes longer than 8', it is permitted to have the upper end above ground level if a suitable means of protection is provided for the grounding electrode conductor attachment; otherwise, the upper end must be flush with the earth surface.

NEC Section 250.53(A)(2) requires a supplemental electrode when a single rod, pipe, or plate electrode of a type specified in *NEC Sections 250.52(A)(2) through 250.52(A)(8)* is used. If a single rod or plate grounding electrode that has a resistance of 25 ohms or less is used, the supplemental electrode shall not be required. Always check with the local inspection authority, including the local utility, for rules that surpass the requirements of the *NEC®*.

- Where multiple rod, pipe, or plate electrodes are installed to meet the requirements of this section, they shall not be less than 6' apart.
- Plate electrodes must be buried at least 30" below the surface of the earth, according to *NEC Section 250.53(H)*.
- Where two or more electrodes are effectively bonded together, they are treated as a single electrode system.

5.1.2 Grounding Electrode Conductors (GECs)

The grounding electrode conductor (GEC) connecting the neutral (grounded conductor of the service) at the panelboard neutral bus to the grounding electrodes must meet the requirements

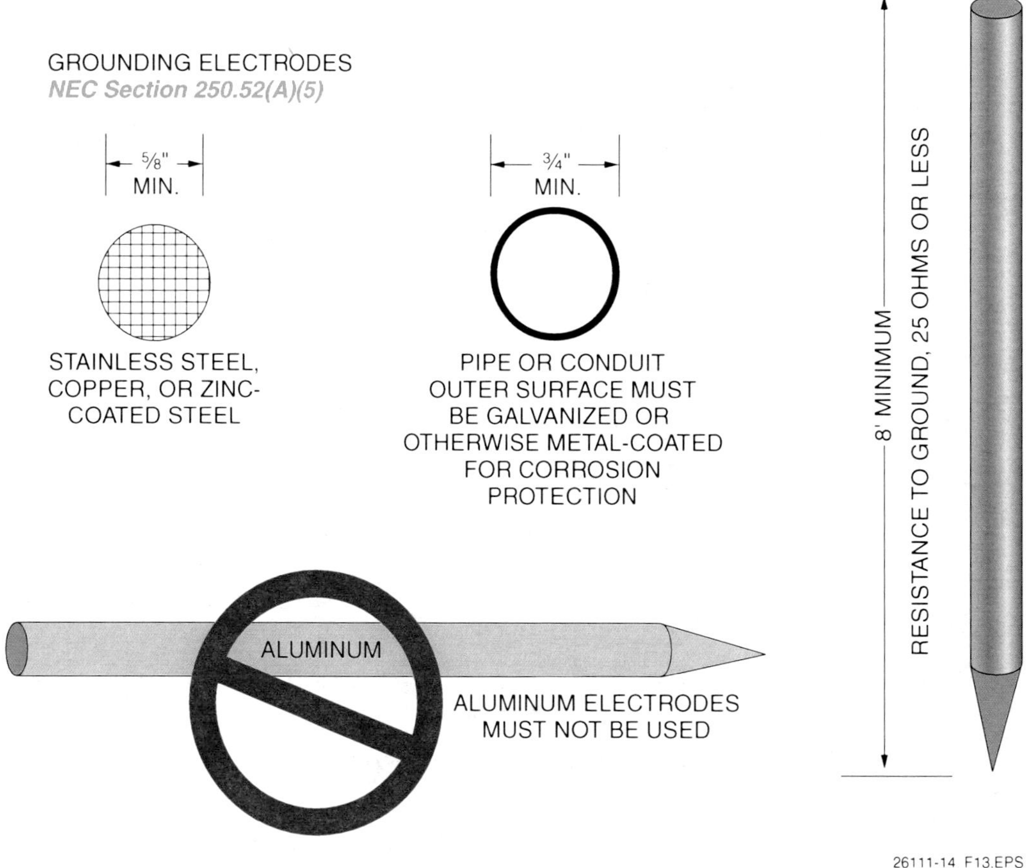

Figure 13 Specifications for rod and pipe grounding electrodes.

of *NEC Section 250.62*. This requires that it be made of copper, aluminum, or copper-clad aluminum. The material selected shall be protected against corrosion. The GEC may be either solid or stranded, covered or bare. Note that the GEC is not an equipment grounding conductor, and thus is not required to be identified by the use of the color green or green with yellow stripes, if insulated.

5.1.3 Installation of GECs

NEC Section 250.64 provides the installation requirements for GECs and does not permit bare aluminum or copper-clad aluminum grounding conductors to be used where in direct contact with masonry, the earth, where subject to corrosive conditions, or where used outside within 18" of the earth at the termination point. Other *NEC®* requirements include the following:

- A GEC or its enclosure is required to be securely fastened to the surface on which it is carried.
- A No. 4 AWG or larger copper or aluminum GEC is required to be protected if it will be exposed to severe physical damage.
- A No. 6 AWG or larger GEC that is free from exposure to physical damage is permitted to be run along the surface of the building without metal covering or protection if it is securely fastened to the building. Otherwise, it must be installed in RMC, IMC, PVC, reinforced thermosetting resin conduit (RTRC), EMT, or a cable armor.
- GECs smaller than No. 6 AWG must be protected by RMC, IMC, PVC, RTRC, EMT, or cable armor.
- The GEC shall be installed in one continuous length without a splice or joint, unless it meets the requirements of *NEC Sections 250.64(C)(1) through (C)(4)*.
- Where a service consists of more than a single enclosure, as permitted in *NEC Section 230.71(A)*, grounding electrode connections shall be made in accordance with *NEC Sections 250.64(D)(1), (D)(2), or (D)(3)*.
- Ferrous metal enclosures for the GEC are required to be electrically continuous from the point of attachment to metal cabinets or metallic equipment enclosures to the GEC. They must also be securely fastened to the ground clamp or fitting.
- Ferrous metal enclosures for the GEC that are not physically continuous from a metal cabinet or metallic equipment enclosure to the grounding electrode must be made electrically continuous by bonding each to the enclosed GEC. Bonding methods must comply with *NEC Section 250.92(B)* for installations at service equipment locations and with *NEC Sections 250.92(B)(2) through (B)(4)* for other-than-service equipment locations.
- GECs may be run to any convenient grounding electrode available in the grounding electrode system, or to one or more grounding electrode(s) individually. The GEC shall be sized for the largest grounding electrode conductor required among all the electrodes connected together.

Think About It

Grounding Conductors

This residential application has a grounding electrode connected to a rod that travels through the floor and into the ground at least 8'. In addition, it is also connected to a metal cold-water pipe (not shown). What type of grounding system is provided at your home? Does it meet *NEC®* requirements?

26111-14_SA02.EPS

5.1.4 Methods of Connecting GECs

NEC Section 250.70 requires the GEC to be connected to electrodes using exothermic welding, listed pressure connectors, listed clamps, listed lugs, or other listed means. Connections that depend on solder must never be used. To prevent corrosion, the ground clamp must be listed for the material of the grounding electrode and the GEC.

Where used on a pipe, ground rod, or other buried electrodes, the fitting must be listed for direct soil burial or concrete encasement. More than one conductor is not permitted to be connected to the grounding electrode using a single clamp or fitting unless the clamp or fitting is specifically listed for the connection of more than one conductor.

Think About It

Grounding Electrode Conductors

Which *NEC*® table would you use to size the minimum GEC required for a typical residential service?

For the connection to an electrode, you must use one of the following:

- A listed, bolted clamp of cast bronze or brass, or plain or malleable iron
- A pipe fitting, pipe plug, or other approved device that is screwed into a pipe or pipe fitting
- For indoor communication purposes only, a listed sheet metal strap-type ground clamp with a rigid metal base that seats on the electrode with a strap that will not stretch during or after installation
- An equally substantial approved means

The connection of a GEC or a **bonding jumper** to a grounding electrode must be accessible unless that connection is to the concrete-encased or buried grounding electrodes permitted in *NEC Section 250.68.* Where it is necessary to ensure the grounding path for metal piping used as a grounding electrode, effective bonding shall be provided around insulated joints and around any equipment likely to be disconnected for repairs or replacement. Bonding conductors shall be of sufficient length to permit removal of such equipment while retaining the integrity of the bond.

NOTE

The UL listing states that "strap-type ground clamps are not suitable for attachment of the grounding electrode conductor of an interior wiring system to a grounding electrode."

As required by *NEC Section 250.96*, coatings on metal piping systems must be removed to ensure that a permanent and effective grounding path is provided. Grounding electrode conductors and bonding jumpers shall be permitted to be connected at the following locations and used to extend the connections to an electrode:

- Interior metal piping located not more than 5 feet from the point of entrance of a building
- Structural frame of a building directly connected to the GEC

For the example house, the point of connection to the water piping is shown in *Figure 12* and would be required to be accessible after any wall coverings are installed. Any nonconductive coatings on the water piping would also have been scraped off or removed prior to installing the clamp on the water pipe.

5.1.5 Sizing GECs

Grounding electrode conductors must be sized per *NEC Section 250.66,* which uses the area of the largest service-entrance conductor (or equivalent area for paralleled conductors). Except as noted below, *NEC Table 250.66* will provide the minimum size GEC and any bonding jumpers used to interconnect grounding electrodes used.

- Where connected to rod, pipe, or plate electrodes, that portion of the GEC that is the sole connection to the grounding electrode shall not be required to be larger than No. 6 AWG copper or No. 4 AWG aluminum.
- Where connected to a concrete-encased electrode, that portion of the GEC that is the sole connection to the grounding electrode shall not be required to be larger than No. 4 AWG copper wire.
- Where the GEC is connected to a ground ring, that portion of the conductor that is the sole connection to the grounding electrode shall not be required to be larger than the conductor used for the ground ring.
- Where multiple sets of service-entrance conductors are used as permitted in *NEC Section 230.40, Exception 2,* the equivalent size of the largest service-entrance conductor is required to be determined by the largest sum of the areas of the corresponding conductors of each set.
- Where there are no service-entrance conductors, the GEC size is required to be determined by the equivalent size of the largest service-entrance conductor required for the load to be served.

For our sample dwelling unit, the size of the service-entrance conductors is No. 2 AWG. Using *NEC Table 250.66,* we can determine that the size of the conductor coming from the service panel to the water pipe (the GEC) must be at least No. 8 AWG copper. This No. 8 AWG may continue on without a splice to the ground rod, as shown in *Figure 12,* or a separate No. 6 AWG could be installed for the ground rod(s). This conductor would have to be connected to the service panel as an individual run or with a separate connector to any portion of the No. 8 AWG. It may not be connected directly to the water piping.

5.1.6 Air Terminals (Lightning Protection)

Air terminal conductors and driven pipes, rods, or plate electrodes used for grounding air terminals

On Site

What Does a Lightning Rod Do?

An interesting fact about grounding is that a lightning rod (air terminal) isn't meant to bring a bolt of lightning to ground. To do this, its conductors would have to be several feet in diameter. The purpose of the rod is to dissipate the negative static charge that would cause the positive lightning charge to strike the house.

are not permitted to be used in lieu of the grounding electrodes covered in *NEC Section 250.50* for grounding wiring systems and equipment. However, *NEC Section 250.106* requires that they be bonded to the wiring and equipment grounding electrode system for the structure.

5.2.0 Main Bonding Jumper

NEC Section 250.24(B) requires that an unspliced main bonding jumper (MBJ) shall be used to connect the equipment grounding conductor(s) and the service disconnect enclosure to the grounded conductor (neutral) of the system within the enclosure of each service disconnect.

The MBJ must be of copper or other corrosion-resistant material. An MBJ may be in the form of a wire, bus, screw, or similar suitable conductor.

Where an MBJ is in the form of a screw, it is required to be identified with a green finish so that the head of the screw is visible for inspection. An MBJ must be attached using exothermic welding, a listed pressure connector, listed clamp, or other listed means.

The MBJ cannot be smaller than the sizes given in *NEC Table 250.66* for grounding electrode conductors. See *NEC Section 250.28(D)* for service conductors that exceed 1,100 kcmil.

The MBJ is the means by which any ground fault in the branch circuits and feeders of the electrical system travels back to the source of supply at the utility. A ground fault will travel along the equipment conductors of the circuits back to the service disconnecting means. Where metallic raceways are used as equipment grounding conductors, there will be no connection to the grounded conductor at the service. Without the MBJ, the path back to the source would be through the grounding electrode system and the earth. This does not provide a low-impedance path, and thus will not allow enough current to flow in the circuit to let the overcurrent devices open.

For example, suppose a phase conductor makes contact with the metallic housing of a 120V, 15A appliance that was wired using EMT. Further suppose that the total combined resistance of the EMT being used as the equipment grounding conductor connected to the appliance and the resistance of the metal water piping and our ground rod in the sample house is 20Ω [less than the 25Ω permitted in *NEC Section 250.53(A)(2), Exception*]. The amount of current that could flow back to the utility source would be 120V ÷ 20 = 6A. The smallest overcurrent device in our electrical system is 15A, and would not trip. With the MBJ installed, the path back to the utility source is through the MBJ to the grounded conductor of the service. This resistance will be much less than 1Ω, and thus would allow enough current to flow to open up the overcurrent devices within the system. The MBJ provides the path back to the source for faults that occur within the service disconnect means.

5.2.1 Bonding at the Service

Electrical continuity is required at the service per *NEC Section 250.92(A)*, which states that all of the following must be bonded:

- The service raceways, auxiliary gutters, or service cable armor or sheaths, except for underground metallic sheaths of continuously underground cables as noted in *NEC Section 250.84*
- All service enclosures containing service-entrance conductors, including meter fittings, boxes, or the like interposed in the service raceway or armor
- Any metallic raceway or armor enclosing a grounding electrode conductor as specified in *NEC Section 250.64(E)*

Bonding shall apply at each end and to all intervening raceways, boxes, and enclosures between the service equipment and the grounding electrode.

The items that typically require bonding include the mast and weatherhead, the meter enclosure, the armor of the SE cable (if it has armor), and the service disconnect.

5.2.2 Methods of Bonding at the Service

The electrical continuity of the service equipment, raceways, and enclosures will be ensured per *NEC Section 250.92(B)* through the use of the following methods:

- Bonding equipment to the grounded service conductor in a manner provided in *NEC Section 250.8*

- Connections utilizing threaded couplings or threaded bosses on enclosures where made up wrenchtight
- Threadless couplings and connectors where made up tight for metal raceways and metal-clad cables
- Other approved devices, such as bonding-type locknuts and bonding bushings

Bonding jumpers must be used around concentric or eccentric knockouts that are punched or otherwise formed so as to impair the electrical connection to ground. Standard locknuts or bushings shall not be the sole means for bonding.

5.2.3 Bonding and Grounding Requirements for Other Systems

An accessible means external to the service equipment enclosure is required for connecting intersystem bonding and grounding conductors and connections for the communications, radio and television (TV), community antenna television (CATV), and network-powered broadband communication system. The intersystem bonding termination must consist of at least three terminals and be installed in accordance with *NEC Section 250.94*. Any one of the following can be used:

- A set of listed terminals for grounding and bonding
- A bonding bar near the service-entrance enclosure, meter enclosure, or raceway for service conductors connected to an equipment grounding conductor in the enclosure or raceway with a minimum No. 6 AWG copper conductor
- A bonding bar near the grounding electrode conductor connected with a minimum No. 6 AWG copper conductor

The intersystem bonding termination must meet the following requirements per *NEC Section 250.94*:

- At the disconnecting means for a building or structure, be securely mounted and electrically connected to the metal enclosure or GEC with a minimum No. 6 AWG copper conductor
- Be accessible for connection and inspection
- Not to interfere with access to service, building, or structure disconnecting means or metering equipment
- Consist of a set of terminals with the capacity for connection of not less than three intersecting bonding conductors

5.2.4 Bonding of Water Piping Systems

Metallic water piping systems in or on a structure must be bonded as required by *NEC Section 250.104(A)*. The metallic water piping system(s) must be bonded by means of a bonding jumper sized in accordance with *NEC Table 250.66* and connected to one of the following:

- The service-entrance enclosures
- The grounded (neutral) conductor at the service
- The grounding electrode conductor where of sufficient size
- The grounding electrode(s) used

The points of attachment of the bonding jumper(s) shall be accessible. It shall be installed in accordance with *NEC Section 250.64(A), (B), and (E)*. Note that while this conductor is sized in the same manner as if the water piping system is a grounding electrode, the point of attachment to the water piping is permitted to be at any convenient point on the water piping system and not just within the first 5' of where the water enters the building.

NEC Section 250.104(A)(2) states that in multi-family dwelling units (or other multiple occupancy buildings) where the metal water piping system(s) installed in or attached to a building or structure for the individual occupancies is metallically isolated from all other occupancies by use of nonmetallic water piping, the metal water piping system(s) for each occupancy shall be permitted to be bonded to the equipment grounding terminal of the panelboard or switchboard enclosure (other than service equipment) supplying that occupancy. The bonding jumper shall be sized in accordance with *NEC Table 250.122*.

5.2.5 Bonding of Other Piping Systems

NEC Section 250.104(B) requires that other piping systems, where installed in or attached to a building or structure, including gas piping, that may become energized shall be bonded to one of the following:

- The service equipment enclosure
- The grounded conductor at the service
- The grounding electrode conductor where of sufficient size
- One or more grounding electrodes used

The bonding jumper(s) shall be sized in accordance with *NEC Table 250.122* using the rating of the circuit that may energize the piping system(s).

The equipment grounding conductor for the circuit that may energize the piping shall be permitted to serve as the bonding means. The points of attachment of the bonding jumper(s) shall be accessible.

NOTE

Bonding all piping and metal air ducts within the premises will provide additional safety.

6.0.0 Installing the Service Entrance

In practical applications, the electric service is normally one of the last components of an electrical system to be installed. However, it is one of the first considerations when laying out a residential electrical system. For instance:

- The electrician must know in which direction and to what location to route the circuit homeruns while **roughing in** the electrical wiring.
- Provisions must be made for sleeves through footings and foundations in cases where underground systems (service laterals) are used.
- The local power company must be notified as to the approximate size of service required so they may plan the best way to furnish a **service drop** to the property.

6.1.0 Service Drop Locations

The location of the service drop, electric meter, and load center should be considered first. It is always wise to consult the local power company to obtain their requirements; where you want the service drop and where they want it may not coincide. A brief meeting with the power company about the location of the service drop can prevent problems later on.

The service drop must be routed so that the service drop conductors have a clearance of not less than 3' horizontally and below windows that open, doors, porches, fire escapes, or similar locations. In addition, they must have a 10' vertical clearance that extends 3' horizontally from porches, fire escapes, balconies, and so forth, as required in *NEC Section 230.9.* Where overhead service conductors pass over rooftops, driveways, yards, and so forth, they must have clearances as specified in *NEC Section 230.24.*

A plot plan (also called a site plan) is often available for new construction. The plot plan shows the entire property, with the building or buildings drawn in their proper location on the plot of land. It also shows sidewalks, driveways, streets, and existing utilities—both overhead and underground.

A plot plan of the sample residence is shown in *Figure 14*. In reviewing this drawing, you can see that the closest power pole is located across a

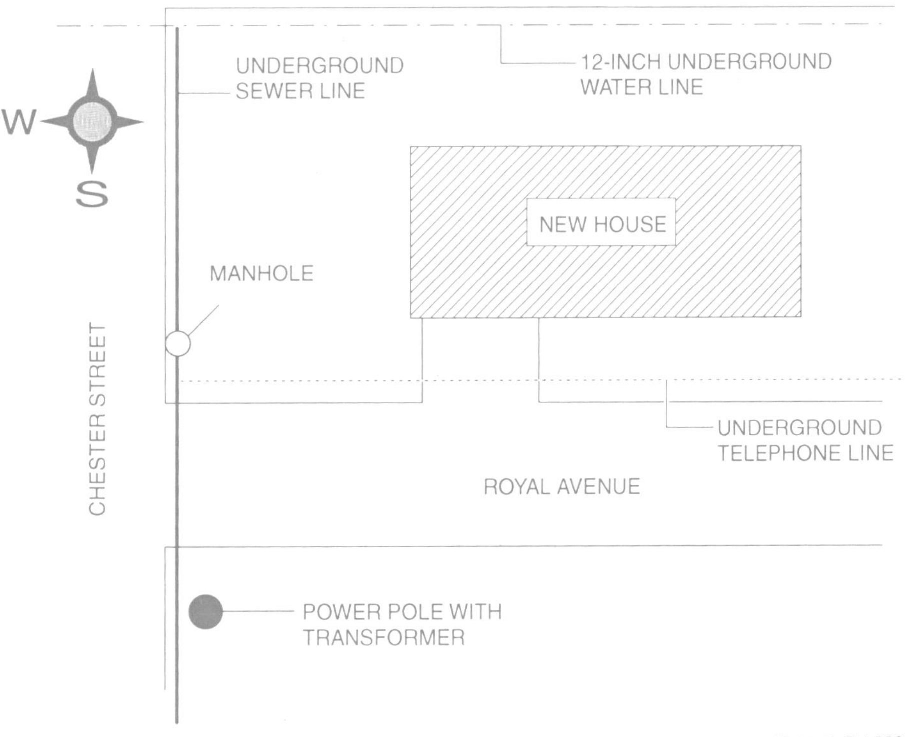

Figure 14 Plot plan of the sample residence.

public street from the house. By consulting with the local power company, it is learned that the service will be brought to the house from this pole by triplex cable, which will connect to the residence at a point on its left (west) end. The steel uninsulated conductor of triplex cable acts as both the grounded conductor (neutral) and as a support for the insulated (ungrounded) conductors. It is also suitable for overhead use.

When service-entrance cable is used, it will run directly from the point of attachment and service head to the meter base. However, since the carport is located on the west side of the building, a service mast (*Figure 15*) will have to be installed.

The *NEC®* requires a clearance of not less than 8' over rooftops, unless the roof has a slope of 4" in 12" or greater, in which case the clearance may be reduced to 3'. Where the service drop conductors pass over only the overhang (eaves) of a roof, the clearance may be reduced to 18" as long as no more than 6' of the conductors travel over no more than 4' of the overhang (eave). This minimum height requirement extends beyond the roof for a distance of not less than 3' in all directions, except the final portion of the span where the service drop conductors attach to the sides of a building.

6.2.0 Vertical Clearances of Service Drop

NEC Section 230.24(B) specifies the distances by which service drop conductors must clear the ground. These distances vary according to the surrounding conditions.

In general, the *NEC®* states that the vertical clearances of all service drop conductors that carry 600V or under are based on a conductor temperature of 60°F (15°C) with no wind and with the

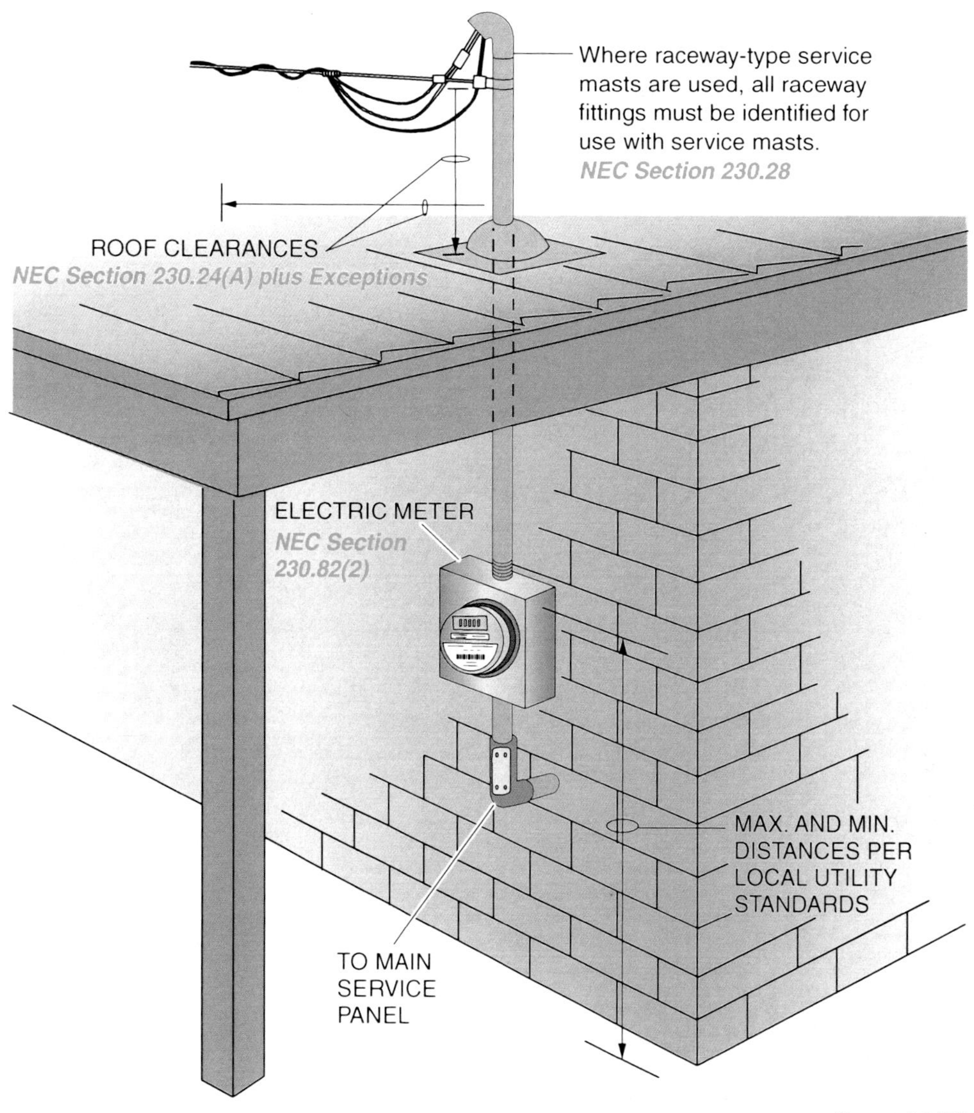

Figure 15 *NEC®* sections governing service mast installations.

final unloaded sag in the wire, conductor, or cable. Service drop conductors must be at least 10' above the ground or other accessible surfaces at all times. More distance is required under most conditions. For example, if the service conductors pass over residential property and driveways or commercial property that is not subject to truck traffic, the conductors must be at least 15' above the ground. However, this distance may be reduced to 12' when the voltage is limited to 300V to ground.

In other areas, such as public streets, alleys, roads, parking areas subject to truck traffic, driveways on other-than-residential property, the minimum vertical distance is 18'. The conditions of the sample residence are shown in *Figure 16*.

6.3.0 Service Drop (Overhead Service Conductor) Clearances for Building Openings

Service conductors that are installed as open conductors or multiconductor cable without an overall outer jacket must have a clearance of not less than 3' from windows that are designed to be opened, doors, porches, balconies, ladders, stairs, fire escapes, or similar locations (*NEC Section 230.9*). However, conductors run above the top level of a window are permitted to be less than 3' from the window opening.

The 3' of clearance is not applicable to raceways or cable assemblies that have an overall outer jacket approved for use as a service conductor. The intention of this requirement is to protect the conductors from physical damage and/or physical contact with unprotected personnel when evacuating a structure through the window opening. The exception allows service conductors, including drip loops and service drop conductors, to be located just above the window openings because they would not interfere with ladders leaning against the structure to the right, left, or below the window opening when used to evacuate people from the building.

Case History

Failure to De-Energize Panelboard

A 31-year-old electrician was finishing the installation of an outdoor floodlight on a new home. He borrowed an aluminum ladder from another contractor and then proceeded with his task. He did not verify that power was removed at the panelboard, and when he used his wire strippers to remove the conductor insulation, his right thumb and index finger contacted a 110V circuit. He received a fatal shock.

The Bottom Line: Always de-energize circuits at the panelboard before beginning any electrical task, and never use aluminum ladders while working in or near electrical devices. In this case, the ladder provided a path to ground.

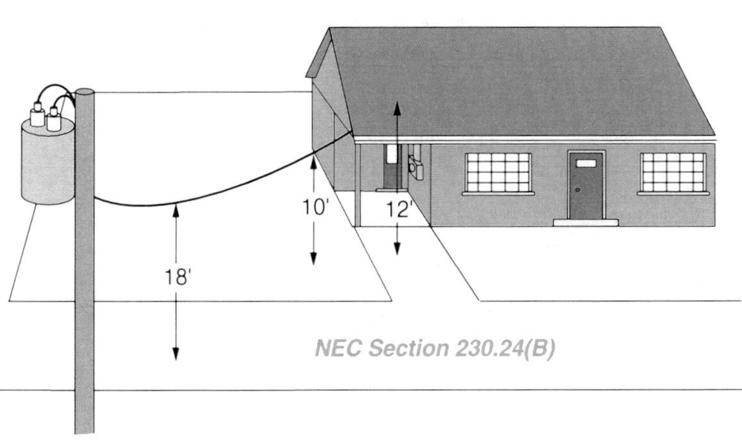

26111-14_F16A.EPS

26111-14_F16B.EPS

Figure 16 Vertical clearances for service drop conductors.

7.0.0 Panelboard Location

The main service disconnect or panelboard is normally located in a portion of an unfinished basement or utility room on an outside wall so that the service cable coming from the electric meter can terminate immediately into the switch or panelboard when the cable enters the building. In the example home, however, there is no basement and the utility room is located in the center of the house with no outside walls. Consequently, a somewhat different arrangement will have to be used. A load center is a type of panelboard that is normally located at the service entrance of a residential installation. The load center usually contains a main circuit breaker, which is the main disconnect. Circuit breakers are provided for equipment such as electric water heaters, ranges, dryers, air conditioning and heating units, and breakers that feed subpanels such as lighting panels.

NEC Section 230.70 requires that the service disconnecting means be installed in a readily accessible location—either outside or inside the building. If located inside the building, it must be located nearest the point of entrance of the service conductors. In the sample home, there are at least two methods of installing the panelboard in the utility room that will comply with this *NEC®* regulation, as well as the requirements in *NEC Sections 110.26 and 240.24.*

The first method utilizes a weatherproof 100A disconnect (safety switch or circuit breaker enclosure) mounted next to the meter base on the outside of the building. With this method, service conductors are provided with overcurrent protection; the neutral conductor is also grounded at this point, as this becomes the main disconnect switch. Three-wire cable with an additional grounding wire is then routed from this main disconnect to the panelboard in the utility room. All three current-carrying conductors (two ungrounded and one neutral) must be insulated with this arrangement; the equipment ground, however, may be bare. The panelboard containing overcurrent protection devices for the branch circuits, which is located in the utility room, now becomes a subpanel. See *Figure 17*.

> **NOTE**
> Local ordinances in some areas may require a disconnect at the meter base, making the panel in the utility room a subpanel.

An alternate method utilizes conduit from the meter base that is routed under the concrete slab and then up to a main panelboard located in the utility room. *NEC Section 230.6* considers conductors to be outside of a building when they are installed under not less than 2" of concrete beneath a building or installed in a conduit not less than 18" deep beneath a building. The sample residence has a 4"-thick reinforced concrete slab—well within the *NEC®* regulations. Therefore, the service conductors from the meter base that are installed under the concrete slab in conduit are considered to be outside the house, and no disconnect is required at the meter base. When this conduit emerges in the utility room, it will run straight up into the bottom of the panelboard, again meeting the *NEC®* requirement that the panel be located nearest the point of entrance of the service conductors. Always check with your local authority having jurisdiction for specific requirements about where services are to be located. Details of this service arrangement are shown in *Figure 18*.

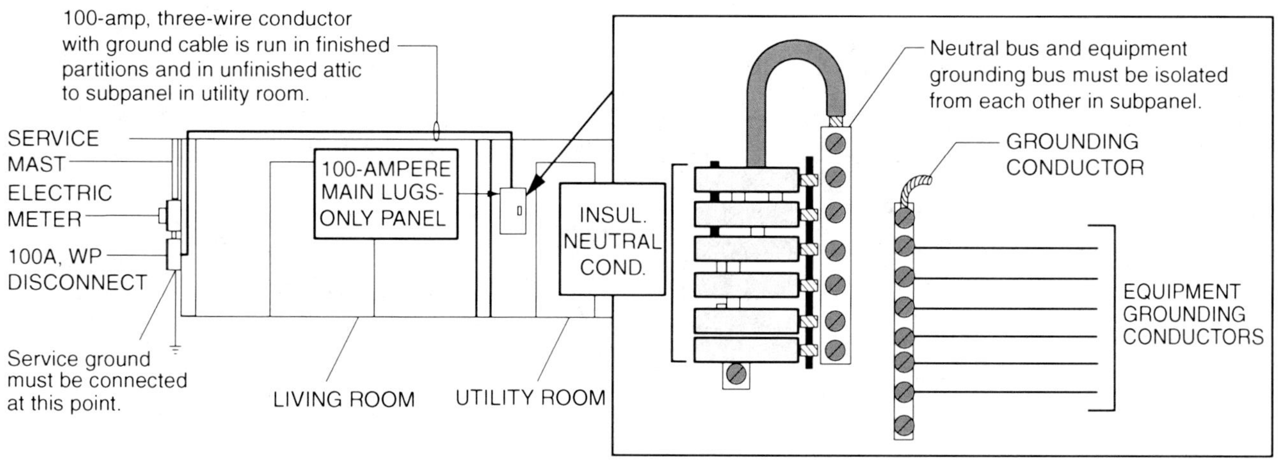

Figure 17 One method of wiring a panelboard for the sample residence.

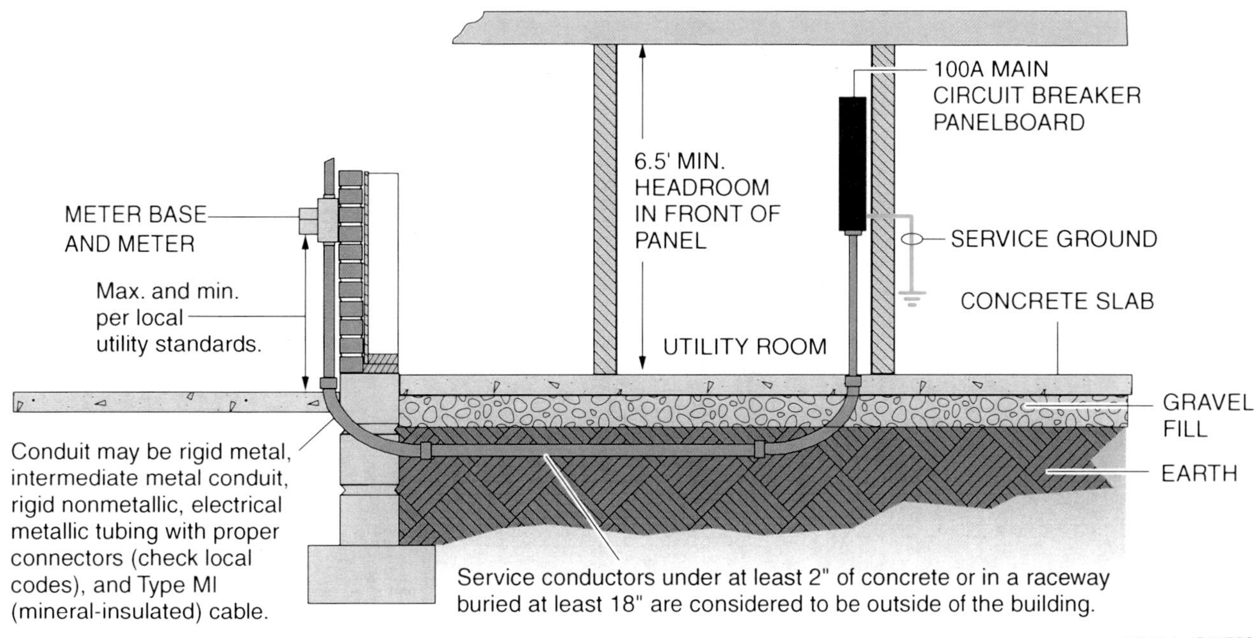

100A MAIN
CIRCUIT BREAKER
PANELBOARD
6.5' MIN.
HEADROOM
IN FRONT OF
PANEL
METER BASE
AND METER
SERVICE GROUND
Max. and min.
per local
utility standards.
CONCRETE SLAB
UTILITY ROOM
GRAVEL
FILL
EARTH
Conduit may be rigid metal, intermediate metal conduit, rigid nonmetallic, electrical metallic tubing with proper connectors (check local codes), and Type MI (mineral-insulated) cable.
Service conductors under at least 2" of concrete or in a raceway buried at least 18" are considered to be outside of the building.
26111-14_F18.EPS

Figure 18 Alternate method of service installation for the sample residence.

8.0.0 Wiring Methods

Branch circuits and feeders are used in residential construction to provide power wiring to operate components and equipment, and control wiring to regulate the equipment. Wiring may be further subdivided into either open or concealed wiring.

In open wiring systems, the cable and/or raceways are installed on the surface of the walls, ceilings, columns, and other areas where they are in view and are readily accessible. Open wiring is often used in areas where appearance is not important, such as in unfinished basements, attics, and garages.

Concealed wiring systems are installed inside walls, partitions, ceilings, columns, and behind baseboards or moldings where they are out of view and are not readily accessible. This type of wiring is generally used in all new construction with finished interior walls, ceilings, and floors, and it is the preferred type of wiring where appearance is important.

In general, there are two basic wiring methods used in the majority of modern residential electrical systems. They are:

- Sheathed cables of two or more conductors
- Raceway (conduit) systems

The method used on a given job is determined by the requirements of the *NEC®*, any amendments made by local authorities, the type of building construction, and the location of the wiring in the building. In most applications, either of the two methods may be used, and both methods are frequently used in combination.

8.1.0 Cable Systems

Several types of cable are used in wiring systems to feed or supply power to equipment. These include nonmetallic-sheathed cable, metal-clad (MC) cable, underground feeder cable, and service-entrance cable.

8.1.1 Nonmetallic-Sheathed Cable

Nonmetallic-sheathed (Type NM) cable (*NEC Article 334*) is manufactured in two- or three-wire configurations with varying sizes of conductors. In both two- and three-wire cables, conductors are color-coded: one conductor is black while the other is white in two-wire cable; in three-wire cable, the additional conductor is red. Both types also have a grounding conductor, which is usually bare, but it is sometimes covered with green plastic insulation, depending upon the manufacturer. Type NMC is basically the same as NM, but the outer nonmetallic sheath is corrosion-resistant. The jacket or covering consists of rubber, plastic, or fiber. Most also have markings on this jacket giving the manufacturer's name or trademark, wire size, and number of conductors (see *Figure 19*). For example, NM 12-2 W/GRD indicates that the jacket contains two No. 12

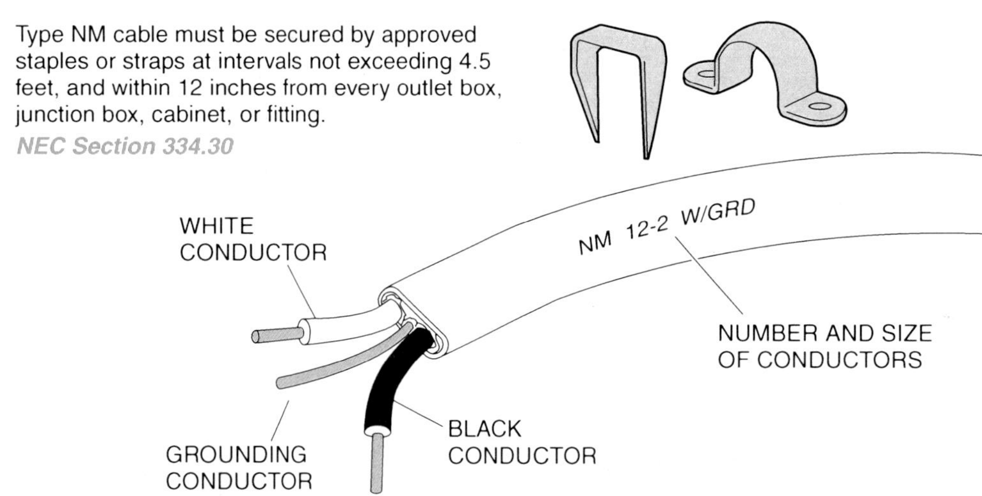
Type NM cable must be secured by approved staples or straps at intervals not exceeding 4.5 feet, and within 12 inches from every outlet box, junction box, cabinet, or fitting.
NEC Section 334.30
WHITE CONDUCTOR
NM 12-2 W/GRD
NUMBER AND SIZE OF CONDUCTORS
GROUNDING CONDUCTOR
BLACK CONDUCTOR
26111-14_F19.EPS

Figure 19 Characteristics of Type NM cable.

AWG conductors along with a grounding wire; NM 12-3 W/GRD indicates three conductors plus a grounding wire. Type NM cable is often referred to as Romex®.

NEC Section 334.10 permits Type NM, NMC, and NMS cable to be used in the following applications:

- Outdoors in dry locations
- One- and two-family dwelling units and attached or detached garages or storage buildings
- Multi-family dwellings when they are of Types III, IV, and V construction
- Other structures if concealed behind a 15-minute finish barrier and are of Types III, IV, and V construction

In addition, Type NMC can be used outdoors in dry or moist locations.

Type NMS is insulated power or control conductors with signaling, data, and communications conductors within an overall nonmetallic jacket. Type NMS cable shall be permitted as follows:

- For both exposed and concealed in normally dry locations
- To be fished in voids in masonry block or tile walls

NEC Section 334.12 prohibits the use of Type NM, NMC, and NMS cable in the following applications:

- As open runs in dropped or suspended ceilings in other-than-dwelling units
- As service-entrance cable
- In commercial garages with hazardous (classified) areas
- In theaters and similar locations, except as permitted by *NEC Section 518.4(B)*
- In motion picture studios
- In storage battery rooms
- In hoistways or on elevators or escalators
- Embedded in poured cement, concrete, or aggregate
- In hazardous (classified) areas
- Where exposed to corrosive fumes or vapors (NM and NMS)
- Embedded in masonry, adobe, fill, or plaster (NM and NMS)
- In a shallow chase in masonry, concrete, or adobe and covered with plaster, adobe, or similar finish (NM and NMS)
- Where exposed or subject to excessive moisture or dampness (NM and NMS)

Type NM cable is the most common type of cable for residential use. *Figure 20* shows additional *NEC®* regulations pertaining to the installation of Type NM cable.

8.1.2 Metal-Clad Cable

Metal-clad (MC) cable is manufactured in two-, three-, and four-wire assemblies with varying sizes of conductors, and is used in locations similar to those for Type NM, NMC, and NMS cable. Unlike Type NM, NMC, and NMS, it can also be used as service-entrance cable and in other locations permitted by *NEC Section 330.10*.

The metallic spiral covering on Type MC cable offers a greater degree of mechanical protection than Type NM cable and also provides a continuous grounding bond without the need for additional grounding conductors.

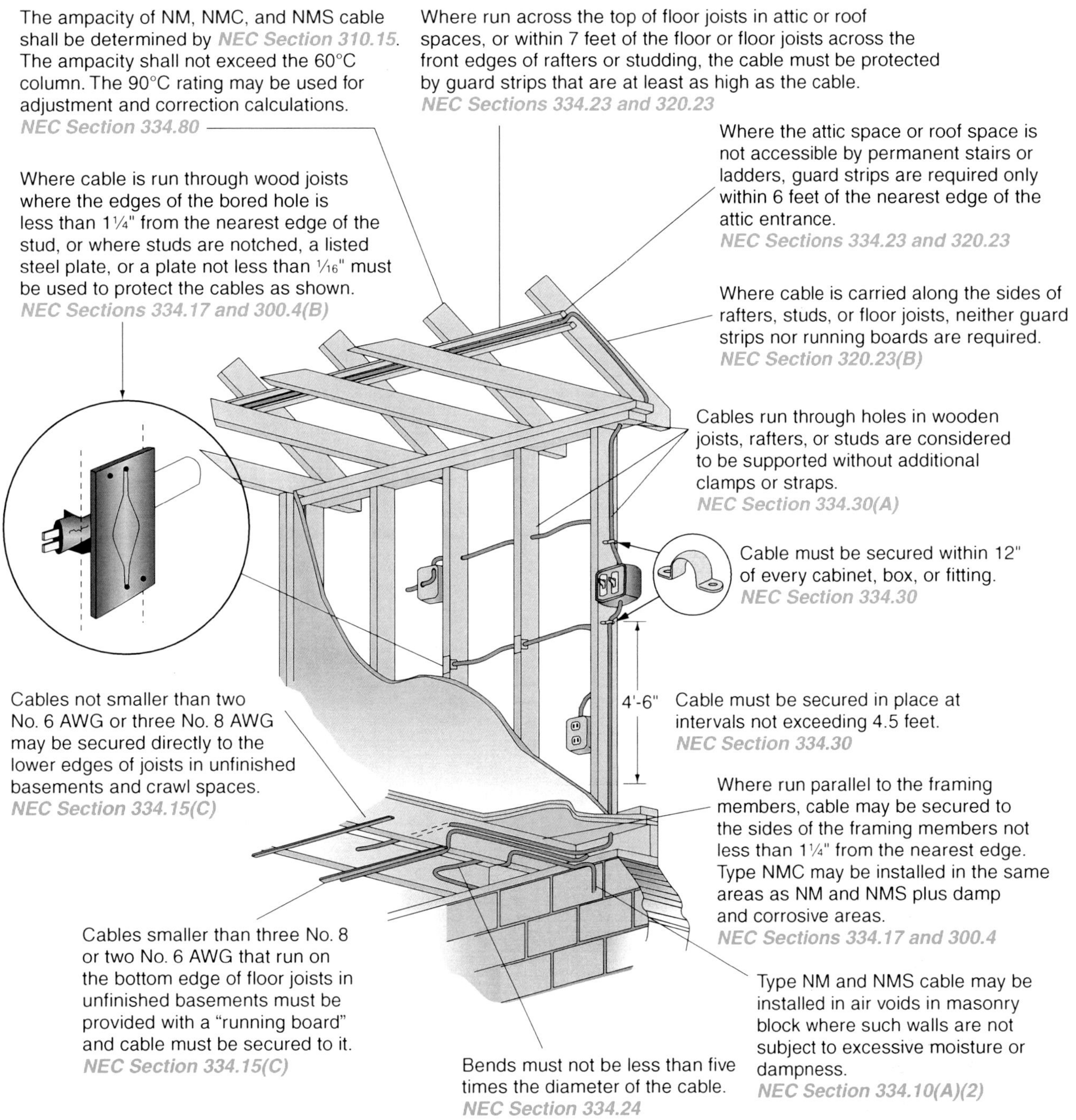

The ampacity of NM, NMC, and NMS cable shall be determined by NEC Section 310.15. The ampacity shall not exceed the 60°C column. The 90°C rating may be used for adjustment and correction calculations.
NEC Section 334.80
Where run across the top of floor joists in attic or roof spaces, or within 7 feet of the floor or floor joists across the front edges of rafters or studding, the cable must be protected by guard strips that are at least as high as the cable.
NEC Sections 334.23 and 320.23
Where the attic space or roof space is not accessible by permanent stairs or ladders, guard strips are required only within 6 feet of the nearest edge of the attic entrance.
NEC Sections 334.23 and 320.23
Where cable is run through wood joists where the edges of the bored hole is less than 1¼" from the nearest edge of the stud, or where studs are notched, a listed steel plate, or a plate not less than 1⁄16" must be used to protect the cables as shown.
NEC Sections 334.17 and 300.4(B)
Where cable is carried along the sides of rafters, studs, or floor joists, neither guard strips nor running boards are required.
NEC Section 320.23(B)
Cables run through holes in wooden joists, rafters, or studs are considered to be supported without additional clamps or straps.
NEC Section 334.30(A)
Cable must be secured within 12" of every cabinet, box, or fitting.
NEC Section 334.30
Cables not smaller than two No. 6 AWG or three No. 8 AWG may be secured directly to the lower edges of joists in unfinished basements and crawl spaces.
NEC Section 334.15(C)
4'-6"
Cable must be secured in place at intervals not exceeding 4.5 feet.
NEC Section 334.30
Where run parallel to the framing members, cable may be secured to the sides of the framing members not less than 1¼" from the nearest edge. Type NMC may be installed in the same areas as NM and NMS plus damp and corrosive areas.
NEC Sections 334.17 and 300.4
Cables smaller than three No. 8 or two No. 6 AWG that run on the bottom edge of floor joists in unfinished basements must be provided with a "running board" and cable must be secured to it.
NEC Section 334.15(C)
Type NM and NMS cable may be installed in air voids in masonry block where such walls are not subject to excessive moisture or dampness.
NEC Section 334.10(A)(2)
Bends must not be less than five times the diameter of the cable.
NEC Section 334.24
26111-14_F20.EPS

Figure 20 NEC® sections governing the installation of Type NM cable.

Type MC cable may be embedded in plaster finish, brick, or other masonry, except in damp or wet locations. It may also be run in the air voids of masonry block or tile walls, except where such walls are exposed or subject to excessive moisture or dampness. It may be used in wet locations if the conditions of *NEC Section 330.10(A)(11)* are met. It may not be used where subject to physical damage. See *Figures 21 and 22*.

NOTE

In the past, armored cable (Type AC), also called BX® cable, was commonly used in residential applications. Today, Type MC cable is used because it has a plastic wrapping to protect the conductors and does not require an insulating bushing at cable terminations.

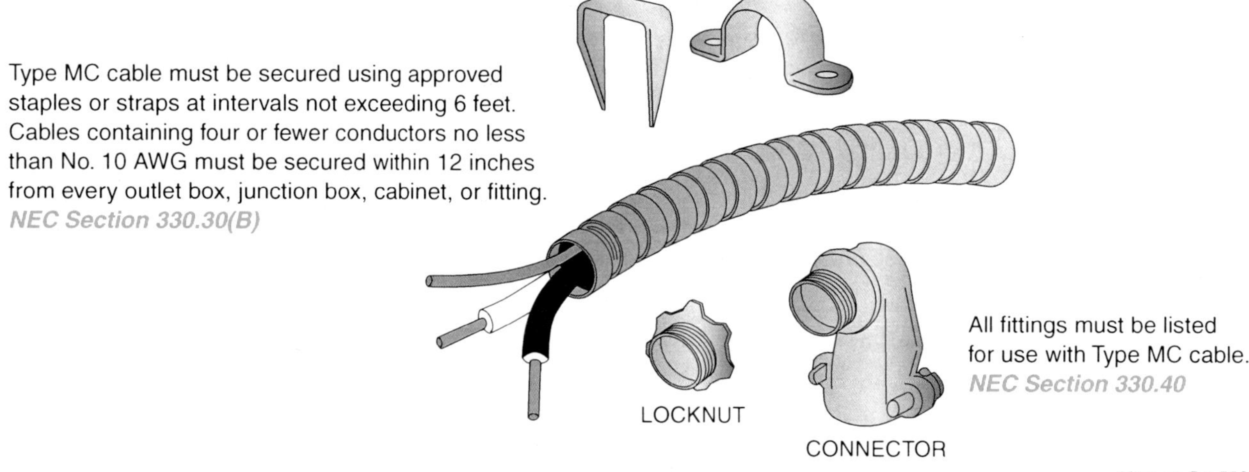

Type MC cable must be secured using approved staples or straps at intervals not exceeding 6 feet. Cables containing four or fewer conductors no less than No. 10 AWG must be secured within 12 inches from every outlet box, junction box, cabinet, or fitting.
NEC Section 330.30(B)
LOCKNUT
CONNECTOR
All fittings must be listed for use with Type MC cable.
NEC Section 330.40
26111-14_F21.EPS

Figure 21 Characteristics of Type MC cable.

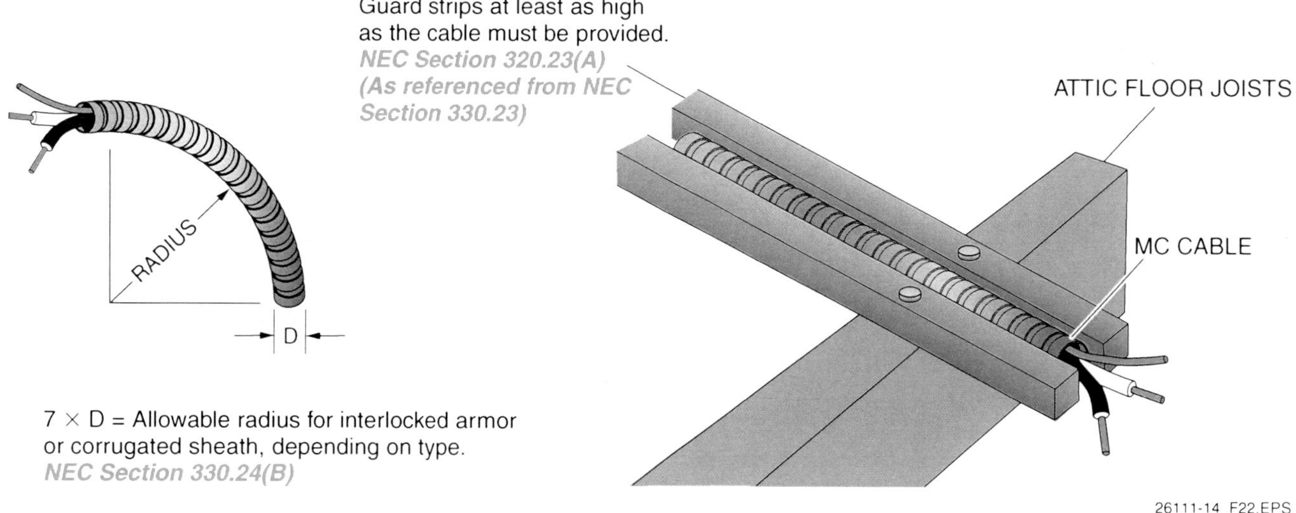

Guard strips at least as high as the cable must be provided.
NEC Section 320.23(A)
(As referenced from NEC Section 330.23)
ATTIC FLOOR JOISTS
MC CABLE
RADIUS
D
7 × D = Allowable radius for interlocked armor or corrugated sheath, depending on type.
NEC Section 330.24(B)
26111-14_F22.EPS

Figure 22 *NEC*® sections governing the installation of Type MC cable.

8.1.3 Underground Feeder Cable

Underground feeder (Type UF) cable *(NEC Article 340)* may be used underground, including direct burial in the earth, as a feeder or branch circuit cable when provided with overcurrent protection at the rated ampacity as required by the *NEC*®. When Type UF cable is used above grade where it will come in direct contact with the rays of the sun, its outer covering must be sun-resistant. Furthermore, where Type UF cable emerges from the ground, some means of mechanical protection must be provided. This protection may be in the form of conduit or guard strips. *NEC Section 300.5(D)(1)* requires that the protection extend from the minimum burial depth below grade to a point at least 8' above grade. *NEC Section 300.5(D)(4)* states that if conduit is used as protection, the permitted types are RMC, IMC, and Schedule 80 PVC, or equivalent. Type UF cable resembles Type NM cable; however, the jacket is constructed of weather-resistant material to provide the required protection for direct-burial wiring installations.

8.1.4 Service-Entrance Cable

Service-entrance (Type SE) and underground service-entrance (Type USE) cable, when used for electrical services, must be installed as specified in *NEC Articles 230 and 338*. Service-entrance cable is available with the grounded conductor bare for outside service conductors, and also with an insulated grounded conductor for interior wiring systems.

On Site

Cable Stripping

Special strippers are used to remove the jackets from Type NM and Type MC cable.

(A) NM CABLE RIPPER

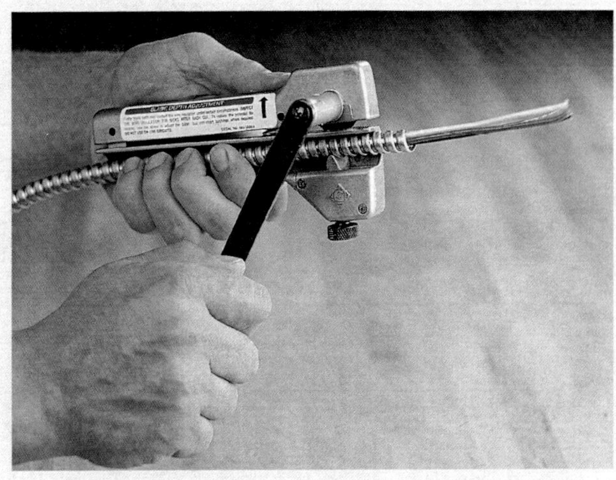

(B) MC CABLE CUTTER

26111-14 SA03.EPS

Type SE cable is permitted for use on branch circuits or feeders provided that all current-carrying conductors are insulated; this includes the grounded or neutral conductor. Where a conductor in the cable is not insulated, it is only permitted to be used as an equipment grounding conductor for branch circuits or feeders. Where used as an interior wiring method, the installation requirements of *NEC Article 334* must be followed, except for determining the ampacity of the cable. Where installed as exterior wiring, the requirements of *NEC Article 225* must be met, with the supports for the cable in accordance with *NEC Section 334.30.*

SE Style R (SER) cable is used in residential applications for subfeeds for ranges, and it is also used for service laterals in multi-family dwellings.

Figure 23 summarizes the installation rules for Type SE cable for both exterior and interior wiring.

8.2.0 Raceways

A raceway is any channel that is designed and used solely for the purpose of holding wires, cables, or busbars. Types of raceways include rigid metal conduit, intermediate metal conduit, rigid nonmetallic conduit, flexible metallic conduit, electrical metallic tubing, and auxiliary gutters. Raceways are constructed of either metal or insulating material, such as polyvinyl chloride or PVC (plastic). Metal raceways are joined using threaded, compression, or setscrew couplings; nonmetallic raceways are joined using cement-coated couplings. Where a raceway terminates in an outlet box, junction box, or other enclosure, an approved connector must be used.

Raceways provide mechanical protection for the conductors that run in them and also prevent accidental damage to insulation and the conducting material. They also protect conductors from corrosive atmospheres and prevent fire hazards to life and property by confining arcs and flames that may occur due to faults in the wiring system. Conduits or raceways are used in residential applications for service masts, underground wiring embedded in concrete, and sometimes in unfinished basements, shops, or garage areas.

Another function of metal raceways is to provide a continuous equipment grounding system throughout the electrical system. To maintain this feature, it is extremely important that all raceway systems be securely bonded together into a continuous conductive path and properly connected to the system ground. The following section explains how this is accomplished.

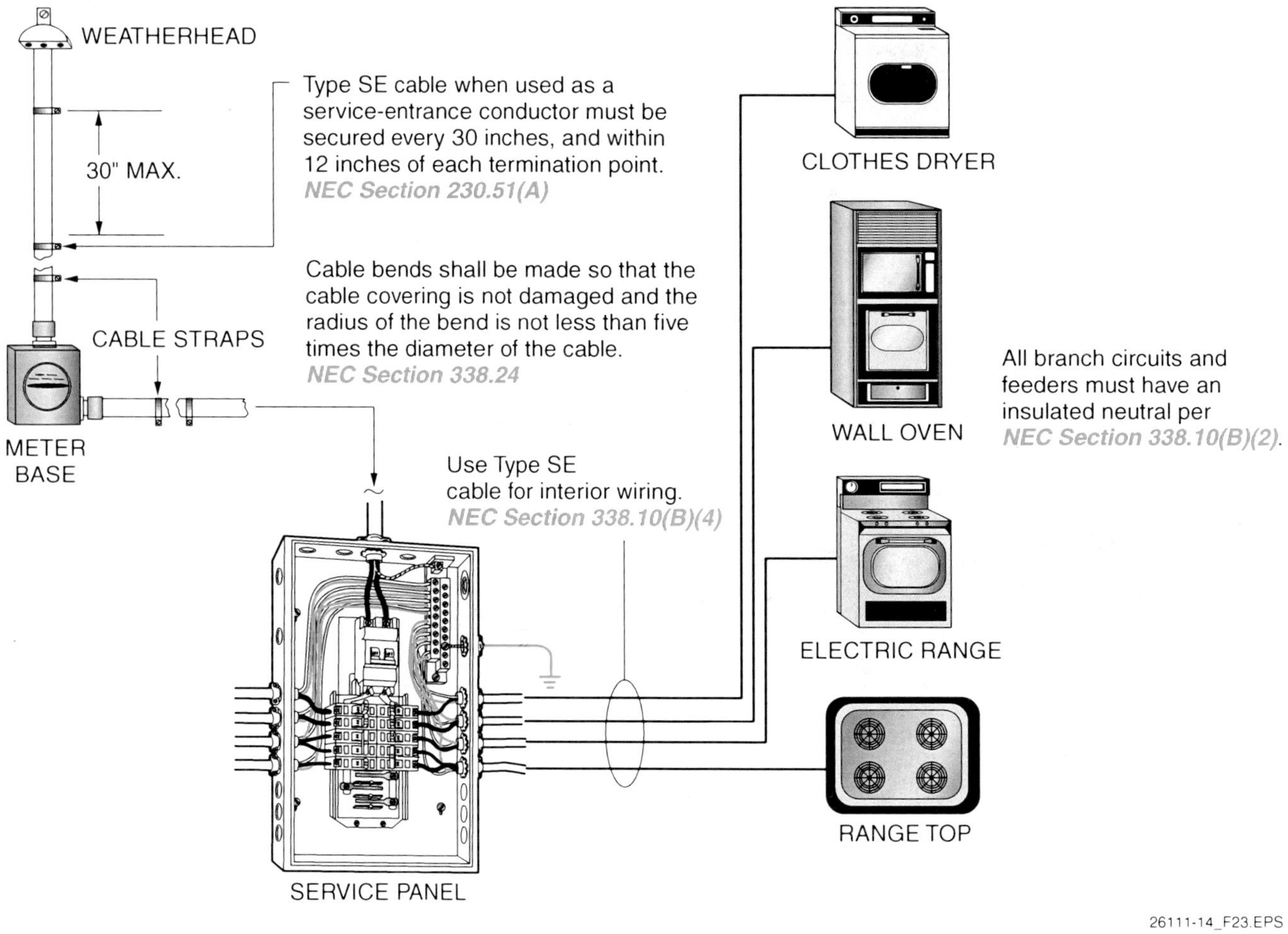

WEATHERHEAD

30" MAX.

CABLE STRAPS

METER BASE

Type SE cable when used as a service-entrance conductor must be secured every 30 inches, and within 12 inches of each termination point. *NEC Section 230.51(A)*

Cable bends shall be made so that the cable covering is not damaged and the radius of the bend is not less than five times the diameter of the cable. *NEC Section 338.24*

Use Type SE cable for interior wiring. *NEC Section 338.10(B)(4)*

All branch circuits and feeders must have an insulated neutral per *NEC Section 338.10(B)(2).*

CLOTHES DRYER

WALL OVEN

ELECTRIC RANGE

RANGE TOP

SERVICE PANEL

26111-14_F23.EPS

Figure 23 NEC® sections governing Type SE cable.

9.0.0 Equipment Grounding System

NEC Article 250, Part IV generally requires that all metallic enclosures, raceways, and cable armor be grounded. The exceptions in *NEC Sections 250.80 and 250.86* allow metal enclosures or short sections of raceways that are used to provide support or physical protection to be ungrounded under specific conditions.

NEC Article 250, Part VI covers equipment grounding and equipment grounding conductors. This section generally requires that the exposed noncurrent-carrying metal parts of fixed equipment likely to become energized be grounded under the following conditions:

- Where within 8' vertically or 5' horizontally of ground or grounded metal objects and subject to contact by occupants or others
- Where located in wet or damp locations
- Where in electrical contact with metal
- Where in hazardous (classified) locations as covered by *NEC Articles 500 through 517*
- Where supplied by a metal-clad, metal-sheathed, or metal raceway, or other wiring method that provides an equipment ground
- Where equipment operates with any terminal at over 150V to ground

Specific equipment that is required to be grounded regardless of the voltage is listed in *NEC Section 250.112* and includes equipment such as motors, motor controllers, and light fixtures. Types of cord- and plug-connected equipment in dwelling units that are required to be grounded are found in *NEC Section 250.114* and include equipment such as refrigerators, freezers, air conditioners, information technology equipment (computers), clothes washers, clothes dryers, and dishwashing machines.

The types of equipment grounding conductors that are acceptable to be used are found in *NEC Section 250.118.* Note that among the list of wiring methods approved for use as equipment grounding conductors, both flexible metal conduit (FMC) and liquidtight flexible metal conduit (LFMC) are permitted to be used. Listed FMC is permitted to be used as an equipment grounding conductor only when the following conditions are met:

- The conduit is terminated in fittings listed for grounding.
- The circuit conductors contained in the conduit are protected by overcurrent devices rated at 20A or less.
- The combined length of FMC, FMT, and LFMC in the same ground return path does not exceed 6'.
- The conduit is not installed for flexibility.

Type LFMC is also used in dwelling units and has slightly different requirements when used as an equipment grounding conductor:

- The conduit is terminated in fittings listed for grounding.
- For trade sizes ⅜ through ½, the circuit conductors contained in the conduit are protected by overcurrent devices rated at 20A or less.
- For trade sizes ¾ through 1¼, the circuit conductors contained in the conduit are protected by overcurrent devices rated at 60A or less and there is no FMC, FMT, or LFMC in trade sizes ⅜ through ½ in the grounding path.
- The combined length of FMC, FMT, and LFMC in the same ground return path does not exceed 6'.
- The conduit is not used for flexibility.

Where external bonding jumpers are used to provide the continuity of the fault current path, *NEC Section 250.102(E)(2)* limits the length to not more than 6', except at outside pole locations for the purposes of bonding or grounding the isolated sections of metal raceways or elbows installed in exposed risers at those pole locations. When installing an equipment grounding conductor in a raceway, *NEC Table 250.122* is used to determine the size of the equipment grounding conductor. It is permitted to install one equipment grounding conductor in a raceway that has several circuits. In that case, the size of the equipment grounding conductor is based on the rating of the largest overcurrent device protecting the circuits contained in the raceway.

NEC Section 250.148 requires that where circuit conductors are spliced within a box, or terminated on equipment within or supported by a box, separate equipment grounding conductors associated with those circuit conductors shall be spliced or joined within the box or to the box with devices suitable for the use. *Figure 24* shows several types of fittings that are suitable for this purpose.

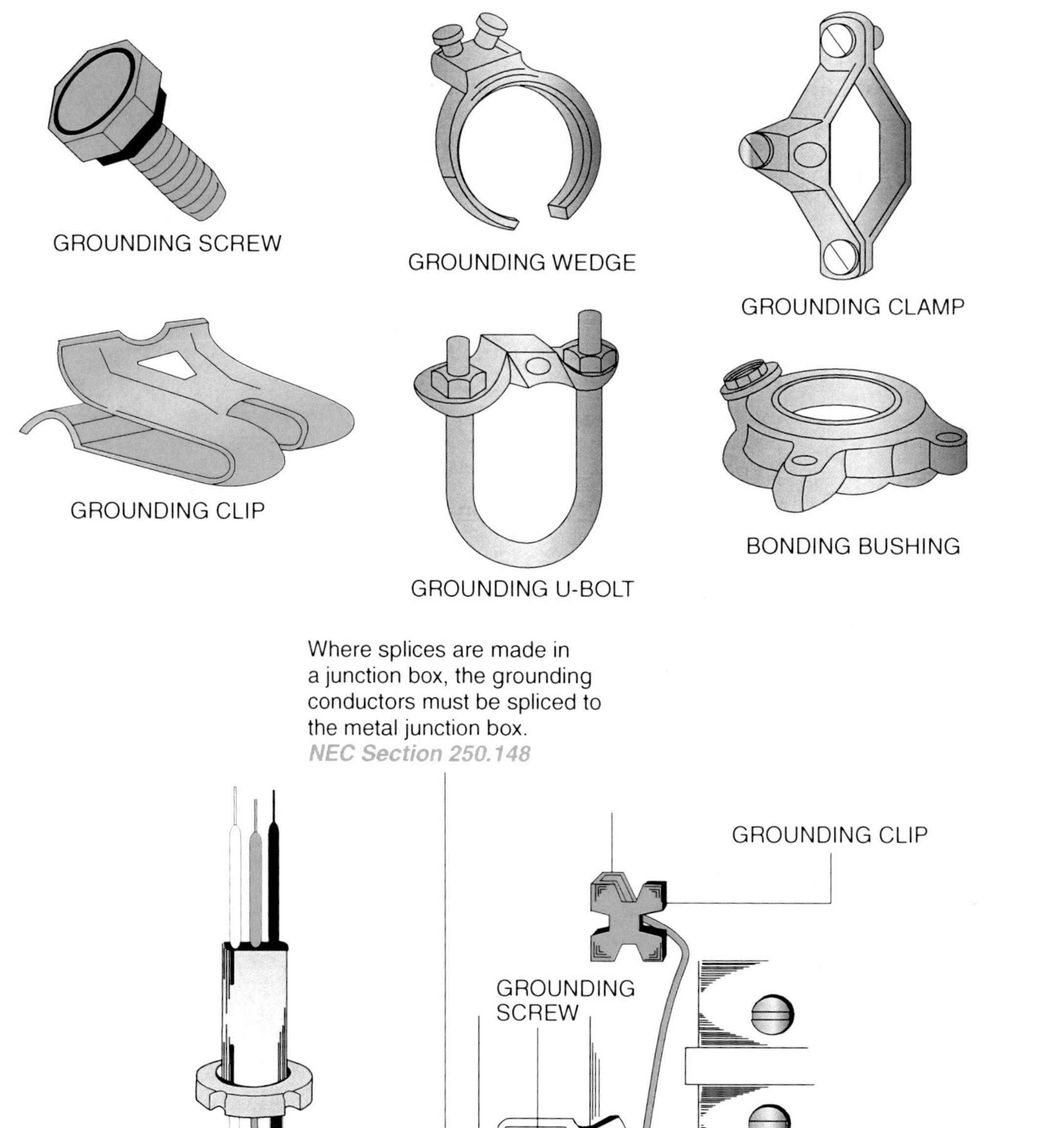

Figure 24 Equipment grounding methods.

10.0.0 Branch Circuit Layout for Power

The point at which electrical equipment is connected to the wiring system is commonly called an outlet. There are many classifications of outlets: lighting, receptacle, motor, appliance, and so forth. This section, however, deals with the power outlets normally found in residential electrical wiring systems.

When viewing an electrical drawing, outlets are indicated by symbols (usually a small circle with appropriate markings to indicate the type of outlet). The most common symbols for receptacles are shown in *Figure 25*.

10.1.0 Branch Circuits and Feeders

The conductors that extend from the panelboard to the various outlets are called branch circuits and are defined by the *NEC*® as the point of a wiring system that extends beyond the final overcurrent device protecting the circuit. See *Figure 26*.

A feeder consists of all conductors between the service equipment and the final overcurrent device. See *Figure 27*.

In general, the size of the branch circuit conductors varies depending upon the load requirements of the electrically operated equipment connected to the outlet. For residential use, most branch circuits consist of either No. 14 AWG, No. 12 AWG, No. 10 AWG, or No. 8 AWG conductors.

The basic branch circuit requires two wires or conductors to provide a continuous path for the flow of electric current, plus a third wire for equipment grounding. The usual receptacle branch circuit operates at 120V.

Fractional horsepower motors and small electric heaters usually operate at 120V and are connected to 120V branch circuits by means of a receptacle, junction box, or direct connection.

With the exception of very large residences and tract-development houses, the size of the average residential electrical system of the past has not been large enough to justify the expense of preparing complete electrical working drawings and specifications. Such electrical systems were usually laid out by the architect in the form of a sketchy outlet arrangement or else laid out by the electrician on the job, often only as the work progressed. However, many technical developments in residential electrical use—such as electric heat

Think About It

Grounding Devices

Identify each of the devices pictured here and explain their function(s). Which of these devices would not be used for equipment grounding?

26111-14_SA04.EPS

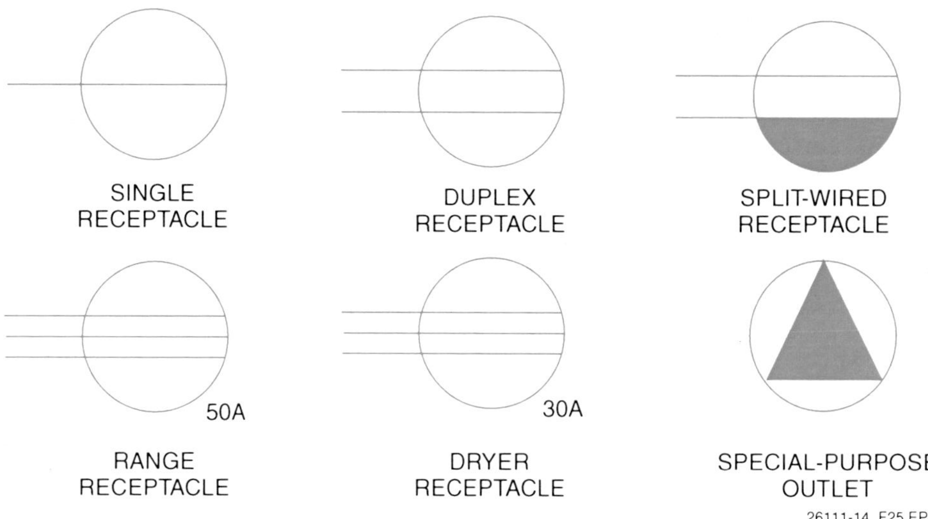

Figure 25 Typical outlet symbols appearing in electrical drawings.

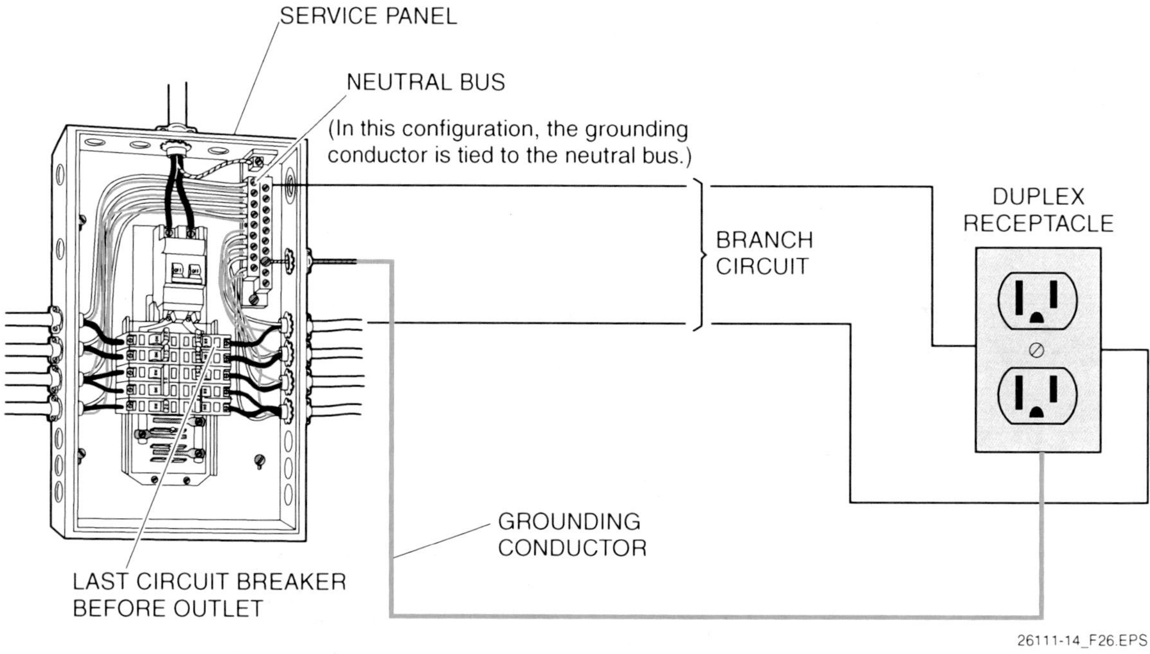

Figure 26 Components of a duplex receptacle branch circuit.

with sophisticated control wiring, increased use of electrical appliances, various electronic alarm systems, new lighting techniques, and the need for energy conservation techniques—have greatly expanded the demand and extended the complexity of today's residential electrical systems.

Each year, the number of homes with electrical systems designed by consulting engineering firms increases. Such homes are provided with complete electrical working drawings and specifications, similar to those frequently provided for commercial and industrial projects. Still, these are more the exception than the rule. Most residential projects will not have a complete set of drawings.

Circuit layout is provided on the drawings to follow for several reasons:

- They provide a visual layout of house wiring circuitry.
- They provide a sample of electrical residential drawings that are prepared by consulting engineering firms, although the number may still be limited.
- They introduce the method of showing electrical systems on working drawings to provide a foundation for tackling advanced electrical systems.

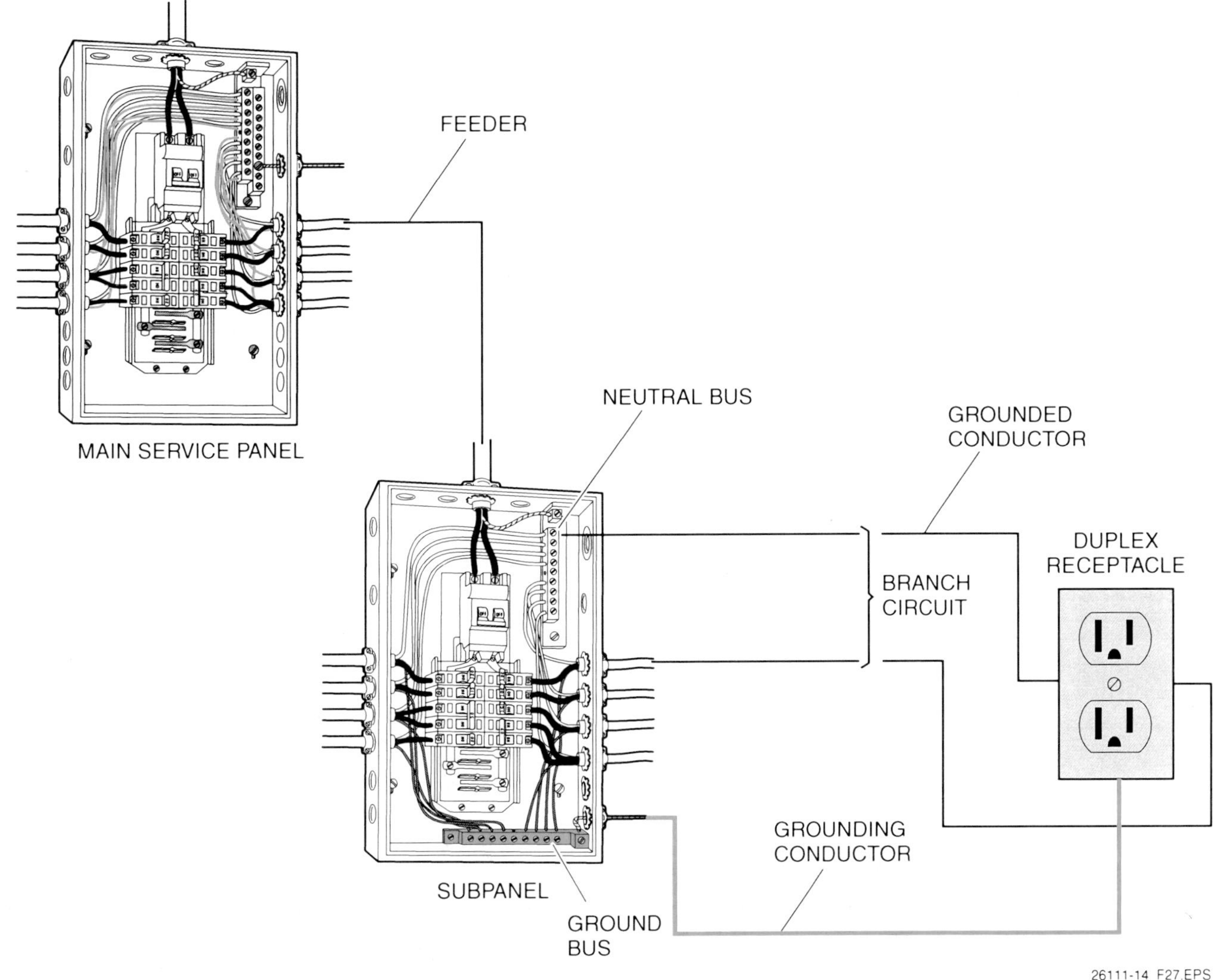

Figure 27 A feeder being used to feed a subpanel from the main service panel.

Branch circuits are shown on electrical drawings by means of a single line drawn from the panelboard (or by homerun arrowheads indicating that the circuit goes to the panelboard) to the outlet or from outlet to outlet where there is more than one outlet on the circuit.

The lines indicating branch circuits can be solid to show that the conductors are to be run concealed in the ceiling or wall; dashed to show that the conductors are to be run in the floor or ceiling below; or dotted to show that the wiring is to be run exposed. *Figure 28* shows examples of these three types of branch circuit lines.

In *Figure 28*, No. 12 indicates the wire size. The slash marks shown through the circuits in *Figure 28* indicate the number of current-carrying conductors in the circuit. Although two slash marks are shown, in actual practice, a branch circuit containing only two conductors usually contains no slash marks; that is, any circuit with no slash marks is assumed to have two conductors. However, three or more conductors are always indicated on electrical working drawings—either by slash marks for each conductor, or else by a note.

Never assume that you know the meaning of any electrical symbol. Although great efforts have been made in recent years to standardize drawing symbols, architects, consulting engineers, and electrical drafters still modify existing symbols or devise new ones to meet their own needs. Always consult the symbol list or legend on electrical working drawings for an exact interpretation of the symbols used.

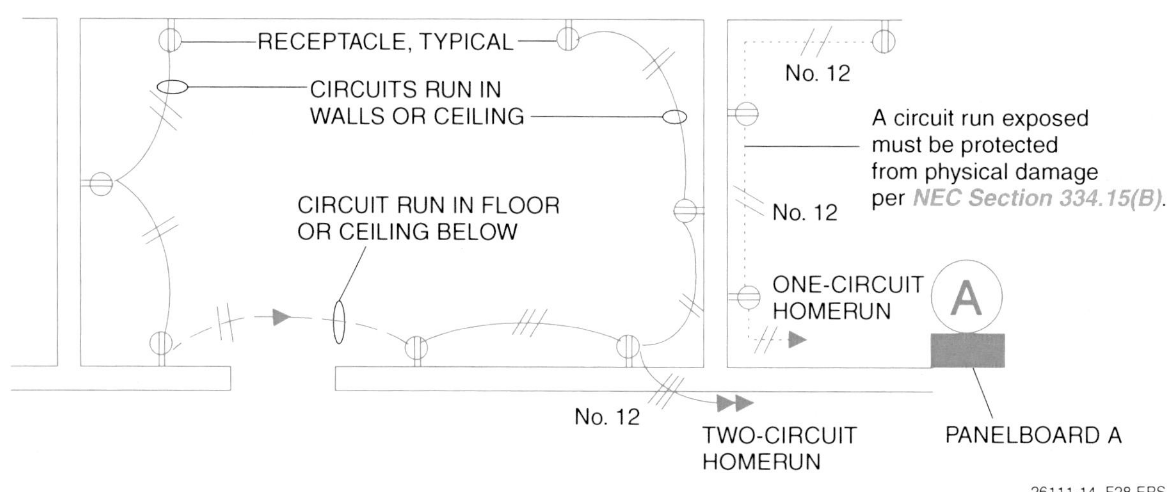

Figure 28 Types of branch circuit lines shown on electrical working drawings.

10.2.0 Locating Receptacles

NEC Section 210.52 states the minimum requirements for the location of receptacles in dwelling units. It specifies that in each kitchen, family room, and dining room, receptacle outlets shall be installed so that no point along the floor line in any wall space is more than 6', measured horizontally, from an outlet in that space, including any wall space 2' or more in width and the wall space occupied by fixed panels in exterior walls, but excluding sliding panels. Receptacle outlets shall, insofar as practicable, be spaced equal distances apart. Receptacle outlets in floors shall not be counted as part of the required number of receptacle outlets unless located within 18" of the wall.

The *NEC®* defines wall space as a wall that is unbroken along the floor line by doorways, fireplaces, or similar openings. Each wall space that is two feet or more in width must be treated individually and separately from other wall spaces within the room.

The purpose of *NEC Section 210.52* is to minimize the use of cords across doorways, fireplaces, and similar openings.

With this *NEC®* requirement in mind, outlets for our sample residence will be laid out (see *Figure 29*). In laying out these receptacle outlets, the floor line of the wall is measured (also around corners), but not across doorways, fireplaces, passageways, or other spaces where a flexible cord extended across the space would be unsuitable.

In general, duplex receptacle outlets must be no more than 12' apart. When spaced in this manner, a 6' extension cord will reach a receptacle from any point along the wall line.

Note that at no point along the wall line are any receptacles more than 12' apart or more than six feet from any door or room opening. Where practical, no more than eight receptacles are connected to one circuit. However, this is just a design consideration since general-purpose receptacles in dwelling units are sized on the basis of 3VA per square foot of dwelling space. A 15A branch circuit is rated at 1,800VA (15A × 120V = 1,800VA) and the *NEC®* requires that for every 600 square feet (1,800VA ÷ 3VA/sq. ft. = 600 sq. ft.), a circuit to supply lighting and receptacles must be installed. Always check with the local authorities about the requirements for the number of branch circuits in a dwelling.

The utility room has at least one receptacle for the laundry on a separate circuit in order to comply with *NEC Sections 210.11(C)(2) and 210.52(F).*

One duplex receptacle is located in the vestibule for cleaning purposes, such as feeding a portable vacuum cleaner or similar appliance. It is connected to the living room circuit. An additional duplex receptacle is required per *NEC Section 210.52(H)* in hallways of 10' or more.

Although this is not shown in the figure, the living room outlets could be split-wired (the lower half of each duplex receptacle is energized all the time, while the upper half can be switched on or off). The reason for this is that a great deal of the illumination for this area will be provided by portable table lamps, and the split-wired receptacles provide a means to control these lamps from several locations, such as at each entry to the living room, if desired. Split receptacles are discussed in more detail in the next section.

To comply with *NEC Sections 210.11(C)(1) and 210.52(B),* the kitchen receptacles are laid out as follows. In addition to the number of branch circuits determined previously, two or more 20A small appliance branch circuits must be provided

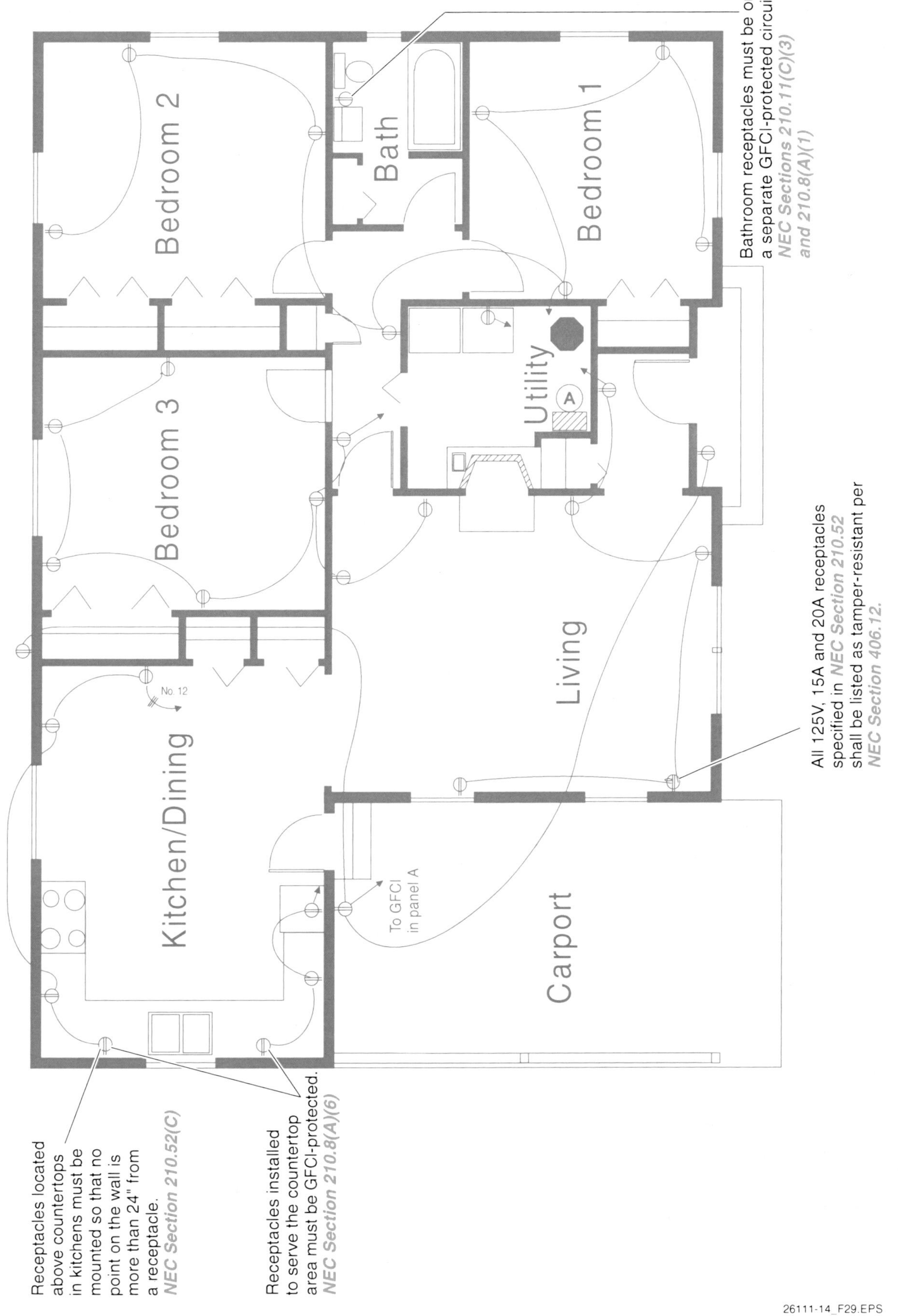
Bathroom receptacles must be on a separate GFCI-protected circuit. NEC Sections 210.11(C)(3) and 210.8(A)(1)
Bedroom 2
Bath
Bedroom 1
Utility
A
Bedroom 3
Living
Kitchen/Dining
No. 12
To GFCI in panel A
Carport
All 125V, 15A and 20A receptacles specified in NEC Section 210.52 shall be listed as tamper-resistant per NEC Section 406.12.
Receptacles located above countertops in kitchens must be mounted so that no point on the wall is more than 24" from a receptacle. NEC Section 210.52(C)
Receptacles installed to serve the countertop area must be GFCI-protected. NEC Section 210.8(A)(6)
26111-14_F29.EPS

Figure 29 Floor plan of the sample residence.

to serve all receptacle outlets (including refrigeration equipment) in the kitchen, pantry, breakfast room, dining room, or similar area of the house. Such circuits, whether two or more are used, must have no other outlets connected to them. All receptacles serving a kitchen countertop require GFCI protection. No small appliance branch circuit shall serve more than one kitchen.

To comply with *NEC Sections 210.11(C)(3) and 210.52(D),* bathroom receptacle(s) must be on a separate branch circuit supplying only bathroom receptacles or on a circuit supplying a single bathroom with no loads other than that bathroom. All receptacles located within a bathroom require GFCI protection. GFCI protection is also required on garage and exterior receptacles. All other branch circuits that supply the lighting and general-purpose receptacles in dwelling units must have arc fault circuit interrupter protection to comply with *NEC Section 210.12.*

10.3.0 Split-Wired Duplex Receptacles

In modern residential construction, it is common to have duplex wall receptacles that have one of the outlets wired as a standard duplex outlet (hot all the time) and the other half controlled by a wall switch. This allows table or floor lamps to be controlled by a wall switch and leaves the other outlet available for items that are not to be switched. This wiring method is commonly referred to as a split receptacle. Note that switched receptacles are installed to provide lighting. Dimmer switches are not permitted to be used per *NEC Section 404.14(E).*

Most duplex 15A and 20A receptacles are provided with a breakoff tab that permits each of the two receptacle outlets to be supplied from a different source or polarity. For example, one outlet would be supplied from the hot leg of a series of outlets and the other outlet supplied from the switch leg of a light switch. A diagram of this arrangement is shown in *Figure 30.*

Another application of split receptacles is shown in *Figure 31.* In this example, one outlet connected from a double-pole circuit breaker supplies 240V for an appliance such as a window air conditioning unit, while the other outlet is connected from one pole of the double-pole circuit breaker and the other side is connected to the neutral or grounded conductor to supply 120V for an appliance such as a lamp. *NEC Section 210.4(B)* requires the use of a two-pole breaker when two circuits are connected to one duplex receptacle so that all ungrounded conductors of the circuit are disconnected simultaneously. This circuit and the split receptacle mentioned above are both considered multiwire branch circuits.

10.4.0 Multiwire Branch Circuits

NEC Article 100 defines a multiwire branch circuit as "two or more ungrounded conductors having a potential difference between them, and a grounded conductor having equal potential

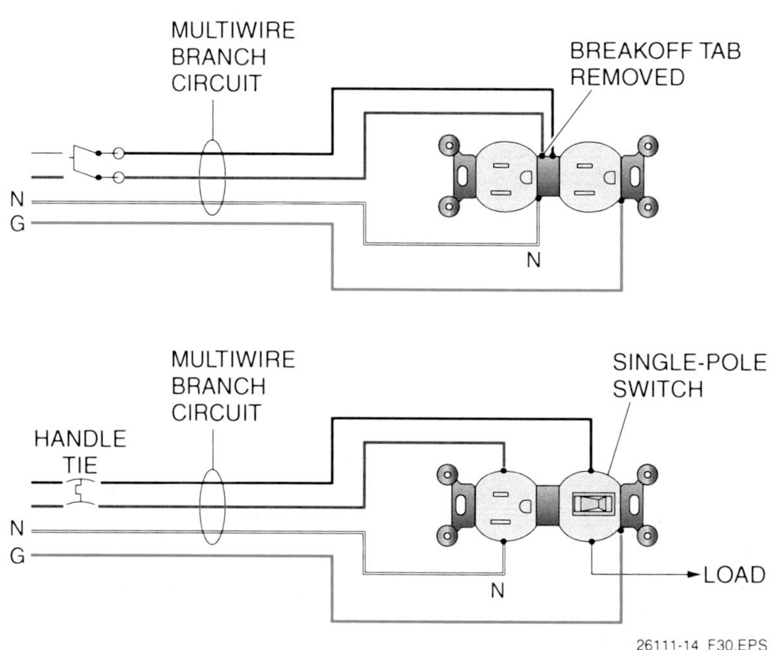

Figure 30 Two 120V receptacle outlets supplied from different sources.

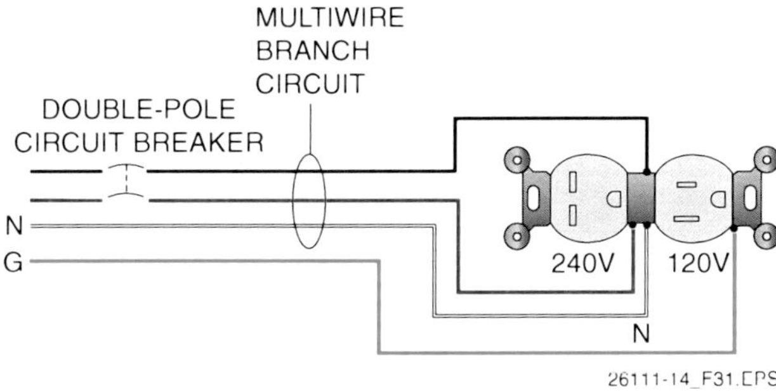

Figure 31 Combination receptacle.

difference between it and each ungrounded conductor of the circuit and that is connected to the neutral conductor of the system."

10.5.0 240-Volt Circuits

The electric range, clothes dryer, and water heater in the sample residence all operate at 240VAC. Each will be fed by a separate circuit and connected to a two-pole circuit breaker of the appropriate rating in the panelboard. To determine the conductor size and overcurrent protection for the range, proceed as follows:

Step 1 Find the nameplate rating of the electric range. This has previously been determined to be 12kVA.

Step 2 Refer to *NEC Table 220.55.* Since Column A of this table applies to ranges rated at 12kVA (12kW) and under, this will be the column to use in this example.

Step 3 Under the Number of Appliances column, locate the appropriate number of appliances (one in this case), and find the maximum demand given for it in Column A. Column A states that the circuit should be sized for 8kVA (not the nameplate rating of 12kVA).

Step 4 Calculate the required conductor ampacity as follows:

$$\frac{8{,}000\text{VA}}{240\text{V}} = 33.33\text{A}$$

The minimum branch circuit must be rated at 40A since common residential circuit breakers are rated in steps of 15A, 20A, 30A, 40A, and so forth. A 30A circuit breaker is too small, so a 40A circuit breaker is selected. The conductors must have a current-carrying capacity that is equal to or greater than the overcurrent protection. Therefore, No. 8 AWG conductors will be used.

If a cooktop and wall oven were used instead of the electric range, the circuit would be sized similarly. The *NEC*® specifies that a branch circuit for a counter-mounted cooking unit and not more than two wall-mounted ovens, all supplied from a single branch circuit and located in the same room, is computed by adding the nameplate ratings of the individual appliances and treating this total as equivalent to one range. Therefore, two appliances of 6kVA each may be treated as a single range with a 12kVA nameplate rating.

Figure 32 shows how the electric range circuit may appear on an electrical drawing. The connection may be made directly to the range junction box, but more often a 50A range receptacle is mounted at the range location and a range cord-and-plug set is used to make the connection. This facilitates moving the appliance later for maintenance or cleaning.

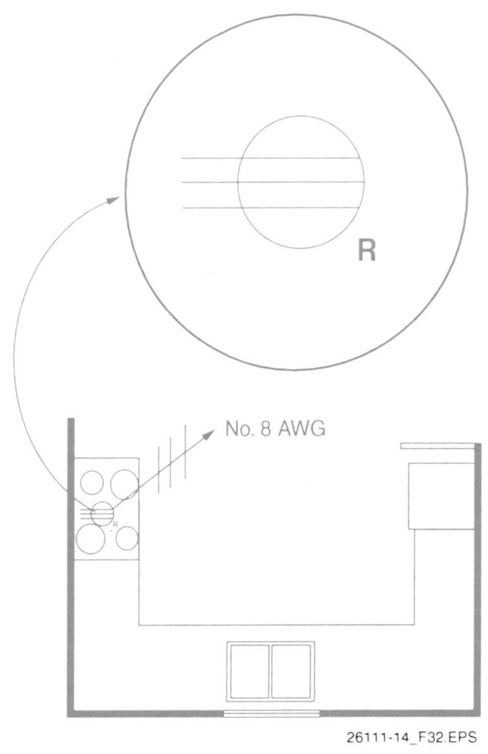

Figure 32 Range circuit shown on an electrical drawing.

Think About It

240V Circuits

Calculate the ampacity required for a kitchen range with an 8kW rating. Now design the practical wiring in a labeled diagram. How will the wires be connected at the service panel and at the appliance? How will the cable be installed?

Figure 33 shows several types of receptacle configurations used in residential wiring applications. You will eventually recognize these configurations at a glance.

The branch circuit for the water heater in the sample residence must be sized for its full capacity because there is no diversity or demand factor for this appliance. Since the nameplate rating on the water heater indicates two heating elements of 4,500W each, the first inclination would be to size the circuit for a total load of 9,000W (volt-amperes). However, only one of the two elements operates at a time. See *Figure 34*. Note that each element is controlled by a separate thermostat. The lower element becomes energized when the thermostat calls for heat, and at the same time, the thermostat opens a set of contacts to prevent the upper element from operating. When the lower element's thermostat is satisfied, the lower contacts open, and at the same time, the thermostat closes the contacts for the upper element to become energized to maintain the water temperature.

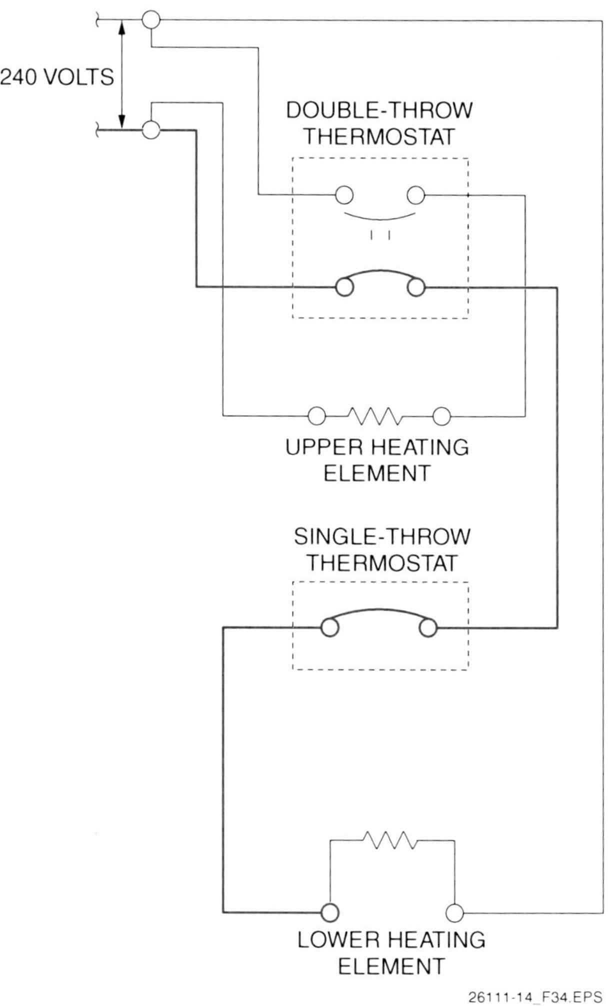

Figure 34 Wiring diagram of water heater controls.

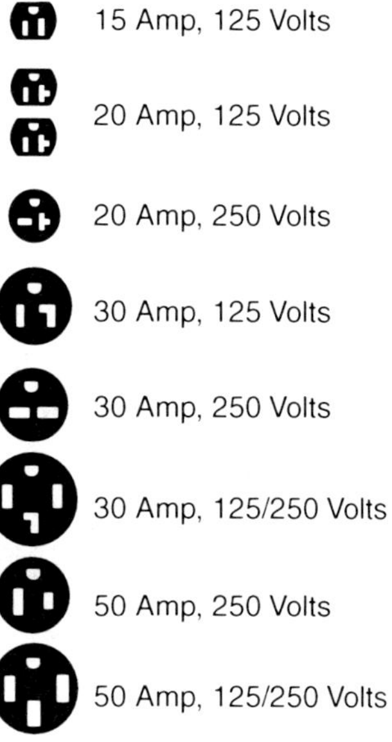

Figure 33 Residential receptacle configurations.

With this information in hand, the circuit for the water heater may be sized as follows:

$$\frac{4{,}500\text{VA}}{240\text{V}} = 18.75\text{A} \times 1.25 = 23.44\text{A}$$

NEC Section 422.13 requires that the branch circuits that supply storage type water heaters having a capacity of 120 gallons or less be rated not less than 125% of the nameplate rating of the water heater. Our calculation shows this to be not less than 23A. Normally, this would require a maximum rating for the branch circuit to be not more than 25A. (See standard ratings of overcurrent devices in *NEC Section 240.6.*) However, *NEC Section 422.11(E)(3)* permits a single nonmotor-operated appliance to be protected

by overcurrent devices rated up to 150% of the nameplate rating of the appliance. In this case, 4,500VA ÷ 240V = 18.75A × 150% = 28.125A. Since the next standard rating is 30A, the water heater will be wired with No. 10 AWG conductors protected by a 30A overcurrent device.

The *NEC*® specifies that electric clothes dryers must be rated at 5kVA or the nameplate rating, whichever is greater. In this case, the dryer is rated at 5.5kVA, and the conductor current-carrying capacity is calculated as follows:

$$\frac{5{,}500\text{VA}}{240\text{V}} = 22.92\text{A}$$

A three-wire, 30A circuit will be provided (No. 10 AWG wire). It is protected by a 30A circuit breaker. The dryer may be connected directly, but a 30A dryer receptacle is normally provided for the same reasons as mentioned for the electric range.

Large appliance outlets rated at 240V are frequently shown on electrical drawings using lines and symbols to indicate the outlets and circuits. In some cases, no drawings are provided.

11.0.0 Branch Circuit Layout for Lighting

A simple lighting branch circuit requires two conductors to provide a continuous path for current flow. The usual lighting branch circuit operates at 120V; the white (grounded) circuit conductor is therefore connected to the neutral bus in the panelboard, while the black (ungrounded) circuit conductor is connected to an overcurrent protection device.

Lighting branch circuits and outlets are shown on electrical drawings by means of lines and symbols; that is, a single line is drawn from outlet to outlet and then terminated with an arrowhead to indicate a homerun to the panelboard. Several methods are used to indicate the number and size of conductors, but the most common is to indicate the number of conductors in the circuit by using slash marks through the circuit lines and then indicate the wire size by a notation adjacent to these slash marks. For example, two slash marks indicate two conductors; three slash marks indicate three conductors. Some electrical designers omit slash marks for two-conductor circuits. In this case, the conductor size is usually indicated in the symbol list or legend.

The circuits used to feed residential lighting must conform to standards established by the *NEC*® as well as by local and state ordinances. Most of the lighting circuits should be calculated to include the total load, although at times this is not possible because the electrician cannot be certain of the exact wattage that might be used by the homeowner. For example, an electrician may install four porcelain lampholders for the unfinished basement area, each to contain one 100-watt (100W) incandescent lamp. However, the homeowners may eventually replace the original lamps with others rated at 150W or even 200W. Thus, if the electrician initially loads the lighting circuit to full capacity, the circuit will probably become overloaded in the future.

It is recommended that no residential branch circuit be loaded to more than 80% of its rated capacity. Since most circuits used for lighting are rated at 15A, the total ampacity (in volt-amperes) for the circuit is as follows:

$$15\text{A} \times 120\text{V} = 1{,}800\text{VA}$$

Therefore, if the circuit is to be loaded to only 80% of its rated capacity, the maximum initial connected load should be no more than 1,440VA.

Figure 35 shows one possible lighting arrangement for the sample residence. All lighting fixtures are shown in their approximate physical location as they should be installed.

Electrical symbols are used to show the fixture types. Switches and lighting branch circuits are also shown by appropriate lines and symbols. The meanings of the symbols used on this drawing are explained in the symbol list in *Figure 36*.

In actual practice, the location of lighting fixtures (luminaires) and their related switches will probably be the extent of the information shown on working drawings. The circuits shown in *Figure 35* are meant to illustrate how lighting circuits are routed, not to imply that such drawings are typical for residential construction. If fixtures are used in a closet, they must meet the requirements of *NEC Section 410.16*.

A box used at fan outlets is not permitted to be used as the sole support for ceiling (paddle) fans, unless it is listed for the application as the sole means of support. Where a ceiling fan does not exceed 70 pounds in weight, it is permitted to be supported by outlet boxes listed and identified for such use. Boxes designed to support more than 35 pounds must be marked with the maximum weight to be supported. See *NEC Section 314.27(C)*. These boxes must be rigidly supported from a structural member of the building. *NEC Section 314.27(C)* also requires that a ceiling-fan rated box be used if a spare conductor is installed to the box and the location of the box is acceptable for a fan installation.

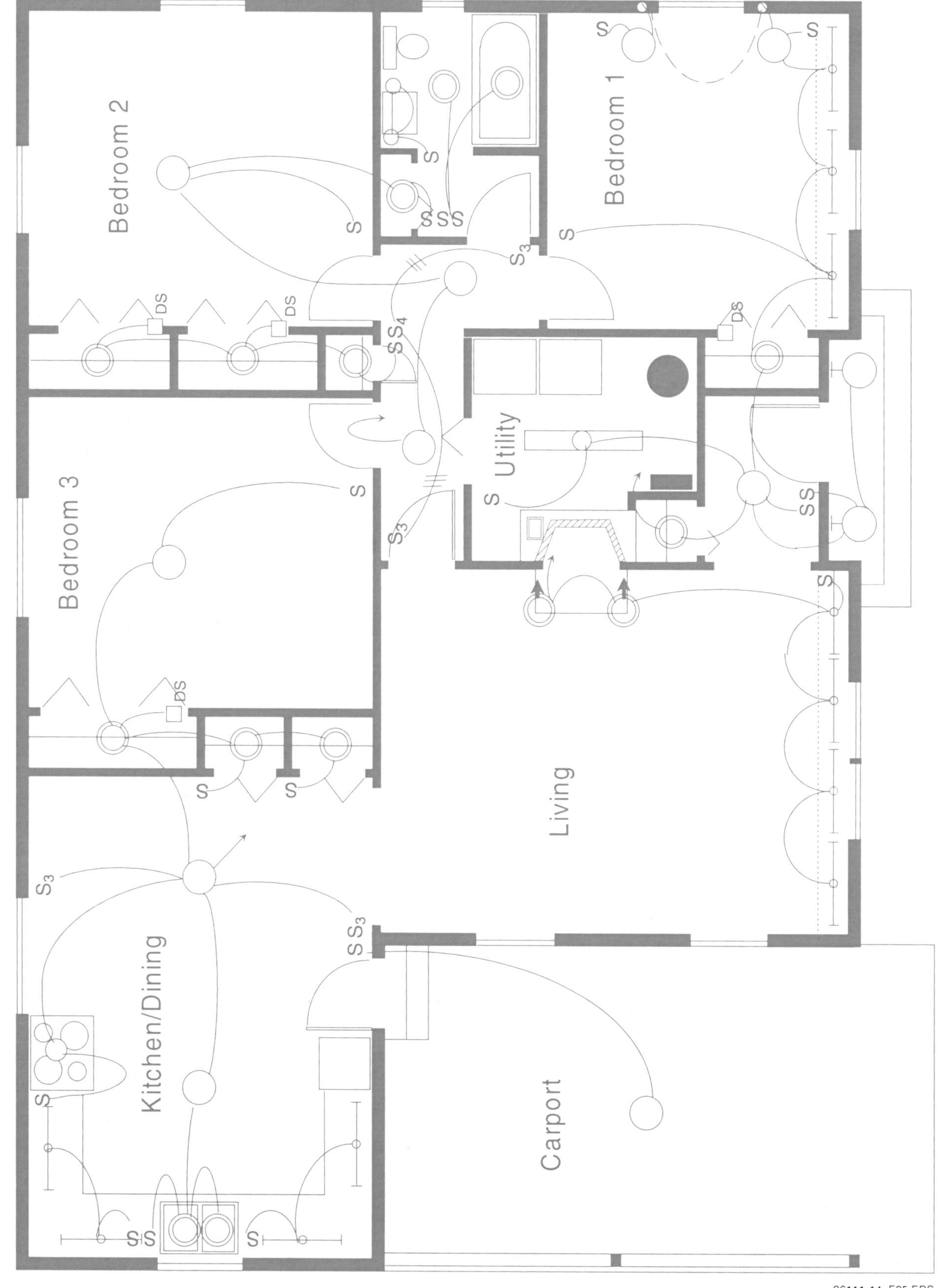

Figure 35 Lighting layout of the sample residence.

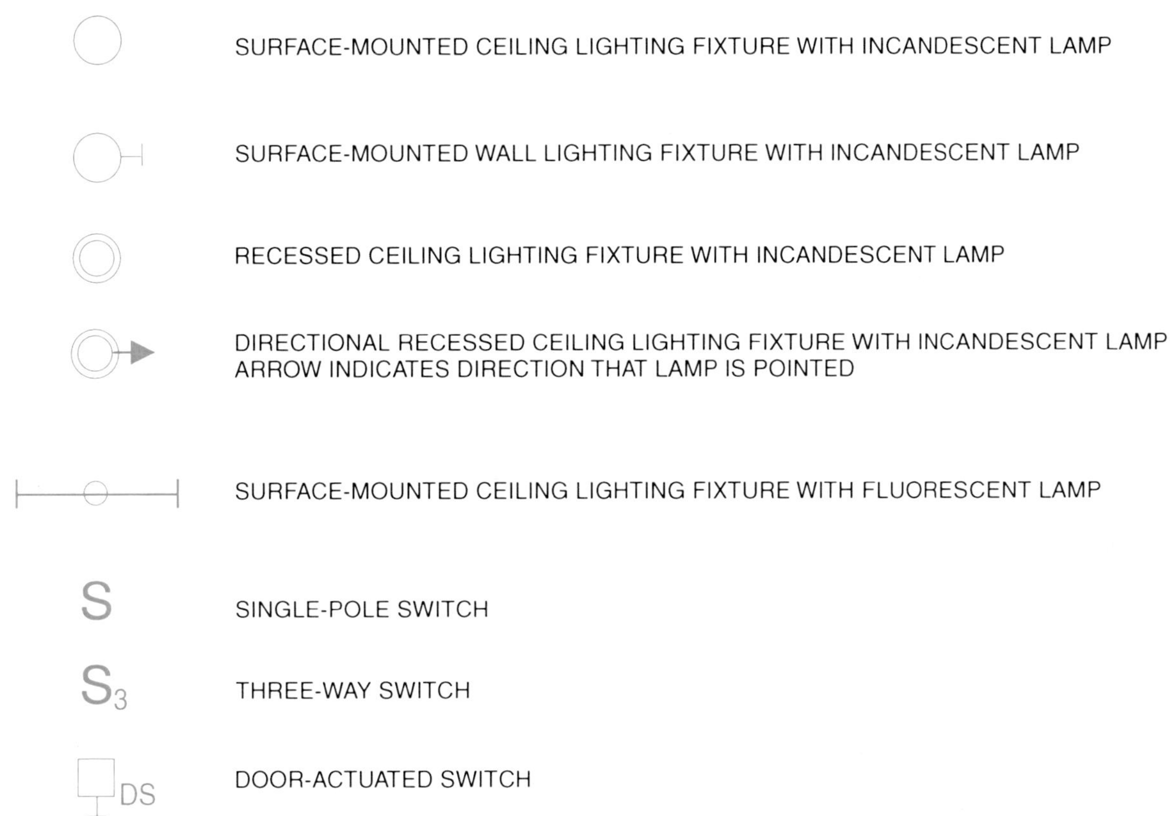

Figure 36 Symbols.

12.0.0 Outlet Boxes

Electricians installing residential electrical systems must be familiar with outlet box capacities, means of supporting outlet boxes, and other requirements of the *NEC*®. Boxes were discussed in detail in an earlier module, but a general review of the rules and necessary calculations is provided here.

The maximum numbers of conductors of the same size permitted in standard outlet boxes are listed in *NEC Table 314.16(A)*. These figures apply where no fittings or devices such as fixture studs, cable clamps, switches, or receptacles are contained in the box and where no grounding conductors are part of the wiring within the box. Obviously, in all modern residential wiring systems there will be one or more of these items contained in every outlet box installed. Therefore, where one or more of the above-mentioned items are present, the total number of conductors will be less than that shown in the table. Also, if the box contains a looped, unbroken conductor 12" or more in length, it must be counted twice.

For example, a deduction of two conductors must be made for each strap containing a wiring device entering the box (based on the largest size conductor connected to the device) such as a switch or duplex receptacle; a further deduction of one conductor must be made for one or more equipment grounding conductors entering the box (based on the largest size grounding conductor). For instance, a 3" × 2" × 2¾" box is listed in the table as containing a maximum of six No. 12 wires. If the box contains cable clamps and a duplex receptacle, three wires will have to be deducted from the total of six, providing for only three No. 12 wires. If a ground wire is used, which is always the case in residential wiring, only two No. 12 wires may be used.

For example, to size a metallic outlet box for two No. 12 AWG conductors with a ground wire, cable clamp, and receptacle, proceed as follows:

Step 1 Calculate the total number of conductors and equivalents [*NEC Section 314.16(B)*]. One ground wire plus one cable clamp plus one receptacle (two wires) plus two No. 12 conductors equals a total of six No. 12 conductors.

Step 2 Determine the amount of space required for each conductor. *NEC Table 314.16(B)* gives the box volume required for each conductor. No. 12 AWG equals 2.25 cubic inches.

Step 3 Calculate the outlet box space required by multiplying the number of cubic inches required for each conductor by the total number of conductors:

$$6 \times 2.25 = 13.5 \text{ cubic inches}$$

Step 4 Once you have determined the required box capacity, again refer to *NEC Table 314.16(A)* and note that a 3" × 2" × 2¾" box comes closest to our requirements. This box is rated for 14 cubic inches.

Now, size the box for two additional conductors. Where four No. 12 conductors enter the box with two ground wires, only the two additional No. 12 conductors must be added to our previous count for a total of 8 conductors (6 + 2 = 8). Remember, any number of ground wires in a box counts as only one conductor; any number of cable clamps also counts as only one conductor. Therefore, the box size required for use with two additional No. 12 conductors may be calculated as follows:

$$8 \times 2.25 = 18 \text{ cubic inches}$$

Again, refer to *NEC Table 314.16(A)* and note that a 3" × 2" × 3½" device box with a rated capacity of 18.0 cubic inches is the closest device box that meets *NEC®* requirements. An alternative is to use a 4" × 1¼" square box with a single-gang plaster ring, as shown in *Figure 37*. This box also has a capacity of 18.0 cubic inches.

Other box sizes are calculated in a similar fashion. When sizing boxes for different size conductors, remember that the box capacity varies as shown in *NEC Table 314.16(B)*.

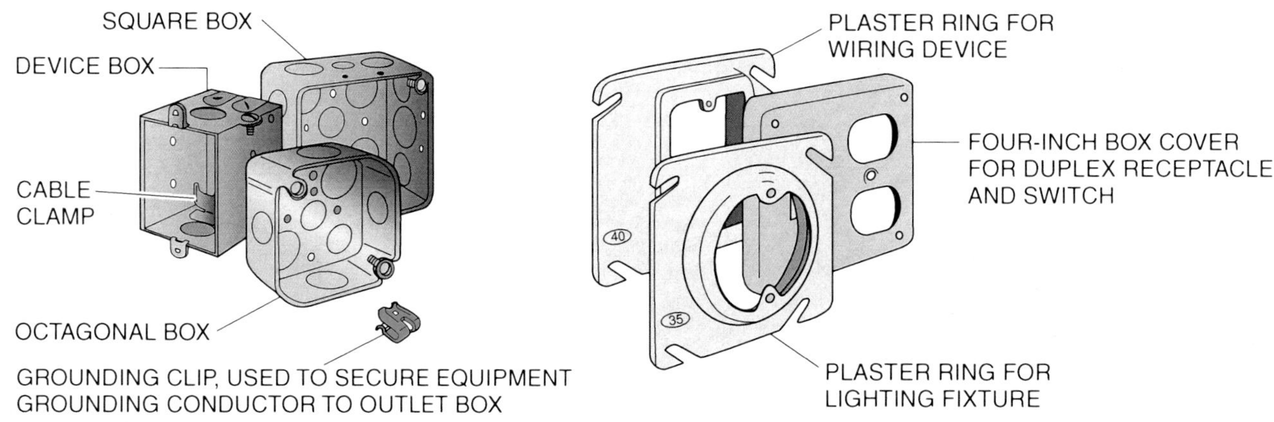

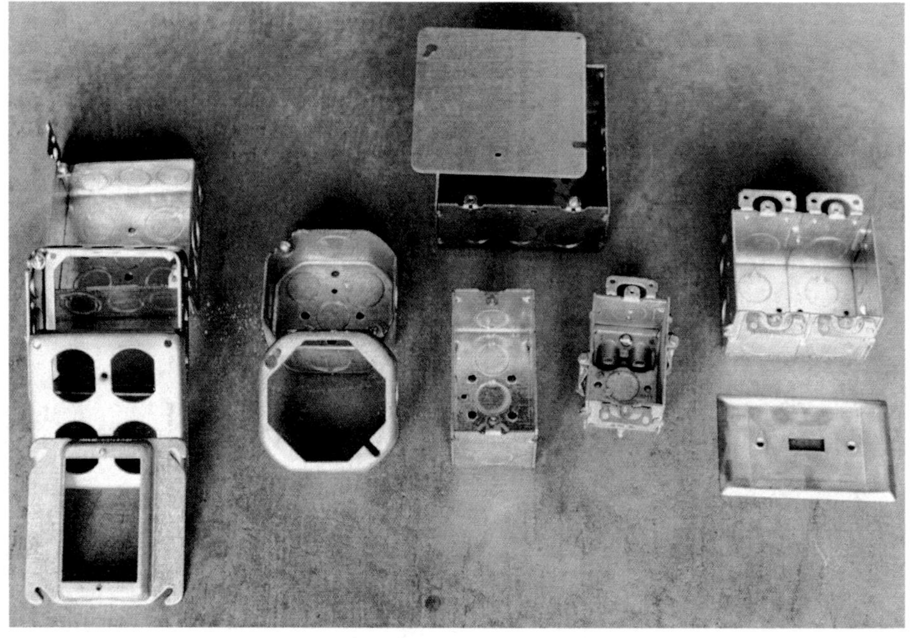

26111-14_F37B.EPS

Figure 37 Typical metallic outlet boxes with extension (plaster) rings.

On Site

Calculating Conductors

In a 4" × 4" × 1½" metal box, one 14/3 cable with ground feeds three 14/2 cables with ground wires. The red wire of the 14/3 cable feeds a receptacle, and the black wire feeds the 14/2 black wires. All of the white wires are spliced together, with one brought out to the receptacle terminal. The ground wires are all spliced, with one brought out to the grounding terminal on the receptacle and one to the ground clip on the box. All four cables are connected with box connectors rather than internal clamps. Using *NEC Section 314.16,* determine whether this wiring violates the code.

26111-14_SA05.EPS

12.1.0 Mounting Outlet Boxes

Outlet box configurations are almost endless, and if you research the various methods of mounting these boxes, you will be astonished. In this section, some common outlet boxes and their mounting considerations will be reviewed.

The conventional metallic device box, which is used for residential duplex receptacles and switches for lighting control, may be mounted to wall studs using 16d (penny) nails placed through the round mounting holes passing through the interior of the box. The nails are then driven into the wall stud. When nails are used for mounting outlet boxes in this manner, the nails must be located within ¼" of the back or ends of the enclosure.

Nonmetallic boxes normally have mounting nails fitted to the box for mounting. Other boxes have mounting brackets. When mounting outlet boxes with brackets, use either wide-head roofing nails or box nails about 1¼" in length. *Figure 38* shows various methods of mounting outlet boxes. Before mounting any boxes during the rough wiring process, first find out what type and thickness of finish will be used on the walls. This will dictate the depth to which the boxes must be mounted to comply with *NEC®* regulations. For example, the finish on plastered walls or ceilings is normally ½" thick; gypsum board or drywall is either ½" or ⅝" thick; and wood paneling is normally only ¼" thick. (Some tongue-and-groove wood paneling is ½" to ⅝" thick.)

The *NEC®* specifies the amount of space permitted from the edge of the outlet box to the finished wall. When a noncombustible wall finish (such as plaster, masonry, or tile) is used, the box may be recessed ¼". However, when combustible finishes are used (such as wood paneling), the box must be flush (even) with the finished wall or ceiling. See *Figure 39* and *NEC Section 314.20.*

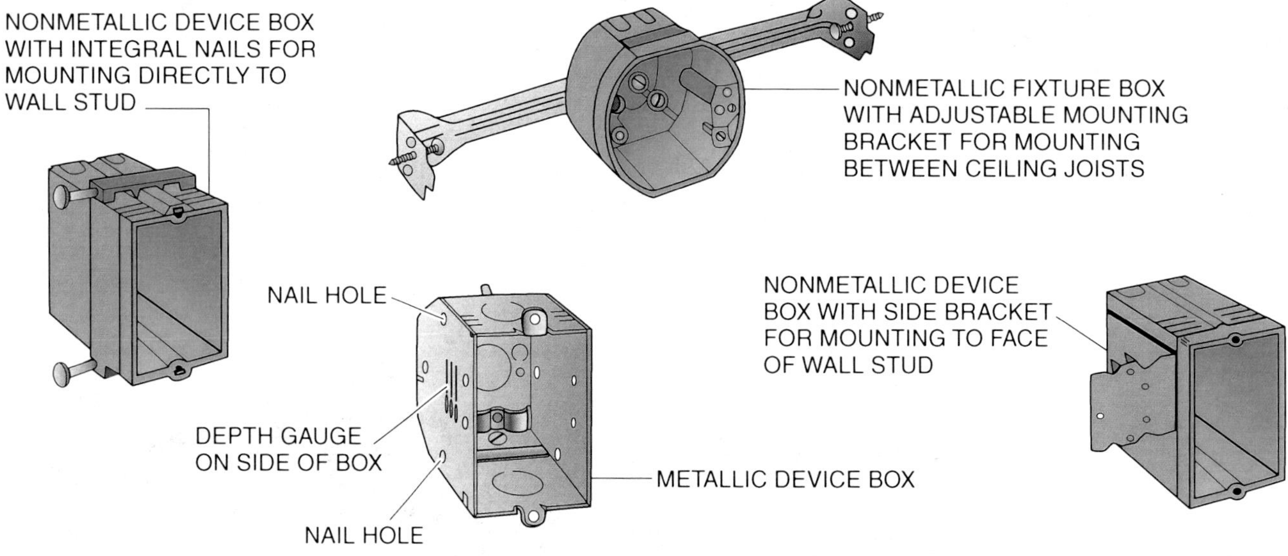

Figure 38 Several methods of mounting outlet boxes.

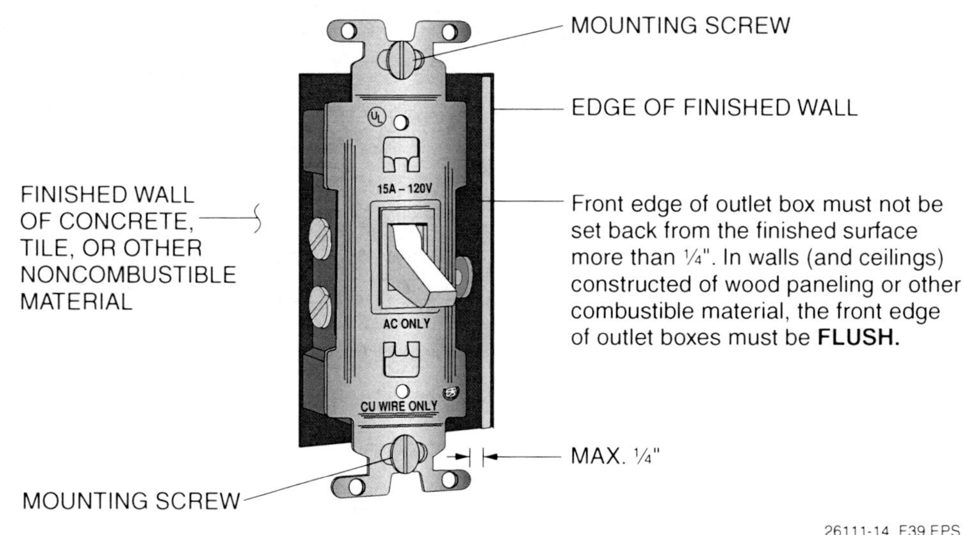

Figure 39 Outlet box installation.

On Site

Mounting Boxes

To quickly mount each box at the same height from the floor, make a simple height template (story pole) and mark it with the receptacle and switch heights. The story pole consists of an L-shaped jig made out of 2 × 2s or 2 × 4s. After installing the boxes, make sure to push the wires well back into the box so that the sheetrock installers will not damage the wires when they rout out a hole for the receptacle.

When Type NM cable is used in either metallic or nonmetallic outlet boxes, the cable assembly, including the sheath, must extend into the box by not less than ¼" [*NEC Section 314.17(C)*]. In all instances, all permitted wiring methods must be secured to the boxes by means of either cable clamps or approved connectors. The one exception to this rule is where Type NM cable is used with 2¼" × 4" (or smaller) nonmetallic boxes where the cable is fastened within eight inches of the box. In this case, the cable does not have to be secured to the box. See *NEC Section 314.17(C), Exception.*

13.0.0 Wiring Devices

Wiring devices include various types of receptacles and switches, the latter being used for lighting control. Switches are covered in *NEC Article 404,* while regulations for receptacles may be found in *NEC Article 406.*

13.1.0 Receptacles

Receptacles are rated by voltage and amperage capacity. *NEC Section 406.3* requires that receptacles connected to a 15A or 20A circuit have the correct voltage and current rating for the application, and be of the grounding type. *NEC Section 406.12* requires that all 15A and 20A, 125V receptacles installed in dwelling units be listed as tamper-resistant.

NEC Section 406.4(D) has several requirements for replacement receptacles:

- *NEC Section 406.4(D)(4)* – The replacement needs to be AFCI-protected if specified elsewhere.
- *NEC Section 406.4(D)(5)* – The replacement shall be tamper-resistant if specified elsewhere.
- *NEC Section 406.4(D)(4)* – The replacement must be weather-resistant if specified elsewhere.

Where there is only one outlet on a circuit, the receptacle's rating must be equal to or greater than the capacity of the conductors feeding it per *NEC Section 210.21(B)(1).* For example, if one receptacle is connected to a 20A residential laundry circuit, the receptacle must be rated at 20A or more. When more than one outlet is on a circuit, the total connected load must be equal to or less than the capacity of the branch circuit conductors feeding the receptacles.

Refer to *Figure 40* for some of the characteristics of a standard 125V, 15A duplex receptacle. Note that the terminals are color coded as follows:

- *Green* – Connection for the equipment grounding conductor
- *Silver* – Connection for the neutral or grounded conductor
- *Brass* – Connection for the ungrounded conductor

A standard 125V, 15A receptacle is also typically imprinted with the following symbols:

- *UL* – Underwriters Laboratories, Inc., listing
- *CSA* – Canadian Standards Association
- *CO/ALR* – Designed for use with both copper and aluminum wire
- *15A* – Receptacle rated for a maximum of 15A
- *125V* – Receptacle rated for a maximum of 125V

The UL label means that the receptacle has undergone testing by Underwriters Laboratories, Inc., and meets minimum safety requirements. Underwriters Laboratories, Inc., was created by the National Board of Fire Underwriters to test electrical devices and materials. The UL label is a safety rating only and does not mean that the device or equipment meets any type of quality standard. The CSA label means that the receptacle is approved by the Canadian Standards Association, the Canadian equivalent to Underwriters

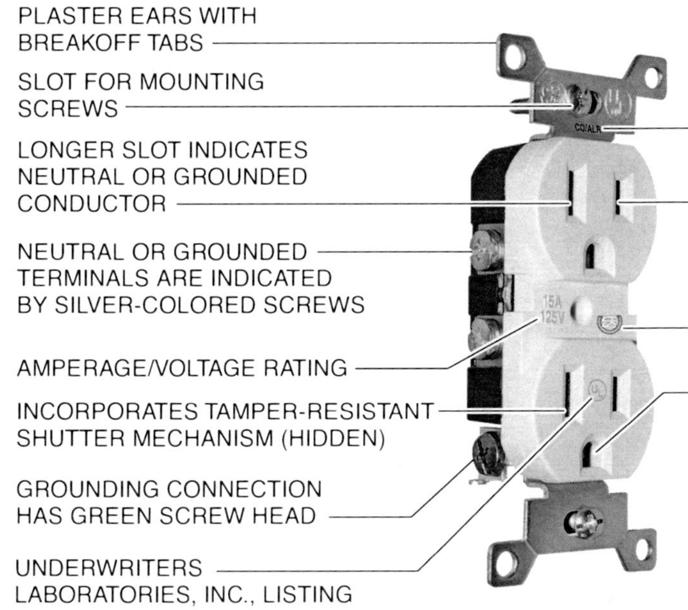

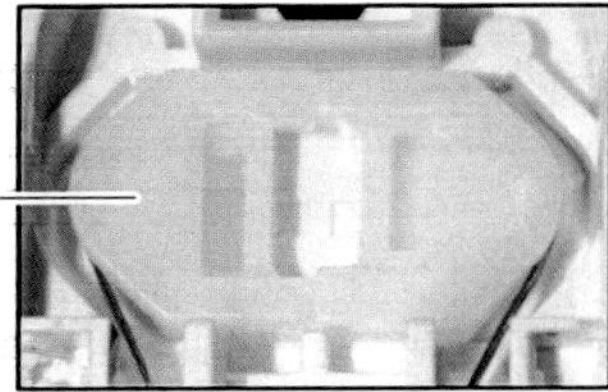

Figure 40 Standard 125V, 15A duplex receptacle.

Laboratories, Inc. The CSA label means that the receptacle is acceptable for use in Canada.

The CO/ALR symbol means that the device is suitable for use with copper, aluminum, or copper-clad aluminum wire. The CO in the symbol stands for copper while ALR stands for aluminum revised. The CO/ALR symbol replaces the earlier CU/AL mark, which appeared on wiring devices that were later found to be inadequate for use with aluminum wire in the 15A to 20A range. Therefore, any receptacle or wall switch marked with the CU/AL configuration or anything other than CO/ALR should be used only for copper wire.

These same configurations also apply to wall switches used for lighting control. These will be discussed next.

14.0.0 Lighting Control

There are many types of lighting control devices. These devices have been designed to make the best use of the lighting equipment provided by the lighting industry. They include:

- Automatic timing devices for outdoor lighting
- Dimmers for residential lighting
- Common single-pole, three-way, and four-way switches

For the purposes of this module, a switch is defined as a device that is used on branch circuits to control lighting. Switches fall into the following basic categories:

- Snap-action switches
- Quiet switches

A single-pole snap-action switch consists of a device containing two stationary current-carrying elements, a moving current-carrying element, a toggle handle, a spring, and a housing. When the contacts are open, as shown in *Figure 41*, the circuit is broken and no current flows. When the moving element is closed by manually flipping the toggle handle, the contacts complete the circuit and the lamp is energized. See *Figure 42*.

The quiet switch (*Figure 43*) is the most common switch for use in lighting applications. Its operation is much quieter than the snap-action switch.

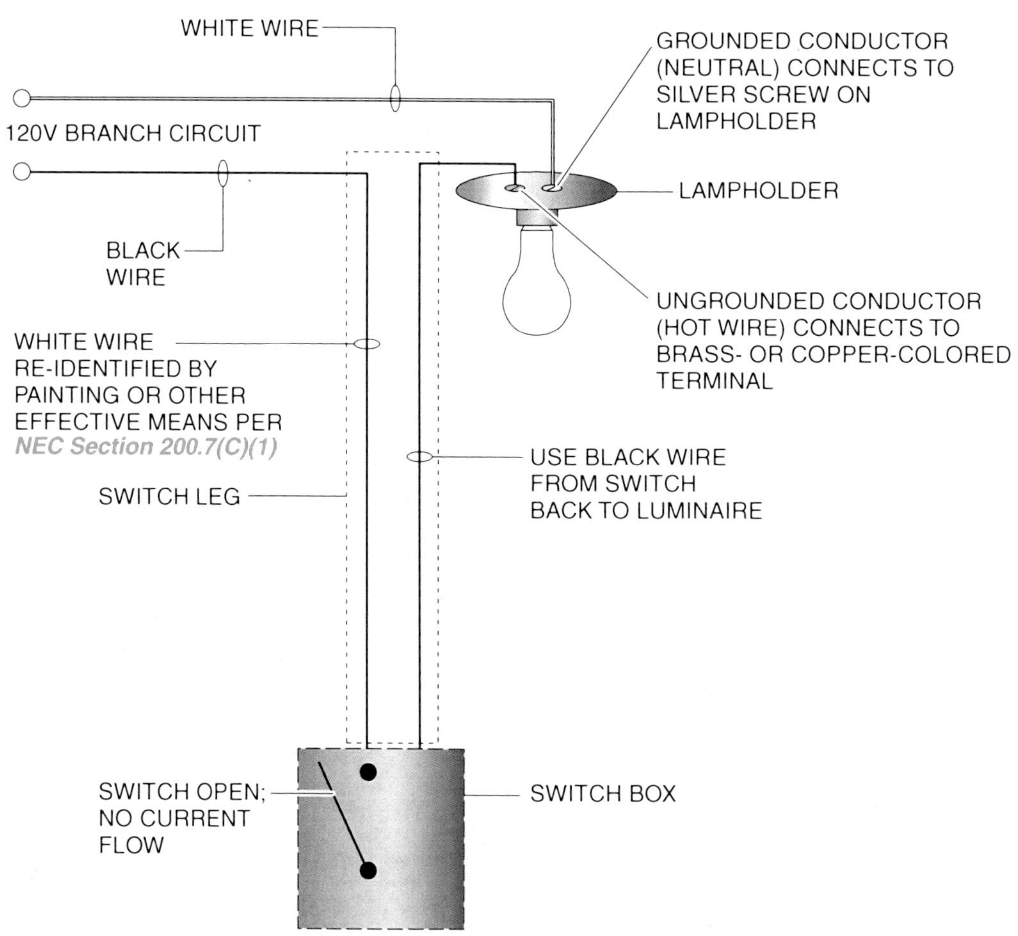

Figure 41 Switch operation, contacts open.

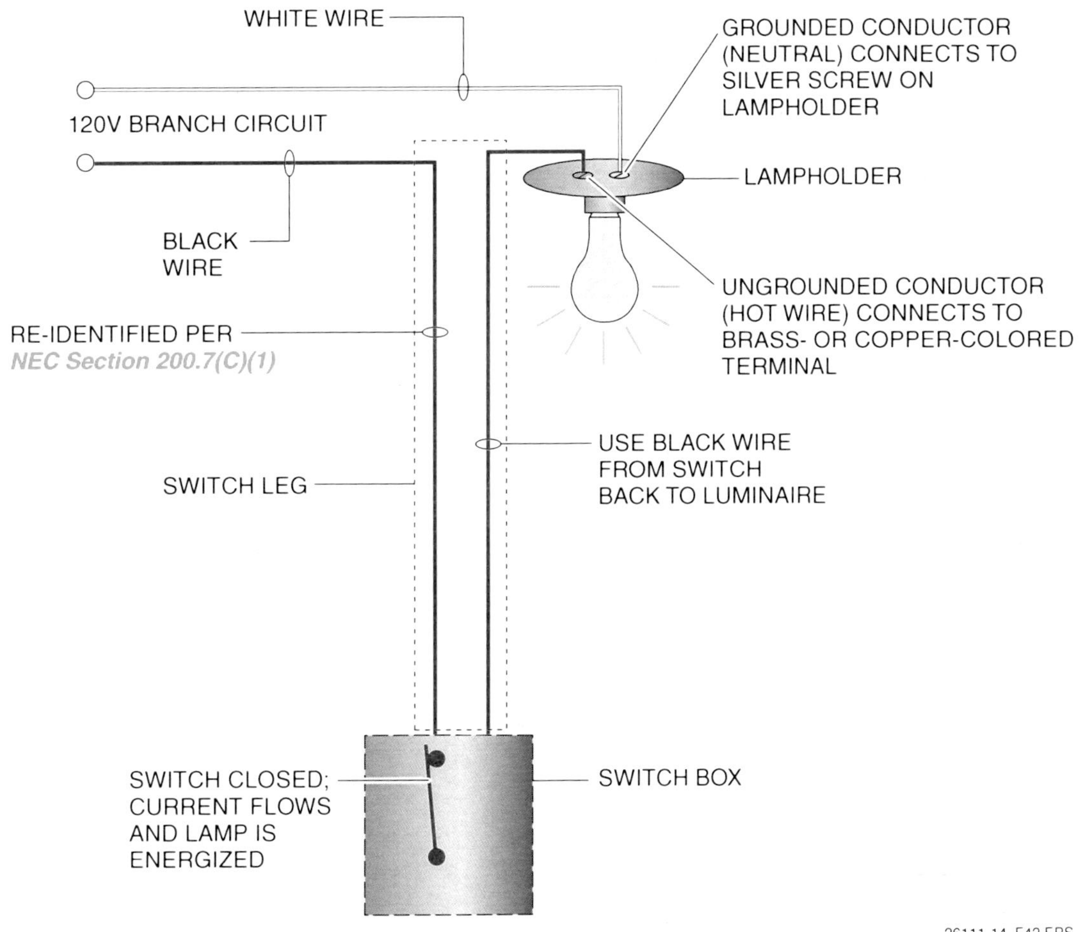

Figure 42 Switch operation, contacts closed.

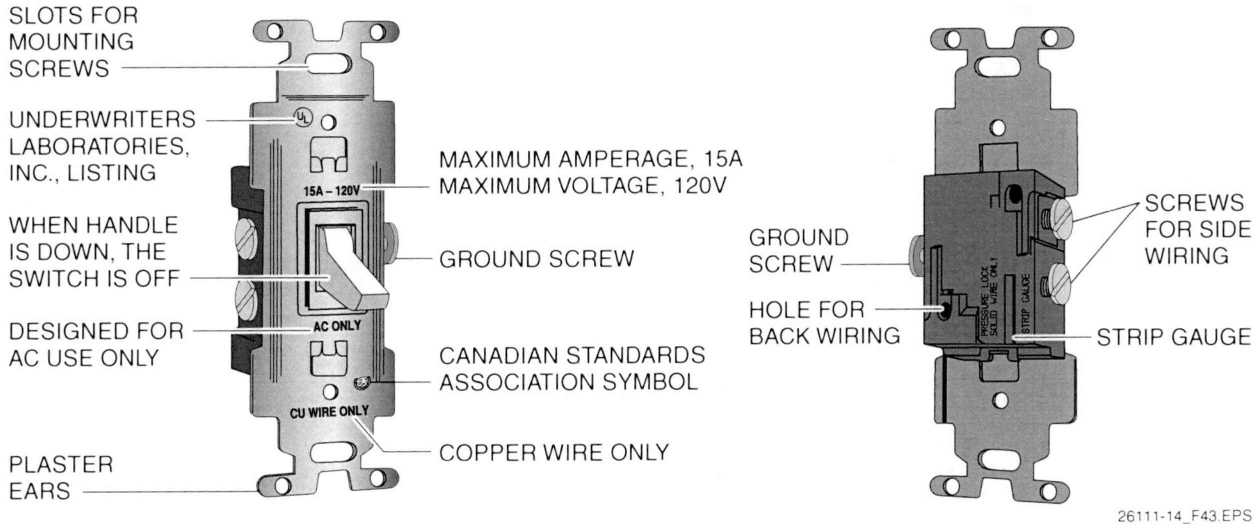

Figure 43 Characteristics of a single-pole quiet switch.

The quiet switch consists of a stationary contact and a moving contact that are close together when the switch is open. Only a short, gentle movement is required to open and close the switch, producing very little noise. This type of switch may be used only on alternating current.

Quiet switches are common for loads from 10A to 20A, and are available in single-pole, three-way, and four-way configurations.

Many other types of switches are available for lighting control. One type of switch used mainly in residential occupancies is the door-actuated switch. It is generally installed in the door jamb of a closet to control a light inside the closet. When the door is open, the light comes on; when the door is closed, the light goes out. Most refrigerator and oven lights are also controlled by door-actuated switches.

Combination switch/indicator light assemblies are available for use where the light cannot be seen from the switch location, such as an attic or garage. Switches are also made with small neon lamps in the handle that light when the switch is off. These low-current-consuming lamps make the switches easy to find in the dark.

14.1.0 Three-Way Switches

Three-way switches are used to control one or more lamps from two different locations, such as at the top and bottom of stairways, in a room that has two entrances, etc. A typical three-way switch is shown in *Figure 44*.

A three-way switch has three terminals. The single terminal at one end of the switch is called the common or hinge point. This terminal is easily identified because it is darker than the other two terminals. The feeder (hot wire) or switch leg is always connected to the common dark or black terminal. The two remaining terminals are called traveler terminals. These terminals are used to connect three-way switches together.

The connection of two three-way switches is shown in *Figure 45*. By means of the two switches, it is possible to control the lamp from two locations. By tracing the circuit, it may be seen how these three-way switches operate.

A 120V circuit emerges from the left side of the drawing. The white or neutral wire connects directly to the neutral terminal of the lamp. The hot wire carries current, in the direction of the arrows, to the common terminal of the three-way switch on the left. Since the handle is in the Up position, the current continues to the top traveler terminal and is carried by this traveler to the other three-way switch. Note that the handle is also in the Up position on this switch; this picks up the current flow and carries it to the common point, which continues to the ungrounded terminal of the lamp to make a complete circuit. The lamp is energized.

Moving the handle to a different position on either three-way switch will break the circuit, which in turn de-energizes the lamp. For example, let's say a person leaves the room at the point of the three-way switch on the left, and the switch handle is flipped down, as shown in *Figure 46*. Note that the current flow is now directed to the bottom traveler terminal, but since the handle of the three-way switch on the right is still in the Up position, no current will flow to the lamp.

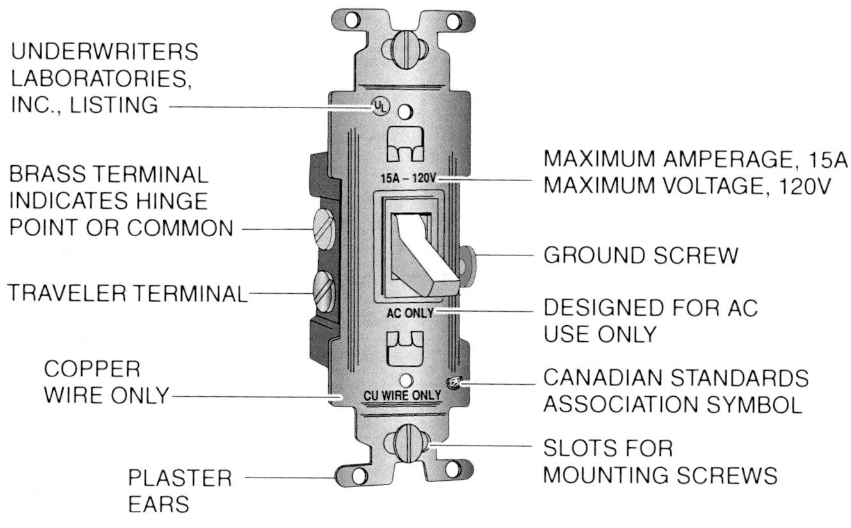

Figure 44 Typical three-way switch.

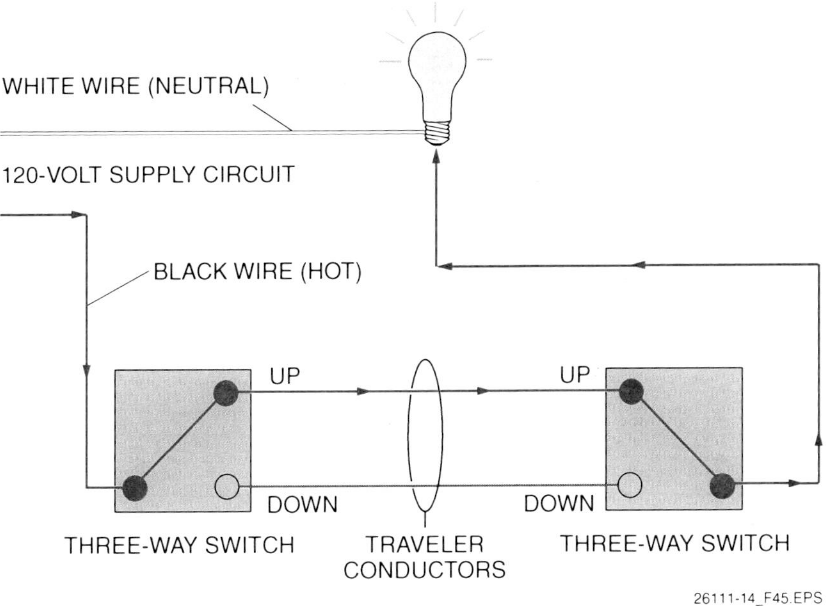

Figure 45 Three-way switches in the On position; both handles are up.

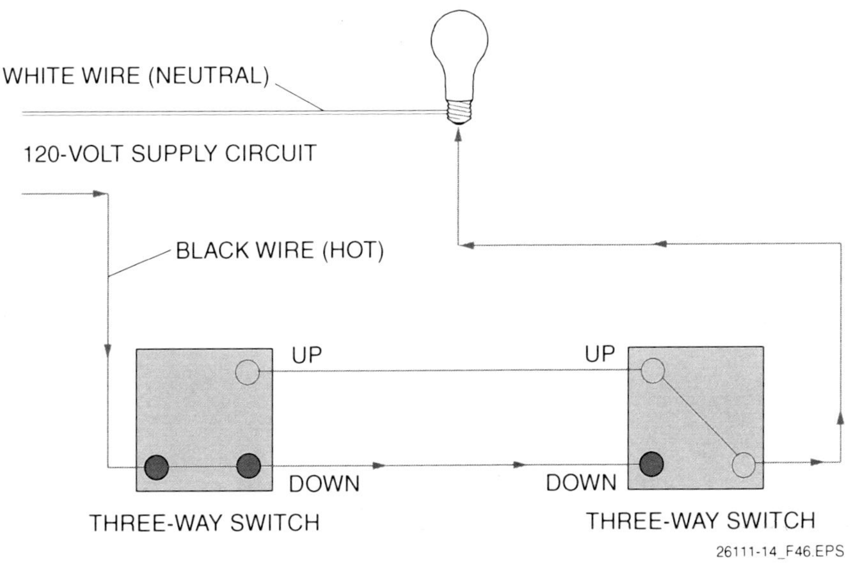

Figure 46 Three-way switches in the Off position; one handle is down, one handle is up.

If another person enters the room at the location of the three-way switch on the right, and the handle is flipped downward, as shown in *Figure 47*, this change provides a complete circuit to the lamp, which causes it to be energized. In this example, current flow is on the bottom traveler. Again, changing the position of the switch handle (pivot point) on either three-way switch will de-energize the lamp.

In actual practice, the exact wiring of the two three-way switches to control the operation of a lamp will be slightly different from the routing shown in these three diagrams. There are several ways that two three-way switches may be connected. One solution is shown in *Figure 48*. In this case, two-wire, Type NM cable is fed to the three-way switch on the left.

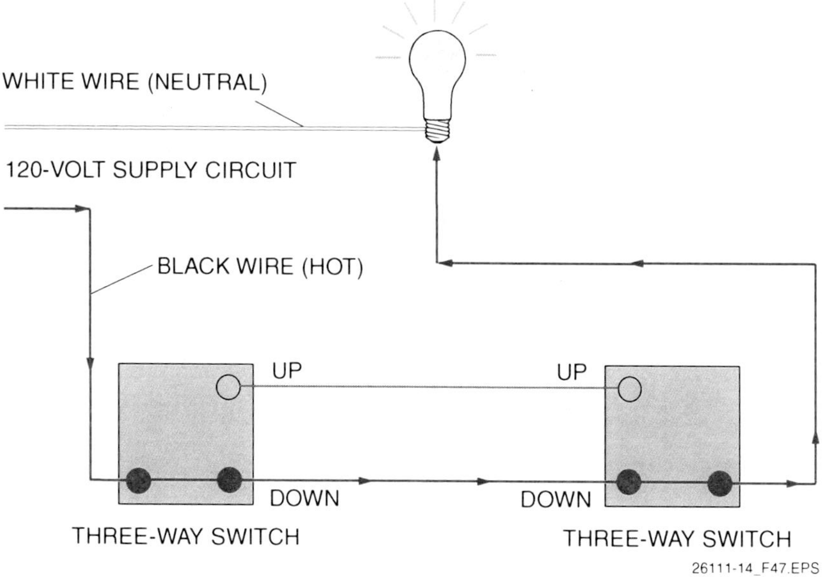

Figure 47 Three-way switches with both handles down; the light is energized.

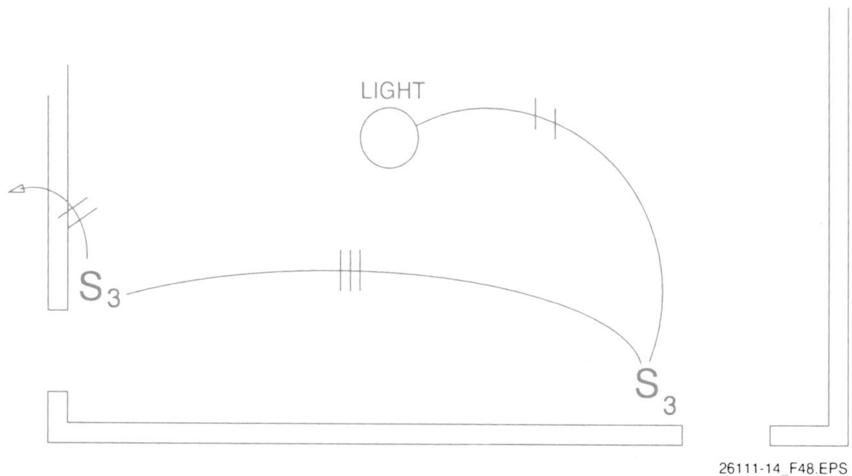

Figure 48 Method of showing the wiring arrangement on a floor plan.

The black or hot conductor is connected to the common terminal on the switch, while the white or neutral conductor is spliced to the white conductor of the three-wire, Type NM cable leaving the switch. This three-wire cable is necessary to carry the two travelers plus the neutral to the three-way switch on the right. At this point, the black and red wires connect to the two traveler terminals, respectively. The white or neutral wire is again spliced—this time to the white wire of another two-wire, Type NM cable. The neutral wire is never connected to the switch itself. The black wire of the two-wire, Type NM cable connects to the common terminal on the three-way switch. This cable, carrying the hot and neutral conductors, is routed to the lighting fixture outlet for connection to the fixture.

Another solution is to feed the lighting fixture outlet with two-wire cable. Run another two-wire cable carrying the hot and neutral conductors to one of the three-way switches. A three-wire cable is pulled between the two three-way switches, and then another two-wire cable is routed from the other three-way switch to the lighting fixture outlet.

Some electricians use a shortcut method that eliminates one of the two-wire cables in the preceding method. In this case, a two-wire cable is run from the lighting fixture outlet to one three-way switch. Three-wire cable is pulled between the two three-way switches—two of the wires for travelers and the third for the common point return. This method is shown in *Figure 49*.

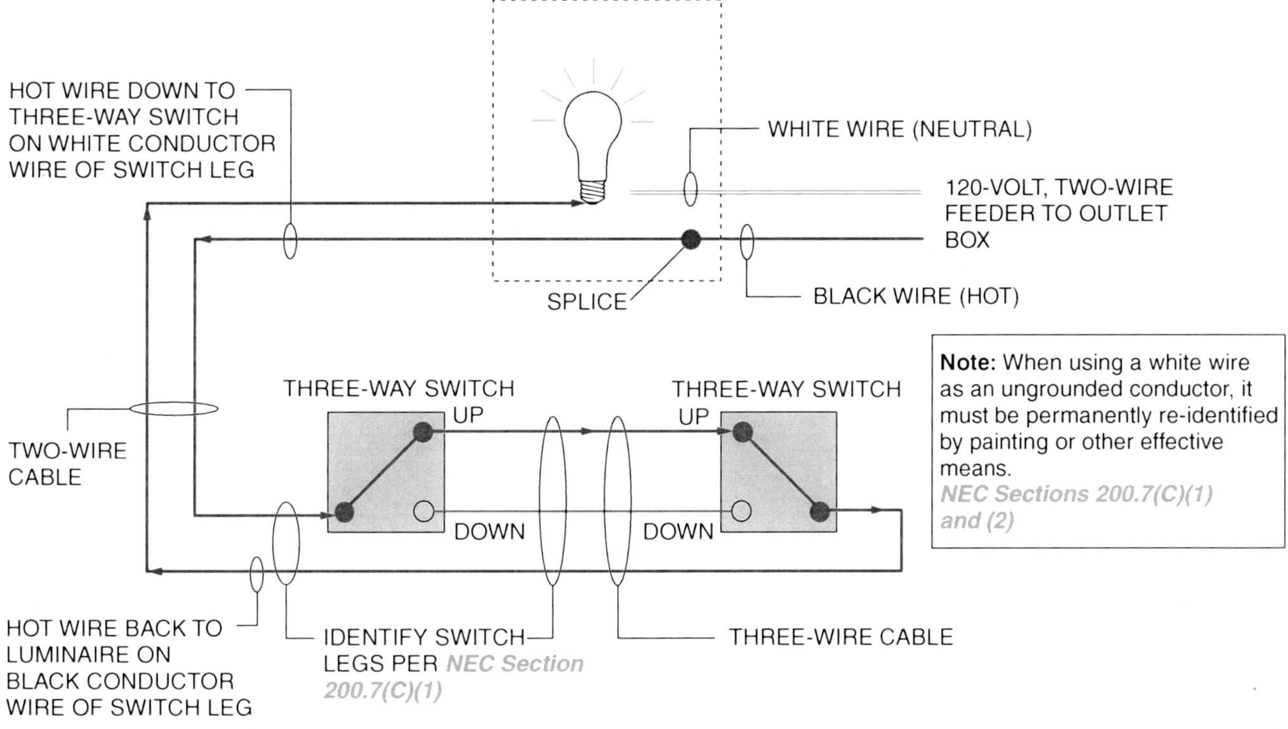

Figure 49 One way to connect a pair of three-way switches to control one lighting fixture.

Think About It

Wiring Three-Way Switches

Using a schematic drawing, explain the actual wiring of two different three-way switches, one in which the load and supply come in from different boxes, and the other in which the load and supply come in from the same box. Be specific about which wires connect to which terminals.

14.2.0 Four-Way Switches

Two three-way switches may be used in conjunction with any number of four-way switches to control a lamp, or a series of lamps, from any number of positions. When connected correctly, the actuation of any one of these switches will change the operating condition of the lamp (i.e., turn the lamp either on or off).

Figure 50 shows how a four-way switch may be used in combination with two three-way switches to control a device from three locations. In this example, note that the hot wire is connected to the common terminal on the three-way switch on the left. Current then travels to the top traveler terminal and continues on the top traveler conductor to the four-way switch. Since the handle is up on the four-way switch, current flows through the top terminals of the switch and into the traveler conductor going to the other three-way switch.

Again, the switch is in the Up position. Therefore, current is carried from the top traveler terminal to the common terminal and then to the lighting fixture to energize it.

If the position of any one of the three switch handles is changed, the circuit will be broken and no current will flow to the lamp. For example, assume that the four-way switch handle is flipped downward. The circuit will now appear as shown in *Figure 51*, and the light will be out.

Remember, any number of four-way switches may be used in combination with two three-way switches, but two three-way switches are always necessary for the correct operation of one or more four-way switches.

14.3.0 Photoelectric Switches

The chief application of the photoelectric switch is to control outdoor lighting, especially the dusk-to-dawn lights found in suburban areas. This switch has an endless number of possible uses and is a great tool for electricians dealing with outdoor lighting situations.

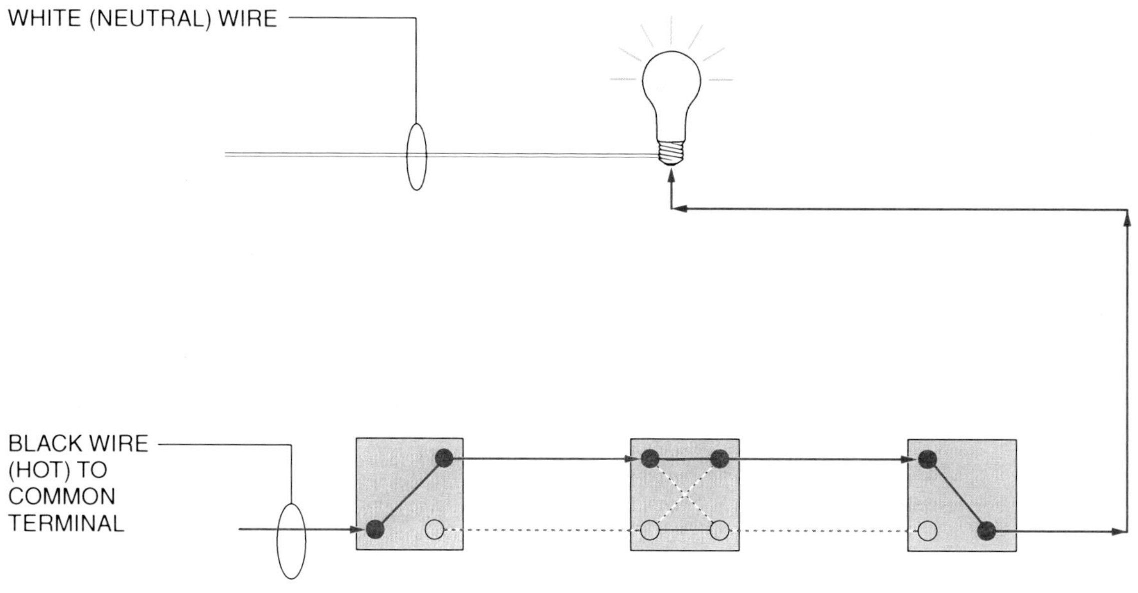

Figure 50 Three- and four-way switches used in combination; the light is on.

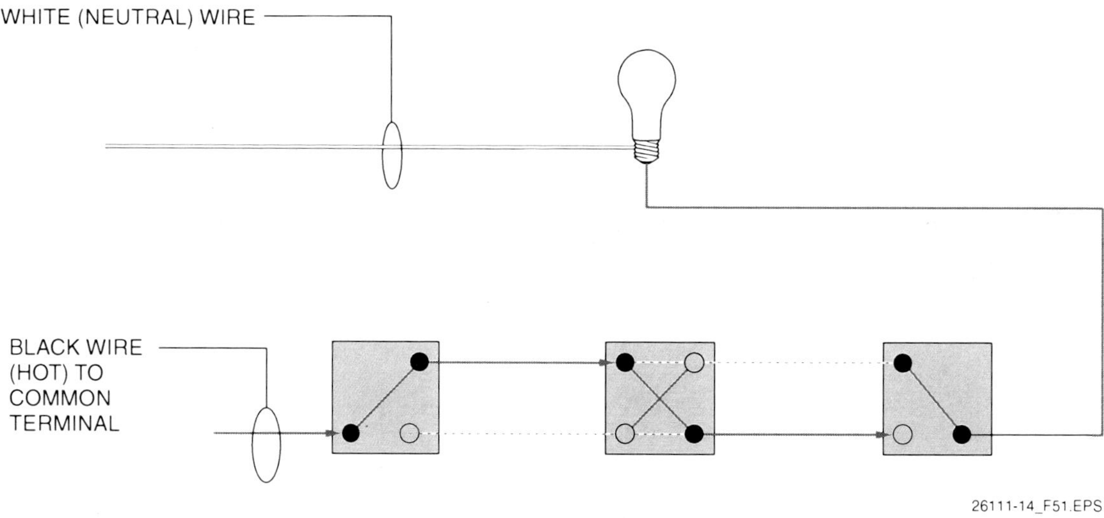

Figure 51 Three- and four-way switches used in combination; the light is off.

14.4.0 Relays

Next to switches, relays play the most important part in the control of light. However, the design and application of relays is a study in itself, and they are far beyond the scope of this module. Still, a brief mention of relays is necessary to round out your knowledge of lighting controls.

An electric relay is a device whereby an electric current causes the opening or closing of one or more pairs of contacts. These contacts are usually capable of controlling much more power than is necessary to operate the relay itself. This is one of the main advantages of relays.

One popular use of the relay in residential lighting systems is that of remote control lighting. In this type of system, all relays are designed to operate on a 24V circuit and are used to control 120V lighting circuits. They are rated at 20A, which is sufficient to control the full load of a normal lighting branch circuit, if desired.

Remote control switching makes it possible to install a switch wherever it is convenient and practical to do so or wherever there is an obvious need for a switch, no matter how remote it is from the lamp or lamps it is to control. This method enables lighting designs to achieve new advances in lighting control convenience at a reasonable cost. Remote control switching is also ideal for rewiring existing homes with finished walls and ceilings.

One relay is required for each fixture or each group of fixtures that are controlled together. Switch locations for remote control follow the same rules as for conventional direct switching. However, since it is easy to add switches to control a given relay, no opportunities should be overlooked for adding a switch to improve the convenience of control.

Remote control lighting also has the advantage of using selector switches at central locations. For example, selector switches located in the master bedroom or in the kitchen of a home enable the owner to control every lighting fixture on the property from this location. For example, the selector switch may be used to control outside or basement lights that might otherwise be left on inadvertently.

14.5.0 Dimmers

Dimming a lighting system provides control of the quantity of illumination. It may be done to create certain moods or to blend the lighting from different sources for various lighting effects.

For example, in homes with formal dining rooms, a chandelier mounted directly above the dining table and controlled by a dimmer switch becomes the centerpiece of the room while providing general illumination. The dimmer adds versatility since it can set the mood for the activity—low brilliance (candlelight effect) for formal dining or bright for an evening of playing cards. When chandeliers with exposed lamps are used, the dimmer is essential to avoid a garish and uncomfortable atmosphere. The chandelier should be sized in proportion to the dining area.

> **NOTE**
> It is very important that dimmers be matched to the wattage of the application. Check the manufacturer's data.

14.6.0 Switch Locations

Although the location of wall switches is usually provided for convenience, the *NEC®* also stipulates certain mandatory locations for lighting fixtures and wall switches. See *NEC Section 210.70(A)* for specific switch locations in dwelling units. These locations are deemed necessary for added safety in the home for both the occupants and service personnel.

For example, the *NEC®* requires adequate light in areas where heating, ventilating, and air conditioning (HVAC) equipment is placed. Furthermore, these lights must be conveniently controlled so that homeowners and service personnel do not have to enter a dark area where they might come in contact with dangerous equipment. Three-way switches are required under certain conditions. The *NEC®* also specifies regulations governing lighting fixtures in clothes closets, along with those governing lighting fixtures that may be mounted directly to the outlet box without further support. *Figure 52* summarizes some of the *NEC®* requirements for light and switch placement in the home. For further details, refer to the appropriate sections in the *NEC®*.

14.7.0 Low-Voltage Electrical Systems

Conventional lighting systems operate and are controlled by the same system voltage, generally 120V in residential lighting circuits. The *NEC®* permits the use of low-voltage systems to control lighting circuits. There are some advantages to low-voltage systems. One advantage is that the control of lighting from several different locations is more easily accomplished, such as with the remote control system discussed earlier. For example, outside flood lighting can be controlled from several different rooms in a house. The cost of the control wiring is less in that it is rated for a lower voltage and only carries a minimum amount of current compared to a standard lighting system. When extensive or complex lighting control is required, low-voltage systems are preferred. Also, since these circuits are low-energy circuits, circuit protection is not required.

14.7.1 NEC® Requirements for Low-Voltage Systems

NEC Article 725 governs the installation of low-voltage system wiring. These provisions apply to remote control circuits, low-voltage relay switching, low-energy power circuits, and low-voltage circuits. The *NEC®* divides these circuits into three categories:

- Remote control
- Signaling
- Power-limited circuits

As mentioned earlier, circuit protection of the low-voltage circuit is not required; however, the high-voltage side of the transformer that supplies the low-voltage system must be protected. *NEC Chapter 9, Tables 11(A) and 11(B)* cover circuits that are inherently limited in power output and

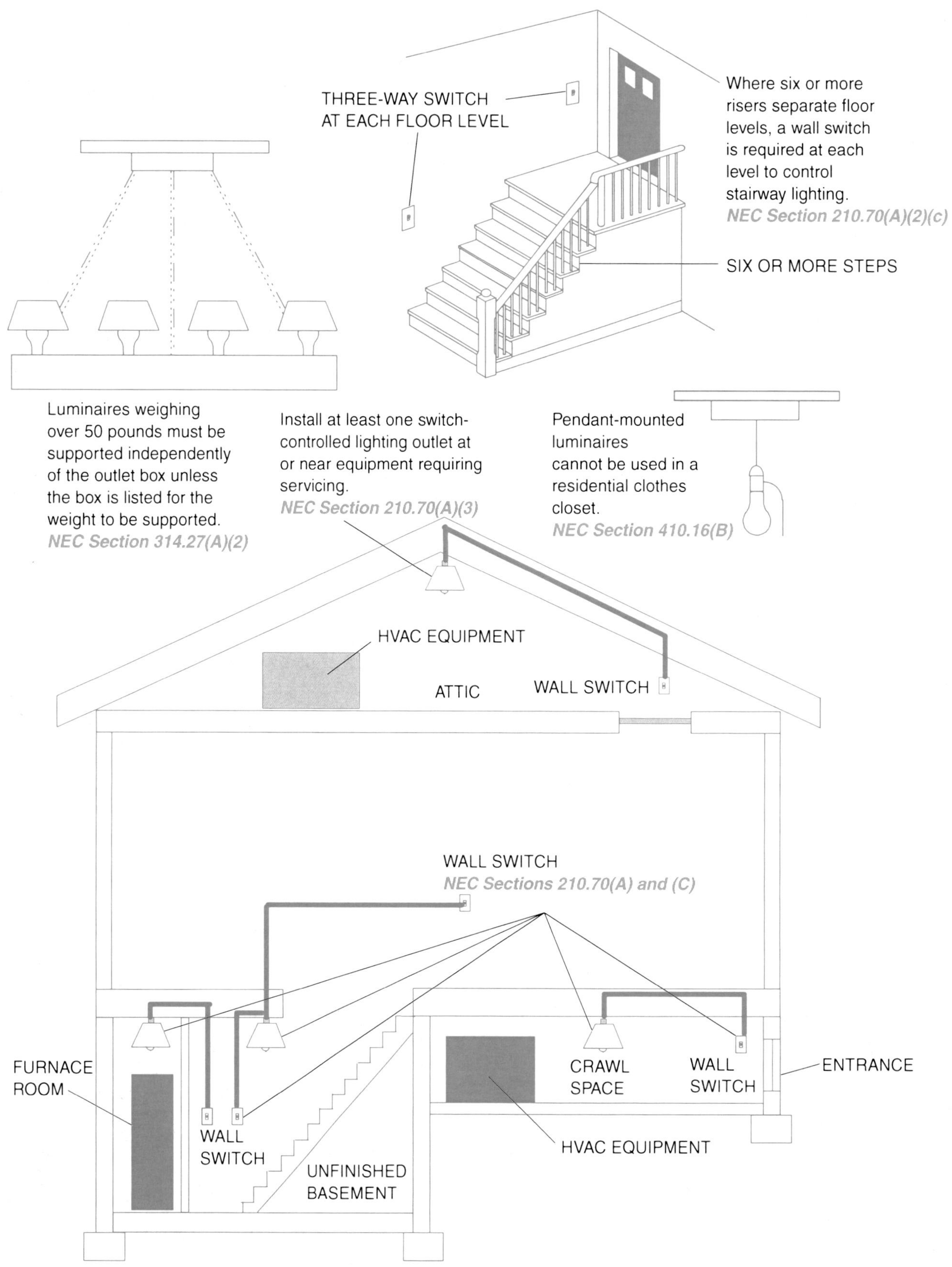

THREE-WAY SWITCH
AT EACH FLOOR LEVEL
Where six or more
risers separate floor
levels, a wall switch
is required at each
level to control
stairway lighting.
NEC Section 210.70(A)(2)(c)
SIX OR MORE STEPS
Luminaires weighing
over 50 pounds must be
supported independently
of the outlet box unless
the box is listed for the
weight to be supported.
NEC Section 314.27(A)(2)
Install at least one switch-
controlled lighting outlet at
or near equipment requiring
servicing.
NEC Section 210.70(A)(3)
Pendant-mounted
luminaires
cannot be used in a
residential clothes
closet.
NEC Section 410.16(B)
HVAC EQUIPMENT
ATTIC
WALL SWITCH
WALL SWITCH
NEC Sections 210.70(A) and (C)
FURNACE
ROOM
WALL
SWITCH
UNFINISHED
BASEMENT
CRAWL
SPACE
WALL
SWITCH
ENTRANCE
HVAC EQUIPMENT
26111-14_F52.EPS

Figure 52 NEC® requirements for light and switch placement.

therefore require no overcurrent protection or are limited by a combination of power source and overcurrent protection.

There are a number of requirements of the power systems described in *NEC Chapter 9, Tables 11(A) and 11(B)* and the notes preceding the tables. You should read and study all applicable portions of the *NEC*® before installing low-voltage power systems.

Low-voltage systems are described in more detail in later modules.

15.0.0 Electric Heating

The use of electric heating in residential occupancies has risen tremendously over the past decade or so, and the practice will no doubt continue. This is due to the following advantages of electric heat over most other heating systems:

- Electric heat is noncombustible and is therefore safer than combustible fuels.
- It requires no storage space, fuel tanks, or chimneys.
- It requires little maintenance.
- The initial installation cost is relatively inexpensive when compared to other types of heating systems.
- The comfort level may be improved since each room may be controlled separately by its own thermostat.

There are also some disadvantages to using electric baseboard heat, especially in northern climates. Some of these disadvantages include:

- Electric heat is often more expensive to operate than other types of fuels.
- Receptacles must not be installed above electric baseboard heaters.
- Electric baseboard heaters tend to discolor the wall area immediately above the heater, especially if there are smokers in the home.

NOTE

It is very important to calculate the extra electric load of an electric heater installation (especially in an add-on situation). Ensure that the extra load does not exceed the maximum amperage draw of either the circuit or the panel.

The type of electric heating system used for a given residence will usually depend on the structural conditions, the kind of room, and the activities for which the room will be used. The homeowner's preference will also enter into the final decision.

Electric heating equipment is available in baseboard, wall, ceiling, kick space, and floor units; in resistance cable embedded in the ceiling or concrete floor; in forced-air duct systems similar to conventional oil- or gas-fired hot air systems; and in electric boilers for hot water baseboard heat.

Electric heat pumps have also become popular for HVAC systems in certain parts of the country. The term *heat pump*, as applied to a year-round air conditioning system, commonly denotes a system in which refrigeration equipment is used in such a manner that heat is taken from a heat source and transferred to the conditioned space when heating is desired; heat is removed from the space and discharged to a heat sink when cooling and dehumidification are desired.

A heat pump has the unique ability to furnish more energy than it consumes. This is due to the fact that under certain outdoor conditions, electrical energy is required only to move the refrigerant and run the fan; thus, a heat pump can attain a heating efficiency of two or more to one; that is, it will put out an equivalent of two or three watts of heat for every watt consumed. For this reason, its use is highly desirable for the conservation of energy.

In general, electric baseboard heating equipment should be located on the outside wall near the areas where the greatest heat loss will occur, such as under windows, etc. The controls for wall-mounted thermostats should be located on an interior wall, about 50 inches above the floor to sense the average room temperature. *Figure 53* shows an electric heating arrangement for the sample residence. *NEC*® regulations governing the installation of these units are also noted.

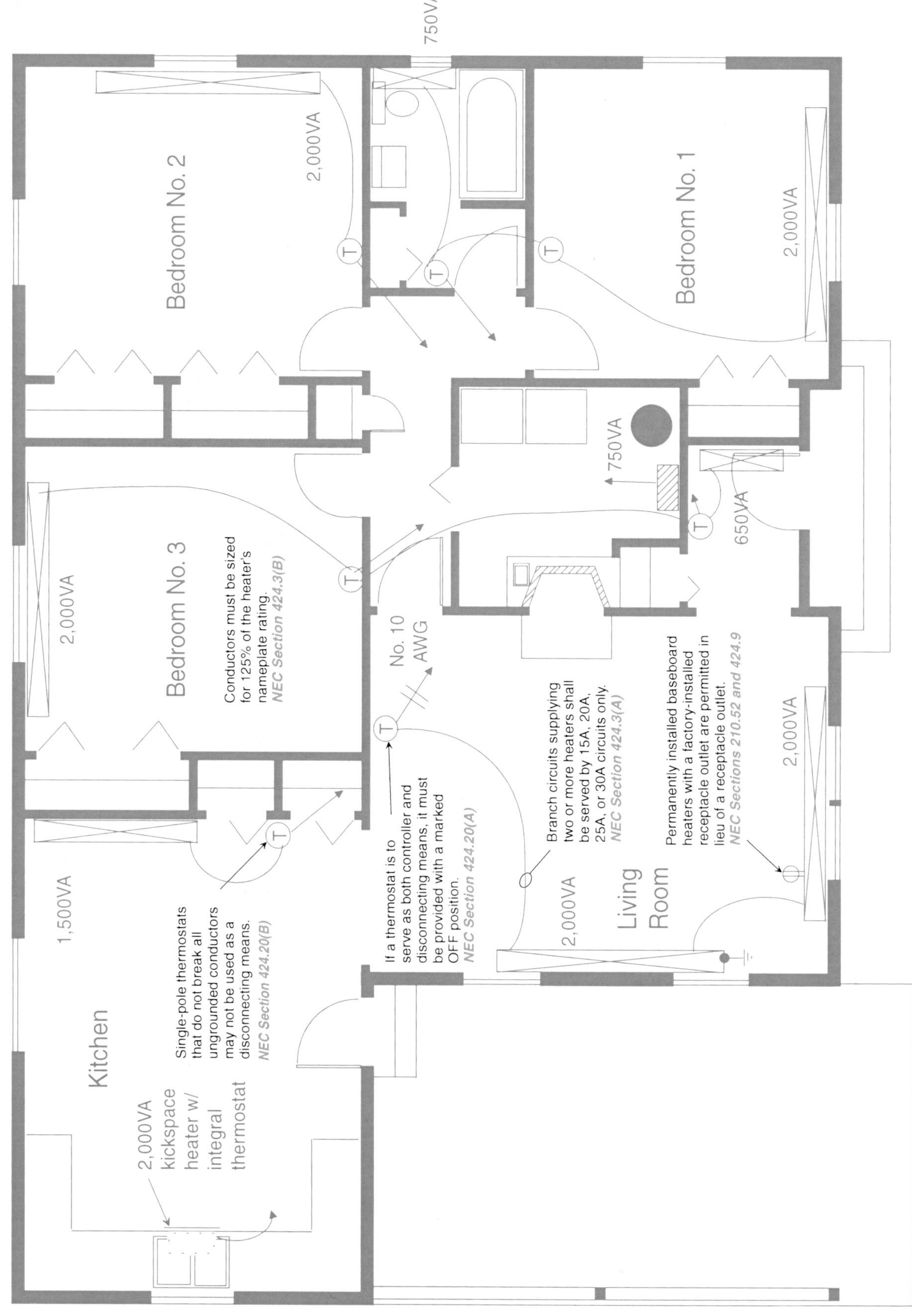
750VA
2,000VA
Bedroom No. 2
Bedroom No. 1
2,000VA
750VA
650VA
Bedroom No. 3
2,000VA
Conductors must be sized for 125% of the heater's nameplate rating. NEC Section 424.3(B)
No. 10 AWG
Branch circuits supplying two or more heaters shall be served by 15A, 20A, 25A, or 30A circuits only. NEC Section 424.3(A)
Permanently installed baseboard heaters with a factory-installed receptacle outlet are permitted in lieu of a receptacle outlet. NEC Sections 210.52 and 424.9
2,000VA
If a thermostat is to serve as both controller and disconnecting means, it must be provided with a marked OFF position. NEC Section 424.20(A)
2,000VA
Living Room
1,500VA
Single-pole thermostats that do not break all ungrounded conductors may not be used as a disconnecting means. NEC Section 424.20(B)
Kitchen
2,000VA kickspace heater w/ integral thermostat
26111-14 F53.EPS

Figure 53 Electric heating arrangement for the sample residence.

16.0.0 Residential Swimming Pools, Spas, and Hot Tubs

The *NEC®* recognizes the potential danger of electric shock to persons in swimming pools, wading pools, and therapeutic pools, or near decorative pools or fountains. This shock could occur from electric potential in the water itself or as a result of a person in the water or a wet area touching an enclosure that is not at ground potential. Accordingly, the *NEC®* provides rules for the safe installation of electrical equipment and wiring in or adjacent to swimming pools and similar locations. *NEC Article 680* covers the specific rules governing the installation and maintenance of swimming pools, spas, and hot tubs.

The electrical installation procedures for hot tubs and swimming pools are too vast to be covered in detail in this module. However, the general requirements for the installation of outlets, overhead fans and lighting fixtures, and other items are summarized in *Figure 54*.

Besides *NEC Article 680* (see *Figure 55*), another good source for learning more about electrical installations in and around swimming pools is from manufacturers of swimming pool equipment, including those who manufacture and distribute underwater lighting fixtures. Many of these manufacturers offer pamphlets detailing the installation of their equipment with helpful illustrations, code explanations, and similar details. This literature is usually available at little or no cost to qualified personnel. You can write directly to manufacturers to request information about available literature, or contact your local electrical supplier or contractor who specializes in installing residential swimming pools.

Think About It

Residential Wiring

Make a mental wiring tour of your home. Picture several rooms, including the kitchen and utility/laundry room. How is each device connected to the power source, and what is the probable amperage and overcurrent protection? What other devices might or might not be included in the circuit? How many branch circuits serve each room? Later, examine the panelboard and exposed wiring to see how accurately you identified the branch circuits.

On Site

Pools

Pools are a common site for homeowners to add lights, receptacles, or heaters, and code violations are common. If you are called in for a service problem, ask the homeowner about any do-it-yourself wiring.

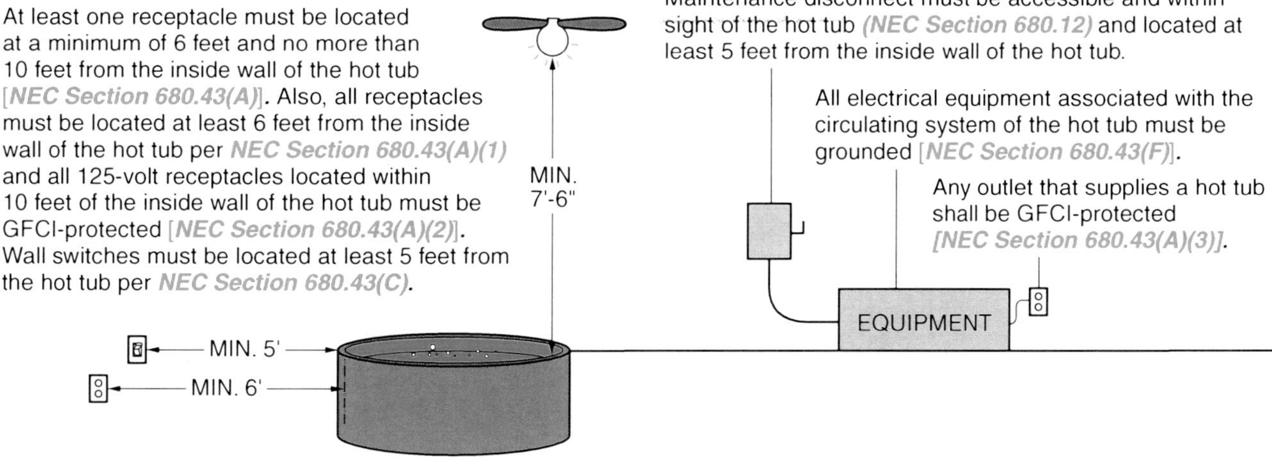

Luminaires, lighting outlets, and ceiling fans located over the hot tub or within 5 feet from its inside walls shall be a minimum of 7 feet 6 inches above the maximum water level and shall be GFCI-protected [NEC Section 680.43(B)].
At least one receptacle must be located at a minimum of 6 feet and no more than 10 feet from the inside wall of the hot tub [NEC Section 680.43(A)]. Also, all receptacles must be located at least 6 feet from the inside wall of the hot tub per NEC Section 680.43(A)(1) and all 125-volt receptacles located within 10 feet of the inside wall of the hot tub must be GFCI-protected [NEC Section 680.43(A)(2)]. Wall switches must be located at least 5 feet from the hot tub per NEC Section 680.43(C).
Maintenance disconnect must be accessible and within sight of the hot tub (NEC Section 680.12) and located at least 5 feet from the inside wall of the hot tub.
All electrical equipment associated with the circulating system of the hot tub must be grounded [NEC Section 680.43(F)].
Any outlet that supplies a hot tub shall be GFCI-protected [NEC Section 680.43(A)(3)].
MIN. 7'-6"
EQUIPMENT
MIN. 5'
MIN. 6'
26111-14_F54.EPS

Figure 54 *NEC®* requirements for packaged indoor hot tubs.

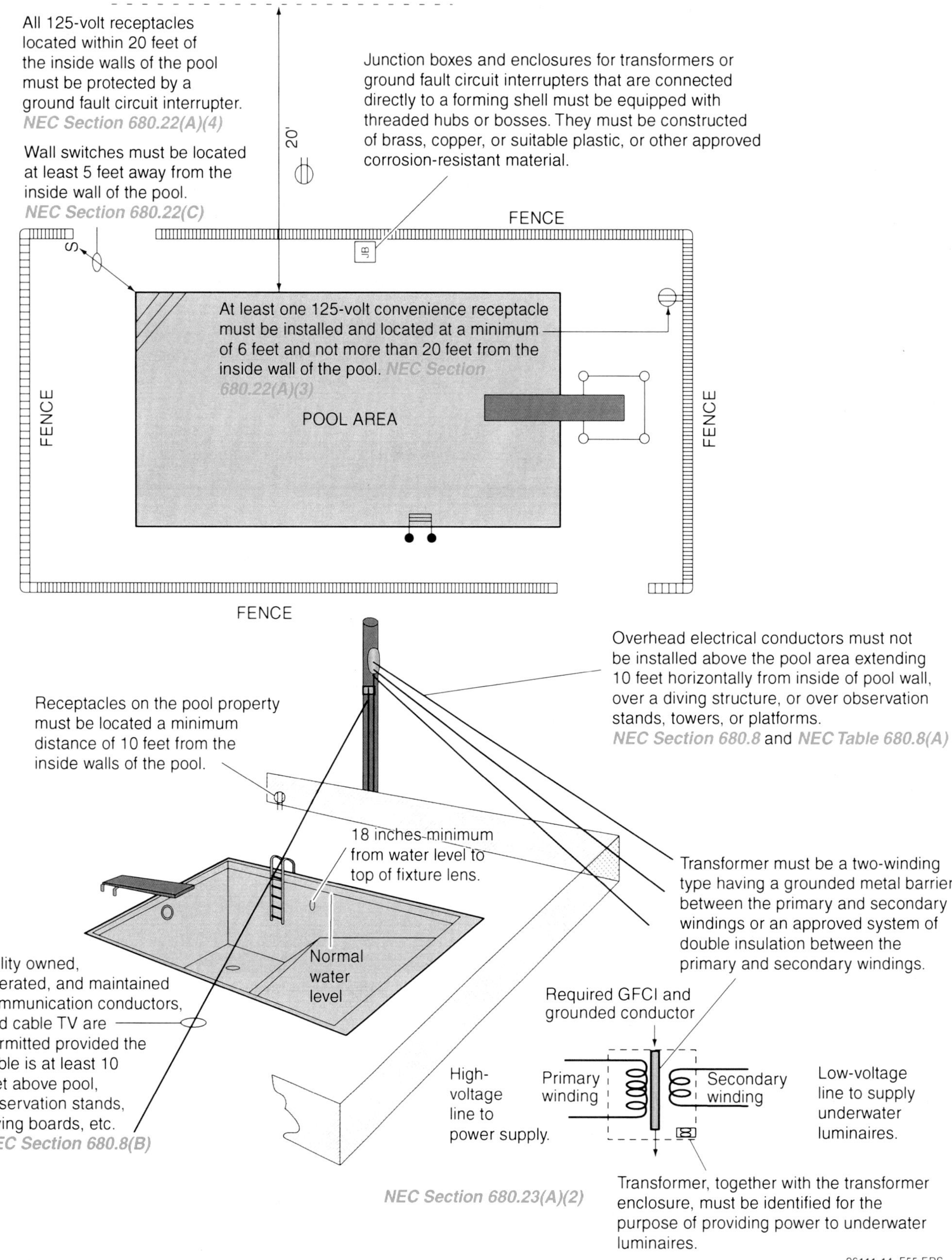

All 125-volt receptacles located within 20 feet of the inside walls of the pool must be protected by a ground fault circuit interrupter.
NEC Section 680.22(A)(4)
Wall switches must be located at least 5 feet away from the inside wall of the pool.
NEC Section 680.22(C)
20'
Junction boxes and enclosures for transformers or ground fault circuit interrupters that are connected directly to a forming shell must be equipped with threaded hubs or bosses. They must be constructed of brass, copper, or suitable plastic, or other approved corrosion-resistant material.
FENCE
S
JB
At least one 125-volt convenience receptacle must be installed and located at a minimum of 6 feet and not more than 20 feet from the inside wall of the pool. NEC Section 680.22(A)(3)
POOL AREA
FENCE
FENCE
FENCE
Overhead electrical conductors must not be installed above the pool area extending 10 feet horizontally from inside of pool wall, over a diving structure, or over observation stands, towers, or platforms.
NEC Section 680.8 and NEC Table 680.8(A)
Receptacles on the pool property must be located a minimum distance of 10 feet from the inside walls of the pool.
18 inches minimum from water level to top of fixture lens.
Transformer must be a two-winding type having a grounded metal barrier between the primary and secondary windings or an approved system of double insulation between the primary and secondary windings.
Normal water level
Utility owned, operated, and maintained communication conductors, and cable TV are permitted provided the cable is at least 10 feet above pool, observation stands, diving boards, etc.
NEC Section 680.8(B)
Required GFCI and grounded conductor
High-voltage line to power supply.
Primary winding
Secondary winding
Low-voltage line to supply underwater luminaires.
NEC Section 680.23(A)(2)
Transformer, together with the transformer enclosure, must be identified for the purpose of providing power to underwater luminaires.
26111-14_F55.EPS

Figure 55 NEC® requirements for typical swimming pool installations.

SUMMARY

This module covered the basics of residential wiring, including load calculations and wiring devices.

Residential electrical system design begins with the floor plan. The square footage of the home is used to calculate the lighting loads. The lighting loads, along with small appliance loads, fixed appliance loads, and other loads must be calculated to determine the service size. Demand factors are applied and the neutral conductor is sized per *NEC Article 220*. GFCI and AFCI breakers must be installed in all required locations, and the system must be grounded and bonded per *NEC Article 250*. Most residences use Type NM or MC cable for branch circuits. Switches must be installed in all locations required by the *NEC*®. Special consideration must be given to electric heating units and circuits supplying swimming pools and hot tubs.

A thorough knowledge of the *NEC*® is essential to the safe and successful installation of residential wiring systems.

Review Questions

1. When sizing electrical services, at what percentage is the first 3,000VA rated?
   a. 20%
   b. 45%
   c. 80%
   d. 100%

2. What section of the *NEC®* requires that fittings be identified for use with service masts?
   a. *NEC Section 230.28*
   b. *NEC Section 230.40*
   c. *NEC Section 250.46*
   d. *NEC Section 250.83*

3. A service conductor without an overall jacket must have a clearance of not less than _____ above a window that can be opened.
   a. two feet
   b. three feet
   c. eight feet
   d. ten feet

4. *NEC Section 230.6* considers conductors installed under at least _____ inch(es) of concrete to be outside the building.
   a. one
   b. two
   c. four
   d. five

5. Type NM cable may *not* be used in _____.
   a. shallow chases of masonry, concrete, or adobe
   b. the framework of a building
   c. protective strips
   d. attic spaces

6. Type MC cable may *not* be used _____.
   a. in concrete or plaster where dry
   b. in dry masonry
   c. in attic spaces
   d. where subject to physical damage

7. Type SE cable is available with _____ for interior wiring systems.
   a. a non-insulated ground or neutral conductor
   b. an insulated grounded conductor
   c. no ground conductor
   d. guard strips

8. Type SER cable may be used _____.
   a. in overhead applications
   b. underground
   c. as a subfeed under certain conditions
   d. in hazardous locations

Identify the following receptacles by numbers shown below for each receptacle.

9. _____ Single receptacle
10. _____ Split-wired receptacle
11. _____ Dryer receptacle
12. _____ Range receptacle
13. _____ Duplex receptacle
14. _____ Special-purpose outlet

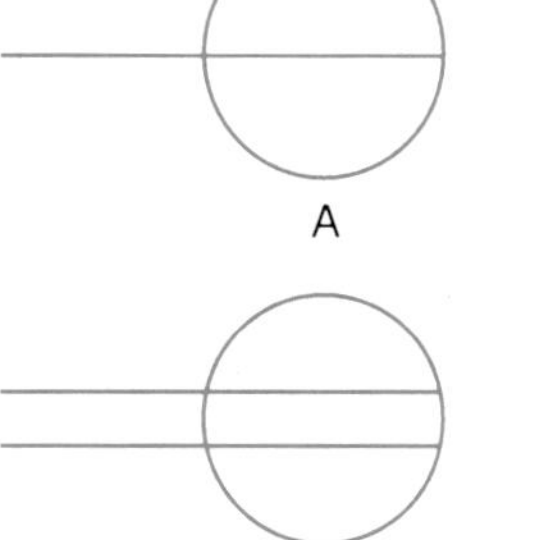

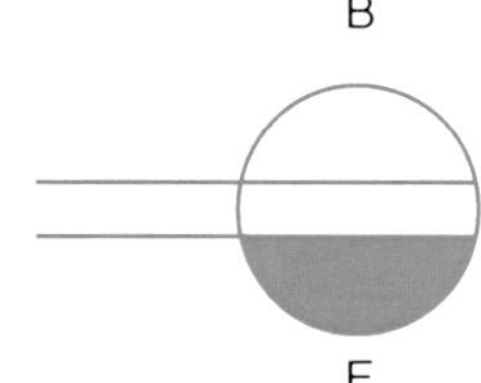

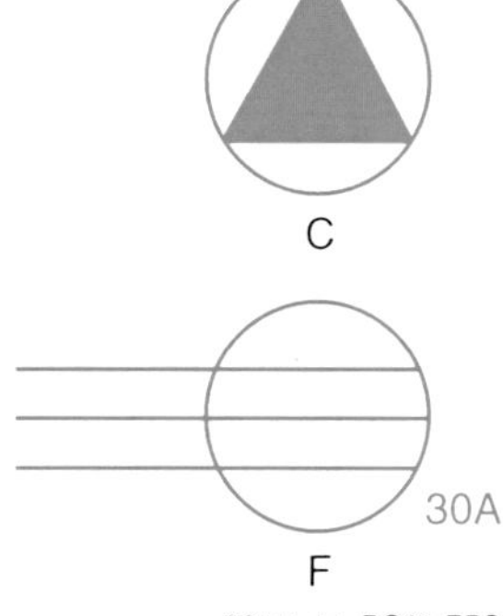

26111-14_RQ01.EPS

15. Using *NEC Table 314.16(A),* calculate the cubic inches required for the receptacle outlets shown in the table below. Then, indicate the size of the metallic box that should be used.

Number and Size of Conductors in Box	Free Space within Box for Each Conductor	Total Cubic Inches of Box Space Required	What Size Metallic Box May Be Used?
A. Six No. 12 conductors and three ground wires	2.25	_____	_____
B. Seven No. 12 conductors and three ground wires with one receptacle	2.25	_____	_____
C. Two No. 14 conductors and one ground wire	2.0	_____	_____
D. Four No. 14 conductors and two ground wires	2.0	_____	_____
E. Six No. 14 conductors and three ground wires with one receptacle	2.0	_____	_____

Trade Terms Quiz

Fill in the blank with the correct term that you learned from your study of this module.

1. A cable that contains insulated circuit conductors enclosed in armor made of metal is ____________ cable.
2. A factory-assembled cable with two or more insulated conductors and a nonmetallic jacket is called ____________ cable.
3. A(n) ____________ is a piece of equipment that has been designed for a particular purpose.
4. A(n) ____________ is used for turning an electrical circuit on and off.
5. The circuit that is routed to a switch box for controlling electric lights is known as a(n) ____________.
6. A(n) ____________ is equipped with a conductor terminal to take a bonding jumper.
7. A(n) ____________ is a bare or green insulated conductor used to ensure conductivity between metal parts that are required to be electrically connected.
8. The ____________ is comprised of the conductors that extend from the last power company pole to the point of connection at the service facilities.
9. The ____________ is the point where power is supplied to a building.
10. ____________ lie between the point of termination of the overhead service drop or underground service lateral and the main disconnecting device in the building.
11. ____________ mainly provides overcurrent protection to the feeder and service conductors.
12. A(n) ____________ is comprised of the underground conductors through which service is supplied between the power company's distribution facilities and their first point of connection to the building.
13. The portion of a wiring system that extends beyond the final overcurrent device is the ____________.
14. A(n) ____________ is a circuit that carries current from the service equipment to a subpanel or a branch circuit panel or to some point in the wiring system.
15. Normally located at the service entrance of a residential installation, a(n) ____________ usually contains the main disconnect.
16. Raceway, cable, wires, boxes, and other equipment are installed during ____________.

Trade Terms

Appliance
Bonding bushing
Bonding jumper
Branch circuit
Feeder
Load center
Metal-clad (Type MC) cable
Nonmetallic-sheathed (Type NM) cable
Romex®
Roughing in
Service drop
Service entrance
Service-entrance conductors
Service-entrance equipment
Service lateral
Switch
Switch leg

Module 26111-14
Supplemental Exercises

1. Because all residential electrical outlets are never used at the same time, the *NEC®* allows a diversity or ______________________ to be used when sizing the general lighting load for electric services.

2. When sizing the general lighting load for electric services, what percentage is the first 3,000VA rated at? ______________________

3. The minimum service disconnecting means for a one-family dwelling is ______________________.

4. The general lighting load in a residence is 3,600VA at 120V. What is the amperage?

   ____

5. A single-pole GFCI breaker is rated at ______________________.

6. True or False? In a residential electric service, the service can be grounded to the underground gas piping system.

7. Service drop conductors must be at least ______________________ feet above the ground or other accessible surface at all times.

8. True or False? GFCI protection is required for receptacles in residential bathrooms.

9. In a noncombustible wall, the outlet box may be recessed ______________________.

10. A duplex receptacle outlet must be installed in all hallways longer than ___________________ feet.

11. Electric ranges, clothes dryers, and water heaters that operate at 240V require a(n) ____________ circuit breaker.

12. In general, there are two basic methods used in the majority of modern residential electrical systems. What are they?

    ____

    ____

13. In a standard 125V receptacle, which wire is connected to the brass terminal?

    ____

14. Three-way switches are used to control lamps from ______________________ different locations.

15. The minimum number of small appliance circuits required by the *NEC®* in a kitchen area is ______________________.

Cornerstone of Craftsmanship

Dan Lamphear

Associated Builders and Contractors, Inc.

Like many other people, Dan Lamphear just fell into his career as an electrician. But once he discovered the electrical trade, he knew he had found a home. Since then, he has progressed from a helper to an apprentice, a journeyman, an independent contractor, an inventor, and finally, a teacher.

It was as much luck as anything else that led Dan toward a career as a professional electrician more than two decades ago. He wasn't sure what he wanted to do with his life after graduating from high school. However, after watching an electrician perform a commercial wiring job at a friend's business—and providing a helping hand—he was hooked. "It seemed like a challenging career, and I was curious to learn more about how electricity works," he recalls.

Dan was hired by that same electrician, under whom he apprenticed for several years before hearing about the NCCER program. He jumped at the chance to further his skills through the program. "Like they say, knowledge is money," he smiles.

After graduating from the program, Dan struck out on his own as an independent electrician, specializing in plant maintenance, industrial, and commercial work. His ability to diagnose and repair electrical problems in factory machinery soon made him a valuable contractor in Milwaukee's industrial sector.

He also discovered his knack for invention, and he has designed and built specialized machinery for a company that hired him as its full-time electrical maintenance supervisor. "Knowing the electrical side of machinery allowed me to understand how they operate mechanically," he says of his work as an inventor.

Dan later returned to the Associated Builders and Contractors (ABC) chapter, which trains out of a local community college, to repay the favor that helped him embark on his career. He teaches Electrical Level 2 courses for students who represent the next generation of professional electricians.

"Knowing how to use test instruments is perhaps the most important aspect of the job," he notes. "I still have some of the same meters I started out with."

Cornerstone of Craftsmanship

David Lewis

Instructor
Putnam Career & Technical Center

David Lewis started his career working in coal mines. After a few years he opened his own electrical business. Now he is an electrical instructor and works with the State Department of Education on curriculum development. He also serves on the NCCER revision team for the Electrical curriculum.

How did you first get interested in the field?
After graduating from high school in 1972 and attending college for a while, I decided that I wanted to work in the coal mines. Electricity interested me, so I became a maintenance foreman/electrician. Eventually, I started my own business.

What kind of training have you been through?
While working in the coal mines, I attended several electrical training classes and obtained my underground electrical license. While in business for myself I got my Master Electrician license and attended many update classes. Since I have started teaching, I have attended classes on PLCs and other topics. I also went back to college and obtained a bachelor of science degree in Career and Technical Education.

What work have you done in your career?
In the coal mines I worked on all types of mining equipment. After starting my own business, I worked mainly in residential and light commercial wiring.

Tell us about your present job and what you like about it.
I enjoy being an instructor in Electrical Technology. I work mostly with high school students and during the two years they are with me, it is great to see them grasp the knowledge of electricity.

What factors have contributed most to your success?
Hard work and the willingness to learn from experienced electricians.

What advice would you give to those new to the field?
Try to learn all you can. Work with an experienced electrician and learn from them. Attend any training or classes that you can. There is always something new to learn.

Trade Terms Introduced in This Module

Appliance: Equipment designed for a particular purpose (for example, using electricity to produce heat, light, or mechanical motion). Appliances are usually self-contained, are generally available for applications other than industrial use, and are normally produced in standard sizes or types.

Bonding bushing: A special conduit bushing equipped with a conductor terminal to take a bonding jumper. It also has a screw or other sharp device to bite into the enclosure wall to bond the conduit to the enclosure without a jumper when there are no concentric knockouts left in the wall of the enclosure.

Bonding jumper: A bare or green insulated conductor used to ensure the required electrical conductivity between metal parts required to be electrically connected. Bonding jumpers are frequently used from a bonding bushing to the service-equipment enclosure to provide a path around concentric knockouts in an enclosure wall, and they may also be used to bond one raceway to another.

Branch circuit: The portion of a wiring system extending beyond the final overcurrent device protecting a circuit.

Feeder: A circuit, such as conductors in conduit or a cable run, that carries current from the service equipment to a subpanel or a branch circuit panel or to some point in the wiring system.

Load center: A type of panelboard that is normally located at the service entrance of a residential installation. It usually contains the main disconnect.

Metal-clad (Type MC) cable: A factory assembly of one or more insulated circuit conductors with or without optical fiber members enclosed in an armor of interlocking metal tape, or a smooth or corrugated metallic sheath.

Nonmetallic-sheathed cable: A factory assembly of two or more insulated conductors enclosed within an overall nonmetallic jacket. Type NM contains insulated conductors enclosed within an overall nonmetallic jacket; Type NMC contains insulated conductors enclosed within an overall, corrosion-resistant, nonmetallic jacket; and Type NMS contains insulated power or control conductors with signaling, data, and communications conductors within an overall nonmetallic jacket.

Romex®: General Cable's trade name for Type NM cable; however, it is often used generically to refer to any nonmetallic-sheathed cable.

Roughing in: The first stage of an electrical installation, when the raceway, cable, wires, boxes, and other equipment are installed. This is the electrical work that must be done before any finishing work can be done.

Service drop: The overhead conductors, through which electrical service is supplied, between the last power company pole and the point of their connection to the service facilities located at the building.

Service entrance: The point where power is supplied to a building (including the equipment used for this purpose). The service entrance includes the service main switch or panelboard, metering devices, overcurrent protective devices, and conductors/raceways for connecting to the power company's conductors.

Service-entrance conductors: The conductors between the point of termination of the overhead service drop or underground service lateral and the main disconnecting device in the building.

Service-entrance equipment: Equipment that provides overcurrent protection to the feeder and service conductors, a means of disconnecting the feeders from energized service conductors, and a means of measuring the energy used.

Service lateral: The underground conductors through which service is supplied between the power company's distribution facilities and the first point of their connection to the building or area service facilities located at the building.

Switch: A mechanical device used for turning an electrical circuit on and off.

Switch leg: A circuit routed to a switch box for controlling electric lights.

Additional Resources

This module presents thorough resources for task training. The following resource material is suggested for further study.

National Electrical Code® Handbook, Latest Edition. Quincy, MA: National Fire Protection Association.

Figure Credits

Associated Builders and Contractors, Inc., Module opener

John Traister, Figure 2, Figures 5–8, Figures 10–13, Figures 19–23, Figures 25–29, Figure 35, Figure 43, Figure 44, Figure 53, Figure 55

Topaz Publications, Inc., Figure 16B, Figure 37B, 111SA01A, 111SA02, 111SA04, 111SA05

Tim Dean, Figure 40, 111SA01B

Greenlee Textron, Inc., a subsidiary of Textron Inc., 111SA03

Other Codes and Standards That Apply to Electrical Installations

Until 2000, there were three model building codes:

- *Standard Building Code (SBC)* – Published by the Southern Building Code Congress International.
- *BOCA National Building Code (NBC)* – Published by the Building Officials and Code Administrators.
- *Uniform Building Code (UBC)* – Published by the International Conference of Building Officials.

The three code writing groups, SBCCI, BOCA, and UBC, combined into one organization called the International Code Council with the purpose of writing one nationally accepted family of building and fire codes. It is known as the *International Building Code.*

The *International Residential Code (IRC)* is adopted as part of the electrical code requirements in many areas of the country. The *IRC* covers one- and two-family dwellings of three stories or less. The *IRC* includes requirements for such things as ventilating fans for bathrooms, requirements for smoke detectors, and other items not specified by the *NEC®*. The *IRC* covers all trades, including building, plumbing, mechanical, gas, energy, and electrical.

The NFPA also publishes its own building code, *NFPA 5000.*

To be thoroughly competent in the electrical trade, you should become familiar with the contents of these codes and the terminology used in them.

NOTE

Always refer to the latest editions of codes in effect in your area.

NCCER CURRICULA — USER UPDATE

NCCER makes every effort to keep its textbooks up-to-date and free of technical errors. We appreciate your help in this process. If you find an error, a typographical mistake, or an inaccuracy in NCCER's curricula, please fill out this form (or a photocopy), or complete the online form at **www.nccer.org/olf**. Be sure to include the exact module ID number, page number, a detailed description, and your recommended correction. Your input will be brought to the attention of the Authoring Team. Thank you for your assistance.

Instructors – If you have an idea for improving this textbook, or have found that additional materials were necessary to teach this module effectively, please let us know so that we may present your suggestions to the Authoring Team.

NCCER Product Development and Revision

13614 Progress Blvd., Alachua, FL 32615

Email: curriculum@nccer.org
Online: www.nccer.org/olf

❑ Trainee Guide ❑ AIG ❑ Exam ❑ PowerPoints Other ______________________

Craft / Level: Copyright Date:

Module ID Number / Title:

Section Number(s):

Description:

Recommended Correction:

Your Name:

Address:

Email: Phone:

Distribution Equipment

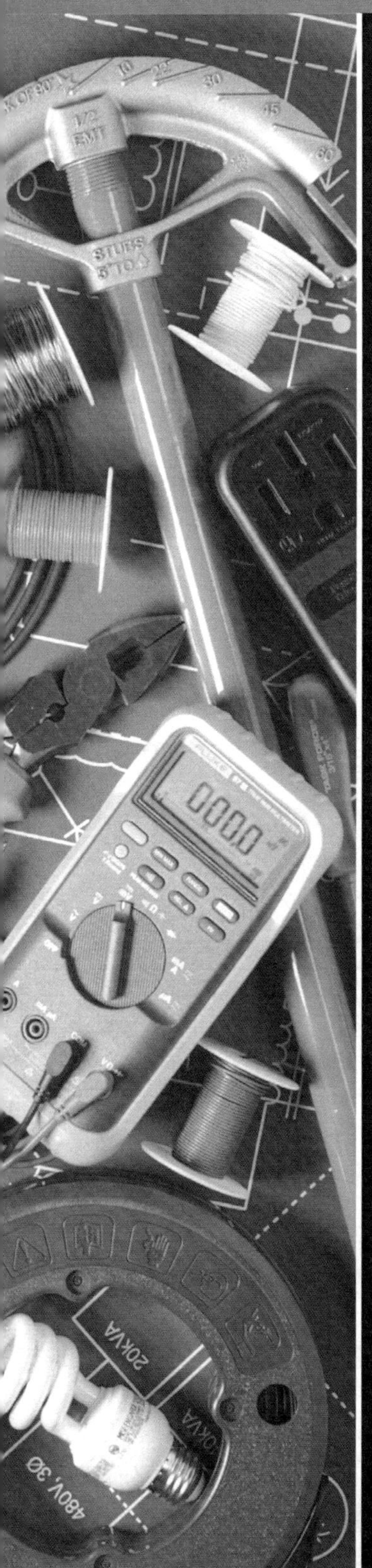

Hoover Dam

Upon completion in 1935, Hoover Dam was the world's largest electric power-producing facility and its largest concrete structure. Today, this National Historic Landmark is the 34th largest hydroelectric generating station on the globe, producing an average 4.4 billion kilowatt-hours per year.

26306-14

Trainees with successful module completions may be eligible for credentialing through NCCER's National Registry. To learn more, go to **www.nccer.org** or contact us at **1.888.622.3720.** Our website has information on the latest product releases and training, as well as online versions of our *Cornerstone* magazine and Pearson's product catalog.

Your feedback is welcome. You may email your comments to **curriculum@nccer.org,** send general comments and inquiries to **info@nccer.org,** or fill in the User Update form at the back of this module.

This information is general in nature and intended for training purposes only. Actual performance of activities described in this manual requires compliance with all applicable operating, service, maintenance, and safety procedures under the direction of qualified personnel. References in this manual to patented or proprietary devices do not constitute a recommendation of their use.

Distribution Equipment

Objectives

When you have completed this module, you will be able to do the following:

1. Describe the purpose of switchgear.
2. Describe the four general classifications of circuit breakers and list the major circuit breaker ratings.
3. Describe switchgear construction, metering layouts, wiring requirements, and maintenance.
4. List *National Electrical Code®* (*NEC®*) requirements pertaining to switchgear.
5. Describe the visual and mechanical inspections and electrical tests associated with low-voltage and medium-voltage cables, metal-enclosed busways, and metering and instrumentation.
6. Describe a ground fault relay system and explain how to test it.

Performance Tasks

This is a knowledge-based module. There are no Performance Tasks.

Trade Terms

Air circuit breaker
Basic impulse insulation level (BIL)
Branch circuit
Bus
Bushing
Capacity
Current transformer (CT)
Distribution system equipment
Distribution transformer
Feeder
Metal-enclosed switchgear
Potential transformer (PT)
Service-entrance equipment
Switchboard
Switchgear

Required Trainee Materials

1. Pencil and paper
2. Appropriate personal protective equipment
3. Copy of the latest edition of the *National Electrical Code®*

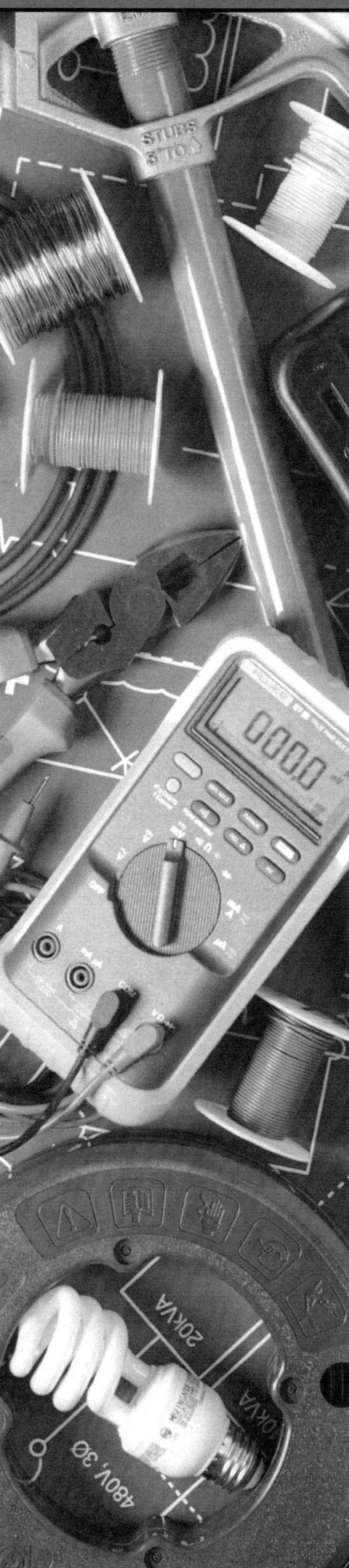

Contents

Topics to be presented in this module include:

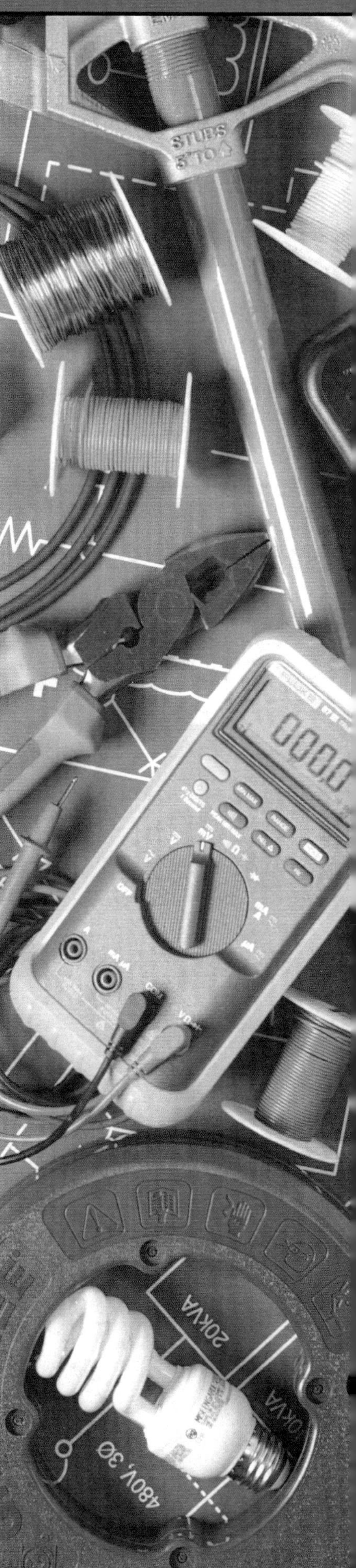

STUBS
20KVA
480V, 3Ø

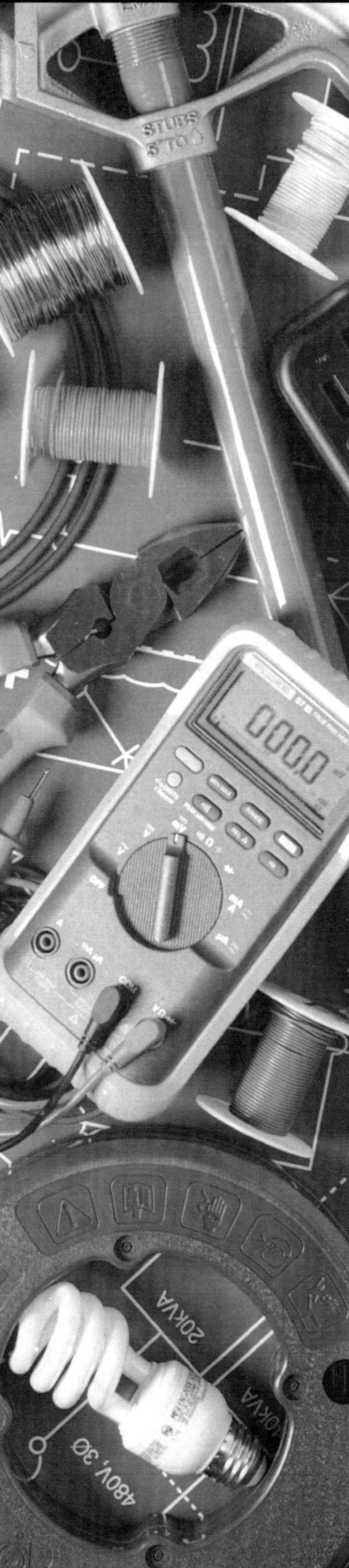

Figures and Tables

1.0.0 Introduction

An electrical power system consists of several subsystems on both the utility (supply) side and the customer (user) side. Electricity generated in power plants is stepped up to transmission voltage and fed into a nationwide grid of transmission lines. This power is then bought, sold, and dispatched as needed. Local utility companies take power from the grid and reduce the voltage to levels suitable for subtransmission and distribution through various substations to the customer. This may range from the common 200A, 120/240V residential service to thousands of amps at voltages from 480V to 69kV in an industrial facility.

From the point of service, customers must control, distribute, and manage the power to supply their electrical needs. This module will discuss how this is done using a typical industrial facility as an example. We will discuss the various components of the distribution system and their interdependence. An understanding of single-line diagrams will allow analysis of a facility's distribution system.

> **NOTE**
> The voltage conventions used in this module are industry standards for distribution systems.

2.0.0 Voltage Classifications

While electrical systems and equipment are often classified by voltage rating, switchgear is classified first by the type of construction and secondly by voltage rating. It is important to note that there is no official industry-wide voltage classification system. For example, the *NEC*® considers anything above 600V as high voltage, while the transmission sector considers anything below 72,500V (72.5kV) as low voltage. In industrial applications, the term *low-voltage* refers to systems rated up to 1,000V, while medium voltage refers to systems rated above 1,000V and up to 38,000V (38kV). This is the range in which metal-clad switchgear and circuit breakers are manufactured in standard configurations. This is also the voltage range in which premolded and shrink-on termination kits are readily available for shielded cable terminations. Above this voltage level, cable is usually run on overhead power lines rather than in raceway or cable tray.

Low-voltage power circuit breaker switchgear, for example, may be rated up to 1,000VAC or 3,200VDC. Metal-clad or metal-enclosed switchgear is applied at voltages over 1,000VAC up to a maximum of 38,000VAC.

3.0.0 Switchboards

According to the *National Electrical Code*®, the term **switchboard** may be defined as a large single panel, frame, or assembly of panels on which switches, overcurrent and other protective devices, **buses**, and instruments may be mounted, either on the face, on the back, or on both the face and back. Switchboards are generally accessible from both the rear and from the front and are not intended to be installed in cabinets.

3.1.0 Applications

Switchboards are used in modern distribution systems to subdivide large blocks of electrical power. One location for switchboards is typically where the main power enters the building. In this location, the switchboard is referred to as **service-entrance equipment**. The other location common for switchboards is downstream from the service-entrance equipment. In the downstream location, the switchboard is commonly referred to as **distribution system equipment**.

3.2.0 General Description

A switchboard consists of a stationary structure that includes one or more freestanding units of uniform height that are mechanically and electrically joined to make a single coordinated installation. These cubicles contain circuit-interrupting devices. They take up less space in a plant, have more eye appeal, and eliminate the need for a separate room to protect personnel from contact with lethal voltages.

The main portion of the switchboard is formed from heavy-gauge steel welded with members across the top and bottom to provide a rigid enclosure. Most switchboard enclosures are divided into three sections: the front section, the bus section, and the cable section. These three sections are physically separated from one another by metal partitions. This confines any damage that may occur to any one section and keeps it from affecting the other sections.

Typical switchboard components include:

- Circuit breakers
- Fuses
- Motor starters
- Ground fault systems
- Instrument transformers
- Switchboard metering
- Control power transformers
- Busbars

Electrical ratings include three-phase, three-wire and three-phase, four-wire systems with voltage ratings up to 600V and current ratings up to 6,000A and above.

A switchboard enclosure is described as a dead front panel, which means that no live parts are exposed on the opening side of the equipment; however, it contains energized breakers. Busbars can be a standard size or customized. Standard sizes are usually made of silver-plated or tin-plated copper or tin-plated aluminum. Conventional bus sizing is 0.25" × 2" through 0.375" × 7". Copper provides an ampacity of 1,000A/sq. in. of cross-sectional area. When using aluminum, the ampacity is 750A/sq. in.

When two busbars are bolted together using Grade S hardware with the proper torque, the ampacity of the connection is 200A/sq. in. of the lapped portion for aluminum or copper bussing. Bussing joints must be bolted together to the specified torque and include Belleville washers or Keps nuts. Aluminum busbars must be tin-plated, and copper busbars over 600A must be plated with tin or silver.

On Site

Busbars

Busbars have very specific spacing requirements. Note the red spacer blocks on the switchgear shown here.

26306-14_SA01.EPS

3.3.0 Switchboard Frame Heating

Table 1 shows guidelines that should be observed in order to keep heat losses in the iron switchboard frame members to a safe minimum. The dimensions are recommended values and should be adhered to whenever possible.

NOTE

Some switchboard frames are engineered differently and will have values other than those shown in *Table 1*.

3.4.0 Low-Voltage Spacing Requirements

To minimize tracking or arcing from energized parts to ground, switchboard construction includes spacing requirements. These spacing requirements are measured between live parts of opposite polarity and between live parts and grounded metal parts. *Figure 1* illustrates typical switchboard spacing requirements.

An isolated dead metal part, such as a screw-head or washer, interposed between uninsulated live parts of opposite polarity or between an uninsulated live part and grounded dead metal, is considered to reduce the spacing by an amount

Table 1 Switchboard Frame Heating Guidelines

Amperes	Minimum Distance from Phase Bus to Closest Steel Member	Minimum Distance from Neutral Bus to Closest Steel Member
3,000	4"	2"
4,000	6"	3"
5,000 and over	12"	see below
5,000 to 6,000	An aluminum or nonmagnetic material should be used in place of steel frame sections. Wherever possible, you must maintain 12" to steel members and 6" to aluminum or nonmagnetic members. Neutral spacing can be 6" and 3", respectively. If the main bus is tapered, it is permissible (at 4,000A and below) to use steel frames for those sections containing the tapered bus.	
6,000 and over	You must use an aluminum or nonmagnetic material for frame sections and maintain 12" to steel members and 6" to aluminum or nonmagnetic members. Neutral spacing can be 6" and 3", respectively. The use of any steel frame members is discouraged. If the main bus is tapered, it is permissible (at 4,000A and below) to use steel frames for those sections containing the tapered bus.	

Note: For amperages above 8,000A, the neutral spacing must be 12" wherever possible.

VOLTAGE INVOLVED		MINIMUM SPACING BETWEEN LIVE PARTS OF OPPOSITE POLARITY		MINIMUM SPACING THROUGH AIR AND OVER SURFACE BETWEEN LIVE PARTS AND GROUNDED METAL PARTS
GREATER THAN	MAX.	THROUGH AIR	OVER SURFACE	BOTH THROUGH AIR AND OVER SURFACE
0	125	½"	¾"	½"
125	250	¾"	1¼"	½"
250	600	1"	2"	*1"

* A through air spacing of not less than ½" is acceptable (1) at a molded-case circuit breaker or a switch other than a snap switch, (2) between uninsulated live parts of a meter mounting or grounded dead metal, and (3) between grounded dead metal and the neutral of a 480Y/277V, three-phase, four-wire switchgear section.

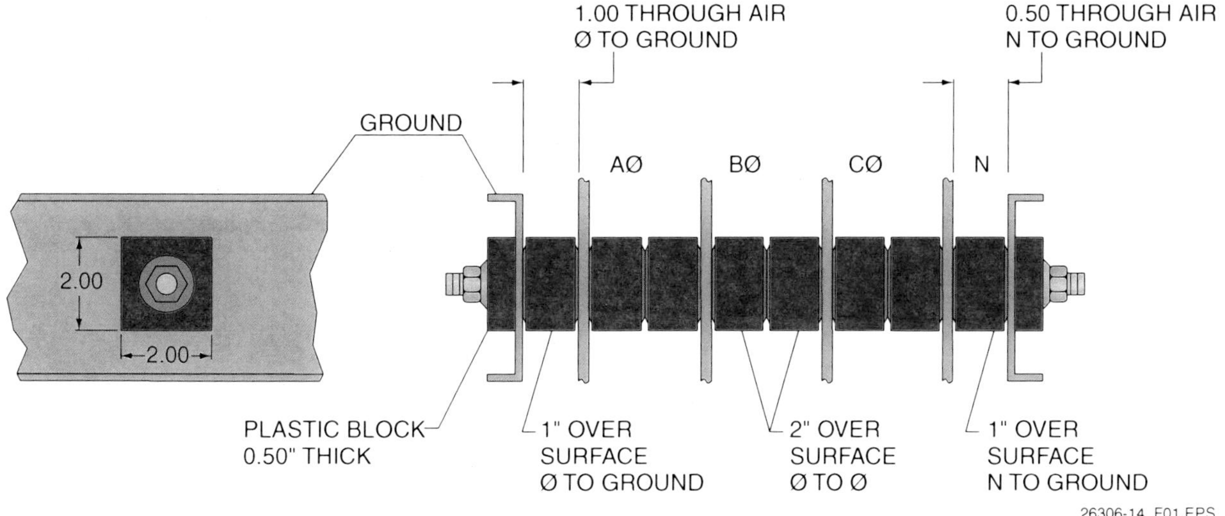

Figure 1 Typical busbar spacing requirements.

equal to the dimension of the interposed part along the path of measurement.

When measuring over-surface spacing, any slot, groove, and the like that is 0.013" (0.33 mm) wide or less and in the contour of the insulating material is to be disregarded.

When measuring spacing, an air space of 0.013" or less between a live part and an insulating surface is to be disregarded, and the live part is to be considered in contact with the insulating material. A pressure wire connector shall be prevented from any turning motion that would result in less than the minimum acceptable spacings. The means used to ensure turn prevention must be reliable, such as a shoulder or boss. A lock washer alone is not acceptable.

A means of turn prevention need not be provided if spacings are not less than the following minimum accepted values:

- When the connector and any connector of opposite polarity have each been turned 30 degrees toward the other
- When the connector has been turned 30 degrees toward other live parts of opposite polarity and toward grounded dead metal parts

3.5.0 Cable Bracing

All construction using conductors and having a short circuit current rating greater than 50,000 rms symmetrical amperes requires a cable brace positioned as close to the supply lugs as possible. The cable brace is intended to be mounted in the same area that is allotted for wire bending. It is not necessary to provide additional mounting height to accommodate the cable brace.

The cable brace requirement does not apply to load-side cables, main breakers, or switches. It only applies when cables are connected directly to an unprotected line-side bus. The bus restrictions for a line-side bus are as follows:

- There can be no splice in edgewise bus mounting of 2,100A or less rated at 50,000 rms symmetrical amperes.

- There can be no splice in flatwise bus mounting of 600A or less rated over 50,000 rms symmetrical amperes.

NOTE

This does not apply to connections made from the through bus to a switch or circuit breaker.

The cable restrictions for a line-side bus include:

- Busing of 600A or less that is rated over 50,000 rms symmetrical amperes cannot use cables; it must be bus connected.
- If cabling is required, 800A minimum busing must be used.

Cable bracing requirements may be excluded if the busing is able to fully withstand the total available short circuit current.

4.0.0 Switchgear

Switchgear is a general term used to describe switching and interrupting devices and assemblies of those devices containing control, metering, protective, and regulatory equipment, along with the associated interconnections and supporting structures. Switchgear performs two basic functions:

- Provides a means of switching or disconnecting power system apparatus
- Provides power system protection by automatically isolating faulty components

Switchgear can be classified as:

- Metal-enclosed switchgear (low voltage)
- Metal-clad switchgear (low and medium voltage)
- Metal-enclosed interrupters
- Unit substations

The low-voltage and medium-voltage switchgear assemblies are completely enclosed on all sides and topped with sheet metal, except for ventilating openings and inspection windows. They contain primary power circuit switching or interrupting devices, buses, connections, and control and auxiliary devices. *Figure 2* shows typical low-voltage, metal-clad switchgear.

The station-type cubicle switchgear consists of indoor and outdoor types with power circuit breakers rated from 14.4kV to 34.5kV, 1,200A to 5,000A, and 1,500kVA with 2,500kVA interrupting capacity. Equipment can be special ordered and built at higher kVA ratings.

26306-14_F02.EPS

Figure 2 Typical low-voltage, metal-clad switchgear.

4.1.0 Switchgear Construction

Switchgear consists of a stationary structure that includes one or more freestanding units of uniform height that are mechanically and electrically joined to make a single coordinated installation. These units, commonly referred to as cubicles, contain circuit-interrupting devices such as circuit breakers.

Switchgear enclosures are formed from heavy-gauge sheet steel that has been welded or bolted together. Structural members across the top, sides, and bottom provide a rigid enclosure. Metal-clad switchgear enclosures are divided into three sections: the front section, the bus section, and the cable or termination section.

These three sections are physically separated from one another by metal partitions. This confines any damage that may occur to any one section and keeps it from affecting the other sections. It also separates power between the sections for ease and safety of maintenance.

The rigid enclosure provides the primary structural strength of the switchgear assembly and the means by which the switchgear is fastened to its foundation. The strength of the enclosure and its mounting system will vary depending on its intended use. For example, switchgear used in a nuclear application must meet certain seismic qualifications.

The enclosure also provides the required supports and mounts for items to be located in the switchgear and provides for the necessary interconnections between the switchgear and other plant systems. The number of sections and physical makeup of switchgear varies depending on the voltage and current ratings, project specifications, and specific manufacturer.

Figures 3 and *4* show external and internal views, respectively, of medium-voltage, metal-clad switchgear. This equipment is available in voltages from 4.76kV to 27kV and current ranges from 1,200A through 3,000A.

4.2.0 Control and Metering Safety Standards

There is a tendency among some people in the industry to use the terms *switchboard* and *switchgear* interchangeably. However, they are not the same. Switchgear is manufactured and tested to more exacting standards and is configured differently than switchboards. For example, in switchgear there are physical barriers between breakers, and between the breakers and the bus. Switchgear is more durable and fault resistant, and is commonly selected for larger applications where low-voltage power circuit breakers and selective coordination are applied, such as computer data centers, manufacturing, and process facilities.

26306-14_F03.EPS

Figure 3 Medium-voltage, metal-clad switchgear (exterior view).

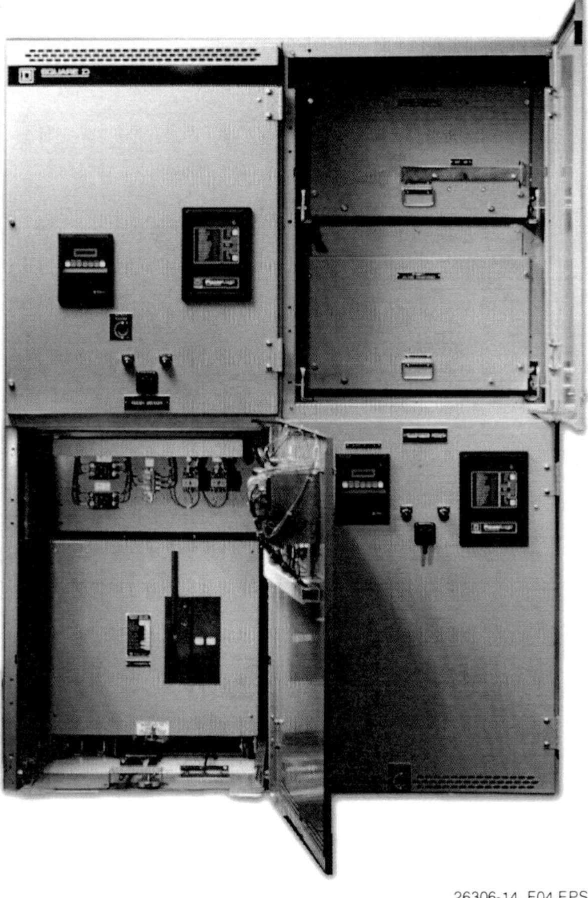

26306-14_F04.EPS

Figure 4 Medium-voltage, metal-clad switchgear (interior view).

4.3.0 Wiring System

The *NEC®* requires wiring to be supported mechanically to keep the wiring in place. Wire harnessing is generally used within the switchboard with the following restrictions:

- Each bundle or cable of wires must be run in a vertical or horizontal direction, securing the harness by means of plastic cable ties or cable clips.
- Plastic wire cable clamps shall be placed at strategic locations along the harnessing to hold the harness firmly in place to prevent interference with the control components' required electrical, mechanical, and arcing clearances.
- Apply wire ties to the harnessed wiring every 3" to 4" with self-adhesive cable ties spaced at every 12".
- Some precautions to be observed when wiring the switchboard electrical components are:
  - Keep control wires at least ½" from moving parts.
  - Avoid running wires across sharp metal edges. To protect the wiring from mechanical damage, use approved cable protectors, such as a nylon clip cable guard, a wire guard for edge protection, or special edge protection molding.
  - Wires must not touch exposed bare electrical parts of opposite polarity.
  - Wires must not interfere with the adjustment or replacement of components.
  - Wires should be as straight and as short as possible.
  - Wires shall not be spliced.
  - To eliminate possible strain on the control wire, a certain amount of slack should be given to the individual or harnessed conductor terminated at a component connection.
  - The equipment ground busbar shall not be used as a portion of the control or metering circuits.
  - Do not use pliers for bending control wiring. Use your hands or an approved wire bending device.

4.3.1 Door-Mounted Wiring Restrictions

No incoming wiring connections may be made directly to the door-mounted devices. Wires from the door-mounted equipment to the panel terminal block should be a minimum of 19-strand wire.

Wires from the door must be neatly cabled so that the door can be opened easily without placing excessive strain on the wire terminal connections. In some cases, the cable must be separated into two bundles to accomplish this. Insulated sleeving, tubing, or vinyl tape must be used to bundle and protect the flexible wires.

4.3.2 Terminal Connections

All control or metering wiring entering or leaving the switchboard should terminate at terminal blocks, leaving one side of the terminal block free for the user's connections. No factory connections are allowed on the user's terminal connection point. For factory wiring, allow a maximum of two control wires on the same side of a terminal block. No more than three connections are allowed on terminals of control transformers, meters, meter selector switches, and metering equipment.

Since bolted pressure switches or any 100% current-rated, molded-case circuit breaker's line and load power terminals are allowed a higher maximum operating temperature than the recommended insulated conductor's operating temperature, the control wires cannot be placed directly on the 100%-rated disconnect device's line and load connections.

In all cases, control wires cannot touch any exposed part of opposite electrical polarity.

4.4.0 Metering Current and Potential Transformers

Ground connections on a potential transformer (PT) or current transformer (CT) secondary terminal must be connected to the ground bus. CT secondary terminals must be shorted if no metering equipment is connected to the current transformer.

PTs are required to have primary and secondary fusing. If protective circuits, such as ground fault or phase failure protective systems, are placed in the secondary circuit of the potential transformer, no secondary fusing is required.

Metering circuit connections made directly to the incoming bus must be provided with current-limiting fuses that are equal in rating to the available interrupting capacity.

> **NOTE**
> CTs and PTs will be discussed later.

4.5.0 Switchgear Handling, Storage, and Installation

The following are basic guidelines for the handling of switchgear. It is important to note that these recommendations only supplement the manufacturer's instructions. Manufacturers include instruction books and drawings with their equipment, and it is absolutely imperative that you read and understand these documents before handling any equipment.

- *Switchgear handling* – Immediately upon receipt of switchgear, an inspection for damage during transit should be performed. If any damage is noted, the transportation company should be notified immediately.
- *Switchgear rigging* – Instructions for switchgear should be found in the manufacturer's instruction books and drawings. Verify that the rigging is suitable for the size and weight of the equipment.
- *Switchgear storage* – Indoor switchgear that is not being installed right away should be stored in a clean, dry location. The equipment should be level and protected from the environment if construction is proceeding. The longer equipment is in storage, the more care is required for protection of the equipment. If a temporary cover is used to protect the equipment, this cover should not prevent air circulation. If the building is not heated or temperature controlled, heaters should be used to prevent moisture/condensation buildup. Outdoor switchgear that cannot be installed immediately must be provided with temporary power. This power will allow operation of the space heaters provided with the equipment.
- *Bus connections* – The main bus that is usually removed during shipping should be reconnected. Ensure that the contact surfaces are clean and pressure is applied in the correct manner. The conductivity of the joints is dependent on the applied pressure at the contact points. The manufacturer's torque instructions should be referenced.
- *Cable connections* – When making cable connections, verify the phasing of each cable. This procedure is done in accordance with the connection diagrams and the cable tags. When forming and mounting cables, ensure that the cables are tightened per the manufacturer's instructions.
- *Grounding* – Any sections of ground bus that were previously disconnected for shipping should be reconnected when the units are installed. In addition, the system must be bonded at this time. The ground bus should be connected to the system ground with as direct a connection as possible. If the system ground is to be run in metal conduit, bonding to the conduit is required. The ground connection is necessary for all switchgear and should be sized per the *NEC*®.

5.0.0 Testing and Maintenance

This section covers general testing and maintenance procedures.

WARNING!

When working on switchgear or any piece of electrical equipment, you must always be aware of and follow all applicable safety procedures. You must also understand the construction and operation of the equipment. You must be specifically trained and qualified to work on or near energized electrical circuits and equipment. National consensus standards such as *NFPA 70E*® and *70B* provide specific guidance for achieving an electrically safe work condition. *NFPA 70E*®, *Standard for Electrical Safety in the Workplace, Article 120*, provides a step-by-step procedure for achieving an electrically safe work condition.

Chapter 7 in *NFPA 70B, Recommended Practice for Electrical Equipment Maintenance*, provides guidelines for personnel safety for qualified electrical workers, while other chapters provide specific direction for maintenance and troubleshooting of various types of equipment.

NOTE

Test values will differ depending on whether you are performing an acceptance test or a maintenance test.

5.1.0 General Maintenance Guidelines

To perform a visual inspection:

Step 1 Check the exterior for the proper fit of doors and covers, paint, etc.

Step 2 Check the interior, particularly the current-carrying parts, including the following items:

- Inspect the busbars for dirt, corrosion, and/or overheating.
- If necessary, perform an infrared or thermographic test. Note any discoloration that would represent a poor bus joint.
- Check the busbar supports for cracks.
- Check for correct electrical spacing.
- Verify the integrity of all bolted connections.

On Site

Protective Grounding

Even after a circuit has been isolated, de-energized, locked out, and verified without voltage, it still may not be safe to work on. This is because there is still a possibility that a circuit or conductor may be inadvertently re-energized through any one of the following means:

- Induced voltages from other energized conductors
- Static buildup from wind on outdoor conductors
- High voltage from lightning strikes
- Any condition that might bring an energized conductor into contact with the de-energized circuit
- Switching errors causing re-energizing of the circuit
- Capacitive charges in equipment or conductors

When any of these conditions are possible, *NFPA 70B, Recommended Practice for Electrical Equipment Maintenance*, requires that temporary grounds be applied before the circuit or equipment is considered safe. In fact, standard practice in overhead line construction and within open substations is that any conductor without a temporary ground connection is considered energized. While the terms *temporary ground, safety ground,* and *protective ground* are often used interchangeably, temporary grounds cover both personal protective grounds and static grounds. Personal protective grounds consist of cable connected to de-energized lines and equipment by jumpering and bonding with appropriate clamps, to limit the voltage difference between accessible points at a work site to safe values if the lines or equipment are accidentally re-energized. Protective grounds are sized to carry the maximum available fault current at the work site for the expected fault duration. Static grounds include any grounding cable or bonding jumper (including clamps) that has an ampacity less than the maximum available fault current at the work site, or is smaller than No. 2 AWG copper equivalent. Static grounds are used for potential equalizing between conductive parts in grounding configurations that cannot subject them to significant current. Therefore, smaller wire that provides adequate mechanical strength is sufficient (e.g., No. 12 AWG).

Low-voltage equipment with only a single source of supply usually does not require temporary grounding for safety. Low-voltage equipment with dual supply and medium-voltage equipment should be grounded at the bus.

ASTM International Standard F855-04, Temporary Protective Grounds to Be Used on De-energized Electric Power Lines and Equipment, is the national consensus standard covering the equipment making up the temporary grounding system. This standard addresses the parts of a temporary grounding system, which include the clamps, ferrules, cables, or a complete protective ground assembly of clamps, ferrules, and cables. These components work together and must be capable of conducting the maximum available fault current that could occur at a work location if lines or equipment become re-energized from any source, and for the expected duration of the fault. Because the circuit is NOT safe until grounding is applied, placing and removing temporary grounds is considered work on live parts, and appropriate PPE and safe work practices must be followed.

This picture shows a temporary protective ground cluster on incoming medium-voltage feeders at equipment. Not shown is the connection to the permanent system and feeder grounding conductors. This arrangement will provide safety for the connected equipment bus. Notice the phase arrangement is from left to right at the front of the equipment (the back of the equipment is shown here).

26306-14_SA02.EPS

To clean the switchboard:

Step 1 Vacuum the interior (do not use compressed air).

Step 2 Wipe down the interior using a clean, lint-free cloth. Use nonconductive, nonresidue solution, such as contact cleaner or denatured alcohol.

To check equipment operation:

Step 1 Manually open and close circuit breakers and switches.

Step 2 Electrically operate all components, such as ground fault detectors, sure trip metering, current transformers, test blocks, ground lights, blown main fuse detectors, and phase failure detectors.

To perform a megger test:

Step 1 Isolate the bus by opening all circuit breakers and switches.

Step 2 Disconnect any devices, such as relays and transformers, that may be connected to the busbars.

Step 3 Make sure all personnel are clear of the switchboard.

Step 4 Use a 1,000V megger to check the phase-to-phase and phase-to-ground resistance. Megger readings should reflect the values listed in the equipment manufacturer's instructions. Typical values are shown in *Table 2*.

5.2.0 Test Guidelines

This section provides typical guidelines for performing various tests on distribution equipment.

WARNING!

This test is performed while the equipment is energized and the covers are removed. This test may only be performed by qualified personnel under the appropriate safe work plan or permit.

5.2.1 Thermographic Survey

A thermographic (infrared) survey (*Figure 5*) involves checking switches, busways, open buses, switchgear, cable and bus connections, circuit breakers, rotating equipment, and load tap changers.

Infrared surveys should be performed during periods of maximum possible loading and not at less than 40% of the rated load of the electrical equipment being inspected. Negative test results include:

- Temperature gradients of 1°C to 3°C indicate a possible deficiency and require investigation.
- Temperature gradients of 4°C to 15°C indicate a deficiency. Repair as time permits.
- Temperature gradients of 16°C and above indicate a major deficiency. Secure power and repair as soon as possible.

5.2.2 Metal-Enclosed Switchgear and Switchboards

WARNING!

You must be qualified and authorized to perform these tests. Ensure that there is no voltage present prior to testing.

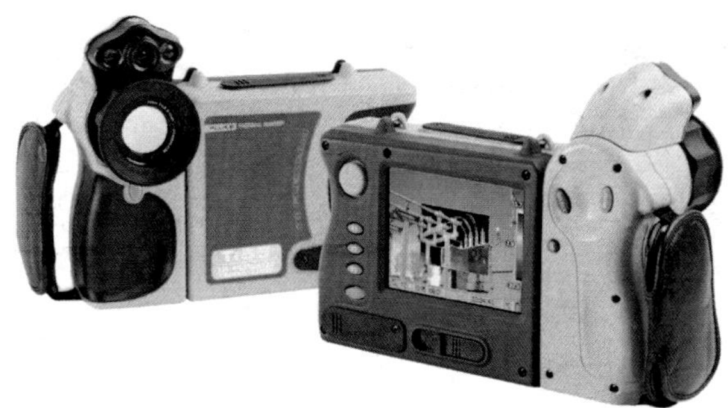

26306-14_F05.EPS

Figure 5 Infrared imager used in thermographic surveys.

Table 2 Typical Insulation Resistance Tests on Electrical Apparatus and Systems at 68°F

Minimum Voltage Rating of Equipment	Minimum Test Voltage (VDC)	Recommended Minimum Insulation Resistance (in Megohms)
2–250V	500	50
251–600V	1,000	100
601–5,000V	2,500	1,000
5,001–15,000V	2,500	5,000
15,001–39,000V	5,000	20,000

On Site

Meggers

To test for potential insulation breakdown, phase-to-phase shorts, or phase-to-ground shorts in switchgear, you need to apply a much higher potential than that supplied by the battery of an ohmmeter. A megohmmeter, or megger, is commonly used for these tests. The megger is a portable instrument consisting of a hand-driven DC generator, which supplies the level of voltage for making the measurement, and the instrument portion, which indicates the value of the resistance being measured.

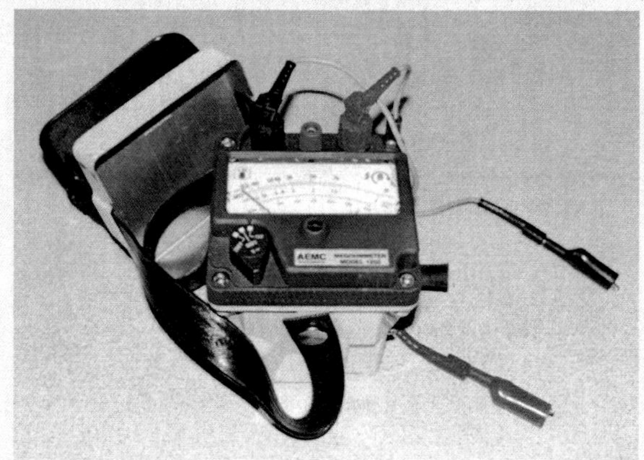

26306-14_SA03.EPS

To perform a visual and mechanical inspection:

Step 1 Inspect the physical, electrical, and mechanical condition of the equipment.

Step 2 Compare the equipment nameplate information with the latest single-line diagram, and report any discrepancies.

Step 3 Check for proper anchorage, required area clearances, physical damage, and proper alignment.

Step 4 Inspect all doors, panels, and sections for missing paint, dents, scratches, fit, and missing hardware.

Step 5 Inspect all bus connections for high resistance. Use a low-resistance ohmmeter or check tightness of bolted bus joints using a calibrated torque wrench.

Step 6 Test all electrical and mechanical interlock systems for proper operation and sequencing:
- A closure attempt must be made on all locked-open devices. An opening attempt must be made on all locked-closed devices.
- A key exchange must be made with all devices operated in normally off positions.

Step 7 Clean the entire switchgear using the manufacturer's approved methods and materials.

Step 8 Inspect insulators for evidence of physical damage or contaminated surfaces.

Step 9 Inspect the lubrication:
- Verify appropriate contact lubricant on moving current-carrying parts.
- Verify appropriate lubrication of moving and sliding surfaces.
- Exercise all active components.
- Inspect all indicating devices for proper operation.

WARNING! Electrical testing may produce hazardous voltages and may only be performed by qualified personnel under the appropriate safe work plan or permit. Prepare the area to avoid any accidental contact with the system under test, and wear appropriate personal protective equipment.

To perform electrical testing:

Step 1 Perform ratio and polarity tests on all current and voltage transformers.

Step 2 Perform ground resistance tests.

Step 3 Perform insulation resistance tests on each bus section (phase-to-phase and phase-to-ground) for one minute. Refer to the specific manufacturer's guidelines, an example of which is shown in *Table 2*.

Step 4 Perform an overpotential test on each bus section (phase-to-ground) for one minute. Refer to specific manufacturer's guidelines, an example of which is shown in *Table 3*.

NOTE The values shown in *Tables 2* and *3* are typical acceptance values. Maintenance values will vary by manufacturer.

Step 5 Perform an insulation resistance test on the control wiring. Do not perform this test on wiring connected to solid-state components.

On Site

Keyed Interlocks

Keyed interlocks, such as the one shown here, ensure that qualified personnel perform operations in the required sequence by preventing or allowing the operation of one part only when another part is locked in a predetermined position. These devices can be used for a variety of safety applications, such as preventing personnel from accessing a high-voltage compartment before opening the disconnect switch.

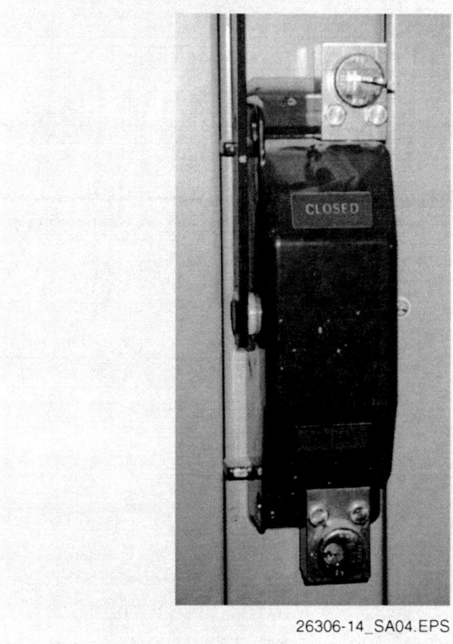

26306-14_SA04.EPS

Step 6 Perform a phasing check on double-ended switchgear to ensure proper bus phasing from each source.

Any values of insulation resistance less than those listed in the manufacturer's literature should be investigated. Overpotential tests should not proceed until insulation resistance levels are raised above minimum values.

Overpotential test voltages must be applied in accordance with the manufacturer's literature. Test results are evaluated on a go/no-go basis by slowly raising the test voltage to the required value. The final test voltage is applied for one minute.

Table 3 Overpotential DC Test Voltages for Electrical Apparatus Other Than Inductive Equipment

	DC Test Voltage Max.	
Nominal Voltage Class	**New**	**Used**
250V	2,500VDC	1,500VDC
600V	3,500VDC	2,000VDC
5,000V	18,000VDC	11,000VDC
15,000V	50,000VDC	30,000VDC

5.2.3 Low-Voltage Cables (600V Maximum)

To perform a visual and mechanical inspection:

Step 1 Inspect cables for physical damage and proper connection in accordance with the single-line diagram.

Step 2 Verify the integrity of all bolted connections.

Step 3 Check color-coded cable against the applicable engineer's specifications and *NEC*® standards.

To perform electrical testing:

Step 1 Perform an insulation resistance test on each conductor with respect to ground and adjacent conductors. The applied potential should be 1,000VDC for one minute.

Step 2 Perform a continuity test to ensure proper cable connection. The minimum insulation resistance values must not be less than two megohms.

5.2.4 Medium-Voltage Cables (15kV Maximum)

To perform a visual and mechanical inspection:

Step 1 Inspect exposed sections for physical damage.

Step 2 Inspect for shield grounding, cable support, and termination.

Step 3 Inspect for proper fireproofing in common cable areas.

Step 4 If cables are terminated through window-type CTs, make an inspection to verify that neutrals and grounds are properly terminated for normal operation of the protective devices.

Step 5 Visually inspect the jacket and insulation condition.

Step 6 Inspect for proper phase identification and arrangement.

On Site

Manufacturer's Data

Never assume anything when it comes to equipment operation, testing, or maintenance. Always refer to the manufacturer's installation, operating, and maintenance instructions for the equipment in use. These materials provide important data that explain the warranty requirements, appropriate test procedures, and specific maintenance and test points.

5.2.5 Metal-Enclosed Busways

To perform a visual and mechanical inspection:

Step 1 Inspect the bus for physical damage.

Step 2 Inspect for proper bracing, suspension, alignment, and enclosure.

Step 3 Check the tightness of bolted joints using a calibrated torque wrench.

Step 4 Check for proper physical orientation per the manufacturer's labels to ensure proper cooling. Perform continuity tests on each conductor to verify that proper phase relationships exist.

Step 5 Check outdoor busways for removal of weep-hole plugs if applicable and also for the proper installation of a joint shield.

To perform electrical testing:

Step 1 Perform an insulation resistance test. Measure the insulation resistance on each bus run (phase-to-phase and phase-to-ground) for one minute.

Step 2 Perform AC or DC overpotential tests on each bus run, both phase-to-phase and phase-to-ground.

Step 3 Perform a contact resistance test on each connection point of the uninsulated bus. On an insulated bus, measure the resistance of the bus section and compare values with adjacent phases.

Step 4 Insulation resistance test voltages and resistance values must be in accordance with the manufacturer's specifications.

Step 5 Apply overpotential test voltages in accordance with the manufacturer's specifications.

5.2.6 Metering and Instrumentation

To perform a visual and mechanical inspection:

Step 1 Examine all devices for broken parts, indication of shipping damage, and wire connection tightness.

Step 2 Verify that meter connections are in accordance with appropriate diagrams.

To perform electrical testing:

Step 1 Check the calibration of meters at all cardinal points.

Step 2 Calibrate watt-hour meters to one-half of one percent (0.5%).

Step 3 Verify all instrument multipliers.

6.0.0 *NEC®* Requirements

This section provides a brief description of the *NEC®* articles that are applicable to switchboard construction, installation, and accessories.

6.1.0 Requirements for Electrical Installations

NEC® requirements for electrical installations include the following:

- *Interrupting rating* – The interrupting rating is the maximum current a device is intended to interrupt under standard test conditions. *NEC Section 110.9* defines an interrupting rating at nominal circuit voltage sufficient for the current that is available at the line terminals of the equipment.
- *Deteriorating agents* – *NEC Section 110.11* provides for the protection of equipment and conductors from environments that could cause deterioration, such as gases, vapors, liquids, or moisture, unless specifically designed for such environments.
- *Mechanical execution of work* – *NEC Section 110.12* states that electrical equipment is to be installed in a neat and professional manner. Any openings provided by the equipment manufacturer or at the time of installation that are not being used must be sealed equivalent to the structure wall. This section also forbids the use of electrical equipment with damaged parts that may affect the safe operation or mechanical strength of the equipment.
- *Mounting and cooling* – *NEC Section 110.13* states that electrical equipment shall be securely fastened to its mounting surface by mechanical fasteners, excluding wooden plugs driven into

concrete, masonry, plaster, or similar materials. Equipment shall be located so as not to restrict air flow required for convection or forced-air cooling.

- *Electrical connections* – Due to the resistive oxidation created when dissimilar metals are connected, splicing devices and pressure connectors must be identified for the conductor material with which they are to be used (*NEC Section 110.14*). Dissimilar metal conductors may not be mixed in terminations or splices. Antioxidation compounds must be suitable for use and must not adversely affect conductors, installation, or equipment. Terminals for use with more than one conductor or aluminum must be identified as such.
- *Markings* – The manufacturer's trademark or logo and system ratings, including voltage, current, and wattage, shall be of sufficient durability to withstand the environment involved. Per *NEC Section 110.24*, field marking of service equipment shall indicate the available fault current, the date the fault current calculation was performed, and the environment. Modifications to equipment that affect available fault current shall be recalculated to ensure service equipment ratings are sufficient for additional fault current, and any field-required markings must be modified.
- *Disconnect identification* – Each disconnecting means, such as circuit breakers, fused switches, **feeders**, or unfused disconnects, must be clearly marked as to its purpose at its point of origin unless located in such a manner that its purpose is evident (*NEC Section 110.22*).
- *Working space* – Suitable access and working space shall be maintained around electrical equipment to permit safe operation and maintenance (*NEC Section 110.26*). Minimum clearances in front of all electrical enclosures must conform to those specified in *NEC Section 110.26;* in all cases, space must be adequate to allow doors or hinged parts to open to a 90-degree angle. In differing conditions, the distances in *NEC Table 110.26(A)(1)* must be adhered to. Storage of any kind is not permitted within the clearance area. In accordance with *NEC Section 110.26(C)(1)*, at least one entrance of ample size must be provided to enter and exit the work area. In cases of services over 1,200A and over 6' wide, two entrances are required. The work space must be adequately illuminated.
- *Flash protection* – *NEC Section 110.16* states that electrical equipment such as switchboards, panelboards, industrial control panels, meter socket enclosures, and motor control centers in other-than-dwelling occupancies that are likely to require examination, adjustment, servicing, or maintenance while energized shall be field or factory marked to warn qualified persons of potential electric arc flash hazards. The marking shall be located so as to be clearly visible to qualified persons before examination, adjustment, servicing, or maintenance of the equipment. It may not be handwritten, and must be durable for the environment.

Case History

How *Not* to Build a Better Mousetrap

The expensive switchgear shown here had an unused opening that was left uncovered after the installation. A rodent entered the compartment, shorting out one of the busbars and causing extensive damage.

The Bottom Line: *NEC Section 110.12(A)* requires that any unused openings must be sealed equivalent to the structure wall.

26306-14_SA05.EPS

6.2.0 Requirements for Conductors

NEC Section 200.6 covers requirements associated with identifying grounded conductors. It includes the following:

- *Neutrals* – Grounded conductors (neutrals) are color coded with a solid white or gray marking or with three white or gray stripes for the entire length of the conductor. Conductors size 4 AWG and larger may be color coded with a white or gray marking tape at termination points at the time of installation. Marking shall encircle the conductor or insulation. Where different electrical systems are run together, each system's grounded conductor must be distinctively identified [NEC Section 200.6(D)].

- *Protection* – Branch circuit conductors must be protected by overcurrent devices, as specified in *NEC Sections 240.4 and 240.21.*
- *Loading* – *NEC Section 210.19(A)(1)* states that the conductor ampacity shall not be less than the noncontinuous load plus 125% of the continuous load, and the minimum conductor size must be based on this load after the application of any adjustment factors per *NEC Section 210.19(A)(1) and NEC Tables 310.15(B)(2)(a) and 310.15(B)(3)(a).*
- *Tap rules* – Tap conductors in switchboards are tapped onto the line-side bus of the switchboard to feed control circuits, control power transformers, and metering devices. Overcurrent devices (typically fuses) are usually connected where the conductor to be protected receives its supply. However, per *NEC Section 240.21(B)(1)*, tap conductors do not require protection if the following conditions are met:
  - The length of the conductor is not over 10'.
  - The ampacity of the conductor is not less than the combined loads supplied by the conductor.
  - The conductors do not extend beyond the switchboard for control devices they supply.
  - The conductors are enclosed in a raceway except at the point of connection to the bus.
  - For field installations where the tap conductors leave the enclosure or vault in which the tap is made, the rating of the overcurrent device on the line side of the tap conductors does not exceed 10 times the tap conductor's ampacity.
- *Markings* – All conductors and cables shall be permanently marked to indicate the manufacturer, voltage, AWG size, and insulation type (*NEC Section 310.120*).
  - Grounding conductors (equipment grounding wires) shall be permitted to be bare wire. In cases of insulated grounding conductors, the conductor will have a continuous marking of green for the entire length of the conductor. Larger conductors may be marked at each end and every point where the conductor is accessible.
  - Ungrounded conductors (phase wires) must be distinguishable from grounded or grounding conductors with colors other than white, gray, or green. Typical ungrounded conductor identification colors are black, red, blue, brown, orange, and yellow. However, the only code-specified colors are for high-leg delta (*NEC Section 110.15*), direct current [(*NEC Section 210.5(C)(2)*)], and isolated power systems [(*NEC Section 517.160(A)(5)*)].
  - In switchboards fed by a four-wire, delta system in which one phase is grounded at its midpoint, the phase having the higher voltage must be marked with an orange color according to *NEC Section 110.15.*
- *Ampacities* – The ampacities of conductors are determined by the tables referenced in *NEC Section 310.15(B)* or with engineering support per *NEC Section 310.15(C).*

6.3.0 Grounding

NEC® grounding requirements include the following:

- *Grounding* – *NEC Section 250.20(B)* states that AC systems between 50V and 1,000V must be grounded when any of the following conditions are met:
  - Where the system can be grounded in such a way that the maximum phase-to-ground voltage does not exceed 150V
  - When the system is three-phase, four-wire, wye-connected and the neutral is used as a circuit conductor
  - When the system is three-phase, four-wire, delta-connected and the midpoint of a phase is used as a conductor (developed neutral)
- *Grounding electrode conductor* – *NEC Sections 250.24 and 250.66* cover the requirements of grounding electrode conductors, including proper sizing of the equipment grounding conductors to the service equipment enclosures. *NEC Section 250.24* states that for grounded systems (delta or wye), an unspliced main bonding jumper in the service equipment must be used to connect the grounding conductor and the service disconnect enclosure to the grounded conductor of the system within the enclosure.
- *Electrodes* – *NEC Sections 250.52 and 250.53* require that when rod or pipe electrodes are used, they must extend a minimum of 8' into the soil. The electrode must be no less than ¾" in diameter for pipe and ⅝" in diameter for rods. It must be galvanized metal or copper-coated to resist corrosion. Underground structures, such as water piping systems, may also be used as an electrode. Underground gas piping systems must not be used. Aluminum electrodes are not permitted. Rod, pipe, or plate electrodes must maintain a resistance of no more than 25Ω to ground. If the resistance is above 25Ω, an additional electrode is required to maintain the minimum resistance.

- *Grounding of ground wire conduits* – *NEC Section 250.64(E)* states that a grounding conductor or its enclosure must be securely mounted to the surface along which it runs. In cases where the conductor is enclosed, the enclosure must be electrically continuous and firmly grounded.
- *Ground connection surfaces* – Nonconducting coatings, such as paint, enamel, or insulating materials, must be thoroughly removed at any point where a grounding connection is made *(NEC Section 250.12)*.

6.4.0 Switchboards and Panelboards

NEC® requirements for switchboards and panelboards include the following:

- *Dedicated space* – *NEC Section 110.26(E)(1)* states that panelboards and switchboards may only be installed in spaces specifically designed for such purposes. No other piping, ducts, or devices may be installed or pass through such areas, except equipment that is necessary to the operation of the electrical equipment.
- *Inductive heating* – *NEC Section 408.3(B)* states that busbars and conductors must be arranged so as to avoid overheating due to inductive effects.
- *Phasing* – *NEC Section 408.3(E)* states that phasing in switchboards must be arranged A, B, C from front to back, top to bottom, and left to right, respectively, when facing the front of the switchboard. In systems containing a high leg, the B phase must be the phase conductor having a higher voltage to ground.
- *Wire bending space* – *NEC Section 408.4(G)* states that the wire bending space must be in accordance with *NEC Tables 312.6(A) and (B)*.
- *Minimum spacing* – *NEC Section 408.56* states that the spacing between bare metal parts and conductors must be as specified in *NEC Table 408.56*. Conductors entering the bottom of switchboards must have the clearances specified in *NEC Table 408.5*.
- *Conductor insulation* – Insulated conductors within switchboards must be listed as flame-retardant and rated at not less than the voltage applied to them or any adjacent conductors they may come in contact with *(NEC Section 408.19)*.

7.0.0 Ground Faults

Ground faults exist when an unintended current path is established between an ungrounded conductor and ground on a solidly grounded service. These faults can occur due to deteriorated insulation, moisture, dirt, rodents, foreign objects (such as tools), and careless installation.

Ground faults are usually high arcing and low level in nature, which conventional breakers will not detect. Ground fault protection is used to protect equipment and cables against these low-level faults. *NEC Section 230.95* addresses ground fault protection of equipment.

Ground fault protection is required per the *NEC®* on solidly-grounded wye services of more than 150V to ground but not exceeding a phase-to-phase voltage of 600V with each service disconnecting means of 1,000A or more.

7.1.0 Ground Fault Systems

The three basic methods of sensing ground faults include:

- Ground-return method
- Residual method
- Zero sequence method

The ground-return method incorporates a sensing coil around the grounding electrode conductor. The residual method uses three individual sensing coils to monitor the current on each phase conductor. The zero sequence method requires a single, specially designed sensor to monitor all the phases and the neutral conductor of a system at the same time, as shown in *Figure 6*.

7.2.0 Sensing Operation

When circuit conditions are normal, the currents from all the phase and neutral (if used) conductors add up to zero, and the sensor current transformer produces no signal. When any ground fault occurs, the currents add up to equal the ground fault current, and the sensor produces a signal proportional to the ground fault. This

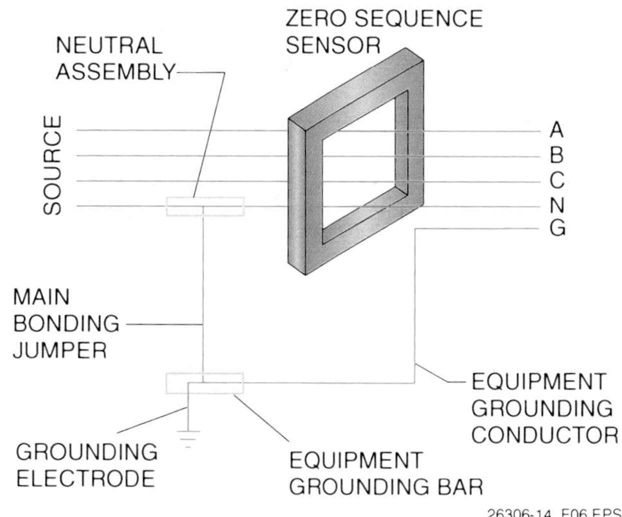

Figure 6 Zero sequencing diagram.

On Site

Transformer Grounding

This is the secondary termination compartment of a 2.5MVA padmount transformer that shows the connection and arrangement of parallel feeders serving downstream 480V switchgear. This is a solidly grounded wye transformer.

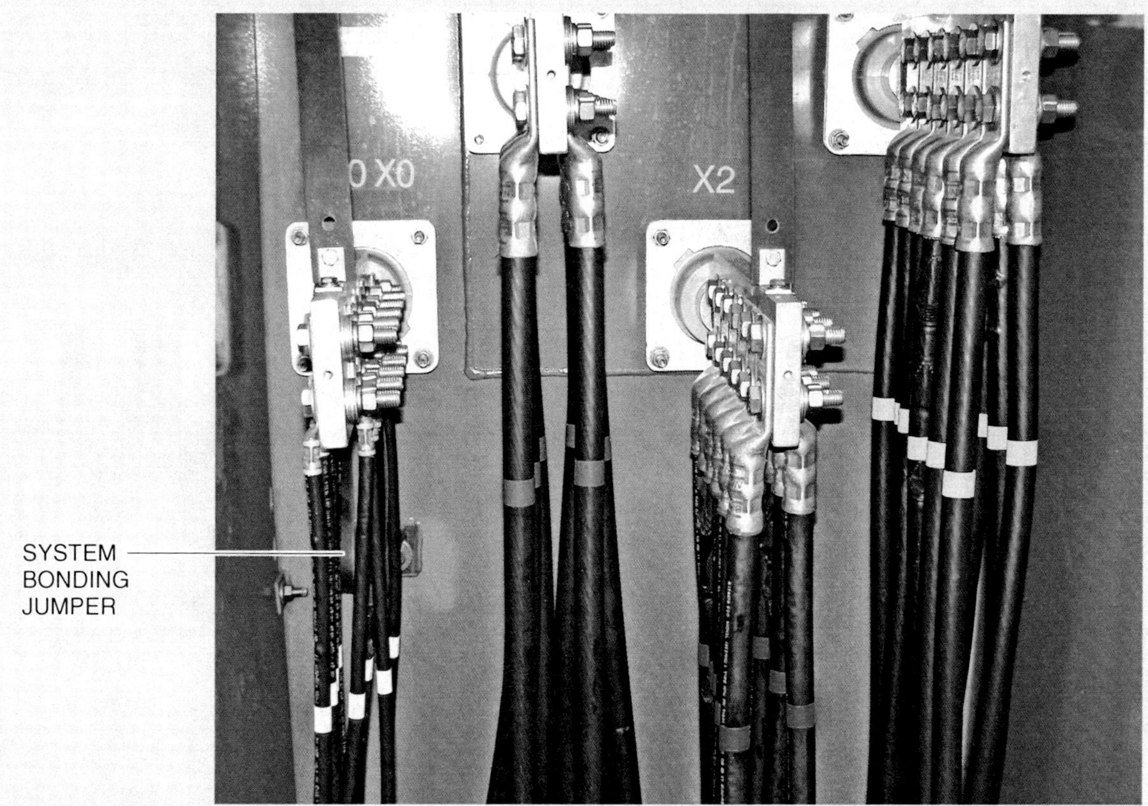

26306-14_SA06.EPS

signal provides power to the ground fault relay, which trips the circuit breaker.

A ground fault lasting for less than the time-delay period will not pick up the ground trip coil, thus eliminating nuisance tripping of self-clearing faults.

The ground fault relay is a high-reliability device due to its solid-state construction. The use of redundant, self-protecting, and high-reliability components further improves the performance. Self-protection against failure is provided through an internal fuse that will blow and result in a tripping function if the solid-state circuitry fails during a ground fault situation.

7.3.0 Zero Sequencing Sensor Mounting

The sensor current transformer (sensor) should be mounted so that all phase and neutral (if used) conductors pass through the core window once. The ground conductor (if used) must not pass through the core window. The neutral conductors must be free of all grounds after passing through the core window (see *Figure 6*).

When so specified by the system design engineer, the sensor may be mounted so that only the conductor connecting the neutral to ground at the service equipment passes through the core window. In such cases, the sensor must provide power to the particular ground fault relay that is associated with the main circuit breaker.

Maintain at least two inches of clearance from the iron core of the sensor to the nearest busbar or cable to avoid false tripping. Cable conductors should be bundled securely and braced to hold them at the center of the core window. The sensor should be mounted within an enclosure and protected from mechanical damage.

7.4.0 Relay Mounting

The ground fault relay should be mounted in a vertical position within an enclosure with the terminal block at the lower end. The location of the relay should be such that the trip setting knob is accessible without exposing the operator to contact with live parts or arcing from disconnect operations.

7.5.0 Connections

Connections for standard applications should be made in accordance with the wiring diagrams in the manufacturer's literature. An example of one circuit is shown in *Figure 7*. Wires from the sensor to the ground fault relay should be no longer than 25' and no smaller than No. 14 AWG wire. Wires from the ground fault relay to the trip coil should be no longer than 50' and no smaller than No. 14 AWG wire. All wires should be protected from arcing fault and physical damage by barriers, conduit, armor, or location in an equipment enclosure. Do not disconnect or short circuit wires to the circuit breaker trip coil at any time when the power is turned on.

7.6.0 Relay Settings

The ground fault relay has an adjustable trip setting. The amount of time delay is factory set and is available in nominal time delays of 0.1, 0.2, 0.3, and 0.5 second. When ground fault protection is used in downstream steps, the feeder should have the next lower time-delay curve than the main, the branch the next lower curve than the feeder, and so on.

High trip settings on main and feeder circuits are desirable to avoid nuisance tripping. High settings usually do not reduce the effectiveness of the protection if the ground path impedance is reasonably low. Ground faults usually quickly reach a value of 40% or more of the available short circuit current in the ground path circuit.

7.6.1 Coordination with Downstream Circuit Breakers

It is recommended that the magnetic trips of any downstream circuit breakers that are not equipped with ground fault protection be set as low as possible. Likewise, the ground fault relay trip settings for main or feeder circuits should be

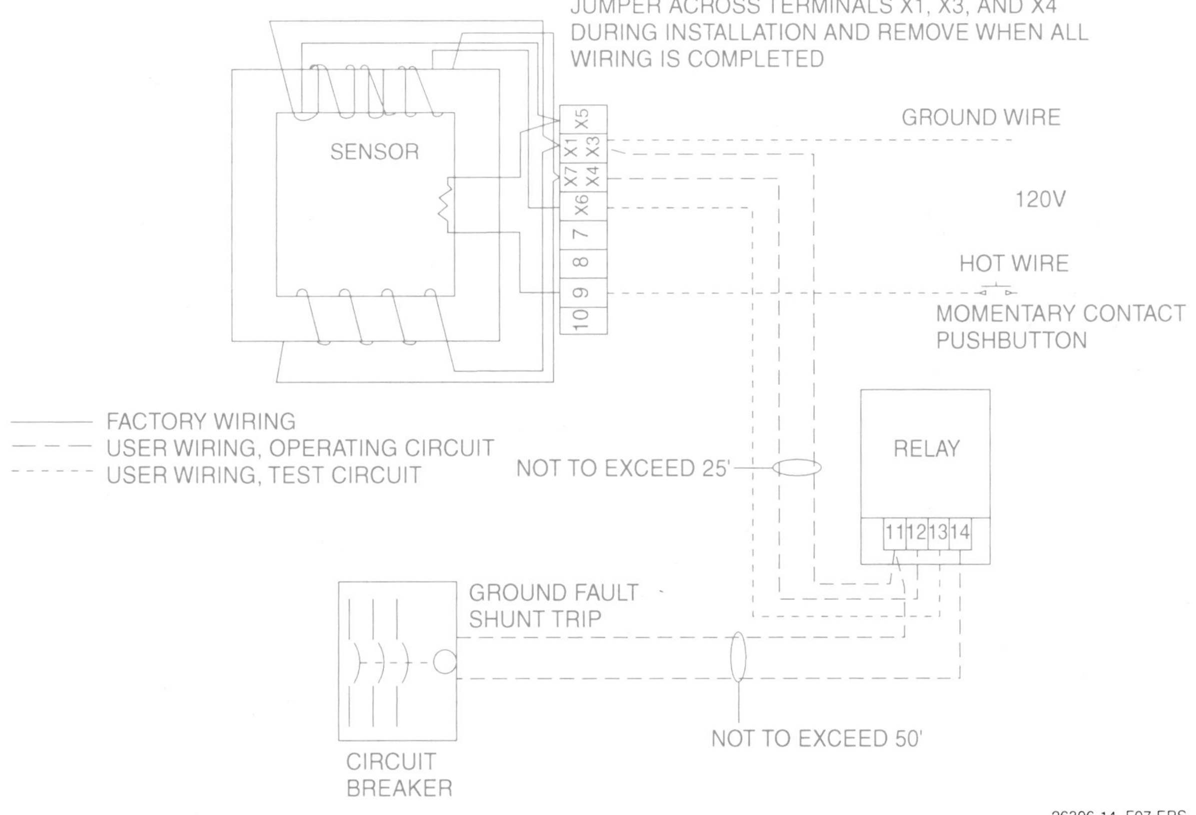

Figure 7 Typical wiring diagram.

higher than the magnetic trip settings for unprotected downstream breakers where possible. This will minimize nuisance tripping of the main or feeder breaker for ground faults occurring on downstream circuits.

7.6.2 Instantaneous Trip Feature

Standard ground-powered ground fault relays have a built-in instantaneous trip feature. This instantaneous trip has a fixed time delay of approximately 1½ cycles, and the fixed trip setting is higher than found on most feeder or branch breakers to avoid nuisance tripping. Its purpose is to interrupt very high-current ground faults on main disconnects as quickly as possible and to protect the ground fault relay components.

7.7.0 Ground Fault System Test

This section provides an overview of a generic visual inspection and electrical test for ground faults. Always follow the procedures specified by the equipment manufacturer for the system being tested.

7.7.1 Procedures

Perform a visual inspection:

Step 1 Inspect the components for physical damage.

Step 2 Determine if a ground sensor was located properly around the appropriate conductor(s):
- Zero sequence sensing requires all phases and the neutral to be encircled by the sensor(s).
- Ground return sensing requires the sensor to encircle the main bonding jumper.

Step 3 Inspect the main bonding jumper to ensure:
- Proper size
- Termination on the line side of the neutral disconnect link
- Termination on the line side of the sensor on zero sequence systems

Step 4 Inspect the grounding electrode conductor to ensure:
- Proper size
- Correct switchboard termination

Step 5 Inspect the ground fault control power transformer for proper installation and size. When the control transformer is supplied from the line side of the ground fault protection circuit interrupting device, overcurrent protection and a circuit disconnecting means must be provided.

Step 6 Visually inspect the switchboard neutral bus downstream of the neutral disconnect line to verify the absence of ground connections.

Perform electrical tests as required by *NEC Section 230.95(C):*

Step 1 Check for proper ground fault system performance, including correct response of the circuit interrupting device confirmed by primary/secondary ground sensor current injection:
- Measure the relay pickup current.
- Ensure that the relay time delay is measured at two values above the pickup current.

Step 2 Test system operation at 57% of the rated voltage.

Step 3 Functionally check the operation of the ground fault monitor panel for:
- Trip test
- No-trip test
- Nonautomatic reset

Step 4 Verify proper sensor polarity on the phase and neutral sensors for residual systems.

Step 5 Measure the system neutral insulation resistance downstream of the neutral disconnect link to verify the absence of grounds.

Step 6 Test systems (zone interlock/time coordinates) by simultaneous ground sensor current injection, and monitor for the proper response.

Test result evaluation:

- The system neutral insulation resistance should be above 100Ω and preferably one megohm or greater.

On Site

Ground Fault Trip Settings

Even minor ground faults will usually arc, causing immediate damage. Major damage can occur in a matter of a second. Ideally, the ground fault relay should respond in less than 30 cycles (½ second in a 60Hz system).

- The maximum pickup setting of the ground fault protection shall be 1,200A and the maximum time delay shall be one second for ground fault currents equal to or greater than 3,000A, according to *NEC Section 230.95(A)*.
- The relay pickup current should be within 10% of the manufacturer's calibration marks or fixed setting.
- The relay timing should be in accordance with the manufacturer's published time-current characteristics.

8.0.0 HVL Switch

Figure 8 shows the general appearance of an HVL (high-voltage limiting) switch. The HVL switch is a switching device for primary circuits up to the full interrupting current of the switch. The switches are single-throw devices designed for use on 2.4kV to 34.5kV systems.

HVL switches may provide both switching and overcurrent protection. HVL switches are commonly used as a service disconnect in unit substations and for sectionalizing medium-voltage feeder systems. The HVL switch is designed to conform to ANSI standards for metal-enclosed switchgear.

26306-14_F08.EPS

Figure 8 High-voltage limiting switch.

8.1.0 Ratings

Switch ratings are as follows:

- *Switch kV* – The design voltage for the switch. Of course, nominal system voltage is the normal application method; thus, a 5kV switch may be used for nominal system voltages of 2.4kV or 4.16kV, etc.
- **Basic impulse insulation level**, *or BIL (kV)* – The maximum voltage pulse that the equipment will withstand.
- *Frequency (Hertz)* – All HVL switches may be used in either 50Hz or 60Hz power systems.
- *Withstand (kV)* – The maximum 60Hz voltage that can be applied to the switch for one minute without causing insulation failure.
- *Capacitor switching (kVAR)* – The maximum capacitance expressed in kVAR that can be switched with the HVL.
- *Fault close* – The maximum, fully offset fault current that the switch can be closed into without sustaining damage. The term *fully offset* means that the fault current will have a delaying DC component in addition to the AC component.
- *Short time current* – The amount of current that the switch will carry for 10 seconds without sustaining any damage.
- *Continuous current (amps)* – The amount of current that the switch will carry continuously.
- *Interrupting current (amps)* – The maximum amount of current that the switch will safely interrupt.

8.2.0 Variations

There are six main types of switches:

- *Upright* – The upright switch design is the most common type. The upright construction of the service entry, jaws, and arc chutes are located near the top of the cubicle. The hinge point is below the jaws and arc chutes.
- *Inverted* – The inverted switch design has the terminals, jaws, and arc chutes located near the bottom of the cubicle. The hinge point is above the jaws and arc chutes. This type of switch is used primarily as a main switch to a lineup of other switches. Its handle operation is identical to that of an upright switch; to close the switch, the handle is moved up, and to open it, the handle is moved down.
- *Fused/unfused* – HVL switches are available in both fused and unfused models. If equipped with fuses, the entire HVL switch has the fault interrupting capacity of the fuse and therefore provides fault protection. Either current-limiting or boric acid fuses may be used in the HVL switch.

- *Duplex* – A duplex switch is actually two switches, each in its own bay. The bays are mechanically connected and the switches are electrically connected on the load side. This switch may be used to supply power to a single load from two different sources.
- *Selector* – A selector allows an HVL switch to have double-throw characteristics. The selector switch is a single switch with a load connected to the moving or switch mechanism. Throwing the switch to one side connects the load to one source, while throwing it the other way connects it to a second source. The selector switch will be interlocked with another switch to prevent the selector switch from interrupting current flow. The selector serves a purpose similar to the duplex switch. However, the selector switch is not an interrupter; it is a disconnect.
- *Motor-operated* – This type of switch is most commonly used as the major component in an automatic transfer scheme. It can also be used when open and close functions are to be initiated from remote locations.

8.3.0 Opening Operation

In the closed position, the main switch blade is engaged on the stationary interrupting contacts. The circuit current flows through the main blades.

As the switch operating handle is moved toward the open position, the stored energy springs are charged. After the springs become fully charged, they toggle over the dead center position, discharging force to the switch operating mechanism.

The action of the switch operating mechanism forces the movable main blade off the stationary main contacts while the interrupting contacts are held closed, momentarily carrying all the current without arcing. Once the main contacts have separated well beyond the striking distance, the interrupting blade contact that was held captive has charged the interrupter blade hub spring, and the interrupter blade is suddenly forced free and flips open.

The resulting arc drawn between the stationary and movable interrupting contacts is elongated and cooled as the plastic arc chute absorbs heat and generates an arc-extinguishing gas to break up and blow out the arc. The combination of arc stretching, arc cooling, and extinguishing gas causes a quick interruption with only minor erosion of the contacts and arc chutes. The movable main and interrupting contacts continue to the fully open position and are maintained there by spring pressure.

8.4.0 Closing

When the switch operating handle is moved toward the closed position, the stored energy springs are being charged and the main blades begin to move. As the main and interrupter blades approach the arc chute, the stored energy springs become fully charged and toggle over the dead center position.

When the main and movable blades approach the main stationary contacts, a high-voltage arc leaps across the diminishing air gap in an attempt to complete the circuit. The arc occurs between the tip of the stationary main contacts and a remote corner of the movable main blades. This arc is short and brief because the fast-closing blades minimize the arcing time.

The spring pressure and momentum of the fast-moving main blades completely close the contacts. The force is great enough to cause the contacts to close even against repelling short circuit magnetic forces if a fault exists. At the same time, the interrupter blade tip is driven through the twin stationary interrupting contacts, definitely latching and preparing them for an interrupting operation when the switch is opened.

WARNING!

Maintenance and testing may only be performed by qualified personnel under the appropriate safe work plan or permit.

8.5.0 Maintenance

Maintenance tasks for an HVL switch include the following:

Step 1 The HVL switch should be operated several times. Observe the mechanism and check for binding.

Step 2 Inspect the interrupting and main blades every 100 operations for excessive wear or damage; replace as necessary. Also, inspect the arc chutes for damage.

Step 3 Clean the switch and its compartment thoroughly. Use a clean cloth and avoid solvents.

Step 4 Lubricate the switch. The pivot points on the switch should be greased. The switch contacts should also be lubricated with a light film of grease after being cleaned.

Step 5 Final maintenance checks include phase-to-ground and phase-to-phase megger testing. If the results are satisfactory, then a DC high-potential test is performed.

8.6.0 Sluggish Operation

A switch that is operating sluggishly hesitates on the opening cycle. This contrasts with the normal snapping action. Observing the interrupter blade during the opening operation is the proper way to determine sluggish operation. Sluggishness must be repaired to prevent the switch from locking up completely. Perform the following procedure:

Step 1 Tease the switch closed and then open again while watching the interrupter blades closely. Sluggishness on close is shown by the main blade's being engaged behind the contacts of the arc chute. On opening, the interrupter blades may hesitate momentarily.

Step 2 Disconnect the links from the operating shaft. Never operate the switch with the links off as this may break the handle crank casting. This is because the main spring energy is absorbed by the handle crank rather than the main blades.

Step 3 Rotate the handle approximately 45 degrees, and hold it in this position while trying to operate the switch by hand. Excessive binding will prevent rotation of the shaft.

Step 4 Check the contact adjustment at the jaw and hinge.

Step 5 Check for binding between the interrupter blade and the arc chute.

Step 6 Remove the front panel over the operating mechanism and disconnect the spring yoke from the cam. Check for binding between the spring pivot and the sides of the operator. Check the spring for breaks.

9.0.0 Bolted Pressure Switches

Bolted pressure switches (*Figure 9*) are used frequently on service-entrance feeders in switchgear such as that shown in *Figure 10*. They are often used instead of circuit breakers because they are inexpensive. Bolted pressure switches can be manually operated or motor operated. However, unlike a circuit breaker, they can only be automatically tripped by three events: a ground fault, a phase failure, or a blown main fuse detector.

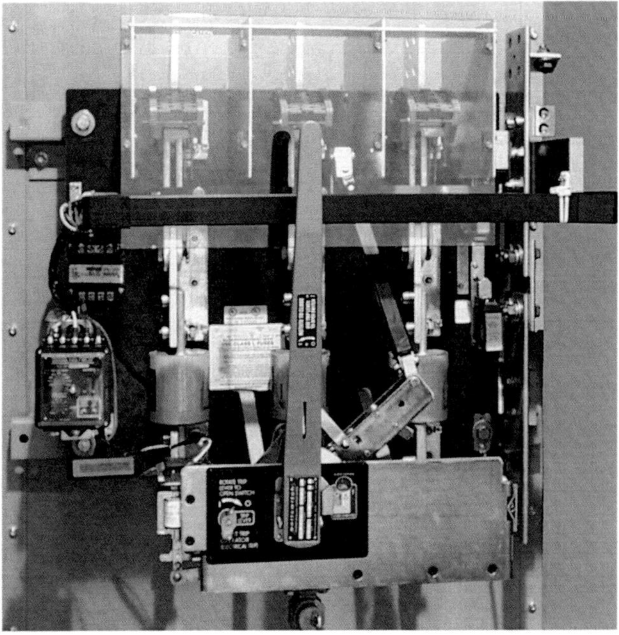

26306-14_F09.EPS

Figure 9 Bolted pressure switch.

26306-14_F10.EPS

Figure 10 Switchgear.

9.1.0 Ground Fault

Under normal conditions, the currents in all conductors surrounded by the ground fault CT equal zero. When a ground fault occurs, this sensed current increases, eventually reaching the ground fault relay pickup point and causing the bolted pressure switch to trip.

The ground fault system may also be tested. By pressing the Test button, a green test light will illuminate, indicating correct circuit operation. To actually test the switch, press the Test and Reset buttons simultaneously. This sends an actual trip signal through the current sensor, thus tripping the switch. Whenever a bolted pressure switch is tripped, a red light or a red flag will trip. Additionally, the ground fault relay must be reset before the switch can be reclosed.

9.2.0 Phase Failure

If a phase failure relay is installed, it will cause a trip of the bolted pressure switch if a phase is lost. This could occur if a tree limb knocks a line down. Under this condition, the phase failure relay will sense the lost phase and trip the bolted pressure switch, preventing a single-phasing condition.

9.3.0 Blown Main Fuse Detector

If one of the in-line main fuses were to blow, the blown main fuse detector would detect it and cause a trip of the bolted pressure switch. The trip signal generated comes from a capacitor trip unit. This ensures that power is always available to trip the switch.

9.4.0 Maintenance

These switches have a high failure rate due to lack of maintenance. All manufacturers of bolted pressure switches recommend annual maintenance. Lack of annual maintenance will eventually result in a switch that is stuck shut. Since these switches are often used as service-entrance equipment, a stuck switch can pose immediate personnel safety hazards, as well as equipment failures.

> **WARNING!**
>
> When performing any maintenance, always follow the safety procedures of your company.

Due to the high interrupting capacity of the switch when operated under load, the grease that is used on the movable blades deteriorates over time and eventually turns into an adhesive. Even when the switch is not operated on a recurring basis, the grease still deteriorates due to the high temperatures associated with the current drawn by the phase. The deterioration of this grease has been shown to cause the switch to stick shut. The grease must be cleaned off yearly with denatured alcohol and replaced.

> **CAUTION**
>
> Regular electrical grease cannot be used; use only the grease specifically recommended by the switch manufacturer.

Additionally, infrared scanning of in-service bolted pressure switches has revealed a marked heating concern in switches. A digital low-resistance ohmmeter (DLRO) is used to ensure that all three phases carry similar current loads. DLRO readings should never be greater than 75 microhms, and there should not be more than a 5% difference between the phases.

Typical annual maintenance includes:

Step 1 De-energize the switch, lock and tag it, and perform a preliminary operational check.

Step 2 Record pre-maintenance DLRO readings.

Step 3 With the switch open, disassemble the crossbar to free all three phases.

Step 4 Clean off all old grease with denatured alcohol or a similar solvent.

Step 5 Inspect the arc tips and arc chutes for damage.

Step 6 Adjust all pivotal connections on each blade to within the manufacturer's recommended tolerances.

Step 7 Apply an appropriate grease to the movable blades and the area where the blades come in contact with the stationary assembly.

Step 8 Check the pullout torque on each individual blade prior to crossbar reassembly. It should be in accordance with the manufacturer's prescribed limits. Too much torque will result in a switch that will be unable to open under load.

Step 9 Record the DLRO readings.

Step 10 Reassemble the crossbar assembly.

Step 11 Close and open the switch manually several times. Ensure that no phases hang up on the arc chute assembly.

Step 12 Megger the switch.

Step 13 Energize and test all accessories, such as the ground fault detector, phase failure detector, and blown main fuse detector.

On Site

High-Resistance Grounding

High-resistance grounding (HRG) is increasingly applied in both medium- and low-voltage distribution systems to limit ground fault energy. Medium-voltage systems have long used low-impedance grounding systems to limit ground fault current. Limiting ground fault current to values of 25A or less increased system reliability by allowing ground faults to be detected and selectively cleared. These systems used either a large resistor or inductance (transformer primary with a shorted secondary or a relay coil in the secondary) connected between the neutral bushing of the service transformer and the system bonding jumper. Detection of a ground fault at certain levels caused a protective relay to open the circuit and clear the fault. The resistors used were mounted in wire cages next to the supply transformers. The resistors were rated at maximum ground fault power for the duration of the fault before it cleared. If the resistors burned up due to failure to clear the fault, the system became an ungrounded wye and extremely dangerous.

In practice, low-resistance grounding for 480V or 600V systems was seldom applied due to the requirements for large resistors and space for enclosures and heat dissipation. The use of high-resistance grounding for low-voltage, high-current systems is becoming common. The high fault currents available on large 480V or 600V systems present a significant arc flash hazard while at the same time the arcing fault may be seen as only an overload by the protective device. High-resistance ground systems allow detection of ground faults and facilitate location of the faulted circuit.

The most common types of faults in power systems are:

- Three-phase (balanced) fault
- Phase to phase
- Phase to phase to ground
- Phase to ground

In industrial facilities it is estimated that 98% or more of all faults begin as a ground fault. If the arcing ground fault current is high enough, the fault develops into a phase-to-phase or three-phase fault. High-resistance grounding in 600V systems limits ground fault current to less than 10A; 5A is a common limit. This level of fault current is too low to present an arc flash hazard or to sustain an arc by itself. This makes development of phase-to-phase faults unlikely. The low fault current also allows continuity of service for a period of time with little risk of equipment damage. Good practice requires that a fault be located and cleared as quickly as possible. The current allowed in the ground fault must be greater than the capacitive coupled charging current in the system in order to avoid false alarms. In low-voltage systems, a sensed ground fault is usually indicated and alarmed but does not send a trip signal to controlling equipment. This is done to allow location of the fault using various features available in HRG panels and cabinets.

In the event of a ground fault in an HRG 480V system, the two non-faulted phases will be at 480V (line potential) to ground and to the faulted phase. If a second phase should fault to ground before an existing fault is cleared, the second fault will NOT be limited and fault currents greater than encountered on a solidly grounded system should be expected. In performing arc hazard analysis, be aware that there is a much lower risk of your actions causing an uncontrolled fault, but you cannot reduce the evaluated incident energy levels or PPE. This is because the risk is not eliminated and a line-to-line or three-phase fault is still possible. Surveys indicate that human error is responsible for most faults that start as line to line or three phase. It should be noted that resistance or reactance grounded systems may NOT supply line-to-neutral loads, but may supply line-to-line loads.

Remember, if the switch is physically stuck shut, de-energize the switch from the incoming power supply, and take extra precautions when trying to unstick the switch. It may be necessary to pry the blades open, but beware of the excessive outward force that will result from a charged opening spring. To alleviate this, discharge the opening spring before starting to work on the switch.

10.0.0 Transformers

Transformers are used to step voltage up and down in the power transmission and distribution system.

The reason for such high transmission voltages is twofold. First, as a transformer increases transmission voltage, the required current decreases in the same proportion; therefore, larger amounts of power can be transmitted and line losses reduced. Second, to send large amounts of power over long distances at a high current and a low voltage requires a very large diameter wire. The reduction in current reduces the conductor size, which results in a cost reduction.

A transformer is an electrical device that uses the process of electromagnetic induction to change the levels of voltage and current in an AC circuit without changing the frequency and with very little loss of power.

10.1.0 Transformer Theory

As current flows through a conductor, a magnetic field is produced around the conductor. This magnetic field begins to form at the instant current begins to flow and expands outward from the conductor as the current increases in magnitude.

When the current reaches its peak value, the magnetic field is also at its peak value. When the current decreases, the magnetic field also decreases.

Alternating current (AC) changes direction twice per cycle. These changes in direction or alternation create an expanding and collapsing magnetic field around the conductor.

If the conductor is wound into a coil, the magnetic field expanding from each turn of the coil cuts across other turns of the coil. When the source current starts to reverse direction, the magnetic field collapses, and again the field cuts across the other turns of the coil.

The result in both cases is the same as if a conductor is passed through a magnetic field. An electromotive force (EMF) is induced in the conductor. This EMF is called a self-induced EMF because it is induced in the conductor carrying the current.

The direction of this induced EMF is always opposite the direction of the EMF that caused the current to flow initially. This principle is known as Lenz's law:

- An induced EMF always has such a direction as to oppose the action that produced it.
- For this reason, the EMF induced is also known as a counter-electromotive force (CEMF).

The counter-electromotive force reaches a value nearly equal to the applied voltage; thus, the primary current is limited when the secondary is open circuited.

10.1.1 No-Load Operation

The operation of a transformer is based on the principle that electrical energy can be transferred efficiently by mutual induction from one winding to another. When the primary winding is energized from an AC source, an alternating magnetic flux is established in the transformer core. This flux links the turns of the primary with the secondary, thereby inducing a voltage in them. Since the same flux cuts both windings, the same voltage is induced in each turn of both windings. Whenever the secondary of a transformer is left disconnected (or open), there is no current drawn by the secondary winding. The primary winding draws the amount of current required to supply the magnetomotive force, which produces the transformer core flux. This current is called the exciting or magnetizing current.

The exciting current is limited by the CEMF in the primary and a small amount of resistance, which cannot be avoided in any current-carrying conductor.

10.1.2 Load Operation

When a load is connected to the secondary winding of a transformer, the secondary current flowing through the secondary turns produces a counter-magnetomotive force. According to Lenz's law, this magnetomotive force is in a direction that opposes the flux that produced it. This opposition tends to reduce the transformer flux and is accompanied by a reduction in the CEMF in the primary. Since the primary current is limited by the internal impedance of the primary winding and the CEMF in the winding, whenever the CEMF is reduced, the primary current continues to increase until the original transformer flux reaches a state of equilibrium.

10.2.0 Transformer Types

Transformers can be divided into two main categories: power transformers and distribution transformers. Power transformers handle large amounts of power and step down from transmission voltages to distribution voltages. Distribution transformers are designed to handle larger currents at lower voltage levels. Distribution transformers have smaller kVA ratings and are physically much smaller than power transformers. Power transformers often have an auxiliary means of cooling, such as fans and radiators. Distribution transformers are usually self-cooled, using no fans or other cooling methods. Whereas distribution transformers may be pole-mounted or pad-mounted, power transformers are always freestanding.

Although there is some overlap between power and distribution transformers, a transformer that is rated at more than 500kVA and/or 34.5kV is generally a power transformer. A transformer rated below these values can be considered a distribution transformer. Remember, there is an overlap in kVA capacity and voltage depending on the system and power requirements.

26306-14_F11.EPS

Figure 11 Dry-type transformer.

10.3.0 Dry Transformers (Air-Cooled)

Many transformers do not use an insulating liquid to immerse the core and windings. Dry or air-cooled transformers are used for many jobs where small, low-kVA transformers are required. Large distribution transformers are usually oil-filled for better cooling and insulating. However, for installations in buildings and other locations where the oil in oil-filled transformers would be a serious fire hazard, dry transformers are used. These transformers are generally of the core form. The core and coils are similar to those of other transformers.

A three-phase, dry-type transformer is shown in *Figure 11*. The case is made of sheet metal and provided with ventilating louvers for the circulation of cooling air. To increase the output, fans can be installed to draw cooling air through the coils at a faster rate than is possible with natural circulation.

Either Class B or Class H insulation is used for the windings. Class B insulation may be operated safely at a hot-spot temperature of 130°C. Class H insulation may be operated safely at a hot-spot temperature of 180°C. The use of these materials makes it possible to manufacture smaller transformers. Both Class B and Class H insulation consist of mica, asbestos, fiberglass, and similar inorganic material. Temperature-resistant organic varnishes are used as the binder for Class B insulation. Silicone or fluorine compounds or similar materials are used as the binder for Class H insulation. Such transformers use high-temperature insulation only in locations where the high temperature requires such insulation.

10.4.0 Sealed Dry Transformers

Hermetically sealed dry transformers are constructed in large sizes for voltages above 15kV. They are used for installations in buildings and other locations where oil-filled transformers would be a serious fire hazard, but they may also be used for lower voltages and kVA ratings and for water-submersible transformers in locations subject to floods. Nitrogen is typically used for the insulation and cooling of sealed dry transformers.

10.5.0 Transformer Nameplate Data

Transformer nameplate data includes the following:

- *Electrical ratings* – The electrical ratings convey information relating to the transformer electrical parameters.
- *Voltage ratings* – The voltage rating identifies the nominal root-mean-square (rms) voltage value at which the transformer is designed to operate. A transformer can operate within a

±5% range of its rated primary voltage. If the primary voltage is increased to more than +5%, the windings of the transformer can overheat. Operation of the transformer at more than –5% decreases its power output proportionally to the percent voltage reduction. Transformer windings are rated as follows:

- Phase-to-phase and phase-to-neutral for wye windings, such as 480Y/277VAC
- Phase-to-phase for delta windings, such as 480VAC
- Dual-voltage windings, such as 480VAC × 240VAC

When transformers are equipped with a tap changer, the voltage ratings in the nameplate indicate the nominal voltages.

- *BIL* – This identifies the maximum impulse voltage the winding insulation can withstand without failure.
- *Phase* – The phase information indicates the number of phase windings contained in a transformer tank.
- *Frequency* – The frequency rating of a transformer is the normal operating system frequency. When a transformer is operated at a lower frequency, the reactance of the primary winding decreases. This causes a higher exciting current and an increase in flux density. In addition, there is an increase in core loss, which results in overall heating.
- *Class* – Transformers are classified by the type of cooling they employ.
- *Temperature rise* – The temperature rise rating is the maximum elevation above ambient temperature that can be tolerated without causing insulation damage.
- *Capacity* – The capacity of a transformer to transfer energy is related to its ability to dissipate the heat produced in the windings. The capacity rating is the product of the rated voltage and the current that can be carried at that voltage without exceeding the temperature rise limitation.
- *Impedance* – Impedance identifies the opposition of a transformer to the passage of short circuit current.
- *Phasor diagrams* – Phasor diagrams show phase and polarity relationships of the high and low windings. They can be used with the schematic connection diagram to provide test connection points and to provide proper external system connections.

10.6.0 Transformer Case Inspections

When inspecting the inside of a dry-type, air-cooled transformer case, look for the following:

- Temporary shipping supports or guards
- Bent, broken, or loose parts
- Debris on the floor or in the coils
- Corrosion of any part
- Worn or frayed insulation
- Shifted core members
- Damaged tap changer mounts or mechanisms
- Misaligned core spacers and loose coil elements
- Broken or loose blocking

Upon the completion of the inspection, replace the covers and bolt securely. All information should be recorded on appropriate inspection sheets.

10.7.0 Transformer Tests

The following tests are the recommended minimum tests that should be included as part of a maintenance program. These tests are conducted to determine and evaluate the present condition of the transformer. From the results of these tests, a determination is made as to whether the transformer is suitable for service. All tests should be performed using the standards and procedures provided by the transformer manufacturer.

- *Continuity and winding resistance test* – There should be a continuity check of all windings. If possible, measure the winding resistance and compare it to the factory test values. An increase of more than 10% could indicate loose internal connections.
- *Insulation resistance test* – To ensure that no grounding of the windings exists, a 1,000V insulation resistance test should be made.
- *Ratio test* – A turns ratio test should be made to ensure proper transformer ratios and to ensure that all connections were made. If equipped with a tap changer, all positions should be checked.
- *Core ground* – This test is performed in the same way as the insulation resistance test, except the measurement is made from the core to the frame and ground bus. Remove the core ground strap before the test.
- *Heat scanning* – After the transformer is energized, a heat scan test should be done to detect loose connections. This test is performed using an infrared scanning device that shows or indicates hot spots.

11.0.0 INSTRUMENT TRANSFORMERS

For all practical purposes, the voltages and currents used in the primary circuits of substations are much too large to be used to provide operating quantities to relaying or metering circuits. In order to reduce voltage and currents to usable levels, instrument transformers are employed. Instrument transformers are used to:

- Protect personnel and equipment from the high voltages and/or currents used in electric power transmission and distribution
- Provide reasonable use of insulation levels and current-carrying capacity in relay and metering systems and other control devices
- Provide a means to combine voltage and/or current phasors to simplify relaying or metering

Instrument transformers are manufactured with a multitude of different ratios to provide a standard output for the many different system primary voltage levels and load currents. There are two types of instrument transformers, potential transformers and current transformers. In general, a potential transformer (*Figure 12*) is used to a supply voltage signal to devices such as voltmeters, frequency meters, power factor meters, watt-hour meters, and protective relays. The voltage is proportional to the primary voltage, but it is small enough to be safe for the test instrument. The secondary of a potential transformer may be designed for several different voltages, but most are designed for 120V. The potential transformer is primarily a distribution transformer especially designed for voltage regulation so that the secondary voltage (under all conditions) will be as close as possible to a specified percentage of the primary voltage.

A current transformer is used to supply current to an instrument connected to its secondary with the current being proportional to the primary current but small enough to be safe for the instrument. The secondary of a current transformer is usually designed for a rated current of 5A.

A current transformer operates in the same way as any other transformer in that the same relationship exists between the primary current and the secondary current. A current transformer uses the circuit conductors as its primary winding. The secondary of the current transformer is connected to current devices such as ammeters, wattmeters, watt-hour meters, power factor meters, some forms of relays, and the trip coils of some types of circuit breakers.

When no instruments or other devices are connected to the secondary of the current transformer, a short circuit device or shunt is placed across the secondary to prevent the secondary circuit from being opened while the primary winding is carrying current.

WARNING!

If the secondary circuit is open, there will be no secondary ampere turns to balance the primary ampere turns, so the total primary current becomes exciting current and magnetizes the core to a high flux density. This produces a high voltage across both the primary and secondary windings and endangers the life of anyone coming in contact with the meters or leads. This is why current transformers should never be fused. A current transformer is the only transformer that may be short-circuited on the secondary while energized.

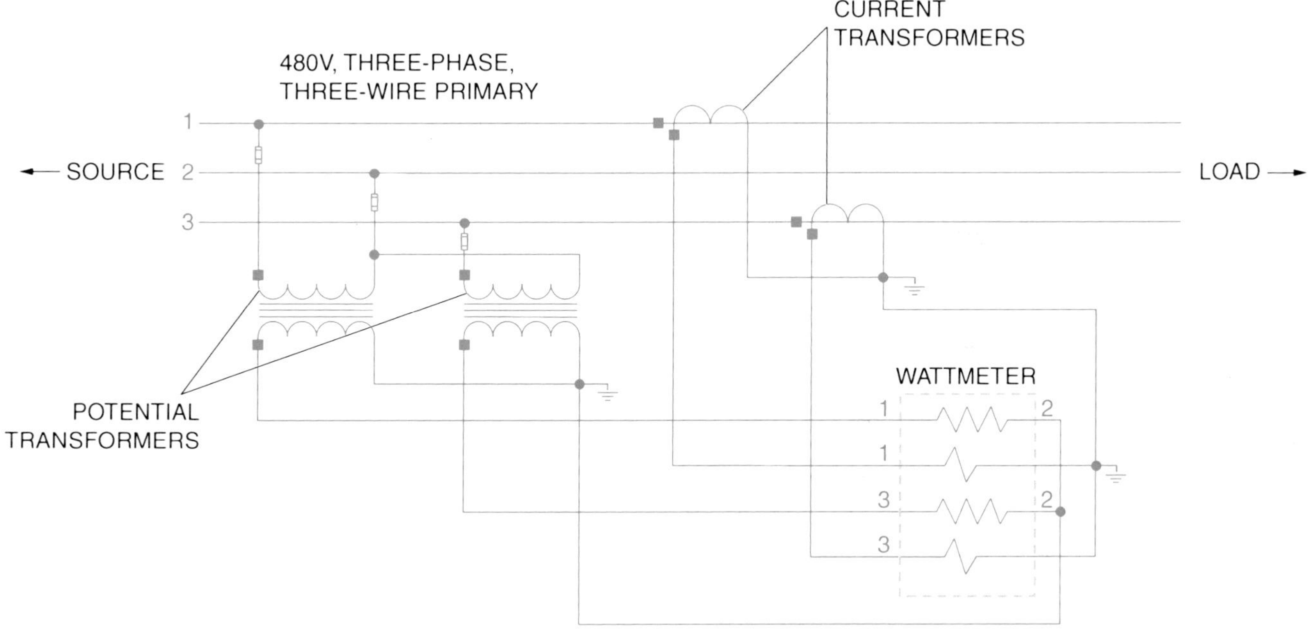

Figure 12 Current and potential transformers connected for power metering of a three-phase circuit.

11.1.0 Potential Transformers

Potential transformers are designed to reduce primary system voltages down to usable levels for metering and are often referred to as voltage transformers or VTs. Potential transformers are often used where the system's primary voltage exceeds 600V and sometimes on 240V and 480V systems.

The standard secondary circuit voltage level for a potential transformer circuit is 120V for circuits below 25kV and 115V for circuits above 25kV at the potential transformer's rated primary voltage. These voltages correspond to typical transformation ratios of standard transmission voltages. The current flowing in the secondary of the potential transformer circuit is very low under normal operating conditions, typically less than one ampere.

Potential transformers are constructed to be lightly loaded with the design emphasis on winding ratio accuracy rather than current rating. Potential transformer construction can be air-insulated dry, case epoxy-insulated, oil-filled, or SF_6-insulated, depending upon the primary circuit voltage level.

The standard output voltage of potential transformers is either 120V or 69.3V, depending on whether its primary winding uses phase-to-phase or phase-to-neutral connections. Understanding the operation of a potential or voltage transformer is simplified by the inspection of its equivalent circuit.

Potential transformers must have their secondary circuits grounded for safety reasons in the event that a short circuit develops between the primary and secondary windings and to negate the effects of parasitic capacitance between the primary and the secondary. *Figure 13* shows the connection of an ideal potential transformer circuit.

11.2.0 Current Transformers

A current transformer is designed to reduce high primary system currents down to usable levels. Current transformers are used whenever system primary voltage isolation is required. The standard secondary circuit current for a current transformer circuit is 5A with full-rated current flowing in the primary circuit.

> **WARNING!**
>
> The voltage level across a current transformer's secondary terminals can rise to a very dangerous level if the secondary circuit opens while the primary circuit is energized.

The primary considerations in current transformer design are the current-carrying capability and saturation characteristics. Insulation systems are of the same generic types as potential transformers; however, SF_6 insulation is infrequently used in current transformer construction.

Current transformers are manufactured in four basic types: oil-filled (for example, donut type), bar, window, and **bushing**. The bushing-type transformer is normally applied on circuit breakers or power transformers. The other types are used for the remaining indoor and outdoor installations. *Figure 14* illustrates some common types of current transformer construction.

The major criteria for the selection of the current transformer for relaying are its primary current rating, maximum burden, and saturation

> **GOING GREEN**
>
> **SF_6 Insulation**
>
> Sulfur hexafluoride (SF_6) is a colorless, odorless, nontoxic, nonflammable gas that is used as an insulating gas in electrical equipment. SF_6 is used as a gaseous dielectric for transformers, condensers, and circuit breakers, often replacing harmful PCBs.

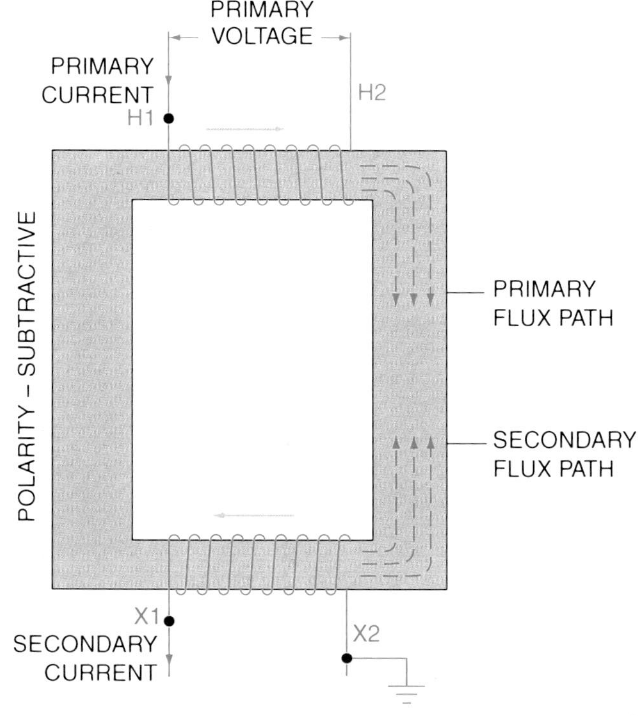

Figure 13 Potential transformer construction.

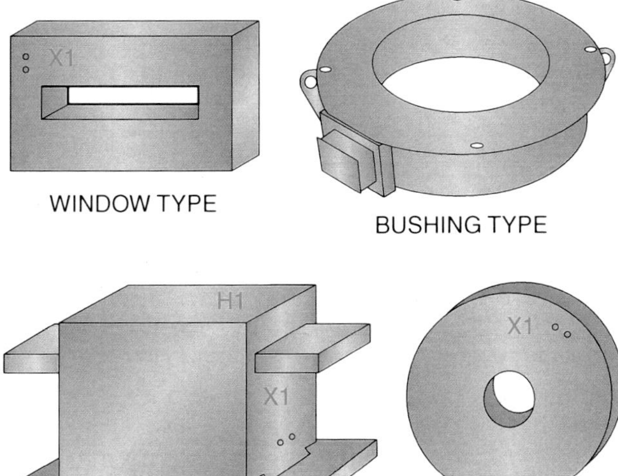

Figure 14 Types of current transformer construction.

characteristics. Saturation is particularly important in relaying due to the fact that many relays are called upon to operate only under fault conditions.

Current transformer circuits operate at a very low voltage. Connected loads (burdens) range from 0.2Ω to 2Ω. These small impedances, together with a maximum continuous current of up to 5A, keep these circuits at low potentials. The voltage can become high momentarily during faults when large secondary currents flow. This voltage is a function of the current, burden, and transformer VA capability.

As with potential transformers, current transformers must also have their secondary windings grounded in the event of an insulation breakdown between the primary and secondary and to negate the effects of parasitic capacitance.

11.3.0 Instrument Transformer Maintenance

Instrument transformers require regular inspection and maintenance. A typical inspection includes the following steps:

Step 1 Inspect for physical damage, and check the nameplate information for compliance with instructions and specification requirements.

Step 2 Verify the proper connection of transformers against the system requirements.

Step 3 Verify the tightness of all bolted connections, and ensure that adequate clearances exist between the primary circuits and the secondary circuit wiring.

Think About It

Transformers

What is the difference between an instrument (potential) transformer and a control transformer? Why can't one device serve both functions?

Step 4 Verify that all required grounding and shorting connections provide good contact.

Step 5 Test for proper operation of the potential transformer isolation (PT tip out) compartment and grounding operation when applicable.

12.0.0 Circuit Breakers

Circuit breakers are the only circuit interrupting devices that combine a full fault current interruption rating and the ability to be manually or automatically opened or closed. A circuit breaker is defined as a mechanical switching device that is capable of making, carrying, and breaking currents under normal circuit conditions and also making, carrying (for a specified time), and breaking currents under specified abnormal circuit conditions, such as a short circuit (according to IEEE). The four general classifications of circuit breakers are:

- Air circuit breakers (ACBs)
- Oil circuit breakers (OCBs)
- Vacuum circuit breakers (VCBs)
- Gas circuit breakers (GCBs)

Circuit breakers may conveniently be divided into low-voltage, medium-voltage, and high-voltage classes. Although there is considerable overlap among these classes, each one has certain characteristic features.

12.1.0 Circuit Breaker Ratings

Circuit breaker ratings are given on the breaker nameplate. The information from the nameplate should be reviewed when considering any breaker selection problem. The same rating information should be included in any documentation for breaker applications. The rating information includes:

- *Rated voltage* – The rated voltage is the maximum voltage for which the circuit breaker is designed.
- *Rated current* – This is the continuous current that the circuit breaker can carry without exceeding a standard temperature rise (usually 55°C).

- *Interrupting rating* – This is the maximum value of current at rated voltage that the circuit breaker is required to successfully interrupt for a limited number of operations under specified conditions. The term is usually applied to abnormal or emergency conditions.

13.0.0 Electrical Drawing Identification

Before looking at actual plant diagrams, it is necessary to understand the symbology used to condense electrical drawings. The designer uses symbols and abbreviations as a type of shorthand. This section will present the standard symbols, abbreviations, and device numbers that make up the designer's shorthand. For IEEE device numbers, see *Appendix A*.

13.1.0 Electrical Diagram Symbology

It is imperative that every line, symbol, figure, and letter in a diagram have a specific purpose and that the information be presented in its most concise form. For example, when the rating of a current transformer is given, a transformer symbol is shown, and an abbreviation such as CT is not needed; the information is implied by the symbol itself. Writing the unit of measure (amp) in this case is also unnecessary, since a current transformer is always rated in amperes. Thus, the numerical rating and the transformer symbol are sufficient.

The key to reading and interpreting electrical diagrams is to understand and use the electrical legend. The legend shows the symbols used in the diagram and also contains general notes and other important information. Most electrical legends are very similar; however, there are some variations between the legends developed by different companies. Only the legend specifically designed for a given set of drawings should be used for those drawings.

The legend precludes the need to memorize all the symbols presented on a diagram, and it can be used as a reference for unfamiliar symbols. Typically, the legend will be found in the bottom right corner of a print or on a separate drawing. In addition to symbols, abbreviations are an important part of the designer's shorthand. For example, a circle can be used to symbolize a meter, relay, motor, or indicating light. A circle's application can generally be distinguished by its location in the circuit; however, the designer uses a set of standard abbreviations to make the distinction clear. The following abbreviations are used to represent meters:

A	Ammeter
AH	Ampere-hour meter
CRO	Oscilloscope
DM	Demand meter
F	Frequency meter
GD	Ground detector
OHM	Ohmmeter
OSC	Oscillograph
PF	Power factor meter
PH	Phase meter
SYN	Synchroscope
TD	Transducer
V	Voltmeter
VA	Volt-ammeter
VAR	VAR meter
VARH	VAR hour meter
W	Wattmeter
WH	Watt-hour meter

As mentioned earlier, indicating lamps may also be represented by a circle. The following abbreviations are used to represent indicating lamps:

A	Amber
B	Blue
C	Clear
G	Green
R	Red
W	White

Case History

Oil-Filled Circuit Breaker (OCB) Testing

An assistant engineer and an electrician had the responsibility of testing the insulation values of the bushings on an OCB. The assistant engineer pulled down the handle and opened the breaker, visually determining that the contacts were open and safe. He instructed the electrician to move the test leads from one bushing to the next as the assistant engineer read the values. On the third and last bushing, the electrician was electrocuted as he placed the test leads on the bushing. The last contact had not opened due to a broken porcelain insulator skirt, which allowed the cap to remain stationary while the rest of the mechanism rotated as the handle was pulled down. This was not noticeable from the assistant engineer's eye level when he determined all contacts were opened.

The Bottom Line: ***Never*** come in contact with switchgear such as this without first testing each and every contact point with the proper meter, and ***never*** rely on someone else's word that the power is off.

Relays are another component commonly represented by a circle. The following abbreviations are used for relays:

CC	Closing coil
CR	Closing/control relay
TC	Trip coil
TR	Trip relay
TD	Time-delay relay
TDE	Time-delay energize
TDD	Time-delay de-energize
X	Auxiliary relay

Still another component that is commonly represented by a circle is the motor. Motors usually have the horsepower rating in or near the circle representing them. The abbreviation for horsepower is hp. Any other piece of equipment represented by a circle will be identified in the legend, notes, or spelled out on the diagram itself.

Contacts and switches are also identified using standard abbreviations. The following is a list of these abbreviations:

A	Breaker A contact
B	Breaker B contact
BAS	Bell alarm switch
BLPB	Backlighted pushbutton
CS	Control switch
FS	Flow switch
LS	Limit switch
PB	Pushbutton
PS	Pressure switch
PSD	Differential pressure switch
TDO	Time-delay open
TDC	Time-delay closed
TS	Temperature switch
XS	Auxiliary switch

The following figures illustrate examples of these abbreviations and symbols. *Figure 15* shows A and B contacts in their normally de-energized state. If relay CR is de-energized, contact A is open and contact B is shut. When relay CR is energized, contact A is shut and contact B is open.

Figure 16 illustrates a control switch and its associated contacts. Contacts 1 through 4 open and close as a result of the operation of control switch 1 (CS1).

In the stop position, contact 2 is shut, and the red indicating lamp is lit. In the start position, contacts 3 and 4 are shut, energizing the M coil and the amber indicating lamp, respectively. When the switch handle is released, the spring returns to the run position, and contact 4 opens, de-energizing the amber lamp and closing contact 1 to energize the green lamp.

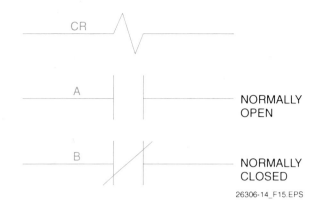

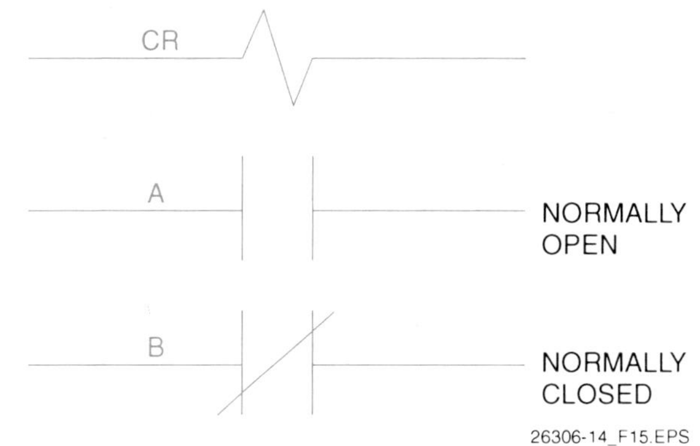

Figure 15 Contact symbols.

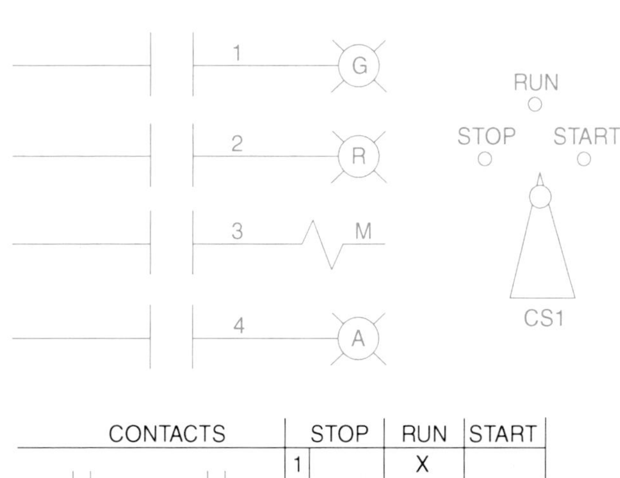

CONTACTS		STOP	RUN	START	
	1		X		
	2	X			
	3		X	X	CS1
	4			X	
SPRING RETURN				←	

X-SHUT

26306-14_F16.EPS

Figure 16 Switch development.

There are many abbreviations used on electrical drawings. The designer makes an effort to use standard abbreviations; however, you will encounter nonstandard abbreviations. Nonstandard abbreviations will typically be defined in the diagram notes or legend. *Figure 17* defines abbreviations commonly used in wiring prints and specifications. The symbols further illustrate descriptions of the abbreviations.

14.0.0 Electrical Prints

This section describes the specific types of electrical prints with which you need to be familiar in order to install and maintain electrical systems.

SPST NO		SPST NC		SPDT	
SINGLE BREAK	DOUBLE BREAK	SINGLE BREAK	DOUBLE BREAK	SINGLE BREAK	DOUBLE BREAK
DPST NO		DPST NC		DPDT	
SINGLE BREAK	DOUBLE BREAK	SINGLE BREAK	DOUBLE BREAK	SINGLE BREAK	DOUBLE BREAK

TERMS	
SPST	SINGLE-POLE SINGLE-THROW
SPDT	SINGLE-POLE DOUBLE-THROW
DPST	DOUBLE-POLE SINGLE-THROW
DPDT	DOUBLE-POLE DOUBLE-THROW
NO	NORMALLY OPEN
NC	NORMALLY CLOSED

26306-14_F17.EPS

Figure 17 Supplementary contact symbols.

14.1.0 Single-Line Diagrams

Analyzing and reading complex electrical circuits can be very difficult. Diagrams are simplified to single-line (one-line) diagrams to aid in reading the prints.

A single-line diagram is defined as a diagram that indicates by means of single lines and standard symbology the paths, interconnections, and component parts of an electric circuit or system of circuits. This type of drawing uses a single line to represent all conductors (phases) of the system. All components of power circuits are represented by symbols and notations. One-line diagrams are valuable tools for system visualization during planning, installation, operation, and maintenance, and they provide a basic understanding of how a portion of the electrical system functions in terms of the physical components of the circuit.

Types of single-line diagrams for industrial facilities include summary (overall facility) diagrams and detailed single-line diagrams. The summary diagrams show each bus and disconnecting device from the point of supply to the line side connection of motor control centers (MCCs). The drawing(s) typically include all voltage levels and power transformers down to the voltage level for three-phase power usage (575V or 480V). The detailed single-line diagrams identify the components and disconnect devices all the way to downstream users. Individual motors or panelboards fed from the MCC will be shown, as well as lighting transformers and lighting panels. The single line of branch circuits and end devices from panelboards is usually called the panel schedule. An example of a summary single-line diagram is shown in *Figure 18*.

14.2.0 Elementary Diagrams

An elementary diagram is a drawing that falls between one-line diagrams and schematics in terms of complexity. An elementary diagram is a wiring diagram showing how each individual conductor is connected. *Figure 19* is an example of an elementary schematic diagram with the circuit powered by the phase voltage between L1 and L2.

Elementary diagrams, interconnection diagrams, and connection diagrams all illustrate individual conductors. Elementary diagrams are used to show the wiring of instrument and electrical control devices in an elementary ladder or schematic form. The elementary diagram reflects the control wiring required to achieve the operation and sequence of operations described in the logic diagram. When presented in ladder form, the vertical lines in each ladder diagram represent the control power wires of a control circuit. If a number of schemes are connected to the same control circuit, the vertical lines are continuous from the top to the bottom of the ladder. The power source wire is always shown on the left side of the ladder and the ground or neutral wire on the right. A ground symbol is normally not shown on the neutral wire.

The control power wire numbers are shown at the top of the vertical lines on each ladder diagram. The circuit identification number and source of the control circuit are also shown at the top center of each ladder. If two or more control circuits are represented in a single ladder, the vertical lines are broken, and the wire numbers and circuit identification are entered at the top of each ladder segment. Each horizontal line in a ladder diagram represents a circuit path. All devices shown on a single horizontal line represent a series circuit path; parallel circuit paths are shown on two or more horizontal lines.

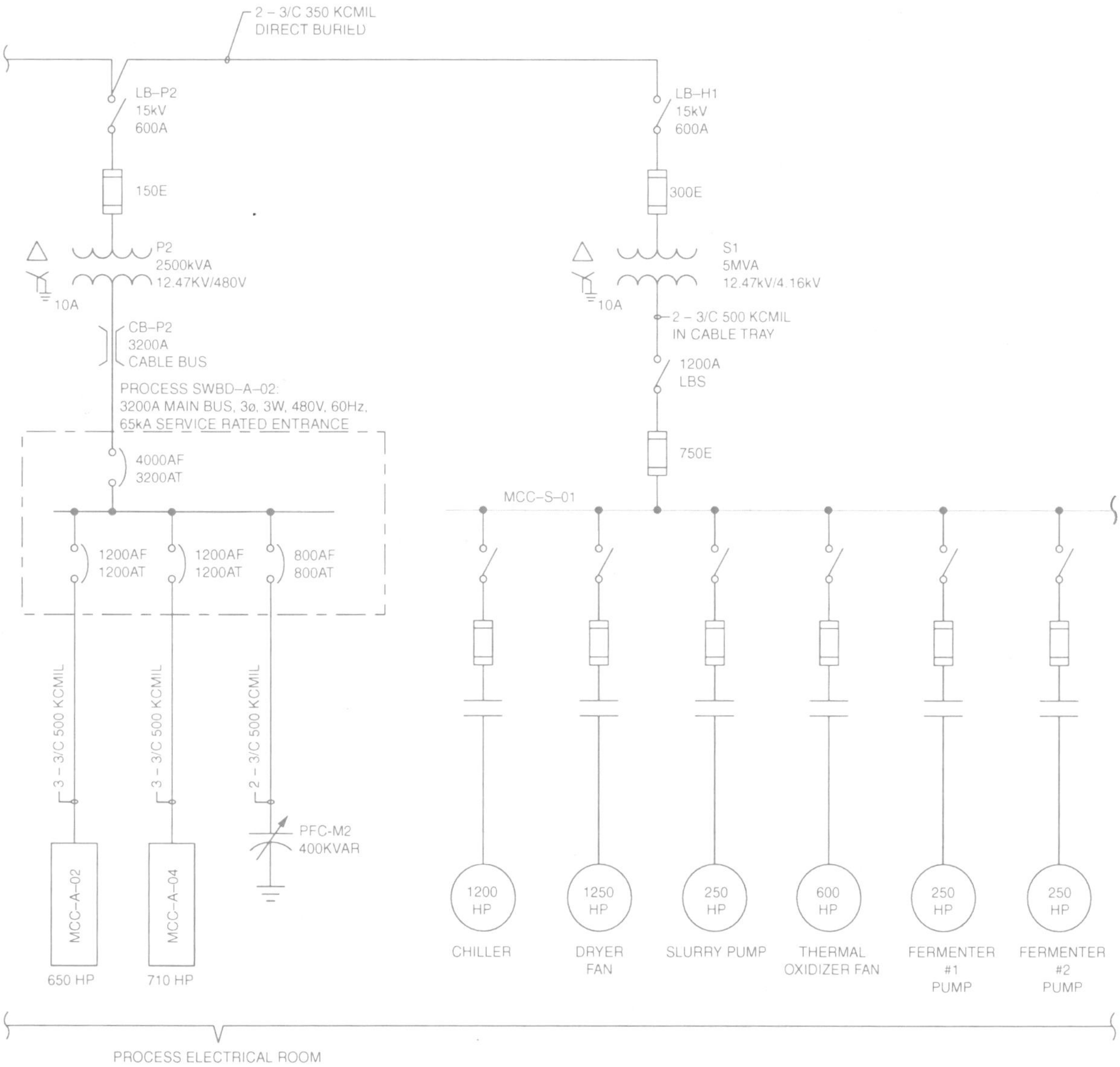

2 – 3/C 350 KCMIL DIRECT BURIED
LB–P2 15kV 600A
150E
P2 2500kVA 12.47KV/480V
10A
CB–P2 3200A CABLE BUS
PROCESS SWBD–A–02: 3200A MAIN BUS, 3ø, 3W, 480V, 60Hz, 65kA SERVICE RATED ENTRANCE
4000AF 3200AT
1200AF 1200AT
1200AF 1200AT
800AF 800AT
3 – 3/C 500 KCMIL
3 – 3/C 500 KCMIL
2 – 3/C 500 KCMIL
MCC–A–02
650 HP
MCC–A–04
710 HP
PFC-M2 400KVAR
LB–H1 15kV 600A
300E
S1 5MVA 12.47kV/4.16kV
10A
2 – 3/C 500 KCMIL IN CABLE TRAY
1200A LBS
750E
MCC–S–01
1200 HP CHILLER
1250 HP DRYER FAN
250 HP SLURRY PUMP
600 HP THERMAL OXIDIZER FAN
250 HP FERMENTER #1 PUMP
250 HP FERMENTER #2 PUMP
PROCESS ELECTRICAL ROOM
26306-14_F18.EPS

Figure 18 Single-line diagram.

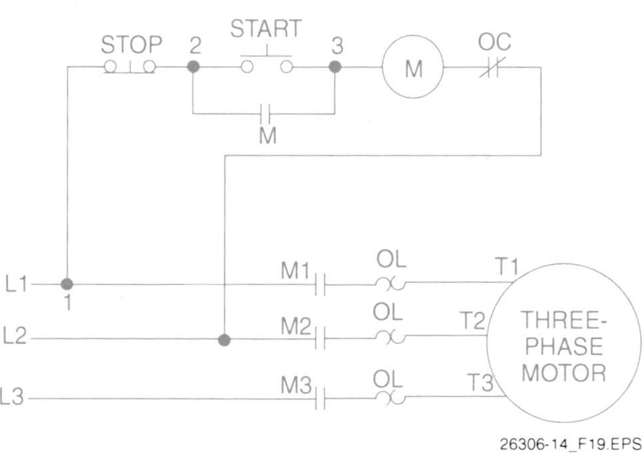

Figure 19 Elementary schematic diagram.

14.3.0 Interconnection Diagrams

When troubleshooting electrical circuits, you may use an elementary circuit diagram to determine the cause of a failure; however, since elementary diagrams are drawn without regard to physical locations, connection diagrams should be used to aid in locating faulty components. Interconnection and connection diagrams are structured in such a way that they present all the wires that were shown in the elementary drawing in their actual locations. These drawings show all electrical connections within an enclosure, with each wire labeled to indicate where each end of the wire is terminated.

The interconnection diagram is made to show the actual wiring connections between unit assemblies or equipment. Internal wiring connections within unit assemblies or equipment are usually omitted. The interconnection diagrams will appear adjacent to the schematic diagram or on a separate drawing, depending on the format chosen when making the schematic diagram. The development of the interconnection diagram is integrated with that of the schematic diagram and only the equipment, terminal blocks, and wiring pertinent to the accompanying schematic diagram appear in the interconnection diagram. A typical interconnection diagram will contain:

- An outline of the equipment involved in its relative physical location
- Terminal blocks in the equipment that are concerned with the wiring illustrated on the schematic
- Wire numbers, cable sizes, cable numbers, cable routing, and cable tray identification (should not be repeated on the interconnection diagram except where necessary)
- Wiring between equipment (normally shown as individual cables but may be combined on complex drawings)
- Equipment identification information

14.4.0 Connection Diagrams

The connection diagram shows the internal wiring connections between the parts that make up an apparatus. It will contain as much detail as necessary to make or trace any electrical connections involved. A connection diagram generally shows the physical arrangement of component electrical connections. It differs from the interconnection diagram by excluding external connections between two or more unit assemblies or pieces of equipment.

The schematic diagram shows the arrangement of a circuit with the components represented by conventional symbols. Its intent is to show the function of a circuit. The schematic, like the elementary drawing, is not laid out with respect to physical locations.

A wiring diagram also shows the physical locations of all electrical equipment and/or components with all interconnecting wiring. It shows the actual connection point of every wire and the color of the wires connected to each terminal of every component. It allows the electrician to easily locate terminals and wires. A wiring diagram in conjunction with a schematic greatly aids in troubleshooting a given piece of equipment. Connection diagrams can be shown in various forms.

The following sections illustrate two types of connection diagrams.

14.4.1 Point-to-Point Method

The point-to-point method is used for the simpler diagrams where sufficient space is available to show each individual wire without sacrificing the clarity of the diagram. Point-to-point diagrams provide accurate information to terminate and troubleshoot the wiring. *Figure 20* is an example of an internal point-to-point connection diagram.

14.4.2 Cable Method

In complex diagrams, only individual cables are shown between devices or terminal strips. Lines from the cable go to each termination point at the device or strip, but individual connections are not identified. Connection diagrams provide adequate information to route the cable, but not to terminate the conductors. *Figure 21* is an example of an internal cable connection diagram.

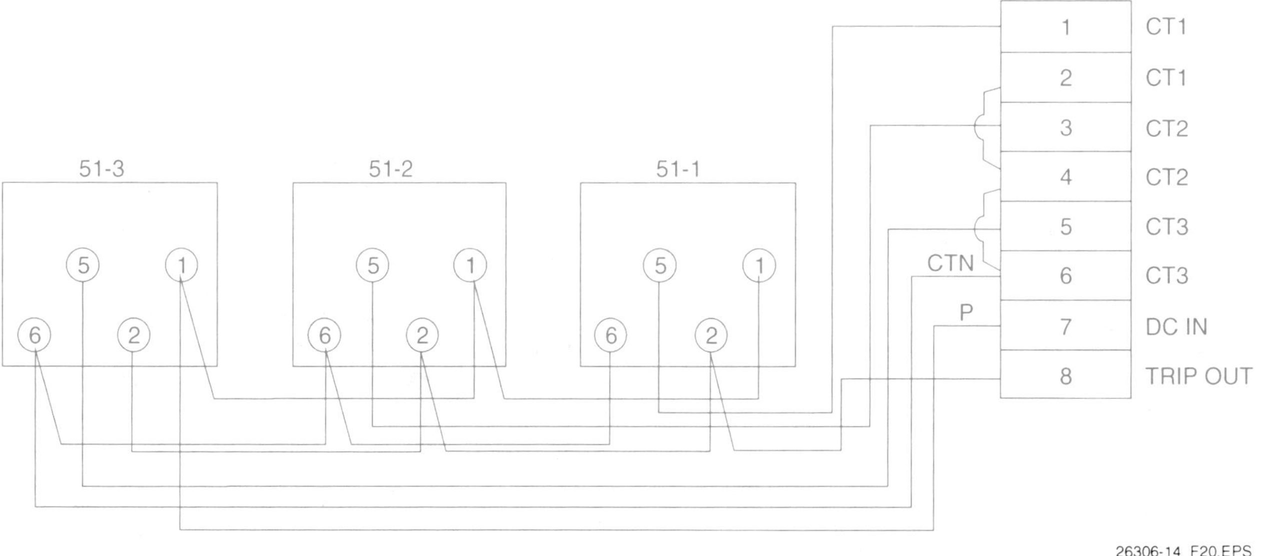

Figure 20 Point-to-point connection diagram.

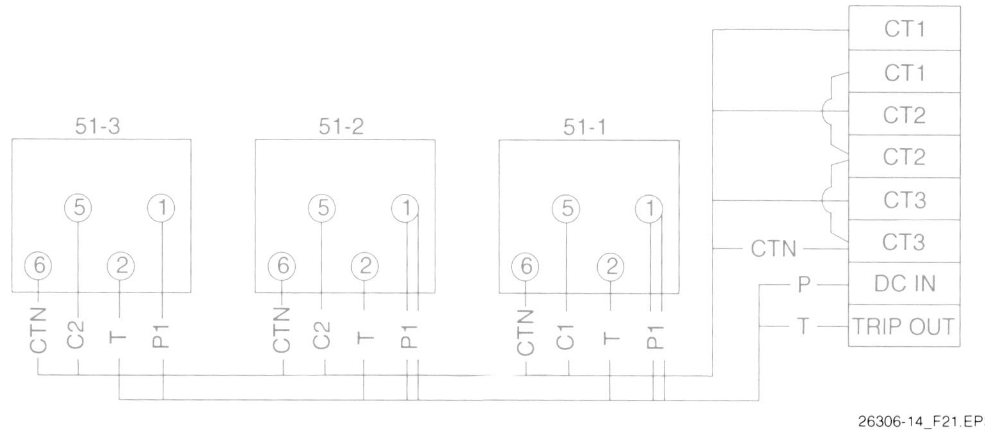

Figure 21 Cable connection diagram.

15.0.0 Manufacturer Drawings

When a project is proposed, there are several different types of drawings involved. The engineer and designer work from manufacturer drawings to determine specific details of the equipment and incorporate them into the design. The electrical worker must also be familiar with the manufacturer drawings because the design drawings don't always include all the manufacturer's information.

This section discusses the information found in manufacturer drawings. *Appendix B* includes an example of one manufacturer's drawings for a new switchboard to distribute power to downstream equipment such as motor control centers, panelboards, and major utilization equipment. In this case, the switchboard may be the service equipment or may be fed from the facility power transformer. A brief description of each sheet of the drawing follows:

- *Title sheet* – This sheet (*not shown*) includes the manufacturer and purchaser reference numbers, location, contact persons, dates, and other identifying information. A table of contents is also included so that the job requirements can be easily navigated.
- *General notes* – This sheet (*Appendix B, Sheet 1*) shows the front view of the switchboard along with dimensions. Descriptive notes are included to describe the equipment. Electrical ratings are noted, as well as physical data such as the enclosure type and weight. References are also made to product literature such as instruction manual(s).
- *Floor plan* – This sheet (*Appendix B, Sheet 2*) provides a top view, side view, and floor plan view. This gives the installer a footprint of the space needed for the installation. The installer must make sure to include the minimum working space around the equipment as required by the *NEC*®.
- *One-line diagram* – This sheet (*Appendix B, Sheet 3*) shows that the project consists of a three-section switchboard. The one-line (single-line) diagram for each section is shown, along with how they are interconnected with the main bus. The sizes of overcurrent devices are listed, along with the trip characteristics. Where interconnecting wiring is to be field-installed, details of that are also listed.
- *Schedule* – The schedule (*Appendix B, Sheet 4*) shows all the equipment that is installed in the switchboard. All the breakers are listed along with their size, frame designation, trip setting, location, function, and lug size. Additional accessories and information are also listed, including a legend.
- *Wiring diagram* – The sheet shows the wiring diagram for each device installed in the switchboard *(Appendix B, Sheet 5)*. Any interconnection between devices is also documented. Any notes for wiring are also included; these may include the wire size and type. This shows both the factory and field wiring.
- *Catalog sheet* – This sheet (*Appendix B, Sheet 6*), sometimes called a Bill of Materials, gives catalog numbers and additional details on the components included in the order.

15.1.0 Shop Drawings

When large pieces of electrical equipment are needed, such as high-voltage switchgear and motor control centers, most are custom-built for each individual project. In doing so, shop drawings are normally furnished by the equipment manufacturer prior to shipment to ensure that the equipment will fit the location at the shop site and to instruct the workers about preparing for such equipment as rough-in conduit and cable trays.

The drawing in *Figure 22* is one page of a shop drawing showing a pictorial view of the enclosure.

Shop drawings will also usually include connection diagrams for all components that must be field wired or connected.

As-built drawings, including detailed factory-wired connection diagrams, are also included to assist workers and maintenance personnel in making the final connections, and in troubleshooting problems once the system is in operation.

Typical drawings are shown in *Figures 23* and *24*.

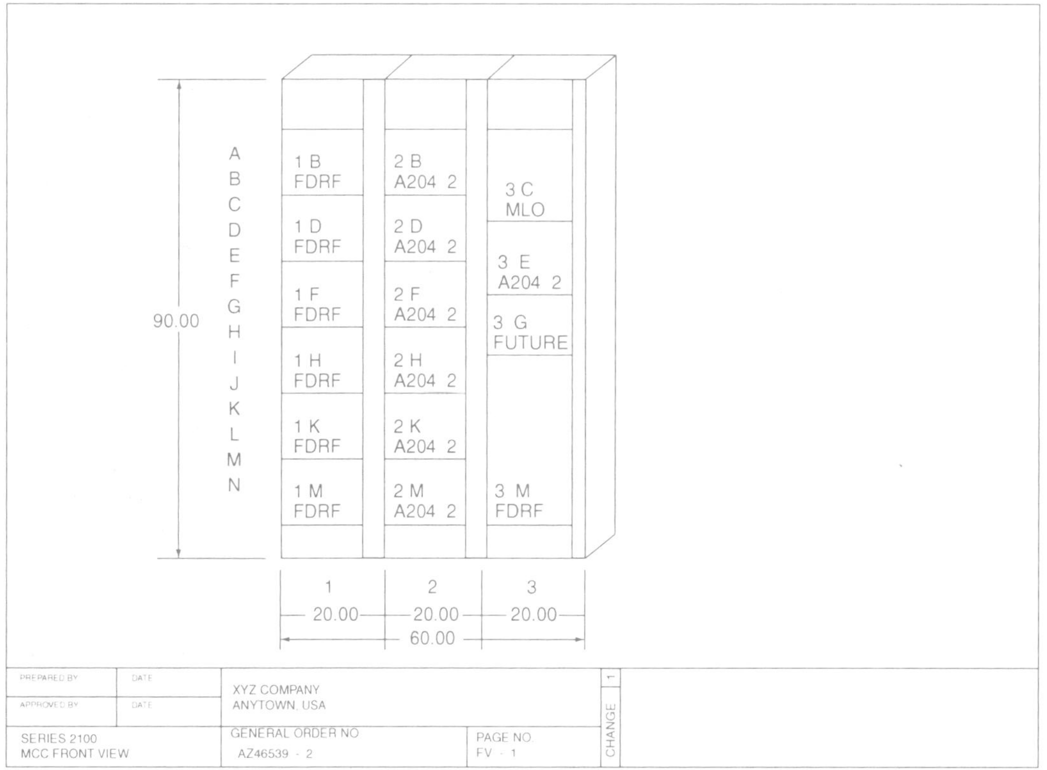

Figure 22 View of a motor control center.

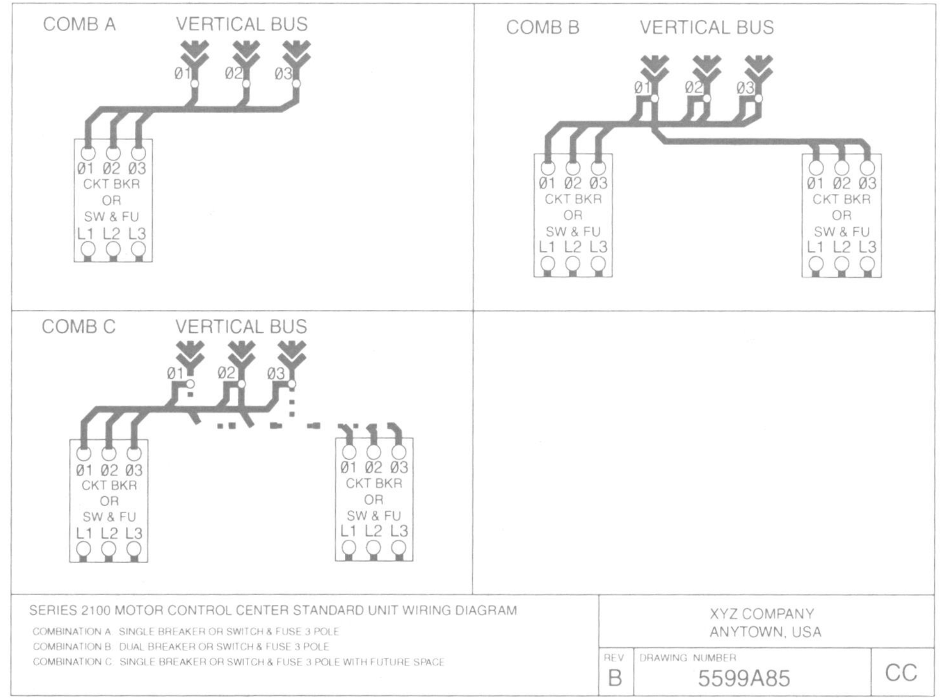

Figure 23 Motor control center standard unit wiring diagram.

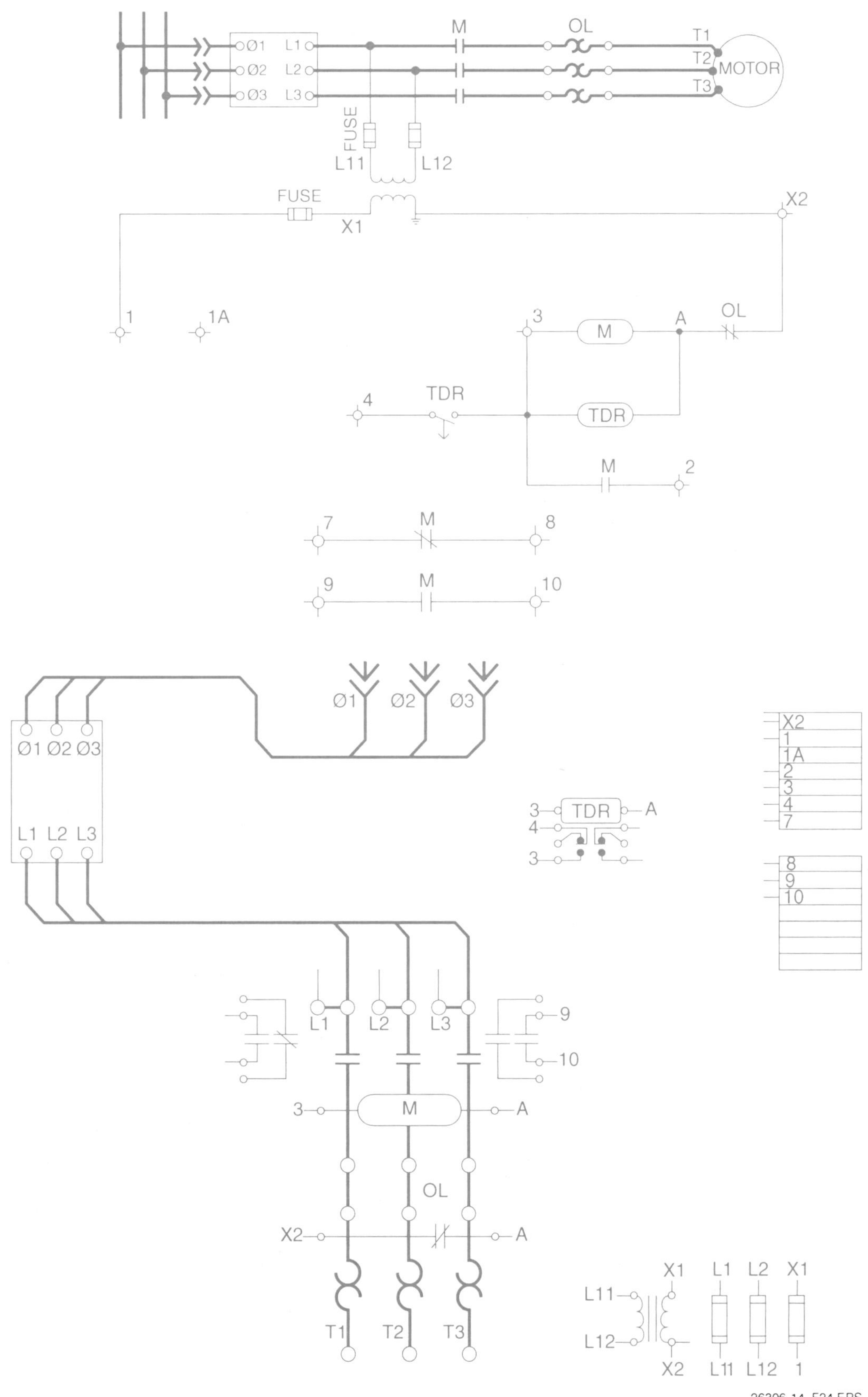

Figure 24 Unit diagrams for motor control center.

16.0.0 Panelboards

This section covers panelboard construction and protective devices.

16.1.0 Lighting and Power Panelboards

Circuit control and overcurrent protection must be provided for all circuits and the power-consuming devices connected to these circuits. Lighting and power panels located throughout large buildings being supplied with electrical energy provide this control and protection. *Figure 25* shows a schedule of fifteen panelboards provided in a typical industrial building to feed electrical energy to the various circuits.

16.2.0 Panelboard Construction

In general, panelboards are constructed so that the main feed busbars run the height of the panelboard. The buses to the branch circuit protective devices are connected to the alternate main buses. In an arrangement of this type, the connections directly across from each other are on the same phase, and the adjacent connections on each side are on different phases. As a result, multiple protective devices can be installed to serve the 208V equipment. An example of a panelboard is shown in *Figure 26*.

16.2.1 Identification of Conductors

The ungrounded conductors may be any color except green (or green with a yellow stripe), which is reserved for grounding purposes only; or white or gray, which are reserved for the grounded circuit conductor. See *NEC Section 200.6.*

NEC Section 210.5(C) requires that where different voltages exist in a building, the ungrounded conductors for each system must be identified at each accessible location. Identification may be by color-coding, marking, tape, tagging, or other approved means. The means of identification must be permanently posted at each branch circuit panelboard, or be readily available.

For example, this situation may occur when the building is served with 277/480V and step-down transformers are used to provide 120/208V for lighting and receptacle outlets. Examples of panelboard wiring connections are shown in *Figures 27, 28, 29,* and *30*.

16.2.2 Number of Circuits

The number of overcurrent devices in a panelboard is determined by the needs of the area being served. Using the bakery panelboard in *Figure 29* as an example, there are 13 single-pole circuits and five three-pole circuits. This is a total of 28 poles. When using a three-phase supply, the incremental number is six (a pole for each of the three phases on both sides of the panelboard). The minimum number of poles that could be specified for the bakery is 30. This would limit the power available for growth and would not permit the addition of a three-pole lead. The reasonable choice is to go to 36 poles, which provides flexibility for growth loads.

16.3.0 Panelboard Protective Devices

The main protective device for a panelboard may be either a fuse or a circuit breaker. This section describes the use of circuit breakers. The selection of a circuit breaker should be based on the following criteria. It must:

- Provide the proper overload protection
- Ensure a suitable voltage rating
- Provide a sufficient interrupting current rating
- Provide short circuit protection
- Coordinate the breaker(s) with other protective devices

The choice of the overload protection is based on the rating of the panelboard. The trip rating of the circuit breaker cannot exceed the amperage capacity of the busbars in the panelboard. The number of branch circuit breakers is generally not a factor in the selection of the main protective device, except in a practical sense. It is a common practice to have the total amperage of the branch breakers greatly exceed the rating of the main breaker; however, it makes little sense for a single branch circuit breaker to be the same size as, or larger than, the main breaker.

The voltage rating of the breaker must be higher than that of the system. Breakers are usually rated at 250V to 600V.

The importance of the proper interrupting rating cannot be overstressed. You should recall that if there is ever any question as to the exact value of the short circuit current available at a point, the circuit breaker with the higher interrupting rating is to be installed.

PANEL NO.	LOCATION	MAINS	VOLTAGE RATING	NO. OF CIRCUITS	BREAKER RATINGS	POLES	PURPOSE
P-1	BASEMENT N. CORRIDOR	BREAKER 100A	208/120V 3Ø, 4W	19 2 5	20A 20A 20A	1 2 1	LIGHTING AND RECEPTACLES SPARES
P-2	BASEMENT N. CORRIDOR	BREAKER 100A	208/120V 3Ø, 4W	24 2 0	20A 20A	1 2	LIGHTING AND RECEPTACLES SPARES
P-3	2ND FLOOR N. CORRIDOR	BREAKER 100A	208/120V 3Ø, 4W	24 2 0	20A 20A	1 2	LIGHTING AND RECEPTACLES SPARES
P-4	BASEMENT S. CORRIDOR	BREAKER 100A	208/120V 3Ø, 4W	24 2 0	20A 20A	1 2 1	LIGHTING AND RECEPTACLES SPARES
P-5	1ST FLOOR S. CORRIDOR	BREAKER 100A	208/120V 3Ø, 4W	23 2 1	20A 20A 20A	1 2 1	LIGHTING AND RECEPTACLES SPARES
P-6	2ND FLOOR S. CORRIDOR	BREAKER 100A	208/120V 3Ø, 4W	22 2 2	20A 20A 20A	1 2 1	LIGHTING AND RECEPTACLES SPARES
P-7	MFG. AREA S. WALL E.	BREAKER 100A	208/120V 3Ø, 4W	5 7 2	20A 20A 20A	1 1 1	LIGHTING AND RECEPTACLES SPARES
P-8	MFG. AREA S. WALL W.	BREAKER 100A	208/120V 3Ø, 4W	5 7 2	20A 20A 20A	1 1 1	LIGHTING AND RECEPTACLES SPARES
P-9	MFG. AREA S. WALL E.	BREAKER 100A	208/120V 3Ø, 4W	5 7 2	50A 20A 20A	1 1 1	LIGHTING AND RECEPTACLES SPARES
P-10	MFG. AREA S. WALL W.	BREAKER 100A	208/120V 3Ø, 4W	5 7 2	50A 20A 20A	1 1 1	LIGHTING AND RECEPTACLES SPARES
P-11	MFG. AREA EAST WALL	LUGS ONLY 225A	208/120V 3Ø, 4W	6	20A	3	BLOWERS AND VENTILATORS
P-12	BOILER ROOM	BREAKER 100A	208/120V 3Ø, 4W	10 4	20A 20A	1 1	LIGHTING AND RECEPTACLES SPARES
P-13	BOILER ROOM	LUGS ONLY 225A	208/120V 3Ø, 4W	6	20A	3	OIL BURNERS AND PUMPS
P-14	MFG. AREA EAST WALL	LUGS ONLY 400A	208/120V 3Ø, 4W	3 2 1	175A 70A 40A	3 3 3	CHILLERS FAN COIL UNITS FAN COIL UNITS
P-15	MFG. AREA WEST WALL	LUGS ONLY 600A	208/120V 3Ø, 4W	5	100A	3	TROLLEY BUSWAY AND ELEVATOR

26306-14_F25.EPS

Figure 25 Schedule of electric panelboards for an industrial building.

26306-14_F26.EPS

Figure 26 Typical panelboard.

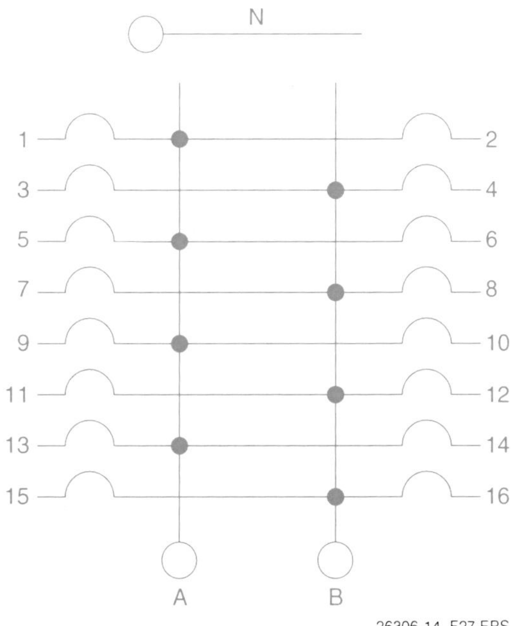

26306-14_F27.EPS

Figure 27 Lighting and appliance branch circuit panelboard—single-phase, three-wire connections.

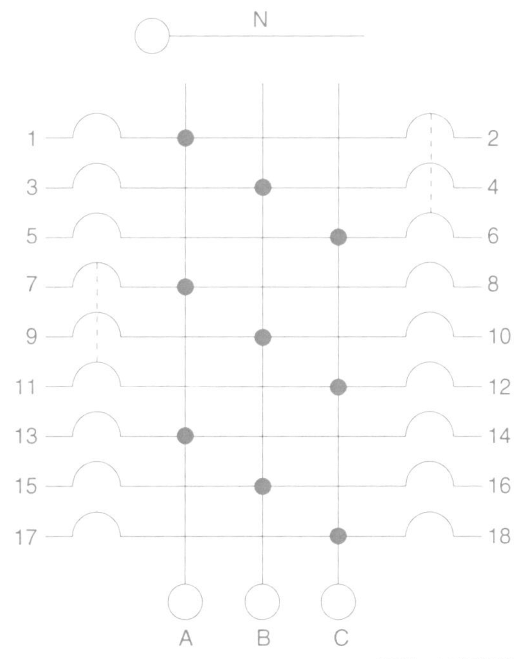

26306-14_F28.EPS

Figure 28 Lighting and appliance branch circuit panelboard—three-phase, four-wire connections.

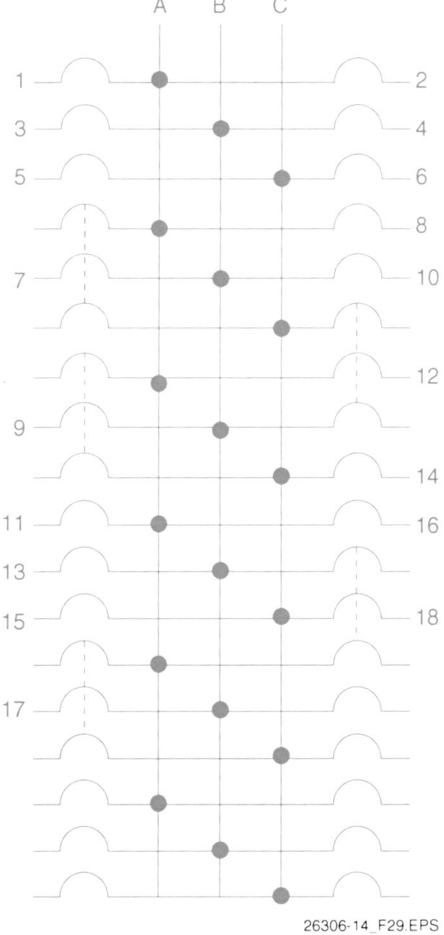

26306-14_F29.EPS

Figure 29 Bakery panelboard circuit showing alternate numbering scheme.

Many circuit breakers used as the main protective device are provided with an electronic trip unit (*Figure 31*). Adjustments of this trip determine the degree of protection provided by the circuit breaker if a short circuit occurs. The manufacturer of this device provides exact information about the adjustments to be made. In general, a low setting may be 10 or 12 times the overload trip rating.

Two rules should be followed whenever the trip is set:

- The trip must be set to the minimum practical setting.
- The setting must be lower than the value of the short circuit current available at that point.

If subfeed lugs are used, ensure that the lugs are suitable for making multiple breaker connections,

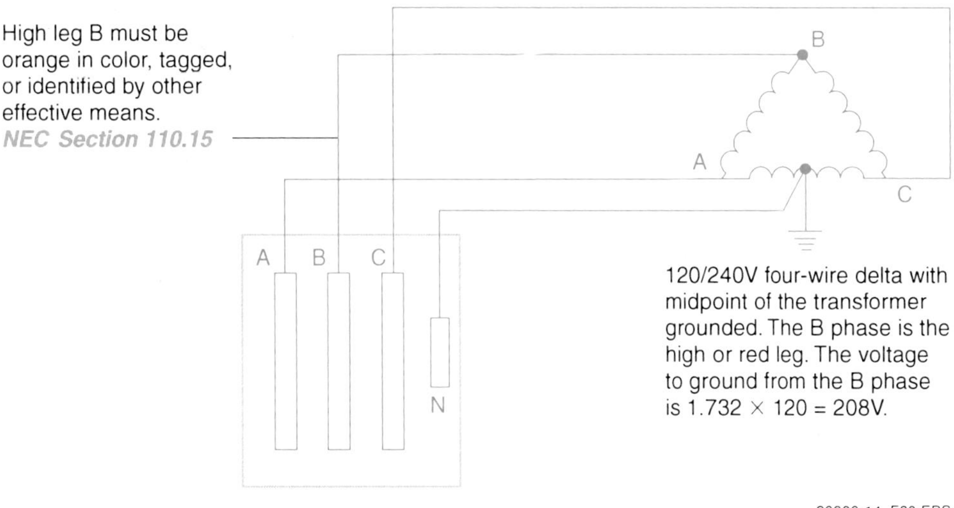
High leg B must be orange in color, tagged, or identified by other effective means.
NEC Section 110.15
B
A
C
A
B
C
N
120/240V four-wire delta with midpoint of the transformer grounded. The B phase is the high or red leg. The voltage to ground from the B phase is 1.732 × 120 = 208V.
26306-14_F30.EPS

Figure 30 Panelboards and switchboards supplied by four-wire, delta-connected system.

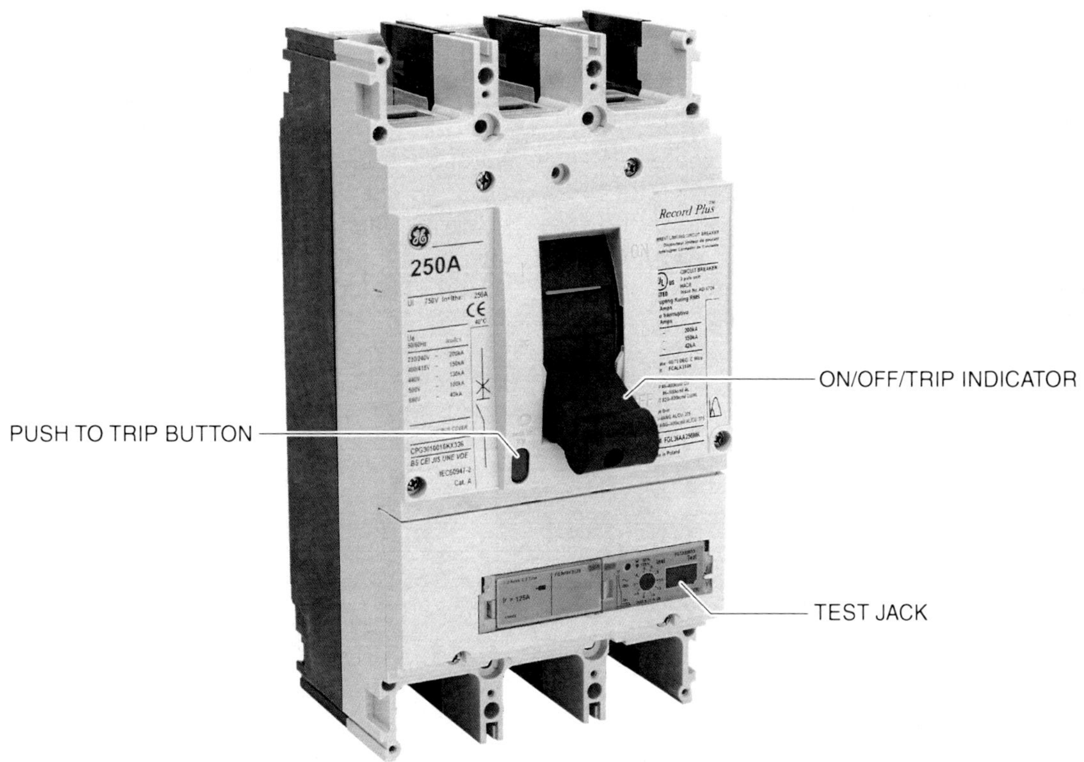
250A
Record Plus
ON/OFF/TRIP INDICATOR
PUSH TO TRIP BUTTON
TEST JACK
26306-14_F31.EPS

Figure 31 Circuit breaker with electronic trip unit.

as required by *NEC Section 110.14(A)*. In general, this means that a separate lug is to be provided for each conductor being connected.

If taps are made to the subfeeder, they can be reduced in size according to *NEC Section 240.21*. This specification is very useful in cases such as that of panel P-12 in *Figure 25*. For this panel, a 100A main breaker is fed by a 350MCM conductor. Within the distances given in *NEC Section 240.21(B)(1)*, a conductor with a 100A rating may be tapped to the subfeeder and connected to the 100A main breaker in the panel.

Per *NEC Section 110.14(C)*, the temperature rating of conductors must be selected and coordinated so as not to exceed the lowest temperature rating of any connected termination, conductor, or device.

16.4.0 Branch Circuit Protective Devices

The schedule of panelboards for the industrial building (*Figure 25*) shows that lighting panels P-1 through P-6 have 20A circuit breakers, including double-pole breakers to supply special receptacle outlets. A double-pole breaker requires the same installation space as two single-pole breakers. Breakers are shown in *Figure 32*.

26306-14_F32.EPS

Figure 32 Branch circuit protective devices.

Summary

This module explained the purpose of switchgear. Switchgear construction, metering layouts, wiring requirements, and maintenance were discussed. It also explained *NEC®* requirements for these systems and provided a basic understanding of how to apply them. Circuit breakers, their four general classifications, and the major circuit breaker ratings were also addressed. Additionally, ground fault relay systems and the testing of such systems were explained. This module also covered visual and mechanical inspections and electrical tests associated with low-voltage and medium-voltage cables, metal-enclosed busways, and metering and instrumentation.

Review Questions

1. In industrial applications, medium-voltage may refer to systems rated over _____.
   a. 50V up to 480V
   b. 600V up to 120,000V
   c. 1,000V up to 38,000V
   d. 2,000V up to 69,000V

2. The term *interrupting rating* refers to the _____.
   a. trip setting of a circuit breaker
   b. voltage rating of a fuse
   c. highest voltage level a device can withstand
   d. maximum current a device will safely interrupt at rated voltage

3. Which of the following is a color that can be used to designate an ungrounded conductor?
   a. Green
   b. White
   c. Gray
   d. Red

4. When an unintended path is established between an ungrounded conductor and ground, it is called a(n) _____.
   a. phase fault
   b. open circuit
   c. ground fault
   d. overload

5. A device that is specifically designed to protect equipment from ground faults through the use of sensors is a _____.
   a. molded-case circuit breaker
   b. dual-element fuse
   c. ground fault relay
   d. ground fault circuit interrupter

6. The maximum voltage that a piece of equipment can withstand is known as its _____.
   a. interrupting capacity
   b. basic impulse insulation level (BIL)
   c. current limit
   d. frequency

7. A transformer rated at more than 500kVA is considered a(n) _____ transformer.
   a. power
   b. control
   c. distribution
   d. isolation

8. The term *capacity* on a transformer nameplate refers to _____.
   a. its voltage rating
   b. its ability to transfer energy
   c. the voltage produced by the secondary
   d. the number of secondary windings

9. The term *class* on a transformer nameplate refers to _____.
   a. its use, such as control or power
   b. the type of cooling it uses
   c. whether it is step-up or step-down
   d. its range of operating frequencies

10. The secondary of a current transformer is usually designed for a rated current of _____.
    a. 5A
    b. 10A
    c. 15A
    d. 20A

11. Of the following types of current transformers, which is normally used with circuit breakers or power transformers?
    a. Bar
    b. Bushing
    c. Oil filled
    d. Window

12. Which of the following is *not* a general classification of circuit breakers?
    a. Fuse circuit breaker
    b. Air circuit breaker
    c. Oil circuit breaker
    d. Gas circuit breaker

13. What type of diagram shows the actual wiring connections between unit assemblies or equipment with each wire labeled to indicate where to terminate it?
    a. Schematic diagram
    b. Front panel diagram
    c. Interconnection diagram
    d. Block diagram

14. The trip rating of a circuit breaker used as the main protective device in a panelboard *cannot* exceed _____.
    a. the total amperage of the branch breakers
    b. the amperage capacity of the busbars in the panelboard
    c. the amperage of the individual branch fuses
    d. 250V

15. According to the IEEE Identification System found in *Appendix A* of this module, if device No. 51 is indicated on an electrical print, it would be a(n) _____.
    a. circuit breaker
    b. reverse power relay
    c. field circuit breaker
    d. AC time overcurrent relay

Module 26306-14
Supplemental Exercises

1. What are the two basic functions performed by switchgear?

____

____

____

2. Switchboard control and meter wiring standards shall meet the requirements of ______________

____.

3. When wiring switchboard electrical components, keep the control wires at least ______________ from moving parts.

4. Specific instructions for handling, storage, installation, testing, and maintenance of distribution equipment is found in ______________.
   a. standard specifications
   b. electrical textbooks
   c. drawing notes
   d. manufacturer's instructions.

5. What is a ground fault?

____

____

____

6. The three generic types of ground fault systems include ______________

____

____.

7. Wires from the sensor to the ground fault relay should be no longer than ______________ and no smaller than ______________ AWG wire.

8. The instantaneous trip feature of a standard ground fault relay has a fixed time delay of approximately ______________ cycles.

9. What is the function of an HVL switch?

____

____

____

10. The standard output voltage of a potential transformer is ______________ or ______________, depending on whether the primary connections are from phase-to-phase or phase-to-neutral.

11. Name the four general classifications of circuit breakers.

12. Define the term *amperes* interrupting rating.

13. What are the standard abbreviations for a time-delay open, pressure switch, auxiliary switch, and backlighted pushbutton?

14. What is the purpose of a single-line (one-line) diagram?

15. What conductors may be any color except green, green with a yellow stripe, white, or gray?

Trade Terms Introduced in This Module

Air circuit breaker: A circuit breaker in which the interruption occurs in air.

Basic impulse insulation level (BIL): The maximum impulse voltage the winding insulation can withstand without failure.

Branch circuit: A set of conductors that extends beyond the last overcurrent device in the low-voltage system of a given building.

Bus: A conductor or group of conductors that serves as a common connection for two or more circuits in a switchgear assembly.

Bushing: An insulating structure including a through conductor, or providing a passageway for such a conductor, for the purpose of insulating the conductor from the barrier and conducting from one side of the barrier to the other.

Capacity: The rated load-carrying ability, expressed in kilovolt-amperes or kilowatts, of generating equipment or other electric apparatus.

Current transformer (CT): A single-phase instrument transformer connected in series in a line that carries the full-load current. The turns ratio is designed to produce a reduced current in the secondary suitable for the current coil of standard measuring instruments and in proportion to the load current.

Distribution system equipment: Switchboard equipment that is downstream from the service-entrance equipment.

Distribution transformer: A transformer that is used for transferring electric energy from a primary distribution circuit to a secondary distribution circuit. Distribution transformers are usually rated between 5kVA and 500kVA.

Feeder: A set of conductors originating at a main distribution center that supply one or more secondary distribution centers, one or more branch circuit distribution centers, or any combination of these two types of load.

Metal-enclosed switchgear: Switchgear that is primarily used in indoor applications up to 600V.

Potential transformer (PT): A special transformer designed for use in measuring high voltage; normally, the secondary voltage is 120V.

Service-entrance equipment: Equipment located at the service entrance of a given building that provides overcurrent protection to the feeder and service conductors and also provides a means of disconnecting the feeders from the energized service equipment.

Switchboard: A large single panel, frame, or assembly of panels on which switches, fuses, buses, and instruments are mounted.

Switchgear: A general term covering switching or interrupting devices and any combination thereof with associated control, instrumentation, metering, protective, and regulating devices.

Additional Resources

This module presents thorough resources for task training. The following resource material is suggested for further study.

National Electrical Code® Handbook, Latest Edition. Quincy, MA: National Fire Protection Association.

Figure Credits

©iStock.com/photoquest7, Module Opener

Topaz Publications, Inc., SA01, Figure 2, SA03, Figures 8, 10, 26, and 32

Square D/Schneider Electric, Figures 3 and 4

Jim Mitchem, SA02, SA06, Figures 12, 18, and Appendix B

Mike Powers, SA04 and SA05

Fluke Corporation, Reproduced with permission, Figure 5

Boltswitch, Inc., Figure 9

Federal Pacific Transformer Co., Figure 11

General Electric Company, Figure 31

Appendix A

IEEE Identification System

The devices in switching equipment are referred to by numbers with appropriate suffix letters when necessary, according to the functions they perform.

These numbers are based on a system adopted as standard for automatic switchgear by IEEE and incorporated in *American Standard C37.2-1970*. This system is used in connection diagrams, instruction books, and specifications.

Device Number	Definition and Function
1	**Master Element** – The initiating device, such as a control switch, voltage relay, float switch, that serves either directly, or through such permissive devices as protective and time-delay relays, to place equipment in or out of operation.
2	**Time-Delay Starting or Closing Relay** – A device that functions to give a desired amount of time delay before or after any point of operation in a switching sequence or protective relay system, except as specifically provided by device functions 48, 62, and 79 described later.
3	**Checking or Interlocking Relay** – A device that operates in response to the position of a number of other devices (or to a number of predetermined conditions) in equipment to allow an operating sequence to proceed, to stop, or to provide a check of the position of these devices or of these conditions for any purpose.
4	**Master Contactor** – A device, generally controlled by device No. 1 or equivalent, and the required permissive and protective devices, that serves to make and break the necessary control circuits to place equipment into operation under the desired conditions and to take it out of operation under other or abnormal conditions.
5	**Stopping Device** – A control device used primarily to shut down equipment and hold it out of operation. [This device may be manually or electrically actuated, but excludes the function of electrical lockout (see device function 86) on abnormal conditions.]
6	**Starting Circuit Breaker** – A device whose principal function is to connect a machine to its source of starting voltage.
7	**Anode Circuit Breaker** – A device used in the anode circuits of a power rectifier for the primary purpose of interrupting the rectifier circuit if an arc-back should occur.
8	**Control Power Disconnecting Device** – A disconnective device, such as a knife switch, circuit breaker, or pullout fuse block, that is used for the purpose of connecting and disconnecting the source of control power to and from the control bus or equipment. ***Note:*** Control power is considered to include auxiliary power which supplies such apparatus as small motors and heaters.
9	**Reversing Device** – A device used for the purpose of reversing a machine field or for performing any other reversing functions.
10	**Unit Sequence Switch** – A device used to change the sequence in which units may be placed in and out of service in multiple-unit equipment.
11	Reserved for future application.
12	**Over-Speed Device** – Usually a direct-connected speed switch that functions on machine over-speed.
13	**Synchronous-Speed Device** – A device such as a centrifugal-speed switch, slip-frequency relay, voltage relay, or undercurrent relay, that operates at approximately the synchronous speed of a machine.
14	**Under-Speed Device** – A device that functions when the speed of a machine falls below a predetermined value.
15	**Speed- or Frequency-Matching Device** – A device that functions to match and hold the speed or frequency of a machine or of a system equal to, or approximately equal to, that of another machine, source, or system.

26306-14_A01.EPS

Device Number	Definition and Function
16	Reserved for future application.
17	**Shunting or Discharge Switch** – A device that serves to open or close a shunting circuit around any piece of apparatus (except a resistor), such as machine field, machine armature, capacitor, or reactor. ***Note:*** This excludes devices that perform such shunting operations as may be necessary in the process of starting a machine by devices 6 or 42, or their equivalent, and also excludes the device 73 function, which serves for the switching of resistors.
18	**Accelerating or Decelerating Device** – A device used to close or to cause the closing of circuits that are used to increase or decrease the speed of a machine.
19	**Starting-to-Running Transition Contactor** – A device that operates to initiate or cause the automatic transfer of a machine from the starting to the running power connection.
20	**Electrically Operated Valve** – An electrically operated, controlled, or monitored valve in a fluid line. ***Note:*** The function of the valve may be indicated by the use of suffixes.
21	**Distance Relay** – A device that functions when the circuit admittance, impedance, or reactance increases or decreases beyond predetermined limits.
22	**Equalizer Circuit Breaker** – A breaker that serves to control or to make and break the equalizer or the current-balancing connections for a field, or for regulating equipment, in a multiple-unit installation.
23	**Temperature Control Device** – A device that functions to raise or lower the temperature of a machine or other apparatus, or of any medium, when its temperature falls below or rises above a predetermined value. ***Note:*** An example is a thermostat that switches on a space heater in a switchgear assembly when the temperature falls to a desired value as distinguished from a device that is used to provide automatic temperature regulation between close limits and would be designated as 90T.
24	Reserved for future application.
25	**Synchronizing or Synchronism-Check Device** – A device that operates when two AC circuits are within the desired limits of frequency, phase angle, or voltage to permit or to cause the paralleling of these two circuits.
26	**Apparatus Thermal Device** – A device that functions when the temperature of the shunt field or the armortisseur winding of a machine or that of a load limiting or load shifting resistor or of a liquid or other medium exceeds a predetermined value; it also functions if the temperature of the protected apparatus, such as a power rectifier, or of any medium decreases below a predetermined value.
27	**Undervoltage Relay** – A device that functions on a given value of undervoltage.
28	**Flame Detector** – A device that monitors the presence of the pilot or main flame in such apparatus as a gas turbine or steam boiler.
29	**Isolating Contactor** – A device used expressly for disconnecting one circuit from another for the purposes of emergency operation, maintenance, or testing.
30	**Annunciator Relay** – A nonautomatic reset device that gives a number of separate visual indications upon the functioning of protective devices and that may also be arranged to perform a lockout function.
31	**Separate Excitation Device** – A device that connects a circuit, such as the shunt field of a synchronous converter, to a source of separate excitation during the starting sequence or one that energizes the excitation and ignition circuits of a power rectifier.

26306-14_A02.EPS

Device Number	Definition and Function
32	**Directional Power Relay** – A device that functions on a desired value of power flow in a given direction or upon reverse power resulting from arc-back in the anode or cathode circuits of a power rectifier.
33	**Position Switch** – A device that makes or breaks its contacts when the main device or piece of apparatus that has no device function number reaches a given position.
34	**Master Sequence Device** – A device, such as a motor-operated multi-contact switch or the equivalent, or a programming device, such as a computer, that establishes or determines the operating sequence of the major devices in equipment during starting and stopping or during other sequential switching operations.
35	**Brush-Operating or Slip-Ring Short-Circuiting Device** – A device used for raising, lowering, or shifting the brushes of a machine; for short-circuiting its slip rings, or for engaging or disengaging the contacts of a mechanical rectifier.
36	**Polarity or Polarizing Voltage Device** – A device that operates or permits the operation of another device on a predetermined polarity only, or one that verifies the presence of a polarizing voltage in equipment.
37	**Undercurrent or Underpower Relay** – A device that functions when the current or power flow decreases below a predetermined value.
38	**Bearing Protective Device** – A device that functions on excessive bearing temperature or on other abnormal mechanical conditions, such as undue wear, that may eventually result in excessive bearing temperature.
39	**Mechanical Condition Monitor** – A device that functions upon the occurrence of an abnormal mechanical condition (except that associated with bearings as covered under device function 38), such as excessive vibration, eccentricity, expansion, shock, tilting, or seal failure.
40	**Field Relay** – A device that functions on a given or abnormally low value or failure of machine field current or on an excessive value of the reactive component of armature current in an AC machine indicating abnormally low field excitation.
41	**Field Circuit Breaker** – A device that functions to apply or remove the field excitation of a machine.
42	**Running Circuit Breaker** – A device whose principal function is to connect a machine to its source of running or operating voltage. This function may also be used for a device, such as a contactor, that is used in series with a circuit breaker or other fault protecting means, primarily for frequent opening and closing of the circuit.
43	**Manual Transfer or Selector Device** – A device that transfers the control circuits so as to modify the plan of operation of the switching equipment or of some of the devices.
44	**Unit Sequence Starting Relay** – A device that functions to start the next available unit in multiple-unit equipment on the failure or non-availability of the normally preceding unit.
45	**Atmospheric Condition Monitor** – A device that functions upon the occurrence of an abnormal atmospheric condition, such as damaging fumes, explosive mixtures, smoke, or fire.
46	**Reverse-Phase or Phase-Balance Current Relay** – A device that functions when the polyphase currents are of reverse-phase sequence or when the polyphase currents are unbalanced or contain negative phase-sequence components above a given amount.
47	**Phase-Sequence Voltage Relay** – A relay that functions upon a predetermined value of polyphase voltage in the desired phase sequence.
48	**Incomplete Sequence Relay** – A relay that generally returns the equipment to the normal or off position and locks it out if the normal starting, operating, or stopping sequence is not properly completed within a predetermined time. If the device is used for alarm purposes only, it should preferably be designated as 48A (alarm).

26306-14_A03.EPS

Device Number	Definition and Function
49	**Machine or Transformer Thermal Relay** – A relay that functions when the temperature of a machine armature, or other load-carrying winding or element of a machine or the temperature of a power rectifier or power transformer (including a power rectifier transformer) exceeds a predetermined value.
50	**Instantaneous Overcurrent or Rate-of-Rise Relay** – A relay that functions instantaneously on an excessive value of current or on an excessive rate of current rise, indicating a fault in the apparatus or circuit being protected.
51	**AC Time Overcurrent Relay** – A relay with either a definite or inverse time characteristic that functions when the current in an AC circuit exceeds a predetermined value.
52	**AC Circuit Breaker** – A device that is used to close and interrupt an AC power circuit under normal conditions or to interrupt this circuit under fault or emergency conditions.
53	**Exciter or DC Generator Relay** – A relay that forces the DC machine field excitation to build up during starting or which functions when the machine voltage has built up to a given value.
54	Reserved for future application.
55	**Power Factor Relay** – A relay that operates when the power factor in an AC circuit rises above or below a predetermined value.
56	**Field Application Relay** – A relay that automatically controls the application of the field excitation to an AC motor at some predetermined point in the slip cycle.
57	**Short-Circuiting or Grounding Device** – A primary circuit switching device that functions to short-circuit or ground a circuit in response to automatic or manual means.
58	**Rectification Failure Relay** – A device that functions if one or more anodes of a power rectifier fail to fire, to detect an arc-back, or on failure of a diode to conduct or block properly.
59	**Overvoltage Relay** – A relay that functions on a given value of overvoltage.
60	**Voltage or Current Balance Relay** – A relay that operates on a given difference in voltage or current input or output of two circuits.
61	Reserved for future application.
62	**Time-Delay Stopping or Opening Relay** – A time-delay relay that serves in conjunction with the device that initiates the shutdown, stopping, or opening operation in an automatic sequence.
63	**Pressure Switch** – A switch that operates on given values or on a given rate of change of pressure.
64	**Ground Protective Relay** – A relay that functions on failure of the insulation of a machine, transformer, or other apparatus to ground or on flashover of a DC machine to ground. ***Note:*** This function is assigned only to a relay that detects the flow of current from the frame of a machine or enclosing case or structure of a piece of apparatus to ground or one that detects a ground on a normally ungrounded winding or circuit. It is not applied to a device connected in the secondary circuit or secondary neutral of a current transformer connected in the power circuit of a normally grounded system.
65	**Governor** – The assembly of fluid, electrical, or mechanical control equipment used for regulating the flow of water, steam, or other medium to the prime mover for such purposes as starting, holding speed or load, or stopping.

26306-14_A04.EPS

Device Number	Definition and Function
66	**Notching or Jogging Device** – A device that functions to allow only a specified number of operations of a given device or equipment or a specified number of successive operations within a given time of each other. It also functions to energize a circuit periodically or for fractions of specified time intervals or that is used to permit intermittent acceleration or jogging of a machine at low speeds for mechanical positioning.
67	**AC Directional Overcurrent Relay** – A relay that functions on a desired value of AC overcurrent flowing in a predetermined direction.
68	**Blocking Relay** – A relay that initiates a pilot signal for blocking of tripping on external faults in a transmission line or in other apparatus under predetermined conditions, or a relay cooperates with other devices to block tripping or to block reclosing on an out-of-step condition or on power swings.
69	**Permissive Control Device** – Generally a two-position, manually operated switch that in one position permits the closing of a circuit breaker or the placing of equipment into operation and in the other position prevents the circuit breaker or the equipment from being operated.
70	**Rheostat** – A variable resistance device used in an electric circuit that is electrically operated or has other electrical accessories, such as auxiliary, position, or limit switches.
71	**Level Switch** – A switch that operates on given values or on a given rate of change of level.
72	**DC Circuit Breaker** – A circuit breaker used to close and interrupt a DC power circuit under normal conditions or to interrupt this circuit under fault or emergency conditions.
73	**Load-Resistor Contactor** – A contactor used to shunt or insert a step of load limiting, shifting, or indicating resistance in a power circuit, to switch a space heater in a circuit, or to switch a light or regenerative load resistor of a power rectifier or other machine in and out of a circuit.
74	**Alarm Relay** – A device other than an annunciator, as covered under device No. 30, that is used to operate or to operate in connection with a visual or audible alarm.
75	**Position Changing Mechanism** – A mechanism that is used for moving a main device from one position to another in equipment (for example, shifting a removable circuit breaker unit to and from the connected, disconnected, and test positions).
76	**DC Overcurrent Relay** – A relay that functions when the current in a DC circuit exceeds a given value.
77	**Pulse Transmitter** – A device used to generate and transmit pulses over a telemetering or pilot-wire circuit to remove the indicating or receiving device.
78	**Phase Angle Measuring or Out-of-Step Protective Relay** – A relay that functions at a predetermined phase angle between two voltages, between two currents, or between voltage and current.
79	**AC Reclosing Relay** – A relay that controls the automatic reclosing and locking out of an AC circuit interrupter.
80	**Flow Switch** – A switch that operates on given values, or a given rate of change of flow.
81	**Frequency Relay** – A relay that functions on a predetermined value of frequency, either under, over, or on normal system frequency or rate of change of frequency.
82	**DC Reclosing Relay** – A relay that controls the automatic closing and reclosing of a DC circuit interrupter, generally in response to load circuit conditions.
83	**Automatic Selective Control or Transfer Relay** – A relay that operates to select automatically between certain sources or conditions in equipment or that performs a transfer operation automatically.

26306-14_A05.EPS

Device Number	Definition and Function
84	**Operating Mechanism** – The complete electrical mechanism or servo-mechanism, including the operating motor, solenoids, position switches, and for a tap changer, induction regulator, or any similar piece of apparatus that has no device function number.
85	**Carrier or Pilot-Wire Receiver Relay** – A relay that is operated or restrained by a signal used in connection with carrier-current or DC pilot-wire fault directional relaying.
86	**Locking-Out Relay** – An electrically operated relay that functions to shut down and hold equipment out of service on the occurrence of abnormal conditions. It may be reset either manually or electrically.
87	**Differential Protective Relay** – A protective relay that functions on a percentage of phase angle or other quantitative difference of two currents or of some other electrical quantities.
88	**Auxiliary Motor or Motor Generator** – A device used for operating auxiliary equipment, such as pumps, blowers, exciters, and rotating magnetic amplifiers.
89	**Line Switch** – A switch used as a disconnecting load-interrupter or isolating switch in an AC or DC power circuit when this device is electrically operated or has electrical accessories, such as an auxiliary switch or magnetic lock.
90	**Regulating Device** – A device that functions to regulate a quantity, or quantities, such as voltage, current, power, speed, frequency, temperature, and load, at a certain value or between certain (generally close) limits for machines, tie lines, or other apparatus.
91	**Voltage Directional Relay** – A relay that operates when the voltage across an open circuit breaker or contactor exceeds a given value in a given direction.
92	**Voltage and Power Directional Relay** – A relay that permits or causes the connection of two circuits when the voltage difference between them exceeds a given value in a predetermined direction and causes these two circuits to be disconnected from each other when the power flowing between them exceeds a given value in the opposite direction.
93	**Field Changing Contactor** – A device that functions to increase or decrease in one step the value of field excitation on a machine.
94	**Tripping or Trip-Free Relay** – A device that functions to trip a circuit breaker, contactor, or equipment, to permit immediate tripping by other devices, or to prevent immediate reclosure of a circuit interrupter in case it should open automatically even though its closing circuit is maintained closed.
95 96 97	Used only for specific applications on individual installations where none of the assigned numbered functions from 1 to 94 is suitable.

26306-14_A06.EPS

Appendix B

TYPICAL MANUFACTURER DRAWINGS

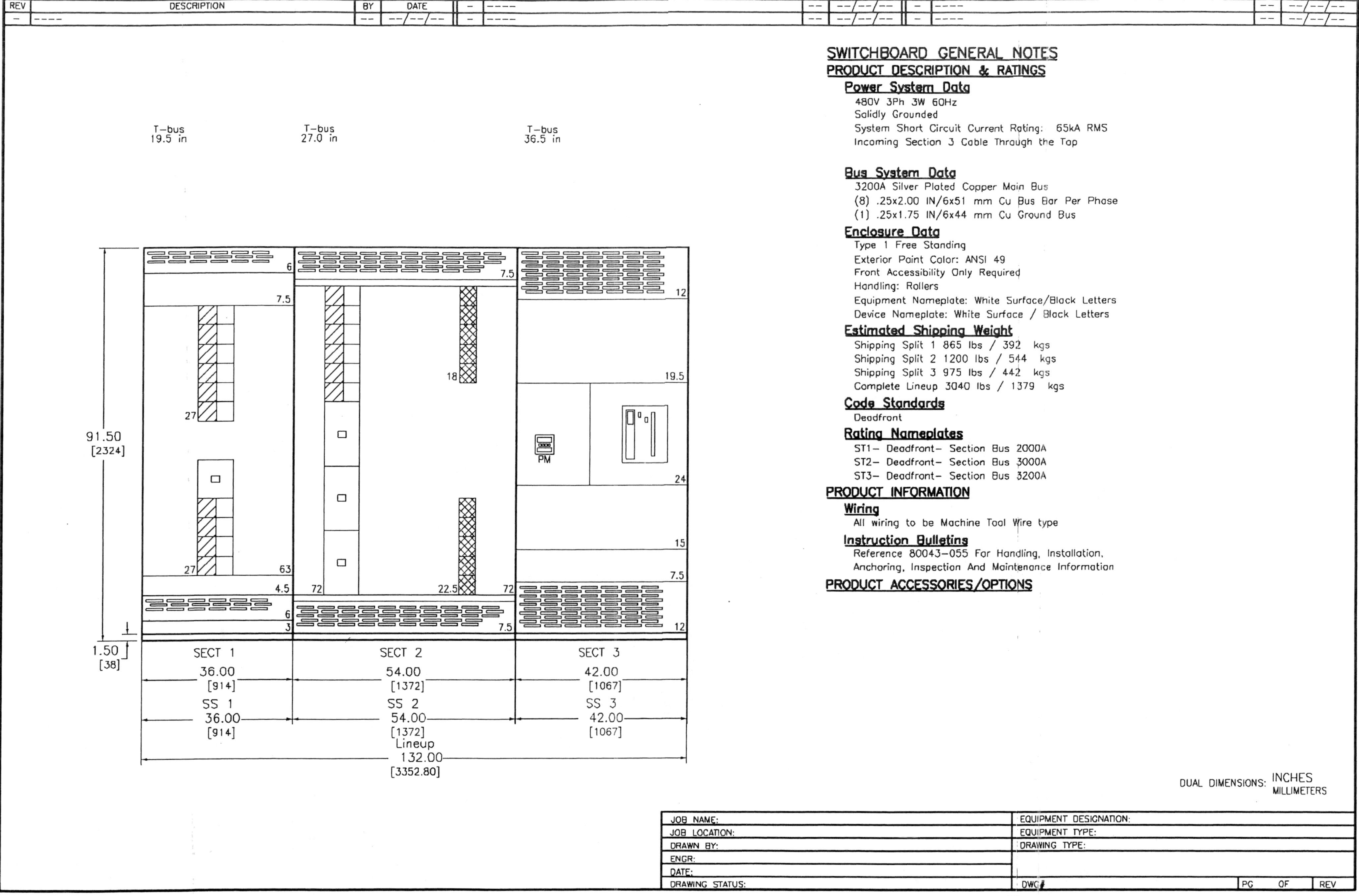

REV
DESCRIPTION
BY
DATE
SWITCHBOARD GENERAL NOTES
PRODUCT DESCRIPTION & RATINGS
Power System Data
480V 3Ph 3W 60Hz
Solidly Grounded
System Short Circuit Current Rating: 65kA RMS
Incoming Section 3 Cable Through the Top
Bus System Data
3200A Silver Plated Copper Main Bus
(8) .25x2.00 IN/6x51 mm Cu Bus Bar Per Phase
(1) .25x1.75 IN/6x44 mm Cu Ground Bus
Enclosure Data
Type 1 Free Standing
Exterior Paint Color: ANSI 49
Front Accessibility Only Required
Handling: Rollers
Equipment Nameplate: White Surface/Black Letters
Device Nameplate: White Surface / Black Letters
Estimated Shipping Weight
Shipping Split 1 865 lbs / 392 kgs
Shipping Split 2 1200 lbs / 544 kgs
Shipping Split 3 975 lbs / 442 kgs
Complete Lineup 3040 lbs / 1379 kgs
Code Standards
Deadfront
Rating Nameplates
ST1- Deadfront- Section Bus 2000A
ST2- Deadfront- Section Bus 3000A
ST3- Deadfront- Section Bus 3200A
PRODUCT INFORMATION
Wiring
All wiring to be Machine Tool Wire type
Instruction Bulletins
Reference 80043-055 For Handling, Installation, Anchoring, Inspection And Maintenance Information
PRODUCT ACCESSORIES/OPTIONS
T-bus 19.5 in
T-bus 27.0 in
T-bus 36.5 in
91.50 [2324]
1.50 [38]
PM
SECT 1
36.00 [914]
SS 1
36.00 [914]
SECT 2
54.00 [1372]
SS 2
54.00 [1372]
SECT 3
42.00 [1067]
SS 3
42.00 [1067]
Lineup
132.00 [3352.80]
DUAL DIMENSIONS: INCHES MILLIMETERS
JOB NAME:
JOB LOCATION:
DRAWN BY:
ENGR:
DATE:
DRAWING STATUS:
EQUIPMENT DESIGNATION:
EQUIPMENT TYPE:
DRAWING TYPE:
DWG#
PG
OF
REV
26306-14 A07.EPS

Appendix B Typical manufacturer drawings (Sheet 1 of 6).

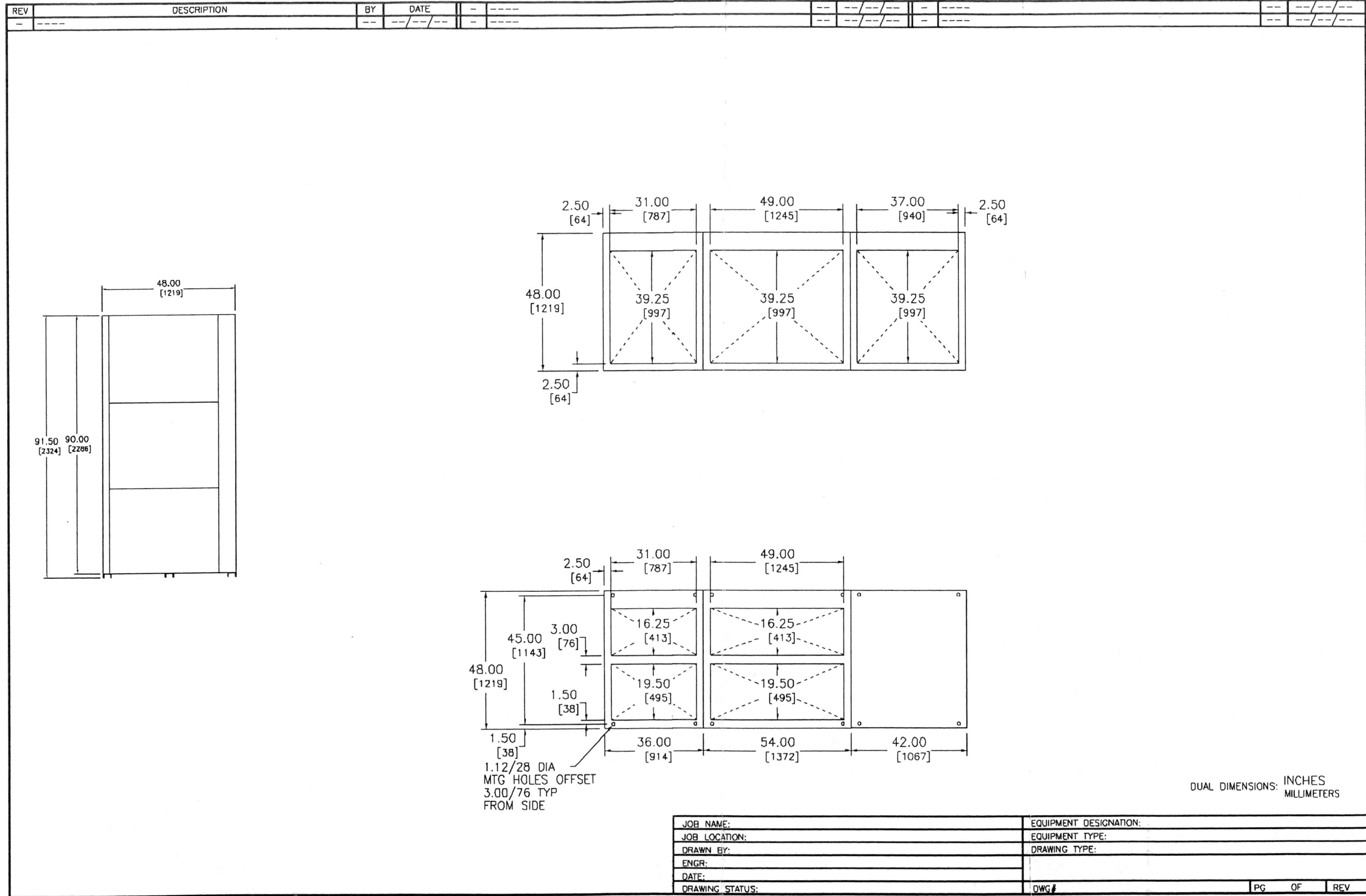

Appendix B Typical manufacturer drawings (Sheet 2 of 6).

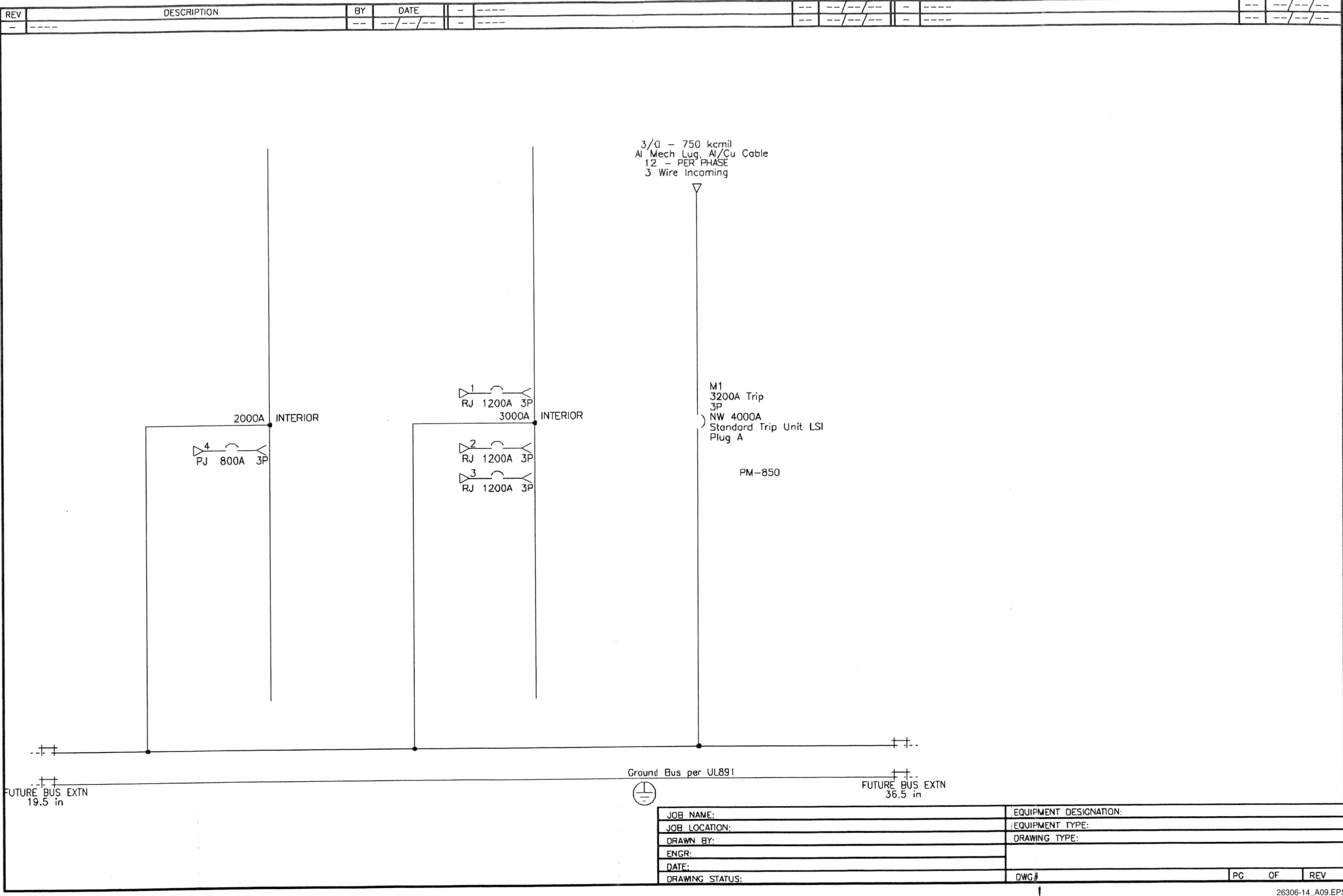

Appendix B Typical manufacturer drawings (Sheet 3 of 6).

Device Number	Definition and Function
84	**Operating Mechanism** – The complete electrical mechanism or servo-mechanism, including the operating motor, solenoids, position switches, and for a tap changer, induction regulator, or any similar piece of apparatus that has no device function number.
85	**Carrier or Pilot-Wire Receiver Relay** – A relay that is operated or restrained by a signal used in connection with carrier-current or DC pilot-wire fault directional relaying.
86	**Locking-Out Relay** – An electrically operated relay that functions to shut down and hold equipment out of service on the occurrence of abnormal conditions. It may be reset either manually or electrically.
87	**Differential Protective Relay** – A protective relay that functions on a percentage of phase angle or other quantitative difference of two currents or of some other electrical quantities.
88	**Auxiliary Motor or Motor Generator** – A device used for operating auxiliary equipment, such as pumps, blowers, exciters, and rotating magnetic amplifiers.
89	**Line Switch** – A switch used as a disconnecting load-interrupter or isolating switch in an AC or DC power circuit when this device is electrically operated or has electrical accessories, such as an auxiliary switch or magnetic lock.
90	**Regulating Device** – A device that functions to regulate a quantity, or quantities, such as voltage, current, power, speed, frequency, temperature, and load, at a certain value or between certain (generally close) limits for machines, tie lines, or other apparatus.
91	**Voltage Directional Relay** – A relay that operates when the voltage across an open circuit breaker or contactor exceeds a given value in a given direction.
92	**Voltage and Power Directional Relay** – A relay that permits or causes the connection of two circuits when the voltage difference between them exceeds a given value in a predetermined direction and causes these two circuits to be disconnected from each other when the power flowing between them exceeds a given value in the opposite direction.
93	**Field Changing Contactor** – A device that functions to increase or decrease in one step the value of field excitation on a machine.
94	**Tripping or Trip-Free Relay** – A device that functions to trip a circuit breaker, contactor, or equipment, to permit immediate tripping by other devices, or to prevent immediate reclosure of a circuit interrupter in case it should open automatically even though its closing circuit is maintained closed.
95 96 97	Used only for specific applications on individual installations where none of the assigned numbered functions from 1 to 94 is suitable.

26306-14_A06.EPS

Appendix B

Typical Manufacturer Drawings

NCCER CURRICULA — USER UPDATE

NCCER makes every effort to keep its textbooks up-to-date and free of technical errors. We appreciate your help in this process. If you find an error, a typographical mistake, or an inaccuracy in NCCER's curricula, please fill out this form (or a photocopy), or complete the online form at **www.nccer.org/olf**. Be sure to include the exact module ID number, page number, a detailed description, and your recommended correction. Your input will be brought to the attention of the Authoring Team. Thank you for your assistance.

Instructors – If you have an idea for improving this textbook, or have found that additional materials were necessary to teach this module effectively, please let us know so that we may present your suggestions to the Authoring Team.

NCCER Product Development and Revision

13614 Progress Blvd., Alachua, FL 32615

Email: curriculum@nccer.org
Online: www.nccer.org/olf

❏ Trainee Guide ❏ AIG ❏ Exam ❏ PowerPoints Other ______________________________

Craft / Level: Copyright Date:

Module ID Number / Title:

Section Number(s):

Description:

Recommended Correction:

Your Name:

Address:

Email: Phone:

Commercial Electrical Services

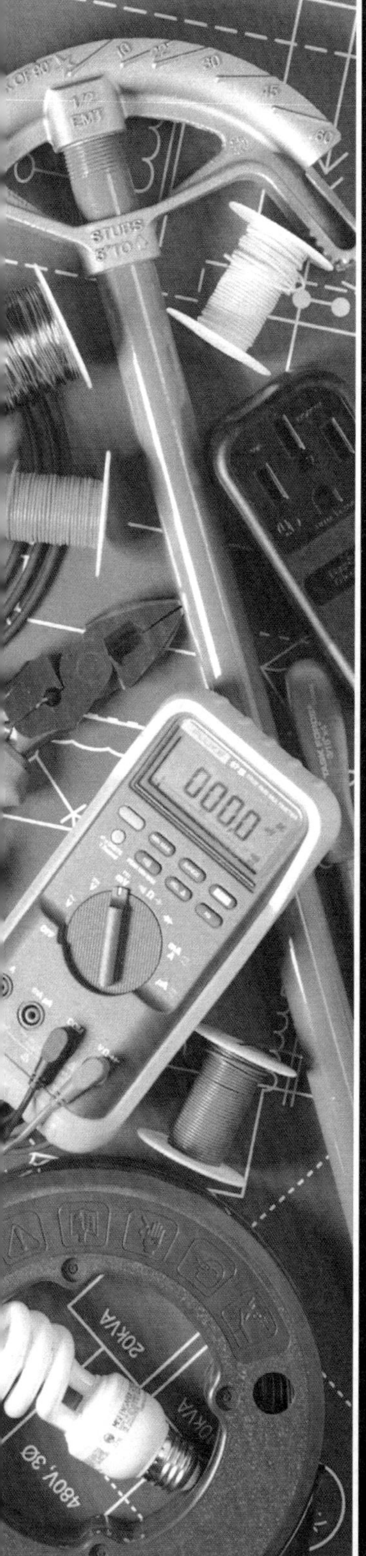

Statue of Liberty goes green

The Statue of Liberty celebrated her 120th birthday in 2006 by going 100 percent green. The Statue is "green powered" by windmill generators in West Virginia and Pennsylvania.

26308-14

Trainees with successful module completions may be eligible for credentialing through NCCER's National Registry. To learn more, go to **www.nccer.org** or contact us at **1.888.622.3720.** Our website has information on the latest product releases and training, as well as online versions of our *Cornerstone* magazine and Pearson's product catalog.

Your feedback is welcome. You may email your comments to **curriculum@nccer.org,** send general comments and inquiries to **info@nccer.org,** or fill in the User Update form at the back of this module.

This information is general in nature and intended for training purposes only. Actual performance of activities described in this manual requires compliance with all applicable operating, service, maintenance, and safety procedures under the direction of qualified personnel. References in this manual to patented or proprietary devices do not constitute a recommendation of their use.

26308-14

Commercial Electrical Services

Objectives

When you have completed this module, you will be able to do the following:

1. Describe various types of electric services for commercial and industrial installations.
2. Read electrical diagrams describing service installations.
3. Select service-entrance equipment for various applications.
4. Explain the role of the *National Electrical Code®* in service installations.
5. Install main disconnect switches, panelboards, and overcurrent protection devices.
6. Identify the *National Electrical Code®* requirements and purposes of service grounding.
7. Describe single-phase service connections.
8. Describe both wye- and delta-connected three-phase services.

Performance Tasks

This is a knowledge-based module. There are no Performance Tasks.

Trade Terms

Cold sequence metering
Delta-connected
Service
Service conductors
Service drop
Service entrance
Service equipment
Service lateral

Required Trainee Materials

1. Pencil and paper
2. Appropriate personal protective equipment
3. Copy of the latest edition of the *National Electrical Code®*

Note:
 All *National Electrical Code®* and *NEC®* references in this module refer to the 2014 edition of the *National Electrical Code®*.

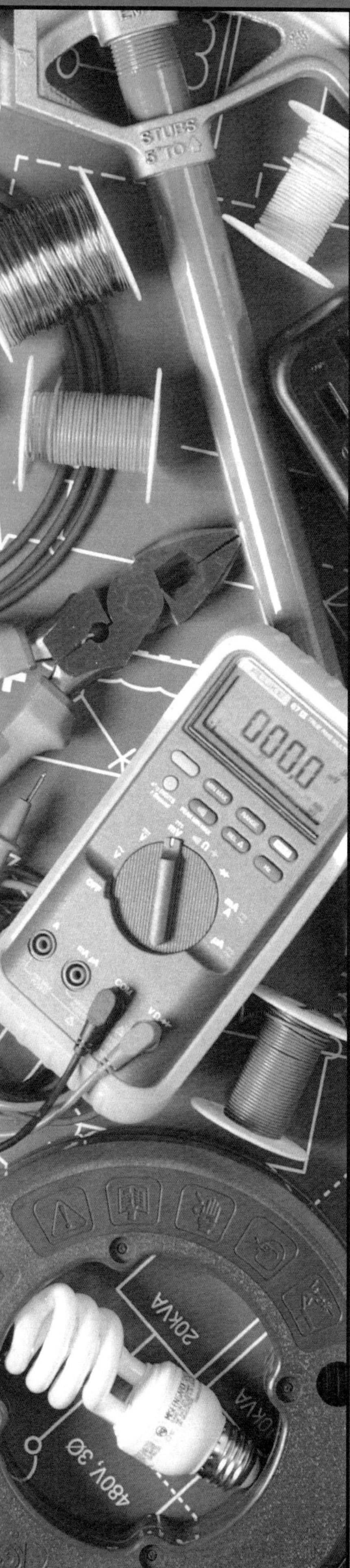

Contents

Topics to be presented in this module include:

Figures and Tables

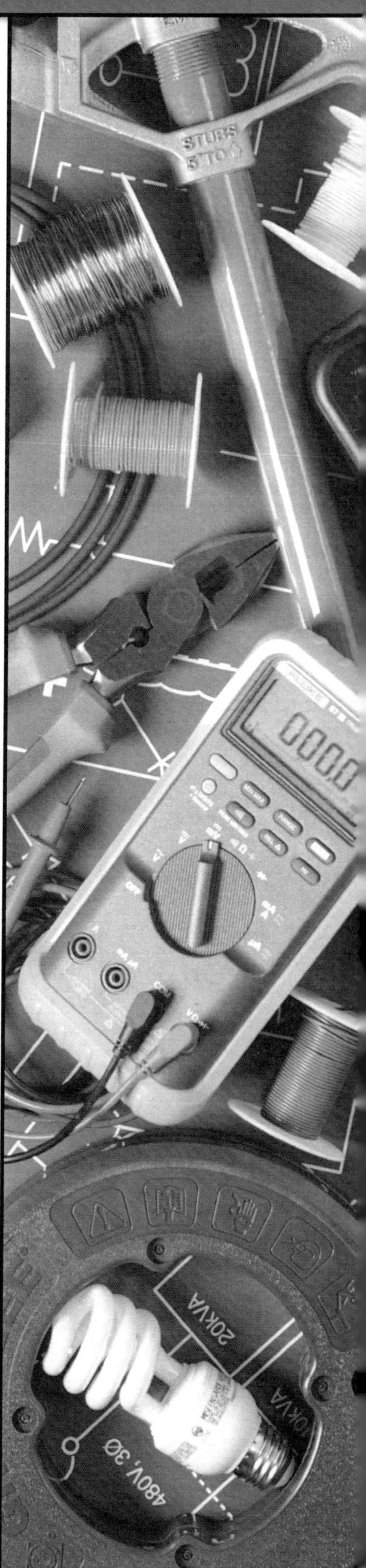

1.0.0 Introduction

The electrical contractor is typically responsible for the installation of all electrical systems including the electric service. Service equipment consists of conduit and service conductors, the panelboard, and the overcurrent protective devices. *NEC Article 230* lists the requirements for service conductors and raceways, along with numerous additional requirements for service installations.

2.0.0 Drawings and Specifications

Electric services are usually designed by qualified electrical engineers who produce drawings and specifications showing the design and installation requirements for the service. The drawings include the floor plan, one-line diagram, site plan, panelboard schedules, and specifications. A service one-line or single-line drawing shows service characteristics including the size and voltage rating, fault current rating, service-entrance conduit and conductor sizes, grounding requirements, transformers, and panelboards. The one-line drawing also shows whether the service is overhead or underground. If the power connects to the electric service overhead, the incoming service supply is referred to as a service drop. If the service is supplied underground, the supply is defined as a service lateral. The one-line for a small installation typically shows the conduit and conductor sizes for the service. Larger service one-line diagrams often include a schedule or table indicating the conduit and conductor sizes for service entrance, distribution, and panelboard feeders.

NOTE

Electricians install the electric service but connections to the utility transformer are typically made by the utility company.

A building layout shows the location of the electric service and the location of distribution and branch circuit panelboards within the structure. It is important to review all of the project drawings and specifications to obtain all of the information needed to install the electric service. For example, the building elevation drawing will show the amount of exterior wall space available at the location where the service equipment might be mounted. It is also important to know the type of construction so that the proper anchoring systems can be ordered for the installation.

3.0.0 General Installation Considerations

A qualified electrician should have the ability to work with the supervisor, the project manager, the utility company, and the electrical engineer to install the service components in a workmanlike, professional, and efficient manner. Safety considerations come first in every installation; this means that the required personal protective equipment must be used to allow the installation to proceed in a safe manner. All equipment must be installed level and plumb and in a manner that meets all *NEC®* requirements and all of the requirements presented in the project electrical drawings and specifications. All equipment and materials must be new and installed per the manufacturer's guidelines. The electrician may be required to install the conduit, service-entrance conductors, wireways, bussed gutter, service disconnects, current transformer (CT) can, meter can, and other fittings as needed to comply with *NEC®* requirements, local building department requirements and codes, project specifications, and even the local fire marshal's requirements.

The location of the bus and ground bars and the service-side entrance compartment are important considerations when installing the service-entrance conductors. The service grounding conductors are usually routed to and bonded in the first service disconnecting means. When service-entrance conductors terminate in a wireway or bussed gutter to serve multiple service disconnecting means, the service grounding conductors may be terminated to and bonded to the grounded service conductor in the wireway or bussed gutter enclosure. In many instances, the local Authority Having Jurisdiction (AHJ) will make the determination regarding specific grounding decisions to ensure that these connections meet *NEC®* requirements. Another important consideration is whether housekeeping pads are required to mount or raise the switchgear or transformers above the finished floor.

In most cases, electricians are not required to design electrical systems except for design-build projects that require a stamped set of drawings and the oversight of an electrical engineer. Usually the electrician is only required to interpret the engineer's drawings and apply them to the installation of the project. Other important factors relating to the installation of service equipment are the inspection and acceptance of service equipment from the delivery service and the megging of the conductors and equipment before energizing the equipment.

On Site

Receiving Equipment

Freight claims for damage caused during shipping must be made by written notation on the freight bill when the equipment is received at the job site. If freight damage is not noted on the freight bill, a claim for damages may not be possible at a later time. All boxes should be examined for hidden damage prior to uncrating.

The following considerations apply to the selection and installation of electric services:

- *Codes and standards* – All services must be designed and installed in accordance with the provisions of the *NEC*® and all local codes. Suitability of service equipment for the intended use is evidenced by listing or labeling.
- *Mechanical protection* – Mechanical strength and durability, including the adequacy of the protection provided, must be considered.
- *Wiring space* – Wire bending and connection space in distribution equipment is provided according to UL standards. When unusual conditions are encountered requiring additional wiring space, larger wireways and/or termination cabinets must be considered.
- *Classification* – Classification according to type, size, voltage rating, current capacity, interrupting rating, and specific use must be considered when selecting service equipment. Loads may be continuous or noncontinuous, and load calculations per *NEC*® requirements must be completed in order to determine the proper sizing of service equipment. All distribution equipment carries labels showing the maximum voltage and current ratings for the equipment. A typical example is shown in *Figure 1*. The supply voltage and current ratings must not be exceeded. In addition, always observe the minimum and maximum values listed for conductor terminations.
- *Heating effects* – All installations must consider heating effects both under normal operating conditions and under any extreme conditions of use that might reasonably be expected. Ambient heat conditions must be considered when specifying conductor insulation for the specific application.
- *Arcing effects* – The normal arcing effects of overcurrent protective devices must be considered when the application is in or near combustible materials or vapors (classified/hazardous locations). Enclosures and wiring methods must be selected based on *NEC*® requirements.
- *Personal protection* – Every service installation should begin with a review of safety policies and a site visit to determine any special safety requirements relating to the specific site and type of construction. Always wear all personal protective equipment required for the installation. Safe work practices are extremely important when installing service equipment that may be heavy and awkward to lift and place. Be aware of potential pinch points as well as all other work site conditions that may present specific safety hazards. Safety should always be a top priority when installing electric services.

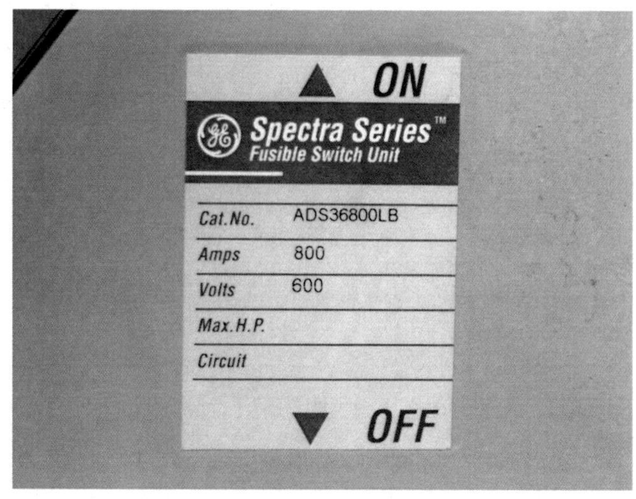

Figure 1 Typical maximum voltage and current rating label.

4.0.0 Service Components

All service components must be carefully selected and coordinated to ensure proper system operation. Common service components include the service disconnect, meter, transformers, wireways, gutters, weatherhead and service mast, and panelboards.

4.1.0 Service Disconnecting Means

Whether a service is single-phase or three-phase, overhead or underground, *NEC Section 230.70* requires that a means be provided to disconnect all conductors in a building from the service-entrance conductors. The service disconnecting means must be in a readily accessible location, marked as a service disconnect, and listed as suitable for use as a service disconnecting means per *NEC Section*

On Site

Dual Services

Some large installations have two or more services. Dual services are provided with separate disconnects, as shown here.

26308-14_SA01.EPS

230.66. The service disconnect can be a fusible switch or a circuit breaker and is typically located at the point where the service-entrance conductors come into the building or structure. In some cases, the utility company requires **cold sequence metering**, in which a disconnect is installed ahead of the electric meter. Cold sequence metering provides the utility company the opportunity to work on the metering equipment with the power disconnected.

4.2.0 Metering

The metering assembly, single meter enclosure, multiple meter enclosures, or CT metering is installed at the point of service entrance. A self-contained meter installation refers to a single meter enclosure with a single watt-hour or demand meter. Typically, the electrician is responsible for the meter enclosure installation and the utility company will provide and install the electric meter. A CT meter installation refers to the installation of a CT enclosure or cabinet. The CT cabinet is a listed piece of manufactured equipment designed to accept the installation of current transformers used to measure electric usage. A CT meter enclosure is installed alongside or within a short distance of the CT cabinet. The electrician is usually responsible for the installation of the CT cabinet and the CT meter base. The utility company will then install the current transformers, the CT meter, and the wiring between the CT meter enclosure and the CT cabinet.

Most watt-hour meters use five dials (see *Figure 2*). The dial farthest to the right on the meter counts the kilowatt-hours singly. The second dial from the right counts by tens, the third dial by hundreds, the fourth dial by thousands, and the left-hand dial by ten thousands. The dials may seem a little strange at first, but they are actually very simple to read. The number that the dial has passed is the reading. For example, look at the dial on the far left. Note that the pointer is about halfway between the number 2 and the number 3. Since it has passed the number 2, but has not yet reached 3, the dial reading is 2. The same is true of the second dial from the left; that is, the pointer is between 2 and 3. Consequently, the reading of this dial is also 2. Following this procedure, the complete reading for the meter in *Figure 2* is 22,179 kilowatt-hours.

Although knowing how to read an electric meter is useful, most electricians will be involved only with installing the meter base and making the connections therein. Once these connections are made and inspected, the local power company will install and seal the meter.

4.3.0 Current Transformers

Meters used to record electric usage normally respond to a current level that varies from 0A to 5A. To respond to the actual current, each meter is provided with current transformers. If the peak demand is 100A, a 100:5 current transformer is used. If the peak demand is expected to be 200A, a 200:5 current transformer is used.

Services rated 400A and above usually utilize a group of current transformers, one for each ungrounded conductor or set of conductors. There are two basic types of current transformers: the busbar type and the doughnut type. The doughnut-type CT encircles the ungrounded conductors in the system to measure the current flow, much the same as a clamp-on ammeter. See *Figure 3*. The busbar type CT has each transformer connected in series with a busbar and does not encircle the conductor.

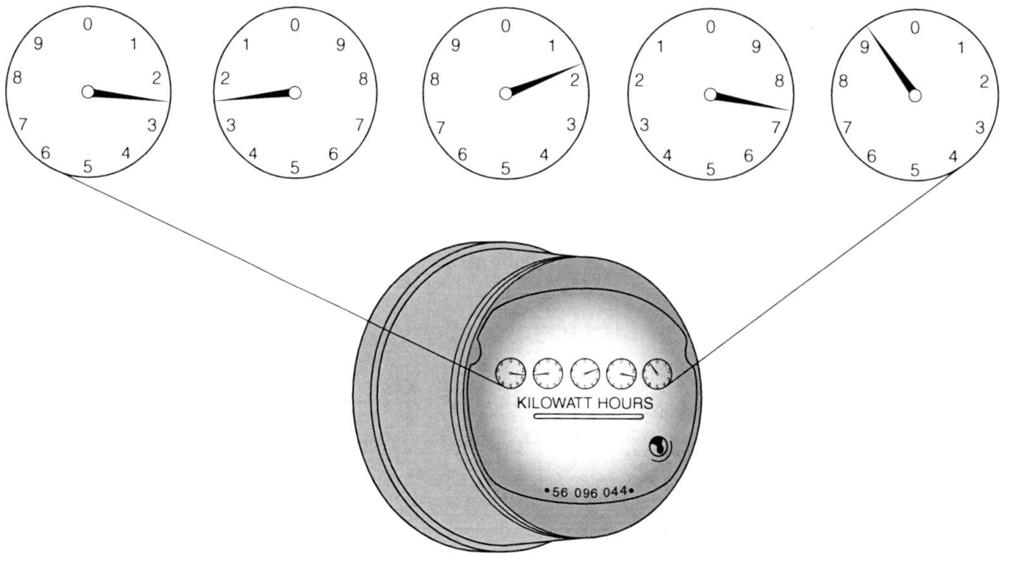

26308-14_F02.EPS

Figure 2 Typical watt-hour meter.

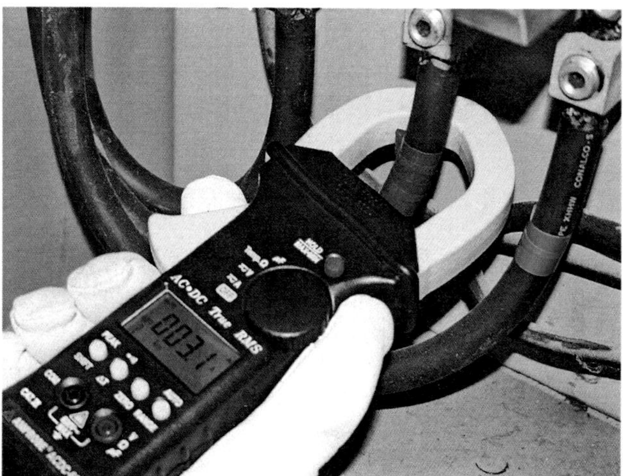

26308-14_F03.EPS

Figure 3 Clamp-on ammeters operate on the same principle as doughnut-type current transformers.

Current transformers are normally enclosed in a CT cabinet. *Figure 4* shows a typical CT cabinet with current transformers and their related wiring. In some cases, the current transformers may be mounted exposed on overhead conductors, but this arrangement is more of an exception than the rule.

Utility companies have specifications for the location and wiring of CTs and CT cabinets, depending upon the location. The following are requirements for one utility company. Always check requirements for the local utility.

- The meter base and meter may be located on either the side or top of the current transformer cabinet, or they may be located at a distance, if approved by the utility company and as long as the conduit containing the instrument wiring is run exposed.

Think About It

Reading a Watt-Hour Meter

What is the reading on this meter?

26308-14_SA02.EPS

On Site

Meter Types

Watt-hour meters are available in both analog and digital forms, as shown here.

ANALOG

26308-14_SA03A.EPS

DIGITAL

26308-14_SA03B.EPS

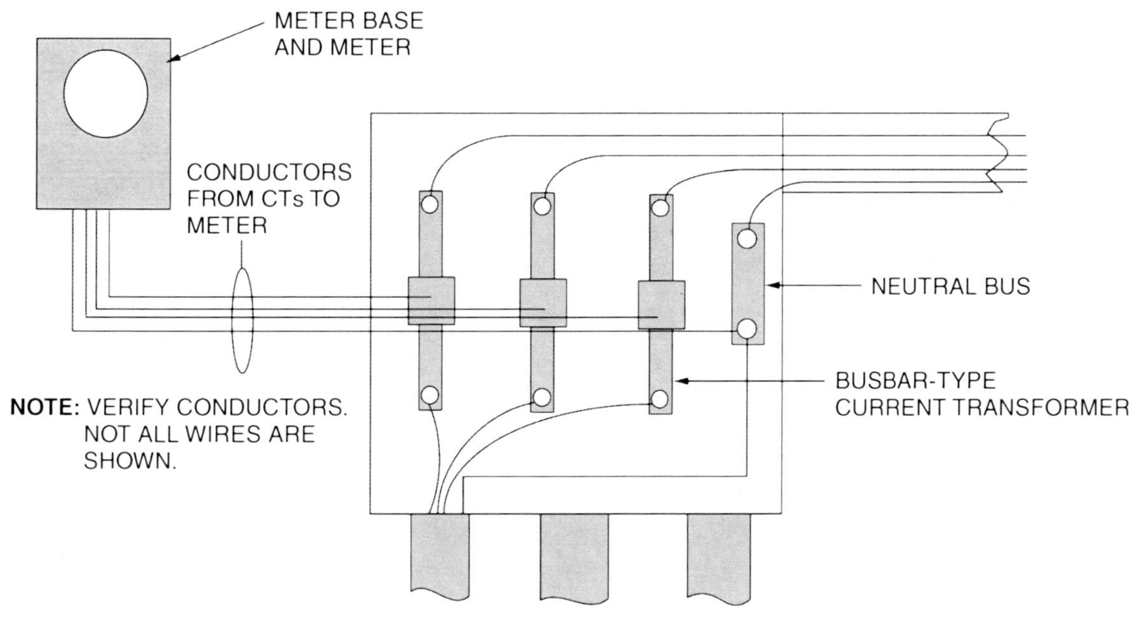

Figure 4 Typical CT cabinet arrangement.

- In no case shall more than one set of conductors terminate in the instrument transformer cabinet. Subfeeders and branch circuits are to terminate at the customer's distribution panel. The instrument transformer cabinet shall not be used as a junction box.
- When service-entrance conductors enter or leave the back of the cabinet, the size of the CT cabinet must be increased to provide additional working space.
- For services at higher voltages, additional space must be provided in the transformer cabinet for mounting potential transformers. Consult the local utility company for dimensions.
- If recording demand instruments are required, increase the height of the meter mounting by 12" to accommodate the recording instrument.

4.4.0 Metal Wireways

Metal wireways are defined in *NEC Section 376.2* as sheet metal troughs with hinged or removable covers for housing and protecting electrical wires. As part of a service installation, wireways are used to provide space for splicing service-entrance conductors to conductors supplying individual metering equipment or service disconnects. Follow *NEC Section 376.22* to determine the appropriate size wireway to use in a particular service installation. Wireways installed outdoors must be listed for outdoor use.

4.5.0 Busways

NEC Section 368.2 defines a busway as a grounded metal enclosure containing factory-mounted bare or insulated conductors, which are usually copper or aluminum bars, rods, or tubes (*Figure 5*). Busways are used to provide a means of tapping the service-entrance conductors or distribution feeders to supply the service disconnecting means, self-contained metering equipment, CT metering equipment, or for other purposes such as disconnects for equipment feeders in an industrial plant or manufacturing facility. Busways are manufactured to meet the project specifications for their intended use. These specifications include the voltage, ampacity, and fault current ratings, along with the NEMA enclosure classification (e.g., NEMA 3R for outdoor use) and the gutter length. Busways can be manufactured with copper bus or plated aluminum bus. It may include factory-installed mechanical lugs of specific sizes to accommodate line and load feeders. Busways may be bottom fed or top fed.

Busways are one of the most common types of wiring methods for use with multi-switch service installations. One advantage of a busway is the ease of installation and modification. Adding disconnect switches or changing switches is relatively easy.

4.5.1 Bus Bracing

One characteristic of fault currents is an induced torque in conductors carrying the fault. Because of this torque, the busbars must be mounted in the enclosure in such a manner as to allow them to withstand the fault current that may be imposed. This is accomplished by the use of bracing. *Figure 6* shows typical busbar bracing. Larger available fault current values require more substantial bracing and braces that are placed closer together. For example, busways may be manufactured with an AIC rating of 20,000 AIC, 30,000 AIC, or 200,000 AIC. Manufacturers typically have standard ratings to accommodate project requirements. The listing for busways must include the fault current rating.

4.6.0 Weatherhead and Service Mast

Overhead services include a weatherhead and a service mast. Weatherheads may be cast aluminum,

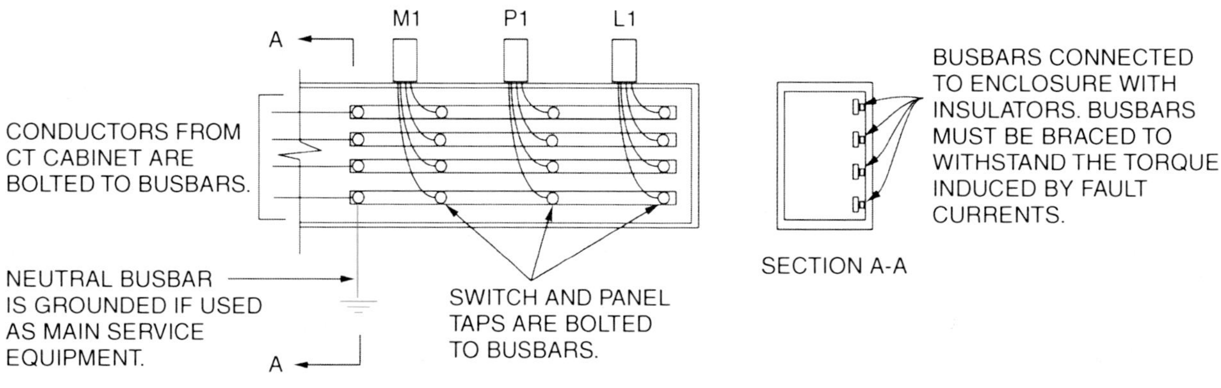
M1
P1
L1
A
CONDUCTORS FROM CT CABINET ARE BOLTED TO BUSBARS.
NEUTRAL BUSBAR IS GROUNDED IF USED AS MAIN SERVICE EQUIPMENT.
A
SWITCH AND PANEL TAPS ARE BOLTED TO BUSBARS.
BUSBARS CONNECTED TO ENCLOSURE WITH INSULATORS. BUSBARS MUST BE BRACED TO WITHSTAND THE TORQUE INDUCED BY FAULT CURRENTS.
SECTION A-A
26308-14_F05.EPS

Figure 5 Three-phase busway.

26308-14_F06.EPS

Figure 6 Typical busbar bracing.

On Site

Panelboards

After the panelboard is assembled, the appropriate number and type of circuit breakers must be ordered separately and installed in the panel.

26308-14_SA04.EPS

galvanized steel, or PVC. Service masts are typically constructed of galvanized steel and supported as required by the *NEC®* and the utility company. The service mast terminates in the hub of the meter housing, CT cabinet, or other service equipment and must use watertight fittings when the components are installed outdoors. The service-entrance riser conductors terminate in the meter housing or the service disconnecting means if the service disconnect is required before the meter (cold sequence metering) or after the meter (hot sequence metering).

4.7.0 Panelboards

The final component in a commercial electric service is the panelboard. Panelboards are designed to distribute electric energy through branch circuit breakers. In a small commercial service, a panelboard may include the service disconnecting means together with all of the branch circuit breakers needed for the building. Panelboards may also be designated as distribution panelboards. Distribution panels are used to provide overcurrent protection for individual panel feeders when the service is large enough to require numerous branch circuit panelboards. The selection of the components used in a panelboard is based on the following criteria:

- Feeder voltage and amperage
- Phase (single or three-phase) and number of conductors
- Type of busbar material (copper or aluminum)
- Number of required spaces or blanks
- Whether the panelboard is configured as a main breaker type of panel or main-lugs only (MLO) type of panel

NOTE

MLO panels do not have a MAIN circuit breaker.

CAUTION

Always install breakers according to the manufacturer's installation instructions. When installing bolt-in breakers, make sure to tighten them to the correct torque. Failure to do so could result in improper operation of the service equipment.

5.0.0 *NEC*® Requirements

NEC Section 230.2 states that a building shall be supplied by only one service except when special conditions listed under *NEC Section 230.2(A) through (D)* are present. Per *NEC Section 230.2(A)*, an additional service is permitted to supply a fire pump, emergency systems, legally required or optional standby systems, parallel power production systems, or systems connected to multiple supply sources. For the purpose of enhanced reliability, additional services are permitted for sufficiently large buildings or certain multiple occupancy buildings per *NEC Section 230.2(B)*, capacity requirements as outlined in *NEC Section 230.2(C)*, and for different characteristics as identified in *NEC Section 230.2(D)*. *NEC Section 230.66* requires service equipment to be marked as suitable for its intended use. All service equipment shall be listed. Distribution panelboards and switchgear assemblies are generally intended to carry and control electric current, but are not intended to dissipate or use energy.

In accordance with *NEC Section 230.82(3)*, a service disconnect switch connected to the supply side of the meter (cold sequence) must be rated at no more than 1,000V. In addition, it must have a short-circuit rating equal to or greater than the available short-circuit current, provided the housings and service enclosures are grounded and bonded in accordance with *NEC Article 250, Parts V and VII*. The switch must be capable of interrupting the load served and be field labeled.

5.1.0 Services Passing Through Buildings

Per *NEC Section 230.3*, service conductors supplying one building cannot pass through the interior of another building or structure. *NEC Section 230.6* states that conductors are considered to be outside of a building if any of the following conditions are met:

- Where installed beneath the building under at least 2" of concrete
- Where buried under at least 18" of earth in conduit
- Located inside the building if encased in at least 2" of concrete or brick
- Installed in a vault that meets the requirements of *NEC Article 450, Part III*
- Where installed within rigid metal conduit (Type RMC) or intermediate metal conduit (Type IMC) used to accommodate the clearance requirements in *NEC Section 230.24* and routed directly through an eave but not a wall of a building.

5.2.0 Grounding and Bonding

NEC Article 250 covers the requirements for grounding and bonding electric services. In general, the *NEC*® requires that a premises AC service be grounded with a grounding electrode conductor connected to a grounding electrode. It follows that all of the requirements for grounding and bonding identified in *NEC Figure 250.1 and Table 250.3* must be considered and applied to every electric service.

The grounding electrode conductor must be grounded to the grounded service conductor (neutral) at any accessible point from the load end of the service drop or service lateral up to and including the terminal bus to which the grounded service conductor is connected at the service disconnecting means. A grounding connection must not be made to any grounded circuit conductor on the load side of the service disconnecting means.

NEC Section 250.50 requires all grounding electrodes to be bonded together to create the grounding electrode system. *NEC Section 250.52* lists the grounding electrodes as metal underground water pipe in direct contact with the earth for 10' or more, the metal frame of the building or structure, concrete-encased electrode, ground ring, rod and pipe electrodes, other listed electrodes, plate electrodes, and other metal grounding systems or structures. These requirements apply to all electric services, regardless of the voltage rating of the service or the size (ampacity rating) of the service. *NEC Section 250.53* guides the installation of the grounding electrode system. *Table 1* gives the required sizes of the grounding electrode conductor for electric services.

5.3.0 High-Leg Marking

The conductor or busbar with a higher voltage to ground in a **delta-connected** four-wire system, also known as the high leg, is required to be durably and permanently marked with an outer finish that is orange in color or by other effective means per *NEC Section 110.15*. If the grounded conductor is also present, this marking must appear at each point where a connection is made. In panelboards, the phase having the higher voltage to ground is the B phase per *NEC Section 408.3(E)*.

5.4.0 Clearances

NEC Section 230.24 lists the minimum service drop clearances for various applications. Service drop conductors require a vertical clearance of no less than 8' above roof surfaces per *NEC Section*

Table 1 Grounding Electrode Conductors for AC Systems (Data from *NEC Table 250.66*)

Size of Largest Service-Entrance Conductor or Equivalent for Parallel Conductors		Size of Grounding Electrode Conductor	
Copper	**Aluminum or Copper-Clad Aluminum**	**Copper**	**Aluminum or Copper-Clad Aluminum**
2 or smaller	1/0 or smaller	8	6
1 or 1/0	2/0 or 3/0	6	4
2/0 or 3/0	4/0 or 250 kcmil	4	2
Over 3/0 through 350 kcmil	Over 250 kcmil through 500 kcmil	2	1/0
Over 350 kcmil through 600 kcmil	Over 500 kcmil through 900 kcmil	1/0	3/0
Over 600 kcmil through 1,100 kcmil	Over 900 kcmil through 1,750 kcmil	2/0	4/0
Over 1,100 kcmil	Over 1,750 kcmil	3/0	250 kcmil

230.24(A) and no less than 10' at the electrical service entrance to buildings, at the lowest point of the drip loop, and over sidewalks accessible to pedestrians only where it does not exceed 150V to ground per *NEC Section 230.24(B)(1)*. Note that this is the minimum for the lowest point of the drip loop and the weatherhead or tie point for the service drop should be a minimum of 13'-6" above grade. This accounts for the height of the weatherhead itself, the insulator that attaches to the mast below the weatherhead, the drip loop, and the conductor sag (lowest point) in a service drop, which varies by conductor size and length of drop. The insulator, whether attached to the mast or to the building, is the point of attachment for the service drop. If the service mast is to support the service drop, it must be well secured per *NEC Section 230.28*. Meter bases should be installed with anchors to hold the weight of the meter as well as the raceway system resting on the meter base.

Service conductor clearances on buildings, porches, and platforms are covered in *NEC Section 230.9*. They may be installed as open conductor or MC cable without an overall outer jacket, and must be located at least 3' from windows, doors, porches, balconies, ladders, stairs, fire escapes, and similar locations. These clearances do not apply to windows that are not designed to be opened, or to locations where the conductor is run above the top level of the window [*NEC Section 230.9(A) Exception*].

6.0.0 Typical Installations

The most common service voltage for small commercial and other small loads is a 120/240V, single-phase, three-wire service. Common services for larger commercial installations are 120/240V, three-phase, four-wire; 120/208V, three-phase, four-wire; and 277/480V, three-phase, four-wire installations. To understand the function of each component of an electrical service, we will examine five specific installations of commercial electric services. These include a single-phase service, a small service utilizing a wireway to connect multiple meters and service disconnects, a bussed gutter installation, a service entrance using switchgear, and a multi-family service.

6.1.0 208Y/120V Overhead Service

Figure 7 shows an overhead 208Y/120V service. The service is rated at 400A and the grounding requirements are established based on a 400A service. The two service-entrance conductors consist of No. 3/0 THWN copper in 2" conduit. Because these are parallel service-entrance conductors, the GEC is sized at No. 2 copper (or 1/0 aluminum) using *NEC Table 250.66*. Note that there are drip loops formed at the weatherheads as required by *NEC Section 230.54(F)*. The parallel service-entrance conductors terminate in a wire-

26308-14_F07.EPS

Figure 7 Overhead service.

way. The service disconnects are connected to the wireway with rigid galvanized steel nipples and the conductors supplying each meter are terminated in the wireway. The terminations in the wireway may be mechanical (split-bolt) type connections or they may be mechanical connections made using a multi-tap insulated connector. In this example, the GEC is bonded to the grounded service conductor (neutral) in the wireway. There are two 200A, 240V three-phase meters and service disconnects, and one 100A, 240V single-phase meter and disconnect. Because the building has a 208Y/120V three-phase service, the voltage to the single-phase meters is also 208V. Note the use of weatherheads, drip loops, conduit supports, and the arrangement of the service equipment. This service illustrates hot sequence metering.

Because this equipment is installed on the exterior of the building, it is rated for outdoor use. In this installation, the point of attachment is bolted through the masonry wall to make it secure enough to support the service drop (also taking into account the wind load and ice weight) and includes a porcelain insulator. Porcelain insulator attachments are preferable and may be required by the local utility. Always check with the local utility before proceeding with any installation. Porcelain insulator attachments provide a separation between the service drop conductors (which may become worn and short over time) and other metal components.

Figure 8 is the one-line diagram for the service just described. Note that the one-line diagram includes sizes for service-entrance conduit and

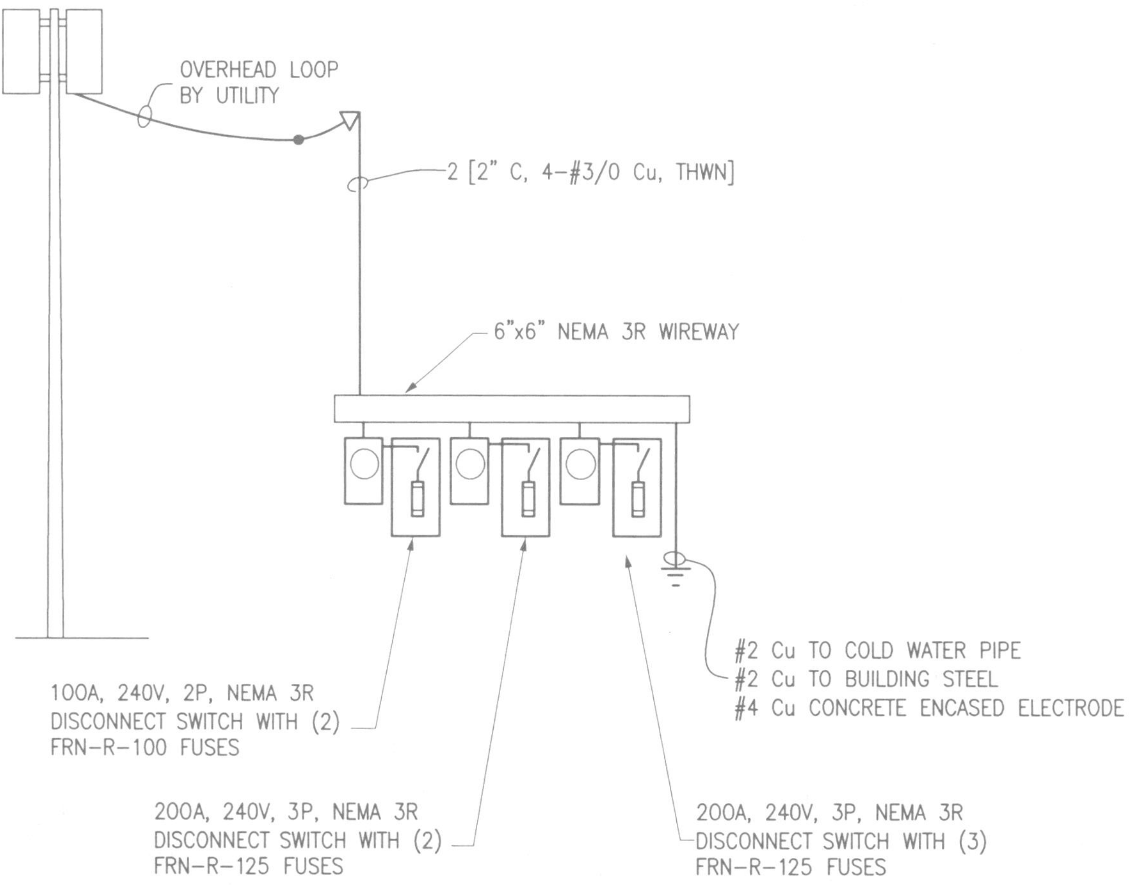

Figure 8 One-line diagram for overhead service.

conductors, sizes and fuse requirements for the service disconnects, the size and length of the wireway, and sizes for the grounding electrode conductors.

6.2.0 208Y/120V Three-Phase Underground Service – Wireway

Figure 9 shows an underground 208Y/120V three-phase service. The service is rated at 800A, and the grounding requirements are established based on an 800A service. The service-entrance conductors consist of three cables, with each cable being four-conductor, 400 kcmil THWN aluminum. Each cable is in an underground 3" conduit (the fourth conduit is a spare). Because these are parallel service-entrance conductors, the GEC is sized at 2/0 copper (or 4/0 aluminum) using *NEC Table 250.66*. The parallel service-entrance conductors terminate in a main service disconnect. The tenant service disconnects are connected to the wireway with EMT conduit with Myers-type hubs used where the conduit terminates into the wireway, and the conductors supplying each tenant disconnect are terminated in the wireway. The terminations in the wireway are mechanical connections made using a multi-tap insulated connector. Per *NEC Section 310.10(H)(2)(5)*, parallel conductors must be terminated in the same manner. In this example, the GEC is bonded to the grounded service conductor (neutral) in the wireway. In this installation, there is one 100A fusible disconnect ahead of (cold sequence) the meter serving panel HP (the house panel) which in turn supplies branch circuit power to the lighting controller for exterior building lighting and parking lot lighting. There is one 200A fusible tenant disconnect ahead of the meter serving a tenant space and one 400A CT cabinet ahead of a 400A fusible disconnect serving a larger tenant space. The vertical line originating at the top of the 200A tenant meter indicates the feeder to the tenant panel located in the tenant space. Note that the feeder to the 400A tenant panel is not shown because it is routed inside the building and terminates into the back of the 400A tenant disconnect.

26308-14_F09.EPS

Figure 9 Underground wireway service.

Note that the *NEC®* would not require a main service disconnect for this installation because there are fewer than six switches to disconnect power to the building and the ampacity of the feeders serving panel HP and the tenant services does not exceed the ampacity of the service-entrance conductors. However, the service for this retail building was designed before any tenants were identified to occupy the building, and provided flexibility to allow a tenant mix that could have required more than six disconnects for tenant services. This design also provides flexibility for future changes in the tenant mix, making it unnecessary to rework the entire service to accommodate changes. Because this equipment is installed on the exterior of the building, all of the equipment is rated for outdoor use.

Figure 10 shows the one-line diagram for the service just described. Note that the one-line diagram includes sizes for service-entrance conduit and conductors, sizes and fuse requirements for the service disconnects, the size and length of the wireway, the sizes of panel feeder conduit and conductors, and sizes for the grounding electrode conductors. The branch circuit panelboard for the lighting contactors is also shown as part of the one-line diagram.

6.3.0 208Y/120V Three-Phase Service – Bussed Gutter with Multiple Service Disconnects

Figure 11 shows an underground 208Y/120V three-phase service. The service is rated at 800A and the grounding requirements are established based on an 800A service. The service-entrance conductors consist of two cables, with each cable being a three-conductor, 500 kcmil THWN copper in 3" conduit. Because these are parallel service-entrance conductors, the GEC is sized at 2/0 copper (or 4/0 aluminum) using *NEC Table 250.66*. The parallel service-entrance conductors terminate in a bussed gutter. The service disconnects are connected to the bussed gutter with RGS nipples and the conductors supplying each meter are terminated in the bussed gutter using mechanical lugs. It is important to follow the manufacturer's requirements for torque when terminating conductors using mechanical lugs.

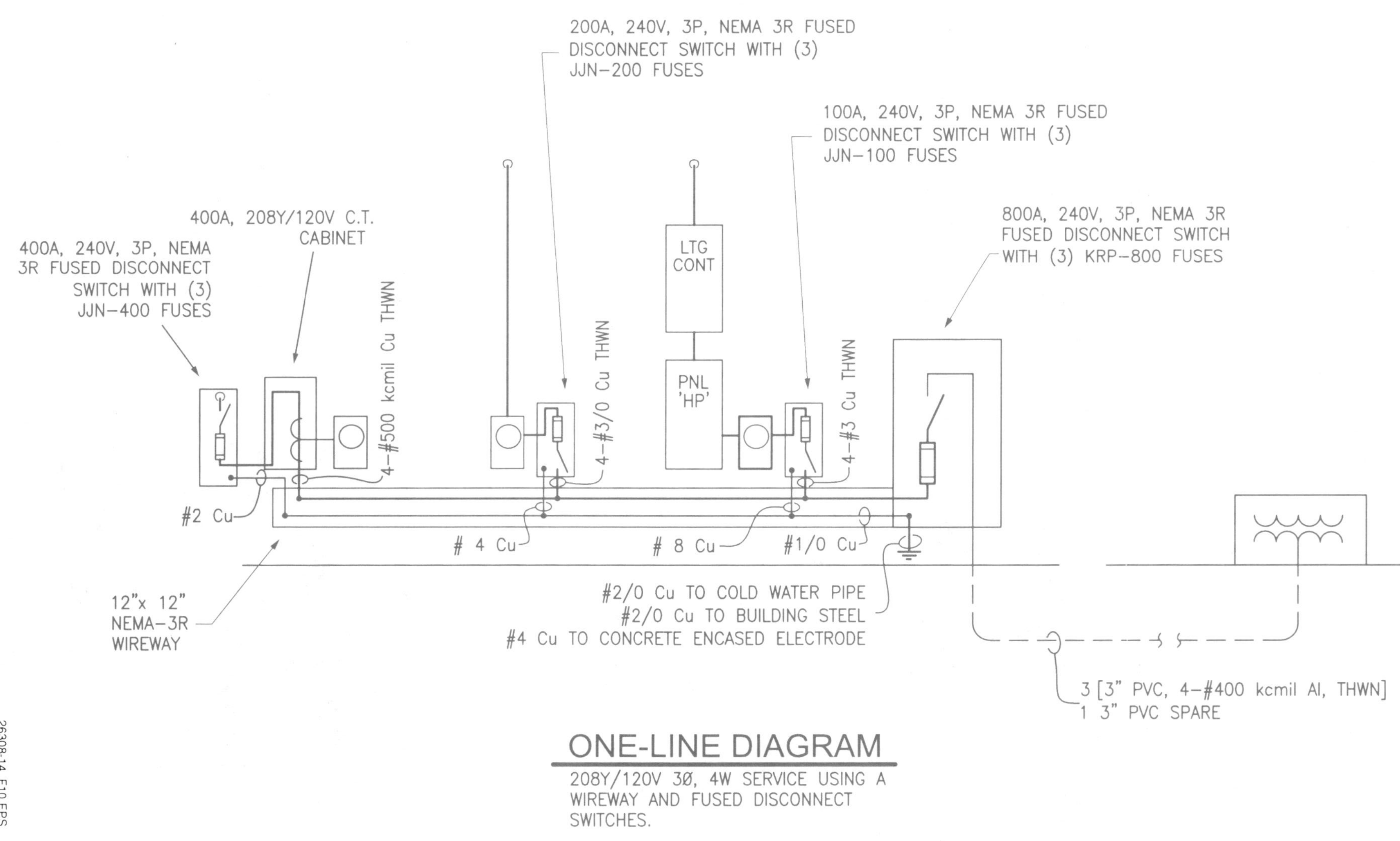

Figure 10 One-line diagram for an underground wireway service.

Because this equipment is installed on the exterior of the building, all of the equipment is rated for outdoor use.

Figure 12 is the one-line diagram for the service just described. Note that the one-line diagram includes sizes for service-entrance conduit and conductors, sizes and fuse requirements for the service disconnects, the size and length of the wireway, the sizes of panel feeder conduit and conductors and sizes for the grounding electrode conductors. The branch circuit panelboards are also shown as part of the one-line diagram.

26308-14_F11A.EPS

26308-14_F11B.EPS

Figure 11 Underground bussed gutter service.

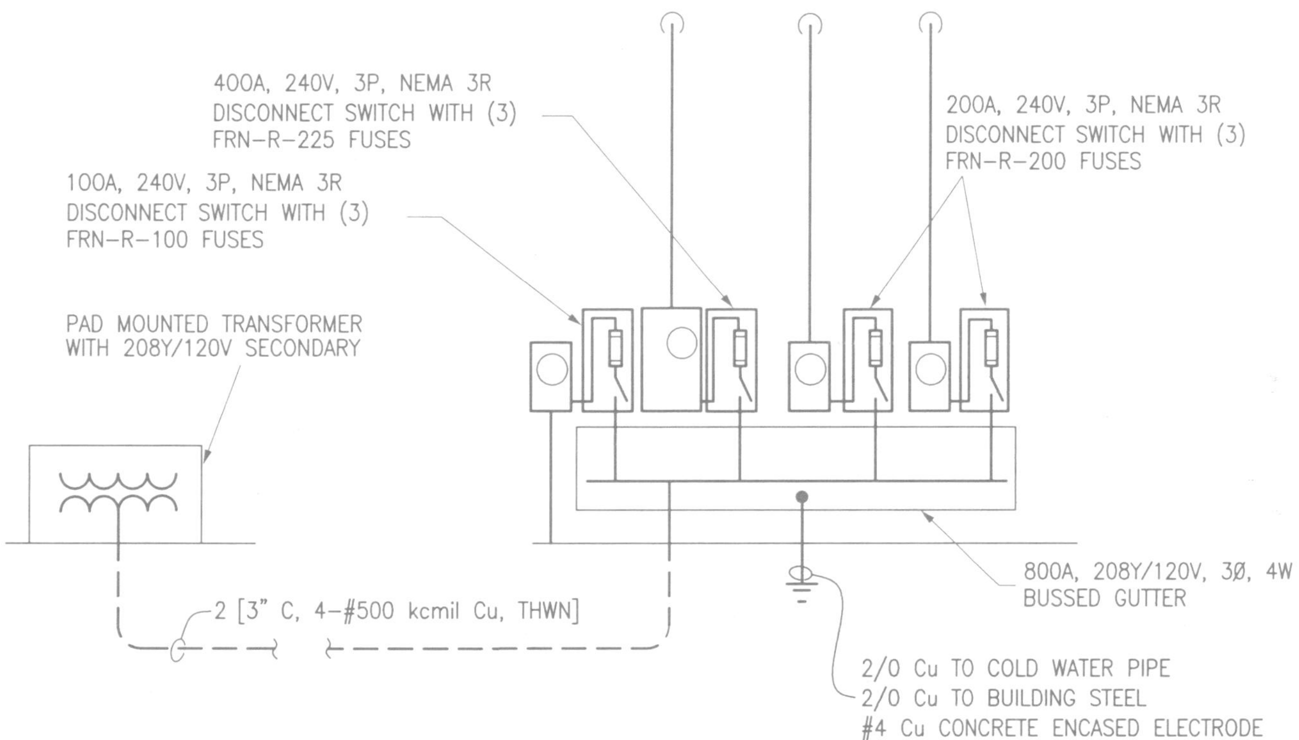

ONE-LINE DIAGRAM

208Y/120V 3Ø, 4W SERVICE USING A
BUSSED GUTTER AND FUSED
DISCONNECT SWITCHES

26308-14_F12.EPS

Figure 12 One-line diagram for an underground bussed gutter service.

6.4.0 480Y/277V Three-Phase Service – Switchgear

Figure 13 shows a switchgear 480Y/277V three-phase service which is a typical industrial plant installation. The service is rated at 2,000A and the grounding requirements are established based upon a 2,000A service. The fault current rating for this equipment is 50,000 AIC. The service-entrance conductors consist of seven cables, with each cable being a four-conductor, 500 kcmil THWN copper in 3½" conduit. Because these are parallel service-entrance conductors, the GEC is sized at 3/0 copper (or 250 kcmil aluminum) using *NEC Table 250.66*. The switchgear consists of a network of busbars installed horizontally. The busbars extend through each metal switchgear cabinet to supply power to individual disconnects. If a service is of sufficient size to require more than six disconnects, a main disconnecting means must be included. The service shown in this example has four service disconnects and spaces for two additional future service disconnects. A main disconnecting means is not required in this configuration.

The service-entrance conductors enter underground and are terminated in a CT metering section that is part of the panel main switchboard (MSB). The metering section includes provisions for terminating the service-entrance conductors to the switchgear bus. The bus then carries current through the switchgear to fusible disconnects supplying power to panelboards (*Figure 14*) serving mechanical equipment loads, a lighting panelboard, a transformer, and a shunt-trip circuit breaker supplying an elevator. Because this equipment is installed on the interior of the building, all of the equipment is rated for indoor use.

Figure 15 is the one-line diagram for the service just described. Note that the 600A switch with 500A fuses feeds a 300kVA transformer to the panel SSB—a 1,200A switchgear supplying power for all 208V and 120V loads. This one-line diagram includes sizes for service-entrance conduit and conductors, the size and ratings for the switchgear, transformers, and panelboard feeders. The branch circuit panelboards are also shown as part of the one-line diagram. *Figure 16* represents panel schedules for two of the panelboards in this installation.

6.5.0 240/120V Multi-Family Service

Figure 17 shows a 240/120V single-phase service for a multi-family apartment building. This is a 24-unit apartment building with individual tenant meters located on each end of the building. Grounding for this service is sized for parallel (3 sets) of 350 kcmil aluminum service-entrance conductors. The service equipment is designed for a fault current rating of 100,000 AIC. The service-entrance conductors consist of three cables with each cable being a three-conductor, 350 kcmil THWN aluminum in 3" PVC conduit. Because these are parallel service-entrance conductors, the GEC is sized at 2/0 copper (or 4/0 aluminum) using *NEC Table 250.66* (3 × 350 kcmil = 1,050 kcmil). The service consists of

26308-14_F13.EPS

Figure 13 MSB and SSB switchgear service.

26308-14_F14.EPS

Figure 14 Panelboards.

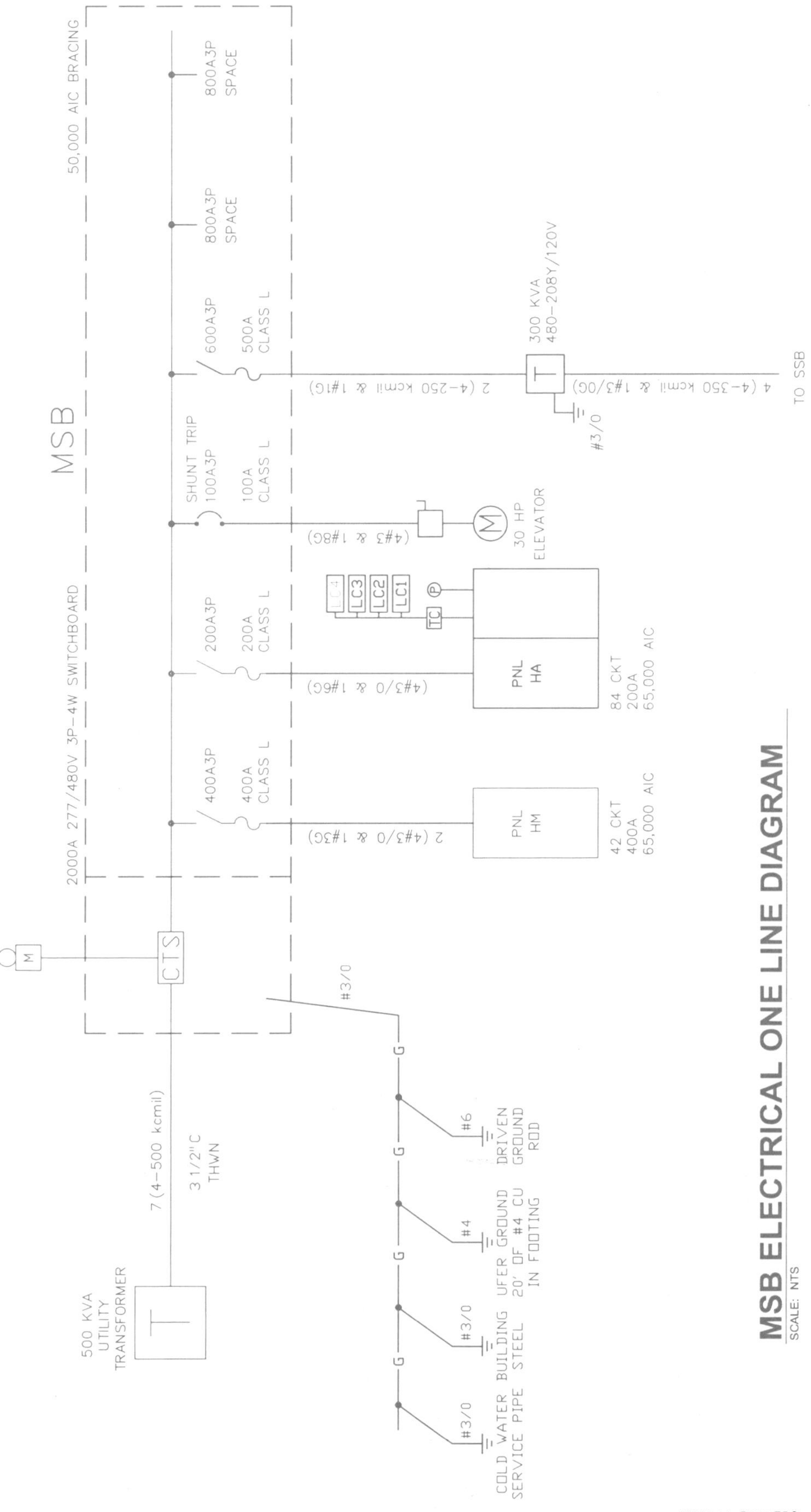

Figure 15 One-line diagram for MSB and SSB switchgear service (1 of 2).

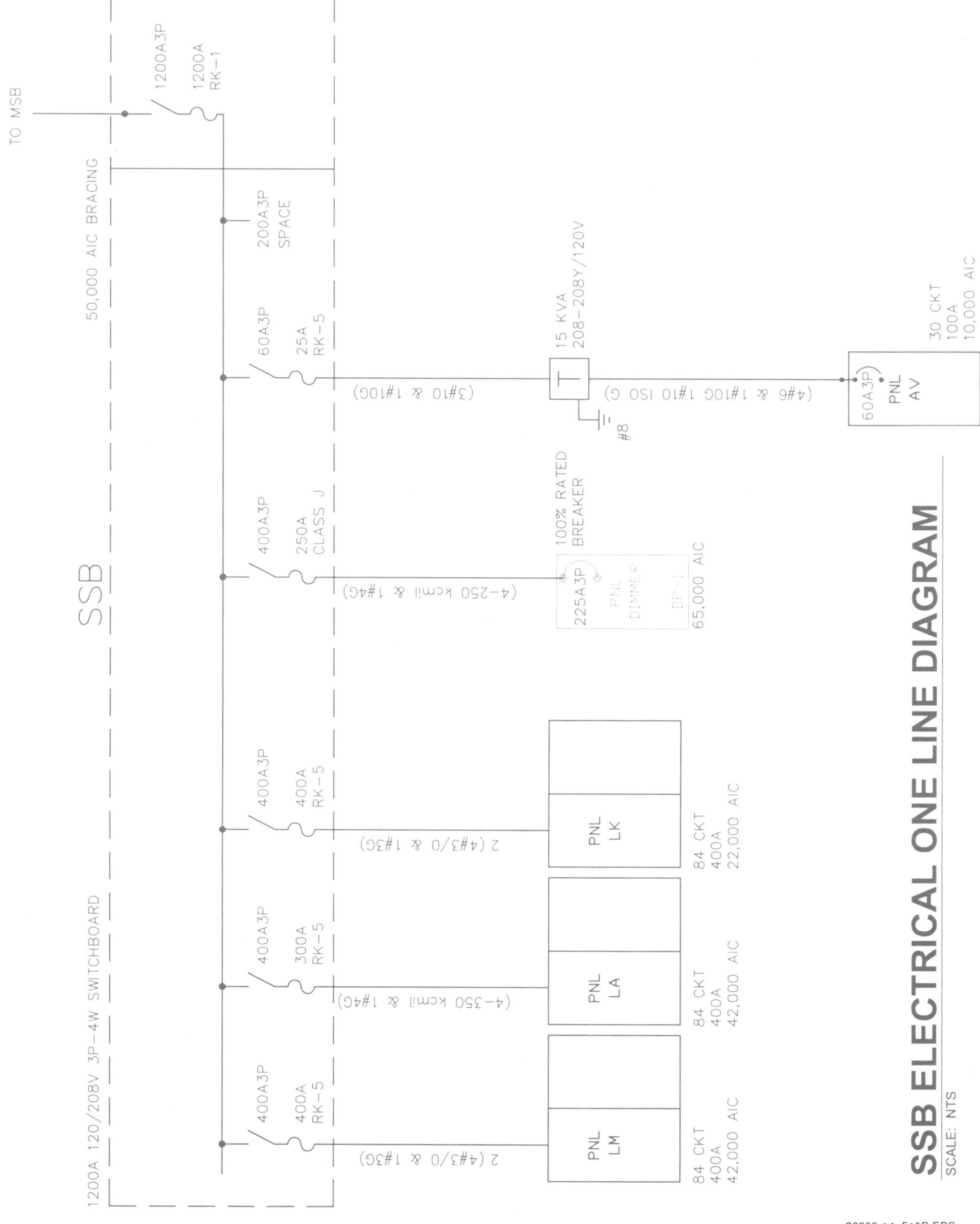

26308-14_F15B.EPS

Figure 15 One-line diagram for MSB and SSB switchgear service (2 of 2).

a main fused disconnect switch and meter stacks connected with horizontal busbars to the main disconnect. The busbars extend horizontally from the main disconnect through each meter stack and then vertical bus is connected to supply power to each meter. Individual meters in the meter stack consist of the meter base and a two-pole, 100A circuit breaker that serves as the overcurrent and short-circuit protection for the feeder supplying the apartment. This circuit

> **On Site**
>
> **Arc Flash**
>
> The service point typically will deliver the greatest level of arc flash potential to the electrician in the customer's electrical system. However onsite backup generation may deliver higher energies than the utility point of service.

PANEL SCHEDULE

PANEL NAME HA

PROJECT:	CROSSROADS CHURCH	VOLTAGE L-L (V):	480
JOB NO.:	M-1904	VOLTAGE L-N (V):	277
LOCATION:	ELECTRICAL ROOM	TYPE:	3P 4W
MINIMUM BUS CAPACITY (A):	200	SHORT CIRCUIT RATING (A):	65000
MAIN O.C. DEVICE (A):	MLO	MOUNTING:	SURFACE
DESIGN CAPACITY (A):	200	COMMENTS:	

DEVICE AMPS	POLE	LTNG (VA)	RCPT (VA)	M/LM/E/A/S (VA)	DESCRIPTION	CKT NO.	PHASE	CKT NO.	DESCRIPTION	M/LM/E/A/S (VA)	RCPT (VA)	LTNG (VA)	POLE	DEVICE AMPS
20	1	1200			SE MONUMENT SIGN	1	A	2	N DRIVE SITE LTG			2530	2	20
20	1	1200			E MONUMENT SIGN	3	B	4	/			2530	/	/
20	1	1200			E MONUMENT SIGN	5	C	6	SE DRIVE SITE LTG			1610	2	20
20	1	1032			BLDG ACCENT LTG	7	A	8	/			1610	/	/
20	1	100			TREE ACCENT LTG	9	B	10	W PARKING LOT LTG			3220	2	20
20	1	683			ARCADE DOWN LTG	11	C	12	/			3220	/	/
20	1	394			ARCADE ACCENT LTG	13	A	14	SPARE				2	20
20	1	200			ENTRY LTG	15	B	16	/				/	/
20	1	3795			CLASSRM #139-#147 LTG	17	C	18	SPARE				2	20
20	1	3566			CORR/STOR/RR/CSRM LTG	19	A	20	/				/	/
20	1	4094			1ST FLR NE LTG	21	B	22	EXTER WALLMNT LTG			72	1	20
20	1	2800			NARTHEX LTG	23	C	24	EXTER WALLMNT LTG			459	1	20
20	1	3108			1ST FLR NW LTG	25	A	26	SPARE				1	20
20	1	3670			1ST FLR N LTG	27	B	28	SPARE				1	20
20	1				SPARE	29	C	30	MULTI RM LTG STEP1			1680	1	20
20	1				SPARE	31	A	32	MULTI RM LTG STEP2			1680	1	20
20	1				SPARE	33	B	34	MULTI RM LTG STEP3			1680	1	20
20	1				SPARE	35	C	36	MULTI RM LTG STEP 4			1680	1	20
20	1	2975			2ND FLR BEV/STAR/CORR LT	37	A	38	MULTI RM LTG STEP1			1680	1	20
20	1	2607			2ND FLR S LTG	39	B	40	MULTI RM LTG STEP2			1680	1	20
20	1	2935			2ND FLR S LTG	41	C	42	MULTI RM LTG STEP3			1680	1	20
20	1	2614			2ND FLR NE LTG	43	A	44	MULTI RM LTG STEP 4			1680	1	20
20	1				SPARE	45	B	46	SPARE				1	20
20	1				SPARE	47	C	48	SPARE				1	20
20	1				SPARE	49	A	50	SPARE				1	20
20	1				SPARE	51	B	52	SPARE				1	20
20	1				SPARE	53	C	54	SPARE				1	20
20	1				SPARE	55	A	56	SPARE				1	20
20	1				SPARE	57	B	58	SPARE				1	20
20	1				SPARE	59	C	60	SPARE				1	20

CONNECTED VA PHASE A:	24069	DEMANDED VA PHASE A:	30086
CONNECTED VA PHASE B:	21053	DEMANDED VA PHASE B:	26316
CONNECTED VA PHASE C:	21742	DEMANDED VA PHASE C:	27178

	CONNECTED	D.F.	DEMAND		
LIGHTING LOAD:	66864	1.25	83580	DEMAND LOAD (A) =	101
RECEPTACLE (FIRST 10 KVA)	0	1.00	0	SPARE CAPACITY (A) =	99
RECEPTACLE (REMAINDER)	0	0.50	0		
LARGEST MOTOR:	0	1.25	0		
REMAINING MOTORS:	0	1.00	0		
APPLIANCES:	0	0.65	0		
EQUIPMENT:	0	1.00	0		
SUB FED PANEL:	0	1.00	0		
TOTAL:	66864		83580		
LOAD (AMPS):	80.4		100.5		

M = MOTOR E = EQUIPMENT S = SUB FEED PANEL
LM = LARGEST MOTOR A = APPLIANCE

NOTES:
1 CONTROL VIA CONTACTOR

26308-14_F16A.EPS

Figure 16 Panel schedules for a 480Y/277V panelboard and a 208Y/120V panelboard (1 of 2).

PANEL SCHEDULE			
PANEL NAME		LA	
PROJECT:	CROSSROADS CHURCH	VOLTAGE L-L (V):	208
JOB NO.:	M-1904	VOLTAGE L-N (V):	120
LOCATION:	ELECTRICAL ROOM	TYPE:	3P 4W
MINIMUM BUS CAPACITY (A):	400	SHORT CIRCUIT RATING (A):	42000
MAIN O.C. DEVICE (A):	MLO	MOUNTING:	SURFACE
DESIGN CAPACITY (A):	300	COMMENTS:	

DEVICE AMPS	POLE	LTNG (VA)	RCPT (VA)	M/LM/E/A/S (VA)	DESCRIPTION	CKT NO.	PHASE	CKT NO.	DESCRIPTION	M/LM/E/A/S (VA)	RCPT (VA)	LTNG (VA)	POLE	DEVICE AMPS
20	1		720		CLASSRM #140		A	2	TOILET #145		180		1	20
20	1		900		CLASSRM #140	3	B	4	EWC-1B	M 244			1	20
20	1		1080		CLASSRM #143	5	C	6	TOILET #133		180		1	20
20	1		1260		CLASSRM #146		A	8	RESTROOMS #149/150		360		1	20
20	1		1260		CLASSRM #147	9	B	10	STORAGE #151		540		1	20
20	1		1260		TODDLERS #135	11	C	12	CORRIDOR #125/129		1440		1	20
20	1		1080		NURSERY #131		3 A	14	MAINT WORKSHP		720		1	20
20	1			M 1582	WASHER	15	B	16	MAINT WORKSHP		900		1	20
50	2			E 4800	DRYER	17	C	18	STOR/ELEC RM		720		1	20
/	/			E 4800	/	19	A	20	YOUTH RM #124, #121		1440		1	20
20	1		1080		EXTERIOR RCPT	21	B	22	SPARE				1	20
20	1		720		RESTROOM #119/120	23	C	24	WELCOME NARTHEX		1080		1	20
20	1			M 244	EWC-1A	25	A	26	MULTI PURPOSE RM		900		1	20
20	1			M 244	EWC-1C	27	B	28	MULTI PURPOSE RM		540		1	20
20	1		1260		LOCKER/STOR/JAN	29	C	30	STORAGE		900		1	20
20	1	555			COFFEE BAR LTG	31	A	32	PA SYSTEM	E 200			1	20
20	1	740			ENTRY LTG	33	B	34	PA SYSTEM	E 200			1	20
20	1			M 1000	ENTRY DOORS	35	C	36	FIRE SMOKE DAMPERS	E 400			1	20
20	1			LM 1656	MOTORIZED HOOP	37	A	38	SPARE				1	20
20	1		1080		YOUTH #224 / STORAGE	39	B	40	SPARE				1	20
20	1			M 1656	MOTORIZED HOOP	41	C	42	SPARE				1	20
20	1		1260		CLASSRM #206	43	A	44	CONF RM #213		540		1	20
20	1		1080		CLASSRM #207	45	B	46	RECEP #214		720		1	20
20	1		1260		CLASSRM #209	47	C	48	KITCHENETTE #211	E 1000	180		1	20
20	1		900		OFFICE #210A	49	A	50	KITCHENETTE #211		180		1	20
20	1				SPARE	51	B	52	WORK ROOM #212		360		1	20
20	1		1080		OFFICE #215/216	53	C	54	COPIER	E 1000			1	20
20	1		900		CLASSRM #204	55	A	56	TELE/COMP RM #205		1080		1	20
20	1		900		CLASSRM #203	57	B	58	STAIR/CORRIDOR		360		1	20
20	1		900		STORAGE/MEDIA RM	59	C	60	RESTROOMS		360		1	20
20	1		1080		YOUTH #225	61	A	62	BEV AREA		360		1	20
20	1		1080		YOUTH #224	63	B	64	BEV AREA		540		1	20
20	1	72			BEV AREA LTG	65	C	66	CORRIDOR /BEV AREA		900		1	20
20	1			M 244	EWC-1D	67	A	68	SPARE		360		1	20
20	1		180		PA SYSTEM	69	B	70	SECURITY GRILL	M 1175			1	20
20	1		180		PA SYSTEM	71	C	72	YOUTH TRACK			1600	1	20
20	1			E 900	BEV AREA REFRIG	73	A	74	YOUTH TRACK			1600	1	20
20	1				SPARE	75	B	76	YOUTH TRACK			1600	1	20
20	1				SPARE	77	C	78	YOUTH TRACK			1600	1	20
20	1				SPARE	79	A	80	YOUTH STAGE			900	1	20
20	1			E 600	CONTACTOR COILS	81	B	82	ROOFTOP RCPT		720		1	20
20	1		540		EXTERIOR RCPT	83	C	84	ROOFTOP RCPT		540		1	20

CONNECTED VA PHASE A:	24419	DEMANDED VA PHASE A:	20573
CONNECTED VA PHASE B:	18625	DEMANDED VA PHASE B:	14187
CONNECTED VA PHASE C:	27708	DEMANDED VA PHASE C:	23503

	CONNECTED	D.F.	DEMAND		
LIGHTING LOAD:	8667	1.25	10834	DEMAND LOAD (A) =	162
RECEPTACLE (FIRST 10 KVA)	10000	1.00	10000	SPARE CAPACITY (A) =	138
RECEPTACLE (REMAINDER)	30140	0.50	15070		
LARGEST MOTOR:	1656	1.25	2070		
REMAINING MOTORS:	6389	1.00	6389		
APPLIANCES:	0	0.65	0		
EQUIPMENT:	13900	1.00	13900		
SUB FED PANEL:	0	1.00	0		
TOTAL:	70752		58263		
LOAD (AMPS):	196.4		161.7		

M = MOTOR E = EQUIPMENT S = SUB FEED PANEL
LM = LARGEST MOTOR A = APPLIANCE

NOTES:

26308-14_F16B.EPS

Figure 16 Panel schedules for a 480Y/277V panelboard and a 208Y/120V panelboard (2 of 2).

On Site

Call First Before Digging

When installing any underground electrical, a call to the local utility should be the first order of business. This allows the utility company's third-party locating service to come out and mark where the existing underground services are present. These may include existing gas, telephone, fiber-optic lines, or other electrical services. 811 is on the way to becoming a national call-before-you-dig number.

Think About It

Putting It All Together

Examine the service at your school or workplace. Is the service entrance properly installed and protected? Is the service-entrance cable cracked or frayed? What about the electrical panel? Are the breakers properly labeled? Is there a main service disconnect switch?

26308-14_F17.EPS

Figure 17 Multi-family service.

breaker is sized for the load to be served. The meter breakers may not be equal size—they are sized for the load to be served and the load for each apartment must be calculated to determine the feeder size. The red sign on the main service disconnect reads: A DISCONNECT ON OTHER END OF BUILDING. This plaque informs the fire department and other authorities that more than one disconnect controls power to the building.

This service complies with *NEC Section 230.72(C)*, which requires that each occupant have access to his or her own service disconnecting means. This exception allows the tenant meters and service disconnecting means to be placed inside the building under the conditions listed. *Figure 18* is a one-line diagram for the multi-family service just described.

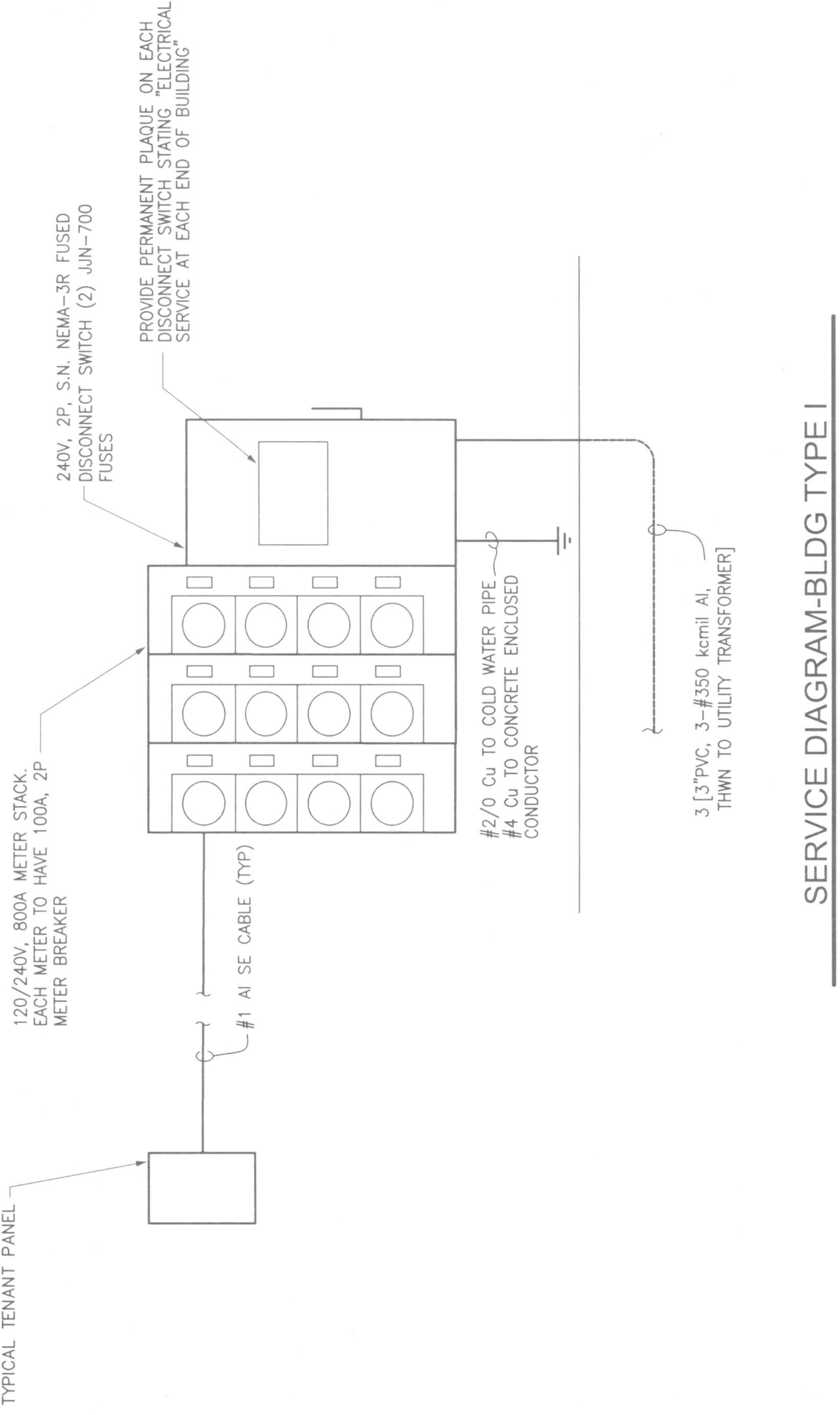

26308-14_F18.EPS

Figure 18 One-line diagram for a multi-family service.

Summary

This module covered typical commercial and small industrial electric service applications, including the installation of service-rated components and their related electrical equipment. Regardless of the size or complexity, all electric services serve the same purpose: to deliver electrical energy safely from the supply system to the wiring system on the premises served. The basic components of a commercial electric service usually include a utility transformer, a service drop or lateral, a service entrance, and service equipment. *NEC Article 230* lists the requirements for electric services.

Review Questions

1. The NEC requirements for services can be found in _____.
   a. *NEC Article 225*
   b. *NEC Article 230*
   c. *NEC Article 240*
   d. *NEC Article 250*

2. All electrical service distribution equipment is labeled with its maximum voltage and current ratings.
   a. True
   b. False

3. Cold sequence metering is accomplished by _____.
   a. unplugging the meter from the meter base
   b. installing the service disconnect after the meter
   c. installing the service disconnect before the meter
   d. placing a switch in CT leads to a meter

4. Most analog watt-hour meters have _____.
   a. four dials
   b. five dials
   c. six dials
   d. seven dials

5. CT metering is typically used in services rated _____.
   a. 200A and above
   b. 300A and above
   c. 400A and above
   d. 500A and above

6. The term *busway* is defined in _____.
   a. *NEC Article 368*
   b. *NEC Article 376*
   c. *NEC Article 378*
   d. *NEC Article 392*

7. Bracing of busways is required primarily to _____.
   a. support the weight of the busbars
   b. allow easier connection of taps
   c. resist the torque of fault current
   d. remove heat from the busbar

8. Service conductors passing through a building are permitted if the conductors are _____.
   a. insulated and fireproofed
   b. in heavy insulated conduit
   c. in conduit encased by 2" of concrete
   d. out of reach

9. The weatherhead for a service drop should be a minimum of _____.
   a. 10' above grade
   b. 13'-6" above grade
   c. 18' above grade
   d. 21'-6" above grade

10. Grounding electrode conductors are sized using _____.
    a. *NEC Table 250.66*
    b. *NEC Table 250.122*
    c. *NEC Table 310.16*
    d. *NEC Table 310.19*

Module 26308-14
Supplemental Exercises

1. Service equipment consists of ____

____.

2. *NEC Article 230* covers service conductors and ______________________.

3. The incoming overhead service supply is referred to as the ______________________.

4. A service ____________ drawing indicates service characteristics such as the voltage rating and grounding requirements.

5. Every service installation begins with a review of ____________ policies and requirements.

6. The location of the bus and ground bars and the ____________ are important in service-entrance conductor installation.

7. True or False? Cold sequence metering allows the utility company to work on metering equipment with the power connected.

8. Most watt-hour meters use ____________ dials.

9. The two basic types of current transformers are the busbar type and the ____________ type.

10. A characteristic of fault currents is a(n) ____________ torque in conductors carrying the fault.

11. True or False? An MLO panelboard has a main circuit breaker.

12. *NEC Section 230.82(3)* requires that a service disconnect switch connected to the supply side of the meter be rated at not more than ____________ volts.

13. According to *NEC Section 230.3*, ____________ supplying one building cannot pass through the interior of another building or structure.

14. The most common service voltage for small commercial loads is ______________________.

15. Equipment installed on the exterior of a building must be rated for ____________ use.

Trade Terms Introduced in This Module

Cold sequence metering: A service installation where the service disconnect is installed ahead of the metering in order for power to be disconnected to allow for safe maintenance of the metering.

Delta-connected: A three-phase transformer connection in which the terminals are connected in a triangular shape like the Greek letter delta (Δ).

Service: The electric power delivered to the premises.

Service conductors: The conductors between the point of termination of the overhead service drop or underground service lateral and the main disconnecting device in the building or on the premises.

Service drop: The overhead conductors through which electrical service is supplied between the last power company pole and the point of their connection to the service-entrance conductors located at the building or other support used for the purpose.

Service entrance: All components between the point of termination of the overhead service drop or underground service lateral and the building's main disconnecting device, except for metering equipment.

Service equipment: The necessary equipment, usually consisting of a circuit breaker or switch and fuses and their accessories, located near the point of entrance of supply conductors to a building and intended to constitute the main control and cutoff means for the electric supply to the building.

Service lateral: The underground service conductors between the street main, including any risers at a pole or other structure or from transformers, and the first point of connection to the service-entrance conductors in a terminal box, meter, or other enclosure with adequate space, inside or outside the building wall.

Additional Resources

This module is intended to present thorough resources for task training. The following resource material is suggested for further study.

National Electrical Code® Handbook, Latest Edition. Quincy, MA: National Fire Protection Association.

Figure Credits

©iStock.com/tpnagasima, Module Opener

Al Hamilton, Figures 1, 6, and 7–18

Topaz Publications, Inc., SA01–SA04

Tim Dean, Figure 3

National Fire Protection Association, Table 1

Reprinted with permission from *NFPA 70®*-2014, *National Electrical Code®* Copyright © 2011, National Fire Protection Association, Quincy, MA. This reprinted material is not the complete and official position of the National Fire Protection Association on the referenced subject, which is represented only by the standard in its entirety.

NCCER CURRICULA — USER UPDATE

NCCER makes every effort to keep its textbooks up-to-date and free of technical errors. We appreciate your help in this process. If you find an error, a typographical mistake, or an inaccuracy in NCCER's curricula, please fill out this form (or a photocopy), or complete the online form at **www.nccer.org/olf**. Be sure to include the exact module ID number, page number, a detailed description, and your recommended correction. Your input will be brought to the attention of the Authoring Team. Thank you for your assistance.

Instructors – If you have an idea for improving this textbook, or have found that additional materials were necessary to teach this module effectively, please let us know so that we may present your suggestions to the Authoring Team.

NCCER Product Development and Revision

13614 Progress Blvd., Alachua, FL 32615

Email: curriculum@nccer.org
Online: www.nccer.org/olf

❑ Trainee Guide ❑ AIG ❑ Exam ❑ PowerPoints Other ______________________________

Craft / Level: Copyright Date:

Module ID Number / Title:

Section Number(s):

Description:

Recommended Correction:

Your Name:

Address:

Email: Phone: